JAVA 2: IN R

STEVEN HOLZNER

560pp; 7.5" × 9"
ISBN: 0-7821-2171-3
$29.99

Java is the talk of the programming world. Covering the JDK 2, Java 2: In Record Time is the most up-to-date book on the language available for every computer user who wants to learn Java by "doing." Chapters focus on skills and let readers learn through tutorials and scores of real-world examples. In no time, the reader moves right into Java's hottest subjects—graphics and sound, animation, applets, database connectivity, debugging, and much more. Unlike other "teach yourself" books, Java 2: In Record Time really delivers on the promise to quickly teach Java proficiency to the newcomer.

JAVA 2 DEVELOPER'S HANDBOOK

PHILIP HELLER AND SIMON ROBERTS

1,248pp; 7.5" × 9"
ISBN: 0-7821-2179-9
$59.99

Hey, developers, don't miss the book that the Java Developer's Journal calls "the most advanced guide to Java available—it will definitely take you to the next level." With extensive coverage of the new advanced Java topics like security, remote method invocation, internationalization, Swing, and more, this book has been completely revised for the latest version of Java. Learn problem-solving and troubleshooting techniques developed and tested by well-respected Java programmers/educators/Sun employees. You'll find plenty of reusable code, both in the book and on the companion CD. The CD also includes timesaving applets, tools, and utilities. If you're building full-scale Java applications, you'll need this book on your desk.

Java™ 2
Complete

SYBEX® SAN FRANCISCO ▸ PARIS ▸ DÜSSELDORF ▸ SOEST ▸ LONDON

Associate Publisher: Gary Masters

Contracts and Licensing Manager: Kristine O'Callaghan

Acquisitions & Developmental Editors: Denise Santoro and Maureen Adams

Project Editor: Gemma O'Sullivan

Compilation Editor: Suzanne Goraj

Editors: Lisa Duran, Kim Wimpsett, Maureen Adams, Shelby Zimmerman, Alison Moncrieff, Steve Gilmartin, Laura Arendal, Krista Reid-McLaughlin

Compilation Technical Editor: Kirky Ringer

Technical Editors: Matthew Fielder, Kirky Ringer, John Zukowski

Book Designer: Maureen Forys, Happenstance Type-O-Rama

Graphic Illustrators: Tony Jonick, Patrick Dintino, Inbar Berman

Electronic Publishing Specialists: Cyndy Johnsen and Maureen Forys

Production Coordinator: Susan Berge

Indexer: Nancy Guenther

Cover Designer: Design Site

Cover Illustrator: Jack D. Myers

Library of Congress Card Number: 99-60006
ISBN: 0-7821-2468-2

Manufactured in the United States of America

10 9 8 7 6 5 4 3

TRADEMARKS:

SYBEX has attempted throughout this book to distinguish proprietary trademarks from descriptive terms by following the capitalization style used by the manufacturer.

The author and publisher have made their best efforts to prepare this book, and the content is based upon final release software whenever possible. Portions of the manuscript may be based upon pre-release versions supplied by software manufacturer(s). The author and the publisher make no representation or warranties of any kind with regard to the completeness or accuracy of the contents herein and accept no liability of any kind including but not limited to performance, merchantability, fitness for any particular purpose, or any losses or damages of any kind caused or alleged to be caused directly or indirectly from this book.

Photographs and illustrations used in this book have been downloaded from publicly accessible file archives and are used in this book for news reportage purposes only to demonstrate the variety of graphics resources available via electronic access. Text and images available over the Internet may be subject to copyright and other rights owned by third parties. Online availability of text and images does not imply that they may be reused without the permission of rights holders, although the Copyright Act does permit certain unauthorized reuse as fair use under 17 U.S.C. Section 107.

Netscape Communications, the Netscape Communications logo, Netscape, and Netscape Navigator are trademarks of Netscape Communications Corporation.

Netscape Communications Corporation has not authorized, sponsored, endorsed, or approved this publication and is not responsible for its content. Netscape and the Netscape Communications Corporate Logos are trademarks and trade names of Netscape Communications Corporation. All other product names and/or logos are trademarks of their respective owners.

ACKNOWLEDGMENTS

This book incorporates the work of many people, inside and outside Sybex.

Maureen Adams, Denise Santoro, and Gary Masters defined the book's overall structure and contents. Suzanne Goraj compiled and adapted all the material for publication in this book. Gemma O'Sullivan was the Project Editor.

David Wall wrote The Essential Java 2 API Reference especially for this book. Kirky Ringer reviewed all programming examples and updated all references to available Java documentation and resources.

A large team of editors, developmental editors, project editors, and technical editors helped to put together the various books from which *Java 2 Complete* was compiled: Denise Santoro, Suzanne Rotondo, and Maureen Adams handled developmental tasks; Alison Moncrieff, Steve Gilmartin, Laura Arendal, Krista Reid-McLaughlin, Shelby Zimmerman, Maureen Adams, Lisa Duran, and Kim Wimpsett all contributed to editing or project editing; and the technical editors were Matthew Fielder, Kirky Ringer, and John Zukowski.

The *Java 2 Complete* production team of electronic publishing specialists Cyndy Johnsen and Maureen Forys, and production coordinator Susan Berge worked with speed and accuracy to turn the manuscript files and illustrations into the handsome book you're now reading. Finally, our most important thanks go to the contributors who agreed to have their work excerpted into *Java 2 Complete*: Steven Holzner, John Zukowski, Philip Heller, Simon Roberts, Peter Seymour, Tom McGinn, and Laurence Vanhelsuwé. Without their efforts, this book would not exist.

NTENTS AT A GLANCE

Contents at a Glance

Table of Contents

Part II ▸ Java Fundamentals   **177**

Part III ▶ Advanced Java   **347**

Chapter 12 ▫ Custom Components   **349**

Chapter 13 ▫ The JFC Swing Components   **409**

INTRODUCTION

J*ava 2 Complete* is a one-of-a-kind computer book—valuable both for the breadth of its content and for its low price. This thousand-page compilation of information from four Sybex books provides comprehensive coverage of the increasingly popular programming language Java. This book, unique in the computer book world, was created with several goals in mind:

- ▶ Offering instruction spanning basic to advanced Java at an affordable price

- ▶ Helping you become familiar with the capabilities and uses of Java so you'll know which additional Java books will best suit your needs

- ▶ Acquainting you with some of our best authors—their writing styles and teaching skills, and the level of expertise they bring to their books—so you can easily find a match for your interests as you delve deeper into Java programming

Java 2 Complete is designed to provide all the essential information you'll need to create user-friendly Web sites and sophisticated programs with Java, while at the same time inviting you to explore the even greater depths and wider coverage of material in the original books.

If you've read other computer "how-to" books, you've seen that there are many possible approaches to the task of showing how to use software and hardware effectively. The books from which *Java 2 Complete* was compiled represent a range of the approaches to teaching that Sybex and its authors have developed—from the quick, concise *In Record Time* style to the exhaustively thorough *Mastering* and high-level *Developer's Handbook* styles. As you read through various chapters of *Java 2 Complete*, you'll see which approach works best for you. You'll also see what these books have in common: a commitment to clarity, accuracy, and practicality.

You'll find in these pages ample evidence of the high quality of Sybex's authors. Unlike publishers who produce "books by committee," Sybex authors are encouraged to write in individual voices that reflect their own experience with programming, with real-world applications, and with the evolution of today's personal computers. Every book represented here is the work of a single writer or a pair of close collaborators. Each author has written and fine-tuned the programs included in his chapters, and has supplied tips and warnings born of his own direct experience.

In adapting the various source materials for inclusion in *Java 2 Complete*, the compiler preserved these individual voices and perspectives. Chapters were edited only to minimize duplication, to add helpful explanations of topics otherwise not covered here in depth, and to update references as needed so you're sure to get the most current information available.

Who Can Benefit from This Book?

Java 2 Complete is designed to meet the needs of a wide range of computer users. Therefore, while you *could* read this book from beginning to end, all of you may not *need* to read every chapter. The Table of Contents and the Index will guide you to the subjects you're looking for.

Beginners   Even if you have only a little familiarity with programming methods and concepts, this book will enable you to build full-featured Web sites and useful Java applets and applications.

Intermediate users   If you already know the basics of Java, this book will give you more sophisticated programming skills and a deeper understanding of the capabilities of Java.

Advanced users   You, too, will find much useful information in this book, including complete explanations of concepts, methods, and processes; useful programming shortcuts and alternatives; and a wealth of references including documentation for all essential Core Java API classes.

How This Book Is Organized

Java 2 Complete has eighteen chapters and one appendix.

Part I: Introducing Java   In the first six chapters of the book, we'll introduce you to basic Java programs, including those for text fields, check boxes, and scroll bars. You will create your own programs immediately, without first having to wade through chapters of concepts and terminology.

Part II: Java Fundamentals   In Part II, you'll explore Java in greater depth. Here you will learn essential programming methods and concepts, amply illustrated with hands-on examples.

Part III: Advanced Java   Part III addresses Java's more advanced uses and methods. We will cover custom and Swing components, thread behavior and database connectivity, and the 2D API graphics capabilities.

Part IV: JavaBeans   Part IV is devoted to JavaBeans, a powerful, flexible programming tool that allows you to create and reuse Java "beans"—self-contained, fully functional components you can plug into any Java application or applet.

Appendix   This appendix is designed for quick lookup—or casual browsing. The Essential Java 2 API Reference describes the most useful classes in the Java 2 Applications Programming Interface.

A Few Typographical Conventions

When an operation requires a series of choices from menus or dialog boxes, the ➢ symbol is used to guide you through the instructions, like this: "Select Programs ➢ Accessories ➢ System Tools ➢ System Information." The items the ➢ symbol separates may be menu names, toolbar icons, check boxes, or other elements of the Windows interface—anyplace you can make a selection.

`This typeface` is used to identify programming code and Internet URLs, and **boldface type** is used whenever you need to type something into a text box.

You'll find these types of special notes throughout the book:

TIP
You'll get a lot of these Tips—for quicker and smarter ways to accomplish tasks—based on the authors' long experience using Java.

NOTE
You'll see these Notes, too. They usually represent alternate ways to accomplish a task or some additional information that needs to be highlighted.

WARNING

In a very few places you'll see a Warning like this one. When you see a Warning, pay attention to it!

YOU'LL ALSO SEE "SIDEBAR" BOXES LIKE THIS

These boxed sections provide added explanation of special topics that are noted briefly in the surrounding discussion, but that you may want to explore separately. Each sidebar has a heading that announces the topic so you can quickly decide whether it's something you need to know about.

For More Information...

See the Sybex Web site, www.sybex.com, to learn more about all the books that went into *Java 2 Complete*. On the site's Catalog page, you'll find links to any book you're interested in.

We hope you enjoy this book and find it useful. Happy programming!

PART i
INTRODUCING JAVA

Chapter 1
BUILDING THE FIRST JAVA EXAMPLES

Welcome to Java 2! An ambitious agenda lies before you: You're going to get a firm grip on Java programming, creating both powerful Java programs and Web pages, and you will take a guided tour through Java 2. There is no more exciting programming package available. As you are probably aware, the popularity of Java has skyrocketed as more and more people have seen how versatile and powerful it is. Web programmers have found it an excellent tool because it allows them to write programs that will run on many different types of computers. They have started using it to make their Web pages actually *do* something.

Adapted from *Java 2: In Record Time* by Steven Holzner
ISBN 0-7821-2171-3   560 pages $29.99

With Java, you will be able to display animation and images, accept mouse clicks and text, use controls like scrollbars and check boxes, print graphics, support pop-up menus, and even support additional windows and menu bars.

We'll start working on your Java skills right away—you won't need to wade through chapters of abstractions first. We will concentrate on examples, on seeing things from the programmer's point of view—on seeing Java at *work*.

Java programs come two ways: as stand-alone applications and as small programs you can embed in Web pages, called *applets*. Of the two, applets are the most popular, and we'll concentrate primarily on them.

BUILDING THE HELLO EXAMPLE

The first example will be a simple one because right now we just want to get you started in Java without too many extra details to weigh you down. You will create a small Java applet, the type of Java program you can embed in a Web page, that will display the words "Hello from Java!"

What's an Applet?

Just what do I mean by an applet? An applet is a special program that you can embed in a Web page such that the applet gains control over a certain part of the Web page. On that part of the page, the applet can display buttons, list boxes, images, and more. Applets make Web pages "come alive."

Each applet is given the amount of space (usually measured in pixels) that it requests in a Web page, such as the amount of space shown in Figure 1.1. (Soon I'll show you how an applet "requests" space.) This is the space that the applet will use for its display. We'll place the words "Hello from Java!" in the applet, as shown in Figure 1.2.

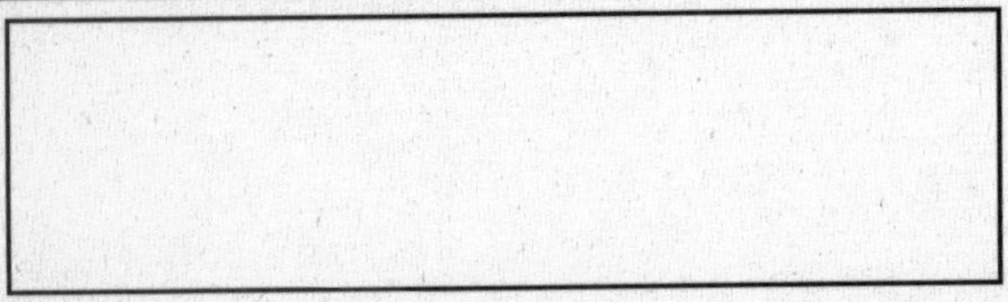

FIGURE 1.1: An applet requests space in a Web page.

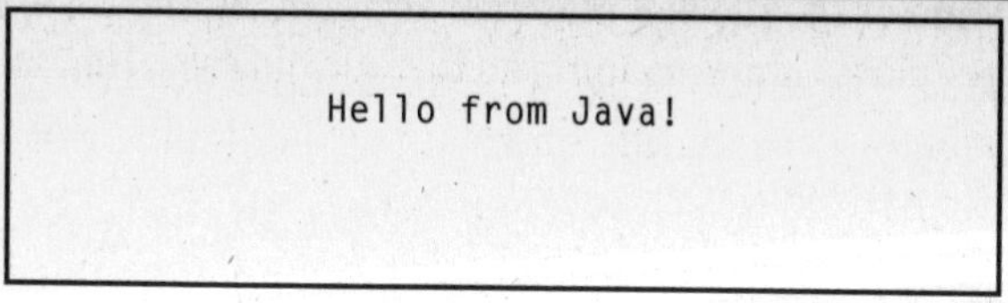

```
Hello from Java!
```

FIGURE 1.2: Hello from Java!

That's how this applet will work; after you create it, you will be able to embed it in a Web page. Let's create and run the applet now.

Creating the Hello Example

Let's call this first applet *hello*. You will store the actual Java code (the lines of text that make up the program) for this applet in a text file named hello.java. You'll need an editor of some kind to create this file (such as Windows WordPad or Notepad). You will be creating .java files throughout the book, so use an editor you are comfortable with. Also notice that, if you are going to use a word processor like Microsoft Word, you'll have to save your .java files as straight text—something you can type out at the DOS prompt and read directly. Check your word processor's Save As menu item or your word processor's documentation to see how to do this. The Sun Java system won't be able to handle anything but straight text files. Now, type the following text into the file hello.java (this is the traditional first program in most Java books):

```
import java.awt.Graphics;
public class hello extends java.applet.Applet
{
  public void paint(Graphics g)
  {
    g.drawString("Hello from Java!", 60, 30 );
  }
}
```

This is the text of your first Java program, and soon you'll see what each line means. Having typed in the text, save it to disk as hello.java.

NOTE

Note that case counts here—make sure you type hello.java, not Hello.java or hello.Java.

In general, the name of the file will match exactly (including case) the name given in the "class" statement in the file; in this case, that is hello:

```
import java.awt.Graphics;

public class hello extends java.applet.Applet
{
  public void paint( Graphics g )
  {
    g.drawString("Hello from Java!", 60, 30 );
  }
}
```

In this book, you will place your programs into subdirectories of a new directory called java1-2 (this is optional—you can choose any name). That means you'll save the hello.java file as c:\java1-2\hello\hello.java.

Now you have created hello.java. This is the source code for your applet, and it contains the Java code that you have written. The next step is to compile this Java code into a working applet and see your applet at work. Applets have the extension .class, making the name of your actual applet hello.class. I'll show you *why* applets have the extension .class shortly.

SETTING UP THE JAVA JDK

Now you'll use Java itself to create your applet, hello.class, from the code hello.java. If you haven't already done so, you should install the Java Development Kit (JDK) 1.2.

With previous versions of Java, you used to have to go through a rather lengthy and involved installation process, but that's all changed now—you just have to run an .EXE file. You get this .EXE file online, from http://java.sun.com/products/jdk/1.2/—just download it and follow the instructions for installation.

The next step is to make sure you can run the JDK from any location in your computer (including the c:\java1-2 directory and its subdirectories, which is where you'll put your Java programs). To do that, make sure the PATH statement in your AUTOEXEC.BAT file (found in the main directory of the C: drive) includes the JDK BIN and LIB directories (here I have installed the JDK in c:\jdk12—use whatever path is appropriate to the way you have installed the JDK):

```
PATH=C:\WINDOWS;C:\JDK12\BIN;C:\JDK12\LIB
```

For Windows NT, the path will need to be entered into Start ➤ Settings ➤ Control Panel ➤ System. In the System Properties window, select the Environment tab and set the PATH variable.

The JDK 1.2 is ready to go.

TIP

If you need more help installing the JDK, check out the Troubleshooting Web page at http://www.javasoft.com.

You can copy the Java documentation from JavaSoft to the same directory—for example, c:\JDK12. Unzip the documentation .zip file, creating a docs subdirectory (your unzipping program must be able to handle long filenames).

NOTE

You'll need a Web browser to look at the Java documentation because it's formatted in HTML.

Now that you've installed Java 2, let's take a look at what's new in this version of Java.

What's New in 2?

If you're familiar with Java 1.0 or Java 1.1, then you'd probably expect there to be some changes in Java 2, and you'd be right. Let's get an overview of the changes in this new edition of Java. If you're not familiar with Java, you should probably skip to the next section and take a look at this material later—much of this won't make any sense unless you've programmed in Java before.

From Java 1.0 to Java 1.1

Many readers will be familiar with Java 1.0, not Java 1.1, so we will start by looking at the changes from Java 1.0 to Java 1.1.

Abstract Windowing Toolkit enhancements   Java 1.1 supports printing, faster scrolling, pop-up menus, the clipboard, a delegation-based event model, imaging and graphics enhancements, and more. In addition, it's faster than Java 1.0 (something Java programmers can definitely appreciate)!

.jar files   .jar (Java Archive) files were introduced in Java 1.1 and let you package a number of files together, zipping them to shrink them, so the user can download many files at once. You can put many applets and the data they need together into one .jar file, making downloading much faster. These files are analogous to .zip files except that your browser will download them and unzip them on-the-fly for you.

Internationalization   Java 1.1 lets you develop *locale-specific applets*, including using Unicode characters, a locale mechanism, localized message support, locale-sensitive date, time, time zone, number handling, and more.

Signed applets and digital signatures   Java 1.1 can create digitally signed Java applications. A digital signature gives your users a "path" back to you in case something goes wrong. This is one of the new security precautions popular on the World Wide Web.

Remote method invocation   In Java 1.1, RMI lets Java objects have their methods invoked from Java code running in other Java sessions. This is sort of similar to Local Remote Procedure Calls (LRPCs).

Object serialization   Serialization was new in Java 1.1, and it lets you store objects and handle them with binary input/output streams. Besides allowing you to store copies of the objects you serialize, serialization is also the basis of communication between objects engaged in RMI. Object serialization is similar to MFC Serialization, for those who are familiar with Microsoft's Foundation Classes.

Reflection   In Java 1.1, reflection lets Java code examine information about the methods and constructors of loaded classes and make use of those reflected methods and constructors.

Inner classes   Java 1.1 makes it easier to create adapter classes. An adapter class is a class that implements an interface required by an API (Applications Programming Interface). An adapter class "delegates" control back to an enclosing main object.

New Java native method interface   Native code is code that is written specifically for a particular machine. In Java 1.1, this interface was introduced to provide a standard programming interface for writing Java native methods. The primary goal is binary compatibility of native method libraries across all Java virtual machine implementations on a given platform. Writing and calling native code can significantly improve execution speeds. Java 1.1 included a powerful new Java native method interface.

Byte, Short, and Void classes   In Java 1.1, Byte and Short values can be handled as "wrapped" numbers when you use the new Java classes Byte and Short. The new Void class is a placeholder class that we can derive classes from, rather than use directly.

Deprecated methods   Quite a number of Java 1.0 methods were considered obsolete in Java 1.1, and they are marked as deprecated in the Java 1.1 documentation. (The Java compiler now displays a warning when it compiles code that uses a deprecated feature.)

Networking enhancements   Networking enhancements in Java 1.1 included support for selected BSD-style socket options in the java.net base classes. With Java 1.1, Socket and Server-Socket are non-final, extendable classes. New subclasses of SocketException were added for finer granularity in reporting and handling network errors.

I/O enhancements   In Java 1.1, the I/O package was extended with character streams, which are like byte streams except that they contain 16-bit Unicode characters rather than eight-bit bytes. Character streams make it easy to write programs that are independent of a specific character encoding and are therefore easier to internationalize. Nearly all of the functionality available for byte streams is also available for character streams.

That completes this overview of what's new in Java 1.1—if you have no idea what I'm talking about, don't worry, it'll become clear later.

From Java 1.1 to Java 2

Now let's have a look at what's new in Java 2.

Security enhancements   When code is loaded, it is assigned permissions based on the security policy currently in effect. Each permission specifies a permitted access to a particular resource (such as "read" and "write" access to a specified file or directory, "connect" access to a given host and port, and so on). The policy, specifying which permissions are available for code from various signers/locations, can be initialized from an external configurable policy file. Unless a permission is explicitly granted to code, it cannot access the resource that is guarded by that permission.

Swing (JFC)   Swing is the part of the Java Foundation Classes (JFC) that implements a new set of GUI components with a "pluggable" look and feel. Swing is implemented in pure Java, and is based on the JDK 1.1 Light-weight UI Framework. The pluggable look and feel lets you design a single set of GUI components that can automatically have the look and feel of any platform (e.g., Windows, Solaris, Macintosh).

Java 2D (JFC)   The Java 2D API is a set of classes for advanced 2D graphics and imaging. It encompasses line art, text, and images in a single comprehensive model.

Accessibility (JFC)   Through the Java Accessibility API, developers will be able to create Java applications that can interact with assistive technologies such as screen readers, speech recognition systems, and Braille terminals.

Drag and Drop (JFC)   Drag and Drop enables data transfer across both Java and native applications, between Java applications, and within a single Java application.

Collections   The Java Collections API is a unified framework for representing and manipulating Java collections (I'll show you more about them later), allowing them to be manipulated independent of the details of their representation.

Java extensions   Framework Extensions are packages of Java classes (and any associated native code) that application developers can use to extend the core platform. The extension mechanism allows the Java Virtual Machine (JVM) to use the extension classes in much the same way it uses the system classes.

JavaBeans enhancements   Java 2 provides developers with standard means to create more sophisticated JavaBeans components and applications that offer their customers more seamless integration with the rest of their runtime environment, such as the desktop of the underlying operating system or the browser.

Input method framework   The input method framework enables all text-editing components to receive Japanese, Chinese, or Korean text input through standard input methods.

Package version identification   "Versioning" introduces package level version control where applications and applets can identify (at runtime) the version of a specific Java Runtime Environment, VM, and class package.

RMI enhancements   Remote Method Invocation (RMI) has several new enhancements including Remote Object Activation, which introduces support for remote objects and automatic object activation, as well as Custom Socket Types that allow a remote object to specify the custom socket type that RMI will use for remote calls to that object. (RMI over a secure transport, such as SSL, can be supported using custom socket types.)

Serialization enhancements   Serialization now includes an API that allows the serialized data of an object to be specified independently of the fields of the class. This allows serialized data fields to be written to and read from the stream using the existing techniques (this ensures compatibility with the default writing and reading mechanisms).

Reference objects   A reference object encapsulates a reference to some other object so that the reference itself may be examined and manipulated like any other object. Reference objects allow a program to maintain a reference to an object that does not prevent the object from being reclaimed by the Java "garbage collector," which manages memory.

Audio enhancements   Audio enhancements include a new sound engine and support for audio in applications as well as applets.

Java IDL   Java IDL adds CORBA (Common Object Request Broker Architecture) capability to Java, providing standards-based interoperability and connectivity. Java IDL enables distributed Web-enabled Java applications to invoke operations transparently on remote network services using the industry standard OMG IDL (Object Management Group Interface Definition Language) and IIOP (Internet Inter-ORB Protocol) defined by the Object Management Group.

JAR enhancements   The enhancements include added functionality for the command-line JAR tool for creating and updating signed JAR files. There are also new standard APIs for reading and writing JAR files.

JNI enhancements   The Java Native Interface (JNI) is a standard programming interface for writing Java native methods and embedding the Java Virtual Machine into native applications. The primary goal is binary compatibility of native method libraries across all Java Virtual Machine implementations on a given platform. Java 2 extends the Java Native Interface to incorporate new features in the Java platform.

JVMDI   A new debugger interface, the Java Virtual Machine, now provides low-level services for debugging. The interface for these services is the Java Virtual Machine Debugger Interface (JVMDI).

JDBC enhancements   Java Database Connectivity (JDBC) is a standard SQL database access interface, providing uniform access to a wide range of relational databases. JDBC also provides a common base on which higher-level tools and interfaces can be built. The Java 2 software bundle includes JDBC and the JDBC-ODBC bridge.

These concepts will become clearer as we proceed. Now, you're ready to compile the hello applet and see it at work.

Compiling the Hello Applet

Now that you have installed the JDK and have your `hello.java` source file ready to go, you can create the actual applet and see it run. To do this, change to the `c:\java1-2\hello` directory now (or wherever you have saved the `hello.java` file); this is how the DOS prompt should look:

```
c:\java1-2\hello>
```

Next, type this to create your applet:

```
c:\java1-2\hello>javac hello.java
```

The name of the Java program that takes your Java code and turns it into `.class` files ready to run in Web pages is `javac.exe`, the Java *compiler* (i.e., it compiles `.java` files into `.class` files). If you type the DOS command `Dir` to look at the current directory contents, you should see both `hello.java` and `hello.class`. Because you've created `hello.class`, your applet is ready to go—but what does that mean? What have you really done?

UNDERSTANDING JAVA

Let's take the time now to get an overview of Java. As in most programming languages, we write Java code using words and numbers that are then translated—that is, *compiled*—into binary files that computers can understand. The `hello.java` program is an example of this—you write it such that you can understand it, but when you want to actually run your program, you have to compile it into something a computer can use. In this case, that means using the Java compiler to produce the file named `hello.class`. `hello.class` is a binary file of *bytecodes* that Java-compatible Web browsers can run to produce the desired result. In this way, several lines of Java program code can be compiled neatly into a few bytes. Those bytes are what is actually downloaded when Web browsers read the Web page in which you have placed your Java applets— that is to say, the actual applet is a `.class` file, like `hello.class`, and those are the files you place on your Internet Service Provider's server so other people's Web browsers can download them, as you'll see very shortly.

Experienced programmers may wonder about these bytecodes—why isn't Java simply compiled into the normal machine code that each computer really runs? Because Java bytecodes were intentionally made machine-independent so that they could be run on a wide variety of machines, and that is what originally made them so popular on the Internet—it doesn't matter what type of machine you're downloading to, as long as the user's Web browser can run Java. The downloaded bytecodes are run by the *Java Virtual Machine*, or JVM, and it is the JVM's task to convert bytecodes into the machine language that users' individual computers can run.

The JVM is actually a hypothetical chip that runs Java—it is almost always software, not hardware, that runs Java. Each Web browser that supports Java has a JVM built right into it, and it loads the `.class` file that makes up your applet with JVM's *class loader* and then runs the applet.

Running the Hello Applet

To see `hello.class`, your first applet, running, you'll need a Web page to place it in. Use your editor again to create a new file, `hello.htm`, which will be your Web page, written in the language of Web pages, *HyperText Markup Language* (HTML) (we'll review HTML in a minute). Enter the following text into `hello.htm` and save it in the same directory as the `hello.class` file:

```
<html>

<!- Web page written for the Sun Applet Viewer>

<head>
<title>hello</title>
</head>

<body>
<hr>

<applet
code=hello.class
width=200
height=200>

</applet>

<hr>
</body>
</html>
```

Now you can run the hello applet by simply viewing this new Web page, `hello.htm`. To do that, use the Applet Viewer that comes with the JDK 1.2. To use the Applet Viewer, go back to the `hello` subdirectory and type the following:

```
c:\java1-2\hello>appletviewer hello.htm
```

Again, capitalization is very important here—make sure your capitalization matches the exact spelling of the Web page name. When you've done this, the Applet Viewer runs, as shown below—and you see your message, "Hello from Java!" Your first applet is a success.

TIP
You can use any Java-enabled Web browser to look at this Web page. For most of the applets in this book, however, you will have to use either a Web browser that supports Java 2 (not just Java 1.0 or Java 1.1) or the Sun Applet Viewer.

Your first applet, `hello.class`, runs—but what exactly did you do? Let's take a look now at the Java code that you entered for `hello.java`, examining it line by line to get a better idea of how Java programming works (even though Java will handle many of these details for you later).

Understanding the Hello Example

Let's take apart your first applet now. Begin with this line:

```
import java.awt.Graphics;
```

```
.
.
.
```

What does this mean? This line actually points out one of the great advantages of Java programming. When you're adding menus and separate windows to your Java applets, you can imagine that it would be a great deal of work to create everything from scratch—that is, write the entire code for menu handling, separate window creation, and so forth. Instead of asking you to do so, Java comes complete with several predefined libraries, and much of this book will be an examination of the routines in these libraries. You'll learn more about this later, but what you're doing is adding support from the main Java graphics library of routines to your applet. In this way, we'll be able to draw the text string, "Hello from Java!", in the applet's window.

NOTE
If you're a C/C++ programmer, you'll notice that the import statement works much like the C/C++ #include statement.

Next, add these lines to hello.java:

```
import java.awt.Graphics;

public class hello extends java.applet.Applet

{
    .
    .
    .
```

You've just created a Java *class* named hello. What does this mean?

OBJECT-ORIENTED PROGRAMMING

Objects and *classes* are two fundamental concepts in object-oriented languages like Java. There's been a lot of hype about object-oriented programming (OOP), and that can make the whole topic seem mysterious and unapproachable. In fact, object-oriented programming was introduced to make longer programs *easier* to create. We'll start a mini-survey of object-oriented programming by looking at objects.

Understanding Java Objects

In long, involved programs, there can be a profusion of both variables and functions, sometimes hundreds of each. Creating and maintaining the program code can become a very cluttered task because you have to keep so many things in mind. There may also be unwanted interaction if various functions use variables of the same name. Object-oriented programming was invented to break up such large programs.

The idea behind objects is quite simple—you just break up your program into the various parts, each of which you can easily conceptualize as performing a discrete task, and those are your objects. For example, you may put all the screen-handling parts of a program together into an object named `screen`. Objects are more powerful than simple functions or sets of variables because an object can hold both functions and variables wrapped up together in a way that makes it easy to use. The `screen` object may hold not only all the data displayed on the screen, but also the functions needed to handle that data, like `drawString()` or `drawLine()`. This means that all the screen handling is hidden from the rest of the program in a convenient way, making the rest of the program easier to handle.

As another example, think of a refrigerator. A refrigerator would be far less useful if you had to regulate all the temperatures and pumps and so forth by hand at all times. Making all those functions internal and automatic to the refrigerator makes it into an easy object to deal with and a useful one: a *refrigerator*. Wrapping up code and data into objects this way is the basis of object-oriented programming.

What's a Java Class?

But how do you create objects? That's where *classes* come in. A class is to an object what a cookie cutter is to a cookie—a template or blueprint. In terms of programming, you might think of the relationship between a data type, like an integer, and the actual variable itself like this, where you set up an integer named `the_data`:

```
int the_data;
```

This is the actual way to create an integer variable in Java. Here, `int` is the type of variable you are declaring and `the_data` is the variable itself. This is the same relationship that a class has to an object, and informally you may think of a class as an object's *type*.

TIP

Java supports all the standard C and C++ primitive data types like `int`, `double`, `long`, `float`, and so forth.

For example, if you had set up a class named, say, `graphicsClass`, you can create an object of that class named `screen` this way:

```
graphicsClass screen;
```

You'll see how to actually create a class soon (creating a class like `graphicsClass` is not hard—when you create a class in code, you will just group all its functions and data inside the class definition), and then you'll see how to create objects of that class. What's important to remember is this: the object itself is what holds the data you want to work with; the class itself holds no data but just describes how the object should be set up.

Object-oriented programming at root is nothing more than a way of grouping functions and the data they work on together to make your program less cluttered. You'll see more about object-oriented programming throughout this book, including how to create a class, how to create an object of that class, and how to reach the functions and data in that object when you want to.

That completes the mini-overview of classes and objects. As you can see, a class is just a programming construct that groups together, or *encapsulates*, functions and data, and an object may be thought of as a variable of that class's type, as the object `screen` is to the class `screenclass`.

As it turns out, Java comes complete with several libraries of predefined classes, which save you a great deal of work. Throughout this book, we will examine these predefined and very useful Java classes. Using these predefined classes, we'll create objects needed to handle buttons, text fields, scroll bars, and much more.

Learning about Java Packages

These class libraries are called *packages* in Java, and one such library is called `java.awt` (where awt stands for Abstract Window Toolkit). This library holds the `Graphics` class, which will handle the graphics work you undertake. So this line in the `hello.java` file:

```
import java.awt.Graphics;
```

actually means that you want to include the Java Graphics class and make use of it in your program. In a minute, you will use an object of the `Graphics` class for your graphics output.

You've added support for graphics handling by including the `java.awt.Graphics` class (and in Java, displaying the text string "Hello from Java!" is considered graphics handling). Next, it's time to set up your hello applet itself. To do so, define a new class named `hello`. This is the standard way of setting up an applet in Java, and in fact, the applet itself has the file extension `.class`. That's because each class defined in a `.java` file ends up being exported to a `.class` file, where you can make use of it. You'll learn more details about this soon.

It would be quite difficult to write all the code an applet class needs from scratch. For example, we'd need to interact with the Web browser, reserve a section of screen, initialize the appropriate Java packages, and much more. It turns out that all that functionality is already built into the Java `Applet` class, which is part of the `java.applet` package. But how do you make use of the `Applet` class? You want to customize the applet to display your text string, and the `java.applet.Applet` class itself knows nothing about that.

Understanding Java Inheritance

You can customize the `java.applet.Applet` class by *deriving* the `hello` class from the `java.applet.Applet` class. This makes `java.applet.Applet` the *base* class of the `hello` class, and it makes `hello` a class derived from `java.applet.Applet`. This gives you all the power of the `java.applet.Applet` class without the worries of writing it yourself, and you can add what you want to this class by adding code to your derived class `hello`.

This is an important part of object-oriented programming, and it's called *inheritance*. In this way, a derived class inherits the functionality of its base class and adds more on top of it. For example, you may have a base class called `chassis`. You can derive various classes from this base class called, say, `car` and `truck`. In this way, two derived classes can share the same base class, saving time and effort programmatically. Although the `car` and `truck` classes share the same base class, `chassis`, they added different items to the base class, ending up as two quite different classes, `car` and `truck`.

Using inheritance, then, you will *extend* the base class `java.applet.Applet` by creating your own class `hello` and adding onto the base class. In the `hello.java` source, you indicate that the `hello` class is derived from the `java.applet.Applet` class like this (note that you use the keyword *class* to indicate that you are defining a new class):

```
import java.awt.Graphics;

public class hello extends java.applet.Applet
{
     .
     .
     .
```

In starting to set up the new class, `hello`, you've given it all the power of the `java.applet.Applet` class (like the ability to request space from the Web browser and to respond to many browser-created commands). But how do you make additions and even alterations to the `java.applet.Applet` class to customize your own `hello` class? How do you display your text string? One way is by *overriding* the base class's built-in functions (overriding is an important part of object-oriented programming). When you redefine a base class's function in a derived class, the new version of the function is the one that takes over. In this way, you can customize the functions from the base class as you like them in the derived class.

For example, one function in the `java.applet.Applet` class is called `paint()`. This is a very important function that is called when the Web browser tells the applet to create its display on the screen. This happens when the applet first begins and every time it has to be redisplayed later (for example, if the Web browser was minimized and then maximized, or if some window was moved and the applet's display area was uncovered after having been covered).

Your goal in the `hello` class is to display the string "Hello from Java!" on the screen, and in fact, you will override the `java.applet.Applet` class's `paint()` function to do so. You override a base class's function simply by redefining it in the new class. Do that now for the `paint()` function, noting first that the built-in functions of a class are called that class's *methods*. In this case, then, you override (that is, redefine) the `paint()` method like this:

```
import java.awt.Graphics;

public class hello extends java.applet.Applet
{
    public void paint( Graphics g )[
    {
        .
        .
        .
```

NOTE

The built-in functions of a class are called *methods*. Classes can also have built-in variables—called *data members*—and even constants. Collectively, all these parts are called a class's *members*.

What Are Java Access Modifiers?

The keyword *public* is called an *access modifier*. A class's methods can be declared public, private, or protected. If they are declared public, then you can call them from anywhere in the program, not just in the class in which they are defined. If they are private, they may be called from only the class in which they are defined. If they are protected, they may be called from only the class in which they are defined and the classes derived from that class.

Next, indicate the *return* type of the paint() method. When you call a method, you can pass parameters to it, and it can return data to you. In this case, paint() has no return value, which you indicate with the return type *void*. Other return types are int for an integer return value (this variable is usually 32 bits long), long for a long integer (this variable is usually 64 bits long), float for a floating point return, or double for a double-precision floating point value. You can also return arrays and objects in Java.

Finally, note that you indicate that the paint() method is automatically passed one parameter—an object of the Graphics class called g:

```
import java.awt.Graphics;

public class hello extends java.applet.Applet
{
  public void paint(Graphics g)
  { .
        .
        .
```

This Graphics object represents the physical display of the applet. That is, you can use the built-in methods of this object—such as drawImage(), drawLine(), drawOval(), and others—to drawn on the screen. In this case, you want to place the string "Hello from Java!" on the screen, and you can do that with the drawString() method.

How do you reach the methods of an object like the Graphics object named g? You do that with a dot operator (.) like this: g.drawString(), where here you are invoking g's drawString() method to "draw" a string of text on the screen (text is handled like any other type of graphics in a windows environment—that is, it is drawn on the screen rather than "printed," just as you would draw a rectangle or circle). Supply three parameters to the drawString() method—the string of text you want to display, and the (x, y) location of that string's lower-left corner (called the starting point of the string's *baseline*) in pixels on the screen, passed in two integer values. As shown in Figure 1.3, you can draw your string at the pixel location (60, 30), where (0, 0) is the upper-left corner of the applet's display.

NOTE

The coordinate system in a Java program is set up with the origin (∅, ∅) at the upper left, with x increasing horizontally to the right and y increasing vertically downwards; this fact will be important throughout the book. If it seems backwards to you, you might try thinking of it in terms of reading a page of text, like this one, where you start at the upper-left and work your way to the right and down. The units of measurement in Java coordinate systems are almost always screen pixels.

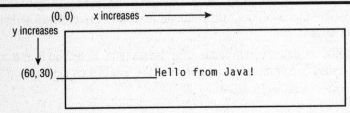

FIGURE 1.3: Drawing a string at (60,30)

This means that you add a call to the drawString() method this way:

```
import java.awt.Graphics;
public class hello extends java.applet.Applet
{
  public void paint( Graphics g )
  {
    g.drawString( "Hello from Java!", 60, 30 );
  }
}
```

Note that Java uses the same convention as C or C++ to indicate that a code statement is finished: it ends the statement with a semicolon (;).

TIP

In general, Java adheres very strongly to C++ coding conventions. If you know C++, you already know a great deal of Java.

You have completed the code necessary for this applet, which is also to say you have completed the code for the new class, `hello`. When the Java compiler creates `hello.class`, the entire specification of the new class will be in that file. This is the actual binary file that you upload to your Internet Service Provider so that it may be included in your Web page. A Java-enabled Web browser takes this class specification and creates an object of that class and then gives it control to display itself and, if applicable, handle user input.

But how? You have not yet completed the dissection of the first example; all you have done so far is to trace the development of `hello.java` into `hello.class`. How did you get the applet to be displayed in the Applet Viewer?

Understanding the Applet's Web Page

The Applet Viewer took the `hello.class` applet and displayed it in a Web page, as shown in Figure 1.4.

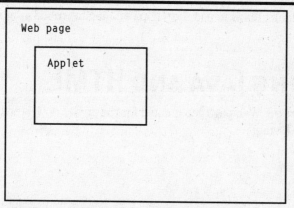

FIGURE 1.4: Displaying an applet in a Web page

How did it get there? You created a Web page for your applet and then opened that Web page in the Applet Viewer, which then displayed your applet. That Web page looks like this:

```
<html>

<!- Web page written for the Sun Applet Viewer>

<head>
```

```
<title>hello</title>
</head>

<body>
<hr>

<applet
code=hello.class
width=200
height=200>

</applet>

<hr>
</body>
</html>
```

Web pages are written in HTML (HyperText Markup Language). Because applets appear in Web pages, we will take the time to briefly work through the above page to make sure you know what's going on. If you're familiar with HTML, you can skip much of this review, but you should take a look at how to use the `<applet>` tag to embed applets in Web pages.

CONNECTING JAVA AND HTML

Let's take apart the Web page you created for the applet now, starting with the `<html>` tag:

```
<html>
  .·
  .
  .
```

Instructions in `.html` pages are placed into tags surrounded by angle brackets: < and >. The tags hold directions to the Web browser and are not displayed on the screen. Here, the `<html>` tag indicates to the Web browser that this `.html` file is written in HTML.

Next comes a comment. Comments in `.html` pages are written using the ! symbol like this: `<! This is a comment.>`. Indicate that this is a Web page written so that we can use the Sun Applet Viewer, like this:

```
<html>

<!- Web page written for the Sun Applet Viewer>
```

Next comes the header portion of the Web page, which you declare with the <head> tag, ending the header section with the corresponding end header tag, </head> (many HTML tags are used in pairs like this, such as <head> and </head>, or <center> and </center> to center text and images). In this case, the .html file gets the title (set up with the <title> tag) *hello*, to match your applet:

```
<html>

<!- Web page written for the Sun Applet Viewer>

<head>
<title>hello</title>
</head>
```

The title is the name given to a Web page, and it's usually displayed in the Web browser's title bar. Next comes the body of the Web page. Here is where all the actual items for display will go. You start the page off with a ruler line (visible in Figure 1.4), using the <hr> tag:

```
<html>

<!- Web page written for the Sun Applet Viewer>

<head>
<title>hello</title>
</head>

<body>
<hr>
```

Now we come to the applet. Applets are embedded with the <applet> tag, and here you use the *code* keyword to indicate that this applet is supported by the hello.class file. You indicate the size of the applet as 200×200 pixels (you can choose any size you like here) this way:

```
<html>

<!- Web page written for the Sun Applet Viewer>
```

```
<head>
<title>hello</title>
</head>

<body>
<hr>
<applet
code=hello.class
width=200
height=200>
</applet>
    .
    .
    .
```

TIP

You can also use the java.applet.Applet.resize() method in your source code to request that the Web browser resize applets.

The <applet> tag is important, so let's take a closer look at it now. Here's how the <applet> tag works in general (the items in square brackets are optional, and the others are required):

```
<APPLET>
  [ALIGN = LEFT or RIGHT or TOP or TEXTTOP or MIDDLE or
     ABSMIDDLE or BASELINE or BOTTOM or ABSBOTTOM]
  [ALT = AlternateText]
  CODE = AppletName.class
  [CODEBASE = URL of .class file]
  HEIGHT = AppletPixelsHeight
  [HSPACE = PixelSpaceToLeftOfApplet]
  [NAME = AppletInstanceName]
  [VSPACE = PixelSpaceAboveApplet]
  WIDTH = AppletPixelsWidth
  >
  [<PARAM NAME = Parameter1 VALUE = VALUE1]
  [<PARAM NAME = Parameter2 VALUE = VALUE2]
    .
    .
    .
</APPLET>
```

TIP

You can specify the URL of the applet's .class file with the CODEBASE keyword. This is often useful if you want to store your applets together in a directory in your ISP, away from the .html files.

Indicate to the Web browser here how much space you'll need for your applet, using the HEIGHT and WIDTH keywords. You can also pass parameters to applets with the PARAM keyword like this: `<applet> PARAM today = "friday" </applet>`. Passing parameters in this way allows you to customize your applets to fit different Web pages because you can read the parameters from inside an applet and make use of them.

TIP

There are enhancements to the `<applet>` tag in Java 2, such as the ability to pass the name of .jar files as parameters. You'll learn more about this later on.

Not all Web browsers support Java. In practice, this means that those browsers just ignore the `<applet>` tag. This, in turn, means that you can place text between the `<applet>` and `</applet>` tags that will be displayed in non-Java browsers (and not in Java-enabled browsers), like this:

```
<applet code=hello>
Your Web browser does not support Java, so you can't see my
applets, sorry!
</applet>
```

Using the `<applet>` tag, you can embed applets in Web pages, as Java has done in this temporary page. Finish off the Web page with the `</body>` and `</html>` tags as follows:

```
<html>

<!- Web page written for the Sun Applet Viewer>

<head>
<title>hello</title>
</head>

<body>
<hr>

<applet
code=hello.class
width=200
```

```
height=200>

</applet>

<hr>
</body>
</html>
```

This completes our first example—you've had a glimpse into the process of creating and running an applet. It was as quick and easy as that—you created and ran your first applet.

WHAT'S NEXT?

In this chapter, the example applet demonstrated the easiest way to get an applet to work. Let's continue on to get a better idea of how you'll be working with Java throughout the book as you give your applet more power in Chapter 2.

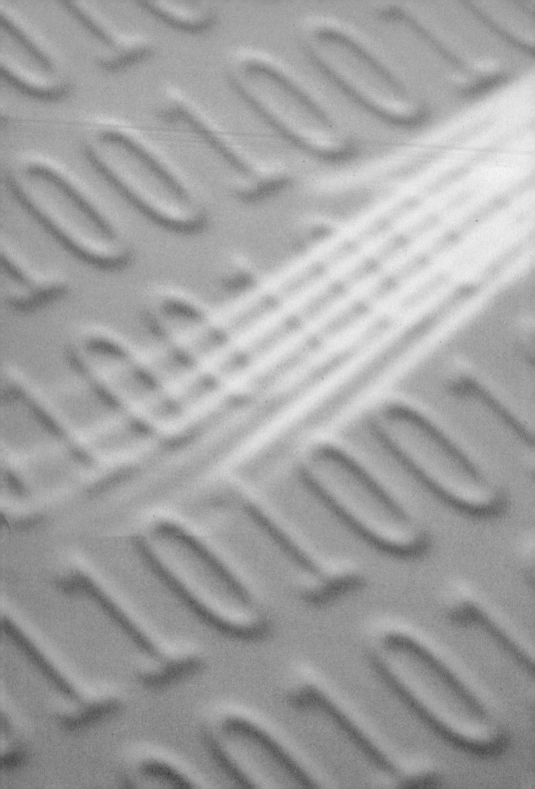

Chapter 2

HANDLING JAVA TEXT FIELDS

I n Chapter 1, you saw the basics of a simple Java applet. In Chapter 2, you're going to add *controls* to programs. Controls are the interactive items you use in applets, like text boxes, buttons, and scrolling list boxes, and they're very powerful parts of Java programs. After exploring text boxes (called *text fields* in Java) in this chapter, we'll see how to integrate them with buttons in Chapter 3. For example, we'll see how to create an applet with a text field and a button marked Click Here, as shown in Figure 2.1. Text fields and buttons are two of the most important and fundamental controls.

Adapted from *Java 2: In Record Time* by Steven Holzner
ISBN 0-7821-2171-3   560 pages $29.99

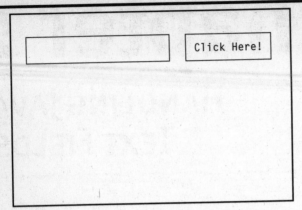

FIGURE 2.1: An applet with a text field and a button

When the user clicks the Click Here button, they will see a new message, "Welcome to Java," in the text field, as shown in Figure 2.2.

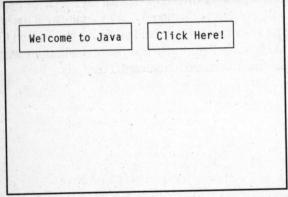

FIGURE 2.2: When the user clicks the Click Here button, a message appears in the text field.

Using controls is a very strong technique in Java—in fact, using controls is often the whole point of an applet.

Declaring a Text Field

In this example, the first control you add to an applet will be the text field. Familiar to all Windows users, a *text field* is just a box that can hold text. (Text fields are also called *text boxes* and *edit controls*.) Your goal might be to place a text field in your applet, as shown in Figure 2.3. You can even start the text field out with the message "Welcome to Java," as shown in Figure 2.4. After this text field appears, the users can edit the text as they like, using the mouse and keyboard.

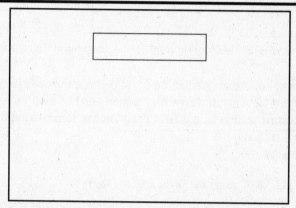

FIGURE 2.3:   An applet with an empty text field

TIP

Sometimes you may not want the user to edit the text you display in a Java program. In that case, you can use the TextField setEditable() method, which allows you to make text fields read-only. In addition, you can use *Label* controls, instead of text fields. Label controls display text that cannot be altered by the user. We'll learn about these controls in Chapter 4.

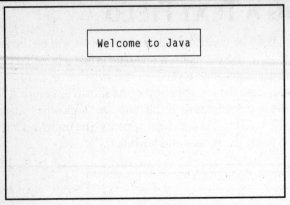

FIGURE 2.4:   The message "Welcome to Java" can be displayed in a text field.

Create a new subdirectory, named `text`, to contain the code for your text field example. Now create a new file, named `text.java`, with your editor. You can start your new text field program the same way you started the `hello.java` file:

```
import java.awt.*;

public class text extends java.applet.Applet
{
    .
    .
    .
}
```

Here, you import all the classes in the Java AWT package with the statement `import java.awt.*`. These are the classes that will let you add text fields and buttons to your applet—for example, two of the classes in this package that you will use are `Button` and `TextField`. In addition, you will declare a new public class named `text` as your applet's main class, based on the `java.applet.Applet` class.

Next, you create your text field. First you have to declare it, setting up an object named, for example, `text1` of the `TextField` class:

```
import java.awt.*;

public class text extends java.applet.Applet
{
    TextField text1;
        .
        .
```

}

The above declares your new text field, named `text1`. The methods of the Java class `TextField`, which is the class you will use for text fields, appear in Table 2.1.

NOTE

Note the distinction between the terms `TextField` and `text1`. `TextField` is a Java class, and `text1` is the object of that class that we will actually work with.

TABLE 2.1: Java `TextField` Class Methods

METHOD	DOES THIS
addActionListener (ActionListener)	Adds `ActionListener` to the text field to receive action events.
addNotify()	Creates the text field's peer.
echoCharIsSet()	Returns true if the text field has echoing.
getColumns()	Returns the number of columns.
getEchoChar()	Returns the echoing character.
getMinimumSize()	Returns minimum dimensions for the text field.
getMinimumSize(int)	Returns minimum dimensions needed for the text field with specified number of columns.
getPreferredSize()	Returns preferred size for the text field.
getPreferredSize(int)	Returns preferred size for the text field with the specified number of columns.
minimumSize()	Deprecated. Replaced by `getMinimumSize()`.
minimumSize(int)	Deprecated. Replaced by `getMinimumSize(int)`.
paramString()	Returns the string of parameters representing the state of the text field.
preferredSize()	Deprecated. Replaced by `getPreferredSize()`.
preferredSize(int)	Deprecated. Replaced by `getPreferredSize(int)`.
processAction-Event(ActionEvent)	Processes action events by dispatching them to `Action-Listener` objects.
processEvent(AWTEvent)	Processes events on the text field.

TABLE 2.1 continued: Java TextField Class Methods

METHOD	DOES THIS
removeActionListener- (ActionListener)	Removes the specified ActionListener Object.
setColumns(int)	Sets number of columns in the text field.
setEchoChar(char)	Sets echo character for the text field.
setEchoCharacter(char)	Deprecated. Replaced by setEchoChar(char).
setText(String)	Sets the text to the specified string.

TIP

Note the getText() and setText() methods in the TextField class; these are the usual ways to get text from a text field or set the text in that text field.

Placing text1 in your applet makes it a *global class variable*. What I mean by global is that it will be available to all the methods (built-in functions) of the text class and to all the code in those methods, because it is declared outside any such method.

As far as variables go, a variable is just a place set aside in memory for data; you will find that variables' numeric data types in Java are just the same as most standard Basic, C, or C++ implementations. For example, to set aside space for integer data, we set up an integer variable of type int:

```
int the_integer;
```

To place values in a variable, just assign them to that variable as follows:

```
the_integer = 5;
```

The built-in Java numeric data types like int and float appear in Table 2.2.

WARNING

It is usually good to restrict the number of global class variables you use to a minimum. Because these variables can be reached anywhere, there is always the possibility of conflict with another variable of the same name in one of your methods. Using too many global variables goes directly against the spirit of object-oriented programming, which was originally developed to handle larger programs by getting variables and methods out of the global space, placing them in objects to clear the global space of clutter.

TABLE 2.2: The Java Numeric Data Types

TYPE	BITS	MEANS
Byte	8	Holds a byte of data
Short	16	Short integer
Int	32	Integer value
Long	64	Long integer
Float	32	Floating point value
Double	64	Double precision floating point value
Char	16	Unicode character
Boolean	—	Takes true or false values

NOTE

You can declare a class's data as private, protected, or public, just as you can for a class's methods.

INITIALIZING WITH THE *INIT()* METHOD

Declaring a text field just sets aside memory for it and does nothing to display it in your applet. You have to handle that yourself in the init() method.

When you want to initialize an applet by adding text fields to it, you do it in the init() method. As you'll see throughout this book, all kinds of initialization can take place in the init() function. It runs automatically when the applet starts, so you should place code that you want run first in the init() function. To use init(), just add it to your class as follows:

```
import java.awt.*;

public class text extends java.applet.Applet
{
  TextField text1;
```

```
            public void init()
            {
                .
                .
                .
            }

        }
```

Note that the `init()` function is like any other function, except that it doesn't return a value (which is why the return type is listed as `void` above) and it runs automatically when the applet starts. Your task in `init()` is to create the new text field and install it in your applet. Creating Java controls is a two-step process: first declare the object as you have done above, and then create the new object in the `init()` function, using the Java new operator.

HANDLING MEMORY WITH THE *NEW* OPERATOR

The Java new operator is just like the C++ new operator; it is used to allocate memory for objects, variables, arrays—for anything you'd like. If you know C, the new operator largely replaces `malloc()`, `calloc()`, and all the memory allocation functions—and it is much easier to work with.

NOTE
While the standard memory-allocating functions like `malloc()` and `calloc()` in C are functions, the new operator is indeed an operator (like +, −, and so on), not a function. This operator is a built-in part of Java and does not come from any class library.

Let's put the new operator to work. Create your new object named `text1` in your applet's `init()` method, using the following syntax:

```
import java.awt.*;

public class text extends java.applet.Applet
{
    TextField text1;

    public void init()
    {
```

```
        text1 = new TextField();
          .
          .
          .

      }


  }
```

This syntax creates a new `TextField` object and places it in the `text1` variable. This is a two-step process that you'll see many times in this book: you first *declare* a control's object and then use the `new` operator to *create* that object in the `init()` method.

The above new line of code creates a new text field, but it's only one character wide. To make the text field, say, 20 characters wide, pass a value of 20 to the `TextField` class's *constructor*.

WHAT ARE JAVA CONSTRUCTORS?

Using constructors is a very popular technique in object-oriented programming; a constructor for a particular class is simply a method that is automatically run when you create an object of that class. Its purpose is to initialize that object as you want it. That is, constructors are used to initialize objects. A class's constructor is called when a new object of that class is being created, and you can set the object up as you like it. Because a constructor is a method, you can pass data to constructors (if they are written to accept such data), allowing you to set up an object as you want when that object is created. In this case, you'll pass a value of 20 to your new text field's constructor. You can do that using the following syntax:

```
import java.awt.*;

public class text extends java.applet.Applet
{
  TextField text1;

  public void init()
  {
    text1 = new TextField(20);
      .
      .
      .

  }
```

This makes your new text field 20 characters wide. If you wanted to set up an initial string in the text field instead of using a set number of characters, you could just pass that string to `TextField`'s constructor as follows:

```
text1 = new TextField("Welcome to Java");
```

OVERLOADING JAVA METHODS

If you are not familiar with C++, this might seem odd—how can you call a function with a numeric value like 20 *or* a string like "Welcome to Java"? The reason is that in Java, as in C++, you can *overload* functions. This means that you can set up a function to be called with different types and numbers of parameters. The Java compiler determines which version of the function to call depending on what parameters—and how many of them—you pass. For that reason, both these lines are valid Java code:

```
text1 = new TextField(20);
text2 = new TextField("Welcome to Java");
```

NOTE

Don't confuse overloading functions with overriding them. Overloading a function means that the function can be called with different parameter lists, while overriding a function redefines the version of the function that appears in the class's base class.

Now that you've created your new text field, the next step is to *add* it to your applet's display. In Chapter 3, I'll show you that Java handles the display (or *layout*) of your controls automatically, although you will take more control of this process as time goes on. To add your text field to your applet's display, use the `add()` method as follows, where you add the new control `text1` to your applet's default layout:

```
import java.awt.*;

public class text extends java.applet.Applet
{
  TextField text1;

  public void init()
  {
      text1 = new TextField(20);
```

```
        add(text1);
            .
            .
            .
    }

}
```

Now your new text field appears in the applet, as shown in Figure 2.5. Figure 2.6 shows the text you'll be adding to the text field.

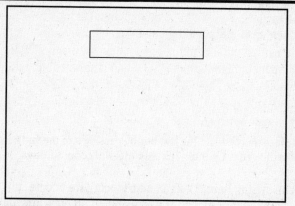

FIGURE 2.5:   Your new text field

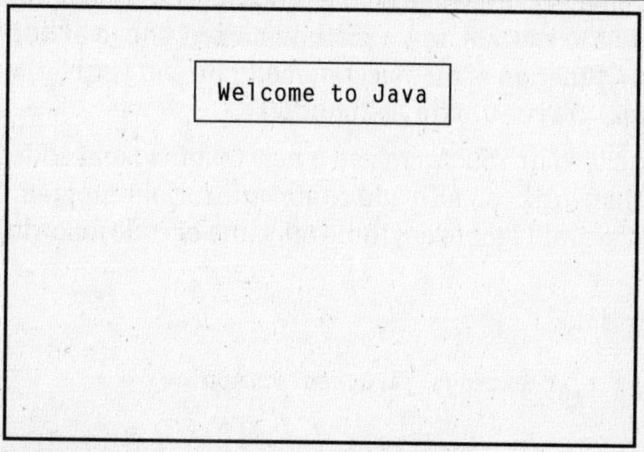

```
                    Welcome to Java
```

FIGURE 2.6:   You want to add the text "Welcome to Java".

Add the text shown in Figure 2.6 to the text field as follows, using the
TextField class's setText() method (see Table 2.1).

```java
import java.awt.*;

public class text extends java.applet.Applet
{
  TextField text1;

  public void init()
  {
    text1 = new TextField(20);
    add(text1);
    text1.setText("Welcome to Java");
  }

}
```

NOTE

You could place this text into the text box by passing it to the text field's constructor, like this: text1 = new TextField("Welcome to Java");.

Note again the syntax here: text1.setText("Welcome to
Java");. This is the standard way of executing an object's internal
method (here, that's the setText() method of the text1 object) with
the dot operator. Again, this is standard C++ terminology, but if you're
not used to it, it might take a while before it becomes second nature. In
general, if you want to execute, say, a method named the_method(),
which is a built-in function of an object named the_object, the correct syntax is: the_object.the_method();.

That's all there is to it! You've created a new text field and added it to
your applet's display. You can also add comments to your program to
make it clearer—Java will ignore anything on a line of code following a //
symbol:

```java
import java.awt.*;

public class text extends java.applet.Applet
{
        //Declare a text field
        TextField text1;
```

```
public void init()
{
    //Create a text field
    text1 = new TextField(20);

    //Add text field to applet
    add(text1);

    //Place text in text
text1.setText("Welcome to Java"); field
    }


}
```

Create the `text.class` file now with javac. You'll need a Web page to display your new class file in the Applet Viewer, so create a new .htm file called `text.htm` now, adding the following HTML code to it:

```
<html>

<!- Web page written for the Sun Applet Viewer>

<head>
<title>text</title>
</head>

<body>
<hr>

<applet
  code=text.class
  width=200
  height=200
>
</applet>

<hr>
</body>
</html>
```

You're ready to run the Applet Viewer with this new Web page. The result appears below—you can see your text field, with your message in it. Your first text field applet is a success. The listing for this applet appears in `text.java`.

LIST 2.1:   text.java

```
import java.awt.*;

public class text extends java.applet.Applet
{
  TextField text1;

  public void init()
  {
      text1 = new TextField(20);
      add(text1);
      text1.setText("Welcome to Java");
  }

}
```

TIP

Java text fields support the standard Windows editing shortcuts like Ctrl+V to paste from the clipboard, Ctrl+X to cut selected text, Ctrl+C to copy selected text, and so on.

WHAT'S NEXT?

Creating and using text fields is a good start. However, it's only a start. Let's turn now to Chapter 3, where we'll work with a new Java control: buttons.

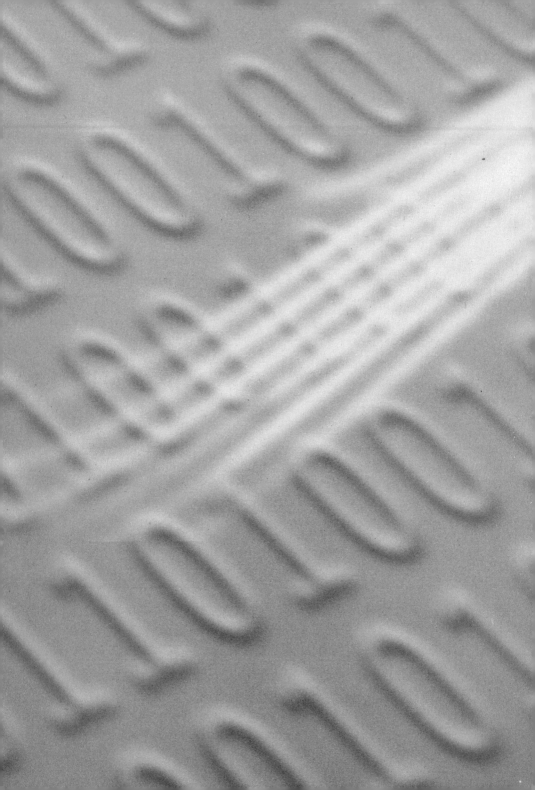

Chapter 3

USING JAVA BUTTONS

In Chapter 2, you got started with Java controls by taking a look at text fields. Here, you're going to flesh out your programs by adding buttons. Every GUI (Graphics User Interface) user is familiar with buttons—you click them to make some action occur. Buttons connect naturally with text fields in Java—when you click a button, you can display something in a text field. These are fundamental GUI controls, so let's start working with buttons now.

Adapted from *Java 2: In Record Time* by Steven Holzner
ISBN 0-7821-2171-3   560 pages $29.99

Working with Buttons in Java

You have already learned a little about handling text fields. Next, you'll see how to have even more control over what happens, by using buttons. For example, you might set up a new applet with a text field and a button that has the caption "Click Here!". (See Figure 3.1.) When the user clicks the button, a message such as "Welcome to Java" might be displayed in your text field, as shown in Figure 3.2.

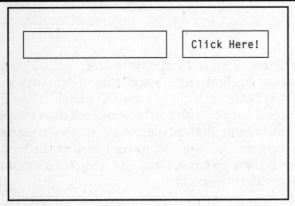

FIGURE 3.1: Using a text field and a button together in an applet

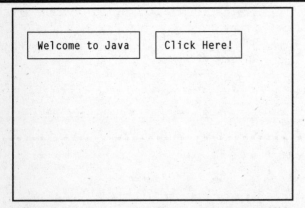

FIGURE 3.2: "Welcome to Java" appears in the text field.

Let's create this example now. Call your new applet *clicker*, create a new file named `clicker.java`, and start with the usual beginning-of-applet code (note that here you import the `java.applet.Applet` class, which means we can then just extend the `Applet` class, without needing to call it by its full name, `java.applet.Applet`):

```
import java.applet.Applet;
import java.awt.*;

public class clicker extends Applet {
  .
  .
  .
}
```

Start by adding the text field for your new applet, which, as before, you can name `text1`. Declare the new control at the beginning of our class's declaration. This is where you will place all your control's declarations, to make them global class variables because you need to reach them from more than one method:

```
import java.applet.Applet;
import java.awt.*;

public class clicker extends Applet {

TextField text1;
  .
  .
  .
```

Next, create the text field with the new operator and add it to your applet's display with the `add()` method, just as you did in the `text` `.java` example in Chapter 2:

```
import java.applet.Applet;
import java.awt.*;

public class clicker extends Applet {

TextField text1;

  public void init(){
    text1 = new TextField(20);
    add(text1);
    .
    .
    .
  }

}
```

Adding a Button to a Program

You've created your text field. Now, add the new button with the caption "Click Here!", as shown in Figure 3.3.

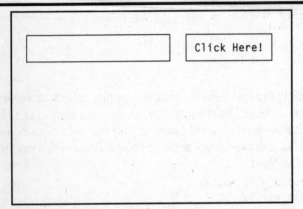

FIGURE 3.3:   Add the Click Here! button to `clicker.java`.

We add a new button with the Java **Button** class, naming our new button object **button1**, and declare it at the beginning of our class, as we do with all controls:

```
import java.applet.Applet;
import java.awt.*;

public class clicker extends Applet {

    TextField text1;
    Button button1;

    public void init(){
        text1 = new TextField(20);
        add(text1);
            .

            .

            .

    }

}
```

The methods of the Java **Button** class appear in Table 3.1.

TABLE 3.1: Java Button Class Methods

METHOD	DOES THIS
Button()	Constructs a button with no label.
Button(String)	Constructs a button with the given label.
addActionListener(ActionListener)	Adds the ActionListener to the button to receive action events.
addNotify()	Creates the button's peer.
getActionCommand()	Returns the command name of the action event fired by a button.
getLabel()	Gets label of a button.
paramString()	Returns parameter string representing the state of the button.
processActionEvent(ActionEvent)	Processes action events occurring by dispatching them to the Action-Listener objects.
processEvent(AWTEvent)	Processes events.
removeActionListener(ActionListener)	Removes the given ActionListener object.
setActionCommand(String)	Sets the command name of the action event fired by the button.
setLabel(String)	Sets the button's label.

TIP

You can set a button's caption on-the-fly with setLabel(), which allows you to change the options you offer to the user as required.

Next, create the button and add it to your applet. Give the button a caption of "Click Here!" by passing that text to the Button class's constructor as follows:

```
import java.applet.Applet;
import java.awt.*;

public class clicker extends Applet {
```

```
TextField text1;
Button button1;

public void init(){
  text1 = new TextField(20);
  add(text1);
  button1 = new Button("Click Here!");
  add(button1);
    .
    .
    .

  }

}
```

Now you have two controls: the text field and the button. The next step is to actually connect the button to the text field in code.

What Are Java Events?

When the user clicks a button, types text, uses the mouse, or performs any other interface-related action in your applet, an interface *event* occurs. If you have programmed in Windows, you probably know about such interface events already. When an event occurs in your applet, such as when the user clicks the mouse, the applet is notified and takes the appropriate action. That's the way programming goes in GUI programs like those written for Windows—the program responds to user events when they happen because the user directs the program flow by manipulating the controls in the applet. In this case, you can find out what events—like mouse movements or button clicks—occur as your applet runs by using the *ActionListener* interface.

If you've programmed in Java 1.0, you were probably expecting us to use an `action()` method here, to handle button clicks, but the `action()` method is now considered *deprecated*—obsolete! This is a fundamental change. The new technique in Java 1.1 and Java 2 is the use of the *delegation-based event model*. To use this technique, we indicate that our applet class will *implement* the ActionListener interface (this is somewhat like saying that we are deriving our applet's class based on ActionListener—You'll learn more about implementing interfaces in Chapter 14, *Threads and Multithreading*).

NOTE

Java does not support multiple inheritance—that is, deriving one class from two others, like the `Applet` class and some hypothetical `ActionListener` class, at the same time. Java declares ActionListener as an interface to let you use the ActionListener methods; this means you can *extend* the `Applet` *class* to create your applet, and *implement* the ActionListener *interface* to use the Action-Listener methods as well. You'll learn more about this later.

Implementing our interface looks like this (note that you also import the `java.awt.event` package that holds the ActionListener interface):

```
import java.applet.Applet;
import java.awt.*;
import java.awt.event.*;

public class clicker extends Applet
  implements ActionListener{

  TextField text1;
  Button button1;

  public void init(){
    text1 = new TextField(20);
    add(text1);
    button1 = new Button("Click Here!");
    add(button1);
    .
    .
    .

  }
}
```

TIP

The class that implements the ActionListener interface does not have to be the applet's main class—you can create an entirely new class to do that. In larger programs it's often a good idea to do so because it helps break up the code. One of the primary differences between Java 1.0 and Java 2 is that in Java 1.0 all the code that handled events had to go into the `action()` method, whereas in Java 2 you can create `Listener` objects to handle events. You can use many `Listener` objects in a Java program to handle a great variety of events.

The delegation-based event model works like this: Events are passed from source controls to `Listener` objects. That means you will connect a

Listener to your button, button1. When an event occurs, the Listener object will "hear" it. In this case, you will make the Listener object the applet object itself by connecting your applet to button1 as a listener; do that with the button's addActionListener() method. But to indicate that you want the applet itself to be the button's listener, you would need to be able to pass the applet itself as an argument to addAction-Listener(). How do you do that?

The *this* Keyword

You do that with the this keyword, which is a keyword that refers to the object you're currently in. This means that you set up your Action-Listener as follows:

```
import java.applet.Applet;
import java.awt.*;
import java.awt.event.*;

public class clicker extends Applet
  implements ActionListener{

  TextField text1;
  Button button1;

  public void init(){
    text1 = new TextField(20);
    add(text1);
    button1 = new Button("Click Here!");
    add(button1);
    button1.addActionListener(this);
  }
}
```

We've set up our ActionListener; now, when there are button events, they will be sent to our applet. But how do we make use of the button events?

Using Button Events

Catch the events sent to you by overriding the ActionListener interface's actionPerformed() method and adding your own version, which looks like this:

```
import java.applet.Applet;
import java.awt.*;
```

```
import java.awt.event.*;

public class clicker extends Applet
  implements ActionListener {

  TextField text1;
  Button button1;

  public void init(){
    text1 = new TextField(20);
    add(text1);
    button1 = new Button("Click Here!");
    add(button1);
    button1.addActionListener(this);
  }

  public void actionPerformed(ActionEvent event){
       .
       .
       .
  }
}
```

This is the method that will be called when the user clicks your button. The ActionEvent object that is passed to you here holds information about the event that occurred. But if you have a number of buttons, clicking any one will call this method—how do you make sure that your button, button1, was clicked?

You can check which button was clicked with the ActionEvent class's getSource() method. This method returns the control that caused the event, and you can check to see if that control is button1:

```
import java.applet.Applet;
import java.awt.*;
import java.awt.event.*;

public class clicker extends Applet
  implements ActionListener {

  TextField text1;
  Button button1;

  public void init(){
    text1 = new TextField(20);
    add(text1);
    button1 = new Button("Click Here!");
```

```
        add(button1);
        button1.addActionListener(this);
    }

    public void actionPerformed(ActionEvent event){
        if(event.getSource() == button1){
            .
            .
            .

        }
    }
}
```

If the control that created the Java event is button1, the code you place in the code block—the code surrounded by the { and } braces following the if statement—will be executed. That's because you use the Java *equality* operator (==) to compare the control returned by event .getSource() and button1.

NOTE

In Java, if statements work the same way they do in just about any other programming language: if the expression in the parentheses of the if statement is true, the code in the code block is executed.

```
    if(conditional){
    [code block]
    }
```

If button1 was indeed clicked, you want to display your message "Welcome to Java," and you do that by first setting up a Java String object named msg (which, since we define it in actionPerformed(), will only be available in that procedure, making it a *local* variable), holding that text, and then displaying that string in the text field using the TextField's setText() method:

```
    import java.applet.Applet;
    import java.awt.*;
    import java.awt.event.*;

    public class clicker extends Applet
        implements ActionListener {

        TextField text1;
        Button button1;
```

```
public void init(){
  text1 = new TextField(20);
  add(text1);
  button1 = new Button("Click Here!");
  add(button1);
  button1.addActionListener(this);
}

public void actionPerformed(ActionEvent event){
  String msg = new String ("Welcome to Java");
  if(event.getSource() == button1){
    text1.setText(msg);
  }
}
}
```

You might also note here that we combined the two usual steps—declaring and creating an object—into one line with the msg variable.

The String class is a super-handy Java class that handles text strings for you. The methods of this class appear in Table 3.2, and it's worth taking a look at that table to see what's available.

TABLE 3.2: The Java String Class Methods

METHOD	DOES THIS
String()	Constructs new string.
String(byte[])	Constructs new string by converting the array of bytes into the string using the platform's default character encoding.
String(byte[], int)	Deprecated. Constructs new string from given array of bytes.
String(byte[], int, int)	Constructs new string by converting the subarray using platform's default character-encoding converter.
String(byte[], int, int, int)	Deprecated. Constructs new string from given subarray of bytes.
String(byte[], int, int, String)	Constructs new string by converting the specified subarray of bytes using the specified character encoding.
String(byte[], String)	Constructs new string by converting the specified array of bytes using the specified character encoding.
String(char[])	Constructs new string from given array of characters.
String(char[], int, int)	Constructs new string from given subarray of characters.
String(String)	Constructs new string by copying the given string.

TABLE 3.2 continued: The Java String Class Methods

METHOD	DOES THIS
String(StringBuffer)	Constructs new string from contents of given string buffer.
charAt(int)	Returns character at the given index.
compareTo(Object)	Compares this string to another object.
compareTo(String)	Compares this string to another string.
compareToIgnoreCase (String)	Compares two strings lexicographically, ignoring case considerations.
concat(String)	Concatenates given string to the end of this string.
copyValueOf(char[])	Returns a string that is equivalent to the given character array.
copyValueOf(char[], int, int)	Returns a string that is equivalent to the specified character array.
endsWith(String)	Determines if the string ends with the given suffix.
equals(Object)	Compares the string to the given object.
equalsIgnoreCase(String)	Compares this string to another object, ignoring case considerations.
getBytes()	Applies the character-encoding converter to string, storing result in a byte array.
getBytes(int, int, byte[], int)	Deprecated. Copies characters from this string into the specified byte array.
getBytes(String)	Converts this string into bytes according to the specified character encoding, storing the result into a new byte array.
getChars(int, int, char[], int)	Copies characters from this string into the specified character array.
hashCode()	Returns a hashcode for the string.
indexOf(int)	Returns index in the string of first occurrence of the given character.
indexOf(int, int)	Returns index in the string of first occurrence of the given character, starting at from Index.
indexOf(String)	Returns index in the string of first occurrence of given substring.
indexOf(String, int)	Returns index in the string of first occurrence of given substring.

TABLE 3.2 continued: The Java String Class Methods

METHOD	DOES THIS
intern()	Returns a string that is equal to this string but that is guaranteed to be from the unique string pool. Returns a canonical representation for the String object.
lastIndexOf(int)	Returns index in the string of last occurrence of given character.
lastIndexOf(int, int)	Returns index in the string of last occurrence of given character, searching backward starting at the given index.
lastIndexOf(String)	Returns index within the string of rightmost occurrence of given substring.
lastIndexOf(String, int)	Returns index in the string of last occurrence of given substring.
length()	Returns length of this string.
regionMatches(boolean, int, String, int, int)	Tests if two string regions are equal.
regionMatches(int, String, int, int)	Determines if a region of the string matches given region of given string.
replace(char, char)	Converts this string by replacing all occurrences of old-Char with newChar.
startsWith(String)	Determines if this string starts with some prefix.
startsWith(String, int)	Determines if this string starts with some prefix beginning a specified index.
substring(int)	Returns substring of a string.
substring(int, int)	Returns substring of a string.
toCharArray()	Converts this string to a new character array.
toLowerCase()	Converts characters in this string to lowercase using the rules of the default locale.
toLowerCase(Locale)	Converts all of the characters in this string to lowercase using the rules of the given locale.
toString()	Converts the object (in this case already a string) to a string.
toUpperCase()	Converts all of the characters in this string to uppercase using the rules of the default locale.

Part i

TABLE 3.2 continued: The Java String Class Methods

Method	Does This
toUpperCase(Locale)	Converts all of the characters in this string to uppercase using the rules of the given locale.
trim()	Trims leading and trailing white space from this string.
valueOf(boolean)	Returns a String object that represents the state of the given boolean.
valueOf(char)	Returns a String object that contains a single character.
valueOf(char[])	Returns a string that is equivalent to the given character array.
valueOf(char[], int, int)	Returns a string that is equivalent to the given character array.
valueOf(double)	Returns a string that represents the value of the double.
valueOf(float)	Returns a string that represents the value of the float.
valueOf(int)	Returns a string that represents the value of the integer.
valueOf(long)	Returns a string that represents the value of the long.
valueOf(Object)	Returns the string representation of the Object argument.

TIP

The String class's methods now make use of the Java 1.1 Internationalization techniques, like using character-encoding converters and being locale-aware. Using the Java Locale class, you can set the formation of Strings with constants like Locale.FRENCH, Locale.GERMAN, and so on.

Your new applet is complete. Compile it now and run it. (Don't forget that you will need to create a clicker.htm file to be able to run your applet.) Click the button and watch the "Welcome to Java" message appear in the text field as shown below. The code for this applet appears in clicker.java and clicker.html.

LIST 3.1: *clicker.java*

```java
import java.applet.Applet;
import java.awt.*;
import java.awt.event.*;

public class clicker extends Applet
  implements ActionListener {

  TextField text1;
  Button button1;

  public void init(){
    text1 = new TextField(20);
    add(text1);
    button1 = new Button("Click Here!");
    add(button1);
    button1.addActionListener(this);
  }

  public void actionPerformed(ActionEvent event){
    String msg = new String ("Welcome to Java");
    if(event.getSource() == button1){
      text1.setText(msg);
    }
  }
}
```

LIST 3.2: clicker.html

```
<HTML>
<HEAD>
  <TITLE>Clicker Applet </TITLE>
</HEAD>
<BODY>
  <HR>
  <APPLET code=clicker.class width=200 height=200> </APPLET>
</BODY>
</HTML>
```

So far, you've seen how to add both a text field and a button to your applet. Now let's turn to the next case—multiple buttons.

HOW TO HANDLE MULTIPLE BUTTONS

Say you want to set up a new applet that has two buttons, labeled "Welcome to" and "Java," along with a text box, as shown in Figure 3.4. When the user clicks the Welcome To button, "Welcome to" is displayed in the text box, as shown in Figure 3.5. When they click the Java button, "Java" is displayed in the text box, as shown in Figure 3.6.

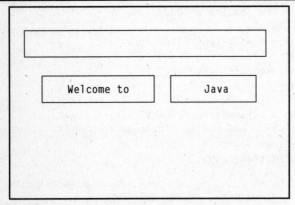

FIGURE 3.4: An applet with a text box and two buttons

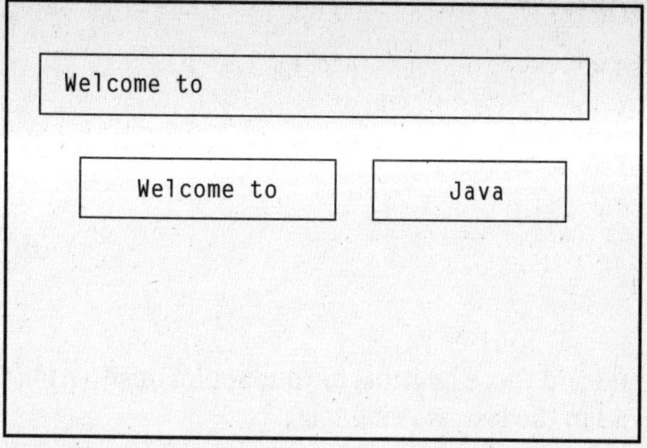

FIGURE 3.5: Click the Welcome To button and "Welcome to" appears in the text box.

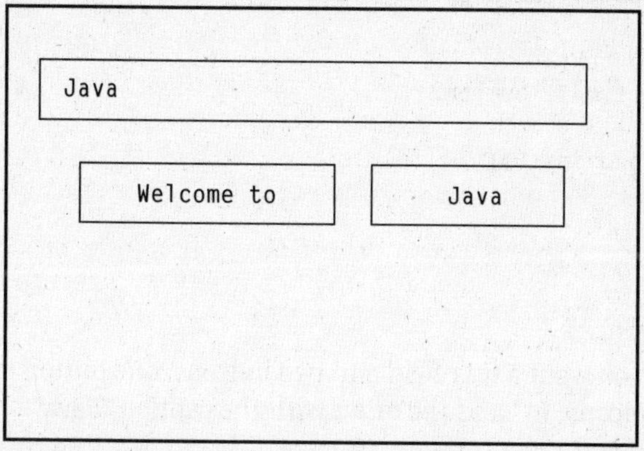

FIGURE 3.6: Click the Java button and "Java" appears in the text box.

Creating *clickers.java*

This exercise will show you how to keep buttons separate and teach you a new and faster method for determining which button was clicked. Let's put this together now. Create a new file called clickers.java. You'll need two buttons, button1 and button2, and a text field, text1. Add those to the beginning of your class definition as follows:

```
import java.applet.Applet;
import java.awt.*;
```

```
import java.awt.event.*;

public class clickers extends Applet {

    TextField text1;
    Button button1, button2;
        .
        .
        .

}
```

Next, create and add those controls to your applet in an init() method, as you did in the last two examples:

```
import java.applet.Applet;
import java.awt.*;
import java.awt.event.*;

public class clickers extends Applet {

    TextField text1;
    Button button1, button2;

    public void init(){
        .
        .
        .

    }
}
```

In this case, you want a text field and two buttons, one button with the caption "Welcome to" and the other with the caption "Java":

```
import java.applet.Applet;
import java.awt.*;
import java.awt.event.*;

public class clickers extends Applet {

    TextField text1;
    Button button1, button2;

    public void init(){
        text1 = new TextField(20);
        add(text1);
        button1 = new Button("Welcome to");
        add(button1);
        button2 = new Button("Java");
```

```
    add(button2);
  }
}
```

At this point, you've added all the controls you'll need to your applet, as shown in Figure 3.7.

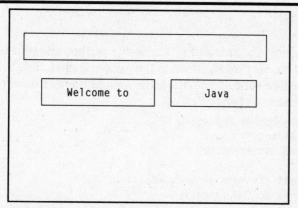

FIGURE 3.7: Your applet contains three controls: two buttons and a text field.

Making *clickers.java* Work

Now it's time to get the controls working. As before, do that by adding the `actionPerformed()` method to our class, along with the keywords `implements ActionListener`:

```
import java.applet.Applet;
import java.awt.*;
import java.awt.event.*;

public class clickers extends Applet
  implements ActionListener{

  TextField text1;
  Button button1, button2;

  public void init(){
    text1 = new TextField(20);
    add(text1);
    button1 = new Button("Welcome to");
    add(button1);
    button2 = new Button("Java");
```

```
        add(button2);
    }

    public void actionPerformed(ActionEvent e){
            .
            .
            .
    }
}
```

As well as adding the `actionPerformed()` method and your keywords, you will connect your buttons to the ActionListener. Note that both buttons will be connected to the same ActionListener this way, as we use `addActionListener()`:

```
import java.applet.Applet;
import java.awt.*;
import java.awt.event.*;

public class clickers extends Applet
    implements ActionListener{

    TextField text1;
    Button button1, button2;

    public void init(){
        text1 = new TextField(20);
        add(text1);
        button1 = new Button("Welcome to");
        add(button1);
        button1.addActionListener(this);
        button2 = new Button("Java");
        add(button2);
        button2.addActionListener(this);
    }

    public void actionPerformed(ActionEvent e){
            .
            .
            .
    }
}
```

Now your buttons are connected to the `actionPerformed()` method. The next step is to determine which button caused the click event that called `actionPerformed()`, and you can do that with the

Part i

ActionEvent class's getSource() method. Here, the two buttons are button1 and button2. Check to see which one was clicked as follows:

```java
import java.applet.Applet;
import java.awt.*;
import java.awt.event.*;

public class clickers extends Applet
  implements ActionListener {

  TextField text1;
  Button button1, button2;

  public void init(){
    text1 = new TextField(20);
    add(text1);
    button1 = new Button("Welcome to");
    add(button1);
    button1.addActionListener(this);
    button2 = new Button("Java");
    add(button2);
    button2.addActionListener(this);
  }

  public void actionPerformed(ActionEvent e){
    if(e.getSource() == button1){
         .
         .
         .
    }
    if(e.getSource() == button2){
         .
         .
         .
    }
  }
}
```

In the case where button1 was clicked, place the text "Welcome to" in the text field text1 like this:

```java
import java.applet.Applet;
import java.awt.*;
import java.awt.event.*;

public class clickers extends Applet
  implements ActionListener {
```

```
     TextField text1;
     Button button1, button2;

  public void init(){
     text1 = new TextField(20);
     add(text1);
     button1 = new Button("Welcome to");
     add(button1);
     button1.addActionListener(this);
     button2 = new Button("Java");
     add(button2);
     button2.addActionListener(this);
  }

  public void actionPerformed(ActionEvent e){
     if(e.getSource() == button1){
       text1.setText("Welcome to");
     }
     if(e.getSource() == button2){
          .

          .

          .
     }
   }
 }
```

We can do the same for **button2**, which places the text "Java" in **text1**, as follows:

```
import java.applet.Applet;
import java.awt.*;
import java.awt.event.*;

public class clickers extends Applet
  implements ActionListener {

  TextField text1;
  Button button1, button2;

  public void init(){
     text1 = new TextField(20);
     add(text1);
     button1 = new Button("Welcome to");
     add(button1);
     button1.addActionListener(this);
     button2 = new Button("Java");
```

```
        add(button2);
        button2.addActionListener(this);
    }

    public void actionPerformed(ActionEvent e){
        if(e.getSource() == button1){
            text1.setText("Welcome to");
        }
        if(e.getSource() == button2){
            text1.setText("Java");
        }
    }
}
```

Your applet is complete. Build that applet now and execute it, as shown below. As you designed it, when the user clicks the Welcome To button, "Welcome to" appears in the text field; when they click the Java button, "Java" appears in the text field. Your applet is working. The listing for this applet appears in `clickers.java` and `clickers.html`.

LIST 3.3: *clickers.java*

```
import java.applet.Applet;
import java.awt.*;
import java.awt.event.*;

public class clickers extends Applet
    implements ActionListener {

    TextField text1;
    Button button1, button2;

    public void init(){
```

```
        text1 = new TextField(20);
        add(text1);
        button1 = new Button("Welcome to");
        add(button1);
        button1.addActionListener(this);
        button2 = new Button("Java");
        add(button2);
        button2.addActionListener(this);
    }

    public void actionPerformed(ActionEvent e){
        if(e.getSource() == button1){
            text1.setText("Welcome to");
        }
        if(e.getSource() == button2){
            text1.setText("Java");
        }
    }
}
```

LIST 3.4: clickers.html

```
<HTML>
<HEAD>
  <TITLE>Clickers Applet</TITLE>
</HEAD>
<BODY>
  <APPLET code=clickers.class width=200 height=200> </APPLET>
</BODY>
</HTML>
```

While we're working on text fields and buttons, let's take a look at the multi-line text field called a *text area*. Java uses a text area to support text that takes up more than one line.

HANDLING JAVA TEXT AREAS

A text area works in almost the same way that a text field does, but it can have several lines, as shown in Figure 3.8.

This is the control to use when you have multiple lines of text to display (such as a set of instructions), or when you let the user edit a large amount of text. Text fields can do the same job, but for large amounts of text—especially text that has carriage returns or paragraphs—text areas are the way to go.

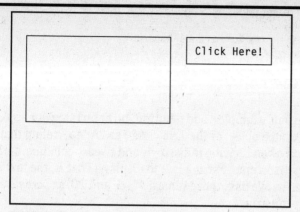

FIGURE 3.8:   An empty text area

Creating *txtarea.java*

Let's put together an example applet using a text area. When the user clicks a button labeled "Click Here," you can place a message saying: "Welcome to Java" in the text area, as shown in Figure 3.9.

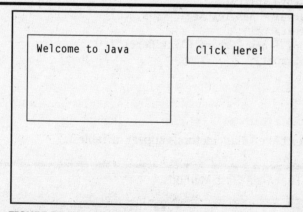

FIGURE 3.9:   When the user clicks the button, "Welcome to Java" appears in the text area.

You handle a text area much as you would handle a text field. Let's see one in action. Create a new file named `txtarea.java`. Open that file and add the usual starting code:

```
import java.applet.Applet;
import java.awt.*;
```

```
import java.awt.event.*;

public class txtarea extends Applet {
    .
    .
    .
}
```

As with previous examples, add a button, button1, to your applet. Next, add a text area object of the Java class TextArea, calling that object, say, textarea1, giving it five rows and twenty columns, and starting it off with an empty string, " ", to display. (That is, the text area will appear blank.) We pass those values, " ", 5, and 20, as *parameters* to the TextArea constructor:

```
import java.applet.Applet;
import java.awt.*;
import java.awt.event.*;

public class txtarea extends Applet {

    TextArea textarea1;
    Button button1;

    public void init(){
        textarea1 = new TextArea("", 5, 20);
        add(textarea1);
        button1 = new Button("Click Here!");
        add(button1);
        .
        .
        .
    }
}
```

The Java TextArea class methods appear in Table 3.3.

TABLE 3.3: TextArea Class Methods

Method	Does This
TextArea()	Constructs a new text area.
TextArea(int, int)	Constructs a new empty text area with the specified number of rows and columns.
TextArea(String)	Constructs a new text area with the specified text.
TextArea(String, int, int)	Constructs a new text area with given text and number of rows and columns.

TABLE 3.3 continued: TextArea Class Methods

METHOD	DOES THIS
TextArea(String, int, int, int)	Constructs a new text area with given text and number of rows, columns, and scrollbar "visibility."
addNotify()	Creates the text area's peer.
append(String)	Appends given text to end of the text area's current text.
appendText(String)	Deprecated. Replaced by append(String).
getColumns()	Returns number of columns in the text area.
getMinimumSize()	Returns minimum size of the text area.
getMinimumSize(int, int)	Returns the minimum dimensions of the text area with the specified number of rows and columns.
getPreferredSize()	Returns the preferred dimensions of the text area.
getPreferredSize(int, int)	Returns the preferred dimensions of the text area with the specified number of rows and columns.
getRows()	Returns the number of rows in the text area.
getScrollbarVisibility()	Returns enumerated value describing which scrollbars the text area uses.
insert(String, int)	Inserts the given text at the given position.
insertText(String, int)	Deprecated. Replaced by insert(String, int).
minimumSize()	Deprecated. Replaced by getMinimumSize().
minimumSize(int, int)	Deprecated. Replaced by getMinimumSize (int, int).
paramString()	Returns the string of parameters for this text area.
preferredSize()	Deprecated. Replaced by getPreferredSize().
preferredSize(int, int)	Deprecated. Replaced by getPreferredSize(int, int).
replaceRange(String, int, int)	Replaces text from the indicated start to end position with the new text given.
replaceText(String, int, int)	Deprecated. Replaced by replaceRange(String, int, int).
setColumns(int)	Sets the number of columns for this text area.
setRows(int)	Sets the number of rows for this text area.

Making *txtarea.java* Work

Now add the keywords `implements ActionListener` and make the applet's main class a listener for the Click Here! button:

```java
import java.applet.Applet;
import java.awt.*;
import java.awt.event.*;

public class txtarea extends Applet
  implements ActionListener{

  TextArea textarea1;
  Button button1;

  public void init(){
    textarea1 = new TextArea("", 5, 20);
    add(textarea1);
    button1 = new Button("Click Here!");
    add(button1);
    button1.addActionListener(this);
  }
}
```

In addition, you'll need an `actionPerformed()` method to catch button clicks:

```java
import java.awt.*;
import java.awt.event.*;

public class txtarea extends Applet
  implements ActionListener {

  TextArea textarea1;
  Button button1;

  public void init(){
    textarea1 = new TextArea("", 5, 20);
    add(textarea1);
    button1 = new Button("Click Here!");
    add(button1);
    button1.addActionListener(this);
  }

  public void actionPerformed (ActionEvent e){
```

```
    }
  }
```

When the button is clicked, the program can place your "Welcome to Java" text into the text area. Instead of using setText() to set the text of your text area as you did for text fields, you will use the TextArea class's insert() method.

TIP

The insert() method, which lets you insert text at a specific location, is unique to text areas—text fields do not have this method. With insert(), you treat all the text in the text area as one long string, each character counting as one place, and you indicate the position at which you want to insert your new text by passing that location as an integer to insert().

You can insert your text at a specified position in the text area. In this case, place the "Welcome to Java" message at the beginning of the text area so you pass a location of 0. We create a new String object named msg and then display that string using insert() to place it into the text area:

```
import java.applet.Applet;
import java.awt.*;
import java.awt.event.*;

public class txtarea extends Applet
  implements ActionListener {

  TextArea textarea1;
  Button button1;

  public void init(){
    textarea1 = new TextArea("", 5, 20);
    add(textarea1);
    button1 = new Button("Click Here!");
    add(button1);
    button1.addActionListener(this);
  }

  public void actionPerformed (ActionEvent e){
    String msg = "Welcome to Java";
      if(e.getSource() == button1){
        textarea1.insert(msg, 0);
      }
```

```
    }
  }
```

Run the new applet, as shown below. As you can see, your new text area is working. Now you're able to support not only buttons and text fields, but text areas as well. If the user were to edit the text in the text area, they'd find out that it supports multiple lines and that they can use the Enter key as they type. The listing for this applet appears in `txtarea.java` and `textarea.html`.

LIST 3.5: txtarea.java

```java
import java.applet.Applet;
import java.awt.*;
import java.awt.event.*;

public class txtarea extends Applet
  implements ActionListener {

  TextArea textarea1;
  Button button1;

  public void init(){
    textarea1 = new TextArea("", 5, 20);
    add(textarea1);
    button1 = new Button("Click Here!");
    add(button1);
    button1.addActionListener(this);
  }

  public void actionPerformed (ActionEvent e){
    String msg = "Welcome to Java";
    if(e.getSource() == button1){
```

```
            textarea1.insert(msg, 0);
        }
    }
}
```

LIST 3.6: *txtarea.html*
```
<HTML>
<HEAD>
  <TITLE>Text Area Applet</TITLE>
</HEAD>
<BODY>
  <APPLET code=txtarea.class width=200 height=200> </APPLET>
</BODY>
</HTML>
```

WHAT'S NEXT?

This completes our guided tour of buttons and text fields. You've learned how to add controls to your programs and use text boxes, buttons, and text areas. Let's turn now to Chapter 4, in which you will start working with a new Java control: check boxes.

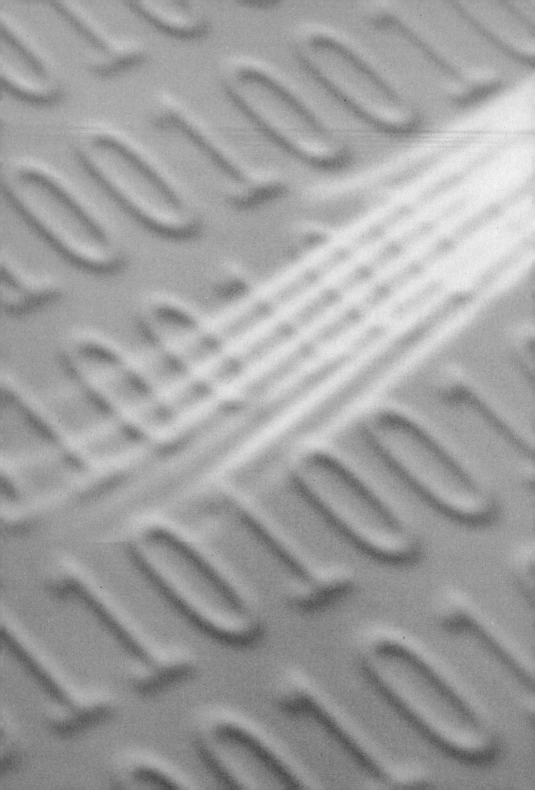

Chapter 4

USING JAVA LAYOUTS AND CHECK BOXES

You've already come far: you've worked with text fields, text areas, and buttons. However, there are many more powerful Java controls, and one of those is the check box. In this skill, we're going to take a look at check boxes. This new control is important by itself, but you'll also learn more about coordinating controls (handling and arranging a number of controls together) in a Java program. You'll need to learn more about coordinating controls because controls like check boxes and radio buttons are meant to be handled in *groups*. You often use check boxes to choose one or more selections among a group of selections, and radio buttons are even more group-oriented—they are used to allow the user to select one option among many.

Java 2

In Record Time

Adapted from *Java 2: In Record Time* by Steven Holzner
ISBN 0-7821-2171-3   560 pages $29.99

What Is a Java Layout?

In Chapters 1 through 3, you did not perform any special placement of text fields and buttons in your applets—Java handled the placement of controls for you. That is both good and bad—it's good if things work out the way you want them, but bad otherwise.

You have been using Java's default *layout manager*, the FlowLayout manager. Layout managers control the placement of controls in an applet. You can select which layout manager to use, and that's a good thing because often the default layout manager will not arrange your controls the way you want them.

Let's take a look at an example. In this case, you want to build a small adding calculator applet. All you'll do is take two integers from the user, add them together, and display the result. This applet will require you to handle both text and numeric input, as well as layout managers. Let's get started now.

Building the Adder Applet

Your goal is simply to create a Java applet that acts as an adding calculator. You can make this calculator up of text fields and buttons: one text field for the first number, one for the second, a button for the equals sign, and another text field for the answer. To add 2 + 2, the user will enter that data into the first two text fields, as shown in Figure 4.1. Then, when they click the button whose caption is "=", they will see the result in the bottom text field, as shown in Figure 4.2.

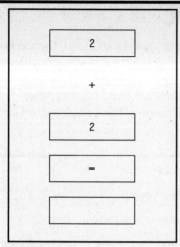

FIGURE 4.1:   The user enters data into the first two text fields of our applet.

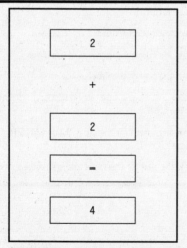

FIGURE 4.2:   When the user clicks the = button, the sum of the first two text fields appears in the third text field.

THE *LABEL* CONTROL

You may wonder at first how to place a plus sign between the top two text boxes, and may assume that you should use the drawString() method as you did in Chapter 1. In fact, you'll place the plus sign in a new type of control: a Label control. This control is a control like any other—it displays text and nothing more. The methods of the Label control appear in Table 4.1.

TABLE 4.1: The Label Class Methods

METHOD	DOES THIS
Label()	Constructs an empty label.
Label(String)	Constructs a label with the specified string of text that is left-justified.
Label(String, int)	Constructs a label with the specified string of text and alignment (Label.RIGHT, Label.CENTER, or Label.LEFT).
addNotify()	Creates the label's peer.
getAlignment()	Gets the current alignment of the label.
getText()	Gets the text of the label.
paramString()	Returns the parameter string representing the state of the label.
setAlignment(int)	Sets alignment for the label (Label.RIGHT, Label.CENTER, or Label.LEFT).
setText(String)	Sets the text for this label to the specified string.

TIP

Note that you can set the text of a Label control with the setText() method just as you can in a text field. You can also align the text in the label to the right, left, or center by passing one of the Label class's pre-defined constants to the constructor or the setAlignment() method: Label.RIGHT, Label.LEFT, or Label.CENTER.

Let's start this project. Create a new file named `adder.java` and add the usual starting code, including a new class named `adder`:

```
import java.applet.Applet;
import java.awt.*;
import java.awt.event.*;

public class adder extends Applet {

}
```

First, add all the controls you'll need, including the new label, `plus-label`, like this:

```
import java.applet.Applet;
import java.awt.*;
import java.awt.event.*;

public class adder extends Applet {

  TextField text1, text2, answertext;
  Label pluslabel;
  Button button1;
      .
      .
      .


}
```

Next, you have to initialize these controls in the `init()` method, so add that method now:

```
import java.applet.Applet;
import java.awt.*;
import java.awt.event.*;

public class adder extends Applet {

  TextField text1, text2, answertext;
  Label pluslabel;
  Button button1;

  public void init(){
      .
      .
      .
  }
```

```
        }
```

Your first job is to add the top text field, `text1`. You do so in the `init()` method as follows:

```
import java.applet.Applet;
import java.awt.*;
import java.awt.event.*;

public class adder extends Applet {

  TextField text1, text2, answertext;
  Label pluslabel;
  Button button1;

  public void init(){

    text1 = new TextField(10);
    add(text1);
        .
        .
        .

  }

}
```

NOTE
When you use the add() method, you are adding controls to your applet using the default layout manager, which is called the *FlowLayout* manager.

You've added the first text field. Next, you can add the plus sign that is supposed to appear between the top two text fields.

Adding a Java *Label* Control

You've already declared the `Label` control that will display your plus sign as an object of the Java class `Label`, and called it `pluslabel`:

```
import java.applet.Applet;
import java.awt.*;
import java.awt.event.*;

public class adder extends Applet implements ActionListener {

  TextField text1, text2, answertext;
  Label pluslabel;
```

```
        Button button1;
           .
           .
           .
```

Now, in the `init()` method, you can create this label object and add it to your applet's layout. Do so as follows:

```
import java.applet.Applet;
import java.awt.*;
import java.awt.event.*;

public class adder extends Applet {

  TextField text1, text2, answertext;
  Label pluslabel;
  Button button1;

  public void init(){

    text1 = new TextField(10);
    add(text1);

    pluslabel = new Label("+");
    add(pluslabel);
       .
       .
       .

}
```

`Label` controls are very useful, as their name indicates, when you want to label anything, including other controls. They present you with an easy way to display text without having to worry about redrawing that text when the applet is uncovered or redisplayed.

Now add the other controls: the second text field, the equals button, and the answer text field. In `init()`, add the controls as follows:

```
import java.applet.Applet;
import java.awt.*;
import java.awt.event.*;

public class adder extends Applet {

  TextField text1, text2, answertext;
  Label pluslabel;
  Button button1;

  public void init(){
```

```
            text1 = new TextField(10);
            add(text1);

            pluslabel = new Label("+");
            add(pluslabel);

            text2 = new TextField(10);
            add(text2);

            button1 = new Button("=");
            add(button1);

            answertext = new TextField(10);
            add(answertext);
        }
    }
```

At this point, then, you've added all the controls we'll need. The next step is to connect the controls to our code and make your adding calculator work.

Writing the Adder Applet

You make your calculator work by responding to the user when they click the = button. To do that, implement the ActionListener interface, connect your button to it, and add the `actionPerformed()` method to your applet:

```
import java.applet.Applet;
import java.awt.*;
import java.awt.event.*;

public class adder extends Applet implements ActionListener {

    TextField text1, text2, answertext;
    Label pluslabel;
    Button button1;

    public void init(){

        text1 = new TextField(10);
        add(text1);

        pluslabel = new Label("+");
        add(pluslabel);
```

```
            text2 = new TextField(10);
            add(text2);

            button1 = new Button("=");
            add(button1);
            button1.addActionListener(this);

            answertext = new TextField(10);
            add(answertext);

        }

        public void actionPerformed(ActionEvent e) {
                 .
                 .
                 .
        }

    }
```

When the user clicks the = button, you want the program to read the two integers in the top two text fields, add them, and display the result in the bottom text field (the answertext text field). Start in the action-Performed() method by making sure that the = button (button1) was the button that was clicked:

```
    import java.applet.Applet;
    import java.awt.*;
    import java.awt.event.*;

    public class adder extends Applet implements ActionListener {

        TextField text1, text2, answertext;
        Label pluslabel;
        Button button1;

        public void init(){

            text1 = new TextField(10);
            add(text1);

            pluslabel = new Label("+");
            add(pluslabel);

            text2 = new TextField(10);
            add(text2);
```

```
            button1 = new Button("=");
            add(button1);
            button1.addActionListener(this);

            answertext = new TextField(10);
            add(answertext);

        }

        public void actionPerformed(ActionEvent e) {
          if(e.getSource() == button1){
                  .
                  .
                  .

          }
        }

      }
```

When the = button is clicked, the program should go on to read the integers the user placed in the top two text fields, text1 and text2. How do you do that?

Reading Numeric Data from Text Fields

You saw in Chapter 3 that you can place text in a text field with the set-Text() method. To read text, it turns out you can use the text field's getText() method like this: text1.getText(). This syntax returns the string of text in the text field text1. For example, if the user has placed "2" in text1, you get "2" back—but that is a text string, and *not* a numeric value. How do you convert the string "2" to the actual number 2? You do that with the Java Integer class.

The Java Integer class has a method called parseInt() that takes text and returns an integer value. For example, you can get the text in the text field text1 this way:

```
    text1.getText()
```
And you can convert that text to an integer value this way:

```
    Integer.parseInt(text1.getText())
```

TIP

Besides the parseInt() method, Java also has a parseLong() method, and a parseNumbers() method for floating-point values. You can do other things with classes like Integer too—if you want to check the maximum or minimum possible values an integer can hold, just look at that class's constants named MAX_VALUE or MIN_VALUE like this: int big_number = Integer.MAX_VALUE;.

In your applet, this means that you can now take the integer in `text1`, add it to the integer in `text2`, and store the result in a new integer called `sum` as follows:

```java
import java.applet.Applet;
import java.awt.*;
import java.awt.event.*;

public class adder extends Applet implements ActionListener {

    TextField text1, text2, answertext;
    Label pluslabel;
    Button button1;

    public void init(){

        text1 = new TextField(10);
        add(text1);

        pluslabel = new Label("+");
        add(pluslabel);

        text2 = new TextField(10);
        add(text2);

        button1 = new Button("=");
        add(button1);
        button1.addActionListener(this);

        answertext = new TextField(10);
        add(answertext);

    }

    public void actionPerformed(ActionEvent e) {
        if(e.getSource() == button1){
            int sum = Integer.parseInt(text1.getText()) +
Integer.parseInt(text2.getText());
```

```
             .
             .
             .
         }
      }

   }
```

TIP

You may be surprised to see (unless you program in C++) that you can declare new variables like sum right in the middle of your code, rather than having to do it at the beginning of the function. This is a very useful aspect of Java—if you declare variables in a specific block of code (blocks of code are set apart with { and }), then the variables you declare inside that block of code are created when you enter that block and destroyed when you leave. In practical terms, that means you can declare variables as you like throughout a Java program.

Now that you have the answer you want to display in the integer named sum, convert that value to a string so you can display it in the answer text field.

Putting Numeric Data into Text Fields

At this point, you need to take an integer value (in the variable named sum) and convert it to a string that you can display in the text field answertext. The Java String class will help you here because it has a method called valueOf() designed for just this case. You can pass a number to the valueOf() method, and receive a string of text representing that number. In code, it looks like this:

```
import java.applet.Applet;
import java.awt.*;
import java.awt.event.*;

public class adder extends Applet implements ActionListener {

   TextField text1, text2, answertext;
   Label pluslabel;
   Button button1;

   public void init(){

      text1 = new TextField(10);
      add(text1);
```

```
        pluslabel = new Label("+");
        add(pluslabel);

        text2 = new TextField(10);
        add(text2);

        button1 = new Button("=");
        add(button1);
        button1.addActionListener(this);

        answertext = new TextField(10);
        add(answertext);

    }

    public void actionPerformed(ActionEvent e) {
        if(e.getSource() == button1){
            int sum = Integer.parseInt(text1.getText()) +
Integer.parseInt(text2.getText());
            answertext.setText(String.valueOf(sum));
        }
    }

}
```

TIP

The `String` class method `valueOf()` is overloaded to handle not only integers, but `longs`, `doubles`, and `floats` as well.

Your applet is ready to go. The listing for this applet appears in `adder.java`.

LIST 4.1: adder.java

```
import java.applet.Applet;
import java.awt.*;
import java.awt.event.*;

public class adder extends Applet implements ActionListener {

    TextField text1, text2, answertext;
    Label pluslabel;
    Button button1;

    public void init(){
```

```
        text1 = new TextField(10);
        add(text1);

        pluslabel = new Label("+");
        add(pluslabel);

        text2 = new TextField(10);
        add(text2);

        button1 = new Button("=");
        add(button1);
        button1.addActionListener(this);

        answertext = new TextField(10);
        add(answertext);

    }

    public void actionPerformed(ActionEvent e) {
        if(e.getSource() == button1){
            int sum = Integer.parseInt(text1.getText()) +
Integer.parseInt(text2.getText());
            answertext.setText(String.valueOf(sum));
        }
    }

}
```

LIST 4.2: adder.html

```
<HTML>
<HEAD>
  <TITLE>Adder Applet Version 1</TITLE>
</HEAD>
<BODY>
  <APPLET code=adder.class width=225 height=200> </APPLET>
</BODY>
</HTML>
```

Build the applet and run it, creating the display shown below. Your results will depend on the width you set for the applet's HTML page in the Applet Viewer; in the figure shown here, the width is 225 and the height 200.

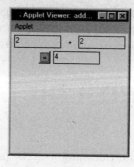

As you can see, the calculator functions, but it looks all wrong—the controls are all on two lines and look scrambled. That's because you are using the default layout manager. As shown in Figure 4.3, this layout manager just adds controls to an applet as you might add text to a document in a word processor—row by row, like words on a page. When it comes to the end of a row, it simply wraps the next controls around to the next line, as shown in Figure 4.4.

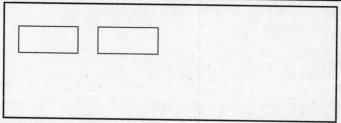

FIGURE 4.3:   The default layout manager adds controls to an applet row by row, like words on a page.

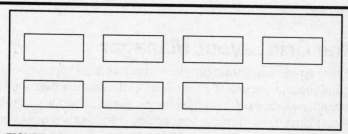

FIGURE 4.4:   When the default layout manager comes to the end of a row, it wraps the next controls.

Part i

Up until now, the default layout manager has given you sufficient layout control, but the adding calculator demands more. Let's take a look at a new layout manager—the *GridLayout* manager—now.

WORKING WITH THE JAVA GRID LAYOUT

The controls on your calculator must be placed as shown in Figure 4.5: vertically, not horizontally. You can place them vertically by replacing the default FlowLayout manager in your applet with another layout manager—the GridLayout manager.

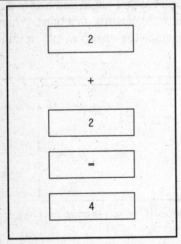

FIGURE 4.5:   Your controls must be arranged vertically.

Using the GridLayout Manager

The FlowLayout manager simply places controls in an applet one by one, wrapping them at the end of a row. The GridLayout manager, on the other hand, is often more useful, because it places controls in a grid, as shown in Figure 4.6. To arrange your adding calculator's controls vertically, add them to your applet in a grid of dimensions 9×3, as shown in Figure 4.7.

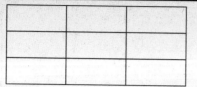

FIGURE 4.6:   The GridLayout manager places controls on a grid.

	2	
	+	
	2	
	=	
	4	

FIGURE 4.7:   Your calculator with padded cells arranged in a grid

To add your calculator's controls to your applet in a 9 × 3 grid, install the GridLayout manager in your applet and then add the controls to it. As you add controls to the layout manager, it will place them in the grid, one after the other, row by row. That means that you have to fill all of the entries in the grid, not just the entries that hold the controls you want to display. One way of solving this problem is to use a set of labels without any text that act as spacers. Add these labels now, giving them the names shown in Figure 4.8.

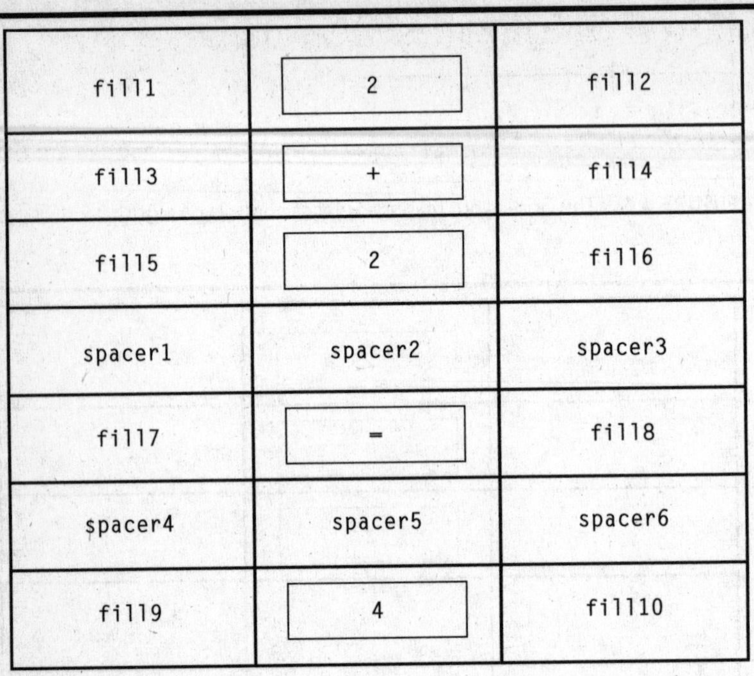

fill1	2	fill2
fill3	+	fill4
fill5	2	fill6
spacer1	spacer2	spacer3
fill7	-	fill8
spacer4	spacer5	spacer6
fill9	4	fill10

FIGURE 4.8: Adding labels to every entry in the grid

Add these spacer labels to the **adder** class as shown below.

```
import java.applet.Applet;
import java.applet.Applet;
import java.awt.*;
import java.awt.event.*;

public class adder2 extends Applet
implements ActionListener {

    TextField text1, text2, answertext;
    Label pluslabel, fill1, fill2, fill3, fill4, fill5,
    fill6, fill7, fill8, fill9, fill10;
    Label spacer1, spacer2, spacer3, spacer4, spacer5, spacer6;
    Button button1;
    .
    .
    .
}
```

Now you can install the GridLayout manager as your new layout manager.

Adding a GridLayout Manager

Install the GridLayout manager (replacing the default FlowLayout manager) in the `init()` method before you have added any controls to the layout. In this case, you want a grid of 9 rows and 3 columns, and you set that up with the `setLayout()` method as follows:

```java
import java.applet.Applet;
import java.awt.*;
import java.awt.event.*;

public class adder2 extends Applet
  implements ActionListener {

    TextField text1, text2, answertext;
    Label pluslabel, fill1, fill2, fill3, fill4, fill5,
    fill6, fill7, fill8, fill9, fill10;
    Label spacer1, spacer2, spacer3, spacer4, spacer5, spacer6;
    Button button1;

    public void init(){

      setLayout(new GridLayout(9, 3));
        .
        .
        .
    }
}
```

Now your applet uses a grid layout. Add the other controls, including the spacer labels, the same way (note in particular that to place the plus sign in the middle of its label you include the class constant `Label.CENTER` in the call to the `Label` class's constructor):

```java
import java.applet.Applet;
import java.awt.*;
import java.awt.event.*;

public class adder2 extends Applet
  implements ActionListener {

    TextField text1, text2, answertext;
    Label pluslabel, fill1, fill2, fill3, fill4, fill5,
    fill6, fill7, fill8, fill9, fill10;
    Label spacer1, spacer2, spacer3, spacer4, spacer5, spacer6;
    Button button1;
```

```java
public void init(){

    setLayout(new GridLayout(9, 3));

    fill1 = new Label();
    add(fill1);
    text1 = new TextField(10);
    add(text1);
    fill2 = new Label();
    add(fill2);

    fill3 = new Label();
    add(fill3);
    pluslabel = new Label("+", Label.CENTER);
    add(pluslabel);
    fill4 = new Label();
    add(fill4);

    fill5 = new Label();
    add(fill5);
    text2 = new TextField(10);
    add(text2);
    fill6 = new Label();
    add(fill6);

    spacer1 = new Label();
    add(spacer1);
    spacer2 = new Label();
    add(spacer2);
    spacer3 = new Label();
    add(spacer3);

    fill7 = new Label();
    add(fill7);
    button1 = new Button("=");
    add(button1);
    button1.addActionListener(this);
    fill8 = new Label();
    add(fill8);

    spacer4 = new Label();
    add(spacer4);
    spacer5 = new Label();
    add(spacer5);
    spacer6 = new Label();
    add(spacer6);
```

```
fill9 = new Label();
add(fill9);
answertext = new TextField(10);
add(answertext);
fill10 = new Label();
add(fill10);
    }
}
```

Now your controls will be aligned vertically. Build and run the new version of the adder applet. As you can see in the graphic below, your controls are placed as you want them—your grid layout example is a success. The code for this applet appears in adder2.java.

LIST 4.3: adder2.java (with layout)

```
import java.applet.Applet;
import java.awt.*;
import java.awt.event.*;

public class adder2 extends Applet
  implements ActionListener {

  TextField text1, text2, answertext;
  Label pluslabel, fill1, fill2, fill3, fill4, fill5,
  fill6, fill7, fill8, fill9, fill10;
  Label spacer1, spacer2, spacer3, spacer4, spacer5, spacer6;
  Button button1;

  public void init(){

    setLayout(new GridLayout(9, 3));
```

```
fill1 = new Label();
add(fill1);
text1 = new TextField(10);
add(text1);
fill2 = new Label();
add(fill2);

fill3 = new Label();
add(fill3);
pluslabel = new Label("+", Label.CENTER);
add(pluslabel);
fill4 = new Label();
add(fill4);

fill5 = new Label();
add(fill5);
text2 = new TextField(10);
add(text2);
fill6 = new Label();
add(fill6);

spacer1 = new Label();
add(spacer1);
spacer2 = new Label();
add(spacer2);
spacer3 = new Label();
add(spacer3);

fill7 = new Label();
add(fill7);
button1 = new Button("=");
add(button1);
button1.addActionListener(this);
fill8 = new Label();
add(fill8);

spacer4 = new Label();
add(spacer4);
spacer5 = new Label();
add(spacer5);
spacer6 = new Label();
add(spacer6);

fill9 = new Label();
add(fill9);
```

```
            answertext = new TextField(10);
            add(answertext);
            fill10 = new Label();
            add(fill10);
        }

        public void actionPerformed(ActionEvent e){
            if(e.getSource() == button1){
                int sum = Integer.parseInt(text1.getText()) +
Integer.parseInt(text2.getText());
                answertext.setText(String.valueOf(sum));
            }
        }
    }
```

LIST 4.4: adder2.html

```
<HTML>
<HEAD>
  <TITLE>Adder Applet Version 2 (With Layout)</TITLE>
</HEAD>
<BODY>
  <HR>
  <APPLET code=adder2.class width=225 height=200> </APPLET>
</BODY>
</HTML>
```

Now that you are somewhat familiar with layouts, let's press on to work with check boxes, which are often used in special layouts, as you'll soon see.

BUILDING PROGRAMS WITH CHECK BOXES

We will begin check boxes with a simple check box example. In this case, you'll just put five check boxes into your applet, as shown in Figure 4.9. When the user clicks one of these check boxes, you can indicate that action in a text field, as shown in Figure 4.10.

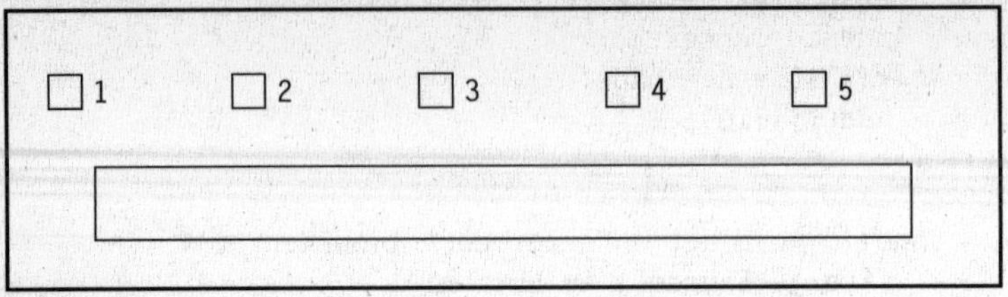

FIGURE 4.9: An applet with five check boxes and a text field

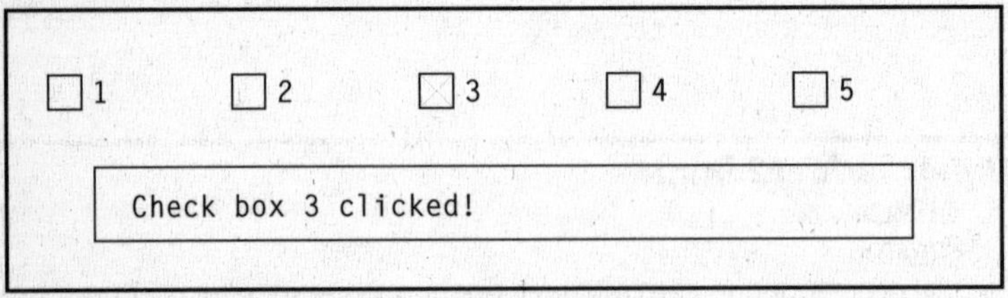

FIGURE 4.10: When the user clicks check box 3, the message "Check box 3 clicked!" appears in the text field.

Now you'll create a new applet called *checker*. Create a new file named checker.java and create a new class named checker as shown below:

```
import java.applet.Applet;
import java.awt.*;
import java.awt.event.*;

public class checker extends Applet {

}
```

Now you can declare the five check boxes you'll need—naming them checkbox1 to checkbox5—and the text field, called text1, that you'll use to report when the user clicks a check box. Check boxes are created with the Java Checkbox class, so declare your five check boxes as follows:

```
import java.applet.Applet;
import java.awt.*;
import java.awt.event.*;

public class checker extends Applet {

Checkbox checkbox1, checkbox2, checkbox3,
        checkbox4, checkbox5;
```

```
    TextField text1;
        .
        .
        .
    }
```

The Java `Checkbox` class methods appear in Table 4.2.

As with other controls, you actually create and add the new check boxes to your applet in the `init()` method, so create that method now:

```
    import java.applet.Applet;
    import java.awt.*;
    import java.awt.event.*;

    public class checker extends Applet {

        Checkbox checkbox1, checkbox2, checkbox3,
                checkbox4, checkbox5;
        TextField text1;

        public void init(){

        }

    }
```

TABLE 4.2: The Checkbox Class Methods

METHOD	DOES THIS
Checkbox()	Constructs a check box with no label.
Checkbox(String)	Constructs a check box with the given label.
Checkbox(String, boolean)	Constructs a check box with the given label and sets the specified boolean state.
Checkbox(String, boolean, CheckboxGroup)	Constructs a check box with the given label, set to the given boolean state, and in the specified check box group.
Checkbox(String, CheckboxGroup, boolean)	Constructs a check box with the given label, set to the specified boolean state, in the specified check box group.
addItemListener(ItemListener)	Adds the given ItemListener to receive item events from this check box.
addNotify()	Creates the check box's peer.
getCheckboxGroup()	Returns the Checkbox group for this check box.

TABLE 4.2 continued: The Checkbox Class Methods

METHOD	DOES THIS
getLabel()	Gets check box's label.
getSelectedObjects()	Returns an array (length 1) containing the selected check box's label or null if the check box is not selected.
getState()	Returns the boolean state of the check box to determine whether this check box is in the "on" or "off" state.
paramString()	Returns the parameter string representing the state of this check box.
processEvent(AWTEvent)	Processes events on this check box.
processItemEvent(ItemEvent)	Processes item events occurring on this check box by dispatching them to any registered Item-Listener objects.
removeItemListener(Item Listener)	Removes the specified ItemListener so that it no longer receives item events from this check box.
setCheckboxGroup(Checkbox-Group)	Sets the check box group to the given check box's group.
setLabel(String)	Sets this check box's label to be the given string.
setState(Boolean)	Sets the check box's state.

All you have to do here is add the check boxes and the text field. Add the check box checkbox1 like this:

```
import java.applet.Applet;
import java.awt.*;
import java.awt.event.*;

public class checker extends Applet {

    Checkbox checkbox1, checkbox2, checkbox3,
            checkbox4, checkbox5;
    TextField text1;

    public void init(){

        checkbox1 = new Checkbox("1");
        add(checkbox1);
```

·
·
·
```
        }
    }
```

Note that you can give the check box a label (here that label is simply "1") by passing a string to the Checkbox class's constructor, as you did above. All that remains now is to add the other check boxes and the text field:

```java
import java.applet.Applet;
import java.awt.*;
import java.awt.event.*;

public class checker extends Applet {

    Checkbox checkbox1, checkbox2, checkbox3,
            checkbox4, checkbox5;
    TextField text1;

    public void init(){

        checkbox1 = new Checkbox("1");
        add(checkbox1);
        checkbox2 = new Checkbox("2");
        add(checkbox2);
        checkbox3 = new Checkbox("3");
        add(checkbox3);
        checkbox4 = new Checkbox("4");
        add(checkbox4);
        checkbox5 = new Checkbox("5");
        add(checkbox5);
        text1 = new TextField(20);
        add(text1);
    }
}
```

Now your new check boxes are installed. The next step is to connect them to the code. You might expect to use an ActionListener interface, but in fact, you use a different interface with check boxes because, unlike buttons, check boxes can be either checked or unchecked (and the way to test their state is with the getState() method). The interface you use here is called ItemListener, and you implement it as follows:

```java
import java.applet.Applet;
import java.awt.*;
import java.awt.event.*;
```

```
public class checker extends Applet implements ItemListener{

    Checkbox checkbox1, checkbox2, checkbox3,
            checkbox4, checkbox5;
    TextField text1;

    public void init(){

        checkbox1 = new Checkbox("1");
        add(checkbox1);
        checkbox2 = new Checkbox("2");
        add(checkbox2);
        checkbox3 = new Checkbox("3");
        add(checkbox3);
        checkbox4 = new Checkbox("4");
        add(checkbox4);
        checkbox5 = new Checkbox("5");
        add(checkbox5);
        text1 = new TextField(20);
        add(text1);
    }
}
```

Make your applet into the listener for your check boxes (that is, your applet will handle the events that occur when the check boxes are clicked or unclicked) with the check box addItemListener() method this way:

```
import java.applet.Applet;
import java.awt.*;
import java.awt.event.*;

public class checker extends Applet implements ItemListener {

    Checkbox checkbox1, checkbox2, checkbox3,
            checkbox4, checkbox5;
    TextField text1;

    public void init(){

        checkbox1 = new Checkbox("1");
        add(checkbox1);
        checkbox1.addItemListener(this);
        checkbox2 = new Checkbox("2");
        add(checkbox2);
        checkbox2.addItemListener(this);
        checkbox3 = new Checkbox("3");
        add(checkbox3);
```

```
    checkbox3.addItemListener(this);
    checkbox4 = new Checkbox("4");
    add(checkbox4);
    checkbox4.addItemListener(this);
    checkbox5 = new Checkbox("5");
    add(checkbox5);
    checkbox5.addItemListener(this);
    text1 = new TextField(20);
    add(text1);
  }
}
```

Now you've added your new check boxes to the applet and connected them up so that check box events will be sent to your applet. You're almost done; all that remains is the handling of the check box events. The method to override when using the ItemListener interface (so that you will be notified when check boxes are checked) is itemStateChanged():

```
import java.applet.Applet;
import java.awt.*;
import java.awt.event.*;

public class checker extends Applet implements ItemListener {

    Checkbox checkbox1, checkbox2, checkbox3,
             checkbox4, checkbox5;
    TextField text1;

    public void init(){

      checkbox1 = new Checkbox("1");
      add(checkbox1);
      checkbox1.addItemListener(this);
      checkbox2 = new Checkbox("2");
      add(checkbox2);
      checkbox2.addItemListener(this);
      checkbox3 = new Checkbox("3");
      add(checkbox3);
      checkbox3.addItemListener(this);
      checkbox4 = new Checkbox("4");
      add(checkbox4);
      checkbox4.addItemListener(this);
      checkbox5 = new Checkbox("5");
      add(checkbox5);
      checkbox5.addItemListener(this);
      text1 = new TextField(20);
      add(text1);
    }
```

```
        public void itemStateChanged(ItemEvent e) {
                .
                .
                .

        }
    }
```

itemStateChanged() is the method that will be called if the user clicks one of your check boxes and you are passed an object of class ItemEvent in that method. You can examine which check box was clicked with the ItemEvent class's getItemSelectable() method for checkbox1, as follows:

```
import java.applet.Applet;
import java.awt.*;
import java.awt.event.*;

public class checker extends Applet implements ItemListener {

    Checkbox checkbox1, checkbox2, checkbox3,
             checkbox4, checkbox5;
    TextField text1;

    public void init(){

        checkbox1 = new Checkbox("1");
        add(checkbox1);
        checkbox1.addItemListener(this);
        checkbox2 = new Checkbox("2");
        add(checkbox2);
        checkbox2.addItemListener(this);
        checkbox3 = new Checkbox("3");
        add(checkbox3);
        checkbox3.addItemListener(this);
        checkbox4 = new Checkbox("4");
        add(checkbox4);
        checkbox4.addItemListener(this);
        checkbox5 = new Checkbox("5");
        add(checkbox5);
        checkbox5.addItemListener(this);
        text1 = new TextField(20);
        add(text1);
    }

    public void itemStateChanged(ItemEvent e) {
        if(e.getItemSelectable() == checkbox1){
```

```
          .
          .
      }
    }
  }
```

For cases where checkbox1 is clicked, you can have a message appear in the text field saying "Check box 1 clicked!" by using the TextField setText() method, as follows:

```java
import java.applet.Applet;
import java.awt.*;
import java.awt.event.*;

public class checker extends Applet implements ItemListener {

    Checkbox checkbox1, checkbox2, checkbox3,
              checkbox4, checkbox5;
    TextField text1;

    public void init(){

        checkbox1 = new Checkbox("1");
        add(checkbox1);
        checkbox1.addItemListener(this);
        checkbox2 = new Checkbox("2");
        add(checkbox2);
        checkbox2.addItemListener(this);
        checkbox3 = new Checkbox("3");
        add(checkbox3);
        checkbox3.addItemListener(this);
        checkbox4 = new Checkbox("4");
        add(checkbox4);
        checkbox4.addItemListener(this);
        checkbox5 = new Checkbox("5");
        add(checkbox5);
        checkbox5.addItemListener(this);
        text1 = new TextField(20);
        add(text1);
    }

    public void itemStateChanged(ItemEvent e) {
        if(e.getItemSelectable() == checkbox1){
            text1.setText("Check box 1 clicked!");
        }
```

.
.
.
```
          }
        }
```

You can set responses to clicks on the other check boxes in the same way:

```
    import java.applet.Applet;
    import java.awt.*;
    import java.awt.event.*;

    public class checker extends Applet implements ItemListener {

        Checkbox checkbox1, checkbox2, checkbox3,
                checkbox4, checkbox5;
        TextField text1;

        public void init(){

          checkbox1 = new Checkbox("1");
          add(checkbox1);
          checkbox1.addItemListener(this);
          checkbox2 = new Checkbox("2");
          add(checkbox2);
          checkbox2.addItemListener(this);
          checkbox3 = new Checkbox("3");
          add(checkbox3);
          checkbox3.addItemListener(this);
          checkbox4 = new Checkbox("4");
          add(checkbox4);
          checkbox4.addItemListener(this);
          checkbox5 = new Checkbox("5");
          add(checkbox5);
          checkbox5.addItemListener(this);
          text1 = new TextField(20);
          add(text1);
        }

        public void itemStateChanged(ItemEvent e) {
          if(e.getItemSelectable() == checkbox1){
            text1.setText("Check box 1 clicked!");
          }
          if(e.getItemSelectable() == checkbox2){
            text1.setText("Check box 2 clicked!");
          }
          if(e.getItemSelectable() == checkbox3){
            text1.setText("Check box 3 clicked!");
```

```
     }
     if(e.getItemSelectable() == checkbox4){
       text1.setText("Check box 4 clicked!");
     }
     if(e.getItemSelectable() == checkbox5){
       text1.setText("Check box 5 clicked!");
     }
   }
 }
```

Your check box example is ready to go. Build the new applet now and run it, as shown below. As you can see, when the user clicks a check box, your applet responds and indicates what happened. Your check box example works exactly as you want it to. The code for this applet appears in checker.java.

TIP

To see at any time whether a check box is clicked or not, you can use the get-State() method like this: checkbox1.getState(), which returns true if the check box is checked and false otherwise.

LIST 4.5: checker.java

```
import java.applet.Applet;
import java.awt.*;
import java.awt.event.*;

public class checker extends Applet implements ItemListener {

   Checkbox checkbox1, checkbox2, checkbox3,
            checkbox4, checkbox5;
   TextField text1;
```

```java
    public void init(){

        checkbox1 = new Checkbox("1");
        add(checkbox1);
        checkbox1.addItemListener(this);
        checkbox2 = new Checkbox("2");
        add(checkbox2);
        checkbox2.addItemListener(this);
        checkbox3 = new Checkbox("3");
        add(checkbox3);
        checkbox3.addItemListener(this);
        checkbox4 = new Checkbox("4");
        add(checkbox4);
        checkbox4.addItemListener(this);
        checkbox5 = new Checkbox("5");
        add(checkbox5);
        checkbox5.addItemListener(this);
        text1 = new TextField(20);
        add(text1);
    }

    public void itemStateChanged(ItemEvent e) {
        if(e.getItemSelectable() == checkbox1){
            text1.setText("Check box 1 clicked!");
        }
        if(e.getItemSelectable() == checkbox2){
            text1.setText("Check box 2 clicked!");
        }
        if(e.getItemSelectable() == checkbox3){
            text1.setText("Check box 3 clicked!");
        }
        if(e.getItemSelectable() == checkbox4){
            text1.setText("Check box 4 clicked!");
        }
        if(e.getItemSelectable() == checkbox5){
            text1.setText("Check box 5 clicked!");
        }
    }
}
```

LIST 4.6: *checker.html*

```html
<HTML>
<HEAD>
  <TITLE>Checker Applet</TITLE>
</HEAD>
<BODY>
```

```
<HR>
<APPLET code=checker.class width=250 height=200> </APPLET>
</BODY>
</HTML>
```

What's Next?

You've had a good introduction to check boxes in the checkers applet. Now you're able to use check boxes in your Java programs. In the next chapter, you will turn to the other control that acts very much like check boxes: radio buttons.

Chapter 5

WORKING WITH RADIO BUTTONS

In Chapter 4, we took a look at Java check boxes. Here, you're going to learn about radio buttons. In addition, you'll start to learn how to group controls together, both with the CheckboxGroup class and the Panel class. You'll bring radio buttons and check boxes together in a relatively large-scale example. Let's start at once with a guided tour of radio buttons.

Java 2
In Record Time
Teach Yourself like 16 Example...

Adapted from *Java 2: In Record Time* by Steven Holzner
ISBN 0-7821-2171-3   560 pages $29.99

Building Programs with Radio Buttons

Radio buttons (also called *option buttons*) are much like check boxes, but there is an important difference. You can check a number of check boxes at the same time, as shown in Figure 5.1. Radio buttons, however, operate in a group, and only one can be clicked at one time, as shown in Figure 5.2.

FIGURE 5.1: You can check more than one check box at a time.

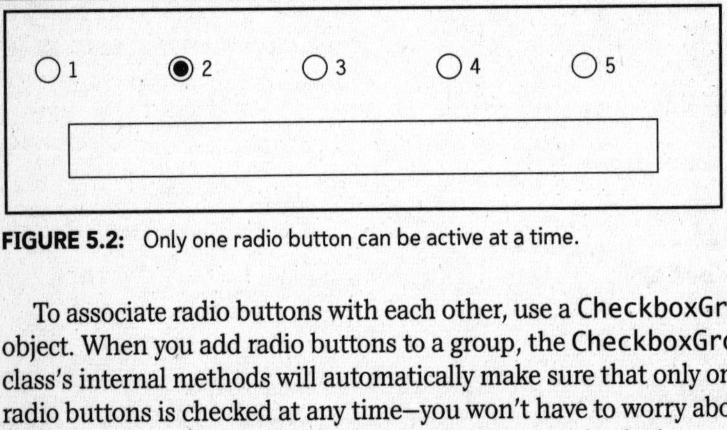

FIGURE 5.2: Only one radio button can be active at a time.

To associate radio buttons with each other, use a CheckboxGroup object. When you add radio buttons to a group, the CheckboxGroup class's internal methods will automatically make sure that only one of the radio buttons is checked at any time—you won't have to worry about "unchecking" radio buttons when one of a group is checked.

The Radios Applet

To see radio buttons at work, let's write a new applet much like Chapter 4's check box applet that will present radio buttons, instead of check boxes, to the user. When the user clicks one of the radio buttons, that fact can be reported, as shown in Figure 5.3.

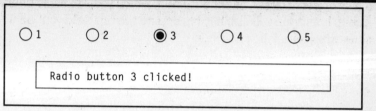

FIGURE 5.3: When the user clicks a button, a message appears in the text field.

Create a new project named radios.java and create the new class named radios, like this:

```
import java.applet.Applet;
import java.awt.*;
import java.awt.event.*;

public class radios extends Applet {
        .
        .
        .
}
```

You might be expecting a new Java class called RadioButton or something like that. However, in Java, radio buttons are actually just check boxes that have been added to a check box group. When you add check boxes to a check box group, they change their appearance automatically and become radio buttons. That means that you can create five new Checkbox objects for your radio controls:

```
import java.applet.Applet;
import java.awt.*;
import java.awt.event.*;


public class radios extends Applet {

Checkbox checkbox1, checkbox2, checkbox3,
        checkbox4, checkbox5;
}
```

Next, you will need an object of class CheckboxGroup to add your check boxes to (so they can act in a coordinated fashion). The CheckboxGroup class methods appear in Table 5.1. In your applet, you declare a new object of class `CheckboxGroup`, which you can name `checkbox-group1`, and you will also need to declare the text field you will use to show which check box is selected:

```
import java.applet.Applet;
import java.awt.*;
import java.awt.event.*;

public class radios extends Applet {

    CheckboxGroup checkboxgroup1;
    Checkbox checkbox1, checkbox2, checkbox3,
             checkbox4, checkbox5;
    TextField text1;

}
```

TABLE 5.1: The CheckboxGroup Class Methods

METHOD	DOES THIS
CheckboxGroup()	Creates a check box group.
getCurrent()	Deprecated. Replaced by getSelectedCheckbox().
getSelectedCheckbox()	Gets current selected check box from this check box group.
setCurrent(Checkbox)	Deprecated. Replaced by setSelectedCheckbox(Checkbox).
setSelectedCheckbox(Checkbox)	Sets the current choice in this check box's group to the specified check box.
toString()	Returns a string representing the value of this check box group's current selection.

Next, set up your controls in the `init()` method by adding that method to your applet:

```
import java.applet.Applet;
import java.awt.*;
import java.awt.event.*;
```

```
public class radios extends Applet {

    CheckboxGroup checkboxgroup1;
    Checkbox checkbox1, checkbox2, checkbox3,
            checkbox4, checkbox5;
    TextField text1;

    public void init(){
        .
        .
        .
    }
}
```

Create your new CheckboxGroup object, checkbox1:

```
import java.applet.Applet;
import java.awt.*;
import java.awt.event.*;

public class radios extends Applet {

    CheckboxGroup checkboxgroup1;
    Checkbox checkbox1, checkbox2, checkbox3,
            checkbox4, checkbox5;
    TextField text1;

    public void init(){

    checkboxgroup1 = new CheckboxGroup();
        .
        .
        .
    }

}
```

Connecting Check Boxes to a *CheckboxGroup*

Now you are ready to add your radio buttons to this new check box group. You do that when you create each check box, by passing your CheckboxGroup object to the constructor of the Checkbox class. This attaches the new check box to the check box group and turns that check box into a radio button. For example, you add the first radio button and give it the simple caption "1," as follows:

NOTE
The last parameter indicates whether the radio button should appear initially checked; you pass a value of `false` to indicate that it should appear unchecked initially.

```java
import java.applet.Applet;
import java.awt.*;
import java.awt.event.*;

public class radios extends Applet {

   CheckboxGroup checkboxgroup1;
   Checkbox checkbox1, checkbox2, checkbox3,
            checkbox4, checkbox5;
   TextField text1;

   public void init(){

     checkboxgroup1 = new CheckboxGroup();

     checkbox1 = new Checkbox("1", false, checkboxgroup1);
     add(checkbox1);
          .
          .
          .

   }

}
```

Now you can add the rest of the radio buttons and the text field you'll use to report on user activities:

```java
import java.applet.Applet;
import java.awt.*;
import java.awt.event.*;

public class radios extends Applet {

   CheckboxGroup checkboxgroup1;
   Checkbox checkbox1, checkbox2, checkbox3,
            checkbox4, checkbox5;
   TextField text1;
```

```
public void init(){

    checkboxgroup1 = new CheckboxGroup();

    checkbox1 = new Checkbox("1", false, checkboxgroup1);
    add(checkbox1);

    checkbox2 = new Checkbox("2", false, checkboxgroup1);
    add(checkbox2);

    checkbox3 = new Checkbox("3", false, checkboxgroup1);
    add(checkbox3);

    checkbox4 = new Checkbox("4", false, checkboxgroup1);
    add(checkbox4);

    checkbox5 = new Checkbox("5", false, checkboxgroup1);
    add(checkbox5);

    text1 = new TextField(20);
    add(text1);

    }
}
```

At this point, then, you've installed your radio buttons. The next step is to report a response when they are clicked, and you do that just as you did in Chapter 4's example on check boxes, in itemStateChanged(). First, make your applet into the ItemListener for the radio buttons and then add the listener for your check boxes with the check box addItemListener() method:

```
import java.applet.Applet;
import java.awt.*;
import java.awt.event.*;

public class radios extends Applet implements ItemListener{

    CheckboxGroup checkboxgroup1;
    Checkbox checkbox1, checkbox2, checkbox3,
             checkbox4, checkbox5;
    TextField text1;

    public void init(){

        checkboxgroup1 = new CheckboxGroup();
```

```
checkbox1 = new Checkbox("1", false, checkboxgroup1);
add(checkbox1);
checkbox1.addItemListener(this);

checkbox2 = new Checkbox("2", false, checkboxgroup1);
add(checkbox2);
checkbox2.addItemListener(this);

checkbox3 = new Checkbox("3", false, checkboxgroup1);
add(checkbox3);
checkbox3.addItemListener(this);

checkbox4 = new Checkbox("4", false, checkboxgroup1);
add(checkbox4);
checkbox4.addItemListener(this);

checkbox5 = new Checkbox("5", false, checkboxgroup1);
add(checkbox5);
checkbox5.addItemListener(this);

text1 = new TextField(20);
add(text1);

    }
}
```

Now add the itemStateChanged() method. Just as in the check box example, you can examine which radio button was clicked with the ItemEvent class's getItemSelectable() method and report back to the user in your text field, using the TextField setText() method:

```
import java.applet.Applet;
import java.awt.*;
import java.awt.event.*;

public class radios extends Applet implements ItemListener{

    CheckboxGroup checkboxgroup1;
    Checkbox checkbox1, checkbox2, checkbox3,
            checkbox4, checkbox5;
    TextField text1;

    public void init(){

        checkboxgroup1 = new CheckboxGroup();

        checkbox1 = new Checkbox("1", false, checkboxgroup1);
```

```
    add(checkbox1);
    checkbox1.addItemListener(this);

    checkbox2 = new Checkbox("2", false, checkboxgroup1);
    add(checkbox2);
    checkbox2.addItemListener(this);

    checkbox3 = new Checkbox("3", false, checkboxgroup1);
    add(checkbox3);
    checkbox3.addItemListener(this);

    checkbox4 = new Checkbox("4", false, checkboxgroup1);
    add(checkbox4);
    checkbox4.addItemListener(this);

    checkbox5 = new Checkbox("5", false, checkboxgroup1);
    add(checkbox5);
    checkbox5.addItemListener(this);

    text1 = new TextField(20);
    add(text1);

}

public void itemStateChanged(ItemEvent e){
  if(e.getItemSelectable() == checkbox1){
    text1.setText("Radio button 1 clicked!");
  }
  if(e.getItemSelectable() == checkbox2){
    text1.setText("Radio button 2 clicked!");
  }
  if(e.getItemSelectable() == checkbox3){
    text1.setText("Radio button 3 clicked!");
  }
  if(e.getItemSelectable() == checkbox4){
    text1.setText("Radio button 4 clicked!");
  }
  if(e.getItemSelectable() == checkbox5){
    text1.setText("Radio button 5 clicked!");
  }
 }
}
```

There you have it. Build this new radio button applet and run it, as shown below. You can see the radio buttons in this applet—and remember, only one may be selected at a time. When the user clicks a new radio button, the one that had been selected before is cleared, and the just-clicked radio button is selected instead. Your radio button example is a success. The code for this applet appears in `radios.java`.

LIST 5.1:   radios.java

```
import java.applet.Applet;
import java.awt.*;
import java.awt.event.*;

public class radios extends Applet implements ItemListener {

    CheckboxGroup checkboxgroup1;
    Checkbox checkbox1, checkbox2, checkbox3,
            checkbox4, checkbox5;
    TextField text1;

    public void init(){

        checkboxgroup1 = new CheckboxGroup();

        checkbox1 = new Checkbox("1", false, checkboxgroup1);
        add(checkbox1);
        checkbox1.addItemListener(this);

        checkbox2 = new Checkbox("2", false, checkboxgroup1);
        add(checkbox2);
        checkbox2.addItemListener(this);

        checkbox3 = new Checkbox("3", false, checkboxgroup1);
        add(checkbox3);
        checkbox3.addItemListener(this);

        checkbox4 = new Checkbox("4", false, checkboxgroup1);
```

```
      add(checkbox4);
      checkbox4.addItemListener(this);

      checkbox5 = new Checkbox("5", false, checkboxgroup1);
      add(checkbox5);
      checkbox5.addItemListener(this);

      text1 = new TextField(20);
      add(text1);

   }

   public void itemStateChanged(ItemEvent e){
      if(e.getItemSelectable() == checkbox1){
         text1.setText("Radio button 1 clicked!");
      }
      if(e.getItemSelectable() == checkbox2){
         text1.setText("Radio button 2 clicked!");
      }
      if(e.getItemSelectable() == checkbox3){
         text1.setText("Radio button 3 clicked!");
      }
      if(e.getItemSelectable() == checkbox4){
         text1.setText("Radio button 4 clicked!");
      }
      if(e.getItemSelectable() == checkbox5){
         text1.setText("Radio button 5 clicked!");
      }
   }
}
```

LIST 5.2: radios.html

```
<HTML>
<HEAD>
  <TITLE>Radios Applet</TITLE>
</HEAD>
<BODY>
  <HR>
  <APPLET code=radios.class width=225 height=200> </APPLET>
</BODY>
</HTML>
```

Now that you have some experience in handling both check boxes and radio buttons in isolation, the next step is to see them at work in an applet, arranged into groups as they normally are. To do so, you'll first learn to arrange controls in *panels* and then arrange the panels themselves.

BUILDING PROGRAMS WITH PANELS

Layout managers are only part of the story of organizing controls in an applet. Another part of the story concerns the Panel class. A panel is just a rectangular region that contains controls. For example, you could design a panel with four check boxes and then display that panel in an applet, as shown in Figure 5.4. In many ways, you can think of a panel as a new control that contains other controls. This means that you could add more panels to your applet just as easily as you added the first one, as shown in Figure 5.5.

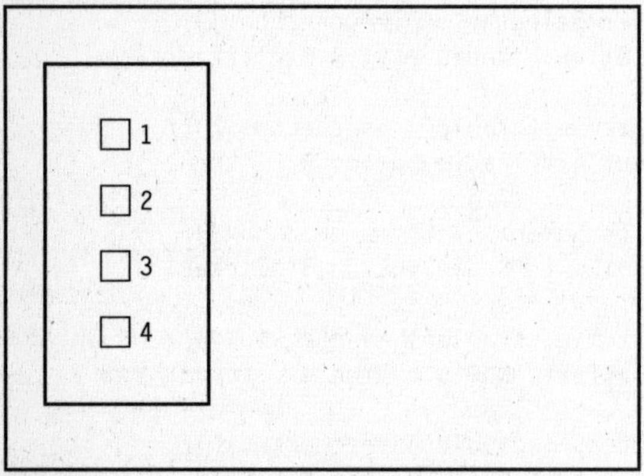

FIGURE 5.4:   A panel with four check boxes

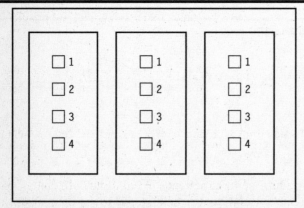

FIGURE 5.5:   Adding several panels to our applet

This technique is perfect for groups of controls like radio buttons or check boxes, because it keeps the group of controls together. Watch this technique at work as you create a new example that uses panels.

Creating a Panel

Create a new file named `checkpanels.java`. To construct the example shown in Figure 5.5, your first job is to create a new type of panel with the four check boxes you want in it. Call this new class `checkboxpanel`, and use this panel in your applet. Create this class by deriving it from the Java `Panel` class—add this code to the `checkpanels.java` file:

```
class checkboxpanel extends Panel {
    .
    .
    .
}
```

This is the first time that you have created a new class in your programs. This new class will be used by the main applet class, and because you are defining this new class in the same file as the applet's code, you won't have to use the Java `import` statement to import this new class. When you compile `checkpanels.java`, two `.class` files will be created: `checkboxpanel.class` (your new class) and the applet class itself, `checkpanels.class`. When the applet is run, the code in the applet, `checkpanels.class`, will load the code in `checkboxpanel.class` as needed.

Add the four check boxes you want in this class as you have added controls in the past—by first declaring them at the beginning of your new class's definition:

```
class checkboxpanel extends Panel {
    Checkbox check1, check2, check3, check4;
    .
    .
    .
}
```

Now create and add the new check boxes to this panel. You do this not in the panel's `init()` method but in its constructor (the `Panel` class does not support an `init()` method). A Java constructor is run when an object of the class is created, and you define it as just a method with the exact same name of the class itself. Constructors never have a return value, but may have parameters used for initializing the new object being created, and can be overloaded based on the number and type of parameters. This is similar to what you see in the Java classes you've already discussed. In this case, it's checkboxpanel, so set up the constructor for this class and name the constructor checkboxpanel():

```
class checkboxpanel extends Panel {

    checkboxpanel(){
        .
        .
        .
    }
}
```

That's your new class's constructor. In that constructor, create and add your new check boxes, as follows:

```
class checkboxpanel extends Panel {
    Checkbox check1, check2, check3, check4;

    checkboxpanel(){
        check1 = new Checkbox("1");
        add(check1);
        check2 = new Checkbox("2");
        add(check2);
        check3 = new Checkbox("3");
        add(check3);
        check4 = new Checkbox("4");
        add(check4);
    }
}
```

Now you've created a new panel class named checkboxpanel. A panel of this class will look like this:

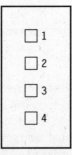

You can treat these new panels much like controls in our applet. For example, to add three of these panels to our applet as, say, `panel1`, `panel2`, and `panel3`, you start by declaring them like this in our applet's main class, `checkpanels`:

```
import java.applet.Applet;
import java.awt.*;

public class checkpanels extends Applet {

  checkboxpanel panel1, panel2, panel3;
    .
    .
    .

      }

class checkboxpanel extends Panel {
  Checkbox check1, check2, check3, check4;

  checkboxpanel(){
    check1 = new Checkbox("1");
    add(check1);
    check2 = new Checkbox("2");
    add(check2);
    check3 = new Checkbox("3");
    add(check3);
    check4 = new Checkbox("4");
    add(check4);
  }
}
```

(Note that there is no `import java.awt.event.*;` declaration in this example. Since this applet doesn't do anything, no events will be handled—this example merely illustrates the panel concept.)

Next, you have to initialize these panels in the `init()` method. You will use the GridLayout manager with one row and three columns to make these panels appear side by side, so start off by installing that manager first:

```
import java.applet.Applet;
import java.awt.*;

public class checkpanels extends Applet {

  checkboxpanel panel1, panel2, panel3;

    public void init(){
```

```
            setLayout(new GridLayout(1, 3));

          .

          .

          .

        }
    }

    class checkboxpanel extends Panel {
      Checkbox check1, check2, check3, check4;

      checkboxpanel(){
        check1 = new Checkbox("1");
        add(check1);
        check2 = new Checkbox("2");
        add(check2);
        check3 = new Checkbox("3");
        add(check3);
        check4 = new Checkbox("4");
        add(check4);
      }
    }
```

Now create and add your three check box panels, panel1, panel2, and panel3 of your new class checkpanels to the applet:

```
    import java.applet.Applet;
    import java.awt.*;

    public class checkpanels extends Applet {

      checkboxpanel panel1, panel2, panel3;

      public void init(){
        setLayout(new GridLayout(1, 3));
        panel1 = new checkboxpanel();
        panel2 = new checkboxpanel();
        panel3 = new checkboxpanel();
        add(panel1);
        add(panel2);
        add(panel3);
      }

    }

    class checkboxpanel extends Panel {
      Checkbox check1, check2, check3, check4;

      checkboxpanel(){
```

```
        check1 = new Checkbox("1");
        add(check1);
        check2 = new Checkbox("2");
        add(check2);
        check3 = new Checkbox("3");
        add(check3);
        check4 = new Checkbox("4");
        add(check4);
    }
}
```

That's all there is to it—now you've created a new panel type, added controls to the panel, and added panels of that type to your applet. As you can see in the graphic below, you have successfully installed three panels in your applet. Your checkpanels applet is a success. The code for this applet appears in checkpanels.java.

LIST 5.3: checkpanels.java

```java
import java.applet.Applet;
import java.awt.*;

public class checkpanels extends Applet {

  checkboxpanel panel1, panel2, panel3;

  public void init(){
    setLayout(new GridLayout(1, 3));
    panel1 = new checkboxpanel();
    panel2 = new checkboxpanel();
    panel3 = new checkboxpanel();
    add(panel1);
    add(panel2);
```

```
        add(panel3);
    }

}

class checkboxpanel extends Panel {
    Checkbox check1, check2, check3, check4;

    checkboxpanel(){
        check1 = new Checkbox("1");
        add(check1);
        check2 = new Checkbox("2");
        add(check2);
        check3 = new Checkbox("3");
        add(check3);
        check4 = new Checkbox("4");
        add(check4);
    }
}
```

LIST 5.4: checkpanels.html

```
<HTML>
<HEAD>
  <TITLE>Check Panels Applet</TITLE>
</HEAD>
<BODY>
  <HR>
  <APPLET code=checkpanels.class width=250 height=200>
  </APPLET>
</BODY>
</HTML>
```

As you can see, panels make up a powerful technique for grouping controls together. You'll use panels in your next example, in which you will bring Chapter 5 together with Chapter 4 by using radio buttons, check boxes, panels, and layouts all in the same applet.

PUTTING CHECK BOXES AND RADIO BUTTONS TOGETHER

Let's say that you decide to set up a sandwich shop on the Web. In particular, you want to embed an applet in a Web page giving customers the price of various sandwiches. That applet might look something like Figure 5.6, in which you let the customer select from one of three sandwich options, and let the applet indicate the ingredients in each sandwich and give the customer a price for what they have selected.

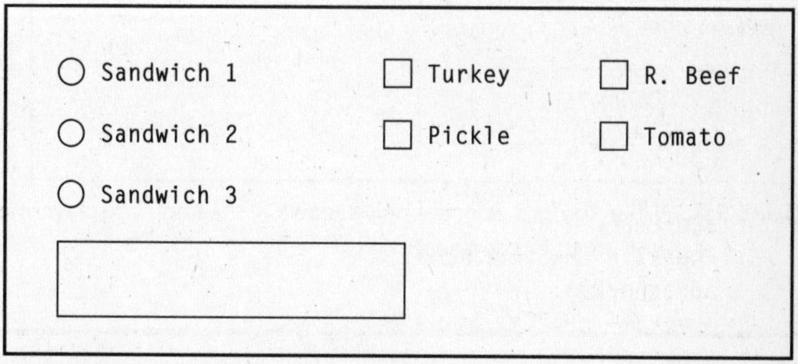

FIGURE 5.6:   An online sandwich shop

For example, if the user clicks the Sandwich 1 radio button, you set the corresponding check boxes to indicate what's in this sandwich, and indicate the total price in a text field, as shown in Figure 5.7. If the user then clicks another radio button, all the other check boxes are cleared, a new set of sandwich ingredients is indicated, and a new price appears, as shown in Figure 5.8.

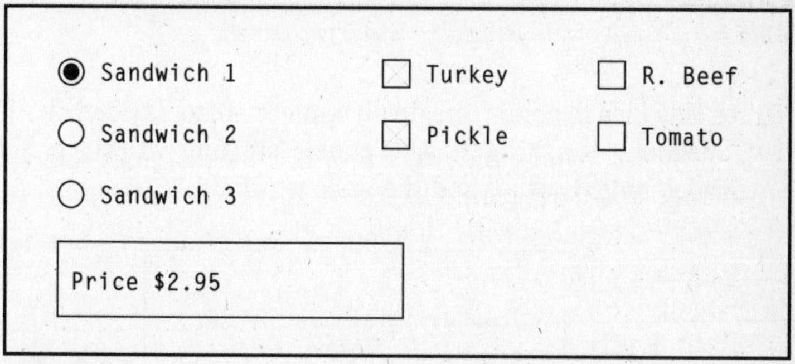

FIGURE 5.7:   When the user selects a sandwich, the applet indicates the ingredients and price of the sandwich.

You can put the controls in your applet into two panels, as shown in Figure 5.9. Panel1 will be the user menu list and price and Panel2 will be the ingredient list.

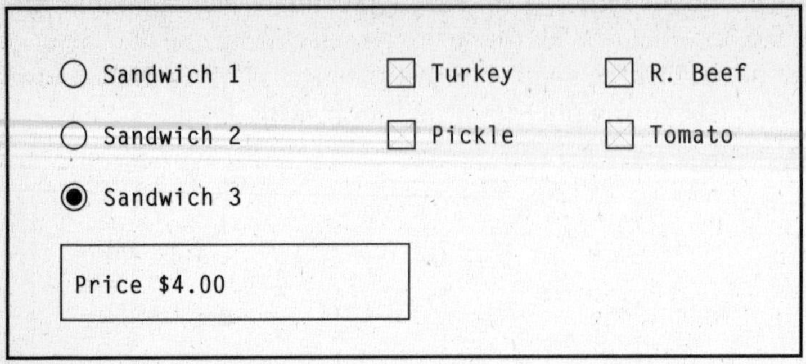

FIGURE 5.8: When the user selects a new sandwich, the applet displays information about the new sandwich.

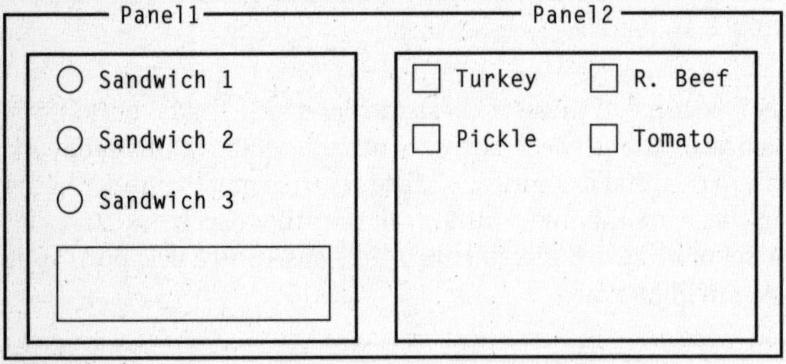

FIGURE 5.9: You'll divide your controls into two panels.

To see this idea in action, create an applet named sandwich.java.
You will begin by designing the new panels, starting with the panel with
the sandwich radio buttons and the price text field.

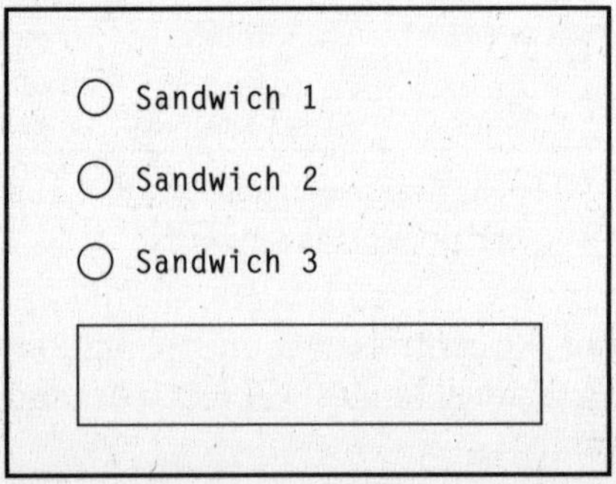

Creating the Menu Panel

You design the new panels as you did in your previous panels applet, by deriving a new class named, for instance, Menu, from the Java Panel class (add this new class to the sandwich.java file):

```
class Menu extends Panel {
    .
    .
    .

}
```

Now add the controls you'll need—note that since this panel holds radio buttons, you'll need a CheckboxGroup object and the text field for reporting the sandwich's price:

```
class Menu extends Panel {
    CheckboxGroup CGroup;
    Checkbox sandwich1, sandwich2, sandwich3;
    TextField Pricebox;
    .
    .
    .

}
```

Now add your controls to the new Panel class in that class's constructor:

```
class Menu extends Panel {
    CheckboxGroup CGroup;
    Checkbox Sandwich1, Sandwich2, Sandwich3;
    TextField Pricebox;

    Menu(){
        CGroup = new CheckboxGroup();
        add(Sandwich1 = new Checkbox("Sandwich 1",
                                CGroup, false));
        add(Sandwich2 = new Checkbox("Sandwich 2",
                                CGroup, false));
        add(Sandwich3 = new Checkbox("Sandwich 3",
                                CGroup, false));
        Pricebox = new TextField(15);
        add(Pricebox);
        }
}
```

Part i

That's it—you've set up your first panel:

```
┌─────────────────────────────┐
│                             │
│   ○  Sandwich 1             │
│                             │
│   ○  Sandwich 2             │
│                             │
│   ○  Sandwich 3             │
│                             │
│    ┌───────────────────┐    │
│    │                   │    │
│    └───────────────────┘    │
│                             │
└─────────────────────────────┘
```

Creating the Ingredients Panel

The other panel you need looks like this, with four labeled check boxes:

```
┌─────────────────────────────┐
│                             │
│                             │
│   □ Turkey     □ R. Beef    │
│                             │
│   □ Pickle     □ Tomato     │
│                             │
│                             │
│                             │
│                             │
└─────────────────────────────┘
```

You can call this new panel class `Ingredients` and add the definition of this new class to the `sandwich.java` file. All you'll need in this new class are four check boxes, labeled with the ingredients in your sandwiches:

```java
class Ingredients extends Panel {
    Checkbox Ingredient1, Ingredient2,
             Ingredient3, Ingredient4;

    Ingredients(){
        add(Ingredient1 = new Checkbox("Turkey"));
        add(Ingredient2 = new Checkbox("R.Beef"));
        add(Ingredient3 = new Checkbox("Pickle"));
        add(Ingredient4 = new Checkbox("Tomato"));
    }
```

}

And that takes care of the Ingredients panel.

Adding Panels to the *sandwich* Class

At this point, our new panels are ready to add to the sandwich class. Add that class now and declare a panel of each of our new panel classes as follows:

```java
import java.applet.Applet;
import java.awt.*;
import java.awt.event.*;

public class sandwich extends Applet {

  Menu Panel1;
  Ingredients Panel2;
      .
      .
      .

}

class Menu extends Panel {
  CheckboxGroup CGroup;
  Checkbox Sandwich1, Sandwich2, Sandwich3;
  TextField Pricebox;

  Menu(){
    CGroup = new CheckboxGroup();
    add(Sandwich1 = new Checkbox("Sandwich 1",
                                 CGroup, false));
    add(Sandwich2 = new Checkbox("Sandwich 2",
                                 CGroup, false));
    add(Sandwich3 = new Checkbox("Sandwich 3",
                                 CGroup, false));
    Pricebox = new TextField(15);
    add(Pricebox);
  }
}

class Ingredients extends Panel {
  Checkbox Ingredient1, Ingredient2,
           Ingredient3, Ingredient4;

  Ingredients(){
```

```
        add(Ingredient1 = new Checkbox("Turkey"));
        add(Ingredient2 = new Checkbox("R.Beef"));
        add(Ingredient3 = new Checkbox("Pickle"));
        add(Ingredient4 = new Checkbox("Tomato"));
    }
}
```

Now you can create and add your Menu and Ingredients panels. To
make sure they appear side by side, you'll use the GridLayout manager.
Install that manager in the applet's init() method:

```
import java.applet.Applet;
import java.awt.*;
import java.awt.event.*;

public class sandwich extends Applet {

  Menu Panel1;
  Ingredients Panel2;

   public void init(){
     setLayout(new GridLayout(1, 2));
        .
        .
        .
     }
}
```

Then simply create and add your two new panels, like this:

```
import java.applet.Applet;
import java.awt.*;
import java.awt.event.*;

public class sandwich extends Applet {

  Menu Panel1;
  Ingredients Panel2;

  public void init(){
     setLayout(new GridLayout(1, 2));
     Panel1 = new Menu();
     Panel2 = new Ingredients();
     add(Panel1);
     add(Panel2);
        .
        .
        .
  }
```

```
    }
```

At this point, your applet will look like Figure 5.10.

○ Sandwich 1	☐ Turkey	☐ R. Beef
○ Sandwich 2	☐ Pickle	☐ Tomato
○ Sandwich 3		

FIGURE 5.10: Your applet so far

NOTE

Panels do not have any predefined outlines that appear around them in an applet. They are really just constructs to arrange controls, not GUI objects.

Connecting the Buttons in Code

You haven't done anything yet to make this applet functional—you still need to connect up the buttons. You start that process as you did in our earlier example, by adding the ItemListener interface to your applet:

```
import java.applet.Applet;
import java.awt.*;
import java.awt.event.*;

public class sandwich extends Applet implements ItemListener{

  Menu Panel1;
  Ingredients Panel2;

  public void init(){
    setLayout(new GridLayout(1, 2));
    Panel1 = new Menu();
    Panel2 = new Ingredients();
    add(Panel1);
```

```
        add(Panel2);
    }

}
```

Now you have to connect the option button's `ItemListener` interfaces to your applet. In code, the option buttons are named `Sandwich1`,
`Sandwich2`, and `Sandwich3`, but you can't just execute a statement
such as

```
    Sandwich1.addItemListener(this)
```

because `Sandwich1` is not an object in your applet, but in the `Panel1`
object. That means you will reach those option buttons another way,
using the Java dot operator (`.`):

```
import java.applet.Applet;
import java.awt.*;
import java.awt.event.*;

public class sandwich extends Applet implements ItemListener{

    Menu Panel1;
    Ingredients Panel2;

    public void init(){
        setLayout(new GridLayout(1, 2));
        Panel1 = new Menu();
        Panel2 = new Ingredients();
        add(Panel1);
        Panel1.Sandwich1.addItemListener(this);
        Panel1.Sandwich2.addItemListener(this);
        Panel1.Sandwich3.addItemListener(this);
        add(Panel2);
    }
}
```

Next, add the `itemStateChanged()` method to handle radio-button
clicks:

```
import java.applet.Applet;
import java.awt.*;
import java.awt.event.*;

public class sandwich extends Applet implements ItemListener{

    Menu Panel1;
    Ingredients Panel2;
```

```
public void init(){
  setLayout(new GridLayout(1, 2));
  Panel1 = new Menu();
  Panel2 = new Ingredients();
  add(Panel1);
  Panel1.Sandwich1.addItemListener(this);
  Panel1.Sandwich2.addItemListener(this);
  Panel1.Sandwich3.addItemListener(this);
  add(Panel2);
}


public void itemStateChanged(ItemEvent e) {
  .
  .
  .
}
}
```

Now you need to handle the case in which the user clicks the radio button marked "Sandwich 1". Use the following syntax to check whether that button was clicked:

```
import java.applet.Applet;
import java.awt.*;
import java.awt.event.*;

public class sandwich extends Applet implements ItemListener{

  Menu Panel1;
  Ingredients Panel2;

  public void init(){
    setLayout(new GridLayout(1, 2));
    Panel1 = new Menu();
    Panel2 = new Ingredients();
    add(Panel1);
    Panel1.Sandwich1.addItemListener(this);
    Panel1.Sandwich2.addItemListener(this);
    Panel1.Sandwich3.addItemListener(this);
    add(Panel2);
  }


    public void itemStateChanged(ItemEvent e){
    if(e.getItemSelectable() == Panel1.Sandwich1){
      .
```

```
      }
    }
  }
```

If, in fact, the Sandwich 1 radio button is clicked, you want the check boxes to indicate what is in the sandwich, as shown in Figure 5.11.

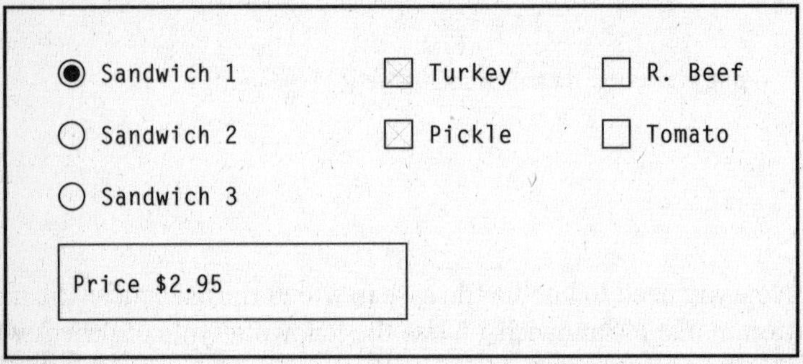

FIGURE 5.11: When the user clicks the Sandwich 1 button, the check boxes should indicate what's in the sandwich.

If the Sandwich 1 radio button was clicked, you will set the check boxes appropriately in Panel2. The check boxes are actually objects internal to the Panel2 object that you have named Ingredient1 to Ingredient4, so address them as Panel2.Ingredient1 to Panel2.Ingredient4. You can use the check box method set-State() to set the check boxes as you want them—passing a value of true makes them appear checked, and a value of false makes them appear unchecked—as well as place the price in the text field:

```
import java.applet.Applet;
import java.awt.*;
import java.awt.event.*;

public class sandwich extends Applet implements ItemListener{

  Menu Panel1;
  Ingredients Panel2;

  public void init(){
    setLayout(new GridLayout(1, 2));
    Panel1 = new Menu();
```

Working with Radio Buttons 143

```
      Panel2 = new Ingredients();
      add(Panel1);
      Panel1.Sandwich1.addItemListener(this);
      Panel1.Sandwich2.addItemListener(this);
      Panel1.Sandwich3.addItemListener(this);
      add(Panel2);
    }


    public void itemStateChanged(ItemEvent e){
      if(e.getItemSelectable() == Panel1.Sandwich1){
        Panel2.Ingredient1.setState(true);
        Panel2.Ingredient2.setState(false);
        Panel2.Ingredient3.setState(true);
        Panel2.Ingredient4.setState(false);
        Panel1.Pricebox.setText("Price: $2.95");
      }
    }
  }
```

That is how you handle the Sandwich 1 button. The other sandwich
buttons are handled similarly, but with different options, so the code to
activate them looks like this:

```
import java.applet.Applet;
import java.awt.*;
import java.awt.event.*;

public class sandwich extends Applet implements ItemListener{

  Menu Panel1;
  Ingredients Panel2;

  public void init(){
    setLayout(new GridLayout(1, 2));
    Panel1 = new Menu();
    Panel2 = new Ingredients();
    add(Panel1);
    Panel1.Sandwich1.addItemListener(this);
    Panel1.Sandwich2.addItemListener(this);
    Panel1.Sandwich3.addItemListener(this);
    add(Panel2);
  }


  public void itemStateChanged(ItemEvent e){
    if(e.getItemSelectable() == Panel1.Sandwich1){
```

```
          Panel2.Ingredient1.setState(true);
          Panel2.Ingredient2.setState(false);
          Panel2.Ingredient3.setState(true);
          Panel2.Ingredient4.setState(false);
          Panel1.Pricebox.setText("Price: $2.95");
       }
       if(e.getItemSelectable() == Panel1.Sandwich2){
          Panel2.Ingredient1.setState(false);
          Panel2.Ingredient2.setState(true);
          Panel2.Ingredient3.setState(true);
          Panel2.Ingredient4.setState(true);
          Panel1.Pricebox.setText("Price: $2.95");
       }
       if(e.getItemSelectable() == Panel1.Sandwich3){
          Panel2.Ingredient1.setState(true);
          Panel2.Ingredient2.setState(true);
          Panel2.Ingredient3.setState(true);
          Panel2.Ingredient4.setState(true);
          Panel1.Pricebox.setText("Price: $4.00");
       }
    }
 }
```

You've completed your `sandwich.java` example applet, which uses panels, check boxes, radio buttons, and a grid layout. The completed applet is shown below. (Your applet may look slightly different than the example, depending on the width settings in your HTML file. The example below was constructed using `<applet code=sandwich.class width=300 height=200>`.) When the user clicks various system options, the applet shows the corresponding price and ingredients. Your applet is a success. The code for this applet appears in `sandwich.java`.

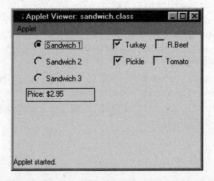

LIST 5.5: sandwich.java

```java
import java.applet.Applet;
import java.awt.*;
import java.awt.event.*;

public class sandwich extends Applet implements ItemListener{

  Menu Panel1;
  Ingredients Panel2;

  public void init(){
    setLayout(new GridLayout(1, 2));
    Panel1 = new Menu();
    Panel2 = new Ingredients();
    add(Panel1);
    Panel1.Sandwich1.addItemListener(this);
    Panel1.Sandwich2.addItemListener(this);
    Panel1.Sandwich3.addItemListener(this);
    add(Panel2);
  }


  public void itemStateChanged(ItemEvent e){
    if(e.getItemSelectable() == Panel1.Sandwich1){
      Panel2.Ingredient1.setState(true);
      Panel2.Ingredient2.setState(false);
      Panel2.Ingredient3.setState(true);
      Panel2.Ingredient4.setState(false);
      Panel1.Pricebox.setText("Price: $2.95");
    }
    if(e.getItemSelectable() == Panel1.Sandwich2){
      Panel2.Ingredient1.setState(false);
      Panel2.Ingredient2.setState(true);
      Panel2.Ingredient3.setState(true);
      Panel2.Ingredient4.setState(true);
      Panel1.Pricebox.setText("Price: $2.95");
    }
    if(e.getItemSelectable() == Panel1.Sandwich3){
      Panel2.Ingredient1.setState(true);
      Panel2.Ingredient2.setState(true);
      Panel2.Ingredient3.setState(true);
      Panel2.Ingredient4.setState(true);
      Panel1.Pricebox.setText("Price: $4.00");
    }
  }
}
```

```
class Menu extends Panel{
  CheckboxGroup CGroup;
  Checkbox Sandwich1, Sandwich2, Sandwich3;
  TextField Pricebox;

  Menu(){
    CGroup = new CheckboxGroup();
    add(Sandwich1 = new Checkbox("Sandwich 1",
                              CGroup, false));
    add(Sandwich2 = new Checkbox("Sandwich 2",
                              CGroup, false));
    add(Sandwich3 = new Checkbox("Sandwich 3",
                              CGroup, false));
    Pricebox = new TextField(15);
    add(Pricebox);
  }
}

class Ingredients extends Panel{
  Checkbox Ingredient1, Ingredient2,
           Ingredient3, Ingredient4;

  Ingredients(){
    add(Ingredient1 = new Checkbox("Turkey"));
    add(Ingredient2 = new Checkbox("R.Beef"));
    add(Ingredient3 = new Checkbox("Pickle"));
    add(Ingredient4 = new Checkbox("Tomato"));
  }
}
```

LIST 5.6: *sandwich.html*

```
<HTML>
<HEAD>
  <TITLE>Sandwich Applet</TITLE>
</HEAD>
<BODY>
  <HR>
  <APPLET code=sandwich.class width=325 height=200> </APPLET>
</BODY>
</HTML>
```

WHAT'S NEXT?

Now you're working with check boxes, radio buttons, and panels. You've also gained some practical experience accessing members of another class by reaching the buttons in your panels from your applet class. Now let's turn to another powerful Java control—scroll bars—in Chapter 6.

Part i

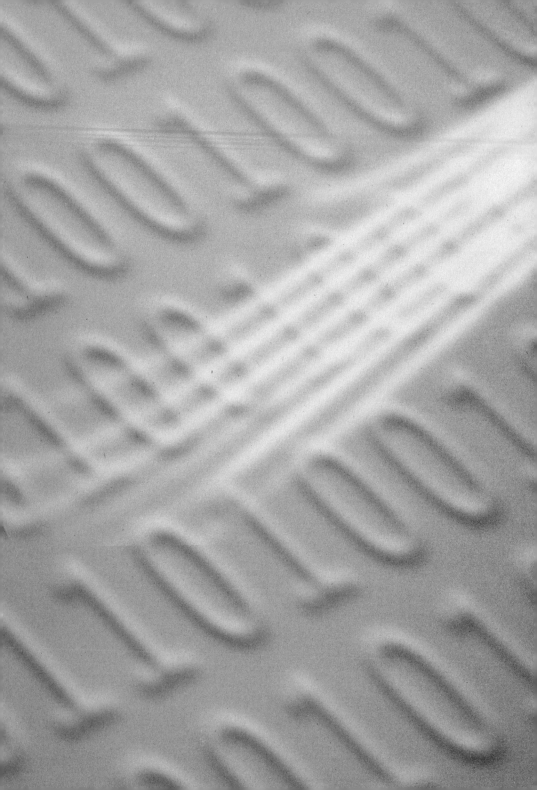

Chapter 6

ADDING SCROLL BARS

Chapter 5 provided you with a good introduction to the use of radio buttons, and showed you how to put radio buttons and check boxes together in the sandwich applet. In this chapter, you're going to continue the guided tour of Java by examining a new control: scroll bars. As any user of a windowed environment can tell you, scroll bars are very important controls. You'll also examine some additional Java layout techniques—layouts are an essential part of Java programming, and here you'll become more familiar with what Java has to offer. You'll also be introduced to the new `ScrollPane` class.

Java 2

In Record Time

Adapted from *Java 2: In Record Time* by Steven Holzner
ISBN 0-7821-2171-3   560 pages $29.99

ADDING SCROLL BARS TO PROGRAMS

Let's start off with a scroll bar example. There are two types of scroll bar controls—horizontal and vertical scroll bars—and you'll see both here. For example, let's create a new applet named scroller that contains both types of scroll bars, as shown in Figure 6.1. When the user moves a scroll bar, we'll get a report on the new horizontal or vertical position of the bars in a text field, as shown in Figure 6.2.

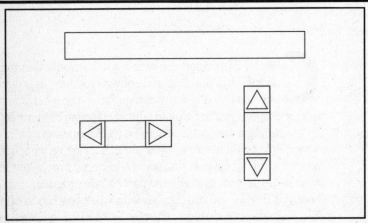

FIGURE 6.1: Our applet will contain a vertical scroll bar and a horizontal scroll bar.

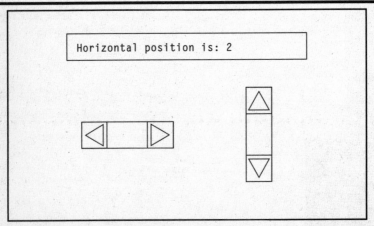

FIGURE 6.2: The text field will report the new position of the scroll bar.

This will be an easy example. Create a new file named `scroller`
`.java`. Begin by adding the text field, `text1`, and the two scroll bars,
`scroll1` and `scroll2`, which are objects of the Java `Scrollbar` class:

```
import java.applet.Applet;
import java.awt.event.*;
import java.awt.*;

public class scroller extends Applet {

    TextField text1;
    Scrollbar scroll1, scroll2;
        .
        .
        .

}
```

The Java `Scrollbar` class's methods appear in Table 6.1.

TABLE 6.1: The `Scrollbar` Class Methods

Method	Does This
`Scrollbar()`	Constructs a new vertical scroll bar.
`Scrollbar(int)`	Constructs a scroll bar with specified orientation: `Scrollbar.HORIZONTAL` or `Scrollbar.VERTICAL`.
`Scrollbar(int, int, int, int, int)`	Constructs a scroll bar with given orientation, initial value, scroll thumb size, minimum and maximum values.
`addAdjustmentListener (AdjustmentListener)`	Adds new `AdjustmentListener` to get adjustment events from this scroll bar.
`addNotify()`	Adds the scroll bar's peer.
`getBlockIncrement()`	Gets block increment for the scroll bar.
`getLineIncrement()`	Deprecated. Replaced by `getUnitIncrement()`.
`getMaximum()`	Gets maximum setting of this scroll bar.
`getMinimum()`	Gets minimum setting of this scroll bar.
`getOrientation()`	Determines the orientation of this scroll bar.
`getPageIncrement()`	Deprecated. Replaced by `getBlockIncrement()`.
`getUnitIncrement()`	Gets the unit increment for this scroll bar.
`getValue()`	Gets the current value of this scroll bar.
`getVisible()`	Deprecated. Replaced by `getVisibleAmount()`.

TABLE 6.1 continued: The Scrollbar Class Methods

METHOD	DOES THIS
getVisibleAmount()	Gets the visible amount of this scroll bar.
paramString()	Gets the string parameters for representing the state of this scroll bar.
process AdjustmentEvent (AdjustmentEvent)	Processes the adjustment events of this scroll bar by dispatching them to AdjustmentListener objects.
processEvent(AWTEvent)	Processes events for this scroll bar.
removeAdjustmentListener (AdjustmentListener)	Removes the specified AdjustmentListener so that it no longer gets adjustment events.
setBlockIncrement(int)	Sets block increment for this scroll bar.
setLineIncrement(int)	Deprecated. Replaced by setUnitIncrement(int).
setMaximum(int)	Sets maximum value for this scroll bar.
setMinimum(int)	Sets minimum value for this scroll bar.
setOrientation(int)	Sets orientation for this scroll bar.
setPageIncrement(int)	Deprecated. Replaced by setBlockIncrement().
setUnitIncrement(int)	Sets the unit increment for this scroll bar.
setValue(int)	Sets the value of this scroll bar to the specified value.
setValues(int, int, int, int)	Sets the values for this scroll bar.
setVisibleAmount(int)	Sets the visible amount of this scroll bar.

Installing Scroll Bars

In the init() method, you will add scroll bars and text fields to the applet. You'll start with the text field needed to report the scroll bars' positions, text1:

```java
import java.applet.Applet;
import java.awt.event.*;
import java.awt.*;

public class scroller extends Applet {
```

```
    TextField text1;
    Scrollbar scroll1, scroll2;

    public void init(){
      text1 = new TextField(20);
      add(text1);
           .
           .
           .

    }
}
```

Now you will continue constructing your horizontal scroll bar,
scroll1, by passing these parameters to its constructor (see Table 6.1):
its orientation (you use the predefined Scrollbar class constants
Scrollbar.HORIZONTAL or Scrollbar.VERTICAL, which are built
into the Scrollbar class), the scroll bar's initial value (i.e., the location
of the scroll box in the scroll bar—called the *thumb*), the size of the scroll
thumb in pixels, and the scroll bar's minimum possible value (use 1) and
its maximum possible value (use 100):

```
    import java.applet.Applet;
    import java.awt.event.*;
    import java.awt.*;


    public class scroller extends Applet {

      TextField text1;
      Scrollbar scroll1, scroll2;

      public void init(){
        text1 = new TextField(20);
        add(text1);

        scroll1 = new Scrollbar(Scrollbar.HORIZONTAL,
                                1, 10, 1, 100);
        add(scroll1);
             .
             .
             .

      }
    }
```

TIP

Using the setValues() method, you can change a scroll bar's maximum and minimum possible values while your applet is running. You can also scroll the scroll bar from code with the setValue() method. (It's a common error to confuse setValue() with setValues(), but note that these are two different methods.)

Using this code, you will create a new horizontal scroll bar whose values can range from 1 to 100, and whose initial value is 1.

In the same way, you can create a similar scroll bar, scroll2, which has the same value range but is vertical:

```java
import java.applet.Applet;
import java.awt.event.*;
import java.awt.*;


public class scroller extends Applet {

    TextField text1;
    Scrollbar scroll1, scroll2;

    public void init(){
        text1 = new TextField(20);
        add(text1);

        scroll1 = new Scrollbar(Scrollbar.HORIZONTAL,
                                1, 10, 1, 100);
        add(scroll1);

        scroll2 = new Scrollbar(Scrollbar.VERTICAL,
                                1, 10, 1, 100);
        add(scroll2);
    }
}
```

That's it—your scroll bars will now appear in your applet.

Connecting Scroll Bars to Code

The next step is to connect the scroll bars to code. You might think that's done with an ActionListener or ItemListener interface—but in fact, the *AdjustmentListener* interface is used this time, because scroll bars are considered *adjustable* controls. Use the addAdjustmentListener()

method of the `Scrollbar` class as you used the `addItemListener()` and `addActionListener()`.

```
import java.applet.Applet;
import java.awt.event.*;
import java.awt.*;


public class scroller extends Applet
    implements AdjustmentListener {

   TextField text1;
   Scrollbar scroll1, scroll2;

   public void init(){
     text1 = new TextField(20);
     add(text1);

     scroll1 = new Scrollbar(Scrollbar.HORIZONTAL,
                        1, 10, 1, 100);
     add(scroll1);
     scroll1.addAdjustmentListener(this);

     scroll2 = new Scrollbar(Scrollbar.VERTICAL,
                        1, 10, 1, 100);
     add(scroll2);
     scroll2.addAdjustmentListener(this);
   }
}
```

You can determine which scroll bar caused the event by overriding the `adjustmentValueChanged()` method. That method takes a parameter of class `AdjustmentEvent`:

```
import java.applet.Applet;
import java.awt.event.*;
import java.awt.*;


public class scroller extends Applet
    implements AdjustmentListener {

   TextField text1;
   Scrollbar scroll1, scroll2;

   public void init(){
     text1 = new TextField(20);
     add(text1);
```

```
            scroll1 = new Scrollbar(Scrollbar.HORIZONTAL,
                            1, 10, 1, 100);
            add(scroll1);
            scroll1.addAdjustmentListener(this);
            scroll2 = new Scrollbar(Scrollbar.VERTICAL,
                            1, 10, 1, 100);
            add(scroll2);
            scroll2.addAdjustmentListener(this);
        }

        public void adjustmentValueChanged(AdjustmentEvent e){
            .
            .
            .

        }
    }
```

You can determine which scroll bar caused the event with the
AdjustableEvent class's getAdjustable() method the following
way, where you check to see if scroll1 caused the scroll event:

```
import java.applet.Applet;
import java.awt.event.*;
import java.awt.*;


public class scroller extends Applet
    implements AdjustmentListener {

    TextField text1;
    Scrollbar scroll1, scroll2;

    public void init(){
        text1 = new TextField(20);
        add(text1);
        scroll1 = new Scrollbar(Scrollbar.HORIZONTAL,
                            1, 10, 1, 100);
        add(scroll1);
        scroll1.addAdjustmentListener(this);
        scroll2 = new Scrollbar(Scrollbar.VERTICAL,
                            1, 10, 1, 100);
        add(scroll2);
        scroll2.addAdjustmentListener(this);
    }

    public void adjustmentValueChanged(AdjustmentEvent e){
        if(e.getAdjustable() == scroll1) {
```

```
        }
      }
    }
```

The first step is to set the scroll bar's thumb position to the place the user scrolled it to. That might seem funny, but it turns out that unless you arrange to update the scroll bar's thumb yourself in the program code, it will spring back when the user releases it to the position it occupied before it was scrolled. The reason that you have to move it yourself is that the user may have moved the thumb to some location you consider "forbidden," and Java allows you the option of not accepting the user's scroll actions in that case. To set the thumb's new location, use the Scrollbar class's setValue() method, and to get its current value, use the getValue() method. To place the thumb at the location the user moved it to, execute this code:

```java
import java.applet.Applet;
import java.awt.event.*;
import java.awt.*;


public class scroller extends Applet
    implements AdjustmentListener {

  TextField text1;
  Scrollbar scroll1, scroll2;

  public void init(){
    text1 = new TextField(20);
    add(text1);
    scroll1 = new Scrollbar(Scrollbar.HORIZONTAL,
                      1, 10, 1, 100);
    add(scroll1);
    scroll1.addAdjustmentListener(this);
    scroll2 = new Scrollbar(Scrollbar.VERTICAL,
                      1, 10, 1, 100);
    add(scroll2);
    scroll2.addAdjustmentListener(this);
  }

  public void adjustmentValueChanged(AdjustmentEvent e){
    if(e.getAdjustable() == scroll1) {
      scroll1.setValue(scroll1.getValue());
```

```
        .
        .
      }
    }
  }
```

WARNING

Don't forget to arrange for the scroll bar thumb to be set to its new value when it has been scrolled, or it will appear to "jump" back on its own when the user releases it.

Because `scroll1`, the horizontal scroll bar, was scrolled, we need to display the new setting of that scroll bar in the text field `text1`. To do so, convert the value of `scroll1` to an integer and display it in `text1` this way:

```java
import java.applet.Applet;
import java.awt.event.*;
import java.awt.*;


public class scroller extends Applet
    implements AdjustmentListener {

  TextField text1;
  Scrollbar scroll1, scroll2;

  public void init(){
    text1 = new TextField(20);
    add(text1);
    scroll1 = new Scrollbar(Scrollbar.HORIZONTAL,
                            1, 10, 1, 100);
    add(scroll1);
    scroll1.addAdjustmentListener(this);
    scroll2 = new Scrollbar(Scrollbar.VERTICAL,
                            1, 10, 1, 100);
    add(scroll2);
    scroll2.addAdjustmentListener(this);
  }

  public void adjustmentValueChanged(AdjustmentEvent e){
    if(e.getAdjustable() == scroll1) {
      scroll1.setValue(scroll1.getValue());
      text1.setText("Horizontal position: "
                    + scroll1.getValue());
```

```
          }
        }
      }
```

TIP

You can concatenate—that is, join—strings in Java with the + operator, as in the line text1.setText("horizontal position: " + scroll1.get-Value());.

Display `scroll2`'s value, as you did for `scroll1`, with the following code:

```
import java.applet.Applet;
import java.awt.event.*;
import java.awt.*;


public class scroller extends Applet
    implements AdjustmentListener {

  TextField text1;
  Scrollbar scroll1, scroll2;

  public void init(){
    text1 = new TextField(20);
    add(text1);
    scroll1 = new Scrollbar(Scrollbar.HORIZONTAL,
                    1, 10, 1, 100);
    add(scroll1);
    scroll1.addAdjustmentListener(this);
    scroll2 = new Scrollbar(Scrollbar.VERTICAL,
                    1, 10, 1, 100);
    add(scroll2);
    scroll2.addAdjustmentListener(this);
  }

  public void adjustmentValueChanged(AdjustmentEvent e){
    if(e.getAdjustable() == scroll1) {
      scroll1.setValue(scroll1.getValue());
      text1.setText("Horizontal position: "
                    + scroll1.getValue());
    }
    if(e.getAdjustable() == scroll2) {
      scroll2.setValue(scroll2.getValue());
```

```
                    text1.setText("Vertical position: "
                                  + scroll2.getValue());
        }
    }
}
```

Your scroll bar applet is ready to go. As shown below, the user can move the scroll bar thumbs, and their new position will be reported in the text fields. Your scrolling applet is a success! The code for this applet appears in scroller.java.

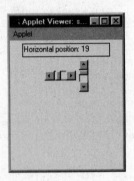

LIST 6.1: scroller.java

```
import java.applet.Applet;
import java.awt.event.*;
import java.awt.*;


public class scroller extends Applet
    implements AdjustmentListener {

    TextField text1;
    Scrollbar scroll1, scroll2;

    public void init(){
        text1 = new TextField(20);
        add(text1);
        scroll1 = new Scrollbar(Scrollbar.HORIZONTAL,
                                1, 10, 1, 100);
        add(scroll1);
        scroll1.addAdjustmentListener(this);
        scroll2 = new Scrollbar(Scrollbar.VERTICAL,
                                1, 10, 1, 100);
```

```
        add(scroll2);
        scroll2.addAdjustmentListener(this);
    }

    public void adjustmentValueChanged(AdjustmentEvent e){
        if(e.getAdjustable() == scroll1) {
            scroll1.setValue(scroll1.getValue());
            text1.setText("Horizontal position: "
                        + scroll1.getValue());
        }
        if(e.getAdjustable() == scroll2) {
            scroll2.setValue(scroll2.getValue());
            text1.setText("Vertical position: "
                        + scroll2.getValue());
    }
    }
}
```

LIST 6.2: scroller.htm
```
<html>
  <head>
    <title>Scroller applet</title>
  </head>
  <body>
    <applet code=scroller.class width=200 height=200>
    </applet>
  </body>
</html>
```

There is a special Java layout manager—the *BorderLayout* manager—
that is perfect for use with scroll bars, although even many Java experts
do not know about it. Let's use this layout to add power to the following
applet.

USING SCROLL BARS AND BORDERLAYOUT

The BorderLayout manager will allow you to surround your applet with
scroll bars, as shown in Figure 6.3. When the user scrolls the horizontal
or vertical scroll bars, you can get a report of the settings of the changed
scroll bar in the text field, as shown in Figure 6.4.

FIGURE 6.3: Using the BorderLayout manager to place the scroll bars

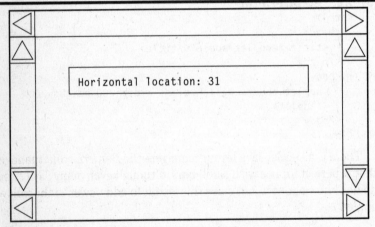

FIGURE 6.4: Reporting the new position of the scroll bar

Let's see this feature in action. Create a new file named, say, scroll-border.java. You declare the controls you need—two horizontal scroll bars, hScroll1 and hScroll2, and two vertical scroll bars, vScroll1 and vScroll2—as follows:

```
import java.applet.Applet;
import java.awt.*;
import java.awt.event.*;

public class scrollborder extends Applet
    implements AdjustmentListener {
```

```
Scrollbar hScroll1, hScroll2, vScroll1, vScroll2;
    .
    .
    .
}
```

You want to display a text field in the center of the applet. To accommodate this, you will place a text field in a panel (named `Panel1`) of a new class named `textpanel`:

```
import java.applet.Applet;
import java.awt.*;
import java.awt.event.*;

public class scrollborder extends Applet
    implements AdjustmentListener {

    Scrollbar hScroll1, hScroll2, vScroll1, vScroll2;
    textPanel Panel1;
    .
    .
    .

}
```

Create your `textpanel` class now. To do so, add this code to the end of the `scrollborder.java` file:

```
class textpanel extends Panel {
    .
    .
    .

}
```

You learned how to work with panels in Chapter 5. All you need to do here is create and add a text field, which you might call `Text1`, to your text panel's contructor method:

```
class textPanel extends Panel {
    TextField Text1;

    textPanel(){
      Text1 = new TextField(20);
      add(Text1);
      }
}
```

Now that your new panel class is ready, you can set up your new layout. This layout will consist of four scroll bars surrounding your central panel, and as you'll see, that's easy to set up with the BorderLayout manager. First, install BorderLayout as your new layout manager in the applet's `init()` method:

```
import java.applet.Applet;
import java.awt.*;
import java.awt.event.*;

public class scrollborder extends Applet
        implements AdjustmentListener {

    Scrollbar hScroll1, hScroll2, vScroll1, vScroll2;
    textPanel Panel1;

    public void init(){
        setLayout(new BorderLayout());
          .
          .
          .
        }

    }
```

You can now add your controls to this new layout. When you add controls to the BorderLayout manager, you specify where the new control goes—around the edges of the applet (which are designated `north`, `south`, `east`, and `west`) or in the `center`, as shown in Figure 6.5.

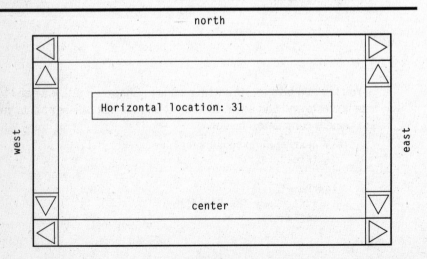

FIGURE 6.5: Locations in the layout are designated as north, south, east, west, and center.

For example, create and add a scroll bar on the top of the applet—the "North" position—like this, where you also connect your applet as its AdjustmentListener:

```
import java.applet.Applet;
import java.awt.*;
import java.awt.event.*;

public class scrollborder extends Applet
    implements AdjustmentListener {

    Scrollbar hScroll1, hScroll2, vScroll1, vScroll2;
    textPanel Panel1;

    public void init(){
      setLayout(new BorderLayout());

      hScroll1 = new Scrollbar(Scrollbar.HORIZONTAL,
                              1, 1, 1, 200);
      add("North", hScroll1);
      hScroll1.addAdjustmentListener(this);
                .
                .
                .
    }
}
```

Continue on, adding the other scroll bars and the Panel1 object in the center of your applet:

```
import java.applet.Applet;
import java.awt.*;
import java.awt.event.*;

public class scrollborder extends Applet
    implements AdjustmentListener {

    Scrollbar hScroll1, hScroll2, vScroll1, vScroll2;
    textPanel Panel1;

    public void init(){
      setLayout(new BorderLayout());

      hScroll1 = new Scrollbar(Scrollbar.HORIZONTAL,
                              1, 1, 1, 200);
      add("North", hScroll1);
      hScroll1.addAdjustmentListener(this);
```

```
                   vScroll1 = new Scrollbar(Scrollbar.VERTICAL,
                                           1, 1, 1, 200)
                   add("West", vScroll1);
                   vScroll1.addAdjustmentListener(this);

                   hScroll2 = new Scrollbar(Scrollbar.HORIZONTAL,
                                           1, 1, 1, 200);
                   add("South", hScroll2);
                   hScroll2.addAdjustmentListener(this);

                   vScroll2 = new Scrollbar(Scrollbar.VERTICAL,
                                           1, 1, 1, 200)
                   add("East", vScroll2);
                   vScroll2.addAdjustmentListener(this);

                   Panel1 = new textPanel();
                   add("Center", Panel1);

             }
       }
```

Now the scroll bars are laid out correctly in the applet. All that remains
is to connect them to the code in the adjustmentValueChanged()
method. To do this, add the following code to scrollborder.java:

```
       import java.applet.Applet;
       import java.awt.*;
       import java.awt.event.*;

       public class scrollborder extends Applet
           implements AdjustmentListener {

           Scrollbar hScroll1, hScroll2, vScroll1, vScroll2;
           textPanel Panel1;

           public void init(){
             setLayout(new BorderLayout());

             hScroll1 = new Scrollbar(Scrollbar.HORIZONTAL,
                                     1, 1, 1, 200);
             add("North", hScroll1);
             hScroll1.addAdjustmentListener(this);

             vScroll1 = new Scrollbar(Scrollbar.VERTICAL,
                                     1, 1, 1, 200);
             add("West", vScroll1);
             vScroll1.addAdjustmentListener(this);
```

```
      hScroll2 = new Scrollbar(Scrollbar.HORIZONTAL,
                               1, 1, 1, 200);
      add("South", hScroll2);
      hScroll2.addAdjustmentListener(this);

      vScroll2 = new Scrollbar(Scrollbar.VERTICAL,
                               1, 1, 1, 200);
      add("East", vScroll2);
      vScroll2.addAdjustmentListener(this);

      Panel1 = new textPanel();
      add("Center", Panel1);
    }

    public void adjustmentValueChanged(AdjustmentEvent e){
               .
               .
               .
    }
}
```

Note that you should keep the scroll bars coordinated (i.e., if the user scrolls one, you should update the other as well):

```
import java.applet.Applet;
import java.awt.*;
import java.awt.event.*;

public class scrollborder extends Applet
    implements AdjustmentListener {

    Scrollbar hScroll1, hScroll2, vScroll1, vScroll2;
    textPanel Panel1;

    public void init(){
      setLayout(new BorderLayout());

      hScroll1 = new Scrollbar(Scrollbar.HORIZONTAL,
                               1, 1, 1, 200);
      add("North", hScroll1);
      hScroll1.addAdjustmentListener(this);

      vScroll1 = new Scrollbar(Scrollbar.VERTICAL,
                               1, 1, 1, 200);
      add("West", vScroll1);
      vScroll1.addAdjustmentListener(this);
```

```
               hScroll2 = new Scrollbar(Scrollbar.HORIZONTAL,
                                   1, 1, 1, 200);
          add("South", hScroll2);
          hScroll2.addAdjustmentListener(this);

               vScroll2 = new Scrollbar(Scrollbar.VERTICAL,
                                   1, 1, 1, 200);
          add("East", vScroll2);
          vScroll2.addAdjustmentListener(this);

          Panel1 = new textPanel();
          add("Center", Panel1);
     }

     public void adjustmentValueChanged(AdjustmentEvent e){
          if(e.getAdjustable() == hScroll1){

          hScroll1.setValue(hScroll1.getValue());
          hScroll2.setValue(hScroll1.getValue());
     }
     if(e.getAdjustable() == vScroll1){
          vScroll1.setValue(vScroll1.getValue());
          vScroll2.setValue(vScroll1.getValue());
     }
      if(e.getAdjustable() == hScroll2){
          hScroll2.setValue(hScroll2.getValue());
          hScroll1.setValue(hScroll2.getValue());
     }
      if(e.getAdjustable() == vScroll2){
          vScroll2.setValue(vScroll2.getValue());
          vScroll1.setValue(vScroll2.getValue());
     }
    }

  }
```

Finally, you can report the new scroll bar positions in the appropriate text field as follows:

```
import java.applet.Applet;
import java.awt.*;
import java.awt.event.*;

public class scrollborder extends Applet
     implements AdjustmentListener {
```

```
Scrollbar hScroll1, hScroll2, vScroll1, vScroll2;
textPanel Panel1;

public void init(){
  setLayout(new BorderLayout());
    .
    .
    .
}

public void adjustmentValueChanged(AdjustmentEvent e){
  if(e.getAdjustable() == hScroll1){
    hScroll1.setValue(hScroll1.getValue());
    hScroll2.setValue(hScroll1.getValue());
    Panel1.Text1.setText("Horizontal location: "
                       + hScroll1.getValue());
  }
  if(e.getAdjustable() == vScroll1){

    vScroll1.setValue(vScroll1.getValue());
    vScroll2.setValue(vScroll1.getValue());
    Panel1.Text1.setText("Vertical location: "
                       + vScroll1.getValue());
  }
  if(e.getAdjustable() == hScroll2){
    hScroll2.setValue(hScroll2.getValue());
    hScroll1.setValue(hScroll2.getValue());
    Panel1.Text1.setText("Horizontal location: "
                       + hScroll2.getValue());
  }
  if(e.getAdjustable() == vScroll2){
    vScroll2.setValue(vScroll2.getValue());
    vScroll1.setValue(vScroll2.getValue());
    Panel1.Text1.setText("Vertical location: "
                       + vScroll2.getValue());
  }
 }
}
```

And that's it—your scrollborder applet is finished. Run the scrollborder applet now. As you can see below, the scroll bars appear surrounding the central panel. When the user scrolls the scroll bars, the new horizontal and vertical positions appear in the text fields. The code for this applet appears in scrollborder.java.

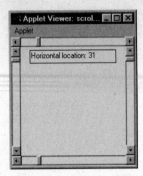

TIP

If you want to move controls around in the central panel in response to the action of the surrounding scroll bars, just use the control's SetLocation() method (which most Java controls have). This can give the user the impression that they are scrolling the controls around inside the applet.

LIST 6.3: *scrollborder.java*

```java
import java.applet.Applet;
import java.awt.*;
import java.awt.event.*;

public class scrollborder extends Applet
    implements AdjustmentListener {

    Scrollbar hScroll1, hScroll2, vScroll1, vScroll2;
    textPanel Panel1;

    public void init(){
      setLayout(new BorderLayout());

      hScroll1 = new Scrollbar(Scrollbar.HORIZONTAL,
                          1, 1, 1, 200);
      add("North", hScroll1);
      hScroll1.addAdjustmentListener(this);

      vScroll1 = new Scrollbar(Scrollbar.VERTICAL,
                          1, 1, 1, 200);
      add("West", vScroll1);
      vScroll1.addAdjustmentListener(this);
```

```
        hScroll2 = new Scrollbar(Scrollbar.HORIZONTAL,
                                 1, 1, 1, 200);
        add("South", hScroll2);
        hScroll2.addAdjustmentListener(this);

        vScroll2 = new Scrollbar(Scrollbar.VERTICAL,
                                 1, 1, 1, 200);
        add("East", vScroll2);
        vScroll2.addAdjustmentListener(this);

        Panel1 = new textPanel();
        add("Center", Panel1);
    }

    public void adjustmentValueChanged(AdjustmentEvent e){
        if(e.getAdjustable() == hScroll1){
            hScroll1.setValue(hScroll1.getValue());
            hScroll2.setValue(hScroll1.getValue());
            Panel1.Text1.setText("Horizontal location: "
                                 + hScroll1.getValue());
        }
        if(e.getAdjustable() == vScroll1){

            vScroll1.setValue(vScroll1.getValue());
            vScroll2.setValue(vScroll1.getValue());
            Panel1.Text1.setText("Vertical location: "
                                 + vScroll1.getValue());
        }
        if(e.getAdjustable() == hScroll2){
            hScroll2.setValue(hScroll2.getValue());
            hScroll1.setValue(hScroll2.getValue());
            Panel1.Text1.setText("Horizontal location: "
                                 + hScroll2.getValue());
        }
        if(e.getAdjustable() == vScroll2){
            vScroll2.setValue(vScroll2.getValue());
            vScroll1.setValue(vScroll2.getValue());
            Panel1.Text1.setText("Vertical location: "
                                 + vScroll2.getValue());
        }
    }

}

class textPanel extends Panel {
    TextField Text1;
```

```
        textPanel(){
          Text1 = new TextField(20);
          add(Text1);
        }
    }
```

LIST 6.4: *scrollborder.html*

```
<html>
  <head>
    <title>Scrollborder applet</title>
  </head>
  <body>
    <applet code=scrollborder.class width=250 height=200>
    </applet>
  </body>
</html>
```

That's it—now you can use scroll bars with the border layout, giving your Java programs a professional air.

WORKING WITH THE *SCROLLPANE* CLASS

Java 1.1 introduced a class called `ScrollPane`, which lets you place a control in the middle of a container object and display it. Scroll bars will appear around the edges of this container as needed. This is something like the example we just developed, except the `ScrollPane` class scrolls the controls placed in its pane automatically, instead of letting you handle the scrolling events yourself. It's easy to implement, so let's see it at work now. Create a file named `scrpane.java`, and start it off as usual:

```
import java.applet.Applet;
import java.awt.*;

public class scrpane extends Applet {

}
```

Now add your `ScrollPane` object, which you might call `scrollpane1`:

```
import java.applet.Applet;
import java.awt.*;

public class scrpane extends Applet {

    ScrollPane scrollpane1;
```

```
    public void init(){
        scrollpane1 = new ScrollPane();
             .
             .
             .
    }

}
```

All you have to do is create a new control and add it to your Scroll-Pane object. You will add a new text field to the ScrollPane object as follows:

```
import java.applet.Applet;
import java.awt.*;

public class scrpane extends Applet {

    ScrollPane scrollpane1;
    TextField text1;

    public void init(){
        scrollpane1 = new ScrollPane();
        text1 = new TextField("Welcome to Java");
        scrollpane1.add(text1);
             .
             .
             .

    }
}
```

The Java ScrollPane class's methods appear in Table 6.2.

TABLE 6.2: The ScrollPane Class Methods

METHOD	DOES THIS
ScrollPane()	Creates a new scroll pane container with a display policy of "as needed."
ScrollPane(int)	Creates a new scroll pane container.
addImpl(Component, Object, int)	Adds the specified component to this scroll pane container.
addNotify()	Creates the scroll pane's peer.
doLayout()	Lays out the container by resizing its child to its preferred size.

TABLE 6.2 continued: The `ScrollPane` Class Methods

METHOD	DOES THIS
getHAdjustable()	Returns the `Adjustable` object that represents the horizontal scroll bar.
getHScrollbarHeight()	Returns the height that would be occupied by a horizontal scroll bar.
getScrollbarDisplayPolicy()	Returns the display policy for the scroll bars.
getScrollPosition()	Returns the current x,y position within the child, which is displayed at the 0,0 location of the scrolled panel's view.
getVAdjustable()	Returns the `Adjustable` object that represents the state of the vertical scroll bar.
getViewportSize()	Returns the current size of the scroll pane's view port.
getVScrollbarWidth()	Returns the width that would be occupied by a vertical scroll bar.
paramString()	Returns the parameter string of this container.
layout	Deprecated. Replaced by doLayout().
printComponents(Graphics)	Prints the component in this scroll pane.
setLayout(LayoutManager)	Sets the layout manager for this container.
setScrollPosition(int, int)	Scrolls to the given position in the child component.
setScrollPosition(Point)	Scrolls to the given position in the child component.

All that's left is to add the `ScrollPane` object to your applet:

```java
import java.applet.Applet;
import java.awt.*;

public class scrpane extends Applet {

    ScrollPane scrollpane1;
    TextField text1;

    public void init(){
        scrollpane1 = new ScrollPane();
        text1 = new TextField("Welcome to Java");
```

```
            scrollpanel.add(text1);
            add(scrollpanel);
        }

    }
```

You can run the applet now, as shown below. As you can see, the
ScrollPane is active, and by using the scroll bar, the user can scroll
your control in the ScrollPane. In this way, you can put controls into a
ScrollPane and let the user scroll as needed. This new applet appears
in scrpane.java.

LIST 6.5: scrpane.java

```java
import java.applet.Applet;
import java.awt.*;

public class scrpane extends Applet {

    ScrollPane scrollpanel;
    TextField text1;

    public void init(){
        scrollpanel = new ScrollPane();
        text1 = new TextField("Welcome to Java");
        scrollpanel.add(text1);
        add(scrollpanel);
    }

}
```

LIST 6.6: scrpane.html

```
<html>
  <head>
    <title>Scrpane applet</title>
  </head>
  <body>
    <applet code=scrpane.class width=150 height=150>
    </applet>
  </body>
</html>
```

That's all there is to it—now you're using the ScrollPane class.

WHAT'S NEXT?

We've come far in Chapter 6, adding scrolling to our arsenal of Java techniques. Now we'll move on to more advanced uses of Java: applets, applications, and the Java Development Kit.

PART ii
JAVA FUNDAMENTALS

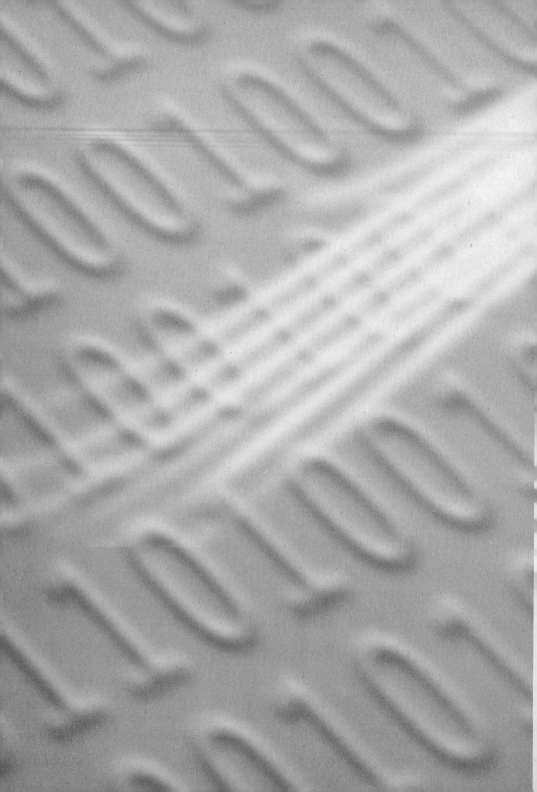

Chapter 7

APPLETS, APPLICATIONS, AND THE JAVA DEVELOPMENT KIT

Java programs come in three flavors: *applets*, *servlets*, and *applications*. Simply speaking, a Java applet is a program that appears embedded in a Web document; a servlet is a special Java program that runs inside a Web server. A Java application is the term applied to all other kinds of Java programs, such as those found on network servers and consumer electronics. Much of this chapter will be devoted to the differences between applets and applications, along with the ways these differences affect the Java software development path.

Adapted from *Mastering Java 2* by John Zukowski
ISBN 0-7821-2180-2   1280 pages $49.99

The Java Development Kit (JDK) from Sun's JavaSoft division contains the basic tools and libraries necessary for creating and executing Java applets and applications. It also contains a number of useful utilities for debugging and documenting Java source code, and for interfacing C to Java code. You will learn how to download, install, and apply the JDK to the construction of both applets and applications. Along the way, you will receive a primer on HTML for applets and get your first taste of Java source code. You'll also learn about the Java Runtime Environment (JRE), which is what you deliver with your Java applications so others can run your programs.

SERVLETS

At a superficial level, a servlet is much like an applet. It does not run as an application or start at a static main() method; rather, it is loaded and an instance is created. When the instance exists, it is given an environment from which it can determine details, such as the parameters with which it has been invoked.

In an Applet class, the behavior is largely determined by a few methods: init(), start(), stop(), destroy(), and paint(). In a class implementing the Servlet interface, the same basic concept is used, but the particular set of implementing methods is slightly different.

A servlet does not need to become active or inactive in the way that an applet does when it moves in and out of the current page. Also, a servlet does not have a GUI of its own. The Servlet interface, therefore, does not define the start(), stop(), or paint() methods. The main behavior of the servlet is required in response to a new connection at the server, and that connection results in a call to the service() method of the servlet.

A servlet, rather than an applet, might be the better choice if any of these considerations apply:

▶ Privileged access to server facilities. An applet generally does not have any special access to services and information on a server, and a server usually cannot distinguish between a request from an applet that it might want to trust and any other request.

CONTINUED ➡

▶ Protection of proprietary algorithms. In a number of ways, Java's byte-code is easier to reverse-engineer than other machine languages. Because of this, a proprietary algorithm of significant value should generally not be entrusted to an applet.

▶ Concerns about browser incompatibility. If you do not know what version of a browser your end user is running, you may not be able to take advantage of some of the latest Java capabilities. Therefore, you may need to move the execution of part of your program to the Web server.

The Java Web Server is Sun's Web server, written in Java, which supports the use of servlets and can be used on any Java-capable platform. It is not part of the JDK distribution, but you can download it from the Sun site: `http://jserv.java.sun.com`. Many other servers already provide support for this mechanism. For an up-to-date list of third-party server implementations, see `http://jserv.java.sun.com/products/java-server/servlets/environments.html`.

JAVA APPLETS VERSUS JAVA APPLICATIONS

Traditionally, the word *applet* has come to mean any small application. In Java, an applet is any Java program that is launched from a Web document—that is, from an HTML file. Java applications, on the other hand, are programs that run from a command line, independent of a Web browser. The size or complexity of a Java applet has no limit. In fact, Java applets are in some ways more powerful than Java applications. However, with the Internet, where communication speed is limited and download times are long, most Java applets are small by necessity.

The technical differences between applets and applications stem from the context in which they run. A Java application runs in the simplest possible environment—its only input from the outside world is a list of command-line parameters. On the other hand, a Java applet receives a lot of information from the Web browser. It needs to know when it is initialized, when and where to draw itself in the browser window, and when it is activated or deactivated. As a consequence of these two very different execution environments, applets and applications have different minimum requirements.

The decision to write a program as an applet versus an application depends on the context of the program and its delivery mechanism. Because Java applets are always presented in the context of a Web browser's graphical user interface (GUI), Java applications are preferred over applets when graphical displays are unnecessary. For example, an HTTP server written in Java needs no graphical display; it requires only file and network access.

The convenience of Web protocols for applet distribution makes applets the preferred program type for Internet applications, although applications can easily be used to perform many of the same tasks. With Java, writing Internet-based software, either as applets or applications, is extremely easy. Non-networked systems and systems with small amounts of memory are much more likely to be written as Java applications than as Java applets.

Table 7.1 summarizes the differences between these two flavors of Java programs.

TABLE 7.1: Differences between Java Applets and Applications

	JAVA APPLICATION	JAVA APPLET
Use of graphics	Optional	Inherently graphical
Memory requirements	Minimal Java application requirements	Java application requirements plus Web browser requirements
Distribution	Loaded from the file system or by a custom class loading process	Linked via HTML and transported via HTTP
Environmental input	Command-line parameters	Browser client location and size; parameters embedded in the host HTML document
Method expected by the Virtual Machine (VM)	main—startup method	init—initialization method start—startup method stop—pause/deactivate method destroy—termination method paint—drawing method

TABLE 7.1 continued: Differences between Java Applets and Applications

	JAVA APPLICATION	JAVA APPLET
Typical applications	Network server; multimedia kiosks; developer tools; appliance and consumer electronics control and navigation	Public-access order-entry systems for the Web; online multimedia presentations; Web page animation

You should consider one other major factor when deciding whether your new program should be an applet or an application. If you are using features of newer Java versions, you need to wait until browsers support the capabilities. With an application, you can provide the Java Runtime Environment (the JRE is discussed later in this chapter). However, within an applet, you can only use the capabilities a browser offers. In an Internet environment, you can expect users to still be using older browser versions, which do not support either Java 1.1 or Java 2. In a corporate intranet environment, where there tends to be more control over software versions, you can know what versions are available and develop accordingly.

USING THE JAVA DEVELOPMENT KIT (JDK)

The JDK was the original Java development environment for many of today's Java professionals. Although many programmers have moved on to third-party alternatives, the JDK is still considered to be the reference implementation of Java. If you can build and test an application with the JDK, it should run on any third-party implementations, such as those in Web browsers, development tools, or device-specific VMs. In fact, Sun has a whole suite of tests to ensure that third-party Java environments conform to the JDK version.

TIP

You can download the latest version of the JDK, version 1.2, for free on the Internet from Sun's Java Web site. For more information, see "Downloading and Installing the JDK," coming up shortly.

The JDK can create and display graphical applications, but the JDK itself has a somewhat primitive command-line interface. For instance, you run the JDK programs by typing commands into a command-shell window (in Windows, a DOS box; on Unix systems, a normal command shell). Do not be discouraged by the apparent complexity of the JDK commands; they are all quite easy to use after a bit of practice.

The JDK consists of a library of standard classes and a collection of utilities for building, testing, and documenting Java programs. The Core Java API (formerly known as the JavaApplet API) is a library of prefabricated classes; classes are grouped by related functionality into *packages*. The `java.lang` package provides classes that are fundamental to the design of the Java programming language, such as object handling and error processing. It is impossible to write a Java program without using this library, since it is the root of the class hierarchy. The other packages contain classes used for utilities, networking, I/O, graphical user interface tools, and Web browser interaction. Packages that deal with security, database access, reusable software components, collections, drag-and-drop, accessibility, and reference objects are also available, and new ones are in development all the time.

The Core API includes some important language constructs (including `String` datatypes and exceptions), as well as graphics, network, and file I/O capabilities. It is generally safe to assume that the Core API is common to all platforms running Java. The EmbeddedJava and PersonalJava APIs specify well-defined subsets for specific environments. For instance, a Java VM in a toaster or other household appliance is unlikely to support the graphics part of the API, but it will almost certainly implement `String` datatypes and other Core API language classes. A Web browser running on a desktop computer will likely implement the complete Core API (and also many of the optional Extension APIs).

TIP

For additional information on the upcoming EmbeddedJava API for small-footprint embedded systems, see http://www.javasoft.com/products /embeddedjava/. For information on the PersonalJava specification for networkable consumer appliances, see http://www.javasoft.com/ products/personaljava/.

JDK Utilities

Version 1.2 of the JDK includes the following utilities:

javac   The Java *compiler*. Converts Java source code into bytecodes.

java   The Java *interpreter*. Executes Java application bytecodes directly from class files.

jre   Alternate Java interpreter. Executes Java application bytecodes directly from class files. Part of Java Runtime Environment.

appletviewer   A Java interpreter that executes Java applet classes hosted by HTML files.

javadoc   Creates HTML documentation based on Java source code and the comments it contains.

jdb   The Java *debugger*. Allows you to step through the program one line at a time, set breakpoints, and examine variables.

javah   Generates C header files that can be used to make C routines that can call Java methods, or to make C routines that can be called by Java programs.

javap   The Java *disassembler*. Displays the accessible functions and data in a compiled class file. It also displays the meaning of the bytecodes.

rmic   Creates class files that support Remote Method Invocation (RMI). See Chapter 17 for information about RMI.

rmiregistry   Registry used to gain access to RMI objects on a specific machine.

rmid   Activation system daemon for RMI object registration and activation.

serialver   Serialization utility. Permits versioning of persistent objects. See Chapter 17 for information about serialization.

native2ascii   Special program used to convert between standard Latin-1 Unicode characters and other international encoding schemes.

jar   Java Archive (JAR) file generator. JAR files allow multiple Java classes and resources to be distributed in one compressed file.

keytool   Used for security key generation and management.

jarsigner   Implements digital signing of JAR and class files. Allows applets to be certified by trusted authorities.

policytool   Allows installation-level security policy configuration.

tnameserv   The Java IDL (Interface Definition Language) transient name server.

servletrunner   A simple Web server to test servlets. The Java Servlet Development Kit (JSDK) contains a simple Servlet engine for developing and testing servlets, the `javax.servlet` package sources, and API documentation. It is free and can be downloaded from `http://java.sun.com/products/servlet/index.html`.

The way these tools are applied to build and run Java applications is illustrated in Figure 7.1. When building applets, the flowchart looks slightly different, as you can see in Figure 7.2.

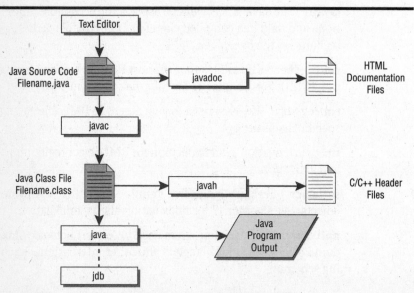

FIGURE 7.1: How Java applications are built using the JDK

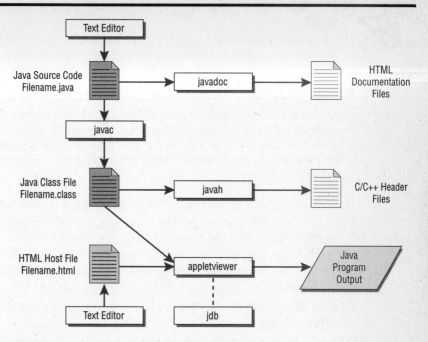

FIGURE 7.2:   How Java applets are built using the JDK

After the descriptions of how to download and install the JDK, you will see how Figure 7.1 applies to a sample Java application. Then you will see how to follow Figure 7.2 for building applets.

Downloading and Installing the JDK

To help get you started with Java, the following sections summarize the steps you need to install the JDK on your machine. You need to install it before you can follow any of the exercises presented in this book.

Downloading the JDK

The latest version (1.2) of the JDK can be downloaded from Sun's Java Web site at `http://java.sun.com/`. The JDK is a self-extracting, compressed, executable file. Version 1.2 is available from Sun for the following platforms:

▶ Solaris 2.5.1, 2.6, and 7 for both SPARC and *x*86 architectures

▶ Windows 95/98 and Windows NT 4 for *x*86 architectures

NOTE

Notice that there is no development platform for Windows 3.1x. Netscape and Microsoft do offer runtime environments for Java under Window 3.1x within their browsers. IBM did create an early development environment called ADK, but progress halted once Netscape and Microsoft announced 16-bit Windows run-time support. Also, while Sun initially provided JDK ports for the Macintosh environment, Apple has taken control of JDK support for this platform. For a list of all the platforms that provide JDKs and where to get them, see http:// java.sun.com/cgi-bin/java-ports.cgi. Although some of these efforts have successfully ported Java 1.0 and 1.1, Java 2 ports may not be immediately available on every one.

The first step in downloading the JDK is to locate the correct binary files at Sun's Java Web site or from the appropriate site if you are using a platform other than those supported by Sun. The complete JDK is distributed as a single file, and the download may take 90 minutes with a 33.6kbps modem, or about half as long with a single-channel ISDN connection, assuming that the server is not busy. It may help to try downloading the file early in the morning or late in the evening when the server is not so busy.

Sun also has a separate distribution file for the JDK documentation. This includes release notes, help files, and documentation for all of the classes and tools distributed with the JDK. It is strongly recommended that you download this as well. It is about 4MB (megabytes) compressed and is well worth the download time. You can also access this documentation online on Sun's Java Web page.

Installing the JDK

The JDK installation process is fairly straightforward but generally takes a little manual setup to finish off. To give you a head start, Table 7.2 summarizes the installation procedure for JDK 1.2 for each platform supported by Sun.

TABLE 7.2: JDK Installation Instructions for Windows and Solaris
Platforms

INSTALLATION PROCEDURES	WINDOWS 95/98 & WINDOWS NT	SUN SOLARIS*
Downloaded file type	Self-extracting executable (`.exe`)	Packed archive (`.sh`)
Where to install the JDK	Usually installed in `c:\jdk1.2`, by the self-extracting executable.	Usually installed in `jdk1.2`, by the self-extracting executable.
If you have already installed a previous version of the JDK	Should install in different directory by default so both versions are available. Otherwise, save any files you have changed or created in the original Java directory tree in a separate directory, and then delete the original installation.	Should install in different directory by default so both versions are available. Otherwise, save any files you have changed or created in the original Java directory tree in a separate directory, and then delete the original installation.
Decompression procedure	Run the executable to decompress and install.	Use `sh` to decompress and run the install script.
Additional setup	Add the `jdk1.2\bin` directory to your path.	Add the `jdk1.2/bin` directory to your path.
If you have already installed a previous** version of the JDK	Check that the `classes.zip` referred to by the CLASSPATH environment variable points to the new version of the JDK.	Check that the `classes.zip` referred to by the CLASSPATH environment variable points to the new version of the JDK.

* Versions 2.5.1, 2.6, and 7 on SPARC-based machines; version 2.5 and 2.6 on *x*86-based machines.

** If you do not have a CLASSPATH environment variable set, by default Java uses `..\lib\classes.zip; .`, starting from the Java executable directory.

Building Applications with the JDK

Now that you have installed the JDK, it's time to take it for a test drive. To smooth the ride, this section describes how to create a small Java application, applying each JDK utility to the code. You will see the same code compiled, executed, disassembled, documented, and interfaced to the C language.

Java Application Source Code

Java source code can be written with a simple text editor. In Unix, vi or emacs will do; in Windows, you can use Notepad or EDIT. Many programmers have a preferred text editor or use the editor shipped with third-party integrated development environments (IDEs).

The first example is a little Java program that you can use to play with the JDK:

```
public class TestDrive {
  public static void main (String args[]) {
  System.out.println ("JDK Test Drive");
  }
}
```

This is a rework of the classic HelloWorld program; it simply prints the words "JDK Test Drive." It is the simplest Java program you can write, but to the uninitiated, it may still look rather cryptic. For the purposes of this chapter, there is no need to understand it all perfectly; don't worry too much about what each keyword means.

The code defines a Java class called TestDrive, which contains a single method called main().When the Java interpreter tries to execute the TestDrive class, it will look for a method called main(). In fact, every Java application must define a function called main as:

```
public static void main (String args[])
```

The VM will execute this function to run the program. Here, args is an array of String (text) variables. When you run the program, the array will be filled with the values of any arguments it was given on the command line.

If you know how to program in C, the main() function will look familiar. The C equivalent:

```
int main (char *argv[], int argc)
```

includes `argc`, an integer variable that tells you how many arguments are in the array. In Java, this is unnecessary because arrays know how many elements they contain. Another difference between Java and C is that in C, the first element in the array, `argv[0]`, contains the name of the program itself. In Java, `args[0]` is the first parameter on the command line.

Type the Java source code for the `TestDrive` class into your text editor and save it under the name `TestDrive.java`.

NOTE

The name of the Java source file is not arbitrary; it must be the same as the name of the public class defined in the `.java` file. Consequently, only one public class can be defined in each source file, although additional nonpublic classes can be defined in each file. If no public classes are defined in the Java source file, the name of the file can be anything you want.

You are now ready to compile your first Java program.

Using *javac*

The `javac` compiler converts Java source code into Java bytecodes, which can then be executed by `java` (the Java interpreter), the `appletviewer`, or any other Java VM, such as within Netscape Communicator.

You can compile your `TestDrive` program by entering the following at the shell prompt:

```
javac TestDrive.java
```

If the Java code is acceptable to the compiler, the file `TestDrive.class` will be created (no messages will be displayed).

If you are curious and would like to see the details of the compilation, you can use the `verbose` option. The `verbose` option is rarely used, but seeing it at least once is instructive. The `verbose` option will cause the `javac` compiler to tell you which other Java classes the compiler needs to create the compiled class file and how long it took to do the compilation. When you enter

```
javac -verbose TestDrive.java
```

it produces something like this (your times and locations may vary):

```
[parsed TestDrive.java in 210 ms]
[loaded C:\jdk1.2\lib\classes.zip(java/lang/Object.class) in
120 ms]
[checking class TestDrive]
```

```
[loaded C:\jdk1.2\lib\classes.zip(java/lang/String.class) in
91 ms]
[loaded C:\jdk1.2\lib\classes.zip(java/lang/System.class) in
50 ms]
[loaded C:\jdk1.2\lib\classes.zip(java/io/PrintStream.class)
in 60 ms]
[loaded C:\jdk1.2\lib\classes.zip(java/io/Serializable.class)
in 0 ms]
[loaded C:\jdk1.2\lib\classes.zip(java/io/FilterOutputStream
.class) in 10 ms]
[loaded C:\jdk1.2\lib\classes.zip(java/io/OutputStream.class)
in 10 ms]
[wrote TestDrive.class]
[done in 8031 ms]
```

Behind the scenes, the compiler must check that the TestDrive
program is consistent with any other classes it uses. String, System,
PrintStream, FilterOutputStream, OutputStream, and Serializable are included in Java's standard class libraries, the Core API. All
of these classes are essential to print a string to the standard output.

 CLASSES

In version 1.2 of the JDK, there are about 900 classes in the standard class library, the Core API, and about 1,600 supplementary
classes provided as a tools and debugging class library. The Core
API contains a wealth of ready-to-use functionality and will save
you a great deal of development time. These classes are stored in
a compressed zip file in the jdk1.2/lib directory. Do not remove
the classes.zip file because the Java compiler and VM access the
library classes from this file directly. If you want to see the source
code for the library classes, how to get at the source varies from
platform to platform: with the Windows 95/98/NT installation,
source code access is an installation-time option. With UNIX, it is
always in the same place. If you want it installed, or it automatically
is, you will find the source code located in the src.zip file in the
jdk1.2 installation directory. When the zip file is expanded,
the source files are placed in the src subdirectory.

After running javac to compile TestDrive.java, the file Test-
Drive.class contains bytecodes that can be executed by any Java VM
on any platform. The class file format is an open standard, and a detailed

specification for it is available at Sun's Web site. If you use a binary file viewer to analyze the file, you will notice that there is text as well as binary data in the file. The names of classes and methods used by the class file must be stored in the bytecodes in order to access those classes and methods on the destination system.

Using *java*

After compiling `TestDrive`, you can run the program with the Java interpreter by entering the following command:

```
java TestDrive
```

The output will be the words "JDK Test Drive," as shown in Figure 7.3.

FIGURE 7.3:   A sample Windows 95/98 command-line session that compiles `TestDrive.java` and executes `TestDrive.class`

The interpreter has many command-line options—most of which are functions likely to be used only by advanced Java programmers. Nevertheless, it is worth your while to look at a useful, relatively simple feature built into the interpreter: a *profiler*. A profiler is used to analyze how much time a program spends in each part of the code. You can use this information to determine which parts of a program to optimize. If you use the `prof` option of the interpreter, with the command

```
java -prof TextDrive
```

a file called `java.prof` will be created. This file shows how many times each method was called and how many milliseconds were spent executing each one. An excerpt of the profile for `TestDrive.class` is shown here:

```
count callee caller time
2 java/lang/System.arraycopy(Ljava/lang/Object;ILjava/lang/
Object;II)V java/lang/String.getChars(II[CI)V 0
```

```
2 java/lang/System.arraycopy(Ljava/lang/Object;ILjava/lang/
Object;II)V java/io/BufferedOutputStream.write([BII)V 0
2 java/io/FileOutputStream.writeBytes([BII)V java/io/
FileOutputStream.write([BII)V 10
1 java/lang/Class.getPrimitiveClass(Ljava/lang/String;)Ljava/
lang/Class; java/lang/Double.<clinit>()V 0
1 java/lang/Double.longBitsToDouble(J)D java/lang/Double
.<clinit>()V 0
1 java/lang/Class.getPrimitiveClass(Ljava/lang/String;)Ljava/
lang/Class; java/lang/Float.<clinit>()V 0
1 java/lang/Double.doubleToLongBits(D)J java/lang/Math
.<clinit>()V 0
1 java/lang/Float.floatToIntBits(F)I java/lang/Math
.<clinit>()V 0
handles_used: 1317, handles_free: 26214, heap-used: 247424,
heap-free: 591432
sig count bytes indx
[C    165  18452    5
[B     5  19200    8
*** tab[987] p=1d18bb8 cb=f80160 cnt=4 ac=0 al=0
   Ljava/lang/Object; 4 0
*** tab[985] p=1d18b98 cb=f80158 cnt=0 ac=1 al=2
 [Ljava/lang/Class; 1 8
*** tab[983] p=1d18b78 cb=f80150 cnt=633 ac=0 al=0
   Ljava/lang/String; 633 7596
*** tab[977] p=1d18b18 cb=f80138 cnt=2 ac=0 al=0
   Ljava/util/Hashtable; 2 32
*** tab[967] p=1d18a78 cb=f80110 cnt=450 ac=3 al=1817
   Ljava/util/Hashtable$HashtableEntry; 450 7200
 [Ljava/util/Hashtable$HashtableEntry; 3 7268
*** tab[931] p=1d18838 cb=f80080 cnt=2 ac=1 al=4
   Ljava/lang/ThreadGroup; 2 80
 [Ljava/lang/ThreadGroup; 1 16
*** tab[907] p=1d186b8 cb=f80020 cnt=1 ac=0 al=0
   Ljava/lang/Ref$RefHandler; 1 40
*** tab[903] p=1d18678 cb=f80010 cnt=2 ac=2 al=8
   Ljava/lang/Thread; 2 80
 [Ljava/lang/Thread; 2 32
   . . .
```

The first section of the file shows which methods were called in order of decreasing frequency. The next section shows how much memory was used, providing handles and heap information. The third section lists the variable types created and how many bytes were necessary to store them.

This output stores plenty of other information; most of it is too compli-cated to go into here.

As you learn more about Java, you will be able to put this information to good use. It is particularly helpful for deciding how to optimize your software. Programs often follow an 80/20 rule: 80 percent of the execu-tion time is spent in 20 percent of the code. The profiler points out which methods are using up the most time so you can optimize the most time-consuming parts of the code.

Using *javadoc*

By adding a few comments to your Java source code, you make it possible for javadoc to automatically generate HTML documentation for your code. Add the following few comments to your TestDrive.java file:

```
/** TestDrive - A test file for demonstration of the JDK. */
public class TestDrive {
  /** This method is called first by the Java interpreter.
   * It prints a message to the console. */
  // javadoc will ignore this comment
  public static void main(String argv[]) {
    /* javadoc will also ignore this comment */
    System.out.println("JDK Test Drive");
  }
}
```

C and C++ programmers will immediately notice the similarities between Java and C syntax. The curly braces ({ }) group code together into blocks. As in C, line indentation is unnecessary, but it helps make the code more readable.

Java also uses the same kind of comments as C++, but a comment beginning with multiple asterisks has a special meaning for javadoc. It signifies the start of a *documentation comment* block, which is a comment block that will be used by javadoc to create documentation. Given our newly commented TestDrive.java, javadoc will produce the files AllNames.html, tree.html, packages.html, and TestDrive .html, all of which can easily be viewed using a standard Web browser, as shown in Figure 7.4. To run javadoc, simply enter the following command:

```
javadoc TestDrive.java
```

Part ii

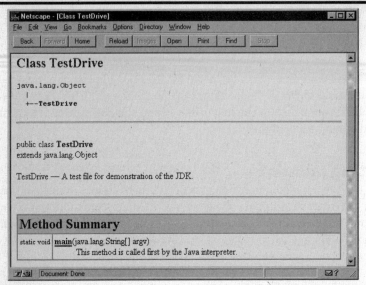

FIGURE 7.4:   Viewing source code documentation in HTML format produced by
javadoc

The graphical titles and bullets shown in Figure 7.4 are provided with
the HTML documentation for the Java API. To see the HTML with the
graphics displayed correctly, you must copy the images directory to the
directory that contains your documentation. The relationship between
the graphics and the HTML will be clearer after you have read the HTML
primer coming up shortly.

Using *javah*

In order for Java to be applied to platform-specific or performance-critical
problems, Java needs the ability to call native code written in C or other
languages. Embedded applications are prime examples of where a Java
program would need to access platform-specific information, such as LED
displays, relays, and sensors. Similarly, until the Java3D API becomes
available, rendering complex 3-D graphics in real-time is an application
that demands the raw speed of C. Because Java was originally based on an
embedded systems language, Java has built-in support for calling native
routines.

To help you write C code that interfaces with Java, the JDK includes
javah, a utility that, given a class file, generates the C header files
needed by C programs to access the class's data.

Using *jdb*

The Java debugger, jdb, monitors and controls the execution of a Java program so that bugs can be found. With jdb, a running program can be stopped at any point so that the variables and internal operation of the program can be examined.

NOTE

Many programmers prefer third-party debuggers, like the ones included with Symantec's Café and Borland's JBuilder development environments. They have all of the features of jdb and allow you to set breakpoints directly in the code and view the program internals with separate windows for variables, threads, and function calls.

Although jdb may seem difficult to use and is poorly documented, it can still be a useful tool. It is worthwhile to take a few moments to learn how to use some of the more basic features of jdb. Once you get started, learning more advanced techniques is much easier. Also, Unix C programmers who are used to using tools such as dbx and gdb will probably find jdb very easy to use.

Here is the procedure to use jdb on TestDrive.class, performing only a few basic functions:

1. Load the TestDrive class into jdb, and set a breakpoint. When the debugger hits a breakpoint in the code, it stops executing the program and allows the user to inspect the state of the program. Tell the debugger to stop when it reaches the main() method.

2. Take a look at the source code for TestDrive. The debugger lists the code and also shows where it is about to execute a new instruction (it uses a => to indicate its current position). If there are many lines of code, you could also have jdb step through the code one line at a time.

3. Clear the breakpoint and allow jdb to finish executing the program.

Here's the output of the jdb session just described:

```
C:\internet\MasteringJava\ch02>jdb TestDrive
Initializing jdb...
0xa50198:class(TestDrive)
> stop in TestDrive.main
```

Part ii

```
Breakpoint set in TestDrive.main
> run
run TestDrive
running ...
main[1]
Breakpoint hit: TestDrive.main (TestDrive:8)
main[1] list
4           * It prints a message to the console. */
5           // javadoc will ignore this comment
6          public static void main (String argv[]) {
7           /* javadoc will ignore this comment */
8    =>     System.out.println("JDK Test Drive");
9          }
10         }
main[1] clear TestDrive.main
Breakpoint cleared at TestDrive.main
main[1] cont
main[1] JDK Test Drive

TestDrive exited
```

Note that this debugger can connect to a VM that is running in another process, even on a remote machine. This could be especially useful when debugging VMs running on remote servers, appliances, or consumer electronics. To learn more about jdb, type ? at the prompt.

Using *javap*

It is possible to examine the bytecodes of a compiled class file and identify its accessible variables and functions. The javap utility creates a report that shows not only what functions and variables are available, but what the code actually does, albeit at a very low level. If you run javap with no command-line arguments:

```
javap TestDrive
```

the output shows from which file the class was compiled and the accessible functions and variables, like this:

```
Compiled from TestDrive.java
public synchronized class TestDrive extends java.lang.Object
{
   public static void main(java.lang.String []);
   public TestDrive();
}
```

In this case, we have no "public" variables, so only the main() and TestDrive() methods are displayed. The TestDrive() function is a *default constructor*, a special function that is automatically created by the compiler if you do not write one. You will learn more about default constructors in the next chapter.

If you use `javap` with the `-c` option to display the meaning of the bytecodes in the file:

```
javap -c TestDrive
```

the output shows each step that will be taken by the VM to execute the methods of the class:

```
Compiled from TestDrive.java
public synchronized class TestDrive extends java.lang.Object
{
    public static void main(java.lang.String[]);
    public TestDrive();
}

Method TestDrive()
   0 aload_0
   1 invokespecial #6 <Method java.lang.Object()>
   4 return

Method void main(java.lang.String[])
   0 getstatic #7 <Field java.io.PrintStream out>
   3 ldc #1 <String "JDK Test Drive">
   5 invokevirtual #8 <Method void println(java.lang.String)>
   8 return
```

This is much more complicated than the original `TestDrive.java` file, but it shows each step that the VM will take when executing the program. As you can see, `javap` is a tool for advanced Java programmers.

BUILDING APPLETS WITH THE JDK

So far, you have seen the process by which you build Java applications using the JDK. In this section, you will learn about creating Java applets and the HTML documents in which you host them.

This section presents a sample Java applet called `FilledBox.java`, whose only function is to display a filled rectangle in an HTML document. The HTML document can control the color of the rectangle by passing a parameter to the applet, which illustrates the relationship of HTML to Java applets.

Before going any further, you may find it helpful to take a minute to understand the following short lesson in HTML. After a brief introduction to HTML, you will be up and running with Java applets in no time. If you're already familiar with HTML, feel free to skip this section.

HTML for Java Applets

HTML files are text files with special character sequences that specify the document-formatting characteristics. The special character sequences are called *tags*, and they consist of symbols placed between left and right angle brackets, as shown in the following excerpt:

```
Here is some normal text. <I>Here is some italic text.</I>
```

The <I> start tag sets the italic formatting, and the </I> end tag unsets it. A Web browser or HTML viewer interprets the HTML file and produces the corresponding output. This excerpt of HTML produces the following output:

```
Here is some normal text. Here is some italic text.
```

Most HTML tags use the <*tag*> and </*tag*> sequences to set and unset their relevant properties. For example, <B> turns on bold, and </B> turns it off. Other tags, such as the paragraph tag, may not require an end tag.

A complete HTML file has both formatting and structure tags:

```
<HTML>
  <HEAD>
      <TITLE>Sample HTML Document</TITLE>
  </HEAD>
  <BODY>
      <H1>HTML Demo</H1>
      This document is a sample of HTML.
  </BODY>
</HTML>
```

The <HTML> tag indicates that the file is an HTML document. The <HEAD> tag marks the start of an invisible header section normally used for recording the title and author of the document. Some programs will only look at the header section of a document. The phrase between the <TITLE> and </TITLE> tags is the name of this document. The body section of the document, marked by the <BODY> tag, contains all the displayed information—in this case, a level-one heading (signified by <H1>

and </H1>) and a line of normal text. The output generated by this HTML file is shown in Figure 7.5.

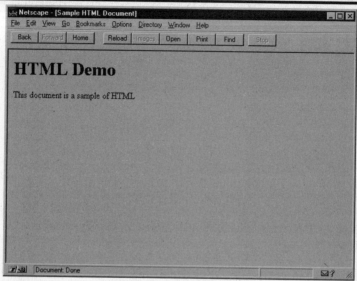

FIGURE 7.5: A sample HTML file displayed in Netscape Navigator

To include an image in an HTML file, use the <IMG> tag and specify the name and location of the image you want to load. You can use the full URL of the image; a simpler relative reference can be used if the graphic is located on the same server as the HTML file itself:

```
<HTML>
  <HEAD>
    <TITLE>Sample HTML Document</TITLE>
  </HEAD>
  <BODY>
    <IMG SRC="sybex.gif">
    <H1>HTML Demo</H1>
    This document is a sample of HTML.
  </BODY>
</HTML>
```

The resulting display is shown in Figure 7.6.

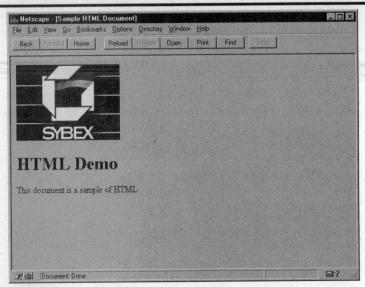

FIGURE 7.6:   An HTML document with an embedded image

NOTE

Web browsers can display image files in GIF and JPEG. GIF means Graphics Interchange Format, and JPEG stands for Joint Photographic Experts Group, the group that created it. Most browsers also support animated and transparent GIF images (also known as GIF89a format). All of these formats are supported by the Core API. In the future, other graphics formats will probably be supported via Extension APIs.

If you want to connect this page to another document via a hypertext link, you must insert an *anchor* tag (<A>). Everything between the anchor tag and the end anchor tag will be highlighted, so the user knows that the highlighted text or graphics can be clicked on. The following will build a hypertext link to Sun's Java home page in the sample document:

```
<HTML>
  <HEAD>
     <TITLE>Sample HTML Document</TITLE>
  </HEAD>
  <BODY>
     <IMG SRC="sybex.gif">
     <H1>HTML Demo</H1>
     This document is a sample of HTML.
```

```
        <P>
        You can get the Java Development Kit from the
        <A HREF="http://java.sun.com">JavaSoft Home Page</A>.
      </BODY>
    </HTML>
```

The paragraph tag (<P>) makes the text easier to read. A Web browser ignores excess spaces and new lines when displaying a document, so if you need to break a line or begin a new paragraph, you must insert <BR> or <P> tags as necessary. Now the HTML document has text, graphics, and a link, as shown in Figure 7.7.

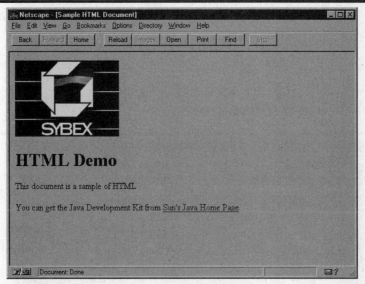

FIGURE 7.7:   A sample HTML document including text, an image, and a hyper-text link

Adding a Java applet to an HTML document is quite straightforward. There is an <APPLET> tag that specifies the location of the class file and the display area allocated to the applet. Suppose you want to add a Clock applet that will display the current time in hours, minutes, and seconds. Here is a simple example of an <APPLET> tag that loads the Clock applet:

```
<APPLET CODE="Clock.class" WIDTH=200 HEIGHT=60> </APPLET>
```

When a browser encounters these tags, it will start the VM and ask it to load Clock.class. It also tells the VM that the applet may draw in a region that is 200 × 60 pixels. The location of the <APPLET> tag in the document determines the coordinate of the top left of the applet's display area. Add the line to load the Clock applet to the HTML file:

```
<HTML>
  <HEAD>
      <TITLE>Sample HTML Document</TITLE>
  </HEAD>
  <BODY>
     <IMG SRC="sybex.gif">
     <H1>HTML Demo</H1>
     This document is a sample of HTML.
     <P>
    You can get the Java Development Kit from the
     <A HREF="http://java.sun.com">JavaSoft Home Page</A>.
     <P>
     <APPLET CODE="Clock.class" WIDTH=200 HEIGHT=60>
     </APPLET>
  </BODY>
</HTML>
```

The output should look like the document in Figure 7.8.

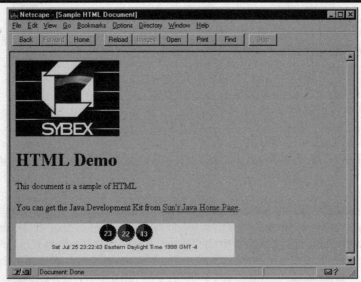

FIGURE 7.8: The Clock applet embedded in an HTML document

As you can see, embedding applets into Web pages is simple. Java is able to create plug-in components that can be used by novices as well as experts. For this component strategy to work, the HTML author must be able to customize the properties and behavior of the applet via HTML. The Java programmer decides which parameters will have meaning for the applet, and the HTML author uses <PARAM> tags to pass initial parameters to the applet.

The Clock applet needs no parameters; telling the time is a universal function. On the other hand, the sample FilledBox applet needs to know what color to make the box. You can write the FilledBox applet to expect a parameter called color in the HTML using the <PARAM> tag:

```
<APPLET CODE="FilledBox.class" WIDTH=50 HEIGHT=50>
<PARAM NAME=color VALUE="blue">
</APPLET>
```

The <PARAM> tag accepts two arguments: NAME and VALUE. NAME is used to specify the name of the parameter, and VALUE defines its value. As far as Java is concerned, all parameters are String objects, although they can be converted to any other Java datatype quite easily. The output of the FilledBox applet is shown in Figure 7.9. Notice that only the applet is displayed.

FIGURE 7.9:   The appletviewer running the FilledBox applet from FilledBox.html

If the Web browser includes a Java VM, it will display the applet and ignore everything but the <PARAM> tags, which lie between <APPLET> and </APPLET>. Web browsers that are not Java-enabled, or have Java disabled, will ignore the <APPLET> and <PARAM> tags and display any valid HTML between the <APPLET> and </APPLET> tags. This allows you to provide an alternative for non-Java-enabled browsers, which is important because some users cannot (or choose not to) run Java applets. If you want your Web page to be accessible to everyone, you need to make it readable by non-Java platforms.

Web Browser Applet Processing

A Java-enabled Web browser follows a specific series of steps when it encounters an <APPLET> tag in an HTML document:

1. The browser reserves space in the document for displaying the applet. The WIDTH and HEIGHT parameters of the <APPLET> tag determine the amount of space used by the applet.

2. The browser reads the parameters from the <PARAM> tags.

3. The VM starts and is asked to load and initialize the applet. The applet has access to the names and values in the <PARAM> tags.

4. The VM creates a running copy of the applet based on the class file.

5. The browser calls the applet's init method so the applet will initialize itself.

6. The VM calls the start method of the applet when it is ready for the applet to start processing. It also calls paint to draw the applet in the browser window.

7. Whenever the applet needs to be redrawn (for example, when the user scrolls the applet into view), the browser calls the applet's paint method.

8. The browser calls the stop method when the user moves on to another HTML document.

9. The browser calls the destroy method when it clears the applet out of memory.

Java Applet Source Code

Java applet source code is written in the same way as Java application source code—with a text editor. The difference is that Java applets do not have a main method. Instead, they have several other methods that are called by the VM when requested by the browser. Here is the source code for the simple FilledBox applet:

```
import java.awt.*;
import java.applet.Applet;
/** FilledBox displays a filled, colored box in the browser
/    window
 */
```

```
public class FilledBox extends Applet {
  // This variable stores the color specified in the HTML
      document Color boxColor;
  /** Get the box color from the host HTML file
   */
  public void init() {
    String s;
    s = getParameter("color");
    // The default color is gray
    boxColor = Color.gray;

    // We expect a parameter called color, which will have
    // the value red, white, or blue. If the parameter
    // is missing, s will be null
    if (s != null) {
      if (s.equals("red")) boxColor = Color.red;
      if (s.equals("white")) boxColor = Color.white;
      if (s.equals("blue")) boxColor = Color.blue;
    }
  }

  /** Paint the box in region assigned to the applet.
   *  Use the color specified in the HTML document
   */
  public void paint(Graphics g) {
    g.setColor (boxColor);
    g.fillRect (0, 0, size().width, size().height);
  }
}
```

It's a little more complicated than the Java application example, but that is because it does more. You will recall that a main method is required by all Java applications; it is conspicuously absent in this applet. In fact, Java applets do not have any required methods at all. However, there are five methods that the VM may call when requested by the Web browser (or appletviewer):

public void init()   Initializes the applet. Called only once.

public void start()   Called when the browser is ready to start executing the initialized applet. Can be called multiple times if user keeps leaving and returning to the Web page. Also called when browser deiconified.

public void stop()   Called when the browser wishes to stop executing the applet. Called whenever the user leaves the Web page. Also called when browser iconified.

public void destroy()   Called when the browser clears the applet out of memory.

public void paint(Graphics g)   Called whenever the browser needs to redraw the applet.

If the applet does not implement any of these methods, the applet will have no functionality for the specific method not implemented. In the example, `init` and `paint` are implemented. The `init` function obtains the desired box color from a parameter in the host document (applet parameters were explained previously in "HTML for Java Applets"). The `paint` method draws the filled box in the browser window.

Save this Java applet source as `FilledBox.java`.

Using *javac*

The `javac` compiler works the same on applets as it does on Java applications:

```
javac FilledBox.java
```

Here are a few tips that may help you get started. First, applet classes must always be declared `public` or they will not get compiled. Also, remember that Java is case-sensitive; `filledbox.java` is *not* the same as `FilledBox.java` and will not be compiled.

If the Java code is acceptable to the compiler, the only message you will see is about a deprecated API:

```
Note: FilledBox.java uses a deprecated API. Recompile with "-
deprecation" for details.
1 warning.
```

For now, ignore the warning. As long as there were no error messages, the file `FilledBox.class` will be created. If there were error messages, you need to go back and fix your code. There are many different types of error messages that the compiler may generate when given a source file. The simplest to fix are syntax errors, such as a missing semicolon or closing brace. Other messages will highlight incorrect use of variable types, invalid expressions, or violation access restrictions. Getting your source code to compile is only the first part of the debugging process; error-free compilation does not guarantee that your program will do what you want. But don't worry about debugging just yet; this example is simple enough that it should run without any problems.

NOTE

Between Java 1.0 and Java 1.1, several method names were renamed. Until everyone upgrades their browsers to support the Java 1.1 version, it still may be necessary to use 1.0 methods. If you happen to be using a 1.1-compliant browser, you can change the `size()` calls to `getSize()` to remove the warning message.

Before you can run your applet, you must create an HTML document to host it.

Creating an HTML File

Now that you know a little about HTML, it is easy to create a simple HTML file to host your applet:

```
<HTML>
  <HEAD>
    <TITLE>Sample HTML Document With Filled Box</TITLE>
  </HEAD>
  <BODY>
    <H1>FilledBox Demo</H1>
    <P>
    <APPLET CODE="FilledBox.class" WIDTH=50 HEIGHT=50>
    <PARAM NAME=color VALUE="blue">
    </APPLET>
  </BODY>
</HTML>
```

You can create this file by simply typing it into a text editor. Save the file as `FilledBox.html`. HTML files can be named anything you like, although it is common practice to name them after the applets they host.

WARNING

If you name the `.html` file after the applet and then run `javadoc` on the source code, the `.html` file will be overwritten.

Using *appletviewer*

The appletviewer utility is used to display the applet as it would be seen by the browser without displaying any of the HTML document itself. In the case of FilledBox.html, appletviewer will display a filled box in its own window:

```
appletviewer FilledBox.html
```

Refer back to Figure 7.9 to see the output. For comparison, you can open the file FilledBox.html using a Java-enabled Web browser. Figure 7.10 shows this output as it would be seen by Netscape Navigator. Both the applet and the text are displayed.

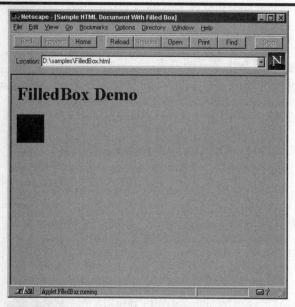

FIGURE 7.10   Netscape Navigator displaying the file FilledBox.html

If there is more than one applet in a page, appletviewer will open a separate window for each applet; a Web browser will show them in their respective locations within the same Web page. One rather nice feature of appletviewer is that it can load classes from across the network, not just from files. Just give appletviewer the URL of the HTML document containing one or more applets, and it will load the applets as if they were on your local disk. Note, however, that the SecurityManager for the appletviewer may expose your system to greater risks from network-loaded applets than would a Web browser like Netscape Navigator.

appletviewer makes it possible to distribute and run Java applets without the aid of a Web browser, so the choice between writing applets versus applications becomes less critical. Most applets are easy to convert into applications and vice versa. The key to this convertibility is to avoid placing a lot of code directly in the main, init, start, stop, and destroy methods, and use calls to generic methods instead.

Using *javadoc* and *javah*

The javadoc and javah utilities work on applet source code, too. The command lines are just like the application command lines:

```
javadoc FilledBox.java
```

and

```
javah FilledBox.class
```

Part II

TIP

Because we commented this example code well, javadoc will produce useful results, which make it easier to keep track of what all of the code does. Although this is not critical for a simple applet like this, it is a valuable lesson to remember as you go on to more complicated applets.

DELIVERING APPLICATIONS WITH THE JAVA RUNTIME ENVIRONMENT (JRE)

The Java Runtime Environment (JRE) is something first introduced with Java 1.1. If you want to distribute a Java application, you need to provide users with a Java platform to run the program. The JRE is just such a program; it provides a Java VM for users to execute your application. You can either package the JRE with your application or let them download it separately. Either way, they should only need to install the JRE once for all the Java applications they want to run. By distributing the JRE, you are assured that the user of your application has a compatible Java VM.

TIP

The latest version of the JRE, for Java version 2, can be downloaded free from Sun's Java Web site. For software development, the JRE is not necessary; however, it is required for application distribution.

WHAT'S NEW IN JDK 1.2

If you're already familiar with writing programs with JDK 1.1, there really aren't any changes in creating general applets and applications with Java 2. However, if you happen to be transitioning from a Java 1.0 environment, you may have noticed some changes introduced with the 1.1 release. Here we present a brief list of these changes. This list consists of changes that affect the JDK tools; it is not meant to be a comprehensive list of the new features of Java 2:

(appletviewer) <APPLET> tag changes   The tag used to load Java applets has been modified. You can now specify resources and other objects to be loaded along with the applet.

(javac) @deprecated tag   The `javac` compiler will now warn you if you use methods that were supported in previous releases of the JDK but are not the preferred ones in the current release. (For details about all deprecated methods, go to the Java Platform 1.2 API Specification section at `http://java.sun.com/products/jdk/1.2/docs/api/index.html`.)

(jar) Java archives   Java classes and resources, such as images and sounds, can now be bundled into compressed archives called JAR files. This facilitates digital signing and reduces download time.

(javah) New native method interface   The interface for calling native methods has been reworked and standardized across all platforms.

The code signing tools changed between Java 1.1 and 2. In Java 1.1, `javakey` managed everything; now there are three tools:

(keytool) Java key generator   Program used to generate keys to digitally sign classes

(jarsigner) Java archive signer   Program used to digitally sign class and JAR files so that they can be authenticated

(policytool) Security policy manager   Application to assist in configuring the security policy for an installation

Three brand new tools introduced with Java 2 are specific to some very advanced concepts:

(tnameserv) IDL Transient Name Server   The name server needs to be started before CORBA COS (Common Object Services) naming services can be used. (See Chapter 1 for more information on this tool.)

(rmid) RMI activation system daemon   The daemon needs to be started before using activatable RMI objects. (See Chapter 17 for further discussion of RMI.)

(servletrunner) Servlet runner   Use this to test-run servlets before installing them in a Web server. (See the sidebar earlier in this chapter for an explanation of servlets.)

WHAT'S NEXT?

In the next chapter, we will move on to object-oriented programming, including use of polymorphic functions, constructors, and finalizers.

Part ii

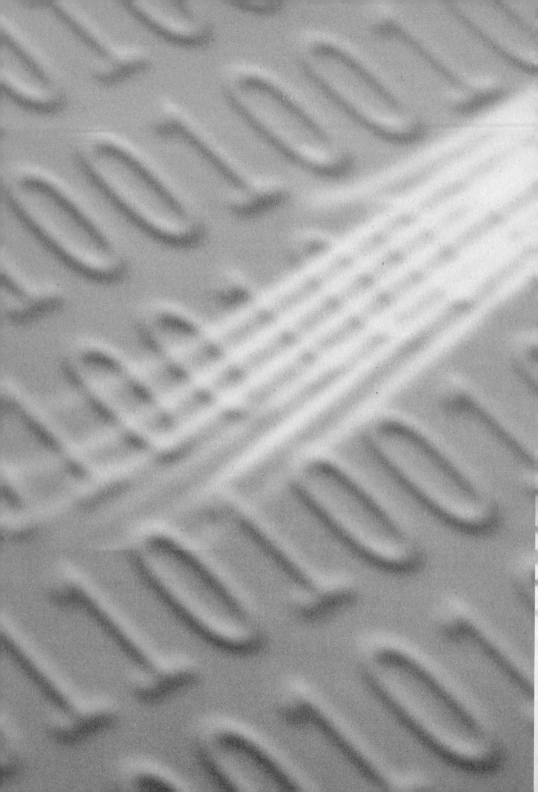

Chapter 8

WORKING WITH JAVA OBJECTS

The object-oriented programming (OOP) paradigm has swept through the software industry over the last decade, bringing with it advances in programmer productivity, software reuse, and maintainability. OOP is now considered "best practice" in the software development business. A fully object-oriented language, Java requires a thorough understanding of object-orientation to be effective. To that end, this chapter begins with an introduction to OOP.

Adapted from *Mastering Java 2* by John Zukowski
ISBN 0-7821-2180-2   1,280 pages $49.99

AN INTRODUCTION TO OOP

At its core, OOP is simply a way of thinking about problems and their solutions. Instead of tackling programs in a top-down, linear fashion (as with traditional programming languages such as Pascal or C), OOP attempts to break a problem into its component parts. The solution focuses on these independent *objects* and their relationships to other objects. This approach is better suited to most tasks because most problems are complex and multifaceted and do not conform easily to a linear approach.

Classes of objects closely resemble structures and record types in non-OOP languages, so this section starts by reviewing simple data structures and by looking at the software development problems inherent in structures. To maintain continuity with the sample code presented in this chapter, as well as to provide an illustrative example of OOP, these concepts will be applied to the design of an air traffic control system.

NOTE

Although C++ is an OOP language, it also supports non-object-oriented techniques. Because C++ and Java syntax are so similar, the examples of non-object-oriented code are in C++.

Data Structures

In almost all programming languages, data is stored in variables that have a specific *datatype*; for example, integer datatypes hold whole numbers, character datatypes hold individual alphanumeric characters, and string datatypes hold groups of alphanumeric characters. Many languages also allow you to create your own datatypes by grouping several simple datatypes together. In C++, these "compound" datatypes are *structures*; in Pascal, they are *record types*. Here is a sample structure written in C++ that represents an aircraft's flight segment:

```
struct Flight {
    int   altitude;
    int   heading;
    int   speed;
    float latitude;
    float longitude;
}
```

The Flight structure is a new datatype made up of built-in C/C++ types, namely integers and floating-point numbers. The components of a structure (the integers and floating-point numbers, in this example) are *members*. The Flight structure could also contain members for the destination of the flight, the type of aircraft, and other pieces of information, but the members listed here are sufficient for these examples.

The structure itself stores no information; it is only a pattern for creating new Flight variables. To declare a new Flight variable called incomingFlight, you would use the following code:

```
struct Flight incomingFlight;
```

You access the members of incomingFlight by using the name of the Flight variable followed by a period and the name of the member:

```
incomingFlight.altitude = 3000;
if (incomingFlight.heading < 180) {. . .}
```

In Pascal or Visual Basic, you would use similar code to create the Flight structure and to access member variables.

In non-OOP (structure-specific programming, referred to here as *structure-oriented code*), the code that accesses the Flight variables is separate and specific to the datatype. For example, a C++ routine that represents a turn of an aircraft might be declared as follows:

```
void turnFlight (Flight &aFlight, int angle) {
  aFlight.heading = (aFlight.heading + angle) % 360;
  // make sure angle is in the range 0-359 degrees
  if (aFlight.heading < 0)
    aFlight.heading = aFlight.heading + 360;
}
```

The turnFlight routine expects to be given variables that are Flight and int datatypes, respectively. Turning an incoming flight 90 degrees to the right is now achieved with this code:

```
turnFlight (incomingFlight, 90);
```

You could write similar routines to descend the aircraft and display it on a computer screen. Figure 8.1 shows a schematic representation of this code and data structure.

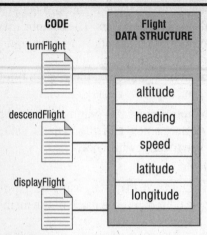

FIGURE 8.1:   A schematic view of the Flight data structure and the code that references it

The next step is to model commercial flights. You create a new structure called CommercialFlight that includes everything that the Flight structure included, plus the flight number and number of passengers:

```
struct CommercialFlight {
    // extra members in CommercialFlight
    int  flightNumber;
    int  passengers;
    // members in Flight
    int  altitude;
    int  heading;
    int  speed;
    float latitude;
    float longitude;
}
```

Again, to create a CommercialFlight variable called incoming-CommercialFlight, you could simply type:

```
struct CommercialFlight incomingCommercialFlight;
```

However, the routines written for generic flights will not work with CommercialFlight variables because CommercialFlight variables have no relationship to Flight variables. For example, the compiler will not allow you to use the turnFlight routine with a Commercial-Flight variable. Therefore, the following call is illegal:

```
turnFlight (incomingCommercialFlight, 90);
```

Figure 8.2 shows a schematic representation of the `Commercial-Flight` datatype and its functions.

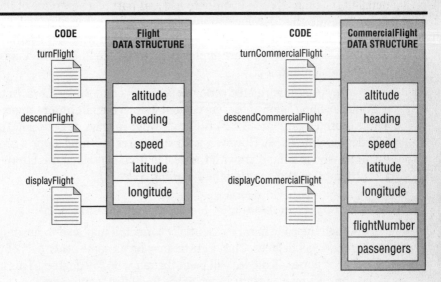

FIGURE 8.2: The `Flight` and `CommercialFlight` data structures and associated routines

Although you can use tricks to circumvent the datatype problem, they make the code harder to read, more complex, and less reliable. The only safe alternative is to create a new routine for commercial flights called `turnCommercialFlight`:

```
void turnCommercialFlight (CommercialFlight &aFlight,
                           int angle) {
  aFlight.heading = (aFlight.heading + angle) % 360;
  // make sure angle is in the range 0-359 degrees
  if (aFlight.heading < 0)
    aFlight.heading = aFlight.heading + 360;
}
```

However, this kind of code duplication presents a maintenance problem. If changes need to be made for 10 different structures, 10 different routines need to be modified. Not only is this hard work, but it is also an opportunity to introduce additional defects into the code.

Maintenance is only one of several problems with non-OOP structures. Traditional structures are also difficult to use more than once. Structures and their associated routines can quickly become entangled, making it difficult for someone to extract the required code for reuse in a new program. In effect, these entanglements force programmers to look at every detail of the original code in order to use it as part of a new piece of program. To avoid this, developers must exercise a lot of discipline to keep the interface of a structure and its routines—in other words, the parts that need to be used by future applications—separate from the details of their implementation.

Finally, structure-oriented code has some inherent safety flaws. In the previous examples, routines were created to turn aircraft by any angle. These routines guaranteed that the angle would always be between 0 and 359 degrees, inclusive. However, with structures, nothing stops a programmer who is unfamiliar with the design from bypassing the `turn-Flight` routine and entering the following code:

```
// right turn 90 degrees
incomingFlight.heading = incomingFlight.heading + 90;
```

Although the code may be essentially correct, it may lead to headings greater than 359 degrees. This, in turn, may break some other part of the code that assumes all angles will be in the range 0–359 degrees. This lack of data protection also contributes to the fragility of source code.

NOTE

From this point forward, Java source code, not C++ source code, is used. But note that in many cases the two may appear similar.

From Structures to Classes: Encapsulation

In OOP, the routines for a structure and the structure itself are combined, or *encapsulated*, into a single entity called a *class*. Here is the Java source code for a `Flight` class, an object-oriented version of the `Flight` structure:

```java
class Flight {
    int   altitude;
    int   heading;
    int   speed;
    float latitude;
    float longitude;
    // change the flight's heading by angle degrees
    void turnFlight (int angle) {
        heading = (heading + angle) % 360;
        // make sure angle is in the range 0-359 degrees
        if (heading < 0)
            heading = heading + 360;
```

```
    }
    // print information about the flight
    void printFlight() {
      System.out.println (altitude + "/" + heading +
                          "/" + speed);
    }
  }
```

The `turnFlight` routine is now a *member function* of the class; that is, the routine is part of the structure itself. You will notice that the code for the function is actually a little cleaner because you no longer need to refer to the heading as a member of a dummy variable—the variable `aFlight` has been eliminated altogether. The routine now also includes a member function, `printFlight`, that prints some flight information on the console.

NOTE

Member functions are more properly referred to as *methods*, although other terms are often used.

Just as with the structure definition, this class definition is a pattern, or template, for variables to be created with the `Flight` class datatype. Variables with the `Flight` class datatype are called `Flight` *objects* (hence the name object-oriented programming). An object is a storage variable that is created based on a class. Objects are said to be an *instance* of a class. Classes define the variables and routines that are members of all objects of that class. This may sound confusing if you've never worked with objects before, but a look at how the sample `Flight` class is applied will help you get a feel for using objects.

The next step is to create a `Flight` object variable based on the `Flight` class (this process is often referred to as *instantiation*). An *object variable* is a reference to an object; creating a reference to an object and creating the object itself are two separate steps. To create the object variable, use:

```
  Flight incomingFlight;
```

The `Flight` variable can have two possible kinds of values: `null` or a `Flight` object. The default value of the previous `incomingFlight` is `null`; it is simply a name and does not yet refer to any object. To create an object referenced by `incomingFlight`, use the new operator:

```
  incomingFlight = new Flight();
```

Part II

Now `incomingFlight` refers to a new `Flight` object, and you can access its member variables:

```
incomingFlight.altitude = 2500;
if (incomingFlight.heading < 180) { … }
```

Methods are called in an analogous way:

```
incomingFlight.turnFlight (90);
```

To understand how this works, imagine that `incomingFlight` points to an object that understands how to turn itself, and that you are sending a message to the object, asking it to turn right by 90 degrees. In fact, in OOP systems, all objects interact by sending messages to each other. The object-oriented equivalent of Figure 8.1 now looks like Figure 8.3.

Encapsulation also allows you to use *data hiding*, which is a way to prevent direct access to the variables in an object. This can force other objects to use methods to alter or read data in member variables, rather than accessing them directly. This is a key strength of encapsulation: it separates the interface to the class from its implementation, so you do not need to know the implementation details of the class to safely reuse the code. You can modify the `Flight` class to hide the `heading` member variable by using the `private` keyword:

```
class Flight {
  int  altitude;
```

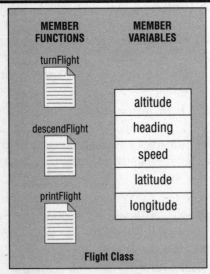

FIGURE 8.3: The `Flight` data structure and associated routines as an encapsulated class

```
    private int  heading;
    int  speed;
    float latitude;
    float longitude;
    void turnFlight (int angle) {
      heading = (heading + angle) % 360;
      // make sure angle is in the range 0-359 degrees
      if (heading < 0)
        heading = heading + 360;
    }
    void setHeading (int angle) {
      heading = angle % 360;
      // make sure angle is in the range 0-359 degrees
      if (heading < 0)
        heading = heading + 360;
    }
    int getHeading() {
      return heading;
    }
    void printFlight() {
      System.out.println (altitude + "/" + heading +
                          "/" + speed);

    }
  }
```

Now that the heading variable is private and hidden to code outside the class, you can no longer access it directly. Two additional functions are needed in order to access the private variable heading: setHeading, in order to set the heading, and getHeading, to obtain the current heading.

It is generally good practice to hide as many variables as possible. This separates the implementation of your class from its interface, making it more difficult for another programmer to break your code by bypassing the safety measures in your methods.

Class Inheritance

Using classes instead of structures also solves the problem of code duplication. Recall that for extended structures, such as CommercialFlight, you need to create a new copy of each function that acts on the original structure (Flight). With classes, you can inherit both the data members and methods when creating a new class:

```
class CommercialFlight extends Flight {
    // extra members in CommercialFlight
    int  flightNumber;
```

```
    int  passengers;
}
```

The `CommercialFlight` class, a *subclass* of `Flight`, automatically inherits all the data members and methods of the `Flight` class, so you can write:

```
// Create the object variable and instantiate it
CommercialFlight incomingCommercialFlight;
incomingCommercialFlight = new CommercialFlight();
// Now access its members and methods
incomingCommercialFlight.altitude = 2500;
incomingCommercialFlight.setHeading (45);
incomingCommercialFlight.flightNumber = 101;
incomingCommercialFlight.passengers = 24;
```

As you can see, inheritance makes life much easier. It also makes code more maintainable because the code to alter the heading of both a `Flight` and a `CommercialFlight` is all in one place, namely in the definition of the parent or *base class*. Figure 8.4 shows a schematic for the relationship of class and subclass.

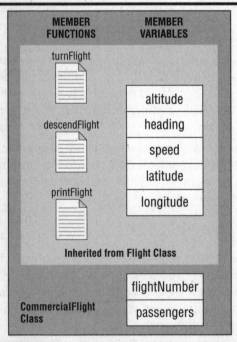

FIGURE 8.4:   The `CommercialFlight` class inherits member variables and functions from `Flight` and then adds its own member variables.

In many cases, you will want a subclass to override one or more methods of a parent class. Continuing with the example, you may want a commercial flight to print in a special way on the console, displaying the flight number in addition to other information. You can easily override the `printFlight` routine of the `Flight` class by reimplementing it in the `CommercialFlight` class:

```java
class Flight {
  int  altitude;
  private int  heading;
  int  speed;
  float latitude;
  float longitude;
  void turnFlight (int angle) {
    heading = (heading + angle) % 360;
    // make sure angle is in the range 0-359 degrees
    if (heading < 0)
      heading = heading + 360;
  }
  void setHeading (int angle) {
    heading = angle % 360;
    // make sure angle is in the range 0-359 degrees
    if (heading < 0)
      heading = heading + 360;
  }
  int getHeading() {
    return heading;
  }
  // print the flight's altitude, heading and speed
  // on the console
  void printFlight() {
    System.out.println (altitude + " ft / " + heading
                        + " degrees / " + speed + " knots");
  }
}
```

```
class CommercialFlight extends Flight {
    // extra members in CommercialFlight
    int flightNumber;
    int passengers;
    // reimplement the printFlight routine to
    // override the previous definition
    void printFlight() {
        System.out.print ("Flight " + flightNumber + " ");
        super.printFlight();
    }
}
```

Notice that the new `printFlight` method calls `super.print-Flight()`. The `super` keyword refers to the *superclass* of `Commercial-Flight` (in this case, the `Flight` class) and so `super.printFlight()` is a call to the original `printFlight` function as defined in the `Flight` class. You will often see the `super` keyword used when overriding methods because the overriding function usually implements supplementary processing—it does all its parent class did and more.

If you call a `Flight` object's `printFlight` function:

```
incomingFlight.printFlight();
```

you will get output like the following:

```
2500 ft / 270 degrees / 240 knots
```

If you call a commercial flight's `printFlight` routine:

```
incomingCommercialFlight.printFlight();
```

the output might look like the following:

```
Flight 101 3000 ft / 185 degrees / 350 knots
```

Figure 8.5 shows how the `CommercialFlight` class reimplements the `printFlight` function.

It is sometimes advantageous to use inheritance even when the base class is so generic that it cannot be implemented. You can do this using the concept of abstract classes.

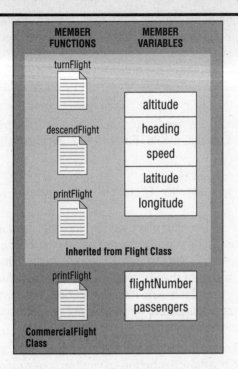

MEMBER FUNCTIONS
MEMBER VARIABLES

turnFlight

altitude
heading
speed
latitude
longitude

descendFlight

printFlight

Inherited from Flight Class

printFlight

flightNumber
passengers

CommercialFlight Class

FIGURE 8.5: The `CommercialFlight` class inherits member variables and functions from `Flight`, adds its own member variables, and overrides
the `printFlight` function.

Abstract Classes

This section describes how to incorporate air traffic control facilities into
the example by including classes for flight control towers (for aircraft fly-
ing, landing, and taking off) and ground control towers (for taxiing aircraft). To begin, you create `ControlFacility` as a parent class, and
then create `FlightControlTower` and `GroundControlTower` as subclasses. Then create a method called `getClearance`, which is called to

see if a facility will clear a flight for landing, taking off, taxiing, and so on. However, you cannot create a generic `ControlFacility` object because you cannot implement `getClearance` without knowing whether you control space on the ground or in the air. On the other hand, you still want to insist that every subclass of `ControlFacility` implements the `getClearance` method.

The solution to this dilemma is provided by Java's ability to define *abstract classes*. The code for the `ControlFacility` class illustrates how abstract classes work:

```
abstract class ControlFacility {
   abstract boolean getClearance (FlightAction request);
}
```

In this piece of code, you declare your new class and the `getClearance` method function that returns a boolean (`true` or `false`) value. The function will accept an object of a class named `FlightAction` (which is not defined here; it is just part of the illustration). However, the function is defined as `abstract`, and it has no implementation. Any class that has such abstract functions is said to be an *abstract class*, and no objects of such classes can ever be created.

The `FlightControlTower` and `GroundControlTower` subclasses must implement the `getClearance` function so you can create objects that represent such facilities:

```
class FlightControlTower extends ControlFacility {
   boolean getClearance (FlightAction request) {
      // implementation of the getClearance function for
      // flight control towers
      .
      .
      .
   }
}
class GroundControlTower extends ControlFacility {
   boolean getClearance (FlightAction request) {
      // implementation of the getClearance function for
      // ground control towers
      .
      .
      .
   }
}
```

Since both of these subclasses—`FlightControlTower` and `Ground-ControlTower`—implement the abstract functions defined in the parent class, they are not abstract classes and can both be instantiated. In addition to formalizing the interface, abstract classes give the programmer other advantages, which are discussed in the next section.

Polymorphism

Polymorphic functions are functions that do not care which variable types are passed to them. The PRINT statement in BASIC and the `writeln` statement in Pascal are examples of polymorphic routines because you can pass any type of variable to them and they always act appropriately. Standard BASIC does not need a PRINTINTEGER or PRINTSTRING statement because PRINT is smart enough to take care of any datatype. However, the PRINT statement has this ability specially coded into the BASIC interpreter, and its ability does not extend to user-defined structures. BASIC also has no provision for creating user-defined polymorphic routines.

Java makes it possible for programmers to simplify their code with polymorphism in three ways:

Inheritance   Allowing subclasses to automatically inherit methods from their parent classes. Also, any method that accepts a particular class as an argument will also accept any subclass of that class as an argument.

Overloading   Implementing identically named methods that take different arguments within the same class.

Interfacing   Implementing identically named methods that take identical arguments in different classes.

Let's look at these three cases in turn.

Inheritance

Inheritance is the simplest kind of polymorphism, as well as one you have already encountered. In the air traffic control example, you can ask any `Flight` object or `Flight`-subclassed object to turn left by calling the method `turnFlight (-90)`. This means that instead of requiring a multitude of function names like `turnFlight`, `turnCommercial-Flight`, or `turnMilitaryFlight` (for a `MilitaryFlight` class), you can use `turnFlight` consistently:

```
incomingFlight.turnFlight (-90);
incomingCommercialFlight.turnFlight (-90);
incomingMilitaryFlight.turnFlight (-90);
```

Better still, you can easily write code that works with the Flight class and all subclasses of the Flight. For example, you can create a new class called Airport that has a method called aircraftInbound; in turn, this adds a flight to the list of inbound flights:

```
class Airport {
   String airportName;
   Flight inboundFlights[], outboundFlights[];
   void aircraftInbound (Flight aFlight) {
     //implementation of aircraftInbound function
     .
     .
     .

   }
}
```

An Airport object will now accept any Flight object or object that is a subclass of Flight. For example, you could type:

```
// Create the object variable cityAirport and instantiate it
Airport cityAirport;
cityAirport = new Airport();
// Name the airport and add flight to its aircraftInbound
// Flight list
cityAirport.airportName = "City National Airport";
cityAirport.aircraftInbound (incomingFlight);
cityAirport.aircraftInbound (incomingCommercialFlight);
cityAirport.aircraftInbound (incomingMilitaryFlight);
```

Polymorphism by inheritance also allows you to take full advantage of abstract classes. Inheriting from a generic abstract class allows you to group together classes that share common functions but not common implementation. Having created the abstract class ControlFacility in the previous section, you can now write code that refers to ControlFacility objects and works with all subclasses of ControlFacility, even though ControlFacility objects themselves can never be created.

Overloading

Another way to add polymorphic functions is known as *function overloading*. In Java, C++, and other languages that support function overloading, it is possible to define the same function twice while using different parameters for each definition. For example, in the previous listing, the aircraftInbound function does the same thing no matter which subclass of Flight is passed to it. Suppose you want to add inbound aircraft to the Airport class's list of the inbound flights with different priorities according to the type of flight. By overloading the aircraftInbound function, you can customize its behavior for each kind of Flight object:

```
class Airport {
  String airportName;
  Flight inboundFlights[], outboundFlights[];
  // aircraftInbound function accepting Flight objects
  void aircraftInbound (Flight aFlight) {
    // implementation of aircraftInbound function for
    // generic flights
    .
    .
    .
  }
  // aircraftInbound function accepting CommercialFlight
  // objects
  void aircraftInbound (CommercialFlight aFlight) {
    // implementation of aircraftInbound function for
    // commercial flights
    .
    .
    .
  }
  // aircraftInbound function accepting MilitaryFlight
  // objects
  void aircraftInbound (MilitaryFlight aFlight) {
    // implementation of aircraftInbound function for
    // military flights
    .
    .
    .
  }
}
```

NOTE

Note that the method signature for polymorphic methods does not include the return type. You cannot have two methods with the same name and parameter list that have different return types.

Just as before, you call the function identically, no matter which type of Flight object is passed to the function:

```
Airport cityAirport;
cityAirport = new Airport();
cityAirport.aircraftInbound (incomingFlight);
```

```
cityAirport.aircraftInbound (incomingCommercialFlight);
cityAirport.aircraftInbound (incomingMilitaryFlight);
```

NOTE

Overloading is not a feature of object-oriented languages per se although it is most commonly implemented in object-oriented languages.

Polymorphism can also be achieved by implementing the same methods in different classes, a technique called *interfacing*.

Interfacing

Suppose you need to create a report that lists both airports and all their incoming and outgoing flights. You can do this by writing a printOn-Report function for both the Airport and Flight classes:

```
class Airport {
    String airportName;
    Flight inboundFlights[], outboundFlights[];
    // printOnReport function prints an Airport entry
    // on the report
    void printOnReport() {
        System.out.println ("Airport: " + airportName);
    }
}
class Flight {
    int  altitude;
    private int  heading;
    int  speed;
    float latitude;
    float longitude;
    // print the flight's altitude, heading, and speed on
    // the console
    void printOnReport() {
      System.out.println("Flight: " + altitude + " ft / " +
                          heading + " degrees / " + speed + "
                          knots");
    }
}
```

You can call these new functions in the following way:

```
incomingFlight.printOnReport();
cityAirport.printOnReport();
```

Informally speaking, these classes now have a common interface as far as printing reports is concerned. Java allows you to formalize the interface so that you can guarantee that a class will support all the functions (there may be more than one) that make up an interface. By using formal interfaces, you can write a function that will accept an argument of any class that implements a particular interface.

Let's define a formal interface for the report printing example. Java's `interface` keyword is used just like the `class` keyword:

```
interface ReportPrintable {
    void printOnReport();
}
```

Note that `ReportPrintable` is not a class and cannot be instantiated; essentially, the methods declared in an interface are abstract. To tell the compiler that the `Airport` and `Flight` classes implement the `ReportPrintable` interface, add an `implements` clause to the class declarations:

```
class Airport implements ReportPrintable {
    .
    .
    .
}
class Flight implements ReportPrintable {
    .
    .
    .
}
```

Next, you can create a `ReportGenerator` class that creates a report from any object that implements the `ReportPrintable` interface:

```
class ReportGenerator {
    void addToReport (ReportPrintable anObject) {
        anObject.printOnReport();
    }
}
```

The `addToReport` function of `ReportGenerator` will accept *any* class that implements the `ReportPrintable` interface.

As you can see, polymorphism greatly simplifies writing code, especially when modeling complex, real-world situations. The programmer does not need to remember as many function names, and the source code becomes much more readable.

Part ii

CONSTRUCTORS AND FINALIZERS

You can define two special kinds of methods:

Constructors   Methods that return new instances of the class. If you do not write a constructor, you can use a default constructor to create instances of the class.

Finalizers   Functions that are called just before an object is garbage-collected.

The following sections describe these special methods, as well as garbage collection.

Constructors

Going back to the `Airport` class, you will recall that you created and initialized the code as follows:

```
Airport cityAirport;
cityAirport = new Airport();
cityAirport.airportName = "City National Airport";
```

After the first line, `cityAirport` has been defined as an object variable. After the second line, an object is created, and `cityAirport` refers to the object. The third line initializes the name of the `Airport` object. The function `Airport()` is the *default constructor* for the `Airport` class.

The default constructor is inherited from `Airport`'s parent class, `Object`, and it is automatically added to the class by the Java compiler. The `Object`'s constructor allocates storage for any member variables that are declared as one of Java's built-in datatypes. In this case, none of the `Airport`'s member variables are allocated because neither the `String` variable nor the `Flight` datatypes are built in. For example, the `airportName` member object variable is `null` until you allocate space for the corresponding `String` or assign an object to it.

To simplify the object creation process, and to protect yourself from uninitialized object variables, you can create your own constructor for the `Airport` class:

```
class Airport {
   String airportName;
   Flight[] inboundFlights, outboundFlights;
   // a new constructor that takes no arguments
   Airport() {
```

```
      super();
    airportName = "Unknown";
  }
    .
    .
    .
}
```

A constructor is defined in the same way as an ordinary method, but it must have the same name as the class and have no return datatype. In this example, the constructor calls super(), which is a reference to the constructor in the parent class, Object. Writing the call to super() is optional because the compiler will implicitly call the parent class's constructor if you do not call it. You can call the new constructor exactly as you called it earlier:

```
Airport cityAirport = new Airport();
cityAirport.airportName = "City National Airport";
```

Now, after calling the new constructor, cityAirport.airport-Name will default to "Unknown." However, because you will always change the airport name, you can save a step by writing another constructor that creates the Airport object and sets the airportName to the caller's choice, as follows:

```
class Airport {
  String airportName;
  Flight inboundFlights[], outboundFlights[];
  // a new constructor that takes no arguments
  Airport() {
    super();
    airportName = "Unknown";
  }
  // a new constructor that takes the new airport's name as
  // an argument
  Airport (String newName) {
    super();
    airportName = newName;
  }
    .
    .
    .
}
```

This is an example of overloading: The two constructors have the same name but accept different parameters. Now you can write the following:

```
Airport cityAirport = new Airport ("City National Airport");
```

Constructors can call other constructors. You can rewrite the Airport() constructor so that it calls the Airport (String newName) constructor by using the this keyword:

```
// a new constructor that takes no arguments
Airport() {
    this ("Unknown");
}
```

The keyword this followed by parentheses (and arguments, if any) refers to a constructor for this class. In this case, the compiler knows you are referring to the Airport (String newName) constructor because it is the only constructor that takes a String as an argument. Since the different constructors of a class typically perform common tasks, you will find the ability to call other constructors very useful.

Garbage Collection

What happens when an object is no longer needed by the system? The following code and Figures 8.6 and 8.7 illustrate what "no longer needed" means:

```
cityAirport = new Airport ("City National Airport");
cityAirport = new Airport ("Potter's Field");
```

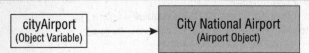

FIGURE 8.6: The object variable cityAirport initially references the object representing City National Airport.

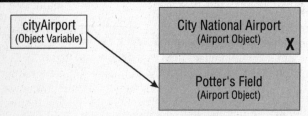

FIGURE 8.7: The object variable then references a new object representing Potter's Field. Since there are no references to the first object, it will be automatically discarded by the garbage collector.

Two objects are created in this code, but only one object variable is here. After the first statement, cityAirport points to the object representing City National Airport. After the second statement, city-Airport points to the other object representing Potter's Field, and nothing points to the first object. Just as you would expect, the original object is lost from the system. Java automatically reclaims memory used by an object when no object variables refer to that object, a process known as *garbage collection*. Consider the following assignments and the corresponding Figures 8.8 and 8.9:

```
localAirport = new Airport ("City National Airport");
cityAirport = localAirport;
cityAirport = new Airport ("Potter's Field");
```

In this instance, the object representing City National Airport is not garbage-collected because localAirport still refers to it.

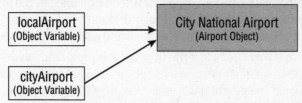

FIGURE 8.8: The object variables localAirport and cityAirport initially reference the new object representing City National Airport.

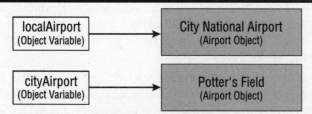

FIGURE 8.9: Next, the object variable cityAirport is used to refer to the new object representing Potter's Field. Since there is still a reference to the first object (localAirport), the original object will not be discarded by the system.

Finalizers

A few situations exist in which a class needs to clean itself up before garbage collection. It can do this by implementing a finalizer method. *Finalizers* are called just before a class is garbage-collected. Finalizers are typically used to close open files or connections, or to ensure that related tasks are completed before the object is forgotten.

To create a finalizer, simply define a method called `finalize`:

```
protected void finalize() throws Throwable {
    System.out.println (
            "This object is about to be garbage collected");
    super.finalize();
}
```

The `protected` keyword (which limits the classes that may call the finalizer function) and the `throws Throwable` clause which describes what to do when the unexpected happens) will be explained in the next chapter. The `super.finalize()` call ensures that the `finalize()` method of your superclass will be called, finalizing its part of the object.

Finalizers are rather tricky to write because it is impossible to determine exactly when an object will be garbage-collected; it could be within microseconds or, if the program is terminated, may never occur. This means that a finalizer should rely as little as possible on the existence of other objects because there is no guarantee that the other objects were not garbage-collected first. It is also possible for an object to avert its own garbage collection by creating a new reference to itself in the finalizer. Therefore, if your class must perform some shutdown or cleanup operation before being garbage-collected, you should write a non-finalizer method to take care of the operation and call that method explicitly before discarding the object.

For example, suppose you write a class called ComLink that handles network communications and a method called close that closes the network channel. You know you need to close the network channel before discarding any ComLink objects, so the simplest solution might appear to be calling close from ComLink's finalize method. However, it is possible that close will not be called for an extended period of time, or perhaps not at all. This could cause the system to exhaust available network channels because channels have not been freed in a timely manner by discarded ComLink objects. The only reliable solution in such cases is to make sure you call the close function explicitly, before any objects are discarded.

WHAT'S NEXT?

In the next chapter, we will discuss exception handling, including the basic classes used in error and exception handling and the creation of custom exception classes.

Part ii

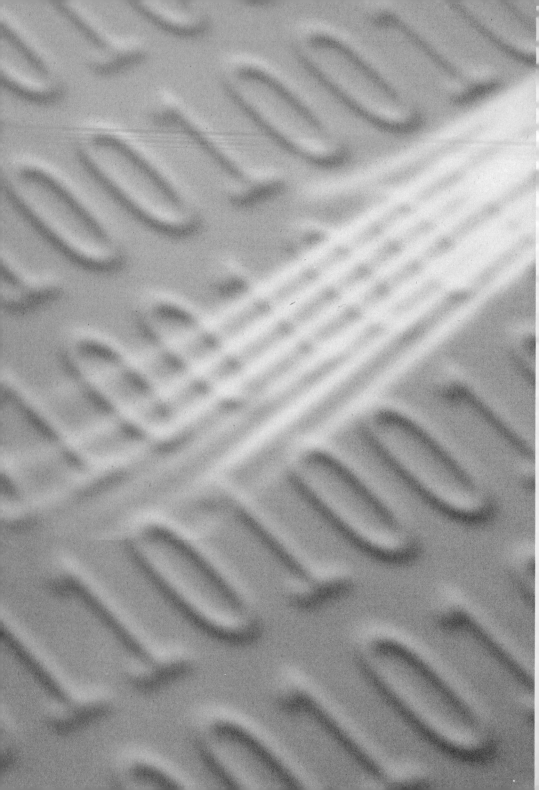

Chapter 9

EXCEPTION HANDLING

A s programs become more complicated, making them robust is a much more difficult task. Traditional programming languages like C rely on the heavy use of `if` statements to detect abnormal conditions, `goto` statements to branch to the error handlers, and cryptic `return` codes for propagating the abnormal conditions back to the calling methods. Thus, normal program flow gets buried in the web of exception detection and handling statements, or robustness is sacrificed for the sake of clarity.

Using an exception-handling mechanism similar to that of C++, Java provides an elegant way to build programs that are both robust and clear. In this chapter, you will learn to use this cleaner mechanism to handle errors and unusual conditions.

Adapted from *Mastering Java 2* by John Zukowski
ISBN 0-7821-2180-2   1,280 pages $49.99

OVERVIEW OF EXCEPTION HANDLING

An *exception* is an abnormal condition that disrupts normal program flow. There are many cases where abnormal conditions happen during program execution, such as the following:

▶ The file you try to open may not exist.

▶ The class file you want to load may be missing or in the wrong format.

▶ The other end of your network connection may be nonexistent.

▶ The network connection may be disrupted for some mysterious reason.

▶ An operand is not in the legal range prescribed for operations or methods. For example, an array element index cannot exceed the size of the array, and a divisor in a division operation cannot be zero.

If these abnormal conditions are not prevented or at least handled properly, either the program will be aborted abruptly or the incorrect results or status will be carried on, causing more and more abnormal conditions. Imagine a program that reads from an unopened file and does computations based on those input values!

The Basic Model

Java follows the basic C++ syntax for exception handling. First, you `try` to execute a block of statements. If an abnormal condition occurs, something will `throw` an exception that you can `catch` with a handler. In addition, `finally`, there may be a block of statements you always want executed—no matter whether an exception occurred and no matter whether the exception is handled if it does occur.

Throwing an exception is friendlier than terminating the program because it provides the programmer with the option of writing a handler to deal with the abnormal condition. For example, the following program fragment causes the program to sleep for 10 seconds (10,000 milliseconds) by calling the `sleep()` class method defined in class `Thread` of the `java.lang` package. If `sleep` is interrupted before the time expires, a message is printed and the execution continues with the statement following this `try-catch` construct:

```
PrintWriter out = new PrintWriter(System.out, true);
try {
```

```
    Thread.sleep(10000);
} catch (InterruptedException e) {
    out.println("Sleeping interrupted.");
}
// reaches here after try-block finished or exception handled
```

The next program, which copies the contents of one file to another, demonstrates exception handling in a more practical setting. The program first takes filenames from the command-line arguments. Then, it opens the files and copies data in 512-byte block increments. The number of bytes copied is tracked, and the byte count is reported once the operation is completed. The program fragment to carry out these operations is as follows:

```
int  byteCount = 0;
byte buffer[] = new byte[512];
String inputFile = null;
String outputFile = null;
PrintWriter out = new PrintWriter(System.out, true);
FileInputStream fin;
FileOutputStream fout;
inputFile = args[0];
outputFile = args[1];
fin = new FileInputStream(inputFile);
fout = new FileOutputStream(outputFile);
int bytesInOneRead;
while ((bytesInOneRead = fin.read(buffer)) != -1) {
  fout.write(buffer, 0, bytesInOneRead);
  byteCount += bytesInOneRead;
}
out.println(byteCount + " written");
```

The FileInputStream and FileOutputStream classes are defined in the java.io package. Their constructors allow you to open files by name, and their methods let you read data from or write data into a single byte or a byte array.

But what if the user does not provide the input and output filenames? Or what if the user provides a nonexistent input file? In Java, these abnormal conditions are system-defined exceptions that will be thrown by the system as they occur. Accessing an array with an index larger than or equal to the array size will cause an ArrayIndexOutOfBoundsException to be thrown. The constructor of the FileInputStream class will throw a FileNotFoundException exception if the file cannot be located. The constructor for FileOutputStream and the read() and write() methods will throw an IOException exception for an I/O error.

Furthermore, exception handlers can be located together. A catch clause is necessary for each exception handler to identify the abnormal condition to which the handler is attending. Three handlers need to be added to the previous program to attend to the abnormal conditions mentioned previously:

▶ One handler will print the usage of the program when the user does not provide both the input and output filenames.

▶ The next handler will notify the user when the input file does not exist.

▶ Another handler will print an error message when other I/O exceptions occur.

The program to print the number of bytes copied is moved to the finally clause so that it will always be executed—even if some abnormal condition disrupts the normal program flow. Here is the full program:

```
import java.io.*;
public class MyCopy {
  public static void main (String args[]) {
    int    byteCount = 0;
    byte buffer[] = new byte[512];
    String inputFile  = null;
    String outputFile = null;
    PrintWriter out = new PrintWriter(System.out, true);
    FileInputStream  fin;
    FileOutputStream fout;
    try {
      inputFile  = args[0];
      outputFile = args[1];
      fin  = new FileInputStream(inputFile);
      fout = new FileOutputStream(outputFile);
      int bytesInOneRead;
      while ((bytesInOneRead = fin.read(buffer)) != -1) {
        fout.write(buffer, 0, bytesInOneRead);
        byteCount += bytesInOneRead;
      }
    } catch (ArrayIndexOutOfBoundsException e) {
      out.println(
          "Usage: java MyCopy [inputFile] [outputFile]");
    } catch (FileNotFoundException e) {
      out.println("Cannot open input file: " + inputFile);
    } catch (IOException e) {
      out.println("I/O exception occurs!");
    } finally {
```

```
        if (byteCount > 0)
          out.println(byteCount + " bytes written");
      }
    }
  }
```

Here is a sample output of the previous program run under different conditions:

```
C:\MasteringJava\Ch07>javac MyCopy.java
C:\MasteringJava\Ch07>java MyCopy
Usage: java MyCopy [inputFile] [outputFile]
C:\MasteringJava\Ch07>java MyCopy MyCopy.java temp.java
1095 bytes written
C:\MasteringJava\Ch07>java MyCopy NoSuchFile.java temp.java
Cannot open input file: NoSuchFile.java
```

Why Use Exception Handling?

You should use exception handling for several reasons. One is that error-handling code is separated from normal program flow to increase the readability and maintainability of the program.

Imagine how you would rewrite the example from the previous section in C if exception handling was not available. You would need an if statement after every I/O operation to make sure they were completed successfully. You would also need to use an if statement to check whether the user provided enough filenames. To handle these abnormal conditions, you would either add more code in place or use goto statements to branch to the code fragment that handles common failures. Add a few more I/O calls, and even you, the author of the program, will not be able to easily recognize what the program was originally intended to accomplish. With Java, there is no need to test if an exception condition happens. Adding more handlers requires adding more catch clauses, but the original program flow is unaffected.

Another reason to use exception handling is so you can easily say where the exception will be handled. Exceptions propagate up the call stack at run time—first up the enclosing try blocks and then back to the calling method—until an exception handler catches them. For example, the previous example can be rewritten as a method with input and output filenames as the arguments. The synopsis of this new method is as follows:

```
int copyFile(String inputFile, String outputFile)
```

The caller of this method may want to handle the abnormal condition itself. For example, an application with a GUI may want to display a dialog box prompting the user for another filename when the input file does not exist. In this case, the error handler for an I/O exception is removed from the method and a throws clause is added to the method declaration. The caller can then have its own error-handling routines for these abnormal conditions. Here is the modified method definition:

```
int copyFile(String inputFile, String outputFile) throws
IOException {
  int bytesInOneRead, byteCount = 0;
  byte buffer[] = new byte[512];
  FileInputStream fin = new FileInputStream(inputFile);
  FileOutputStream fout= new FileOutputStream(outputFile);
  while ((bytesInOneRead = fin.read(buffer)) != -1) {
    fout.write(buffer, 0, bytesInOneRead);
    byteCount += bytesInOneRead;
  }
  return byteCount;
}
```

Here is a code fragment to call this method and handle the abnormal conditions itself:

```
int byteCount = 0;
String inputFile = null;
String outputFile = null;
PrintWriter out = new PrintWriter(System.out, true);
try {
  inputFile  = args[0];
  outputFile = args[1];
  byteCount = copyFile(inputFile, outputFile);
} catch (ArrayIndexOutOfBoundsException e) {
  out.println(
      "Usage: java MyCopy [inputFile] [outputFile]");
} catch (FileNotFoundException e) {
  out.println("Cannot open input file: " + inputFile);
} catch (IOException e) {
  out.println("I/O exception occurs!");
} finally {
  if (byteCount > 0)
    out.println(byteCount + " bytes written");
}
```

Exceptions are objects with hierarchical relationships. You can create a single exception handler to catch all exceptions from a class and its subclasses, or you can create a series of exception handlers, each handling exceptions from individual subclasses. The MyCopy example demonstrates another option. The second `catch` clause deals with `FileNotFoundException`, and the next one catches any other `IOException`. `FileNotFoundException` is a subclass of `IOException`, so you can check for both subclass and superclass exceptions.

Here is the full program:

```java
import java.io.*;
public class MyCopy {
   public static void main (String args[]) {
      int byteCount = 0;
      String inputFile = null;
      String outputFile = null;
      PrintWriter out = new PrintWriter(System.out, true);
      try {
         inputFile  = args[0];
         outputFile = args[1];
         byteCount = copyFile(inputFile, outputFile);
      } catch (ArrayIndexOutOfBoundsException e) {
      out.println(
            "Usage:. java MyCopy [inputFile] [outputFile]");
      } catch (FileNotFoundException e) {
      out.println("Cannot open input file: " + inputFile);
      } catch (IOException e) {
      out.println("I/O exception occurs!");
      } finally {
      if (byteCount > 0)
         out.println(byteCount + " bytes written");
      }
    }
   static int copyFile(String inputFile, String outputFile)
                  throws IOException      {
      int  bytesInOneRead, byteCount = 0;
      byte buffer[] = new byte[512];
      FileInputStream  fin = new FileInputStream(inputFile);
      FileOutputStream fout= newFileOutputStream(outputFile);
```

```
        while ((bytesInOneRead = fin.read(buffer)) != -1) {
          fout.write(buffer, 0, bytesInOneRead);
          byteCount += bytesInOneRead;
        }
        return byteCount;
    }
}
```

Hierarchy of Exception Classes

Just like nearly everything else in Java, exceptions are either objects or class instances. Exception classes form their own class hierarchy. The root class of all the exception classes is the Throwable class, which is an immediate subclass of the Object class. Methods are defined in the Throwable class to retrieve the error message associated with the exception and to print the stack trace showing where the exception occurs (see the next section for more details).

Class Throwable has two immediate subclasses: class Error and class Exception. Subclasses of class Exception have the suffix Exception. Subclasses of class Error have the suffix Error (and then there is ThreadDeath, a subclass of Error). The subclasses of Error are basically used for signaling abnormal system conditions. For example, an OutOfMemoryError signals that the Java Virtual Machine has run out of memory and that the garbage collector is unable to claim any more free memory. A StackOverflowError signals a stack overflow in the interpreter. These Error exceptions are, in general, unrecoverable and should not be handled.

The subclasses of the Exception class are, in general, recoverable. For example, an EOFException signals that a file you have opened has no more data for reading. A FileNotFoundException signals that a file you want to open does not exist in the file system. You can choose to handle the exceptions by using a try-catch block to enclose the statements whose exceptional conditions will be handled.

Figure 9.1 illustrates the hierarchical relationships among some of the more common errors and exceptions. Many more exceptions exist, but they are not important at this point and will be explained as they are used in examples. Additional information about exceptions can be found in the online documentation at http://www.java.sun.com/products/jdk/1.2/docs/api/index.html.

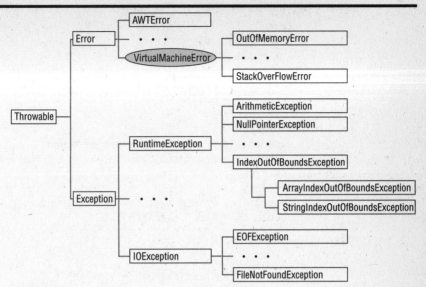

FIGURE 9.1: Hierarchy of common exceptions

The following example loops through four pathological cases in which the system throws four types of `RuntimeException`:

`ArithmeticException` For exceptional arithmetic conditions like integer division by zero

`NullPointerException` For accessing a field or invoking a method of a null object

`ArrayIndexOutOfBoundsException` For accessing an array element by providing an index value less than zero or greater than or equal to the array size

`StringIndexOutOfBoundsException` For accessing a character of a `String` or `StringBuffer` with an index less than zero or greater than or equal to the length of the string

Here is the test program:

```
import java.io.*;
public class ExceptionTest {
  public static void main(String args[]) {
    PrintWriter out = new PrintWriter(System.out, true);
    for (int i = 0; i < 4; i++) {
      int k;
      try {
```

```
          switch (i) {
            case 0:      // divided by zero
              int zero = 0;
              k = 911 / zero;
              break;
            case 1:      // null pointer
              int b[] = null;
              k = b[0];
              break;
            case 2:      // array index out of bound
              int c[] = new int[2];
              k = c[9];
              break;
            case 3:      // string index out of bound
              char ch = "abc".charAt(99);
              break;
          }
        } catch (Exception e) {
          out.println("\nTest case #" + i + "\n");
          out.println(e);
        }
      }
    }
  }
```

The output of the previous test program is shown here:

```
C:\MasteringJava\Ch07>javac ExceptionTest.java
C:\MasteringJava\Ch07>java ExceptionTest
Test case #0
java.lang.ArithmeticException: / by zero
Test case #1
java.lang.NullPointerException
Test case #2
java.lang.ArrayIndexOutOfBoundsException: 9
Test case #3
java.lang.StringIndexOutOfBoundsException: String index out
of range: 99
```

EXCEPTION-HANDLING CONSTRUCTS

The general form of an exception-handling construct (the try statement) is:

```
try {
    normalProgramBody
} catch (ExceptionClass1 exceptionVariable1) {
    exceptionHandlerProgramBody1
```

```
} catch (ExceptionClass2 exceptionVariable2) {
    exceptionHandlerProgramBody2
. . .
} finally {
    exitProgramBody
}
```

TIP

Early versions of the JDK (before 1.0.2) did not require curly braces in the body of a try-catch-finally construct if the program body consisted of only a single statement. However, curly braces are always required in JDK versions 1.0.2 and newer.

The `try` keyword is used to specify a block of statements whose exceptions will be handled by the succeeding `catch` clauses. There can be any number of `catch` clauses. When an exception condition occurs, the body of the first exception handler whose exception class type is the same class as or is a superclass of the thrown exception will be executed.

Since exception matching is done sequentially, an exception handler may never be reached if its `catch` clause is placed after the `catch` clause for its superclass exception handler. For example, in an earlier example, the handler for `FileNotFoundException` needed to be placed before the handler for `IOException`, the immediate superclass of `FileNotFoundException`. The compiler checks to ensure all exception handlers are reachable. If you exchange the order of the handlers for `FileNotFoundException` and `IOException`, the compiler will issue the following error message:

```
C:\MasteringJava\Ch07>javac MyCopy.java
MyCopy.java:16: catch not reached.
    } catch (FileNotFoundException e) {
      ^
1 error
```

The exit program block after the `finally` keyword will be executed before the program control is transferred outside the programming construct. This will eventually happen when the execution of the program body or the exception handler is finished, a flow-breaking statement (a `break`, `continue`, or `return` statement) is encountered, or an exception is thrown with no handler inside the construct capable of catching it.

Part ii

The `catch` clause is optional, as is the `finally` clause. However, at least one of the `catch` or `finally` clauses must exist in a `try-catch-finally` construct. The exit program body comes in handy for freeing resources like file handles allocated in the normal program body.

The following example demonstrates the effects of `break` and `continue` statements on a `finally` clause. Inside the nested `for` loop, labeled and unlabeled `break` and `continue` statements are executed, and the flow is traced:

```java
import java.io.*;
public class FinallyTest {
  public static void main(String args[]) {
    PrintWriter out = new PrintWriter(System.out, true);
outerLoop:
  for (int i = 0; i < 3; i++)
    for (int j = 0; j < 3; j++)
      try {
        out.println("try before if: i=" +
                        i + ", j=" + j);
        if ((i == 0) && (j == 1))
          continue;
        else if ((i == 0) && (j == 2))
          continue outerLoop;
        else if ((i == 1) && (j == 0))
          break;
        else if ((i == 2) && (j == 1))
          break outerLoop;
        out.println("try after if:  i=" +
                        i + ", j=" + j);
      } finally {
        out.println("finally:      i=" +
                        i + ", j=" + j + "\n");
      }
    }
  }
}
```

The output of the program is shown next. You can see that the `finally` clause is always executed once the `try` block is entered:

```
C:\MasteringJava\Ch07>javac FinallyTest.java
C:\MasteringJava\Ch07>java FinallyTest
try before if: i=0, j=0
try after  if: i=0, j=0
finally:       i=0, j=0

try before if: i=0, j=1
finally:       i=0, j=1
```

```
try before if: i=0, j=2
finally:       i=0, j=2

try before if: i=1, j=0
finally:       i=1, j=0

try before if: i=2, j=0
try after  if: i=2, j=0
finally:       i=2, j=0

try before if: i=2, j=1
finally:       i=2, j=1
```

If the exception is not caught in the current try-catch-finally construct, it will be propagated up the program stack. The same exception-matching process will be repeated for all the enclosing try-catch-finally constructs, from the innermost construct to the outermost one, until a matching exception handler can be found. If no match can be found in the current method, the same process will be repeated for all the try-catch-finally constructs of the calling method, again from the innermost construct to the outermost one, until a match is found.

As the system tries to find a handler for the exception, from innermost to outermost, it executes the finally clauses of the try-catch-finally construct, from the innermost to the outermost. When the program runs out of try-catch-finally constructs and does not find a matching exception handler, it will print the message associated with the exception and a stack trace showing where the exception occurred; then it will terminate.

Here is a sample output of a program with an uncaught exception:

```
java.lang.ArithmeticException: / by zero
    at NoHandler.inner(NoHandler.java:6)
    at NoHandler.outer(NoHandler.java:11)
    at NoHandler.main(NoHandler.java:15)
```

Even if an exception is caught, the handler can rethrow the exception or throw another exception, and the exception-matching process will continue. The next example generates three different exceptions in the for loop of the method() method. The first exception, Arithmetic-Exception, is caught in the inner try-catch-finally construct because of an exact match in exception type. The second exception, ArrayIndexOutOfBoundsException, is caught in the inner try-catch-finally construct because it is a subclass of IndexOutOf-BoundsException, but then it is rethrown and caught by the outer try-catch-finally construct. The last exception, StringIndexOut-OfBoundsException, is caught in the inner try-catch-finally construct because it is also a subclass of IndexOutOfBoundsException. It is then rethrown, but no handler in the outer try-catch-finally construct can catch it. It is thus propagated to the calling method and caught because it is a subclass of RuntimeException.

Here's the example:

```java
import java.io.*;
public class NestedException {
  static PrintWriter out = new PrintWriter(
      System.out, true);
  public static void method() {
    for (int i = 0; i < 3; i++) {
      int k;
      try {
        out.println("\nOuter try block; Test Case #" + i);
        try {
          out.println("Inner try block");
          switch (i) {
            case 0:     // divided by zero
              int zero = 0;
              k = 911 / zero;
              break;
            case 1:     // array index out of bound
              int c[] = new int[2];
              k = c[9];
              break;
            case 2:     // string index out of bound
              char ch = "abc".charAt(99);
              break;
          }
        } catch (ArithmeticException e) {
          out.println("Inner ArithmeticException>" + e);
        } catch (IndexOutOfBoundsException e) {
          out.println(
              "Inner IndexOutOfBoundsException>" + e);
          throw e;
        } finally {
          out.println("Inner finally block");
        }
      } catch (ArrayIndexOutOfBoundsException e) {
        out.println("Outer ArrayIndexOutOfBound>" + e);
      }
      finally {
        out.println("Outer finally block");
```

```
          }
        }
      }
      public static void main(String args[]) {
        try {
          method();
        } catch (RuntimeException e) {
          out.println("main() RuntimeException>" + e);
        } finally {
          out.println("\nmain() finally block");
        }
      }
    }
```

Here is the output of the program:

```
C:\MasteringJava\Ch07>javac NestedException.java
C:\MasteringJava\Ch07>java NestedException

Outer try block; Test Case #0
Inner try block
Inner ArithmeticException>java.lang.ArithmeticException: /
by zero
Inner finally block
Outer finally block

Outer try block; Test Case #1
Inner try block
Inner IndexOutOfBoundsException>java.lang.ArrayIndexOutOf
BoundsException:
Inner finally block
Outer ArrayIndexOutOfBound>java.lang.ArrayIndexOutOfBounds
Exception:
Outer finally block

Outer try block; Test Case #2
Inner try block
Inner
IndexOutOfBoundsException>java.lang.StringIndexOutOfBounds
Exception: String index out of range: 99
Inner finally block
Outer finally block
main() RuntimeException>java.lang.StringIndexOutOfBounds
Exception: String index out of range: 99

main() finally block
```

Methods Available to Exceptions

All errors and exceptions are subclasses of class `Throwable` and thus can access the methods defined in it.

getMessage()   To obtain the error message associated with the exception or error

printStackTrace()   To print a stack trace showing where the exception occurs

toString()   To show the exception name along with the message returned by `getMessage()`

getLocalizedMessage()   To create a localized description of the exception or error that can be used by a `subClass` to override this method in order to produce a locale-specific message

fillInStackTrace()   To record within the exception object information about the current state of the stack frames for the current thread

printStackTrace(PrintStream s)   To print a stack trace showing where the exception occurs to the specified print stream

Most exception classes have two constructors: one with a `String` argument to set the error message that can later be fetched through the `getMessage()` method; the other with no argument. In the second case, the `getMessage()` method will return `null`. The same error message will be embedded in the return of the `toString()` method or be a part of the stack trace output by the `printStackTrace()` method. An example of output or return from these methods is listed here:

```
*** example of return from getMessage() ***
/ by zero
*** example of return from toString() ***
java.lang.ArithmeticException: / by zero
*** example of output by printStackTrace() ***
java.lang.ArithmeticException: / by zero
    at NoHandler.inner(NoHandler.java:6)
    at NoHandler.outer(NoHandler.java:11)
    at NoHandler.main(NoHandler.java:16)
```

The *throw* Statement

A throw statement causes an exception to be thrown. The synopsis of a throw statement is:

```
throw expression;
```

where the expression must be evaluated to an instance of class Throwable or its many subclasses.

In the most common usage, a new statement is used to create an instance in the expression. For example, the following statement will throw an IOException with "cannot find the directory" as the error message:

```
throw new IOException("cannot find the directory");
```

The *throws* Clause

A method that throws an exception within it must catch that exception or have that exception declared in its throws clause unless the exception is a subclass of either the Error class or the RuntimeException class. When multiple exceptions are to be put in one throws clause, use commas to separate them. For example, the following program segment declares a method that propagates out IOException and InterruptedException:

```
int readModel(String filename) throws IOException,
InterruptedException
```

There are four reasons why exceptions that are subclasses of the Error or RuntimeException class need not be declared or handled in a method:

▶ If you need to catch or declare a throws clause for every such exception that might occur in the method, the program will look very cumbersome.

▶ It is difficult to check at compile time whether such exceptions will occur. For example, every reference to an object potentially can throw a NullPointerException. It is a formidable task for a compiler to make sure that every object referred to will be non-null at run time, especially when the object is passed in as an argument of the method.

▶ Most of the errors can occur beyond the programmer's control. It does not make much sense to ask the programmer to be responsible for handling these errors.

▶ Most of the runtime exceptions tend to be the result of programmer error. Correct code will not generate them.

The compiler relies on the declaration of throws clauses to determine if an exception may occur in an expression, a statement, or a method. The exceptions that may occur in a method are the union of all the exceptions that can be generated by the throw statements within the method and all the exceptions contained in the throws clauses of the methods that might be called within the method. The compiler issues an error message for any method that does not declare all (non-error/non-runtime) exceptions in its throws clause. A sample output for such an error message is shown here:

```
DontCompile.java:8:
Exception java.io.FileNotFoundException must be caught,
or it must be declared in the throws clause of this method.
FileInputStream fin = new FileInputStream
("BasicException.java");
                 ^
```

CREATING YOUR OWN EXCEPTION CLASSES

When writing a method, there are two ways to report abnormal conditions to the calling method: Use a predefined error code as the return value or throw an exception.

If an exception is thrown, the calling method is automatically handed the convenience and power of the whole exception-handling mechanism to respond to the abnormal conditions. It will also be possible for the compiler to check if these abnormal conditions are dealt with properly, since these abnormal conditions are declared in the throws clause of the method.

When throwing an exception, you can create an instance from an exception class already defined in the language or from one you define on your own. It may be difficult to find a predefined exception that is designed for your particular situation. By using an exception already prescribed for other conditions, you may complicate the exception handler's task. The reason is that the exception handler may need to differentiate your abnormal condition from ones the exception class is originally prescribed for, if they can both occur in the method.

The common practice in creating a customized exception class is to subclass the Exception class. This ensures the compiler checks if it is dealt with properly. However, if you are writing system- or hardware-related utilities, you may be justified in creating subclasses from either Error or RuntimeException classes. You should not subclass Error or RuntimeException just so you do not need to create throws clauses for your methods. That defeats the whole purpose of using exceptions.

Because exception classes are class objects, they can have data members and methods defined within them. As an example, Interrupted-IOException, defined in the java.io package, has a public instance variable, bytesTransferred, to hold the number of bytes read or written before the operation is interrupted. You may choose to create customized exception classes in a hierarchy so that the handler has the option of handling the superclass as a whole, handling the subclasses individually, or handling both classes simultaneously.

AN EXAMPLE: AGE EXCEPTIONS

The example presented in this section demonstrates how to create a hierarchy of user-defined exception classes for abnormal conditions and how to write a program using these user-defined exceptions for abnormal condition handling. In the first part of the example, you construct a hierarchy of exception classes to report age-related anomalies, as shown in Figure 9.2.

FIGURE 9.2: The class hierarchy for the AgeException class

The root of this hierarchy is the AgeException class. It has a data member, age, to hold the age causing the occurrence of the exception. It has two subclasses: OutOfAgeLimitException for cases where the age given is too young or too old to perform a certain activity and Illegal-AgeFormatException for cases where the age given is out of the legal age range or in the wrong format. The former class has a data member, ageLimit, to hold the limit being violated. The program for defining these classes is listed below. Place this exception hierarchy into a file named AgeException.java:

```java
class AgeException extends Exception {
  int age;
  AgeException(String message) {
    super(message);
  }
  AgeException() {
    super();
  }
}
class OutOfAgeLimitException extends AgeException {
  int ageLimit;
  OutOfAgeLimitException(int ageLimit, String message) {
    super(message);
    this.ageLimit = ageLimit;
  }
  OutOfAgeLimitException(String message) {
    super(message);
  }
}
class TooYoungException extends OutOfAgeLimitException {
  TooYoungException(int age, int ageLimit, String message) {
    super(ageLimit, "You are too young to " +
                    message + ".");
    this.age = age;
  }
  TooYoungException() {
    super("too young");
  }
}
class TooOldException extends OutOfAgeLimitException {
  TooOldException(int age, int ageLimit, String message) {
    super(ageLimit, "You are too old to " + message + ".");
    this.age = age;
  }
  TooOldException() {
    super("too old");
  }
}
class IllegalAgeFormatException extends AgeException {
  IllegalAgeFormatException(String message) {
    super(message);
  }
  IllegalAgeFormatException() {
    super("Illegal age format");
```

```
  }
}
class NegativeAgeException extends IllegalAgeFormatException
{
  NegativeAgeException(String message) {
    super(message);
  }
  NegativeAgeException(int age) {
    super("Age must be nonnegative.");
    this.age = age;
  }
}
```

TIP

As with all Java classes, the only classes that need to go into separate files are public Java classes. Therefore, all these exception classes could go into one file, into separate files, or into the same file as the AgeExceptionTest program below.

The second part of the example is a program to use the previous exception hierarchy. The program will loop through different ages to see if a person of the age specified can ride a roller coaster. The method ride-RollerCoasterAtAge() will throw TooYoungException, TooOld-Exception, or NegativeAgeException if it finds an age that is too young, too old, or negative, respectively. The program listing for the Age-ExceptionTest.java file is as follows:

```
import java.io.*;
public class AgeExceptionTest {
  static PrintWriter out = new PrintWriter(System.out, true);
  static void rideRollerCoasterAtAge(int age)
     throws NegativeAgeException, OutOfAgeLimitException {
    out.println("Trying to ride a roller coaster at age " +
      age + "...");
    if (age < 0)
      throw new NegativeAgeException(age);
    else if (age < 5)
      throw new TooYoungException(age, 5,
        "ride a roller coaster");
    else if (age > 45)
      throw new TooOldException(age, 45,
        "ride a roller coaster");
    out.println("Riding the roller coaster....");
  }
  public static void main(String args[]) {
```

```
            int ages[] = {-3, 2, 10, 35, 65};
            for (int i = 0; i < ages.length; i++)
              try {
                rideRollerCoasterAtAge(ages[i]);
                out.println("Wow! What an experience!");
              } catch (OutOfAgeLimitException e) {
                out.println(e.getMessage());
                if (ages[i] < e.ageLimit)
                  out.println((e.ageLimit - ages[i]) +
                    " more years and you'll be able to try it.");
                else
                  out.println((ages[i] - e.ageLimit) +
                    " years ago riding it was like a piece of
cake.");
              } catch (NegativeAgeException e) {
                out.println(e.getMessage());
              } finally {
                out.println();
              }
          }
        }
```

The output of the sample program is listed here:

```
C:\MasteringJava\Ch07>javac AgeException.java
C:\MasteringJava\Ch07>javac AgeExceptionTest.java
C:\MasteringJava\Ch07>java AgeExceptionTest
Trying to ride a roller coaster at age -3...
Age must be nonnegative.

Trying to ride a roller coaster at age 2...
You are too young to ride a roller coaster.
3 more years and you'll be able to try it.

Trying to ride a roller coaster at age 10...
Riding the roller coaster....
Wow! What an experience!

Trying to ride a roller coaster at age 35...
Riding the roller coaster....
Wow! What an experience!

Trying to ride a roller coaster at age 65...
You are too old to ride a roller coaster.
20 years ago riding it was like a piece of cake.
```

WHAT'S NEXT?

The next chapter will cover the most frequently used standard Java packages, including those that support languages, graphics, Internet programming, and Swing.

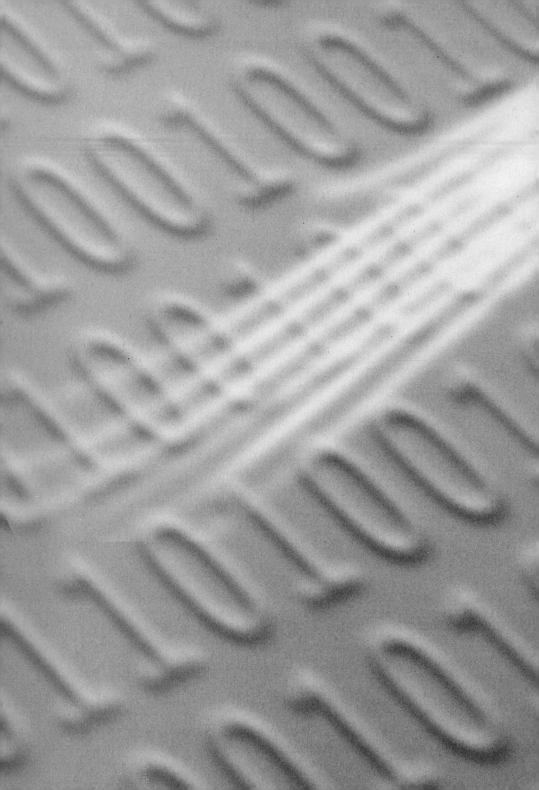

Chapter 10

STANDARD JAVA PACKAGES

This chapter introduces the Java packages, focusing on seven of the most commonly used ones. But before learning about the individual packages, you will see how these packages relate to Java's class hierarchy.

Adapted from *Mastering Java 2* by John Zukowski
ISBN 0-7821-2180-2   1,280 pages $49.99

Java Packages and the Class Hierarchy

Java has been object-oriented from day one. And as befits real object-oriented languages, Java comes with a standard set of support classes, versus hybrids like C++, which are only now getting standardized support libraries. Java's classes are very different from the familiar libraries that accompany procedural languages like C or Pascal. Because these support classes exploit the full potential of object-oriented languages, they transcend simple libraries. Class inheritance is by far the most common and most powerful feature used. (See Chapters 1 and 8 for more information about class inheritance.)

The entire Java hierarchy can be viewed from two organizational angles: as an object-oriented inheritance hierarchy and as groups of classes in packages. The inheritance hierarchy groups classes that share common implementation aspects (that is, code or variables). Java packages simply collect classes on a more pragmatic basis: Classes with related functionality are bundled together in the same package, whether they share code, data, or neither. In addition to their obvious structuring benefits, packages use namespace partitioning, which means that every class contained in a package has a unique name that cannot conflict (collide) with class names defined elsewhere. For example, two companies could safely sell code for classes with identical names. A bubble-sorting class from Mango Macrosystems might be called `mango.utilities.Bubble`, while a similar product from Sun-So-Soft Inc. might be called `sosoft.utils.Bubble`. The class names are the same, but Java uses the package names and subpackage names to distinguish one class from another.

The language's strict single inheritance scheme determines the way Java's standard classes relate to one another in terms of object-oriented inheritance. The resulting inheritance tree is, therefore, a pure tree, and not a graph, as is the case with multiple inheritance, object-oriented hierarchies. Multiple inheritance, of sorts, is employed within the Java classes by using the language's powerful interface mechanism.

MULTIPLE INHERITANCE VERSUS SINGLE INHERITANCE

Multiple inheritance is a mechanism that allows one class to inherit from more than one superclass. This produces the net effect of mixing characteristics of multiple classes into a new class.

Multiple inheritance was introduced to solve single inheritance's straightjacket effect. For example, say that you have a single inheritance hierarchy branching into two fundamental subtrees, `Living` and `InAnimate`. From `Living` grows the successive subclass branch `Plant`–`FruitTree`–`Banana`. The `InAnimate` branch could have a `Valuable`–`Food` subbranch. Now, `Food` might quite understandably want to have `Banana` as its subclass as well. Single inheritance does not let you have both. Class `Banana` is either a `FruitTree` or a `Food`; it can inherit from only one superclass hierarchy, not two (or more). The single inheritance tree shown here illustrates the limitations of pure single inheritance.

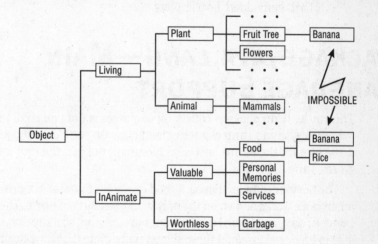

Since packages give you an easy handle on the entire hierarchy, they will now be your guides as you explore the Java class hierarchy. The Java 2 release has about 60 `java.*` packages. This chapter examines the seven most commonly used packages:

▶ Package `java.lang` contains the main language support classes. These deal with object wrappers, strings, multithreading, and related areas.

- ▶ Package `java.util` contains language support classes of a more utilitarian nature. These include collection and calendar classes, as well as some useful abstract designs codified by the interfaces `Comparator`, `Iterator`, and `Observer`.

- ▶ Package `java.io` provides device-independent file and stream I/O services.

- ▶ Package `java.awt` hides the bulk of all graphical classes. Because it contains Java's Abstract Window Toolkit (AWT) and twelve subpackages, this package should really be considered as the heart of the entire hierarchy.

- ▶ Package `javax.swing` offers classes for components, higher-level controls, and pluggable look-and-feel.

- ▶ Package `java.net` combines the classes supporting low-level Internet programming plus World Wide Web and HTML support.

- ▶ Package `java.applet` contains a single class with support for HTML embedded Java applets.

PACKAGE *JAVA.LANG* — MAIN LANGUAGE SUPPORT

The `java.lang` package collection of classes is flat and shallow. The majority of `java.lang` classes extend class `Object` directly, which is the root for the entire Java class hierarchy, not just the root for `java.lang`.

The `Number` subhierarchy is a good example of how object-oriented inheritance works and when to apply it. Classes `Byte`, `Short`, `Integer`, `Long`, `Float`, and `Double` have things in common, so a superclass was created to hold (*encapsulate*) these shared traits. Note that class `Number` is also declared `abstract`. You cannot make (*instantiate*) objects directly from an abstract class—you can do this from only concrete classes. Although having an abstract parent class (*superclass*) is common, it is by no means necessary. Concrete classes can be the local roots of entire subhierarchies (class `Object` is a prime example).

Of all the packages, package `java.lang` is exceptional, because it is the only package you never need to explicitly import in your programs.

The compiler does so by implicitly adding the following line at the top of all your source files:

```
import java.lang.*;
```

The asterisk in this line means that all of the package's classes are imported. This does not import classes in subpackages.

Package `java.lang` gets special treatment because some of its classes are so low-level that they are considered part of the Java language proper. The dividing line between language and external libraries might be important to language designers, but to application programmers the difference is mostly academic. BASIC, for example, has its string-manipulation commands defined as part of the language definition. C, on the other hand, relies on an external (and internationally recognized) standard library of functions to accomplish those tasks. Since Java adheres more to the C philosophy of keeping a language core as simple as possible, it too relies on an external collection of methods for anything beyond the simplest data processing or algorithmic control.

The following types of classes are contained in package `java.lang`:

▶ Type wrapper classes

▶ String support classes

▶ A math library class

▶ Multithreading support classes

▶ Low-level system-access classes

▶ Error and exception classes

The following sections look at these classes in more detail.

The Type Wrapper Classes

Java deals with two different types of entities: primitive types and true objects. Numbers, booleans, and characters behave very much like the familiar equivalents of procedural languages such as Pascal, C, or even C++. Other object-oriented languages, like Smalltalk, do not handle these primitive types in the same way. Smalltalk, for example, uses objects for everything—numbers are objects, booleans are objects, characters are objects, and so on.

NOTE

Although the Smalltalk language originated in an era when the punched card ruled the world (1972), it still manages to be the reference by which new object-oriented languages are judged. Every object-oriented language since has tried to improve on Smalltalk, but most barely manage to equal it. Viewed purely as an object-oriented language, Java comes very close indeed.

Although Java is truly object-oriented, it does not use objects for the most primitive types for the usual reason: performance. Manipulating primitive types without any object-oriented overhead is quite a bit more efficient. However, a uniform and consistent playing field, made up of only objects, is simpler and can be significantly more powerful.

Java contains many subsystems that can work only with objects. With many of these subsystems, the need frequently arises to have the system handle numbers, flags (booleans), or characters. How does Java get around this dilemma? By wrapping the primitive types up in some object sugar coating. You can easily create a class, for example, whose sole purpose is encapsulating a single integer. The net effect would be to obtain an integer object, giving you the universality and power that come with dealing with only objects (at the cost of some performance degradation).

Package `java.lang` contains such "type wrapper" classes for every Java primitive type:

- ▶ Class `Integer` for primitive type `int`
- ▶ Class `Long` for primitive type `long`
- ▶ Class `Byte` for primitive type `byte`
- ▶ Class `Short` for primitive type `short`
- ▶ Class `Float` for primitive type `float`
- ▶ Class `Double` for primitive type `double`
- ▶ Class `Character` for primitive type `char`
- ▶ Class `Boolean` for primitive type `boolean`
- ▶ Class `Void` for primitive type `void`

Among the numeric types, classes `Integer`, `Long`, `Byte`, `Short`, `Float`, and `Double` are so similar that they all descend from an abstract superclass called `Number`. Essentially, every one of these classes allows you to create an object from the equivalent primitive type, and vice versa.

The String Classes

Two string-support classes exist in java.lang: String and String-Buffer. Class String supports "read-only" strings; class String-Buffer supports modifiable strings. Although both classes obviously have a few things in common, they are unrelated in that neither inherits from a common "string" superclass.

Class String contains the following core functionality:

▶ String length function

▶ Substring extraction

▶ Substring finding and matching

▶ String comparison, using the Comparable interface, among many other means

▶ Uppercase and lowercase conversion

▶ Leading and trailing whitespace elimination

▶ Conversion to and from char arrays

▶ Conversion from primitive types to String type

▶ Appending strings (converted from any type, including objects)

▶ Inserting strings (again converted from any type)

The conversion and whitespace-stripping methods might seem contradictory in view of the read-only nature of String strings. This is true, but class String does not break its own rules. During these operations, String creates new read-only strings from the old ones, which it unceremoniously discards in the process. Class StringBuffer, conversely, concentrates on operations that typically modify the string or change its length.

The *Math* Library Class

Class Math groups together a typical and quite conservative collection of mathematical functions. The functions provided can be classified as follows:

▶ Absolute value, ceiling, floor, min, and max functions. These are suitably overloaded so that you can pass in any numeric type without having your arguments automatically cast to different types, thereby possibly losing accuracy.

▶ Square root, power, logarithm, and exponential functions. All of these take and return `double` values only (`double`, not `float`, is the default floating-point accuracy used by Java). You do not need to use casts when passing other numeric types, like `int` or `float`, because Java's compiler will automatically convert (compatible) argument types for you. A constant for the natural logarithm base is defined as a double precision value in the constant `Math.E`.

▶ Trigonometric functions (sin, cos, tan, asin, acos, atan). All of these functions work with angles expressed in radians instead of degrees. A full circle in radians is 2*PI radians (as opposed to 360 degrees). Pi is conveniently defined to double precision as the `Math` class constant `Math.PI`.

▶ A pseudo-random number generator function. One method, `random()`, is provided as a basis for randomness in applications. Random numbers are very important in simulations, statistical analysis, and, of course, games.

The Multithreading Support Classes

Two classes, `Thread` and `ThreadGroup`, and one interface, `Runnable`, are the gateways to adding multithreaded behavior in your applications or applets. Multithreading amounts to having a multitasking operating system within your own application. Several program threads can execute in parallel and at the same time.

Similar to the way that a multitasking operating system is more powerful and flexible than a single-tasking operating system, users greatly benefit from multithreaded applications. For example, a printing command can be handled in the background, repaginating a long document can be done while the user carries on editing that same document, and so on. Java is one of the rarer languages that provide multithreading from within the language itself (Ada is another example; C, C++, LISP, Pascal, and BASIC all lack built-in multithreading support).

The `java.lang` class `Thread` is the more important class of the two. It provides a collection of methods that allows you to perform the following tasks:

▶ Create new threads. This lets your applications spread independent jobs over several internal "subprograms." Overall application performance increases when several of these threads need to do I/O operations.

▶ Start threads. When a thread is initially created, it does not start running immediately. You need to start it explicitly with a `start()` command. To stop a thread, it should periodically check a status variable and return in an orderly fashion. This ensures all resources used are released properly.

▶ Put threads to sleep for a given amount of time, or yield execution. When a thread has no more work to do while sitting in a loop, the thread should put itself to sleep to let other threads use more of the processor's resources. Also, CPU-intensive threads should periodically pause to permit other threads to execute.

▶ Change thread priority, name, or daemon status. Threads have several attributes that can be dynamically altered as the thread runs. The priority attribute in particular will affect the proportion of processing resources the thread receives from the processor. Threads can also be flagged as being daemon threads.

▶ Query thread attributes. Any thread can find out what its priority, name, or daemon status is. This is useful when you launch several thread clones (differentiated only by name, for example) who nevertheless need to act as individuals (like twins in real life).

▶ Use the `Runnable` interface to tell the thread what to do.

▶ Use `ThreadLocal` and `InheritableThreadLocal` class instances to provide thread-level, private, static variables.

Class `ThreadGroup` encapsulates methods similar to those listed for `Thread`, except that a thread group is just that—a scope for related threads to operate in. They allow a number of related threads to share attributes and be affected in bulk by thread group changes. See Chapter 14 for more information about threads and multithreading.

The Low-Level System-Access Classes

A handful of classes offer access to system information and resources: `System`, `Runtime`, and `Process`.

Class `System` encapsulates the classic file handles `stdin` (as `System.in`), `stdout` (as `System.out`), and `stderr` (as `System.err`). These allow you to write output to or get input from the console in the usual way. In addition to these class variables, the following method types are contained in `System`:

Part ii

- ▶ Platform-optimized array copying

- ▶ Catastrophic exit (terminates application and the Java interpreter subsystem!)

- ▶ System properties querying

- ▶ Security policy related methods

Class Runtime offers specific runtime-environment access via the following method types:

- ▶ Available system memory and memory usage advice

- ▶ Platform-specific program launching, with the help of the Process class

Class Process provides access to stdin, stdout, and stderr for the executing program's process, as well as the return value of the program.

The Error and Exception Classes

The difference between errors and exceptions is that errors signify trouble in the Java VM (Virtual Machine), and exceptions signify trouble in an executing program. There are about 20 error classes and more than 25 exception classes in JDK 1.2.

Throwable is the root class of all the exception classes; it is an immediate subclass of the Object class. The methods in class Throwable retrieve error messages associated with exceptions and note where exceptions occur.

The immediate subclasses of class Throwable are class Error and class Exception. The subclasses of Error are basically used for signaling abnormal system conditions, such as when the Java VM runs out of memory or when there is a stack overflow in the interpreter. In general, these error conditions are unrecoverable and should not be handled.

On the other hand, the subclasses of class Exception represent conditions that are potentially recoverable. For example, an Exception subclass signals the end of file input; a program that encounters this condition should not crash—it should simply cease reading from the file.

See Chapter 9 for more information about Java exceptions and exception handling.

PACKAGE *JAVA.UTIL*—UTILITARIAN LANGUAGE SUPPORT

Package java.util contains more abstract datatype (ADT) classes plus 13 interfaces, most of which are being introduced in Java 2 to support the Collections Framework (see sidebar, below). Package java.util uses inheritance more than package java.lang. For example, the Properties class is an extension (subclass) of class Hashtable, which itself is an extension of Dictionary. As we discuss more packages later, you will see that the hierarchies gradually become deeper and more complex.

NOTE

Stack is implemented as a subclass of a Vector. One class you would expect to see alongside Stack is some form of the Queue class. However, queue support (first-in, first-out or FIFO) is provided via the LinkedList class.

The following are the main classes contained in package java.util:

- ▶ Core collection interfaces: Collection, Set, SortedSet, List, Map, and SortedMap

- ▶ Concrete implementations: ArrayList, HashMap, HashSet, Hashtable, LinkedList, Properties, Stack, TreeMap, TreeSet, Vector, and WeakHashMap

- ▶ Abstract implementations: AbstractCollection, Abstract-List, AbstractMap, AbstractSequentialList, Abstract-Set, and Dictionary

- ▶ Infrastructure interfaces: Iterator, ListIterator, Comparable (from java.lang), and Comparator

- ▶ Infrastructure classes: Collections and Arrays

- ▶ Date and its supporting calendar and time classes

- ▶ Locale and its supporting resource bundle classes

- ▶ BitSet

This package also includes three other interfaces:

- ▶ Enumeration

Part ii

▸ Observer (and class Observable)

▸ EventListener

The following sections look at these classes and interfaces in more detail.

THE COLLECTIONS FRAMEWORK

The JDK 1.2 release includes a new Java platform feature, the Collections Framework. A collection is an object that represents a group of objects, such as a vector or list. The Collections Framework creates a unified architecture for representing and manipulating any type of collection. It reduces programming time and effort while increasing performance and allowing for better software reuse. The new Collections Framework is based on six collection interfaces and the algorithms needed to manipulate them. The most basic interface is Collection. There are three interfaces—Set, List, and SortedSet—that extend Collection, and two other interfaces—Map and SortedMap– that represent mappings and contain collection-view operations, allowing them to be manipulated as collections.

The Core Collection Interfaces

The interfaces Collection, Set, SortedSet, List, Map, and SortedMap offer the basis for the Collection Framework. They provide unordered groups via Collection, collections without duplicates via Set, ordered groups via List, and key-value pair collections via Map, as well as sorted groups with SortedSet and SortedMap. The methods of these interfaces are used for the following tasks:

▸ Adding elements

▸ Finding elements

▸ Accessing elements

▸ Removing elements

▸ Listing elements

▸ Getting size information

TIP

You may notice that several interfaces and classes in the java.util package provide duplicate functionality. Prior to Java 2, the Enumeration interface with the Vector, Hashtable, and Dictionary classes were the basis for collection-oriented support. The Collections Framework introduced in Java 2 provides a more complete basis for working with groups of objects. New programs should use the newer classes, instead of older ones.

The Concrete Collection Implementation Classes

The ArrayList, HashMap, HashSet, Hashtable, LinkedList, Properties, Stack, TreeMap, TreeSet, Vector, and WeakHashMap classes are what you will most frequently use from java.util. They represent the actual implementations of the core collection interfaces:

▶ ArrayList is a resizable array that implements the List interface. The Vector class acts like an ArrayList, while Stack offers a last-in, first-out vector of objects.

▶ HashMap and HashSet offer hash table–backed collections that implement the Map and Set interfaces, respectively. Hashtable functions similarly to a HashMap, while Properties is a specific String hash table that can be easily saved and restored. WeakHashMap offers a hash table of weak references.

▶ LinkedList is a doubly linked list and implements the List interface. It can be used for queues and stacks.

▶ TreeMap and TreeSet are balanced binary tree implementations that implement the Map and Set interfaces, respectively.

Vector and Hashtable provide synchronized access to their elements, while the remaining new classes offer unsynchronized access. For the new classes, access can be synchronized externally with synchronizing wrappers provided for you. See Chapter 14 for additional information on thread synchronization and communications between threads.

The Abstract Collection Implementations

The AbstractCollection, AbstractList, AbstractMap, AbstractSequentialList, and AbstractSet classes offer skeleton implementations of the collections. When creating your own collections, you will almost definitely subclass one of these, instead of implementing the repeatable, basic operations of the interfaces yourself. For instance, for the `AbstractCollection` interface, only `iterator()` and `size()` have to be written. Operations like add and remove are common for all implementations.

Also, while `Dictionary` falls into this category, the `Map` interface and `AbstractMap` class supersede its usage in the 1.2 JDK.

The Infrastructure Interfaces and Classes

There are three infrastructure interfaces in `java.util`: `Iterator`, `List-Iterator`, and `Comparator`. With the addition of the `Comparable` interface in `java.lang`, these interfaces offer the framework for iterating through the list and ordering the elements.

NOTE

The `Iterator` interface is meant to eventually replace `Enumeration`. New code should try to avoid the `Enumeration` interface in favor of `Iterator`.

When it is necessary to examine all the elements of a collection, you will use `Iterator` and `ListIterator`. Interface `Iterator` provides an impressive example of Java's powerful interface feature. It defines the behavior (in terms of methods to be supported) of being able to enumerate every component, element, object, or entry—in short, everything contained by any class having some "container" quality. `ListIterator` extends `Iterator` to permit changing of the underlying collection and bidirectional walkthroughs. The `Iterator` interface forces any class to implement three methods: `hasNext()`, `next()`, and an optional `remove()`. The key two methods mean that any object that supports enumerating its components via this standard (method) interface can be explored using the following standard Java `while` loop:

```
iter = someCollection.iterator();
while (iter.hasNext()) {
  containedObj = iter.next();
  // process this object
}
```

The `Comparable` and `Comparator` interfaces provide sort order control. Many classes, like `String`, `Date`, and URL, already implement the

Comparable interface, so sorting internal Java classes is relatively easy. When it comes time to order your own classes, you will use these interfaces.

The infrastructure classes, Collections and Arrays, use the infrastructure interfaces to sort and search the collections. The simplicity of the interfaces permits amazing results, all depending on the collection used:

▶ Sorting using a tuned quick-sort algorithm

▶ Searching using a binary search algorithm

▶ Finding the minimum or maximum element of a collection

▶ Sorting and searching using a provided Comparator

The Date and Support Classes

Class Date encapsulates the representation of an instant of time, with millisecond precision. The date support classes are TimeZone, SimpleTimeZone, Calendar, and GregorianCalendar. These provide the following types of methods for interpreting and modifying date information:

▶ Altering year, month, day, hour, minute, and second components

▶ Querying year, month, day, hour, minute, and second components

▶ Converting to and from strings and long integers

▶ Comparing date and time values (including calendar arithmetic)

▶ Time-zone support

The Locale and Supporting Classes

Class Locale provides the basis for internationalization of Java programs. The locale support classes are ResourceBundle, ListResourceBundle, and PropertyResourceBundle. Through these classes, you can provide runtime customization of text messages for different languages and localities.

The java.text package also contains many classes for internationalization support: for instance, DateFormat, MessageFormat, and NumberFormat. These classes permit formatting of text to be in the local customs with respect to month, day, and year ordering and monetary symbols, among many other things.

The *BitSet* Class

Class BitSet implements a set of bits. Unlike many other bit set classes or language features in other languages, this bit set has no limits. You can therefore go way beyond the typical 32- or 256-bit limits imposed by other implementations. BitSet operations include the following:

▶ Setting, clearing, and getting single bits

▶ ANDing, ORing, and XORing bit sets together

▶ Comparing bit sets

The *Observer* Interface and *Observable* Class

Interface Observer and class Observable together exemplify the way Java's designers have tried to avoid reinventing the wheel, an all-too-common occurrence in software development. The Observer-Observable metaphor addresses a design obstacle slightly more abstract than the enumeration problem solved by the Iterator interface.

Sometimes, within an application, it is necessary for a change in an object to trigger changes in other objects; these changes may, in turn, trigger changes in yet other objects. In short, you have a number of objects that are in some way dependent on other objects; this is called a *dependency network*. Java's class hierarchy designers developed the Observer-Observable duo to solve this design obstacle.

The mechanism enforced by this duo is quite simple: Any root object that needs to send some kind of notification to other objects should be subclassed from class Observable, and any objects that need to receive such notifications should implement interface Observer. The following is the sole method interface Observer requires:

```
public void update(Observable o, Object arg)
```

To establish the dependency, any observer objects (that is, any objects implementing interface Observer) are added to the observable object (that is, the object subclassed from class Observable). Whenever this observable object changes, it can then call its Observable method notifyObservers( ).

PACKAGE *JAVA.IO*—FILE AND STREAM I/O SERVICES

Package `java.io` contains a whole arsenal of I/O-related classes. A top-level classification organizes them as follows:

- ▶ Byte input and output streams
- ▶ Character readers and writers
- ▶ Stream, reader, and writer filtering
- ▶ Stream tokenization
- ▶ Class `RandomAccessFile`

As you can see from the inheritance tree, the I/O stream branches form the bulk of the tree. A *stream* is an abstract concept used frequently in the context of I/O programming. It represents a linear, sequential flow of bytes of input or output data. Streams can be "flowing toward you," in which case you have an *input stream*, or they can "flow away from you," in which case you refer to an *output stream*. You read from input streams (that is, you read the data a stream delivers to you), and you write to output streams (that is, you transfer data to a stream).

The key point about streams is that they shield you from the input or output devices to which you are ultimately talking. If your code deals with these abstract objects (streams) instead, you can easily switch to different physical I/O devices without changing any of the I/O processing code in your application. This is the main raison d'être of streams.

Readers and writers are similar to input and output streams, but their basic unit of data is a Unicode character.

The stream, reader, and writer classes in package `java.io` can be classified into two types according to their main concern:

- ▶ Classes linking a stream, reader, or writer to a concrete I/O data source or destination
- ▶ Classes enhancing stream, reader, or writer functionality

The java.io package and its classes are discussed in detail in Chapter 11. The following sections provide an overview of the functionality of this package.

The *InputStream* Class

Class InputStream is an abstract class from which the entire input stream subhierarchy inherits. Essentially, any input stream can simply read one or more bytes (and only bytes) of data from whatever data source it supports (the mark/reset-related functionality is not supported by default). Five subclasses deal with specific data sources for the input stream:

▶ An array of bytes

▶ An external file

▶ Piped stream (of type PipedInputStream)

▶ Two or more other input streams concatenated together

▶ A String (and not a StringBuffer as you could be forgiven for thinking) passed as the constructor's argument

WARNING

LineNumberInputStream and StringBufferInputStream are not recommended. Their usage is functionally replaced with LineNumberReader and the more appropriately named StringReader.

Figure 10.1 will help you visualize the relationship between an input stream and its data source. The figure depicts class ByteArrayInput-Stream, an input stream that lets you read from the stream, as usual, a single byte or a block of bytes at a time (as defined by class Input-Stream). In the case of class ByteArrayInputStream, the bytes read in this way originated from an array of bytes. Other classes will have other data sources; for example, class FileInputStream will take its data from a file.

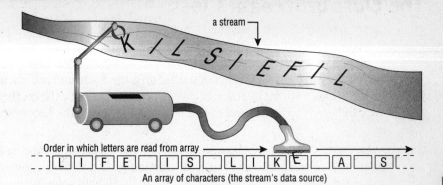

FIGURE 10.1: Data source and input stream

The input streams you have seen so far read bytes from various sources of data; you might think of them as low-level input streams. The remaining input streams in the java.io package read bytes from low-level streams and organize the input into higher-level information. The abstract class FilterInputStream is the root for the subtree grouping together most of these extra classes, which perform the following functions:

▶ Insert a performance-enhancing input buffering mechanism between the InputStream class's standard reading functionality and your application

▶ Add support for reading all of Java's primitive types previously saved to a stream

▶ Add the option of undoing the last single-byte read operation

▶ Read objects from a low-level stream

NOTE

The FilterInputStream subclasses can be powerfully combined with other InputStream classes. For example, you could create a ByteArrayDataInput-Stream or a FilePushbackInputStream. To do this, you would pass an instance of a data source–type InputStream (Byte, File, Pipe, Sequence, or String) object as argument to the constructor of the filter-type InputStream (Buffered, DataInput, LineNumber, or Pushback). Because these FilterInputStream subclasses are themselves InputStreams, you could even combine several filtering types. You could therefore conceivably create a BufferingPushback-LineNumberingStringInputStream (although by then you would be breaking every readability rule in the book). This same technique is possible with OutputStreams.

The *OutputStream* Class

Class OutputStream is an abstract class from which the entire output stream subhierarchy inherits. An output stream's sole requirement is to be able to write a single byte or write an array of bytes. (Flushing and closing the stream are peripheral to what an output stream is all about.) As is the case with input streams, output streams cannot exist on their own; they need to be connected to a data destination before becoming useful.

OutputStream's subclasses can be similarly classified according to their main concern: choice of data destination (called *sink*) or choice of enhanced stream writing behavior. Figure 10.2 will help you visualize the relationship between an output stream and its data sink. The figure depicts the scenario for class FileOutputStream. All the bytes that were written to the stream end up stored in an external file; you specify the file when you create the output stream.

The output stream classes that enhance output stream behavior almost all descend from the output equivalent of FilterInputStream (described in the previous section): FilterOutputStream.

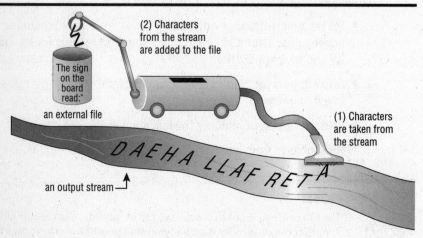

FIGURE 10.2:   An output stream and a data sink

The *Reader* and *Writer* Classes

Class Reader is the abstract character-oriented counterpart of Input-Stream. Reader has nine subclasses. Like input streams, these classes fall into two categories: low-level readers that take raw character input from various sources and high-level filtering readers that organize the data delivered by low-level readers.

Class Writer is the abstract character-oriented counterpart of Output-Stream. Writer has eight subclasses, which also fall into the low-level and high-level categories. Low-level writers deliver character output to various destinations. High-level filtering writers convert organized input to characters that are delivered to other writers.

The *RandomAccessFile* Class

Class RandomAccessFile encapsulates full byte-level read and write access to files. This class is rather odd when compared to the other classes in the I/O hierarchy. You would expect the class to be derived from both an abstract input class and an abstract output class (plus some seeking functionality), but since RandomAccessFile descends directly from Object, a rather conventional (that is, not object-oriented) design approach was used instead.

The methods implemented by RandomAccessFile can be summarized into the following groups:

- ▸ Reading of primitive types and byte arrays (in binary form)
- ▸ Writing of primitive types and byte arrays (in binary form)
- ▸ Positioning of the file pointer (seeking)

The *StreamTokenizer* Class

Class StreamTokenizer extracts identifiable substrings and punctuation from an input stream according to user-defined rules. This process is called *tokenizing* because the stream is reduced to tokens. Tokens typically represent keywords, variable names, numerical constants, string literals, and syntactic punctuation (like brackets, equals signs, and so on). StreamTokenizer includes various methods that affect the rules for parsing the input stream into tokens. It also contains the nextToken() method to extract the next token from the input stream.

Text tokenizing is a common technique used to reduce the complexity of textual input. The archetypal application that uses text tokenizing is the programming-language compiler. Compilers do not analyze your source file as is, because that would lead to an onslaught of independent characters. Instead, compilers analyze a stream of tokens representing and extracted from your source file. Keywords, identifiers, punctuation, comments, strings, and so on are first compressed into easy-to-manipulate tokens. Only after this lexical-analysis stage does a compiler start to check the complex grammar of any programming (or other) language. The Java compiler (javac) uses the StreamTokenizer class for this purpose.

NOTE

The java.util.zip and java.util.jar packages contain classes that support the reading and writing of compressed .GZ, .ZIP and .JAR files.

PACKAGE *JAVA.AWT*—HEART OF THE HIERARCHY

The package java.awt is organized into the following main groups.

- ▶ Two GUI component branches
    - ▶ The Component subtree, with another important subtree, the Container subtree buried slightly deeper within it
    - ▶ The MenuComponent subtree
- ▶ Layout manager classes
    - ▶ FlowLayout
    - ▶ BorderLayout
    - ▶ CardLayout
    - ▶ GridLayout
    - ▶ GridBagLayout and GridBagConstraints
    - ▶ Insets
- ▶ Graphics classes
    - ▶ Graphics, Graphics2D, and PrintGraphics
    - ▶ Image

- ▶ Color and SystemColor
- ▶ Font
- ▶ FontMetrics
- ▶ AlphaComposite and Composite
- ▶ BasicStroke and Stroke
- ▶ GraphicsConfigTemplate, GraphicsConfiguration, GraphicsDevice, and GraphicsEnvironment
- ▶ GradientPaint and TexturePaint
- ▶ RenderingHints

▶ Geometry classes

- ▶ Point
- ▶ Polygon
- ▶ Dimension
- ▶ Rectangle
- ▶ Shape

▶ Event classes

- ▶ Event
- ▶ AWTEvent
- ▶ AWEventMulticaster
- ▶ EventQueue
- ▶ ActiveEvent

▶ Miscellaneous classes

- ▶ MediaTracker
- ▶ Toolkit
- ▶ PrintJob
- ▶ Cursor
- ▶ ComponentOrientation

Part ii

Java's AWT package is the largest and most important package of the entire hierarchy. This is what you would expect in an age when the design and implementation of application GUIs can easily consume more than one-third of software-development resources. The AWT aims to significantly reduce this proportion by allowing GUIs to be platform independent in a hassle-free way—a revolutionary step. The whole hierarchy is there to make the lives of application developers easier, but in particular it was meant to make GUI development quick and painless.

All the classes outlined next are 100 percent hardware and software independent. This means your Java GUI-based applications will run on every Java-capable platform.

GUI Classes

The bulk of the classes within the package `java.awt` relate to GUI creation and management. The classes can be classified into the following groups:

- Widget classes
- Container classes
- Widget layout classes
- Menu classes

Widget Classes

The fundamental building blocks of GUI designs are called *widgets*, *gadgets*, or *buttons*, depending on the GUI school of thought that invented them. The most common term, and the one used in this book, is widgets (for window gadgets). Java implements a nice variety of them; they are easily deployed in your GUI designs, as you have seen in earlier chapters.

- Class `Button` implements that bread-and-butter widget: the button. The simplest and by far most common incarnation is the labeled variety. You can also have buttons with iconic identification (not supported by class `Button`, but provided by the `javax.swing.JButton` class, described later).

- A `Canvas` component provides a drawable area. As such, it is invisible (it has no graphical representation) but can detect mouse click and move events, which can then be used by the application.

▶ Classes `Checkbox` and `CheckboxGroup` implement checkable items. The latter class forces the former into a mutually exclusive grouping, commonly known as *radio buttons*.

▶ Class `Choice` implements a multiple-choice component, typically with only a few choices (use `List` for more items). The graphical implementation for a `Choice` usually looks like a pop-up menu.

▶ The `Component` class is an abstract superclass for widgets.

▶ A `Label` is used to give GUI zones a title or to label other widgets. It just encapsulates a single line of read-only text.

▶ A `List` is a heavy-duty list display and item selection widget. It comes with a vertical scrollbar and allows selection of multiple items at the same time.

▶ A `Scrollbar` component is the Java slider control, which can be either horizontal or vertical. If a `List` object does not provide enough listing functionality, you could design your own custom lister by incorporating a vertical `Scrollbar` object, in a `Panel` subclass, for example. This widget represents a continuous range of values that can be "sampled" at any time by the application. Clicks on the scrollbar's arrow icons are treated as "line increment" commands that move the scrollbar cursor according to a defined line increment. Similarly, clicks above or below the cursor are interpreted as "page increment" commands with analogous results.

▶ The text-entry components start with `TextComponent`, which is the abstract superclass of `TextField` and `TextArea`. The `TextField` widget is the pillar of GUI form screens. It allows you to enter any text within a short, single-line input window. `TextArea` is a variant of the `TextField` widget. It allows multiple lines of text, such as for free-form "memo" type fields. Both `TextField` and `TextArea` allow unconstrained data entry, which often isn't what an application needs. To implement entry fields that accept only strict types of data (text only, numbers only, dates only, and so on), you need to subclass either `TextField` or `TextArea` (depending on your requirements) and enhance their behavior by validating the user's input to the type of data allowed.

Part ii

While some of these components are used in various examples, the Swing component set is what is described in more detail in Chapter 13. Newly created programs should use those components instead.

Container Classes

An application's window typically is not just an unstructured heap of clickable or selectable components. Well-designed GUIs are highly structured to aid you in navigating the interface. This structuring can be in part achieved by using component containers. A window can be subdivided into areas or zones, each containing related buttons, choices, lists, and so on. When you use containers to implement these visual and logical areas, you mirror the hierarchy in your code. This is just another example of the key object-oriented principle of projecting the vocabulary and structures of the problem domain into your code. The container classes in Java's AWT are also the entities on which the layout manager classes work (see the following section).

WARNING

Do not confuse the term *container*, as used by Java's AWT, with the more general term *container class*, as used by other object-oriented frameworks. AWT containers are GUI component containers. Generic container classes, on the other hand, are abstract datatype classes that can contain other objects (for example, linked lists, stacks, bags, and vectors).

The AWT containers include the following:

▶ A class, Container, which is the generic widget container on which layout managers act. All the other container classes are derived from this superclass.

▶ The Panel class, which is a concrete incarnation of class Container. It does not have a graphic representation—not even a simple outline. You typically subclass a Panel, or Container, to define and control a logical grouping of widgets.

▶ Class Frame, which is the building block class for producing full-fledged windows. (There is also a Window class, which produces "windows" without any borders or a menu bar.) Frames have titles, background colors, optional menu bars, and layout managers.

▶ Class `Dialog`, which is used for implementing direct application-to-user feedback or questions. Typical uses include pop-up warning dialog windows, quit confirmation dialog boxes, and so on. The `Dialog` class is not a self-contained component like, for example, `Frame`. In fact, it relies on class `Frame` to provide it with a display medium in which to display itself.

▶ Class `FileDialog`, which implements the indispensable file Open/Save/Save As dialog window, complete with filename filtering capability, plus any transparent extras provided by the native operating system. On Windows 95/98, for example, the Java `FileDialog` widget allows the user to create new directories on the fly, before saving a file.

▶ The `ScrollPane` class, which implements a container with scrollbars so that a large component can be viewed through a small viewport.

Widget Layout Classes

One of Java's innovations in the field of GUI programming is its GUI component-placement strategy. With other GUI frameworks, you usually need to specify pixel coordinates for all of your components. Even with GUI building tools, you need to position your components absolutely. Java was designed to be platform independent, but since AWT still relies on the host's native windowing system to provide it with its window and button building blocks, it is not possible to specify component dimensions and placement with absolute precision. The AWT uses an automatic layout system based on layout managers instead:

▶ With the `FlowLayout` class, every component is positioned and sized in the same way flowing text is in a WYSIWYG word processor: from left to right, and then overflowing to the next line when the first line is filled, and so on.

▶ The `BorderLayout` class positions and scales components according to the conventional distribution of components around a generic window. It allows components to be laid out along the top, bottom, left, or right edges of a window and leaves one large central area for the remainder of the components. The other areas will recover any unassigned areas.

▶ The `GridLayout` class, as the name suggests, enforces a simple grid layout. But unlike what you would expect from a grid layout, you cannot specify the positions of your components using two-dimensional coordinates; you must use a one-dimensional index. (You can use GridBagLayout to avoid this annoying situation.)

▶ The GridBagLayout class extends the approach taken by class GridLayout. It basically allows any one component to use up more than one grid cell, in either a horizontal or vertical direction. Extra control over the precise layout process is provided by instances of a helper class: class GridBagConstraints. This is the most powerful layout manager of all the standard offerings.

▶ Class CardLayout embodies the concept of a number of cards that can be flipped through, with only one card visible at any one time. This layout management style is most commonly used to implement multiple "pages" (or cards) that the user can view by selecting their "tabs." Since class CardLayout does not go beyond laying out the components, the trendy rendering of the card tabs themselves should be handled by another class. The standard component to do this is JTabbedPane, found in the javax.swing package.

▶ The Insets class encapsulates information about how close to a container's edge a component may be placed.

Menu Classes

Drop-down or pop-up menus associated with windows are part of any modern application. Java's AWT supports complete menu functionality (submenus and checkable menu items are included) using a small and surprisingly easy-to-use set of menu classes:

▶ Class MenuBar acts as the anchor for the entire collection of menus connected to an application, or to be more precise, connected to a Frame. Every Java Frame can have its own menu bar with menu items responding to selections private to its context.

▶ The Menu class is the logical building block for any menu system. Menus hold logically related menu items and/or submenus. A menu is identified primarily by a simple menu title.

▶ The PopupMenu class implements a menu that can be popped up at any point of a GUI.

▶ The `MenuComponent` class is the abstract superclass of `Menu-Item` and `CheckboxMenuItem`, which represent the menu items that a user selects on a menu.

▶ The `MenuShortcut` class encapsulates a keyboard shortcut for a menu item.

NOTE

Don't let the class hierarchy confuse you. A `MenuItem` (or `CheckboxMenuItem`) is *logically* the leaf component in a final, concrete menu system. But as far as the object-oriented hierarchy is concerned, a `MenuItem` must be a `Menu` object's parent. This is totally counterintuitive, but can be understood as follows: Wherever you have a menu item, you can in fact substitute an entire submenu for it. So, class `Menu` must be a subclass of `MenuItem`. In any case, this admittedly chicken-and-egg type situation does not in any way complicate AWT menu programming. The fact is that adding menus to applications is probably the easiest thing you can do within AWT.

The Graphics Classes

For animation or special effects, you need something very different from standard GUI classes. You need to be able to control colors and imagery without any of the window-metaphor constraints imposed by a set of GUI classes. Java provides both elementary rendering classes and more sophisticated rendering; `Graphics` is the core class in the elementary area, while `Graphics2D` is for the more sophisticated variety. The following sections provide an overview of the functionality of these classes.

The *Graphics* and *Graphics2D* Classes and *PrintGraphics* Interface

`Graphics` is an abstract class that supports a simple 2D painting model with the usual rendering primitives. Specifically, the following classes of methods are provided:

▶ Text rendering

▶ Rectangular area copying (also called blitting)

▶ Filled and outlined rectangles, ovals, polygons, and arcs

▶ Lines

▶ Coordinate system translation

▶ Clipping rectangle support

▶ Changing current drawing color

▶ Various graphics state querying functions

`PrintGraphics` is an interface that closely resembles `Graphics` but renders to a printer.

`Graphics2D` is an extension of `Graphics` that supports a more complex 2D painting model. The class supports the following capabilities:

▶ Drawing images while performing transformations

▶ Drawing shapes with support for various rendering qualities like antialiasing, rendering for speed versus quality, wide lines, and gradient file, among many others

▶ Text rendering with support for things like clipping the draw region

▶ Coordinate system translation

▶ Various graphics state querying functions

The `Graphics2D`-related classes are explored in Chapter 16, which examines the Java-2D framework, introduced with Java 2.

The *Image* Class

Class `Image` encapsulates a platform-independent image data structure. This approach shields you from the profusion of hardware- or software-dependent bitmap "standards" (bitplane, chunky, interleaved, etc.). The methods provided by class `Image` allow you to perform the following tasks:

▶ Query the image's dimensions

▶ Query the image's properties (for example, source image format, copyright information, and so on)

▶ Create a graphics context for the image so you can use the `Graphics` rendering methods on this image

The *Color* and *SystemColor* Classes

Class Color encapsulates a platform-independent color data structure. As with bitmapped images, a color can be implemented in a variety of ways. The Color class shields you from these platform dependencies. The provided methods support the following:

- ▸ Conversion between RGB (Red, Green, Blue) and HSB (Hue, Saturation, Brightness) color models

- ▸ Accessing the red, green, and blue color components

- ▸ Increasing or decreasing the brightness of a color

The SystemColor class is a subclass of Color. It provides access to prevailing Desktop colors.

The *Font* and *FontMetrics* Classes

The Font and FontMetrics classes give you a platform-independent way of accessing and querying the platform local fonts. The methods let you do the following:

- ▸ Specify a font family, style, and point size

- ▸ Query font attributes and metrics (family name, style, point size, character and string widths, ascender and descender lengths)

The *AlphaComposite* Class and *Composite* Interface

The Composite interface describes how to blend images to implement effects like transparency. AlphaComposite is a specific effect for the blending to produce transparency, while other effects are possible by implementing the interface on your own.

The *BasicStroke* Class and *Stroke* Interface

The Stroke interface provides the means to describe the logical pen to use for drawing operations. While the Graphics primitives only support drawing single pixel-wide colored lines, Graphics2D operations support a more rules-based approach. BasicStroke is a specific implementation that supports pen width, dash attributes, end caps, and line join decorations.

Part iii

The *GraphicsConfigTemplate, Graphics-Configuration, GraphicsDevice,* and *Graphics-Environment* Classes

These four classes describe the makeup of the Graphics2D operation destinations, whether they are a printer, monitor, or other display type. Each graphics environment may consist of a number of graphic devices. Then, each graphics device has one or more graphics configuration.

The *GradientPaint* and *TexturePaint* Classes

Along with the Color class, the GradientPaint and TexturePaint classes provide the pattern for Graphics2D operations. Gradient-Paint provides a linear color gradient, while TexturePaint offers an image to use as the fill pattern. Color is used for the simple, solid, case.

The *RenderingHints* Class

You use the RenderingHints class to enable optional drawing attributes, like antialiasing, for the Graphics2D object.

Geometry Classes

Package java.awt contains four geometry classes. These encapsulate the mathematical concepts point, polygon, rectangle, and dimension:

▶ The Point class represents a simple (x,y) data structure along with two methods: setLocation() and translate(). As with all geometry classes, integers are used instead of floating-point numbers. This reflects the main use of these classes as helper classes for GUI programming (and not pure math, which assumes numbers and shapes to have infinite precision).

NOTE
There is a floating-point version of setLocation() for Point. However, it only rounds the floating-point number to the nearest integer.

▶ The Polygon class represents an ordered collection of points treated as the definition of a polygon. Three methods enhance the data structure: addPoint() modifies the polygon to include the new point, getBounds() calculates the smallest rectangle enclosing all points of the polygon, and `contains()` tests whether a given point lies inside or outside the polygon.

▶ The `Dimension` class is a pure data structure holding a width and height variable. No methods enhance the raw data structure (in other words, this is really equivalent to a C structure or a Pascal record).

▶ The `Rectangle` class represents a rectangle at a certain (x,y) position. The class adds several methods to manipulate rectangles (move, shrink, grow, calculate intersection with other rectangles, and test whether a point is inside a rectangle).

▶ The `Shape` interface implemented by `Polygon`, `Rectangle`, and several classes in the `java.awt.geom` package describes the path that forms a geometric shape. The shape can then be drawn with the `draw(Shape)` method of `Graphics2D`.

Although these classes have nothing to do with rendering or with GUI programming per se, they are used by those higher-level classes to improve code reuse, robustness, and readability. Since GUI programming constantly involves dealing with positions and rectangular component dimensions or outlines, it makes sense to localize (abstract) some representation and a set of common operations for those positions and dimensions. This way, you avoid scattering your code with bits of identical functionality with slightly differing implementations.

WARNING

If you are familiar with the geometry classes prior to Java 2, you might want to look at them again. Their inheritance hierarchy, and capabilities, changed significantly between Java 1.1 and Java 2. Also, you may want to look into the subpackage `java.awt.geom` for additional geometry support classes.

Miscellaneous AWT Classes

The following `java.awt` classes do not fall neatly into any category:

▶ The classes that support event handling are `AWTEvent`, `AWTMulticasterEvent`, and `EventQueue`. The `Event` class supports the earlier (before version 1.1) Java event model, which is incompatible with the more modern 1.1 model. Event handling is discussed in detail in Chapter 12.

- The Cursor class allows you to specify an appearance for the mouse cursor.

- The MediaTracker class keeps track of images loaded from a server.

- The PrintJob class mediates between a Java program and a printer.

- The Toolkit class allows you to access specific resources of the underlying window system, which includes binding to AWT components, as well as querying for system font names or for the best size for a cursor image.

- The ComponentOrientation class helps you position components in a language-sensitive manner. While Western European alphabets are left to right, others are right to left or top to bottom.

PACKAGE JAVAX.SWING

Introduced in the 1.2 Java Development Kit, the javax.swing packages compose the second generation of Java graphical widgets.

NOTE
While most things like AWT are acronyms, Swing is not. Supposedly, it involves a loose association of the Java character "Duke" to Duke Ellington and his saying "It don't mean a thing if it ain't got that swing." Also, a Sun engineer commented about swing music being the "in" sound now.

The javax.swing classes can be grouped into the following responsibility areas:

- The JComponent branch for widgets

- Layout manager classes

  - BoxLayout

  - OverlayLayout

  - ScrollPaneLayout

  - ViewportLayout

  - SizeRequirements

- ▶ The Model classes and interfaces
- ▶ The Manager classes
  - ▶ `DesktopManager` and `DefaultDesktopManager`
  - ▶ `FocusManager` and `DefaultFocusManager`
  - ▶ `MenuSelectionManager`
  - ▶ `RepaintManager`
  - ▶ `ToolTipManager`
  - ▶ `UIManager`
- ▶ The `AbstractAction` and `KeyStroke` classes and `Action` interface
- ▶ Miscellaneous classes
  - ▶ `BorderFactory`
  - ▶ `ImageIcon` and `Icon` interface
  - ▶ `LookAndFeel`
  - ▶ `ProgressMonitor` and `ProgressMonitorInput-Stream`
  - ▶ `SwingUtilities`
  - ▶ `GrayFilter`
  - ▶ `Timer`

In addition to the above core `javax.swing` package, many subpackages provide additional support:

`javax.swing.border`	Defines various border rendering styles
`javax.swing.colorchooser`	Support classes for color choosing component
`javax.swing.event`	Swing-specific event classes
`javax.swing.filechooser`	Support classes for choosing files
`javax.swing.plaf.*`	Pluggable Look-and-Feel support classes

Part ii

javax.swing.table	Table usage support classes
javax.swing.text.*	Text component support classes, including HTML and Rich Text Format (RTF)
javax.swing.tree	Tree component support classes
javax.swing.undo	Undo/redo implementation support classes

The Swing components and architecture will be described more fully in Chapter 13, which describes the Swing architecture in more detail. While this chapter describes the common pieces shared with the AWT widgets, like Component, Container, the layout managers, and the events, using the AWT widgets is not described and is discouraged.

NOTE

The com.sun.* APIs represent interfaces that Sun has fully committed to supporting and whose stability you can rely on. They just may not be available from all Java runtimes. If you happen to be using a Java 1.1+ runtime without support for the Swing packages, you can download them from Sun at http://java.sun.com/products/jfc/.

JComponent Classes

Like java.awt, the majority of classes within package javax.swing are related to GUI creation.

- ▶ JButton and JLabel   The Swing button and label widgets, providing support for a single line of text, an image, and pop-up tool tips.

- ▶ JPanel and Box   The container widgets, providing support for buffering of painting operations, user-defined borders, and much more.

- ▶ JMenu, JMenuItem, JSeparator, JCheckBoxMenuItem, JRadioButtonMenuItem, JMenuBar, and JPopupMenu   The menu widgets: menu, menu item, menu separator, toggleable menu items, menu bar, and pop-up menu. Each can have a single line of text, an image, and pop-up tool tips.

▶ JToggleButton, JRadioButton, JCheckBox, and Button-Group   The toggleable widgets: alone, in a group, or out. The last class is for grouping support.

▶ JColorChooser   A pop-up widget for the selection of color values.

▶ JComboBox and JList   The widgets offering a group of choices, no longer limited to just text. Also, the JComboBox provides support for entering a choice when the desired choice is not offered.

▶ JFileChooser   Widget for directory and file selection.

▶ JInternalFrame, JDesktopPane, and JDesktopIcon Widgets that provide a desktop to work with, which support opening, closing, and resizing internal frame, like a desktop manager.

▶ JLayeredPane and JRootPane   Widgets that offer a layering effect when displaying components on top of components on top of components.

▶ JOptionPane   For creating and displaying standard dialog boxes with icons signifying type of message shown.

▶ JProgressBar   Widgets for showing progress of a multi-step operation.

▶ JSlider and JScrollBar   Widgets for selecting a range of values, with and without labels to show available range.

▶ JScrollPane and JViewPort   Widgets to display a single large component within a smaller area. JScrollPane offers scrollbars, while JViewPort doesn't.

▶ JSplitPane   A widget that holds two widgets. Once created, the user can resize each.

▶ JTabbedPane   A tabbed widget that offers access to multiple panels.

▶ JTable   A widget for the display of multi-columnar data.

▶ JTextComponent, JTextField, JPasswordField, JText-Area, JTextPane, and JEditorPane   The widgets for text input and display. JTextComponent is the parent of all, while the rest offer single or multiline text support. The most sophisticated are JTextPane for the display of formatted text and images and JEditorPane for a lightweight HTML renderer.

▶ JToolBar and JToolTip   Widgets to create tool bars and help text in the form of pop-up tool tips.

▶ JTree   A widget to display hierarchical data.

▶ JApplet   The Swing applet widget, this adds support for displaying menus within applets.

▶ JWindow, JDialog, and JFrame   The Swing window, dialog box, and frame widgets, extending upon the base AWT widgets.

Layout Manager Classes

In addition to the half dozen or so layout manager classes in AWT, there are more available in javax.swing. These offer the same benefits available with the java.awt layout managers, which are basically platform-independent applications:

▶ With the BoxLayout class, components are laid out either vertically or horizontally in a single column or row. Each component does not have to be the same size and there is support for providing spacers between components.

▶ The OverlayLayout class offers support for arranging components one on top of another.

▶ Class ScrollPaneLayout provides the layout manager used by the JScrollPane with areas for your own scrollbars, headers, and corner images. Usually, you will never use this outside of the one created for you when you use JScrollPane.

▶ The ViewportLayout class is similar to ScrollPaneLayout in that it exists for the JViewport class's benefit. It offers sizing and alignment support for when objects in viewport are larger than space permits.

▶ Class SizeRequirements is a support class for the layout managers, to help calculate component sizes and positions.

Model Classes and Interfaces

The Swing widgets offer two means of operations. You can store their data internally and let them act accordingly, or you can store the data externally. When the data is truly stored outside the widget, the means used is the model classes provided within the javax.swing package. By storing the data externally, you can change the widget used and the view of the data, without worrying about losing anything. While working in this manner creates more robust and maintainable programs, it takes longer to set up initially.

Manager Classes

Like just about everything in Swing, you can customize the behavior of almost everything. The various manager classes in javax.swing offer help in allowing you to customize the user's experiences with your programs. For instance, if you don't like the way those little tool tip messages are displayed when you rest your mouse over a widget, you can use the ToolTipManager to adjust behavior like the delay time. Each of the Manager classes is responsible for its own area of the Swing experience.

AbstractAction and *KeyStroke* Classes and *Action* Interface

The AbstractAction, KeyStroke, and Action classes (and interface) provide an alternative to the simple-minded approach of handling events within the AWT widgets. Normally, developers would program responses to specific user behavior during the course of an application. This is fine for things that live in isolated worlds. However, by declaring a well-defined services protocol, developers can define services related to objects, register them with the objects, and then let others use the services when they need them. For instance, if you define how to save a JTextArea, a multiline-input field, you would normally associate that behavior with the File ➢ Save menu. However, if you were to register the "save" Action with the JTextArea, when you want to save the text somewhere else, you would just ask the JTextArea how to do it. Through the registration process, JTextArea knows what Action operations it supports. In this case, your AbstractAction implementation that supports the "save" Action would be available and could be associated to some other interface.

The KeyStroke class is also available, to support keyboard-oriented events.

Miscellaneous Swing Classes

The following javax.swing classes do not fall neatly into any category:

- ▶ The BorderFactory class works with the border subpackage. Using the Abstract Factory creation pattern, the BorderFactory class creates Border objects without your specifying the actual concrete class that implements the Border interface.

- ▶ The ImageIcon class provides an implementation of the Icon interface for Image objects. You use icons for displaying images with labels, buttons, and menus, among many other places.

- ▶ Along with several .plaf subpackages, the LookAndFeel class provides the basis for Swing's pluggable look-and-feel support.

- ▶ The ProgressMonitor and ProgressMonitorInput-Stream pair provides a prebuilt generic pop-up window to permit users to interrupt the loading of files.

- ▶ The SwingUtilities class provides a set of convenience routines for common operations. Among many others, methods exist for finding a component's top-level window and checking which mouse button a mouse event is for.

- ▶ The GrayFilter represents an image-related support class used by Swing that the development team thought other developers would welcome. GrayFilter turns any image into a "grayscale" image.

- ▶ The Timer class provides the means to signal periodic operations.

PACKAGE *JAVA.NET*—INTERNET, WEB, AND HTML SUPPORT

The java.net package is one of the other main features of the Core Java API. It provides very high-level interfaces to the rather less sophisticated set of data-communication protocols (and their associated APIs) called TCP/IP and UDP/IP. The java.net classes hide many of the technical quagmires inherent to low-level Internet programming.

The java.net classes can be grouped according to the following responsibilities.

Internet Addressing (Classes *InetAddress* and *URL*)

- ▶ TCP/IP connection-oriented classes (various Socket classes)

- ▶ UDP/IP connectionless classes (DatagramPacket, Datagram-Socket, and MulticastSocket)

- ▶ URL Authentication classes (Authenticator, Password-Authentication, URLDecoder, and URLEncoder)

- ▶ MIME content type handlers (ContentHandler and URL-StreamHandler)

- ▶ Web-related classes (various URLConnection classes)

NOTE

In terms of complexity—and, therefore, ease of use—the UDP protocol lies between the Transmission Control Protocol (TCP) protocol (the low-level protocol) and the Internet Protocol (IP) protocol (the high-level protocol). UDP is a datagram-oriented protocol, which means data packets travel individually (like letters in the postal system), without any guarantees of delivery. This is because—unlike TCP—UDP does not attempt to detect or correct loss of packets. This lack of protocol overhead is what makes UDP interesting for certain types of applications, such as broadcasting currency exchange rates, to gain speed at the cost of an occasional lost update. However, most Internet applications do not use the UDP protocol to achieve their functionality, but instead use the TCP protocol, which supports a guaranteed delivery end-to-end link.

The following is a brief overview of the commonly used java.net classes:

- ▶ The InetAddress class deals with Internet addresses in their mnemonic (*host.domain*) form and their 32-bit numeric form (*byte.byte.byte.byte*).

- ▶ The URL class encapsulates a Uniform Resource Locator (URL) specification plus associated methods, including opening a connection to the URL resource (a Web page, a file, or telnet port), retrieving the URL resource, and querying URL fields (protocol, host, filenames, and port number).

▶ The `ServerSocket` and `Socket` classes together provide complete TCP/IP connectivity support. Each class supports one side of the client/server application model. Class `Socket` is used to implement a client; class `ServerSocket` is used to implement a server. Class `Socket` provides methods to connect any stream (as input or output) to a socket to communicate through. This way, you can essentially separate internetworking technicalities (and pitfalls!) from your application by working at the abstract stream level instead.

NOTE

Sockets are the software interfaces that connect an application to the network beyond. On the Internet, each machine has 65,536 (64K) addressable sockets it can use. All standard Internet services (like e-mail, FTP, and so on) use agreed-upon socket numbers, colloquially termed "well-known port numbers." Server programs listen to these sockets for any incoming service request. A client program needs to open a socket of its own before it can connect to a server socket at the other end.

▶ The `DatagramPacket` and `DatagramSocket` together provide User Datagram Protocol (UDP) Internet services. Through class `DatagramPacket`, you can specify a packet's Internet host destination (using an `InetAddress` instance), the port (or socket) to connect to on that host, and the binary contents of the packet. You can then send or receive datagrams via an instance of class `DatagramSocket`.

▶ The `Authenticator` class provides access to password-protected URLs. By providing `PasswordAuthentication`, you can easily read from destinations requiring challenge-confirm access.

PACKAGE *JAVA.APPLET*—HTML EMBEDDED APPLETS

A big reason for Java's runaway success is that it's a highly efficient and easy-to-learn language for distributed software components. Java applets are nothing more or less than distributed software components. Even so, the standard class framework contains little that explicitly deals with those instrumental applets.

The `java.applet` package looks very barren compared to the other packages. Its sole contents are one class and three interfaces. Class `java.applet.Applet` is the main repository for methods supporting applet functionality.

The methods it makes available can be grouped into the following categories:

▸ Applet initialization, restarting, and freezing

▸ Embedded HTML applet parameter support

▸ High-level image loading

▸ High-level audio loading and playing for applets and applications

▸ Origins querying (`getDocumentBase()` and `getCodeBase()`)

▸ Simple status displaying (`showStatus(String)`)

MISCELLANEOUS JAVA PACKAGES

Other Java packages support more advanced or less commonly used features. Here is a brief summary of their functionality:

> `javax.swing.accessibility` This package provides developers easy access to assistive technologies like screen readers and Braille terminals.

> `java.awt.color`, `java.awt.font`, and `java.awt.geom` These packages support the Java 2D framework. They will be covered in Chapter 16.

> `java.awt.datatransfer` The classes in this package support clipboard data-transfer models.

> `java.awt.dnd` Drag-and-drop functionality is now provided in version 2. Using a series of drag sources and drop targets, Java programs can interact with Java and native applications.

> `java.awt.event` This extensive package supports event delegation.

`java.awt.im`   This small package adds support for native input methods of Asian languages.

`java.awt.image`   The classes in this package are related to image processing.

`java.awt.peer`   This package contains classes that "glue" AWT components to the underlying window system. If you are writing Java programs, you will never need to use these interfaces.

`java.awt.print`   The classes in this package extend the printing capabilities introduced in Java 1.1 to include support for printing pages and books.

`java.beans`   This package supports development of components, called "Beans," that are so reusable that they can interact with non-Java systems such as ActiveX and LiveConnect. JavaBeans are covered in Chapters 17 and 18.

`java.beans.beancontext`   The classes here represent the JavaBeans Runtime Containment and Services Protocol for the discovery of services available from the surrounding environment.

`java.lang.ref`   This package describes a set of classes that offer weak references, or caching. Use with the reference objects does not count as usage when it comes time for garbage collection.

`java.lang.reflect`   The classes in this package support *object reflection*. This is a feature whereby it is possible to inspect the makeup of the class of an arbitrary object.

`java.math`   This package is very different from the more commonly used `java.lang.Math` class, which provides standard mathematical functions in the form of static methods. The `java.math` package contains two rarely used classes that represent decimal and integer numbers of arbitrarily high precision.

`java.rmi`, `java.rmi.activation`, `java.rmi.dgc`, `java.rmi.registry`, and `java.rmi.server`   These packages support Remote Method Invocation (RMI), which permits an object to make a method call on an object running on a different machine. RMI is covered in Chapter 17.

`java.security`, `java.security.acl`, `java.security` `.cert`, `java.security.interfaces`, and `java.security` `.spec`   The classes in these packages support secure data communication.

`javax.servlet`   This package provides the means to embed Java servlet programs within Web servers, to replace CGI (Common Gateway Interface) scripts.

`java.sql`   This package provides classes and interfaces that support Java Database Connectivity (JDBC), which is discussed in Chapter 15.

`java.text`   This package provides classes that format internationalized text.

`java.util.mime`   This package provides support for describing Multipurpose Internet Mail Extension (MIME) types.

WHAT'S NEXT?

We will now move on to input/output (I/O) support classes and the stream-based model of reading and writing files and organizing data.

Part II

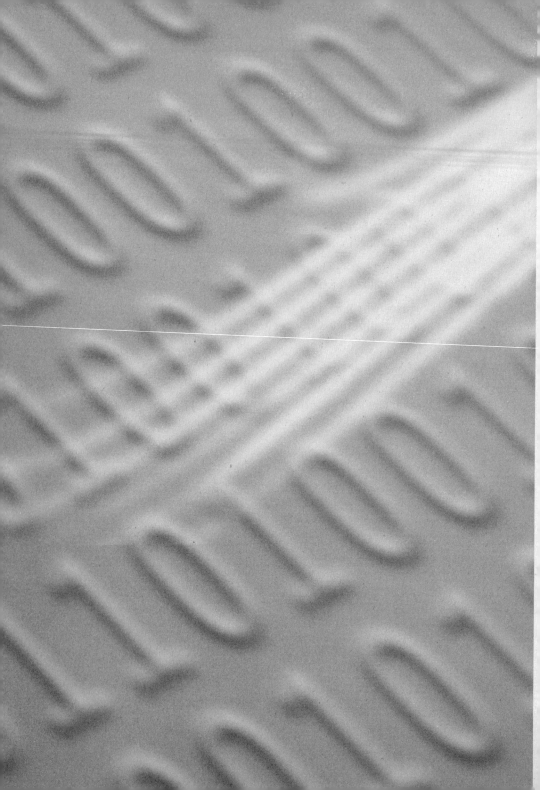

Chapter 11

FILE I/O AND STREAMS

Java's file input/output (I/O) support classes reside in the java.io package. Most of these classes support a stream-based model of reading and writing files. There are low-level stream classes for communicating with disk files and high-level classes for organizing the information that moves through the low-level streams. The high-level streams are also useful for organizing information sent to or received from the network.

This chapter investigates all the low-level and high-level stream classes, as well as the few classes that communicate with disk files without using the streams mechanism.

Adapted from *Java 2 Developer's Handbook* by Philip Heller and Simon Roberts
ISBN 0-7821-2179-9   1,248 pages $59.99

An Overview of Streams

A *stream* can be thought of as a conduit for data, somewhat like a straw or a siphon, with a *source* at one end and a *consumer* at the other end. For example, a Java program can read bytes from a disk file with the `FileInputStream` class, as shown in Figure 11.1. In the figure, the Java program makes a read call to the `FileInputStream`, which reads bytes from the disk and delivers them to the caller. In Figure 11.2, a program writes to a file with the `FileOutputStream` class.

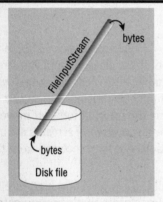

FIGURE 11.1:   A simple input stream

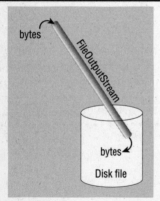

FIGURE 11.2:   A simple output stream

In practice, this mechanism is not particularly useful. Files usually contain highly structured information. The bytes are to be construed as numbers, text, source code, and so on. The `java.io` package provides a number of high-level input streams that read bytes from a low-level stream and return more sophisticated data. For example, the `DataInputStream` class consumes bytes and produces Java primitive types and strings, as illustrated in Figure 11.3. The technique of attaching a sophisticated stream to a lower-level one, as shown in the figure, is called *chaining*.

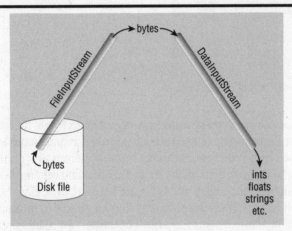

FIGURE 11.3:   Two levels of input streams

Similarly, writing bytes to a file is cumbersome. Usually, a program needs to write structured information to a file. The `DataOutputStream` class has methods for writing primitive data types and strings. The data-output stream converts its source data to bytes, which are passed to the stream's output. In Figure 11.4, the data-output stream's output is chained to a file-output stream; the result is that when a program writes primitives to the data-output stream, the corresponding bytes are written to the disk. The bytes are written in a platform-independent order; thus a file written by a big-endian machine can be read on a little-endian machine.

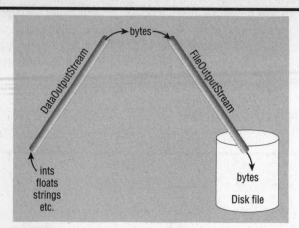

FIGURE 11.4:   Two levels of output streams

Traditionally, Java's low-level streams have operated on bytes. Release 1.1 of the JDK introduced character-based streams. These stream classes look very similar to their byte-based counterparts, but they permit programmers to operate on a level independent of any character-encoding scheme because all translations between characters and bytes are hidden by the class methods. This makes it easier to develop programs that are simple to internationalize. Moreover, character streams have been optimized for reading and writing multiple characters at a time. For these reasons, for character-based I/O, it is generally preferable to use character streams rather than byte streams whenever possible.

THE ABSTRACT SUPERCLASSES

Java's byte-oriented input and output streams are derived from the InputStream and OutputStream abstract classes. The character-oriented classes are derived from the Reader and Writer abstract classes.

The *InputStream* Class

Most of the InputStream class methods interact with system resources and have the potential for encountering platform-specific system problems and throwing an IOException.

The constructor for InputStream is:

InputStream()   Constructs an instance of the class.

The following are the methods of `InputStream`:

int read() throws IOException   Reads one byte from the data source. Returns the byte in the low-order 8 bits of the return value. If no more data is available, returns –1. If data is not available at the moment of the call, the calling thread is blocked (see Chapter 14 for more information about blocking).

int read(byte[] dest) throws IOException   Reads bytes from the data source into the `dest` array. Returns when the array is full or when the data source has no more data. The return value is the number of bytes read. Note that you can convert an array of bytes to a string by calling the `String(byte)` constructor.

int read(byte[] dest, int offset, int length) throws IOException   Just like read(byte[] dest) above, but only attempts to read `length` bytes into the portion of the byte array beginning at `offset`. Returns –1 at the end of the input.

void close() throws IOException   Releases system resources associated with the data source. For example, on a UNIX platform, a file-input stream consumes one file descriptor. The `close()` call releases this file descriptor, and the stream then becomes permanently unavailable for reading.

int available() throws IOException   Returns the number of bytes that may be read immediately without blocking. This call is not reliable on all systems; some implementations of Java are known to return 0.

long skip(long nbytes) throws IOException   Attempts to skip over and discard `nbytes` bytes from the data source. It skips fewer bytes if no more data is available. It returns the number of bytes skipped.

boolean markSupported()   Returns `true` if the mark/reset mechanism is supported; otherwise, returns `false`. (See the `mark()` method description below.)

void mark(int readlimit)   Sets a mark in the input
stream. If in the future a reset() call is made and mark-
Supported() is true, subsequent reads from the input
stream will repeat all bytes read since the mark call. If more
than readlimit bytes are read before the next reset() call,
the mark is lost.

void reset() throws IOException   Repositions the
stream so that subsequent reads repeat the values read since
the last mark() call. Throws IOException if the file has not
been marked.

The *OutputStream* Class

As with input streams, most of the OutputStream class methods interact with system resources and inform the caller of platform-specific system problems by throwing an IOException.

The constructor for OutputStream is:

OutputStream()   Constructs an instance of the class.

The following are the methods of OutputStream:

void write(int b) throws IOException   Writes the
byte that appears in the low-order 8 bits of the argument, discarding the higher 24 bits.

void write(byte b[]) throws IOException   Writes
an array of bytes. Note that a string can be converted to a char
array by calling the getBytes() method, but any information
in the high-order byte of each Unicode character will be lost.

**void write(byte b[],int offset, int length)
throws IOException**   Writes the subset of the byte array
beginning at offset and is length bytes long.

void flush() throws IOException   Writes any bytes
that the stream has buffered.

void close() throws IOException   Releases system
resources associated with the data source. The stream becomes
permanently unavailable for writing. An output stream should
be flushed before it is closed.

The *Reader* Class

The character-oriented abstract classes `Reader` and `Writer` both define two constructors in addition to their various methods. The following are the constructors for `Reader`:

Reader()   Constructs an instance of the class.

Reader(Object lock)   Constructs an instance of the class. Critical sections of class methods will synchronize on `lock`.

The following are the methods of the `Reader` class. Only two of these methods—read(char[], int, int) and close()—are abstract and must be supplied by concrete subclasses. All of the other methods are implemented.

int read() throws IOException   Reads one character from the data source into the low-order 16 bits of the return value. If the data source has no more data, returns the int -1. If data is not available at the moment of the call, the calling thread is blocked (see Chapter 14 for more information about threads and blocking).

int read(char[] dest) throws IOException   Reads characters from the data source into the `dest` array. Returns when the array is full or when the data source has no more data. The return value is the number of characters read, or -1 if there is no more data.

int read(char[] dest, int offset, int length) throws IOException   Just like read(char[] dest) (above), but attempts to read `length` characters into the portion of the character array beginning at `offset`. Returns -1 when there is no more data.

void close() throws IOException   Releases system resources associated with the data source. For example, on a UNIX platform, a file-input stream consumes one file descriptor. The close() call releases this file descriptor, and the stream then becomes permanently unavailable for reading.

long skip(long nchars) throws IOException   Attempts to skip over and discard `nchars` bytes from the data source. It skips fewer bytes if no more data is available. It returns the number of bytes skipped.

boolean markSupported()   Returns true if the mark/reset mechanism is supported; otherwise, returns false. (See the mark() method description below.)

void mark(int readlimit)   Sets a mark in the input stream. If in the future a reset() call is made and mark-Supported() returns true, subsequent reads from the input stream will repeat all characters read since the mark call. If more than readlimit characters are read before the next reset() call, the mark is lost.

void reset() throws IOException   Repositions the stream so that subsequent reads repeat the values read since the last mark() call.

boolean ready() throws IOException   Returns true if the stream has data immediately available, so that a read() call will not block. Returns false if block prevention cannot be assured.

The *Writer* Class

Like Reader, the Writer class has an overloaded constructor that offers the option of synchronizing on any arbitrary object. Writer has two constructors:

Writer()   Constructs an instance of the class.

Writer(Object lock)   Constructs an instance of the class. Critical sections of class methods will synchronize on lock.

The following are the methods of the Writer class. Three of these methods—write(char[], int, int), flush(), and close()—are abstract and must be supplied by concrete subclasses. All of the other methods are implemented.

void write(int c) throws IOException   Writes the character that appears in the low-order 16 bits of the argument.

void write(char[] c) throws IOException   Writes an array of characters.

void write(char[] c, int offset, int length) throws IOException   Writes a subset of an array of characters.

void write(String s) throws IOException   Writes a string.

void write(byte[] b,int offset, int length) throws IOException   Writes a subset of a string.

void flush() throws IOException   Writes any characters that the stream has buffered. A single call to flush() will flush all the buffers in a chain of Writers and OutputStreams.

void close() throws IOException   Releases system resources associated with the data source. The stream becomes permanently unavailable for writing. Writers should be flushed before they are closed.

THE LOW-LEVEL STREAM CLASSES

The java.io package provides four low-level stream classes for file access. These classes are FileInputStream for byte input, FileOutputStream for byte output, FileReader for character input, and FileWriter for character output.

The *FileInputStream* Class

The FileInputStream class is a byte-based input stream that reads from a file. In addition to the inherited methods described in the previous sections, this class has three constructors. All three constructors require arguments to specify the file to be opened:

FileInputStream(String path) throws FileNotFoundException   Attempts to open a stream to the file described by path. Throws an exception if the file does not exist.

FileInputStream(File file) throws FileNotFoundException   Attempts to open a stream to the file described by file. Throws an exception if the file described by file does not exist.

FileInputStream(FileDescriptor fdObj)   Opens a stream to the file described by using the file descriptor, which represents an existing connection to a file.

NOTE

On Windows machines, a file path can use either forward or backward slashes as separators.

The *FileOutputStream* Class

The FileOutputStream class is an output stream that writes to a file. This class has four constructors:

FileOutputStream(String path) throws FileNot-FoundException   Attempts to open a stream to the file described by path. The file is created if it does not already exist.

FileOutputStream(String path, boolean append) throws FileNotFoundException   Attempts to open a stream to the file described by path. If append is true, the file will be opened in append mode; this means that if the file already exists, data will be written to the end of the file rather than replacing the file's existing contents. The file is created if it does not already exist.

FileOutputStream(File file) throws FileNot-FoundException   Attempts to open a stream to the file described by file. The file is created if it does not already exist.

FileOutputStream(FileDescriptor fdObj)   Opens a stream to the file described by using the file descriptor, which represents an existing connection to a file.

NOTE

In an applet, permission to access files is granted or denied by the browser's security manager. If permission is denied, all the FileOutputStream class constructors throw a SecurityException. Because SecurityException is a type of runtime exception, it does not need to be caught.

The *FileReader* Class

The FileReader class is a character-based stream for reading from a file. It is a subclass of the Reader and InputStreamReader classes (discussed later, in the "The InputStreamReader and OutputStream-Writer Classes" section) and adds no methods of its own except for the following three constructors:

FileReader(String path) throws FileNotFound-Exception   Attempts to open a stream to the file described by path.

FileReader(File file) throws FileNotFound-Exception   Attempts to open a stream to the file described by file.

FileReader(FileDescriptor fd)   Opens a stream to the file described by using the file descriptor, which represents an existing connection to a file.

The *FileWriter* Class

The FileWriter class is a character-based stream for writing to a file. It is a subclass of the Writer and OutputStreamWriter classes (discussed later, in the "The InputStreamReader and OutputStreamWriter Classes" section) and adds no methods of its own except for the following four constructors:

FileWriter(String path) throws IOException   Attempts to open a stream to the file described by path.

FileWriter(String path, boolean append) throws IOException   Attempts to open a stream to the file described by path. If append is true, the file will be opened in append mode; this means that if the file already exists, data will be written to the end of the file rather than replacing the file's existing contents.

FileWriter(File file) throws IOException   Attempts to open a stream to the file described by file.

FileWriter(FileDescriptor fd)   Opens a stream to the file described by using the file descriptor, which represents an existing connection to a file.

OTHER LOW-LEVEL STREAM CLASSES

In addition to FileInputStream, the java.io package contains several other low-level input stream classes: ByteArrayInputStream and PipedInputStream for byte input; and CharArrayReader, PipedReader, and StringReader for character input. These classes read from sources other than a disk file. Otherwise, they are similar to FileInputStream and StringReader—they inherit from the InputStream or Reader class, and they read bytes or characters from a data source. A program may use the data directly, or it may chain a high-level input stream for more sophisticated processing.

There are several low-level output classes in addition to FileOutputStream: ByteArrayOutputStream and PipedOutputStream for byte output; and CharArrayWriter, PipedWriter, and StringWriter for character output. These classes write to destinations that are not files. Otherwise, they are similar to FileOutputStream and Writer—they inherit from the OutputStream or Writer class, and they write bytes or characters. A program may write data to any of these classes, or it may chain a higher-level output stream to facilitate writing of more structured information.

The following sections examine these classes in more detail.

Stream Classes That Connect to Arrays

The ByteArrayInputStream class takes its input from a byte array or from a piece of a byte array. There are two constructors:

ByteArrayInputStream(byte[] buf) Constructs an input stream that reads bytes from array buf.

ByteArrayInputStream(byte[] buf, int offset, int length) Constructs an input stream that reads bytes from a subset of array buf. The subset begins at offset and is length bytes long.

The ByteArrayOutputStream class writes to a byte array. The array grows automatically as needed. There are two constructors:

ByteArrayOutputStream() Creates a new instance.

ByteArrayOutputStream(int size)   Creates a new
instance with an initial destination array of the specified size.
If the number of bytes written to the stream exceeds size, the
destination array will grow automatically.

There are three methods for converting a byte array output stream into
more accessible data:

String toString()   Returns a String consisting of all
the bytes written to the stream so far.

String toString(String encoding) throws
UnsupportedEncodingException   Returns a String
consisting of all the bytes written to the stream so far. The
string is created using the specified encoding.

byte[] toByteArray()   Returns an array containing all
bytes written to the stream so far. This array is a copy of the
stream's contents, so it may be modified without corrupting
the original data.

These two classes (ByteArrayInputStream and ByteArray-
OutputStream) have character-based analogues that extend the Reader
and Writer abstract superclasses. The CharArrayReader class
reads characters from a character array; the CharArrayWriter class
writes characters to a character array.

The following are the constructors for CharArrayReader:

CharArrayReader(char[] chars)   Creates a character
array reader from the array of characters.

CharArrayReader(char[] chars, int start, int
length)   Creates a character array reader from a subset of
the specified array of characters. The subset begins at start
and is length characters long.

The following are the constructors for CharArrayWriter:

CharArrayWriter()   Creates a character array writer.

CharArrayWriter(int length)   Creates a character
array writer whose internal array has the initial size of length.
Throws IllegalArgumentException if initialSize is
negative.

Stream Classes That Connect to Strings

The StringReader and StringWriter classes communicate with
Java strings and string buffers. The StringReader class reads characters from a string. The StringWriter class writes characters to a string
buffer (*not* a string!).

The StringReader class has the following constructor:

StringReader(String s)   Constructs an input stream
that reads characters from the specified string.

The StringWriter class accumulates its characters in a string
buffer. It has two constructors.

StringWriter()   Constructs a string writer with a default-
sized internal buffer.

StringWriter(int size)   Constructs a string writer with
an internal string buffer whose initial size is specified by size.

NOTE

Release 1.1 of the JDK included a StringBufferInputStream class. This class
is deprecated as of release 1.2.

Stream Classes That Connect to Each Other

The java.io package contains four *piped* classes that operate in pairs
and in tandem. A piped input stream reads bytes that are written to a corresponding piped output stream; a piped reader reads characters that are
written to a corresponding piped writer. The most common use for these
classes is for interthread communications: One thread writes to a piped
writer or output stream, while another thread reads the same data from
a piped reader input stream. For character-based communication, it is
generally preferable to use a reader/writer pair because those classes are
optimized for block transfers. Each of these classes has two constructors.

The PipedInputStream class has the following constructors:

PipedInputStream()   Constructs a piped input stream
with no data source. The stream is useless until it is associated
with a piped output stream. This is accomplished by calling the
connect(PipedOutputStream) method.

PipedInputStream(PipedOutputStream source) throws IOException Constructs a piped input stream whose data source is the bytes written to the source output stream. Data written to source will then be available as input from this stream. If an I/O error occurs, an IOException will be thrown.

The PipedOutputStream class has these two constructors:

PipedOutputStream() Constructs a piped output stream with no data source. The stream is useless until it is associated with a piped input stream. This is accomplished by calling the connect(PipedInputStream) method.

PipedOutputStream(PipedInputStream receiver) throws IOException Constructs a piped output stream whose data is written into the receiver piped input stream. Data bytes written to this stream will then be available as input from the receiver. If an I/O error occurs, an IOException will be thrown.

The following are the constructors for PipedReader:

PipedReader() Constructs a piped reader with no data source. The stream is useless until it is associated with a piped writer. This is accomplished by calling the connect(Piped-Writer) method.

PipedReader(PipedWriter source) throws IO-Exception Constructs a piped reader whose data source is the characters written to the source writer. Data written to source will then be available as input from this stream. If an I/O error occurs, an IOException will be thrown.

The following are the constructors for PipedWriter:

PipedWriter() Constructs a piped writer with no data receiver. The stream is useless until it is associated with a piped reader. This is accomplished by calling the connect(Piped-Reader) method.

PipedWriter(PipedReader receiver) throws IO-Exception Constructs a piped writer whose data is written into the receiver reader. Data written to source will then be available as input from this stream. If an I/O error occurs, an IOException will be thrown.

A stream of any type can be associated with a stream of the opposite type by calling the connect() method.

There are two ways to create a paired set of piped streams. The first way is to start with a piped input stream, open a piped output stream, and connect the piped input stream to the piped output stream:

```
PipedInputStream instream = new PipedInputStream();
PipedOutputStream outstream = new
PipedOutputStream(instream);
instream.connect(outstream);
```

The alternative way is to start with a piped output stream, then open a piped input stream and connect the piped output stream to the input stream:

```
PipedOutputStream outstream = new PipedOutputStream();
PipedInputStream instream = new PipedInputStream(outstream);
outstream.connect(instream);
```

The same principle applies to creating a piped reader/writer pair. One way is to start with a reader:

```
PipedReader reader = new PipedReader();
PipedWriter writer = new PipedWriter(reader);
instream.connect(writer);
```

The alternative is to start with a piped writer:

```
PipedWriter writer = new PipedWriter();
PipedReader reader = new PipedReader(writer);
outstream.connect(instream);
```

THE HIGH-LEVEL STREAM CLASSES

High-level input streams take their input from other input streams. High-level output streams direct their output to other output streams.

Each of these classes is constructed by passing as an argument to the constructor an instance of another stream type. The new stream is chained onto the argument stream; a high-level input stream will read bytes from the argument stream, and a high-level output stream will write bytes to the argument stream. The argument stream may itself be a high-level stream.

The following sections discuss each of the high-level input and output stream classes.

The *BufferedInputStream* and *Buffered-OutputStream* Classes

The BufferedInputStream class maintains an internal array of characters in which it buffers the data it reads from its source. The default size of the buffer is 2048 bytes. The first time one of the read() methods is called on the buffered input stream, it fills its buffer from its own data source. Subsequent reads on the buffered input stream return bytes from the buffer until the buffer is empty. At this point, the buffered input stream again fills its buffer from the data source.

A buffered input stream is beneficial in situations where reading a large number of consecutive bytes from a data source is not significantly more costly than reading a single byte. For example, when reading from a disk file, a large amount of time is spent in positioning the disk drive's read head and in waiting for the disk to spin into position under the read head. This time expenditure must be made no matter how many consecutive bytes are to be read. In this case, it would be advantageous to read an entire block of disk data (512 or 1048 bytes on most systems) and buffer the undesired bytes in case they are needed in the future.

There are two constructors for the BufferedInputStream class. One version creates a buffer with a default size of 2048 bytes; the other version lets the caller specify the buffer size:

> **BufferedInputStream(InputStream source)** Creates a buffered input stream with a 2048-byte buffer. The input stream uses source as its data source.

> **BufferedInputStream(InputStream source, int bufsize)** Creates a buffered input stream with an internal buffer of bufsize bytes. The input stream uses source as its data source. Will throw an IllegalArgumentException if bufsize is less than 0.

The BufferedReader class is the character-based analogue of the buffered input stream. Because of the benefit conferred by the buffer, this class is the preferred tool for reading lines of input. Not surprisingly, there are two constructors:

> **BufferedReader(Reader source)** Creates a buffered reader with an 8192-character buffer. The reader uses source as its data source.

BufferedReader(Reader source int bufsize) Creates a buffered reader with a buffer of `bufsize` characters. The reader uses `source` as its data source. Will throw an `Illegal-ArgumentException` if `bufsize` is less than 0.

The `BufferedOutputStream` class also maintains a buffer of bytes. Data written to a buffered output stream is accumulated in the buffer until the buffer is full. Then the bytes are written in a single operation to whatever output stream is chained to the buffered output stream.

Like `BufferedInputStream`, the `BufferedOutputStream` class has two constructors. One version creates a buffer with a default size of 512 bytes; the other version lets the caller specify the buffer size:

BufferedOutputStream(OutputStream dest) Creates a buffered output stream with a default 512-byte buffer. The stream writes its data to the output stream `dest`.

BufferedOutputStream(OutputStream dest, int bufsize) Creates a buffered output stream with a buffer of `bufsize` bytes. The stream writes its data to the output stream `dest`. Will throw an `IllegalArgumentException` if `bufsize` is less than 0.

The `BufferedWriter` class is analogous:

BufferedWriter(Writer dest) Creates a buffered writer with a 512-byte buffer. The writer writes its data to `dest`.

BufferedWriter(Writer dest, int bufsize) Creates a buffered writer with a buffer of `bufsize` characters. The stream writes its data to `dest`. Will throw an `IllegalArgument-Exception` if `bufsize` is less than 0.

NOTE
The largest network packet size is 64KB. If a buffered writer is to be used for network output, there is no benefit to creating it with a buffer larger than 64KB.

The *DataInputStream* and *DataOutputStream* Classes

The `DataInputStream` class reads bytes from another stream and interprets them as Java primitives, char arrays, and strings. There is no corresponding character-oriented reader class, because it makes no sense to write primitives in character form. The constructor expects to be passed an input stream:

DataInputStream(InputStream source) Creates a `FilterInputStream` that takes its data from the input stream `source`.

In addition to the usual inherited `read` methods, data-input streams support the following methods:

int read(byte[] dest) throws IOException Reads bytes from the data source into the `dest` array. Returns when the array is full or when the data source has no more data. The return value is the number of bytes read. Note that you can convert an array of bytes to a string by calling the `String(byte)` constructor.

int read(byte[] dest, int offset, int length) throws IOException Just like `read(byte[] dest)` above, but only attempts to read `length` bytes into the portion of the byte array beginning at `offset`. Returns –1 at the end of the input.

boolean readBoolean() throws IOException Reads a boolean value.

byte readByte() throws IOException Reads a signed 2's-complement byte from the input stream.

int readUnsignedByte() throws IOException Reads an unsigned byte from the input stream. Returns the next byte of this input stream, interpreted as an unsigned 8-bit integer.

short readShort() throws IOException Reads a signed 2's-complement short from the input stream. Returns the next two bytes of this input stream, interpreted as a signed 16-bit number.

int readUnsignedShort() throws IOException Reads an unsigned short from the input stream. Returns the next two bytes of this input stream, interpreted as an unsigned 16-bit integer.

char readChar() throws IOException Reads a 2-byte Unicode char from the input stream. The first byte read is

Part ii

interpreted as the high-order byte of the char. Returns the next two bytes of this input stream as a Unicode character.

`int readInt() throws IOException`   Reads a signed 2's-complement 4-byte Java int from the input stream. The first byte read is interpreted as the high-order byte of the int. Returns the next four bytes of this input stream, interpreted as an integer.

`long readLong() throws IOException`   Reads a signed 2's-complement 8-byte Java long from the input stream. The first byte read is interpreted as the high-order byte of the long. Returns the next eight bytes of this input stream, interpreted as a long.

`float readFloat() throws IOException`   Reads a 4-byte representation of a Java float from the input stream.

`double readDouble() throws IOException`   Reads an 8-byte representation of a Java double from the input stream.

`String readUTF() throws IOException`   Reads a series of bytes from the input stream and interprets them as a Java modified Universal Text Format (UTF-8) string.

NOTE

UTF is an emerging international standard that uses one, two, or three bytes to represent each character. There are no string-termination issues because a UTF string includes length information.

`static String readUTF(DataInput din) throws IOException`   A static method. Reads a UTF string from the specified data input stream and interprets it as a Java modified Universal Text Format (UTF-8) string.

`void readFully(byte[] dest) throws IOException`   Attempts to fill byte array `dest` with bytes from the data source. The executing thread blocks if enough bytes are not available, and it throws an `EOFException` if the data source is depleted before destination buffer `dest` is filled, otherwise an `IOException` is thrown.

`void readFully(byte[] dest, int offset, int length) throws IOException`   Like `readFully()`

(above), but only attempts to fill a subset of the destination buffer `dest`. The subset begins at index `offset` and is `length` bytes long.

void skipBytes(int offset) throws IOException
Like `readFully()` (above), but discards the number of bytes specified by the offset rather than storing them in an array. The executing thread blocks if not enough bytes are available.

The `DataOutputStream` class supports the writing of Java's primitive data types to an output stream. Strings and byte arrays may also be written. There is no analogous character-oriented writer class. Both `DataOutputStream` and `DataInputStream` communicate in a platform-independent way. The constructor expects to be passed an output stream:

DataOutputStream(OutputStream dest) Creates a new data-output stream that writes its data to specified output stream `dest`.

The data written to a data-output stream is broken up into its constituent bytes, which are written to whatever output stream is chained to the data-output stream. In addition to the various byte-writing methods inherited from its `DataOutput` superclass, the `DataOutputStream` class supports the following methods for writing:

void writeBoolean(boolean b) throws IOException Writes a boolean value to the output stream. A value of `true` is represented by `(byte)0`; a value of `false` is represented by `(byte)1`.

void writeByte(int i) throws IOException Writes the low-order byte of `i` to the output stream. If no exception is thrown, the counter is incremented by 1.

void writeChar(int i) throws IOException Writes a character to the output stream as a 2-byte value, high byte first. If no exception is thrown, the counter is incremented by 2.

void writeShort(int i) throws IOException Writes the two low-order bytes of specified integer `i` to the output stream. Of the two bytes written, the higher-order byte is written first (bits 8 to 15), followed by the lower-order byte (bits 0 to 7). If no exception is thrown, the counter is incremented by 2.

Part ii

void writeInt(int i) throws IOException   Writes all four bytes of the specified integer i to the output stream, starting with the highest-order byte (bits 24 to 31). If no exception is thrown, the counter is incremented by 4.

void writeLong(long theLong) throws IOException Writes all four bytes of the specified Long to the output stream, starting with the highest-order byte (bits 56 to 63). If no exception is thrown, the counter is incremented by 8.

void writeFloat(float f) throws IOException Writes the 4-byte representation of f to the output stream. If no exception is thrown, the counter is incremented by 4.

void writeDouble(double d) throws IOException Writes the 8-byte representation of d to the output stream. If no exception is thrown, the counter is incremented by 8.

void writeBytes(String s) throws IOException Writes s as a series of bytes. Only the low-order byte of each 2-byte Unicode character is written; the high eight bits are discarded. If no exception is thrown, the counter is incremented by the length of s.

void writeChars(String s) throws IOException Writes s as a series of Unicode characters. Starting with the high-order byte, two bytes are written for each Unicode character. If no exception is thrown, the counter is incremented by twice the length of s.

void writeUTF(String s) throws IOException Writes the string s to the output stream as a Java modified Universal Text Format (UTF-8) string. If no exception is thrown, the counter is incremented by the total number of bytes written to the output stream.

void write(int b) throws IOException   Writes the byte that appears in the low-order 8 bits of the argument, discarding the higher 24 bits. If no exception is thrown, the counter written is incremented by 1.

void write(byte b[],int offset, int length) throws IOException   Writes the subset of the array that is length bytes long beginning at the specified offset.

void flush() throws IOException   Writes any bytes that the stream currently has buffered.

int size()   Returns the current value of the counter written which specifies the number of bytes written to the data output stream so far.

The *LineNumberReader* Class

The LineNumberReader class maintains an internal count of the number of lines it has read. A line is considered to be any number of bytes, terminated by a return character ('\r'), a newline character ('\n'), or a return followed by a newline. This class is a subclass of BufferedReader.

The constructors expect to be passed a reader:

LineNumberReader(Reader source)   Creates a line-number reader that takes its data from the specified input reader source.

LineNumberReader(Reader source, int size)   Creates a line-number reader that takes its data from the specified input reader source. The internal buffer size is given by size.

This class introduces the following new methods and inherits the read(), read(char[] buf, int offset, int length), mark-(int readlimit), reset(), and skip(long nchar) methods described earlier in the java.io.Reader class:

int getLineNumber()   Returns the current line number.

void setLineNumber(int newvalue)   Sets the current line number to the specified newvalue.

public String readLine() throws IOException
Returns the next line of input, not including any line-termination characters, or null if the end of the stream has been reached.

NOTE

Release 1.0 of the JDK provided a LineNumberInputStream class. This class is deprecated in releases 1.1 and 1.2.

Part ii

The *PrintStream* and *PrintWriter* Classes

The PrintStream and PrintWriter classes have methods that support printing text. This support consists of data-type conversion and automatic flushing.

The PrintStream class has two constructors:

PrintStream(OutputStream dest)   Constructs a print stream and chains its output to dest. Automatic flushing is not supported in this method.

PrintStream(OutputStream dest, boolean auto-Flush)   Constructs a print stream and chains its output to dest. If the boolean specified is true, the output buffer will automatically be flushed whenever a byte array is written.

The PrintStream class has numerous methods for converting and writing different data types. For each data type, there is a print() method, which writes the data as a string, and a println() method, which writes the data as a string and appends a newline character. The supported methods are listed in Table 11.1.

TABLE 11.1: PrintStream Methods for Data Types

METHOD	DESCRIPTION
void print(char c)	Prints a character.
void println(char c)	Prints a character followed by a newline character.
void print(int i)	Prints an int.
void println(int i)	Prints an int followed by a newline character.
void print(long ln)	Prints a long.
void println(long ln)	Prints a long followed by a newline character.
void print(float f)	Prints a float.
void println(float f)	Prints a float followed by a newline character.
void print(double d)	Prints a double.
void println(double d)	Prints a double followed by a newline character.
void print(boolean b)	Prints a boolean. If the boolean value is true, prints the string true, otherwise prints the string false.
void println(boolean b)	Prints a boolean followed by a newline character.

TABLE 11.1 continued: PrintStream Methods for Data Types

METHOD	DESCRIPTION
void print(char[] c)	Prints a character array.
void println(char[] c)	Prints a character array followed by a newline character.
void print(String s)	Prints a string.
void println(String s)	Prints a string followed by a newline character.
void print(Object ob)	Prints an object. The string that is printed is the result of calling ob.toString().
void println(Object ob)	Prints a character followed by a newline character.
void println()	Terminates the current line by writing the line separator string.
boolean checkError()	Flushes the stream and checks its error state.
void setError()	Sets the error state of the stream to true.

WARNING

Print streams should be used only in programs based on pre-1.1 versions of the JDK. Since JDK 1.1, the entire class has been periodically deprecated and rehabilitated. Print writers are the preferred choice. The one exception is the phenomenally useful System.out, which is a PrintStream.

The PrintWriter class has four constructors:

PrintWriter(Writer dest)   Constructs a print writer and chains its output to dest. Automatic flushing is not supported.

PrintWriter(Writer dest, boolean autoflush)   Constructs a print writer and chains its output to dest. The value of autoflush determines whether automatic flushing is supported; if this value is true, the print stream will be flushed whenever a newline character is written.

PrintWriter(OutputStream out)   Constructs a print writer and chains its output to dest (which doesn't support autoflushing) from an existing output stream specified in out. This convenience constructor creates the necessary intermediate OutputStreamWriter, which will convert characters into bytes using the default character encoding.

PrintWriter(OutputStream out, boolean autoflush)
Constructs a print writer which supports autoflushing and chains
its output to existing output stream specified in out.

The names of the writing methods for this class precisely match those
of the PrintStream class (see Table 11.1). The only functional difference is that a print writer writes characters rather than bytes.

There is nothing inherent in PrintStream or PrintWriter that
requires that the output be a printing device. A print writer might, for
example, be chained to a string writer (which writes to a string buffer,
not to a string!); when output to the print writer is completed, the string
buffer can be converted to a string and written to a text-area component.

The *Pushback* Classes

The PushbackInputStream and PushbackReader classes permit
data to be *unread* or *pushed back* into the data source. The classes maintain internal stacks for pushed-back bytes and chars. Read operations
pop data from the stack until the stack is empty—only then is the data
source accessed again.

The following are the constructors for PushbackInputStream:

PushbackInputStream(InputStream source)   Creates
a pushback input stream connected to source. The stream's
buffer accommodates a single byte.

**PushbackInputStream(InputStream source, int
bufsize)**   Creates a pushback input stream connected to
source. The stream's buffer accommodates bufsize bytes.
This constructor is not supported in pre-1.1 releases of the
JDK. It will throw an IllegalArgumentException if size is
less than or equal to 0.

The following are the constructors for PushbackReader:

PushbackReader(Reader source)   Creates a pushback
reader connected to source. The stream's buffer accommodates a single byte.

PushbackReader(Reader source, int bufsize)   Creates a reader stream connected to source. The stream's buffer
accommodates bufsize bytes. It will throw an Illegal-
ArgumentException if size is less than or equal to 0.

For pushback input streams, the following methods support pushing back:

void unread(int ch) throws IOException Stores the low-order byte of ch in an internal buffer. The next read operation from the stream will return ch as a byte.

void unread(byte bytes[]) throws IOException Undoes the reading of all the bytes in array bytes[]. Not supported in pre-1.1 releases of the JDK.

void unread(byte bytes[], int start, int length) throws IOException Unreads a subset of array bytes[] which is length bytes long starting at the byte specified in start. Not supported in pre-1.1 releases of the JDK.

The pushback readers have the following methods:

void unread(int ch) throws IOException Pushes back the low-order two bytes of ch.

void unread(char chars[]) throws IOException Undoes the reading of all the characters in array chars[].

void unread(char bytes[], int start, int length) throws IOException Undoes the reading of a subset of array chars[] which is length bytes long starting at the byte specified in start.

All the pushback methods for both classes throw an IOException if the internal pushback buffer does not have space to accommodate the operation. This can happen if the operation pushes more data than the capacity of the buffer or if there have not been enough reads since the last pushback to create sufficient buffer space. In addition to the above specified pushback methods, the classes also support the inherited methods discussed previously: available(), close(), markSupported(), read(), read(byte[] b, int offset, int length), and skip(long nbytes).

Finding Fields within Nondelimited Input

The pushback input classes are useful for finding fields within nondelimited input. Consider the problem of finding a field within delimited input. Suppose that an input stream consists of various nonnumeric data, followed by a single slash character (/), followed by a number. Now suppose that the stream is currently somewhere in the nonnumeric data, and it is necessary to skip to the numeric field. Because the input is delimited (the fields are separated), this is easy to do, as shown in the following code fragment. This code fragment assumes that the input stream is called `inreader`.

```
// Assume inreader is somewhere in nonnumeric field.
int intchar;
while ((intchar=inreader.read()) != -1)
{
  if (intchar == '/')
    break;
}
// Now inreader is positioned at 1st char after '/'
```

Unfortunately, not all input is delimited. If the input data does not have a slash between its two fields, it is tempting to do something like the following:

```
int intchar;
while ((intchar=inreader.read()) != -1)
{
  if (Character.isDigit((char)intchar))
    break;
}
```

This code fails because, by the time the loop is exited, the first character of the numeric field has been read and the input stream is positioned at the second character. The code must undo the reading of the first numeric character. Reading is undone by chaining a pushback input stream onto `inreader`.

```
int intchar;
PushbackInputStream pbis = new PushbackInputStream(inreader);
while ((intchar=pbis.read()) != -1)
{
  if (Character.isDigit((char)intchar))
  {
    pbis.unread(intchar);
    break;
  }
}
```

The ability to push a single byte back into the data source does not seem impressive, but it permits the easy parsing of structured, nondelimited input.

The *SequenceInputStream* Class

The SequenceInputStream class is a mechanism for combining two or more input streams. There is no corresponding character-based reader class. A sequence input stream reads from its first input stream until that stream is exhausted; it then reads from its second input stream, continuing until the last input stream is emptied. Only then does a read of the sequence input stream return –1.

This class has two constructors:

SequenceInputStream(InputStream s1, Input-Stream s2)   Creates a sequence input stream out of s1 and s2 that will be read in order, first s1 and then s2, to provide the bytes to be read from this SequenceInputStream.

SequenceInputStream(Enumeration enum)   Creates a sequence input stream out of the list of input streams given by enum. The input streams that are produced by the enumeration will be read, in order, to provide the bytes to be read from this SequenceInputStream. After each input stream from the enumeration is exhausted, it is closed by calling its close method.

The second constructor requires an enumeration—that is, an object that implements the Enumeration interface. The easiest way to build an enumeration is to add all the input streams to a vector and then have the vector return an enumeration of its elements. Thus, the following code constructs a sequence input stream out of input streams s1, s2, s3, s4, and s5:

```
Vector vec = new Vector();
vec.addElement(s1);
vec.addElement(s2);
vec.addElement(s3);
vec.addElement(s4);
vec.addElement(s5);
SequenceInputStream sis = new
                SequenceInputStream(vec.elements());
```

The *InputStreamReader* and *Output-StreamWriter* Classes

The InputStreamReader class, when chained onto any subclass of InputStream, reads bytes from the input stream and converts them to characters. The `OutputStreamWriter` class, when chained onto any subclass of `OutputStream`, converts characters written to it into bytes and writes the bytes to the output stream. The conversion is illustrated in Figure 11.5.

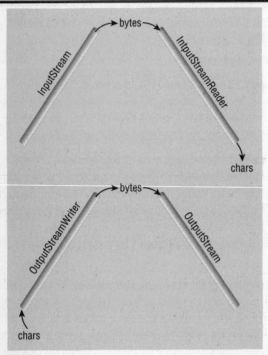

FIGURE 11.5: Converting with InputStreamReader and OutputStreamWriter

Both classes need to know how to convert between 16-bit characters and 8-bit bytes. Conversion mappings are represented by string names. Either of these classes may be constructed with an optional string argument to specify a mapping other than the default.

TIP

If you have downloaded the JDK 1.2 documentation in addition to the JDK 1.2 software, you can find a list of encodings in docs/tooldocs/win32/native2ascii.html.

The following are the constructors for InputStreamReader:

InputStreamReader(InputStream source)   Constructs an input stream reader whose data source is source. Note that the recommended way to read standard input is to use this constructor to create an InputStreamReader that reads from System.in.

InputStreamReader(InputStream source, String encodingName) throws UnsupportedEncoding-Exception   Constructs an input stream reader whose data source is source. Bytes will be converted to chars using the encoding specified by encodingName.

The constructors for OutputStreamWriter offer the same combinations of options:

OutputStreamWriter(OutputStream out)   Constructs an output stream writer connected to out.

OutputStreamWriter(OutputStream out, String encodingName) throws UnsupportedEncoding-Exception   Constructs an output stream writer connected to out. Bytes will be converted to chars using the encoding specified by encodingName.

THE NON-STREAM CLASSES

The java.io package contains several classes that are not streams. These include File, FileDescriptor, RandomAccessFile, and Stream-Tokenizer. File and FileDescriptor are straightforward and are adequately described in Sun's API documentation. The next two sections discuss the RandomAccessFile and StreamTokenizer classes.

The *RandomAcce/file* Class

The RandomAccessFile class supports reading and writing of a file, as well as file-pointer positioning. Because it does not treat the file as an ordered sequence of pure input or pure output, it operates outside the streams model.

There are two constructors for RandomAccessFile:

RandomAccessFile(String path, String permissions) throws FileNotFoundException   Creates a random-access file connected to the file path. A new FileDescriptor object is created to represent the connection to the file. Access permission is described by the string permissions, which must be either "r" for read-only mode or "rw" for read-write mode.

RandomAccessFile(File file, String permissions) throws IOException   Same as above, but the file path is taken from an instance of the File class and a new File-Descriptor object is created to represent this file connection. Access permission is described by the string permissions, which must be either "r" for read-only mode or "rw" for read-write mode.

Random-access files support a wide variety of methods for reading and writing various data types. These methods have the same names as the methods for the DataInputStream and DataOutputStream classes, which are listed earlier in this chapter.

UNIX programmers who are accustomed to the standard I/O library are used to being able to position a file pointer relative to the start of the file, the end of the file, or the current file-pointer position. The Random-AccessFile class offers only a single seek() method, which positions with respect to the start of the file. In order to achieve the other two modes of seeking, it is necessary to retrieve the file length or the current position and do an explicit subtraction.

The following methods support positioning:

void seek(long newPosition)   Sets the file's pointer to newPosition.

long length()   Returns the current length of the file in bytes.

long getFilePointer()   Returns the current location of the file pointer.

FileDescriptor getFD()   Returns the opaque file descriptor object associated with this stream.

The *StreamTokenizer* Class

The `StreamTokenizer` class is a parser, useful for analyzing input whose format is similar to Java, C, or C++ source code.

The first step in using a stream tokenizer is, of course, to construct one:

StreamTokenizer(Reader reader)   Constructs a stream tokenizer that takes its input from `reader`.

NOTE

In release 1.1 of the JDK, the preferred way to tokenize an input stream was to convert it into a character stream using the `StreamTokenizer(InputStream is)` constructor. This class is deprecated as of JDK release 1.2.

The next step is to parse the input reader `reader`. Parsing is typically done in a `while` loop, calling the tokenizer's `nextToken()` method until the end of the input is reached. The `nextToken()` method returns an int that describes the type of the next token. There are four possible return values for `nextToken()`:

StreamTokenizer.TT_NUMBER   Indicates that the token just read was a number. The number's value may be read from the tokenizer's `nval` instance variable, which is of type double.

StreamTokenizer.TT_WORD   Indicates that the token just read was a nonnumerical word (an identifier, for example). The word may be read from the tokenizer's `sval` instance variable, which is of type String.

StreamTokenizer.TT_EOL   Indicates that the token just read was an end-of-line character.

StreamTokenizer.TT_EOF   Indicates that the end of the input stream has been reached.

A stream tokenizer can be customized to recognize caller-specified characters, such as whitespace, comment delimiters, string delimiters, and other format-specific values. The customization methods are listed in Table 11.2.

Part II

TABLE 11.2: StreamTokenizer Customization Methods

METHOD	DESCRIPTION
void commentChar(int comment)	Specifies that comment is to denote the first character of a single-line comment.
void quoteChar(int quote)	Specifies that quote is to delimit the beginning and end of string constants.
void whitespaceChars (int low, int high)	Specifies that all input characters in the range low through high (inclusive) are to be interpreted as whitespace.
void wordChars(int low, int high)	Specifies that all input characters in the range low through high (inclusive) are to be interpreted as word characters.
void ordinaryChar(int ord)	Specifies that ord is an ordinary character and is not a quote delimiter, comment-line delimiter, whitespace character, word character, or number character. This "turns off" any special significance previously assigned using the calls listed above.
void ordinaryChars (int low, int high)	Specifies that all input characters in the range low through high (inclusive) are to be interpreted as ordinary characters.
void eolIsSignificant- (boolean flag)	If flag is true, specifies that the parser will recognize end-of-line characters as tokens. If flag is false, end-of-line characters will not be recognized.
void parseNumbers (boolean flag)	If flag is true, specifies that the parser will recognize numbers as tokens. If flag is false, numbers will not be recognized.
void slashStarComments (boolean flag)	If flag is true, specifies that the parser will recognize C-style comments and skip over the comment body. If flag is false, C-style comments will not be recognized. C-style comments begin with a slash character followed by an asterisk character (/*) and end with an asterisk followed by a slash (*/); they may span multiple lines.
void slashSlash- Comments(boolean flag)	If flag is true, specifies that the parser will recognize C++-style comments. If flag is false, C++-style comments will not be recognized. C++-style comments begin with two slash characters (//) and end at the end of the current line.
void resetSyntax()	Resets the significance of all characters to be ordinary.
int lineno()	Return the current line number.
void lowerCaseMode (boolean flag)	Determines whether or not word tokens are automatically lowercased.

TABLE 11.2 continued: StreamTokenizer Customization Methods

METHOD	DESCRIPTION
int nextToken()	Parses the next token from the input stream of this tokenizer. The return values are discussed above.
string toString()	Returns the string representation of the current stream token.

NOTE

Notice that the values for the StreamTokenizer customization methods listed in Table 11.2, such as comment, quote, low, and high, are ints, not bytes or chars. However, the values should certainly represent characters.

With the methods listed in Table 11.2, the StreamTokenizer class can be configured as a flexible and moderately powerful parser for an input stream whose format resembles Java, C, or C++ source code. Parsing of more general formats would require a powerful lexical analyzer and compiler generator, similar to the lex and yacc tools found in UNIX.

WHAT'S NEXT?

In the next chapter, we will advance beyond the use of standard Java components and discuss designing and creating your own custom components.

PART iii

ADVANCED JAVA

Chapter 12

CUSTOM COMPONENTS

J ava's AWT (Abstract Windowing Toolkit) provides a small but reasonable set of user interface components. The JFC (Java Foundation Classes), which were introduced with release 2, substantially extend the toolkit (the new JFC components are discussed in Chapter 13). However, you still may find that the standard set of components does not provide the functionality you need for certain applications. In such cases, you will need to develop your own custom components.

A major consideration in the development of custom components is the handling of events. This chapter begins with a quick review of event delegation, and then focuses on three alternative strategies for creating custom components, along with criteria for selecting the most appropriate strategy for your situation. We'll develop three examples of custom components based on each of the design strategies.

Adapted from *Java 2 Developer's Handbook*
by Philip Heller and Simon Roberts
ISBN 0-7821-2179-9   1,248 pages $59.99

THE EVENT DELEGATION MODEL

The event delegation model is based on the concept of the *event listener*. An event listener is an object that receives notification when a GUI event takes place. There are ten categories of GUI events, each represented by a different class, and there is almost a one-to-one correspondence between event types and listener types (the correspondence breaks down in the case of mouse events, as explained later in the chapter). The event class hierarchy is shown in Figure 12.1.

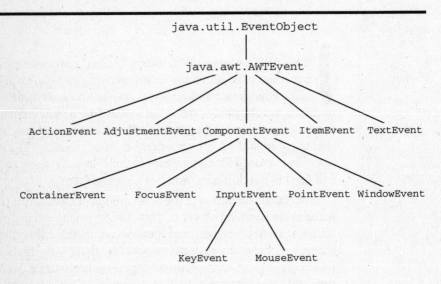

All classes belong to `java.awt.event` package unless otherwise noted.

FIGURE 12.1: The event class hierarchy

At the top of the hierarchy is the event object class. `EventObject` is perhaps an inelegant class name, but the name `Event` was already taken by the `java.awt.Event` class, which is deprecated. The `EventObject` superclass is intended to be the parent of all imaginable event types. AWT events (those that are triggered by the components of the AWT) are only one subset of all possible event types; AWT events are represented by subclasses of `java.awt.AWTEvent`. Other families of events include Bean events and application-specific events. The subclasses of `java .awt.AWTEvent` belong to the `java.awt.event` package.

NOTE

This book is based on the event delegation model introduced with Java release 1.1. The older 1.0 propagation model, in which events ripple outward through the containment hierarchy, has been deprecated.

All event subclasses inherit the getSource() method from Event-Object. This method returns the object that originated the event. For the AWTEvent subclasses, getSource() returns the component in which user input took place.

Listener Interfaces and Methods

When a user stimulates a GUI component with a keyboard key or with a mouse click, a method call is made to all objects that have registered with the component as listeners for the type of event that took place. The method has a parameter whose type is one of the subclasses of java.awt.AWTEvent. Additional information about what occurred can be obtained by making method calls on the event.

For example, the key event category is represented by the KeyEvent class. When a user triggers a key event by pressing a keyboard key while the mouse is in a canvas, the system creates an instance of java.awt .event.KeyEvent and calls keyPressed() on all of the canvas's key listeners, passing the key event as a parameter. Any implementation of keyPressed() that is interested in the event's data—for instance, to discover which key was pressed—can call getKeyCode() on the key event.

In order to be eligible to become a listener for a certain type of event, an object must implement an interface that corresponds to the event type of interest. For any event type XXX, the name of the corresponding listener interface is xxxListener. To register an object as an xxx listener of a particular component, call the component's addxxxListener() method, passing the listener as the method argument.

NOTE

There are two listener interfaces that handle mouse events: MouseListener and MouseMotionListener. A mouse listener is notified when a mouse button is used, or when the mouse cursor enters or leaves a component. A mouse-motion listener is notified when the mouse is moved or dragged.

The various listener interface types, interface methods, and add methods are listed in Table 12.1.

TABLE 12.1: Listener Interfaces

INTERFACE	INTERFACE METHODS	ADD METHOD
ActionListener	actionPerformed(ActionEvent)	addActionListener (ActionListener)
AdjustmentListener	adjustmentValueChanged (AdjustmentEvent)	addAdjustmentListener (AdjustmentListener)
ComponentListener	componentHidden(ComponentEvent) componentMoved(ComponentEvent) componentResized(ComponentEvent) componentShown(ComponentEvent)	addComponentListener (ComponentListener)
ContainerListener	componentAdded(ContainerEvent) componentRemoved(ContainerEvent)	addContainerListener (ContainerListener)
FocusListener	focusGained(FocusEvent) focusLost(FocusEvent)	addFocusListener (FocusListener)
InputMethodListener	caretPositionChanged (InputMethodEvent) inputMethodTextChanged (InputMethodEvent)	addInputMethodListener (InputMethodListener)
ItemListener	itemStateChanged(ItemEvent)	addItemListener (ItemListener)
KeyListener	keyPressed(KeyEvent) keyReleased(KeyEvent) keyTyped(KeyEvent)	addKeyListener (KeyListener)
MouseListener	mouseClicked(MouseEvent) mouseEntered(MouseEvent) mouseExited(MouseEvent) mousePressed(MouseEvent) mouseReleased(MouseEvent)	addMouseListener (MouseListener)
MouseMotionListener	mouseDragged(MouseEvent) mouseMoved(MouseEvent)	addMouseMotionListener (MouseMotionListener)
TextListener	textValueChanged(TextEvent)	addTextListener (TextListener)

TABLE 12.1 continued: Listener Interfaces

INTERFACE	INTERFACE METHODS	ADD METHOD
WindowListener	windowActivated(WindowEvent)	addWindowListener (WindowListener)
	windowClosed(WindowEvent)	
	windowClosing(WindowEvent)	
	windowDeactivated(WindowEvent)	
	windowDeiconified(WindowEvent)	
	windowIconified(WindowEvent)	
	windowOpened(WindowEvent)	
AWTEventListener	eventDispatched(AWTEvent event)	addAWTEventListener (AWTEventListener, long)

Explicit Event Enabling

As an alternative to delegating a component's events, you can use another technique called *explicit event enabling*. Components have a method called enableEvents(), which can be invoked to detect events before listeners are notified. The argument to the enableEvents() call is an int value that specifies the type or types of events to be enabled; constants for these values are defined in the AWTEvent class.

When a component has explicitly enabled events of type *xxx*, an *xxx* event causes a call to the component's processxxxEvent(xxxevent) method. By default, these methods notify all of the component's registered event listeners. Component subclasses can override the process-xxxEvent() methods to perform desired event processing.

For example, to explicitly enable action events, a subclass of Button can call enableEvents(AWTEvent.ACTION_EVENT_MASK) in its constructor and override processActionEvent(ActionEvent). To explicitly enable both key and action events, a subclass of TextField can call enableEvents(AWTEvent.KEY_EVENT_MASK | AWTEvent .ACTION_EVENT_MASK) in its constructor and override both process-ActionEvent(ActionEvent) and processKeyEvent(KeyEvent).

Part iii

In all cases, the subclass version of the method should call the super-class version, so that registered listeners will be notified. A `process-KeyEvent()` method, for example, should look something like this:

```
public void processKeyEvent(KeyEvent e) {
    // Subclass-specific processing goes here.
    super.processKeyEvent(e);
}
```

As you will see later in this chapter, explicit event enabling provides custom components with a convenient mechanism for handling events.

STRATEGIES FOR DESIGNING CUSTOM COMPONENTS

The decision to create a custom component class should not be undertaken lightly. By far, the most important GUI design consideration is user convenience, and user convenience is usually best served by providing the smallest possible learning curve. A standard component that does an adequate job can be preferable to a custom component that does a spectacular job, because users already know how to use the standard version.

However, you may still encounter situations where no standard component will be adequate. In these cases, once you have decided to create a custom component class, you have three options:

▶ You can subclass `Component` and have the subclass take care of all painting and event handling. The result is a completely new look and feel.

▶ You can subclass `Container` and populate the subclass with standard components. These will interact with each other to provide higher-level behavior. The result is an aggregation of preexisting components.

▶ You can subclass one of the noncontainer components such as `Button` or `Checkbox`. The subclass will enhance the inherited behavior.

Each of these approaches has its pros and cons. When judging an approach, the primary consideration is ease of mastery. Users should be able to quickly figure out how to use a new component, and the component should assist users in doing productive work. Any feature of a component that is difficult to understand or difficult to use should be considered a serious liability.

Component Class Subclassing

In general, components designed with the first strategy—subclassing Component—will be the most difficult for the user to master. Because the look and the feel are completely new, the user has no experience with similar components to suggest how to interact with this new one.

Because the user will need to learn how to use this new component, its use should be as intuitive as possible. Thus, the component should match the user's mental image of the data to be entered as closely as possible. Subclassing Component works best when the user's job is to enter a new kind of data, which is not well represented as text, a checkbox state, or a scrollbar position.

As an example of creating a custom component using this method, we'll develop a new component for entering a value in polar coordinates (see the "Subclassing Component: The Polar Component" section later in this chapter).

Aggregation

The second strategy—aggregation—is most likely to result in a component that the user will be able to learn to use easily. Everything the container contains is already well known. Only the interactions among the subcomponents within the container are new. Since users already know how to use checkboxes, textfields, and scrollbars, there is little for them to learn.

By using this approach, you take advantage of all the expensive usability research that has been done over the years to refine the subcomponents. This strategy is useful when a component must combine both input and output functionality or when you want to offer multiple input paradigms.

As an example of using the aggregation strategy, we'll develop a custom component that offers three options for entering a numeric value. The example includes a choice of checkboxes, a textfield, or a scrollbar for inputting a value (see the "Aggregation: The ThreeWay Component" section later in this chapter).

Standard Component Subclassing

The third strategy provides a familiar look with a new feel. When you sub-class a component, the user sees something familiar and approaches it with the expectation that it will behave like its standard superclass. Users will need some education so that they realize that this is not the case.

This strategy works best when you must restrict the set of valid inputs to a component. As an example, we'll develop two versions of a validating textfield component (see the "Subclassing a Standard Component: Validating Textfields" section later in this chapter).

Design Considerations

Before deciding on a design strategy—subclassing Component, aggregating in a container, or subclassing a primitive component—there are two questions that you need to consider:

- ▶ How should the component display its value?

- ▶ How should the user specify new values?

Once these look-and-feel issues are decided, the best subclassing strategy will generally be obvious. At this point, the following list of issues can help you to organize your thoughts and make well-founded design decisions:

- ▶ How can the programmer modify the component's appearance?

- ▶ What limits should be set on the component's possible values?

- ▶ How should the value be stored, set, and retrieved?

- ▶ What events should the component send? Will custom event types and listener interfaces be required?

- ▶ Will the component behave properly in a multithreaded environment?

- ▶ Will the component behave properly if it is resized?

As we work through the examples of custom components in this chapter, you will see that the answers to these questions provide the basis for a sound design plan.

SUBCLASSING *COMPONENT*: THE *POLAR* COMPONENT

The first example is a component called `Polar`, which is used for inputting a point in polar coordinates. Polar coordinates describe a point in terms of its distance from the origin (usually called ρ, or rho for radius) and the angle it makes with the right-pointing horizontal (usually called θ, or theta).

NOTE

Polar coordinates are an alternative way of using two numbers to describe a point in a two-dimensional space. It is easy to translate between the polar (ρ, θ) coordinates and the familiar (x,y) coordinates of rectangular Cartesian space: x = ρ cos θ; y = ρ sin θ.

Polar's Look-and-Feel Issues

As you learned in the previous section, before you can develop a custom component, you need to consider how the user should see and use the component.

Displaying Values

The first consideration is appearance: How should the component display its value? Because the component is to represent a point in 2-D space, the only reasonable choice is a square region or a squarish rectangle. It is not necessary to force the component to be perfectly square, but neither dimension should be particularly narrow. We can decide somewhat arbitrarily that the component will declare its minimum and preferred size to be 50×50 pixels (minimum and preferred size are of concern to layout managers). As with other components, the minimum and preferred size of a `Polar` component are likely to be overruled by the prevailing layout manager.

As for what is to be drawn in the component's region, the appearance should match as closely as possible the picture in the user's mind's eye. Probably, the user's mental picture is a textbook illustration: a pair of axes with a dot superimposed, possibly with an arrow from the origin to the dot, as shown in Figure 12.2.

Part iii

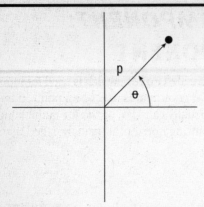

FIGURE 12.2:   Mental picture of polar coordinates

The `Polar` component should resemble Figure 12.2 as closely as possible. However, in practice ease-of-use considerations will suggest some modifications and compromises. The current point should certainly be represented by a circular dot. In practice, rendering an arrowhead at the tip of the line would produce visual clutter and obscure the dot, so there will not be an arrowhead.

The user should be cued that this device operates in the polar domain and not the Cartesian, so drawing a circle would be preferable to drawing a rectangle. If there is to be a circle, where should it go? If we draw a ring that passes through the current point, the user will receive additional feedback about the distance from the center. The result is shown in Figure 12.3, which is a screenshot of the finished product. Note how the ring cues the value of rho, while the line cues the value of theta.

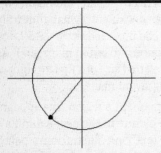

FIGURE 12.3:   The `Polar` component

Specifying Values

How should the user specify new values? The `Polar` component clearly wants to be clicked.

The simplest interface lets the user grab the ring by holding down the mouse button anywhere inside the component. The current point and the ring will jump to the mouse cursor location. Subsequently, as long as the mouse button is down, the value will track the mouse. When the user releases the mouse button, the value ceases tracking. As long as the user is dragging the mouse, the dot, the line, and the ring will be rendered in (arbitrarily) blue, so the component can tell the user, "I'm listening." At times when the component is not responding to the mouse (which is almost always), it will be rendered in black. Because the axes never change and do not communicate information about the current value, they will be rendered in their own constant color. Proliferation of colors is dangerous because a GUI with too many colors is confusing. Therefore, it is best to take a conservative approach and draw the axes in gray.

This process gives satisfactory graphical feedback. Because numerical feedback is also required, the values of rho and theta will be displayed in the upper-left corner of the component.

Choosing a Subclassing Strategy

Now that we have defined a look and a feel, it is time to choose a subclassing strategy. Clearly, there are no standard components that render a ring or an arrow, so aggregation and simple subclassing are out of the question. To create the `Polar` component, we will need to subclass Component and write all the rendering and event-handling code from scratch:

```
public class Polar extends Component
```

Polar's Design Issues

We can now continue developing the `Polar` component by addressing the design issues: modifying the component's appearance, limiting values, handling value input, handling events, and providing for multi-threading and resizing behavior.

Modifying the Component's Appearance

How can the programmer modify the component's appearance? Consider those aspects of the appearance that are susceptible to change. The numeric value display comes to mind—you may want to disable it or modify its font.

You should also be able to change the drawing colors and the component's background color. For the most part, the programmer can be given control over these aspects with no extra effort.

Every component has a background color, a foreground color, and a font. When a component is told to repaint(), the GUI thread will eventually call the component's update() method; update() clears the component using the background color, sets the current color to the foreground color, and calls paint(). So, if the paint() method assumes that the component has been cleared using some appropriate background color, you can change a Polar component's background by calling its set-Background() method. Since this method is inherited from the Component class, programmers have nothing extra to learn.

Similarly, it is reasonable for you to expect that the ring, dot, and ray will be rendered using the foreground color. With this arrangement, you can simply call setForeground() to change the rendering color.

If the paint() code does not explicitly set the font used to render the textual value, i, the value will default to the component's own font. Thus, you can control this font by calling setFont() on the component.

The only conditions that cannot be modified by using the component's inherited methods are the color of the display during dragging and the presence or absence of the textual feedback. For such modification, two public methods are needed: setDragColor() and setShowText().

Limiting the Value

Next, we need to consider the component's ability to put limits on its value. Theta is inherently constrained to the range 0 to 360 degrees.

Rho, on the other hand, needs limits. There needs to be a maximum value for rho, represented by a ring that fills the component; this dictates a scale for translating distance in pixels into values for rho. This maximum is to be provided as an argument to the Polar component's constructor, and it is stored in an instance variable called maxRho. In theory, the maxRho value should correspond to a ring whose diameter (in pixels) is the lesser of the component's width and its height. In practice, a ring that grazes the boundary of the component is unsightly, so maxRho will actually correspond to a ring that is 10 percent smaller than the smaller dimension of the component.

There are many points within the Polar component—especially near the corners—that represent illegal values because rho would be greater than maxRho. When the user drags through these regions, the ring should refuse to follow; it should instead remain at its maximum legal size.

Storing, Setting, and Retrieving Values

The next issue is how the value should be stored, set, and retrieved. Rho and theta should be represented by floats or doubles. Doubles are more convenient because the component will need to make numerous calls to the trigonometric methods of the Math class, which uses doubles. Programmers who use the Polar class will be likely to do trigonometric operations on the results and will likewise prefer values that are doubles. An auxiliary class called PolarPoint will be defined to encapsulate doubles for rho and theta.

NOTE

If you use the Polar class, remember that all of Java's trigonometric functions deal in radians. For conversion to and from degrees, the Math class defines a static final double called PI.

The PolarPoint class definition follows. The source code for the PolarPoint class appears below.

LIST 12.1: *PolarPoint.java*

```
/*
 * The PolarPoint class describes a point in polar
   *coordinates. Used by the Polar component class for
   *storing its value.
 */

public class PolarPoint
{
  private double      rho;
  private double      theta;


  public PolarPoint(double rho, double theta)
  {
    this.rho = rho;
    this.theta = theta;
  }


  public PolarPoint(PolarPoint p)
  {
```

```
          this.rho = p.getRho();
          this.theta = p.getTheta();
      }

      public double getRho()                 { return rho; }
      public void setRho(double rho)         { this.rho = rho; }
      public double getTheta()               { return theta; }
      public void setTheta(double theta) { this.theta = theta; }

      public String toString()
      {
          return "RHO = " + rho + " ... THETA = " + theta;
      }
  }
```

This class stores `rho` and `theta` as private doubles, with public accessor and mutator methods. The nomenclature of the accessors and mutators (or *getters* and *setters*) is in keeping with the Beans naming discipline. (See Chapter 18 for more information about the Beans naming conventions.)

Now the `Polar` class can be given a private instance variable called `value`, of type `PolarPoint`, and public methods to get and set the value. These methods will be called `getPolarValue()` and `setPolarValue()`, again in keeping with the Beans naming convention. Setting the value should force a repaint, so that the component's appearance will reflect its new value. The `paint()` method can assume that `value` is valid; it also assumes the validity of a scale factor called `unitsPerPixel`, which correlates rho units to screen pixels, and of a boolean called `dragging`, which tells whether a mouse drag is in progress. The `paint()` method looks like this:

```
      public void paint(Graphics g)
      {
          int        radiusPix;
          int        centerX;
          int        centerY;
          Dimension  size;

          radiusPix = (int)(value.getRho() / unitsPerPixel);
          size = getSize();
          centerX = size.width / 2;
          centerY = size.height / 2;
          int ulx = centerX - radiusPix;
          int uly = centerY - radiusPix;

          // Draw axes in light gray.
          g.setColor(Color.lightGray);
```

```
g.drawLine(centerX, 0, centerX, size.height);
g.drawLine(0, centerY, size.width, centerY);

// Draw label string in upper-left corner.
g.setColor(getForeground());
if (showTextValue)
{
  g.drawString((value.getRho() + ", "
               + value.getTheta()),
               5, size.height-5);
}

// If dragging, subsequent drawing will use
// the drag color.
if (dragging)
{
  g.setColor(dragColor);
}

// Draw ring.
g.drawOval(ulx, uly, 2*radiusPix, 2*radiusPix);

// Draw dot.
int arrowTipX = centerX +
    (int)(radiusPix * Math.cos(value.getTheta()));
int arrowTipY = centerY -
    (int)(radiusPix * Math.sin(value.getTheta()));
g.fillOval(arrowTipX-3, arrowTipY-3, 7, 7);

// Draw line from center to dot, space permitting.
if (radiusPix > 5)
{
  g.drawLine(centerX, centerY, arrowTipX, arrowTipY);
}
}
```

The `Mouse` and `MouseMotion` event handlers have the job of updating the `value` and `dragging` instance variables. The `Polar` class will serve as its own `MouseListener` and `MouseMotionListener`. The code fragment below lists the event-handling portion of the class. Note that the class declaration has been modified to declare implementation of the two listener interfaces.

```
public class Polar extends Component
              implements MouseListener,
                         MouseMotionListener
{
  private PolarPoint    value;
```

```
    private double          maxRho;
    private double          unitsPerPixel;
    private boolean         dragging = false;
    private Color           dragColor = Color.blue;
    private boolean         showTextValue = true;

  {
    value = xyToPolar(e.getX(), e.getY());
    repaint();
  }

  public void mouseDragged(MouseEvent e)
  {
    dragging = true;
    value = xyToPolar(e.getX(), e.getY());
    repaint();
  }

  public void mouseReleased(MouseEvent e)
  {
    dragging = false;
    value = xyToPolar(e.getX(), e.getY());
    repaint();
  }

  private PolarPoint xyToPolar(int x, int y)
  {
    double    newRho;
    double    newTheta;

    int deltaX = x - getSize().width/2;
    int deltaY = getSize().height/2 - y;
    double deltaLen = Math.sqrt(deltaX*deltaX +
                                deltaY*deltaY);
    double rho = unitsPerPixel * deltaLen;
    rho = Math.min(rho, maxRho);
    double theta = Math.atan2(deltaY, deltaX);
    while (theta < 0.0)
      theta += 2*Math.PI;

    return new PolarPoint(rho, theta);
  }

  public void mouseClicked(MouseEvent e)    { }
  public void mouseMoved(MouseEvent e)      { }
  public void mouseEntered(MouseEvent e)    { }
  public void mouseExited(MouseEvent e)     { }
}
```

The xyToPolar() method converts pixel coordinates to polar coordinates, returning an instance of PolarPoint. The four empty methods at the end are present so that the two interfaces will be completely implemented.

So far, the new component class has an appearance and a value, both of which are appropriately adjusted when a user provides mouse input. Now it is time to consider event handling.

Handling Events

The next issue is the kind of event that the Polar component will send out when activated by a user.

It would be convenient if the custom component could send one of the standard event types. The type that comes to mind is the Adjustment event, since a Polar component is a kind of round two-dimensional scrollbar. Unfortunately, Adjustment events are not quite adequate because the AdjustmentEvent class has a getValue() method that returns an int, and the value of a Polar component is a PolarPoint.

Since there is no truly appropriate event type, we must invent one: PolarEvent. The listing for the PolarEvent class follows.

LIST 12.2: PolarEvent.java

```
import java.awt.AWTEvent;

public class PolarEvent extends AWTEvent
{
  private PolarPoint    polarValue;

  public PolarEvent(Polar source, PolarPoint p)
  {
    super(source, RESERVED_ID_MAX+1);
    polarValue = p;
  }

  public PolarPoint getPolarValue()       { return polarValue; }
  public void setPolarValue(PolarPoint p) { polarValue = p; }
}
```

In the first line of the constructor, the second parameter passed to the superclass constructor is the ID for the event. Values up to and including AWTEvent.RESERVED_ID_MAX should not be used by programmers creating new event classes.

The PolarEvent class is simple, but inventing a new event type requires more work. First, there must be a listener interface. It seems natural to call this interface PolarListener. The interface will have a single method, called polarValueChanged(), whose argument will be an instance of PolarEvent. The listing for the PolarListener interface follows.

LIST 12.3:   PolarListener.java

```java
public interface PolarListener
        extends java.util.EventListener
{
    public void polarValueChanged(PolarEvent pe);
}
```

Now any object that wants to receive notification from a polar component can implement the PolarListener interface and provide a polarValueChanged() method.

The Polar class will need to provide addPolarListener() and removePolarListener() methods. An easy way to keep track of listeners is with a vector. We give the Polar class a vector instance variable called listeners, as shown in the code fragment below.

```java
public class Polar extends Component
                   implements MouseListener,
                                MouseMotionListener
{
    private Vector listeners = new Vector();

    public void addPolarListener(PolarListener listener)
    {
        if (!listeners.contains(listener))
            listeners.addElement(listener);
    }

    public void removePolarListener(PolarListener listener)
    {
        listeners.removeElement(listener);
    }


        . . .

}
```

When the mouse is clicked or dragged, the event handlers (which already update the value and call repaint()) should also notify all listeners. They do so by calling the method listed below, which constructs an instance of `PolarEvent` and then calls `polarValueChanged()` on all registered `Polar` listeners.

```
private void notifyListeners()
{
  // Clone vector of listeners in case a listener's
  // polarValueChanged modifies the original vector.
  Vector copyOfListeners = (Vector)(listeners.clone());

  // Create a Polar event that encapsulates
  // the current value.
  PolarPoint pp = new PolarPoint(value);
  PolarEvent event = new PolarEvent(this, pp);

  // Notify each listener.
  Enumeration enum = copyOfListeners.elements();
  while (enum.hasMoreElements())
  {
    PolarListener listener =
                  (PolarListener)enum.nextElement();
    listener.polarValueChanged(event);
  }
}
```

Notice that notification is performed by cloning the vector of listeners and working from the clone rather than from the original. The reason for this will be made clear in the next section.

So far, we have examined the issues of how the new component class handles its value and appearance, and how it notifies its listeners. These are the central issues, and considering them will result in a class that behaves well under most circumstances. The remaining two considerations have to do with how the class behaves in stressful environments: multithreading and resizing.

Behaving in a Multithreading Environment

The first stressful consideration is multithreading. A multithreaded situation is always a potential threat to shared data (data that might simultaneously be accessed by two different threads). In our example, there are two pieces of shared data that need to be considered:

▶ The single `PolarEvent` that is sent as an argument to all `Polar` listeners. This object contains a reference to a `PolarPoint` that reflects the current value.

▶ The vector of listeners. `Polar` listeners can register and unregister with a `Polar` component asynchronously.

The `PolarEvent` is created and written by the `Polar` class and read by the registered listeners. The danger is that one of the listeners could corrupt the event. This is a general hazard of the event propagation model. By convention, the problem is solved by alerting programmers of listener methods that could present a threat. Listener methods that need to modify events should copy the events and modify the copies, leaving the originals alone. Since this is good practice in general, it is not really necessary to take further precautions.

The vector of listeners, on the other hand, requires special attention. This vector is traversed when a user modifies the component, so that listeners can be notified. The main danger is that a listener's `polarValueChanged()` method might deregister the listener from the component's listener list. If this were to happen, traversal of the vector would be corrupted. It is also conceivable that independent threads could register or deregister other listeners, again corrupting traversal of the vector. The safest solution is to clone the vector of listeners and notify by traversing the clone rather than traversing the original.

NOTE

All methods of the `Vector` class that modify the internal data are synchronized, so there is no danger that the vector might be corrupted at times other than event notification.

Behaving during Resizing

The final question is what to do when the component resizes. It has already been decided that the constructor should specify a maximum value for rho, which will define a scale conversion factor from rho's units to pixels. This conversion factor will be consulted whenever the value changes, so it should be stored as an instance variable.

Appropriate variable naming is always important, but this is a case where it is doubly so. If the conversion factor is called `conversionFactor`, future developers who maintain this code will need to work out for themselves whether converting from pixels to units requires multiplying or dividing by `conversionFactor`. A mistake here could introduce a very subtle bug. It is much better to eliminate all possible confusion by calling the instance variable either `pixelsPerUnit` or `unitsPerPixel`. Here, `unitsPerPixel` is used because the example converts from pixels to units, and this entails multiplication rather than division. Multiplication is commutative, so there is no possibility that in the future somebody will introduce a maintenance bug by getting the operands in the wrong order.

When the component resizes, `unitsPerPixel` is recomputed:

```
private void adjustScale(int w, int h)
  unitsPerPixel = 2.0 * maxRho / Math.min(w, h);
  unitsPerPixel *= 1.1;
}
```

Multiplying by 1.1 ensures that when the component represents the maximum allowable rho, the ring occupies only about 90 percent of the entire component, and will never get so close to the edges that the component is difficult to read or use.

```
public void setBounds(int x, int y, int w, int h)
{
  adjustScale(w, h);
  super. setBounds(x, y, w, h);
}
```

The *Polar* Component Class and Test Applet

The full `Polar` class listing follows.

LIST 12.4: Polar.java

```
import java.awt.*;
import java.awt.event.*;
import java.util.*;


/*
 * Our home-made component for specifying a point in polar
 * coordinates. Gives constant graphical and textual
 * feedback of its current value. Posts a PolarEvent to all
 * Polar listeners when the mouse is dragged or released.
 */

public class Polar extends Component
                   implements MouseListener,
                              MouseMotionListener
{
  private Vector        listeners = new Vector();
  private PolarPoint    value;
  private double        maxRho;
```

```
private double      unitsPerPixel;
private boolean     dragging = false;
private Color       dragColor = Color.blue;
private boolean     showTextValue = true;


public Polar()
{
  this(100.0, 0.0, 100.0);
}
public Polar(double initRho, double initTheta, double maxRho)
{
  value = new PolarPoint(initRho, initTheta);
  this.maxRho = maxRho;
  setBackground(Color.white);

  addMouseListener(this);
  addMouseMotionListener(this);
}


public void setDragColor(Color c)
{
  dragColor = c;
}


public void setShowText(boolean b)
{
  showTextValue = b;
}


public void setValue(PolarPoint newValue)
{
  value = newValue;
  repaint();
}


public PolarPoint getValue()
{
  return value;
}


public void addPolarListener(PolarListener listener)
```

```
{
    if (!listeners.contains(listener))
        listeners.addElement(listener);
}

public void removePolarListener(PolarListener listener)
{
    listeners.removeElement(listener);
}


private void notifyListeners()
{
    // Clone vector of listeners in case a listener's
    // polarValueChanged modifies the original vector.
    Vector copyOfListeners = (Vector)(listeners.clone());

    // Create a Polar event that encapsulates the
    // current value.
    PolarPoint pp = new PolarPoint(value);
    PolarEvent event = new PolarEvent(this, pp);

    // Notify each listener.
    Enumeration enum = copyOfListeners.elements();
    while (enum.hasMoreElements())
    {
        PolarListener listener =
                    (PolarListener)enum.nextElement();
        listener.polarValueChanged(event);
    }
}


/*
 * Adjust scale so that the largest permissible value takes up
 * not quite the entire component.
 */
private void adjustScale(int w, int h)
{
    unitsPerPixel = 2.0 * maxRho / Math.min(w, h);
    unitsPerPixel *= 1.1;
}



/*
 * When the component resizes, we need to adjust our scale.
```

```
 * Note that we do not need to override setSize(), because
 * setSize() calls setBounds().
 */
public void setBounds(int x, int y, int w, int h)
{
  adjustScale(w, h);
  super.setBounds(x, y, w, h);
}


public void paint(Graphics g)
{
  int       radiusPix;
  int       centerX;
  int       centerY;
  Dimension size;

  radiusPix = (int)(value.getRho() / unitsPerPixel);
  size = getSize();
  centerX = size.width / 2;
  centerY = size.height / 2;
  int ulx = centerX - radiusPix;
  int uly = centerY - radiusPix;

  // Draw axes in light gray.
  g.setColor(Color.lightGray);
  g.drawLine(centerX, 0, centerX, size.height);
  g.drawLine(0, centerY, size.width, centerY);

  // Draw label string in upper-left corner.
  g.setColor(getForeground());
  if (showTextValue)
  {
    g.drawString((value.getRho() + ", " +
                 value.getTheta()),
                 5, size.height-5);
  }

  // If dragging, subsequent drawing will use the drag color.
  if (dragging)
  {
    g.setColor(dragColor);
  }

  // Draw ring.
  g.drawOval(ulx, uly, 2*radiusPix, 2*radiusPix);
```

```
    // Draw dot.
    int arrowTipX = centerX +
                    (int)(radiusPix *
                    Math.cos(value.getTheta()));
    int arrowTipY = centerY -
                    (int)(radiusPix *
                    Math.sin(value.getTheta()));
    g.fillOval(arrowTipX-3, arrowTipY-3, 7, 7);

    // Draw line from center to dot, space permitting.
    {
      g.drawLine(centerX, centerY, arrowTipX, arrowTipY);
    }
}


public void mousePressed(MouseEvent e)
{
    value = xyToPolar(e.getX(), e.getY());
    repaint();
}


public void mouseDragged(MouseEvent e)
{
    dragging = true;
    value = xyToPolar(e.getX(), e.getY());
    repaint();
    notifyListeners();
}


public void mouseReleased(MouseEvent e)
{
    dragging = false;
    value = xyToPolar(e.getX(), e.getY());
    repaint();
    notifyListeners();
}


private PolarPoint xyToPolar(int x, int y)
{
    double    newRho;
    double    newTheta;
```

```
        int deltaX = x - getSize().width/2;
        int deltaY = getSize().height/2 - y;
        double deltaLen = Math.sqrt(deltaX*deltaX + deltaY*deltaY);
        double rho = unitsPerPixel * deltaLen;
        rho = Math.min(rho, maxRho);
        double theta = Math.atan2(deltaY, deltaX);
        while (theta < 0.0)
          theta += 2*Math.PI;

        return new PolarPoint(rho, theta);
      }


      public void mouseClicked(MouseEvent e)    {  }
      public void mouseMoved(MouseEvent e)      {  }
      public void mouseEntered(MouseEvent e)    {  }
      public void mouseExited(MouseEvent e)     {  }


      public Dimension getMinimumSize()
      {
        return getPreferredSize();
      }


      public Dimension getPreferredSize()
      {
        return new Dimension(50, 50);
      }
    }
```

The Polar component class may now be used like any other component. The source code for the PolarTest program follows.

LIST 12.5: *PolarTest.java*

```
    import java.awt.*;
    import java.applet.Applet;


    public class PolarTest extends Applet
                           implements PolarListener
    {
      private TextField   tf;
```

```
public void init()
{
  setLayout(new BorderLayout());

  Polar polar = new Polar();
  polar.setShowText(true);
  polar.addPolarListener(this);
  add(polar, BorderLayout.CENTER);
  tf = new TextField("RHO = 0.0 ...  THETA = 0.0");
  tf.setEditable(false);
  add(tf, BorderLayout.SOUTH);
}


public void polarValueChanged(PolarEvent e)
{
  tf.setText(e.getPolarValue().toString());
}
}
```

LIST 12.6:   PolarTest.html

```
<HTML>
<HEAD>
  <TITLE>Polar Applet </TITLE>
</HEAD>
<BODY>
  <APPLET code=PolarTest.class width=500 height=500> </APPLET>
</BODY>
</HTML>
```

Part iii

In order to compile and run the PolarTest applet, create the following files in any text editor: PolarPoint.java (List 12.1), PolarEvent.java (List 12.2), PolarListener.java (List 12.3), Polar.java (List 12.4), PolarTest.java (List 12.5), and PolarTest.html (List 12.6). Here is a sample compile transcript. Notice that when Polar.java is compiled, four classes are created: Polar.class, PolarEvent.class, PolarListener.class, and PolarPoint.class. Once the Polar classes have been compiled, compile the PolarTest applet and run it in the Applet Viewer (as shown in Figure 12.4).

```
C:\JavaDevHdbk\Ch03>javac Polar.java
C:\JavaDevHdbk\Ch03>javac PolarTest.java
C:\JavaDevHdbk\Ch03>appletviewer PolarTest.html
```

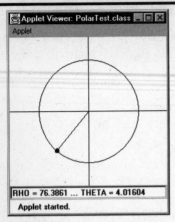

FIGURE 12.4: Polar test program

Aggregation: The *ThreeWay* Component

Sometimes absolute precision is required when specifying a number; other times a fair approximation is good enough. The `Polar` component we described in the previous section is inherently imprecise, because it receives freehand input and its resolution is limited to radius increments of one pixel.

The next example offers users a choice of three different levels of precision for entering an int: the complete accuracy of a textfield, the moderate accuracy of a scrollbar, and the vagueness of a set of radio buttons. The less accurate components will be easier to use. The resulting component will be called a `ThreeWay`.

The `ThreeWay` class goes a few steps beyond the traditional numeric scrollbar coupled with a nearby label or read-only textfield to reflect its value. We want three ways to write a number *and* three ways to read one. Again, the design issues listed earlier in the "Design Considerations" section provide a way in which to move through the process.

ThreeWay's Look-and-Feel Issues

Because it uses familiar elements, the decisions of how to display the component and how to specify its values are easier to make for the ThreeWay component than for the Polar component.

Displaying Values

First, we need to consider how the ThreeWay component should display its value. Of the three elements—scrollbar, textfield, and set of radio button checkboxes—the visually dominant one is the scrollbar. The textfield goes to the right of the scrollbar to conserve screen space. Above the scrollbar is a row of five radio checkboxes.

If the component's value is at or near its minimum, the leftmost radio button will be selected, and this button is to be positioned above the left end of the scrollbar, which, of course, is the slider position that represents the scrollbar's own minimum value. The rightmost radio button is positioned above the extreme right-hand position of the scrollbar, and it is selected if the component's value is at or near its maximum. The three radio buttons in the middle designate values that are approximately the half and quarter marks of the component's range. Simply stated, every subcomponent will do its best to reflect the ThreeWay component's current value. Figure 12.5 shows a ThreeWay component.

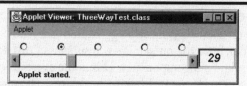

FIGURE 12.5: The ThreeWay component

NOTE

The screenshot shown in Figure 12.5 comes from a Windows 95 machine. Note that scrollbar and checkbox appearances vary greatly from platform to platform.

Part iii

SCROLLBAR CAUTIONS

On Motif platforms such as Sun workstations, the triangular arrow buttons of a scrollbar can grow without bounds. A very tall horizontal scrollbar will have very tall arrow buttons, and the buttons are equilateral triangles, so the width will be about 0.9 times the height. This encroaches on space that would otherwise be available to the slider. A tall scrollbar, no matter how wide it might be, could be useless because its slider's range is only a few pixels, and so it is important to restrict a horizontal scrollbar's vertical growth.

On Windows platforms, the scrollbar arrows are well-behaved. They lie inside rectangular boxes, and while the boxes grow taller, the arrows do not. A tall scrollbar has tall, narrow buttons that contain small triangles.

Specifying Values

With the manner in which the ThreeWay component will display its value established, it is now time to decide how users should interact with the new component. In this example, the answer is simple: Users should manipulate the scrollbar, the textfield, and the checkboxes in the expected way.

Choosing a Subclassing Strategy

Next, we need to decide on a subclassing strategy. In this case, the best approach has been obvious from the outset: We will subclass Container and populate it with standard subcomponents. This is the aggregation strategy, which allows users to interact with familiar devices. The programming task benefits from object reuse; the main task is to get the subcomponents to interact properly with each other, and there is more to this than may be immediately obvious. The components will be referenced by instance variables called textfield, scrollbar, and checkboxes[].

ThreeWay's Design Issues

Now we can move on to the remaining design issues, which guide us through the development of the custom component.

Modifying the Component's Appearance

Let's consider programmatically modifying the component's appearance. As with the `Polar` class example, the `setForeground()`, `setBackground()`, and `setFont()` methods can be made available to clients.

There is a bit of work to be done to support `setForeground()` and `setBackground()`. Because panels are likely to be used to lay out `ThreeWay`'s subcomponents, there will be a modest containment hierarchy, and any intermediate panels will need to have their foreground and background colors set. Consider `setForeground()`, which must be overridden. One could simply call `setForeground()` on everything, component by component, but this would introduce a maintenance risk. Somebody could change the containment structure, introduce a new subpanel, and forget to modify `setForeground()` accordingly. Hence, a recursive algorithm will be used to call `setForeground()` on all components within the `ThreeWay` panel:

```java
public void setForeground(Color color)
{
  super.setForeground(color);
  setForegndRecursive(this, color);
}

private void setForegndRecursive(Container parent, Color color)
{
  Component children[] = parent.getComponents();
  for (int i=0; i<children.length; i++)
  {
    children[i].setForeground(color);
    if (children[i] instanceof Container)
    {
      setForegndRecursive((Container)children[i], color);
    }
  }
}
```

We do much the same thing for the overridden `setBackground()` method. There is no need to go this far for `setFont()`, because the only child that actually uses this font is the textfield.

Limiting the Value

Next, we need to consider how to limit input values. The `ThreeWay` class is not so different from the `Scrollbar` class; certainly there should be an upper limit and a lower limit.

In the constructor for `Scrollbar`, the initial value appears before the minimum value, which comes before the maximum. This is the order maintained in `ThreeWay`'s constructor. The constructor's calling sequence is `ThreeWay(int value, int minValue, int maxValue)`.

Storing, Setting, and Retrieving Values

The next issues are storing, setting, and retrieving the component's value. Storing and retrieving the value are simple. There is a private instance variable called `value` and a public accessor called `getValue()`:

```
private int    value;
       . . .
public int getValue()
{
   return(value);
}
```

Setting the value requires updating the visible subcomponents. Setting the scrollbar and textfield values is easy. For the checkboxes, a float instance variable called `spreadPerRadio` is needed to help decide which checkbox is to be turned on. Because there are five checkboxes, the computation of `spreadPerRadio` (performed in the constructor) is:

```
spreadPerRadio = (float)(maxValue-minValue) / 4.0f;
```

The methods to revise the visible components are as follows:

```
private void reviseScrollbar()
{
   scrollbar.setValue(value);
}

private void reviseTextfield()
{
   textfield.setText((new Integer(value)).toString());
}

private void reviseRadios()
{
   float f = (value - minValue) / spreadPerRadio;
   int nth = Math.round(f);
   if (nth < 0)
   {
     nth = 0;
   }
   else if (nth > 4)
   {
     nth = 4;
```

```
        }

        cbgroup.setSelectedCheckbox(checkboxes[nth]);
    }
```

Handling Events

Next to be addressed is the question of event handling. When any of the subcomponents is activated, the `ThreeWay` component should fire some kind of event to its listeners. With the `Polar` component of the previous example, we needed to invent a new event type (along with a new listener interface) because the `Adjustment` event was not quite appropriate. In this case, however, the `Adjustment` event will do the job perfectly, so it will not be necessary to develop a custom event type.

However, the `Container` class, from which `ThreeWay` inherits, does not provide support for adding, removing, or notifying `Adjustment` listeners. We need to write this support explicitly, much as we added support for adding, removing, or notifying `Polar` listeners to the `Polar` component.

The `ThreeWay` class's event support code is shown here. It is nearly identical to the event support for the `Polar` class; the only difference is that `Adjustment` events are sent rather than `Polar` events.

```
    public void addAdjustmentListener(AdjustmentListener listener)
    {
        if (!listeners.contains(listener))
            listeners.addElement(listener);
    }


    public void removeAdjustmentListener(
                AdjustmentListener listener)
    {
        listeners.removeElement(listener);
    }


    private void notifyListeners()
    {
        AdjustmentListener listener;

        AdjustmentEvent event = new AdjustmentEvent(this,
            AWTEvent.RESERVED_ID_MAX+1,
            AdjustmentEvent.ADJUSTMENT_VALUE_CHANGED,
            value);
```

```
Vector copyOfListeners = (Vector)(listeners.clone());
Enumeration enum = copyOfListeners.elements();
while (enum.hasMoreElements())
{
    listener = (AdjustmentListener)enum.nextElement();
    listener.adjustmentValueChanged(event);
}
}
```

When input occurs in any of the components, the other components need to be updated to reflect the new value. The code that supports this behavior follows. The only unusual part of the code is the Action-Performed() method, which is called when the user presses the Enter key in the textfield. Since nonnumerical input is meaningless, the code makes sure that the input is valid and restores the old value if the input does not represent a positive integer.

```
private void reviseScrollbar()
{
    bar.setValue(value);
}


private void reviseTextfield()
{
    textfield.setText((new Integer(value)).toString());
}


private void reviseRadios()
{
    float f = (value - minValue) / spreadPerRadio;
    int nth = Math.round(f);
    if (nth < 0)
    {
        nth = 0;
    }
    else if (nth > 4)
    {
        nth = 4;
    }

    cbgroup.setSelectedCheckbox(checkboxes[nth]);
}

//
```

```
// Called when the scrollbar is moved.
//
public synchronized void adjustmentValueChanged(
                        (AdjustmentEvent e)
{
  value = e.getValue();
  reviseRadios();
  reviseTextfield();
  notifyListeners();
}


//
// Called when one of the checkboxes is clicked.
//
public synchronized void itemStateChanged(ItemEvent e)
{
  int   newValue = 0;

  // Only react to selected checkbox.
  if (e.getStateChange() != ItemEvent.SELECTED)
      return;

  // Determine new value.
  for (int i=0; i<checkboxes.length; i++)
  {
    if (e.getSource() == checkboxes[i])
        break;
    newValue += spreadPerRadio;
  }

  value = newValue;
  reviseTextfield();
  reviseScrollbar();
  notifyListeners();
}


//
// Called when the user hits ENTER in the textfield.
//
public synchronized void actionPerformed(ActionEvent e)
{
  // Only accept valid numeric input.
  int   newValue = 0;
  try
```

Part iii

```
{
  newValue = Integer.parseInt(textfield.getText());
}
catch (NumberFormatException x)
{
  textfield.setText("" + value);
  return;
}

// Normalize to within bounds.
newValue = Math.min(newValue, maxValue);
newValue = Math.max(newValue, minValue);

value = newValue;
reviseScrollbar();
reviseRadios();
reviseTextfield();
notifyListeners();
}
```

Our final considerations are how the ThreeWay component behaves when it is stressed by multithreading or by resizing.

Behaving in a Multithreading Environment

The ThreeWay component, like the Polar component, clones its vector of listeners and notifies via the clone, rather than via the original. Aside from the listeners vector, there is no other data that is subject to modification (and hence corruption) from external objects, so multithreading will not present any problems.

Behaving during Resizing

What should be done when the component resizes? The Polar class had to adjust its scale factor. Here, there is no comparable internal state to revise. The scrollbar has an internal scale factor, but the Scrollbar class takes care of it automatically. Our only responsibility is to ensure that the layout looks reasonable no matter how the ThreeWay component is resized. This means we do not need to override setSize(), but we must build a robust containment hierarchy in our constructor.

As mentioned at the beginning of this section, scrollbars should be constrained in the vertical direction. On the other hand, when the `ThreeWay` component grows horizontally, all the new pixels should be given to the scrollbar; the textfield is always wide enough, and there is no benefit in making it any wider. This suggests a border layout manager, with the scrollbar occupying the South region. On the other hand, we need to align a row of checkboxes above the scrollbar, and this suggests a grid layout with two rows of one column. As usual, there are probably several feasible solutions. Here, the checkboxes are put in a panel (called `cboxPanel`), and the `cboxPanel` is placed above the scrollbar in a 2×1 grid. (See Chapter 4 for more information about layout managers and how they constrain components.)

The `cboxPanel` uses a grid bag layout manager to keep the checkboxes centered in the bottoms of their cells. So far, we have the structure shown in Figure 12.6, which introduces a new informal notation. Each container is labeled reasonably close to its upper-left corner. The label's format is *name @ position u layout*, where:

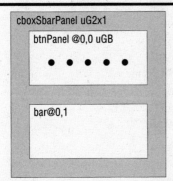

FIGURE 12.6: Containment of `cboxSbarPanel`

- ▶ *name* is the container instance variable handle
- ▶ *position* is its position within its own container (for example, N for North in a border or 2,1 for column 2, row 1 in a grid)
- ▶ *u* stands for uses

▶ *layout* is the type of layout manager used by the container (B for border, G for grid, F for flow, GB for grid bag, or C for card)

Noncontainer components are labeled near the center, if at all.

The `cboxSbarPanel` will ensure that the checkboxes stay above the scrollbar. The checkboxes will be put at South of some other panel, whose only job is to constrain `cboxSbarPanel` from vertical growth. This new panel is called `restrictorPanel` and it contains only the single child.

The `restrictorPanel` is put at Center of the `ThreeWay` so that it can grow in both directions. Horizontal growth will be passed to `cboxSbar-Panel`. In the case of vertical growth, `restrictorPanel` will grow taller, but `btnSbarPanel` will not; `btnSbarPanel` will stick to the bottom of `restrictorPanel`. This produces the structure shown in Figure 12.7.

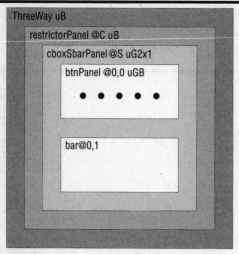

FIGURE 12.7:   Containment: more details

The textfield should go at East, to restrict its horizontal. But it would also be convenient if it could go at South, so that it is horizontally aligned with the scrollbar. An extra panel, called `tfPanel`, is needed. If `tfPanel` had to contain several components, a grid bag layout manager might be in order; however, in this simple case, a border with the textfield inside `tfPanel` at South is sufficient. This completes our design of the `ThreeWay` component's containment hierarchy, which is shown in Figure 12.8.

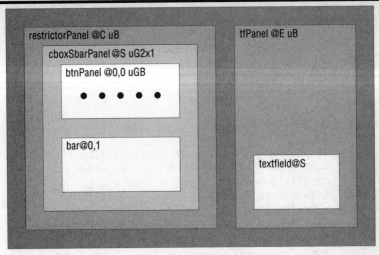

FIGURE 12.8: Complete containment of ThreeWay

The *ThreeWay* Component and Test Applet

Here is the full listing of ThreeWay example ThreeWay.java:

LIST 12.7: ThreeWay.java

```
import java.awt.*;
import java.awt.event.*;
import java.util.*;


public class ThreeWay
  extends Container
  implements ActionListener, AdjustmentListener,
             ItemListener, Adjustable
{
  private Vector          listeners = new Vector();
  private Scrollbar       bar;
  private TextField       textfield;
  private CheckboxGroup   cbgroup;
  private Checkbox        checkboxes[];
  private int             minValue;
  private int             maxValue;
  private int             value;
  private float           spreadPerRadio;
```

```
public ThreeWay(int value, int minValue, int maxValue)
{
    this.minValue = minValue;
    this.maxValue = maxValue;
    this.value = value;

    setLayout(new BorderLayout());

    // Build and add textfield.
    Panel tfPanel = new Panel();
    tfPanel.setLayout(new BorderLayout());
    textfield = new TextField(" " + value);
    textfield.addActionListener(this);
    tfPanel.add(textfield, BorderLayout.SOUTH);
    add(tfPanel, BorderLayout.EAST);

    // Build and add checkboxes.
    Panel cboxPanel = new Panel();
    GridBagLayout gbl = new GridBagLayout();
    cboxPanel.setLayout(gbl);
    GridBagConstraints gbc = new GridBagConstraints();
    gbc.gridwidth = gbc.gridheight = 1;
    gbc.weightx = gbc.weighty = 1;
    gbc.gridy = 0;
    gbc.fill = GridBagConstraints.NONE;
    gbc.anchor = GridBagConstraints.SOUTH;
    checkboxes = new Checkbox[5];
    cbgroup = new CheckboxGroup();
    for (int i=0; i<5; i++)
    {
        checkboxes[i] = new Checkbox("", (i==0), cbgroup);
        checkboxes[i].addItemListener(this);
        gbc.gridx = i;
        if (i > 2)
            gbc.anchor = GridBagConstraints.SOUTHEAST;
        gbl.setConstraints(checkboxes[i], gbc);
        cboxPanel.add(checkboxes[i]);
    }
    spreadPerRadio = (float)(maxValue-minValue) / 4.0f;

    // Build and add scrollbar.
    Panel cboxSbarPanel = new Panel();
    cboxSbarPanel.setLayout(new GridLayout(2, 1));
    cboxSbarPanel.add(cboxPanel);
    bar = new Scrollbar(Scrollbar.HORIZONTAL, value, 0,
                        minValue, maxValue);
```

```
        bar.addAdjustmentListener(this);
        cboxSbarPanel.add(bar);
        Panel restrictorPanel = new Panel();
        restrictorPanel.setLayout(new BorderLayout());
        restrictorPanel.add(cboxSbarPanel, BorderLayout.SOUTH);
        add(restrictorPanel, BorderLayout.CENTER);

        // Make all subordinate components reflect current value.
        reviseScrollbar();
        reviseTextfield();
        reviseRadios();
    }


public int getValue()
   {
      return(value);
   }


   public synchronized void setValue(int newValue)
   {
     value = newValue;
     reviseScrollbar();
     reviseTextfield();
     reviseRadios();
     notifyListeners();
   }


   public void addAdjustmentListener(
             AdjustmentListener listener)
   {
     if (!listeners.contains(listener))
         listeners.addElement(listener);
   }


   public void removeAdjustmentListener(
             AdjustmentListener listener)
   {
     listeners.removeElement(listener);
   }


   private void notifyListeners()
   {
```

```
        AdjustmentListener listener;

        AdjustmentEvent event = new AdjustmentEvent(this,
                                   0, 0, value);
        Vector copyOfListeners = (Vector)(listeners.clone());
        Enumeration enum = copyOfListeners.elements();
        while (enum.hasMoreElements())
        {
          listener = (AdjustmentListener)enum.nextElement();
          listener.adjustmentValueChanged(event);
        }
      }


    private void reviseScrollbar()
    {
      bar.setValue(value);
    }


    private void reviseTextfield()
    {
      textfield.setText((new Integer(value)).toString());
    }


    private void reviseRadios()
    {
      float f = (value - minValue) / spreadPerRadio;
      int nth = Math.round(f);
      if (nth < 0)
      {
        nth = 0;
      }
      else if (nth > 4)
      {
        nth = 4;
      }

      cbgroup.setSelectedCheckbox(checkboxes[nth]);
    }


  //
  // Called when the scrollbar is moved.
  //
```

```
public synchronized void adjustmentValueChanged(
                         AdjustmentEvent e)
{
  value = e.getValue();
  reviseRadios();
  reviseTextfield();
  notifyListeners();
}


//
// Called when one of the checkboxes is clicked.
//
public synchronized void itemStateChanged(ItemEvent e)
{
  // Only react to selected checkbox.
  if (e.getStateChange() != ItemEvent.SELECTED)
      return;

  // Determine new value.
  int newValue = minValue;
  for (int i=0; i<checkboxes.length; i++)
  {
    if (e.getSource() == checkboxes[i])
        break;
    newValue += spreadPerRadio;
  }

  value = newValue;
  reviseTextfield();
  reviseScrollbar();
  notifyListeners();
}


//
// Called when the user hits ENTER in the textfield.
//
public synchronized void actionPerformed(ActionEvent e)
{
  // Only accept valid numeric input.
  int   newValue = 0;
  try
  {
    newValue = Integer.parseInt(textfield.getText());
  }
  catch (NumberFormatException x)
```

Part iii

```
    {
      textfield.setText("" + value);
      return;
    }

    // Normalize to within bounds.
    newValue = Math.min(newValue, maxValue);
    newValue = Math.max(newValue, minValue);

    value = newValue;
    reviseScrollbar();
    reviseRadios();
    notifyListeners();
  }


  /*
   * Set background color of everything by setting it on this
   * container and recursively on all children.
   */
  public void setBackground(Color color)
  {
    super.setBackground(color);
    setBackgndRecursive(this, color);
  }


  private void setBackgndRecursive(Container parent,
                                   Color color)
  {
    Component children[] = parent.getComponents();
    for (int i=0; i<children.length; i++)
    {
      children[i].setBackground(color);
      if (children[i] instanceof Container)
      {
        setBackgndRecursive((Container)children[i], color);
      }
    }
  }


  /*
   * Set foreground color of everything by setting it on this
   * container and recursively on all children.
   */
```

```
public void setForeground(Color color)
{
  super.setForeground(color);
  setForegndRecursive(this, color);
}


private void setForegndRecursive(Container parent,
                                 Color color)
{
  Component children[] = parent.getComponents();
  for (int i=0; i<children.length; i++)
  {
    children[i].setForeground(color);
    if (children[i] instanceof Container)
    {
      setForegndRecursive((Container)children[i], color);
    }
  }
}


public void setFont(Font font)
{
  textfield.setFont(font);
}

//
// Methods of interface Adjustable.
//
public int getBlockIncrement()
          { return (int)spreadPerRadio;   }
public int getMaximum()
          { return maxValue;              }
public int getMinimum()
          { return minValue;              }
public int getOrientation()
          { return Scrollbar.HORIZONTAL;  }
public int getUnitIncrement()
          { return bar.getUnitIncrement(); }
public int getVisibleAmount()
          { return bar.getVisibleAmount(); }
public void setBlockIncrement(int b) { }
public void setMaximum(int m)        { }
public void setMinimum(int m)        { }
public void setUnitIncrement(int m)  { }
```

```
    public void setVisibleAmount(int v)
                { bar.setVisibleAmount(v); }
}
```

Because all the complexity has been encapsulated inside `ThreeWay`, the class is very easy to use. The following applet code updates its textfield with the value of its `ThreeWay` component whenever the user clicks the Show button. The applet is shown in Figure 12.9.

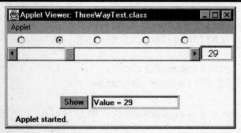

FIGURE 12.9: A simple applet that uses the `ThreeWay` component

LIST 12.8: *ThreeWayTest.java*

```java
import java.awt.*;
import java.awt.event.*;
import java.applet.Applet;


public class ThreeWayTest extends Applet
                implements ActionListener
{
  ThreeWay    threeway;
  Button      button;
  TextField   textfield;

  public void init()
  {
    setLayout(new BorderLayout());
    threeway = new ThreeWay(23, 0, 100);
    threeway.setFont(new Font("Helvetica", Font.ITALIC, 14));
    add(threeway, BorderLayout.NORTH);
    Panel panel = new Panel();
    button = new Button("Show");
    button.addActionListener(this);
    panel.add(button);
    textfield = new TextField("Value = 23", 15);
    panel.add(textfield);
```

```
        add(panel, BorderLayout.SOUTH);
    }


    public void actionPerformed(ActionEvent e)
    {
        textfield.setText("Value = " + threeway.getValue());
    }
}
```

LIST 12.9: ThreeWayTest.html

```
<HTML>
<HEAD>
    <TITLE>Three Way Test Applet </TITLE>
</HEAD>
<BODY>
    <APPLET code=ThreeWayTest.class width=500 height=500>
    </APPLET>
</BODY>
</HTML>
```

Compile an output listing:

```
C:\JavaDevHdbk\Ch03>javac ThreeWay.java
C:\JavaDevHdbk\Ch03>javac ThreeWayTest.java
C:\JavaDevHdbk\Ch03>appletviewer ThreeWayTest.html
```

SUBCLASSING A STANDARD COMPONENT: VALIDATING TEXTFIELDS

Many programs require text validation. For example, the information typed into a textfield may need to be numeric, may be required to fall within a certain range, or may need to match a certain pattern. Because the standard AWT TextField class has no facilities for validation, you must create a custom component to incorporate this capability. For this example, we'll develop two alternatives: a simple IntTextField component for validating numeric input and a more sophisticated ValidatingTextField component that can check for specific input formats.

Part iii

IntTextField's Look-and-Feel Issues

Obviously, a validating textfield should display its value in the same way that any textfield displays its value, and users should enter new values by typing. Our subclassing strategy is also obvious: A single component, TextField, requires enhancement. To begin, we will create a TextField subclass called IntTextField, which accepts only nonnegative integer input.

IntTextField's Design Issues

As with our previous examples, we will work through the list of design decisions to develop the validating textfield component.

Modifying the Component's Appearance

Programmatically modifying an IntTextField component's appearance is straightforward. Because IntTextField is a simple subclass, the setForeground(), setBackground(), and setFont() methods are inherited from TextField and will function as required without any additional effort.

Limiting the Value

The next issue is how to restrict values. For now, the class will insist on nonnegative integer values, and that will be the only restriction. When the user presses the Enter key, the input is checked to see if it represents a nonnegative integer; if it does not, the component is restored to its previous value.

Storing, Setting, and Retrieving Values

The new component will need to store its last valid value, so it will be able to restore itself if the user enters invalid input. The last valid value will be stored as an int, in an instance variable called intValue.

You may want to set the component's value from an int or from a string. To support setting from an int, the class has a setIntValue() method that takes an int argument and takes no action if the argument is negative. For setting from a string, the setText() method is overridden; again, the method has no effect if the argument is not valid. Both methods update the component's text as well as the `intValue` instance variable. These methods are listed here:

```
public void setText(String s)
{
  // Check for valid nonnegative int.
  int   newintval = 0;
  try
  {
    newintval = Integer.parseInt(s);
  }
  catch (NumberFormatException nfex)
  {
    return;
  }
  if (newintval < 0)
  {
    return;
  }

  // Valid input, update value and textfield.
  intValue = newintval;
  super.setText("" + newintval);
}


public void setIntValue(int newintval)
{
  if (newintval < 0)
  {
    return;
  }

  intValue = newintval;
  super.setText("" + newintval);
}
```

The value can be retrieved as a string by calling the inherited `getText()` method. However, that string most likely would be immediately converted to an int; therefore, an additional accessor called `getIntValue()` is provided:

```
public int getIntValue()
{
  return intValue;
}
```

Part III

Handling Events

Now consider the type of event that the IntTextField component should send. Programmers expect textfields to send Action events when the user presses Enter, so it is reasonable to expect the IntTextField component to do the same.

The new component will need to detect action events sent by itself and validate its contents. If the contents are valid, all Action listeners must be notified. If the contents are not valid, the value must be restored. This is a perfect opportunity to exploit the explicit event-enabling mechanism. The IntTextField class can enable Action events and request notification of listeners only if the input is valid. Recall that the way to request notification of listeners is simply to call the inherited version of the event-handler method.

The first step is to enable detection of Action events at construction time. Our class will provide two constructors, one that specifies just an initial int value and one that specifies both an initial int value and a width:

```
public IntTextField(int val)
{
  super((new Integer(val<0 ? 0 : val)).toString());
  intValue = val;
  enableEvents(AWTEvent.KEY_EVENT_MASK);
}

public IntTextField(int val, int width)
{
  super((new Integer(val<0 ? 0 : val)).toString(), width);
  intValue = val;
  enableEvents(AWTEvent.ACTION_EVENT_MASK);
}
```

Both constructors set the initial value to zero if the requested value is negative. It is difficult to check for this condition while still leaving the first line for the superclass constructor call, but the ternary operator comes to the rescue.

Now that explicit detection of Action events has been enabled, it is time to write a processActionEvent() method:

```
public void processActionEvent(ActionEvent e)
    int       newintval = 0;
    boolean   trouble = false;
```

```
                try
                {
                  newintval = Integer.parseInt(getText());
                  if (newintval < 0)
                  {
                    trouble = true;
                  }
                }
                catch (NumberFormatException nfex)
                {
                  trouble = true;
                }

                // Invalid char => undo.
                if (trouble)
                {
                  setText("" + intValue);
                }

                // All is well.
                else
                {
                  intValue = newintval;
                  super.processActionEvent(e);
                }
            }
```

Behaving under Stress

The issues of the component's behavior during multithreading and resizing are trivial for this example. The benefit of inheriting so much behavior from an industrial-strength superclass is that these matters have already been taken care of. No precautions need to be taken.

The *IntTextField* Component

The following is the complete listing for IntTextField example IntTextField.java:

LIST 12.10: *IntTextField.java*

```
import java.awt.*;
import java.awt.event.*;
```

```java
public class IntTextField extends TextField
{
  private int    intValue;


  public IntTextField(int val)
  {
    super((new Integer(val<0 ? 0 : val)).toString());
    intValue = val;
    enableEvents(AWTEvent.KEY_EVENT_MASK);
  }


  public IntTextField(int val, int width)
  {
    super((new Integer(val<0 ? 0 : val)).toString(), width);
    intValue = val;
    enableEvents(AWTEvent.ACTION_EVENT_MASK);
  }


  public synchronized void setText(String s)
  {
    // Check for valid nonnegative int.
    int    newintval = 0;
    try
    {
      newintval = Integer.parseInt(s);
    }
    catch (NumberFormatException nfex)
    {
      return;
    }
    if (newintval < 0)
    {
      return;
    }

    // Valid input, update value and textfield.
    intValue = newintval;
    super.setText("" + newintval);
  }

  public synchronized void setIntValue(int newintval)
  {
    if (newintval < 0)
    {
```

```
      return;
    }

    intValue = newintval;
    super.setText("" + newintval);
  }


  public int getIntValue()
  {
    return intValue;
  }


  public void processActionEvent(ActionEvent e)
  {
    int      newintval = 0;
    boolean  trouble = false;

    try
    {
      newintval = Integer.parseInt(getText());
      if (newintval < 0)
      {
        trouble = true;
      }
    }
    catch (NumberFormatException nfex)
    {
      trouble = true;
    }

    // Invalid char => undo.
    if (trouble)
    {
      setText("" + intValue);
    }

    // All is well.
    else
    {
      intValue = newintval;
      super.processActionEvent(e);
    }
  }
}
```

External Validation:
The *ValidatingTextField* Component

The IntTextField subclass accepts only nonnegative integer input. Our next example is a variation that can check for other input formats. For the ValidatingTextField component, validation is provided by an external object. An arbitrary validator is passed into the constructor and called upon to perform validation when the user presses the Enter key.

We begin by defining an interface called Validator, containing a single method:

LIST 12.11: Validator.java

```
public interface Validator
{
  public boolean  validate(String s);
}
```

The ValidatingTextField class is similar to the IntTextField class, with the following differences:

▶ The new class has a private instance variable, of type Validator, which is supplied via the constructor; when an Action event is detected, this object is consulted.

▶ No int value is maintained, since the class may not represent an int. Instead, the class has a string variable called lastValid-TextValue, which is only used for restoring a previous value when invalid input is detected.

The source for the ValidatingTextField class is listed in List 12.12.

LIST 12.12: ValidatingTextField.java

```
import java.awt.*;
import java.awt.event.*;

public class ValidatingTextField extends TextField
{
  private Validator  validator;
  private String     lastValidTextValue;
```

```
public ValidatingTextField(String value,
                           int width,
                           Validator validator)
{
  super(value, width);
  lastValidTextValue = value;
  this.validator = validator;
  if (!validator.validate(value))
  {
    lastValidTextValue = "";
    setText(lastValidTextValue);
  }
  enableEvents(AWTEvent.ACTION_EVENT_MASK);
}


public void processActionEvent(ActionEvent e)
{
  String textValue = getText();
  if (!validator.validate(textValue))
  {
    // Invalid input. Reset text, do not notify listeners.
    setText(lastValidTextValue);
    return;
  }

  // Valid input. Notify action listeners.
  lastValidTextValue = textValue;
  super.processActionEvent(e);
}
}
```

Validating Textfields: Test Applet and Validator Classes

Figure 12.10 shows an applet that has three custom components. At the top is an instance of IntTextField. The other two components are instances of ValidatingTextField. The middle textfield uses a validator that checks for a U.S. social security number format (as in 123-45-6789); the bottom textfield uses a validator that checks for a float value.

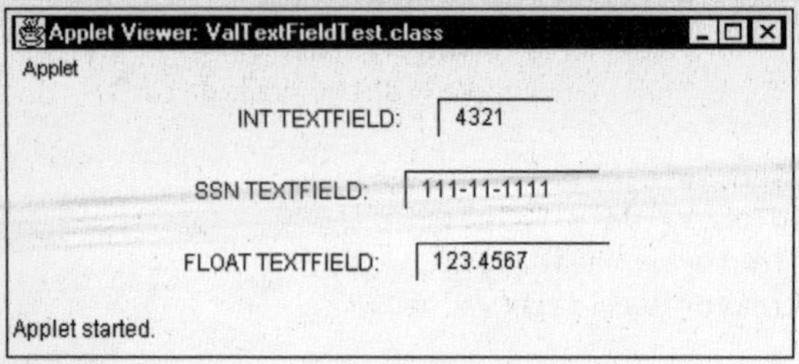

FIGURE 12.10: Three subclasses of TextField

The code that produced Figure 12.10 is listed in List 12.13 along with the two validator classes, SSNValidator.java (List 12.14) and Float-Validator.java (List 12.15). You will also need IntTextField.java (List 12.10), Validator.java (List 12.11), ValidatingTextField .java (List 12.12), and ValTextFieldTest.html (List 12.16).

LIST 12.13: ValTextFieldTest.java

```java
import java.awt.*;
import java.applet.Applet;


public class ValTextFieldTest extends Applet
{

  public void init()
  {
    setSize(420, 120);
    setLayout(new GridLayout(3, 1));

    Panel p = new Panel();
    p.add(new Label("INT TEXTFIELD:"));
    p.add(new IntTextField(4321, 6));
    add(p);

    p = new Panel();
    p.add(new Label("SSN TEXTFIELD:"));
    Validator val = new SSNValidator();
    p.add(new ValidatingTextField("111-11-1111", 12, val));
```

```
        add(p);

        p = new Panel();
        p.add(new Label("FLOAT TEXTFIELD:"));
        val = new FloatValidator();
        p.add(new ValidatingTextField("123.4567", 12, val));
        add(p);
    }
}
```

LIST 12.14: SSNValidator.java

```java
/*
 * A validator that checks if a string is a valid United States
 * social security number. The format is three digits, a hyphen,
 * two digits, another hyphen, and four more digits, e.g.
 * 123-45-6789.
 */

public class SSNValidator implements Validator
{
    public boolean validate(String s)
    {
        char    ch;

        if (s.length() != 11)                    // Check string length
            return false;

        for (int i=0; i<11; i++)
        {
            ch = s.charAt(i);
            if (i == 3 || i == 6)                // Hyphen expected
            {
                if (ch != '-')
                {
                    return(false);               // Not a hyphen
                }
            }
```

```
            else if (!Character.isDigit(ch))  // Digit expected
            {
              return(false);                  // Not a digit
            }
        }


        return true;                          // Valid
    }
}
```

LIST 12.15:   FloatValidator.java

```
/*
 * A validator that checks if a string is a valid float.
 */

public class FloatValidator implements Validator
{
  public boolean validate(String s)
  {
    try
    {
      Float.valueOf(s);
    }
    catch (NumberFormatException x)
    {
      return false;  // Invalid
    }

    return true;     // Valid
  }
}
```

LIST 12.16:   ValTextFieldTest.html

```
<HTML>
<HEAD>
  <TITLE>Validating Text Field Test Applet </TITLE>
</HEAD>
<BODY>
  <APPLET code=ValTextFieldTest.class width=500 height=500>
  </APPLET>
</BODY>
</HTML>
```

Compile an output listing:

```
C:\JavaDevHdbk\Ch03>javac IntTextField.java.java
C:\JavaDevHdbk\Ch03>javac ValidatingTextField.java
C:\JavaDevHdbk\Ch03>javac ValTextFieldTest.java
C:\JavaDevHdbk\Ch03>appletviewer ValTextFieldTest.html
```

WHAT'S NEXT?

In the next chapter, we'll explore the Java Swing components, including frames and menus, labels and buttons, password fields, and toolbars.

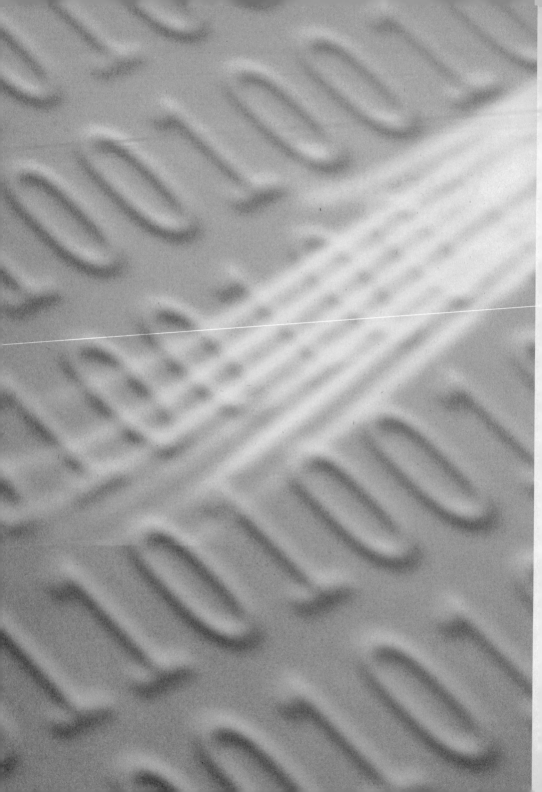

Chapter 13

THE JFC SWING COMPONENTS

The functionality of the Java Foundation Classes (JFC) includes an event propagation model, drag-and-drop support, handicapped accessibility, a wide variety of obscure specialty capabilities, and a package of components known as the Swing components or Swing Set. Even the Swing Set by itself is enormous. The `java.awt.swing` package contains eight subordinate packages, more than 20 interfaces, and more than 75 classes. (Obviously, we won't be examining all the details here, which would require several hundred pages!)

The most important thing to remember about the Swing components is that they are just components. They're complicated, they're richly featured, and there are a lot of them, but they're just components. As a Java programmer, you already have plenty of experience using components.

Adapted from *Java 2 Developer's Handbook*
by Philip Heller and Simon Roberts
ISBN 0-7821-2179-9   1248 pages $59.99

This chapter introduces the following common Swing components:

JFrame	JToggleButton	JSlider
JTabbedPane	JCheckBox	JPasswordField
JTextField	JRadioButton	JToolbar
JButton	JComboBox	JTable
Jlabel		

A Sampler of Swing Components

As an introduction to programming with Swing components, we will examine a single, large program. The SwingDemo application displays several types of components, organized into eight tabbed panels. The panels appear in a frame, as shown in Figure 13.1.

The first thing to observe about the SwingDemo window is that it appears to show a perfectly ordinary frame, which in turn appears to contain a perfectly ordinary text field. In fact, the frame is an instance of the JFrame class, and the text field is an instance of the JTextField class. All the familiar AWT components have corresponding JFC classes. In general, there are four differences between the AWT classes and the JFC classes:

▶ The JFC classes have names that begin with the letter *J*.

▶ The JFC classes typically provide more functionality than the corresponding AWT classes.

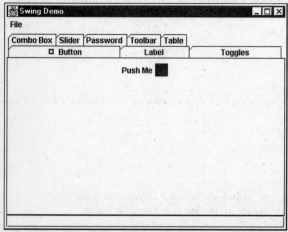

FIGURE 13.1: The SwingDemo program

▶ The JFC classes reside in the `java.awt.swing` package.

▶ The JFC classes bypass the AWT peer mechanism.

For example, the JFC version of the `java.awt.Button` class is the `java.awt.swing.JButton` class. This class has no peer; a `JButton` interacts directly with the mouse and screen and has the same appearance and behavior on all platforms.

JFC Textfields, Frames, and Menus

The constructor for the `SwingDemo` program adds a `JTextField` to the frame. The main method and constructor are as follows:

```
public static void main(String[] args)
{
  SwingDemo that = new SwingDemo();
  that.setVisible(true);
}

public SwingDemo()
{
  super("Swing Demo");
  setSize(450, 350);

  addWindowListener(new WindowAdapter() {
    public void windowClosing(WindowEvent e)
    {
      System.exit(0);
    }
  });

  textfield = new JTextField();
  getContentPane().add(textfield, BorderLayout.SOUTH);

  addMenu();
  addTabbedPane();
}
```

Note that the `JFrame` class has one more level of containment than the AWT `Frame` class; a `JFrame` contains a subordinate container called a *content pane*, which can be obtained by calling `getContentPane()` on the `JFrame`. Child components should always be added to the content pane, rather than to the `JFrame` itself.

After inserting the `JTextField`, the constructor calls two methods that add a menu and a tabbed pane. Both methods appear in `SwingDemo`, just below the constructor.

The `addMenu()` method inserts a File menu with two choices:

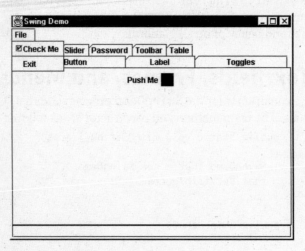

The code for the `addMenu()` method is:

```
private void addMenu()
{
  JMenuBar mbar = new JMenuBar();
  JMenu menu = new JMenu("File");
  menu.add(new JCheckBoxMenuItem("Check Me"));
  menu.addSeparator();
  JMenuItem item = new JMenuItem("Exit");
  item.addActionListener(new ActionListener() {
    public void actionPerformed(ActionEvent e)
    {
      System.exit(0);
    }
  });
  menu.add(item);
  mbar.add(menu);
  setJMenuBar(mbar);
}
```

This code is easy to understand, even if you don't know anything about JFC components. If you take away all the *J*s in the class names, you have classic AWT code. Note that the `JMenuItem` takes an `ActionListener`, just like a `MenuItem`. The `JCheckBoxMenuItem` could have been given an `ItemListener`, just like a `CheckBoxMenuItem`.

JFC Tabbed Panes

The SwingDemo constructor calls a method named addTabbedPane().
This method builds and installs a JTabbedPane. The code for add-
TabbedPane() appears below.

```
private void addTabbedPane()
{
    JTabbedPane tabbedPane = new JTabbedPane();

    // addTab(Title, Icon, Component, Tooltip)
    tabbedPane.addTab("Button",
            new TabIcon(),
            new ButtonPanel(textfield),
            "Click here for Button demo");

    tabbedPane.addTab("Label",
            null,
            new LabelPanel(),
            "Click here for Label demo");

    tabbedPane.addTab("Toggles",
            null,
            new TogglePanel(textfield),
            "Click here for Toggle demo");

    tabbedPane.addTab("Combo Box",
            null,
            new ComboPanel(textfield),
            "Click here for Combo Box demo");

    tabbedPane.addTab("Slider",
            null,
            new SliderPanel(textfield),
            "Click here for Slider demo");

    tabbedPane.addTab("Password",
            null,
            new PasswordPanel(textfield),
            "Click here for Password Field demo");

    tabbedPane.addTab("Toolbar",
            null,
            new ToolbarPanel(textfield),
            "Click here for Toolbar demo");
```

```
tabbedPane.addTab("Table",
        null,
        new TablePanel(),
        "Click here for Table demo");

    getContentPane().add(tabbedPane, BorderLayout.CENTER);
}
```

Adding Tabs

A JTabbedPane is a kind of container that presents its contents in a tabbed-pane format. The addTab() method is overloaded. The version used here takes four arguments:

- ▶ A string that appears as the label of the tab being added
- ▶ An optional icon (null specifies that no icon should appear)
- ▶ The component that appears when the tab is selected
- ▶ A string that appears as a rollover tooltip

Adding an Icon to a Tab

In the code for the tabbed pane, only the first call to addTab() specifies an icon. The icon can be seen on the Button tab (see Figure 13.1). An icon is an instance of a class that implements the Icon interface, which has three methods:

public int getIconWidth()   Returns the width of the icon, in pixels.

public int getIconHeight()   Returns the height of the icon, in pixels.

public void paintIcon(Component c, Graphics g, int x, int y)   Paints the icon within component c, starting at (x, y), using graphics contact g.

The icon that appears on the Button tab is an instance of TabIcon, which is an inner class within the SwingDemo class:

```
class TabIcon implements Icon
{
  public int getIconWidth()  { return 16; }
  public int getIconHeight() { return 16; }
```

```
        public void paintIcon(Component c, Graphics g,
                               int x, int y)
        {
          g.setColor(Color.black);
          g.fillRect(x+4, y+4,
                     getIconWidth()-8, getIconHeight()-8);
          g.setColor(Color.cyan);
          g.fillRect(x+6, y+6,
                     getIconWidth()-12, getIconHeight()-12);
        }
      }
```

The *SwingDemo* Class

The source code for the SwingDemo class follows. The complete program appears at the end of this chapter.

LIST 13.1: *SwingDemo.java*

```
import javax.swing.*;
import java.awt.*;
import java.awt.event.*;

public class SwingDemo extends JFrame
{
  private JTextField   textfield;
  private JTabbedPane  tabbedPane;


  public static void main(String[] args)
  {
    SwingDemo that = new SwingDemo();
    that.setVisible(true);
  }

  public SwingDemo()
  {
    super("Swing Demo");
    setSize(450, 350);

    addWindowListener(new WindowAdapter() {
      public void windowClosing(WindowEvent e)
      {
        System.exit(0);
      }
    });
```

```java
        textfield = new JTextField();
        getContentPane().add(textfield, BorderLayout.SOUTH);

        // Tabbed pane contains panels for the
        // various Jcomponents.
        tabbedPane = new JTabbedPane();
        populateTabbedPane();
        getContentPane().add(tabbedPane, BorderLayout.CENTER);
        addMenu();
    }


    private void addMenu()
    {
      JMenuBar mbar = new JMenuBar();
      JMenu menu = new JMenu("File");
      menu.add(new JCheckBoxMenuItem("Check Me"));
      menu.addSeparator();
      JMenuItem item = new JMenuItem("Exit");
      item.addActionListener(new ActionListener() {
        public void actionPerformed(ActionEvent e)
        {
          System.exit(0);
        }
      });
      menu.add(item);
      mbar.add(menu);
      setJMenuBar(mbar);
    }


    private void populateTabbedPane()
    {


    // addTab(Title, Icon, Component, help)
    tabbedPane.addTab("Button",
            new TabIcon(),
            new ButtonPanel(textfield),
            "Click here for Button demo");

    tabbedPane.addTab("Label",
            null,
            new LabelPanel(),
```

```
                    "Click here for Label demo");

        tabbedPane.addTab("Toggles",
                null,
                new TogglePanel(textfield),
                "Click here for Toggle demo");

        tabbedPane.addTab("Combo Box",
                null,
                new ComboPanel(textfield),
                "Click here for Combo Box demo");

        tabbedPane.addTab("Slider",
                null,
                new SliderPanel(textfield),
                "Click here for Slider demo");

        tabbedPane.addTab("Password",
                null,
                new PasswordPanel(textfield),
                "Click here for Password Field demo");

        tabbedPane.addTab("Toolbar",
                null,
                new ToolbarPanel(textfield),
                "Click here for Toolbar demo");

        tabbedPane.addTab("Table",
                null,
                new TablePanel(),
                "Click here for Table demo");


    }


class TabIcon implements Icon
{
  public int getIconWidth() { return 16; }
  public int getIconHeight() { return 16; }

  public void paintIcon(Component c, Graphics g,
                        int x, int y)
  {
  g.setColor(Color.black);
  g.fillRect(x+4, y+4,
```

```
                              getIconWidth()-8, getIconHeight()-8);
        g.setColor(Color.cyan);
        g.fillRect(x+6, y+6,
                              getIconWidth()-12, getIconHeight()-12);
        }
    }
}
```

The remainder of this chapter investigates the various panes that appear within the SwingDemo program. Each pane illustrates one or more JFC components. Many of the components in the panes report status changes to the JTextField that appears at the bottom of the frame.

IMPROVED COMPONENTS

This section examines labels and several variations on the button theme: plain buttons, toggle buttons, and checkboxes. We'll take a look at the Label, Button, and Toggles panes of the SwingDemo program.

JFC Labels

The Label pane, shown in Figure 13.2, is extremely simple. It contains a single instance of the JLabel class, as you can see in the following listing.

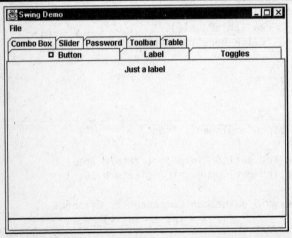

FIGURE 13.2: The Label pane of the SwingDemo program

LIST 13.2:   ***LabelPanel.java***

```java
import javax.swing.*;

public class LabelPanel extends JPanel
{
  public LabelPanel()
  {
    add(new JLabel("Just a label"));
  }
}
```

In its simplest form, a JLabel just displays a text message. The JLabel class has facilities for adding an optional icon and for specifying the relative positions of the text and icon.

JFC Buttons

The Button pane (shown earlier in Figure 13.1) demonstrates how the JButton class provides more features than the java.awt.Button class. The source code for ButtonPanel is shown below.

LIST 13.3:   *ButtonPanel.java*

```java
import javax.swing.*;
import java.awt.*;
import java.awt.event.*;


public class ButtonPanel extends JPanel
{
  private JTextField log;

  public ButtonPanel(JTextField tf)
  {
    this.log = tf;

    // Create button.
    JButton btn = new JButton("Push Me",
                new BoxIcon(Color.blue, 2));

    // Set alternative icons.
    btn.setRolloverIcon(new BoxIcon(Color.cyan, 3));
    btn.setPressedIcon(new BoxIcon(Color.yellow, 4));

    // Set text to left of icon.
```

```
      btn.setHorizontalTextPosition(JButton.LEFT);

      // Set border.
      btn.setBorder(BorderFactory.createEtchedBorder());

      // Set listener.
      btn.addActionListener(new ActionListener() {
        public void actionPerformed(ActionEvent e)
        {
          log.setText("Button was pressed.");
        }
      });      // Visual cue: end of anonymous inner class.

      // Add button to panel.
      add(btn);
  }


  class BoxIcon implements Icon
  {
      private Color  color;
      private int    borderWidth;

      BoxIcon(Color color, int borderWidth)
      {
        this.color = color;
        this.borderWidth = borderWidth;
      }

      public int getIconWidth() { return 20; }
      public int getIconHeight() { return 20; }

      public void paintIcon(Component c, Graphics g,
                            int x, int y)
      {
        g.setColor(Color.black);
        g.fillRect(x, y, getIconWidth(), getIconHeight());
        g.setColor(color);
        g.fillRect(x + borderWidth,
                   y + borderWidth,
                   getIconWidth() - 2*borderWidth,
                   getIconHeight() - 2*borderWidth);
      }
  }
}
```

The `BoxIcon` inner class is another implementation of the `Icon` interface, which was discussed earlier in the chapter. The `BoxIcon` constructor takes two arguments: a color and a border width.

The `JButton` constructor used here takes two arguments: a text string and a default icon. The default icon is blue, with a two-pixel black border. The `JButton` constructor call is:

```
JButton btn = new JButton("Push Me",
                          new BoxIcon(Color.blue, 2));
```

A `JButton` can specify alternate icons to be displayed when the `JButton` is in non-default states. The code at hand provides two alternate icons: one for when the cursor rolls over the button and one for when the button is pressed. The code that specifies these icons is:

```
// Set alternate icons.
btn.setRolloverIcon(new BoxIcon(Color.cyan, 3));
btn.setPressedIcon(new BoxIcon(Color.yellow, 4));
```

The code specifies that the button's text should appear to the left of the icon. This is done with the following call:

```
btn.setHorizontalTextPosition(JButton.LEFT);
```

The `JButton` class has several constants that allow you to set all of the possible text/icon relative locations.

The code also specifies that the button should have an etched border. The border is created with the following call:

```
btn.setBorder(BorderFactory.createEtchedBorder());
```

The `BorderFactory` class has several `createXXXBorder()` methods for specifying various border styles.

Note the comment near the end of the constructor:

```
// Visual cue: end of anonymous inner class.
```

Anonymous inner classes are a useful way to add a lightweight listener to a component. The syntax appears a bit strange at first. There are two ways to recognize an anonymous inner class:

▶ The class definition appears where you would expect an object reference. Instead of a reference, you see new *Typename()*, where *Typename* is either a class name or an interface name.

▶ The class definition ends with `})`;. This combination is rarely seen in Java except at the end of the definition of an anonymous inner class.

Part iii

JFC Toggles and Checkboxes

The Toggles pane, shown in Figure 13.3, displays a Toggle button, a plain checkbox, and three checkboxes organized as a radio group. The complete code for the `TogglePanel` class is shown below.

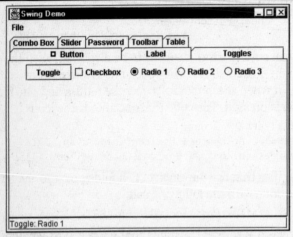

FIGURE 13.3: The Toggles pane of the `SwingDemo` program

LIST 13.4: *TogglePanel.java*

```java
import java.awt.event.*;
import javax.swing.*;

public class TogglePanel extends JPanel
{
  private JTextField   log;

  public TogglePanel(JTextField tf)
  {
    this.log = tf;

    // Toggle button.
    JToggleButton tog = new JToggleButton("Toggle");
    ItemListener listener = new ItemListener() {
      public void itemStateChanged(ItemEvent e)
```

```
      {
        AbstractButton src = (AbstractButton)(e.getSource());
        log.setText("Toggle: " + src.getText());
      }
    };
    tog.addItemListener(listener);
    add(tog);


    // Checkbox.
    JCheckBox cbox = new JCheckBox("Checkbox");
    cbox.addItemListener(listener);
    add(cbox);


    // Radio button boxes.
    ButtonGroup btngroup = new ButtonGroup();
    for (int i=1; i<=3; i++)
    {
      JRadioButton radio = new JRadioButton("Radio " + i);
      btngroup.add(radio);
      radio.addItemListener(listener);
      add(radio);
    }
  }
}
```

JToggleButtons announce state changes by sending ItemEvents to ItemListeners. The Toggle button is created with the following code:

```
    // Toggle button.
    JToggleButton tog = new JToggleButton("Toggle");
    ItemListener listener = new ItemListener() {
      public void itemStateChanged(ItemEvent e)
      {
        AbstractButton src = (AbstractButton)(e.getSource());
        log.setText("Toggle: " + src.getText());
      }
    };
    tog.addItemListener(listener);
    add(tog);
```

A JCheckbox is similar to a JToggleButton, but its appearance and state change display are different. A JToggleButton looks like a button and displays its state by altering the appearance of the entire button. A JCheckbox looks like a label next to a check region and displays its state by drawing or not drawing a checkmark in the check region.

The first JCheckbox in the panel is created with the following code:

```
// Checkbox.
JCheckBox cbox = new JCheckBox("Checkbox");
cbox.addItemListener(listener);
add(cbox);
```

The three JRadioButtons on the right side of the Toggles pane are organized as a radio group. The following code creates them:

```
// Radio button boxes.
ButtonGroup btngroup = new ButtonGroup();
for (int i=1; i<=3; i++)
{
  JRadioButton radio = new JRadioButton("Radio " + i);
  btngroup.add(radio);
  radio.addItemListener(listener);
  add(radio);
}
```

New Components

The remainder of this chapter looks at four of the new JFC components that are not related to AWT components:

▶ A combo box, which adds functionality to the AWT Choice component

▶ A slider, which adds functionality to the AWT Scrollbar component

▶ A password field, which provides a secure way to enter text data

▶ A toolbar, which contains other components and supports user positioning at runtime

Each of these component types appears on its own tabbed pane in the SwingDemo application.

JFC Combo Boxes

The JComboBox class is a lot like the java.awt.Choice class. The user is prompted to select one item from a list, and the list is only visible

during selection. A JComboBox, like a Choice, announces activity by
sending ItemEvents to its ItemListeners. The main difference is
that with a JComboBox, the programmer can specify the number of visible items in the list; the list will display a scrollbar if it contains more
than the visible number of items.

You can set the number of visible items in a JComboBox by calling
setMaximumRowCount() after construction. Here is an example of a
combo box with five visible items and a scrollbar:

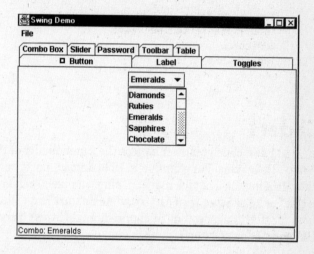

The source code for the ComboPanel portion of the SwingDemo program is listed below.

LIST 13.5: *ComboPanel.java*

```
import java.awt.event.*;
import javax.swing.*;


public class ComboPanel extends JPanel
{
    private JTextField          log;

    final static String[] treasure = { "Gold", "Silver",
                        "Diamonds", "Rubies", "Emeralds",
                        "Sapphires", "Chocolate"};

    public ComboPanel(JTextField tf)
```

Part iii

```
    {
        this.log = tf;

        final JComboBox combo = new JComboBox(treasure);
        combo.setMaximumRowCount(5);
        combo.addItemListener(new ItemListener() {
          public void itemStateChanged(ItemEvent e)
          {
            log.setText("Combo: " + combo.getSelectedItem());
          }
        });
        combo.setSelectedIndex(4);
        add(combo);
        log.setText("");
    }
}
```

JFC Sliders

The JSlider class greatly enhances the functionality of the java.awt
.Scrollbar class. For example, a JSlider supports both major and
minor tick marks. The tick mark spacing (in pixels) can be set by calling
setMajorTickSpacing(int) and setMinorTickSpacing(int).
If you set tick marks, you must explicitly enable their display by calling
setPaintTicks(true).

TIP

Of course, JSlider components have extensive functionality beyond tick
marks. You can learn about the features of the JSlider and the other Swing
components by reading their class APIs.

When a user moves a JSlider, the JSlider sends ChangeEvents
to its ChangeListeners. The source code for the SliderPanel class
is listed below. The SliderPanel code produces the display shown in
Figure 13.4.

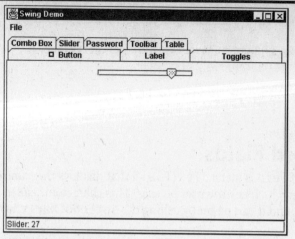

FIGURE 13.4: The JSlider component

LIST 13.6: SliderPanel.java

```java
import java.awt.event.*;
import javax.swing.*;
import javax.swing.event.*;


public class SliderPanel extends JPanel
{
  JTextField        log;
  JSlider           slider;

  public SliderPanel(JTextField tf)
  {
    this.log = tf;
    slider = new JSlider(JSlider.HORIZONTAL, -50, 50, 35);
    slider.setPaintTicks(true);
    slider.setMajorTickSpacing(10);
    add(slider);
```

```
slider.addChangeListener(new ChangeListener() {
  public void stateChanged(ChangeEvent e)
  {
    log.setText("Slider: " + slider.getValue());
  }
});
    }
  }
```

JFC Password Fields

A `JPasswordField` is just a `JTextField` that displays the same char-acter, no matter which key the user presses. This character is called the *echo character*, and it can be set by calling the `setEchoChar(char)` method.

Figure 13.5 shows a `JPasswordField` that uses the pound character (#) for its echo character.

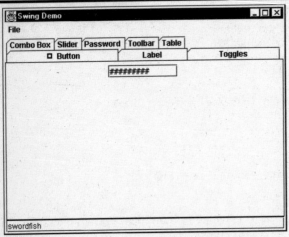

FIGURE 13.5: The `JPasswordField` component

The source code for the `PasswordPanel` class is listed below.

LIST 13.7: *PasswordPanel.java*

```
import javax.swing.*;

public class PasswordPanel extends JPanel
{
```

```
public PasswordPanel()
{
  // Construct a field that is 10 chars wide.
  JPasswordField pwf = new JPasswordField(10);
  pwf.setEchoChar('#');
  add(pwf);
}
}
```

JFC Toolbars

A JToolBar is a rectangular area that can contain other components. A user can detach a JToolBar from the window in which it resides and place it on the Desktop as a detached window. A JToolBar can also be placed into another region of the window in which it originated.

Figure 13.6 shows a JFC toolbar that contains three checkboxes. Figure 13.7 shows the same toolbar after a user has detached it. Each of the checkboxes sends an ActionEvent to an ActionListener, which logs the event to the JTextField.

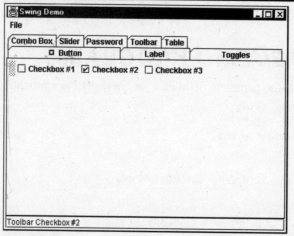

FIGURE 13.6: The JToolBar component with three checkboxes

FIGURE 13.7: A detached JToolBar component

Part iii

The code for the ToolbarPanel class appears below.

LIST 13.8: *ToolbarPanel.java*

```java
import javax.swing.*;
import java.awt.*;

public class ToolbarPanel extends JPanel
{
  public ToolbarPanel()
  {
    setLayout(new BorderLayout());
    JToolBar toolbar = new JToolBar();

    // Put 3 Jcheckboxes in the toolbar.
    for (int i=1; i<4; i++)
    {
      toolbar.add(new JCheckBox("Checkbox #" + i));
    }

    add(toolbar, BorderLayout.NORTH);
  }
}
```

THE *SWINGDEMO* PROGRAM

The following is the complete listing for the SwingDemo application.

```java
import javax.swing.*;
import java.awt.*;
import java.awt.event.*;


public class SwingDemo extends JFrame
{
  private JTextField    textfield;
  private JTabbedPane   tabbedPane;

  public static void main(String[] args)
  {
    SwingDemo that = new SwingDemo();
    that.setVisible(true);
  }

  public SwingDemo()
```

[handwritten annotations: "MainFrame" above class SwingDemo; "Driver" to the left of main method; "MainFrame" above public SwingDemo()]

```java
{
    super("Swing Demo");
    setSize(450, 350);

    // Listen for close command from title bar.
    addWindowListener(new WindowAdapter() {
        public void windowClosing(WindowEvent e)
        {
            System.exit(0);
        }
    });

    // Textfield at south is for status messages. The
    // Jcomponents use it to report events.
    textfield = new JTextField();
    getContentPane().add(textfield, BorderLayout.SOUTH);

    // Tabbed pane contains panels for the
    // various Jcomponents.
    tabbedPane = new JTabbedPane();
    populateTabbedPane();
    getContentPane().add(tabbedPane, BorderLayout.CENTER);

    addMenu();
}

private void addMenu()
{
    JMenuBar mbar = new JMenuBar();
    JMenu menu = new JMenu("File");
    menu.add(new JCheckBoxMenuItem("Check Me"));
    menu.addSeparator();
    JMenuItem item = new JMenuItem("Exit");
    item.addActionListener(new ActionListener() {
        public void actionPerformed(ActionEvent e)
        {
            System.exit(0);
        }
    });
    menu.add(item);
    mbar.add(menu);
    setJMenuBar(mbar);
}

private void populateTabbedPane()
```

Part III

```
{
// addTab(Title, Icon, Component, Tooltip)
tabbedPane.addTab("Button",
        new TabIcon(),
        new ButtonPanel(textfield),
        "Click here for Button demo");

   tabbedPane.addTab("Label",
           null,
           new LabelPanel(),
           "Click here for Label demo");

   tabbedPane.addTab("Toggles",
           null,
           new TogglePanel(textfield),
           "Click here for Toggle demo");


   tabbedPane.addTab("Combo Box",
           null,
           new ComboPanel(textfield),
           "Click here for Combo Box demo");

   tabbedPane.addTab("Sliders",
           null,
           new SliderPanel(textfield),
           "Click here for Slider demo");
   tabbedPane.addTab("Password",
           null,
           new PasswordPanel(),
           "Click here for Password Field demo");
   tabbedPane.addTab("Toolbar",
           null,
           new ToolbarPanel(),
           "Click here for Toolbar demo");
   tabbedPane.addTab("Table",
           null,
           new TablePanel(),
           "Click here for Table demo");
}


//
// This icon appears on the "Button" tab.
//
class TabIcon implements Icon
{
  public int getIconWidth()  { return 16; }
```

```
        public int getIconHeight() { return 16; }

        public void paintIcon(Component c, Graphics g,
                              int x, int y)
        {
          g.setColor(Color.black);
          g.fillRect(x+4, y+4, getIconWidth()-8,
                     getIconHeight()-8);
          g.setColor(Color.cyan);
          g.fillRect(x+6, y+6, getIconWidth()-12,
                     getIconHeight()-12);
        }
      }
    }
```

ButtonPanel.java

```
import javax.swing.*;
import java.awt.*;
import java.awt.event.*;


public class ButtonPanel extends JPanel
{
  private JTextField   log;

  public ButtonPanel(JTextField tf)
  {
    this.log = tf;

    // Create button.
    JButton btn = new JButton("Push Me",
                    new BoxIcon(Color.blue, 2));

    // Set alternative icons.
    btn.setRolloverIcon(new BoxIcon(Color.cyan, 3));
    btn.setPressedIcon(new BoxIcon(Color.yellow, 4));

    // Set text to left of icon.
    btn.setHorizontalTextPosition(JButton.LEFT);

    // Set border.
    btn.setBorder(BorderFactory.createEtchedBorder());

    // Set listener.
```

```java
      btn.addActionListener(new ActionListener() {
        public void actionPerformed(ActionEvent e)
        {
          log.setText("Button was pressed.");
        }
      });      // Visual cue: end of anonymous inner class

      // Add button to panel.
      add(btn);
  }


  //
  // Inner class creates a 20x20 icon with a black
  // border. The border width and the color of the
  // interior are specified to the constructor.
  //
  class BoxIcon implements Icon
  {
    private Color  color;
    private int    borderWidth;

    BoxIcon(Color color, int borderWidth)
    {
      this.color = color;
      this.borderWidth = borderWidth;
    }

    public int getIconWidth()  { return 20; }
    public int getIconHeight() { return 20; }

    public void paintIcon(Component c, Graphics g,
                          int x, int y)
    {
      g.setColor(Color.black);
      g.fillRect(x, y, getIconWidth(), getIconHeight());
      g.setColor(color);
      g.fillRect(x + borderWidth,
                 y + borderWidth,
                 getIconWidth() - 2*borderWidth,
                 getIconHeight() - 2*borderWidth);
    }
  }
}
```

LabelPanel.java

```java
import javax.swing.*;


public class LabelPanel extends JPanel
{
  public LabelPanel()
  {
    add(new JLabel("Just a label"));
  }
}
```

TogglePanel.java

```java
import java.awt.event.*;
import javax.swing.*;


public class TogglePanel extends JPanel
{
  private JTextField    log;

  public TogglePanel(JTextField tf)
  {
    this.log = tf;

    // Toggle button.
    JToggleButton tog = new JToggleButton("Toggle");

    // Listener for all 3 varieties.
    ItemListener listener = new ItemListener() {
      public void itemStateChanged(ItemEvent e)
      {
        AbstractButton src = (AbstractButton)(e.getSource());
        log.setText("Toggle: " + src.getText());
      }
    };
    tog.addItemListener(listener);
    add(tog);

    // Checkbox.
    JCheckBox cbox = new JCheckBox("Checkbox");
    cbox.addItemListener(listener);
    add(cbox);
```

```java
    // Radio button boxes.
    ButtonGroup btngroup = new ButtonGroup();
    for (int i=1; i<=3; i++)
    {
      JRadioButton radio = new JRadioButton("Radio " + i);
      btngroup.add(radio);
      radio.addItemListener(listener);
      add(radio);
    }
  }
}
```

ComboPanel.java

```java
import java.awt.event.*;
import javax.swing.*;


public class ComboPanel extends JPanel
{
  private JTextField      log;

  // Initialization strings.
  final static String[] treasure = { "Gold", "Silver",
                      "Diamonds", "Rubies", "Emeralds",
                      "Sapphires", "Chocolate"};

  public ComboPanel(JTextField tf)
  {
    this.log = tf;

    // Construct. Has to be final so the inner class
    // can have access.
    final JComboBox combo = new JComboBox(treasure);
    combo.setMaximumRowCount(5);

    // Combo box is like java.awt.Choice: it
    // sends ItemEvents.
    combo.addItemListener(new ItemListener() {
      public void itemStateChanged(ItemEvent e)
      {
        log.setText("Combo: " + combo.getSelectedItem());
      }
    });
    add(combo);
```

```
    }
}


SliderPanel.java

import java.awt.*;
import javax.swing.*;
import javax.swing.event.*;


public class SliderPanel extends JPanel
{
  private JTextField        log;
  private JSlider           slider;

  public SliderPanel(JTextField tf)
  {
    this.log = tf;
    setLayout(new BorderLayout());
    slider = new JSlider(JSlider.HORIZONTAL, -50, 50, 35);
    // Draw both major and minor tick marks.
    slider.setMajorTickSpacing(20);
    slider.setMinorTickSpacing(5);
    slider.setPaintTicks(true);
    slider.setPaintLabels(true);
    add(slider, BorderLayout.NORTH);
    slider.addChangeListener(new ChangeListener() {
      public void stateChanged(ChangeEvent e)
      {
        log.setText("Value = " + slider.getValue());
      }
    });
  }
}


PasswordPanel.java

import javax.swing.*;


public class PasswordPanel extends JPanel
{
  public PasswordPanel()
  {
```

```
    // Construct a field that is 10 chars wide.
    JPasswordField pwf = new JPasswordField(10);
    pwf.setEchoChar('#');
    add(pwf);
  }
}
```

ToolbarPanel.java

```
import javax.swing.*;
import java.awt.*;


public class ToolbarPanel extends JPanel
{
  public ToolbarPanel()
  {
    setLayout(new BorderLayout());
    JToolBar toolbar = new JToolBar();

    // Put 3 Jcheckboxes in the toolbar.
    for (int i=1; i<4; i++)
    {
      toolbar.add(new JCheckBox("Checkbox #" + i));
    }
    add(toolbar, BorderLayout.NORTH);
  }
}
```

TablePanel.java

```
import java.awt.event.*;
import javax.swing.*;


public class TablePanel extends JPanel
{
  public TablePanel()
  {
    String[] columnTitles =
    {
      "col1", "col2", "col3"
    };
```

```
String[][] rows =
{
    { "AAA", "Bbb", "Ccc" },
    { "ddd", "EeE", "FfF" },
    { "GGG", "HHH", "iii" },
    { "jjj", "KKk", "LLL" },
    { "Mmm", "NNN", "OoO" }
};

add(new JTable(rows, columnTitles));
    }
}
```

WHAT'S NEXT?

The next chapter will cover threads and multithreading, including creating and controlling threads, inter-thread communication, and thread synchronization, priorities, and scheduling.

Part iii

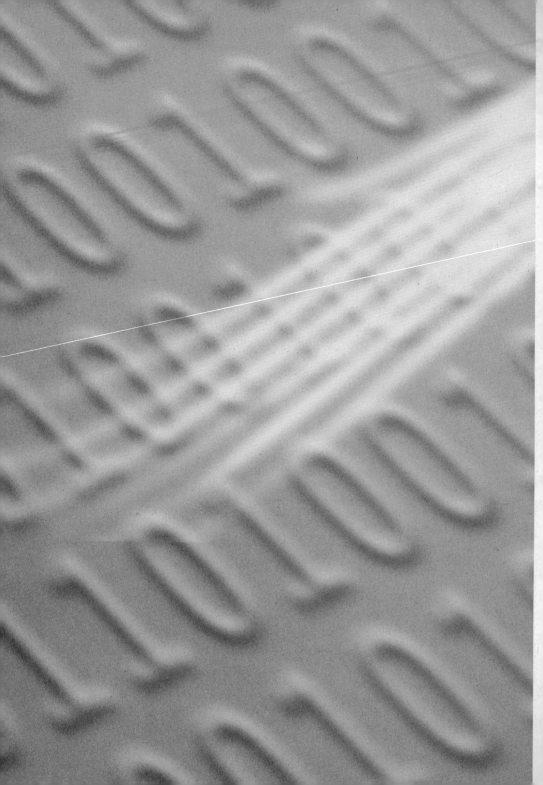

Chapter 14

THREADS AND MULTITHREADING

U p until now, all of our sample programs have been single-threaded; that is, they have had only one line of execution. If the program execution is blocked while waiting for the completion of some I/O operation, no other portion of the program can proceed. However, users of today's modern operating systems are accustomed to starting multiple programs and watching them work concurrently, even if there is only a single CPU available to run all the applications. Multithreading allows multiple tasks to execute concurrently within a single program.

Adapted from *Mastering Java 2* by John Zukowski
ISBN 0-7821-2180-2   1,280 pages $49.99

The advantage of multithreading is twofold. First, programs with multiple threads will, in general, better utilize system resources, including the CPU, because another line of execution can grab the CPU when one line of execution is blocked. Second, multiple threads solve numerous problems better. For example, how would you write a single-threaded program to show animation, play music, display documents, and download files from the network at the same time?

Java was designed from the beginning with multithreading in mind. Not only does the language itself have multithreading support built in, allowing for easy creation of robust, multithreaded applications, but the virtual machine relies on multithreading to concurrently provide multiple services—like garbage collection—to the application. In this chapter, you will learn to use multiple threads in your Java programs.

OVERVIEW OF MULTITHREADING

A thread is a single flow of control within a program. It is sometimes called the *execution context* because each thread must have its own resources—like the program counter and the execution stack—as the context for execution. However, all threads in a program still share many resources, such as memory space and opened files. Therefore, a thread may also be called a *lightweight process*. It is a single flow of control like a process (or a running program), but it is easier to create and destroy than a process because less resource management is involved.

TIP

The terms *parallel* and *concurrent* occur frequently in computer literature, and the difference between them can be confusing. When two threads run in parallel, they are both being executed at the same time on different CPUs. However, two concurrent threads are both in progress, or trying to get some CPU time for execution, at the same time, but are not necessarily being executed simultaneously on different CPUs.

A program may spend a big portion of its execution time just waiting. For example, it may wait for some resource to become accessible in an I/O operation, or it may wait for some time-out to occur to start drawing the next scene of an animation sequence. To improve CPU utilization, all the tasks with potentially long waits can run as separate threads. Once a task starts waiting for something to happen, the Java run time can choose another runnable task for execution.

The first example demonstrates the difference between a single-threaded program and its multithreaded counterpart. In the first program, a `run()` method in the `NoThreadPseudoIO` class is created to simulate a 10-second I/O operation. The main program will first perform the simulated I/O operation, then start another task. The method `show-ElapsedTime()` is defined to print the elapsed time in seconds since the program started, together with a user-supplied message. The `current-TimeMillis()` method of the `System` class in the `java.lang` package will return a `long` integer for the time difference, measured in milliseconds, between the current time and 00:00:00 GMT on January 1, 1970. The single-threaded program is listed here:

LIST 14.1:   WithoutThread.java

```
import java.io.*;
public class WithoutThread {
  static PrintWriter out = new PrintWriter
        (System.out, true);
  public static void main (String args[]) {
    // first task: some pseudo-I/O operation
    NoThreadPseudoIO pseudo = new NoThreadPseudoIO();
    pseudo.run();
    //  second task: some random task
    showElapsedTime ("Another task starts");
  }
  static long baseTime = System.currentTimeMillis();
  // show the time elapsed since the program started
  static void showElapsedTime (String message) {
    long elapsedTime = System.currentTimeMillis()
                      - baseTime;
    out.println (message + " at " +
      (elapsedTime / 1000.0) + " seconds");
  }
}
// pseudo-I/O operation run in caller's thread
class NoThreadPseudoIO {
  int data = -1;
  NoThreadPseudoIO() {    // constructor
    WithoutThread.showElapsedTime (
                "NoThreadPseudoIO created");
  }
  public void run() {
    WithoutThread.showElapsedTime (
                "NoThreadPseudoIO starts");
    try {
```

```
Thread.sleep (10000);   //. 10 seconds
data = 999;              // the data is ready
WithoutThread.showElapsedTime (
                "NoThreadPseudoIO finishes");
} catch (InterruptedException e) {}
}
}
```

Even if the second task does not refer to any data generated or modified by the pseudo-I/O operation, the task cannot start until the I/O operation is finished. For most real I/O operations, the CPU will be sitting idle most of the time waiting for a response from the peripheral device, which is really a waste of precious CPU cycles. A sample output of this program is shown here (the times shown will vary depending on your machine types and environments):

```
C:\MasteringJava\Ch08>javac WithoutThread.java
C:\MasteringJava\Ch08>java WithoutThread
NoThreadPseudoIO created at 1.642 seconds
NoThreadPseudoIO starts at 2.113 seconds
NoThreadPseudoIO finishes at 10.044 seconds
Another task starts at 10.044 seconds
```

The multithreaded second program declares the class for the pseudo-I/O operation as a subclass of the Thread class:

```
class ThreadedPseudoIO extends Thread {
```

After the thread is created, it uses the start() method of the Thread class to start the I/O operation:

```
ThreadedPseudoIO pseudo = new ThreadedPseudoIO();
pseudo.start();
```

The thread's start() method in turn calls the run() method of the subclass.

TIP

Up through JDK version 1.0.2, there is a bug in the code for running multiple threads under Windows 95/98 and NT: Programs that start multiple threads will not automatically exit. The workaround is to either have the last running thread call the System.exit() method or have a thread monitor other threads by calling the join() methods of the monitored threads. exit() is a class method defined in the System class of the java.lang package for terminating Java run time. For security reasons, an applet is not allowed to call exit(). Forcibly calling exit() from an applet will cause a SecurityException to be thrown. The workaround is not necessary for other platforms or with Java 1.1 or 2.

A full listing of this multithreaded program is as follows:

LIST 14.2: *WithThread.java*

```java
import java.io.*;
public class WithThread {
  static PrintWriter out = new PrintWriter(
        System.out, true);
  public static void main (String args[]) {
    // first task: some pseudo-I/O operation
    ThreadedPseudoIO pseudo = new ThreadedPseudoIO();
    pseudo.start();
    // second task: some random task
    showElapsedTime ("Another task starts");
  }
  static long baseTime = System.currentTimeMillis();
  // show the time elapsed since the program started
  static void showElapsedTime (String message) {
    long elapsedTime = System.currentTimeMillis()
                     - baseTime;
    out.println (message + " at " +
      (elapsedTime / 1000.0) + " seconds");
  }
}
// pseudo-I/O operation run in a separate thread
class ThreadedPseudoIO extends Thread {
  int data = -1;
  ThreadedPseudoIO() {  // constructor
    WithThread.showElapsedTime ("ThreadedPseudoIO created");
  }
  public void run() {
    WithThread.showElapsedTime ("ThreadedPseudoIO starts");
    try {
      Thread.sleep (10000);   // 10 seconds
      data = 999;             // data ready
      WithThread.showElapsedTime (
                "ThreadedPseudoIO finishes");
    } catch (InterruptedException e) {}
  }
}
```

Here is the output of the multithreaded program. You will notice that the second task starts even before the pseudo-I/O operation starts; this is natural when you have only one CPU running two threads. The run() method of the newly created thread will not be executed until the currently running thread relinquishes program control.

```
C:\MasteringJava\Ch08>javac WithThread.java
C:\MasteringJava\Ch08>java WithThread
ThreadedPseudoIO created at 0.11 seconds
Another task starts at 0.25 seconds
ThreadedPseudoIO starts at 0.27 seconds
ThreadedPseudoIO finishes at 10.025 seconds
```

THREAD BASICS

The following sections introduce the basics of working with threads, including how to create and run threads, control thread executions, and get information about threads and thread groups. You will also learn about the life cycle of a thread and thread groups.

Creating and Running a Thread

When you have a task you want to run concurrently with other tasks, there are two ways to do this: create a new class as a subclass of the Thread class or declare a class implementing the Runnable interface.

Using a Subclass of the *Thread* Class

When you create a subclass of the Thread class, this subclass should define its own run() method to override the run() method of the Thread class. This run() method is where the task is performed.

Just as the main() method is the first user-defined method the Java run time calls to start an application, the run() method is the first user-defined method the Java run time calls to start a thread. An instance of this subclass is then created by a new statement, followed by a call to the thread's start() method to have the run() method executed. This is exactly what was done with the ThreadedPseudoIO class in the previous example.

Implementing the Runnable Interface

The Runnable interface requires only one method to be implemented—the run() method. You first create an instance of this class with a new statement, followed by the creation of a Thread instance with another new statement, and finally a call to this thread instance's start() method to start performing the task defined in the run() method. A class instance with the run() method defined within it must be passed in as an argument in creating the Thread instance, so that when the start() method of this Thread instance is called, Java run time knows which run() method to execute.

This alternative way of creating a thread comes in handy when the class defining the run() method needs to be a subclass of another class. The class can inherit all the data and methods of the superclass, and the Thread instance just created can be used for thread control.

The previous multithreaded example can be reimplemented using the Runnable interface by first changing the class definition to implement the Runnable interface, instead of subclassing the Thread class:

```
class RunnablePseudoIO implements Runnable {
```

Then, an instance of the class is created and passed to a newly created Thread instance, followed by a call to the start() method to start the execution of the run() method as follows:

```
RunnablePseudoIO pseudo = new RunnablePseudoIO();
Thread thread = new Thread (pseudo);
thread.start();
```

A full listing of the program is included here:

LIST 14.3:   RunnableThread.java

```
import java.io.*;
public class RunnableThread {
  static PrintWriter out = new PrintWriter
          (System.out, true);
  public static void main (String args[]) {
    //  first task: some pseudo-I/O operation
    RunnablePseudoIO pseudo = new RunnablePseudoIO();
    Thread thread = new Thread (pseudo);
    thread.start();
    //  second task: some random task
    showElapsedTime ("Another task starts");
  }
  static long baseTime = System.currentTimeMillis();
  // show the time elapsed since the program started
  static void showElapsedTime (String message) {
    long elapsedTime = System.currentTimeMillis()
                    - baseTime;
    out.println (message + " at " +
      (elapsedTime / 1000.0) + " seconds");
  }
```

Part iii

```
    }
// pseudo I/O operation run in a separate thread
class RunnablePseudoIO implements Runnable {
  int data = -1;
  RunnablePseudoIO() {   // constructor
    RunnableThread.showElapsedTime(
                "RunnablePseudoIO created");
  }
  public void run() {
    RunnableThread.showElapsedTime(
                "RunnablePseudoIO starts");
    try {
      Thread.sleep (10000);  // 10 seconds
      data = 999;            // data ready
      RunnableThread.showElapsedTime (
                "RunnablePseudoIO finishes");
    } catch (InterruptedException e) {}
  }
}
```

The output of the program is similar to that of the earlier program:

```
C:\MasteringJava\Ch08>javac RunnableThread.java
C:\MasteringJava\Ch08>java RunnableThread
RunnablePseudoIO created at 0.01 seconds
Another task starts at 0.11 seconds
RunnablePseudoIO starts at 0.11 seconds
RunnablePseudoIO finishes at 10.145 seconds
```

The Thread-Control Methods

Many methods defined in the `java.lang.Thread` class control the running of a thread. Java 2 deprecated several of them to prevent data inconsistencies or deadlocks. If you are just starting with Java 2, avoid the deprecated methods and use the equivalent behavior described later in the chapter. However, if you are transitioning from Java 1.0 or 1.1, you will need to modify your code to avoid the deprecated methods if you used them. Here are some of the ones that were most commonly used:

> **void start() throw IllegalThreadStateException**
> Used to start the execution of the thread body defined in the
> run() method. Program control will be immediately returned
> to the caller, and a new thread will be scheduled to execute the
> run() method concurrently with the caller's thread.

void stop() Deprecated. Used to stop the execution of the thread no matter what the thread is doing. The thread is then considered dead, the internal states of the thread are cleared, and the resources allocated are reclaimed. Using this method has the potential to leave data in an inconsistent state and should be avoided.

void suspend() Deprecated. Used to temporarily stop the execution of the thread. All the states and resources of the thread are retained. The thread can later be restarted by another thread calling the `resume()` method. Using this method has a strong potential for deadlocks and should be avoided. You should use the `Object.wait()` method described later instead.

void resume() Deprecated. Used to resume the execution of a suspended thread. The suspended thread will be scheduled to run. If it has a higher priority than the running thread, the running thread will be preempted; otherwise, the just-resumed thread will wait in the queue for its turn to run. Using this method has a strong potential for deadlocks and should be avoided. You should use the `Object.notify()` method described later instead.

static void sleep(long sleepTimeInMilliseconds) throws InterruptedException A class method that causes the Java run time to put the caller thread to sleep for a minimum of the specified time period. The `Interrupted-Exception` may be thrown while a thread is sleeping or any-time if you `interrupt()` it. Either a `try-catch` statement needs to be defined to handle this exception or the enclosing method needs to have this exception in the `throws` clause.

void join()throws InterruptedException Used for the caller's thread to wait for this thread to die—for example, by coming to the end of the `run()` method.

static void yield() A class method that temporarily stops the caller's thread and puts it at the end of the queue to wait for another turn to be executed. It is used to make sure other threads of the same priority have the chance to run.

TIP

All the class methods defined in the Thread class, such as sleep() and yield(), will act on the caller's thread. That is, it is the caller's thread that will sleep for a while or yield to others. The reason is that a class method can never access an instance's data or method members unless the instance is passed in as an argument, created inside the method, or stored in a class variable visible to the method.

The following example shows how some of the above methods are used. The main thread creates two threads, then waits for the first thread to finish by calling the first thread's join() method. The first thread calls the sleep() method to be asleep for 10 seconds. Meanwhile, the second thread calls its own wait() method to suspend itself until the main thread calls its notify() method. After the first thread comes to an end, the main thread will resume its execution, wake up the second thread by calling the second thread's resume() method, and wait until the second thread also comes to an end by calling the second thread's join() method. The program is as follows:

LIST 14.4:   MethodTest.java

```java
import java.io.*;
public class MethodTest {
  static PrintWriter out = new PrintWriter
        (System.out, true);
  public static void main (String args[]) {
    FirstThread  first  = new FirstThread();
    SecondThread second = new SecondThread();
    first.start();
    second.start();
    try {
      out.println ("Waiting for first thread to finish...");
      first.join();
      out.println ("It's a long wait!");
      out.println ("Waking up second thread...");
      synchronized (second) {
        second.notify();
      }
      out.println ("Waiting for second thread to finish...");
      second.join();
    } catch (InterruptedException e) {
    }
    out.println("I'm ready to finish too.");
  }
}
```

```
class FirstThread extends Thread {
  public void run() {
    try {
      MethodTest.out.println (
               " First thread starts running.");
      sleep (10000);
      MethodTest.out.println (
               " First thread finishes running.");
    } catch (InterruptedException e) {
    }
  }
}
class SecondThread extends Thread {
  public synchronized void run() {
    try {
      MethodTest.out.println (
               " Second thread starts running.");
      MethodTest.out.println (
               " Second thread suspends itself.");
      wait();
      MethodTest.out.println (
               " Second thread runs again and finishes.");
    } catch (InterruptedException e) {
    }
  }
}
```

The output of this program is shown here:

```
C:\MasteringJava\Ch08>javac MethodTest.java
C:\MasteringJava\Ch08>java MethodTest
Waiting for first thread to finish...
  First thread starts running.
  Second thread starts running.
  Second thread suspends itself.
  First thread finishes running.
It's a long wait!
Waking up second thread...
Waiting for second thread to finish...
  Second thread runs again and finishes.
I'm ready to finish too.
```

NOTE

If you are not familiar with the synchronized keyword, it will be explained shortly in the "Advanced Multithreading" section.

The Thread Life Cycle

Every thread, after creation and before destruction, will always be in one of four states: newly created, runnable, blocked, or dead. These states are illustrated in Figure 14.1 and described in the following sections.

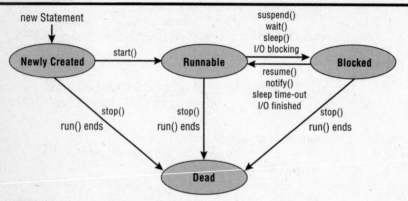

FIGURE 14.1:   The thread life cycle

Newly Created Threads

A thread enters the newly created state immediately after creation; that is, it enters the state right after the thread-creating new statement is executed. In this state, the local data members are allocated and initialized, but execution of the run() method will not begin until its start() method is called. After the start() method is called, the thread will be put into the runnable state.

Runnable Threads

When a thread is in the runnable state, the execution context exists and the thread can be scheduled to run at any time; that is, the thread is not waiting for any event to happen.

For the sake of explanation, this state can be subdivided into two sub-states: the running and queued states. When a thread is in the running state, it is assigned CPU cycles and is actually running. When a thread is in the queued state, it is waiting in the queue and competing for its turn to spend CPU cycles. The transition between these two substates is controlled by the virtual machine scheduler. However, a thread can call the yield() method to voluntarily move itself to the queued state from the running state.

Blocked Threads

The blocked state is entered when one of the following events occurs:

- ▶ The thread itself or another thread calls the `suspend()` method.

- ▶ The thread calls an object's `wait()` method.

- ▶ The thread itself calls the `sleep()` method.

- ▶ The thread is waiting for some I/O operation to complete.

- ▶ The thread will `join()` with another thread.

A thread in a blocked state will not be scheduled for running. It will go back to the runnable state, competing for CPU cycles, when the counter-event for the blocking event occurs:

- ▶ If the thread is suspended, another thread calls its `resume()` method.

- ▶ If the thread is blocked by calling an object's `wait()` method, the object's `notify()` or `notifyAll()` method is called.

- ▶ If the thread is put to sleep, the specified sleeping time elapses.

- ▶ If the thread is blocked on I/O, the specified I/O operation completes.

TIP

Keep in mind you should never call suspend() or resume(), even before Java 2. Java 2 strongly discourages their usage by deprecating the methods.

Dead Threads

The dead state is entered when a thread finishes its execution or is stopped by another thread calling its `stop()` method.

To avoid the use of `stop()`, the proper way to exit out of a `while (true)` loop is to maintain a state variable that is used as the `while` loop condition check. So, instead of `run()` looking like the following and using `stop()` to halt the thread:

```
public void run () {
  while (true) {
    ...
  }
}
```

you would change the test case to be some boolean condition. Then, when you want the thread to stop, instead of calling `stop()`, you change the state of the boolean. This causes the thread to stop on the next pass and ensures that the thread doesn't leave data in an inconsistent state.

```
public void run () {
    while (aBooleanVariable) {
        ...
    }
}
```

TIP

Under the JDK 1.1 and earlier implementations of the Java virtual machine, `stop()` will be ignored if a thread is created but not yet started.

To find out whether a thread is alive—that is, currently runnable or blocked—use the thread's `isAlive()` method. It will return `true` if the thread is alive. If a thread is alive, it does not mean that it is running, just that it can run.

Thread Groups

Every thread instance is a member of exactly one thread group. A thread group can have both threads and other thread groups as its members. In fact, every thread group, except the system thread group, is a member of some other thread group. All the threads and thread groups in an application form a tree, with the system thread group as the root.

When a Java application is started, the Java virtual machine creates the main thread group as a member of the system thread group. A main thread is created in this main thread group to run the `main()` method of the application. By default, all new user-created threads and thread groups will become the members of this main thread group unless another thread group is passed as the first argument of the new statement's constructor method. A new thread group is created by instantiating the `ThreadGroup` class. For example, the following statements create a thread group named `MyThread-Group` as a member of the default main thread group, and then create a thread named `MyThread` as a member of the newly created thread group:

```
ThreadGroup group = new ThreadGroup ("MyThreadGroup");
Thread thread = new Thread (group, "MyThread");
```

Three methods are defined in the `ThreadGroup` class to manipulate all the threads in the `Thread` class group and its subthread groups at once: `stop()`, `suspend()`, and `resume()`. As with `Thread`, the `stop()`, `suspend()`, and `resume()` methods are now deprecated and should be avoided. (Basically, the methods had a use that didn't work properly, so Sun deprecated them.) Proper use of condition variables should diminish the dependency on these methods.

Getting Information about Threads and Thread Groups

Many methods are defined in `Thread` and `ThreadGroup` for getting information about threads and thread groups.

Thread Information

The following are some of the most commonly used methods for getting information about threads:

`java.lang.thread` methods:

> **static thread currentThread()**   Returns the caller's thread.

> **string getName()**   Returns the current name of the thread.

> **ThreadGroup getThreadGroup()**   Returns the parent thread group of the thread.

> **int getPriority()**   Returns the current priority of the thread.

> **boolean isAlive()**   Returns `true` if the thread is started but not dead yet.

> **boolean isDaemon()**   Returns `true` if the thread is a daemon thread.

Thread Group Information

The following are some of the most commonly used methods for getting information about thread groups:

`java.lang.ThreadGroup` methods:

> **string getName()**   Returns the name of the thread group.

ThreadGroup getParent()   Returns the parent thread group of the thread group.

int getMaxPriority()   Returns the current maximum priority of the thread group.

int activeCount()   Returns the number of active threads in the thread group.

int activeGroupCount()   Returns the number of active thread groups in the thread group.

int enumerate(Thread list[], boolean recursive)
Adds all the active threads in this thread group into the list array. If recursive is true, all the threads in the subthread groups will be copied over as well. This method will return the number of threads copied. The activeCount() method is often used to size the list when the space of this thread array is to be allocated.

Thread priorities and daemon threads will be discussed in later sections.

A Program to Get and Print Thread Information

This section presents an example that uses the methods described in the previous sections to show information about all the threads and thread groups in an application. The program creates a thread group named MyThreadGroup and creates four threads in the thread group. It then continues on to print all the information by calling the printAllThreadInfo() method.

The printAllThreadInfo() method first locates the root thread group of all the running threads and thread groups. It then prints the information about the underlying threads and thread groups recursively from the root. The output is indented to show the depth of individual threads or thread groups in the tree. The full program is as follows:

LIST 14.5:   ThreadInfo.java

```
import java.io.*;
public class ThreadInfo {
  static PrintWriter out = new PrintWriter
          (System.out, true);
  public static void main (String args[]) {
    Thread[] threads = new Thread[4];
    ThreadGroup group = new ThreadGroup ("MyThreadGroup");
    if (args.length > 0) {
```

```
      Thread thread = Thread.currentThread();
      thread.setName (args[0]);
    }
    for (int i = 0; i < 4; i++)
      threads[i] = new Thread (group, "MyThread#" + i);
    ThreadInfo.printAllThreadInfo();
  }
  // list information about all the threads and thread groups
  // in the application
  public static void printAllThreadInfo() {
    ThreadGroup parent, root;
    // find the root of all running threads
    root = parent = Thread.currentThread().getThreadGroup();
    while ((parent = parent.getParent()) != null)
      root = parent;
    // print information recursively from the root
    out.println();
    printThreadGroupInfo ("", root);
  }
  // print information about a thread group
  public static void printThreadGroupInfo
      (String indent, ThreadGroup group) {
    final int SAFETY = 5;
    if (group == null)
      return;
    out.println (indent +
      "THREAD GROUP: " + group.getName() +
      "; Max Priority: " + group.getMaxPriority() +
      (group.isDaemon() ? " [Daemon]" : ""));
    // print information about component threads
    int numThreads = group.activeCount();
    Thread threads[]  = new Thread[numThreads+SAFETY];
    numThreads = group.enumerate (threads, false);
    for (int i = 0; i < numThreads; i++)
      printThreadInfo(indent + "   ", threads[i]);
    // print information about component thread groups
    int numGroups  = group.activeGroupCount();
    ThreadGroup groups[] = new ThreadGroup[
                        numGroups+SAFETY];
    numGroups = group.enumerate (groups, false);
    for (int i = 0; i < numGroups; i++)
      printThreadGroupInfo (indent + "   ", groups[i]);
  }
  // print information about a single thread
  public static void printThreadInfo
      (String indent, Thread thread) {
```

```
    if (thread == null)
      return;
    out.println (indent +
      "THREAD: " + thread.getName() +
      "; Priority: " + thread.getPriority() +
      (thread.isDaemon() ? " [Daemon]" : "") +
      (thread.isAlive() ? " [Alive]" : " [NotAlive]") +
      ((Thread.currentThread() == thread) ?
                            " <== current" : ""));
  }
}
```

NOTE

Since the number of threads running may change between the `activeGroup-Count()` call and the `enumerate()` call, a safety margin is added in case the count increases. The "Advanced Multithreading" section later in this chapter discusses ways to solve this problem.

The output of the previous program run under Windows NT is as follows:

```
C:\MasteringJava\Ch08>javac ThreadInfo.java
C:\MasteringJava\Ch08>java ThreadInfo
THREAD GROUP: system; Max Priority: 10
  THREAD: Signal dispatcher; Priority 10 [Daemon] [Alive]
  THREAD: Reference handler; Priority 10 [Daemon] [Alive]
  THREAD: Finalizer; Priority: 8 [Daemon] [Alive]
  THREAD GROUP: main; Max Priority: 10
    THREAD: main; Priority: 5 [Alive] <== current
    THREAD GROUP: MyThreadGroup; Max Priority: 10
```

The same program run under Solaris 2.5 produces similar output, as follows:

```
harpoon:/users/me/java/examples/ch8>javac ThreadInfo.java
harpoon:/users/me/java/examples/ch8>java ThreadInfo
THREAD GROUP: system; Max Priority: 10
  THREAD: Clock; Priority: 12 [Daemon] [Alive]
  THREAD: Idle thread; Priority: 0 [Daemon] [Alive]
  THREAD: Async Garbage Collector; Priority: 1 [Daemon] [Alive]
  THREAD: Reference handler; Priority: 10 [Daemon] [Alive]
  THREAD: Finalizer; Priority: 8 [Daemon] [Alive]
  THREAD: SoftReference sweeper; Priority: 9 [Daemon] [Alive]
  THREAD GROUP: main; Max Priority: 10
    THREAD: main; Priority: 5 [Alive] <== current
```

```
THREAD GROUP: MyThreadGroup; Max Priority: 10
```

Your output may differ slightly, depending on how the vendor of your Java implementation manages system-threading resources.

ADVANCED MULTITHREADING

The following sections introduce some advanced multithreading topics: thread synchronization, inter-thread communications, thread priorities and scheduling, and daemon threads.

Thread Synchronization

Synchronization is the way to avoid data corruption caused by simultaneous access to the same data. Because all the threads in a program share the same memory space, it is possible for two threads to access the same variable or run the same method of the same object at the same time. Problems may occur when multiple threads are accessing the same data concurrently. Threads may race each other, and one thread may overwrite the data just written by another thread. Or one thread may work on another thread's intermediate result and break the consistency of the data. Some mechanism is needed to block one thread's access to the critical data, if the data is being worked on by another thread.

For example, suppose that you have a program to handle a user's bank account. There are three subtasks in making a deposit for the user:

- ▶ Get the current balance from some remote server, which may take as long as five seconds.

- ▶ Add the newly deposited amount into the just-acquired balance.

- ▶ Send the new balance back to the same remote server, which again may take as long as five seconds to complete.

If two depositing threads, each making a $1,000 deposit, are started at roughly the same time on a current balance of $1,000, the final balance of these two deposits may reflect the result of only one deposit. A possible scenario is depicted in Table 14.1.

TABLE 14.1: Two Depositing Threads Running Concurrently

TIME	THREAD #1	THREAD #2	BALANCE IN REMOTE SERVER
a	Getting balance		$1,000
b	Waiting...	Getting balance	$1,000
c	Get balance = $1,000	Waiting...	$1,000
d	Compute new balance = $2,000	Waiting...	$1,000
e	Setting new balance	Waiting...	$1,000
f	Waiting...	Get balance = $1,000	$1,000
g	Waiting...	Compute new balance = $2,000	$1,000
h	Waiting...	Setting new balance	$1,000
i	New balance set	Waiting...	$2,000
j		New balance set	$2,000

The balance stored in the remote server increases by only one deposit amount!

The following sample program simulates the scenario in Table 14.1. An `Account` class is defined with three methods: `getBalance()` to fetch the current balance from some pseudo-server, with a simulated five-second delay; `setBalance()` to write back the new balance to the same pseudo-server, with (again) a simulated five-second delay; and `deposit()` to use the other two methods to complete a deposit transaction. A `DepositThread` class is declared to start the deposit operation on the account passed in. The main program creates an account instance and then starts two threads to make a deposit of $1,000 each to that account. The full program listing is as follows:

LIST 14.6:   Deposit.java

```
import java.io.*;
public class Deposit {
  // simulate balance kept remotely
  static int balance = 1000;
  public static void main (String args[]) {
    PrintWriter out = new PrintWriter (System.out, true);
    Account account = new Account (out);
```

```
        DepositThread first, second;
        first  = new DepositThread (account, 1000, "#1");
        second = new DepositThread (account,
                        1000, "\t\t\t\t#2");
        // start the transactions
        first.start();
        second.start();
        // wait for both transactions to finish
        try {
            first.join();
            second.join();
        } catch (InterruptedException e) {}
        // print the final balance
        out.println ("*** Final balance is " + balance);
    }
}
class Account {
    PrintWriter out;
    Account (PrintWriter out) {
        this.out = out;
    }
    void deposit (int amount, String name) {
        int balance;
        out.println (name + " trying to deposit " + amount);
        out.println (name + " getting balance...");
        balance = getBalance();
        out.println (name + " balance got is " + balance);
        balance += amount;
        out.println (name + " setting balance...");
        setBalance (balance);
        out.println (name + " new balance set to "
                        + Deposit.balance);
    }
    int getBalance() {
        // simulate the delay in getting balance remotely
        try {
            Thread.sleep (5000);
        } catch (InterruptedException e) {}
        return Deposit.balance;
    }
    void setBalance (int balance) {
        // simulate the delay in setting new balance remotely
        try {
            Thread.sleep (5000);
        } catch (InterruptedException e) {}
        Deposit.balance = balance;
    }
```

Part iii

```
    }
    class DepositThread extends Thread {
        Account account;
        int    depositAmount;
        String message;
        DepositThread (Account account, int amount,
                       String message) {
            this.message  = message;
            this.account  = account;
            this.depositAmount = amount;
        }
        public void run() {
            account.deposit (depositAmount, message);
        }
    }
}
```

An example of the output of the above program is as follows:

```
C:\MasteringJava\Ch08>javac Deposit.java
C:\MasteringJava\Ch08>java Deposit
#1 trying to deposit 1000
#1 getting balance...
                                    #2 trying to deposit 1000
                                    #2 getting balance...

#1 balance got is 1000
#1 setting balance...
                                    #2 balance got is 1000
                                    #2 setting balance...

#1 new balance set to 2000
                                    #2 new balance set to 2000

*** Final balance is 2000
```

Java's Monitor Model for Synchronization

Java uses the idea of monitors to synchronize access to data. A *monitor* is like a guarded place where all the protected resources have the same locks. Only a single key fits all the locks inside a monitor, and a thread must get the key to enter the monitor and access these protected resources. If many threads want to enter the monitor simultaneously, only one thread is handed the key; the others must wait outside until the key-holding thread finishes its use of the resources and hands the key back to the Java virtual machine.

Once a thread gets a monitor's key, the thread can access any of the resources controlled by that monitor countless times, as long as the thread still owns the key. However, if this key-holding thread wants to access the resources controlled by another monitor, the thread must get that particular monitor's key. At any time, a thread can hold many monitors' keys. Different threads can hold keys for different monitors at the same time. Deadlock may occur if threads are waiting for each other's key to proceed.

In Java, the resources protected by monitors are program fragments in the form of methods or blocks of statements enclosed in curly braces. If some data can be accessed only through methods or blocks protected by the same monitor, access to the data is indirectly synchronized. You use the keyword `synchronized` to indicate that the following method or block of statements is to be synchronized by a monitor. When a block of statements is to be synchronized, an object instance enclosed in parentheses immediately following the `synchronized` keyword is required so the Java virtual machine knows which monitor to check.

You can think of a monitor as a guarded parking lot, where all the synchronized methods or blocks are just like cars you can drive (or execute, if you are a thread). All the cars share the same key. You need to get this unique key to enter the parking lot and drive any of the cars until you hand back the key. At that time, one of the persons waiting to get in will get the key and be able to drive the car(s) of their choice. This concept is illustrated in Figure 14.2.

For example, the `deposit()` method in the previous example can be synchronized to allow only one thread to run at a time. The only change needed is a `synchronized` keyword before the method definition, as follows:

```
synchronized void deposit(int amount, String name) {
```

Part iii

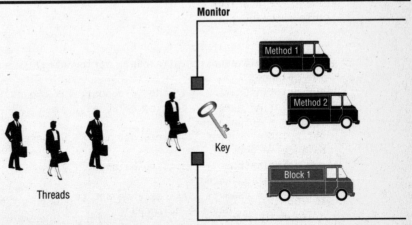

FIGURE 14.2: Threads need a unique key to access resources protected by a Java monitor.

Here is the full program listing:

LIST 14.7:   *Deposit.java (version 2)*

```java
import java.io.*;
public class Deposit {
  // simulate balance kept remotely
  static int balance = 1000;
  public static void main (String args[]) {
    PrintWriter out = new PrintWriter (System.out, true);
    Account account = new Account (out);
    DepositThread first, second;
    first  = new DepositThread (account, 1000, "#1");
    second = new DepositThread (account,
              1000, "\t\t\t\t#2");
    // start the transactions
    first.start();
    second.start();
    // wait for both transactions to finish
    try {
      first.join();
      second.join();
    } catch (InterruptedException e) {}
    // print the final balance
    out.println ("*** Final balance is " + balance);
  }
}

class Account {
  PrintWriter out;
  Account (PrintWriter out) {
    this.out = out;
  }

  synchronized void deposit(int amount, String name) {
    int balance;
    out.println (name + " trying to deposit " + amount);
    out.println (name + " getting balance...");
    balance = getBalance();
    out.println (name + " balance got is " + balance);
    balance += amount;
    out.println (name + " setting balance...");
    setBalance (balance);
    out.println (name + " new balance set to "
                  + Deposit.balance);
  }
```

```
    int getBalance() {
      // simulate the delay in getting balance remotely
      try {
        Thread.sleep (5000);
      } catch (InterruptedException e) {}
      return Deposit.balance;
    }
    void setBalance (int balance) {
      // simulate the delay in setting new balance remotely
      try {
        Thread.sleep (5000);
      } catch (InterruptedException e) {}
      Deposit.balance = balance;
    }
  }

  class DepositThread extends Thread {
    Account account;
    int     depositAmount;
    String  message;
    DepositThread (Account account, int amount,
                   String message) {
      this.message = message;
      this.account = account;
      this.depositAmount = amount;
    }
    public void run() {
      account.deposit (depositAmount, message);
    }
  }
```

A sample output of the modified program is as follows:

```
C:\MasteringJava\Ch08>javac Deposit.java
C:\MasteringJava\Ch08>java Deposit
#1 trying to deposit 1000
#1 getting balance...
#1 balance got is 1000
#1 setting balance...
#1 new balance set to 2000
                              #2 trying to deposit 1000
                              #2 getting balance...
                              #2 balance got is 2000
                              #2 setting balance...
                              #2 new balance set to 3000
*** Final balance is 3000
```

Part iii

Alternatively, a block of statements in the `deposit()` method can be synchronized on the called object, as follows:

```
void deposit (int amount, String name) {
  int balance;
  out.println (name + " trying to deposit " + amount);
  synchronized (this) {
    out.println (name + " getting balance...");
    balance = getBalance();
    out.println (name + " gets balance = " + balance);
    balance += amount;
    out.println (name + " setting balance...");
    setBalance (balance);
  }
  out.println (name + " set new balance = " + balance);
}
```

The output of this program is almost the same as the previous one, except the first message from the second thread will be interleaved in the messages from the first thread, because the first `println()` method is not inside the synchronized block. Here is the full program listing:

LIST 14.8:   Deposit.java (Version 3)

```
import java.io.*;

public class Deposit {
  // simulate balance kept remotely
  static int balance = 1000;
  public static void main (String args[]) {
    PrintWriter out = new PrintWriter (System.out, true);
    Account account = new Account (out);
    DepositThread first, second;
    first  = new DepositThread (account, 1000, "#1");
    second = new DepositThread (account,
                               1000, "\t\t\t\t#2");
    // start the transactions
    first.start();
    second.start();
    // wait for both transactions to finish
    try {
      first.join();
      second.join();
    } catch (InterruptedException e) {}
    // print the final balance
    out.println ("*** Final balance is " + balance);
  }
```

```
}
class Account {
  PrintWriter out;
  Account (PrintWriter out) {
    this.out = out;
  }

void deposit (int amount, String name) {
  int balance;
  out.println (name + " trying to deposit " + amount);
  synchronized (this) {
    out.println (name + " getting balance...");
    balance = getBalance();
    out.println (name + " gets balance = " + balance);
    balance += amount;
    out.println (name + " setting balance...");
    setBalance (balance);
  }
  out.println (name + " set new balance = " + balance);
}

  int getBalance() {
    // simulate the delay in getting balance remotely
    try {
      Thread.sleep (5000);
    } catch (InterruptedException e) {}
    return Deposit.balance;
  }
  void setBalance (int balance) {
    // simulate the delay in setting new balance remotely
    try {
      Thread.sleep (5000);
    } catch (InterruptedException e) {}
    Deposit.balance = balance;
  }
}
class DepositThread extends Thread {
  Account account;
  int    depositAmount;
  String message;
  DepositThread (Account account, int amount,
                 String message) {
    this.message = message;
    this.account = account;
    this.depositAmount = amount;
  }
```

```
  public void run() {
    account.deposit (depositAmount, message);
  }
}
```

Here is an example of the output:

```
C:\MasteringJava\Ch08>javac Deposit.java
C:\MasteringJava\Ch08>java Deposit
#1 trying to deposit 1000
#1 getting balance...
                                    #2 trying to deposit 1000

#1 balance got is 1000
#1 setting balance...
#1 new balance set to 2000
                                    #2 getting balance...
                                    #2 balance got is 2000
                                    #2 setting balance...
                                    #2 new balance set to 3000
  *** Final balance is 3000
```

One unique key will be issued to every object containing any synchronized instance method or being referred by any synchronized block. For synchronized class methods, the key is issued to the class because the method may be called before any class instances exist. This means that every object and every class can have a monitor if there are any synchronized methods or blocks of statements associated with it. Furthermore, a class monitor's key is different from any of the keys of its class instance monitors.

Differences in Synchronization Techniques

The next example demonstrates the difference between a synchronized method and a synchronized block, and the difference between class-based synchronization and object-based synchronization. Class SyncToken contains three methods, all synchronized differently and all calling the ticker() method to print out three ticks in random intervals. Class SyncTestRunner is a thread class that will choose different methods of class SyncToken to run based on the ID given. The main() method of the SyncTest class will generate 10 threads running the tickers with different synchronization schemes so the comparison can be made. The program listing is as follows:

LIST 14.9:   SyncTest.java

```
import java.io.*;
public class SyncTest {
```

```
      public static void main (String args[]) {
        SyncToken token = new SyncToken();
        SyncTestRunner runners[] = new SyncTestRunner[10];
        for (int i = 0; i < 10; i++) {
          runners[i] = new SyncTestRunner (token, i);
          runners[i].start();
        }
      }
    }
    class SyncTestRunner extends Thread {
      SyncToken token;
      int       id;
      SyncTestRunner (SyncToken token, int id) {
        this.token = token;
        this.id   = id;
      }
      public void run() {
        switch (id % 3) {
          case 0:
            SyncToken.classTicker ("\t\t\tClass #" + id, token);
            break;
          case 1:
            token.methodTicker ("Method #" + id);
            break;
          case 2:
            token.blockTicker ("Block  #" + id);
            break;
        }
      }
    }
    class SyncToken {
      PrintWriter out = new PrintWriter (System.out, true);
      // the ticker method: give three ticks in random interval
      void ticker (String message) {
        for (int i = 0; i < 3; i++) {
          try {
            Thread.sleep ((int) (800 * Math.random()));
          } catch (InterruptedException e) {
          }
          out.println(message + ", tick #" + i);
        }
      }
      // class-based synchronization
      static synchronized void classTicker (String message,
                                            SyncToken token) {
        token.ticker(message);
```

```
    }
    // object-based synchronization: synchronized block
    void blockTicker (String message) {
      synchronized(this) {
        ticker (message);
      }
    }
    // object-based synchronization: synchronized method
    synchronized void methodTicker (String message) {
      ticker (message);
    }
  }
```

The output of this program is as follows:

```
C:\MasteringJava\Ch08>javac SyncTest.java
C:\MasteringJava\Ch08>java SyncTest
                        Class #0, tick #0
Method #1, tick #0
                        Class #0, tick #1
Method #1, tick #1
Method #1, tick #2
Block #2, tick #0
                        Class #0, tick #2
                        Class #3, tick #0
Block #2, tick #1
                        Class #3, tick #1
                        Class #3, tick #2
Block #2, tick #2
Method #4, tick #0
Method #4, tick #1
Method #4, tick #2
                        Class #6, tick #0
Block #5, tick #0
                        Class #6, tick #1
Block #5, tick #1
Block #5, tick #2
                        Class #6, tick #2
Method #7, tick #0
Method #7, tick #1
                        Class #9, tick #0
Method #7, tick #2
                        Class #9, tick #1
                        Class #9, tick #2
Block #8, tick #0
Block #8, tick #1
Block #8, tick #2
```

Your output may differ slightly, depending on how the vendor of your Java implementation manages resources.

You can see that object-based synchronized methods and synchronized blocks share the same monitor key if they are for the same object. Also, class-based synchronization and object-based synchronization do use different keys because their output interleaves each other.

Synchronization is an expensive operation, and the use of it should be kept to a minimum, especially for frequently executed methods or blocks of statements. However, synchronization can help reduce the interference among different threads. Good use of it will definitely improve the stability and robustness of the program.

Inter-thread Communications

Inter-thread communications allow threads to talk to or wait for each other. You can have threads communicate with each other through shared data or by using thread-control methods to have threads wait for each other.

Threads Sharing Data

All the threads in the same program share the same memory space. If the reference to an object is visible to different threads by the syntactic rules of scopes, or explicitly passed to different threads, these threads share access to the data members of that object. As explained in the previous section, synchronization is sometimes necessary to enforce exclusive access to the data to avoid racing conditions and data corruption.

Threads Waiting for Other Threads

By using thread-control methods, you can have threads communicate by waiting for each other. For example, the join() method can be used for the caller thread to wait for the completion of the called thread. Also, a thread can suspend itself and wait at a rendezvous point using the suspend() method; another thread can wake it up through the waiting thread's resume() method, and both threads can run concurrently thereafter.

Deadlock may occur when a thread holding the key to a monitor is suspended or waiting for another thread's completion. If the other thread it is waiting for needs to get into the same monitor, both threads will be waiting forever. This is why the suspend() and resume() methods are now deprecated and should not be used. The wait(), notify(), and notifyAll() methods defined in class Object of the java.lang package can be used to solve this problem.

The wait() method will make the calling thread wait until either a time-out occurs or another thread calls the same object's notify() or notifyAll() method. The synopsis of the wait() method is:

```
wait()
```

or

```
wait (long timeoutPeriodInMilliseconds)
```

The former will wait until the thread is notified. The latter will wait until either the specified time-out expires or the thread is notified, whichever comes first.

When a thread calls the wait() method, the key it is holding will be released for another waiting thread to enter the monitor. The notify() method will wake up only one waiting thread, if any. The notifyAll() method will wake up all the threads that have been waiting in the monitor. After being notified, the thread will try to re-enter the monitor by requesting the key again and may need to wait for another thread to release the key.

Note that these methods can be called only within a monitor, or synchronized block. The thread calling an object's notify() or notifyAll() method needs to own the key to that object's monitor; otherwise, IllegalMonitorStateException, a type of RuntimeException, will be thrown.

The next example demonstrates the use of the wait() and notify() methods to solve the classical producer and consumer problem. In this problem, the producer will generate data for the consumer to consume. However, if the producer produces data faster than the consumer can consume, the newly created data may be overwritten before it is consumed. On the other hand, if the consumer consumes faster than the producer can produce, the consumer may keep using already processed data. Synchronization alone will not solve the problem because it only guarantees exclusive access to the data, not availability.

The first implementation uses a monitor, an instance of the NoWait-Monitor class, to control the access to the data, token. The producer and consumer will set and get, respectively, the token value in random intervals, with the maximum interval length regulated by the speed argument passed to their constructors. The main program accepts up to two command-line arguments for setting the producing and consuming speed, creates an instance of the monitor, creates a producer and a consumer, and watches them run for 10 seconds. The program is listed as follows:

LIST 14.10:   NoWaitPandC.java

```
import java.io.*;
public class NoWaitPandC {
  static int produceSpeed = 200;
  static int consumeSpeed = 200;
  public static void main (String args[]) {
    if (args.length > 0)
      produceSpeed = Integer.parseInt (args[0]);
    if (args.length > 1)
      consumeSpeed = Integer.parseInt (args[1]);
    NoWaitMonitor monitor = new NoWaitMonitor();
    new NoWaitProducer (monitor, produceSpeed);
    new NoWaitConsumer (monitor, consumeSpeed);
    try {
      Thread.sleep (1000);
    } catch (InterruptedException e) {
    }
    System.exit(0);
  }
}
class NoWaitMonitor {
  int token = -1;
  PrintWriter out = new PrintWriter (System.out, true);
  // get token value
  synchronized int get () {
    out.println ("Got: " + token);
    return token;
  }
  // put token value
  synchronized void set (int value) {
    token = value;
    out.println ("Set: " + token);
  }
}
class NoWaitProducer implements Runnable {
  NoWaitMonitor monitor;
  int    speed;
  NoWaitProducer (NoWaitMonitor monitor, int speed) {
    this.monitor = monitor;
    this.speed = speed;
    new Thread (this, "Producer").start();
  }
```

```
        public void run() {
          int i = 0;
          while (true) {
            monitor.set (i++);
            try {
              Thread.sleep ((int) (Math.random() * speed));
            } catch (InterruptedException e) {
            }
          }
        }
      }
      class NoWaitConsumer implements Runnable {
        NoWaitMonitor monitor;
        int    speed;
        NoWaitConsumer (NoWaitMonitor monitor, int speed) {
          this.monitor = monitor;
          this.speed = speed;
          new Thread (this, "Consumer").start();
        }
        public void run() {
          while (true) {
            monitor.get();
            try {
              Thread.sleep((int) (Math.random() * speed));
            } catch (InterruptedException e) {}
          }
        }
      }
```

Here is an example of the type of output of this program where the producer outpaces the consumer:

```
C:\MasteringJava\Ch08>javac NoWaitPandC.java
C:\MasteringJava\Ch08>java NoWaitPandC 100 400
Set: 0
Got: 0
Set: 1
Set: 2
Set: 3
Set: 4
Got: 4
Set: 5
Set: 6
Set: 7
Set: 8
Set: 9
```

```
Set: 10
Got: 10
Set: 11
Set: 12
```

You can see there is a lot of data generated (shown as Set) but overwritten before it is processed (shown as Got).

Here is an example of the program's output where the consumer is faster than the producer:

```
C:\MasteringJava\Ch08>java NoWaitPandC 400 100
Set: 0
Got: 0
Got: 0
Got: 0
Got: 0
Got: 0
Got: 0
Set: 1
Set: 2
Got: 2
Set: 3
Got: 3
Got: 3
Got: 3
Got: 3
Got: 3
Set: 4
Got: 4
Got: 4
Got: 4
Got: 4
Got: 4
```

This time, some of the data is processed multiple times.

The second implementation of the sample program uses the wait() and notify() methods to make sure all data is created and used exactly once. The program is the same as the previous one, except for the implementation of the monitor. A boolean variable, valueSet, is added to indicate whether the data is ready for consumption or already used. The get() method will first test if the data is ready for consumption. If not, the calling thread will wait until some other thread sets the data and notifies the current thread. The boolean variable is then set to indicate that the data is consumed. Any thread waiting to produce new data will then be notified to start the production. If there is no thread waiting to produce, the notify() method will be ignored. The get() method is shown here:

```
synchronized int get() {
  if (! valueSet)
    try {
      wait();
    } catch (InterruptedException e) {
    }
  valueSet = false;
  out.println ("Got: " + token);
  notify();
  return token;
}
```

Symmetrically, the set() method will first test whether the data is already used. If not, the calling thread will wait until some other thread uses the data and notifies the current thread. The boolean variable is then set to indicate that the data is ready for consumption. Any thread waiting to consume the data will then be notified to start the consumption. If there is no thread waiting, the notify() method will be ignored. The set() method is shown here:

```
synchronized void set (int value) {
  if (valueSet)
    try {
      wait();
    } catch (InterruptedException e) {
    }
  valueSet = true;
  token = value;
  out.println ("Set: " + token);
  notify();
}
```

The full program listing is shown here:

LIST 14.11: PandC.java

```
import java.io.*;
public class PandC {
  static int produceSpeed = 200;
  static int consumeSpeed = 200;
  public static void main (String args[]) {
    if (args.length > 0)
      produceSpeed = Integer.parseInt (args[0]);
    if (args.length > 1)
```

```
          consumeSpeed = Integer.parseInt (args[1]);
      Monitor monitor = new Monitor();
      new Producer(monitor, produceSpeed);
      new Consumer(monitor, consumeSpeed);
      try {
        Thread.sleep(1000);
      } catch (InterruptedException e) {
      }
      System.exit(0);
    }
  }
class Monitor {
  PrintWriter out = new PrintWriter (System.out, true);
  int token;
  boolean valueSet = false;
  // get token value
  synchronized int get () {
    if (! valueSet)
      try {
        wait();
      } catch (InterruptedException e) {
      }
    valueSet = false;
    out.println ("Got: " + token);
    notify();
    return token;
  }
  // set token value
  synchronized void set (int value) {
    if (valueSet)
      try {
        wait();
      } catch (InterruptedException e) {
      }
    valueSet = true;
    token = value;
    out.println ("Set: " + token);
    notify();
  }
}
class Producer implements Runnable {
  Monitor monitor;
  int speed;
  Producer (Monitor monitor, int speed) {
    this.monitor = monitor;
    this.speed = speed;
```

```
            new Thread (this, "Producer").start();
        }
        public void run() {
            int i = 0;
            while (true) {
                monitor.set (i++);
                try {
                    Thread.sleep ((int) (Math.random() * speed));
                } catch (InterruptedException e) {
                }
            }
        }
    }
    class Consumer implements Runnable {
        Monitor monitor;
        int speed;
        Consumer (Monitor monitor, int speed) {
            this.monitor = monitor;
            this.speed = speed;
            new Thread (this, "Consumer").start();
        }
        public void run() {
            while (true) {
                monitor.get();
                try {
                    Thread.sleep ((int) (Math.random() * speed));
                } catch (InterruptedException e) {
                }
            }
        }
    }
```

Here is an example of the output of this program:

```
C:\MasteringJava\Ch08>javac PandC.java
C:\MasteringJava\Ch08>java PandC 400 100
Set: 0
Got: 0
Set: 1
Got: 1
Set: 2
Got: 2
Set: 3
Got: 3
Set: 4
Got: 4
```

This time, every piece of data generated is consumed exactly once.

Priorities and Scheduling

Priorities are the way to make sure important or time-critical threads are executed frequently or immediately. *Scheduling* is the means to make sure priorities and fairness are enforced.

If you have only one CPU, all of the runnable threads must take turns executing. Scheduling is the activity of determining the execution order of multiple threads.

Thread Priority Values

Every thread in Java is assigned a priority value. When more than one thread is competing for CPU time, the thread with the highest priority value is given preference. Thread priority values that can be assigned to user-created threads are simple integers ranging between `Thread .MIN_PRIORITY` and `Thread.MAX_PRIORITY`. User applications are normally run with the priority value of `Thread.NORM_PRIORITY`. Through JDK 1.2, the following constants of the `Thread` class—MIN_ PRIORITY, MAX_PRIORITY, and NORM_PRIORITY—have the values of 1, 10, and 5, respectively. Every thread group has a maximum priority value assigned. This is a cap to the priority values of member threads and thread groups when they are created or want to change their priority values.

When a thread is created, it will inherit the priority value of the creating thread if the priority value doesn't exceed the limit imposed by its parent thread group. The `setPriority()` method of `Thread` class can be used to set the priority value of a thread. If the value to be set is outside the legal range, an `IllegalArgumentException` will be thrown. If the value is larger than the maximum priority value of its parent thread group, the maximum priority value will be used.

The `setMaxPriority()` method of class `ThreadGroup` can be used to set the maximum priority value of a thread group. For security reasons (so that a user-created thread will not monopolize the CPU), a Web browser may not allow an applet to change its priority.

Preemptive Scheduling and Time-Slicing

Java's scheduling is *preemptive*; that is, if a thread with a higher priority than the currently running thread becomes runnable, the higher priority thread should be executed immediately, pushing the currently running thread back to the queue to wait for its next turn. A thread can voluntarily pass the CPU execution privilege to waiting threads of the same priority by calling the `yield()` method.

Part iii

In some implementations, thread execution is *time-sliced*; that is, threads with equal priority values will have equal opportunities to run in a round-robin manner. Even threads with lower priorities will still get a small portion of the execution time slots, roughly proportional to their priority values. Therefore, no threads will be starving in the long run.

Other implementations do not have time-slicing. A thread will relinquish its control only when it finishes its execution, is preempted by a higher-priority thread, or is blocked by I/O operations or the `sleep()`, `wait()`, or `suspend()` method calls. For computation-intensive threads, it is a good idea to occasionally call the `yield()` method to give other threads a chance to run. It may improve the overall interactive responsiveness of graphical user interfaces.

TIP

Up to JDK 1.1, the Java virtual machine for Windows 95/98 and NT is time-sliced; the Java virtual machine for Solaris 2 is not time-sliced. However, in Java 2, a time-sliced variety is available for Solaris. It does require several patches to be installed and, because of this, is not enabled by default. See the README file that comes with the JDK for the list of patches to install for Solaris 2.5.1 and Solaris-x86. Once the patches are installed, to change thread scheduling from non-time-sliced to time-sliced, set the environment variable THREADS_FLAG to native for time-sliced, or set it to green (or leave it unset) for the default behavior. You can also specify runtime options of -native or -green to the command-line tools, like java and javac.

Scheduling Threads with Different Priorities

The next example demonstrates the effect of scheduling on threads with different priorities. The main program will accept an optional command-line argument to indicate whether the threads created will yield to each other regularly.

The main program starts four threads with priority values of 1, 2, 4, and 4, respectively. Each thread will increment its counter 600,001 times and optionally yield to threads with equal priority on every three-thousandth increment. Because the main thread has a higher priority value, 5, than these computation-intensive threads, the main thread may grab the CPU every 0.3 second to print the counter values of these four computing threads. The program is listed as follows:

LIST 14.12:   *PriorityTest.java*

```java
import java.io.*;
public class PriorityTest {
  static int    NUM_THREADS = 4;
  static boolean yield = true;
  static int counter[] = new int[NUM_THREADS];
  public static void main (String args[]) {
    PrintWriter out = new PrintWriter (System.out, true);
    int numIntervals = 10;
    if (args.length > 0)
      yield = false;
    out.println ("Using yield()? "
                  + (yield ? "YES" : "NO"));
    for (int i = 0; i < NUM_THREADS; i++)
      (new PrTestThread ((i > 1) ? 4 : (i + 1), i)).start();
    ThreadInfo.printAllThreadInfo();
    out.println();
    //   repeatedly print out the counter values
    int step = 0;
    while (true) {
      boolean allDone = true;
      try {
        Thread.sleep (300);
      } catch (InterruptedException e) {
      }
      out.print ("Step " + (step++) + ": COUNTERS:");
      for (int j = 0; j < NUM_THREADS; j++) {
        out.print (" " + counter[j]);
        if (counter[j] < 2000000)
          allDone = false;
      }
      out.println();
      if (allDone)
        break;
    }
    System.exit(0);
  }
}
class PrTestThread extends Thread {
  int   id;
  PrTestThread (int priority, int id) {
    super ("PrTestThread#" + id);
    this.id = id;
    setPriority(priority);
```

```
    }
  public void run() {
    for (int i = 0; i <= 2000000; i++) {
      if (((i % 3000) == 0) && PriorityTest.yield)
        yield();
      PriorityTest.counter[id] = i;
    }
  }
}
```

Here is an example of the output when the program is run on a time-sliced system (Windows 95/98/NT or Solaris with native threads), with the computing threads frequently yielding to each other:

```
C:\MasteringJava\Ch08>javac PriorityTest.java
C:\MasteringJava\Ch08>java PriorityTest
Using yield()? YES
THREAD GROUP: system; Max Priority: 10
    THREAD: Signal dispatcher; Priority: 10 [Daemon] [Alive]
    THREAD: Reference handler; Priority: 10 [Daemon] [Alive]
    THREAD: Finalizer; Priority: 8 [Daemon] [Alive]
    THREAD GROUP: main; Max Priority: 10
      THREAD: main; Priority: 5 [Alive] <== current
      THREAD: PrTestThread#0; Priority: 1 [Alive]
      THREAD: PrTestThread#1; Priority: 2 [Alive]
      THREAD: PrTestThread#0; Priority: 4 [Alive]
      THREAD: PrTestThread#1; Priority: 4 [Alive]

Step 0: COUNTERS: 2999 0 530999 533999
Step 1: COUNTERS: 5999 2999 1073999 1085999
Step 2: COUNTERS: 8999 5999 1607999 1637999
Step 3: COUNTERS: 149999 149999 2000000 2000000
Step 4: COUNTERS: 704999 701999 2000000 2000000
Step 5: COUNTERS: 1249866 1259999 2000000 2000000
Step 6: COUNTERS: 1796999 1817999 2000000 2000000
Step 7: COUNTERS: 2000000 2000000 2000000 2000000
```

From the output, you can see some surprising results. The two threads with the highest priority tend to hog most of the CPU time. However, since the priority 1 thread is so close to priority 2, there is a closer splitting of CPU time.

Here is an example of the output when the same program is run on a Java virtual machine, with no time-slicing and, again, the threads yielding to each other regularly.

```
harpoon:/users/me/java/examples/ch8> javac PriorityTest.java
harpoon:/users/me/java/examples/ch8> java PriorityTest
```

```
Using yield()? YES
THREAD GROUP: system; Max Priority: 10
  THREAD: Clock; Priority: 12 [Daemon] [Alive]
  THREAD: Idle thread; Priority: 0 [Daemon] [Alive]
  THREAD: Async Garbage Collector; Priority: 1 [Daemon] [Alive]
  THREAD: Reference handler; Priority: 10 [Daemon] [Alive]
  THREAD: Finalizer; Priority: 8 [Daemon] [Alive]
  THREAD: SoftReference sweeper; Priority: 9 [Daemon] [Alive]
  THREAD GROUP: main; Max Priority: 10
    THREAD: main; Priority: 5 [Alive] <== current
    THREAD: PrTestThread#0; Priority: 1 [Alive]
    THREAD: PrTestThread#1; Priority: 2 [Alive]
    THREAD: PrTestThread#0; Priority: 4 [Alive]
    THREAD: PrTestThread#1; Priority: 4 [Alive]

Step 0: COUNTERS: 0 0 103563 101999
Step 1: COUNTERS: 0 0 206999 208476
Step 2: COUNTERS: 0 0 314999 312189
Step 3: COUNTERS: 0 0 419999 416889
Step 4: COUNTERS: 0 0 527999 520335
Step 5: COUNTERS: 0 67070 600000 600000
Step 6: COUNTERS: 0 295645 600000 600000
Step 7: COUNTERS: 0 521522 600000 600000
Step 8: COUNTERS: 145375 600000 600000 600000
Step 9: COUNTERS: 374097 600000 600000 600000
Step 10: COUNTERS: 515023 600000 600000 600000
Step 11: COUNTERS: 600000 600000 600000 600000
```

From the output, it is obvious that lower-priority threads do not have any chance to run until all the higher-priority threads finish their execution.

NOTE

You'll have to play with the maximum value setting for the counters to get reasonable results for your machine. Do not use a value so low that everything is done in two or three steps. However, anything taking over 20 steps may be a little much.

Here is the output when the same program is run on a time-sliced system with no yielding:

```
C:\MasteringJava\Ch08>java PriorityTest 0
Using yield()? NO
THREAD GROUP: system; Max Priority: 10
  THREAD: Signal dispatcher; Priority: 10 [Daemon] [Alive]
  THREAD: Reference handler; Priority: 10 [Daemon] [Alive]
  THREAD: Finalizer; Priority: 8 [Daemon] [Alive]
  THREAD GROUP: main; Max Priority: 10
```

```
THREAD: main; Priority: 5 [Alive] <== current
THREAD: PrTestThread#0; Priority: 1 [Alive]
THREAD: PrTestThread#1; Priority: 2 [Alive]
THREAD: PrTestThread#0; Priority: 4 [Alive]
THREAD: PrTestThread#1; Priority: 4 [Alive]

Step 0: COUNTERS: 60965 61129 546422 441717
Step 1: COUNTERS: 126821 123038 1052759 951456
Step 2: COUNTERS: 188446 182858 1555466 1484050
Step 3: COUNTERS: 252345 246123 2000000 2000000
Step 4: COUNTERS: 764587 861142 2000000 2000000
Step 5: COUNTERS: 1302086 1435581 2000000 2000000
Step 6: COUNTERS: 1900295 1977578 2000000 2000000
Step 7: COUNTERS: 2000000 2000000 2000000 2000000
```

NOTE

Running the program on a different operating system may generate a different pattern of output. You are at the mercy of the scheduling algorithm of the operating system and/or the particular port of the JDK.

Interestingly, the lower-priority threads get more chances to run than in the previous run with yielding. This is probably because yielding disturbs the scheduler's original plan to execute lower-priority threads by forcing the scheduler to look for threads with equal priority first. With no yielding, all the schedules for lower-priority threads can be smoothly exercised.

Finally, the program is run with no yielding on an implementation with no time-slicing:

```
harpoon:/users/me/java/examples/ch8> java PriorityTest 0
Using yield()? NO
THREAD GROUP: system; Max Priority: 10
  THREAD: Clock; Priority: 12 [Daemon] [Alive]
  THREAD: Idle thread; Priority: 0 [Daemon] [Alive]
  THREAD: Async Garbage Collector; Priority: 1 [Daemon] [Alive]
  THREAD: Reference handler; Priority: 10 [Daemon] [Alive]
  THREAD: Finalizer; Priority: 8 [Daemon] [Alive]
  THREAD: SoftReference sweeper; Priority: 9 [Daemon] [Alive]
THREAD GROUP: main; Max Priority: 10
  THREAD: main; Priority: 5 [Alive] <== current
  THREAD: PrTestThread#0; Priority: 1 [Alive]
  THREAD: PrTestThread#1; Priority: 2 [Alive]
```

```
THREAD: PrTestThread#2; Priority: 4 [Alive]
THREAD: PrTestThread#3; Priority: 4 [Alive]

Step 0: COUNTERS: 0 0 203552 0
Step 1: COUNTERS: 0 0 203552 210978
Step 2: COUNTERS: 0 0 413376 210978
Step 3: COUNTERS: 0 0 413376 422790
Step 4: COUNTERS: 0 0 600000 444539
Step 5: COUNTERS: 0 57353 600000 600000
Step 6: COUNTERS: 0 272848 600000 600000
Step 7: COUNTERS: 0 488745 600000 600000
Step 8: COUNTERS: 100596 600000 600000 600000
Step 9: COUNTERS: 314749 600000 600000 600000
Step 10: COUNTERS: 587513 600000 600000 600000
Step 11: COUNTERS: 600000 600000 600000 600000
```

The lower-priority threads have no chance to run until all the higher-priority threads finish. Even threads with equal priority values do not have the chance to run until the main thread preempts the running thread. When a thread is preempted, it will be put to the end of the waiting queue. When the main thread relinquishes program control after printing the counter values, the previously waiting thread that is ahead in the queue will get the chance to run. You can see proof of this in the output listing: only one of the highest-priority threads advances its counter between each printing.

Thread Local Variables

Introduced into the Core API in Java 2, the concept of thread local variables is actually not new to Java. A similar class existed within the internal `sun.server.util` package of the Java Web Server product. Apparently, there was enough demand to make the design pattern a standard part of Java, so the concept has moved into the `java.lang.ThreadLocal` and `java.lang.InheritableThreadLocal` classes. So, what exactly are they? Well, thread local variables permit individual thread instances to have independent copies of variables.

Normally you will rarely need to use `ThreadLocal` variables, although `InheritableThreadLocal` is more likely. They become important when you need static variables to store an identifier, probably for database access or a session identifier. Then, you share the variable only within a particular running thread or a thread and all its descendants.

Part iii

NOTE

A ThreadLocal variable is initialized via its protected initialValue() method. The default initial value of a ThreadLocal variable is null. So, to provide a different initial value, you must subclass ThreadLocal and override the method. You can also change the value at a later time with the set() method.

The following example demonstrates the differences between class variables and ThreadLocal variables. Using multithreading, the program creates several instances of a class and counts the number created in the counter class variable. For each thread, the static threadLocal variable is also available. The value of threadLocal is used as the amount of time to sleep. The inner class, MyThreadLocal, offers up to 1,000 milliseconds for the thread to sleep via its initialValue() method. Notice that both variables are static, meaning one would expect there to be one copy of each variable for all instances of the class.

LIST 14.13:   LocalThreadVars.java

```java
import java.io.*;
public class LocalThreadVars implements Runnable {
  static private class MyThreadLocal extends ThreadLocal {
    protected Object initialValue() {
      return new Double (Math.random() * 1000.0);
    }
  }
  static ThreadLocal threadLocal = new MyThreadLocal();
  static int counter = 0;
  private LocalThreadVars() {
    counter++;
  }
  public void run() {
    LocalThreadVars myLTV = new LocalThreadVars();
    displayValues();
    try {
      Thread.currentThread().sleep (
        ((Double)threadLocal.get()).longValue());
      myLTV.displayValues();
    } catch (InterruptedException e) {
      e.printStackTrace();
    }
  }
  private void displayValues() {
    System.out.println (threadLocal.get() + "\t" + counter +
      "\t" + Thread.currentThread().getName());
```

```
    }
    public static void main (String args[]) {
      LocalThreadVars ltv = new LocalThreadVars();
      ltv.displayValues();
      for (int i=0;i<5;i++) {
        Thread t = new Thread (ltv);
        t.start();
      }
    }
  }
```

After running the program, you'll think otherwise. Here is an example of the output the program produces. As the program utilizes random numbers, your output will most likely differ.

```
C:\MasteringJava\Ch08>javac LocalThreadVars.java
C:\MasteringJava\Ch08>java LocalThreadVars
353.6782033483381      1    main
607.6189861951625      2    Thread-0
204.82242103443437     3    Thread-1
216.68547449023978     4    Thread-2
960.1210961092618      5    Thread-3
221.4544981562063      6    Thread-4
204.82242103443437     6    Thread-1
216.68547449023978     6    Thread-2
221.4544981562063      6    Thread-4
607.6189861951625      6    Thread-0
960.1210961092618      6    Thread-3
```

Notice how the `counter` variable is shared across threads, but the `threadLocal` variable isn't. If the `ThreadLocal` static variable was shared across threads, you would see the same value repeated for all values, instead of just for multiple classes within the same thread.

You'll appreciate the `ThreadLocal` class more once you are doing network programming. For now, just be aware of its existence and keep it in the back of your mind for when you need it.

Daemon Threads

Daemon threads are service threads. They exist to provide services to other threads. They normally enter an endless loop waiting for clients requesting services. When all the active threads remaining are daemon threads, the Java virtual machine will exit.

For example, a timer thread that wakes up in regular intervals is a good candidate for daemon threads. This timer thread can notify other threads regularly about the time-outs. When no other thread is running, there is no need for the timer thread's existence.

To create a daemon thread, call the `setDaemon()` method immediately after the thread's creation and before the execution is started. The constructor of the thread is a good candidate for making this method call. By default, all the threads created by a daemon thread are also daemon threads. The synopsis of the `setDaemon()` method is:

```
setDaemon (boolean isDaemon)
```

When `isDaemon` is `true`, the thread is marked as a daemon thread; otherwise, it is marked as a non-daemon thread.

WHAT'S NEXT?

Next, we'll move on to Java Database Connectivity (JDBC) and explore Java as a database front-end application.

Chapter 15

JAVA DATABASE CONNECTIVITY (JDBC)

In the current information age, a database is the tool used to collect and manipulate data. The database forms the foundation of the infrastructure of many companies. While the database system is well suited to the storage and retrieval of data, people need some sort of visual front-end application to see and use the data stored.

The problem is complicated by the existence of heterogeneous computers in most companies. The art and marketing departments may have Macintosh systems, the engineers could have high-end Unix workstations, while the sales force is probably using some variation of Microsoft Windows (Windows 95/98, Windows NT 4, Windows NT 3.51, or Windows 3.1) on PCs. To expose the data in a corporate database, developers must consider all of the various system permutations on which they wish to deploy.

Adapted from *Mastering Java 2* by John Zukowski
ISBN 0-7821-2180-2   1,280 pages $49.99

This chapter will look at Java as the way to solve the database front-end Tower of Babel, by providing a single and consistent application programming interface: the Java Database Connectivity API.

Java as a Database Front End

Java offers several benefits to the developer creating a front-end application for a database server. Java is a "write once, run anywhere" language. This means that Java programs may be deployed without recompilation on any of the computer architectures and operating systems that possess a Java Virtual Machine. For large corporations, just having a common development platform is a big savings: no longer are programmers required to write separate applications for the many platforms a large corporation may have. Java is also attractive to third-party developers—a single Java program can answer the needs of both small and large customers.

In addition, there is a cost associated with the deployment and maintenance of the hardware and software of any system (client) the corporation owns. Systems such as Windows PCs, Macintosh, and Unix desktop-centric clients (*fat clients*) can cost corporations between $10,000 and $15,000 per installation seat. Java technology now makes it possible for any company to use a smaller system footprint. These systems are based on a Java chip set and can run any and all Java programs from a built-in Java operating system.

Java-based clients (*thin clients*) that operate with a minimum of hardware resources, yet run the complete Java environment, are expected to cost around $750 per seat. According to various studies, the savings for a corporation moving 10,000 fat client systems to thin client systems could be as much as $100 million annually. While Pentium systems are available for under $1,000 too, the cost to configure and maintain them, with their local storage, is where the higher costs come from.

It follows, then, that the incentive to create Java-based solutions for corporate systems is big. Corporations are extremely interested in shifting their applications from architecture- and operating-system-specific models to network-centric models. Java represents a long-term strategy in saving resource costs.

For the developer, Java represents a huge market opportunity. There are very few medium-to-large organizations that do not use databases for some portion of their business operation, while most use databases for *every* aspect of their business, from human resources to front-line customer sales.

This chapter examines Java Database Connectivity (JDBC), including how to use the current JDBC API to connect Java applications and applets to database servers.

DATABASE CLIENT/SERVER METHODOLOGY

The evolution of relational data storage began in 1970 with the work of Dr. E. F. Codd, who proposed a set of 12 rules for identifying relationships between pieces of data. Codd's rules formed the basis for the development of systems to manage data. Today, Relational Database Management Systems (RDBMS) are the result of Codd's vision.

Data in an RDBMS are stored as rows of distinct information in tables. A structured language is used to query (retrieve), store, and change the data. The Structured Query Language (SQL) is an ANSI standard, and all major commercial RDBMS vendors provide mechanisms for issuing SQL commands.

The early development of RDBMS applications utilized an integrated model of user interface code, application code, and database libraries. This single binary model ran only on a local machine, typically a mainframe. The applications were simple but inefficient and did not work over LANs. The model did not scale, and the application and user interface code was tightly coupled to the database libraries. Figure 15.1 illustrates the monolithic single-tier database design.

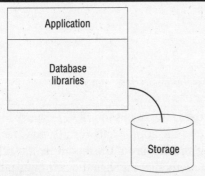

FIGURE 15.1: The monolithic single-tier database design

Part iii

Further, the monolithic approach did not allow multiple instances of the application to communicate with *each other*. So there was often contention between instances of the application.

NOTE

It is typical for RDBMS and DBMS (Database Management System) to be used interchangeably because most major commercial databases are relational and support some form of SQL to allow the user to query the relations between data tables.

Two-Tier Database Design

Two-tier models appeared with the advent of server technology. Communication-protocol development and extensive use of local and wide area networks allowed the database developer to create an application front end that accessed data through a connection (*socket*) to the backend server. Figure 15.2 illustrates a two-tier database design, where the client software is connected to the database through a socket connection.

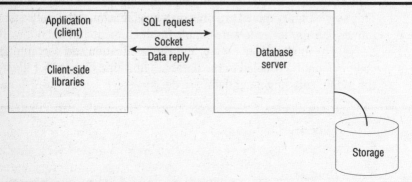

FIGURE 15.2: The two-tier database design

Client programs (applying a user interface) send SQL requests to the database server. The server returns the appropriate results, and the client is responsible for the formatting and display of the data. Clients still use a vendor-provided library of functions that manage the communication between client and server. Most of these libraries are written in either the C language or Perl.

Commercial database vendors realized the potential for adding intelligence to the database server. They created proprietary techniques that allowed the database designer to develop macro programs for simple data manipulation. These macros, called *stored procedures*, can cause problems relating to version control and maintenance. Because a stored procedure is an executable program living on the database, it is possible for the stored procedure to attempt to access named columns of a database table after the table has been changed. For example, if a column with the name id is changed to cust_id, the meaning of the original stored procedure is lost. The advent of *triggers*, which are stored procedures executed automatically when some action (such as insert) happens with a particular table or tables, can compound these difficulties when the data returned from a query are not expected. Again, this can be the result of the trigger reading a table column that has been altered.

Despite the success of client/server architectures, two-tier database models suffer a number of limitations:

▶ The vendor-provided library limits them. Switching from one database vendor to another requires a rewrite of a significant amount of code to the client application.

▶ Version control is an issue. When the vendor updates the client-side libraries, the applications that utilize the database must be recompiled and redistributed.

▶ Vendor libraries deal with low-level data manipulation. Typically, the base library only deals with queries and updates of single rows or columns of data. This can be enhanced on the server side by creating a stored procedure, but the complexity of the system then increases.

▶ All of the intelligence associated with using and manipulating the data is implemented in the client application, creating large client-side runtimes. This drives up the cost of each client set.

THREE-TIER DATABASE DESIGN

Today there is a great deal of interest in multi-tier design. In a multi-tier design, the client communicates with an intermediate server that provides a layer of abstraction from the RDBMS. There does not have to be just three tiers, but conceptually this is the next step. Figure 15.3 illustrates a three-tier database design.

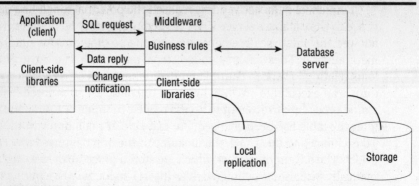

FIGURE 15.3:   A three-tier database design

The intermediate layer is designed to handle multiple client requests and manage the connection to one or more database servers. The three-tier design gives the middle tier the following advantages over the two-tier design:

▶ It is multithreaded to manage multiple client connections simultaneously.

▶ It can accept connections from clients over a variety of vendor-neutral protocols (from HTTP to TCP/IP), then hand off the requests to the appropriate vendor-specific database servers, returning the replies to the appropriate clients.

▶ It can be programmed with a set of "business rules" that manage the manipulation of the data. Business rules could include anything from restricting access to certain portions of data to making sure that data is properly formatted before being inserted or updated.

▶ It prevents the client from becoming too heavy by centralizing process-intensive tasks and abstracting data representation to a higher level.

▶ It isolates the client application from the database system and frees a company to switch database systems without having to rework the business rules.

▶ It can asynchronously provide the client with the status of a current data table or row.

As an example of this last point, suppose that a client application had just completed a query of a particular table. If a subsequent action by another distinct client *changed* that data, the first client could receive notification from an intelligent middle-tier program.

THE JDBC API

The JDBC API is designed to allow developers to create database front ends without having to continually rewrite their code. Despite standards set by the ANSI committee, each database system vendor has a unique way of connecting and, in some cases, communicating with their system.

The ability to create robust, platform-independent applications and Web-based applets prompted developers to consider using Java to develop front-end connectivity solutions. At the outset, third-party software developers met the need by providing proprietary solutions, using native methods to integrate client-side libraries or creating a third tier and a new protocol.

The Java Software Division, Sun Microsystems' division responsible for the development of Java products, worked in conjunction with database and database-tool vendors to create a DBMS-independent mechanism that would allow developers to write their client-side applications without concern for the particular database being used. The result is the JDBC API, which is part of the core JDK 1.2.

JDBC provides application developers with a *single* API that is uniform and database independent. The API provides a standard to write to, and a standard that takes all of the various application designs into account. The secret is a set of Java interfaces that are implemented by a driver. The driver takes care of the translation of the standard JDBC calls into the specific calls required by the database it supports. In the following figure, the application is written once and moved to the various drivers. The application remains the same; the drivers change. Drivers may be used to develop the middle tier of a multi-tier database design, also known as *middleware*, as illustrated in Figure 15.4.

In addition to providing developers with a uniform and DBMS-independent framework, JDBC also provides a means of allowing developers to retain the specific functionality that their database vendor offers. JDBC drivers must support the ANSI SQL-2 Entry Level standard, but JDBC allows developers to pass query strings directly to the connected driver. These strings may or may not be ANSI SQL, or even SQL at all. The use of these strings is up to the underlying driver. Of course, use of this feature limits the freedom of the application developer to change database back ends.

Part iii

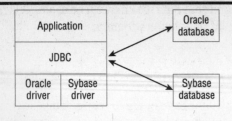

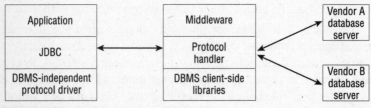

FIGURE 15.4: JDBC database designs

NOTE

For additional information on SQL, you may want to get Martin Gruber's *SQL Instant Reference* book from Sybex or purchase the standards documents from ANSI at http://www.ansi.org.

JDBC is *not* a derivative of Microsoft's Open Database Connectivity specification (ODBC). JDBC is written entirely in Java and ODBC is a C interface. While ODBC is usable by non-C languages, like Visual Basic, it has the inherent development risks of C, such as memory leaks. However, both JDBC and ODBC are based on the X/Open SQL Command Level Interface (CLI). Having the same conceptual base allowed work on the API to proceed quickly and makes acceptance and learning of the API easier. Sun provides a JDBC-ODBC bridge that translates JDBC to ODBC. This implementation, done with native methods, is very small and efficient.

NOTE

While still small and efficient, the 1.2 JDK includes a new version of the JDBC-ODBC bridge.

In general, there are two levels of interfaces in the JDBC API: the Application Layer, where the developer uses the API to make calls to the database via SQL and retrieve the results, and the Driver Layer, which handles all communication with a specific Driver implementation.

Every JDBC application (or applet) must have at least one JDBC driver, and each driver is specific to the type of DBMS used. A driver does not, however, need to be directly associated with a database.

The API Components

As mentioned earlier, there are two distinct layers within the JDBC API: the Application Layer, which database-application developers use, and the Driver Layer, which the driver vendors implement. It is important to understand the Driver Layer, if only to realize that the driver creates some of the objects used at the Application Layer. Figure 15.5 illustrates the connection between the Driver and Application layers.

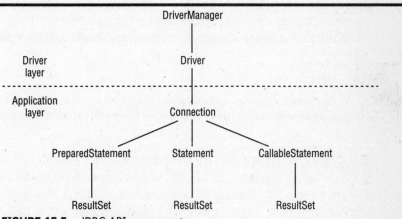

FIGURE 15.5: JDBC API components

Fortunately, the application developer need only use the standard API interfaces in order to guarantee JDBC compliance. The driver developer is responsible for developing code that interfaces to the database and supports the JDBC application level calls.

There are four main interfaces that every driver layer must implement, and one class that bridges the Application and Driver layers. The four interfaces are the `Driver`, `Connection`, `Statement`, and `ResultSet`. The `Driver` interface implementation is where the connection to the database is made. In most applications, the `Driver` is accessed through the `DriverManager` class—providing one more layer of abstraction for the developer.

Part III

The Connection, Statement, and ResultSet interfaces are implemented by the driver vendor, but these interfaces represent the methods that the application developer will treat as real object classes and allow the developer to create statements and retrieve results. So the distinction in this section between Driver and Application layers is artificial—but it allows the developer to create database applications without having to think about where the objects are coming from or worry about what specific driver the application will use.

The Driver Layer

There is a one-to-one correspondence between the database and the JDBC Driver. This approach is common in multi-tier designs. The Driver class is an interface implemented by the driver vendor. The other important class is the DriverManager class, which sits above the Driver and Application layers. The DriverManager is responsible for loading and unloading drivers and making connections through drivers. The Driver-Manager also provides features for logging and database login timeouts.

NOTE

As shown in Figure 15.4, the driver does not have to connect directly to a database and can support a new protocol for a multi-tier database design.

The _Driver_ Interface   Every JDBC program must have at least one JDBC driver implementation. The Driver interface allows the Driver-Manager and JDBC Application layers to exist independently of the particular database used. A JDBC driver is an implementation of the Driver interface class. Drivers use a string to locate and access databases. The syntax of this string is very similar to a URL string. The purpose of a JDBC URL string is to separate the application developer from the driver developer. Sun defines the following goals for driver URLs:

▶ The name of the driver-access URL should define the type of database being used.

▶ The user (application developer) should be free from any of the administration of creating the database connection. Therefore, any database connection information (host, port, database name, user access, and passwords) should be encoded in the URL.

► A network naming system may be used in order to prevent the user from having to specifically encode the exact hostname and port number of the database.

The URL syntax used by the World Wide Web supports a standard syntax that satisfies these goals. A JDBC URL has the following syntax and structure:

```
jdbc:<subprotocol>:<subname>
```

where *<subprotocol>* defines the type of driver, and *<subname>* provides the network encoded name. For example:

```
jdbc:oracle:products
```

Here the database driver is an Oracle driver and the subname is a local database called `products`. This driver is designed to know how to use the subname when making the connection to the Oracle database.

A network naming service may also be specified as the subprotocol, rather than using a specific database driver name. In this case, the subprotocol would define the naming service:

```
jdbc:localnaming:human-resources
```

Here the subprotocol defines a local service that can resolve the subname `human-resources` to a database server. This approach can be useful when the application developer wants to isolate the user from the actual location, name, database username, and database password. This URL specifies that a driver named `localnaming` be specified. This could be a Java program that contains a simple flat-file lookup, translates `human-resources` into `hrdatabase1.eng:888/personnel`, and knows to use the username `user` and password `matilda`. The details of the connection are kept hidden from the user.

Typically, the application developer will know specifically where the database is located and may not wish to use redirection to locate the database. In this case, the URL may be expanded to include the location of the host and specific port and database information:

```
jdbc:msql://dbserver.eng:1112/bugreports
```

Here an `msql` database driver type is used to locate a server named `dbserver` in the `eng` domain and attempt to connect to a database server on port 1112 that contains a `bugreports` database, using the default username and password to connect.

NOTE

It is possible for subprotocol names to overlap. To help prevent this, Sun informally maintains a registry of reserved names. For more information on registering a JDBC subprotocol name, consult the JDBC Specification.

The driver vendor implements the `Driver` interface by creating methods for each of the following interface methods:

Signature: `public interface java.sql.Driver`

public abstract Connection connect(String url, Properties info) throws SQLException The driver implementation of this method should check the subprotocol name of the URL string passed for a match with this driver. If there is a match, the driver should then attempt to connect to the database using the information passed in the remainder of the URL. A successful database connection will return an instance of the driver's implementation of a `Connection` interface (object). The `SQLException` should be thrown only if the driver recognizes the URL subprotocol but cannot make the database connection. A `null` is returned if the URL does not match a URL the driver expected. The username and password are included in a container class called `Properties`.

public abstract DriverPropertyInfo[] getPropertyInfo(String url, Properties info) throws SQLException If you are not aware of which properties to use when calling `connect()`, you can ask the `Driver` if the supplied properties are sufficient to establish a connection. If they aren't, an array of necessary properties is provided with the help of the `DriverPropertyInfo` class.

public abstract boolean acceptsURL(String url) throws SQLException It is also possible to explicitly "ask" the driver if a URL is valid. But note that the implementation of this method (typically) only checks if the subprotocol specified in the URL is valid, not whether a connection can be made.

public int getMajorVersion() Returns the driver's major version number. If the driver's version was at 4.3, this would return the integer 4.

MORE ON *DRIVERPROPERTYINFO*

For each possible property, a *DriverPropertyInfo* instance is provided. There are five instance variables available to describe the property, enabling the automated creation of a graphical screen to prompt for information:

name	name of property
description	short description of property (may be null)
required	boolean value describing if property is required
value	current/default property value (may be null)
choices	array of possible values for property (may be null)

public int getMinorVersion()   Returns the driver's minor version number. If the driver's version was at 4.3, this would return the integer 3.

public boolean jdbcCompliant()   Returns whether or not the driver is a complete JDBC implementation. For legacy systems or lightweight solutions, it may not be possible, or necessary, to have a complete implementation.

The connect() method of Driver is the most important method and is called by the DriverManager to obtain a Connection object. As Figure 15.5 previously showed, the Connection object is the starting point of the JDBC Application layer. The Connection object is used to create Statement objects that perform queries.

The connect() method typically performs the following steps:

1. Checks to see if the URL string provided is valid

2. Opens a TCP connection to the host and port number specified

3. Attempts to access the named database table (if any)

4. Returns an instance of a Connection object

NOTE

Connection is a Java interface, so the object returned is actually a reference to the driver's implementation of the Connection interface.

The *DriverManager* Class   The DriverManager class is really a utility class used to manage JDBC drivers. The class provides methods to obtain a connection through a driver, register and de-register drivers, set up logging, and set login timeouts for database access. All of the methods in the DriverManager class listed below are static and may be referenced through the following class name:

Signature: `public class java.sql.DriverManager`

public static synchronized Connection getConnection(String url, Properties info) throws SQLException   This method (and the other getConnection() methods) attempts to return a reference to an object implementing the Connection interface. The method sweeps through an internal collection of stored Driver classes, passing the URL string and Properties object info to each in turn. The first Driver class that returns a Connection is used. info is a reference to a Properties container object of tag/value pairs, typically username/password. This method allows several attempts to make an authorized connection for each driver in the collection.

public static synchronized Connection getConnection(String url) throws SQLException
This method calls getConnection (url, info) above with an empty Properties object (info).

public static synchronized Connection getConnection(String url, String user, String password) throws SQLException   This method creates a Properties object (info), stores the user and password strings in it, and then calls getConnection (url, info) above.

public static synchronized void registerDriver (java.sql.Driver driver) throws SQLException
This method stores the instance of the Driver interface implementation into a collection of drivers, along with the program's current security context to identify where the driver came from.

public static void setLogStream(PrintStream out)   Deprecated. This method sets a logging/tracing PrintStream that is used by the DriverManager.

public static void setLoginTimeout(int seconds)
This method sets the permissible delay a driver should wait when attempting a database login. Drivers are registered with the DriverManager class either at initialization of the Driver-Manager class or when an instance of the driver is created.

When the DriverManager class is loaded, a section of static code (in the class) is run, and the class names of drivers listed in a Java property named jdbc.drivers are loaded. This property can be used to define a list of colon-separated driver class names, such as:

```
jdbc.drivers=imaginary.sql.Driver:oracle.sql.Driver:weblogic
.sql.Driver
```

Each driver name is a class file name (including the package declaration) that the DriverManager will attempt to load through the current CLASSPATH. The DriverManager uses the following call to locate, load, and link the named class:

```
Class.forName(driver);
```

If the jdbc.drivers property is empty (unspecified), then the application programmer must create an instance of a driver class.

In both cases, the Driver class implementation must explicitly register itself with the DriverManager by calling:

```
DriverManager.registerDriver (this);
```

Here is a segment of code from the imaginary Driver (for the Mini-SQL database). The Driver registers itself whenever an instance of the imaginary driver is created:

```
...
public class iMsqlDriver implements java.sql.Driver
{
  static {
    try {
      new iMsqlDriver();
    }
    catch( SQLException e ) {
      e.printStackTrace();
    }
  }
  /**
   * Constructs a new driver and registers it with
   * java.sql.DriverManager.registerDriver() as specified
   * by the JDBC draft protocol.
   */
  public iMsqlDriver() throws SQLException {
```

```
        java.sql.DriverManager.registerDriver(this);
    }
    ...
```

The primary use of the DriverManager is to get a Connection object reference through the getConnection method:

```
Connection conn;
conn = DriverManager.getConnection (
        "jdbc:sybase://dbserver:8080/billing",
        dbuser, dbpasswd);
```

This method goes through the list of registered drivers and passes the URL string and parameters to each driver in turn through the driver's connect() method. If the driver supports the subprotocol and subname information, a Connection object reference is returned.

The DriverManager class is not required to create JDBC applications, as it is possible to get a Connection object directly from the Driver:

```
Connection conn;
Driver sybDriver = new SybaseDriver();
conn = sybDriver.connect(
        "jdbc:sybase://dbserver:8080/billing", props);
```

This means of obtaining a connection is not as clean and leaves the application developer dependent on the Driver implementation class to provide security checks.

The Application Layer

The Application Layer encompasses three interfaces that are implemented at the Driver Layer but are used by the application developer. In Java, the interface provides a means of using a general name to indicate a specific object. The general name defines methods that *must* be implemented by the specific object classes. For the application developer, this means that the specific Driver class implementation is irrelevant. Just coding to the standard JDBC APIs will be sufficient. This is, of course, assuming that the driver is JDBC compliant. Recall that this means the database at least supports ANSI SQL-2 Entry Level.

The three main interfaces are Connection, Statement, and ResultSet. A Connection object is obtained from the driver implementation through the DriverManager.getConnection() method call. Once a Connection object is returned, the application developer may create a Statement object to issue against the database. The result of a Statement is a ResultSet object, which contains the results of the particular statement (if any).

Connection Basics   The `Connection` interface represents a session with the database connection provided by the `Driver`. Typical database connections include the ability to control changes made to the actual data stored through transactions. A *transaction* is a set of operations that are completed in order. A *commit* action makes the operations store (or change) data in the database. A *rollback* action undoes the previous transaction before it has been committed. On creation, JDBC `Connections` are in an *auto-commit* mode; there is no rollback possible. So after getting a `Connection` object from the driver, the developer should consider setting auto-commit to `false` with the `setAutoCommit (boolean b)` method.

When auto-commit is disabled, the `Connection` will support both `Connection.commit()` and `Connection.rollback()` method calls. The level of support for transaction isolation depends on the underlying support for transactions in the database.

A portion of the `Connection` interface definition follows:

Signature: `public interface Connection`

> **Statement createStatement() throws SQLException**
> The `Connection` object implementation will return an instance of an implementation of a `Statement` object. The `Statement` object is then used to issue queries.
>
> **PreparedStatement prepareStatement(String sql) throws SQLException** The `Connection` object implementation will return an instance of a `PreparedStatement` object that is configured with the `sql` string passed. The driver may then send the statement to the database, if the database (driver) handles precompiled statements. Otherwise the driver may wait until the `PreparedStatement` is executed by an execute method. An exception may be thrown if the driver and database do not implement precompiled statements.
>
> **CallableStatement prepareCall(String sql) throws SQLException** The `Connection` object implementation will return an instance of a `CallableStatement`. `CallableStatements` are optimized for handling stored procedures. The driver implementation may send the `sql` string immediately when `prepareCall()` is complete or may wait until an `execute()` method occurs.

Part iii

void setAutoCommit(boolean autoCommit) throws SQLException   Sets a flag in the driver implementation that enables commit/rollback (`false`) or makes all transactions commit immediately (`true`).

void commit() throws SQLException   Makes all changes made since the beginning of the current transaction (either the opening of the `Connection` or since the last `commit()` or `rollback()`).

void rollback() throws SQLException   Drops all changes made since the beginning of the current transaction.

The primary use of the `Connection` interface is to create a statement:

```
Connection msqlConn;
Statement stmt;

msqlConn = DriverManager.getConnection (url);
stmt = msqlConn.createStatement();
```

This statement may be used to send SQL queries that return a single result set in a `ResultSet` object reference or a count of the number of records affected by the statement. Statements that need to be called a number of times with slight variations may be executed more efficiently using a `PreparedStatement`. The `Connection` interface is also used to create a `CallableStatement` whose primary purpose is to execute stored procedures.

TIP

The primary difference between `Statement`, `PreparedStatement`, and `CallableStatement` is that `Statement` does not permit any parameters within the SQL statement to be executed, `PreparedStatement` permits In parameters, and `CallableStatement` permits Inout and Out parameters. In parameters are parameters that are passed into an operation. Out parameters are parameters passed by reference; they are expected to return a result of the reference type. Inout parameters are Out parameters that contain an initial value that may change as a result of the operation. JDBC supports all three parameter types.

Most of the time, the developer knows the database specifics beforehand and creates the application accordingly. However, JDBC provides an interface that may be used to dynamically determine database-specific information. The `Connection` interface `getMetaData` method will return a `DatabaseMetaData` object. The instance of the class that implements the interface provides information about the database as a whole, including access information about tables and procedures, column names, data types, and so on. The implementation details of `DatabaseMetaData` are dependent upon the database vendor's ability to return this type of information.

Statement Basics   A *statement* is the vehicle for sending SQL queries to the database and retrieving a set of results. Statements can be SQL updates, inserts, deletes, or queries (via Select). The `Statement` interface provides a number of methods designed to make the job of writing queries to the database easier. There are other methods to perform other operations with a `Statement`.

Signature: `public interface Statement`

ResultSet executeQuery(String sql) throws SQLException   Executes a single SQL query and returns the results in an object of type `ResultSet`.

int executeUpdate(String sql) throws SQLException Executes a single SQL query that does not return a set of results, but a count of rows affected.

boolean execute(String sql) throws SQLException A general SQL statement that may return multiple result sets and/or update counts. This method is most frequently used when you do not know what can be returned, probably because of a user entering the SQL statement directly. The `getResultSet()`, `getUpdateCount()`, and `getMoreResults()` methods are used to retrieve the data returned.

ResultSet getResultSet() throws SQLException Returns the current data as the result of a statement execution as a `ResultSet` object. Note that if there are no results to be read or if the result is an update count, this method returns `null`. Also note that once read, the results are cleared.

int getUpdateCount() throws SQLException   Returns the status of an `Update`, `Insert`, or `Delete` query or a stored procedure. The value returned is the number of rows affected. A -1 is returned if there is no update count or if the data returned is a result set. Once read, the update count is cleared.

boolean getMoreResults() throws SQLException
Moves to the next result in a set of multiple results/update
counts. This method returns true if the next result is a Result-
Set object. This method will also close any previous ResultSet
read.

Statements may or may not return a ResultSet object, depending on
the Statement method used. The executeUpdate() method, for
example, is used to execute SQL statements that do not expect a result
(except a row count status):

```
int rowCount;
rowCount = stmt.executeUpdate (
"DELETE FROM customer WHERE CustomerID = 'McG10233'");
```

SQL statements that return a single set of results can use the execute-
Query() method. This method returns a single ResultSet object. The
object represents the row information returned as a result of the query:

```
ResultSet results;
results = stmt.executeQuery ("SELECT * FROM stock");
```

SQL statements that execute stored procedures (or trigger a stored procedure) may return more than one set of results. The execute() method is a
general-purpose method that can return a single result set, a result count, or
some combination thereof. The method returns a boolean flag that is used
to determine whether there are more results. Because a result set could
contain either data or the count of an operation that returns a row count,
the getResultSet(), getMoreResults(), and getUpdateCount()
methods are used.

For example:

```
// Assume SQLString returns multiple result sets
// true if a ResultSet is returned
boolean result = stmt.execute (SQLString);
int count = stmt.getUpdateCount();

// Now loop until there are no more results or update counts
while (result || (count != -1)) {
  // Is the result a ResultSet?
  if (result) {
    results = stmt.getResultSet();
    // Process result set
  } else if (count != -1) {
    // Do something with count
  }
  result = stmt.getMoreResults();
```

```
    count = stmt.getUpdateCount();
}
```

The `PreparedStatement` interface extends the `Statement` interface. When there is a SQL statement that requires repetition with minor variations, the `PreparedStatement` provides an efficient mechanism for passing a precompiled SQL statement that uses input parameters.

Signature: `public interface PreparedStatement extends Statement`

`PreparedStatement` parameters are used to pass data into a SQL statement, so they are considered `In` parameters and are filled in by using `setType` methods:

NOTE

The `setType` methods fill the value of parameters (marked by question marks) in a `PreparedStatement`. These parameters are indexed from 1 to *n*.

```
// Assume priceList is an array of prices that needs
// to be reduced for a 10% off sale, and reducedItems
// is an array of item IDs
int reduction = 10;
PreparedStatement ps = msqlConn.prepareStatment (
    "UPDATE Catalog SET Price = ? WHERE ItemID = ?");
// Do the updates in a loop
for (int i = 0; i < reducedItems.length(); i++) {
    // Note that the setType methods set the value of the
    // parameters noted in the SQL statement with question
    // marks (?). They are indexed, starting from 1 to n.
    ps.setFloat (1,
                (priceList[i]*((float)(100-reduction)/100)));
    ps.setString (2, reducedItems[i]);
    if (ps.executeUpdate() == 0) {
        throw new SQLException ("No Item ID: "
                                + reducedItems[i]);
    }
}
```

Parameters hold their current values until either a new `setType` method is called or the method `clearParameters()` is called for the `PreparedStatement` object. In addition to the `execute` methods inherited from `Statement`, `PrepareStatement` declares the following `setType` methods. Each method takes two arguments: a parameter index and the primitive or class type, as illustrated in Table 15.1.

The `CallableStatement` interface is used to execute SQL stored procedures. `CallableStatement` inherits from the `PreparedStatement` interface, so all of the `execute` and `setType` methods are available. Stored procedures have a varying syntax among database vendors, so JDBC defines a standard way for all RDBMSs to call stored procedures.

Signature: `public interface CallableStatement extends PreparedStatement`

The JDBC uses an escape syntax that allows parameters to be passed as In parameters and Out parameters. The syntax also allows a result to be returned; and if this syntax is used, the parameter must be registered as an Out parameter.

Here is an example of a `CallableStatement` returning an Out parameter:

```
CallableStatement cs = conn.prepareCall(
                       "{call getQuote (?, ?)}");
cs.setString (1, stockName);
// java.sql.Types defines SQL data types that are returned
// as Out parameters
cs.registerOutParameter (2, Types.FLOAT);
stmt.executeUpdate();
float quote = stmt.getFloat (2);
```

TABLE 15.1: setType Methods

METHOD SIGNATURE	JAVA TYPE	SQL TYPE FROM THE DATABASE
void setByte (int index, byte b)	byte	TINYINT
void setShort (int index, short s)	short	SMALLINT
void setInt (int index, int i)	int	INTEGER
void setLong (int index, long l)	long	BIGINT
void setFloat (int index, float f)	float	FLOAT
void setDouble (int index, double d)	double	DOUBLE
void setBigDecimal (int index, BigDecimal bd)	java.math.BigDecimal	NUMERIC
void setString (int index, String s)	java.lang.String	VARCHAR
void setCharacterStream (int index, Reader r, int length)	java.io.Reader	LONGVARCHAR
void setBytes (int index, byte b[])	byte array	VARBINARY

TABLE 15.1 continued: setType Methods

METHOD SIGNATURE	JAVA TYPE	SQL TYPE FROM THE DATABASE
void setBinaryStream (int index, InputStream is, int length)	java.io.InputStream	LONGVARBINARY
void setString(int parameterIndex, String x)	String	CHAR, VARCHAR or LONGVARCHAR
void setDate (int index, Date d)	java.sql.Date	DATE
void setTime (int index, Time t)	java.sql.Time	TIME
void setTimestamp (int index, Timestamp ts)	java.sql.Timestamp	TIMESTAMP
void setNull (int index, int sqlType)	—	java.sql.types lists SQL types by number, and NULL is integer 0 (zero)
void setBoolean (int index, boolean b)	boolean	BIT

CallableStatement defines a set of getType methods that convert the SQL types returned from the database to Java types. These methods match the setType methods declared by PreparedStatement, as shown in Table 15.2.

NOTE

The getType methods access data in each column as the result of a query. Each column can be accessed by either its position in the row, numbered from 1 to *n* columns, or its name, like custID.

TABLE 15.2: getType Methods

METHOD SIGNATURE	JAVA TYPE	SQL TYPE FROM THE DATABASE
boolean getBoolean (int index)	boolean	BIT
byte getByte (int index)	byte	TINYINT
short getShort (int index)	short	SMALLINT
int getInt (int index)	int	INTEGER

TABLE 15.2 continued: getType Methods

Method Signature	Java Type	SQL Type from the Database
`long getLong (int index)`	long	BIGINT
`float getFloat (int index)`	float	FLOAT
`double getDouble (int index)`	double	DOUBLE
`BigDecimal getBigDecimal (int index, int scale)`	java.math.BigDecimal	NUMERIC
`String getString (int index)`	String	CHAR, VARCHAR or LONGVARCHAR
`byte[] getBytes (int index)`	byte array	BINARY or VARBINARY
`Date getDate (int index)`	java.sql.Date	DATE
`Time getTime (int index)`	java.sql.Time	TIME
`Timestamp getTimestamp (int index)`	java.sql.Timestamp	TIMESTAMP

NOTE

Note that it is the responsibility of the JDBC driver to convert the data passed from the database as SQL data types into Java values.

***ResultSet* Basics**   The `ResultSet` interface defines methods for accessing tables of data generated as the result of executing a `Statement`. `ResultSet` column values may be accessed in any order; they are indexed and may be selected by either the name or the number (numbered from 1 to *n*) of the column. `ResultSet` maintains the position of the current row, starting with the first row of data returned. The `next()` method moves to the next row of data.

A partial look at the `ResultSet` interface follows:

Signature: `public interface ResultSet`

> **boolean next() throws SQLException**   Positions the `ResultSet` to the next row; `ResultSet` row position is initially the first row of the result set.

ResultSetMetaData getMetaData() throws SQL-Exception   Returns an object that contains a description of the current result set: the number of columns, the type of each column, and properties of the results.

void close() throws SQLException   Normally a ResultSet is closed when another Statement is executed, but it may be desirable to release the resources earlier.

As with the CallableStatement above, the resulting data can be read through getType methods. For example:

```
// Pass a query to the statement object
ResultSet rs = stmt.executeQuery(
                "SELECT * FROM stock WHEREquantity = 0");

// Get the results as their Java types
// Note that columns are indexed by an integer starting with 1,
// or by the name of column, as in "ItemID"
System.out.println ("Stock replenishment list");
while (rs.next()) {

  System.out.println ("Item ID: " + rs.getString("ItemID"));
  System.out.println ("Next ship date: " + rs.getDate(2));
  System.out.println ("");
}
```

The 1.2 JDK introduces several methods with the JDBC 2.0 API. With JDBC 2.0, additional capabilities are available that permit non-sequential reading of rows, as well as updating of rows, while reading. A partial look at the JDBC 2.0 methods of ResultSet follows:

int getType() throws SQLException   Returns the type of result set, determining the manner in which you can read the results. Valid return values are TYPE_FORWARD_ONLY, TYPE_STATIC, TYPE_KEYSET, or TYPE_DYNAMIC. If TYPE_FORWARD_ONLY is returned, most of the remaining methods will throw a SQLException if they are attempted.

boolean first() throws SQLException   Positions the ResultSet at the first row. Returns true if on a valid row, false otherwise.

boolean last() throws SQLException   Positions the ResultSet at the last row. Returns true if on a valid row, false otherwise.

boolean previous() throws SQLException   Positions
the ResultSet at the previous row. Returns true if on a valid
row, false otherwise.

boolean absolute(int row) throws SQLException
Positions the ResultSet at the designated row. If row requested
is negative, positions ResultSet at row relative to end of set.

**boolean relative(int row) throws
SQLException**   Positions the ResultSet at the row, relative to the current position.

boolean isFirst() throws SQLException   JDBC 2.0
Indicates whether the cursor is on the first row of the result set.

boolean isLast() throws SQLException   JDBC 2.0
Indicates whether the cursor is on the last row of the result set.

NOTE

The JDBC 2.0 API also permits the updating of rows, as you read each row from the
ResultSet. You can delete the current row with deleteRow() or update the
columns of the current row with methods like updateInt(int col, int value)
or updateFloat(String columnName, float value). There are two methods for each datatype: one accessing columns by column number, the other by
column name. Once you are done updating a row, you tell the system to update
the actual database with updateRow().

ResultSetMetaData   Besides being able to read data from a
ResultSet object, JDBC provides an interface to allow the developer to
determine what type of data was returned. The ResultSetMetaData
interface is similar to the DatabaseMetaData interface in concept, but
is specific to the current ResultSet. As with DatabaseMetaData, it is
unlikely that many developers will use this interface, since most applications are written with an understanding of the database schema and column names and values. However, ResultSetMetaData is useful in
dynamically determining the meta-data of a ResultSet returned from a
stored procedure or from a user-supplied SQL statement.

The following code demonstrates the displaying of results with the
help of ResultSetMetaData when the contents are unknown:

```
ResultSet results = stmt.executeQuery (sqlString);
ResultSetMetaData meta = results.getMetaData();
```

```
int columns = 0;
boolean first = true;
while (results.next()) {
  if (first) {
    columns = meta.getColumnCount();
    for (int i=1; i<=columns; i++) {
      System.out.print (meta.getColumnName(i) + "\t");
    }
    System.out.println();
    first=false;
  }
  for (int i=1; i<=columns; i++) {
    System.out.print (results.getString (i) + "\t");
  }
  System.out.println();
}
```

Sending and Receiving Large Data Chunks   SQL LONGVARBINARY
and LONGVARCHAR data types can be of arbitrary size. The getBytes()
and getString() methods can read these types up to the limits imposed
by the driver. The limits can be read through the Statement.getMax-
FieldSize() method. For larger blocks of data, the JDBC allows developers to use input streams to return the data in chunks.

TIP

Streams must be read immediately following the query execution. They are
automatically closed at the next receipt of a ResultSet.

Sending large blocks of data is also possible using java.io.Output-
Stream as parameters. When a statement is executed, the JDBC driver
makes repeated calls to read and transmit the data in the streams.

NOTE

The JDBC 2.0 API also adds the ability to use locator type objects Array, Blob,
Clob, and Struct for reading and storing large objects. These are part of the
emerging SQL3 standard. For a more complete description of these JDBC 2 capabilities, visit http://java.sun.com/products/jdbc/jdbcsw2.html.

Part iii

Limitations Using JDBC (Applications vs. Applets)

There are two types of programs in the Java world: applications and applets. Each program type provides benefits, and the use of each is generally determined by the way in which the developer wishes the user to access the program.

Applications

Applications are Java programs that are developed as stand-alone executables. The user is expected to have access to the program executable (`.class` file) and the Java interpreter locally. For an intranet-based database front end, this strategy offers the benefits of faster startup (class files are local) and local disk utilization.

In addition, Java applications are trusted and are allowed greater flexibility with socket connections, making it possible for the client program to access multiple database systems on remote servers.

Java applications are becoming more prevalent as tools become available for GUI development and speed improvements are made possible through Just-In-Time (JIT) compilers/interpreters. Applications can also reduce or eliminate issues with browser security models and their differing Java implementations.

Applets

Applets are mini Java programs that require a Java-enabled browser to run. The browser provides an environment in which the applet can run, including drawing and viewing resources directly on the browser page. When a user moves or "surfs" to a browser page that contains an applet, the applet is automatically executed.

The process involves downloading the necessary Java applet code, including JDBC drivers and application layer software, automatically checking security restrictions on the code, and, if OK, running the applet.

Applets provide several key benefits over applications:

▶ Version control. It is possible to modify an applet almost on the fly by replacing the class file in the HTML page references.

▶ Easier execution model. It takes very little effort to learn to use even the most sophisticated browsers and to execute a front-end client. The user simply navigates to the page where the application is located.

▶ Online help. Creating the running program on a browser HTML page makes it extremely easy to embed Help links that can be developed separately from the running program.

A typical use of applets might be for training within a large organization, where the data being delivered is not critical and access can be limited to a two-tier model. (Three-tier models are possible but involve more complex layering schemes). Another use may be the simple presentation of data to the Internet community, again where the quantity of data is not great and security of the data message is not paramount.

Applets, however, are severely constrained by the browser environment in the following ways:

▶ They cannot access any local files. This limits the use of local caching and table manipulation and storage to in-memory during the life of the applet.

▶ They cannot connect to arbitrary hosts. Socket connections are only allowed between the applet and the host that the applet originated from.

▶ They cannot load or run drivers that contain native methods (C language calls).

Additionally there is a considerable performance hit involved in loading applet code across an Internet (wide area) network connection.

Some of these constraints may be lifted or reduced with the introduction of trusted applets and browsers that accept them. Trusted applets may be code signed with a cryptographic key or may be stored in a trusted location. If the browser environment believes that the applets' source is trusted, then for security purposes they may be treated like applications. However, there may still be limits regarding the location of databases on an Internet that are not related to the Java security manager. Trusted applets are the subject of future consideration in the development of the Java security model.

The other alternative that is more tangible and available today is the use of a three-tier model. In this approach, the applet is loaded from a middleware tier that provides the HTML page and HTTP server, and a multithreaded application (Java, C, or C++) that supports socket connections for multiple clients and, in turn, contacts remote database systems.

Calls to the third tier can be managed by developing a custom (proprietary) protocol, by using Remote Method Invocation (RMI), or by using an Object Request Broker (ORB). See the "Alternative Connectivity Strategies" section later in this chapter.

Security Considerations

The JDBC API follows the standard Java security model. In short, applications are considered trusted code, and applets are considered untrusted. In general, the job of writing a secure JDBC driver is left to the driver vendor.

The Java Virtual Machine employs its own well-documented security checks for untrusted applets, including the aforementioned restrictions. However, if a JDBC driver vendor wants to extend the model by adding features to their driver—for example, allowing multiple applets to use the same TCP socket connection to talk to a database—then it becomes the responsibility of the vendor to check that each applet is allowed to use the connection.

In addition to maintaining the integrity of the Java security model, both the JDBC driver vendor and JDBC application developer need to keep in mind that the JDBC API defines a means of executing database calls and does not define a network security model. The data sent over the wire to the database and the resulting table information (for example, to request customer credit card information) are exposed and can be read by any terminal that is capable of snooping the network.

A JDBC Database Example

The following is an example that uses the concepts presented in this chapter. It is artificial and only meant to illustrate the use of `Statement`, `PreparedStatement`, and `CallableStatement`.

The simple database has a table called *Customers*, which has the schema shown in Table 15.3.

TABLE 15.3: Customer Data Table

CustomerID	VARCHAR
LastName	VARCHAR
FirstName	VARCHAR
PhoneNumber	VARCHAR
StreetAddress	VARCHAR
Zipcode	VARCHAR

Table 15.3 is part of a larger database that stores information related to a large catalog ordering system. Here is the definition of a simple `Customer` object with two primary methods, `insertNewCustomer()` and `getCustomer()`:

Signature: `public class Customer`

`public Customer(Connection conn)` The constructor for the class. The `Customer` constructor receives a `Connection` object, which it uses to create `Statement` references. In addition, the constructor creates a `PreparedStatement` and three `CallableStatement` objects.

`public String insertNewCustomer(String lname, String fname, String pnum, String addr, String zip) throws insertFailedException, SQLException` Creates a new customer record, including a new ID. The ID is created through a stored procedure that reads the current list of customer IDs and creates a new reference. The method returns the new ID created or throws an exception if the insert failed.

`public CustomerInfo getCustomer(String custID) throws selectException, SQLException` Returns an object that contains the data in the Customer table. An exception is thrown if the customer ID passed does not exist or is not properly formatted, or if the SQL statement fails.

`public static synchronized boolean validateZip (String zip) throws SQLException` Is a utility method to validate the zip code. A `true` value is returned if the zip code exists in the ZipCode table in the database.

Part iii

public static synchronized boolean validateID (String id) throws SQLException   Is a utility method to validate a customer ID. If the ID exists, the method returns true.

The source is as follows:

LIST 15.1: Customer.java

```java
// Customer record class
// This class is used to store and access customer
// data from the database
import java.sql.*;

public class Customer {

  private Connection conn;
  private PreparedStatement insertNewCustomer;
  private CallableStatement getNewID;
  public static CallableStatement checkZip;
  public static CallableStatement checkID;

  // Customer constructor: store a local copy of the
  // Connection object create statements for use later
  public Customer (Connection c) {
    conn = c;

    try {
      insertNewCustomer = conn.prepareStatement(
        "INSERT INTO customers VALUES (?, ?, ?, ?, ?, ?)");

      getNewID = conn.prepareCall ("{call getNewID (?)}");
      checkID = conn.prepareCall ("{call checkID (?,?)}");
      checkZip = conn.prepareCall (
                  "{call checkZip (?, ?)}");
    } catch (SQLException e) {
      System.err.println ("Cannot create statements");
    }
  }

  // Method for creating a new customer record.
  // The customerID is generated by a stored procedure
  // call on the database
  public String insertNewCustomer (String lname,
          String fname, String pnum, String addr,
          String zip)
        throws InsertFailedException, SQLException {
```

```java
String newID;

// Get a new customer ID through the stored procedure
if ((newID = getNewID ()) == null) {
  throw new InsertFailedException (
            "could not get new ID");
}

// Insert the new customer ID
insertNewCustomer.setString (1, newID);
insertNewCustomer.setString (2, lname);
insertNewCustomer.setString (3, fname);
insertNewCustomer.setString (4, pnum);
insertNewCustomer.setString (5, addr);
insertNewCustomer.setString (6, zip);

// Execute the statement
if (insertNewCustomer.executeUpdate() != 1) {
  throw new InsertFailedException (
            "could not execute insert");
}
return (newID);
}

// Get a single customer record with this ID
// Note: this method maps the returned data onto a
// CustomerInfo container object
public CustomerInfo getCustomer (String custID)
    throws SelectException, SQLException {

// Check the ID first
if (!validateID (custID)) {
  throw new SelectException ("no customer with ID: "
                            + custID);
}

// Create the select statement
Statement stmt = conn.createStatement();

// Get the results
ResultSet rs = stmt.executeQuery (
  "SELECT *FROM Customer WHERE CustID = " + custID);

// Create a CustomerInfo container object
CustomerInfo info = new CustomerInfo ();
```

```
    // Populate the CustomerInfo object
    // Columns are indexed starting with 1
    info.CustomerID = rs.getString (1);
    info.LastName = rs.getString (2);
    info.FirstName = rs.getString (3);
    info.PhoneNumber = rs.getString (4);
    info.StreetAddress = rs.getString (5);
    info.Zip = rs.getString (6);

    return (info);
}


// Method for validation of a customer's zip code
// This method is public so that it can be called
// from a user interface
public static synchronized boolean validateZip
    (String zip) throws SQLException {

    // Make call to stored procedure to validate zip code
    checkZip.setString (1, zip);
    checkZip.registerOutParameter (2, Types.BIT);
    checkZip.executeUpdate();
    return (checkZip.getBoolean(2));

}

// Method for validating a customer ID
// This method is public so that it can be called
// from a user interface
public static synchronized boolean validateID (String id)
    throws SQLException {

    // Make call to stored procedure to validate customer id
    checkID.setString (1, id);
    checkID.registerOutParameter (2, Types.BIT);
    checkID.executeUpdate();
    return (checkID.getBoolean(2));
}

// Method for retrieving a new customer ID from
// the database
private String getNewID () throws SQLException {

    // Make call to stored procedure to get
    // customer ID from DB
    getNewID.registerOutParameter (1, Types.VARCHAR);
    getNewID.executeUpdate();
```

```
      return (getNewID.getString(1));
    }
  }


  // Exceptions

  // InsertFailedException is a general exception for
  // SQL insert problems
  class InsertFailedException extends SQLException {
    public InsertFailedException () {
    }
    public InsertFailedException (String reason) {
      super (reason);
    }
  }

  // SelectException is a general exception for
  // SQL select problems
  class SelectException extends SQLException {

    public SelectException (String reason) {
      super (reason);
    }
    public SelectException () {
    }
  }
```

The CustomerInfo class is a simple container object. Container classes make it easier to pass a complete customer record to and from any method that manipulates the Customer table in the database. Data can be stored in the container class and passed as a single object reference, rather than having to pass each element as a single reference. The code for the class follows:

LIST 15.2: CustomerInfo.java

```
// A container object for the Customer table
public class CustomerInfo {
  String CustomerID;
  String LastName;
  String FirstName;
  String PhoneNumber;
  String StreetAddress;
  String Zip;
}
```

Finally, to test the simple `Customer` class, here is a simple Java application that illustrates loading a Sybase driver, making a connection, and passing the `Connection` object returned to a new instance of a `Customer` object. The code for the example program follows:

LIST 15.3: Example.java

```java
// A simple Java application that illustrates the use of
// DriverManager, Driver, Connection, Statement
// and ResultSet

import java.sql.*;

public class Example {

  Connection sybaseConn;

  public static void main (String arg[]) {

    // Look for the url, username and password
    if (arg.length < 3) {
      System.err.println ("Example use:");
      System.err.println (
              "java Example <url> <username> <password>");
      System.exit (1);
    }

    // Create an instance of the class
    Example ex = new Example ();

    // Initialize the connection
    ex.initdb (arg[0], arg[1], arg[2]);

    // Test the connection-write a customer and
    // then read it back
    ex.testdb ();
  }

  // method to initialize the database connection
  // The Connection object reference is kept globally
  public void initdb (String url, String user,
                      String passwd) {
    // Try to open the database and get the connection
    try {
```

```java
      // Note that this example assumes that
      // Java property "jdbc.drivers"
      // is loading the appropriate driver(s) for
      // the url passed in the getConnection call.
      // It is possible to explicitly create an
      // instance of a driver as well, for example:
      // new sybase.sql.driver ();

      // Create a connection
      sybaseConn = DriverManager.getConnection
        (url, user, passwd);

    } catch (SQLException e) {
      System.err.println ("Database connection failed:");
      System.err.println (e.getMessage());
      System.exit (2);
    }
  }

// Simple method to test the Customer class methods
public void testdb () {
  String custID = null;

  // Create the instance of the Customer class
  Customer cust = new Customer (sybaseConn);

  try {
    // Now insert a new Customer
    custID = cust.insertNewCustomer (
             "Jones", "Bill", "555-1234",
             "5 Main Street", "01234");

  } catch (SQLException e) {

    System.err.println ("Insert failed:");
    System.err.println (e.getMessage());
    System.exit (3);
  }

  try {
    // Read it back from the database
    CustomerInfo info = cust.getCustomer (custID);

  } catch (SQLException e) {
```

```
        System.err.println ("Read failed:");
        System.err.println (e.getMessage());
        System.exit (4);
    }
  }
}
```

Compile the example program (remember to substitute the path to your database for the path shown below):

```
C:\MasteringJava\Ch21>javac Example.java
C:\MasteringJava\Ch21>java Example

Example Use:
java Example <url> <username> <password>

C:\MasteringJava\Ch21>java Example
jdbc:sybase://dbserver:8080/billing john MyPassword
```

This example illustrates the use of the CallableStatements to issue stored procedure calls that validate the zip code and validate the customer ID, and the use of the PreparedStatement to issue an Insert SQL statement with parameters that will change with each insert.

This example also illustrates code that will run with any JDBC driver that will support the stored procedures used in the Customer class. The driver class names are loaded from the jdbc.drivers property, so code recompilation is not required.

JDBC DRIVERS

One of the real attractions of the JDBC API is the ability to develop applications with the knowledge that all of the major database vendors are working in parallel to create drivers. A number of drivers are available both from database vendors and from third-party developers. In most cases, it is wise to shop around for the best features, cost, and support.

Drivers come in a variety of flavors according to their construction and the type of database they are intended to support. Sun categorizes database drivers in four ways:

1. A JDBC-ODBC bridge driver, shown in Figure 15.6, implemented with ODBC binary code and, in some cases, a client library as well. The bridge driver is made up of three parts: a set of C libraries that connect the JDBC to the ODBC driver manager, the ODBC driver manager, and the ODBC driver.

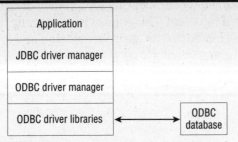

FIGURE 15.6: JDBC-ODBC bridge driver

NOTE

ODBC is a database access API introduced by Microsoft that is very common on PCs. ODBC drivers are available for most PC-based database systems, enabling migration to JDBC without waiting for the ODBC driver vendor to create a JDBC driver.

2. A native library-to-Java implementation, as shown in Figure 15.7. This driver uses native C language library calls to translate JDBC to the native client library. These drivers use C language libraries that provide vendor-specific functionality and tie these libraries (through native method calls) to the JDBC. These drivers were the first available for Oracle, Sybase, Informix, DB2, and other client-library-based RDBMSs.

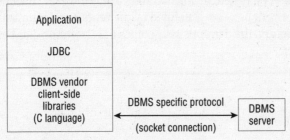

FIGURE 15.7: Native library-to-Java driver

3. Figure 15.8 shows the structure of a network-protocol Java driver. JDBC calls are translated by this driver into a DBMS-independent protocol and sent to a middle-tier server over a

socket. The middle-tier code can contact a variety of databases on behalf of the client. This approach is becoming the most popular and is by far the most flexible. It also deals specifically with issues relating to network security, including passing data through firewalls.

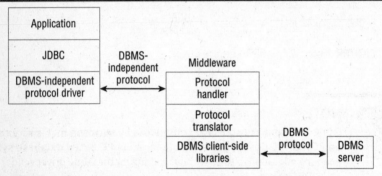

FIGURE 15.8: DBMS-independent network protocol driver

4. A native-protocol Java driver, shown in Figure 15.9. JDBC calls are converted directly to the network protocol used by the DBMS server. In this driver scenario, the database vendor supports a network socket, and the JDBC driver communicates over a socket connection directly to the database server. The client-side code can be written in Java. This solution has the benefit of being one of the easiest to implement and is very practical for intranet use. However, because the network protocol is defined by the vendor and is typically proprietary, the driver usually comes only from the database vendor.

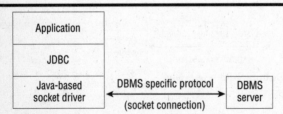

FIGURE 15.9: DBMS-protocol all-Java driver

JDBC-ODBC BRIDGE

The JDBC-ODBC bridge is a JDBC driver that provides translation of JDBC calls to ODBC operations. There are a number of DBMSs that support ODBC. When a company the size of Microsoft creates a standard for database access, there are sure to be vendors that follow. In fact, there are more than 50 different ODBC drivers available.

As mentioned earlier, both JDBC and ODBC are based upon the X/Open SQL CLI, so the translation between JDBC and ODBC is relatively straightforward. ODBC is a client-side set of libraries and a driver that is specific to the client's operating system and, in some cases, machine architecture.

From the developer's perspective, using a JDBC-ODBC bridge driver is an easy choice. Applications will still speak directly to the JDBC interface classes, so it is exactly the same as using any other JDBC driver. However, the implementation of a JDBC-ODBC bridge requires that the developer be aware of what is required to run the application. Because ODBC calls are made using binary C calls, the client must have a local copy of the ODBC driver, the ODBC driver manager, and the client-side libraries.

For these reasons, Sun makes the recommendation that the JDBC-ODBC bridge not be used for Web-based database access. For intranet access, the developer must distribute the Java program to the client machines as either a Java application or Java applet (which would run as a trusted source from the local client file system).

CURRENT JDBC DRIVERS

JDBC drivers are being released from so many vendors and at such a rapid rate that a definitive list is just not practical and would be obsolete by the time it was printed. For information on current driver vendors, their product names, and what databases they support, a good source is `http://java.sun.com/products/jdbc/jdbc.drivers.html`.

ALTERNATIVE CONNECTIVITY STRATEGIES

JDBC represents a very easy way to save time and future investment when developing database applications. The API guarantees that a client program written to the JDBC standard will work with any JDBC-compliant driver and database combination. This next section discusses two alternative technologies coming from Sun that also provide a flexible way to preserve a development investment: Remote Method Invocation (RMI) and the Common Object Request Broker Architecture (CORBA).

Remote Method Invocation (RMI)

Both RMI and CORBA can also be used to connect client applications to databases, although there are some caveats to consider. RMI is analogous to Remote Procedure Calls (RPC), the ability to call and run a procedure in another executing program. However, while RPC was not designed for distributed object systems, this is RMI's strength. RMI is designed to allow client applications to execute the methods of objects that exist on a remote server and execute these methods in such a way that it *appears* that the objects are local.

For database connectivity, this means that the developer can create an application that accesses database objects directly, even though these objects are actually implemented on the database server host. Because RMI provides mechanisms for allowing objects to be passed as serialized streams, it also supports protocols for passing these streams through firewalls.

Because RMI is a Java-to-Java solution, it is also possible to combine the best of JDBC and RMI for a multi-tier solution. For example, if the JDBC driver is written using RMI, then it becomes possible to write to a standard database interface definition *and* use object persistence and remote method calls via RMI, thereby extending the JDBC model.

The Common Object Request Broker Architecture (CORBA)

The Common Object Request Broker Architecture (CORBA) is the result of years of work by the Object Management Group (OMG). The OMG is a consortium of more than 500 companies that have compiled a specification for a communications infrastructure that allows different computer languages on different computer architectures to access a distributed collection of objects.

For the database application developer, CORBA provides the ultimate flexibility in a heterogeneous development environment. The server could be developed in C or C++ and the client could be a Java applet. Currently, Sun is in the process of providing a Java Interface Definition Language (IDL) compiler that takes a CORBA 2.0 IDL file and creates the necessary support files, called *stubs*, for a client implementation.

CORBA is a standard (at version 2.3 as of this writing) that defines a definition language that is vendor- and language-neutral. The IDL is used to create a contract between a client and server implementation. IDL is not an implementation language itself; it merely describes object services and operations that may be performed on an implementation of those services.

At the core of CORBA is the Object Request Broker (ORB). The ORB is the principal component for the transmission of information (requests for operations and their results) between the client and server of a CORBA application. The ORB manages marshaling requests, establishes a connection to the server, sends the data, and executes the requests on the server side. The same process occurs when the server returns the results of the operation.

The CORBA 2.0 specification also defines an Internet interoperability protocol (IIOP) that defines the protocol of the connection between the client and the server through the ORB. This allows developers to choose a client IDL compiler and server IDL compiler from two different vendors.

Besides Sun, there are several vendors that provide CORBA 2.0 compliance, including IIOP and Java IDL compilers.

For a wealth of additional information on the OMG consortium, consult the http://www.omg.org/ Web page.

Part iii

Connectivity to Object Databases

Besides RMI and CORBA, another alternative is to use an object database, specifically one that supports Java's object model. There are several object database products for Java and, as a result of the Object Database Management Group (ODMG), a specification for storing Java objects in databases. The specification is called ODMG 2.0; Java object database vendors are shipping products that support it.

NOTE

To read about the ODMG 2.0 standard, consult the ODMG's Web site http://www.odmg.org/ or *The Object Database Standard: ODMG 2.0* book (Morgan Kaufmann Publishers, 1997, ISBN: 1-55860-463-4).

Connectivity with Web-Based Database Systems

While not specifically JDBC, and not always related to Java, there is another alternative to accessing databases from Web pages. It is possible to use HTML pages to send information to Common Gateway Interface (CGI) scripts. The CGI scripts then connect to the database and return results to the HTML page. Vendors in the Web-based database market have a variety of strategies for improving the performance of CGI with multithreaded applications written in C or C++ that handle the database connection and queries.

The 1.2 JDK provides a technology called *servlets* that replaces the need to use C, C++, or Perl for CGI scripts. The servlet can be instructed to open a database connection, retrieve a result, and return the data to the applet. See Chapter 7 for more information on servlet technology.

WHAT'S NEXT?

In the next chapter, we will explore the high-level graphics capabilities of the 2D API.

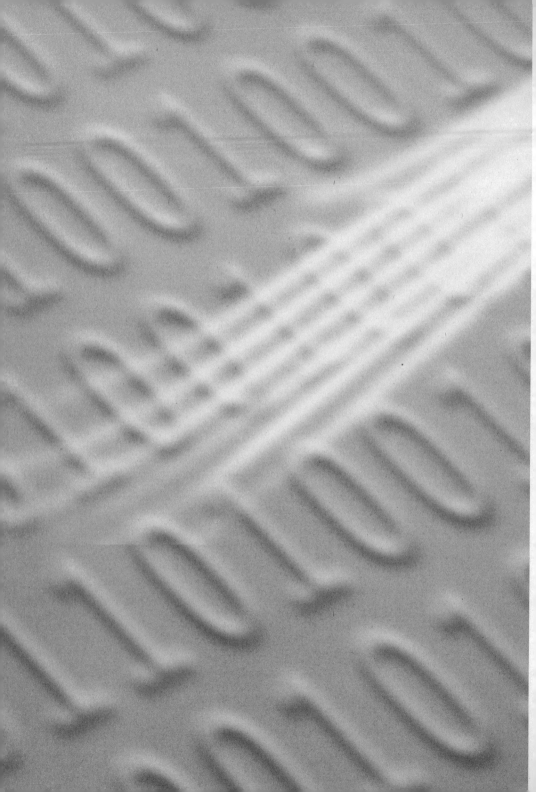

Chapter 16

THE 2D API

J ava's original two-dimensional rendering facilities were a bit primitive. You could draw a line of minimal width. You could outline or fill a rectangle, an oval, or (with slightly more work) an irregular polygon. If you wanted to get fancy, you had to dabble with images. For example, if you wanted a diagonal line that was 25 pixels wide, your only hope was to do the math and create a suitable `MemoryImageSource`. If somebody in the marketing department changed the spec to 28 pixels wide and a slightly steeper slope, you had to go back to the drawing board.

If you wanted to blend colors, use sophisticated line-join styles, or rotate your coordinate system, you found yourself in the same predicament—you had to do a lot of geometric or color-oriented coding, just to get an effect that is pretty much standard on non-Java platforms.

Adapted from *Java 2 Developer's Handbook*
by Philip Heller and Simon Roberts
ISBN 0-7821-2179-9   1,248 pages $59.99

The JDK 1.1 functionality was simply not made to support high-level graphics design. The 2D API changes all that. This chapter introduces you to some of the basic concepts of the new API, including curves, transforms, strokes, and fills.

VISUAL ASPECTS

One reason for Java's popularity as a programming language is its ability to create graphical user interfaces (GUI) quickly and easily. As programmers are aware, the design and visual effect of the GUI are among the most important elements of any application, since they determine how the users interact with the program. There are two visual aspects that go into creating a GUI that are worth noting here: fonts and color models.

java.awt.Font   Fonts vary depending on the hardware platform, but all ports of Java are supposed to support Helvetica, Times Roman, Courier, and Dialog fonts, in addition to mappings to any font they choose. The java.awt.Font package provides classes and interfaces relating to fonts. It contains support for representing Type 1, Type 1 Multiple Master, OpenType, and TrueType fonts.

java.awt.Color   As with fonts, colors vary depending on the user's hardware. Java's color model supports 32-bit or true color and has two built-in common color models: DirectColorModel and IndexColorModel. The java.awt.Color package provides classes for using existing color spaces or for designing your own. It contains an implementation of a color space based on the International Color Consortium (ICC) Profile Format Specification.

The subject matter of this chapter is extremely visual. The goal of this chapter is to get you familiar with the 2D rendering options that are available to you. In order to give you the best possible visual exposure to the new concepts, this chapter includes several "lab" programs. The labs let you try out a lot of options without having to go through the traditional write/compile/debug/execute/observe cycle. The source code for these labs is listed in the text of this chapter, and you are encouraged to read the sources and understand what they do. But it is equally important to execute the programs and play with the parameters until you get a visual/kinesthetic feel for the concepts being illustrated.

THE *Graphics2D* CLASS AND SHAPES

In the JDK 1.1 model, you could draw or fill a rectangle or an oval because the Graphics class had (and still has) methods called drawRect(), fillOval(), and so on. In other words, you could draw a particular shape only if the Graphics class had a method to support that shape.

With the new 2D API, more shapes are available, and you can define your own shapes. You can draw the outline of a shape or you can fill it. You can even use a shape as a stencil. However, in order to do all this, you need to understand how to use the Graphics2D class and the Shape interface.

The *Graphics2D* Class

The java.awt.Graphics class has been extended. The new subclass is java.awt.Graphics2D. In JDK 1.2, when a component's paint() method is called, the method's argument is still declared to be an instance of Graphics, but at runtime what gets passed is really an instance of the Graphics2D subclass. If you don't want the functionality of the 2D API, you can proceed as you would with JDK 1.1: Call setColor(), draw-Line(), and so forth on the argument. On the other hand, if you want to take advantage of the new 2D features, you need to begin by casting the method argument to Graphics2D:

```
public void paint(Graphics g)
{
  Graphics2D g2d = (Graphics2D)g;
  // various method calls on g2d
```

Of course, all the inherited methods from the Graphics class are still available in the Graphics2D subclass. Additionally, there is extensive new functionality. In this chapter, we'll examine the following methods:

clip(Shape)	setRenderingHint (RenderingHint)
draw(Shape)	setStroke(Stroke)
fill(Shape)	shear(double, double)
rotate(double)	transform(AffineTransform)
scale(double, double)	translate(double, double)
setPaint(Paint)	

Many of these methods operate on Shapes, which are discussed in the next section.

The *Shape* Interface and Its Implementors

The Shape interface was introduced in JDK 1.1, but it was not used. This interface has been extensively modified for JDK 1.2. Actually, it is very unlikely that you will ever implement the interface. Most likely, you will use one of the following implementing classes:

Arc2D	Ellipse2D
Line2D	QuadCurve2D
Rectangle2D	CubicCurve2D
RoundRectangle2D	GeneralPath

These eight classes all reside in the java.awt.geom package. The first seven classes correspond to specific curve types; the eighth, General-Path, represents a do-it-yourself curve that goes anywhere you want it to go. The first seven shapes are discussed in this section. GeneralPath is an extensive topic, and is covered in its own section at the end of this chapter.

NOTE
Many of the new classes introduced by the 2D API are in the java.awt package. The remainder reside in the new package java.awt.geom. If you are going to write much 2D code, you might want to get in the habit of importing java.geom.*.

In JDK 1.1, you could only use ints to specify shape parameters. With the exception of GeneralPath, all of the classes listed above require you to specify either float or double parameters. Each of the seven classes is abstract and has two inner classes, named Float and Double. You never instantiate the abstract class; you instantiate one of the inner classes. If, for example, you want the double-precision version of Rectangle2D, you need to do something like the following:

```
double dx = 10.5;
double dy = 15.51;
double dw = 500.043;
double dh = 350.53;
Rectangle2D r2d = new Rectangle2D.Double(dx, dy, dw, dh);
```

Each of the inner classes is a subclass of its containing class. This sounds convoluted but is actually useful, because it allows the conversion performed in the last line of the code fragment above. The declarations of the outer and inner classes look like this:

```
public abstract class Rectangle2D extends RectangularShape
                                    implements Shape
{
  public static class Rectangle2D.Double extends Rectangle2D {
    ...
  }
}
```

You might wonder why it is necessary to support double or float precision for parameters whose units are pixels. In JDK 1.1, there would have been no benefit. However, in JDK 1.2 you can scale, rotate, and translate your coordinate system. You might create a space in which x ranges from -.0001 to +.0001. For such situations, you need to provide parameters with floating-point precision or, for extreme cases, double precision.

The application listed below draws a simple Rectangle2D.

LIST 16.1: RectDemo.java

```
import java.awt.*;
import java.awt.geom.*;

public class RectDemo extends Frame
{
  public static void main(String[] args)
  {
    (new RectDemo()).setVisible(true);
  }

  public RectDemo()
  {
    setSize(150, 150);
  }

  public void paint(Graphics g)
  {
    Graphics2D g2d = (Graphics2D)g;
```

```
        Rectangle2D r2d =
            new Rectangle2D.Float(10f, 10f, 130f, 130f);
        g2d.draw(r2d);
    }
}
```

The Line2D and Ellipse2D shapes are straightforward. The RoundRectangle2D, Arc2D, QuadCurve2D, and CubicCurve2D shapes require some explanation.

The RoundRectangle2D shape is a rectangle with rounded corners. The constructor takes the usual x/y/width/height arguments, as well as the width and height of the rounded portion of the corners. The sample code listed below draws a round rectangle at (20, 30) that is 100 pixels wide and 200 pixels high. The rounded portion of each corner is 10 pixels wide and 15 pixels high.

```
RoundRectangle2D rr =
    new RoundRectangle2D.Float(20, 30, 100, 200, 10, 15);
```

The Arc2D shape is a segment of a circle or an ellipse. The constructor for the Float inner subclass is shown below. (The Double inner subclass constructor is identical.)

```
Public Arc2D.Float(float x, float y, float width, float height,
                   float arcStart, float arcExtent, int type)
```

The circle or ellipse is specified by providing the x, y, width, and height of the bounding square or rectangle. The arc itself begins at angle arcStart (measured from the right in counterclockwise degrees) and extends for arcExtent degrees. The type is one of the following:

Arc2D.CHORD   The arc is closed with a straight-line segment that connects the arc's endpoints.

Arc2D.PIE   The arc is closed with two straight-line segments that connect the arc's endpoints to the center of the circle or ellipse.

Arc2D.ARC   The arc is not closed.

The QuadCurve2D and CubicCurve2D shapes support smooth curves. A quad curve is specified by providing the curve's two endpoints and a third control point that tells the curve how to curve. A cubic curve is similar, but there are two control points. The Float subclasses have the following constructors:

```
QuadCurve2D.Float(float x0, float y0,
                  float ctrlX, float ctrlY,
```

```
                         float x1, float y1)
      CubicCurve2D.Float(float x0, float y0,
                         float ctrlX0, float ctrlY0,
                         float ctrlX1, float ctrlY1,
                         float x1, float y1)
```

The `Double` inner classes have identical constructors, aside from the fact that the arguments are of type `double`.

The `ShapeSampler` application listed below draws a round rectangle in the upper left-hand corner, three kinds of arcs in the upper right-hand quadrant, and, below, a quad curve and a cubic curve, as shown in Figure 16.1.

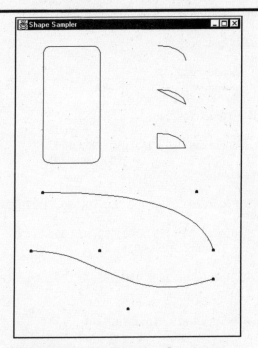

FIGURE 16.1:   The ShapeSampler program

LIST 16.2: ShapeSampler.java

```
import java.awt.*;
import java.awt.geom.*;


public class ShapeSampler extends Frame
{
  public static void main(String[] args)
```

```
{
  (new ShapeSampler()).setVisible(true);
}


public ShapeSampler()
{
  super("Shape Sampler");
  setSize(400, 550);
}


public void paint(Graphics g)
{
  RoundRectangle2D  rrect;
  Arc2D          arc;
  QuadCurve2D       quadcurve;
  CubicCurve2D      cubcurve;

  Graphics2D g2d = (Graphics2D)g;

  rrect = new RoundRectangle2D.Float(50, 50, 100,
                                   200, 30, 20);
  g2d.draw(rrect);

  arc = new Arc2D.Float(200, 50, 100, 50, 0, 90, Arc2D.OPEN);
  g2d.draw(arc);
  arc = new Arc2D.Float(200, 125, 100, 50, 0, 90,
                        Arc2D.CHORD);
  g2d.draw(arc);
  arc = new Arc2D.Float(200, 200, 100, 50, 0, 90, Arc2D.PIE);
  g2d.draw(arc);

  quadcurve = new QuadCurve2D.Float(50, 300,
                                    320, 300,
                                    350, 400);
  g2d.draw(quadcurve);
  g2d.fillOval(48, 298, 5, 5);
  g2d.fillOval(318, 298, 5, 5);
  g2d.fillOval(348, 398, 5, 5);

  cubcurve = new CubicCurve2D.Float(30, 400,
                                    150, 400,
                                    200, 500,
                                    350, 450);
```

```
        g2d.fillOval(28, 398, 5, 5);
        g2d.fillOval(148, 398, 5, 5);
        g2d.fillOval(198, 498, 5, 5);
        g2d.fillOval(348, 448, 5, 5);
        g2d.draw(cubcurve);
    }
}
```

Compile and run the `ShapeSampler` application as shown below:

```
C:\javadevhdbk\ch16\javac ShapeSampler.java
C:\javadevhdbk\ch16\java ShapeSampler
```

DRAWING OPERATIONS

The three major operations that you can perform on a shape are drawing, filling, and clipping. You can also transform a shape, which allows you to manipulate the coordinate space of your drawing region. The basic transformations are rotation, translation, and scaling.

Stroking

In the JDK 1.1 model, the only kind of line you could draw was a solid line of infinitesimal width. With the 2D API, you can specify the line width, cap style, join style, and dash pattern.

Line style is specified in two steps:

1. Create an instance of `BasicStroke`.

2. Call `setStroke()` on the current `Graphics2D`, passing in the `BasicStroke` that you created.

There are several constructors for `BasicStroke`, offering various options for specifying or ignoring the various line qualities. The richest constructor is:

```
public BasicStroke(float width, int cap, int join, float
                    miterLimit, float dash[], float dashphase)
```

The constructor arguments have the following effects:

width Sets the line width.

cap Sets the cap style: `BasicStroke.BUTT`, `Basic-Stroke.ROUND`, or `BasicStroke.SQUARE`.

join   Sets the join style: BasicStroke.BEVEL, Basic-Stroke.MITER, or BasicStroke.ROUND.

miterLimit   Specifies the maximum extension of a miter join; only relevant if join is BasicStroke.MITER.

dash   Specifies an array of floats that describes the dash pattern.

dashphase   Sets the starting point within the dash array.

The StrokeLab program lets you vary the line width, caps type, and join style of a Graphics2D. Figure 16.2 shows the program configured to use a line width of 10, round caps, and beveled joins.

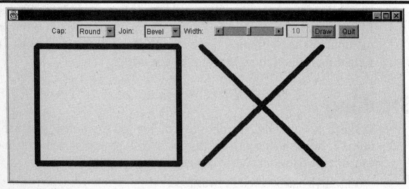

FIGURE 16.2:   The StrokeLab program

If you execute the application, you can experiment with different line widths, caps, and joins. The code is listed below. The most important lines are the ones in paint() that construct a BasicStroke and then call setStroke() on the Graphics2D object:

```
BasicStroke stroke = new BasicStroke(width, cap, join);
g.setStroke(stroke);
```

LIST 16.3: *StrokeLab.java*

```
import java.awt.*;
import java.awt.event.*;


public class StrokeLab extends Frame
                        implements ActionListener,
                                   AdjustmentListener
```

```
{
  private Choice                    capChoice;
  private Choice                    joinChoice;
  private Choice                    dashCountChoice;
  private Scrollbar                 widthBar;
  private TextField                 widthTF;
  private Button                    drawBtn;
  private Button                    quitBtn;
  private StrokeCanvas              strokeCanvas;

  private final static int          WIDTH_MIN   = 0;
  private final static int          WIDTH_MAX   = 21;

  private final static String[]  CAP_TYPE_NAMES =
  {
    "Butt", "Round", "Square"
  };
  private final static int[]     CAP_TYPES =
  {
    BasicStroke.CAP_BUTT,
    BasicStroke.CAP_ROUND,
    BasicStroke.CAP_SQUARE
  };

  private final static String[]  JOIN_TYPE_NAMES =
  {
    "Bevel", "Miter", "Round"
  };
  private final static int[]     JOIN_TYPES =
  {
    BasicStroke.JOIN_BEVEL,
    BasicStroke.JOIN_MITER,
    BasicStroke.JOIN_ROUND
  };


  class WideScrollbar extends Scrollbar
  {
    private int   widthPix;

    WideScrollbar(int min, int max, int widthPix)
    {
      super(Scrollbar.HORIZONTAL, 0, 1,
            WIDTH_MIN, WIDTH_MAX);
      this.widthPix = widthPix;
```

```
    }

  public Dimension getPreferredSize()
  {
    int prefHt = super.getPreferredSize().height;
    return new Dimension(widthPix, prefHt);
  }
}


public static void main(String[] args)
{
  (new StrokeLab()).setVisible(true);
}


StrokeLab()
{
  setSize(700, 300);
  Panel panel = new Panel();
  capChoice = new Choice();
  for (int i=0; i<CAP_TYPE_NAMES.length; i++)
    capChoice.addItem(CAP_TYPE_NAMES[i]);
  panel.add(new Label("Cap:"));
  panel.add(capChoice);
  joinChoice = new Choice();
  for (int i=0; i<CAP_TYPE_NAMES.length; i++)
    joinChoice.addItem(JOIN_TYPE_NAMES[i]);
  panel.add(new Label("Join:"));
  panel.add(joinChoice);
  widthBar = new WideScrollbar(WIDTH_MIN, WIDTH_MAX, 120);
  widthBar.addAdjustmentListener(this);
  widthTF = new TextField(" 0");
  widthTF.setEnabled(false);
  panel.add(new Label("Width:"));
  panel.add(widthBar);
  panel.add(widthTF);
  drawBtn = new Button("Draw");
  drawBtn.addActionListener(this);
  panel.add(drawBtn);
  quitBtn = new Button("Quit");
  quitBtn.addActionListener(this);
  panel.add(quitBtn);
  add(panel, BorderLayout.NORTH);

  strokeCanvas = new StrokeCanvas();
```

```
         add(strokeCanvas, BorderLayout.CENTER);

         addWindowListener(new WindowAdapter() {
           public void windowClosing(WindowEvent e) {
             System.exit(0);
           }
         });
       }


       public void actionPerformed(ActionEvent e)
       {
         if (e.getSource() == quitBtn)
             System.exit(0);

         strokeCanvas.repaint();
       }


       public void adjustmentValueChanged(AdjustmentEvent e)
       {
         widthTF.setText("" + widthBar.getValue());
       }


       class StrokeCanvas extends Canvas
       {
         public void paint(Graphics graphics)
         {
           Graphics2D g = (Graphics2D)graphics;
           g.setColor(Color.blue);
           float width = widthBar.getValue();
           int cap = CAP_TYPES[capChoice.getSelectedIndex()];
           int join = JOIN_TYPES[joinChoice.getSelectedIndex()];
           BasicStroke stroke = new BasicStroke(width, cap, join);

           g.setStroke(stroke);
           g.drawRect(50, 10, 250, 200);
           g.drawLine(340, 10, 550, 210);
           g.drawLine(340, 210, 550, 10);
         }
       }
     }
```

Compile and run the `StrokeLab` application as shown below:

```
C:\javadevhdbk\ch16\javac StrokeLab.java
C:\javadevhdbk\ch16\java StrokeLab
```

Filling

The 2D API offers a variety of options for filling shapes. You can still fill with solid colors, as you could in JDK 1.1, and now you can fill with a texture pattern or with a color gradient.

You tell a `Graphics2D` how to fill by calling its `setPaint()` method. The argument is of type `java.awt.Paint`, which is an interface. There are three classes that implement the `Paint` interface and are eligible to be passed into `setPaint()`:

- `java.awt.Color`
- `java.awt.TexturePaint`
- `java.awt.GradientPaint`

Passing in a `Color` produces the same result as calling `setColor()`: Filling is performed with a solid color.

Passing in a `TexturePaint` results in a repeating fill pattern based on a buffered image. The constructor for `TexturePaint` is:

```
TexturePaint(BufferedImage image, Rectangle control)
```

This specifies a fill pattern based on repeating copies of `image`. The control rectangle specifies the portion of the image to be used and the positioning of the repeated image.

Passing a `GradientPaint` into `setPaint()` results in a smooth gradient of color. There are several constructors for `GradientPaint`. The general approach is to provide two control points and two colors. The first point will appear in the first color, and the second point will appear in the second color. All intermediate points will appear in a color that is a blend of the two original colors. The proportions of the original colors in the blend are derived from each point's distance from the two original control points.

The simplest `GradientPaint` constructor is:

```
GradientPaint(float x0, float y0, Color color0,
              float x1, float y1, Color color1)
```

The `GradientLab` application lets you specify the two control points and associate a color with each point. To begin, you click the mouse to

define the first control point. A dialog box pops up to let you associate a
color with that control point. Then you repeat the process to define the
position and color of the second control point. As soon as you define the
second point, the program fills in its entire area using a `Gradient-`
`Paint`, as shown in Figure 16.3.

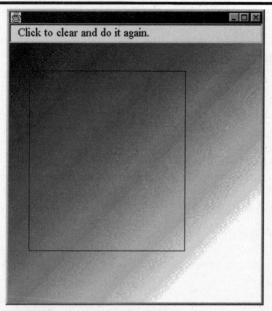

FIGURE 16.3:   The GradientLab program

The complete listing for `GradientLab` appears below.

LIST 16.4:   *GradientLab.java*

```java
import java.awt.*;
import java.awt.event.*;


public class GradientLab extends Canvas
                         implements MouseListener
{
    private TextField            logTF;
    private int                  nClicks;
    private int[]                xs, ys;
    private Color[]              colors;
    private ColorDialog          colorDialog;
```

```
private final static String[]  messages =
{
  "Click to define first point.",
  "Click to define second point.",
  "Click to fill with gradient.",
  "Click to clear and do it again."
};


public static void main(String[] args)
{
  Frame frame = new Frame();
  TextField tf = new TextField();
  frame.add(tf, BorderLayout.NORTH);
  tf.setFont(new Font("Serif", Font.PLAIN, 18));
  frame.add(new GradientLab(tf), BorderLayout.CENTER);
  frame.pack();
  frame.setVisible(true);
  frame.addWindowListener(new WindowAdapter() {
    public void windowClosing(WindowEvent e)
    {
      System.exit(0);
    }
  });
}


GradientLab(TextField logTF)
{
  this.logTF = logTF;
  logTF.setText(messages[0]);
  setBackground(Color.white);
  addMouseListener(this);
  xs = new int[2];
  ys = new int[2];
  colors = new Color[2];

  Component c = logTF;
  while (!(c instanceof Frame))
    c = c.getParent();
  colorDialog = new ColorDialog((Frame)c);
}


public Dimension getPreferredSize()
```

```
{
  return new Dimension(400, 400);
}


public void mouseClicked(MouseEvent e)
{
  if (nClicks <= 1)
  {
    xs[nClicks] = e.getX();
    ys[nClicks] = e.getY();
    colorDialog.setVisible(true);
    colors[nClicks] = colorDialog.getColor();
  }

  nClicks = ++nClicks % 4;
  logTF.setText(messages[nClicks]);
  repaint();
}


private void clear(Graphics g)
{
  g.setColor(Color.white);
  g.fillRect(0, 0, getSize().width, getSize().height);
}


public void paint(Graphics graphics)
{
  Graphics2D g = (Graphics2D)graphics;

  g.setColor(Color.white);
  g.fillRect(0, 0, getSize().width, getSize().height);

  switch(nClicks)
  {
    case 0:     // Clear
      break;

    case 1:     // 1st point
      g.setColor(Color.black);
      g.fillOval(xs[0]-5, ys[0]-5, 10, 10);
      g.setColor(colors[0]);
      g.fillOval(xs[0]-4, ys[0]-4, 8, 8);
      break;
```

```
  case 2:      // 2nd point
    g.setColor(Color.black);
    g.fillOval(xs[0]-5, ys[0]-5, 10, 10);
    g.setColor(colors[0]);
    g.fillOval(xs[0]-4, ys[0]-4, 8, 8);
    g.setColor(Color.black);
    g.fillOval(xs[1]-5, ys[1]-5, 10, 10);
    g.setColor(colors[1]);
    g.fillOval(xs[1]-4, ys[1]-4, 8, 8);
    break;

  case 3:      // 3rd point
    GradientPaint gradi = new GradientPaint(xs[0], ys[0],
                                colors[0],
                                xs[1], ys[1],
                                colors[1]);

    g.setPaint(gradi);
    g.fillRect(0, 0, getSize().width, getSize().height);
    g.setColor(Color.black);
    g.drawRect(Math.min(xs[0], xs[1]),
               Math.min(ys[0], ys[1]),
               Math.abs(xs[0]-xs[1]),
               Math.abs(ys[0]-ys[1]));

    break;
  }
}


public void mousePressed(MouseEvent e)  { }
public void mouseReleased(MouseEvent e) { }
public void mouseEntered(MouseEvent e)  { }
public void mouseExited(MouseEvent e)   { }


class ColorDialog extends Dialog
                  implements ActionListener, ItemListener
{
  Canvas        swatch;
  Choice        choice;
  Scrollbar[]   bars;
  TextField[]   tfs;

  final String[] colorNames =
  {
    "Red", "Blue", "Green", "Yellow", "Orange",
    "Cyan", "Magenta", "White", "Black"
```

```
    };
    final Color[] colors =
    {
      Color.red, Color.blue, Color.green, Color.yellow,
      Color.orange, Color.cyan, Color.magenta,
      Color.white, Color.black
    };


    ColorDialog(Frame parent)
    {
      super(parent, true);
      setSize(200, 100);
      Panel panel = new Panel();
      choice = new Choice();
      for (int i=0; i<colorNames.length; i++)
        choice.addItem(colorNames[i]);
      choice.select(8);
      choice.addItemListener(this);
      panel.add(choice);
      Button btn = new Button("Apply");
      btn.addActionListener(this);
      panel.add(btn);
      add(panel, BorderLayout.NORTH);
      swatch = new Canvas();
      swatch.setBackground(Color.black);
      add(swatch, BorderLayout.CENTER);
    }

    Color getColor() {return colors[choice.getSelectedIndex()];}

    public void itemStateChanged(ItemEvent e)
    {
      swatch.setBackground(getColor());
      swatch.repaint();
    }

    public void actionPerformed(ActionEvent e)
    {
      setVisible(false);
    }
  }
}
```

Compile and run the GradientLab application as shown below:

```
C:\javadevhdbk\ch16\javac GradientLab.java
C:\javadevhdbk\ch16\java GradientLab
```

Clipping

When you use a shape as a stencil outline, the shape acts like a clipping rectangle—pixels outside the clip region are not modified by any subsequent painting operations. You specify a clip shape by calling the `clip()` method of the `Graphics2D` class, passing in the clipping shape as the method's parameter.

Figure 16.4 shows a filled rectangle with a circular clip region. The code that generated Figure 16.4 is listed below.

FIGURE 16.4: Circular clip region

LIST 16.5:   ClipDemo.java

```
import java.awt.*;
import java.awt.geom.*;

public class ClipDemo extends Frame
{
  public static void main(String[] args)
  {
    (new ClipDemo()).setVisible(true);
  }

  public ClipDemo()
  {
    setSize(250, 250);
  }

  public void paint(Graphics g)
  {
    Graphics2D g2d = (Graphics2D)g;
    Ellipse2D e = new Ellipse2D.Float(10, 10, 200, 200);
```

```
        g2d.clip(e);
        g2d.fillRect(40, 60, 500, 500);
    }
}
```

Compile and run the ClipDemo application as shown below:

```
C:\javadevhdbk\ch16\javac ClipDemo.java
C:\javadevhdbk\ch16\java ClipDemo
```

Transforming

The JDK 1.1 drawing model used a rigid coordinate system. The origin was always in a component's upper-left corner; x increased to the right, and y increased downward.

The 2D API allows you to transform your coordinate space. The Graphics2D class has a method called setTransform(), which takes as its argument an instance of the java.awt.geom.AffineTransform class.

If you are familiar with the mathematics of coordinate transformation, you can use the AffineTransform constructors to create very intricate effects. The class also contains a number of static methods that make it much easier to create the following common transforms:

Rotation   Keeps the origin in place but turns the axes so that they can point in arbitrary directions. (The axes remain perpendicular to each other.)

Scaling   Changes the unit size so that, for example, a width of 100 means 100 arbitrary units rather than 100 pixels. The horizontal and vertical scales can be adjusted independently.

Translation   Moves the origin.

Shearing   Manipulates the axes so that they are no longer perpendicular.

The static methods of AffineTransform that create these transformations are:

```
getRotateInstance(double theta)
getRotateInstance(double theta, double x, double y)
getScaleInstance(double scaleX, double scaleY)
getTranslateInstance(double translateX, double translateY)
getShearInstance(double shearX, double shearY)
```

The second version of getRotateInstance() returns a transform that both translates and rotates.

Figures 16.5 through 16.9 show frames whose `paint()` methods all call `fillRect (50, 50, 150, 250)`. Figure 16.5 shows the rectangle with no transformation. The others show a transform applied before drawing the rectangle. The figures illustrate how transforming coordinate space changes the appearance of the rectangle. The frames were all displayed by the `TransformLab` application, which is listed below.

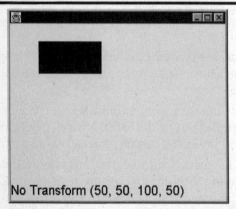

No Transform (50, 50, 100, 50)

FIGURE 16.5:   Rectangle without transformation

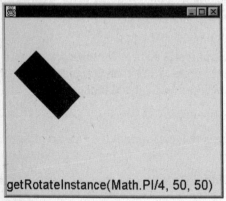

getRotateInstance(Math.PI/4, 50, 50)

FIGURE 16.6:   Rectangle with rotation

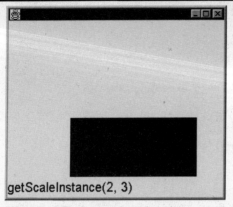

FIGURE 16.7:   Rectangle with scaling

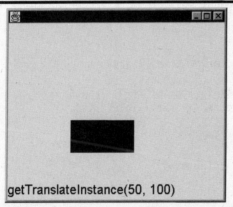

FIGURE 16.8:   Rectangle with translation

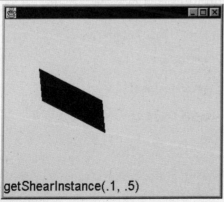

FIGURE 16.9:   Rectangle with shear

LIST 16.6: *TransformLab.java*

```java
import java.awt.*;
import java.awt.geom.*;


public class TransformLab extends Frame
{
  private int       nth;

  private final static String[]  info =
  {
    "No Transform (50, 50, 100, 50)",
    "getRotateInstance(Math.PI/4, 50, 50)",
    "getScaleInstance(2, 3)",
    "getTranslateInstance(50, 100)",
    "getShearInstance(.1, .5)"
  };


  public static void main(String[] args)
  {
    for (int i=0; i<info.length; i++)
      (new TransformLab(i)).setVisible(true);
  }


  public TransformLab(int nth)
  {
    this.nth = nth;
    setSize(350, 300);
    setFont(new Font("Monspaced", Font.PLAIN, 20));
    add(new Label(info[nth]), BorderLayout.SOUTH);
  }


  public void paint(Graphics g)
  {
    AffineTransform    atrans = null;

    Graphics2D g2d = (Graphics2D)g;
    switch (nth)
    {
      case 1:
        atrans = AffineTransform.getRotateInstance(Math.PI/4,
                 50, 50);
        break;
```

```
            case 2:
              atrans = AffineTransform.getScaleInstance(2, 3);
              break;
            case 3:
              atrans =
        AffineTransform.getTranslateInstance(50, 100);
              break;
            case 4:
              atrans = AffineTransform.getShearInstance(.1, .5);
              break;
        }

        if (atrans != null)
            g2d.setTransform(atrans);

        g2d.fillRect(50, 50, 100, 50);
    }
  }
```

Compile and run the TransformLab application as shown below:

```
C:\javadevhdbk\ch16\javac TransformLab.java
C:\javadevhdbk\ch16\java TransformLab
```

GENERAL PATHS FOR YOUR OWN CURVES

The shapes discussed so far are hard-coded. Each class represents a different kind of curve. When you want to draw a curve that is not represented by a standard shape, you need to use the java.awt.geom.GeneralPath class to create your own curve. After creating a GeneralPath, you can use it as you would any other shape (for example, Ellipse2D or Round-Rectangle2D), which means that you can draw it, fill it, or clip to it.

Specifying a Shape

The GeneralPath class has several constructors, the simplest form being the no-args constructor. After you create an instance, there are numerous methods for specifying a shape. The most common approach to specifying a shape is based on an analogy to freehand drawing. When you draw, you move your pencil to a point on your paper, you draw a straight line or a curve, and then you move to another point and repeat

Part iii

the process. With a `GeneralPath`, you use the following methods to simulate this activity:

`public void moveTo(float x, float y)`   Moves to the specified point.

`public void lineTo(float x, float y)`   Extends the curve by drawing a line segment to the specified point.

`public void closePath()`   Extends the curve by drawing a line segment to the point specified by the most recent `moveTo()` call.

The `GeneralPath` class has many more methods than those listed above. However, you can do a lot with just `moveTo()`, `lineTo()`, and `closePath()`, so we will pause here and look at some examples.

The `paint()` method listed below creates a `GeneralPath` that represents an isosceles (but not equilateral) triangle.

```
public void paint(Graphics g)
{
  Graphics2D g2d = (Graphics2D)g;
  GeneralPath path = new GeneralPath();
  path.moveTo(100, 100);
  path.lineTo(200, 100);
  path.lineTo(150, 150);
  path.closePath();
  g2d.draw(path);
}
```

NOTE
The Greek philosopher Isosceles was a contemporary of Pythagoras. He is credited with the invention of the triangle. His daughter Scalene refined the concept.

Transforming a General Path

The `GeneralPath` class has a `transform()` method that takes as its argument an instance of `AffineTransform`. With this method, you can create a path that can draw a regular polygon with any desired number of sides. The next example shows how to do this.

It would be ideal if we could extend `GeneralPath`. The subclass could be called `PolygonPath`, and its constructor could be passed the desired number of sides. Unfortunately, `GeneralPath` is a final class, so extending it is out of the question. We will have to be content with writing a method that creates and returns an appropriate GeneralPath. The method's arguments will take the polygon's number of sides, radius, and center:

```
GeneralPath makePoly(int nSides, float radius,
                     float centerX, float centerY) {…}
```

The method will use the moveTo() and lineTo() methods to draw the desired polygon. The geometric calculations are straightforward, provided that the polygon can be centered on the origin. This can be made to happen with the use of an AffineTransform. We have already seen transforms in the context of the Graphics2D class. The following code shows how to apply a transform to a path so that the path's origin becomes (centerX, centerY):

```
AffineTransform atrans =
    AffineTransform.getTranslateInstance(centerX, centerY);
thePath.transform(centerX, centerY);
```

Any two adjacent points of the polygon sweep out an angle of 360/nPoints degrees. It is standard to measure angles counterclockwise from the right. If the first point of the polygon is placed at zero degrees (that is, precisely to the right of the center), then the nth point sweeps out n*360/nPoints degrees. The coordinates of the point itself are easily determined. If the angle from the horizontal is theta, then x = radius*cos(theta), and y = radius*sin(theta).

The makePoly() method needs to move to the first point, draw a line to each successive point, and finally close the path. The complete method listing is shown below.

```
GeneralPath makePoly(int nSides, float radius,
                     float centerX, float centerY)
{
  GeneralPath path = new GeneralPath();

    // Move to first point.
    path.moveTo(radius, 0);

    // Line to remaining points.
    float deltaTheta = (float)(2*Math.PI/nSides);
    float theta = deltaTheta;
    for (int i=1; i<nSides; i++)
    {
      float x = (float)(radius * Math.cos(theta));
      float y = (float)(radius * Math.sin(theta));
      path.lineTo(x, y);
```

```
        theta += deltaTheta;
    }

    // Close the path.
    path.closePath();

    // Translate to center of polygon.
    AffineTransform atrans =
        AffineTransform.getTranslateInstance(centerX, centerY);
    path.transform(atrans);

    return path;
}
```

Figure 16.10 shows four polygons that were drawn with paths created by the makePoly() method. The paths were created in the following paint() method:

```
public void paint(Graphics g)
{
    Graphics2D g2d = (Graphics2D)g;
    g2d.draw(makePoly( 5, 70, 100, 100));
    g2d.draw(makePoly( 6, 70, 300, 100));
    g2d.draw(makePoly( 8, 70, 100, 300));
    g2d.draw(makePoly(10, 70, 300, 300));
}
```

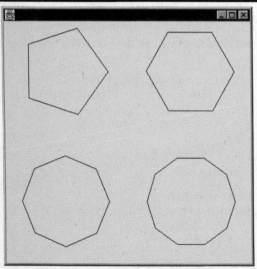

FIGURE 16.10: General path for polygons

The complete listing for the program that creates Figure 16.10 is listed below.

LIST 16.7:   Poly.java

```java
import java.awt.*;
import java.awt.event.*;
import java.awt.geom.*;


public class Poly extends Frame
{
  GeneralPath makePoly(int nSides, float radius,
                       float centerX, float centerY)
  {
    GeneralPath path = new GeneralPath();

    // Move to first point.
    path.moveTo(radius, 0);

    // Line to remaining ponts.
    float deltaTheta = (float)(2*Math.PI/nSides);
    float theta = deltaTheta;
    for (int i=1; i<nSides; i++)
    {
      float x = (float)(radius * Math.cos(theta));
      float y = (float)(radius * Math.sin(theta));
      path.lineTo(x, y);
      theta += deltaTheta;
    }

    // Close the path.
    path.closePath();

    // Translate to center of polygon.
    AffineTransform atrans =
      AffineTransform.getTranslateInstance(centerX, centerY);
    path.transform(atrans);

    return path;
  }


  public void paint(Graphics g)
  {
    Graphics2D g2d = (Graphics2D)g;
```

```
        g2d.draw(makePoly( 5, 70, 100, 100));
        g2d.draw(makePoly( 6, 70, 300, 100));
        g2d.draw(makePoly( 8, 70, 100, 300));
        g2d.draw(makePoly(10, 70, 300, 300));
    }


    public static void main(String[] args)
    {
        Poly p = new Poly();
        p.setSize(400, 400);
        p.setVisible(true);
    }
}
```

Compile and run the Poly application as shown below:

```
C:\javadevhdbk\ch16\javac Poly.java
C:\javadevhdbk\ch16\java Poly
```

Drawing a Bezier Curve

A bezier curve is a smooth curve defined by two endpoints and two control points. The control points tell the curve where to go. The curve passes near the control points but generally does not pass through them. The precise effect of the control points is difficult to describe but is easily grasped intuitively if you look at enough examples. The BezLab program draws a bezier curve and allows you to drag the endpoints and control points to see the effect on the curve. Figure 16.11 shows BezLab in its initial state.

The paint() method in BezLab creates a general path and then makes two calls on that path: moveTo() and curveTo(). You are already familiar with moveTo(). The curveTo() method has the following signature:

```
public void curveTo(float control0x, float control0y,
    float control1x, float control1y, float endx, float endy)
```

The arguments specify two control points and an endpoint. The other endpoint is the current point of the general path.

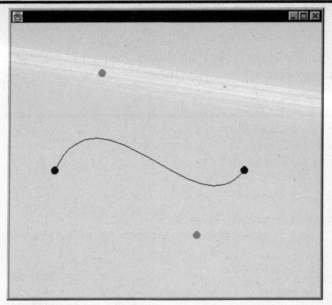

FIGURE 16.11: The BezLab program in its initial state

BezLab maintains two arrays that each contains four floats. The arrays are called xs and ys. The arrays contain the coordinates of the first endpoint, the first control point, the second control point, and the second endpoint. The paint() method in BezLab uses the arrays as follows:

```
public void paint(Graphics g)
{
    // Color in all points.
    for (int i=0; i<4; i++)
    {
        if (i==0 || i==3)
            g.setColor(Color.blue);
        else
            g.setColor(Color.cyan);
            g.fillOval(xs[i]-6, ys[i]-6, 12, 12);
    }
    // Draw curve.
    Graphics2D g2d = (Graphics2D)g;
    g2d.setColor(Color.black);
    GeneralPath path = new GeneralPath();
    path.moveTo(xs[0], ys[0]);
```

```
      path.curveTo(xs[1], ys[1], xs[2], ys[2], xs[3], ys[3]);
      g2d.draw(path);
   }
```

The complete listing for BezLab follows. Experiment with the effects that moving the control points and the end points have on the shape of the bezier curve.

LIST 16.8: *BezLab.java*

```java
import java.awt.*;
import java.awt.event.*;
import java.awt.geom.*;


class BezLab extends Frame
              implements MouseListener, MouseMotionListener
{                                               (

  private int[]                xs = {  75, 150, 300, 375 };
  private int[]                ys = { 250, 100, 350, 250 };
  private int                  dragIndex = NOT_DRAGGING;

  private final static int     NEIGHBORHOOD = 15;
  private final static int     NOT_DRAGGING = -1;


  public static void main(String[] args)
  {
    (new BezLab()).setVisible(true);
  }


  BezLab()
  {
    setSize(500, 450);
    addMouseListener(this);
    addMouseMotionListener(this);
    addWindowListener(new WindowAdapter() {
      public void windowClosing(WindowEvent e)
      {System.exit(0);}
    });
  }


  public void paint(Graphics g)
```

```
{
  // Color in all points.
  for (int i=0; i<4; i++)
                {
    if (i==0 || i==3)
        g.setColor(Color.blue);
    else
        g.setColor(Color.cyan);
    g.fillOval(xs[i]-6, ys[i]-6, 12, 12);
                }

  // Draw curve.
  Graphics2D g2d = (Graphics2D)g;
  g2d.setColor(Color.black);
  GeneralPath path = new GeneralPath();
  path.moveTo(xs[0], ys[0]);
  path.curveTo(xs[1], ys[1], xs[2], ys[2], xs[3], ys[3]);
  g2d.draw(path);
                }


public void mousePressed(MouseEvent e)
{
  // Determine index of point being dragged.
  dragIndex = NOT_DRAGGING;
  int minDistance = Integer.MAX_VALUE;
  int indexOfClosestPoint = -1;
  for (int i=0; i<4; i++)
  {
    int deltaX = xs[i] - e.getX();
    int deltaY = ys[i] - e.getY();
    int distance =
      (int)(Math.sqrt(deltaX*deltaX + deltaY*deltaY));
    if (distance < minDistance)
    {
        minDistance = distance;
        indexOfClosestPoint = i;
    }
  }

  // Must be close enough.
  if (minDistance > NEIGHBORHOOD)
      return;

  dragIndex = indexOfClosestPoint;
}
```

Part III

```java
public void mouseReleased(MouseEvent e)
{
    if (dragIndex == NOT_DRAGGING)
        return;
    xs[dragIndex] = e.getX();
    ys[dragIndex] = e.getY();
    dragIndex = NOT_DRAGGING;
    repaint();
}


public void mouseDragged(MouseEvent e)
{
    if (dragIndex == NOT_DRAGGING)
        return;

    xs[dragIndex] = e.getX();
    ys[dragIndex] = e.getY();
    repaint();
}


public void mouseClicked(MouseEvent e)    { }
public void mouseEntered(MouseEvent e)    { }
public void mouseExited(MouseEvent e)     { }
public void mouseMoved(MouseEvent e)      { }
}
```

Compile and run the BezLab application as shown below:

```
C:\javadevhdbk\ch16\javac BezLab.java
C:\javadevhdbk\ch16\java BezLab
```

Drawing Fractals

To demonstrate a more detailed example that makes heavy use of general paths, we will develop a program called FracLabTriangle, which renders a convoluted triangle-based fractal.

NOTE

The word *fractal* was coined by Benoit Mandelbrot to describe curves that are so convoluted that their dimension exceeds two. However, the curves are definitely not three-dimensional. Mandelbrot proposed using nonintegral numbers to describe the dimensions of convoluted curves. Fractal is an abbreviation of fractional dimension.

One way to generate a fractal is to start with a simple shape such as a triangle. The shape should consist of line segments. You then apply a transformation to each line segment to turn each line segment into a strand of connected line segments, beginning where the original segment began and ending where the original segment ended. Thus, each line segment is transformed into a slightly more convoluted path. You repeat the process on the new (smaller) segments. A fractal is the result of reiterating the process infinitely many times. In practice, four or five iterations are enough to draw a very convoluted picture that does a good job of expressing the strangeness of fractals.

FracLabTriangle begins with a triangle, as shown in Figure 16.12. The transformation removes the middle third of each line segment and replaces that third with the pointy part of an equilateral triangle. The transformation is difficult to describe in words but easy to understand from a picture. Figure 16.13 shows the result of applying the transformation to each segment of the original triangle.

In the next step, the same transformation is applied to each of the new small line segments, resulting in Figure 16.14. After one more iteration, the shape begins to look quite convoluted, as shown in Figure 16.15. After a fourth iteration, the convolutions almost fit between the pixels, as shown in Figure 16.16.

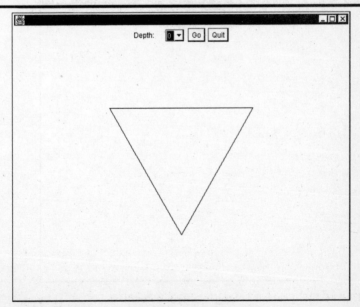

FIGURE 16.12: FracLabTriangle before iteration

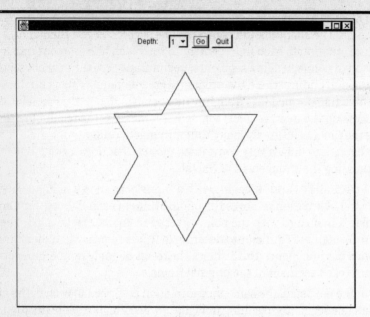

FIGURE 16.13: FracLabTriangle after one iteration

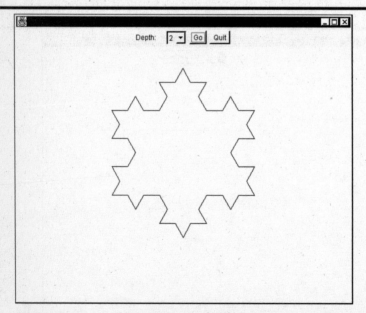

FIGURE 16.14: FracLabTriangle after two iterations

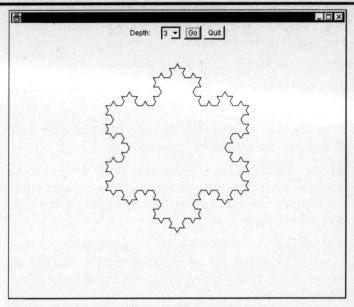

FIGURE 16.15: FracLabTriangle after three iterations

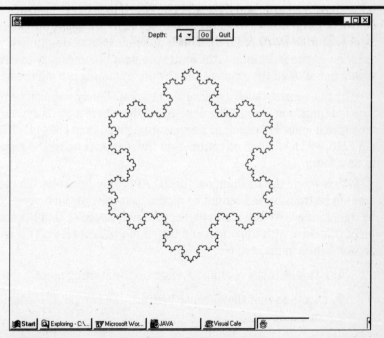

FIGURE 16.16: FracLabTriangle after four iterations

Part iii

FracLabTriangle supports up to five iterations, but the fifth iteration takes a long time and produces tiny convolutions that can be appreciated only on a very large screen.

FracLabTriangle consists of four classes:

FracLabTriangle   The main application class. It extends Frame and contains a control panel.

FracCanvas   A canvas that is contained in the main frame. FracCanvas knows how to draw a fractal.

Xform   Represents a transformation. FracCanvas uses an instance of Xform as instructions on how to convert a line segment during iteration. An Xform contains some number of XformStep values.

XformStep   Represents a single piece of a transformation. Our transformation changes a line segment into four line segments, so the corresponding Xform object will contain four XformStep values.

The easiest way to understand the application is to start from the bottom, with Xform and XformStep. The Xform class encapsulates instructions on how to transform a line segment, *assuming the line segment goes from (0, 0) to (1, 0)*. This is an enormous assumption. If we are allowed the assumption, the entire program becomes easy to write. (If we are not allowed the assumption, the programming is a nightmare.)

Why can we make such a radical assumption? Surely, we must be prepared to transform *any* line segment, no matter where it starts and no matter where it ends. For example, a segment might go from (14.4141, 75) to (15.5115, 76.1). We have no control over the segments we will be required to transform.

This is where the flexibility of the 2D API comes into play. The segment to be transformed cannot be moved, but the coordinate system can be transformed. We can manipulate coordinate space so that the starting point coincides with the origin and the endpoint is at (1, 0). This is accomplished in three steps:

1. Translate the coordinate origin to the starting point.

2. Scale so that the distance between the two points becomes one unit.

3. Rotate so that the endpoint is directly to the right of the starting point.

Now we only need to solve the problem of how to transform a line segment that joins the points (0, 0) and (1, 0). Figure 16.17 illustrates the transformation.

Before:

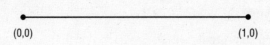

After:

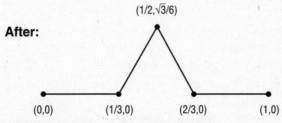

FIGURE 16.17: The basic transformation

Figure 16.17 shows that a line segment joining (0, 0) and (1, 0) needs to be transformed into four line segments:

▶ From (0, 0) to (1/3, 0)

▶ From (1/3, 0) to (1/2, $\sqrt{3}$/6)

▶ From (1/2, $\sqrt{3}$/6) to (2/3, 0)

▶ From (2/3, 0) to (1, 0)

Now that we can describe a transformation in words, we can develop a corresponding class. Actually, we will use two classes: Xform and XformStep. The XformStep class represents a single entry in the list above. This class only needs to encapsulate the coordinates of the next point along the strand:

```
float    x;
float    y;
```

In addition to these instance variables, the class contains a constructor, some numeric constants, and a static array of the steps that describe our transform.

LIST 16.9: XformStep.java

```java
public class XformStep
{
    private final static float        ONE_HALF = 1f / 2f;
    private final static float        ONE_THIRD = 1f / 3f;
    private final static float        ROOT_3_OVER_6 =
                                      (float)(Math.sqrt(3)) / 6;

    public final static XformStep[]  TRIANGLE_STEPS =
    {
        new XformStep(ONE_THIRD,     0),
        new XformStep(ONE_HALF,      ROOT_3_OVER_6),
        new XformStep(2*ONE_THIRD,   0),
        new XformStep(1,             0)
    };


    float    x;
    float    y;


    public XformStep(float x, float y)
    {
        this.x = x;
        this.y = y;
    }
}
```

The Xform class is simply a collection of instances of XformStep.
The collection is implemented as an array. There is one constructor,
which takes as input an array of XformStep values:

LIST 16.10:   Xform.java

```java
public class Xform
{
    public final static Xform     TRIANGLE_XFORM =
        new Xform(XformStep.TRIANGLE_STEPS);


    public XformStep[]        steps;


    public Xform(XformStep[] steps)
    {
        this.steps = steps;
```

```
      }
   }
```

Now the data representation problem is solved. The next step is to develop the FracCanvas class. The job of this class is to draw a fractal, given a set of parameters:

▶ The initial shape

▶ The transformation to apply to each line segment

▶ The number of iterations

The heart of FracCanvas is a method called recurse(), which has the following signature:

```
public void recurse(int depth, float x0, float y0,
                               float x1, float y1)
```

This method deals with the line segment from (x0, y0) to (x1, y1). "Dealing with" a line segment may mean simply drawing it, or it may mean expanding it by applying the transformation; it may even mean iteratively applying the transformation multiple times. The depth argument tells the method how many times to iterate. The figures shown at the beginning of this section were created with different depth arguments: Figure 16.14 shows a depth of 2, and Figure 16.16 shows a depth of 4.

As you can guess from the name, recurse() is a recursive method. If depth is 0, the method just draws a line segment that joins the two endpoints. If depth is greater than zero, the method adjusts coordinate space so that the segment goes from (0, 0) to (1, 0). The method then determines the new set of line segments (there will be four of them); for each of these segments, the recurse() method calls itself, with depth decremented by one.

The recurse() method looks like this:

```
private void recurse(int depth, float x0, float y0,
                                float x1, float y1)
{
   XformStep[]      steps;
   XformStep        step;
   int              nPieces;
   float            x, y;
   float            nextX, nextY;
   float            range, bearing;

   // Check for bottom of recursion.
   if (depth == 0)
   {
```

Part iii

```
            path.moveTo(x0, y0);
            path.lineTo(x1, y1);
            g.setStroke(thinStroke);
            g.draw(path);
            return;
        }

        // Recurse on each line segment.
        depth-;
        normalize(x0, y0, x1, y1);
        x = y = 0f;
        steps = xform.steps;
        for (int i=0; i<steps.length; i++)  // For each step ...
        {
            step = steps[i];
            nextX = step.x;
            nextY = step.y;
            recurse(depth, x, y, nextX, nextY);
            x = nextX;
            y = nextY;
        }

        // Undo temporary transformation.
        unNormalize();
    }
```

The `normalize()` method adjusts coordinate space so that the starting point is at $(0, 0)$ and the endpoint is at $(1, 0)$. The `unNormalize()` method undoes the most recent `normalize()` call. Undoing a normalization operation is not trivial. The program maintains three stacks, called `scaleStack`, `rotationStack`, and `translationStack`. These data structures store the information that describes the various operations. Each stack is serviced by two methods.

The scale stack stores scale factors and is serviced by the `scale()` and `unScale()` methods:

```
        private void scale(double scaleBy)
        {
            g.scale(scaleBy, scaleBy);
            scaleStack.push(new Double(scaleBy));
        }

        private void unScale()
        {
            Double d = (Double)scaleStack.pop();
            double factor = 1 / d.doubleValue();
```

```
        g.scale(factor, factor);
    }
```

The rotation stack stores degrees and is serviced by the `rotate()` and `unRotate()` methods:

```
    private void rotate(double radians)
    {
        g.rotate(radians);
        rotationStack.push(new Double(radians));
    }

    private void unRotate()
    {
        Double d = (Double)rotationStack.pop();
        g.rotate(-(d.doubleValue()));
    }
```

The translation stack stores x and y translation factors and is serviced by the `translate()` and `unTranslate()` methods:

```
    private void translate(double x, double y)
    {
        g.translate(x, y);
        translationStack.push(new Double(x));
        translationStack.push(new Double(y));
    }

    private void unTranslate()
    {
        Double y = (Double)translationStack.pop();
        Double x = (Double)translationStack.pop();
        g.translate(-(x.doubleValue()), -(y.doubleValue()));
    }
```

With this infrastructure in place, it becomes easy to write the normalization method. There are two special cases that avoid numerical singularities; otherwise, the code is straightforward:

```
    private void normalize(float x0, float y0, float x1, float y1)
    {
        // Translate
        translate(x0, y0);              // Translate

        // Rotate
        double deltaX = x1 - x0;
        double deltaY = y1 - y0;
        if (deltaX == 0)               // Special case
        {
```

```
          if (y0 < y1)
              rotate(Math.PI / 2);
          else
              rotate(3 * Math.PI / 2);
      }
      else if (deltaY == 0)          // Special case
      {
          if (x0 > x1)
              rotate(Math.PI);
          else
              rotate(0);
      }
      else
      {
          double slope = deltaY / deltaX;
          double theta = Math.atan(slope);
          rotate(theta);
      }

      // Scale
      double length = Math.sqrt(deltaX*deltaX + deltaY*deltaY);
      scale(length);
  }
```

At this point, the unNormalize() method is trivial:

```
  private void unNormalize()
  {
      unScale();
      unRotate();
      unTranslate();
  }
```

That is almost all of the FracCanvas class. There needs to be a paint() method to tie everything together. This method begins by translating the origin to the center of the canvas and scaling so that the smaller of the two dimensions (width and height) goes from −1 to +1. The code then creates an initial shape and calls recurse(). The paint() code is listed here:

```
  public void paint(Graphics g1d)
  {
      g = (Graphics2D)g1d;
      g.setColor(Color.blue);
      g.setStroke(new BasicStroke(0));

      scaleStack = new Stack();
      rotationStack = new Stack();
      translationStack = new Stack();
```

```
        path = new GeneralPath();
        centerAndScale2x2();

        g.setColor(Color.blue);
        for (int i=0; i<INITIAL_XS.length-1; i++)
        {
            recurse(depth, INITIAL_XS[i],  INITIAL_YS[i],
                    INITIAL_XS[i+1], INITIAL_YS[i+1]);
        }
    }


    public void centerAndScale2x2()
    {
        // Center the origin
        Dimension size = getSize();
        translate(size.width/2, size.height/2);

        // Scale
        int mindim = Math.min(size.width, size.height);
        scale(mindim/2);
    }
```

The complete listing of FracCanvas appears below, followed by
FracLabTriangle. You will also need XformStep.java (List 16.9)
and Xform.java (List 16.10).

LIST 16.11:   *FracCanvas.java*

```
import java.awt.*;
import java.awt.event.*;
import java.awt.geom.*;
import java.util.*;


public class FracCanvas extends Canvas
{
    private Xform           xform = Xform.TRIANGLE_XFORM;
    private int             depth = 0;
    private Stack           scaleStack;
    private Stack           rotationStack;
    private Stack           translationStack;
    private Graphics2D      g;
    private GeneralPath     path;
    private BasicStroke     thinStroke;
```

```
//
// These coords define the initial shape in a space with
// origin at the center, extending from -1 to +1
// in the smaller of the x and y dimensions.
//
private final static float    ROOT_ONE_THIRD =
                                    (float)(Math.sqrt(1d/3d));
private final static float[]  INITIAL_XS =
{
  -ROOT_ONE_THIRD, 0f, +ROOT_ONE_THIRD, -ROOT_ONE_THIRD
};
private final static float[]  INITIAL_YS =
{
  -.5f, +.5f, -.5f , -.5f
};


public FracCanvas()
{
  setBackground(Color.white);
  thinStroke = new BasicStroke(0);
}


public Dimension getPreferredSize()
{
  return new Dimension(700, 700);
}


void go(int depth)
{
  this.depth = depth;
  repaint();
}


public void paint(Graphics g1d)
{
  g = (Graphics2D)g1d;
  g.setColor(Color.blue);
  g.setStroke(new BasicStroke(0));

  scaleStack = new Stack();
  rotationStack = new Stack();
  translationStack = new Stack();
```

```
        path = new GeneralPath();
        centerAndScale2x2();

        g.setColor(Color.blue);
        for (int i=0; i<INITIAL_XS.length-1; i++)
        {
          recurse(depth, INITIAL_XS[i], INITIAL_YS[i],
                  INITIAL_XS[i+1], INITIAL_YS[i+1]);
        }
      }

    private void recurse(int depth, float x0, float y0,
                         float x1, float y1)
    {
      XformStep[]    steps;
      XformStep      step;
      int            nPieces;
      float          x, y;
      float          nextX, nextY;
      float          range, bearing;

      // Check for bottom of recursion.
      if (depth == 0)
      {
        path.moveTo(x0, y0);
        path.lineTo(x1, y1);
        g.setStroke(thinStroke);
        g.draw(path);
        return;
      }

      // Recurse on each line segment.
      depth--;
      normalize(x0, y0, x1, y1);
      x = y = 0f;
      steps = xform.steps;
      for (int i=0; i<steps.length; i++)  // For each step ...
      {
        step = steps[i];
        nextX = step.x;
        nextY = step.y;
        recurse(depth, x, y, nextX, nextY);
        x = nextX;
        y = nextY;
      }
```

```
  // Undo temporary transformation.
  unNormalize();
}


//
//  Translates to (x0, y0). Rotates so that (x1, x1) is
//  to the right. Scales so that the two points are 1
//  unit apart.
//
private void normalize(float x0, float y0, float x1, float y1)
{
  // Translate
  translate(x0, y0);            // Translate

  // Rotate
  double deltaX = x1 - x0;
  double deltaY = y1 - y0;
  if (deltaX == 0)              // Special case
  {
    if (y0 < y1)
      rotate(Math.PI / 2);
    else
      rotate(3 * Math.PI / 2);
  }
  else if (deltaY == 0)         // Special case
  {
    if (x0 > x1)
      rotate(Math.PI);
    else
      rotate(0);
  }
  else
  {
    double slope = deltaY / deltaX;
    double theta = Math.atan(slope);
    rotate(theta);
  }

  // Scale
  double length = Math.sqrt(deltaX*deltaX + deltaY*deltaY);
  scale(length);
}
```

```
private void unNormalize()
{
  unScale();
  unRotate();
  unTranslate();
}


private void scale(double scaleBy)
{
  g.scale(scaleBy, scaleBy);
  scaleStack.push(new Double(scaleBy));
}


private void rotate(double radians)
{
  g.rotate(radians);
  rotationStack.push(new Double(radians));
}

private void translate(double x, double y)
{
  g.translate(x, y);
  translationStack.push(new Double(x));
  translationStack.push(new Double(y));
}


private void unScale()
{
  Double d = (Double)scaleStack.pop();
  double factor = 1 / d.doubleValue();
  g.scale(factor, factor);
}
```

```java
    private void unRotate()
    {
      Double d = (Double)rotationStack.pop();
      g.rotate(-(d.doubleValue()));
    }


    private void unTranslate()
    {
      Double y = (Double)translationStack.pop();
      Double x = (Double)translationStack.pop();
      g.translate(-(x.doubleValue()), -(y.doubleValue()));
    }


    //
    //   Scale a graphics context so that the origin is at the
    //   center and the smaller dimension is from -1 to +1.
    //
    public void centerAndScale2x2()
    {
      // Center the origin
      Dimension size = getSize();
      translate(size.width/2, size.height/2);

      // Scale
      int mindim = Math.min(size.width, size.height);
      scale(mindim/2);
    }
}
```

LIST 16.12:   *FracLabTriangle.java*

```java
import java.awt.*;
import java.awt.event.*;
import java.awt.geom.*;
import java.util.Vector;

public class FracLabTriangle extends Frame
                                implements ActionListener
{
  private FracCanvas              fracCanvas;
  private Choice                  depthChoice;
  private Button                  goBtn, quitBtn;
  private final static int        MIN_DEPTH = 0;
```

```
private final static int          MAX_DEPTH = 5;

public static void main(String[] args)
{
  FracLabTriangle lab = new FracLabTriangle();
  lab.pack();
  lab.setVisible(true);
}

FracLabTriangle()
{
  fracCanvas = new FracCanvas();
  add(fracCanvas, BorderLayout.CENTER);

  Panel controls = new Panel();
  controls.add(new Label("Depth:"));
  depthChoice = new Choice();
  for (int i=MIN_DEPTH; i<=MAX_DEPTH; i++)
       depthChoice.addItem(""+i);
  controls.add(depthChoice);
  goBtn = new Button("Go");
  goBtn.addActionListener(this);
  controls.add(goBtn);
  quitBtn = new Button("Quit");
  quitBtn.addActionListener(this);
  controls.add(quitBtn);
  add(controls, BorderLayout.NORTH);
}

public void actionPerformed(ActionEvent e)
{
  if (e.getSource() == quitBtn)
       System.exit(0);
    fracCanvas.go(depthChoice.getSelectedIndex());
}
}
```

Compile and run the `FracLabTriangle` application as shown below:

```
C:\javadevhdbk\ch16\javac FracLabTriangle.java
C:\javadevhdbk\ch16\java FracLabTriangle
```

Extending the Triangular Fractal

The triangular fractal is just one of a large family of curves. In theory, you can create a fractal by starting with any initial shape and applying any transformation.

The application is an advanced version of the `FracLabTriangle` application. The advanced application is called simply `FracLab`, and it should reside in its own subdirectory because it has its own versions of the support classes. It is similar to `FracLab`, but its GUI has a `Choice` component to allow you to choose other fractals.

The `FracLab` version presents the triangle fractal, as well as two other fractals. Both new shapes start with a square, as shown in Figure 16.18.

The program has two transformations that can operate on this shape. The Box transformation indents each line segment. This transformation is illustrated in Figure 16.19. Figure 16.20 shows the result of applying the transformation four times.

A more sophisticated transformation can be applied to the initial square shape. The new transformation still indents each line segment. In addition, an "island" is drawn within the indentation. Figure 16.21 shows the transformation, which is called the Coast transformation. Figure 16.22 shows the result of applying the Coast transformation four times.

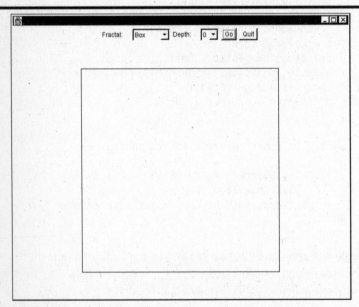

FIGURE 16.18:   The FracLab program starting with a square

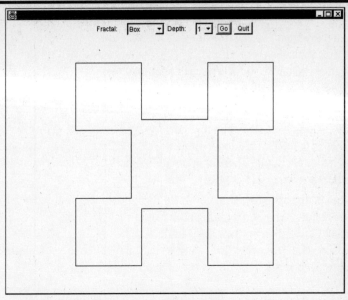

FIGURE 16.19:   FracLab's Box transformation

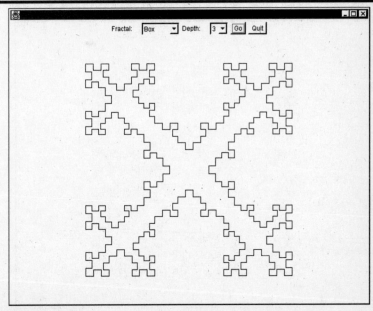

FIGURE 16.20:   FracLab's Box transformation after four iterations

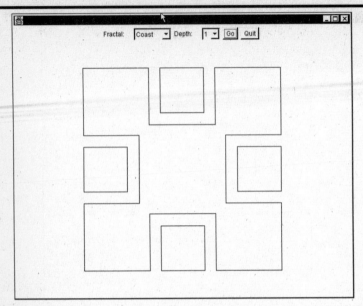

FIGURE 16.21: FracLab's Coast transformation

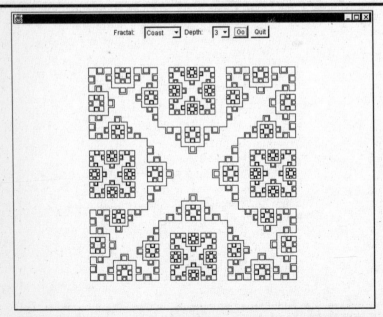

FIGURE 16.22: FracLab's Coast transformation after four iterations

LIST 16.13:   FracLab.java

```java
import java.awt.*;
import java.awt.event.*;
import java.awt.geom.*;
import java.util.Vector;


public class FracLab extends Frame
                     implements ActionListener
{
  private FracCanvas            fracCanvas;
  private Choice                fractalChoice;
  private Choice                depthChoice;
  private Button                goBtn, quitBtn;

  private final static int      MIN_DEPTH = 0;
  private final static int      MAX_DEPTH = 5;


  public static void main(String[] args)
  {
    FracLab lab = new FracLab();
    lab.pack();
    lab.setVisible(true);
  }

  FracLab()
  {
    fracCanvas = new FracCanvas();
    add(fracCanvas, BorderLayout.CENTER);

    Panel controls = new Panel();
    controls.add(new Label("Fractal:"));
    fractalChoice = new Choice();
    for (int i=0; i<FracCanvas.FRACTAL_NAMES.length; i++)
         fractalChoice.addItem(FracCanvas.FRACTAL_NAMES[i]);
    controls.add(fractalChoice);
    controls.add(new Label("Depth:"));
    depthChoice = new Choice();
    for (int i=MIN_DEPTH; i<=MAX_DEPTH; i++)
         depthChoice.addItem(""+i);
    controls.add(depthChoice);
    goBtn = new Button("Go");
    goBtn.addActionListener(this);
    controls.add(goBtn);
    quitBtn = new Button("Quit");
```

```
        quitBtn.addActionListener(this);
        controls.add(quitBtn);
        add(controls, BorderLayout.NORTH);
    }


    public void actionPerformed(ActionEvent e)
    {
      if (e.getSource() == quitBtn)
          System.exit(0);
              fracCanvas.go(fractalChoice.getSelectedIndex(),
              depthChoice.getSelectedIndex());
    }
}
```

Compile and run the FracLab application as shown below:

```
C:\javadevhdbk\ch16\FracLab\javac FracLab.java
C:\javadevhdbk\ch16\FracLab\java FracLab
```

WHAT'S NEXT?

We now move on to JavaBeans. Chapter 17 will give you an overview of this powerful programming tool, and Chapter 18 will cover properties, methods, and categories of beans.

PART iv

JavaBeans

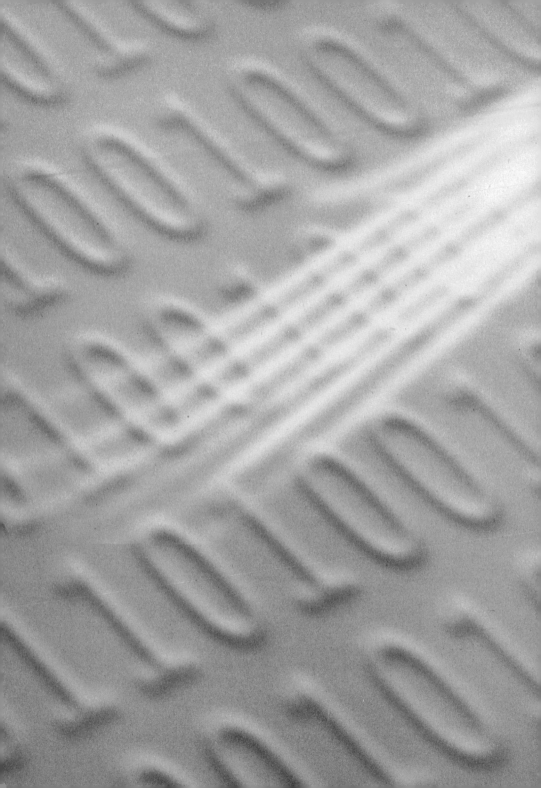

Chapter 17

JavaBeans: An Overview

Adapted from *Mastering JavaBeans*
by Laurence Vanhelsuwé
ISBN 0-7821-2097-0   799 pages $49.99

INTRODUCTION

What exactly *is* a Java bean?

A Java bean is a reusable platform-neutral software component that
can be visually manipulated in a software development tool.

This rather odd definition really consists of two totally independent parts:

- ▶ First, a Java bean is a platform-neutral software component.
  Full stop.

- ▶ Second, a Java bean "knows" about the tools that will manipulate
  it, and is compatible with those tools.

NOTE

If the word "bean" does not conjure up any images of reusable software components or tool-awareness, mentally substitute bean with *IC* (integrated circuit) or *Lego* instead (but ignore the toy connotation of Lego).

The JavaBeans standard is a *low-level* component model tailored to the
Java language. It is low-level because it does not hint at or specify the kind
of *compound document* or *application framework* architectures that some
other component standards specify (CORBA, OpenDOC, Taligent, and so
on). JavaBeans, in its initial (and current) 1.0 form at least, concentrates
purely on the *interface* a Java software building block should present, but
does not venture into the endless landscape of how such building blocks
can or should be combined to create any type of application. However, it
does specify how two or more beans can communicate information, but
without imposing any semantic rules on the information exchanged or on
the topography of any bean communication networks.

While you would expect the definition of a Java bean to simply concentrate on software components, it also includes the development tool
aspect. Without the proper tools, modern software development would
grind to a halt. We need (very) powerful tools to tackle the very complex
applications we are asked to create, and today this means tools with a
pronounced visual element. Java beans are explicitly defined to be "tool-
aware" in the sense that much of a Java bean's interface is designed with
a modern software developer in mind, manipulating the bean via visual
interactions.

Both these JavaBeans aspects boil down to how a bean presents itself to the outside world, whether at runtime communicating with fellow beans, or at design time being manipulated by a designer via the intermediary of a tool.

What Does a Bean Boil Down to in Practice?

Before we delve into yet more abstract pictures of beans, their attributes, and environments, we should quickly demystify the entire bean concept by telling you very concretely what a bean consists of, in everyday practice.

A Java bean, much like a Java applet, is quite simply a Java *class* that obeys some strict protocol (like an applet's `init()`, `start()`, `stop()`, and `paint()`). And like an applet, a bean usually consists of a whole troupe of (support) classes and resource files (images, sounds, data files, and so on) that normally get packaged into Java Archive (JAR) files.

Unlike applets, which need to be concerned only with a single, simple Java API class, `java.applet.Applet`, beans are implemented with the help of some 15 classes and six interfaces that form part of the far-from-trivial new `java.beans` Core API package.

THE BLACK BOX VIEW OF A JAVA BEAN

Primarily, you should think of a Java bean as a *black box*; that is, a software device with known *functionality* but unknown internal *functioning*. As such, black boxes are only defined or discussed in terms of their external characteristics (that is, their interface) with the rest of the world: knobs, buttons, numeric or analog readouts, color, shape, openings, handles, and so on.

If you are not familiar with the concept of a black box, then here is a mental image for you: the typical black box is a... black, box-shaped "thing" with a button and a light that magically produces $50 bills when you press its button. For every press of the button, one $50 bill is produced, but only after the light switches on and off seven times. How this black box achieves its magic of dubious legality is a total mystery, but its function is perfectly clear: to produce $50 bills. How to get it to produce these notes is also crystal clear: by pressing the button and waiting for the light activity to finish. To complete your image of the typical black box, you should also imagine the box to be made of some extraterrestrial alloy, a material

Part iv

that no drill, X-ray machine, or explosive can pierce. This indestructibility is purely so that its internal machinery remains forever an unknown and, as you shall come to appreciate, a wholly unimportant detail.

The concept of a black box in engineering is a very important and valuable one because it allows us to

- ▶ simplify something of arbitrary complexity down to a *single* object of childlike simplicity, and

- ▶ think of large systems as being a collection of black boxes that communicate purely via their black box interfaces.

Being able to mentally reduce the complexity of *anything* down to the toy-like simplicity of an opaque "box" is vitally important during analysis, design, and implementation phases of any complex system because people, research tells us, can only juggle about seven (plus or minus two) concepts in their mind at the same time. This is the reason why we have to create systems built of hierarchical levels; each level shields our mortal intellect from a numerous (more than seven) collection of lower-level entities and magically transforms this collection into a single mental "handle," thus allowing us to cope with more complexity (but only at that new abstraction level).

By thinking of large systems as communication networks that bind together black boxes, we succeed in controlling system complexity by basically ignoring the bulk of a system's complexity that resides *inside* its black boxes. An excellent example is an everyday desktop PC. While inherently hugely complex (not a single person on this planet can explain every aspect of its internal operation to you), a PC can still be understood by treating it as a collection of very clearly defined components (black boxes) that communicate with each other using very clearly defined communication protocols. Each PC component can in turn be viewed as a smaller network of components, again communicating via rigid protocols, and so on, until you reach some microscopic level where the hierarchy *logically* ends.

Viewed as black boxes, Java beans have three interface facets that can be developed to independent degrees:

1. The methods that can be invoked on a bean

2. The readable and/or writable properties that a bean exposes

3. The events a bean can signal to the outside world or accept from it

We will now explore these three key aspects in a bit more detail.

Bean Methods

Because any bean essentially boils down to a Java object (like applets do), invoking methods on this object is the only way of interacting with it. A Java bean sticks rigidly to objected-oriented class design philosophy and does not make any of its instance fields accessible to the outside world (no `public` fields); thus, method invocations are the only way to address a bean, its parts, or its behavior.

However, unlike normal classes, the low-level mechanism of invoking an instance method on some bean is not the main way of manipulating or using a bean. Public bean methods are delegated to a secondary role for bean manipulation because two higher-level bean aspects—properties and events—are the preferred way of interacting with a bean.

Therefore, your beans can provide `public` methods you would like your bean's clients to use, but you should realize that bean designers expect to see most of a bean's functionality reflected in its properties and events, and not in separate methods to be invoked manually. This book will spend very little time on demonstrating plain `public` methods because they can be added as you would any other `public` method; `public` methods do not need to be "enabled" or "registered" by any JavaBeans API mechanisms.

Bean Properties

Beans feature the high-level concept of *properties*. Properties are conceptually nothing more than the classic attributes objects have, in object-oriented speak, but are formally supported by a properties-reading and -setting API.

A clock bean could have "time zone" and "alarm" properties; a calendar bean could have "year" and "month" properties; a mailbox bean could have "mailbox overflow alarm" and "junk mail filter" properties; and so on. Each of these properties would formally come to life by sticking to some simple method naming conventions. This way tools and end-users can find out which properties a bean features, and can then query their values or change them to manipulate the bean.

Changing properties usually results in an immediate change in the bean to reflect the change. So, using our previous examples, if you changed the clock's time zone, the clock face would immediately redraw itself, showing the current time in the selected time zone. Also, if you changed the year property of the calendar to some year in the future, the calendar would redraw itself to show the current month in that year. Finally, if you lowered the mailbox's overflow alarm below the current level of messages it contained, the mailbox could generate an alarm then and there.

Bean Events

The main way beans communicate information with other software components is by firing and receiving events. You should think of a bean's event support as the pins of an IC: in the electronics world, engineers connect pins together to let their components communicate. Some pins are purely for output (event firing) while others are purely for input (event receiving). Beans can be thought of as having that same type of input/output pins that are to be connected together to create communicating networks of beans. Figure 17.1 shows this analogy.

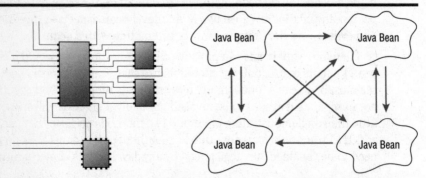

FIGURE 17.1:   Electronic components are connected via their peripheral pins to form higher-level systems. Java beans similarly use event firing and receiving mechanisms to communicate and thus form higher-level software systems.

BEAN ENVIRONMENTS

An everyday light is flexible and robust enough to be used in a NASA R&D laboratory, a Las Vegas casino, your kitchen, or outdoors to help light an advertising sign. Generic components get deployed in a vast number of wildly differing environments. As such, they should perform equally well in every one of those environments. The same is true for Java beans: you cannot predict how, where, or when your bean is going to be used or in what kind of application it will be embedded. However, there are some general facts that we can state:

▶ A bean always runs in a single Java Virtual Machine (the Java-Beans standard is not a *distributed* software components standard, like CORBA).

▶ A bean lives in a multithreaded environment and can therefore be addressed by multiple threads at the same time.

The first bulleted item above means that JavaBeans really does not compete with the CORBA industry standard because CORBA is a component standard for *distributed objects*. Systems built with JavaBeans can still be CORBA-compliant via a JavaBeans-CORBA *bridge*. Because the Java bean does not concern itself with network issues, the standard is more efficient (within its intended application domains) because all bean manipulations and communications are defined to be local.

The second bulleted item above is simply a consequence of the first, and is true for any Java entity (applet, application, bean...). Chapter 18, *Bean Properties*, explains some detailed multithreaded scenarios to be aware of when designing your beans.

WARNING

Understanding how to use Java's multithreading API and the language's syn-chronized keyword should be considered a fundamental skill for serious Java programmers. In the same vein, understanding how race conditions arise, how to use various synchronization mechanisms to guard against race conditions, and how to implement safe and efficient interthread communication should not be considered an advanced skill, but a basic one. Consult any good book on modern operating systems to understand the often thorny issues surrounding multithreading (and multitasking). A good book on Java's multithreading is *Java Threads* by Scott Oaks and Henry Wong (O'Reilly, 1997).

Design-Time Environment

While it is perfectly obvious that Java beans will come to life in applications at runtime, it may come as a surprise that Java beans are equally alive when still on the designer's workbench. Unlike routine or module software libraries of previous generations, JavaBeans components are actually instantiated and allowed to perform their usual functions at *design time*.

This is a very important difference from the electronic circuit design analogy: when an electronics engineer wires components together, all components are "cold"—no electric current passes through them and their functions are consequently dormant and disabled. When a software designer picks a Java bean off his or her tools "components shelf," this bean is already "hot" because it is functioning as if it were embedded in an application. If you were to pick a clock bean and a light bean and position them on your tool's design surface, the clock bean would be ticking away (using a separate Java thread) while the light bean might be on. If these two beans were somehow compatible, you could connect them up, and as soon as the connection is made, the light would pulse at the same rate the clock is ticking.

Clearly, this design-time "live" behavior of beans is *very* different from the code libraries of the past that remained "dead" throughout the development cycle, only to come to life when the application is run. It is this JavaBeans aspect that warranted its mention in the definition of a Java bean that introduced this chapter: beans need to be designed to allow this design-time live interaction between designer, tool, and bean.

This new software development model has some really far-reaching implications: unlike with classic software construction, where we compile, link, and then see if the monolithic end result can stand on its own feet, designing software using JavaBeans does not have this clearly defined boundary between "dead" and "alive" software. With JavaBeans, when you work in your visual design tool you are gradually breathing life into your software. The process lends itself much more to an iterative development approach where you evolve a system, and where you can quickly turn ideas into prototypes.

Because beans, by definition, already start "running" while they are manipulated by a designer and his or her tools, several aspects of the JavaBeans standard are concerned with formalizing some types of design-time interactions that are expected to be commonplace.

Therefore, beans usually (but do not have to) come with explicit information that describes their black box interfaces. Bean properties, for example, come in different, tool-recognized flavors. For example, a property can be classed as an expert or a normal property. Depending on the designer's level of experience, the tool can then hide or include the expert properties in the list of properties it displays for each bean. A single property and a single (fired) event can also be marked as being the default property or event, respectively. This tells the designer that this property or event is probably the one most frequently used.

Now, imagine designers who have spent an entire day laying out components, interconnecting them, and tuning their properties. At the end of the day these designers face a problem that their electronics colleagues do not have: If they switch their computers off their designs vanish, whereas a physical design or prototype obviously stays put until the next morning. Therefore, Java beans should be able to be made *persistent*—that is, stored in some permanent storage device. Prior to the 1.1 release of Java there did not exist any standard way of doing this, so it would have been impossible for a tool to tell all the beans to "go store yourselves in this file." With the addition of Java's Serialization API, all Java objects (not only Java beans) can now be converted into (serial) data streams that can be stored in files, transmitted over networks, and so on. To support a tool's Load/Save and Cut/Copy/Paste functions, Java beans therefore need to be serializable objects, too.

Runtime Environment

As we said earlier, a Java bean can be deployed in almost any Java environment. One harsh and extreme example of a possible environment is an embedded system that does not have a display (say, a NASA interplanetary probe). Beans that are part of such embedded software would not be able to use the AWT at all because

- ▶ no one could see the result of the bean's renderings or GUI, and

- ▶ the AWT package would not even be available in the ROMs of the system.

A bean clearly needs to know whether it can use a GUI or not, so the JavaBeans standard caters to this, too.

Another runtime issue is the end-user's culture and language. Today's software market is a global one, like almost every other market, and so beans need to be flexible enough to serve a/an French Canadian, Brazilian, English, Japanese, Zairese, Vietnamese, Austrian, and so on...user.

This implies that if a bean displays a time or date, this time or date should be formatted in the user's *locale*-dependent style (believe it or not, the vast majority of the world does not know what AM and PM mean because they use a 24-hour clock convention). If a bean manipulates local currencies, then this should be displayed in the standard form for that currency. For example, Indian Rupees have a major magnitude point at 100,000, called a Lakh, so one million Rupees is never displayed as 1,000,000 Rupees but as 10 Lakh. Internationalization of software is a complex topic because the world counts so many permutations of cultures and languages, so this book will only mention it as an issue to keep in mind.

Part iv

Applet versus Application Environments

The core goal of JavaBeans is to make software development easier, faster, and cheaper chiefly by encouraging code reuse on a scale that the software industry has not yet been able to employ. Therefore, there is no reason why Java applets cannot be built from Java beans as well.

This implies that beans can be constrained by the same security rules that are imposed on applets. A bean might not be able to access the local machine's filing system, or open network connections to any Internet host. As with the availability or non-availability of a windowing system to communicate with users, beans might need to know whether they are running as part of (or just as) an applet so that they avoid actions that a browser's `SecurityManager` would block, usually leading to the applet's instant termination.

In addition, the JavaBeans standard does not restrict Java applets from being beans (or vice versa). The distinction between applet and bean disappears when an applet is enhanced with the core traits of any bean (bean properties and bean events) or when a bean gets enhanced to comply to the well-known applet `init()/start()/stop()/paint()` protocol. This means you could as easily use such applet-bean hybrids in a bean development environment (or a final bean-based product) as you could embed one in a WWW page.

THE BEAN DEVELOPMENT KIT AND THE BEANBOX BEAN TESTING APPLICATION

JavaSoft, the Sun Microsystems subsidiary responsible for evolving Java and its related APIs, designs, implements, and makes available various Java *reference* implementations so that licensees and other third parties can *validate* their own Java ports or those of third-party suppliers. The main Java reference product that JavaSoft produces is the Java Development Kit (JDK). The JDK comprises the reference Java Virtual Machine (JVM), a Java compiler, debugger, profiler, and so on.

If a Java program produces different results when run on different platforms, then one of the platforms is not 100 percent Java compatible. To determine which implementation is in error, it is simply a matter of comparing the results with those produced when executing the program using a JDK; the third-party Java implementation that produces the same output as the JDK is correct, any third-party implementations that produce deviating output are flawed.

NOTE

The only way to *comprehensively* test the level of Java compatibility of a third-party Java implementation is to pass JavaSoft's suite of validation tests. These are collections of Java programs that, collectively, rely on every single aspect of the Java language (as specified by *The Java Language Specification*) and the underlying JVM (as specified by *The Java Virtual Machine Specification*) to work as laid down in the standards documents. Both specifications are available from the JavaSoft Web site `http://java.sun.com`.

JavaSoft also produces the Bean Development Kit (BDK). The BDK plays the same role for the JavaBeans standard as the JDK does for Java itself: it is a reference environment in which to develop and test beans. (Both the 1.2 JDK and the 1.0 BDK are available from JavaSoft's site: `http://www.javasoft.com/products/jdk/1.2/` and `http://www.javasoft.com/beans/`, respectively.)

The BeanBox

When you start up the BeanBox application using the provided run batch file, you should see three windows pop up, as shown in Figure 17.2.

The largest window is where all the action happens: it is the BeanBox itself, where you can drop your beans and exercise them in various ways. The smaller ToolBox window represents a bean palette from which you can pick any bean to work with, as if from a physical box full of components. The last window, called PropertySheet, lists the currently selected bean's properties and their values. In the case of Figure 17.2, the BeanBox is itself the currently selected bean (because it too is a bean), so the foreground, background, font, and name properties you see are its current properties. Note also how some beans listed in the ToolBox are flanked by a small icon representing those beans. The Juggler bean's icon is probably the most representative of those shown.

Part iv

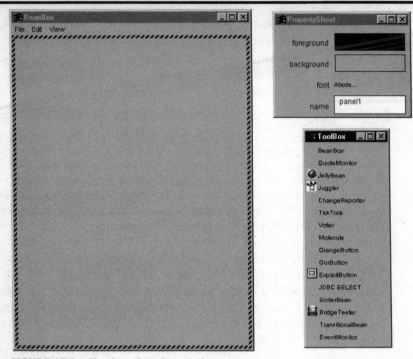

FIGURE 17.2:   The three BeanBox windows

The BDK Demonstration Beans

The ToolBox window is where the BeanBox application lists all the beans that you may select for use within your JavaBeans-based application. After running the BeanBox for the first time (after a fresh install of the BDK), all the beans listed by the ToolBox are JavaBeans demonstration beans. Their main purpose is to demonstrate features of the JavaBeans standard; they are *not* meant to be used as real software building blocks within any real-life application. As a result, most of the BDK demonstration beans come across as odd and thoroughly dysfunctional. It is worth reiterating that this is because these beans each concentrate on one or more aspects of the JavaBeans standard and not on the loftier concerns of rapid application development using interoperable software components.

The full source for these demonstration beans is included in the BDK, as is the complete source code for the BeanBox itself. I strongly encourage you to study these sources. Initially, you can read the source for the demonstration beans; later on, once you have a clearer picture of the tool's key role in the JavaBeans standard, you should definitely invest the time to see how the BeanBox itself ticks.

The remainder of this section will give you a brief introduction to the main BDK demonstration beans.

The Button Beans

The BDK comes with no less than four demonstration button beans: OurButton, OrangeButton, BlueButton, and ExplicitButton. Although all four can be used as button click event sources, they primarily serve to demonstrate the following JavaBeans API aspects:

- ▶ OurButton is a vanilla bean implemented as a subclass of `Canvas`.

- ▶ OrangeButton is an instance of OurButton that was serialized (that is, saved) while its background color property was set to orange.

- ▶ BlueButton is an instance of OurButton that was externalized and had its background color property set to blue.

- ▶ ExplicitButton shows how beans can control their black box interface. While OurButton has background, foreground, font, and name properties that it inherited from `Canvas`, Explicit-Button explicitly controls its set of properties so that the inherited `Canvas` name property, for example, does not appear in its list of properties. ExplicitButton also features its own tool palette icon and a customizer.

All these buttons export properties of the *bound* type, meaning that other entities can be notified when any of the buttons' properties change.

Note that none of these buttons have anything to do with `java.awt.Button`; they are not subclasses of `Button`. Figure 17.3 shows the BeanBox containing an instance of each button bean type. These button beans are actually useful sources of the AWT `ActionEvent` event type, so the BDK demo buttons are frequently used to drive beans that require `ActionEvent` inputs like the Juggler demo bean (explained next).

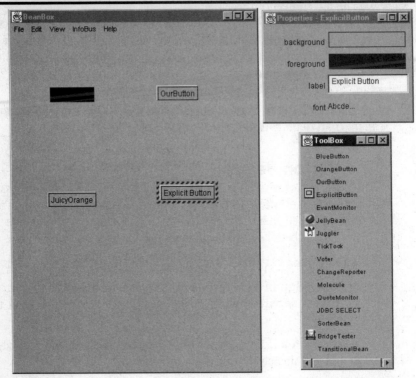

FIGURE 17.3:   The four types of BDK demo buttons are shown here. The button at bottom-right is currently selected (the BeanBox adds an outline to the currently selected bean).

The Juggler Bean

The Juggler bean is a self-contained animation that can be started and stopped via two of its bean methods: start() and stop(). The Juggler bean is useful to test the correct propagation of ActionEvent bean events. If you construct a system of several bean components, but none produce any visual feedback when working correctly, you may be able to hook up a Juggler to the last "stage" of your bean chain or network so that the juggler starts animating (or stops animating) to confirm the correct operation of your design. Figure 17.4 shows an animated Duke juggling Java beans, which you can start and stop using the provided buttons.

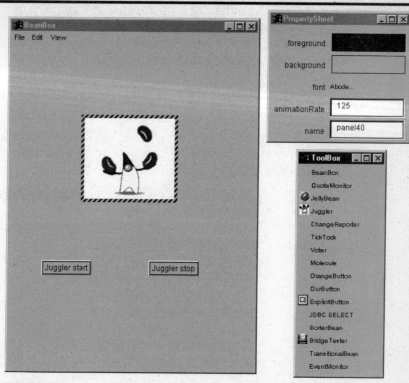

FIGURE 17.4: The Juggler bean with two buttons to control its animating behavior

The TickTock Bean

The TickTock bean is useful because it demonstrates that beans do not have to be graphical or GUI entities; they can also be totally invisible. Of course, complete invisibility at design time would be rather impractical, so the BeanBox simply uses the name of the bean as a handle for the otherwise invisible bean. This can be seen in Figure 17.5.

The TickTock bean produces a steady stream of clock events, at a programmable rate. Like a clock crystal in an electronic circuit, you could use this bean as a timing source in any design that requires a clock to synchronize events. The source code for the TickTock bean (included in the BDK) is very short, and you are encouraged to analyze it once you have read the next chapter. The TickTock bean is a simple example that combines two simple properties (interval and seconds), event firing, and the use of a thread. Note that the PropertySheet in Figure 17.5 only shows the interval property because the BeanBox only shows read-write properties (see Chapter 18, "Bean Properties"). TickTock's seconds property happens to be read-only, so it is not displayed.

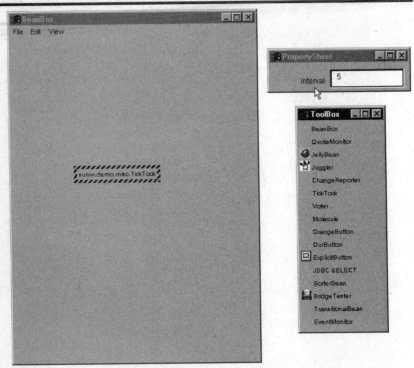

FIGURE 17.5: The TickTock bean made visible courtesy of the BeanBox's "Show Invisible Beans" viewing mode

The ChangeReporter Bean

The ChangeReporter bean's sole function is to display property change events as fired by other beans (Chapter 18, "Bean Properties", has all the details on property change events). The large number of properties listed in the PropertySheet (see Figure 17.6) are actually unrelated to ChangeReporter's core function, but are a result of it being a subclass of TextField. In other words, the properties you see are inherited TextField properties.

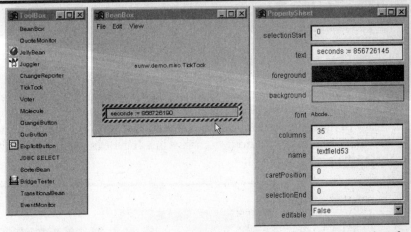

FIGURE 17.6: A ChangeReporter bean displaying the periodic change in value of a TickTock bean's hidden seconds property

The JellyBean Bean

The JellyBean bean (shown in Figure 17.7) contains the property `price-InCents`, which is an example of a special type of property called a *constrained* property. This bean has no other uses beyond demonstrating a constrained property.

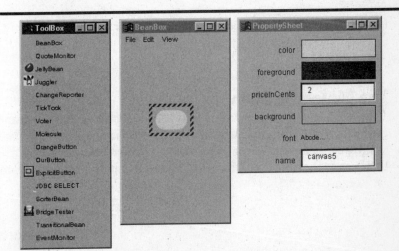

FIGURE 17.7: The JellyBean demonstration bean with its `priceInCents` constrained property

Part iv

The Voter Bean

The Voter bean is used to demonstrate how constrained properties, also known as vetoable properties, can be prevented from changing. The Voter bean has a `vetoAll` property that you can use to control its binary (yes or no) voting behavior. If the `vetoAll` property is set to true and if you connect this bean up to any bean that has constrained properties (such as the JellyBean demonstration bean), then the Voter bean will prevent any of those properties from being changed. Figure 17.8 demonstrates a Voter bean instance vetoing a change in a JellyBean instance's `priceIn-Cents` property.

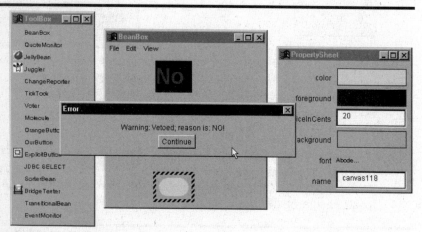

FIGURE 17.8:   The Voter bean vetoes a change in the `PriceInCents` value of a JellyBean

The Molecule Bean

The Molecule bean (see Figure 17.9) is used to demonstrate how beans can control the appearance and editing style for any of their properties, as presented in any tool's property sheet. Another interesting aspect of this bean is that it is the JDK MoleculeViewer applet transformed into a Java bean.

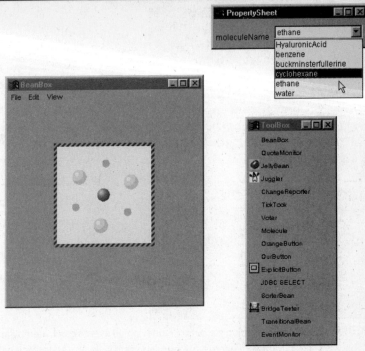

FIGURE 17.9: The Molecule bean with its customized property editor (the Choice menu)

The EventMonitor Bean

The EventMonitor bean is used to capture any events fired by a bean. Bean event dynamics are the most important runtime activity within any bean network, so the ability to view, log, and monitor bean events is a very important development and debugging tool.

While EventMonitor is very powerful in that it can monitor event types that it does not yet know about, its power comes with a hefty price tag: the bean's implementation is dauntingly complex as it relies on very low-level Java aspects that few Java programmers will want to deal with (the Java `.class` file format, among other things). Figure 17.10 shows the event log produced by the EventMonitor bean when you attach the monitor to any of the bean's event sources. In this example, an OurButton bean, a ChangeReporter bean, and a TickTock bean have been used.

Part iv

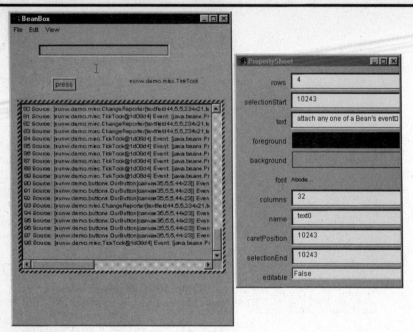

FIGURE 17.10:   An EventMonitor bean monitoring all events generated by an OurButton bean, a ChangeReporter bean, and a TickTock bean

More BDK Demonstration Beans

The 1.0 BeanBox comes with a couple of other beans that further touch on the potential of JavaBeans. For example, the JDBC Select bean can connect itself up to an SQL database and allow a user to perform SQL SELECT statements to query the database. Although impressive, it will not be demonstrated here because few readers will have access to an SQL database server, either locally or remotely.

The QuoteMonitor bean is another bean that relies on data communications to perform its specific task: it uses the Remote Method Invocation (RMI) API to access a remote financial quotes server. Again, while this is impressive, initializing the RMI runtime environment to be able to run this bean is not something that most readers will have experience doing (or might not even be able to execute; to start RMI up on Windows platforms, you need a proprietary MAKE utility that is not part of the JDK or BDK releases).

The TransitionalBean is an example bean that does not make use of any 1.2 methods (including any JavaBeans API methods!) and could therefore have been developed in a pure 1.0.2 Java environment. Or, viewed from a user's perspective, the TransitionalBean is an example of a bean that could be deployed in Java applications that need to be backwards-compatible with the currently ubiquitous 1.0.2-compatible environments.

PACKAGE *JAVA.BEANS*

Many applet writers are hardly aware that their `Applet` base class is part of a separate applet package called `java.applet`. To JavaBeans writers, there will be no doubt that a package devoted purely to bean development exists. You cannot overlook the `java.beans` package, as it is large and complex. The contents of package `java.beans` are shown in Figure 17.11.

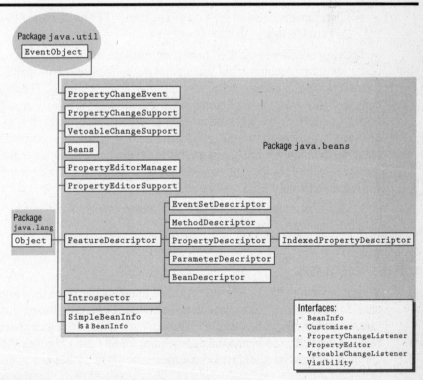

FIGURE 17.11:   Package `java.beans` class hierarchy and interfaces

Part iv

Figure 17.11 might seem imposing at first sight, but you actually do not *need* to use *any* of the shown classes to write a legal Java bean, as the TransitionalBean demonstration bean clearly proves (it relies purely on the 1.0.2 Core API). As far as the standard specifies, any Java class can be viewed as a legal Java bean, although such a bean will probably not have any bean properties or bean event support, just public methods that can be invoked on it.

The real heart of the `java.beans` package is not its class hierarchy but the interfaces it specifies, especially the `BeanInfo` interface.

The concrete classes of the `java.beans` package can be grouped into the following:

▶ Support classes (`PropertyChangeSupport`, `VetoableChange-Support`, `PropertyEditorSupport`, `SimpleBeanInfo`)

▶ Descriptor classes (all classes ending in `-Descriptor`)

▶ Miscellaneous (`Beans`, `PropertyChangeEvent`, `Property-EditorManager`, `Introspector`)

The support classes, as their name suggests, are there to simplify your task as bean implementor, but you are not obliged to use them. Similarly, the descriptor classes are completely optional, at least initially. The miscellaneous classes can also be ignored when you are writing legal beans. What this means is that you can make your JavaBeans API learning curve as easy or as hard as you wish. Initially, we will be writing JavaBeans-compliant beans that do not rely on any `java.beans` classes or interfaces, and only gradually will we explore the more advanced possibilities that do rely on the use of extra classes and/or interfaces.

At this early stage, we will take a look at just one class of the `java.beans` package: class `Beans`.

Class *Beans*

With a name like `Beans` you might think that this has to be the super-class from which all beans have to be subclassed. But Java beans do not have to descend from any mother class, or even implement a single interface. So, class `Beans` is not the parent class for all beans because there is no such thing as an almighty bean superclass. Class `Beans` is a global class containing only a few important methods that beans or tools might wish to use. Here is the definition of class `Beans`:

```
public class Beans extends Object {
  public Beans();
  public static Object instantiate(ClassLoader cls, String
beanName) throws IOException, ClassNotFoundException;
  public static Object getInstanceOf(Object bean, Class
targetType);
  public static boolean isInstanceOf(Object bean, Class
targetType);
  public static boolean isDesignTime();
  public static boolean isGuiAvailable();
  public static void setDesignTime(boolean isDesignTime)
throws SecurityException;
  public static void setGuiAvailable(boolean isGuiAvailable)
throws SecurityException;
}
```

The `xxxDesignTime()` and `xxxGuiAvailable()` methods should be clear to you. The `isXxx()` methods allow beans to find out whether they have been instantiated in a tool or not and whether a GUI can be used (in case they were instantiated by the final application they are part of). The `setXxx()` methods allow tools or applications (but never applets) to set these global flags.

The `isInstanceOf()` and `getInstanceOf()` methods need some explanation: Java beans are expected to be embedded in other "standard" component-based environments such as Apple/IBM's OpenDOC or Microsoft's COM/OLE. To facilitate this interoperability, some Java beans will have to wear different interface masks at different times. These masks concretely map to Java interface types. For this reason, you should never use Java's `instanceof` operator to determine whether some object is or is not a bean.

WARNING

You cannot use the `instanceof` operator on beans to check whether an object is of bean type X, Y, or Z. Instead, you should use the `Beans.isInstanceOf()` method.

For reasons similar to the ones listed above, you should never use a plain class instance creation expression (`new`) to obtain a new instance of a bean.

WARNING

You cannot use new to create a new bean object. Instead, you should use the Beans.instantiate() method.

To obtain different "type views" of a single bean, you should use Beans.getInstanceOf().

WHAT'S NEXT?

Now that you have a general understanding of JavaBeans, we'll get into bean properties and methods.

Chapter 18

BEAN PROPERTIES

Adapted from *Mastering JavaBeans*
by Laurence Vanhelsuwé
ISBN 0-7821-2097-0   799 pages $49.99

INTRODUCTION

The easiest and most visible aspect of a Java bean is its set of *properties*. Bean properties allow a beginning programmer to customize a bean at design time without any coding excursions; you can purely shape or tune a Java bean via the intermediary of the GUI of your chosen visual development environment. A typical design tool would list a bean's properties in a *property sheet*, and allow interactive editing of these properties. Any change made to a property is immediately reflected in the bean currently being customized.

Bean properties typically mirror the type of class fields that define the internal state of an object; for example:

```
class StuffContainer {
    // some Container properties
    Color color;
    Shape shape;
    Volume volume;
}
```

Instances of this example `StuffContainer` class would be defined by their color, shape, and volume properties. To turn these properties into true JavaBeans properties, all you need to do is to apply the standard object-oriented information hiding technique of providing *accessor methods* (also called `getters` and `setters`) for these fields, and protecting the fields themselves from direct (that is, `public`) access:

```
public class StuffContainerBean {
    // the "physical" properties of a StuffContainerBean
    // are inaccessible
    protected Color color;
    protected Shape shape;
    protected Volume volume;

    // but they are made available "logically" through
    // accessor methods
    public Color getColor() {…}
    public Shape getShape() {…}
    public Volume getVolume() {…}
    public void setColor(Color color) {…}
    public void setShape(Shape shape) {…}
    public void setVolume(Volume volume) {…}
}
```

The original fields are now marked `protected`, which means normal clients have no access to them; only subclasses retain direct access. As the `StuffContainerBean` class name suggests, the above class would actually amount to a legal bean, so, clearly, beans can be very simple software entities. For example, take the bean class declaration: a bean does not have to be a subclass of some super parent bean class. The JavaBeans standard deliberately does not require beans to be subclassed from some primeval bean class. This is so that beans can be as lightweight as possible. Our `StuffContainerBean` simply extends `Object` by default, so it is very lightweight indeed.

I sneaked one extra modification in: I declared the `StuffContainerBean` class `public` because all bean classes have to be `public`. However, the `setXXX()`/`getXXX()` methods are the heart of the JavaBeans properties mechanism, so let us study them in detail.

THE *SETXXX()* AND *GETXXX()* ACCESSOR METHODS

Bean properties are defined entirely by the presence or absence of accessor methods. In our above `StuffContainerBean` example, it would not make any difference if we removed the actual physical `color`, `shape`, and `volume` fields. As far as the JavaBeans standard goes, the modified bean would have exactly the same appearance (that is, interface) to users and tools alike: it would still have its three color, shape, and volume *properties*.

A given bean property comes to life purely as a result of adhering to a simple naming convention for get and/or set accessor methods.

NOTE

The people at JavaSoft like to call these conventions *design patterns*. Because design patterns are usually a lot more than a few conventions on how to name methods, I'll most often refer to them as *naming conventions* or simply *templates*. For more information on design patterns, see *Design Patterns* by Gamma, Helm, Johnson, and Vlissides (Addison-Wesley, 1995).

Defining Read Properties

A *read* property is defined by the presence of a method with the following signature:

```
public <propertyType> get<propertyName>( )
```

All accessor methods have to be declared `public`. Package, `protected`, or `private` scoped methods are not exported to the bean's interface; only public methods are.

The `propertyType` returned by a `getXXX()` method defines the Java type of the property. Here are some examples:

```
// define a 'width' read property of type 'int'
public int getWidth() { … }

// define a 'backgroundColor' read property
public Color getBackgroundColor() { … }
```

You need to be careful when defining your properties so that you do not deviate from the template for a `getter` or `setter` method; for example, the following method looks like a bean `getter` method, but is not:

```
// ERROR: this does NOT define a 'fontMetrics' read property
public FontMetrics getFontMetrics(Font font) { … }
```

The added, harmless-looking formal parameter `font` is what disqualifies this method as a bean property `getter`. A property `getter` takes no arguments (but see the section "Indexed Properties," later in this chapter).

Note also the capitalization of the property name when used on its own and when used within the accessor method name. A property name always follows this rule:

▶ A property name starts with a lowercase letter (e.g., "color"),

▶ except when used within a method name, when the first letter is capitalized (e.g., "getColor").

This capitalization rule simply follows the standard Java convention for naming program identifiers that consist of several concatenated words.

If you happen to have an anarchic streak, and dislike conventions, you need to know that JavaBeans *relies* on these naming conventions to identify properties (and events, too).

Defining Write Properties

A *write* property is defined by the presence of a method with the following signature:

```
public void set<propertyName>( <propertyType> formalParamName)
```

Here are some examples:

```
// define a 'width' write property of type 'int'
public void setWidth(int width) { ... }

// define a 'backgroundColor' write property
public void setBackgroundColor(Color color) { ... }
```

The following examples do *not* define write properties:

```
// ERROR: this does NOT define a 'polarPosition' write property
public void setPolarPosition(float angle, float distance) { ... }

// ERROR: this does NOT define a 'position' write property
public void setPosition(int x, int y, int z) { ... }
```

Properties are atomic entities and can only be set by passing a single parameter to the `setter` method. Zero, two, or more parameters disqualifies the method as a valid bean `setter` method (but see the "Indexed Properties" section, later in this chapter). Here is one additional trap:

```
// ERROR: this does NOT define a 'turboMode' write property
public boolean setTurboMode( boolean turboOn ) { ... }
```

Although the `setter` method correctly accepts one argument, it returns a `boolean` value instead of specifying `void`. `Setter` methods are not allowed to return anything. Note that write-only properties do not occur frequently in real-life beans. Most properties are either read/write or read-only.

Defining Read/Write Properties

I have introduced you to `getXXX()` and `setXXX()` methods to explain the separate definitions of read *or* write properties, but in reality properties are most often both readable *and* writable.

For a JavaBean property to be recognized as such, a property requires *matching* `getter` and `setter` methods. Here is the template again:

```
// a read/write property requires a getter and
// a matching setter
public <propertyType> get<propertyName>( )
public void set<propertyName>( <propertyType> formalParamName)
```

The matching criteria are that the property name embedded in the method names and the property's Java type be identical in both `getter` and `setter`. Here are some examples of valid read/write properties:

```
// define a 'discountedValue' read/write property
public Price getDiscountedValue( ) {...}
public void setDiscountedValue( Price bargainValue ) {...}
```

```
// define a 'sex' read/write property
public Sex getSex( ) {...}
public void setSex(Sex maleOrFemale ) {...}
```

Here are some examples of erroneous read/write property definitions:

```
// ERROR: does NOT define a 'discountedValue'
// read/write property
public Price getDiscountedValue( ) {...}
public void setDiscountValue( Price bargainValue ) {...}
```

This example fails because the property names are not identical; the `getter` method uses `discountedValue` and the `setter` method uses `discountValue`. The net result of this mistake would be that the bean that used these methods would export two *different* properties: a read property called `discountedValue` and a separate and totally unrelated write property called `discountValue`.

The following example would result in a similar "duplicate property" error, but for a different reason:

```
// ERROR: does NOT define a 'sex' read/write property
public Sex getSex( ) {...}
public void setSex(boolean maleOrFemale ) {...}
```

In this example, the property name is correctly spelled in both methods but the property type is not identical. This time you would get two properties with the same name, but with differing types: one readable and the other write-only.

WARNING

The matching of `setter` and `getter` does not always have to be in one and the same class (although most of the time it is). If a class containing only a `setter` method (that is, containing a write-only property) is subclassed, and the subclass adds a matching `getter` method, then that subclass will effectively export a readable *and* writable bean property, and not, as you might have thought, just a read-only property.

PROGRAMMER TEMPLATES AND MACROS

This tip will save you many, many days of debugging: If you use a programmer's editor capable of inserting whole chunks of user-defined text, either as you type or when hitting a configured macro hotkey, then you should define a template for a pair of get/set methods. You'll want something like this:

```
public TYPE getNAME( ) {}public void setNAME(TYPE
➥ value) {}
```

Whenever you are about to add a new property to a bean, you can then simply call up the template and fill in the blanks TYPE and NAME. Depending on the editor you use, this can be done in seconds, without introducing a bug. Even better, if your editor supports user-definable prompting dialogs and macro field expansion, you can write a macro that starts by asking the property name and type, thus making it totally impossible to ever mismatch the property's name or type again. And last but not least, if your current editor is incapable of these basic programmer's editor functions, consider replacing your current editor with a more powerful one.

BEAN PROPERTY CATEGORIES

The previous section introduced you to the absolute basics of bean properties: their getter and setter methods. This basic get/set scheme has been further refined to cater to real-life programming and to simplify the programmer's task.

For example, as a convenience for programmers, there is explicit support for boolean-typed properties, which, by an already established Java method naming convention, should be readable using an isXXX()method instead of getXXX().

JavaBeans also recognizes that properties can come in the shape of arrays. Indexed properties explicitly support this category of properties.

Two other real-life scenarios that JavaBeans takes in its stride are properties that automatically notify the outside world when they get modified (by a user or by a program at runtime *or* design time), and properties that have the ability to refuse being set to particular values. The latter two types of properties are called *bound properties* and *constrained properties*, respectively, and are, as you might already suspect, the most complex to put into action. In the next sections, we will have a closer look at these property types.

WARNING

Do not confuse the Java language-level type of a property (for example, int, String, double, Color, Applet) with the higher level classification presented in this section.

Simple Properties

The basic set/get method naming convention that you saw in the previous sections defines *simple* properties. Simple properties are no-frills properties that are, by definition, neither bound nor constrained.

Boolean Properties

Boolean properties are simple properties that use a convenient alternative naming convention for getters that return a Java boolean. The modified template for a getter method becomes:

```
public boolean is<propertyName>( )
```

Some examples from the 1.1 API for class java.awt.Component are:

```
public boolean isValid( ) { ... }
public boolean isVisible( ) { ... }
```

Because these two boolean getter methods are matched by their partner setter methods:

```
public void setValid(boolean x ) { ... }
public void setVisible(boolean x ) { ... }
```

both valid and visible are by definition bean read/write properties within class java.awt.Component. Therefore, it follows that standard Java API classes can themselves be beans. There is nothing that prevents this. Indeed, by the time you read this, all AWT components might have been upgraded to full-fledged beans!

Indexed Properties

Indexed properties exist to handle arrays and/or their individual elements in an intuitive manner. Strictly speaking, arrays proper do not need any extra mechanisms beyond the conventions for simple properties:

```
public void set<PropertyName>(<PropertyType>[] array)
// array setter
public <PropertyType>[] get<PropertyName>()
// array getter
```

The following example demonstrates the use of an array as a bean read/write property:

```
public class GameManager {
  protected Score[] playersTop10;

  public void setTop10(Score[] scores) {
      playersTop10 = scores;
  }
   public Score[] getTop10() {
      return playersTop10;
  }
} // End of Class/Bean GameManager
```

The GameManager bean exports a top10 read/write property as an array of Scores. You could enhance this bean by giving users access to the individual elements of the array. Since the simple property naming convention alone does not support this, an *indexed property* method signature pattern is provided:

```
// indexed setter
public void set<PropertyName>(int index,
                             <PropertyType> value);

// indexed getter
<PropertyType> get<PropertyName>(int index);
```

The following example code enhances the GameManager bean by adding an *indexable* property top10Score:

```
    public void setTop10Score(int index, Score aScore) {
        playersTop10[index] = aScore;
    }
    public Score getTop10Score(int index) {
        return playersTop10[index];
    }
```

Indexed properties are primarily intended for scripting environments (like Netscape's proprietary JavaScript). As such, JavaSoft is not including

Part iv

support for indexed properties in the BeanBox's PropertySheet. The Bean-Box's Report option does output information on indexed properties, but only as part of a complete dump of bean information that is truly reminiscent of core dumps, in the sense that the dump lacks even minimal formatting to make the information more palatable. (On Windows 95/98 hosts, the Report function is of very limited use because a DOS box does not allow you to scroll back the information that scrolled off the top of the window, and most bean "reports" are longer than one window.)

NOTE

While a Windows DOS box *itself* does not allow you to scroll back information as every modern UNIX shell does, you can pipe the output of a BeanBox session to the more utility (" | more "). While this addresses the problem, it sure feels like a patch applied to a CLI that was inadequately primitive in the first place.

NOTE

JavaScript is not compatible with Java. In fact, it is simply Netscape's LiveScript language that they (no doubt the marketing department...) renamed to ride the popularity explosion of Java!

Bound Properties

Bound properties rely on event broadcasting to signal other parts of a program that their value has changed. Such behavior is frequently needed and simplifies the overall design of a program. Here are some example uses:

- ▶ In a spreadsheet program with a graph showing, altering any cell that is directly or indirectly part of the graph would automatically redraw the graph to reflect the change. This would be implemented by having the graph component listen for any changes in the spreadsheet's cells and rescale and repaint itself when a change happens.

- ▶ In a complex dialog window, an entire subpanel can enable or disable itself depending on the state of a tickbox-controlled flag. The panel could listen for a property change event on the flag and reflect the new state by disabling or enabling itself.

- ▶ In a visual development environment, a change in a component's property results in an immediate visual change of the component itself (reflecting the new property), and also a change in the *source code* for the component that is being maintained in parallel. The source code management subsystem would be listening for any changes in bean properties so it could reflect the changes in the source code.

You might ask yourself why you should go to such lengths when some of these examples could be handled "more simply" by "direct" means. The answer comes in two parts:

▶ Strong (direct) coupling of program parts makes brittle and impossible to maintain systems. Strong coupling is a Bad Thing to have in your software.

▶ Loose coupling makes programs more flexible and easier to maintain. Loose coupling is a Good Thing to have in your software.

Using anonymous listeners to act on property changes means a clean, loose coupling of subsystems. The alternative of having a property itself "reach out" into the software around it and modify or update parts not intimately related to itself, runs counter to the object-oriented philosophy of composing programs from loosely coupled, highly (internally) coherent subsystems.

Bound properties can be viewed from two vantage points: that of the bean client (from the outside), and that of the bean implementor (from the inside). We are now going to explore both views.

Bound Properties: The Bean Client's Perspective

The bean property change event system is a straightforward use of the event model. As such, the following two methods, to be present in any bean supporting bound properties, should have a familiar look:

```
public void  addPropertyChangeListener(PropertyChange
                                       Listener x);
public void removePropertyChangeListener(PropertyChange
                                       Listener x);
```

These two methods allow any interested parties to register (and deregister) with a bean so as to receive PropertyChangeEvent notifications whenever any bound property changes. Note that the granularity of registration is coarse: registration is per bean, not per property (later in this chapter I will show how to register on a per-property basis). The way you determine which property has changed will become clear in a minute.

Before registering as a property change listener, your client class has to implement the **PropertyChangeListener** interface:

```
public interface PropertyChangeListener extends EventListener {
  public void propertyChange(PropertyChangeEvent evt);
}
```

It is via the **PropertyChangeEvent** argument that you can find out which property changed, and how. Here is class **PropertyChangeEvent**'s definition:

```
public class PropertyChangeEvent extends EventObject {

    // constructor
    public PropertyChangeEvent(Object src, String propertyName,
                               Object oldValue, Object
                               newValue);

    // instance methods
    public String getPropertyName();
    public Object getNewValue();
    public Object getOldValue();
    public void setPropagationId(Object propagationId);
    public Object getPropagationId();
}
```

The various get methods are all that you need to identify the changed property and find out its old and new values. The following example program relies on one of the BDK demo beans, OurButton, to demonstrate these methods by listening and acting on a property change fired by the bean as a result of our test program changing one of its properties.

To compile the **PropertyChangeDemo** program, you will have to unpack the OurButton bean from its JAR file (**/Bdk/jars/buttons.jar**) and ensure that your CLASSPATH environment variable can reach class **sunw.demo.buttons.OurButton**. To unpack the bean from its JAR, first go to the **jars** directory and then invoke the **jar** tool using its extract option, as follows:

```
jar xf buttons.jar
```

This will unpack all files from the **buttons.jar** file and create two new directory trees in your current directory: META-INF and sunw. Here is how your current directory should look at this stage:

```
Directory of E:\Bdk\jars

  .                  <DIR>        19/02/97  10:53 .
  ..                 <DIR>        19/02/97  10:53 ..
  META-INF           <DIR>        22/02/97  16:41 META-INF
```

```
SUNW          <DIR>            22/02/97   16:41 sunw
BUTTONS   JAR       10,887     17/02/97   18:04 buttons.jar
EVENTM~1  JAR       43,010     17/02/97   18:04 eventmonitor.jar
JELLY     JAR        6,886     17/02/97   18:04 jelly.jar
JUGGLER   JAR       19,960     17/02/97   18:04 juggler.jar
MISC      JAR        3,293     17/02/97   18:04 misc.jar
MOLECULE  JAR       14,725     17/02/97   18:05 molecule.jar
QUOTE     JAR       30,138     17/02/97   18:05 quote.jar
SELECT    JAR       12,617     17/02/97   18:05 select.jar
SORT      JAR        7,516     17/02/97   18:06 sort.jar
TEST      JAR       16,235     17/02/97   18:06 test.jar
TRANSI~1  JAR        4,030     17/02/97   18:06 transitional.jar
         11 file(s)          169,297 bytes
          4 dir(s)         7,071,744 bytes free
```

The META-INF directory is of no use to us, so delete it entirely to avoid future confusion. The sunw directory holds the branch of the sunw package that contains the OurButton bean. You need to move this entire directory tree to a location that gets visited by your CLASSPATH (because many Java programmers customize their CLASSPATH to suit their particular machine and filing hierarchy, I will assume that you know how to perform this step). If you correctly unpacked the OurButton bean and moved it to a directory where javac can "see" it, you can now compile the following program without errors:

BEFORE YOU START...

To access the classes needed for these examples, you need to make sure that your CLASSPATH is set correctly and that it includes both the sunw package directory and your source directory for these examples. For example, if your file system looked something like this:

```
C:
        ...
Jdk1.2
        \bin
        \demo
        ...
Bdk
        \beanbox
        \jars
        ...
MasteringBeans
        \appendix
                \utilities
```

CONTINUED ➡

```
                \ch01
                ...
        JavaComplete
                \sunw
                class
                PropertyChangeDemo.java
                PropertyChangeDemo.class
```

in addition to the normal settings for the JDK and BDK, your CLASS-PATH would have to include

```
        CLASSPATH =<CLASSPATH>;c:\MasteringBeans\utilities;
        c:\JavaComplete ;c:\JavaComplete\sunw;
```

If you have difficulties running these examples, or need further explanations, please see the Sybex Web site for *Mastering JavaBeans* (http://www.sybex.com/cgi-bin/rd_bookpg.pl?2097back.html).

LIST 18.1: *PropertyChangeDemo.java*

```java
import sunw.demo.buttons.OurButton;
import java.beans.*;
import java.awt.*;
import java.awt.event.*;
import java.io.*;
import utilities.*;

public class PropertyChangeDemo extends Frame
                implements PropertyChangeListener {

protected OurButton aButtonBean;

public static void main (String[] args) {
  new PropertyChangeDemo();
}
//--------------------------------
// Constructor: create window with single bean button
//--------------------------------
public PropertyChangeDemo() {

  super("Just sit back and watch..");
  setLayout(new FlowLayout());
```

```
            // instantiate a test bean (never with "new" !!)
            try {
              aButtonBean = (sunw.demo.buttons.OurButton)
                            Beans.instantiate(null,
                              "sunw.demo.buttons.OurButton");

            } catch (ClassNotFoundException noSuchBean) {
              System.out.println("OurButton bean not found: " +
                                  noSuchBean);
              System.exit(10);
            } catch (IOException beanIOerror) {
              System.out.println("I/O error while loading bean: " +
                                  beanIOerror);
              System.exit(10);
            }

            // unlike normal Buttons, we cant give an OurButton
            // an initial label, so set the label now.
            aButtonBean.setLabel("When my properties change...");

            add(aButtonBean);

            // register us as interested in button property changes
            aButtonBean.addPropertyChangeListener(this);

            // pop open window with button
            setSize(new Dimension(300,75));
            setVisible(true);

            // wait a bit, then modify one of the button's properties
            System.out.println("No need to push that button..
                                I'll do that.");
            MiscKit.delay(6*1000);

            aButtonBean.setLabel("anyone can know about it !");

            MiscKit.delay(12*1000);

            // close window, quit
            setVisible(false);
            System.exit(0);
          }
//-------------------------------
// propertyChange() is the method we have to implement from
// interface PropertyChangeListener. This is where we hear of
// OurButton properties changing.
```

Part iv

```
//---------------------------------
public void propertyChange(PropertyChangeEvent pcEvent) {
String changedProperty;
Object oldPropertyValue, newPropertyValue;

  changedProperty    = pcEvent.getPropertyName();
  oldPropertyValue   = pcEvent.getOldValue();
  newPropertyValue   = pcEvent.getNewValue();

  System.out.println("OurButton property '"+
                     changedProperty +"'");
  System.out.println(".. changed from    '"+
                     oldPropertyValue +"'");
  System.out.println(".. to              '"+
                     newPropertyValue +"'");
}
} // End of Class PropertyChangeDemo
```

When run from the console, you should see the following text output:

```
C:\MasteringBeans\ch04>javac PropertyChangeDemo.java
C:\ MasteringBeans\ch04>java PropertyChangeDemo
No need to push that button.. I'll do that.
OurButton property 'label'
.. changed from    'When my properties change...'
.. to              'anyone can know about it !'
```

while Figure 18.1 shows a snapshot of the window and button that PropertyChangeDemo creates.

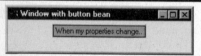

FIGURE 18.1:   The OurButton BDK demo bean about to broadcast a property change

To be able to hear the PropertyChangeEvent generated by the OurButton bean, class PropertyChangeDemo has to implement the PropertyChangeListener interface.

Before the bean can fire any events, we have to instantiate it via Beans .instantiate(). As we remarked in Chapter 17, "Java Beans: An Overview," you should never instantiate a bean with a plain new to invoke a bean's default constructor.

The `Beans.instantiate()` method can throw two checked exceptions, so we have to embed it in a `try-catch` statement that includes the necessary error handling. The first parameter of the `instantiate()` method denotes the `ClassLoader` to use for this bean instantiation. Unless you have compelling reasons to use a different class loader than the system default class loader, you can set the argument to `null`. The second argument specifies the bean class itself as a fully qualified class name. Currently, `instantiate()` first assumes that the bean is stored as a serialized instance, which is a file ending in `.ser`. Only if it cannot find the bean in this serialized form does it assume a plain `.class` file. In this case, the OurButton bean is stored as a `.class` file (its colorful alternative, OrangeButton, is stored as a `.ser` file so you can easily test bean instantiation from serialized beans by changing the `String` passed to `instantiate()` to be `sunw.demo.buttons.OrangeButton`).

Note that there is no way to instantiate a bean to a particular state (unless you serialized a bean in the past, complete with any desired state), as you could if you were allowed to use `new` to invoke non-default constructors (that is, constructors taking parameters). This is why we use `setlabel()` on the bean to set its button label after we have created it. Compare this to a normal `java.awt.Button` that can have its label specified at instantiation time (but *not* if it is used within a bean environment and it is treated as a proper bean).

Once the button is created and initialized, we register the `Property-ChangeDemo` object with the bean as a `PropertyChangeListener`. If we now change any of OurButton's properties (as we do with a second `setLabel()`), the bean will fire a `PropertyChangeEvent` that our program catches in its `propertyChange()` method, the sole method that it had to implement to comply with the `PropertyChangeListener` interface. There it uses `getPropertyName()`, `getOldValue()`, and `get-NewValue()` to print some information on the event.

Note that in this simple example, `PropertyChangeDemo` itself changes the property for which it later receives the change event. In real-life programs, there would rarely be such a reflective relationship between the property-changing entity and that which receives and acts on the change event.

Bound Properties: The Bean Implementor's Perspective

Now that we have seen how to deal with bound properties as fired by existing beans, we will look at how to add bound properties to our own beans. To turn a simple property into a bound property, you need to add a couple of methods to your bean. First, you need the listener management methods that your bean clients will expect to see if the bean contains any bound properties:

```
public void  addPropertyChangeListener(
                 PropertyChangeListener x);
public void  removePropertyChangeListener(
                 PropertyChangeListener x);
```

THE ASYMMETRY BETWEEN EVENT SOURCES AND EVENT LISTENERS

Note the asymmetry that exists between event sources and event listeners: Event listeners are (naturally) required to implement a Java interface, but event sources are not. Event source-side interfaces are not necessary for the listener metaphor to work, although they could come in handy for at least a couple of reasons:

▶ Event listeners can treat sources in generic ways, via their "EventSource" interface type, rather than as a more rigid concrete class type. As is always the case when using such interfaces, this would allow for more flexible programming.

▶ Currently, without event source-side interfaces, a single spelling mistake when coding the listener management methods' signatures leads to a bug. If interfaces were involved, then the compiler would immediately flag the error by stating that the event source interface was not implemented. Even though the JavaBeans standard does not use event source-side interfaces, there is no reason why you cannot rely on them to make your life easier.

Second, you need to modify the setter method(s) for the property(ies) that you are promoting from simple to bound, to notify all the registered listeners of a change in property value. Note that property change events are multicast events, so you need to manage the possibility of a long list of listeners registering and needing notification. Luckily, because bound properties are very common, there is a support class (analogous to AWT-EventMulticaster for firing AWT events) to help you manage all this without having to worry about linked lists and so on. Class Property-ChangeSupport comes to our rescue:

```
public class PropertyChangeSupport extends Object
                implements Serializable {

    public PropertyChangeSupport(Object sourceBean);
      // constructor

      // instance methods
    public synchronized void
    addPropertyChangeListener(PropertyChangeListener
                              listener);
    public synchronized void
    removePropertyChangeListener(PropertyChangeListener
                                 listener);
    public void firePropertyChange(String propertyName,
                                   Object oldValue,
                                   Object newValue);
}
```

As you can see, PropertyChangeSupport already implements the multicast addPropertyChangeListener() and removeProperty-ChangeListener() so you do not have to anymore. And as icing on the cake, it also provides a firePropertyChange() so your property set-ter method can be upgraded to support firing property change events by adding just one simple, convenient statement.

Because PropertyChangeSupport is a class and not an interface, there are two ways you can use it:

▶ You can subclass your bean from it.

▶ Your bean can contain an instance of PropertyChangeSupport and delegate property change management to it.

The first option is very restrictive and might be impossible in many cases (Java does not allow multiple implementation inheritance, only multiple interface inheritance), so I will show an example of the second approach:

LIST 18.2: TestBean.java

```
import java.beans.*;

public class TestBean {
```

```
// an instance of PropertyChangeSupport to give all the
// hard work to
  protected PropertyChangeSupport butler = new
  PropertyChangeSupport(this);

// the guts of the 'glitzyProperty' property
protected int starValue;

//----------------------------------
// Constructor
//----------------------------------
public TestBean() {
  starValue = 99;
// give our property a dummy starting value
}
//----------------------------------
// set()/get() for 'glitzyProperty' property
//----------------------------------
public void setGlitzyProperty(int newValue) {
int oldValue = starValue;

  starValue = newValue;
  butler.firePropertyChange("glitzyProperty",
                            new Integer(oldValue),
                            new Integer(newValue));
}
public int getGlitzyProperty() {
  return starValue;
}
//----------------------------------
// the listener (de)registration methods are trivial:
// just let the PropertyChangeSupport class do all
// the hard work for us.
//----------------------------------
public void addPropertyChangeListener(PropertyChangeListener
                                           listener) {
  butler.addPropertyChangeListener(listener);
}
public void removePropertyChangeListener(
            PropertyChangeListener listener) {
  butler.removePropertyChangeListener(listener);
    butler.removePropertyChangeListener(listener);
}
} // End of Class TestBean
```

This TestBean exports a single (integer) bound property called `glitzy-Property`. Remember that vanilla property change listener registration is done on a per-bean basis, so there is no way to determine whether a specific property is bound or simple. Because our TestBean only contains a single property, and it signals the outside world that it can fire property change events, it follows that `glitzyProperty` must be bound. But if we added a second property, then clients would have no way of knowing which one is bound or if both are. If this is a problem for your bean, you will find a solution in the section "Registering on a Per-Property Basis," later in this chapter.

WARNING

Note the sequence of actions in the `setter` method: (1) the property gets updated *first*, and (2) *then* the notification events are transmitted. This order is a required part of a bound property conforming to the JavaBeans standard!

Another aspect of our TestBean is that it is not a graphical bean: it has no visible representation whatsoever. JavaBean-compatible environments should have no problems with such beans. If a user is to be able to manipulate an invisible bean, then the tool or program should just provide a surrogate graphical handle to the bean. The BeanBox, for example, uses the rendered name of an invisible bean as a handle. The BeanBox can also hide all nongraphical beans via the View ➤ Hide Invisible Beans menu option. While invisible beans are perfectly legal bean manifestations, we will usually create beans with at least a minimal graphical appearance. This is achieved simply by extending from `java.awt.Canvas` and rendering something in the `Canvas`, or extending from `java.awt.Panel` and adding some AWT or custom components to the `Panel`.

Now that you understand why TestBean is written the way it is, we will use a test harness to check the correct functioning of the property change event mechanism:

LIST 18.3: *TestBeanPropertyChangeDemo.java*

```
import java.beans.*;
import java.io.*;

public class TestBeanPropertyChangeDemo implements
                PropertyChangeListener {

protected TestBean ourBean;
```

```
//-------------------------------
// main() entry point
//-------------------------------
public static void main (String[] args) {
  new TestBeanPropertyChangeDemo();
}
//-------------------------------
// TestBeanPropertyChangeDemo Constructor
//-------------------------------
public TestBeanPropertyChangeDemo() {

  ourBean = (TestBean) newBean("TestBean");
  if ( ourBean == null ) {
    System.out.println("Could not instantiate
TestBean.");
    System.exit(10);
  }

  // register us as interested in button property
changes
  ourBean.addPropertyChangeListener(this);

  // modify one of our bean's properties
  ourBean.setGlitzyProperty(1234);

  // quit
  System.exit(0);
}
//-------------------------------
// propertyChange() is the method we have to implement
from
// interface PropertyChangeListener. Here we hear of
// OurButton properties changing.
//-------------------------------
public void propertyChange(PropertyChangeEvent pcEvent)
{
String changedProperty;
Object oldPropertyValue, newPropertyValue;

  changedProperty    = pcEvent.getPropertyName();
  oldPropertyValue   = pcEvent.getOldValue();
  newPropertyValue   = pcEvent.getNewValue();

    System.out.println("TestBean property '"+
                        changedProperty +"'");
    System.out.println(".. changed from   '"+
                        oldPropertyValue +"'");
```

```
        System.out.println(".. to              '"+
                          newPropertyValue +"'");
}
//----------------------------------
// Utility method to instantiate a bean.
//----------------------------------
public static Object newBean(String beanName) {
Object aBean;

   try {
     aBean = Beans.instantiate(null, beanName);

   } catch (ClassNotFoundException noSuchBean) {
     System.out.println("newBean() failed: "+
noSuchBean);
       return null;
   } catch (IOException beanIOerror) {
     System.out.println("newBean() I/O error while
loading bean: " + beanIOerror);
       return null;
   }
   return aBean;

}
} // End of Class TestBeanPropertyChangeDemo
```

If you run this program from the console (it does not pop up any GUI because TestBean is a nongraphical bean), you can see that our bean's bound property is correctly notifying the outside world when it gets changed:

```
C:\MasteringBeans\ch04>javac TestBean.java
C:\MasteringBeans\ch04>javac TestBeanPropertyChangeDemo.java
C:\ MasteringBeans\ch04>java TestBeanPropertyChangeDemo
TestBean property 'glitzyProperty'
.. changed from    '99'
.. to              '1234'
```

Note how we turned the clumsy bean instantiation process (normally involving Beans.instantiate() embedded in a try-catch statement) into a single utility method newBean(). This method is in fact generic enough to qualify for promotion to our utilities package. For future reuse, we will store the newBean() method in a new utilities class called BeansKit, itself stored in a utilities.beans subpackage.

Part iv

NOTE

The utilities package that goes with *Mastering JavaBeans* is downloadable from the Sybex Web site (http://www.sybex.com/cgi-bin/disclaim.pl?2097 sup.html) and must be installed before you can run these examples.

Testing Bound Properties in the BDK BeanBox

Instead of handcrafting an entire program to test the bound properties of a bean under development, as we did earlier, you can also use the BDK's BeanBox to test its functioning.

To test any bean in the BeanBox, you should package your bean up as a JAR file by performing the following procedure:

Create a file called `TestBean.mf` with the following content:

```
Name: TestBean.class
Java-Bean: True
```

Capitalization is important, so watch out for this detail. Next, you create the actual JAR file by invoking the `jar` tool as follows:

```
jar cvfm TestBean.jar TestBean.mf TestBean.class
```

This invocation commands the `jar` tool to create a `TestBean.jar` file using `TestBean.mf` as a template and storing the `TestBean.class` file as the only file in the newly created JAR file. You should see the following output on your console, confirming the correct creation of the JAR file:

```
adding: manifest
adding: TestBean.class (in=1002) (out=546) (deflated 45%)
```

All that remains to be done is to copy or move the obtained JAR file to the `jars` directory of the BDK directory tree. On a DOS-based machine, this could be done using the following command:

```
copy TestBean.jar \Bdk\jars
```

This would assume your working directory is located on the same partition as your copy of the BDK, and that you installed the BDK in the root of that partition.

If you now start the BeanBox, you should see our TestBean listed in the ToolBox window. Figure 18.2 depicts the initial situation.

Your next step is to pick our TestBean and place an instance somewhere on the BeanBox design panel.

To test the property change event, you need to connect our bean to a BDK ChangeReporter demo bean, so pick this from the ToolBox palette and place it alongside the TestBean. If you select the TestBean, you will see the PropertySheet window reflect its properties again along with the properties' current values. Figure 18.3 shows a screenshot of the current situation.

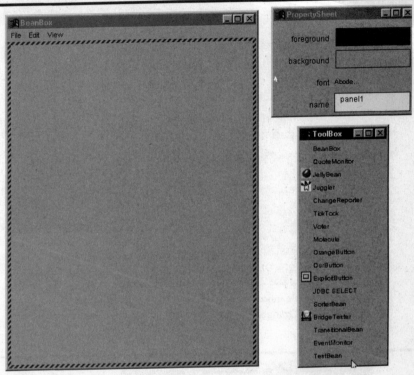

FIGURE 18.2: BeanBox showing our TestBean in the ToolBox window

You now need to hook up the ChangeReporter to our TestBean. ChangeReporter's sole aim in life is to echo PropertyChangeEvents in a TextField. Hookups are effected by telling the source to connect to the destination listener, and not vice versa (which might have been a bit more in line with the listener's active role). So, select the TestBean and, using the Edit ≻ Events ≻ PropertyChange menu items, select the PropertyChange menu item. Figure 18.4 shows how to navigate the menus.

The BeanBox now lets you specify the destination listener for our TestBean's PropertyChangeEvent. A rubber-band line allows you to draw a connecting line between the two beans. Figure 18.5 shows where to place the line's endpoint and click to freeze the line and define the connection.

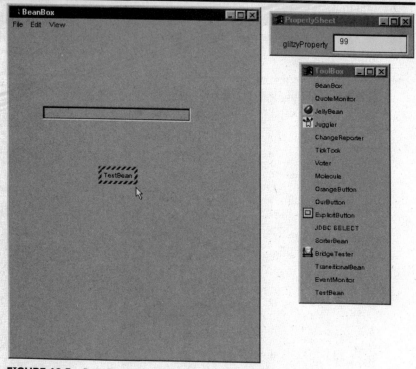

FIGURE 18.3: BeanBox panel containing a selected TestBean and a ChangeReporter, ready to be hooked up

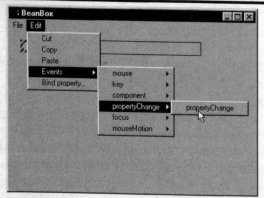

FIGURE 18.4: Selecting the TestBean's `propertyChange` event

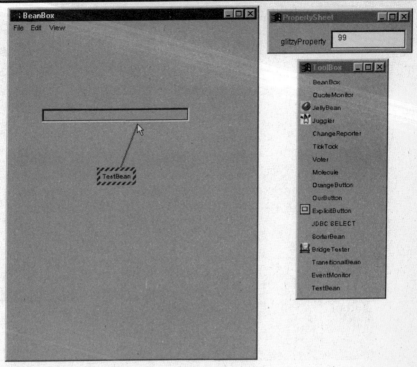

FIGURE 18.5: Specifying the connection between event source and event listener

The BeanBox now pops open an EventTargetDialog window listing all the possible methods in the target listener that are compatible with the type of event generated. In the case of the demo ChangeReporter bean, it only contains one method interested in `PropertyChangeEvents`: `reportChange()`. So, select the method and confirm with OK (see Figure 18.6).

At this stage, the hookup is completed and any property changes in our TestBean will be echoed in the ChangeReporter bean's `TextField`. If you select the TestBean again, and edit the `glitzyProperty` property in the PropertySheet window, then you will see that our bean successfully transmits property change events to any interested listeners (you can add more `ChangeReporters` to satisfy yourself that the multicasting aspect also works). Figure 18.7 is proof of our TestBean's correct functioning.

Part iv

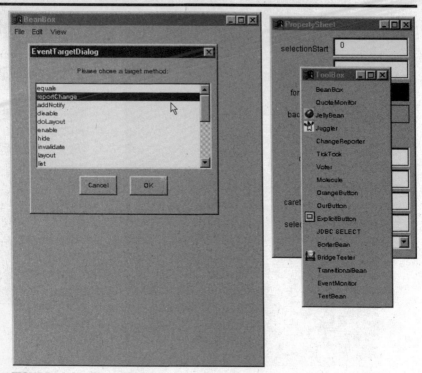

FIGURE 18.6:   The target listener may contain several compatible methods able to receive a certain event. The EventTargetDialog window lets you pick the right method.

Registering on a Per-Property Basis

Earlier we said that when a listener registers for property change events, that listener will receive notifications for *any* changed bound properties through the one `propertyChange()` method. In most cases, listeners are only really interested in a small subset of a bean's bound properties. For example, one listener might only be interested in dimension-related properties, while another might only be interested in a `debug` property. Under the scheme presented so far, if any bound property gets modified in a bean, then all listeners are notified of the change, even though many listeners will always ignore the event, after having wasted processing cycles to find out that they are not interested in that particular property.

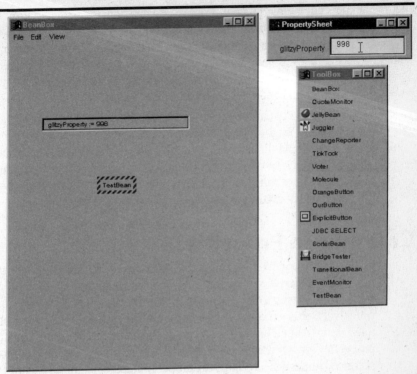

FIGURE 18.7: The `glitzyProperty` is correctly transmitting property change events to any interested listener.

To cut down on (expensive) change events that fall on deaf ears, beans can provide listener management methods on a *per-property* basis. The method template to use is:

```
void add<PropertyName>Listener(PropertyChangeListener p);
void remove<PropertyName>Listener(PropertyChangeListener p);
```

or

```
void add<PropertyName>Listener(VetoableChangeListener p);
void remove<PropertyName>Listener(VetoableChangeListener p);
```

(The second two method signatures are intended for constrained properties, which we will study in the next section.)

Notice that these methods require as an input parameter the same `<TypeName>ChangeListener` argument (`PropertyChangeListener` and `VetoableChangeListener`, respectively); in other words, the notification is still done purely through the single `Change()` method on the listener's side. Providing per-property registration and deregistration methods is therefore a performance optimization to cut down on unnecessary events being broadcast to uninterested listeners. It does not, however, mean that listeners can have a per-property event *receive* methods; all events still arrive at Grand Central, also known as method `property-Change()`, and need to be sorted out on arrival.

When property changes are multicast to many listeners, one or more of these listeners might have very strong objections to the property's new value. A particular listener might not be able to reflect the new property value in its black box because, as far as the listener is concerned, the value is illegal or out of range. To deal with such situations, bean properties can support one last feature—which is the subject of the next section.

Constrained Properties

Constrained properties are the most advanced and, unfortunately, the most complex type of property. They can refuse to take on certain new values by throwing a `java.beans.PropertyVetoException`. Counter-intuitively, this exception does *not* usually originate within the bean itself, but within a listener who vetoes the change. Therefore, constrained properties are a more complex form of bound properties because constrained properties also support property change listeners, except that these are of the vetoing variety. The methods template for constrained properties consists of four methods:

```
public <propertyType> get<propertyName>( );
public void set<propertyName>( <propertyType>
formalParamName) throws PropertyVetoException;

public void  addVetoableChangeListener(VetoableChange
Listener x);
public void removeVetoableChangeListener(VetoableChange
Listener x);
```

The first two methods are the standard accessor methods, except that the `setter` has an additional `throws` clause so it can refuse the set operation by vetoing it. The second two methods are the listener management methods; they are essentially similar to the `add/removeProperty-ChangeListener()` methods of plain (non-vetoable) bound properties.

By recognizing the above `setter` method template in a bean's class definition, you can deduce that the bean can throw a veto—but how does a listener throw a veto? The answer lies in the relevant listener interface, `VetoableChangeListener`:

```
public interface VetoableChangeListener extends EventListener {
    public void vetoableChange(PropertyChangeEvent evt) throws
PropertyVetoException;
}
```

Any listener interested in hearing about constrained property changes has to implement method `vetoableChange()`; and here is where the listener can cast its veto by throwing a `PropertyVetoException`.

WARNING

Note that the actual transmitted event object is still of type `Property-ChangeEvent`. There is no such thing as a VetoableChangeEvent to differentiate the two types of events. Only the listener methods `propertyChange()` and `vetoableChange()` make this distinction.

Because throwing vetoes around is central to using or implementing constrained properties, let us analyze the thrown "veto" itself: class `PropertyVetoException`.

```
public class PropertyVetoException extends Exception {
    // constructor
    public PropertyVetoException(String mess,
PropertyChangeEvent evt);
    // instance methods
    public PropertyChangeEvent getPropertyChangeEvent();
}
```

To veto a vetoable property change, you will have to construct a new instance of `PropertyVetoException`. The class constructor requires a message explaining the reason behind the veto and an instance of the `PropertyChangeEvent` that caused your method to want to veto the change. Because the latter is passed to you as an argument to `vetoable-Change()`, this means you can simply pass this argument on to the exception's constructor.

As an example of multiple listeners assessing a vetoable property change, and possibly one or more of them vetoing the change, imagine the following scenario. A small but very important country wishes to modify its political status by abandoning its usual neutrality and seeking to ally itself with a big superpower. At the next virtual United Nations meeting, the permanent members hold a vote on this newly arisen, tricky situation. The following program, `PrimitiveGames`, simulates the scenario by relying on the mechanism of constrained properties.

The first component of the program is class `Country`, implemented as a bean with the following two exported properties:

- ► countryName

- ► countryStatus

CountryName is a plain bound property while `countryStatus` is the constrained property around which the entire simulation is built. Here is the class implementation:

LIST 18.4: Country.java

```java
import java.beans.*;

public class Country {

// instances of Property- and VetoableChangeSupport to
// give all the hard work of listener management to.
protected PropertyChangeSupport changesButler;
protected VetoableChangeSupport vetosButler;

// the guts of the vetoable 'countryStatus' property
protected String countryStatus;

// the guts of the 'countryName' property
protected String countryName;

//------------------------------
// Country Constructors
//------------------------------
public Country() {
// all beans need default constructors!
  this("Atlantis", "hidden");
}
public Country(String name, String status) {

  this.countryName   = name;
  this.countryStatus = status;

  changesButler  = new PropertyChangeSupport(this);
  vetosButler    = new VetoableChangeSupport(this);
}
//------------------------------
// set()/get() for 'CountryName' property
//------------------------------
```

```
public void setCountryName( String newValue) {
String oldName = countryName;

  countryName = newValue;
  changesButler.firePropertyChange("countryName", oldName,
                                   newValue);

}
public String getCountryName() {
  return countryName;
}
//--------------------------------
// set()/get() for 'CountryStatus' vetoable property
//--------------------------------
public void setCountryStatus(String newValue)
             throws PropertyVetoException {

  // see if any listener objects first. Note that the
  // property has not yet changed at this time.
  vetosButler.fireVetoableChange("countryStatus",
                                 countryStatus, newValue);

  // if any listener vetoed the change, then this line will
  // never be executed: the veto exception would have
  // aborted the method and returned to the caller of
  // setCountryStatus().
  // if no listener vetoed, then we just change
  // the property value.
  countryStatus = newValue;
}
public String getCountryStatus() {
  return countryStatus;
}
//--------------------------------
// the listener (de)registration methods are trivial:
// just let the Property- or VetoableChangeSupport class
// do all the hard work for us.
//--------------------------------
public void addPropertyChangeListener
             (PropertyChangeListener 1) {
  changesButler.addPropertyChangeListener(1);
}
public void removePropertyChangeListener
             (PropertyChangeListener 1) {
  changesButler.removePropertyChangeListener(1);
}
```

```
public void addVetoableChangeListener
            (VetoableChangeListener l) {
  vetosButler.addVetoableChangeListener(l);
}
public void removeVetoableChangeListener
            (VetoableChangeListener l) {
  vetosButler.removeVetoableChangeListener(l);
}
} // End of Class Country
```

The heart of the class (within the context of our discussion on constrained properties) is setCountryStatus(), the setter method for property countryStatus. Every setter of a constrained property first notifies all registered listeners about the impending change (while the change has *not* yet been made for real). If no listener vetoes the change, then only the internal property can be changed.

LIES, DAMN LIES...AND VETOABLE CHANGES

The algorithmic sequence of only changing the property after listeners have been notified of its change means beans lie when they tell listeners that a change has already happened. The bean-side delay between lying to listeners about a new change and the true changing of the property value means that listeners should rely entirely on the new value carried by the PropertyChangeEvent object and *never* rely on the "proper" getter method because the getter will not yet be able to reflect the true value. Vetoable property getter methods should never be used within event notification methods dealing with those properties.

Another source of nasty bugs would be for a listener to use the old value from a PropertyChangeEvent. As you will see when we run the PrimitiveGames simulation, the *old* value parameter can legally take on values that a listener would have vetoed, had it been presented as the *new* value. So, never use the old value either, just restrict your code to look at the new value.

As with plain property changes, I have used a JavaBeans API helper class, VetoableChangeSupport:

```
public class VetoableChangeSupport extends Object implements
Serializable {
```

```
    public VetoableChangeSupport(Object sourceBean);

    public synchronized void addVetoableChangeListener(Vetoable
ChangeListener listener);
    public synchronized void removeVetoableChangeListener
(VetoableChangeListener listener);
    public void fireVetoableChange(String propertyName,
Object oldValue, Object newValue)
                        throws PropertyVetoException;
}
```

This support class, like `PropertyChangeSupport`, manages the low-level details of registering listeners and iterating through a list of listeners when a vetoable change event needs to be fired. However, this time around method `VetoableChangeSupport.fireVetoableChange()` does a lot more than its non-vetoable relative `PropertyChangeSupport.firePropertyChange()`. While the latter simply goes through every registered listener and sends it a `PropertyChangeEvent`, the veto-aware version has to do the following, in pseudo-code:

```
vetoed = false
while (listeners) {
  send listener a PropertyChangeEvent (old, new)
  if listener vetoed change
    vetoed = true
    break out of while loop
}
if (vetoed) {
  reset iterator
  while (listeners) {
    send listener a PropertyChangeEvent (new, old)
  }
}
```

In plain English, this means that the method starts off like its noncon-strained counterpart, but breaks out of its event-sending loop as soon as a listener vetoes the change. It then has to go through all the listeners again, to inform everyone that the property is being reset to its old value.

Now that you understand how our `Country` bean's `countryStatus` constrained property is implemented, we can have a look at the `Super-Power` class, where the property change listening gets done and where some conditional vetoing occurs.

LIST 18.5: SuperPower.java

```java
import java.beans.*;
import java.util.*;

public class SuperPower extends Country
                        implements VetoableChangeListener {

protected static Vector bigGuys = new Vector();

protected static final int SALT_LIMIT = 2000000;
// S.A.L.T

// some extra attribute thats makes a Country
// that bit special
protected int numNuclearWarHeads;

//---------------------------------
// SuperPower Constructors
//---------------------------------
public SuperPower() {
// all beans need default constructors!
   this("Unnamed superpower", 0);
}
public SuperPower(String name, int destructivePower) {

   super(name, "Independent");
   this.numNuclearWarHeads = destructivePower;

   // add new superpower to list of superpowers
   bigGuys.addElement(this);
}
//---------------------------------
// set()/get() for 'ArsenalSize' property
//---------------------------------
public void setArsenalSize(int size) {
   numNuclearWarHeads = size;
}
public int getArsenalSize() {
   // if real arsenal is smaller than many believe,
   // adjust upwards
   if ( numNuclearWarHeads < 500000 ) {
     return (int) (numNuclearWarHeads * 2.5);
     }
   // if real arsenal is larger than allowed by treaty,
   // adjust down
   if ( numNuclearWarHeads > SALT_LIMIT ) {
```

```
      return (int) (SALT_LIMIT * 1.1);
   }
   return numNuclearWarHeads;
}
//-----------------------------
// method vetoableChange() is similar to propertyChange()
// except that the listener can VETO the change. This is
// done by throwing the PropertyVetoException.
//-----------------------------
public void vetoableChange(PropertyChangeEvent
              countryChanged)throws PropertyVetoException {
String howChanged;

  // extract details of property change
  howChanged  = (String) countryChanged.getNewValue();

    System.out.print("UN member "+ countryName + "
                    assesses the situation.. '");
    System.out.println(countryChanged.getOldValue() +"'
                    -> '"+howChanged+"'");

    // if a sensitive country wants to change its independent
    // status, then all superpowers pay attention...
    if ( ! howChanged.equals("Independent") ) {

       // if the country wants to ally itself to another
       // superpower, and that superpower has more
       // firepower than itself, then the smaller superpower
       // vetos the shift
       int allyPosition = howChanged.indexOf("ally of");
       if ( allyPosition != -1 ) {

          for (int i=0; i < bigGuys.size(); i++) {
             String allyName = howChanged.substring(
                             allyPosition+8);

             SuperPower ally = (SuperPower)
                             (bigGuys.elementAt(i));
             if ( ! ally.getCountryName().equals(allyName) )
             {
                continue;
             }

             if ( ally.getArsenalSize() >
                 numNuclearWarHeads ) {
```

```
                  System.out.println(countryName +
                                " vetos change!");

                  String reason = countryName +
                                " will not allow "+
                                "Kuwait to become "+
                                howChanged;
                  throw new PropertyVetoException(
                                reason, countryChanged);
                }
            } // endfor
        } // endif tricky country wants to change color
    } // endif geopolitical trigger
  }
} // End of Class SuperPower
```

Let's give class SuperPower an in-depth walk-through. SuperPower declares itself as a subclass of Country so that it inherits the country-Name and countryStatus properties. It also declares itself to be a VetoableChangeListener, meaning that it implements the method

```
vetoableChange(PropertyChangeEvent x) throws
PropertyVetoException
```

SuperPower uses one static (that is, shared by all instances of the class) java.util.Vector to store references to every SuperPower object it creates. The only extra instance field it adds is NumNuclear-WarHeads, an int holding a SuperPower's firepower. Associated with this firepower is a class constant, SALT_LIMIT, an upper limit for nuclear stockpiles.

The SuperPower constructor is straightforward: given a country name and its firepower, it records these details and stores a reference to the newly created object in its bigGuys database (the static Vector).

Next, SuperPower adds one simple read/write property of its own, arsenalSize, for which it provides accessor methods. The get-ArsenalSize() is a bit tongue-in-cheek, so I leave it to you to analyze.

Finally, we have method vetoableChange(), the heart of class SuperPower. This is where a SuperPower, as a VetoableChange-Listener, gets to cast its vote on whether a Country bean can change its constrained property, countryStatus. The change event is encapsulated in a standard PropertyChangeEvent object, so a call to get-NewValue() lets us find out the new countryStatus property. The rest of the logic boils down to determining whether the ally chosen by the previously independent country has a bigger declared nuclear arsenal, and if so, we veto the change (this is exactly the same kind of sad "logic" used by our species ever since we could judge the size of an opponent's stick).

With classes Country and SuperPower in place, all we need is a main program that sets up the United Nations scenario and lets the superpowers vote:

LIST 18.6:   *PrimitiveGames.java*

```
import java.beans.*;
import utilities.beans.*;


public class PrimitiveGames extends Object {


//------------------------------------------------------------
// main() entry point
//------------------------------------------------------------
public static void main (String[] args) {
  new PrimitiveGames();
}
//------------------------------------------------------------
// PrimitiveGames Constructor
//------------------------------------------------------------
public PrimitiveGames() {
Country valuable;
SuperPower a,b,c;

  // create one mortal country and 3 superpowers
  valuable = (Country)    BeansKit.newBean("Country");
  a        = (SuperPower) BeansKit.newBean("SuperPower");
  b        = (SuperPower) BeansKit.newBean("SuperPower");
  c        = (SuperPower) BeansKit.newBean("SuperPower");

  // give each country its attributes
  valuable.setCountryName("Kuwait");

  try {
    valuable.setCountryStatus("Independent");
  } catch (PropertyVetoException impossibleAtThisStage) {
    System.out.println("Caught impossible
                        PropertyVetoException!");
    System.exit(10);
  }

  a.setCountryName("Britain");
  a.setArsenalSize(600000);
```

Part iv

```
    b.setCountryName("France");
    b.setArsenalSize(3000000);

    c.setCountryName("China");
    c.setArsenalSize(12000000);

    // let all superpowers keep a close watch on mortal country
    valuable.addVetoableChangeListener(a);
    valuable.addVetoableChangeListener(b);
    valuable.addVetoableChangeListener(c);

    System.out.println("");

    // and now the moment of truth..
    // Kuwait wants to become an ally of China
    try {
      System.out.println("Attempting to have Kuwait become an
                          ally of China\n");

      valuable.setCountryStatus("ally of China");

    } catch (PropertyVetoException notAcceptable) {
      System.out.println("");
      System.out.println("Kuwait not allowed to change status
                          because:");
      System.out.println(notAcceptable);
    }
  }
} // End of Class PrimitiveGames
```

The core of the program is the successive registration of Super-
Powers a, b, and c as listeners of any vetoable property changes
attempted by country valuable, and the attempt of valuable to
change its countryStatus to "ally of China." When run from the
console, you should see the following output:

```
C:\MasteringBeans\ch04>javac PrimitiveGames.java
C:\MasteringBeans\ch04>java PrimitiveGames
Attempting to have Kuwait become an ally of China

UN member Britain assesses the situation.. 'Independent' ->
'ally of China'
Britain vetos change!
UN member Britain assesses the situation.. 'ally of China' ->
'Independent'
UN member France assesses the situation.. 'ally of China' ->
'Independent'
```

```
UN member China assesses the situation.. 'ally of China' ->
'Independent'
```

```
Kuwait not allowed to change status because:
java.beans.PropertyVetoException: Britain will not allow
Kuwait to become ally of China
```

The output can be explained as follows: Britain was the first country to be notified of the change and immediately vetoed it (because China has more firepower than Britain). `VetoableChangeSupport` `.fireVetoableChange()` then abandoned notifying the rest of its registered listeners because one listener would not accept the change. It then proceeds by notifying *all* its listeners that it is retracing its steps by resetting the property to its original value.

Here we clearly see that a listener *can* be informed of an old-to-new value change where the old value could never have been accepted in the first place, without someone vetoing the change. Hence, the warning to never have your code look at, or use, the old value from a `Property-ChangeEvent`.

Remember that the order in which listeners are notified is not specified, so, without changing the program, the above output could equally have been:

```
UN member China assesses the situation.. 'Independent' ->
'ally of China'
UN member France assesses the situation.. 'Independent' ->
'ally of China'
UN member Britain assesses the situation.. 'Independent' ->
'ally of China'
Britain vetos change!
UN member Britain assesses the situation.. 'ally of China' ->
'Independent'
UN member France assesses the situation.. 'ally of China' ->
'Independent'
UN member China assesses the situation.. 'ally of China' ->
'Independent'
```

If the vetoing listener happens to be notified last, as in this example, then a lot of work will have been wasted by the previous listeners, who will already have propagated the change into their code and data structures, only to be ordered to undo everything some moments later. One technique to lessen this effect could be to slightly delay any actions flowing from a *vetoable* change, and seeing if a reverse change event arrives soon after. If so, the two events can be treated as self-annihilating and no action needs to be taken. However, be very careful with such an approach because it will only work if the do-undo steps do not leave *any* side effects behind. If they do, then the events have to be acted upon, each individually so that the side effect (that is, presumably a designed one!) does get left behind. Another serious problem with the delaying technique is that interactive performance suffers. As always, you will need to find the correct balance when deciding which option to go for.

NOTE

In fact, when I was questioning JavaSoft engineers on the topic of wasteful do/undo steps due to vetoes, they informed me that vetoable properties are extremely specialized forms of properties and that they should not be used lightly. For the majority of beans, you probably should never even think about adding vetoable properties support.

Testing Constrained Properties in the BDK BeanBox

The BDK contains a demo bean, Voter, that can veto every vetoable change or accept them, depending on Voter's defining boolean property: veto-All. We can therefore also test the Country bean's vetoable country-Status property in the BeanBox.

To add the Country bean to the BeanBox, proceed as you did in the section *Testing Bound Properties in the BDK BeanBox*:

Create a file named Country.mf that contains:

```
Name: Country.class
Java-Bean: True
```

Create the jar file:

```
jar cvfm Country.jar Country.mf Country.class
```

and copy it into the BeanBox jars directory:

```
copy Country.jar \Bdk\jars
```

Next, follow these steps:

1. Pick the Country bean from the ToolBox palette and drop it on the design surface.

2. Pick the Voter demo bean and drop it alongside our Country bean.

3. Hook up the Voter to the `Country` bean, as follows:

▶ Select the `Country` bean

▶ Pick the `vetoableChange` event from the Events menu

▶ Connect the two together via the rubber-band line

▶ Pick the `vetoableChange` method in the EventTarget-Dialog window

If you now select the `Country` bean and attempt to edit its `country-Status` property, the BeanBox will pop open a veto error dialog, meaning that the `Voter` has vetoed the change. Figure 18.8 shows the situation at that point. If you dismiss the dialog you will see that the property has not been changed.

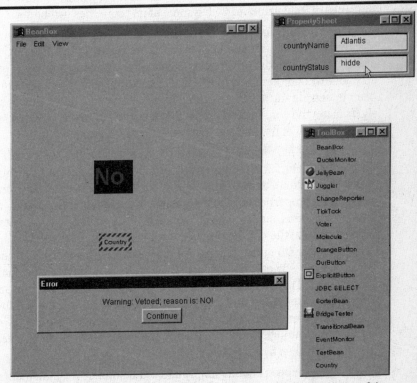

FIGURE 18.8: The BDK Voter demo bean vetoed the attempted change of the Country's `countryStatus` property (although its reason for doing so is rather simplistic).

Part iv

You can change the vetoAll `Voter` property from `true` to `false`, and now the `Voter` will allow any vetoable changes.

Letting Beans Check Property Values Using Constrained Properties

The design of the constrained property system is clearly listener-centric: it exists to let all registered listeners on a property agree on the acceptability of a property's new value. But we can use the system for a very different purpose: letting a bean *itself* veto a new value for one of its properties.

So far, writable bean properties have accepted any legal value within their type's domain. An integer property, for example, will accept all possible Java `int` values, from minus four billion to plus four billion. The same goes for all other types, so the need often arises for a bean to narrow down the range of legal values to which some of its properties can be set.

Take, for example, a bean that exports an `age` property. Ages are strictly positive values, and because Java has no unsigned integer types, using `int` as type for the property would allow clients, if the bean property code did not include any checks, to corrupt the internal state of the bean by setting the age to a negative value. You can counter this possibility by using the constrained properties mechanism to let the bean "self-constrain" any of its properties, by vetoing the change.

One elegant-looking solution would be to have a bean be a `Vetoable-ChangeListener` for its own vetoable properties. The bean could implement the required `vetoableChange()` method, where it validates changes to any of its properties, and register itself, at constructor time, as its own listener! However, such a "clever" solution hides one serious flaw: it would involve, at best, the notification of every *real* (external) listener once, and at worst, twice (to undo changes if a veto occurs). This is because the bean itself would not necessarily be the first to be notified of the change it vetoed itself! This could amount to an enormous amount of CPU power wasted because no external listener really needs to be bothered in the first place. (One event notification can trigger an avalanche of further events propagating through a system, and any event can mean expensive actions being undertaken by a receiver.)

Instead, the bean should simply add old-fashioned `if` statements at the beginning of the property's `setter` method and instantly veto (that is, throw an exception) the value if inappropriate. Only the caller will feel the effects of the veto, and all registered listeners will remain blissfully unaware of the failed property change.

Relying on some simple `if` checks before the normal `fireVetoable-Change()` of a vetoable property `setter` method does mean you need to construct a `PropertyChangeEvent` object that will be passed to the `PropertyVetoException`'s constructor. Here is an example `setter` method for an `age` property in some imaginary bean:

```
public void setAge(int newAge) throws PropertyVetoException {

    if (newAge < 0 || newAge > 200) {
        PropertyChangeEvent pcEvt = new PropertyChange
Event(this,
                        "age", age, newAge);
        throw new PropertyVetoException(
            "age has to be positive and less than 200 years",
pcEvt);
    }

    vetoChangeSuppObj.fireVetoableChange("age", age, newAge);
    // if we arrive here, no vetos happened, so change property
    age = newAge;
}
```

If you found this last section on constrained properties difficult to follow, you might want to remind yourself that keeping your designs as simple as possible (that is, possibly not using any vetoable properties at all) is a wise rule of thumb. This should become even more apparent when you factor in the complexity that Java's omnipresent multithreading adds to the picture. The issues surrounding properties and multithreading are explained in the next section.

PROPERTIES AND MULTITHREADING

Java is a very dynamic language and includes easy-to-use multithreading language constructs and support classes. Many Java programs rely on multithreading to exploit internal application parallelism, improve networking performance, or speed up user feedback response. Most Java runtimes use multithreading to implement Java's garbage collection feature. Finally, the AWT also relies on separate threads for its functioning. In short: even the simplest of Java programs are born in an actively multithreading environment.

Java beans, therefore, are also deployed in such a dynamic, multiple-threads environment, and herein lies the classic danger of *race conditions*. Race conditions are timing-dependent program flow scenarios that can lead to state (program data) corruption (you will see one such scenario, in detail, in the following section). Every Java bean needs to be designed with race conditions in mind so that a bean can withstand simultaneous use by several client threads.

Multithreading Issues with Simple Properties

Bean implementations have to assume that multiple threads are accessing and/or modifying a single bean instance at the same time. As an example of an improperly implemented bean (as it relates to multithreading awareness), consider the following BrokenProperties bean and its associated MTProperties test program:

LIST 18.7: BrokenProperties.java

```java
import java.awt.Point;

// Demo Bean that does not guard against multiple thread use.

public class BrokenProperties extends Point {

//---------------------------------------------------------------
// set()/get() for 'Spot' property
//---------------------------------------------------------------
public void setSpot(Point point) {    // 'spot' setter
   this.x = point.x;
   this.y = point.y;
}
public Point getSpot() {               // 'spot' getter
   return this;
}
} // End of Bean/Class BrokenProperties
```

LIST 18.8: MTProperties.java

```java
import java.awt.Point;
import utilities.*;
import utilities.beans.*;

public class MTProperties extends Thread {

protected BrokenProperties myBean;
// the target bean to bash..
```

```
protected int myID;
// each thread carries a bit of ID


//------------------------------
// main() entry point
//------------------------------
public static void main (String[] args) {
BrokenProperties bean;
Thread thread;

  bean = (BrokenProperties) BeansKit.newBean(
                            "BrokenProperties");

  for (int i=0; i < 20; i++) {
    // start 10 threads to bash bean
    thread = new MTProperties(bean, i);
    // threads get access to bean
    thread.start();
  }
}
//------------------------------
// MTProperties Constructor
//------------------------------
public MTProperties(BrokenProperties bean, int id) {
  this.myBean = bean;          // note the bean to address
  this.myID   = id;            // note who we are
}
//------------------------------
// the thread main loop:
// do forever
//    create new random Point with x == y
//    tell bean to adopt Point as its new 'spot' property
//    ask bean what its 'spot' property is now set to
//    throw a wobbly if spot x does not equal spot y
//------------------------------
public void run() {
int someInt;
Point point = new Point();

  while ( true ) {
    someInt = (int) (Math.random()*100);
    point.x = someInt;
    point.y = someInt;
    myBean.setSpot( point );

    point = myBean.getSpot();
```

```
            if ( point.x != point.y ) {
              System.out.println("Bean corrupted ! x= " +
                                point.x +", y= " + point.y);
              System.exit(10);
            }
            System.out.print( (char) ('A' + myID) );
            System.out.flush();
        }
    }
} // End of Class MTProperties
```

The two source codes define a bean called `BrokenProperties` and a class `MTProperties` used to exercise the bean from within 20 running threads. Let us follow `MTProperties'` `main()` entry point: a `Broken-Properties` bean is instantiated, followed by the creation and starting of 20 threads. Class `MTProperties` extends `java.lang.Thread`, so all we need to do to turn class `MTProperties` into a thread is to implement a `run()` method (as per the `java.lang.Runnable` interface). The constructor for our threads take two arguments: the bean object they will communicate with and a unique identification, so that the threads can easily be differentiated at runtime.

The business end of this demo is the `run()` method in class `MT-Properties`. Here we loop forever, creating random new (x,y) points, but with the following characteristic: their x coordinate always equals their y coordinate. These random points are passed to the bean's `setSpot()` setter method and then immediately read back using the `getSpot()` getter method. One would always expect the read `spot` property to be identical to the earlier created random point, some milliseconds ago.

Here is a sample output of the program when invoked at the command line:

```
C:\MasteringBeans\ch04>javac MTProperties.java
C:\MasteringBeans\ch04>java MTProperties
ABBBBBBBBBBBBBBBBBBBBDJJJJJJJJJJJJJJJJJJJJEGHHHHHHHHHHHHHHHHHHHS
SSSSSSSSSSSSSS
IICCBBBBBBBBBBBBBBBBBBBKBDLJMBOPLQNRTPHHHHHHHHFFFFFFFFFFFFFSSSSS
SSSSSSSSSSSSSS
FFFFFFFFFFFFFFFFAAAAAACCCCCCCCKKKKKKKKKKKKKKKKKKMMMMMMMMMMMMMMMM
MMMMMMMMMMMMMDD
JEOQQQQQQQQQQQQQQQQRRRRRRRRRRRRRRRRRRBBBBBBBBBBBBBBBBBBTTTTTTTTTTT
TTTTTLPPPPPPP
PPPPGGHHHFFFFFFFFFIIIIIIIIIIIIIIIIISSSSSSSSSSSSSSSSSSSSSSSACCCCCCCC
CCCCCCCCCCCKMD
```

```
QQQQQQQNNNNNNNNNNNNNNNNNRRRRRTRRHHHHHHHHHHFFFFFFFFFFFFFFFFFFFFIIII
IIIIIIIIIIIII
MMMJEEEEEEEEEEEDDDDEEEEEEEEEO0000000000000000000000000000QNNNNNNN
NNBTLPLRGFFFF
FFFFFFFFFIIAAAAAAAAAAAAAAAAAAASSSSSSSSSSSSSSSSSSSKKKKKKKKKKKKKKKK
KCCCCCCCMMJAA
AACBean corrupted ! x = 67, y = 13
OOOOOOOOOOOOOOOOOOOO
```

The output shows the 20 threads running in parallel (as far as a human observer goes); each thread uses the ID it received at construction time to print one of the letters 'A' to 'T,' the first 20 letters of the alphabet. As soon as any thread discovers that the read back spot property does not conform to the programmed characteristic of x = y, the thread prints a "Bean corrupted" message and halts the experiment.

What you are seeing is the state-corrupting side effect of a race condition within the bean's setSpot() code. Here is that method again:

```
public void setSpot(Point point) {
// 'spot' setter
this.x = point.x;
this.y = point.y;
}
```

What could ever go wrong in such a simple bit of code? Imagine thread A calling setSpot() with a point argument equal to (67,67). If we now slow down the clock of the Universe so that we can see the JVM execute each Java statement, slowly, one at a time, we can imagine thread A executing the x coordinate copy statement (this.x = point.x;) and then... suddenly, thread A gets frozen by the operating system, and thread C is scheduled to run for a while. In its previous running state, thread C had just created its own new random point (13,13), called setSpot(), and then got frozen to make room for thread M, right after it had set the x coordinate to 13. So, the resumed thread C now carries on with its programmed logic, setting y to 13 and checking if the spot property is equal (13,13)—but finds that it has mysteriously changed to an illegal state of (67,13), the x coordinate being half the state of what thread A was setting spot to and the y coordinate being half the state of what thread C *had set* spot to. The end result is that the BrokenProperties bean ends up with an internally inconsistent state: a broken property.

Whenever a *non-atomic* data structure (that is, a structure consisting of more than one part) can be modified by more than one thread at a time, you need to protect the structure using a lock. In Java, this is done using the synchronized keyword.

WARNING

Unlike all other Java types, Java does *not* guarantee that `long` and `double` are treated atomically! This is because `long` and `double` require 64 bits, which is twice the length of most modern CPU architectures' word length (32 bits). Loading or storing single machine words are intrinsically atomical operations, but moving 64-bit entities requires two such moves, and these are not protected by Java for the usual reason: performance. (Some CPUs allow the system bus to be locked to perform multiword transfers atomically, but this facility is not available on all CPUs and would in any case be incredibly expensive to apply to all `long` or `double` manipulations!) So, even when a property consists of just a *single* `long` or a *single* `double`, you should use full locking precautions to protect your longs or doubles from suddenly getting totally corrupted.

The `synchronized` keyword marks a block of code as being an atomic step. The code cannot be "divided," as when another thread interrupts the code to potentially reenter that block itself (hence the term *reentrant* code; all Java code is reentrant). The solution for our Broken-Properties bean is trivial: just replace its `setSpot()` method by:

```
public void setSpot(Point point) {           // 'spot' setter
    synchronized (this) {
        this.x = point.x;
        this.y = point.y;
    }
}
```

or alternatively,

```
public synchronized void setSpot(Point point) {  // 'spot'
setter
    this.x = point.x;
    this.y = point.y;
}
```

Both replacements are perfectly equivalent, although I prefer the first since it shows more clearly what the exact function of the `synchronized` keyword is: a synchronized block is *always* linked to an object that gets locked. By *locked*, I mean that the JVM first tries to obtain a lock on the object (that is, obtain exclusive access to it), or waits until the object becomes unlocked if it is already locked. The locking process guarantees that any object can only be locked (or owned) by one thread at a time.

So, the `synchronized (this)` syntax clearly echoes the internal mechanism: the argument inside the parentheses is the object to be locked (the current object) before the code block is entered. The alternative syntax, where the `synchronized` keyword is used as a modifier in a method signature, is simply a shorthand version of the former.

WARNING

When `static` methods are marked `synchronized`, then there is no current object to lock for these methods. Only instance methods are associated with a current object (the `this` object instance). So, when class methods are synchronized, the `java.lang.Class` object corresponding to the method's class is used to lock on instead. This has serious performance implications, because a collection of class instances *share* a single associated `Class` object; whenever that `Class` object gets locked, all objects of that class (whether 3, 50, or 1000!) are barred from invoking the same `static` method. With this in mind, you should think twice before using synchronization with `static` methods.

In practice, always remember the explicit `synchronized` form because it allows you to "atomize" the smallest possible block of code within a method. The shorthand form "atomizes" the entire method, and, for performance reasons, this is frequently not what you want: while a thread has entered an atomic block of code, no other thread that needs to execute the same bit of code on an object can enter it.

NOTE

When a lock is obtained on an object, then *all* synchronized code for that object's class will become atomic. Therefore, if your class contains more than one data structure that needs to be treated atomically, but those data structures are otherwise *independent* of each other, then another performance bottleneck can arise. Clients calling synchronized methods that manipulate one internal data structure will block all other clients that call the other methods that deal with any other atomic data structures of your class. Clearly, such situations should be avoided by splitting the class up into smaller classes that only deal with one data structure to be treated atomically at a time.

The JVM deals with this by creating queues of threads waiting for an object to become unlocked. While this is great from the point of view of protecting the consistency of composite data structures, it can result in multithreaded traffic jams when a less-than-efficient section of code is marked as `synchronized`.

Therefore, always pay attention to just how much code you synchronize: it should be the absolute minimum necessary. For example, imagine that our `setSpot()` method originally consisted of:

```
public void setSpot(Point point) {    // 'spot' setter
```

```
        log.println("setSpot() called on " + this.toString() );
        this.x = point.x;
        this.y = point.y;
    }
```

Although the `println` statement might *logically* belong in the `setSpot()` method, it is not a part of the statement sequence that needs to be grouped into an atomic whole. Therefore, in this case the right way to use the `synchronized` keyword would be as follows:

```
    public void setSpot(Point point) {    // 'spot' setter
        log.println("setSpot() called on " + this.toString() );
        synchronized (this) {
            this.x = point.x;
            this.y = point.y;
        }
    }
```

And *not* the "lazy" way, like this:

```
    public synchronized void setSpot(Point point) {
    // 'spot' setter
        log.println("setSpot() called on " + this.toString() );
        this.x = point.x;
        this.y = point.y;
    }
```

The first approach will lock out other threads for the absolute minimum amount of time, whereas the second approach will force other threads to also wait for something that is totally irrelevant to the locking operation: the `println` statement.

If, under the pressures of modern product schedules, you decided to use the lazy approach and made all your bean methods synchronized *in toto*, then all of your bean users would, in turn, end up with an equally lazy (that is, low performance) bean.

Property Listeners and Multithreading

Multithreading introduces a whole spectrum of possible scenarios to complicate your life as a bean developer. Here is another scenario to be aware of: Race conditions (those again!) can result in some unexpected behavior resulting from incorrect *expectations* linked to the order of calling add- and remove<*ListenerType*> and the actual timing of incoming events. Imagine a whole bunch of threads and a single bean with a bound property. If these threads constantly register, deregister, and modify that single bean's property (for reasons better known to themselves!), you can end up with a thread *legally* receiving a property change event while it has just recently deregistered itself (and therefore does not expect to receive any events). The following `UnexpectedEvents` bean and its `MTListeners` test program demonstrates this phenomenon:

LIST 18.9: *UnexpectedEvents.java*

```java
import java.beans.*;

public class UnexpectedEvents {

protected PropertyChangeSupport butler;
// butler does all the work

//----------------------------------
// UnexpectedEvents Constructor
//----------------------------------
public UnexpectedEvents() {
  butler = new PropertyChangeSupport(this);
}
//----------------------------------
// set()/get() for 'Property' dummy property
//----------------------------------
public void setProperty( int value) {

  System.out.println("Bean changing property.
                     Firing PC event.");

  butler.firePropertyChange("property", new Integer(0),
                     new Integer(1));
}
public int getProperty() {
  return 1;
}
//----------------------------------
// Listener registration methods
//----------------------------------
public void addPropertyChangeListener(
              PropertyChangeListener l) {
  butler.addPropertyChangeListener(l);
}
public void removePropertyChangeListener(
              PropertyChangeListener l) {
  butler.removePropertyChangeListener(l);
}
} // End of Bean/Class UnexpectedEvents
```

LIST 18.10:   MTListeners.java

```java
import java.beans.*;
import utilities.*;
import utilities.beans.*;

public class MTListeners extends Thread
                implements PropertyChangeListener {

protected UnexpectedEvents myBean;
// the target bean to bash..

protected int myID;
// each thread carries a bit of ID

protected boolean readyForEvents = false;
// have we registered yet ?

//-----------------------------
// main() entry point
//-----------------------------
public static void main (String[] args) {
UnexpectedEvents bean;
Thread thread;

  bean = (UnexpectedEvents) BeansKit.newBean(
                         "UnexpectedEvents");

  for (int i=0; i < 5; i++) {
    // start N threads to bash bean
    thread = new MTListeners(bean, i);
    // threads get access to bean
    thread.start();
  }
}
//-----------------------------
// MTListeners Constructor
//-----------------------------
public MTListeners(UnexpectedEvents bean, int id) {
  this.myBean = bean;          // note the bean to address
  this.myID   = id;            // note who we are
}
//-----------------------------
// the thread main loop:
// do forever
//    register as listener, set flag to accept events
```

```
//    deregister as listener, set flag to refuse events
//    change bean property
//
// if we ever get an event while we shouldn't get one,
// say so and halt
//-----------------------------------
public void run() {

  while ( true ) {
    // register with bean, this means we might expect
    // events from now on.
    synchronized (this) {
      System.out.println(myID +" registering.");
      myBean.addPropertyChangeListener(this);
      readyForEvents = true;
    }

    // let other threads run for a bit
    randomSleep();

    // now deregister ourselves with bean, meaning we should
    // not receive any more events from bean from now on.
    synchronized (this) {
      System.out.println(myID +" un-registering.");
      myBean.removePropertyChangeListener(this);
      readyForEvents = false;
    }
    // let other threads run for a bit
    randomSleep();

    // then modify the bean's property:
    System.out.println(myID +"
                        about to change bean property..");
    myBean.setProperty( (int) (Math.random()*50));
  }
}
//-----------------------------------
// the implementation of the PropertyChangeListener interface
//-----------------------------------
public void propertyChange(PropertyChangeEvent pcEvent) {

  if ( readyForEvents == false ) {
    System.out.println("I ("+ myID +") got an event while I
                        did not" +" expect to receive one!!");
    System.exit(0);
  }
```

```
        System.out.println(myID +" heard of property change.");
    }
    //------------------------------------------
    // utility function to put a thread to sleep for a random
    // period of less than 1 second.
    //------------------------------------------
    protected void randomSleep() {
      MiscKit.delay( (int) (Math.random()*1000));
    }
    } // End of Class MTListeners
```

As with our earlier MTProperties multithreading demonstration
class, the heart of this demonstration is class MTListeners' run()
method, where the thread's logic hides. What it does is very banal: it
keeps registering and deregistering its thread as a listener for the bean's
property change event source, while also changing the bean's property
and doing a lot of random sleeping. When you run MTListeners from
the console, here is one possible output:

```
C:\MasteringBeans\ch04>javac MTListeners.java
C:\MasteringBeans\ch04>java MTListeners
0 registering.
2 registering.
1 registering.
3 registering.
4 registering.
4 un-registering.
4 about to change bean property..
Bean changing property. Firing PC event.
0 heard of property change.
2 heard of property change.
1 heard of property change.
3 heard of property change.
1 un-registering.
4 registering.
0 un-registering.
3 un-registering.
2 un-registering.
2 about to change bean property..
Bean changing property. Firing PC event.
4 heard of property change.
2 registering.
1 about to change bean property..
Bean changing property. Firing PC event.
```

```
4 heard of property change.
2 heard of property change.
1 registering.
0 about to change bean property..
Bean changing property. Firing PC event.
4 heard of property change.
1 un-registering.
2 heard of property change.
I (1) got an event while I did not expect to receive one!!
```

The program starts by spawning its thread clones, so the output starts with a sequence of threads telling us that they are registering as a listener with the bean. Note that even though the `for` loop spawns the threads in a strict 0-1-2-3... order, the output is already scrambled. This is due to the underlying host operating system's task or process scheduling decisions *at that time* (that is, when you run this program the output will almost definitely be totally different), and is exactly the cause of the often unpredictable sequence of *precise* events in multithreaded systems. (Of course, multithreaded systems taken as a whole are totally deterministic, like purely sequential systems, but this is only so by relying on critical synchronization points.)

Next in the output is thread 4, which is lucky enough to run long enough to register, deregister, and change the bean's property, all in the same time slice. Its changing of the bean's sole bound property triggers the firing of a `PropertyChangeEvent` to all currently registered listeners (threads 0, 1, 2, and 3). You can see this happening in the successive lines "x heard of property change."

As time goes on, the threads display their free-running character by running more and more interleaved (as seen in the output).

I now need you to pick up the thread again (pun intended) at the line reading "0 about to change bean property.." At that point, threads 1, 2, and 4 are in a registered state, and shortly afterward thread 4 already hears of the change, but thread 1 now unregisters itself before having heard of the change. Next, thread 2 receives the event and then Bang! ... thread 1, which is totally disinterested in any change events at this time because it deregistered itself, receives the property change event that thread 0 triggered all those steps ago.

Thread 1 was not registered as a listener for the event and still it received an event that it did not expect at the time. Now, if this were a bug in the `PropertyChangeSupport.firePropertyChange()` method, I would not go to such lengths pointing it out. The crux of the matter is that this is a *legal* side effect of the freedom of implementation given to implementors of event firing methods. While iterating over the list of listeners, a firing method may or may not have previously frozen the list to protect it from changes *while* it is notifying the set of listeners. It is clear that in the case of `PropertyChangeSupport.fireProperty-Change()`, it does freeze the list (by `clone()`ing the `Vector` containing all the listeners). This explains why thread 1 could remove itself as listener, and yet still receive an event moments later.

WARNING

It is clear that multithreading can seriously stress the implementation of a bean. Therefore, it is of critical importance that you stress-test your beans to the full, using aggressive, far-fetched, and ruthless scenarios like the ones demonstrated here. Reality is usually even more creative when it comes to finding unlikely scenarios! If you have attempted to reproduce the output of both test programs, you will have seen how impossible this is, due to the multithreading's unpredictable scheduling. The two test programs can run for minutes without showing up the race conditions. This reason alone should convince you that beans should always be tested in a fully multithreaded environment, and allocated enough simulation time to uncover problems.

Appendix

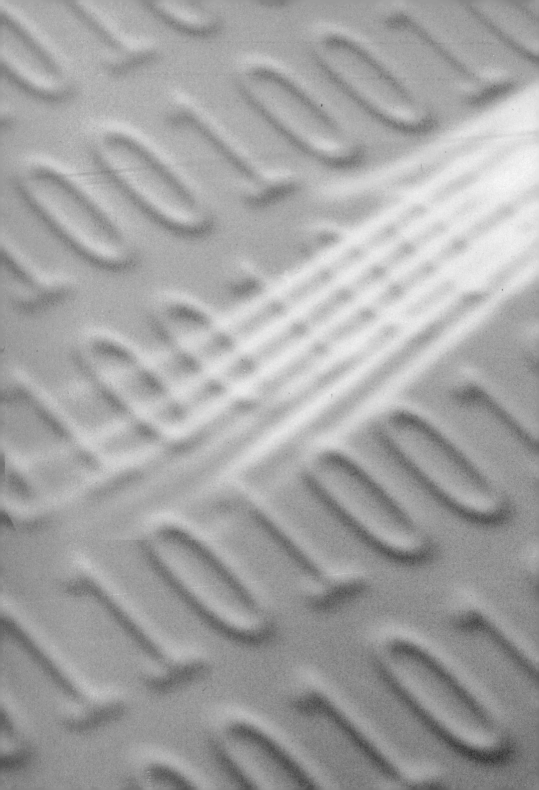

THE ESSENTIAL JAVA 2 API REFERENCE

This reference documents the inheritances, fields, constructors, and methods of the most useful classes in the Java 2 Applications Programming Interface: java.applet.*, java.awt.*, java.beans.*, java.io.*, java.lang.*, java.math.*, java.net.*, java.rmi.*, java.security.*, java.sql.*, java.text.*, and java.util.*.

►ABSTRACTACTION

public abstract class javax.swing.
  AbstractAction
implements javax.swing.Action
implements java.lang.Cloneable
implements java.io.Serializable
extends java.lang.Object

Fields

protected javax.swing.event.
  SwingPropertyChangeSupport
  changeSupport
protected boolean enabled

Constructors

public AbstractAction()
public AbstractAction(String name)
public AbstractAction(String name,Icon
  icon)

Methods

public synchronized void
  addPropertyChangeListener(
  PropertyChangeListener listener)
protected Object clone()
protected void firePropertyChange(String
  propertyName,Object oldValue,Object
  newValue)
public Object getValue(String key)
public boolean isEnabled()
public synchronized void putValue(String
  key,Object newValue)
public synchronized void
  removePropertyChangeListener(
  PropertyChangeListener listener)
public synchronized void setEnabled(
  boolean newValue)

►ABSTRACTBORDER

public abstract class javax.swing.border.
  AbstractBorder
implements javax.swing.border.Border
implements java.io.Serializable
extends java.lang.Object

Methods

public Insets getBorderInsets(Component
  c)
public Insets getBorderInsets(Component
  c,Insets insets)
public Rectangle getInteriorRectangle(
  Component c,int x,int y,int width,int
  height)
public static Rectangle
  getInteriorRectangle(Component c,Border
  b,int x,int y,int width,int height)
public boolean isBorderOpaque()
public void paintBorder(Component c,
  Graphics g,int x,int y,int width,int
  height)

►ABSTRACTBUTTON

public abstract class javax.swing.
  AbstractButton
implements java.awt.ItemSelectable
implements javax.swing.SwingConstants

extends javax.swing.JComponent
extends java.awt.Container
extends java.awt.Component
extends java.lang.Object

Fields

protected java.awt.event.ActionListener
  actionListener
public final static java.lang.String
  BORDER_PAINTED_CHANGED_PROPERTY
protected transient javax.swing.event.
  ChangeEvent changeEvent
protected javax.swing.event.
  ChangeListener changeListener
public final static java.lang.String
  CONTENT_AREA_FILLED_CHANGED_PROPERTY
public final static java.lang.String
  DISABLED_ICON_CHANGED_PROPERTY
public final static java.lang.String
  DISABLED_SELECTED_ICON_CHANGED_PROPERTY
public final static java.lang.String
  FOCUS_PAINTED_CHANGED_PROPERTY
public final static java.lang.String
  HORIZONTAL_ALIGNMENT_CHANGED_PROPERTY
public final static java.lang.String
  HORIZONTAL_TEXT_POSITION_CHANGED_
  PROPERTY
public final static java.lang.String
  ICON_CHANGED_PROPERTY
protected java.awt.event.ItemListener
  itemListener
public final static java.lang.String
  MARGIN_CHANGED_PROPERTY
public final static java.lang.String
  MNEMONIC_CHANGED_PROPERTY
protected javax.swing.ButtonModel model
public final static java.lang.String
  MODEL_CHANGED_PROPERTY
public final static java.lang.String
  PRESSED_ICON_CHANGED_PROPERTY
public final static java.lang.String
  ROLLOVER_ENABLED_CHANGED_PROPERTY
public final static java.lang.String
  ROLLOVER_ICON_CHANGED_PROPERTY
public final static java.lang.String
  ROLLOVER_SELECTED_ICON_CHANGED_PROPERTY
public final static java.lang.String
  SELECTED_ICON_CHANGED_PROPERTY
public final static java.lang.String
  TEXT_CHANGED_PROPERTY
public final static java.lang.String
  VERTICAL_ALIGNMENT_CHANGED_PROPERTY
public final static java.lang.String
  VERTICAL_TEXT_POSITION_CHANGED_PROPERTY

Methods

public void addActionListener(
  ActionListener l)
public void addChangeListener(
  ChangeListener l)
public void addItemListener(ItemListener
  l)
protected int checkHorizontalKey(int key,
  String exception)

```
protected int checkVerticalKey(int key,
    String exception)
protected ActionListener
    createActionListener()
protected ChangeListener
    createChangeListener()
protected ItemListener
    createItemListener()
public void doClick()
public void doClick(int pressTime)
protected void fireActionPerformed(
    ActionEvent event)
protected void fireItemStateChanged(
    ItemEvent event)
protected void fireStateChanged()
public String getActionCommand()
public Icon getDisabledIcon()
public Icon getDisabledSelectedIcon()
public int getHorizontalAlignment()
public int getHorizontalTextPosition()
public Icon getIcon()
public String getLabel()
public Insets getMargin()
public int getMnemonic()
public ButtonModel getModel()
public Icon getPressedIcon()
public Icon getRolloverIcon()
public Icon getRolloverSelectedIcon()
public Icon getSelectedIcon()
public synchronized Object
    getSelectedObjects()
public String getText()
public ButtonUI getUI()
public int getVerticalAlignment()
public int getVerticalTextPosition()
protected void init(String text,Icon
    icon)
public boolean isBorderPainted()
public boolean isContentAreaFilled()
public boolean isFocusPainted()
public boolean isRolloverEnabled()
public boolean isSelected()
protected void paintBorder(Graphics g)
protected String paramString()
public void removeActionListener(
    ActionListener l)
public void removeChangeListener(
    ChangeListener l)
public void removeItemListener(
    ItemListener l)
public void setActionCommand(String
    actionCommand)
public void setBorderPainted(boolean b)
public void setContentAreaFilled(boolean
    b)
public void setDisabledIcon(Icon
    disabledIcon)
public void setDisabledSelectedIcon(Icon
    disabledSelectedIcon)
public void setEnabled(boolean b)
public void setFocusPainted(boolean b)
```

```
public void setHorizontalAlignment(int
    alignment)
public void setHorizontalTextPosition(
    int textPosition)
public void setIcon(Icon defaultIcon)
public void setLabel(String label)
public void setMargin(Insets m)
public void setMnemonic(int mnemonic)
public void setMnemonic(char mnemonic)
public void setModel(ButtonModel
    newModel)
public void setPressedIcon(Icon
    pressedIcon)
public void setRolloverEnabled(boolean b)
public void setRolloverIcon(Icon
    rolloverIcon)
public void setRolloverSelectedIcon(Icon
    rolloverSelectedIcon)
public void setSelected(boolean b)
public void setSelectedIcon(Icon
    selectedIcon)
public void setText(String text)
public void setUI(ButtonUI ui)
public void setVerticalAlignment(int
    alignment)
public void setVerticalTextPosition(int
    textPosition)
public void updateUI()
```

►ABSTRACTCOLLECTION

```
public abstract class java.util.
    AbstractCollection
implements java.util.Collection
extends java.lang.Object
```

Constructors

```
protected  AbstractCollection()
```

Methods

```
public boolean add(Object o)
public boolean addAll(Collection c)
public void clear()
public boolean contains(Object o)
public boolean containsAll(Collection c)
public boolean isEmpty()
public abstract Iterator iterator()
public boolean remove(Object o)
public boolean removeAll(Collection c)
public boolean retainAll(Collection c)
public abstract int size()
public Object toArray()
public Object toArray(Object a)
public String toString()
```

►ABSTRACTCOLORCHOOSERPANEL

```
public abstract class javax.swing.
    colorchooser.AbstractColorChooserPanel
extends javax.swing.JPanel
extends javax.swing.JComponent
extends java.awt.Container
extends java.awt.Component
extends java.lang.Object
```

Methods

```
protected abstract void buildChooser()
```

```
protected Color getColorFromModel()
public ColorSelectionModel
  getColorSelectionModel()
public abstract String getDisplayName()
public abstract Icon getLargeDisplayIcon(
  )
public abstract Icon getSmallDisplayIcon(
  )
public void installChooserPanel(
  JColorChooser enclosingChooser)
public void paint(Graphics g)
public void uninstallChooserPanel(
  JColorChooser enclosingChooser)
public abstract void updateChooser()
```

▶ABSTRACTDOCUMENT

```
public abstract class javax.swing.text.
  AbstractDocument
implements javax.swing.text.Document
implements java.io.Serializable
extends java.lang.Object
```

Fields

```
protected final static java.lang.String
  BAD_LOCATION
public final static java.lang.String
  BidiElementName
public final static java.lang.String
  ContentElementName
public final static java.lang.String
  ElementNameAttribute
protected javax.swing.event.
  EventListenerList listenerList
public final static java.lang.String
  ParagraphElementName
public final static java.lang.String
  SectionElementName
```

Constructors

```
protected  AbstractDocument(Content data)
protected  AbstractDocument(Content data,
  AttributeContext context)
```

Methods

```
public void addDocumentListener(
  DocumentListener listener)
public void addUndoableEditListener(
  UndoableEditListener listener)
protected Element createBranchElement(
  Element parent,AttributeSet a)
protected Element createLeafElement(
  Element parent,AttributeSet a,int p0,int
  p1)
public synchronized Position
  createPosition(int offs)
public void dump(PrintStream out)
protected void fireChangedUpdate(
  DocumentEvent e)
protected void fireInsertUpdate(
  DocumentEvent e)
protected void fireRemoveUpdate(
  DocumentEvent e)
protected void fireUndoableEditUpdate(
  UndoableEditEvent e)
public int getAsynchronousLoadPriority()
```

```
protected final AttributeContext
  getAttributeContext()
public Element getBidiRootElement()
protected final Content getContent()
protected final synchronized Thread
  getCurrentWriter()
public abstract Element
  getDefaultRootElement()
public Dictionary getDocumentProperties()
public final Position getEndPosition()
public int getLength()
public abstract Element
  getParagraphElement(int pos)
public final Object getProperty(Object
  key)
public Element getRootElements()
public final Position getStartPosition()
public String getText(int offset,int
  length)
public void getText(int offset,int
  length,Segment txt)
public void insertString(int offs,String
  str,AttributeSet a)
protected void insertUpdate(
  DefaultDocumentEvent chng,AttributeSet
  attr)
protected void postRemoveUpdate(
  DefaultDocumentEvent chng)
public final void putProperty(Object key,
  Object value)
public final synchronized void readLock()
public final synchronized void
  readUnlock()
public void remove(int offs,int len)
public void removeDocumentListener(
  DocumentListener listener)
public void removeUndoableEditListener(
  UndoableEditListener listener)
protected void removeUpdate(
  DefaultDocumentEvent chng)
public void render(Runnable r)
public void setAsynchronousLoadPriority(
  int p)
public void setDocumentProperties(
  Dictionary x)
protected final synchronized void
  writeLock()
protected final synchronized void
  writeUnlock()
```

▶ABSTRACTLAYOUTCACHE

```
public abstract class javax.swing.tree.
  AbstractLayoutCache
implements javax.swing.tree.RowMapper
extends java.lang.Object
```

Fields

```
protected NodeDimensions nodeDimensions
protected boolean rootVisible
protected int rowHeight
protected javax.swing.tree.TreeModel
  treeModel
protected javax.swing.tree.
  TreeSelectionModel treeSelectionModel
```

Methods
```
public abstract Rectangle getBounds(
  TreePath path,Rectangle placeIn)
public abstract boolean getExpandedState(
  TreePath path)
public TreeModel getModel()
public NodeDimensions getNodeDimensions()
protected Rectangle getNodeDimensions(
  Object value,int row,int depth,boolean
  expanded,Rectangle placeIn)
public abstract TreePath
  getPathClosestTo(int x,int y)
public abstract TreePath getPathForRow(
  int row)
public int getPreferredHeight()
public int getPreferredWidth(Rectangle
  bounds)
public abstract int getRowCount()
public abstract int getRowForPath(
  TreePath path)
public int getRowHeight()
public int getRowsForPaths(TreePath
  paths)
public TreeSelectionModel
  getSelectionModel()
public abstract int getVisibleChildCount(
  TreePath path)
public abstract Enumeration
  getVisiblePathsFrom(TreePath path)
public abstract void
  invalidatePathBounds(TreePath path)
public abstract void invalidateSizes()
public abstract boolean isExpanded(
  TreePath path)
protected boolean isFixedRowHeight()
public boolean isRootVisible()
public abstract void setExpandedState(
  TreePath path,boolean isExpanded)
public void setModel(TreeModel newModel)
public void setNodeDimensions(
  NodeDimensions nd)
public void setRootVisible(boolean
  rootVisible)
public void setRowHeight(int rowHeight)
public void setSelectionModel(
  TreeSelectionModel newLSM)
public abstract void treeNodesChanged(
  TreeModelEvent e)
public abstract void treeNodesInserted(
  TreeModelEvent e)
public abstract void treeNodesRemoved(
  TreeModelEvent e)
public abstract void
  treeStructureChanged(TreeModelEvent e)
```

▶**ABSTRACTLIST**
```
public abstract class java.util.
  AbstractList
implements java.util.List
extends java.util.AbstractCollection
extends java.lang.Object
```

Fields
```
protected transient int modCount
```
Constructors
```
protected AbstractList()
```
Methods
```
public boolean add(Object o)
public void add(int index,Object element)
public boolean addAll(int index,
  Collection c)
public void clear()
public boolean equals(Object o)
public abstract Object get(int index)
public int hashCode()
public int indexOf(Object o)
public Iterator iterator()
public int lastIndexOf(Object o)
public ListIterator listIterator()
public ListIterator listIterator(int
  index)
public Object remove(int index)
protected void removeRange(int fromIndex,
  int toIndex)
public Object set(int index,Object
  element)
public List subList(int fromIndex,int
  toIndex)
```

▶**ABSTRACTLISTMODEL**
```
public abstract class javax.swing.
  AbstractListModel
implements javax.swing.ListModel
implements java.io.Serializable
extends java.lang.Object
```
Fields
```
protected javax.swing.event.
  EventListenerList listenerList
```
Methods
```
public void addListDataListener(
  ListDataListener l)
protected void fireContentsChanged(
  Object source,int index0,int index1)
protected void fireIntervalAdded(Object
  source,int index0,int index1)
protected void fireIntervalRemoved(
  Object source,int index0,int index1)
public void removeListDataListener(
  ListDataListener l)
```

▶**ABSTRACTMAP**
```
public abstract class java.util.
  AbstractMap
implements java.util.Map
extends java.lang.Object
```
Constructors
```
protected AbstractMap()
```
Methods
```
public void clear()
public boolean containsKey(Object key)
public boolean containsValue(Object
  value)
public abstract Set entrySet()
```

public boolean equals(Object o)
public Object get(Object key)
public int hashCode()
public boolean isEmpty()
public Set keySet()
public Object put(Object key,Object
  value)
public void putAll(Map t)
public Object remove(Object key)
public int size()
public String toString()
public Collection values()

▸ABSTRACTMETHODERROR
public class java.lang.
  AbstractMethodError
extends java.lang.
  IncompatibleClassChangeError
extends java.lang.LinkageError
extends java.lang.Error
extends java.lang.Throwable
extends java.lang.Object

Constructors
public AbstractMethodError()
public AbstractMethodError(String s)

▸ABSTRACTSEQUENTIALLIST
public abstract class java.util.
  AbstractSequentialList
extends java.util.AbstractList
extends java.util.AbstractCollection
extends java.lang.Object

Constructors
protected AbstractSequentialList()

Methods
public void add(int index,Object element)
public boolean addAll(int index,
  Collection c)
public Object get(int index)
public Iterator iterator()
public abstract ListIterator
  listIterator(int index)
public Object remove(int index)
public Object set(int index,Object
  element)

▸ABSTRACTSET
public abstract class java.util.
  AbstractSet
implements java.util.Set
extends java.util.AbstractCollection
extends java.lang.Object

Constructors
protected AbstractSet()

Methods
public boolean equals(Object o)
public int hashCode()

▸ABSTRACTTABLEMODEL
public abstract class javax.swing.table.
  AbstractTableModel
implements java.io.Serializable

implements javax.swing.table.TableModel
extends java.lang.Object

Fields
protected javax.swing.event.
  EventListenerList listenerList

Methods
public void addTableModelListener(
  TableModelListener l)
public int findColumn(String columnName)
public void fireTableCellUpdated(int row,
  int column)
public void fireTableChanged(
  TableModelEvent e)
public void fireTableDataChanged()
public void fireTableRowsDeleted(int
  firstRow,int lastRow)
public void fireTableRowsInserted(int
  firstRow,int lastRow)
public void fireTableRowsUpdated(int
  firstRow,int lastRow)
public void fireTableStructureChanged()
public Class getColumnClass(int
  columnIndex)
public String getColumnName(int column)
public boolean isCellEditable(int
  rowIndex,int columnIndex)
public void removeTableModelListener(
  TableModelListener l)
public void setValueAt(Object aValue,int
  rowIndex,int columnIndex)

▸ABSTRACTUNDOABLEEDIT
public class javax.swing.undo.
  AbstractUndoableEdit
implements java.io.Serializable
implements javax.swing.undo.
  UndoableEdit
extends java.lang.Object

Fields
protected final static java.lang.String
  RedoName
protected final static java.lang.String
  UndoName

Constructors
public AbstractUndoableEdit()

Methods
public boolean addEdit(UndoableEdit
  anEdit)
public boolean canRedo()
public boolean canUndo()
public void die()
public String getPresentationName()
public String getRedoPresentationName()
public String getUndoPresentationName()
public boolean isSignificant()
public void redo()
public boolean replaceEdit(UndoableEdit
  anEdit)
public String toString()
public void undo()

►**ABSTRACTWRITER**
public abstract class javax.swing.text.
  AbstractWriter
extends java.lang.Object
Fields
protected final static char NEWLINE
Constructors
protected AbstractWriter(Writer w,
  Document doc)
protected AbstractWriter(Writer w,
  Document doc,int pos,int len)
protected AbstractWriter(Writer w,
  Element root)
protected AbstractWriter(Writer w,
  Element root,int pos,int len)
Methods
protected void decrIndent()
protected Document getDocument()
protected ElementIterator
  getElementIterator()
protected String getText(Element elem)
protected void incrIndent()
protected void indent()
protected boolean inRange(Element next)
protected void setIndentSpace(int space)
protected void setLineLength(int l)
protected void text(Element elem)
protected abstract void write()
protected void write(char ch)
protected void write(String str)
protected void writeAttributes(
  AttributeSet attr)

►**ACCESSCONTROLCONTEXT**
public final class java.security.
  AccessControlContext
extends java.lang.Object
Constructors
public AccessControlContext(
  ProtectionDomain context)
  AccessControlContext()
Methods
public void checkPermission(Permission
  perm)
public boolean equals(Object obj)
public int hashCode()

►**ACCESSCONTROLEXCEPTION**
public class java.security.
  AccessControlException
extends java.lang.SecurityException
extends java.lang.RuntimeException
extends java.lang.Exception
extends java.lang.Throwable
extends java.lang.Object
Constructors
public AccessControlException(String s)
public AccessControlException(String s,
  Permission p)
Methods
public Permission getPermission()

►**ACCESSCONTROLLER**
public final class java.security.
  AccessController
extends java.lang.Object
Constructors
private AccessController()
Methods
public static void checkPermission(
  Permission perm)
public static native Object doPrivileged(
  PrivilegedAction action)
public static native Object doPrivileged(
  PrivilegedAction action,
  AccessControlContext context)
public static native Object doPrivileged(
  PrivilegedExceptionAction action)
public static native Object doPrivileged(
  PrivilegedExceptionAction action,
  AccessControlContext context)
public static AccessControlContext
  getContext()

►**ACCESSEXCEPTION**
public class java.rmi.AccessException
extends java.rmi.RemoteException
extends java.io.IOException
extends java.lang.Exception
extends java.lang.Throwable
extends java.lang.Object
Constructors
public AccessException(String s)
public AccessException(String s,
  Exception ex)

►**ACCESSIBLEBUNDLE**
public abstract class javax.
  accessibility.AccessibleBundle
extends java.lang.Object
Fields
protected java.lang.String key
Methods
protected String toDisplayString(String
  resourceBundleName,Locale locale)
public String toDisplayString(Locale
  locale)
public String toDisplayString()
public String toString()

►**ACCESSIBLECONTEXT**
public abstract class javax.
  accessibility.AccessibleContext
extends java.lang.Object
Fields
protected java.lang.String
  accessibleDescription
protected java.lang.String
  accessibleName
protected javax.accessibility.Accessible
  accessibleParent
public final static java.lang.String
  ACCESSIBLE_ACTIVE_DESCENDANT_PROPERTY

public final static java.lang.String
  ACCESSIBLE_CARET_PROPERTY
public final static java.lang.String
  ACCESSIBLE_CHILD_PROPERTY
public final static java.lang.String
  ACCESSIBLE_DESCRIPTION_PROPERTY
public final static java.lang.String
  ACCESSIBLE_NAME_PROPERTY
public final static java.lang.String
  ACCESSIBLE_SELECTION_PROPERTY
public final static java.lang.String
  ACCESSIBLE_STATE_PROPERTY
public final static java.lang.String
  ACCESSIBLE_TEXT_PROPERTY
public final static java.lang.String
  ACCESSIBLE_VALUE_PROPERTY
public final static java.lang.String
  ACCESSIBLE_VISIBLE_DATA_PROPERTY

Methods
public void addPropertyChangeListener(
  PropertyChangeListener listener)
public void firePropertyChange(String
  propertyName,Object oldValue,Object
  newValue)
public AccessibleAction
  getAccessibleAction()
public abstract Accessible
  getAccessibleChild(int i)
public abstract int
  getAccessibleChildrenCount()
public AccessibleComponent
  getAccessibleComponent()
public String getAccessibleDescription()
public abstract int
  getAccessibleIndexInParent()
public String getAccessibleName()
public Accessible getAccessibleParent()
public abstract AccessibleRole
  getAccessibleRole()
public AccessibleSelection
  getAccessibleSelection()
public abstract AccessibleStateSet
  getAccessibleStateSet()
public AccessibleText getAccessibleText()
public AccessibleValue
  getAccessibleValue()
public abstract Locale getLocale()
public void removePropertyChangeListener(
  PropertyChangeListener listener)
public void setAccessibleDescription(
  String s)
public void setAccessibleName(String s)
public void setAccessibleParent(
  Accessible a)

▶**ACCESSIBLEHYPERLINK**
public abstract class javax.
  accessibility.AccessibleHyperlink
implements javax.accessibility.
  AccessibleAction
extends java.lang.Object

Methods
public abstract boolean
  doAccessibleAction(int i)
public abstract Object
  getAccessibleActionAnchor(int i)
public abstract int
  getAccessibleActionCount()
public abstract String
  getAccessibleActionDescription(int i)
public abstract Object
  getAccessibleActionObject(int i)
public abstract int getEndIndex()
public abstract int getStartIndex()
public abstract boolean isValid()

▶**ACCESSIBLEOBJECT**
public class java.lang.reflect.
  AccessibleObject
extends java.lang.Object

Constructors
protected AccessibleObject()

Methods
public boolean isAccessible()
public static void setAccessible(
  AccessibleObject array,boolean flag)
public void setAccessible(boolean flag)

▶**ACCESSIBLERESOURCEBUNDLE**
public class javax.accessibility.
  AccessibleResourceBundle
extends java.util.ListResourceBundle
extends java.util.ResourceBundle
extends java.lang.Object

Methods
public Object getContents()

▶**ACCESSIBLEROLE**
public class javax.accessibility.
  AccessibleRole
extends javax.accessibility.
  AccessibleBundle
extends java.lang.Object

Fields
public final static javax.accessibility.
  AccessibleRole ALERT
public final static javax.accessibility.
  AccessibleRole AWT_COMPONENT
public final static javax.accessibility.
  AccessibleRole CHECK_BOX
public final static javax.accessibility.
  AccessibleRole COLOR_CHOOSER
public final static javax.accessibility.
  AccessibleRole COLUMN_HEADER
public final static javax.accessibility.
  AccessibleRole COMBO_BOX
public final static javax.accessibility.
  AccessibleRole DESKTOP_ICON
public final static javax.accessibility.
  AccessibleRole DESKTOP_PANE
public final static javax.accessibility.
  AccessibleRole DIALOG

public final static javax.accessibility.
  AccessibleRole DIRECTORY_PANE
public final static javax.accessibility.
  AccessibleRole FILE_CHOOSER
public final static javax.accessibility.
  AccessibleRole FILLER
public final static javax.accessibility.
  AccessibleRole FRAME
public final static javax.accessibility.
  AccessibleRole GLASS_PANE
public final static javax.accessibility.
  AccessibleRole INTERNAL_FRAME
public final static javax.accessibility.
  AccessibleRole LABEL
public final static javax.accessibility.
  AccessibleRole LAYERED_PANE
public final static javax.accessibility.
  AccessibleRole LIST
public final static javax.accessibility.
  AccessibleRole MENU
public final static javax.accessibility.
  AccessibleRole MENU_BAR
public final static javax.accessibility.
  AccessibleRole MENU_ITEM
public final static javax.accessibility.
  AccessibleRole OPTION_PANE
public final static javax.accessibility.
  AccessibleRole PAGE_TAB
public final static javax.accessibility.
  AccessibleRole PAGE_TAB_LIST
public final static javax.accessibility.
  AccessibleRole PANEL
public final static javax.accessibility.
  AccessibleRole PASSWORD_TEXT
public final static javax.accessibility.
  AccessibleRole POPUP_MENU
public final static javax.accessibility.
  AccessibleRole PROGRESS_BAR
public final static javax.accessibility.
  AccessibleRole PUSH_BUTTON
public final static javax.accessibility.
  AccessibleRole RADIO_BUTTON
public final static javax.accessibility.
  AccessibleRole ROOT_PANE
public final static javax.accessibility.
  AccessibleRole ROW_HEADER
public final static javax.accessibility.
  AccessibleRole SCROLL_BAR
public final static javax.accessibility.
  AccessibleRole SCROLL_PANE
public final static javax.accessibility.
  AccessibleRole SEPARATOR
public final static javax.accessibility.
  AccessibleRole SLIDER
public final static javax.accessibility.
  AccessibleRole SPLIT_PANE
public final static javax.accessibility.
  AccessibleRole SWING_COMPONENT
public final static javax.accessibility.
  AccessibleRole TABLE
public final static javax.accessibility.
  AccessibleRole TEXT

public final static javax.accessibility.
  AccessibleRole TOGGLE_BUTTON
public final static javax.accessibility.
  AccessibleRole TOOL_BAR
public final static javax.accessibility.
  AccessibleRole TOOL_TIP
public final static javax.accessibility.
  AccessibleRole TREE
public final static javax.accessibility.
  AccessibleRole UNKNOWN
public final static javax.accessibility.
  AccessibleRole VIEWPORT
public final static javax.accessibility.
  AccessibleRole WINDOW

Constructors
protected AccessibleRole(String key)

▶ACCESSIBLESTATE
public class javax.accessibility.
  AccessibleState
extends javax.accessibility.
  AccessibleBundle
extends java.lang.Object

Fields
public final static javax.accessibility.
  AccessibleState ACTIVE
public final static javax.accessibility.
  AccessibleState ARMED
public final static javax.accessibility.
  AccessibleState BUSY
public final static javax.accessibility.
  AccessibleState CHECKED
public final static javax.accessibility.
  AccessibleState COLLAPSED
public final static javax.accessibility.
  AccessibleState EDITABLE
public final static javax.accessibility.
  AccessibleState ENABLED
public final static javax.accessibility.
  AccessibleState EXPANDABLE
public final static javax.accessibility.
  AccessibleState EXPANDED
public final static javax.accessibility.
  AccessibleState FOCUSABLE
public final static javax.accessibility.
  AccessibleState FOCUSED
public final static javax.accessibility.
  AccessibleState HORIZONTAL
public final static javax.accessibility.
  AccessibleState ICONIFIED
public final static javax.accessibility.
  AccessibleState MODAL
public final static javax.accessibility.
  AccessibleState MULTISELECTABLE
public final static javax.accessibility.
  AccessibleState MULTI_LINE
public final static javax.accessibility.
  AccessibleState OPAQUE
public final static javax.accessibility.
  AccessibleState PRESSED
public final static javax.accessibility.
  AccessibleState RESIZABLE

public final static javax.accessibility.
AccessibleState SELECTABLE
public final static javax.accessibility.
AccessibleState SELECTED
public final static javax.accessibility.
AccessibleState SHOWING
public final static javax.accessibility.
AccessibleState SINGLE_LINE
public final static javax.accessibility.
AccessibleState TRANSIENT
public final static javax.accessibility.
AccessibleState VERTICAL
public final static javax.accessibility.
AccessibleState VISIBLE

Constructors
protected AccessibleState(String key)

►ACCESSIBLESTATESET
public class javax.accessibility.
AccessibleStateSet
extends java.lang.Object

Fields
protected java.util.Vector states

Constructors
public AccessibleStateSet()
public AccessibleStateSet(
AccessibleState states)

Methods
public boolean add(AccessibleState state)
public void addAll(AccessibleState
states)
public void clear()
public boolean contains(AccessibleState
state)
public boolean remove(AccessibleState
state)
public AccessibleState toArray()
public String toString()

►ACLNOTFOUNDEXCEPTION
public class java.security.acl.
AclNotFoundException
extends java.lang.Exception
extends java.lang.Throwable
extends java.lang.Object

Constructors
public AclNotFoundException()

►ACTIONEVENT
public class java.awt.event.ActionEvent
extends java.awt.AWTEvent
extends java.util.EventObject
extends java.lang.Object

Fields
public final static int ACTION_FIRST
public final static int ACTION_LAST
public final static int ACTION_
PERFORMED
public final static int ALT_MASK
public final static int CTRL_MASK
public final static int META_MASK
public final static int SHIFT_MASK

Constructors
public ActionEvent(Object source,int id,
String command)
public ActionEvent(Object source,int id,
String command,int modifiers)

Methods
public String getActionCommand()
public int getModifiers()
public String paramString()

►ACTIVATABLE
public abstract class java.rmi.
activation.Activatable
extends java.rmi.server.RemoteServer
extends java.rmi.server.RemoteObject
extends java.lang.Object

Constructors
protected Activatable(String location,
MarshalledObject data,boolean restart,
int port)
protected Activatable(String location,
MarshalledObject data,boolean restart,
int port,RMIClientSocketFactory csf,
RMIServerSocketFactory ssf)
protected Activatable(ActivationID id,
int port)
protected Activatable(ActivationID id,
int port,RMIClientSocketFactory csf,
RMIServerSocketFactory ssf)

Methods
public static ActivationID exportObject(
Remote obj,String location,
MarshalledObject data,boolean restart,
int port)
public static ActivationID exportObject(
Remote obj,String location,
MarshalledObject data,boolean restart,
int port,RMIClientSocketFactory csf,
RMIServerSocketFactory ssf)
public static Remote exportObject(Remote
obj,ActivationID id,int port)
public static Remote exportObject(Remote
obj,ActivationID id,int port,
RMIClientSocketFactory csf,
RMIServerSocketFactory ssf)
protected ActivationID getID()
public static boolean inactive(
ActivationID id)
public static Remote register(
ActivationDesc desc)
public static boolean unexportObject(
Remote obj,boolean force)
public static void unregister(
ActivationID id)

►ACTIVATEFAILEDEXCEPTION
public class java.rmi.activation.
ActivateFailedException
extends java.rmi.RemoteException
extends java.io.IOException
extends java.lang.Exception
extends java.lang.Throwable

extends java.lang.Object

Constructors

public ActivateFailedException(String s)

public ActivateFailedException(String s, Exception ex)

►**ACTIVATIONDESC**

public final class java.rmi.activation. ActivationDesc

implements java.io.Serializable

extends java.lang.Object

Constructors

public ActivationDesc(String className, String location,MarshalledObject data)

public ActivationDesc(String className, String location,MarshalledObject data, boolean restart)

public ActivationDesc(ActivationGroupID groupID,String className,String location, MarshalledObject data)

public ActivationDesc(ActivationGroupID groupID,String className,String location, MarshalledObject data,boolean restart)

Methods

public boolean equals(Object obj)

public String getClassName()

public MarshalledObject getData()

public ActivationGroupID getGroupID()

public String getLocation()

public boolean getRestartMode()

public int hashCode()

►**ACTIVATIONEXCEPTION**

public class java.rmi.activation. ActivationException

extends java.lang.Exception

extends java.lang.Throwable

extends java.lang.Object

Fields

public java.lang.Throwable detail

Constructors

public ActivationException()

public ActivationException(String s)

public ActivationException(String s, Throwable ex)

Methods

public String getMessage()

public void printStackTrace(PrintStream ps)

public void printStackTrace()

public void printStackTrace(PrintWriter pw)

►**ACTIVATIONGROUP**

public abstract class java.rmi. activation.ActivationGroup

implements java.rmi.activation. ActivationInstantiator

extends java.rmi.server. UnicastRemoteObject

extends java.rmi.server.RemoteServer

extends java.rmi.server.RemoteObject

extends java.lang.Object

Constructors

protected ActivationGroup(ActivationGroupID groupID)

Methods

public abstract void activeObject(ActivationID id,Remote obj)

protected void activeObject(ActivationID id,MarshalledObject mobj)

public static synchronized ActivationGroup createGroup(ActivationGroupID id,ActivationGroupDesc desc,long incarnation)

public static synchronized ActivationGroupID currentGroupID()

public static synchronized ActivationSystem getSystem()

protected void inactiveGroup()

public boolean inactiveObject(ActivationID id)

public static synchronized void setSystem(ActivationSystem system)

►**ACTIVATIONGROUPDESC**

public final class java.rmi.activation. ActivationGroupDesc

implements java.io.Serializable

extends java.lang.Object

Constructors

public ActivationGroupDesc(Properties overrides,CommandEnvironment cmd)

public ActivationGroupDesc(String className,String location, MarshalledObject data,Properties overrides,CommandEnvironment cmd)

Methods

public boolean equals(Object obj)

public String getClassName()

public CommandEnvironment getCommandEnvironment()

public MarshalledObject getData()

public String getLocation()

public Properties getPropertyOverrides()

public int hashCode()

►**ACTIVATIONGROUPID**

public class java.rmi.activation. ActivationGroupID

implements java.io.Serializable

extends java.lang.Object

Constructors

public ActivationGroupID(ActivationSystem system)

Methods

public boolean equals(Object obj)

public ActivationSystem getSystem()

public int hashCode()

►**ACTIVATIONID**

public class java.rmi.activation. ActivationID

implements java.io.Serializable

extends java.lang.Object

Constructors

public ActivationID(Activator activator)

Methods

public Remote activate(boolean force)
public boolean equals(Object obj)
public int hashCode()

►**AdjustmentEvent**

public class java.awt.event.
  AdjustmentEvent
extends java.awt.AWTEvent
extends java.util.EventObject
extends java.lang.Object

Fields

public final static int ADJUSTMENT_
  FIRST
public final static int ADJUSTMENT_LAST
public final static int ADJUSTMENT_VALUE_
  CHANGED
public final static int BLOCK_DECREMENT
public final static int BLOCK_INCREMENT
public final static int TRACK
public final static int UNIT_DECREMENT
public final static int UNIT_INCREMENT

Constructors

public AdjustmentEvent(Adjustable
  source,int id,int type,int value)

Methods

public Adjustable getAdjustable()
public int getAdjustmentType()
public int getValue()
public String paramString()

►**Adler32**

public class java.util.zip.Adler32
implements java.util.zip.Checksum
extends java.lang.Object

Constructors

public static Adler32()

Methods

public long getValue()
public void reset()
public void update(int b)
public void update(byte b,int off,int
  len)
public void update(byte b)

►**AffineTransform**

public class java.awt.geom.
  AffineTransform
implements java.lang.Cloneable
implements java.io.Serializable
extends java.lang.Object

Fields

public final static int TYPE_FLIP
public final static int TYPE_GENERAL_
  ROTATION
public final static int TYPE_GENERAL_
  SCALE
public final static int TYPE_GENERAL_
  TRANSFORM

public final static int TYPE_IDENTITY
public final static int TYPE_MASK_
  ROTATION
public final static int TYPE_MASK_SCALE
public final static int TYPE_QUADRANT_
  ROTATION
public final static int TYPE_
  TRANSLATION
public final static int TYPE_UNIFORM_
  SCALE

Constructors

private AffineTransform()
public AffineTransform()
public AffineTransform(AffineTransform
  Tx)
public AffineTransform(float m00,float
  m10,float m01,float m11,float m02,float
  m12)
public AffineTransform(float flatmatrix)
public AffineTransform(double m00,
  double m10,double m01,double m11,double
  m02,double m12)
public AffineTransform(double
  flatmatrix)

Methods

public Object clone()
public void concatenate(AffineTransform
  Tx)
public AffineTransform createInverse()
public Shape createTransformedShape(
  Shape pSrc)
public Point2D deltaTransform(Point2D
  ptSrc,Point2D ptDst)
public void deltaTransform(double srcPts,
  int srcOff,double dstPts,int dstOff,int
  numPts)
public boolean equals(Object obj)
public double getDeterminant()
public void getMatrix(double flatmatrix)
public static AffineTransform
  getRotateInstance(double theta)
public static AffineTransform
  getRotateInstance(double theta,double x,
  double y)
public static AffineTransform
  getScaleInstance(double sx,double sy)
public double getScaleX()
public double getScaleY()
public static AffineTransform
  getShearInstance(double shx,double shy)
public double getShearX()
public double getShearY()
public static AffineTransform
  getTranslateInstance(double tx,double ty)
public double getTranslateX()
public double getTranslateY()
public int getType()
public int hashCode()
public Point2D inverseTransform(Point2D
  ptSrc,Point2D ptDst)

```
public void inverseTransform(double
  srcPts,int srcOff,double dstPts,int
  dstOff,int numPts)
public boolean isIdentity()
public void preConcatenate(
  AffineTransform Tx)
public void rotate(double theta)
public void rotate(double theta,double x,
  double y)
public void scale(double sx,double sy)
public void setToIdentity()
public void setToRotation(double theta)
public void setToRotation(double theta,
  double x,double y)
public void setToScale(double sx,double
  sy)
public void setToShear(double shx,double
  shy)
public void setToTranslation(double tx,
  double ty)
public void setTransform(AffineTransform
  Tx)
public void setTransform(double m00,
  double m10,double m01,double m11,double
  m02,double m12)
public void shear(double shx,double shy)
public String toString()
public Point2D transform(Point2D ptSrc,
  Point2D ptDst)
public void transform(Point2D ptSrc,int
  srcOff,Point2D ptDst,int dstOff,int
  numPts)
public void transform(float srcPts,int
  srcOff,float dstPts,int dstOff,int
  numPts)
public void transform(double srcPts,int
  srcOff,double dstPts,int dstOff,int
  numPts)
public void transform(float srcPts,int
  srcOff,double dstPts,int dstOff,int
  numPts)
public void transform(double srcPts,int
  srcOff,float dstPts,int dstOff,int
  numPts)
public void translate(double tx,double
  ty)
```

►AFFINETRANSFORMOP
```
public class java.awt.image.
  AffineTransformOp
implements java.awt.image.
  BufferedImageOp
implements java.awt.image.RasterOp
extends java.lang.Object
```
Fields
```
public final static int TYPE_BILINEAR
public final static int TYPE_NEAREST_
  NEIGHBOR
```
Constructors
```
public AffineTransformOp(
  AffineTransform xform,RenderingHints
  hints)
```
```
public AffineTransformOp(
  AffineTransform xform,int
  interpolationType)
```
Methods
```
public BufferedImage
  createCompatibleDestImage(BufferedImage
  src,ColorModel destCM)
public WritableRaster
  createCompatibleDestRaster(Raster src)
public final BufferedImage filter(
  BufferedImage src,BufferedImage dst)
public final WritableRaster filter(
  Raster src,WritableRaster dst)
public final Rectangle2D getBounds2D(
  BufferedImage src)
public final Rectangle2D getBounds2D(
  Raster src)
public final int getInterpolationType()
public final Point2D getPoint2D(Point2D
  srcPt,Point2D dstPt)
public final RenderingHints
  getRenderingHints()
public final AffineTransform
  getTransform()
```

►ALGORITHMPARAMETERGENERATOR
```
public class java.security.
  AlgorithmParameterGenerator
extends java.lang.Object
```
Constructors
```
protected AlgorithmParameterGenerator(
  AlgorithmParameterGeneratorSpi
  paramGenSpi,Provider provider,String
  algorithm)
```
Methods
```
public final AlgorithmParameters
  generateParameters()
public final String getAlgorithm()
public static
  AlgorithmParameterGenerator getInstance(
  String algorithm)
public static
  AlgorithmParameterGenerator getInstance(
  String algorithm,String provider)
public final Provider getProvider()
public final void init(int size)
public final void init(int size,
  SecureRandom random)
public final void init(
  AlgorithmParameterSpec genParamSpec)
public final void init(
  AlgorithmParameterSpec genParamSpec,
  SecureRandom random)
```

►ALGORITHMPARAMETERGENERATORSPI
```
public abstract class java.security.
  AlgorithmParameterGeneratorSpi
extends java.lang.Object
```
Methods
```
protected abstract AlgorithmParameters
  engineGenerateParameters()
```

```
protected abstract void engineInit(int
  size,SecureRandom random)
protected abstract void engineInit(
  AlgorithmParameterSpec genParamSpec,
  SecureRandom random)
```

►ALGORITHMPARAMETERS
```
public class java.security.
  AlgorithmParameters
extends java.lang.Object
```
Constructors
```
protected AlgorithmParameters(
  AlgorithmParametersSpi paramSpi,Provider
  provider,String algorithm)
```
Methods
```
public final String getAlgorithm()
public final byte getEncoded()
public final byte getEncoded(String
  format)
public static AlgorithmParameters
  getInstance(String algorithm)
public static AlgorithmParameters
  getInstance(String algorithm,String
  provider)
public final AlgorithmParameterSpec
  getParameterSpec(Class paramSpec)
public final Provider getProvider()
public final void init(
  AlgorithmParameterSpec paramSpec)
public final void init(byte params)
public final void init(byte params,
  String format)
public final String toString()
```

►ALGORITHMPARAMETERSSPI
```
public abstract class java.security.
  AlgorithmParametersSpi
extends java.lang.Object
```
Methods
```
protected abstract byte engineGetEncoded(
  )
protected abstract byte engineGetEncoded(
  String format)
protected abstract
  AlgorithmParameterSpec
  engineGetParameterSpec(Class paramSpec)
protected abstract void engineInit(
  AlgorithmParameterSpec paramSpec)
protected abstract void engineInit(byte
  params)
protected abstract void engineInit(byte
  params,String format)
protected abstract String engineToString(
  )
```

►ALLPERMISSION
```
public final class java.security.
  AllPermission
extends java.security.Permission
extends java.lang.Object
```
Constructors
```
public AllPermission()
```
```
public AllPermission(String name,String
  actions)
```
Methods
```
public boolean equals(Object obj)
public String getActions()
public int hashCode()
public boolean implies(Permission p)
public PermissionCollection
  newPermissionCollection()
```

►ALPHACOMPOSITE
```
public final class java.awt.
  AlphaComposite
implements java.awt.Composite
extends java.lang.Object
```
Fields
```
public final static int CLEAR
public final static java.awt.
  AlphaComposite Clear
public final static java.awt.
  AlphaComposite DstIn
public final static java.awt.
  AlphaComposite DstOut
public final static java.awt.
  AlphaComposite DstOver
public final static int DST_IN
public final static int DST_OUT
public final static int DST_OVER
public final static int SRC
public final static java.awt.
  AlphaComposite Src
public final static java.awt.
  AlphaComposite SrcIn
public final static java.awt.
  AlphaComposite SrcOut
public final static java.awt.
  AlphaComposite SrcOver
public final static int SRC_IN
public final static int SRC_OUT
public final static int SRC_OVER
```
Constructors
```
private AlphaComposite()
private AlphaComposite()
```
Methods
```
public CompositeContext createContext(
  ColorModel srcColorModel,ColorModel
  dstColorModel,RenderingHints hints)
public boolean equals(Object obj)
public float getAlpha()
public static AlphaComposite getInstance(
  int rule)
public static AlphaComposite getInstance(
  int rule,float alpha)
public int getRule()
public int hashCode()
```

►ALREADYBOUNDEXCEPTION
```
public class java.rmi.
  AlreadyBoundException
extends java.lang.Exception
extends java.lang.Throwable
extends java.lang.Object
```

Constructors

```
public  AlreadyBoundException()
public  AlreadyBoundException(String s)
```

►ANCESTOREVENT

```
public class javax.swing.event.
  AncestorEvent
extends java.awt.AWTEvent
extends java.util.EventObject
extends java.lang.Object
```

Fields

```
public final static int ANCESTOR_ADDED
public final static int ANCESTOR_MOVED
public final static int ANCESTOR_
  REMOVED
```

Constructors

```
public  AncestorEvent(JComponent source,
  int id,Container ancestor,Container
  ancestorParent)
```

Methods

```
public Container getAncestor()
public Container getAncestorParent()
public JComponent getComponent()
```

►ANNOTATION

```
public class java.text.Annotation
extends java.lang.Object
```

Constructors

```
public  Annotation(Object value)
```

Methods

```
public Object getValue()
public String toString()
```

►APPLET

```
public class java.applet.Applet
extends java.awt.Panel
extends java.awt.Container
extends java.awt.Component
extends java.lang.Object
```

Methods

```
public void destroy()
public AppletContext getAppletContext()
public String getAppletInfo()
public AudioClip getAudioClip(URL url)
public AudioClip getAudioClip(URL url,
  String name)
public URL getCodeBase()
public URL getDocumentBase()
public Image getImage(URL url)
public Image getImage(URL url,String
  name)
public Locale getLocale()
public String getParameter(String name)
public String getParameterInfo()
public void init()
public boolean isActive()
public final static AudioClip
  newAudioClip(URL url)
public void play(URL url)
public void play(URL url,String name)
public void resize(int width,int height)
public void resize(Dimension d)
```

```
public final void setStub(AppletStub
  stub)
public void showStatus(String msg)
public void start()
public void stop()
```

►ARC2D

```
public abstract class java.awt.geom.
  Arc2D
extends java.awt.geom.RectangularShape
extends java.lang.Object
```

Fields

```
public final static int CHORD
public final static int OPEN
public final static int PIE
```

Constructors

```
protected  Arc2D(int type)
```

Methods

```
public boolean contains(double x,double
  y)
public boolean contains(double x,double
  y,double w,double h)
public boolean contains(Rectangle2D r)
public boolean containsAngle(double
  angle)
public abstract double getAngleExtent()
public abstract double getAngleStart()
public int getArcType()
public Rectangle2D getBounds2D()
public Point2D getEndPoint()
public PathIterator getPathIterator(
  AffineTransform at)
public Point2D getStartPoint()
public boolean intersects(double x,
  double y,double w,double h)
protected abstract Rectangle2D
  makeBounds(double x,double y,double w,
  double h)
public abstract void setAngleExtent(
  double angExt)
public void setAngles(double x1,double
  y1,double x2,double y2)
public void setAngles(Point2D p1,Point2D
  p2)
public abstract void setAngleStart(
  double angSt)
public void setAngleStart(Point2D p)
public abstract void setArc(double x,
  double y,double w,double h,double angSt,
  double angExt,int closure)
public void setArc(Point2D loc,
  Dimension2D size,double angSt,double
  angExt,int closure)
public void setArc(Rectangle2D rect,
  double angSt,double angExt,int closure)
public void setArc(Arc2D a)
public void setArcByCenter(double x,
  double y,double radius,double angSt,
  double angExt,int closure)
public void setArcByTangent(Point2D p1,
  Point2D p2,Point2D p3,double radius)
public void setArcType(int type)
```

```
public void setFrame(double x,double y,
  double w,double h)
```

►AREA
public class java.awt.geom.Area
implements java.lang.Cloneable
implements java.awt.Shape
extends java.lang.Object

Constructors
public Area()
public Area(Shape g)
 Area()

Methods
public void add(Area rhs)
public Object clone()
public boolean contains(double x,double
  y)
public boolean contains(Point2D p)
public boolean contains(double x,double
  y,double w,double h)
public boolean contains(Rectangle2D r)
public Area createTransformedArea(
  AffineTransform t)
public boolean equals(Area rhs)
public void exclusiveOr(Area rhs)
public Rectangle getBounds()
public Rectangle2D getBounds2D()
public PathIterator getPathIterator(
  AffineTransform t)
public PathIterator getPathIterator(
  AffineTransform t,double f)
public void intersect(Area rhs)
public boolean intersects(double x,
  double y,double w,double h)
public boolean intersects(Rectangle2D r)
public boolean isEmpty()
public boolean isPolygonal()
public boolean isRectangular()
public boolean isSingular()
public void reset()
public void subtract(Area rhs)
public void transform(AffineTransform t)

►AREAAVERAGINGSCALEFILTER
public class java.awt.image.
  AreaAveragingScaleFilter
extends java.awt.image.
  ReplicateScaleFilter
extends java.awt.image.ImageFilter
extends java.lang.Object

Constructors
public AreaAveragingScaleFilter(int
  width,int height)

Methods
public void setHints(int hints)
public void setPixels(int x,int y,int w,
  int h,ColorModel model,byte pixels,int
  off,int scansize)
public void setPixels(int x,int y,int w,
  int h,ColorModel model,int pixels,int
  off,int scansize)

►ARITHMETICEXCEPTION
public class java.lang.
  ArithmeticException
extends java.lang.RuntimeException
extends java.lang.Exception
extends java.lang.Throwable
extends java.lang.Object

Constructors
public ArithmeticException()
public ArithmeticException(String s)

►ARRAY
public final class java.lang.reflect.
  Array
extends java.lang.Object

Constructors
private Array()

Methods
public static native Object get(Object
  array,int index)
public static native boolean getBoolean(
  Object array,int index)
public static native byte getByte(Object
  array,int index)
public static native char getChar(Object
  array,int index)
public static native double getDouble(
  Object array,int index)
public static native float getFloat(
  Object array,int index)
public static native int getInt(Object
  array,int index)
public static native int getLength(
  Object array)
public static native long getLong(Object
  array,int index)
public static native short getShort(
  Object array,int index)
public static Object newInstance(Class
  componentType,int length)
public static Object newInstance(Class
  componentType,int dimensions)
public static native void set(Object
  array,int index,Object value)
public static native void setBoolean(
  Object array,int index,boolean z)
public static native void setByte(Object
  array,int index,byte b)
public static native void setChar(Object
  array,int index,char c)
public static native void setDouble(
  Object array,int index,double d)
public static native void setFloat(
  Object array,int index,float f)
public static native void setInt(Object
  array,int index,int i)
public static native void setLong(Object
  array,int index,long l)
public static native void setShort(
  Object array,int index,short s)
```
```

▶**ARRAYINDEXOUTOFBOUNDSEXCEPTION**
public class java.lang.
   ArrayIndexOutOfBoundsException
extends java.lang.
   IndexOutOfBoundsException
extends java.lang.RuntimeException
extends java.lang.Exception
extends java.lang.Throwable
extends java.lang.Object

Constructors
public ArrayIndexOutOfBoundsException()
public ArrayIndexOutOfBoundsException(
   int index)
public ArrayIndexOutOfBoundsException(
   String s)

▶**ARRAYLIST**
public class java.util.ArrayList
implements java.lang.Cloneable
implements java.util.List
implements java.io.Serializable
extends java.util.AbstractList
extends java.util.AbstractCollection
extends java.lang.Object

Constructors
public ArrayList(int initialCapacity)
public ArrayList()
public ArrayList(Collection c)

Methods
public boolean add(Object o)
public void add(int index,Object element)
public boolean addAll(Collection c)
public boolean addAll(int index,
   Collection c)
public void clear()
public Object clone()
public boolean contains(Object elem)
public void ensureCapacity(int
   minCapacity)
public Object get(int index)
public int indexOf(Object elem)
public boolean isEmpty()
public int lastIndexOf(Object elem)
public Object remove(int index)
protected void removeRange(int fromIndex,
   int toIndex)
public Object set(int index,Object
   element)
public int size()
public Object toArray()
public Object toArray(Object a)
public void trimToSize()

▶**ARRAYS**
public class java.util.Arrays
extends java.lang.Object

Constructors
private Arrays()

Methods
public static List asList(Object a)
public static int binarySearch(long a,
   long key)

public static int binarySearch(int a,int
   key)
public static int binarySearch(short a,
   short key)
public static int binarySearch(char a,
   char key)
public static int binarySearch(byte a,
   byte key)
public static int binarySearch(double a,
   double key)
public static int binarySearch(float a,
   float key)
public static int binarySearch(Object a,
   Object key)
public static int binarySearch(Object a,
   Object key,Comparator c)
public static boolean equals(long a,long
   a2)
public static boolean equals(int a,int
   a2)
public static boolean equals(short a,
   short a2)
public static boolean equals(char a,char
   a2)
public static boolean equals(byte a,byte
   a2)
public static boolean equals(boolean a,
   boolean a2)
public static boolean equals(double a,
   double a2)
public static boolean equals(float a,
   float a2)
public static boolean equals(Object a,
   Object a2)
public static void fill(long a,long val)
public static void fill(long a,int
   fromIndex,int toIndex,long val)
public static void fill(int a,int val)
public static void fill(int a,int
   fromIndex,int toIndex,int val)
public static void fill(short a,short
   val)
public static void fill(short a,int
   fromIndex,int toIndex,short val)
public static void fill(char a,char val)
public static void fill(char a,int
   fromIndex,int toIndex,char val)
public static void fill(byte a,byte val)
public static void fill(byte a,int
   fromIndex,int toIndex,byte val)
public static void fill(boolean a,
   boolean val)
public static void fill(boolean a,int
   fromIndex,int toIndex,boolean val)
public static void fill(double a,double
   val)
public static void fill(double a,int
   fromIndex,int toIndex,double val)
public static void fill(float a,float
   val)
public static void fill(float a,int
   fromIndex,int toIndex,float val)

```
public static void fill(Object a,Object
  val)
public static void fill(Object a,int
  fromIndex,int toIndex,Object val)
public static void sort(long a)
public static void sort(long a,int
  fromIndex,int toIndex)
public static void sort(int a)
public static void sort(int a,int
  fromIndex,int toIndex)
public static void sort(short a)
public static void sort(short a,int
  fromIndex,int toIndex)
public static void sort(char a)
public static void sort(char a,int
  fromIndex,int toIndex)
public static void sort(byte a)
public static void sort(byte a,int
  fromIndex,int toIndex)
public static void sort(double a)
public static void sort(double a,int
  fromIndex,int toIndex)
public static void sort(float a)
public static void sort(float a,int
  fromIndex,int toIndex)
public static void sort(Object a)
public static void sort(Object a,int
  fromIndex,int toIndex)
public static void sort(Object a,
  Comparator c)
public static void sort(Object a,int
  fromIndex,int toIndex,Comparator c)
```

►ARRAYSTOREEXCEPTION
```
public class java.lang.
  ArrayStoreException
extends java.lang.RuntimeException
extends java.lang.Exception
extends java.lang.Throwable
extends java.lang.Object
```
Constructors
```
public  ArrayStoreException()
public  ArrayStoreException(String s)
```

►ATTRIBUTEDSTRING
```
public class java.text.AttributedString
extends java.lang.Object
```
Constructors
```
public  AttributedString(String text)
public  AttributedString(String text,Map
  attributes)
public  AttributedString(
  AttributedCharacterIterator text)
public  AttributedString(
  AttributedCharacterIterator text,int
  beginIndex,int endIndex)
public  AttributedString(
  AttributedCharacterIterator text,int
  beginIndex,int endIndex,Attribute
  attributes)
```

Methods
```
public void addAttribute(Attribute
  attribute,Object value)
public void addAttribute(Attribute
  attribute,Object value,int beginIndex,
  int endIndex)
public void addAttributes(Map attributes,
  int beginIndex,int endIndex)
public AttributedCharacterIterator
  getIterator()
public AttributedCharacterIterator
  getIterator(Attribute attributes)
public AttributedCharacterIterator
  getIterator(Attribute attributes,int
  beginIndex,int endIndex)
```

►ATTRIBUTELIST
```
public final class javax.swing.text.html.
  parser.AttributeList
implements javax.swing.text.html.parser.
  DTDConstants
implements java.io.Serializable
extends java.lang.Object
```
Fields
```
public int modifier
public java.lang.String name
public javax.swing.text.html.parser.
  AttributeList next
public int type
public java.lang.String value
public java.util.Vector values
```
Constructors
```
 AttributeList()
public  AttributeList(String name)
public  AttributeList(String name,int
  type,int modifier,String value,Vector
  values,AttributeList next)
```
Methods
```
public int getModifier()
public String getName()
public AttributeList getNext()
public int getType()
public String getValue()
public Enumeration getValues()
public static int name2type(String nm)
public String toString()
public static String type2name(int tp)
```

►ATTRIBUTES
```
public class java.util.jar.Attributes
implements java.lang.Cloneable
implements java.util.Map
extends java.lang.Object
```
Fields
```
protected java.util.Map map
```
Constructors
```
public  Attributes()
public  Attributes(int size)
public  Attributes(Attributes attr)
```
Methods
```
public void clear()
public Object clone()
```

```
public boolean containsKey(Object name)
public boolean containsValue(Object
  value)
public Set entrySet()
public boolean equals(Object o)
public Object get(Object name)
public String getValue(String name)
public String getValue(Name name)
public int hashCode()
public boolean isEmpty()
public Set keySet()
public Object put(Object name,Object
  value)
public void putAll(Map attr)
public String putValue(String name,
  String value)
public Object remove(Object name)
public int size()
public Collection values()
```

►Authenticator

```
public abstract class java.net.
  Authenticator
extends java.lang.Object
```

Methods
```
protected PasswordAuthentication
  getPasswordAuthentication()
protected final int getRequestingPort()
protected final String
  getRequestingPrompt()
protected final String
  getRequestingProtocol()
protected final String
  getRequestingScheme()
protected final InetAddress
  getRequestingSite()
public static PasswordAuthentication
  requestPasswordAuthentication(
  InetAddress addr,int port,String
  protocol,String prompt,String scheme)
public static synchronized void
  setDefault(Authenticator a)
```

►AWTError

```
public class java.awt.AWTError
extends java.lang.Error
extends java.lang.Throwable
extends java.lang.Object
```

Constructors
```
public  AWTError(String msg)
```

►AWTEvent

```
public abstract class java.awt.AWTEvent
extends java.util.EventObject
extends java.lang.Object
```

Fields
```
public final static long ACTION_EVENT_
  MASK
public final static long ADJUSTMENT_
  EVENT_MASK
public final static long COMPONENT_EVENT_
  MASK
```

```
protected boolean consumed
public final static long CONTAINER_EVENT_
  MASK
public final static long FOCUS_EVENT_
  MASK
protected int id
public final static long INPUT_METHOD_
  EVENT_MASK
public final static long ITEM_EVENT_
  MASK
public final static long KEY_EVENT_MASK
public final static long MOUSE_EVENT_
  MASK
public final static long MOUSE_MOTION_
  EVENT_MASK
public final static int RESERVED_ID_MAX
public final static long TEXT_EVENT_
  MASK
public final static long WINDOW_EVENT_
  MASK
```

Constructors
```
public  AWTEvent(Event event)
public  AWTEvent(Object source,int id)
```

Methods
```
protected void consume()
protected void finalize()
public int getID()
protected boolean isConsumed()
public String paramString()
public String toString()
```

►AWTEventMulticaster

```
public class java.awt.
  AWTEventMulticaster
implements java.awt.event.
  ActionListener
implements java.awt.event.
  AdjustmentListener
implements java.awt.event.
  ComponentListener
implements java.awt.event.
  ContainerListener
implements java.awt.event.FocusListener
implements java.awt.event.
  InputMethodListener
implements java.awt.event.ItemListener
implements java.awt.event.KeyListener
implements java.awt.event.MouseListener
implements java.awt.event.
  MouseMotionListener
implements java.awt.event.TextListener
implements java.awt.event.
  WindowListener
extends java.lang.Object
```

Fields
```
protected final java.util.EventListener
  a
```

Constructors
```
protected  AWTEventMulticaster(
  EventListener a,EventListener b)
```

Methods

public void actionPerformed(ActionEvent
  e)
public static ComponentListener add(
  ComponentListener a,ComponentListener b)
public static ContainerListener add(
  ContainerListener a,ContainerListener b)
public static FocusListener add(
  FocusListener a,FocusListener b)
public static KeyListener add(
  KeyListener a,KeyListener b)
public static MouseListener add(
  MouseListener a,MouseListener b)
public static MouseMotionListener add(
  MouseMotionListener a,
  MouseMotionListener b)
public static WindowListener add(
  WindowListener a,WindowListener b)
public static ActionListener add(
  ActionListener a,ActionListener b)
public static ItemListener add(
  ItemListener a,ItemListener b)
public static AdjustmentListener add(
  AdjustmentListener a,AdjustmentListener
  b)
public static TextListener add(
  TextListener a,TextListener b)
public static InputMethodListener add(
  InputMethodListener a,
  InputMethodListener b)
protected static EventListener
  addInternal(EventListener a,
  EventListener b)
public void adjustmentValueChanged(
  AdjustmentEvent e)
public void caretPositionChanged(
  InputMethodEvent e)
public void componentAdded(
  ContainerEvent e)
public void componentHidden(
  ComponentEvent e)
public void componentMoved(
  ComponentEvent e)
public void componentRemoved(
  ContainerEvent e)
public void componentResized(
  ComponentEvent e)
public void componentShown(
  ComponentEvent e)
public void focusGained(FocusEvent e)
public void focusLost(FocusEvent e)
public void inputMethodTextChanged(
  InputMethodEvent e)
public void itemStateChanged(ItemEvent e)
public void keyPressed(KeyEvent e)
public void keyReleased(KeyEvent e)
public void keyTyped(KeyEvent e)
public void mouseClicked(MouseEvent e)
public void mouseDragged(MouseEvent e)
public void mouseEntered(MouseEvent e)
public void mouseExited(MouseEvent e)
public void mouseMoved(MouseEvent e)
public void mousePressed(MouseEvent e)

public void mouseReleased(MouseEvent e)
protected EventListener remove(
  EventListener oldl)
public static ComponentListener remove(
  ComponentListener l,ComponentListener
  oldl)
public static ContainerListener remove(
  ContainerListener l,ContainerListener
  oldl)
public static FocusListener remove(
  FocusListener l,FocusListener oldl)
public static KeyListener remove(
  KeyListener l,KeyListener oldl)
public static MouseListener remove(
  MouseListener l,MouseListener oldl)
public static MouseMotionListener remove(
  MouseMotionListener l,
  MouseMotionListener oldl)
public static WindowListener remove(
  WindowListener l,WindowListener oldl)
public static ActionListener remove(
  ActionListener l,ActionListener oldl)
public static ItemListener remove(
  ItemListener l,ItemListener oldl)
public static AdjustmentListener remove(
  AdjustmentListener l,AdjustmentListener
  oldl)
public static TextListener remove(
  TextListener l,TextListener oldl)
public static InputMethodListener remove(
  InputMethodListener l,
  InputMethodListener oldl)
protected static EventListener
  removeInternal(EventListener l,
  EventListener oldl)
protected static void save(
  ObjectOutputStream s,String k,
  EventListener l)
protected void saveInternal(
  ObjectOutputStream s,String k)
public void textValueChanged(TextEvent e)
public void windowActivated(WindowEvent
  e)
public void windowClosed(WindowEvent e)
public void windowClosing(WindowEvent e)
public void windowDeactivated(
  WindowEvent e)
public void windowDeiconified(
  WindowEvent e)
public void windowIconified(WindowEvent
  e)
public void windowOpened(WindowEvent e)

▶**AWTEXCEPTION**

public class java.awt.AWTException
extends java.lang.Exception
extends java.lang.Throwable
extends java.lang.Object

Constructors

public AWTException(String msg)

▶**AWTPERMISSION**
public final class java.awt.
  AWTPermission
extends java.security.BasicPermission
extends java.security.Permission
extends java.lang.Object
Constructors
public AWTPermission(String name)
public AWTPermission(String name,String
  actions)

▶**BADLOCATIONEXCEPTION**
public class javax.swing.text.
  BadLocationException
extends java.lang.Exception
extends java.lang.Throwable
extends java.lang.Object
Constructors
public BadLocationException(String s,
  int offs)
Methods
public int offsetRequested()

▶**BANDCOMBINEOP**
public class java.awt.image.
  BandCombineOp
implements java.awt.image.RasterOp
extends java.lang.Object
Constructors
public BandCombineOp(float matrix,
  RenderingHints hints)
Methods
public WritableRaster
  createCompatibleDestRaster(Raster src)
public WritableRaster filter(Raster src,
  WritableRaster dst)
public final Rectangle2D getBounds2D(
  Raster src)
public final float getMatrix()
public final Point2D getPoint2D(Point2D
  srcPt,Point2D dstPt)
public final RenderingHints
  getRenderingHints()

▶**BANDEDSAMPLEMODEL**
public final class java.awt.image.
  BandedSampleModel
extends java.awt.image.
  ComponentSampleModel
extends java.awt.image.SampleModel
extends java.lang.Object
Constructors
public BandedSampleModel(int dataType,
  int w,int h,int numBands)
public BandedSampleModel(int dataType,
  int w,int h,int scanlineStride,int
  bankIndices,int bandOffsets)
Methods
public SampleModel
  createCompatibleSampleModel(int w,int h)
public DataBuffer createDataBuffer()

public SampleModel
  createSubsetSampleModel(int bands)
public Object getDataElements(int x,int
  y,Object obj,DataBuffer data)
public int getPixel(int x,int y,int
  iArray,DataBuffer data)
public int getPixels(int x,int y,int w,
  int h,int iArray,DataBuffer data)
public int getSample(int x,int y,int b,
  DataBuffer data)
public int getSamples(int x,int y,int w,
  int h,int b,int iArray,DataBuffer data)
public void setDataElements(int x,int y,
  Object obj,DataBuffer data)
public void setPixel(int x,int y,int
  iArray,DataBuffer data)
public void setPixels(int x,int y,int w,
  int h,int iArray,DataBuffer data)
public void setSample(int x,int y,int b,
  int s,DataBuffer data)
public void setSamples(int x,int y,int w,
  int h,int b,int iArray,DataBuffer data)

▶**BASICARROWBUTTON**
public class javax.swing.plaf.basic.
  BasicArrowButton
implements javax.swing.SwingConstants
extends javax.swing.JButton
extends javax.swing.AbstractButton
extends javax.swing.JComponent
extends java.awt.Container
extends java.awt.Component
extends java.lang.Object
Fields
protected int direction
Constructors
public BasicArrowButton(int direction)
Methods
public int getDirection()
public Dimension getMaximumSize()
public Dimension getMinimumSize()
public Dimension getPreferredSize()
public boolean isFocusTraversable()
public void paint(Graphics g)
public void paintTriangle(Graphics g,int
  x,int y,int size,int direction,boolean
  isEnabled)
public void setDirection(int dir)

▶**BASICBORDERS**
public class javax.swing.plaf.basic.
  BasicBorders
extends java.lang.Object

▶**BASICBUTTONLISTENER**
public class javax.swing.plaf.basic.
  BasicButtonListener
implements javax.swing.event.
  ChangeListener
implements java.awt.event.FocusListener
implements java.awt.event.MouseListener

implements java.awt.event.
  MouseMotionListener
implements java.beans.
  PropertyChangeListener
extends java.lang.Object

Constructors
public BasicButtonListener(
  AbstractButton b)

Methods
protected void checkOpacity(
  AbstractButton b)
public void focusGained(FocusEvent e)
public void focusLost(FocusEvent e)
public void installKeyboardActions(
  JComponent c)
public void mouseClicked(MouseEvent e)
public void mouseDragged(MouseEvent e)
public void mouseEntered(MouseEvent e)
public void mouseExited(MouseEvent e)
public void mouseMoved(MouseEvent e)
public void mousePressed(MouseEvent e)
public void mouseReleased(MouseEvent e)
public void propertyChange(
  PropertyChangeEvent e)
public void stateChanged(ChangeEvent e)
public void uninstallKeyboardActions(
  JComponent c)

▶**BASICBUTTONUI**
public class javax.swing.plaf.basic.
  BasicButtonUI
extends javax.swing.plaf.ButtonUI
extends javax.swing.plaf.ComponentUI
extends java.lang.Object

Fields
protected int defaultTextIconGap
protected int defaultTextShiftOffset

Methods
protected void clearTextShiftOffset()
protected BasicButtonListener
  createButtonListener(AbstractButton b)
public static ComponentUI createUI(
  JComponent c)
public int getDefaultTextIconGap(
  AbstractButton b)
public Dimension getMaximumSize(
  JComponent c)
public Dimension getMinimumSize(
  JComponent c)
public Dimension getPreferredSize(
  JComponent c)
protected String getPropertyPrefix()
protected int getTextShiftOffset()
protected void installDefaults(
  AbstractButton b)
protected void installKeyboardActions(
  AbstractButton b)
protected void installListeners(
  AbstractButton b)
public void installUI(JComponent c)
public void paint(Graphics g,JComponent
  c)

protected void paintButtonPressed(
  Graphics g,AbstractButton b)
protected void paintFocus(Graphics g,
  AbstractButton b,Rectangle viewRect,
  Rectangle textRect,Rectangle iconRect)
protected void paintIcon(Graphics g,
  JComponent c,Rectangle iconRect)
protected void paintText(Graphics g,
  JComponent c,Rectangle textRect,String
  text)
protected void setTextShiftOffset()
protected void uninstallDefaults(
  AbstractButton b)
protected void uninstallKeyboardActions(
  AbstractButton b)
protected void uninstallListeners(
  AbstractButton b)
public void uninstallUI(JComponent c)

▶**BASICCHECKBOXMENUITEMUI**
public class javax.swing.plaf.basic.
  BasicCheckBoxMenuItemUI
extends javax.swing.plaf.basic.
  BasicMenuItemUI
extends javax.swing.plaf.MenuItemUI
extends javax.swing.plaf.ButtonUI
extends javax.swing.plaf.ComponentUI
extends java.lang.Object

Methods
public static ComponentUI createUI(
  JComponent c)
protected String getPropertyPrefix()
protected void installDefaults()
public void processMouseEvent(JMenuItem
  item,MouseEvent e,MenuElement path,
  MenuSelectionManager manager)

▶**BASICCHECKBOXUI**
public class javax.swing.plaf.basic.
  BasicCheckBoxUI
extends javax.swing.plaf.basic.
  BasicRadioButtonUI
extends javax.swing.plaf.basic.
  BasicToggleButtonUI
extends javax.swing.plaf.basic.
  BasicButtonUI
extends javax.swing.plaf.ButtonUI
extends javax.swing.plaf.ComponentUI
extends java.lang.Object

Methods
public static ComponentUI createUI(
  JComponent b)
public String getPropertyPrefix()

▶**BASICCOLORCHOOSERUI**
public class javax.swing.plaf.basic.
  BasicColorChooserUI
extends javax.swing.plaf.ColorChooserUI
extends javax.swing.plaf.ComponentUI
extends java.lang.Object

Fields

```
protected javax.swing.colorchooser.
  AbstractColorChooserPanel
  defaultChoosers
protected javax.swing.event.
  ChangeListener previewListener
protected java.beans.
  PropertyChangeListener
  propertyChangeListener
```

Methods

```
protected AbstractColorChooserPanel
  createDefaultChoosers()
protected PropertyChangeListener
  createPropertyChangeListener()
public static ComponentUI createUI(
  JComponent c)
protected void installDefaults()
protected void installListeners()
protected void installPreviewPanel()
public void installUI(JComponent c)
protected void uninstallDefaultChoosers()
protected void uninstallDefaults()
protected void uninstallListeners()
public void uninstallUI(JComponent c)
```

▶BasicComboBoxEditor

```
public class javax.swing.plaf.basic.
  BasicComboBoxEditor
implements javax.swing.ComboBoxEditor
implements java.awt.event.FocusListener
extends java.lang.Object
```

Fields

```
protected javax.swing.JTextField editor
```

Constructors

```
public  BasicComboBoxEditor()
```

Methods

```
public void addActionListener(
  ActionListener l)
public void focusGained(FocusEvent e)
public void focusLost(FocusEvent e)
public Component getEditorComponent()
public Object getItem()
public void removeActionListener(
  ActionListener l)
public void selectAll()
public void setItem(Object anObject)
```

▶BasicComboBoxRenderer

```
public class javax.swing.plaf.basic.
  BasicComboBoxRenderer
implements javax.swing.ListCellRenderer
implements java.io.Serializable
extends javax.swing.JLabel
extends javax.swing.JComponent
extends java.awt.Container
extends java.awt.Component
extends java.lang.Object
```

Fields

```
protected static javax.swing.border.
  Border noFocusBorder
```

Constructors

```
public  BasicComboBoxRenderer()
```

Methods

```
public Component
  getListCellRendererComponent(JList list,
  Object value,int index,boolean
  isSelected,boolean cellHasFocus)
```

▶BasicComboBoxUI

```
public class javax.swing.plaf.basic.
  BasicComboBoxUI
extends javax.swing.plaf.ComboBoxUI
extends javax.swing.plaf.ComponentUI
extends java.lang.Object
```

Fields

```
protected javax.swing.JButton
  arrowButton
protected java.awt.Dimension
  cachedMinimumSize
protected javax.swing.JComboBox
  comboBox
protected javax.swing.CellRendererPane
  currentValuePane
protected java.awt.Component editor
protected java.awt.event.FocusListener
  focusListener
protected boolean hasFocus
protected boolean isMinimumSizeDirty
protected java.awt.event.ItemListener
  itemListener
protected java.awt.event.KeyListener
  keyListener
protected javax.swing.JList listBox
protected javax.swing.event.
  ListDataListener listDataListener
protected javax.swing.plaf.basic.
  ComboPopup popup
protected java.awt.event.KeyListener
  popupKeyListener
protected java.awt.event.MouseListener
  popupMouseListener
protected java.awt.event.
  MouseMotionListener
  popupMouseMotionListener
protected java.beans.
  PropertyChangeListener
  propertyChangeListener
```

Methods

```
public void addEditor()
public void configureArrowButton()
protected void configureEditor()
protected JButton createArrowButton()
protected ComboBoxEditor createEditor()
protected FocusListener
  createFocusListener()
protected ItemListener
  createItemListener()
protected KeyListener createKeyListener()
protected LayoutManager
  createLayoutManager()
protected ListDataListener
  createListDataListener()
```

protected ComboPopup createPopup()
protected PropertyChangeListener
  createPropertyChangeListener()
protected ListCellRenderer
  createRenderer()
public static ComponentUI createUI(
  JComponent c)
public Accessible getAccessibleChild(
  JComponent c,int i)
public int getAccessibleChildrenCount(
  JComponent c)
protected Dimension getDefaultSize()
protected Dimension getDisplaySize()
protected Insets getInsets()
public Dimension getMaximumSize(
  JComponent c)
public Dimension getMinimumSize(
  JComponent c)
public Dimension getPreferredSize(
  JComponent c)
protected void installComponents()
protected void installDefaults()
protected void installKeyboardActions()
protected void installListeners()
public void installUI(JComponent c)
public boolean isFocusTraversable(
  JComboBox c)
protected boolean isNavigationKey(int
  keyCode)
public boolean isPopupVisible(JComboBox
  c)
public void paint(Graphics g,JComponent
  c)
public void paintCurrentValue(Graphics g,
  Rectangle bounds,boolean hasFocus)
public void paintCurrentValueBackground(
  Graphics g,Rectangle bounds,boolean
  hasFocus)
protected Rectangle
  rectangleForCurrentValue()
public void removeEditor()
protected void selectNextPossibleValue()
protected void
  selectPreviousPossibleValue()
public void setPopupVisible(JComboBox c,
  boolean v)
protected void toggleOpenClose()
public void unconfigureArrowButton()
protected void unconfigureEditor()
protected void uninstallComponents()
protected void uninstallDefaults()
protected void uninstallKeyboardActions()
protected void uninstallListeners()
public void uninstallUI(JComponent c)

▶BASICCOMBOPOPUP

public class javax.swing.plaf.basic.
  BasicComboPopup
implements javax.swing.plaf.basic.
  ComboPopup
extends javax.swing.JPopupMenu
extends javax.swing.JComponent
extends java.awt.Container
extends java.awt.Component
extends java.lang.Object

Fields
protected javax.swing.Timer
  autoscrollTimer
protected javax.swing.JComboBox
  comboBox
protected boolean hasEntered
protected boolean isAutoScrolling
protected java.awt.event.ItemListener
  itemListener
protected java.awt.event.KeyListener
  keyListener
protected javax.swing.JList list
protected javax.swing.event.
  ListDataListener listDataListener
protected java.awt.event.MouseListener
  listMouseListener
protected java.awt.event.
  MouseMotionListener
  listMouseMotionListener
protected javax.swing.event.
  ListSelectionListener
  listSelectionListener
protected java.awt.event.MouseListener
  mouseListener
protected java.awt.event.
  MouseMotionListener mouseMotionListener
protected java.beans.
  PropertyChangeListener
  propertyChangeListener
protected int scrollDirection
protected javax.swing.JScrollPane
  scroller
protected final static int SCROLL_DOWN
protected final static int SCROLL_UP
protected boolean valueIsAdjusting

Constructors
public BasicComboPopup(JComboBox combo)

Methods
protected void autoScrollDown()
protected void autoScrollUp()
protected Rectangle computePopupBounds(
  int px,int py,int pw,int ph)
protected void configureList()
protected void configurePopup()
protected void configureScroller()
protected MouseEvent convertMouseEvent(
  MouseEvent e)
protected ItemListener
  createItemListener()
protected KeyListener createKeyListener()
protected JList createList()
protected ListDataListener
  createListDataListener()
protected MouseListener
  createListMouseListener()
protected MouseMotionListener
  createListMouseMotionListener()
protected ListSelectionListener
  createListSelectionListener()

```
protected MouseListener
  createMouseListener()
protected MouseMotionListener
  createMouseMotionListener()
protected PropertyChangeListener
  createPropertyChangeListener()
protected JScrollPane createScroller()
protected void delegateFocus(MouseEvent
  e)
public KeyListener getKeyListener()
public JList getList()
public MouseListener getMouseListener()
public MouseMotionListener
  getMouseMotionListener()
protected int getPopupHeightForRowCount(
  int maxRowCount)
public void hide()
protected void installComboBoxListeners()
protected void
  installComboBoxModelListeners(
  ComboBoxModel model)
protected void installKeyboardActions()
protected void installListListeners()
public boolean isFocusTraversable()
public void show()
protected void startAutoScrolling(int
  direction)
protected void stopAutoScrolling()
protected void togglePopup()
protected void
  uninstallComboBoxModelListeners(
  ComboBoxModel model)
public void uninstallingUI()
protected void uninstallKeyboardActions()
protected void
  updateListBoxSelectionForEvent(
  MouseEvent anEvent,boolean shouldScroll)
```

►BasicDesktopIconUI

```
public class javax.swing.plaf.basic.
  BasicDesktopIconUI
extends javax.swing.plaf.DesktopIconUI
extends javax.swing.plaf.ComponentUI
extends java.lang.Object
```

Fields
```
protected JInternalFrame.JDesktopIcon
  desktopIcon
protected javax.swing.JInternalFrame
  frame
```

Constructors
```
public  BasicDesktopIconUI()
```

Methods
```
protected MouseInputListener
  createMouseInputListener()
public static ComponentUI createUI(
  JComponent c)
public void deiconize()
public Insets getInsets(JComponent c)
public Dimension getMaximumSize(
  JComponent c)
public Dimension getMinimumSize(
  JComponent c)
```

```
public Dimension getPreferredSize(
  JComponent c)
protected void installComponents()
protected void installDefaults()
protected void installListeners()
public void installUI(JComponent c)
protected void uninstallComponents()
protected void uninstallDefaults()
protected void uninstallListeners()
public void uninstallUI(JComponent c)
```

►BasicDesktopPaneUI

```
public class javax.swing.plaf.basic.
  BasicDesktopPaneUI
extends javax.swing.plaf.DesktopPaneUI
extends javax.swing.plaf.ComponentUI
extends java.lang.Object
```

Fields
```
protected javax.swing.KeyStroke
  closeKey
protected javax.swing.JDesktopPane
  desktop
protected javax.swing.DesktopManager
  desktopManager
protected javax.swing.KeyStroke
  maximizeKey
protected javax.swing.KeyStroke
  minimizeKey
protected javax.swing.KeyStroke
  navigateKey
```

Constructors
```
public  BasicDesktopPaneUI()
```

Methods
```
public static ComponentUI createUI(
  JComponent c)
public Dimension getMaximumSize(
  JComponent c)
public Dimension getMinimumSize(
  JComponent c)
public Dimension getPreferredSize(
  JComponent c)
protected void installDefaults()
protected void installDesktopManager()
protected void installKeyboardActions()
public void installUI(JComponent c)
public void paint(Graphics g,JComponent
  c)
protected void registerKeyboardActions()
protected void uninstallDefaults()
protected void uninstallDesktopManager()
protected void uninstallKeyboardActions()
public void uninstallUI(JComponent c)
protected void unregisterKeyboardActions(
  )
```

►BasicDirectoryModel

```
public class javax.swing.plaf.basic.
  BasicDirectoryModel
implements java.beans.
  PropertyChangeListener
extends javax.swing.AbstractListModel
extends java.lang.Object
```

Constructors
```
public  BasicDirectoryModel(JFileChooser
  filechooser)
```
Methods
```
public boolean contains(Object o)
public void fireContentsChanged()
public Vector getDirectories()
public Object getElementAt(int index)
public Vector getFiles()
public int getSize()
public int indexOf(Object o)
public void intervalAdded(ListDataEvent
  e)
public void intervalRemoved(
  ListDataEvent e)
public void invalidateFileCache()
protected boolean lt(File a,File b)
public void propertyChange(
  PropertyChangeEvent e)
protected void sort(Vector v)
public void validateFileCache()
```

▸BASICEDITORPANEUI
```
public class javax.swing.plaf.basic.
  BasicEditorPaneUI
extends javax.swing.plaf.basic.
  BasicTextUI
extends javax.swing.plaf.TextUI
extends javax.swing.plaf.ComponentUI
extends java.lang.Object
```
Constructors
```
public  BasicEditorPaneUI()
```
Methods
```
public static ComponentUI createUI(
  JComponent c)
public EditorKit getEditorKit(
  JTextComponent tc)
protected String getPropertyPrefix()
```

▸BASICFILECHOOSERUI
```
public class javax.swing.plaf.basic.
  BasicFileChooserUI
extends javax.swing.plaf.FileChooserUI
extends javax.swing.plaf.ComponentUI
extends java.lang.Object
```
Fields
```
protected int cancelButtonMnemonic
protected java.lang.String
  cancelButtonText
protected java.lang.String
  cancelButtonToolTipText
protected javax.swing.Icon computerIcon
protected javax.swing.Icon
  detailsViewIcon
protected javax.swing.Icon
  directoryIcon
protected javax.swing.Icon fileIcon
protected javax.swing.Icon
  floppyDriveIcon
protected javax.swing.Icon
  hardDriveIcon
protected int helpButtonMnemonic
```

```
protected java.lang.String
  helpButtonText
protected java.lang.String
  helpButtonToolTipText
protected javax.swing.Icon
  homeFolderIcon
protected javax.swing.Icon listViewIcon
protected javax.swing.Icon
  newFolderIcon
protected int openButtonMnemonic
protected java.lang.String
  openButtonText
protected java.lang.String
  openButtonToolTipText
protected int saveButtonMnemonic
protected java.lang.String
  saveButtonText
protected java.lang.String
  saveButtonToolTipText
protected int updateButtonMnemonic
protected java.lang.String
  updateButtonText
protected java.lang.String
  updateButtonToolTipText
protected javax.swing.Icon upFolderIcon
```
Constructors
```
public  BasicFileChooserUI(JFileChooser
  b)
```
Methods
```
public void clearIconCache()
protected MouseListener
  createDoubleClickListener(JFileChooser
  fc,JList list)
public ListSelectionListener
  createListSelectionListener(JFileChooser
  fc)
protected void createModel()
public PropertyChangeListener
  createPropertyChangeListener(
  JFileChooser fc)
public void ensureFileIsVisible(
  JFileChooser fc,File f)
public FileFilter getAcceptAllFileFilter(
  JFileChooser fc)
public JPanel getAccessoryPanel()
protected JButton getApproveButton(
  JFileChooser fc)
public int getApproveButtonMnemonic(
  JFileChooser fc)
public String getApproveButtonText(
  JFileChooser fc)
public String
  getApproveButtonToolTipText(JFileChooser
  fc)
public Action getApproveSelectionAction()
public Action getCancelSelectionAction()
public Action
  getChangeToParentDirectoryAction()
public String getDialogTitle(
  JFileChooser fc)
public String getDirectoryName()
public JFileChooser getFileChooser()
```

public String getFileName()
public FileView getFileView(JFileChooser fc)
public Action getGoHomeAction()
public BasicDirectoryModel getModel()
public Action getNewFolderAction()
public Action getUpdateAction()
public void installComponents(JFileChooser fc)
protected void installDefaults(JFileChooser fc)
protected void installIcons(JFileChooser fc)
protected void installListeners(JFileChooser fc)
protected void installStrings(JFileChooser fc)
public void installUI(JComponent c)
public void rescanCurrentDirectory(JFileChooser fc)
public void setDirectoryName(String dirname)
public void setFileName(String filename)
public void uninstallComponents(JFileChooser fc)
protected void uninstallDefaults(JFileChooser fc)
protected void uninstallIcons(JFileChooser fc)
protected void uninstallListeners(JFileChooser fc)
protected void uninstallStrings(JFileChooser fc)
public void uninstallUI(JComponent c)

▸BASICGRAPHICSUTILS
public class javax.swing.plaf.basic.
  BasicGraphicsUtils
extends java.lang.Object
Methods
public static void drawBezel(Graphics g, int x,int y,int w,int h,boolean isPressed,boolean isDefault,Color shadow, Color darkShadow,Color highlight,Color lightHighlight)
public static void drawDashedRect(Graphics g,int x,int y,int width,int height)
public static void drawEtchedRect(Graphics g,int x,int y,int w,int h,Color shadow,Color darkShadow,Color highlight, Color lightHighlight)
public static void drawGroove(Graphics g, int x,int y,int w,int h,Color shadow, Color highlight)
public static void drawLoweredBezel(Graphics g,int x,int y,int w,int h,Color shadow,Color darkShadow,Color highlight, Color lightHighlight)
public static void drawString(Graphics g, String text,int underlinedChar,int x,int y)

public static Insets getEtchedInsets()
public static Insets getGrooveInsets()
public static Dimension getPreferredButtonSize(AbstractButton b, int textIconGap)

▸BASICICONFACTORY
public class javax.swing.plaf.basic.
  BasicIconFactory
implements java.io.Serializable
extends java.lang.Object
Methods
public static Icon createEmptyFrameIcon()
public static Icon getCheckBoxIcon()
public static Icon getCheckBoxMenuItemIcon()
public static Icon getMenuArrowIcon()
public static Icon getMenuItemArrowIcon()
public static Icon getMenuItemCheckIcon()
public static Icon getRadioButtonIcon()
public static Icon getRadioButtonMenuItemIcon()

▸BASICINTERNALFRAMETITLEPANE
public class javax.swing.plaf.basic.
  BasicInternalFrameTitlePane
extends javax.swing.JComponent
extends java.awt.Container
extends java.awt.Component
extends java.lang.Object
Fields
protected javax.swing.Action closeAction
protected javax.swing.JButton closeButton
protected javax.swing.Icon closeIcon
protected final static java.lang.String CLOSE_CMD
protected javax.swing.JInternalFrame frame
protected javax.swing.JButton iconButton
protected javax.swing.Icon iconIcon
protected javax.swing.Action iconifyAction
protected final static java.lang.String ICONIFY_CMD
protected javax.swing.JButton maxButton
protected javax.swing.Icon maxIcon
protected javax.swing.Action maximizeAction
protected final static java.lang.String MAXIMIZE_CMD
protected javax.swing.JMenuBar menuBar
protected javax.swing.Icon minIcon
protected javax.swing.Action moveAction
protected final static java.lang.String MOVE_CMD
protected java.awt.Color notSelectedTextColor
protected java.awt.Color notSelectedTitleColor

protected java.beans.
  PropertyChangeListener
  propertyChangeListener
protected javax.swing.Action
  restoreAction
protected final static java.lang.String
  RESTORE_CMD
protected java.awt.Color
  selectedTextColor
protected java.awt.Color
  selectedTitleColor
protected javax.swing.Action sizeAction
protected final static java.lang.String
  SIZE_CMD
protected javax.swing.JMenu windowMenu

Constructors

public BasicInternalFrameTitlePane(
  JInternalFrame f)

Methods

protected void addSubComponents()
protected void addSystemMenuItems(JMenu
  systemMenu)
protected void assembleSystemMenu()
protected void createActions()
protected void createButtons()
protected LayoutManager createLayout()
protected PropertyChangeListener
  createPropertyChangeListener()
protected JMenu createSystemMenu()
protected JMenuBar createSystemMenuBar()
protected void enableActions()
protected void installDefaults()
protected void installListeners()
protected void installTitlePane()
public void paintComponent(Graphics g)
protected void postClosingEvent(
  JInternalFrame frame)
protected void setButtonIcons()
protected void showSystemMenu()
protected void uninstallDefaults()

►BasicInternalFrameUI

public class javax.swing.plaf.basic.
  BasicInternalFrameUI
extends javax.swing.plaf.
  InternalFrameUI
extends javax.swing.plaf.ComponentUI
extends java.lang.Object

Fields

protected javax.swing.event.
  MouseInputAdapter borderListener
protected java.awt.event.
  ComponentListener componentListener
protected javax.swing.JComponent
  eastPane
protected javax.swing.JInternalFrame
  frame
protected javax.swing.event.
  MouseInputListener glassPaneDispatcher
protected java.awt.LayoutManager
  internalFrameLayout

protected javax.swing.JComponent
  northPane
protected javax.swing.KeyStroke
  openMenuKey
protected java.beans.
  PropertyChangeListener
  propertyChangeListener
protected javax.swing.JComponent
  southPane
protected javax.swing.plaf.basic.
  BasicInternalFrameTitlePane titlePane
protected javax.swing.JComponent
  westPane

Constructors

public BasicInternalFrameUI(
  JInternalFrame b)

Methods

protected void activateFrame(
  JInternalFrame f)
protected void closeFrame(JInternalFrame
  f)
protected MouseInputAdapter
  createBorderListener(JInternalFrame w)
protected ComponentListener
  createComponentListener()
protected DesktopManager
  createDesktopManager()
protected JComponent createEastPane(
  JInternalFrame w)
protected MouseInputListener
  createGlassPaneDispatcher()
protected void
  createInternalFrameListener()
protected LayoutManager
  createLayoutManager()
protected JComponent createNorthPane(
  JInternalFrame w)
protected PropertyChangeListener
  createPropertyChangeListener()
protected JComponent createSouthPane(
  JInternalFrame w)
public static ComponentUI createUI(
  JComponent b)
protected JComponent createWestPane(
  JInternalFrame w)
protected void deactivateFrame(
  JInternalFrame f)
protected void deiconifyFrame(
  JInternalFrame f)
protected void deinstallMouseHandlers(
  JComponent c)
protected DesktopManager
  getDesktopManager()
public JComponent getEastPane()
public Dimension getMaximumSize(
  JComponent x)
public Dimension getMinimumSize(
  JComponent x)
public JComponent getNorthPane()
public Dimension getPreferredSize(
  JComponent x)
public JComponent getSouthPane()

```
public JComponent getWestPane()
protected void iconifyFrame(
  JInternalFrame f)
protected void installComponents()
protected void installDefaults()
protected void installKeyboardActions()
protected void installListeners()
protected void installMouseHandlers(
  JComponent c)
public void installUI(JComponent c)
public final boolean isKeyBindingActive()
protected final boolean
  isKeyBindingRegistered()
protected void maximizeFrame(
  JInternalFrame f)
protected void minimizeFrame(
  JInternalFrame f)
protected void replacePane(JComponent
  currentPane,JComponent newPane)
public void setEastPane(JComponent c)
protected final void setKeyBindingActive(
  boolean b)
protected final void
  setKeyBindingRegistered(boolean b)
public void setNorthPane(JComponent c)
public void setSouthPane(JComponent c)
protected void setupMenuCloseKey()
protected void setupMenuOpenKey()
public void setWestPane(JComponent c)
protected void uninstallComponents()
protected void uninstallDefaults()
protected void uninstallKeyboardActions()
protected void uninstallListeners()
public void uninstallUI(JComponent c)
```

▶BasicLabelUI
```
public class javax.swing.plaf.basic.
  BasicLabelUI
implements java.beans.
  PropertyChangeListener
extends javax.swing.plaf.LabelUI
extends javax.swing.plaf.ComponentUI
extends java.lang.Object
```

Fields
```
protected static javax.swing.plaf.basic.
  BasicLabelUI labelUI
```

Methods
```
public static ComponentUI createUI(
  JComponent c)
public Dimension getMaximumSize(
  JComponent c)
public Dimension getMinimumSize(
  JComponent c)
public Dimension getPreferredSize(
  JComponent c)
protected void installComponents(JLabel
  c)
protected void installDefaults(JLabel c)
protected void installKeyboardActions(
  JLabel l)
protected void installListeners(JLabel c)
public void installUI(JComponent c)
```

```
protected String layoutCL(JLabel label,
  FontMetrics fontMetrics,String text,Icon
  icon,Rectangle viewR,Rectangle iconR,
  Rectangle textR)
public void paint(Graphics g,JComponent
  c)
protected void paintDisabledText(JLabel
  l,Graphics g,String s,int textX,int
  textY)
protected void paintEnabledText(JLabel l,
  Graphics g,String s,int textX,int textY)
public void propertyChange(
  PropertyChangeEvent e)
protected void uninstallComponents(
  JLabel c)
protected void uninstallDefaults(JLabel
  c)
protected void uninstallKeyboardActions(
  JLabel c)
protected void uninstallListeners(JLabel
  c)
public void uninstallUI(JComponent c)
```

▶BasicListUI
```
public class javax.swing.plaf.basic.
  BasicListUI
extends javax.swing.plaf.ListUI
extends javax.swing.plaf.ComponentUI
extends java.lang.Object
```

Fields
```
protected int cellHeight
protected int cellHeights
protected final static int
  cellRendererChanged
protected int cellWidth
protected final static int
  fixedCellHeightChanged
protected final static int
  fixedCellWidthChanged
protected java.awt.event.FocusListener
  focusListener
protected final static int fontChanged
protected javax.swing.JList list
protected javax.swing.event.
  ListDataListener listDataListener
protected javax.swing.event.
  ListSelectionListener
  listSelectionListener
protected final static int modelChanged
protected javax.swing.event.
  MouseInputListener mouseInputListener
protected java.beans.
  PropertyChangeListener
  propertyChangeListener
protected final static int
  prototypeCellValueChanged
protected javax.swing.CellRendererPane
  rendererPane
protected final static int
  selectionModelChanged
protected int updateLayoutStateNeeded
```

Methods

```
protected int convertRowToY(int row)
protected int convertYToRow(int y0)
protected FocusListener
  createFocusListener()
protected ListDataListener
  createListDataListener()
protected ListSelectionListener
  createListSelectionListener()
protected MouseInputListener
  createMouseInputListener()
protected PropertyChangeListener
  createPropertyChangeListener()
public static ComponentUI createUI(
  JComponent list)
public Rectangle getCellBounds(JList
  list,int index1,int index2)
public Dimension getMaximumSize(
  JComponent c)
public Dimension getMinimumSize(
  JComponent c)
public Dimension getPreferredSize(
  JComponent c)
protected int getRowHeight(int row)
public Point indexToLocation(JList list,
  int index)
protected void installDefaults()
protected void installKeyboardActions()
protected void installListeners()
public void installUI(JComponent c)
public int locationToIndex(JList list,
  Point location)
protected void maybeUpdateLayoutState()
public void paint(Graphics g,JComponent
  c)
protected void paintCell(Graphics g,int
  row,Rectangle rowBounds,ListCellRenderer
  cellRenderer,ListModel dataModel,
  ListSelectionModel selModel,int
  leadIndex)
protected void selectNextIndex()
protected void selectPreviousIndex()
protected void uninstallDefaults()
protected void uninstallKeyboardActions()
protected void uninstallListeners()
public void uninstallUI(JComponent c)
protected void updateLayoutState()
```

▶BASICLOOKANDFEEL

```
public abstract class javax.swing.plaf.
  basic.BasicLookAndFeel
implements java.io.Serializable
extends javax.swing.LookAndFeel
extends java.lang.Object
```

Methods

```
public UIDefaults getDefaults()
protected void initClassDefaults(
  UIDefaults table)
protected void initComponentDefaults(
  UIDefaults table)
protected void initSystemColorDefaults(
  UIDefaults table)
```

```
protected void loadSystemColors(
  UIDefaults table,String systemColors,
  boolean useNative)
```

▶BASICMENUBARUI

```
public class javax.swing.plaf.basic.
  BasicMenuBarUI
extends javax.swing.plaf.MenuBarUI
extends javax.swing.plaf.ComponentUI
extends java.lang.Object
```

Fields

```
protected javax.swing.event.
  ChangeListener changeListener
protected java.awt.event.
  ContainerListener containerListener
protected javax.swing.JMenuBar menuBar
```

Methods

```
protected ChangeListener
  createChangeListener()
protected ContainerListener
  createContainerListener()
public static ComponentUI createUI(
  JComponent x)
public Dimension getMaximumSize(
  JComponent c)
public Dimension getMinimumSize(
  JComponent c)
public Dimension getPreferredSize(
  JComponent c)
protected void installDefaults()
protected void installKeyboardActions()
protected void installListeners()
public void installUI(JComponent c)
protected void uninstallDefaults()
protected void uninstallKeyboardActions()
protected void uninstallListeners()
public void uninstallUI(JComponent c)
```

▶BASICMENUITEMUI

```
public class javax.swing.plaf.basic.
  BasicMenuItemUI
extends javax.swing.plaf.MenuItemUI
extends javax.swing.plaf.ButtonUI
extends javax.swing.plaf.ComponentUI
extends java.lang.Object
```

Fields

```
protected java.awt.Font acceleratorFont
protected java.awt.Color
  acceleratorForeground
protected java.awt.Color
  acceleratorSelectionForeground
protected javax.swing.Icon arrowIcon
protected javax.swing.Icon checkIcon
protected int defaultTextIconGap
protected java.awt.Color
  disabledForeground
protected javax.swing.event.
  MenuDragMouseListener
  menuDragMouseListener
protected javax.swing.JMenuItem
  menuItem
```

protected javax.swing.event.
  MenuKeyListener menuKeyListener
protected javax.swing.event.
  MouseInputListener mouseInputListener
protected boolean oldBorderPainted
protected java.awt.Color
  selectionBackground
protected java.awt.Color
  selectionForeground

Methods

protected MenuDragMouseListener
  createMenuDragMouseListener(JComponent c)
protected MenuKeyListener
  createMenuKeyListener(JComponent c)
protected MouseInputListener
  createMouseInputListener(JComponent c)
public static ComponentUI createUI(
  JComponent c)
public Dimension getMaximumSize(
  JComponent c)
public Dimension getMinimumSize(
  JComponent c)
public MenuElement getPath()
protected Dimension
  getPreferredMenuItemSize(JComponent c,
  Icon checkIcon,Icon arrowIcon,int
  defaultTextIconGap)
public Dimension getPreferredSize(
  JComponent c)
protected String getPropertyPrefix()
protected void installDefaults()
protected void installKeyboardActions()
protected void installListeners()
public void installUI(JComponent c)
public void paint(Graphics g,JComponent
  c)
protected void paintMenuItem(Graphics g,
  JComponent c,Icon checkIcon,Icon
  arrowIcon,Color background,Color
  foreground,int defaultTextIconGap)
protected void uninstallDefaults()
protected void uninstallKeyboardActions()
protected void uninstallListeners()
public void uninstallUI(JComponent c)
public void update(Graphics g,JComponent
  c)

▶BASICMENUUI

public class javax.swing.plaf.basic.
  BasicMenuUI
extends javax.swing.plaf.basic.
  BasicMenuItemUI
extends javax.swing.plaf.MenuItemUI
extends javax.swing.plaf.ButtonUI
extends javax.swing.plaf.ComponentUI
extends java.lang.Object

Fields

protected javax.swing.event.
  ChangeListener changeListener
protected javax.swing.event.MenuListener
  menuListener

protected java.beans.
  PropertyChangeListener
  propertyChangeListener

Methods

protected ChangeListener
  createChangeListener(JComponent c)
protected MenuDragMouseListener
  createMenuDragMouseListener(JComponent c)
protected MenuKeyListener
  createMenuKeyListener(JComponent c)
protected MenuListener
  createMenuListener(JComponent c)
protected MouseInputListener
  createMouseInputListener(JComponent c)
protected PropertyChangeListener
  createPropertyChangeListener(JComponent
  c)
public static ComponentUI createUI(
  JComponent x)
public Dimension getMaximumSize(
  JComponent c)
protected String getPropertyPrefix()
protected void installDefaults()
protected void installKeyboardActions()
protected void installListeners()
protected void setupPostTimer(JMenu menu)
protected void uninstallDefaults()
protected void uninstallKeyboardActions()
protected void uninstallListeners()

▶BASICOPTIONPANEUI

public class javax.swing.plaf.basic.
  BasicOptionPaneUI
extends javax.swing.plaf.OptionPaneUI
extends javax.swing.plaf.ComponentUI
extends java.lang.Object

Fields

protected boolean hasCustomComponents
protected java.awt.Component
  initialFocusComponent
protected javax.swing.JComponent
  inputComponent
public final static int MinimumHeight
protected java.awt.Dimension
  minimumSize
public final static int MinimumWidth
protected javax.swing.JOptionPane
  optionPane
protected java.beans.
  PropertyChangeListener
  propertyChangeListener

Methods

protected void addButtonComponents(
  Container container,Object buttons,int
  initialIndex)
protected void addIcon(Container top)
protected void addMessageComponents(
  Container container,GridBagConstraints
  cons,Object msg,int maxll,boolean
  internallyCreated)
protected void burstStringInto(Container
  c,String d,int maxll)

```
public boolean containsCustomComponents(
  JOptionPane op)
protected ActionListener
  createButtonActionListener(int
  buttonIndex)
protected Container createButtonArea()
protected LayoutManager
  createLayoutManager()
protected Container createMessageArea()
protected PropertyChangeListener
  createPropertyChangeListener()
protected Container createSeparator()
public static ComponentUI createUI(
  JComponent x)
protected Object getButtons()
protected Icon getIcon()
protected Icon getIconForType(int
  messageType)
protected int getInitialValueIndex()
protected int
  getMaxCharactersPerLineCount()
public Dimension getMaximumSize(
  JComponent c)
protected Object getMessage()
public Dimension
  getMinimumOptionPaneSize()
public Dimension getMinimumSize(
  JComponent c)
public Dimension getPreferredSize(
  JComponent c)
protected boolean
  getSizeButtonsToSameWidth()
protected void installComponents()
protected void installDefaults()
protected void installKeyboardActions()
protected void installListeners()
public void installUI(JComponent c)
protected void resetInputValue()
public void selectInitialValue(
  JOptionPane op)
protected void uninstallComponents()
protected void uninstallDefaults()
protected void uninstallKeyboardActions()
protected void uninstallListeners()
public void uninstallUI(JComponent c)
```

►BASICPANELUI
```
public class javax.swing.plaf.basic.
  BasicPanelUI
extends javax.swing.plaf.PanelUI
extends javax.swing.plaf.ComponentUI
extends java.lang.Object
```
Methods
```
public static ComponentUI createUI(
  JComponent c)
protected void installDefaults(JPanel p)
public void installUI(JComponent c)
protected void uninstallDefaults(JPanel
  p)
public void uninstallUI(JComponent c)
```

►BASICPASSWORDFIELDUI
```
public class javax.swing.plaf.basic.
  BasicPasswordFieldUI
extends javax.swing.plaf.basic.
  BasicTextFieldUI
extends javax.swing.plaf.basic.
  BasicTextUI
extends javax.swing.plaf.TextUI
extends javax.swing.plaf.ComponentUI
extends java.lang.Object
```
Methods
```
public View create(Element elem)
public static ComponentUI createUI(
  JComponent c)
protected String getPropertyPrefix()
```

►BASICPERMISSION
```
public abstract class java.security.
  BasicPermission
implements java.io.Serializable
extends java.security.Permission
extends java.lang.Object
```
Constructors
```
public  BasicPermission(String name)
public  BasicPermission(String name,
  String actions)
```
Methods
```
public boolean equals(Object obj)
public String getActions()
public int hashCode()
public boolean implies(Permission p)
public PermissionCollection
  newPermissionCollection()
```

►BASICPOPUPMENUSEPARATORUI
```
public class javax.swing.plaf.basic.
  BasicPopupMenuSeparatorUI
extends javax.swing.plaf.basic.
  BasicSeparatorUI
extends javax.swing.plaf.SeparatorUI
extends javax.swing.plaf.ComponentUI
extends java.lang.Object
```
Methods
```
public static ComponentUI createUI(
  JComponent c)
public Dimension getPreferredSize(
  JComponent c)
public void paint(Graphics g,JComponent
  c)
```

►BASICPOPUPMENUUI
```
public class javax.swing.plaf.basic.
  BasicPopupMenuUI
extends javax.swing.plaf.PopupMenuUI
extends javax.swing.plaf.ComponentUI
extends java.lang.Object
```
Fields
```
protected javax.swing.JPopupMenu
  popupMenu
```
Methods
```
public static ComponentUI createUI(
  JComponent x)
```

```
public Dimension getMaximumSize(
  JComponent c)
public Dimension getMinimumSize(
  JComponent c)
public Dimension getPreferredSize(
  JComponent c)
public void installDefaults()
protected void installKeyboardActions()
protected void installListeners()
public void installUI(JComponent c)
protected void uninstallDefaults()
protected void uninstallKeyboardActions()
protected void uninstallListeners()
public void uninstallUI(JComponent c)
```

▶BASICPROGRESSBARUI

```
public class javax.swing.plaf.basic.
  BasicProgressBarUI
extends javax.swing.plaf.ProgressBarUI
extends javax.swing.plaf.ComponentUI
extends java.lang.Object
```

Fields

```
protected javax.swing.event.
  ChangeListener changeListener
protected javax.swing.JProgressBar
  progressBar
```

Methods

```
public static ComponentUI createUI(
  JComponent x)
protected int getAmountFull(Insets b,int
  width,int height)
protected int getCellLength()
protected int getCellSpacing()
public Dimension getMaximumSize(
  JComponent c)
public Dimension getMinimumSize(
  JComponent c)
protected Dimension
  getPreferredInnerHorizontal()
protected Dimension
  getPreferredInnerVertical()
public Dimension getPreferredSize(
  JComponent c)
protected Color getSelectionBackground()
protected Color getSelectionForeground()
protected Point getStringPlacement(
  Graphics g,String progressString,int x,
  int y,int width,int height)
protected void installDefaults()
protected void installListeners()
public void installUI(JComponent c)
public void paint(Graphics g,JComponent
  c)
protected void paintString(Graphics g,
  int x,int y,int width,int height,int
  amountFull,Insets b)
protected void setCellLength(int cellLen)
protected void setCellSpacing(int
  cellSpace)
protected void uninstallDefaults()
protected void uninstallListeners()
public void uninstallUI(JComponent c)
```

▶BASICRADIOBUTTONMENUITEMUI

```
public class javax.swing.plaf.basic.
  BasicRadioButtonMenuItemUI
extends javax.swing.plaf.basic.
  BasicMenuItemUI
extends javax.swing.plaf.MenuItemUI
extends javax.swing.plaf.ButtonUI
extends javax.swing.plaf.ComponentUI
extends java.lang.Object
```

Methods

```
public static ComponentUI createUI(
  JComponent b)
protected String getPropertyPrefix()
protected void installDefaults()
public void processMouseEvent(JMenuItem
  item,MouseEvent e,MenuElement path,
  MenuSelectionManager manager)
```

▶BASICRADIOBUTTONUI

```
public class javax.swing.plaf.basic.
  BasicRadioButtonUI
extends javax.swing.plaf.basic.
  BasicToggleButtonUI
extends javax.swing.plaf.basic.
  BasicButtonUI
extends javax.swing.plaf.ButtonUI
extends javax.swing.plaf.ComponentUI
extends java.lang.Object
```

Fields

```
protected javax.swing.Icon icon
```

Methods

```
public static ComponentUI createUI(
  JComponent b)
public Icon getDefaultIcon()
public Dimension getPreferredSize(
  JComponent c)
protected String getPropertyPrefix()
protected void installDefaults(
  AbstractButton b)
public synchronized void paint(Graphics
  g,JComponent c)
protected void paintFocus(Graphics g,
  Rectangle textRect,Dimension size)
protected void uninstallDefaults(
  AbstractButton b)
```

▶BASICSCROLLBARUI

```
public class javax.swing.plaf.basic.
  BasicScrollBarUI
implements java.awt.LayoutManager
implements javax.swing.SwingConstants
extends javax.swing.plaf.ScrollBarUI
extends javax.swing.plaf.ComponentUI
extends java.lang.Object
```

Fields

```
protected ArrowButtonListener
  buttonListener
protected javax.swing.JButton
  decrButton
protected final static int DECREASE_
  HIGHLIGHT
```

```
protected javax.swing.JButton
  incrButton
protected final static int INCREASE_
  HIGHLIGHT
protected boolean isDragging
protected java.awt.Dimension
  maximumThumbSize
protected java.awt.Dimension
  minimumThumbSize
protected ModelListener modelListener
protected final static int NO_HIGHLIGHT
protected java.beans.
  PropertyChangeListener
  propertyChangeListener
protected javax.swing.JScrollBar
  scrollbar
protected ScrollListener scrollListener
protected javax.swing.Timer scrollTimer
protected java.awt.Color thumbColor
protected java.awt.Color
  thumbDarkShadowColor
protected java.awt.Color
  thumbHighlightColor
protected java.awt.Color
  thumbLightShadowColor
protected java.awt.Rectangle thumbRect
protected java.awt.Color trackColor
protected int trackHighlight
protected java.awt.Color
  trackHighlightColor
protected TrackListener trackListener
protected java.awt.Rectangle trackRect
```
Methods
```
public void addLayoutComponent(String
  name,Component child)
protected void configureScrollBarColors()
protected ArrowButtonListener
  createArrowButtonListener()
protected JButton createDecreaseButton(
  int orientation)
protected JButton createIncreaseButton(
  int orientation)
protected ModelListener
  createModelListener()
protected PropertyChangeListener
  createPropertyChangeListener()
protected ScrollListener
  createScrollListener()
protected TrackListener
  createTrackListener()
public static ComponentUI createUI(
  JComponent c)
public Dimension getMaximumSize(
  JComponent c)
protected Dimension getMaximumThumbSize()
public Dimension getMinimumSize(
  JComponent c)
protected Dimension getMinimumThumbSize()
public Dimension getPreferredSize(
  JComponent c)
protected Rectangle getThumbBounds()
protected Rectangle getTrackBounds()
protected void installComponents()
```

```
protected void installDefaults()
protected void installKeyboardActions()
protected void installListeners()
public void installUI(JComponent c)
public void layoutContainer(Container
  scrollbarContainer)
protected void layoutHScrollbar(
  JScrollBar sb)
protected void layoutVScrollbar(
  JScrollBar sb)
public Dimension minimumLayoutSize(
  Container scrollbarContainer)
public void paint(Graphics g,JComponent
  c)
protected void paintDecreaseHighlight(
  Graphics g)
protected void paintIncreaseHighlight(
  Graphics g)
protected void paintThumb(Graphics g,
  JComponent c,Rectangle thumbBounds)
protected void paintTrack(Graphics g,
  JComponent c,Rectangle trackBounds)
public Dimension preferredLayoutSize(
  Container scrollbarContainer)
public void removeLayoutComponent(
  Component child)
protected void scrollByBlock(int
  direction)
protected void scrollByUnit(int
  direction)
protected void setThumbBounds(int x,int
  y,int width,int height)
protected void uninstallComponents()
protected void uninstallDefaults()
protected void uninstallKeyboardActions()
protected void uninstallListeners()
public void uninstallUI(JComponent c)
```

▶BASICSCROLLPANEUI
```
public class javax.swing.plaf.basic.
  BasicScrollPaneUI
implements javax.swing.
  ScrollPaneConstants
extends javax.swing.plaf.ScrollPaneUI
extends javax.swing.plaf.ComponentUI
extends java.lang.Object
```
Fields
```
protected javax.swing.event.
  ChangeListener hsbChangeListener
protected javax.swing.JScrollPane
  scrollpane
protected java.beans.
  PropertyChangeListener
  spPropertyChangeListener
protected javax.swing.event.
  ChangeListener viewportChangeListener
protected javax.swing.event.
  ChangeListener vsbChangeListener
```
Methods
```
protected ChangeListener
  createHSBChangeListener()
```

```
protected PropertyChangeListener
  createPropertyChangeListener()
public static ComponentUI createUI(
  JComponent x)
protected ChangeListener
  createViewportChangeListener()
protected ChangeListener
  createVSBChangeListener()
public Dimension getMaximumSize(
  JComponent c)
public Dimension getMinimumSize(
  JComponent c)
public Dimension getPreferredSize(
  JComponent c)
protected void installDefaults(
  JScrollPane scrollpane)
protected void installKeyboardActions(
  JScrollPane c)
protected void installListeners(
  JScrollPane c)
public void installUI(JComponent x)
public void paint(Graphics g,JComponent
  c)
protected void
  syncScrollPaneWithViewport()
protected void uninstallDefaults(
  JScrollPane c)
protected void uninstallKeyboardActions(
  JScrollPane c)
protected void uninstallListeners(
  JComponent c)
public void uninstallUI(JComponent c)
protected void updateColumnHeader(
  PropertyChangeEvent e)
protected void updateRowHeader(
  PropertyChangeEvent e)
protected void
  updateScrollBarDisplayPolicy(
  PropertyChangeEvent e)
protected void updateViewport(
  PropertyChangeEvent e)
```

▶**BASICSEPARATORUI**
```
public class javax.swing.plaf.basic.
  BasicSeparatorUI
extends javax.swing.plaf.SeparatorUI
extends javax.swing.plaf.ComponentUI
extends java.lang.Object
```
Fields
```
protected java.awt.Color highlight
protected java.awt.Color shadow
```
Methods
```
public static ComponentUI createUI(
  JComponent c)
public Dimension getMaximumSize(
  JComponent c)
public Dimension getMinimumSize(
  JComponent c)
public Dimension getPreferredSize(
  JComponent c)
protected void installDefaults(
  JSeparator s)
```

```
protected void installListeners(
  JSeparator s)
public void installUI(JComponent c)
public void paint(Graphics g,JComponent
  c)
protected void uninstallDefaults(
  JSeparator s)
protected void uninstallListeners(
  JSeparator s)
public void uninstallUI(JComponent c)
```

▶**BASICSLIDERUI**
```
public class javax.swing.plaf.basic.
  BasicSliderUI
extends javax.swing.plaf.SliderUI
extends javax.swing.plaf.ComponentUI
extends java.lang.Object
```
Fields
```
protected javax.swing.event.
  ChangeListener changeListener
protected java.awt.event.
  ComponentListener componentListener
protected java.awt.Rectangle
  contentRect
protected java.awt.Insets focusInsets
protected java.awt.event.FocusListener
  focusListener
protected java.awt.Rectangle focusRect
protected java.awt.Insets insetCache
protected java.awt.Rectangle labelRect
public final int MAX_SCROLL
public final int MIN_SCROLL
public final int NEGATIVE_SCROLL
public final int POSITIVE_SCROLL
protected java.beans.
  PropertyChangeListener
  propertyChangeListener
protected ScrollListener scrollListener
protected javax.swing.Timer scrollTimer
protected javax.swing.JSlider slider
protected java.awt.Rectangle thumbRect
protected java.awt.Rectangle tickRect
protected int trackBuffer
protected TrackListener trackListener
protected java.awt.Rectangle trackRect
```
Constructors
```
public  BasicSliderUI(JSlider b)
```
Methods
```
protected void calculateContentRect()
protected void calculateFocusRect()
protected void calculateGeometry()
protected void calculateLabelRect()
protected void calculateThumbLocation()
protected void calculateThumbSize()
protected void calculateTickRect()
protected void calculateTrackBuffer()
protected void calculateTrackRect()
protected ChangeListener
  createChangeListener(JSlider slider)
protected ComponentListener
  createComponentListener(JSlider slider)
```

protected FocusListener
  createFocusListener(JSlider slider)
protected PropertyChangeListener
  createPropertyChangeListener(JSlider
  slider)
protected ScrollListener
  createScrollListener(JSlider slider)
protected TrackListener
  createTrackListener(JSlider slider)
public static ComponentUI createUI(
  JComponent b)
protected Color getFocusColor()
protected int getHeightOfHighValueLabel()
protected int getHeightOfLowValueLabel()
protected int getHeightOfTallestLabel()
protected Component getHighestValueLabel(
)
protected Color getHighlightColor()
protected Component getLowestValueLabel()
public Dimension getMaximumSize(
  JComponent c)
public Dimension
  getMinimumHorizontalSize()
public Dimension getMinimumSize(
  JComponent c)
public Dimension getMinimumVerticalSize()
public Dimension
  getPreferredHorizontalSize()
public Dimension getPreferredSize(
  JComponent c)
public Dimension
  getPreferredVerticalSize()
protected Color getShadowColor()
protected Dimension getThumbSize()
protected int getTickLength()
protected int getWidthOfHighValueLabel()
protected int getWidthOfLowValueLabel()
protected int getWidthOfWidestLabel()
protected void installDefaults(JSlider
  slider)
protected void installKeyboardActions(
  JSlider slider)
protected void installListeners(JSlider
  slider)
public void installUI(JComponent c)
public void paint(Graphics g,JComponent
  c)
public void paintFocus(Graphics g)
protected void paintHorizontalLabel(
  Graphics g,int value,Component label)
public void paintLabels(Graphics g)
protected void
  paintMajorTickForHorizSlider(Graphics g,
  Rectangle tickBounds,int x)
protected void
  paintMajorTickForVertSlider(Graphics g,
  Rectangle tickBounds,int y)
protected void
  paintMinorTickForHorizSlider(Graphics g,
  Rectangle tickBounds,int x)
protected void
  paintMinorTickForVertSlider(Graphics g,
  Rectangle tickBounds,int y)

public void paintThumb(Graphics g)
public void paintTicks(Graphics g)
public void paintTrack(Graphics g)
protected void paintVerticalLabel(
  Graphics g,int value,Component label)
protected void
  recalculateIfInsetsChanged()
public void scrollByBlock(int direction)
public void scrollByUnit(int direction)
protected void scrollDueToClickInTrack(
  int dir)
public void setThumbLocation(int x,int y)
protected void uninstallKeyboardActions(
  JSlider slider)
protected void uninstallListeners(
  JSlider slider)
public void uninstallUI(JComponent c)
public int valueForXPosition(int xPos)
public int valueForYPosition(int yPos)
protected int xPositionForValue(int
  value)
protected int yPositionForValue(int
  value)

▶BASICSPLITPANEDIVIDER

public class javax.swing.plaf.basic.
  BasicSplitPaneDivider
implements java.beans.
  PropertyChangeListener
extends java.awt.Container
extends java.awt.Component
extends java.lang.Object

Fields

protected int dividerSize
protected DragController dragger
protected java.awt.Component
  hiddenDivider
protected javax.swing.JButton
  leftButton
protected MouseHandler mouseHandler
protected final static int ONE_TOUCH_
  OFFSET
protected final static int ONE_TOUCH_
  SIZE
protected int orientation
protected javax.swing.JButton
  rightButton
protected javax.swing.JSplitPane
  splitPane
protected javax.swing.plaf.basic.
  BasicSplitPaneUI splitPaneUI

Constructors

public BasicSplitPaneDivider(
  BasicSplitPaneUI ui)

Methods

protected Jbutton
  createLeftOneTouchButton()
protected JButton
  createRightOneTouchButton()
protected void dragDividerTo(int
  location)

```
protected void finishDraggingTo(int
  location)
public BasicSplitPaneUI
  getBasicSplitPaneUI()
public int getDividerSize()
public Dimension getPreferredSize()
protected void oneTouchExpandableChanged(
  )
public void paint(Graphics g)
protected void prepareForDragging()
public void propertyChange(
  PropertyChangeEvent e)
public void setBasicSplitPaneUI(
  BasicSplitPaneUI newUI)
public void setDividerSize(int newSize)
```

▶BASICSPLITPANEUI

```
public class javax.swing.plaf.basic.
  BasicSplitPaneUI
extends javax.swing.plaf.SplitPaneUI
extends javax.swing.plaf.ComponentUI
extends java.lang.Object
```

Fields

```
protected int beginDragDividerLocation
protected javax.swing.plaf.basic.
  BasicSplitPaneDivider divider
protected javax.swing.KeyStroke
  dividerResizeToggleKey
protected int dividerSize
protected javax.swing.KeyStroke downKey
protected boolean draggingHW
protected javax.swing.KeyStroke endKey
protected java.awt.event.FocusListener
  focusListener
protected javax.swing.KeyStroke homeKey
protected java.awt.event.ActionListener
  keyboardDownRightListener
protected java.awt.event.ActionListener
  keyboardEndListener
protected java.awt.event.ActionListener
  keyboardHomeListener
protected java.awt.event.ActionListener
  keyboardResizeToggleListener
protected java.awt.event.ActionListener
  keyboardUpLeftListener
protected static int KEYBOARD_DIVIDER_
  MOVE_OFFSET
protected BasicHorizontalLayoutManager
  layoutManager
protected javax.swing.KeyStroke leftKey
protected java.awt.Component
  nonContinuousLayoutDivider
protected final static java.lang.String
  NON_CONTINUOUS_DIVIDER
protected java.beans.
  PropertyChangeListener
  propertyChangeListener
protected javax.swing.KeyStroke
  rightKey
protected javax.swing.JSplitPane
  splitPane
protected javax.swing.KeyStroke upKey
```

Methods

```
public BasicSplitPaneDivider
  createDefaultDivider()
protected Component
  createDefaultNonContinuousLayoutDivider()
protected FocusListener
  createFocusListener()
protected ActionListener
  createKeyboardDownRightListener()
protected ActionListener
  createKeyboardEndListener()
protected ActionListener
  createKeyboardHomeListener()
protected ActionListener
  createKeyboardResizeToggleListener()
protected ActionListener
  createKeyboardUpLeftListener()
protected PropertyChangeListener
  createPropertyChangeListener()
public static ComponentUI createUI(
  JComponent x)
protected void dragDividerTo(int
  location)
protected void finishDraggingTo(int
  location)
public void finishedPaintingChildren(
  JSplitPane jc,Graphics g)
public BasicSplitPaneDivider getDivider()
protected int getDividerBorderSize()
public int getDividerLocation(JSplitPane
  jc)
public Insets getInsets(JComponent jc)
public int getLastDragLocation()
public int getMaximumDividerLocation(
  JSplitPane jc)
public Dimension getMaximumSize(
  JComponent jc)
public int getMinimumDividerLocation(
  JSplitPane jc)
public Dimension getMinimumSize(
  JComponent jc)
public Component
  getNonContinuousLayoutDivider()
public int getOrientation()
public Dimension getPreferredSize(
  JComponent jc)
public JSplitPane getSplitPane()
protected void installDefaults()
protected void installKeyboardActions()
protected void installListeners()
public void installUI(JComponent c)
public boolean isContinuousLayout()
public void paint(Graphics g,JComponent
  jc)
protected void resetLayoutManager()
public void resetToPreferredSizes(
  JSplitPane jc)
public void setContinuousLayout(boolean
  b)
public void setDividerLocation(
  JSplitPane jc,int location)
public void setLastDragLocation(int l)
```

```
protected void
  setNonContinuousLayoutDivider(Component
  newDivider)
protected void
  setNonContinuousLayoutDivider(Component
  newDivider,boolean rememberSizes)
public void setOrientation(int
  orientation)
protected void startDragging()
protected void uninstallDefaults()
protected void uninstallKeyboardActions()
protected void uninstallListeners()
public void uninstallUI(JComponent c)
```

▸BASICSTROKE

```
public class java.awt.BasicStroke
implements java.awt.Stroke
extends java.lang.Object
```

Fields

```
public final static int CAP_BUTT
public final static int CAP_ROUND
public final static int CAP_SQUARE
public final static int JOIN_BEVEL
public final static int JOIN_MITER
public final static int JOIN_ROUND
```

Constructors

```
public  BasicStroke(float width,int cap,
  int join,float miterlimit,float dash,
  float dash_phase)
public  BasicStroke(float width,int cap,
  int join,float miterlimit)
public  BasicStroke(float width,int cap,
  int join)
public  BasicStroke(float width)
public  BasicStroke()
```

Methods

```
public Shape createStrokedShape(Shape s)
public boolean equals(Object obj)
public float getDashArray()
public float getDashPhase()
public int getEndCap()
public int getLineJoin()
public float getLineWidth()
public float getMiterLimit()
public int hashCode()
```

▸BASICTABBEDPANEUI

```
public class javax.swing.plaf.basic.
  BasicTabbedPaneUI
implements javax.swing.SwingConstants
extends javax.swing.plaf.TabbedPaneUI
extends javax.swing.plaf.ComponentUI
extends java.lang.Object
```

Fields

```
protected java.awt.Insets
  contentBorderInsets
protected java.awt.Color darkShadow
protected javax.swing.KeyStroke downKey
protected java.awt.Color focus
protected java.awt.event.FocusListener
  focusListener
protected java.awt.Color highlight
```

```
protected javax.swing.KeyStroke leftKey
protected java.awt.Color lightHighlight
protected int maxTabHeight
protected int maxTabWidth
protected java.awt.event.MouseListener
  mouseListener
protected java.beans.
  PropertyChangeListener
  propertyChangeListener
protected java.awt.Rectangle rects
protected javax.swing.KeyStroke
  rightKey
protected int runCount
protected int selectedRun
protected java.awt.Insets
  selectedTabPadInsets
protected java.awt.Color shadow
protected java.awt.Insets tabAreaInsets
protected javax.swing.event.
  ChangeListener tabChangeListener
protected java.awt.Insets tabInsets
protected javax.swing.JTabbedPane
  tabPane
protected int tabRunOverlay
protected int tabRuns
protected int textIconGap
protected javax.swing.KeyStroke upKey
```

Methods

```
protected void assureRectsCreated(int
  tabCount)
protected int calculateMaxTabHeight(int
  tabPlacement)
protected int calculateMaxTabWidth(int
  tabPlacement)
protected int calculateTabAreaHeight(int
  tabPlacement,int horizRunCount,int
  maxTabHeight)
protected int calculateTabAreaWidth(int
  tabPlacement,int vertRunCount,int
  maxTabWidth)
protected int calculateTabHeight(int
  tabPlacement,int tabIndex,int fontHeight)
protected int calculateTabWidth(int
  tabPlacement,int tabIndex,FontMetrics
  metrics)
protected ChangeListener
  createChangeListener()
protected FocusListener
  createFocusListener()
protected LayoutManager
  createLayoutManager()
protected MouseListener
  createMouseListener()
protected PropertyChangeListener
  createPropertyChangeListener()
public static ComponentUI createUI(
  JComponent c)
protected void expandTabRunsArray()
protected Insets getContentBorderInsets(
  int tabPlacement)
protected FontMetrics getFontMetrics()
protected Icon getIconForTab(int
  tabIndex)
```

public Dimension getMaximumSize(
  JComponent c)
public Dimension getMinimumSize(
  JComponent c)
protected int getNextTabIndex(int base)
public Dimension getPreferredSize(
  JComponent c)
protected int getPreviousTabIndex(int
  base)
protected int getRunForTab(int tabCount,
  int tabIndex)
protected Insets getSelectedTabPadInsets(
  int tabPlacement)
protected Insets getTabAreaInsets(int
  tabPlacement)
public Rectangle getTabBounds(
  JTabbedPane pane,int i)
protected Insets getTabInsets(int
  tabPlacement,int tabIndex)
protected int getTabLabelShiftX(int
  tabPlacement,int tabIndex,boolean
  isSelected)
protected int getTabLabelShiftY(int
  tabPlacement,int tabIndex,boolean
  isSelected)
public int getTabRunCount(JTabbedPane
  pane)
protected int getTabRunIndent(int
  tabPlacement,int run)
protected int getTabRunOffset(int
  tabPlacement,int tabCount,int tabIndex,
  boolean forward)
protected int getTabRunOverlay(int
  tabPlacement)
protected Component getVisibleComponent()
protected void installDefaults()
protected void installKeyboardActions()
protected void installListeners()
public void installUI(JComponent c)
protected int lastTabInRun(int tabCount,
  int run)
protected void layoutLabel(int
  tabPlacement,FontMetrics metrics,int
  tabIndex,String title,Icon icon,
  Rectangle tabRect,Rectangle iconRect,
  Rectangle textRect,boolean isSelected)
protected void navigateSelectedTab(int
  direction)
public void paint(Graphics g,JComponent
  c)
protected void paintContentBorder(
  Graphics g,int tabPlacement,int
  selectedIndex)
protected void
  paintContentBorderBottomEdge(Graphics g,
  int tabPlacement,int selectedIndex,int x,
  int y,int w,int h)
protected void
  paintContentBorderLeftEdge(Graphics g,
  int tabPlacement,int selectedIndex,int x,
  int y,int w,int h)

protected void
  paintContentBorderRightEdge(Graphics g,
  int tabPlacement,int selectedIndex,int x,
  int y,int w,int h)
protected void paintContentBorderTopEdge(
  Graphics g,int tabPlacement,int
  selectedIndex,int x,int y,int w,int h)
protected void paintFocusIndicator(
  Graphics g,int tabPlacement,Rectangle
  rects,int tabIndex,Rectangle iconRect,
  Rectangle textRect,boolean isSelected)
protected void paintIcon(Graphics g,int
  tabPlacement,int tabIndex,Icon icon,
  Rectangle iconRect,boolean isSelected)
protected void paintTab(Graphics g,int
  tabPlacement,Rectangle rects,int
  tabIndex,Rectangle iconRect,Rectangle
  textRect)
protected void paintTabBackground(
  Graphics g,int tabPlacement,int tabIndex,
  int x,int y,int w,int h,boolean
  isSelected)
protected void paintTabBorder(Graphics g,
  int tabPlacement,int tabIndex,int x,int
  y,int w,int h,boolean isSelected)
protected void paintText(Graphics g,int
  tabPlacement,Font font,FontMetrics
  metrics,int tabIndex,String title,
  Rectangle textRect,boolean isSelected)
protected static void rotateInsets(
  Insets topInsets,Insets targetInsets,int
  targetPlacement)
protected void selectAdjacentRunTab(int
  tabPlacement,int tabIndex,int offset)
protected void selectNextTab(int current)
protected void selectPreviousTab(int
  current)
protected void setVisibleComponent(
  Component component)
protected boolean shouldPadTabRun(int
  tabPlacement,int run)
protected boolean shouldRotateTabRuns(
  int tabPlacement)
public int tabForCoordinate(JTabbedPane
  pane,int x,int y)
protected void uninstallDefaults()
protected void uninstallKeyboardActions()
protected void uninstallListeners()
public void uninstallUI(JComponent c)

▶BasicTableHeaderUI
public class javax.swing.plaf.basic.
  BasicTableHeaderUI
extends javax.swing.plaf.TableHeaderUI
extends javax.swing.plaf.ComponentUI
extends java.lang.Object
Fields
protected javax.swing.table.JTableHeader
  header
protected javax.swing.event.
  MouseInputListener mouseInputListener

protected javax.swing.CellRendererPane
  rendererPane

Methods

protected MouseInputListener
  createMouseInputListener()
public static ComponentUI createUI(
  JComponent h)
public Dimension getMaximumSize(
  JComponent c)
public Dimension getMinimumSize(
  JComponent c)
public Dimension getPreferredSize(
  JComponent c)
protected void installDefaults()
protected void installKeyboardActions()
protected void installListeners()
public void installUI(JComponent c)
public void paint(Graphics g,JComponent
  c)
protected void uninstallDefaults()
protected void uninstallKeyboardActions()
protected void uninstallListeners()
public void uninstallUI(JComponent c)

►BASICTABLEUI

public class javax.swing.plaf.basic.
  BasicTableUI
extends javax.swing.plaf.TableUI
extends javax.swing.plaf.ComponentUI
extends java.lang.Object

Fields

protected java.awt.event.FocusListener
  focusListener
protected java.awt.event.KeyListener
  keyListener
protected javax.swing.event.
  MouseInputListener mouseInputListener
protected javax.swing.CellRendererPane
  rendererPane
protected javax.swing.JTable table

Methods

protected FocusListener
  createFocusListener()
protected KeyListener createKeyListener()
protected MouseInputListener
  createMouseInputListener()
public static ComponentUI createUI(
  JComponent c)
public Dimension getMaximumSize(
  JComponent c)
public Dimension getMinimumSize(
  JComponent c)
public Dimension getPreferredSize(
  JComponent c)
protected void installDefaults()
protected void installKeyboardActions()
protected void installListeners()
public void installUI(JComponent c)
public void paint(Graphics g,JComponent
  c)
protected void uninstallDefaults()
protected void uninstallKeyboardActions()

protected void uninstallListeners()
public void uninstallUI(JComponent c)

►BASICTEXTAREAUI

public class javax.swing.plaf.basic.
  BasicTextAreaUI
extends javax.swing.plaf.basic.
  BasicTextUI
extends javax.swing.plaf.TextUI
extends javax.swing.plaf.ComponentUI
extends java.lang.Object

Constructors

public BasicTextAreaUI()

Methods

public View create(Element elem)
public static ComponentUI createUI(
  JComponent ta)
protected String getPropertyPrefix()
protected void propertyChange(
  PropertyChangeEvent evt)

►BASICTEXTFIELDUI

public class javax.swing.plaf.basic.
  BasicTextFieldUI
extends javax.swing.plaf.basic.
  BasicTextUI
extends javax.swing.plaf.TextUI
extends javax.swing.plaf.ComponentUI
extends java.lang.Object

Constructors

public BasicTextFieldUI()

Methods

public View create(Element elem)
protected Caret createCaret()
public static ComponentUI createUI(
  JComponent c)
protected String getPropertyPrefix()

►BASICTEXTPANEUI

public class javax.swing.plaf.basic.
  BasicTextPaneUI
extends javax.swing.plaf.basic.
  BasicEditorPaneUI
extends javax.swing.plaf.basic.
  BasicTextUI
extends javax.swing.plaf.TextUI
extends javax.swing.plaf.ComponentUI
extends java.lang.Object

Constructors

public BasicTextPaneUI()

Methods

public static ComponentUI createUI(
  JComponent c)
public EditorKit getEditorKit(
  JTextComponent tc)
protected String getPropertyPrefix()
protected void propertyChange(
  PropertyChangeEvent evt)

►BASICTEXTUI

public abstract class javax.swing.plaf.
  basic.BasicTextUI

implements javax.swing.text.ViewFactory
extends javax.swing.plaf.TextUI
extends javax.swing.plaf.ComponentUI
extends java.lang.Object

Constructors
public BasicTextUI()

Methods
public View create(Element elem)
public View create(Element elem,int p0,
  int p1)
protected Caret createCaret()
protected Highlighter createHighlighter()
protected Keymap createKeymap()
public void damageRange(JTextComponent
  tc,int p0,int p1)
public void damageRange(JTextComponent t,
  int p0,int p1,Bias p0Bias,Bias p1Bias)
protected final JTextComponent
  getComponent()
public EditorKit getEditorKit(
  JTextComponent tc)
protected String getKeymapName()
public Dimension getMaximumSize(
  JComponent c)
public Dimension getMinimumSize(
  JComponent c)
public int getNextVisualPositionFrom(
  JTextComponent t,int pos,Bias b,int
  direction,Bias biasRet)
public Dimension getPreferredSize(
  JComponent c)
protected abstract String
  getPropertyPrefix()
public View getRootView(JTextComponent
  tc)
protected Rectangle getVisibleEditorRect(
)
protected void installDefaults()
protected void installKeyboardActions()
protected void installListeners()
public void installUI(JComponent c)
protected void modelChanged()
public Rectangle modelToView(
  JTextComponent tc,int pos)
public Rectangle modelToView(
  JTextComponent tc,int pos,Bias bias)
public final void paint(Graphics g,
  JComponent c)
protected void paintBackground(Graphics
  g)
protected void paintSafely(Graphics g)
protected void propertyChange(
  PropertyChangeEvent evt)
protected final void setView(View v)
protected void uninstallDefaults()
protected void uninstallKeyboardActions()
protected void uninstallListeners()
public void uninstallUI(JComponent c)
public int viewToModel(JTextComponent tc,
  Point pt)
public int viewToModel(JTextComponent tc,
  Point pt,Bias biasReturn)

▶**BasicToggleButtonUI**
public class javax.swing.plaf.basic.
  BasicToggleButtonUI
extends javax.swing.plaf.basic.
  BasicButtonUI
extends javax.swing.plaf.ButtonUI
extends javax.swing.plaf.ComponentUI
extends java.lang.Object

Methods
public static ComponentUI createUI(
  JComponent b)
protected String getPropertyPrefix()
public void paint(Graphics g,JComponent
  c)
protected void paintButtonPressed(
  Graphics g,AbstractButton b)
protected void paintFocus(Graphics g,
  AbstractButton b,Rectangle viewRect,
  Rectangle textRect,Rectangle iconRect)
protected void paintIcon(Graphics g,
  AbstractButton b,Rectangle iconRect)
protected void paintText(Graphics g,
  AbstractButton b,Rectangle textRect,
  String text)

▶**BasicToolBarSeparatorUI**
public class javax.swing.plaf.basic.
  BasicToolBarSeparatorUI
extends javax.swing.plaf.basic.
  BasicSeparatorUI
extends javax.swing.plaf.SeparatorUI
extends javax.swing.plaf.ComponentUI
extends java.lang.Object

Methods
public static ComponentUI createUI(
  JComponent c)
public Dimension getMaximumSize(
  JComponent c)
public Dimension getMinimumSize(
  JComponent c)
public Dimension getPreferredSize(
  JComponent c)
protected void installDefaults(
  JSeparator s)
public void paint(Graphics g,JComponent
  c)

▶**BasicToolBarUI**
public class javax.swing.plaf.basic.
  BasicToolBarUI
implements javax.swing.SwingConstants
extends javax.swing.plaf.ToolBarUI
extends javax.swing.plaf.ComponentUI
extends java.lang.Object

Fields
protected java.awt.Color
  dockingBorderColor
protected java.awt.Color dockingColor
protected javax.swing.event.
  MouseInputListener dockingListener
protected javax.swing.KeyStroke downKey
protected DragWindow dragWindow

protected java.awt.Color
  floatingBorderColor
protected java.awt.Color floatingColor
protected int focusedCompIndex
protected javax.swing.KeyStroke leftKey
protected java.beans.
  PropertyChangeListener propertyListener
protected javax.swing.KeyStroke
  rightKey
protected javax.swing.JToolBar toolBar
protected java.awt.event.
  ContainerListener toolBarContListener
protected java.awt.event.FocusListener
  toolBarFocusListener
protected javax.swing.KeyStroke upKey

Methods
public boolean canDock(Component c,Point
  p)
protected MouseInputListener
  createDockingListener()
protected DragWindow createDragWindow(
  JToolBar toolbar)
protected JFrame createFloatingFrame(
  JToolBar toolbar)
protected WindowListener
  createFrameListener()
protected PropertyChangeListener
  createPropertyListener()
protected ContainerListener
  createToolBarContListener()
protected FocusListener
  createToolBarFocusListener()
public static ComponentUI createUI(
  JComponent c)
protected void dragTo(Point position,
  Point origin)
protected void floatAt(Point position,
  Point origin)
public Color getDockingColor()
public Color getFloatingColor()
public Dimension getMaximumSize(
  JComponent c)
public Dimension getMinimumSize(
  JComponent c)
public Dimension getPreferredSize(
  JComponent c)
protected void installComponents()
protected void installDefaults()
protected void installKeyboardActions()
protected void installListeners()
public void installUI(JComponent c)
public boolean isFloating()
protected void navigateFocusedComp(int
  direction)
public void setDockingColor(Color c)
public void setFloating(boolean b,Point
  p)
public void setFloatingColor(Color c)
public void setFloatingLocation(int x,
  int y)
public void setOrientation(int
  orientation)
protected void uninstallComponents()

protected void uninstallDefaults()
protected void uninstallKeyboardActions()
protected void uninstallListeners()
public void uninstallUI(JComponent c)

▶BASICTOOLTIPUI
public class javax.swing.plaf.basic.
  BasicToolTipUI
extends javax.swing.plaf.ToolTipUI
extends javax.swing.plaf.ComponentUI
extends java.lang.Object

Constructors
public BasicToolTipUI()

Methods
public static ComponentUI createUI(
  JComponent c)
public Dimension getMaximumSize(
  JComponent c)
public Dimension getMinimumSize(
  JComponent c)
public Dimension getPreferredSize(
  JComponent c)
protected void installDefaults(
  JComponent c)
protected void installListeners(
  JComponent c)
public void installUI(JComponent c)
public void paint(Graphics g,JComponent
  c)
protected void uninstallDefaults(
  JComponent c)
protected void uninstallListeners(
  JComponent c)
public void uninstallUI(JComponent c)

▶BASICTREEUI
public class javax.swing.plaf.basic.
  BasicTreeUI
extends javax.swing.plaf.TreeUI
extends javax.swing.plaf.ComponentUI
extends java.lang.Object

Fields
protected transient javax.swing.tree.
  TreeCellEditor cellEditor
protected transient javax.swing.Icon
  collapsedIcon
protected boolean createdCellEditor
protected boolean createdRenderer
protected transient javax.swing.tree.
  TreeCellRenderer currentCellRenderer
protected int depthOffset
protected java.util.Hashtable
  drawingCache
protected java.awt.Component
  editingComponent
protected javax.swing.tree.TreePath
  editingPath
protected int editingRow
protected boolean
  editorHasDifferentSize
protected transient javax.swing.Icon
  expandedIcon

protected boolean largeModel
protected int lastSelectedRow
protected int leftChildIndent
protected AbstractLayoutCache.
  NodeDimensions nodeDimensions
protected java.awt.Dimension
  preferredMinSize
protected java.awt.Dimension
  preferredSize
protected javax.swing.CellRendererPane
  rendererPane
protected int rightChildIndent
protected boolean
  stopEditingInCompleteEditing
protected int totalChildIndent
protected javax.swing.JTree tree
protected javax.swing.tree.TreeModel
  treeModel
protected javax.swing.tree.
  TreeSelectionModel treeSelectionModel
protected javax.swing.tree.
  AbstractLayoutCache treeState
protected boolean
  validCachedPreferredSize

Constructors
public BasicTreeUI()

Methods
public void cancelEditing(JTree tree)
protected void
  checkForClickInExpandControl(TreePath
  path,int mouseX,int mouseY)
protected void completeEditing()
protected void completeEditing(boolean
  messageStop,boolean messageCancel,
  boolean messageTree)
protected void completeUIInstall()
protected void completeUIUninstall()
protected void configureLayoutCache()
protected CellEditorListener
  createCellEditorListener()
protected CellRendererPane
  createCellRendererPane()
protected ComponentListener
  createComponentListener()
protected TreeCellEditor
  createDefaultCellEditor()
protected TreeCellRenderer
  createDefaultCellRenderer()
protected FocusListener
  createFocusListener()
protected KeyListener createKeyListener()
protected AbstractLayoutCache
  createLayoutCache()
protected MouseListener
  createMouseListener()
protected NodeDimensions
  createNodeDimensions()
protected PropertyChangeListener
  createPropertyChangeListener()
protected PropertyChangeListener
  createSelectionModelProperty
  ChangeListener()

protected TreeExpansionListener
  createTreeExpansionListener()
protected TreeModelListener
  createTreeModelListener()
protected TreeSelectionListener
  createTreeSelectionListener()
public static ComponentUI createUI(
  JComponent x)
protected void drawCentered(Component c,
  Graphics graphics,Icon icon,int x,int y)
protected void drawDashedHorizontalLine(
  Graphics g,int y,int x1,int x2)
protected void drawDashedVerticalLine(
  Graphics g,int x,int y1,int y2)
protected void ensureRowsAreVisible(int
  beginRow,int endRow)
protected TreeCellEditor getCellEditor()
protected TreeCellRenderer
  getCellRenderer()
public TreePath
  getClosestPathForLocation(JTree tree,int
  x,int y)
public Icon getCollapsedIcon()
public TreePath getEditingPath(JTree
  tree)
public Icon getExpandedIcon()
protected Color getHashColor()
protected int getHorizontalLegBuffer()
protected TreePath getLastChildPath(
  TreePath parent)
public int getLeftChildIndent()
public Dimension getMaximumSize(
  JComponent c)
public Dimension getMinimumSize(
  JComponent c)
protected TreeModel getModel()
public Rectangle getPathBounds(JTree
  tree,TreePath path)
public TreePath getPathForRow(JTree tree,
  int row)
public Dimension getPreferredMinSize()
public Dimension getPreferredSize(
  JComponent c)
public Dimension getPreferredSize(
  JComponent c,boolean checkConsistancy)
public int getRightChildIndent()
public int getRowCount(JTree tree)
public int getRowForPath(JTree tree,
  TreePath path)
protected int getRowHeight()
protected TreeSelectionModel
  getSelectionModel()
protected boolean getShowsRootHandles()
protected int getVerticalLegBuffer()
protected void handleExpandControlClick(
  TreePath path,int mouseX,int mouseY)
protected void installComponents()
protected void installDefaults()
protected void installKeyboardActions()
protected void installListeners()
public void installUI(JComponent c)
protected boolean isEditable()

public boolean isEditing(JTree tree)
protected boolean isLargeModel()
protected boolean isLeaf(int row)
protected boolean
  isLocationInExpandControl(TreePath path,
  int mouseX,int mouseY)
protected boolean isMultiSelectEvent(
  MouseEvent event)
protected boolean isRootVisible()
protected boolean isToggleEvent(
  MouseEvent event)
protected boolean isToggleSelectionEvent(
  MouseEvent event)
public void paint(Graphics g,JComponent
  c)
protected void paintExpandControl(
  Graphics g,Rectangle clipBounds,Insets
  insets,Rectangle bounds,TreePath path,
  int row,boolean isExpanded,boolean
  hasBeenExpanded,boolean isLeaf)
protected void paintHorizontalLine(
  Graphics g,JComponent c,int y,int left,
  int right)
protected void paintHorizontalPartOfLeg(
  Graphics g,Rectangle clipBounds,Insets
  insets,Rectangle bounds,TreePath path,
  int row,boolean isExpanded,boolean
  hasBeenExpanded,boolean isLeaf)
protected void paintRow(Graphics g,
  Rectangle clipBounds,Insets insets,
  Rectangle bounds,TreePath path,int row,
  boolean isExpanded,boolean
  hasBeenExpanded,boolean isLeaf)
protected void paintVerticalLine(
  Graphics g,JComponent c,int x,int top,
  int bottom)
protected void paintVerticalPartOfLeg(
  Graphics g,Rectangle clipBounds,Insets
  insets,TreePath path)
protected void pathWasCollapsed(TreePath
  path)
protected void pathWasExpanded(TreePath
  path)
protected void prepareForUIInstall()
protected void prepareForUIUninstall()
protected void selectPathForEvent(
  TreePath path,MouseEvent event)
protected void setCellEditor(
  TreeCellEditor editor)
protected void setCellRenderer(
  TreeCellRenderer tcr)
public void setCollapsedIcon(Icon newG)
protected void setEditable(boolean
  newValue)
public void setExpandedIcon(Icon newG)
protected void setHashColor(Color color)
protected void setLargeModel(boolean
  largeModel)
public void setLeftChildIndent(int
  newAmount)
protected void setModel(TreeModel model)
public void setPreferredMinSize(
  Dimension newSize)

public void setRightChildIndent(int
  newAmount)
protected void setRootVisible(boolean
  newValue)
protected void setRowHeight(int
  rowHeight)
protected void setSelectionModel(
  TreeSelectionModel newLSM)
protected void setShowsRootHandles(
  boolean newValue)
protected boolean
  shouldPaintExpandControl(TreePath path,
  int row,boolean isExpanded,boolean
  hasBeenExpanded,boolean isLeaf)
protected boolean startEditing(TreePath
  path,MouseEvent event)
public void startEditingAtPath(JTree
  tree,TreePath path)
public boolean stopEditing(JTree tree)
protected void toggleExpandState(
  TreePath path)
protected void uninstallComponents()
protected void uninstallDefaults()
protected void uninstallKeyboardActions()
protected void uninstallListeners()
public void uninstallUI(JComponent c)
protected void updateCachedPreferredSize(
)
protected void updateCellEditor()
protected void updateDepthOffset()
protected void updateExpandedDescendants(
  TreePath path)
protected void
  updateLayoutCacheExpandedNodes()
protected void updateRenderer()
protected void updateSize()

►BasicViewportUI
public class javax.swing.plaf.basic.
  BasicViewportUI
extends javax.swing.plaf.ViewportUI
extends javax.swing.plaf.ComponentUI
extends java.lang.Object
Methods
public static ComponentUI createUI(
  JComponent c)
protected void installDefaults(
  JComponent c)
public void installUI(JComponent c)
protected void uninstallDefaults(
  JComponent c)
public void uninstallUI(JComponent c)

►BatchUpdateException
public class java.sql.
  BatchUpdateException
extends java.sql.SQLException
extends java.lang.Exception
extends java.lang.Throwable
extends java.lang.Object

Constructors

public BatchUpdateException(String
  reason,String SQLState,int vendorCode,
  int updateCounts)
public BatchUpdateException(String
  reason,String SQLState,int updateCounts)
public BatchUpdateException(String
  reason,int updateCounts)
public BatchUpdateException(int
  updateCounts)
public BatchUpdateException()

Methods

public int getUpdateCounts()

▶BEANCONTEXTCHILDSUPPORT

public class java.beans.beancontext.
  BeanContextChildSupport
implements java.beans.beancontext.
  BeanContextChild
implements java.beans.beancontext.
  BeanContextServicesListener
implements java.io.Serializable
extends java.lang.Object

Fields

protected transient java.beans.
  beancontext.BeanContext beanContext
public java.beans.beancontext.
  BeanContextChild beanContextChildPeer
protected java.beans.
  PropertyChangeSupport pcSupport
protected transient boolean
  rejectedSetBCOnce
protected java.beans.
  VetoableChangeSupport vcSupport

Constructors

public BeanContextChildSupport()
public BeanContextChildSupport(
  BeanContextChild bcc)

Methods

public void addPropertyChangeListener(
  String name,PropertyChangeListener pcl)
public void addVetoableChangeListener(
  String name,VetoableChangeListener vcl)
public void firePropertyChange(String
  name,Object oldValue,Object newValue)
public void fireVetoableChange(String
  name,Object oldValue,Object newValue)
public synchronized BeanContext
  getBeanContext()
public BeanContextChild
  getBeanContextChildPeer()
protected void
  initializeBeanContextResources()
public boolean isDelegated()
protected void
  releaseBeanContextResources()
public void removePropertyChangeListener(
  String name,PropertyChangeListener pcl)
public void removeVetoableChangeListener(
  String name,VetoableChangeListener vcl)
public void serviceAvailable(
  BeanContextServiceAvailableEvent bcsae)

public void serviceRevoked(
  BeanContextServiceRevokedEvent bcsre)
public synchronized void setBeanContext(
  BeanContext bc)
public boolean
  validatePendingSetBeanContext(
  BeanContext newValue)

▶BEANCONTEXTEVENT

public abstract class java.beans.
  beancontext.BeanContextEvent
extends java.util.EventObject
extends java.lang.Object

Fields

protected java.beans.beancontext.
  BeanContext propagatedFrom

Constructors

protected BeanContextEvent(BeanContext
  bc)

Methods

public BeanContext getBeanContext()
public synchronized BeanContext
  getPropagatedFrom()
public synchronized boolean isPropagated(
)
public synchronized void
  setPropagatedFrom(BeanContext bc)

▶BEANCONTEXTMEMBERSHIPEVENT

public class java.beans.beancontext.
  BeanContextMembershipEvent
extends java.beans.beancontext.
  BeanContextEvent
extends java.util.EventObject
extends java.lang.Object

Fields

protected java.util.Collection children

Constructors

public BeanContextMembershipEvent(
  BeanContext bc,Collection changes)
public BeanContextMembershipEvent(
  BeanContext bc,Object changes)

Methods

public boolean contains(Object child)
public Iterator iterator()
public int size()
public Object toArray()

▶BEANCONTEXTSERVICEAVAILABLEEVENT

public class java.beans.beancontext.
  BeanContextServiceAvailableEvent
extends java.beans.beancontext.
  BeanContextEvent
extends java.util.EventObject
extends java.lang.Object

Fields

protected java.lang.Class serviceClass

Constructors

public BeanContextServiceAvailableEvent(
  BeanContextServices bcs,Class sc)

Methods
```
public Iterator
  getCurrentServiceSelectors()
public Class getServiceClass()
public BeanContextServices
  getSourceAsBeanContextServices()
```

▶**BEANCONTEXTSERVICEREVOKEDEVENT**
```
public class java.beans.beancontext.
  BeanContextServiceRevokedEvent
extends java.beans.beancontext.
  BeanContextEvent
extends java.util.EventObject
extends java.lang.Object
```

Fields
```
protected java.lang.Class serviceClass
```

Constructors
```
public  BeanContextServiceRevokedEvent(
  BeanContextServices bcs,Class sc,boolean
  invalidate)
```

Methods
```
public Class getServiceClass()
public BeanContextServices
  getSourceAsBeanContextServices()
public boolean
  isCurrentServiceInvalidNow()
public boolean isServiceClass(Class
  service)
```

▶**BEANCONTEXTSERVICESSUPPORT**
```
public class java.beans.beancontext.
  BeanContextServicesSupport
implements java.beans.beancontext.
  BeanContextServices
extends java.beans.beancontext.
  BeanContextSupport
extends java.beans.beancontext.
  BeanContextChildSupport
extends java.lang.Object
```

Fields
```
protected transient java.util.ArrayList
  bcsListeners
protected transient
  BCSSProxyServiceProvider proxy
protected transient int serializable
protected transient java.util.HashMap
  services
```

Constructors
```
public  BeanContextServicesSupport(
  BeanContextServices peer,Locale lcle,
  boolean dTime,boolean visible)
public  BeanContextServicesSupport(
  BeanContextServices peer,Locale lcle,
  boolean dtime)
public  BeanContextServicesSupport(
  BeanContextServices peer,Locale lcle)
public  BeanContextServicesSupport(
  BeanContextServices peer)
public  BeanContextServicesSupport()
```

Methods
```
public void
  addBeanContextServicesListener(
  BeanContextServicesListener bcsl)
public boolean addService(Class
  serviceClass,BeanContextServiceProvider
  bcsp)
protected boolean addService(Class
  serviceClass,BeanContextServiceProvider
  bcsp,boolean fireEvent)
protected synchronized void
  bcsPreDeserializationHook(
  ObjectInputStream ois)
protected synchronized void
  bcsPreSerializationHook(
  ObjectOutputStream oos)
protected void childJustRemovedHook(
  Object child,BCSChild bcsc)
protected BCSChild createBCSChild(Object
  targetChild,Object peer)
protected BCSSServiceProvider
  createBCSSServiceProvider(Class sc,
  BeanContextServiceProvider bcsp)
protected final void fireServiceAdded(
  Class serviceClass)
protected final void fireServiceAdded(
  BeanContextServiceAvailableEvent bcssae)
protected final void fireServiceRevoked(
  BeanContextServiceRevokedEvent bcsre)
protected final void fireServiceRevoked(
  Class serviceClass,boolean revokeNow)
public BeanContextServices
  getBeanContextServicesPeer()
protected final static
  BeanContextServicesListener
  getChildBeanContextServicesListener(
  Object child)
public Iterator getCurrentServiceClasses(
  )
public Iterator
  getCurrentServiceSelectors(Class
  serviceClass)
public Object getService(
  BeanContextChild child,Object requestor,
  Class serviceClass,Object
  serviceSelector,
  BeanContextServiceRevokedListener bcsrl)
public synchronized boolean hasService(
  Class serviceClass)
public void initialize()
protected synchronized void
  initializeBeanContextResources()
protected synchronized void
  releaseBeanContextResources()
public void releaseService(
  BeanContextChild child,Object requestor,
  Object service)
public void
  removeBeanContextServicesListener(
  BeanContextServicesListener bcsl)
public void revokeService(Class
  serviceClass,BeanContextServiceProvider
  bcsp,boolean revokeCurrentServicesNow)
```

public void serviceAvailable(
  BeanContextServiceAvailableEvent bcssae)
public void serviceRevoked(
  BeanContextServiceRevokedEvent bcssre)

▶BeanContextSupport

public class java.beans.beancontext.
  BeanContextSupport
implements java.beans.beancontext.
  BeanContext
implements java.beans.
  PropertyChangeListener
implements java.io.Serializable
implements java.beans.
  VetoableChangeListener
extends java.beans.beancontext.
  BeanContextChildSupport
extends java.lang.Object

Fields

protected transient java.util.ArrayList
  bcmListeners
protected transient java.util.HashMap
  children
protected boolean designTime
protected java.util.Locale locale
protected boolean okToUseGui

Constructors

public BeanContextSupport(BeanContext
  peer,Locale lcle,boolean dTime,boolean
  visible)
public BeanContextSupport(BeanContext
  peer,Locale lcle,boolean dtime)
public BeanContextSupport(BeanContext
  peer,Locale lcle)
public BeanContextSupport(BeanContext
  peer)
public BeanContextSupport()

Methods

public boolean add(Object targetChild)
public boolean addAll(Collection c)
public void
  addBeanContextMembershipListener(
  BeanContextMembershipListener bcml)
public boolean avoidingGui()
protected Iterator bcsChildren()
protected void bcsPreDeserializationHook(
  ObjectInputStream ois)
protected void bcsPreSerializationHook(
  ObjectOutputStream oos)
protected void childDeserializedHook(
  Object child,BCSChild bcsc)
protected void childJustAddedHook(Object
  child,BCSChild bcsc)
protected void childJustRemovedHook(
  Object child,BCSChild bcsc)
protected final static boolean
  classEquals(Class first,Class second)
public void clear()
public boolean contains(Object o)
public boolean containsAll(Collection c)
public boolean containsKey(Object o)
protected final Object copyChildren()

protected BCSChild createBCSChild(Object
  targetChild,Object peer)
protected final void deserialize(
  ObjectInputStream ois,Collection coll)
public synchronized void dontUseGui()
protected final void fireChildrenAdded(
  BeanContextMembershipEvent bcme)
protected final void fireChildrenRemoved(
  BeanContextMembershipEvent bcme)
public BeanContext getBeanContextPeer()
protected final static BeanContextChild
  getChildBeanContextChild(Object child)
protected final static
  BeanContextMembershipListener
  getChildBeanContextMembershipListener(
  Object child)
protected final static
  PropertyChangeListener
  getChildPropertyChangeListener(Object
  child)
protected final static Serializable
  getChildSerializable(Object child)
protected final static
  VetoableChangeListener
  getChildVetoableChangeListener(Object
  child)
protected final static Visibility
  getChildVisibility(Object child)
public synchronized Locale getLocale()
public URL getResource(String name,
  BeanContextChild bcc)
public InputStream getResourceAsStream(
  String name,BeanContextChild bcc)
protected synchronized void initialize()
public Object instantiateChild(String
  beanName)
public synchronized boolean isDesignTime(
)
public boolean isEmpty()
public boolean isSerializing()
public Iterator iterator()
public synchronized boolean needsGui()
public synchronized void okToUseGui()
public void propertyChange(
  PropertyChangeEvent pce)
public final void readChildren(
  ObjectInputStream ois)
public boolean remove(Object targetChild)
protected boolean remove(Object
  targetChild,boolean callChildSetBC)
public boolean removeAll(Collection c)
public void
  removeBeanContextMembershipListener(
  BeanContextMembershipListener bcml)
public boolean retainAll(Collection c)
protected final void serialize(
  ObjectOutputStream oos,Collection coll)
public synchronized void setDesignTime(
  boolean dTime)
public synchronized void setLocale(
  Locale newLocale)
public int size()

```
public Object toArray()
public Object toArray(Object arry)
protected boolean validatePendingAdd(
  Object targetChild)
protected boolean validatePendingRemove(
  Object targetChild)
public void vetoableChange(
  PropertyChangeEvent pce)
public final void writeChildren(
  ObjectOutputStream oos)
```

▶**BEANDESCRIPTOR**

```
public class java.beans.BeanDescriptor
extends java.beans.FeatureDescriptor
extends java.lang.Object
```

Constructors

```
public  BeanDescriptor(Class beanClass)
public  BeanDescriptor(Class beanClass,
  Class customizerClass)
 BeanDescriptor()
```

Methods

```
public Class getBeanClass()
public Class getCustomizerClass()
```

▶**BEANS**

```
public class java.beans.Beans
extends java.lang.Object
```

Methods

```
public static Object getInstanceOf(
  Object bean,Class targetType)
public static Object instantiate(
  ClassLoader cls,String beanName)
public static Object instantiate(
  ClassLoader cls,String beanName,
  BeanContext beanContext)
public static Object instantiate(
  ClassLoader cls,String beanName,
  BeanContext beanContext,
  AppletInitializer initializer)
public static boolean isDesignTime()
public static boolean isGuiAvailable()
public static boolean isInstanceOf(
  Object bean,Class targetType)
public static void setDesignTime(boolean
  isDesignTime)
public static void setGuiAvailable(
  boolean isGuiAvailable)
```

▶**BEVELBORDER**

```
public class javax.swing.border.
  BevelBorder
extends javax.swing.border.
  AbstractBorder
extends java.lang.Object
```

Fields

```
protected int bevelType
protected java.awt.Color highlightInner
protected java.awt.Color highlightOuter
public final static int LOWERED
public final static int RAISED
protected java.awt.Color shadowInner
protected java.awt.Color shadowOuter
```

Constructors

```
public  BevelBorder(int bevelType)
public  BevelBorder(int bevelType,Color
  highlight,Color shadow)
public  BevelBorder(int bevelType,Color
  highlightOuter,Color highlightInner,
  Color shadowOuter,Color shadowInner)
```

Methods

```
public int getBevelType()
public Insets getBorderInsets(Component
  c)
public Insets getBorderInsets(Component
  c,Insets insets)
public Color getHighlightInnerColor(
  Component c)
public Color getHighlightOuterColor(
  Component c)
public Color getShadowInnerColor(
  Component c)
public Color getShadowOuterColor(
  Component c)
public boolean isBorderOpaque()
public void paintBorder(Component c,
  Graphics g,int x,int y,int width,int
  height)
protected void paintLoweredBevel(
  Component c,Graphics g,int x,int y,int
  width,int height)
protected void paintRaisedBevel(
  Component c,Graphics g,int x,int y,int
  width,int height)
```

▶**BIGDECIMAL**

```
public class java.math.BigDecimal
implements java.lang.Comparable
extends java.lang.Number
extends java.lang.Object
```

Fields

```
public final static int ROUND_CEILING
public final static int ROUND_DOWN
public final static int ROUND_FLOOR
public final static int ROUND_HALF_DOWN
public final static int ROUND_HALF_EVEN
public final static int ROUND_HALF_UP
public final static int ROUND_
  UNNECESSARY
public final static int ROUND_UP
```

Constructors

```
public  BigDecimal(String val)
public  BigDecimal(double val)
public  BigDecimal(BigInteger val)
public  BigDecimal(BigInteger
  unscaledVal,int scale)
```

Methods

```
public BigDecimal abs()
public BigDecimal add(BigDecimal val)
public int compareTo(BigDecimal val)
public int compareTo(Object o)
public BigDecimal divide(BigDecimal val,
  int scale,int roundingMode)
public BigDecimal divide(BigDecimal val,
  int roundingMode)
```

```
public double doubleValue()
public boolean equals(Object x)
public float floatValue()
public int hashCode()
public int intValue()
public long longValue()
public BigDecimal max(BigDecimal val)
public BigDecimal min(BigDecimal val)
public BigDecimal movePointLeft(int n)
public BigDecimal movePointRight(int n)
public BigDecimal multiply(BigDecimal
  val)
public BigDecimal negate()
public int scale()
public BigDecimal setScale(int scale,int
  roundingMode)
public BigDecimal setScale(int scale)
public int signum()
public BigDecimal subtract(BigDecimal
  val)
public BigInteger toBigInteger()
public String toString()
public BigInteger unscaledValue()
public static BigDecimal valueOf(long
  unscaledVal,int scale)
public static BigDecimal valueOf(long
  val)
```

▶BigInteger
```
public class java.math.BigInteger
implements java.lang.Comparable
extends java.lang.Number
extends java.lang.Object
```
Fields
```
public final static java.math.BigInteger
  ONE
public final static java.math.BigInteger
  ZERO
```
Constructors
```
public  BigInteger(byte val)
public  BigInteger(int signum,byte
  magnitude)
public  BigInteger(String val,int radix)
public  BigInteger(String val)
public  BigInteger(int numBits,Random
  rnd)
public  BigInteger(int bitLength,int
  certainty,Random rnd)
private BigInteger()
```
Methods
```
public BigInteger abs()
public BigInteger add(BigInteger val)
public BigInteger and(BigInteger val)
public BigInteger andNot(BigInteger val)
public int bitCount()
public int bitLength()
public BigInteger clearBit(int n)
public int compareTo(BigInteger val)
public int compareTo(Object o)
public BigInteger divide(BigInteger val)
public BigInteger divideAndRemainder(
  BigInteger val)
```

```
public double doubleValue()
public boolean equals(Object x)
public BigInteger flipBit(int n)
public float floatValue()
public BigInteger gcd(BigInteger val)
public int getLowestSetBit()
public int hashCode()
public int intValue()
public boolean isProbablePrime(int
  certainty)
public long longValue()
public BigInteger max(BigInteger val)
public BigInteger min(BigInteger val)
public BigInteger mod(BigInteger m)
public BigInteger modInverse(BigInteger
  m)
public BigInteger modPow(BigInteger
  exponent,BigInteger m)
public BigInteger multiply(BigInteger
  val)
public BigInteger negate()
public BigInteger not()
public BigInteger or(BigInteger val)
public BigInteger pow(int exponent)
public BigInteger remainder(BigInteger
  val)
public BigInteger setBit(int n)
public BigInteger shiftLeft(int n)
public BigInteger shiftRight(int n)
public int signum()
public BigInteger subtract(BigInteger
  val)
public boolean testBit(int n)
public byte toByteArray()
public String toString(int radix)
public static String toString()
public static BigInteger valueOf(long
  val)
public BigInteger xor(BigInteger val)
```

▶BindException
```
public class java.net.BindException
extends java.net.SocketException
extends java.io.IOException
extends java.lang.Exception
extends java.lang.Throwable
extends java.lang.Object
```
Constructors
```
public  BindException(String msg)
public  BindException()
```

▶BitSet
```
public class java.util.BitSet
implements java.lang.Cloneable
implements java.io.Serializable
extends java.lang.Object
```
Constructors
```
public  BitSet()
public  BitSet(int nbits)
```
Methods
```
public void and(BitSet set)
public void andNot(BitSet set)
```

```
public void clear(int bitIndex)
public Object clone()
public boolean equals(Object obj)
public boolean get(int bitIndex)
public int hashCode()
public int length()
public void or(BitSet set)
public void set(int bitIndex)
public int size()
public String toString()
public void xor(BitSet set)
```

▸BLOCKVIEW

```
public class javax.swing.text.html.
  BlockView
extends javax.swing.text.BoxView
extends javax.swing.text.CompositeView
extends javax.swing.text.View
extends java.lang.Object
```

Constructors

```
public BlockView(Element elem,int axis)
```

Methods

```
public float getAlignment(int axis)
public AttributeSet getAttributes()
public int getResizeWeight(int axis)
protected StyleSheet getStyleSheet()
public void paint(Graphics g,Shape
  allocation)
protected void
  setPropertiesFromAttributes()
```

▸BOOK

```
public class java.awt.print.Book
implements java.awt.print.Pageable
extends java.lang.Object
```

Constructors

```
public Book()
```

Methods

```
public void append(Printable painter,
  PageFormat page)
public void append(Printable painter,
  PageFormat page,int numPages)
public int getNumberOfPages()
public PageFormat getPageFormat(int
  pageIndex)
public Printable getPrintable(int
  pageIndex)
public void setPage(int pageIndex,
  Printable painter,PageFormat page)
```

▸BOOLEAN

```
public final class java.lang.Boolean
implements java.io.Serializable
extends java.lang.Object
```

Fields

```
public final static java.lang.Boolean
  FALSE
public final static java.lang.Boolean
  TRUE
public final static java.lang.Class
  TYPE
```

Constructors

```
public Boolean(boolean value)
public Boolean(String s)
```

Methods

```
public boolean booleanValue()
public boolean equals(Object obj)
public static boolean getBoolean(String
  name)
public int hashCode()
public String toString()
public static Boolean valueOf(String s)
```

▸BORDERFACTORY

```
public class javax.swing.BorderFactory
extends java.lang.Object
```

Constructors

```
private BorderFactory()
```

Methods

```
public static Border createBevelBorder(
  int type)
public static Border createBevelBorder(
  int type,Color highlight,Color shadow)
public static Border createBevelBorder(
  int type,Color highlightOuter,Color
  highlightInner,Color shadowOuter,Color
  shadowInner)
public static CompoundBorder
  createCompoundBorder()
public static CompoundBorder
  createCompoundBorder(Border
  outsideBorder,Border insideBorder)
public static Border createEmptyBorder()
public static Border createEmptyBorder(
  int top,int left,int bottom,int right)
public static Border createEtchedBorder()
public static Border createEtchedBorder(
  Color highlight,Color shadow)
public static Border createLineBorder(
  Color color)
public static Border createLineBorder(
  Color color,int thickness)
public static Border
  createLoweredBevelBorder()
public static MatteBorder
  createMatteBorder(int top,int left,int
  bottom,int right,Color color)
public static MatteBorder
  createMatteBorder(int top,int left,int
  bottom,int right,Icon tileIcon)
public static Border
  createRaisedBevelBorder()
public static TitledBorder
  createTitledBorder(String title)
public static TitledBorder
  createTitledBorder(Border border)
public static TitledBorder
  createTitledBorder(Border border,String
  title)
public static TitledBorder
  createTitledBorder(Border border,String
  title,int titleJustification,int
  titlePosition)
```

```
public static TitledBorder
  createTitledBorder(Border border,String
  title,int titleJustification,int
  titlePosition,Font titleFont)
public static TitledBorder
  createTitledBorder(Border border,String
  title,int titleJustification,int
  titlePosition,Font titleFont,Color
  titleColor)
```

▶BORDERLAYOUT

```
public class java.awt.BorderLayout
implements java.awt.LayoutManager2
implements java.io.Serializable
extends java.lang.Object
```

Fields

```
public final static java.lang.String
  AFTER_LAST_LINE
public final static java.lang.String
  AFTER_LINE_ENDS
public final static java.lang.String
  BEFORE_FIRST_LINE
public final static java.lang.String
  BEFORE_LINE_BEGINS
public final static java.lang.String
  CENTER
public final static java.lang.String
  EAST
public final static java.lang.String
  NORTH
public final static java.lang.String
  SOUTH
public final static java.lang.String
  WEST
```

Constructors

```
public  BorderLayout()
public  BorderLayout(int hgap,int vgap)
```

Methods

```
public void addLayoutComponent(Component
  comp,Object constraints)
public void addLayoutComponent(String
  name,Component comp)
public int getHgap()
public float getLayoutAlignmentX(
  Container parent)
public float getLayoutAlignmentY(
  Container parent)
public int getVgap()
public void invalidateLayout(Container
  target)
public void layoutContainer(Container
  target)
public Dimension maximumLayoutSize(
  Container target)
public Dimension minimumLayoutSize(
  Container target)
public Dimension preferredLayoutSize(
  Container target)
public void removeLayoutComponent(
  Component comp)
public void setHgap(int hgap)
public void setVgap(int vgap)
```

```
public String toString()
```

▶BORDERUIRESOURCE

```
public class javax.swing.plaf.
  BorderUIResource
implements javax.swing.border.Border
implements java.io.Serializable
implements javax.swing.plaf.UIResource
extends java.lang.Object
```

Constructors

```
public  BorderUIResource(Border delegate)
```

Methods

```
public static Border
  getBlackLineBorderUIResource()
public Insets getBorderInsets(Component
  c)
public static Border
  getEtchedBorderUIResource()
public static Border
  getLoweredBevelBorderUIResource()
public static Border
  getRaisedBevelBorderUIResource()
public boolean isBorderOpaque()
public void paintBorder(Component c,
  Graphics g,int x,int y,int width,int
  height)
```

▶Box

```
public class javax.swing.Box
implements javax.accessibility.
  Accessible
extends java.awt.Container
extends java.awt.Component
extends java.lang.Object
```

Fields

```
protected javax.accessibility.
  AccessibleContext accessibleContext
```

Constructors

```
public  Box(int axis)
```

Methods

```
public static Component createGlue()
public static Box createHorizontalBox()
public static Component
  createHorizontalGlue()
public static Component
  createHorizontalStrut(int width)
public static Component createRigidArea(
  Dimension d)
public static Box createVerticalBox()
public static Component
  createVerticalGlue()
public static Component
  createVerticalStrut(int height)
public AccessibleContext
  getAccessibleContext()
public void setLayout(LayoutManager l)
```

▶BOXLAYOUT

```
public class javax.swing.BoxLayout
implements java.awt.LayoutManager2
implements java.io.Serializable
extends java.lang.Object
```

Fields
public final static int X_AXIS
public final static int Y_AXIS

Constructors
public BoxLayout(Container target,int
  axis)
BoxLayout()

Methods
public void addLayoutComponent(String
  name,Component comp)
public void addLayoutComponent(Component
  comp,Object constraints)
public float getLayoutAlignmentX(
  Container target)
public float getLayoutAlignmentY(
  Container target)
public void invalidateLayout(Container
  target)
public void layoutContainer(Container
  target)
public Dimension maximumLayoutSize(
  Container target)
public Dimension minimumLayoutSize(
  Container target)
public Dimension preferredLayoutSize(
  Container target)
public void removeLayoutComponent(
  Component comp)

▶BoxView
public class javax.swing.text.BoxView
extends javax.swing.text.CompositeView
extends javax.swing.text.View
extends java.lang.Object

Constructors
public BoxView(Element elem,int axis)

Methods
protected void baselineLayout(int
  targetSpan,int axis,int offsets,int
  spans)
protected SizeRequirements
  baselineRequirements(int axis,
  SizeRequirements r)
protected SizeRequirements
  calculateMajorAxisRequirements(int axis,
  SizeRequirements r)
protected SizeRequirements
  calculateMinorAxisRequirements(int axis,
  SizeRequirements r)
public void changedUpdate(DocumentEvent
  e,Shape a,ViewFactory f)
protected void childAllocation(int index,
  Rectangle alloc)
protected boolean flipEastAndWestAtEnds(
  int position,Bias bias)
public float getAlignment(int axis)
public final int getHeight()
public float getMaximumSpan(int axis)
public float getMinimumSpan(int axis)
protected final int getOffset(int axis,
  int childIndex)
public float getPreferredSpan(int axis)

public int getResizeWeight(int axis)
protected final int getSpan(int axis,int
  childIndex)
protected View getViewAtPoint(int x,int
  y,Rectangle alloc)
public final int getWidth()
public void insertUpdate(DocumentEvent e,
  Shape a,ViewFactory f)
protected boolean isAfter(int x,int y,
  Rectangle innerAlloc)
protected boolean isAllocationValid()
protected boolean isBefore(int x,int y,
  Rectangle innerAlloc)
protected void layout(int width,int
  height)
protected void layoutMajorAxis(int
  targetSpan,int axis,int offsets,int
  spans)
protected void layoutMinorAxis(int
  targetSpan,int axis,int offsets,int
  spans)
public Shape modelToView(int pos,Shape a,
  Bias b)
public void paint(Graphics g,Shape
  allocation)
protected void paintChild(Graphics g,
  Rectangle alloc,int index)
public void preferenceChanged(View child,
  boolean width,boolean height)
public void removeUpdate(DocumentEvent e,
  Shape a,ViewFactory f)
public void replace(int offset,int
  length,View elems)
public void setSize(float width,float
  height)
public int viewToModel(float x,float y,
  Shape a,Bias bias)

▶BreakIterator
public abstract class java.text.
  BreakIterator
implements java.lang.Cloneable
extends java.lang.Object

Fields
public final static int DONE

Constructors
protected BreakIterator()

Methods
public Object clone()
public abstract int current()
public abstract int first()
public abstract int following(int offset)
public static synchronized Locale
  getAvailableLocales()
public static BreakIterator
  getCharacterInstance()
public static BreakIterator
  getCharacterInstance(Locale where)
public static BreakIterator
  getLineInstance()
public static BreakIterator
  getLineInstance(Locale where)

```
public static BreakIterator
  getSentenceInstance()
public static BreakIterator
  getSentenceInstance(Locale where)
public abstract CharacterIterator
  getText()
public static BreakIterator
  getWordInstance()
public static BreakIterator
  getWordInstance(Locale where)
public boolean isBoundary(int offset)
public abstract int last()
public abstract int next(int n)
public abstract int next()
public int preceding(int offset)
public abstract int previous()
public void setText(String newText)
public abstract void setText(
  CharacterIterator newText)
```

▶**BUFFEREDIMAGE**
```
public class java.awt.image.
  BufferedImage
implements java.awt.image.
  WritableRenderedImage
extends java.awt.Image
extends java.lang.Object
```

Fields
```
public final static int TYPE_3BYTE_BGR
public final static int TYPE_4BYTE_ABGR
public final static int TYPE_4BYTE_ABGR_
  PRE
public final static int TYPE_BYTE_
  BINARY
public final static int TYPE_BYTE_GRAY
public final static int TYPE_BYTE_
  INDEXED
public final static int TYPE_CUSTOM
public final static int TYPE_INT_ARGB
public final static int TYPE_INT_ARGB_
  PRE
public final static int TYPE_INT_BGR
public final static int TYPE_INT_RGB
public final static int TYPE_USHORT_555_
  RGB
public final static int TYPE_USHORT_565_
  RGB
public final static int TYPE_USHORT_
  GRAY
```

Constructors
```
public static  BufferedImage(int width,
  int height,int imageType)
public  BufferedImage(int width,int
  height,int imageType,IndexColorModel cm)
public  BufferedImage(ColorModel cm,
  WritableRaster raster,boolean
  isRasterPremultiplied,Hashtable
  properties)
```

Methods
```
public void addTileObserver(TileObserver
  to)
public void coerceData(boolean
  isAlphaPremultiplied)
public WritableRaster copyData(
  WritableRaster outRaster)
public Graphics2D createGraphics()
public void flush()
public WritableRaster getAlphaRaster()
public ColorModel getColorModel()
public Raster getData()
public Raster getData(Rectangle rect)
public Graphics getGraphics()
public int getHeight()
public int getHeight(ImageObserver
  observer)
public int getMinTileX()
public int getMinTileY()
public int getMinX()
public int getMinY()
public int getNumXTiles()
public int getNumYTiles()
public Object getProperty(String name,
  ImageObserver observer)
public Object getProperty(String name)
public String getPropertyNames()
public WritableRaster getRaster()
public int getRGB(int x,int y)
public int getRGB(int startX,int startY,
  int w,int h,int rgbArray,int offset,int
  scansize)
public SampleModel getSampleModel()
public ImageProducer getSource()
public Vector getSources()
public BufferedImage getSubimage(int x,
  int y,int w,int h)
public Raster getTile(int tileX,int
  tileY)
public int getTileGridXOffset()
public int getTileGridYOffset()
public int getTileHeight()
public int getTileWidth()
public int getType()
public int getWidth()
public int getWidth(ImageObserver
  observer)
public WritableRaster getWritableTile(
  int tileX,int tileY)
public Point getWritableTileIndices()
public boolean hasTileWriters()
public boolean isAlphaPremultiplied()
public boolean isTileWritable(int tileX,
  int tileY)
public void releaseWritableTile(int
  tileX,int tileY)
public void removeTileObserver(
  TileObserver to)
public void setData(Raster r)
public synchronized void setRGB(int x,
  int y,int rgb)
public void setRGB(int startX,int startY,
  int w,int h,int rgbArray,int offset,int
  scansize)
public String toString()
```

▶BUFFEREDIMAGEFILTER
public class java.awt.image.
  BufferedImageFilter
implements java.lang.Cloneable
extends java.awt.image.ImageFilter
extends java.lang.Object

Constructors
public BufferedImageFilter(
  BufferedImageOp op)

Methods
public BufferedImageOp
  getBufferedImageOp()
public void imageComplete(int status)
public void setColorModel(ColorModel
  model)
public void setDimensions(int width,int
  height)
public void setPixels(int x,int y,int w,
  int h,ColorModel model,byte pixels,int
  off,int scansize)
public void setPixels(int x,int y,int w,
  int h,ColorModel model,int pixels,int
  off,int scansize)

▶BUFFEREDINPUTSTREAM
public class java.io.
  BufferedInputStream
extends java.io.FilterInputStream
extends java.io.InputStream
extends java.lang.Object

Fields
protected byte buf
protected int count
protected int marklimit
protected int markpos
protected int pos

Constructors
public BufferedInputStream(InputStream
  in)
public BufferedInputStream(InputStream
  in,int size)

Methods
public synchronized int available()
public synchronized void close()
public synchronized void mark(int
  readlimit)
public boolean markSupported()
public synchronized int read()
public synchronized int read(byte b,int
  off,int len)
public synchronized void reset()
public synchronized long skip(long n)

▶BUFFEREDOUTPUTSTREAM
public class java.io.
  BufferedOutputStream
extends java.io.FilterOutputStream
extends java.io.OutputStream
extends java.lang.Object

Fields
protected byte buf
protected int count

Constructors
public BufferedOutputStream(
  OutputStream out)
public BufferedOutputStream(
  OutputStream out,int size)

Methods
public synchronized void flush()
public synchronized void write(int b)
public synchronized void write(byte b,
  int off,int len)

▶BUFFEREDREADER
public class java.io.BufferedReader
extends java.io.Reader
extends java.lang.Object

Constructors
public BufferedReader(Reader in,int sz)
public BufferedReader(Reader in)

Methods
public void close()
public void mark(int readAheadLimit)
public boolean markSupported()
public int read()
public int read(char cbuf,int off,int
  len)
public String readLine()
public boolean ready()
public void reset()
public long skip(long n)

▶BUFFEREDWRITER
public class java.io.BufferedWriter
extends java.io.Writer
extends java.lang.Object

Constructors
public BufferedWriter(Writer out)
public BufferedWriter(Writer out,int sz)

Methods
public void close()
public void flush()
public void newLine()
public void write(int c)
public void write(char cbuf,int off,int
  len)
public void write(String s,int off,int
  len)

▶BUTTON
public class java.awt.Button
extends java.awt.Component
extends java.lang.Object

Constructors
public Button()
public Button(String label)

Methods
public synchronized void
  addActionListener(ActionListener l)
public void addNotify()
public String getActionCommand()
public String getLabel()
protected String paramString()

```
protected void processActionEvent(
  ActionEvent e)
protected void processEvent(AWTEvent e)
public synchronized void
  removeActionListener(ActionListener l)
public void setActionCommand(String
  command)
public void setLabel(String label)
```

▶BUTTONGROUP
```
public class javax.swing.ButtonGroup
implements java.io.Serializable
extends java.lang.Object
```
Fields
```
protected java.util.Vector buttons
```
Constructors
```
public  ButtonGroup()
```
Methods
```
public void add(AbstractButton b)
public Enumeration getElements()
public ButtonModel getSelection()
public boolean isSelected(ButtonModel m)
public void remove(AbstractButton b)
public void setSelected(ButtonModel m,
  boolean b)
```

▶BUTTONUI
```
public abstract class javax.swing.plaf.
  ButtonUI
extends javax.swing.plaf.ComponentUI
extends java.lang.Object
```

▶BYTE
```
public final class java.lang.Byte
implements java.lang.Comparable
extends java.lang.Number
extends java.lang.Object
```
Fields
```
public final static byte MAX_VALUE
public final static byte MIN_VALUE
public final static java.lang.Class
  TYPE
```
Constructors
```
public  Byte(byte value)
public  Byte(String s)
```
Methods
```
public byte byteValue()
public int compareTo(Byte anotherByte)
public int compareTo(Object o)
public static Byte decode(String nm)
public double doubleValue()
public boolean equals(Object obj)
public float floatValue()
public int hashCode()
public int intValue()
public long longValue()
public static byte parseByte(String s)
public static byte parseByte(String s,
  int radix)
public short shortValue()
public static String toString(byte b)
public String toString()
```

```
public static Byte valueOf(String s,int
  radix)
public static Byte valueOf(String s)
```

▶BYTEARRAYINPUTSTREAM
```
public class java.io.
  ByteArrayInputStream
extends java.io.InputStream
extends java.lang.Object
```
Fields
```
protected byte buf
protected int count
protected int mark
protected int pos
```
Constructors
```
public  ByteArrayInputStream(byte buf)
public  ByteArrayInputStream(byte buf,
  int offset,int length)
```
Methods
```
public synchronized int available()
public synchronized void close()
public void mark(int readAheadLimit)
public boolean markSupported()
public synchronized int read()
public synchronized int read(byte b,int
  off,int len)
public synchronized void reset()
public synchronized long skip(long n)
```

▶BYTEARRAYOUTPUTSTREAM
```
public class java.io.
  ByteArrayOutputStream
extends java.io.OutputStream
extends java.lang.Object
```
Fields
```
protected byte buf
protected int count
```
Constructors
```
public  ByteArrayOutputStream()
public  ByteArrayOutputStream(int size)
```
Methods
```
public synchronized void close()
public synchronized void reset()
public int size()
public synchronized byte toByteArray()
public String toString()
public String toString(String enc)
public String toString(int hibyte)
public synchronized void write(int b)
public synchronized void write(byte b,
  int off,int len)
public synchronized void writeTo(
  OutputStream out)
```

▶BYTELOOKUPTABLE
```
public class java.awt.image.
  ByteLookupTable
extends java.awt.image.LookupTable
extends java.lang.Object
extends java.lang.Object
```

Constructors
public ByteLookupTable(int offset,byte
  data)
public ByteLookupTable(int offset,byte
  data)

Methods
public final byte getTable()
public int lookupPixel(int src,int dst)
public byte lookupPixel(byte src,byte
  dst)

▶**CALENDAR**
public abstract class java.util.
  Calendar
implements java.lang.Cloneable
implements java.io.Serializable
extends java.lang.Object

Fields
public final static int AM
public final static int AM_PM
public final static int APRIL
protected boolean areFieldsSet
public final static int AUGUST
public final static int DATE
public final static int DAY_OF_MONTH
public final static int DAY_OF_WEEK
public final static int DAY_OF_WEEK_IN_
  MONTH
public final static int DAY_OF_YEAR
public final static int DECEMBER
public final static int DST_OFFSET
public final static int ERA
public final static int FEBRUARY
protected int fields
public final static int FIELD_COUNT
public final static int FRIDAY
public final static int HOUR
public final static int HOUR_OF_DAY
protected boolean isSet
protected boolean isTimeSet
public final static int JANUARY
public final static int JULY
public final static int JUNE
public final static int MARCH
public final static int MAY
public final static int MILLISECOND
public final static int MINUTE
public final static int MONDAY
public final static int MONTH
public final static int NOVEMBER
public final static int OCTOBER
public final static int PM
public final static int SATURDAY
public final static int SECOND
public final static int SEPTEMBER
public final static int SUNDAY
public final static int THURSDAY
protected long time
public final static int TUESDAY
public final static int UNDECIMBER
public final static int WEDNESDAY
public final static int WEEK_OF_MONTH

public final static int WEEK_OF_YEAR
public final static int YEAR
public final static int ZONE_OFFSET

Constructors
protected Calendar()
protected Calendar(TimeZone zone,Locale
  aLocale)

Methods
public abstract void add(int field,int
  amount)
public boolean after(Object when)
public boolean before(Object when)
public final void clear()
public final void clear(int field)
public Object clone()
protected void complete()
protected abstract void computeFields()
protected abstract void computeTime()
public boolean equals(Object obj)
public final int get(int field)
public int getActualMaximum(int field)
public int getActualMinimum(int field)
public static synchronized Locale
  getAvailableLocales()
public int getFirstDayOfWeek()
public abstract int getGreatestMinimum(
  int field)
public static synchronized Calendar
  getInstance()
public static synchronized Calendar
  getInstance(TimeZone zone)
public static synchronized Calendar
  getInstance(Locale aLocale)
public static synchronized Calendar
  getInstance(TimeZone zone,Locale aLocale)
public abstract int getLeastMaximum(int
  field)
public abstract int getMaximum(int field)
public int getMinimalDaysInFirstWeek()
public abstract int getMinimum(int field)
public final Date getTime()
protected long getTimeInMillis()
public TimeZone getTimeZone()
public int hashCode()
protected final int internalGet(int
  field)
public boolean isLenient()
public final boolean isSet(int field)
public abstract void roll(int field,
  boolean up)
public void roll(int field,int amount)
public final void set(int field,int
  value)
public final void set(int year,int month,
  int date)
public final void set(int year,int month,
  int date,int hour,int minute)
public final void set(int year,int month,
  int date,int hour,int minute,int second)
public void setFirstDayOfWeek(int value)
public void setLenient(boolean lenient)

```
public void setMinimalDaysInFirstWeek(
  int value)
public final void setTime(Date date)
protected void setTimeInMillis(long
  millis)
public void setTimeZone(TimeZone value)
public String toString()
```

►CANNOTREDOEXCEPTION
```
public class javax.swing.undo.
  CannotRedoException
extends java.lang.RuntimeException
extends java.lang.Exception
extends java.lang.Throwable
extends java.lang.Object
```

►CANNOTUNDOEXCEPTION
```
public class javax.swing.undo.
  CannotUndoException
extends java.lang.RuntimeException
extends java.lang.Exception
extends java.lang.Throwable
extends java.lang.Object
```

►CANVAS
```
public class java.awt.Canvas
extends java.awt.Component
extends java.lang.Object
```
Constructors
```
public  Canvas()
public  Canvas(GraphicsConfiguration
  config)
```
Methods
```
public void addNotify()
public void paint(Graphics g)
```

►CARDLAYOUT
```
public class java.awt.CardLayout
implements java.awt.LayoutManager2
implements java.io.Serializable
extends java.lang.Object
```
Constructors
```
public  CardLayout()
public  CardLayout(int hgap,int vgap)
```
Methods
```
public void addLayoutComponent(Component
  comp,Object constraints)
public void addLayoutComponent(String
  name,Component comp)
public void first(Container parent)
public int getHgap()
public float getLayoutAlignmentX(
  Container parent)
public float getLayoutAlignmentY(
  Container parent)
public int getVgap()
public void invalidateLayout(Container
  target)
public void last(Container parent)
public void layoutContainer(Container
  parent)
```

```
public Dimension maximumLayoutSize(
  Container target)
public Dimension minimumLayoutSize(
  Container parent)
public void next(Container parent)
public Dimension preferredLayoutSize(
  Container parent)
public void previous(Container parent)
public void removeLayoutComponent(
  Component comp)
public void setHgap(int hgap)
public void setVgap(int vgap)
public void show(Container parent,String
  name)
public String toString()
```

►CARETEVENT
```
public abstract class javax.swing.event.
  CaretEvent
extends java.util.EventObject
extends java.lang.Object
```
Constructors
```
public  CaretEvent(Object source)
```
Methods
```
public abstract int getDot()
public abstract int getMark()
```

►CELLRENDERERPANE
```
public class javax.swing.
  CellRendererPane
implements javax.accessibility.
  Accessible
extends java.awt.Container
extends java.awt.Component
extends java.lang.Object
```
Fields
```
protected javax.accessibility.
  AccessibleContext accessibleContext
```
Constructors
```
public  CellRendererPane()
```
Methods
```
protected void addImpl(Component x,
  Object constraints,int index)
public AccessibleContext
  getAccessibleContext()
public void invalidate()
public void paint(Graphics g)
public void paintComponent(Graphics g,
  Component c,Container p,int x,int y,int
  w,int h,boolean shouldValidate)
public void paintComponent(Graphics g,
  Component c,Container p,int x,int y,int
  w,int h)
public void paintComponent(Graphics g,
  Component c,Container p,Rectangle r)
public void update(Graphics g)
```

►CERTIFICATE
```
public abstract class java.security.cert.
  Certificate
extends java.lang.Object
```

Constructors
protected Certificate(String type)

Methods
public boolean equals(Object other)
public abstract byte getEncoded()
public abstract PublicKey getPublicKey()
public final String getType()
public int hashCode()
public abstract String toString()
public abstract void verify(PublicKey
  key)
public abstract void verify(PublicKey
  key,String sigProvider)

▸**CERTIFICATEENCODINGEXCEPTION**
public class java.security.cert.
  CertificateEncodingException
extends java.security.cert.
  CertificateException
extends java.security.
  GeneralSecurityException
extends java.lang.Exception
extends java.lang.Throwable
extends java.lang.Object

Constructors
public CertificateEncodingException()
public CertificateEncodingException(
  String message)

▸**CERTIFICATEEXCEPTION**
public class java.security.cert.
  CertificateException
extends java.security.
  GeneralSecurityException
extends java.lang.Exception
extends java.lang.Throwable
extends java.lang.Object

Constructors
public CertificateException()
public CertificateException(String msg)

▸**CERTIFICATEEXPIREDEXCEPTION**
public class java.security.cert.
  CertificateExpiredException
extends java.security.cert.
  CertificateException
extends java.security.
  GeneralSecurityException
extends java.lang.Exception
extends java.lang.Throwable
extends java.lang.Object

Constructors
public CertificateExpiredException()
public CertificateExpiredException(
  String message)

▸**CERTIFICATEFACTORY**
public class java.security.cert.
  CertificateFactory
extends java.lang.Object

Constructors
protected CertificateFactory(
  CertificateFactorySpi certFacSpi,
  Provider provider,String type)

Methods
public final Certificate
  generateCertificate(InputStream inStream)
public final Collection
  generateCertificates(InputStream
  inStream)
public final CRL generateCRL(InputStream
  inStream)
public final Collection generateCRLs(
  InputStream inStream)
public final static CertificateFactory
  getInstance(String type)
public final static CertificateFactory
  getInstance(String type,String provider)
public final Provider getProvider()
public final String getType()

▸**CERTIFICATEFACTORYSPI**
public abstract class java.security.cert.
  CertificateFactorySpi
extends java.lang.Object

Methods
public abstract Certificate
  engineGenerateCertificate(InputStream
  inStream)
public abstract Collection
  engineGenerateCertificates(InputStream
  inStream)
public abstract CRL engineGenerateCRL(
  InputStream inStream)
public abstract Collection
  engineGenerateCRLs(InputStream inStream)

▸**CERTIFICATENOTYETVALIDEXCEPTION**
public class java.security.cert.
  CertificateNotYetValidException
extends java.security.cert.
  CertificateException
extends java.security.
  GeneralSecurityException
extends java.lang.Exception
extends java.lang.Throwable
extends java.lang.Object

Constructors
public CertificateNotYetValidException()
public CertificateNotYetValidException(
  String message)

▸**CERTIFICATEPARSINGEXCEPTION**
public class java.security.cert.
  CertificateParsingException
extends java.security.cert.
  CertificateException
extends java.security.
  GeneralSecurityException
extends java.lang.Exception
extends java.lang.Throwable
extends java.lang.Object

Constructors
```
public  CertificateParsingException()
public  CertificateParsingException(
  String message)
```

►**CHANGEDCHARSETEXCEPTION**
```
public class javax.swing.text.
  ChangedCharSetException
extends java.io.IOException
extends java.lang.Exception
extends java.lang.Throwable
extends java.lang.Object
```
Constructors
```
public  ChangedCharSetException(String
  charSetSpec,boolean charSetKey)
```
Methods
```
public String getCharSetSpec()
public boolean keyEqualsCharSet()
```

►**CHANGEEVENT**
```
public class javax.swing.event.
  ChangeEvent
extends java.util.EventObject
extends java.lang.Object
```
Constructors
```
public  ChangeEvent(Object source)
```

►**CHARACTER**
```
public final class java.lang.Character
implements java.lang.Comparable
implements java.io.Serializable
extends java.lang.Object
extends java.lang.Object
```
Fields
```
public final static int MAX_RADIX
public final static char MAX_VALUE
public final static int MIN_RADIX
public final static char MIN_VALUE
public final static java.lang.Class
  TYPE
public final static byte UNASSIGNED
```
Constructors
```
public  Character(char value)
```
Methods
```
public char charValue()
public int compareTo(Character
  anotherCharacter)
public int compareTo(Object o)
public static int digit(char ch,int
  radix)
public boolean equals(Object obj)
public static char forDigit(int digit,
  int radix)
public static int getNumericValue(char
  ch)
public static int getType(char ch)
public int hashCode()
public static boolean isDefined(char ch)
public static boolean isDigit(char ch)
public static boolean
  isIdentifierIgnorable(char ch)
```

```
public static boolean isISOControl(char
  ch)
public static boolean
  isJavaIdentifierPart(char ch)
public static boolean
  isJavaIdentifierStart(char ch)
public static boolean isJavaLetter(char
  ch)
public static boolean
  isJavaLetterOrDigit(char ch)
public static boolean isLetter(char ch)
public static boolean isLetterOrDigit(
  char ch)
public static boolean isLowerCase(char
  ch)
public static boolean isSpace(char ch)
public static boolean isSpaceChar(char
  ch)
public static boolean isTitleCase(char
  ch)
public static boolean
  isUnicodeIdentifierPart(char ch)
public static boolean
  isUnicodeIdentifierStart(char ch)
public static boolean isUpperCase(char
  ch)
public static boolean isWhitespace(char
  ch)
public static char toLowerCase(char ch)
public String toString()
public static char toTitleCase(char ch)
public static char toUpperCase(char ch)
```

►**CHARARRAYREADER**
```
public class java.io.CharArrayReader
extends java.io.Reader
extends java.lang.Object
```
Fields
```
protected char buf
protected int count
protected int markedPos
protected int pos
```
Constructors
```
public  CharArrayReader(char buf)
public  CharArrayReader(char buf,int
  offset,int length)
```
Methods
```
public void close()
public void mark(int readAheadLimit)
public boolean markSupported()
public int read()
public int read(char b,int off,int len)
public boolean ready()
public void reset()
public long skip(long n)
```

►**CHARARRAYWRITER**
```
public class java.io.CharArrayWriter
extends java.io.Writer
extends java.lang.Object
```
Fields
```
protected char buf
```

protected int count

Constructors

public CharArrayWriter()
public CharArrayWriter(int initialSize)

Methods

public void close()
public void flush()
public void reset()
public int size()
public char toCharArray()
public String toString()
public void write(int c)
public void write(char c,int off,int len)
public void write(String str,int off,int len)
public void writeTo(Writer out)

►CharConversionException

public class java.io.
  CharConversionException
extends java.io.IOException
extends java.lang.Exception
extends java.lang.Throwable
extends java.lang.Object

Constructors

public CharConversionException()
public CharConversionException(String s)

►Checkbox

public class java.awt.Checkbox
implements java.awt.ItemSelectable
extends java.awt.Component
extends java.lang.Object

Constructors

public Checkbox()
public Checkbox(String label)
public Checkbox(String label,boolean
  state)
public Checkbox(String label,boolean
  state,CheckboxGroup group)
public Checkbox(String label,
  CheckboxGroup group,boolean state)

Methods

public synchronized void addItemListener(
  ItemListener l)
public void addNotify()
public CheckboxGroup getCheckboxGroup()
public String getLabel()
public Object getSelectedObjects()
public boolean getState()
protected String paramString()
protected void processEvent(AWTEvent e)
protected void processItemEvent(
  ItemEvent e)
public synchronized void
  removeItemListener(ItemListener l)
public void setCheckboxGroup(
  CheckboxGroup g)
public void setLabel(String label)
public void setState(boolean state)

►CheckboxGroup

public class java.awt.CheckboxGroup
implements java.io.Serializable
extends java.lang.Object

Constructors

public CheckboxGroup()

Methods

public Checkbox getCurrent()
public Checkbox getSelectedCheckbox()
public synchronized void setCurrent(
  Checkbox box)
public void setSelectedCheckbox(Checkbox
  box)
public String toString()

►CheckboxMenuItem

public class java.awt.CheckboxMenuItem
implements java.awt.ItemSelectable
extends java.awt.MenuItem
extends java.awt.MenuComponent
extends java.lang.Object

Constructors

public CheckboxMenuItem()
public CheckboxMenuItem(String label)
public CheckboxMenuItem(String label,
  boolean state)

Methods

public synchronized void addItemListener(
  ItemListener l)
public void addNotify()
public synchronized Object
  getSelectedObjects()
public boolean getState()
public String paramString()
protected void processEvent(AWTEvent e)
protected void processItemEvent(
  ItemEvent e)
public synchronized void
  removeItemListener(ItemListener l)
public synchronized void setState(
  boolean b)

►CheckedInputStream

public class java.util.zip.
  CheckedInputStream
extends java.io.FilterInputStream
extends java.io.InputStream
extends java.lang.Object

Constructors

public CheckedInputStream(InputStream
  in,Checksum cksum)

Methods

public Checksum getChecksum()
public int read()
public int read(byte buf,int off,int len)
public long skip(long n)

►CheckedOutputStream

public class java.util.zip.
  CheckedOutputStream
extends java.io.FilterOutputStream
extends java.io.OutputStream

extends java.lang.Object
Constructors
public CheckedOutputStream(OutputStream
  out,Checksum cksum)
Methods
public Checksum getChecksum()
public void write(int b)
public void write(byte b,int off,int len)

►CHOICE
public class java.awt.Choice
implements java.awt.ItemSelectable
extends java.awt.Component
extends java.lang.Object
Constructors
public Choice()
Methods
public void add(String item)
public void addItem(String item)
public synchronized void addItemListener(
  ItemListener l)
public void addNotify()
public int countItems()
public String getItem(int index)
public int getItemCount()
public int getSelectedIndex()
public synchronized String
  getSelectedItem()
public synchronized Object
  getSelectedObjects()
public void insert(String item,int index)
protected String paramString()
protected void processEvent(AWTEvent e)
protected void processItemEvent(
  ItemEvent e)
public void remove(String item)
public void remove(int position)
public void removeAll()
public synchronized void
  removeItemListener(ItemListener l)
public synchronized void select(int pos)
public synchronized void select(String
  str)

►CHOICEFORMAT
public class java.text.ChoiceFormat
extends java.text.NumberFormat
extends java.text.Format
extends java.lang.Object
Constructors
public ChoiceFormat(String newPattern)
public ChoiceFormat(double limits,
  String formats)
Methods
public void applyPattern(String
  newPattern)
public Object clone()
public boolean equals(Object obj)
public StringBuffer format(long number,
  StringBuffer toAppendTo,FieldPosition
  status)

public StringBuffer format(double number,
  StringBuffer toAppendTo,FieldPosition
  status)
public Object getFormats()
public double getLimits()
public int hashCode()
public final static double nextDouble(
  double d)
public static double nextDouble(double d,
  boolean positive)
public Number parse(String text,
  ParsePosition status)
public final static double
  previousDouble(double d)
public void setChoices(double limits,
  String formats)
public String toPattern()

►CLASS
public final class java.lang.Class
implements java.io.Serializable
extends java.lang.Object
Constructors
private static Class()
Methods
public static Class forName(String
  className)
public static Class forName(String name,
  boolean initialize,ClassLoader loader)
public Class getClasses()
public ClassLoader getClassLoader()
public native Class getComponentType()
public Constructor getConstructor(Class
  parameterTypes)
public Constructor getConstructors()
public Class getDeclaredClasses()
public Constructor
  getDeclaredConstructor(Class
  parameterTypes)
public Constructor
  getDeclaredConstructors()
public Field getDeclaredField(String
  name)
public Field getDeclaredFields()
public Method getDeclaredMethod(String
  name,Class parameterTypes)
public Method getDeclaredMethods()
public native Class getDeclaringClass()
public Field getField(String name)
public Field getFields()
public native Class getInterfaces()
public Method getMethod(String name,
  Class parameterTypes)
public Method getMethods()
public native int getModifiers()
public native String getName()
public Package getPackage()
public ProtectionDomain
  getProtectionDomain()
public URL getResource(String name)
public InputStream getResourceAsStream(
  String name)

```
public native Object getSigners()
public native Class getSuperclass()
public native boolean isArray()
public native boolean isAssignableFrom(
  Class cls)
public native boolean isInstance(Object
  obj)
public native boolean isInterface()
public native boolean isPrimitive()
public Object newInstance()
public String toString()
```

►**CLASSCASTEXCEPTION**
```
public class java.lang.
  ClassCastException
extends java.lang.RuntimeException
extends java.lang.Exception
extends java.lang.Throwable
extends java.lang.Object
```
Constructors
```
public  ClassCastException()
public  ClassCastException(String s)
```

►**CLASSCIRCULARITYERROR**
```
public class java.lang.
  ClassCircularityError
extends java.lang.LinkageError
extends java.lang.Error
extends java.lang.Throwable
extends java.lang.Object
```
Constructors
```
public  ClassCircularityError()
public  ClassCircularityError(String s)
```

►**CLASSFORMATERROR**
```
public class java.lang.ClassFormatError
extends java.lang.LinkageError
extends java.lang.Error
extends java.lang.Throwable
extends java.lang.Object
```
Constructors
```
public  ClassFormatError()
public  ClassFormatError(String s)
```

►**CLASSLOADER**
```
public abstract class java.lang.
  ClassLoader
extends java.lang.Object
```
Constructors
```
protected  ClassLoader(ClassLoader
  parent)
protected  ClassLoader()
```
Methods
```
protected final Class defineClass(byte b,
  int off,int len)
protected final Class defineClass(String
  name,byte b,int off,int len)
protected final Class defineClass(String
  name,byte b,int off,int len,
  ProtectionDomain protectionDomain)
protected Package definePackage(String
  name,String specTitle,String specVersion,
```

```
  String specVendor,String implTitle,
  String implVersion,String implVendor,URL
  sealBase)
protected Class findClass(String name)
protected String findLibrary(String
  libname)
protected final native Class
  findLoadedClass(String name)
protected URL findResource(String name)
protected Enumeration findResources(
  String name)
protected final Class findSystemClass(
  String name)
protected Package getPackage(String name)
protected Package getPackages()
public final ClassLoader getParent()
public URL getResource(String name)
public InputStream getResourceAsStream(
  String name)
public final Enumeration getResources(
  String name)
public static ClassLoader
  getSystemClassLoader()
public static URL getSystemResource(
  String name)
public static InputStream
  getSystemResourceAsStream(String name)
public static Enumeration
  getSystemResources(String name)
public Class loadClass(String name)
protected synchronized Class loadClass(
  String name,boolean resolve)
protected final void resolveClass(Class
  c)
protected final void setSigners(Class c,
  Object signers)
```

►**CLASSNOTFOUNDEXCEPTION**
```
public class java.lang.
  ClassNotFoundException
extends java.lang.Exception
extends java.lang.Throwable
extends java.lang.Object
```
Constructors
```
public  ClassNotFoundException()
public  ClassNotFoundException(String s)
public  ClassNotFoundException(String s,
  Throwable ex)
```
Methods
```
public Throwable getException()
public void printStackTrace()
public void printStackTrace(PrintStream
  ps)
public void printStackTrace(PrintWriter
  pw)
```

►**CLIPBOARD**
```
public class java.awt.datatransfer.
  Clipboard
extends java.lang.Object
```

Fields
protected java.awt.datatransfer.
  Transferable contents
protected java.awt.datatransfer.
  ClipboardOwner owner

Constructors
public Clipboard(String name)

Methods
public synchronized Transferable
  getContents(Object requestor)
public String getName()
public synchronized void setContents(
  Transferable contents,ClipboardOwner
  owner)

▶**CloneNotSupportedException**
public class java.lang.
  CloneNotSupportedException
extends java.lang.Exception
extends java.lang.Throwable
extends java.lang.Object

Constructors
public CloneNotSupportedException()
public CloneNotSupportedException(
  String s)

▶**CMMException**
public class java.awt.color.
  CMMException
extends java.lang.RuntimeException
extends java.lang.Exception
extends java.lang.Throwable
extends java.lang.Object

Constructors
public CMMException(String s)

▶**CodeSource**
public class java.security.CodeSource
implements java.io.Serializable
extends java.lang.Object

Constructors
public CodeSource(URL url,Certificate
  certs)

Methods
public boolean equals(Object obj)
public final Certificate getCertificates(
)
public final URL getLocation()
public int hashCode()
public boolean implies(CodeSource
  codesource)
public String toString()

▶**CollationElementIterator**
public final class java.text.
  CollationElementIterator
extends java.lang.Object

Fields
public final static int NULLORDER

Constructors
 CollationElementIterator()

 CollationElementIterator()

Methods
public int getMaxExpansion(int order)
public int getOffset()
public int next()
public int previous()
public final static int primaryOrder(int
  order)
public void reset()
public final static short secondaryOrder(
  int order)
public void setOffset(int newOffset)
public void setText(String source)
public void setText(CharacterIterator
  source)
public final static short tertiaryOrder(
  int order)

▶**CollationKey**
public final class java.text.
  CollationKey
implements java.lang.Comparable
extends java.lang.Object

Constructors
 CollationKey()

Methods
public int compareTo(CollationKey target)
public int compareTo(Object o)
public boolean equals(Object target)
public String getSourceString()
public int hashCode()
public byte toByteArray()

▶**Collator**
public abstract class java.text.
  Collator
implements java.lang.Cloneable
implements java.util.Comparator
extends java.lang.Object

Fields
public final static int CANONICAL_
  DECOMPOSITION
public final static int FULL_
  DECOMPOSITION
public final static int IDENTICAL
public final static int NO_
  DECOMPOSITION
public final static int PRIMARY
public final static int SECONDARY
public final static int TERTIARY

Constructors
protected Collator()

Methods
public Object clone()
public abstract int compare(String
  source,String target)
public int compare(Object o1,Object o2)
public boolean equals(String source,
  String target)
public boolean equals(Object that)

```
public static synchronized Locale
  getAvailableLocales()
public abstract CollationKey
  getCollationKey(String source)
public synchronized int getDecomposition(
  )
public static synchronized Collator
  getInstance()
public static synchronized Collator
  getInstance(Locale desiredLocale)
public synchronized int getStrength()
public abstract int hashCode()
public synchronized void
  setDecomposition(int decompositionMode)
public synchronized void setStrength(int
  newStrength)
```

►COLLECTIONS

```
public class java.util.Collections
extends java.lang.Object
```

Fields

```
public final static java.util.List EMPTY_
  LIST
public final static java.util.Set EMPTY_
  SET
```

Constructors

```
private  Collections()
```

Methods

```
public static int binarySearch(List list,
  Object key)
public static int binarySearch(List list,
  Object key,Comparator c)
public static void copy(List dest,List
  src)
public static Enumeration enumeration(
  Collection c)
public static void fill(List list,Object
  o)
public static Object max(Collection coll)
public static Object max(Collection coll,
  Comparator comp)
public static Object min(Collection coll)
public static Object min(Collection coll,
  Comparator comp)
public static List nCopies(int n,Object
  o)
public static void reverse(List l)
public static Comparator reverseOrder()
public static void shuffle(List list)
public static void shuffle(List list,
  Random rnd)
public static Set singleton(Object o)
public static void sort(List list)
public static void sort(List list,
  Comparator c)
public static Collection
  synchronizedCollection(Collection c)
public static List synchronizedList(List
  list)
public static Map synchronizedMap(Map m)
public static Set synchronizedSet(Set s)
```

```
public static SortedMap
  synchronizedSortedMap(SortedMap m)
public static SortedSet
  synchronizedSortedSet(SortedSet s)
public static Collection
  unmodifiableCollection(Collection c)
public static List unmodifiableList(List
  list)
public static Map unmodifiableMap(Map m)
public static Set unmodifiableSet(Set s)
public static SortedMap
  unmodifiableSortedMap(SortedMap m)
public static SortedSet
  unmodifiableSortedSet(SortedSet s)
```

►COLOR

```
public class java.awt.Color
implements java.awt.Paint
implements java.io.Serializable
extends java.lang.Object
```

Fields

```
public final static java.awt.Color
  black
public final static java.awt.Color blue
public final static java.awt.Color cyan
public final static java.awt.Color
  darkGray
public final static java.awt.Color gray
public final static java.awt.Color
  green
public final static java.awt.Color
  lightGray
public final static java.awt.Color
  magenta
public final static java.awt.Color
  orange
public final static java.awt.Color pink
public final static java.awt.Color red
public final static java.awt.Color
  white
public final static java.awt.Color
  yellow
```

Constructors

```
public  Color(int r,int g,int b)
public  Color(int r,int g,int b,int a)
public  Color(int rgb)
public  Color(int rgba,boolean hasalpha)
public  Color(float r,float g,float b)
public  Color(float r,float g,float b,
  float a)
public  Color(ColorSpace cspace,float
  components,float alpha)
```

Methods

```
public Color brighter()
public synchronized PaintContext
  createContext(ColorModel cm,Rectangle r,
  Rectangle2D r2d,AffineTransform xform,
  RenderingHints hints)
public Color darker()
public static Color decode(String nm)
public boolean equals(Object obj)
public int getAlpha()
```

```
public int getBlue()
public static Color getColor(String nm)
public static Color getColor(String nm,
  Color v)
public static Color getColor(String nm,
  int v)
public float getColorComponents(float
  compArray)
public float getColorComponents(
  ColorSpace cspace,float compArray)
public ColorSpace getColorSpace()
public float getComponents(float
  compArray)
public float getComponents(ColorSpace
  cspace,float compArray)
public int getGreen()
public static Color getHSBColor(float h,
  float s,float b)
public int getRed()
public int getRGB()
public float getRGBColorComponents(float
  compArray)
public float getRGBComponents(float
  compArray)
public int getTransparency()
public int hashCode()
public static int HSBtoRGB(float hue,
  float saturation,float brightness)
public static float RGBtoHSB(int r,int g,
  int b,float hsbvals)
public String toString()
```

►ColorChooserComponentFactory

```
public class javax.swing.colorchooser.
  ColorChooserComponentFactory
extends java.lang.Object
```

Constructors
```
private  ColorChooserComponentFactory()
```

Methods
```
public static AbstractColorChooserPanel
  getDefaultChooserPanels()
public static JComponent getPreviewPanel(
  )
```

►ColorChooserUI

```
public abstract class javax.swing.plaf.
  ColorChooserUI
extends javax.swing.plaf.ComponentUI
extends java.lang.Object
```

►ColorConvertOp

```
public class java.awt.image.
  ColorConvertOp
implements java.awt.image.
  BufferedImageOp
implements java.awt.image.RasterOp
extends java.lang.Object
```

Constructors
```
public static  ColorConvertOp(
  RenderingHints hints)
public  ColorConvertOp(ColorSpace cspace,
  RenderingHints hints)
```

```
public  ColorConvertOp(ColorSpace
  srcCspace,ColorSpace dstCspace,
  RenderingHints hints)
public  ColorConvertOp(ICC_Profile
  profiles,RenderingHints hints)
```

Methods
```
public BufferedImage
  createCompatibleDestImage(BufferedImage
  src,ColorModel destCM)
public WritableRaster
  createCompatibleDestRaster(Raster src)
public final BufferedImage filter(
  BufferedImage src,BufferedImage dest)
public final WritableRaster filter(
  Raster src,WritableRaster dest)
public final Rectangle2D getBounds2D(
  BufferedImage src)
public final Rectangle2D getBounds2D(
  Raster src)
public final ICC_Profile getICC_Profiles(
  )
public final Point2D getPoint2D(Point2D
  srcPt,Point2D dstPt)
public final RenderingHints
  getRenderingHints()
```

►ColorModel

```
public abstract class java.awt.image.
  ColorModel
implements java.awt.Transparency
extends java.lang.Object
```

Fields
```
protected int pixel_bits
protected int transferType
```

Constructors
```
public  ColorModel(int bits)
protected  ColorModel(int pixel_bits,int
  bits,ColorSpace cspace,boolean hasAlpha,
  boolean isAlphaPremultiplied,int
  transparency,int transferType)
```

Methods
```
public ColorModel coerceData(
  WritableRaster raster,boolean
  isAlphaPremultiplied)
public SampleModel
  createCompatibleSampleModel(int w,int h)
public WritableRaster
  createCompatibleWritableRaster(int w,int
  h)
public boolean equals(Object obj)
public void finalize()
public abstract int getAlpha(int pixel)
public int getAlpha(Object inData)
public WritableRaster getAlphaRaster(
  WritableRaster raster)
public abstract int getBlue(int pixel)
public int getBlue(Object inData)
public final ColorSpace getColorSpace()
public int getComponents(int pixel,int
  components,int offset)
public int getComponents(Object pixel,
  int components,int offset)
```

```
public int getComponentSize(int
  componentIdx)
public int getComponentSize()
public int getDataElement(int components,
  int offset)
public Object getDataElements(int rgb,
  Object pixel)
public Object getDataElements(int
  components,int offset,Object obj)
public abstract int getGreen(int pixel)
public int getGreen(Object inData)
public float getNormalizedComponents(int
  components,int offset,float
  normComponents,int normOffset)
public int getNumColorComponents()
public int getNumComponents()
public int getPixelSize()
public abstract int getRed(int pixel)
public int getRed(Object inData)
public int getRGB(int pixel)
public int getRGB(Object inData)
public static ColorModel getRGBdefault()
public int getTransparency()
public int getUnnormalizedComponents(
  float normComponents,int normOffset,int
  components,int offset)
public final boolean hasAlpha()
public final boolean
  isAlphaPremultiplied()
public boolean isCompatibleRaster(Raster
  raster)
public boolean isCompatibleSampleModel(
  SampleModel sm)
public String toString()
```

►COLORSPACE

```
public abstract class java.awt.color.
  ColorSpace
extends java.lang.Object
```

Fields

```
public final static int CS_CIEXYZ
public final static int CS_GRAY
public final static int CS_LINEAR_RGB
public final static int CS_PYCC
public final static int CS_sRGB
public final static int TYPE_2CLR
public final static int TYPE_3CLR
public final static int TYPE_4CLR
public final static int TYPE_5CLR
public final static int TYPE_6CLR
public final static int TYPE_7CLR
public final static int TYPE_8CLR
public final static int TYPE_9CLR
public final static int TYPE_ACLR
public final static int TYPE_BCLR
public final static int TYPE_CCLR
public final static int TYPE_CMY
public final static int TYPE_CMYK
public final static int TYPE_DCLR
public final static int TYPE_ECLR
public final static int TYPE_FCLR
public final static int TYPE_GRAY
public final static int TYPE_HLS
```

```
public final static int TYPE_HSV
public final static int TYPE_Lab
public final static int TYPE_Luv
public final static int TYPE_RGB
public final static int TYPE_XYZ
public final static int TYPE_YCbCr
public final static int TYPE_Yxy
```

Constructors

```
protected  ColorSpace(int type,int
  numcomponents)
```

Methods

```
public abstract float fromCIEXYZ(float
  colorvalue)
public abstract float fromRGB(float
  rgbvalue)
public static ColorSpace getInstance(int
  colorspace)
public String getName(int idx)
public int getNumComponents()
public int getType()
public boolean isCS_sRGB()
public abstract float toCIEXYZ(float
  colorvalue)
public abstract float toRGB(float
  colorvalue)
```

►COLORUIRESOURCE

```
public class javax.swing.plaf.
  ColorUIResource
implements javax.swing.plaf.UIResource
extends java.awt.Color
extends java.lang.Object
```

Constructors

```
public  ColorUIResource(int r,int g,int
  b)
public  ColorUIResource(int rgb)
public  ColorUIResource(float r,float g,
  float b)
public  ColorUIResource(Color c)
```

►COMBOBOXUI

```
public abstract class javax.swing.plaf.
  ComboBoxUI
extends javax.swing.plaf.ComponentUI
extends java.lang.Object
```

Methods

```
public abstract boolean
  isFocusTraversable(JComboBox c)
public abstract boolean isPopupVisible(
  JComboBox c)
public abstract void setPopupVisible(
  JComboBox c,boolean v)
```

►COMPILER

```
public final class java.lang.Compiler
extends java.lang.Object
```

Constructors

```
private  Compiler()
```

Methods

```
public static native Object command(
  Object any)
```

```
public static native boolean
  compileClass(Class clazz)
public static native boolean
  compileClasses(String string)
public static native void disable()
public static native void enable()
```

►**COMPONENT**

```
public abstract class java.awt.
  Component
implements java.awt.image.ImageObserver
implements java.awt.MenuContainer
implements java.io.Serializable
extends java.lang.Object
```

Fields

```
public final static float BOTTOM_
  ALIGNMENT
public final static float CENTER_
  ALIGNMENT
public final static float LEFT_
  ALIGNMENT
public final static float RIGHT_
  ALIGNMENT
public final static float TOP_ALIGNMENT
```

Constructors

```
protected  Component()
```

Methods

```
public boolean action(Event evt,Object
  what)
public synchronized void add(PopupMenu
  popup)
public synchronized void
  addComponentListener(ComponentListener l)
public synchronized void
  addFocusListener(FocusListener l)
public synchronized void
  addInputMethodListener(
  InputMethodListener l)
public synchronized void addKeyListener(
  KeyListener l)
public synchronized void
  addMouseListener(MouseListener l)
public synchronized void
  addMouseMotionListener(
  MouseMotionListener l)
public void addNotify()
public synchronized void
  addPropertyChangeListener(
  PropertyChangeListener listener)
public synchronized void
  addPropertyChangeListener(String
  propertyName,PropertyChangeListener
  listener)
public Rectangle bounds()
public int checkImage(Image image,
  ImageObserver observer)
public int checkImage(Image image,int
  width,int height,ImageObserver observer)
protected AWTEvent coalesceEvents(
  AWTEvent existingEvent,AWTEvent newEvent)
public boolean contains(int x,int y)
public boolean contains(Point p)
```

```
public Image createImage(ImageProducer
  producer)
public Image createImage(int width,int
  height)
public void deliverEvent(Event e)
public void disable()
protected final void disableEvents(long
  eventsToDisable)
public final void dispatchEvent(AWTEvent
  e)
public void doLayout()
public void enable()
public void enable(boolean b)
protected final void enableEvents(long
  eventsToEnable)
public void enableInputMethods(boolean
  enable)
protected void firePropertyChange(String
  propertyName,Object oldValue,Object
  newValue)
public float getAlignmentX()
public float getAlignmentY()
public Color getBackground()
public Rectangle getBounds()
public Rectangle getBounds(Rectangle rv)
public ColorModel getColorModel()
public Component getComponentAt(int x,
  int y)
public Component getComponentAt(Point p)
public ComponentOrientation
  getComponentOrientation()
public Cursor getCursor()
public synchronized DropTarget
  getDropTarget()
public Font getFont()
public FontMetrics getFontMetrics(Font
  font)
public Color getForeground()
public Graphics getGraphics()
public int getHeight()
public InputContext getInputContext()
public InputMethodRequests
  getInputMethodRequests()
public Locale getLocale()
public Point getLocation()
public Point getLocation(Point rv)
public Point getLocationOnScreen()
public Dimension getMaximumSize()
public Dimension getMinimumSize()
public String getName()
public Container getParent()
public ComponentPeer getPeer()
public Dimension getPreferredSize()
public Dimension getSize()
public Dimension getSize(Dimension rv)
public Toolkit getToolkit()
public final Object getTreeLock()
public int getWidth()
public int getX()
public int getY()
public boolean gotFocus(Event evt,Object
  what)
```

```
public boolean handleEvent(Event evt)
public boolean hasFocus()
public void hide()
public boolean imageUpdate(Image img,int
  flags,int x,int y,int w,int h)
public boolean inside(int x,int y)
public void invalidate()
public boolean isDisplayable()
public boolean isDoubleBuffered()
public boolean isEnabled()
public boolean isFocusTraversable()
public boolean isLightweight()
public boolean isOpaque()
public boolean isShowing()
public boolean isValid()
public boolean isVisible()
public boolean keyDown(Event evt,int key)
public boolean keyUp(Event evt,int key)
public void layout()
public void list()
public void list(PrintStream out)
public void list(PrintStream out,int
  indent)
public void list(PrintWriter out)
public void list(PrintWriter out,int
  indent)
public Component locate(int x,int y)
public Point location()
public boolean lostFocus(Event evt,
  Object what)
public Dimension minimumSize()
public boolean mouseDown(Event evt,int x,
  int y)
public boolean mouseDrag(Event evt,int x,
  int y)
public boolean mouseEnter(Event evt,int
  x,int y)
public boolean mouseExit(Event evt,int x,
  int y)
public boolean mouseMove(Event evt,int x,
  int y)
public boolean mouseUp(Event evt,int x,
  int y)
public void move(int x,int y)
public void nextFocus()
public void paint(Graphics g)
public void paintAll(Graphics g)
protected String paramString()
public boolean postEvent(Event e)
public Dimension preferredSize()
public boolean prepareImage(Image image,
  ImageObserver observer)
public boolean prepareImage(Image image,
  int width,int height,ImageObserver
  observer)
public void print(Graphics g)
public void printAll(Graphics g)
protected void processComponentEvent(
  ComponentEvent e)
protected void processEvent(AWTEvent e)
protected void processFocusEvent(
  FocusEvent e)

protected void processInputMethodEvent(
  InputMethodEvent e)
protected void processKeyEvent(KeyEvent
  e)
protected void processMouseEvent(
  MouseEvent e)
protected void processMouseMotionEvent(
  MouseEvent e)
public synchronized void remove(
  MenuComponent popup)
public synchronized void
  removeComponentListener(
  ComponentListener l)
public synchronized void
  removeFocusListener(FocusListener l)
public synchronized void
  removeInputMethodListener(
  InputMethodListener l)
public synchronized void
  removeKeyListener(KeyListener l)
public synchronized void
  removeMouseListener(MouseListener l)
public synchronized void
  removeMouseMotionListener(
  MouseMotionListener l)
public void removeNotify()
public synchronized void
  removePropertyChangeListener(
  PropertyChangeListener listener)
public synchronized void
  removePropertyChangeListener(String
  propertyName,PropertyChangeListener
  listener)
public void repaint()
public void repaint(long tm)
public void repaint(int x,int y,int
  width,int height)
public void repaint(long tm,int x,int y,
  int width,int height)
public void requestFocus()
public void reshape(int x,int y,int
  width,int height)
public void resize(int width,int height)
public void resize(Dimension d)
public void setBackground(Color c)
public void setBounds(int x,int y,int
  width,int height)
public void setBounds(Rectangle r)
public void setComponentOrientation(
  ComponentOrientation o)
public synchronized void setCursor(
  Cursor cursor)
public synchronized void setDropTarget(
  DropTarget dt)
public void setEnabled(boolean b)
public void setFont(Font f)
public void setForeground(Color c)
public void setLocale(Locale l)
public void setLocation(int x,int y)
public void setLocation(Point p)
public void setName(String name)
public void setSize(int width,int height)
public void setSize(Dimension d)
```

```
public void setVisible(boolean b)
public void show()
public void show(boolean b)
public Dimension size()
public String toString()
public void transferFocus()
public void update(Graphics g)
public void validate()
```

►**COMPONENTADAPTER**
```
public abstract class java.awt.event.
  ComponentAdapter
implements java.awt.event.
  ComponentListener
extends java.lang.Object
```
Methods
```
public void componentHidden(
  ComponentEvent e)
public void componentMoved(
  ComponentEvent e)
public void componentResized(
  ComponentEvent e)
public void componentShown(
  ComponentEvent e)
```

►**COMPONENTCOLORMODEL**
```
public class java.awt.image.
  ComponentColorModel
extends java.awt.image.ColorModel
extends java.lang.Object
```
Constructors
```
public  ComponentColorModel(ColorSpace
  colorSpace,int bits,boolean hasAlpha,
  boolean isAlphaPremultiplied,int
  transparency,int transferType)
```
Methods
```
public ColorModel coerceData(
  WritableRaster raster,boolean
  isAlphaPremultiplied)
public SampleModel
  createCompatibleSampleModel(int w,int h)
public WritableRaster
  createCompatibleWritableRaster(int w,int
  h)
public boolean equals(Object obj)
public int getAlpha(int pixel)
public int getAlpha(Object inData)
public WritableRaster getAlphaRaster(
  WritableRaster raster)
public int getBlue(int pixel)
public int getBlue(Object inData)
public int getComponents(int pixel,int
  components,int offset)
public int getComponents(Object pixel,
  int components,int offset)
public int getDataElement(int components,
  int offset)
public Object getDataElements(int rgb,
  Object pixel)
public Object getDataElements(int
  components,int offset,Object obj)
public int getGreen(int pixel)
```

```
public int getGreen(Object inData)
public int getRed(int pixel)
public int getRed(Object inData)
public int getRGB(int pixel)
public int getRGB(Object inData)
public boolean isCompatibleRaster(Raster
  raster)
public boolean isCompatibleSampleModel(
  SampleModel sm)
```

►**COMPONENTEVENT**
```
public class java.awt.event.
  ComponentEvent
extends java.awt.AWTEvent
extends java.util.EventObject
extends java.lang.Object
```
Fields
```
public final static int COMPONENT_FIRST
public final static int COMPONENT_
  HIDDEN
public final static int COMPONENT_LAST
public final static int COMPONENT_MOVED
public final static int COMPONENT_
  RESIZED
public final static int COMPONENT_SHOWN
```
Constructors
```
public  ComponentEvent(Component source,
  int id)
```
Methods
```
public Component getComponent()
public String paramString()
```

►**COMPONENTORIENTATION**
```
public final class java.awt.
  ComponentOrientation
implements java.io.Serializable
extends java.lang.Object
```
Fields
```
public final static java.awt.
  ComponentOrientation LEFT_TO_RIGHT
public final static java.awt.
  ComponentOrientation RIGHT_TO_LEFT
public final static java.awt.
  ComponentOrientation UNKNOWN
```
Constructors
```
private  ComponentOrientation()
```
Methods
```
public static ComponentOrientation
  getOrientation(Locale locale)
public static ComponentOrientation
  getOrientation(ResourceBundle bdl)
public boolean isHorizontal()
public boolean isLeftToRight()
```

►**COMPONENTSAMPLEMODEL**
```
public class java.awt.image.
  ComponentSampleModel
extends java.awt.image.SampleModel
extends java.lang.Object
```
Fields
```
protected int bandOffsets
```

protected int bankIndices
protected int numBands
protected int numBanks
protected int pixelStride
protected int scanlineStride

Constructors

public static ComponentSampleModel(int
    dataType,int w,int h,int pixelStride,int
    scanlineStride,int bandOffsets)
public ComponentSampleModel(int
    dataType,int w,int h,int pixelStride,int
    scanlineStride,int bankIndices,int
    bandOffsets)

Methods

public SampleModel
    createCompatibleSampleModel(int w,int h)
public DataBuffer createDataBuffer()
public SampleModel
    createSubsetSampleModel(int bands)
public final int getBandOffsets()
public final int getBankIndices()
public Object getDataElements(int x,int
    y,Object obj,DataBuffer data)
public final int getNumDataElements()
public int getOffset(int x,int y)
public int getOffset(int x,int y,int b)
public int getPixel(int x,int y,int
    iArray,DataBuffer data)
public int getPixels(int x,int y,int w,
    int h,int iArray,DataBuffer data)
public final int getPixelStride()
public int getSample(int x,int y,int b,
    DataBuffer data)
public int getSamples(int x,int y,int w,
    int h,int b,int iArray,DataBuffer data)
public final int getSampleSize()
public final int getSampleSize(int band)
public final int getScanlineStride()
public void setDataElements(int x,int y,
    Object obj,DataBuffer data)
public void setPixel(int x,int y,int
    iArray,DataBuffer data)
public void setPixels(int x,int y,int w,
    int h,int iArray,DataBuffer data)
public void setSample(int x,int y,int b,
    int s,DataBuffer data)
public void setSamples(int x,int y,int w,
    int h,int b,int iArray,DataBuffer data)

►**COMPONENTUI**

public abstract class javax.swing.plaf.
    ComponentUI
extends java.lang.Object

Methods

public boolean contains(JComponent c,int
    x,int y)
public static ComponentUI createUI(
    JComponent c)
public Accessible getAccessibleChild(
    JComponent c,int i)
public int getAccessibleChildrenCount(
    JComponent c)

public Dimension getMaximumSize(
    JComponent c)
public Dimension getMinimumSize(
    JComponent c)
public Dimension getPreferredSize(
    JComponent c)
public void installUI(JComponent c)
public void paint(Graphics g,JComponent
    c)
public void uninstallUI(JComponent c)
public void update(Graphics g,JComponent
    c)

►**COMPONENTVIEW**

public class javax.swing.text.
    ComponentView
extends javax.swing.text.View
extends java.lang.Object

Constructors

public ComponentView(Element elem)

Methods

protected Component createComponent()
public float getAlignment(int axis)
public final Component getComponent()
public float getMaximumSpan(int axis)
public float getMinimumSpan(int axis)
public float getPreferredSpan(int axis)
public Shape modelToView(int pos,Shape a,
    Bias b)
public void paint(Graphics g,Shape a)
public void setParent(View p)
public void setSize(float width,float
    height)
public int viewToModel(float x,float y,
    Shape a,Bias bias)

►**COMPOSITEVIEW**

public abstract class javax.swing.text.
    CompositeView
extends javax.swing.text.View
extends java.lang.Object

Constructors

public CompositeView(Element elem)

Methods

public void append(View v)
protected abstract void childAllocation(
    int index,Rectangle a)
protected boolean flipEastAndWestAtEnds(
    int position,Bias bias)
protected final short getBottomInset()
public Shape getChildAllocation(int
    index,Shape a)
protected Rectangle getInsideAllocation(
    Shape a)
protected final short getLeftInset()
protected int
    getNextEastWestVisualPositionFrom(int
    pos,Bias b,Shape a,int direction,Bias
    biasRet)
protected int
    getNextNorthSouthVisualPositionFrom(int

pos,Bias b,Shape a,int direction,Bias biasRet)
public int getNextVisualPositionFrom(int pos,Bias b,Shape a,int direction,Bias biasRet)
protected final short getRightInset()
protected final short getTopInset()
public View getView(int n)
protected abstract View getViewAtPoint(int x,int y,Rectangle alloc)
protected View getViewAtPosition(int pos, Rectangle a)
public int getViewCount()
protected int getViewIndexAtPosition(int pos)
public void insert(int offs,View v)
protected abstract boolean isAfter(int x, int y,Rectangle alloc)
protected abstract boolean isBefore(int x,int y,Rectangle alloc)
protected void loadChildren(ViewFactory f)
public Shape modelToView(int pos,Shape a, Bias b)
public Shape modelToView(int p0,Bias b0, int p1,Bias b1,Shape a)
public void removeAll()
public void replace(int offset,int length,View views)
protected final void setInsets(short top, short left,short bottom,short right)
protected final void setParagraphInsets(AttributeSet attr)
public void setParent(View parent)
public int viewToModel(float x,float y, Shape a,Bias bias)

▶**COMPOUNDBORDER**
public class javax.swing.border. CompoundBorder
extends javax.swing.border. AbstractBorder
extends java.lang.Object
Fields
protected javax.swing.border.Border insideBorder
protected javax.swing.border.Border outsideBorder
Constructors
public CompoundBorder()
public CompoundBorder(Border outsideBorder,Border insideBorder)
Methods
public Insets getBorderInsets(Component c,Insets insets)
public Insets getBorderInsets(Component c)
public Border getInsideBorder()
public Border getOutsideBorder()
public boolean isBorderOpaque()

public void paintBorder(Component c, Graphics g,int x,int y,int width,int height)

▶**COMPOUNDEDIT**
public class javax.swing.undo. CompoundEdit
extends javax.swing.undo. AbstractUndoableEdit
extends java.lang.Object
Fields
protected java.util.Vector edits
Constructors
public CompoundEdit()
Methods
public boolean addEdit(UndoableEdit anEdit)
public boolean canRedo()
public boolean canUndo()
public void die()
public void end()
public String getPresentationName()
public String getRedoPresentationName()
public String getUndoPresentationName()
public boolean isInProgress()
public boolean isSignificant()
protected UndoableEdit lastEdit()
public void redo()
public String toString()
public void undo()

▶**CONCURRENTMODIFICATIONEXCEPTION**
public class java.util. ConcurrentModificationException
extends java.lang.RuntimeException
extends java.lang.Exception
extends java.lang.Throwable
extends java.lang.Object
Constructors
public ConcurrentModificationException()
public ConcurrentModificationException(String message)

▶**CONNECTEXCEPTION**
public class java.net.ConnectException
extends java.net.SocketException
extends java.io.IOException
extends java.lang.Exception
extends java.lang.Throwable
extends java.lang.Object
Constructors
public ConnectException(String msg)
public ConnectException()

▶**CONNECTEXCEPTION**
public class java.rmi.ConnectException
extends java.rmi.RemoteException
extends java.io.IOException
extends java.lang.Exception
extends java.lang.Throwable
extends java.lang.Object

Constructors
```
public  ConnectException(String s)
public  ConnectException(String s,
  Exception ex)
```

▶**CONNECTIOEXCEPTION**
```
public class java.rmi.
  ConnectIOException
extends java.rmi.RemoteException
extends java.io.IOException
extends java.lang.Exception
extends java.lang.Throwable
extends java.lang.Object
```

Constructors
```
public  ConnectIOException(String s)
public  ConnectIOException(String s,
  Exception ex)
```

▶**CONSTRUCTOR**
```
public final class java.lang.reflect.
  Constructor
implements java.lang.reflect.Member
extends java.lang.reflect.
  AccessibleObject
extends java.lang.Object
```

Constructors
```
private  Constructor()
```

Methods
```
public boolean equals(Object obj)
public Class getDeclaringClass()
public Class getExceptionTypes()
public int getModifiers()
public String getName()
public Class getParameterTypes()
public int hashCode()
public native Object newInstance(Object
  initargs)
public String toString()
```

▶**CONTAINER**
```
public class java.awt.Container
extends java.awt.Component
extends java.lang.Object
```

Constructors
```
public  Container()
```

Methods
```
public Component add(Component comp)
public Component add(String name,
  Component comp)
public Component add(Component comp,int
  index)
public void add(Component comp,Object
  constraints)
public void add(Component comp,Object
  constraints,int index)
public synchronized void
  addContainerListener(ContainerListener l)
protected void addImpl(Component comp,
  Object constraints,int index)
public void addNotify()
public int countComponents()
public void deliverEvent(Event e)
```

```
public void doLayout()
public Component findComponentAt(int x,
  int y)
public Component findComponentAt(Point p)
public float getAlignmentX()
public float getAlignmentY()
public Component getComponent(int n)
public Component getComponentAt(int x,
  int y)
public Component getComponentAt(Point p)
public int getComponentCount()
public Component getComponents()
public Insets getInsets()
public LayoutManager getLayout()
public Dimension getMaximumSize()
public Dimension getMinimumSize()
public Dimension getPreferredSize()
public Insets insets()
public void invalidate()
public boolean isAncestorOf(Component c)
public void layout()
public void list(PrintStream out,int
  indent)
public void list(PrintWriter out,int
  indent)
public Component locate(int x,int y)
public Dimension minimumSize()
public void paint(Graphics g)
public void paintComponents(Graphics g)
protected String paramString()
public Dimension preferredSize()
public void print(Graphics g)
public void printComponents(Graphics g)
protected void processContainerEvent(
  ContainerEvent e)
protected void processEvent(AWTEvent e)
public void remove(int index)
public void remove(Component comp)
public void removeAll()
public synchronized void
  removeContainerListener(
  ContainerListener l)
public void removeNotify()
public void setFont(Font f)
public void setLayout(LayoutManager mgr)
public void update(Graphics g)
public void validate()
protected void validateTree()
```

▶**CONTAINERADAPTER**
```
public abstract class java.awt.event.
  ContainerAdapter
implements java.awt.event.
  ContainerListener
extends java.lang.Object
```

Methods
```
public void componentAdded(
  ContainerEvent e)
public void componentRemoved(
  ContainerEvent e)
```

▶**CONTAINEREVENT**
public class java.awt.event.
  ContainerEvent
extends java.awt.event.ComponentEvent
extends java.awt.AWTEvent
extends java.util.EventObject
extends java.lang.Object
Fields
public final static int COMPONENT_ADDED
public final static int COMPONENT_
  REMOVED
public final static int CONTAINER_FIRST
public final static int CONTAINER_LAST
Constructors
public ContainerEvent(Component source,
  int id,Component child)
Methods
public Component getChild()
public Container getContainer()
public String paramString()

▶**CONTENTHANDLER**
public abstract class java.net.
  ContentHandler
extends java.lang.Object
Methods
public abstract Object getContent(
  URLConnection urlc)

▶**CONTENTMODEL**
public final class javax.swing.text.html.
  parser.ContentModel
implements java.io.Serializable
extends java.lang.Object
Fields
public java.lang.Object content
public javax.swing.text.html.parser.
  ContentModel next
public int type
Constructors
public ContentModel()
public ContentModel(Element content)
public ContentModel(int type,
  ContentModel content)
public ContentModel(int type,Object
  content,ContentModel next)
Methods
public boolean empty()
public boolean first(Object token)
public Element first()
public void getElements(Vector elemVec)
public String toString()

▶**CONVOLVEOP**
public class java.awt.image.ConvolveOp
implements java.awt.image.
  BufferedImageOp
implements java.awt.image.RasterOp
extends java.lang.Object
Fields
public final static int EDGE_NO_OP

public final static int EDGE_ZERO_FILL
Constructors
public ConvolveOp(Kernel kernel,int
  edgeCondition,RenderingHints hints)
public ConvolveOp(Kernel kernel)
Methods
public BufferedImage
  createCompatibleDestImage(BufferedImage
  src,ColorModel destCM)
public WritableRaster
  createCompatibleDestRaster(Raster src)
public final BufferedImage filter(
  BufferedImage src,BufferedImage dst)
public final WritableRaster filter(
  Raster src,WritableRaster dst)
public final Rectangle2D getBounds2D(
  BufferedImage src)
public final Rectangle2D getBounds2D(
  Raster src)
public int getEdgeCondition()
public final Kernel getKernel()
public final Point2D getPoint2D(Point2D
  srcPt,Point2D dstPt)
public final RenderingHints
  getRenderingHints()

▶**CRC32**
public class java.util.zip.CRC32
implements java.util.zip.Checksum
extends java.lang.Object
Constructors
public static CRC32()
Methods
public long getValue()
public void reset()
public void update(int b)
public void update(byte b,int off,int
  len)
public void update(byte b)

▶**CRL**
public abstract class java.security.cert.
  CRL
extends java.lang.Object
Constructors
protected CRL(String type)
Methods
public final String getType()
public abstract boolean isRevoked(
  Certificate cert)
public abstract String toString()

▶**CRLEXCEPTION**
public class java.security.cert.
  CRLException
extends java.security.
  GeneralSecurityException
extends java.lang.Exception
extends java.lang.Throwable
extends java.lang.Object

Constructors

```
public  CRLException()
public  CRLException(String message)
```

▶**CROPIMAGEFILTER**

```
public class java.awt.image.
  CropImageFilter
extends java.awt.image.ImageFilter
extends java.lang.Object
```

Constructors

```
public  CropImageFilter(int x,int y,int
  w,int h)
```

Methods

```
public void setDimensions(int w,int h)
public void setPixels(int x,int y,int w,
  int h,ColorModel model,byte pixels,int
  off,int scansize)
public void setPixels(int x,int y,int w,
  int h,ColorModel model,int pixels,int
  off,int scansize)
public void setProperties(Hashtable
  props)
```

▶**CSS**

```
public class javax.swing.text.html.CSS
extends java.lang.Object
```

Methods

```
public static Attribute
  getAllAttributeKeys()
public final static Attribute
  getAttribute(String name)
```

▶**CUBICCURVE2D**

```
public abstract class java.awt.geom.
  CubicCurve2D
implements java.lang.Cloneable
implements java.awt.Shape
extends java.lang.Object
```

Constructors

```
protected  CubicCurve2D()
```

Methods

```
public Object clone()
public boolean contains(double x,double
  y)
public boolean contains(Point2D p)
public boolean contains(double x,double
  y,double w,double h)
public boolean contains(Rectangle2D r)
public Rectangle getBounds()
public abstract Point2D getCtrlP1()
public abstract Point2D getCtrlP2()
public abstract double getCtrlX1()
public abstract double getCtrlX2()
public abstract double getCtrlY1()
public abstract double getCtrlY2()
public static double getFlatness(double
  x1,double y1,double ctrlx1,double ctrly1,
  double ctrlx2,double ctrly2,double x2,
  double y2)
public static double getFlatness(double
  coords,int offset)
public double getFlatness()
```

```
public static double getFlatnessSq(
  double x1,double y1,double ctrlx1,double
  ctrly1,double ctrlx2,double ctrly2,
  double x2,double y2)
public static double getFlatnessSq(
  double coords,int offset)
public double getFlatnessSq()
public abstract Point2D getP1()
public abstract Point2D getP2()
public PathIterator getPathIterator(
  AffineTransform at)
public PathIterator getPathIterator(
  AffineTransform at,double flatness)
public abstract double getX1()
public abstract double getX2()
public abstract double getY1()
public abstract double getY2()
public boolean intersects(double x,
  double y,double w,double h)
public boolean intersects(Rectangle2D r)
public abstract void setCurve(double x1,
  double y1,double ctrlx1,double ctrly1,
  double ctrlx2,double ctrly2,double x2,
  double y2)
public void setCurve(double coords,int
  offset)
public void setCurve(Point2D p1,Point2D
  cp1,Point2D cp2,Point2D p2)
public void setCurve(Point2D pts,int
  offset)
public void setCurve(CubicCurve2D c)
public static int solveCubic(double eqn)
public void subdivide(CubicCurve2D left,
  CubicCurve2D right)
public static void subdivide(
  CubicCurve2D src,CubicCurve2D left,
  CubicCurve2D right)
public static void subdivide(double src,
  int srcoff,double left,int leftoff,
  double right,int rightoff)
```

▶**CURSOR**

```
public class java.awt.Cursor
implements java.io.Serializable
extends java.lang.Object
```

Fields

```
public final static int CROSSHAIR_
  CURSOR
public final static int CUSTOM_CURSOR
public final static int DEFAULT_CURSOR
public final static int E_RESIZE_CURSOR
public final static int HAND_CURSOR
public final static int MOVE_CURSOR
protected java.lang.String name
public final static int NE_RESIZE_
  CURSOR
public final static int NW_RESIZE_
  CURSOR
public final static int N_RESIZE_CURSOR
protected static java.awt.Cursor
  predefined
public final static int SE_RESIZE_
  CURSOR
```

public final static int SW_RESIZE_
  CURSOR
public final static int S_RESIZE_CURSOR
public final static int TEXT_CURSOR
public final static int WAIT_CURSOR
public final static int W_RESIZE_CURSOR

Constructors
public Cursor(int type)
protected Cursor(String name)

Methods
public static Cursor getDefaultCursor()
public String getName()
public static Cursor getPredefinedCursor(
  int type)
public static Cursor
  getSystemCustomCursor(String name)
public int getType()
public String toString()

▶**DATABUFFER**
public abstract class java.awt.image.
  DataBuffer
extends java.lang.Object

Fields
protected int banks
protected int dataType
protected int offset
protected int offsets
protected int size
public final static int TYPE_BYTE
public final static int TYPE_DOUBLE
public final static int TYPE_FLOAT
public final static int TYPE_INT
public final static int TYPE_SHORT
public final static int TYPE_UNDEFINED
public final static int TYPE_USHORT

Constructors
protected DataBuffer(int dataType,int
  size)
protected DataBuffer(int dataType,int
  size,int numBanks)
protected DataBuffer(int dataType,int
  size,int numBanks,int offset)
protected DataBuffer(int dataType,int
  size,int numBanks,int offsets)

Methods
public int getDataType()
public static int getDataTypeSize(int
  type)
public int getElem(int i)
public abstract int getElem(int bank,int
  i)
public double getElemDouble(int i)
public double getElemDouble(int bank,int
  i)
public float getElemFloat(int i)
public float getElemFloat(int bank,int i)
public int getNumBanks()
public int getOffset()
public int getOffsets()
public int getSize()

public void setElem(int i,int val)
public abstract void setElem(int bank,
  int i,int val)
public void setElemDouble(int i,double
  val)
public void setElemDouble(int bank,int i,
  double val)
public void setElemFloat(int i,float val)
public void setElemFloat(int bank,int i,
  float val)

▶**DATABUFFERBYTE**
public final class java.awt.image.
  DataBufferByte
extends java.awt.image.DataBuffer
extends java.lang.Object

Constructors
public DataBufferByte(int size)
public DataBufferByte(int size,int
  numBanks)
public DataBufferByte(byte dataArray,
  int size)
public DataBufferByte(byte dataArray,
  int size,int offset)
public DataBufferByte(byte dataArray,
  int size)
public DataBufferByte(byte dataArray,
  int size,int offsets)

Methods
public byte getBankData()
public byte getData()
public byte getData(int bank)
public int getElem(int i)
public int getElem(int bank,int i)
public void setElem(int i,int val)
public void setElem(int bank,int i,int
  val)

▶**DATABUFFERINT**
public final class java.awt.image.
  DataBufferInt
extends java.awt.image.DataBuffer
extends java.lang.Object

Constructors
public DataBufferInt(int size)
public DataBufferInt(int size,int
  numBanks)
public DataBufferInt(int dataArray,int
  size)
public DataBufferInt(int dataArray,int
  size,int offset)
public DataBufferInt(int dataArray,int
  size)
public DataBufferInt(int dataArray,int
  size,int offsets)

Methods
public int getBankData()
public int getData()
public int getData(int bank)
public int getElem(int i)
public int getElem(int bank,int i)
public void setElem(int i,int val)

```
public void setElem(int bank,int i,int
  val)
```

►DATABUFFERSHORT

```
public final class java.awt.image.
  DataBufferShort
extends java.awt.image.DataBuffer
extends java.lang.Object
```

Constructors

```
public DataBufferShort(int size)
public DataBufferShort(int size,int
  numBanks)
public DataBufferShort(short dataArray,
  int size)
public DataBufferShort(short dataArray,
  int size,int offset)
public DataBufferShort(short dataArray,
  int size)
public DataBufferShort(short dataArray,
  int size,int offsets)
```

Methods

```
public short getBankData()
public short getData()
public short getData(int bank)
public int getElem(int i)
public int getElem(int bank,int i)
public void setElem(int i,int val)
public void setElem(int bank,int i,int
  val)
```

►DATABUFFERUSHORT

```
public final class java.awt.image.
  DataBufferUShort
extends java.awt.image.DataBuffer
extends java.lang.Object
```

Constructors

```
public DataBufferUShort(int size)
public DataBufferUShort(int size,int
  numBanks)
public DataBufferUShort(short dataArray,
  int size)
public DataBufferUShort(short dataArray,
  int size,int offset)
public DataBufferUShort(short dataArray,
  int size)
public DataBufferUShort(short dataArray,
  int size,int offsets)
```

Methods

```
public short getBankData()
public short getData()
public short getData(int bank)
public int getElem(int i)
public int getElem(int bank,int i)
public void setElem(int i,int val)
public void setElem(int bank,int i,int
  val)
```

►DATAFLAVOR

```
public class java.awt.datatransfer.
  DataFlavor
implements java.lang.Cloneable
implements java.io.Externalizable
```

```
extends java.lang.Object
```

Fields

```
public final static java.awt.
  datatransfer.DataFlavor
  javaFileListFlavor
public final static java.lang.String
  javaJVMLocalObjectMimeType
public final static java.lang.String
  javaRemoteObjectMimeType
public final static java.lang.String
  javaSerializedObjectMimeType
public final static java.awt.
  datatransfer.DataFlavor plainTextFlavor
public final static java.awt.
  datatransfer.DataFlavor stringFlavor
```

Constructors

```
private DataFlavor()
public DataFlavor(Class
  representationClass,String
  humanPresentableName)
public DataFlavor(String mimeType,
  String humanPresentableName)
public DataFlavor(String mimeType,
  String humanPresentableName,ClassLoader
  classLoader)
public DataFlavor(String mimeType)
private DataFlavor()
public DataFlavor()
```

Methods

```
public Object clone()
public boolean equals(Object o)
public boolean equals(DataFlavor
  dataFlavor)
public boolean equals(String s)
public String getHumanPresentableName()
public String getMimeType()
public String getParameter(String
  paramName)
public String getPrimaryType()
public Class getRepresentationClass()
public String getSubType()
public boolean isFlavorJavaFileListType()
public boolean isFlavorRemoteObjectType()
public boolean
  isFlavorSerializedObjectType()
public boolean isMimeTypeEqual(String
  mimeType)
public final boolean isMimeTypeEqual(
  DataFlavor dataFlavor)
public boolean
  isMimeTypeSerializedObject()
public boolean
  isRepresentationClassInputStream()
public boolean
  isRepresentationClassRemote()
public boolean
  isRepresentationClassSerializable()
protected String normalizeMimeType(
  String mimeType)
protected String
  normalizeMimeTypeParameter(String
  parameterName,String parameterValue)
```

```
public synchronized void readExternal(
  ObjectInput is)
public void setHumanPresentableName(
  String humanPresentableName)
protected final static Class
  tryToLoadClass(String className,
  ClassLoader fallback)
public synchronized void writeExternal(
  ObjectOutput os)
```

► **DATAFORMATEXCEPTION**
```
public class java.util.zip.
  DataFormatException
extends java.lang.Exception
extends java.lang.Throwable
extends java.lang.Object
```
Constructors
```
public  DataFormatException()
public  DataFormatException(String s)
```

► **DATAGRAMPACKET**
```
public final class java.net.
  DatagramPacket
extends java.lang.Object
```
Constructors
```
public  DatagramPacket(byte buf,int
  offset,int length)
public  DatagramPacket(byte buf,int
  length)
public  DatagramPacket(byte buf,int
  offset,int length,InetAddress address,
  int port)
public  DatagramPacket(byte buf,int
  length,InetAddress address,int port)
```
Methods
```
public synchronized InetAddress
  getAddress()
public synchronized byte getData()
public synchronized int getLength()
public synchronized int getOffset()
public synchronized int getPort()
public synchronized void setAddress(
  InetAddress iaddr)
public synchronized void setData(byte
  buf,int offset,int length)
public synchronized void setData(byte
  buf)
public synchronized void setLength(int
  length)
public synchronized void setPort(int
  iport)
```

► **DATAGRAMSOCKET**
```
public class java.net.DatagramSocket
extends java.lang.Object
```
Constructors
```
public static  DatagramSocket()
public  DatagramSocket(int port)
public  DatagramSocket(int port,
  InetAddress laddr)
```
Methods
```
public void close()
```

```
public void connect(InetAddress address,
  int port)
public void disconnect()
public InetAddress getInetAddress()
public InetAddress getLocalAddress()
public int getLocalPort()
public int getPort()
public synchronized int
  getReceiveBufferSize()
public synchronized int
  getSendBufferSize()
public synchronized int getSoTimeout()
public synchronized void receive(
  DatagramPacket p)
public void send(DatagramPacket p)
public synchronized void
  setReceiveBufferSize(int size)
public synchronized void
  setSendBufferSize(int size)
public synchronized void setSoTimeout(
  int timeout)
```

► **DATAGRAMSOCKETIMPL**
```
public abstract class java.net.
  DatagramSocketImpl
implements java.net.SocketOptions
extends java.lang.Object
```
Fields
```
protected java.io.FileDescriptor fd
protected int localPort
```
Methods
```
protected abstract void bind(int lport,
  InetAddress laddr)
protected abstract void close()
protected abstract void create()
protected FileDescriptor
  getFileDescriptor()
protected int getLocalPort()
protected abstract int getTimeToLive()
protected abstract byte getTTL()
protected abstract void join(InetAddress
  inetaddr)
protected abstract void leave(
  InetAddress inetaddr)
protected abstract int peek(InetAddress
  i)
protected abstract void receive(
  DatagramPacket p)
protected abstract void send(
  DatagramPacket p)
protected abstract void setTimeToLive(
  int ttl)
protected abstract void setTTL(byte ttl)
```

► **DATAINPUTSTREAM**
```
public class java.io.DataInputStream
implements java.io.DataInput
extends java.io.FilterInputStream
extends java.io.InputStream
extends java.lang.Object
```
Constructors
```
public  DataInputStream(InputStream in)
```

Methods

```
public final int read(byte b)
public final int read(byte b,int off,int
  len)
public final boolean readBoolean()
public final byte readByte()
public final char readChar()
public final double readDouble()
public final float readFloat()
public final void readFully(byte b)
public final void readFully(byte b,int
  off,int len)
public final int readInt()
public final String readLine()
public final long readLong()
public final short readShort()
public final int readUnsignedByte()
public final int readUnsignedShort()
public final String readUTF()
public final static String readUTF(
  DataInput in)
public final int skipBytes(int n)
```

▶**DATAOUTPUTSTREAM**

```
public class java.io.DataOutputStream
implements java.io.DataOutput
extends java.io.FilterOutputStream
extends java.io.OutputStream
extends java.lang.Object
```

Fields

```
protected int written
```

Constructors

```
public  DataOutputStream(OutputStream
  out)
```

Methods

```
public void flush()
public final int size()
public synchronized void write(int b)
public synchronized void write(byte b,
  int off,int len)
public final void writeBoolean(boolean v)
public final void writeByte(int v)
public final void writeBytes(String s)
public final void writeChar(int v)
public final void writeChars(String s)
public final void writeDouble(double v)
public final void writeFloat(float v)
public final void writeInt(int v)
public final void writeLong(long v)
public final void writeShort(int v)
public final void writeUTF(String str)
```

▶**DATATRUNCATION**

```
public class java.sql.DataTruncation
extends java.sql.SQLWarning
extends java.sql.SQLException
extends java.lang.Exception
extends java.lang.Throwable
extends java.lang.Object
```

Constructors

```
public  DataTruncation(int index,boolean
  parameter,boolean read,int dataSize,int
  transferSize)
```

Methods

```
public int getDataSize()
public int getIndex()
public boolean getParameter()
public boolean getRead()
public int getTransferSize()
```

▶**DATE**

```
public class java.sql.Date
extends java.util.Date
extends java.lang.Object
```

Constructors

```
public  Date(int year,int month,int day)
public  Date(long date)
```

Methods

```
public int getHours()
public int getMinutes()
public int getSeconds()
public void setHours(int i)
public void setMinutes(int i)
public void setSeconds(int i)
public void setTime(long date)
public String toString()
public static Date valueOf(String s)
```

▶**DATE**

```
public class java.util.Date
implements java.lang.Cloneable
implements java.lang.Comparable
implements java.io.Serializable
extends java.lang.Object
```

Constructors

```
public  Date()
public  Date(long date)
public  Date(int year,int month,int date)
public  Date(int year,int month,int date,
  int hrs,int min)
public  Date(int year,int month,int date,
  int hrs,int min,int sec)
public  Date(String s)
```

Methods

```
public boolean after(Date when)
public boolean before(Date when)
public Object clone()
public int compareTo(Date anotherDate)
public int compareTo(Object o)
public boolean equals(Object obj)
public int getDate()
public int getDay()
public int getHours()
public int getMinutes()
public int getMonth()
public int getSeconds()
public long getTime()
public int getTimezoneOffset()
public int getYear()
public int hashCode()
public static long parse(String s)
```

```
public void setDate(int date)
public void setHours(int hours)
public void setMinutes(int minutes)
public void setMonth(int month)
public void setSeconds(int seconds)
public void setTime(long time)
public void setYear(int year)
public String toGMTString()
public String toLocaleString()
public String toString()
public static long UTC(int year,int
  month,int date,int hrs,int min,int sec)
```

►DATEFORMAT

```
public abstract class java.text.
  DateFormat
extends java.text.Format
extends java.lang.Object
```

Fields

```
public final static int AM_PM_FIELD
protected java.util.Calendar calendar
public final static int DATE_FIELD
public final static int DAY_OF_WEEK_
  FIELD
public final static int DAY_OF_WEEK_IN_
  MONTH_FIELD
public final static int DAY_OF_YEAR_
  FIELD
public final static int DEFAULT
public final static int ERA_FIELD
public final static int FULL
public final static int HOUR0_FIELD
public final static int HOUR1_FIELD
public final static int HOUR_OF_DAY0_
  FIELD
public final static int HOUR_OF_DAY1_
  FIELD
public final static int LONG
public final static int MEDIUM
public final static int MILLISECOND_
  FIELD
public final static int MINUTE_FIELD
public final static int MONTH_FIELD
protected java.text.NumberFormat
  numberFormat
public final static int SECOND_FIELD
public final static int SHORT
public final static int TIMEZONE_FIELD
public final static int WEEK_OF_MONTH_
  FIELD
public final static int WEEK_OF_YEAR_
  FIELD
public final static int YEAR_FIELD
```

Constructors

```
protected  DateFormat()
```

Methods

```
public Object clone()
public boolean equals(Object obj)
public final StringBuffer format(Object
  obj,StringBuffer toAppendTo,
  FieldPosition fieldPosition)
```

```
public abstract StringBuffer format(Date
  date,StringBuffer toAppendTo,
  FieldPosition fieldPosition)
public final String format(Date date)
public static Locale getAvailableLocales(
  )
public Calendar getCalendar()
public final static DateFormat
  getDateInstance()
public final static DateFormat
  getDateInstance(int style)
public final static DateFormat
  getDateInstance(int style,Locale aLocale)
public final static DateFormat
  getDateTimeInstance()
public final static DateFormat
  getDateTimeInstance(int dateStyle,int
  timeStyle)
public final static DateFormat
  getDateTimeInstance(int dateStyle,int
  timeStyle,Locale aLocale)
public final static DateFormat
  getInstance()
public NumberFormat getNumberFormat()
public final static DateFormat
  getTimeInstance()
public final static DateFormat
  getTimeInstance(int style)
public final static DateFormat
  getTimeInstance(int style,Locale aLocale)
public TimeZone getTimeZone()
public int hashCode()
public boolean isLenient()
public Date parse(String text)
public abstract Date parse(String text,
  ParsePosition pos)
public Object parseObject(String source,
  ParsePosition pos)
public void setCalendar(Calendar
  newCalendar)
public void setLenient(boolean lenient)
public void setNumberFormat(NumberFormat
  newNumberFormat)
public void setTimeZone(TimeZone zone)
```

►DATEFORMATSYMBOLS

```
public class java.text.
  DateFormatSymbols
implements java.lang.Cloneable
implements java.io.Serializable
extends java.lang.Object
```

Constructors

```
public  DateFormatSymbols()
public  DateFormatSymbols(Locale locale)
```

Methods

```
public Object clone()
public boolean equals(Object obj)
public String getAmPmStrings()
public String getEras()
public String getLocalPatternChars()
public String getMonths()
public String getShortMonths()
```

```
public String getShortWeekdays()
public String getWeekdays()
public String getZoneStrings()
public int hashCode()
public void setAmPmStrings(String
  newAmpms)
public void setEras(String newEras)
public void setLocalPatternChars(String
  newLocalPatternChars)
public void setMonths(String newMonths)
public void setShortMonths(String
  newShortMonths)
public void setShortWeekdays(String
  newShortWeekdays)
public void setWeekdays(String
  newWeekdays)
public void setZoneStrings(String
  newZoneStrings)
```

▶DateFormatZoneData

```
public final class java.text.resources.
  DateFormatZoneData
extends java.util.ListResourceBundle
extends java.util.ResourceBundle
extends java.lang.Object
```

Methods
```
public Object getContents()
```

▶DateFormatZoneData_en

```
public final class java.text.resources.
  DateFormatZoneData_en
extends java.util.ListResourceBundle
extends java.util.ResourceBundle
extends java.lang.Object
```

Methods
```
public Object getContents()
```

▶DebugGraphics

```
public class javax.swing.DebugGraphics
extends java.awt.Graphics
extends java.lang.Object
```

Fields
```
public final static int BUFFERED_OPTION
public final static int FLASH_OPTION
public final static int LOG_OPTION
public final static int NONE_OPTION
```

Constructors
```
public  DebugGraphics()
public  DebugGraphics(Graphics graphics,
  JComponent component)
public  DebugGraphics(Graphics graphics)
```

Methods
```
public void clearRect(int x,int y,int
  width,int height)
public void clipRect(int x,int y,int
  width,int height)
public void copyArea(int x,int y,int
  width,int height,int destX,int destY)
public Graphics create()
public Graphics create(int x,int y,int
  width,int height)
public void dispose()
```

```
public void draw3DRect(int x,int y,int
  width,int height,boolean raised)
public void drawArc(int x,int y,int
  width,int height,int startAngle,int
  arcAngle)
public void drawBytes(byte data,int
  offset,int length,int x,int y)
public void drawChars(char data,int
  offset,int length,int x,int y)
public boolean drawImage(Image img,int x,
  int y,ImageObserver observer)
public boolean drawImage(Image img,int x,
  int y,int width,int height,ImageObserver
  observer)
public boolean drawImage(Image img,int x,
  int y,Color bgcolor,ImageObserver
  observer)
public boolean drawImage(Image img,int x,
  int y,int width,int height,Color bgcolor,
  ImageObserver observer)
public boolean drawImage(Image img,int
  dx1,int dy1,int dx2,int dy2,int sx1,int
  sy1,int sx2,int sy2,ImageObserver
  observer)
public boolean drawImage(Image img,int
  dx1,int dy1,int dx2,int dy2,int sx1,int
  sy1,int sx2,int sy2,Color bgcolor,
  ImageObserver observer)
public void drawLine(int x1,int y1,int
  x2,int y2)
public void drawOval(int x,int y,int
  width,int height)
public void drawPolygon(int xPoints,int
  yPoints,int nPoints)
public void drawPolyline(int xPoints,int
  yPoints,int nPoints)
public void drawRect(int x,int y,int
  width,int height)
public void drawRoundRect(int x,int y,
  int width,int height,int arcWidth,int
  arcHeight)
public void drawString(String aString,
  int x,int y)
public void drawString(
  AttributedCharacterIterator iterator,int
  x,int y)
public void fill3DRect(int x,int y,int
  width,int height,boolean raised)
public void fillArc(int x,int y,int
  width,int height,int startAngle,int
  arcAngle)
public void fillOval(int x,int y,int
  width,int height)
public void fillPolygon(int xPoints,int
  yPoints,int nPoints)
public void fillRect(int x,int y,int
  width,int height)
public void fillRoundRect(int x,int y,
  int width,int height,int arcWidth,int
  arcHeight)
public static Color flashColor()
public static int flashCount()
public static int flashTime()
```

```
public Shape getClip()
public Rectangle getClipBounds()
public Color getColor()
public int getDebugOptions()
public Font getFont()
public FontMetrics getFontMetrics()
public FontMetrics getFontMetrics(Font f)
public boolean isDrawingBuffer()
public static PrintStream logStream()
public void setClip(int x,int y,int
  width,int height)
public void setClip(Shape clip)
public void setColor(Color aColor)
public void setDebugOptions(int options)
public static void setFlashColor(Color
  flashColor)
public static void setFlashCount(int
  flashCount)
public static void setFlashTime(int
  flashTime)
public void setFont(Font aFont)
public static void setLogStream(
  PrintStream stream)
public void setPaintMode()
public void setXORMode(Color aColor)
public void translate(int x,int y)
```

▶**DECIMALFORMAT**

```
public class java.text.DecimalFormat
extends java.text.NumberFormat
extends java.text.Format
extends java.lang.Object
```

Constructors

```
public  DecimalFormat()
public  DecimalFormat(String pattern)
public  DecimalFormat(String pattern,
  DecimalFormatSymbols symbols)
```

Methods

```
public void applyLocalizedPattern(String
  pattern)
public void applyPattern(String pattern)
public Object clone()
public boolean equals(Object obj)
public StringBuffer format(double number,
  StringBuffer result,FieldPosition
  fieldPosition)
public StringBuffer format(long number,
  StringBuffer result,FieldPosition
  fieldPosition)
public DecimalFormatSymbols
  getDecimalFormatSymbols()
public int getGroupingSize()
public int getMultiplier()
public String getNegativePrefix()
public String getNegativeSuffix()
public String getPositivePrefix()
public String getPositiveSuffix()
public int hashCode()
public boolean
  isDecimalSeparatorAlwaysShown()
public Number parse(String text,
  ParsePosition parsePosition)
```

```
public void setDecimalFormatSymbols(
  DecimalFormatSymbols newSymbols)
public void
  setDecimalSeparatorAlwaysShown(boolean
  newValue)
public void setGroupingSize(int newValue)
public void setMaximumFractionDigits(int
  newValue)
public void setMaximumIntegerDigits(int
  newValue)
public void setMinimumFractionDigits(int
  newValue)
public void setMinimumIntegerDigits(int
  newValue)
public void setMultiplier(int newValue)
public void setNegativePrefix(String
  newValue)
public void setNegativeSuffix(String
  newValue)
public void setPositivePrefix(String
  newValue)
public void setPositiveSuffix(String
  newValue)
public String toLocalizedPattern()
public String toPattern()
```

▶**DECIMALFORMATSYMBOLS**

```
public final class java.text.
  DecimalFormatSymbols
implements java.lang.Cloneable
implements java.io.Serializable
extends java.lang.Object
```

Constructors

```
public  DecimalFormatSymbols()
public  DecimalFormatSymbols(Locale
  locale)
```

Methods

```
public Object clone()
public boolean equals(Object obj)
public String getCurrencySymbol()
public char getDecimalSeparator()
public char getDigit()
public char getGroupingSeparator()
public String getInfinity()
public String
  getInternationalCurrencySymbol()
public char getMinusSign()
public char getMonetaryDecimalSeparator()
public String getNaN()
public char getPatternSeparator()
public char getPercent()
public char getPerMill()
public char getZeroDigit()
public int hashCode()
public void setCurrencySymbol(String
  currency)
public void setDecimalSeparator(char
  decimalSeparator)
public void setDigit(char digit)
public void setGroupingSeparator(char
  groupingSeparator)
public void setInfinity(String infinity)
```

public void
  setInternationalCurrencySymbol(String
  currency)
public void setMinusSign(char minusSign)
public void setMonetaryDecimalSeparator(
  char sep)
public void setNaN(String NaN)
public void setPatternSeparator(char
  patternSeparator)
public void setPercent(char percent)
public void setPerMill(char perMill)
public void setZeroDigit(char zeroDigit)

▶DEFAULTBOUNDEDRANGEMODEL

public class javax.swing.
  DefaultBoundedRangeModel
implements javax.swing.
  BoundedRangeModel
implements java.io.Serializable
extends java.lang.Object

Fields

protected transient javax.swing.event.
  ChangeEvent changeEvent
protected javax.swing.event.
  EventListenerList listenerList

Constructors

public DefaultBoundedRangeModel()
public DefaultBoundedRangeModel(int
  value,int extent,int min,int max)

Methods

public void addChangeListener(
  ChangeListener l)
protected void fireStateChanged()
public int getExtent()
public int getMaximum()
public int getMinimum()
public int getValue()
public boolean getValueIsAdjusting()
public void removeChangeListener(
  ChangeListener l)
public void setExtent(int n)
public void setMaximum(int n)
public void setMinimum(int n)
public void setRangeProperties(int
  newValue,int newExtent,int newMin,int
  newMax,boolean adjusting)
public void setValue(int n)
public void setValueIsAdjusting(boolean
  b)
public String toString()

▶DEFAULTBUTTONMODEL

public class javax.swing.
  DefaultButtonModel
implements javax.swing.ButtonModel
implements java.io.Serializable
extends java.lang.Object

Fields

protected java.lang.String
  actionCommand
public final static int ARMED

protected transient javax.swing.event.
  ChangeEvent changeEvent
public final static int ENABLED
protected javax.swing.ButtonGroup group
protected javax.swing.event.
  EventListenerList listenerList
protected int mnemonic
public final static int PRESSED
public final static int ROLLOVER
public final static int SELECTED
protected int stateMask

Constructors

public DefaultButtonModel()

Methods

public void addActionListener(
  ActionListener l)
public void addChangeListener(
  ChangeListener l)
public void addItemListener(ItemListener
  l)
protected void fireActionPerformed(
  ActionEvent e)
protected void fireItemStateChanged(
  ItemEvent e)
protected void fireStateChanged()
public String getActionCommand()
public int getMnemonic()
public Object getSelectedObjects()
public boolean isArmed()
public boolean isEnabled()
public boolean isPressed()
public boolean isRollover()
public boolean isSelected()
public void removeActionListener(
  ActionListener l)
public void removeChangeListener(
  ChangeListener l)
public void removeItemListener(
  ItemListener l)
public void setActionCommand(String
  actionCommand)
public void setArmed(boolean b)
public void setEnabled(boolean b)
public void setGroup(ButtonGroup group)
public void setMnemonic(int key)
public void setPressed(boolean b)
public void setRollover(boolean b)
public void setSelected(boolean b)

▶DEFAULTCARET

public class javax.swing.text.
  DefaultCaret
implements javax.swing.text.Caret
implements java.awt.event.FocusListener
implements java.awt.event.MouseListener
implements java.awt.event.
  MouseMotionListener
extends java.awt.Rectangle
extends java.awt.geom.Rectangle2D
extends java.awt.geom.RectangularShape
extends java.lang.Object

Fields

```
protected transient javax.swing.event.
  ChangeEvent changeEvent
protected javax.swing.event.
  EventListenerList listenerList
```

Constructors

```
public  DefaultCaret()
```

Methods

```
public void addChangeListener(
  ChangeListener l)
protected void adjustVisibility(
  Rectangle nloc)
protected synchronized void damage(
  Rectangle r)
public void deinstall(JTextComponent c)
protected void fireStateChanged()
public void focusGained(FocusEvent e)
public void focusLost(FocusEvent e)
public int getBlinkRate()
protected final JTextComponent
  getComponent()
public int getDot()
public Point getMagicCaretPosition()
public int getMark()
protected HighlightPainter
  getSelectionPainter()
public void install(JTextComponent c)
public boolean isSelectionVisible()
public boolean isVisible()
public void mouseClicked(MouseEvent e)
public void mouseDragged(MouseEvent e)
public void mouseEntered(MouseEvent e)
public void mouseExited(MouseEvent e)
public void mouseMoved(MouseEvent e)
public void mousePressed(MouseEvent e)
public void mouseReleased(MouseEvent e)
protected void moveCaret(MouseEvent e)
public void moveDot(int dot)
public void paint(Graphics g)
protected void positionCaret(MouseEvent
  e)
public void removeChangeListener(
  ChangeListener l)
protected final synchronized void
  repaint()
public void setBlinkRate(int rate)
public void setDot(int dot)
public void setMagicCaretPosition(Point
  p)
public void setSelectionVisible(boolean
  vis)
public void setVisible(boolean e)
public String toString()
```

▶DEFAULTCELLEDITOR

```
public class javax.swing.
  DefaultCellEditor
implements java.io.Serializable
implements javax.swing.table.
  TableCellEditor
implements javax.swing.tree.
  TreeCellEditor
```

```
extends java.lang.Object
```

Fields

```
protected transient javax.swing.event.
  ChangeEvent changeEvent
protected int clickCountToStart
protected EditorDelegate delegate
protected javax.swing.JComponent
  editorComponent
protected javax.swing.event.
  EventListenerList listenerList
```

Constructors

```
public  DefaultCellEditor(JTextField x)
public  DefaultCellEditor(JCheckBox x)
public  DefaultCellEditor(JComboBox x)
```

Methods

```
public void addCellEditorListener(
  CellEditorListener l)
public void cancelCellEditing()
protected void fireEditingCanceled()
protected void fireEditingStopped()
public Object getCellEditorValue()
public int getClickCountToStart()
public Component getComponent()
public Component
  getTableCellEditorComponent(JTable table,
  Object value,boolean isSelected,int row,
  int column)
public Component
  getTreeCellEditorComponent(JTree tree,
  Object value,boolean isSelected,boolean
  expanded,boolean leaf,int row)
public boolean isCellEditable(
  EventObject anEvent)
public void removeCellEditorListener(
  CellEditorListener l)
public void setClickCountToStart(int
  count)
public boolean shouldSelectCell(
  EventObject anEvent)
public boolean stopCellEditing()
```

▶DEFAULTCOLORSELECTIONMODEL

```
public class javax.swing.colorchooser.
  DefaultColorSelectionModel
implements javax.swing.colorchooser.
  ColorSelectionModel
implements java.io.Serializable
extends java.lang.Object
```

Fields

```
protected transient javax.swing.event.
  ChangeEvent changeEvent
protected javax.swing.event.
  EventListenerList listenerList
```

Constructors

```
public  DefaultColorSelectionModel()
public  DefaultColorSelectionModel(Color
  color)
```

Methods

```
public void addChangeListener(
  ChangeListener l)
protected void fireStateChanged()
```

```
public Color getSelectedColor()
public void removeChangeListener(
  ChangeListener l)
public void setSelectedColor(Color color)
```

▶**DEFAULTCOMBOBOXMODEL**
```
public class javax.swing.
  DefaultComboBoxModel
implements javax.swing.
  MutableComboBoxModel
implements java.io.Serializable
extends javax.swing.AbstractListModel
extends java.lang.Object
```
Constructors
```
public  DefaultComboBoxModel()
public  DefaultComboBoxModel(Object
  items)
public  DefaultComboBoxModel(Vector v)
```
Methods
```
public void addElement(Object anObject)
public Object getElementAt(int index)
public int getIndexOf(Object anObject)
public Object getSelectedItem()
public int getSize()
public void insertElementAt(Object
  anObject,int index)
public void removeAllElements()
public void removeElement(Object
  anObject)
public void removeElementAt(int index)
public void setSelectedItem(Object
  anObject)
```

▶**DEFAULTDESKTOPMANAGER**
```
public class javax.swing.
  DefaultDesktopManager
implements javax.swing.DesktopManager
implements java.io.Serializable
extends java.lang.Object
```
Methods
```
public void activateFrame(JInternalFrame
  f)
public void beginDraggingFrame(
  JComponent f)
public void beginResizingFrame(
  JComponent f,int direction)
public void closeFrame(JInternalFrame f)
public void deactivateFrame(
  JInternalFrame f)
public void deiconifyFrame(
  JInternalFrame f)
public void dragFrame(JComponent f,int
  newX,int newY)
public void endDraggingFrame(JComponent
  f)
public void endResizingFrame(JComponent
  f)
protected Rectangle getBoundsForIconOf(
  JInternalFrame f)
protected Rectangle getPreviousBounds(
  JInternalFrame f)
```

```
public void iconifyFrame(JInternalFrame
  f)
public void maximizeFrame(JInternalFrame
  f)
public void minimizeFrame(JInternalFrame
  f)
public void openFrame(JInternalFrame f)
protected void removeIconFor(
  JInternalFrame f)
public void resizeFrame(JComponent f,int
  newX,int newY,int newWidth,int newHeight)
public void setBoundsForFrame(JComponent
  f,int newX,int newY,int newWidth,int
  newHeight)
protected void setPreviousBounds(
  JInternalFrame f,Rectangle r)
protected void setWasIcon(JInternalFrame
  f,Boolean value)
protected boolean wasIcon(JInternalFrame
  f)
```

▶**DEFAULTEDITORKIT**
```
public class javax.swing.text.
  DefaultEditorKit
extends javax.swing.text.EditorKit
extends java.lang.Object
```
Fields
```
public final static java.lang.String
  backwardAction
public final static java.lang.String
  beepAction
public final static java.lang.String
  beginAction
public final static java.lang.String
  beginLineAction
public final static java.lang.String
  beginParagraphAction
public final static java.lang.String
  beginWordAction
public final static java.lang.String
  copyAction
public final static java.lang.String
  cutAction
public final static java.lang.String
  defaultKeyTypedAction
public final static java.lang.String
  deleteNextCharAction
public final static java.lang.String
  deletePrevCharAction
public final static java.lang.String
  downAction
public final static java.lang.String
  endAction
public final static java.lang.String
  endLineAction
public final static java.lang.String
  EndOfLineStringProperty
public final static java.lang.String
  endParagraphAction
public final static java.lang.String
  endWordAction
public final static java.lang.String
  forwardAction
```

public final static java.lang.String
  insertBreakAction
public final static java.lang.String
  insertContentAction
public final static java.lang.String
  insertTabAction
public final static java.lang.String
  nextWordAction
public final static java.lang.String
  pageDownAction
public final static java.lang.String
  pageUpAction
public final static java.lang.String
  pasteAction
public final static java.lang.String
  previousWordAction
public final static java.lang.String
  readOnlyAction
public final static java.lang.String
  selectAllAction
public final static java.lang.String
  selectionBackwardAction
public final static java.lang.String
  selectionBeginAction
public final static java.lang.String
  selectionBeginLineAction
public final static java.lang.String
  selectionBeginParagraphAction
public final static java.lang.String
  selectionBeginWordAction
public final static java.lang.String
  selectionDownAction
public final static java.lang.String
  selectionEndAction
public final static java.lang.String
  selectionEndLineAction
public final static java.lang.String
  selectionEndParagraphAction
public final static java.lang.String
  selectionEndWordAction
public final static java.lang.String
  selectionForwardAction
public final static java.lang.String
  selectionNextWordAction
public final static java.lang.String
  selectionPreviousWordAction
public final static java.lang.String
  selectionUpAction
public final static java.lang.String
  selectLineAction
public final static java.lang.String
  selectParagraphAction
public final static java.lang.String
  selectWordAction
public final static java.lang.String
  upAction
public final static java.lang.String
  writableAction

Methods
public Object clone()
public Caret createCaret()
public Document createDefaultDocument()

public Action getActions()
public String getContentType()
public ViewFactory getViewFactory()
public void read(InputStream in,Document
  doc,int pos)
public void read(Reader in,Document doc,
  int pos)
public void write(OutputStream out,
  Document doc,int pos,int len)
public void write(Writer out,Document
  doc,int pos,int len)

▸**DefaultFocusManager**
public class javax.swing.
  DefaultFocusManager
extends javax.swing.FocusManager
extends java.lang.Object
Methods
public boolean compareTabOrder(Component
  a,Component b)
public void focusNextComponent(Component
  aComponent)
public void focusPreviousComponent(
  Component aComponent)
public Component getComponentAfter(
  Container aContainer,Component
  aComponent)
public Component getComponentBefore(
  Container aContainer,Component
  aComponent)
public Component getFirstComponent(
  Container aContainer)
public Component getLastComponent(
  Container aContainer)
public void processKeyEvent(Component
  focusedComponent,KeyEvent anEvent)

▸**DefaultHighlighter**
public class javax.swing.text.
  DefaultHighlighter
extends javax.swing.text.
  LayeredHighlighter
extends java.lang.Object
Fields
public static LayeredHighlighter.
  LayerPainter DefaultPainter
Constructors
public DefaultHighlighter()
Methods
public Object addHighlight(int p0,int p1,
  HighlightPainter p)
public void changeHighlight(Object tag,
  int p0,int p1)
public void deinstall(JTextComponent c)
public boolean getDrawsLayeredHighlights(
)
public Highlight getHighlights()
public void install(JTextComponent c)
public void paint(Graphics g)
public void paintLayeredHighlights(
  Graphics g,int p0,int p1,Shape

viewBounds,JTextComponent editor,View
view)
public void removeAllHighlights()
public void removeHighlight(Object tag)
public void setDrawsLayeredHighlights(
boolean newValue)

► **DEFAULTLISTCELLRENDERER**
public class javax.swing.
DefaultListCellRenderer
implements javax.swing.ListCellRenderer
implements java.io.Serializable
extends javax.swing.JLabel
extends javax.swing.JComponent
extends java.awt.Container
extends java.awt.Component
extends java.lang.Object

Fields
protected static javax.swing.border.
Border noFocusBorder

Constructors
public DefaultListCellRenderer()

Methods
public Component
getListCellRendererComponent(JList list,
Object value,int index,boolean
isSelected,boolean cellHasFocus)

► **DEFAULTLISTMODEL**
public class javax.swing.
DefaultListModel
extends javax.swing.AbstractListModel
extends java.lang.Object

Methods
public void add(int index,Object element)
public void addElement(Object obj)
public int capacity()
public void clear()
public boolean contains(Object elem)
public void copyInto(Object anArray)
public Object elementAt(int index)
public Enumeration elements()
public void ensureCapacity(int
minCapacity)
public Object firstElement()
public Object get(int index)
public Object getElementAt(int index)
public int getSize()
public int indexOf(Object elem)
public int indexOf(Object elem,int index)
public void insertElementAt(Object obj,
int index)
public boolean isEmpty()
public Object lastElement()
public int lastIndexOf(Object elem)
public int lastIndexOf(Object elem,int
index)
public Object remove(int index)
public void removeAllElements()
public boolean removeElement(Object obj)
public void removeElementAt(int index)

public void removeRange(int fromIndex,
int toIndex)
public Object set(int index,Object
element)
public void setElementAt(Object obj,int
index)
public void setSize(int newSize)
public int size()
public Object toArray()
public String toString()
public void trimToSize()

► **DEFAULTLISTSELECTIONMODEL**
public class javax.swing.
DefaultListSelectionModel
implements java.lang.Cloneable
implements javax.swing.
ListSelectionModel
implements java.io.Serializable
extends java.lang.Object

Fields
protected boolean
leadAnchorNotificationEnabled
protected javax.swing.event.
EventListenerList listenerList

Methods
public void addListSelectionListener(
ListSelectionListener l)
public void addSelectionInterval(int
index0,int index1)
public void clearSelection()
public Object clone()
protected void fireValueChanged(boolean
isAdjusting)
protected void fireValueChanged(int
firstIndex,int lastIndex)
protected void fireValueChanged(int
firstIndex,int lastIndex,boolean
isAdjusting)
public int getAnchorSelectionIndex()
public int getLeadSelectionIndex()
public int getMaxSelectionIndex()
public int getMinSelectionIndex()
public int getSelectionMode()
public boolean getValueIsAdjusting()
public void insertIndexInterval(int
index,int length,boolean before)
public boolean
isLeadAnchorNotificationEnabled()
public boolean isSelectedIndex(int index)
public boolean isSelectionEmpty()
public void removeIndexInterval(int
index0,int index1)
public void removeListSelectionListener(
ListSelectionListener l)
public void removeSelectionInterval(int
index0,int index1)
public void setAnchorSelectionIndex(int
anchorIndex)
public void
setLeadAnchorNotificationEnabled(boolean
flag)

```
public void setLeadSelectionIndex(int
  leadIndex)
public void setSelectionInterval(int
  index0,int index1)
public void setSelectionMode(int
  selectionMode)
public void setValueIsAdjusting(boolean
  isAdjusting)
public String toString()
```

▶DEFAULTMENULAYOUT

```
public class javax.swing.plaf.basic.
  DefaultMenuLayout
implements javax.swing.plaf.UIResource
extends javax.swing.BoxLayout
extends java.lang.Object
```

Constructors

```
public DefaultMenuLayout(Container
  target,int axis)
```

▶DEFAULTMETALTHEME

```
public class javax.swing.plaf.metal.
  DefaultMetalTheme
extends javax.swing.plaf.metal.
  MetalTheme
extends java.lang.Object
```

Constructors

```
public DefaultMetalTheme()
```

Methods

```
public FontUIResource getControlTextFont(
  )
public FontUIResource getMenuTextFont()
public String getName()
protected ColorUIResource getPrimary1()
protected ColorUIResource getPrimary2()
protected ColorUIResource getPrimary3()
protected ColorUIResource getSecondary1()
protected ColorUIResource getSecondary2()
protected ColorUIResource getSecondary3()
public FontUIResource getSubTextFont()
public FontUIResource getSystemTextFont()
public FontUIResource getUserTextFont()
public FontUIResource getWindowTitleFont(
  )
```

▶DEFAULTMUTABLETREENODE

```
public class javax.swing.tree.
  DefaultMutableTreeNode
implements java.lang.Cloneable
implements javax.swing.tree.
  MutableTreeNode
implements java.io.Serializable
extends java.lang.Object
extends java.lang.Object
```

Fields

```
protected boolean allowsChildren
protected java.util.Vector children
public final static java.util.
  Enumeration EMPTY_ENUMERATION
protected javax.swing.tree.
  MutableTreeNode parent
```

```
protected transient java.lang.Object
  userObject
```

Constructors

```
public DefaultMutableTreeNode()
public DefaultMutableTreeNode(Object
  userObject)
public DefaultMutableTreeNode(Object
  userObject,boolean allowsChildren)
```

Methods

```
public void add(MutableTreeNode newChild)
public Enumeration
  breadthFirstEnumeration()
public Enumeration children()
public Object clone()
public Enumeration depthFirstEnumeration(
  )
public boolean getAllowsChildren()
public TreeNode getChildAfter(TreeNode
  aChild)
public TreeNode getChildAt(int index)
public TreeNode getChildBefore(TreeNode
  aChild)
public int getChildCount()
public int getDepth()
public TreeNode getFirstChild()
public DefaultMutableTreeNode
  getFirstLeaf()
public int getIndex(TreeNode aChild)
public TreeNode getLastChild()
public DefaultMutableTreeNode
  getLastLeaf()
public int getLeafCount()
public int getLevel()
public DefaultMutableTreeNode
  getNextLeaf()
public DefaultMutableTreeNode
  getNextNode()
public DefaultMutableTreeNode
  getNextSibling()
public TreeNode getParent()
public TreeNode getPath()
protected TreeNode getPathToRoot(
  TreeNode aNode,int depth)
public DefaultMutableTreeNode
  getPreviousLeaf()
public DefaultMutableTreeNode
  getPreviousNode()
public DefaultMutableTreeNode
  getPreviousSibling()
public TreeNode getRoot()
public TreeNode getSharedAncestor(
  DefaultMutableTreeNode aNode)
public int getSiblingCount()
public Object getUserObject()
public Object getUserObjectPath()
public void insert(MutableTreeNode
  newChild,int childIndex)
public boolean isLeaf()
public boolean isNodeAncestor(TreeNode
  anotherNode)
public boolean isNodeChild(TreeNode
  aNode)
```

```
public boolean isNodeDescendant(
  DefaultMutableTreeNode anotherNode)
public boolean isNodeRelated(
  DefaultMutableTreeNode aNode)
public boolean isNodeSibling(TreeNode
  anotherNode)
public boolean isRoot()
public Enumeration
  pathFromAncestorEnumeration(TreeNode
  ancestor)
public Enumeration postorderEnumeration()
public Enumeration preorderEnumeration()
public void remove(int childIndex)
public void remove(MutableTreeNode
  aChild)
public void removeAllChildren()
public void removeFromParent()
public void setAllowsChildren(boolean
  allows)
public void setParent(MutableTreeNode
  newParent)
public void setUserObject(Object
  userObject)
public String toString()
```

▶**DEFAULTSINGLESELECTIONMODEL**

```
public class javax.swing.
  DefaultSingleSelectionModel
implements java.io.Serializable
implements javax.swing.
  SingleSelectionModel
extends java.lang.Object
```

Fields

```
protected transient javax.swing.event.
  ChangeEvent changeEvent
protected javax.swing.event.
  EventListenerList listenerList
```

Methods

```
public void addChangeListener(
  ChangeListener l)
public void clearSelection()
protected void fireStateChanged()
public int getSelectedIndex()
public boolean isSelected()
public void removeChangeListener(
  ChangeListener l)
public void setSelectedIndex(int index)
```

▶**DEFAULTSTYLEDDOCUMENT**

```
public class javax.swing.text.
  DefaultStyledDocument
implements javax.swing.text.
  StyledDocument
extends javax.swing.text.
  AbstractDocument
extends java.lang.Object
```

Fields

```
protected ElementBuffer buffer
public final static int BUFFER_SIZE_
  DEFAULT
```

Constructors

```
public DefaultStyledDocument(Content c,
  StyleContext styles)
public DefaultStyledDocument(
  StyleContext styles)
public DefaultStyledDocument()
```

Methods

```
public void addDocumentListener(
  DocumentListener listener)
public Style addStyle(String nm,Style
  parent)
protected void create(ElementSpec data)
protected AbstractElement
  createDefaultRoot()
public Color getBackground(AttributeSet
  attr)
public Element getCharacterElement(int
  pos)
public Element getDefaultRootElement()
public Font getFont(AttributeSet attr)
public Color getForeground(AttributeSet
  attr)
public Style getLogicalStyle(int p)
public Element getParagraphElement(int
  pos)
public Style getStyle(String nm)
public Enumeration getStyleNames()
protected void insert(int offset,
  ElementSpec data)
protected void insertUpdate(
  DefaultDocumentEvent chng,AttributeSet
  attr)
public void removeDocumentListener(
  DocumentListener listener)
public void removeStyle(String nm)
protected void removeUpdate(
  DefaultDocumentEvent chng)
public void setCharacterAttributes(int
  offset,int length,AttributeSet s,boolean
  replace)
public void setLogicalStyle(int pos,
  Style s)
public void setParagraphAttributes(int
  offset,int length,AttributeSet s,boolean
  replace)
protected void styleChanged(Style style)
```

▶**DEFAULTTABLECELLRENDERER**

```
public class javax.swing.table.
  DefaultTableCellRenderer
implements java.io.Serializable
implements javax.swing.table.
  TableCellRenderer
extends javax.swing.JLabel
extends javax.swing.JComponent
extends java.awt.Container
extends java.awt.Component
extends java.lang.Object
```

Fields

```
protected static javax.swing.border.
  Border noFocusBorder
```

Constructors

public DefaultTableCellRenderer()

Methods

public Component
  getTableCellRendererComponent(JTable
  table,Object value,boolean isSelected,
  boolean hasFocus,int row,int column)
public void setBackground(Color c)
public void setForeground(Color c)
protected void setValue(Object value)
public void updateUI()

▶**DEFAULTTABLECOLUMNMODEL**

public class javax.swing.table.
  DefaultTableColumnModel
implements javax.swing.event.
  ListSelectionListener
implements java.beans.
  PropertyChangeListener
implements java.io.Serializable
implements javax.swing.table.
  TableColumnModel
extends java.lang.Object

Fields

protected transient javax.swing.event.
  ChangeEvent changeEvent
protected int columnMargin
protected boolean
  columnSelectionAllowed
protected javax.swing.event.
  EventListenerList listenerList
protected javax.swing.ListSelectionModel
  selectionModel
protected java.util.Vector tableColumns
protected int totalColumnWidth

Constructors

public DefaultTableColumnModel()

Methods

public void addColumn(TableColumn
  aColumn)
public void addColumnModelListener(
  TableColumnModelListener x)
protected ListSelectionModel
  createSelectionModel()
protected void fireColumnAdded(
  TableColumnModelEvent e)
protected void fireColumnMarginChanged()
protected void fireColumnMoved(
  TableColumnModelEvent e)
protected void fireColumnRemoved(
  TableColumnModelEvent e)
protected void
  fireColumnSelectionChanged(
  ListSelectionEvent e)
public TableColumn getColumn(int
  columnIndex)
public int getColumnCount()
public int getColumnIndex(Object
  identifier)
public int getColumnIndexAtX(int
  xPosition)
public int getColumnMargin()

public Enumeration getColumns()
public boolean getColumnSelectionAllowed(
)
public int getSelectedColumnCount()
public int getSelectedColumns()
public ListSelectionModel
  getSelectionModel()
public int getTotalColumnWidth()
public void moveColumn(int columnIndex,
  int newIndex)
public void propertyChange(
  PropertyChangeEvent evt)
protected void recalcWidthCache()
public void removeColumn(TableColumn
  column)
public void removeColumnModelListener(
  TableColumnModelListener x)
public void setColumnMargin(int
  newMargin)
public void setColumnSelectionAllowed(
  boolean flag)
public void setSelectionModel(
  ListSelectionModel newModel)
public void valueChanged(
  ListSelectionEvent e)

▶**DEFAULTTABLEMODEL**

public class javax.swing.table.
  DefaultTableModel
implements java.io.Serializable
extends javax.swing.table.
  AbstractTableModel
extends java.lang.Object

Fields

protected java.util.Vector
  columnIdentifiers
protected java.util.Vector dataVector

Constructors

public DefaultTableModel()
public DefaultTableModel(int numRows,
  int numColumns)
public DefaultTableModel(Vector
  columnNames,int numRows)
public DefaultTableModel(Object
  columnNames,int numRows)
public DefaultTableModel(Vector data,
  Vector columnNames)
public DefaultTableModel(Object data,
  Object columnNames)

Methods

public void addColumn(Object columnName)
public void addColumn(Object columnName,
  Vector columnData)
public void addColumn(Object columnName,
  Object columnData)
public void addRow(Vector rowData)
public void addRow(Object rowData)
protected static Vector convertToVector(
  Object anArray)
protected static Vector convertToVector(
  Object anArray)
public int getColumnCount()

```
public String getColumnName(int column)
public Vector getDataVector()
public int getRowCount()
public Object getValueAt(int row,int
  column)
public void insertRow(int row,Vector
  rowData)
public void insertRow(int row,Object
  rowData)
public boolean isCellEditable(int row,
  int column)
public void moveRow(int startIndex,int
  endIndex,int toIndex)
public void newDataAvailable(
  TableModelEvent event)
public void newRowsAdded(TableModelEvent
  event)
public void removeRow(int row)
public void rowsRemoved(TableModelEvent
  event)
public void setColumnIdentifiers(Vector
  newIdentifiers)
public void setColumnIdentifiers(Object
  newIdentifiers)
public void setDataVector(Vector newData,
  Vector columnNames)
public void setDataVector(Object newData,
  Object columnNames)
public void setNumRows(int newSize)
public void setValueAt(Object aValue,int
  row,int column)
```

▸DEFAULTTEXTUI

```
public abstract class javax.swing.text.
  DefaultTextUI
extends javax.swing.plaf.basic.
  BasicTextUI
extends javax.swing.plaf.TextUI
extends javax.swing.plaf.ComponentUI
extends java.lang.Object
```

▸DEFAULTTREECELLEDITOR

```
public class javax.swing.tree.
  DefaultTreeCellEditor
implements java.awt.event.
  ActionListener
implements javax.swing.tree.
  TreeCellEditor
implements javax.swing.event.
  TreeSelectionListener
extends java.lang.Object
```

Fields

```
protected java.awt.Color
  borderSelectionColor
protected boolean canEdit
protected transient java.awt.Component
  editingComponent
protected java.awt.Container
  editingContainer
protected transient javax.swing.Icon
  editingIcon
protected java.awt.Font font
```

```
protected transient javax.swing.tree.
  TreePath lastPath
protected transient int lastRow
protected transient int offset
protected javax.swing.tree.
  TreeCellEditor realEditor
protected javax.swing.tree.
  DefaultTreeCellRenderer renderer
protected transient javax.swing.Timer
  timer
protected transient javax.swing.JTree
  tree
```

Constructors

```
public DefaultTreeCellEditor(JTree tree,
  DefaultTreeCellRenderer renderer)
public DefaultTreeCellEditor(JTree tree,
  DefaultTreeCellRenderer renderer,
  TreeCellEditor editor)
```

Methods

```
public void actionPerformed(ActionEvent
  e)
public void addCellEditorListener(
  CellEditorListener l)
public void cancelCellEditing()
protected boolean canEditImmediately(
  EventObject event)
protected Container createContainer()
protected TreeCellEditor
  createTreeCellEditor()
protected void determineOffset(JTree
  tree,Object value,boolean isSelected,
  boolean expanded,boolean leaf,int row)
public Color getBorderSelectionColor()
public Object getCellEditorValue()
public Font getFont()
public Component
  getTreeCellEditorComponent(JTree tree,
  Object value,boolean isSelected,boolean
  expanded,boolean leaf,int row)
protected boolean inHitRegion(int x,int
  y)
public boolean isCellEditable(
  EventObject event)
protected void prepareForEditing()
public void removeCellEditorListener(
  CellEditorListener l)
public void setBorderSelectionColor(
  Color newColor)
public void setFont(Font font)
protected void setTree(JTree newTree)
public boolean shouldSelectCell(
  EventObject event)
protected boolean
  shouldStartEditingTimer(EventObject
  event)
protected void startEditingTimer()
public boolean stopCellEditing()
public void valueChanged(
  TreeSelectionEvent e)
```

▶**DefaultTreeCellRenderer**
public class javax.swing.tree.
  DefaultTreeCellRenderer
implements javax.swing.tree.
  TreeCellRenderer
extends javax.swing.JLabel
extends javax.swing.JComponent
extends java.awt.Container
extends java.awt.Component
extends java.lang.Object
Fields
protected java.awt.Color
  backgroundNonSelectionColor
protected java.awt.Color
  backgroundSelectionColor
protected java.awt.Color
  borderSelectionColor
protected transient javax.swing.Icon
  closedIcon
protected transient javax.swing.Icon
  leafIcon
protected transient javax.swing.Icon
  openIcon
protected boolean selected
protected java.awt.Color
  textNonSelectionColor
protected java.awt.Color
  textSelectionColor
Constructors
public DefaultTreeCellRenderer()
Methods
public Color
  getBackgroundNonSelectionColor()
public Color getBackgroundSelectionColor(
)
public Color getBorderSelectionColor()
public Icon getClosedIcon()
public Icon getDefaultClosedIcon()
public Icon getDefaultLeafIcon()
public Icon getDefaultOpenIcon()
public Icon getLeafIcon()
public Icon getOpenIcon()
public Dimension getPreferredSize()
public Color getTextNonSelectionColor()
public Color getTextSelectionColor()
public Component
  getTreeCellRendererComponent(JTree tree,
  Object value,boolean sel,boolean
  expanded,boolean leaf,int row,boolean
  hasFocus)
public void paint(Graphics g)
public void setBackground(Color color)
public void
  setBackgroundNonSelectionColor(Color
  newColor)
public void setBackgroundSelectionColor(
  Color newColor)
public void setBorderSelectionColor(
  Color newColor)
public void setClosedIcon(Icon newIcon)
public void setFont(Font font)
public void setLeafIcon(Icon newIcon)

public void setOpenIcon(Icon newIcon)
public void setTextNonSelectionColor(
  Color newColor)
public void setTextSelectionColor(Color
  newColor)

▶**DefaultTreeModel**
public class javax.swing.tree.
  DefaultTreeModel
implements java.io.Serializable
implements javax.swing.tree.TreeModel
extends java.lang.Object
Fields
protected boolean asksAllowsChildren
protected javax.swing.event.
  EventListenerList listenerList
protected javax.swing.tree.TreeNode
  root
Constructors
public DefaultTreeModel(TreeNode root)
public DefaultTreeModel(TreeNode root,
  boolean asksAllowsChildren)
Methods
public void addTreeModelListener(
  TreeModelListener l)
public boolean asksAllowsChildren()
protected void fireTreeNodesChanged(
  Object source,Object path,int
  childIndices,Object children)
protected void fireTreeNodesInserted(
  Object source,Object path,int
  childIndices,Object children)
protected void fireTreeNodesRemoved(
  Object source,Object path,int
  childIndices,Object children)
protected void fireTreeStructureChanged(
  Object source,Object path,int
  childIndices,Object children)
public Object getChild(Object parent,int
  index)
public int getChildCount(Object parent)
public int getIndexOfChild(Object parent,
  Object child)
public TreeNode getPathToRoot(TreeNode
  aNode)
protected TreeNode getPathToRoot(
  TreeNode aNode,int depth)
public Object getRoot()
public void insertNodeInto(
  MutableTreeNode newChild,MutableTreeNode
  parent,int index)
public boolean isLeaf(Object node)
public void nodeChanged(TreeNode node)
public void nodesChanged(TreeNode node,
  int childIndices)
public void nodeStructureChanged(
  TreeNode node)
public void nodesWereInserted(TreeNode
  node,int childIndices)
public void nodesWereRemoved(TreeNode
  node,int childIndices,Object
  removedChildren)

public void reload()
public void reload(TreeNode node)
public void removeNodeFromParent(
  MutableTreeNode node)
public void removeTreeModelListener(
  TreeModelListener l)
public void setAsksAllowsChildren(
  boolean newValue)
public void setRoot(TreeNode root)
public void valueForPathChanged(TreePath
  path,Object newValue)

▶DEFAULTTREESELECTIONMODEL

public class javax.swing.tree.
  DefaultTreeSelectionModel
implements java.lang.Cloneable
implements java.io.Serializable
implements javax.swing.tree.
  TreeSelectionModel
extends java.lang.Object
extends java.lang.Object

Fields

protected javax.swing.event.
  SwingPropertyChangeSupport
  changeSupport
protected int leadIndex
protected javax.swing.tree.TreePath
  leadPath
protected int leadRow
protected javax.swing.event.
  EventListenerList listenerList
protected javax.swing.
  DefaultListSelectionModel
  listSelectionModel
protected transient javax.swing.tree.
  RowMapper rowMapper
protected javax.swing.tree.TreePath
  selection
protected int selectionMode
public final static java.lang.String
  SELECTION_MODE_PROPERTY

Constructors

public DefaultTreeSelectionModel()

Methods

public synchronized void
  addPropertyChangeListener(
  PropertyChangeListener listener)
public void addSelectionPath(TreePath
  path)
public void addSelectionPaths(TreePath
  paths)
public void addTreeSelectionListener(
  TreeSelectionListener x)
protected boolean arePathsContiguous(
  TreePath paths)
protected boolean canPathsBeAdded(
  TreePath paths)
protected boolean canPathsBeRemoved(
  TreePath paths)
public void clearSelection()
public Object clone()

protected void fireValueChanged(
  TreeSelectionEvent e)
public TreePath getLeadSelectionPath()
public int getLeadSelectionRow()
public int getMaxSelectionRow()
public int getMinSelectionRow()
public RowMapper getRowMapper()
public int getSelectionCount()
public int getSelectionMode()
public TreePath getSelectionPath()
public TreePath getSelectionPaths()
public int getSelectionRows()
protected void insureRowContinuity()
protected void insureUniqueness()
public boolean isPathSelected(TreePath
  path)
public boolean isRowSelected(int row)
public boolean isSelectionEmpty()
protected void notifyPathChange(Vector
  changedPaths,TreePath oldLeadSelection)
public synchronized void
  removePropertyChangeListener(
  PropertyChangeListener listener)
public void removeSelectionPath(TreePath
  path)
public void removeSelectionPaths(
  TreePath paths)
public void removeTreeSelectionListener(
  TreeSelectionListener x)
public void resetRowSelection()
public void setRowMapper(RowMapper
  newMapper)
public void setSelectionMode(int mode)
public void setSelectionPath(TreePath
  path)
public void setSelectionPaths(TreePath
  pPaths)
public String toString()
protected void updateLeadIndex()

▶DEFLATER

public class java.util.zip.Deflater
extends java.lang.Object

Fields

public final static int BEST_
  COMPRESSION
public final static int BEST_SPEED
public final static int DEFAULT_
  COMPRESSION
public final static int DEFAULT_
  STRATEGY
public final static int DEFLATED
public final static int FILTERED
public final static int HUFFMAN_ONLY
public final static int NO_COMPRESSION

Constructors

public static Deflater(int level,
  boolean nowrap)
public Deflater(int level)
public Deflater()

Methods
```
public synchronized int deflate(byte b,
  int off,int len)
public int deflate(byte b)
public synchronized void end()
protected void finalize()
public synchronized void finish()
public synchronized boolean finished()
public synchronized int getAdler()
public synchronized int getTotalIn()
public synchronized int getTotalOut()
public boolean needsInput()
public synchronized void reset()
public synchronized void setDictionary(
  byte b,int off,int len)
public void setDictionary(byte b)
public synchronized void setInput(byte b,
  int off,int len)
public void setInput(byte b)
public synchronized void setLevel(int
  level)
public synchronized void setStrategy(int
  strategy)
```

▶DEFLATEROUTPUTSTREAM
```
public class java.util.zip.
  DeflaterOutputStream
extends java.io.FilterOutputStream
extends java.io.OutputStream
extends java.lang.Object
```
Fields
```
protected byte buf
protected java.util.zip.Deflater def
```
Constructors
```
public DeflaterOutputStream(
  OutputStream out,Deflater def,int size)
public DeflaterOutputStream(
  OutputStream out,Deflater def)
public DeflaterOutputStream(
  OutputStream out)
```
Methods
```
public void close()
protected void deflate()
public void finish()
public void write(int b)
public void write(byte b,int off,int len)
```

▶DESKTOPICONUI
```
public abstract class javax.swing.plaf.
  DesktopIconUI
extends javax.swing.plaf.ComponentUI
extends java.lang.Object
```

▶DESKTOPPANEUI
```
public abstract class javax.swing.plaf.
  DesktopPaneUI
extends javax.swing.plaf.ComponentUI
extends java.lang.Object
```

▶DIALOG
```
public class java.awt.Dialog
extends java.awt.Window
```
```
extends java.awt.Container
extends java.awt.Component
extends java.lang.Object
```
Constructors
```
public  Dialog(Frame owner)
public  Dialog(Frame owner,boolean modal)
public  Dialog(Frame owner,String title)
public  Dialog(Frame owner,String title,
  boolean modal)
public  Dialog(Dialog owner)
public  Dialog(Dialog owner,String title)
public  Dialog(Dialog owner,String title,
  boolean modal)
```
Methods
```
public void addNotify()
public String getTitle()
public boolean isModal()
public boolean isResizable()
protected String paramString()
public void setModal(boolean b)
public void setResizable(boolean
  resizable)
public synchronized void setTitle(String
  title)
public void show()
```

▶DICTIONARY
```
public abstract class java.util.
  Dictionary
extends java.lang.Object
```
Constructors
```
public  Dictionary()
```
Methods
```
public abstract Enumeration elements()
public abstract Object get(Object key)
public abstract boolean isEmpty()
public abstract Enumeration keys()
public abstract Object put(Object key,
  Object value)
public abstract Object remove(Object key)
public abstract int size()
```

▶DIGESTEXCEPTION
```
public class java.security.
  DigestException
extends java.security.
  GeneralSecurityException
extends java.lang.Exception
extends java.lang.Throwable
extends java.lang.Object
```
Constructors
```
public  DigestException()
public  DigestException(String msg)
```

▶DIGESTINPUTSTREAM
```
public class java.security.
  DigestInputStream
extends java.io.FilterInputStream
extends java.io.InputStream
extends java.lang.Object
```

Fields

```
protected java.security.MessageDigest
  digest
```

Constructors

```
public  DigestInputStream(InputStream
  stream,MessageDigest digest)
```

Methods

```
public MessageDigest getMessageDigest()
public void on(boolean on)
public int read()
public int read(byte b,int off,int len)
public void setMessageDigest(
  MessageDigest digest)
public String toString()
```

▶DIGESTOUTPUTSTREAM

```
public class java.security.
  DigestOutputStream
extends java.io.FilterOutputStream
extends java.io.OutputStream
extends java.lang.Object
```

Fields

```
protected java.security.MessageDigest
  digest
```

Constructors

```
public  DigestOutputStream(OutputStream
  stream,MessageDigest digest)
```

Methods

```
public MessageDigest getMessageDigest()
public void on(boolean on)
public void setMessageDigest(
  MessageDigest digest)
public String toString()
public void write(int b)
public void write(byte b,int off,int len)
```

▶DIMENSION

```
public class java.awt.Dimension
implements java.io.Serializable
extends java.awt.geom.Dimension2D
extends java.lang.Object
```

Fields

```
public int height
public int width
```

Constructors

```
public static  Dimension()
public  Dimension(Dimension d)
public  Dimension(int width,int height)
```

Methods

```
public boolean equals(Object obj)
public double getHeight()
public Dimension getSize()
public double getWidth()
public void setSize(double width,double
  height)
public void setSize(Dimension d)
public void setSize(int width,int height)
public String toString()
```

▶DIMENSION2D

```
public abstract class java.awt.geom.
  Dimension2D
```

```
implements java.lang.Cloneable
extends java.lang.Object
```

Constructors

```
protected  Dimension2D()
```

Methods

```
public Object clone()
public abstract double getHeight()
public abstract double getWidth()
public abstract void setSize(double
  width,double height)
public void setSize(Dimension2D d)
```

▶DIMENSIONUIRESOURCE

```
public class javax.swing.plaf.
  DimensionUIResource
implements javax.swing.plaf.UIResource
extends java.awt.Dimension
extends java.awt.geom.Dimension2D
extends java.lang.Object
```

Constructors

```
public  DimensionUIResource(int width,
  int height)
```

▶DIRECTCOLORMODEL

```
public class java.awt.image.
  DirectColorModel
extends java.awt.image.PackedColorModel
extends java.awt.image.ColorModel
extends java.lang.Object
```

Constructors

```
public  DirectColorModel(int bits,int
  rmask,int gmask,int bmask)
public  DirectColorModel(int bits,int
  rmask,int gmask,int bmask,int amask)
public  DirectColorModel(ColorSpace
  space,int bits,int rmask,int gmask,int
  bmask,int amask,boolean
  isAlphaPremultiplied,int transferType)
```

Methods

```
public final ColorModel coerceData(
  WritableRaster raster,boolean
  isAlphaPremultiplied)
public final WritableRaster
  createCompatibleWritableRaster(int w,int
  h)
public final int getAlpha(int pixel)
public int getAlpha(Object inData)
public final int getAlphaMask()
public final int getBlue(int pixel)
public int getBlue(Object inData)
public final int getBlueMask()
public final int getComponents(int pixel,
  int components,int offset)
public final int getComponents(Object
  pixel,int components,int offset)
public int getDataElement(int components,
  int offset)
public Object getDataElements(int rgb,
  Object pixel)
public Object getDataElements(int
  components,int offset,Object obj)
public final int getGreen(int pixel)
```

```
public int getGreen(Object inData)
public final int getGreenMask()
public final int getRed(int pixel)
public int getRed(Object inData)
public final int getRedMask()
public final int getRGB(int pixel)
public int getRGB(Object inData)
public boolean isCompatibleRaster(Raster
  raster)
public String toString()
```

▶DnDConstants
```
public final class java.awt.dnd.
  DnDConstants
extends java.lang.Object
```

Fields
```
public final static int ACTION_COPY
public final static int ACTION_COPY_OR_
  MOVE
public final static int ACTION_LINK
public final static int ACTION_MOVE
public final static int ACTION_NONE
public final static int ACTION_
  REFERENCE
```

Constructors
```
private  DnDConstants()
```

▶DocumentParser
```
public class javax.swing.text.html.
  parser.DocumentParser
extends javax.swing.text.html.parser.
  Parser
extends java.lang.Object
```

Constructors
```
public  DocumentParser(DTD dtd)
```

Methods
```
protected void handleComment(char text)
protected void handleEmptyTag(TagElement
  tag)
protected void handleEndTag(TagElement
  tag)
protected void handleError(int ln,String
  errorMsg)
protected void handleStartTag(TagElement
  tag)
protected void handleText(char data)
public void parse(Reader in,
  ParserCallback callback,boolean
  ignoreCharSet)
```

▶Double
```
public final class java.lang.Double
implements java.lang.Comparable
extends java.lang.Number
extends java.lang.Object
```

Fields
```
public final static double MAX_VALUE
public final static double MIN_VALUE
public final static double NaN
public final static double NEGATIVE_
  INFINITY
```
```
public final static double POSITIVE_
  INFINITY
public final static java.lang.Class
  TYPE
```

Constructors
```
public  Double(double value)
public  Double(String s)
```

Methods
```
public byte byteValue()
public int compareTo(Double
  anotherDouble)
public int compareTo(Object o)
public static native long
  doubleToLongBits(double value)
public double doubleValue()
public boolean equals(Object obj)
public float floatValue()
public int hashCode()
public int intValue()
public static boolean isInfinite(double
  v)
public boolean isInfinite()
public static boolean isNaN(double v)
public boolean isNaN()
public static native double
  longBitsToDouble(long bits)
public long longValue()
public static double parseDouble(String
  s)
public short shortValue()
public static String toString(double d)
public String toString()
public static Double valueOf(String s)
```

▶DragGestureEvent
```
public class java.awt.dnd.
  DragGestureEvent
extends java.util.EventObject
extends java.lang.Object
```

Constructors
```
public  DragGestureEvent(
  DragGestureRecognizer dgr,int act,Point
  ori,List evs)
```

Methods
```
public Component getComponent()
public int getDragAction()
public Point getDragOrigin()
public DragSource getDragSource()
public DragGestureRecognizer
  getSourceAsDragGestureRecognizer()
public InputEvent getTriggerEvent()
public Iterator iterator()
public void startDrag(Cursor dragCursor,
  Transferable transferable,
  DragSourceListener dsl)
public void startDrag(Cursor dragCursor,
  Image dragImage,Point imageOffset,
  Transferable transferable,
  DragSourceListener dsl)
public Object toArray()
public Object toArray(Object array)
```

►DRAGGESTURERECOGNIZER
public abstract class java.awt.dnd.
  DragGestureRecognizer
extends java.lang.Object

Fields
protected java.awt.Component component
protected java.awt.dnd.
  DragGestureListener dragGestureListener
protected java.awt.dnd.DragSource
  dragSource
protected java.util.ArrayList events
protected int sourceActions

Constructors
protected DragGestureRecognizer(
  DragSource ds,Component c,int sa,
  DragGestureListener dgl)
protected DragGestureRecognizer(
  DragSource ds,Component c,int sa)
protected DragGestureRecognizer(
  DragSource ds,Component c)
protected DragGestureRecognizer(
  DragSource ds)

Methods
public synchronized void
  addDragGestureListener(
  DragGestureListener dgl)
protected synchronized void appendEvent(
  InputEvent awtie)
protected synchronized void
  fireDragGestureRecognized(int dragAction,
  Point p)
public synchronized Component
  getComponent()
public DragSource getDragSource()
public synchronized int getSourceActions(
)
public InputEvent getTriggerEvent()
protected abstract void
  registerListeners()
public synchronized void
  removeDragGestureListener(
  DragGestureListener dgl)
public void resetRecognizer()
public synchronized void setComponent(
  Component c)
public synchronized void
  setSourceActions(int actions)
protected abstract void
  unregisterListeners()

►DRAGSOURCE
public class java.awt.dnd.DragSource
extends java.lang.Object

Fields
public final static java.awt.Cursor
  DefaultCopyDrop
public final static java.awt.Cursor
  DefaultCopyNoDrop
public final static java.awt.Cursor
  DefaultLinkDrop
public final static java.awt.Cursor
  DefaultLinkNoDrop

public final static java.awt.Cursor
  DefaultMoveDrop
public final static java.awt.Cursor
  DefaultMoveNoDrop

Constructors
public DragSource()

Methods
public DragGestureRecognizer
  createDefaultDragGestureRecognizer(
  Component c,int actions,
  DragGestureListener dgl)
public DragGestureRecognizer
  createDragGestureRecognizer(Class
  recognizerAbstractClass,Component c,int
  actions,DragGestureListener dgl)
protected DragSourceContext
  createDragSourceContext(
  DragSourceContextPeer dscp,
  DragGestureEvent dgl,Cursor dragCursor,
  Image dragImage,Point imageOffset,
  Transferable t,DragSourceListener dsl)
public static DragSource
  getDefaultDragSource()
public FlavorMap getFlavorMap()
public static boolean
  isDragImageSupported()
public void startDrag(DragGestureEvent
  trigger,Cursor dragCursor,Image
  dragImage,Point imageOffset,Transferable
  transferable,DragSourceListener dsl,
  FlavorMap flavorMap)
public void startDrag(DragGestureEvent
  trigger,Cursor dragCursor,Transferable
  transferable,DragSourceListener dsl,
  FlavorMap flavorMap)
public void startDrag(DragGestureEvent
  trigger,Cursor dragCursor,Image
  dragImage,Point dragOffset,Transferable
  transferable,DragSourceListener dsl)
public void startDrag(DragGestureEvent
  trigger,Cursor dragCursor,Transferable
  transferable,DragSourceListener dsl)

►DRAGSOURCECONTEXT
public class java.awt.dnd.
  DragSourceContext
implements java.awt.dnd.
  DragSourceListener
extends java.lang.Object

Fields
protected final static int CHANGED
protected final static int DEFAULT
protected final static int ENTER
protected final static int OVER

Constructors
public DragSourceContext(
  DragSourceContextPeer dscp,
  DragGestureEvent trigger,Cursor
  dragCursor,Image dragImage,Point offset,
  Transferable t,DragSourceListener dsl)

Methods

```
public synchronized void
  addDragSourceListener(DragSourceListener
  dsl)
public synchronized void dragDropEnd(
  DragSourceDropEvent dsde)
public synchronized void dragEnter(
  DragSourceDragEvent dsde)
public synchronized void dragExit(
  DragSourceEvent dse)
public synchronized void dragOver(
  DragSourceDragEvent dsde)
public synchronized void
  dropActionChanged(DragSourceDragEvent
  dsde)
public Component getComponent()
public Cursor getCursor()
public DragSource getDragSource()
public int getSourceActions()
public Transferable getTransferable()
public DragGestureEvent getTrigger()
public synchronized void
  removeDragSourceListener(
  DragSourceListener dsl)
public void setCursor(Cursor c)
public void transferablesFlavorsChanged()
protected void updateCurrentCursor(int
  dropOp,int targetAct,int status)
```

▶DRAGSOURCEDRAGEVENT

```
public class java.awt.dnd.
  DragSourceDragEvent
extends java.awt.dnd.DragSourceEvent
extends java.util.EventObject
extends java.lang.Object
```

Constructors

```
public DragSourceDragEvent(
  DragSourceContext dsc,int dropAction,int
  actions,int modifiers)
```

Methods

```
public int getDropAction()
public int getGestureModifiers()
public int getTargetActions()
public int getUserAction()
```

▶DRAGSOURCEDROPEVENT

```
public class java.awt.dnd.
  DragSourceDropEvent
extends java.awt.dnd.DragSourceEvent
extends java.util.EventObject
extends java.lang.Object
```

Constructors

```
public DragSourceDropEvent(
  DragSourceContext dsc,int action,boolean
  success)
public DragSourceDropEvent(
  DragSourceContext dsc)
```

Methods

```
public int getDropAction()
public boolean getDropSuccess()
```

▶DRAGSOURCEEVENT

```
public class java.awt.dnd.
  DragSourceEvent
extends java.util.EventObject
extends java.lang.Object
```

Constructors

```
public DragSourceEvent(
  DragSourceContext dsc)
```

Methods

```
public DragSourceContext
  getDragSourceContext()
```

▶DRIVERMANAGER

```
public class java.sql.DriverManager
extends java.lang.Object
```

Constructors

```
private DriverManager()
```

Methods

```
public static synchronized void
  deregisterDriver(Driver driver)
public static synchronized Connection
  getConnection(String url,Properties info)
public static synchronized Connection
  getConnection(String url,String user,
  String password)
public static synchronized Connection
  getConnection(String url)
public static synchronized Driver
  getDriver(String url)
public static synchronized Enumeration
  getDrivers()
public static int getLoginTimeout()
public static PrintStream getLogStream()
public static PrintWriter getLogWriter()
public static synchronized void println(
  String message)
public static synchronized void
  registerDriver(Driver driver)
public static void setLoginTimeout(int
  seconds)
public static synchronized void
  setLogStream(PrintStream out)
public static synchronized void
  setLogWriter(PrintWriter out)
```

▶DRIVERPROPERTYINFO

```
public class java.sql.
  DriverPropertyInfo
extends java.lang.Object
```

Fields

```
public java.lang.String choices
public java.lang.String description
public java.lang.String name
public boolean required
public java.lang.String value
```

Constructors

```
public DriverPropertyInfo(String name,
  String value)
```

▶DROPTARGET

```
public class java.awt.dnd.DropTarget
```

```
implements java.awt.dnd.
  DropTargetListener
implements java.io.Serializable
extends java.lang.Object
```

Constructors
```
public  DropTarget(Component c,int ops,
  DropTargetListener dtl,boolean act,
  FlavorMap fm)
public  DropTarget(Component c,int ops,
  DropTargetListener dtl,boolean act)
public  DropTarget()
public  DropTarget(Component c,
  DropTargetListener dtl)
public  DropTarget(Component c,int ops,
  DropTargetListener dtl)
```

Methods
```
public synchronized void
  addDropTargetListener(DropTargetListener
  dtl)
public void addNotify(ComponentPeer peer)
protected void clearAutoscroll()
protected DropTargetAutoScroller
  createDropTargetAutoScroller(Component c,
  Point p)
protected DropTargetContext
  createDropTargetContext()
public synchronized void dragEnter(
  DropTargetDragEvent dtde)
public synchronized void dragExit(
  DropTargetEvent dte)
public synchronized void dragOver(
  DropTargetDragEvent dtde)
public synchronized void drop(
  DropTargetDropEvent dtde)
public void dropActionChanged(
  DropTargetDragEvent dtde)
public synchronized Component
  getComponent()
public synchronized int
  getDefaultActions()
public DropTargetContext
  getDropTargetContext()
public FlavorMap getFlavorMap()
protected void initializeAutoscrolling(
  Point p)
public synchronized boolean isActive()
public synchronized void
  removeDropTargetListener(
  DropTargetListener dtl)
public void removeNotify(ComponentPeer
  peer)
public synchronized void setActive(
  boolean isActive)
public synchronized void setComponent(
  Component c)
public synchronized void
  setDefaultActions(int ops)
public void setFlavorMap(FlavorMap fm)
protected void updateAutoscroll(Point
  dragCursorLocn)
```

▶DROPTARGETCONTEXT
```
public class java.awt.dnd.
  DropTargetContext
extends java.lang.Object
```

Constructors
```
DropTargetContext()
```

Methods
```
protected void acceptDrag(int
  dragOperation)
protected void acceptDrop(int
  dropOperation)
public synchronized void addNotify(
  DropTargetContextPeer dtcp)
protected Transferable
  createTransferableProxy(Transferable t,
  boolean local)
public void dropComplete(boolean success)
public Component getComponent()
protected DataFlavor
  getCurrentDataFlavors()
protected List
  getCurrentDataFlavorsAsList()
public DropTarget getDropTarget()
protected int getTargetActions()
protected synchronized Transferable
  getTransferable()
protected boolean isDataFlavorSupported(
  DataFlavor df)
protected void rejectDrag()
protected void rejectDrop()
public synchronized void removeNotify()
protected void setTargetActions(int
  actions)
```

▶DROPTARGETDRAGEVENT
```
public class java.awt.dnd.
  DropTargetDragEvent
extends java.awt.dnd.DropTargetEvent
extends java.util.EventObject
extends java.lang.Object
```

Constructors
```
public  DropTargetDragEvent(
  DropTargetContext dtc,Point cursorLocn,
  int dropAction,int srcActions)
```

Methods
```
public void acceptDrag(int dragOperation)
public DataFlavor getCurrentDataFlavors()
public List getCurrentDataFlavorsAsList()
public int getDropAction()
public Point getLocation()
public int getSourceActions()
public boolean isDataFlavorSupported(
  DataFlavor df)
public void rejectDrag()
```

▶DROPTARGETDROPEVENT
```
public class java.awt.dnd.
  DropTargetDropEvent
extends java.awt.dnd.DropTargetEvent
extends java.util.EventObject
extends java.lang.Object
```

Constructors
```
public  DropTargetDropEvent(
  DropTargetContext dtc,Point cursorLocn,
  int dropAction,int srcActions)
public  DropTargetDropEvent(
  DropTargetContext dtc,Point cursorLocn,
  int dropAction,int srcActions,boolean
  isLocal)
```
Methods
```
public void acceptDrop(int dropAction)
public void dropComplete(boolean success)
public DataFlavor getCurrentDataFlavors()
public List getCurrentDataFlavorsAsList()
public int getDropAction()
public Point getLocation()
public int getSourceActions()
public Transferable getTransferable()
public boolean isDataFlavorSupported(
  DataFlavor df)
public boolean isLocalTransfer()
public void rejectDrop()
```

▶DROPTARGETEVENT
```
public class java.awt.dnd.
  DropTargetEvent
extends java.util.EventObject
extends java.lang.Object
```
Fields
```
protected java.awt.dnd.DropTargetContext
  context
```
Constructors
```
public  DropTargetEvent(
  DropTargetContext dtc)
```
Methods
```
public DropTargetContext
  getDropTargetContext()
```

▶DSAPARAMETERSPEC
```
public class java.security.spec.
  DSAParameterSpec
implements java.security.spec.
  AlgorithmParameterSpec
implements java.security.interfaces.
  DSAParams
extends java.lang.Object
```
Constructors
```
public  DSAParameterSpec(BigInteger p,
  BigInteger q,BigInteger g)
```
Methods
```
public BigInteger getG()
public BigInteger getP()
public BigInteger getQ()
```

▶DSAPRIVATEKEYSPEC
```
public class java.security.spec.
  DSAPrivateKeySpec
implements java.security.spec.KeySpec
extends java.lang.Object
```
Constructors
```
public  DSAPrivateKeySpec(BigInteger x,
  BigInteger p,BigInteger q,BigInteger g)
```

Methods
```
public BigInteger getG()
public BigInteger getP()
public BigInteger getQ()
public BigInteger getX()
```

▶DSAPUBLICKEYSPEC
```
public class java.security.spec.
  DSAPublicKeySpec
implements java.security.spec.KeySpec
extends java.lang.Object
```
Constructors
```
public  DSAPublicKeySpec(BigInteger y,
  BigInteger p,BigInteger q,BigInteger g)
```
Methods
```
public BigInteger getG()
public BigInteger getP()
public BigInteger getQ()
public BigInteger getY()
```

▶DTD
```
public class javax.swing.text.html.
  parser.DTD
implements javax.swing.text.html.parser.
  DTDConstants
extends java.lang.Object
```
Fields
```
public final javax.swing.text.html.
  parser.Element applet
public final javax.swing.text.html.
  parser.Element base
public final javax.swing.text.html.
  parser.Element body
public java.util.Hashtable elementHash
public java.util.Vector elements
public java.util.Hashtable entityHash
public static int FILE_VERSION
public final javax.swing.text.html.
  parser.Element head
public final javax.swing.text.html.
  parser.Element html
public final javax.swing.text.html.
  parser.Element isindex
public final javax.swing.text.html.
  parser.Element meta
public java.lang.String name
public final javax.swing.text.html.
  parser.Element p
public final javax.swing.text.html.
  parser.Element param
public final javax.swing.text.html.
  parser.Element pcdata
public final javax.swing.text.html.
  parser.Element title
```
Constructors
```
protected  DTD(String name)
```
Methods
```
protected AttributeList defAttributeList(
  String name,int type,int modifier,String
  value,String values,AttributeList atts)
protected ContentModel defContentModel(
  int type,Object obj,ContentModel next)
```

```
protected Element defElement(String name,
  int type,boolean omitStart,boolean
  omitEnd,ContentModel content,String
  exclusions,String inclusions,
  AttributeList atts)
public Entity defEntity(String name,int
  type,int ch)
protected Entity defEntity(String name,
  int type,String str)
public void defineAttributes(String name,
  AttributeList atts)
public Element defineElement(String name,
  int type,boolean omitStart,boolean
  omitEnd,ContentModel content,BitSet
  exclusions,BitSet inclusions,
  AttributeList atts)
public Entity defineEntity(String name,
  int type,char data)
public static DTD getDTD(String name)
public Element getElement(String name)
public Element getElement(int index)
public Entity getEntity(String name)
public Entity getEntity(int ch)
public String getName()
public static void putDTDHash(String
  name,DTD dtd)
public void read(DataInputStream in)
public String toString()
```

▶EDITORKIT
```
public abstract class javax.swing.text.
  EditorKit
implements java.lang.Cloneable
implements java.io.Serializable
extends java.lang.Object
```
Methods
```
public abstract Object clone()
public abstract Caret createCaret()
public abstract Document
  createDefaultDocument()
public void deinstall(JEditorPane c)
public abstract Action getActions()
public abstract String getContentType()
public abstract ViewFactory
  getViewFactory()
public void install(JEditorPane c)
public abstract void read(InputStream in,
  Document doc,int pos)
public abstract void read(Reader in,
  Document doc,int pos)
public abstract void write(OutputStream
  out,Document doc,int pos,int len)
public abstract void write(Writer out,
  Document doc,int pos,int len)
```

▶ELEMENT
```
public final class javax.swing.text.html.
  parser.Element
implements javax.swing.text.html.parser.
  DTDConstants
implements java.io.Serializable
extends java.lang.Object
```

Fields
```
public javax.swing.text.html.parser.
  AttributeList atts
public javax.swing.text.html.parser.
  ContentModel content
public java.lang.Object data
public java.util.BitSet exclusions
public java.util.BitSet inclusions
public int index
public java.lang.String name
public boolean oEnd
public boolean oStart
public int type
```
Constructors
```
Element()
Element()
```
Methods
```
public AttributeList getAttribute(String
  name)
public AttributeList getAttributeByValue(
  String name)
public AttributeList getAttributes()
public ContentModel getContent()
public int getIndex()
public String getName()
public int getType()
public boolean isEmpty()
public static int name2type(String nm)
public boolean omitEnd()
public boolean omitStart()
public String toString()
```

▶ELEMENTITERATOR
```
public class javax.swing.text.
  ElementIterator
implements java.lang.Cloneable
extends java.lang.Object
```
Constructors
```
public ElementIterator(Document
  document)
public ElementIterator(Element root)
```
Methods
```
public synchronized Object clone()
public Element current()
public int depth()
public Element first()
public Element next()
public Element previous()
```

▶ELLIPSE2D
```
public abstract class java.awt.geom.
  Ellipse2D
extends java.awt.geom.RectangularShape
extends java.lang.Object
```
Constructors
```
protected Ellipse2D()
```
Methods
```
public boolean contains(double x,double
  y)
public boolean contains(double x,double
  y,double w,double h)
```

```
public PathIterator getPathIterator(
    AffineTransform at)
public boolean intersects(double x,
    double y,double w,double h)
```

►**EMPTYBORDER**
```
public class javax.swing.border.
    EmptyBorder
implements java.io.Serializable
extends javax.swing.border.
    AbstractBorder
extends java.lang.Object
```
Fields
```
protected int left
```
Constructors
```
public  EmptyBorder(int top,int left,int
    bottom,int right)
public  EmptyBorder(Insets insets)
```
Methods
```
public Insets getBorderInsets(Component
    c)
public Insets getBorderInsets(Component
    c,Insets insets)
public boolean isBorderOpaque()
public void paintBorder(Component c,
    Graphics g,int x,int y,int width,int
    height)
```

►**EMPTYSTACKEXCEPTION**
```
public class java.util.
    EmptyStackException
extends java.lang.RuntimeException
extends java.lang.Exception
extends java.lang.Throwable
extends java.lang.Object
```
Constructors
```
public  EmptyStackException()
```

►**ENCODEDKEYSPEC**
```
public abstract class java.security.spec.
    EncodedKeySpec
implements java.security.spec.KeySpec
extends java.lang.Object
```
Constructors
```
public  EncodedKeySpec(byte encodedKey)
```
Methods
```
public byte getEncoded()
public abstract String getFormat()
```

►**ENTITY**
```
public final class javax.swing.text.html.
    parser.Entity
implements javax.swing.text.html.parser.
    DTDConstants
extends java.lang.Object
```
Fields
```
public char data
public java.lang.String name
public int type
```

Constructors
```
public  Entity(String name,int type,char
    data)
```
Methods
```
public char getData()
public String getName()
public String getString()
public int getType()
public boolean isGeneral()
public boolean isParameter()
public static int name2type(String nm)
```

►**EOFEXCEPTION**
```
public class java.io.EOFException
extends java.io.IOException
extends java.lang.Exception
extends java.lang.Throwable
extends java.lang.Object
```
Constructors
```
public  EOFException()
public  EOFException(String s)
```

►**ERROR**
```
public class java.lang.Error
extends java.lang.Throwable
extends java.lang.Object
```
Constructors
```
public  Error()
public  Error(String s)
```

►**ETCHEDBORDER**
```
public class javax.swing.border.
    EtchedBorder
extends javax.swing.border.
    AbstractBorder
extends java.lang.Object
```
Fields
```
protected int etchType
protected java.awt.Color highlight
public final static int LOWERED
public final static int RAISED
protected java.awt.Color shadow
```
Constructors
```
public  EtchedBorder()
public  EtchedBorder(int etchType)
public  EtchedBorder(Color highlight,
    Color shadow)
public  EtchedBorder(int etchType,Color
    highlight,Color shadow)
```
Methods
```
public Insets getBorderInsets(Component
    c)
public Insets getBorderInsets(Component
    c,Insets insets)
public int getEtchType()
public Color getHighlightColor(Component
    c)
public Color getShadowColor(Component c)
public boolean isBorderOpaque()
public void paintBorder(Component c,
    Graphics g,int x,int y,int width,int
    height)
```

►EVENT

```
public class java.awt.Event
implements java.io.Serializable
extends java.lang.Object
```

Fields

```
public final static int ACTION_EVENT
public final static int ALT_MASK
public java.lang.Object arg
public final static int BACK_SPACE
public final static int CAPS_LOCK
public int clickCount
public final static int CTRL_MASK
public final static int DELETE
public final static int DOWN
public final static int END
public final static int ENTER
public final static int ESCAPE
public java.awt.Event evt
public final static int F1
public final static int F10
public final static int F11
public final static int F12
public final static int F2
public final static int F3
public final static int F4
public final static int F5
public final static int F6
public final static int F7
public final static int F8
public final static int F9
public final static int GOT_FOCUS
public final static int HOME
public int id
public final static int INSERT
public int key
public final static int KEY_ACTION
public final static int KEY_ACTION_
  RELEASE
public final static int KEY_PRESS
public final static int KEY_RELEASE
public final static int LEFT
public final static int LIST_DESELECT
public final static int LIST_SELECT
public final static int LOAD_FILE
public final static int LOST_FOCUS
public final static int META_MASK
public int modifiers
public final static int MOUSE_DOWN
public final static int MOUSE_DRAG
public final static int MOUSE_ENTER
public final static int MOUSE_EXIT
public final static int MOUSE_MOVE
public final static int MOUSE_UP
public final static int NUM_LOCK
public final static int PAUSE
public final static int PGDN
public final static int PGUP
public final static int PRINT_SCREEN
public final static int RIGHT
public final static int SAVE_FILE
public final static int SCROLL_ABSOLUTE
public final static int SCROLL_BEGIN
```

```
public final static int SCROLL_END
public final static int SCROLL_LINE_
  DOWN
public final static int SCROLL_LINE_UP
public final static int SCROLL_LOCK
public final static int SCROLL_PAGE_
  DOWN
public final static int SCROLL_PAGE_UP
public final static int SHIFT_MASK
public final static int TAB
public java.lang.Object target
public final static int UP
public long when
public final static int WINDOW_
  DEICONIFY
public final static int WINDOW_DESTROY
public final static int WINDOW_EXPOSE
public final static int WINDOW_ICONIFY
public final static int WINDOW_MOVED
public int x
public int y
```

Constructors

```
public  Event(Object target,long when,
  int id,int x,int y,int key,int modifiers,
  Object arg)
public  Event(Object target,long when,
  int id,int x,int y,int key,int modifiers)
public  Event(Object target,int id,
  Object arg)
```

Methods

```
public boolean controlDown()
public boolean metaDown()
protected String paramString()
public boolean shiftDown()
public String toString()
public void translate(int x,int y)
```

►EVENTLISTENERLIST

```
public class javax.swing.event.
  EventListenerList
implements java.io.Serializable
extends java.lang.Object
```

Fields

```
protected transient java.lang.Object
  listenerList
```

Methods

```
public synchronized void add(Class t,
  EventListener l)
public int getListenerCount()
public int getListenerCount(Class t)
public Object getListenerList()
public synchronized void remove(Class t,
  EventListener l)
public String toString()
```

►EVENTOBJECT

```
public class java.util.EventObject
implements java.io.Serializable
extends java.lang.Object
```

Fields

```
protected transient java.lang.Object
  source
```

Constructors

```
public  EventObject(Object source)
```

Methods

```
public Object getSource()
public String toString()
```

►EVENTQUEUE

```
public class java.awt.EventQueue
extends java.lang.Object
```

Constructors

```
public  EventQueue()
```

Methods

```
protected void dispatchEvent(AWTEvent
  event)
public synchronized AWTEvent
  getNextEvent()
public static void invokeAndWait(
  Runnable runnable)
public static void invokeLater(Runnable
  runnable)
public static boolean isDispatchThread()
public synchronized AWTEvent peekEvent()
public synchronized AWTEvent peekEvent(
  int id)
protected void pop()
public synchronized void postEvent(
  AWTEvent theEvent)
public synchronized void push(EventQueue
  newEventQueue)
```

►EVENTSETDESCRIPTOR

```
public class java.beans.
  EventSetDescriptor
extends java.beans.FeatureDescriptor
extends java.lang.Object
```

Constructors

```
public  EventSetDescriptor(Class
  sourceClass,String eventSetName,Class
  listenerType,String listenerMethodName)
public  EventSetDescriptor(Class
  sourceClass,String eventSetName,Class
  listenerType,String listenerMethodNames,
  String addListenerMethodName,String
  removeListenerMethodName)
public  EventSetDescriptor(String
  eventSetName,Class listenerType,Method
  listenerMethods,Method addListenerMethod,
  Method removeListenerMethod)
public  EventSetDescriptor(String
  eventSetName,Class listenerType,
  MethodDescriptor
  listenerMethodDescriptors,Method
  addListenerMethod,Method
  removeListenerMethod)
EventSetDescriptor()
EventSetDescriptor()
```

Methods

```
public Method getAddListenerMethod()
public MethodDescriptor
  getListenerMethodDescriptors()
public Method getListenerMethods()
public Class getListenerType()
```

```
public Method getRemoveListenerMethod()
public boolean isInDefaultEventSet()
public boolean isUnicast()
public void setInDefaultEventSet(boolean
  inDefaultEventSet)
public void setUnicast(boolean unicast)
```

►EXCEPTION

```
public class java.lang.Exception
extends java.lang.Throwable
extends java.lang.Object
```

Constructors

```
public  Exception()
public  Exception(String s)
```

►EXCEPTIONININITIALIZERERROR

```
public class java.lang.
  ExceptionInInitializerError
extends java.lang.LinkageError
extends java.lang.Error
extends java.lang.Throwable
extends java.lang.Object
```

Constructors

```
public  ExceptionInInitializerError()
public  ExceptionInInitializerError(
  Throwable thrown)
public  ExceptionInInitializerError(
  String s)
```

Methods

```
public Throwable getException()
public void printStackTrace()
public void printStackTrace(PrintStream
  ps)
public void printStackTrace(PrintWriter
  pw)
```

►EXPANDVETOEXCEPTION

```
public class javax.swing.tree.
  ExpandVetoException
extends java.lang.Exception
extends java.lang.Throwable
extends java.lang.Object
```

Fields

```
protected javax.swing.event.
  TreeExpansionEvent event
```

Constructors

```
public  ExpandVetoException(
  TreeExpansionEvent event)
public  ExpandVetoException(
  TreeExpansionEvent event,String message)
```

►EXPORTEXCEPTION

```
public class java.rmi.server.
  ExportException
extends java.rmi.RemoteException
extends java.io.IOException
extends java.lang.Exception
extends java.lang.Throwable
extends java.lang.Object
```

Constructors

```
public  ExportException(String s)
```

public ExportException(String s,
  Exception ex)

▶FEATUREDESCRIPTOR
public class java.beans.
  FeatureDescriptor
extends java.lang.Object

Constructors
public FeatureDescriptor()
 FeatureDescriptor()
 FeatureDescriptor()

Methods
public Enumeration attributeNames()
public String getDisplayName()
public String getName()
public String getShortDescription()
public Object getValue(String
  attributeName)
public boolean isExpert()
public boolean isHidden()
public boolean isPreferred()
public void setDisplayName(String
  displayName)
public void setExpert(boolean expert)
public void setHidden(boolean hidden)
public void setName(String name)
public void setPreferred(boolean
  preferred)
public void setShortDescription(String
  text)
public void setValue(String
  attributeName,Object value)

▶FIELD
public final class java.lang.reflect.
  Field
implements java.lang.reflect.Member
extends java.lang.reflect.
  AccessibleObject
extends java.lang.Object

Constructors
private Field()

Methods
public boolean equals(Object obj)
public native Object get(Object obj)
public native boolean getBoolean(Object
  obj)
public native byte getByte(Object obj)
public native char getChar(Object obj)
public Class getDeclaringClass()
public native double getDouble(Object
  obj)
public native float getFloat(Object obj)
public native int getInt(Object obj)
public native long getLong(Object obj)
public int getModifiers()
public String getName()
public native short getShort(Object obj)
public Class getType()
public int hashCode()
public native void set(Object obj,Object
  value)

public native void setBoolean(Object obj,
  boolean z)
public native void setByte(Object obj,
  byte b)
public native void setChar(Object obj,
  char c)
public native void setDouble(Object obj,
  double d)
public native void setFloat(Object obj,
  float f)
public native void setInt(Object obj,int
  i)
public native void setLong(Object obj,
  long l)
public native void setShort(Object obj,
  short s)
public String toString()

▶FIELDPOSITION
public class java.text.FieldPosition
extends java.lang.Object

Constructors
public FieldPosition(int field)

Methods
public boolean equals(Object obj)
public int getBeginIndex()
public int getEndIndex()
public int getField()
public int hashCode()
public void setBeginIndex(int bi)
public void setEndIndex(int ei)
public String toString()

▶FIELDVIEW
public class javax.swing.text.FieldView
extends javax.swing.text.PlainView
extends javax.swing.text.View
extends java.lang.Object

Constructors
public FieldView(Element elem)

Methods
protected Shape adjustAllocation(Shape a)
protected FontMetrics getFontMetrics()
public float getPreferredSpan(int axis)
public int getResizeWeight(int axis)
public void insertUpdate(DocumentEvent
  changes,Shape a,ViewFactory f)
public Shape modelToView(int pos,Shape a,
  Bias b)
public void paint(Graphics g,Shape a)
public void removeUpdate(DocumentEvent
  changes,Shape a,ViewFactory f)
public int viewToModel(float fx,float fy,
  Shape a,Bias bias)

▶FILE
public class java.io.File
implements java.lang.Comparable
implements java.io.Serializable
extends java.lang.Object

Fields
```
public final static java.lang.String
  pathSeparator
public final static char
  pathSeparatorChar
public final static java.lang.String
  separator
public final static char separatorChar
```
Constructors
```
private  File()
public  File(String pathname)
public  File(String parent,String child)
public  File(File parent,String child)
```
Methods
```
public boolean canRead()
public boolean canWrite()
public int compareTo(File pathname)
public int compareTo(Object o)
public boolean createNewFile()
public static File createTempFile(String
  prefix,String suffix,File directory)
public static File createTempFile(String
  prefix,String suffix)
public boolean delete()
public void deleteOnExit()
public boolean equals(Object obj)
public boolean exists()
public File getAbsoluteFile()
public String getAbsolutePath()
public File getCanonicalFile()
public String getCanonicalPath()
public String getName()
public String getParent()
public File getParentFile()
public String getPath()
public int hashCode()
public boolean isAbsolute()
public boolean isDirectory()
public boolean isFile()
public boolean isHidden()
public long lastModified()
public long length()
public String list()
public String list(FilenameFilter filter)
public File listFiles()
public File listFiles(FilenameFilter
  filter)
public File listFiles(FileFilter filter)
public static File listRoots()
public boolean mkdir()
public boolean mkdirs()
public boolean renameTo(File dest)
public boolean setLastModified(long time)
public boolean setReadOnly()
public String toString()
public URL toURL()
```

►FILECHOOSERUI
```
public abstract class javax.swing.plaf.
  FileChooserUI
extends javax.swing.plaf.ComponentUI
extends java.lang.Object
```

Methods
```
public abstract void ensureFileIsVisible(
  JFileChooser fc,File f)
public abstract FileFilter
  getAcceptAllFileFilter(JFileChooser fc)
public abstract String
  getApproveButtonText(JFileChooser fc)
public abstract String getDialogTitle(
  JFileChooser fc)
public abstract FileView getFileView(
  JFileChooser fc)
public abstract void
  rescanCurrentDirectory(JFileChooser fc)
```

►FILEDESCRIPTOR
```
public final class java.io.
  FileDescriptor
extends java.lang.Object
```
Fields
```
public final static java.io.
  FileDescriptor err
public final static java.io.
  FileDescriptor in
public final static java.io.
  FileDescriptor out
```
Constructors
```
public  FileDescriptor(int fd)
```
Methods
```
public native void sync()
public boolean valid()
```

►FILEDIALOG
```
public class java.awt.FileDialog
extends java.awt.Dialog
extends java.awt.Window
extends java.awt.Container
extends java.awt.Component
extends java.lang.Object
```
Fields
```
public final static int LOAD
public final static int SAVE
```
Constructors
```
public  FileDialog(Frame parent)
public  FileDialog(Frame parent,String
  title)
public  FileDialog(Frame parent,String
  title,int mode)
```
Methods
```
public void addNotify()
public String getDirectory()
public String getFile()
public FilenameFilter getFilenameFilter()
public int getMode()
protected String paramString()
public void setDirectory(String dir)
public void setFile(String file)
public synchronized void
  setFilenameFilter(FilenameFilter filter)
public void setMode(int mode)
```

►**FILEFILTER**
public abstract class javax.swing.
  filechooser.FileFilter
extends java.lang.Object
Methods
public abstract boolean accept(File f)
public abstract String getDescription()

►**FILEINPUTSTREAM**
public class java.io.FileInputStream
extends java.io.InputStream
extends java.lang.Object
Constructors
public FileInputStream(String name)
public FileInputStream(File file)
public FileInputStream(FileDescriptor
  fdObj)
Methods
public native int available()
public native void close()
protected static void finalize()
public final FileDescriptor getFD()
public native int read()
public int read(byte b)
public int read(byte b,int off,int len)
public native long skip(long n)

►**FILENOTFOUNDEXCEPTION**
public class java.io.
  FileNotFoundException
extends java.io.IOException
extends java.lang.Exception
extends java.lang.Throwable
extends java.lang.Object
Constructors
public FileNotFoundException()
public FileNotFoundException(String s)
private FileNotFoundException()

►**FILEOUTPUTSTREAM**
public class java.io.FileOutputStream
extends java.io.OutputStream
extends java.lang.Object
Constructors
public FileOutputStream(String name)
public FileOutputStream(String name,
  boolean append)
public FileOutputStream(File file)
public FileOutputStream(FileDescriptor
  fdObj)
Methods
public native void close()
protected void finalize()
public final FileDescriptor getFD()
public native void write(int b)
public void write(byte b)
public void write(byte b,int off,int len)

►**FILEPERMISSION**
public final class java.io.
  FilePermission
implements java.io.Serializable

extends java.security.Permission
extends java.lang.Object
Constructors
public FilePermission(String path,
  String actions)
 FilePermission()
Methods
public boolean equals(Object obj)
public String getActions()
public int hashCode()
public boolean implies(Permission p)
public PermissionCollection
  newPermissionCollection()

►**FILEREADER**
public class java.io.FileReader
extends java.io.InputStreamReader
extends java.io.Reader
extends java.lang.Object
Constructors
public FileReader(String fileName)
public FileReader(File file)
public FileReader(FileDescriptor fd)

►**FILESYSTEMVIEW**
public abstract class javax.swing.
  filechooser.FileSystemView
extends java.lang.Object
Methods
public File createFileObject(File dir,
  String filename)
public File createFileObject(String path)
public abstract File createNewFolder(
  File containingDir)
public File getFiles(File dir,boolean
  useFileHiding)
public static FileSystemView
  getFileSystemView()
public File getHomeDirectory()
public File getParentDirectory(File dir)
public abstract File getRoots()
public abstract boolean isHiddenFile(
  File f)
public abstract boolean isRoot(File f)

►**FILEVIEW**
public abstract class javax.swing.
  filechooser.FileView
extends java.lang.Object
Methods
public abstract String getDescription(
  File f)
public abstract Icon getIcon(File f)
public abstract String getName(File f)
public abstract String
  getTypeDescription(File f)
public abstract Boolean isTraversable(
  File f)

►**FILEWRITER**
public class java.io.FileWriter
extends java.io.OutputStreamWriter

extends java.io.Writer
extends java.lang.Object

Constructors

public FileWriter(String fileName)
public FileWriter(String fileName,
  boolean append)
public FileWriter(File file)
public FileWriter(FileDescriptor fd)

▶FILTEREDIMAGESOURCE

public class java.awt.image.
  FilteredImageSource
implements java.awt.image.ImageProducer
extends java.lang.Object

Constructors

public FilteredImageSource(
  ImageProducer orig,ImageFilter imgf)

Methods

public synchronized void addConsumer(
  ImageConsumer ic)
public synchronized boolean isConsumer(
  ImageConsumer ic)
public synchronized void removeConsumer(
  ImageConsumer ic)
public void
  requestTopDownLeftRightResend(
  ImageConsumer ic)
public void startProduction(
  ImageConsumer ic)

▶FILTERINPUTSTREAM

public class java.io.FilterInputStream
extends java.io.InputStream
extends java.lang.Object

Fields

protected java.io.InputStream in

Constructors

protected FilterInputStream(InputStream
  in)

Methods

public int available()
public void close()
public synchronized void mark(int
  readlimit)
public boolean markSupported()
public int read()
public int read(byte b)
public int read(byte b,int off,int len)
public synchronized void reset()
public long skip(long n)

▶FILTEROUTPUTSTREAM

public class java.io.FilterOutputStream
extends java.io.OutputStream
extends java.lang.Object

Fields

protected java.io.OutputStream out

Constructors

public FilterOutputStream(OutputStream
  out)

Methods

public void close()
public void flush()
public void write(int b)
public void write(byte b)
public void write(byte b,int off,int len)

▶FILTERREADER

public abstract class java.io.
  FilterReader
extends java.io.Reader
extends java.lang.Object

Fields

protected java.io.Reader in

Constructors

protected FilterReader(Reader in)

Methods

public void close()
public void mark(int readAheadLimit)
public boolean markSupported()
public int read()
public int read(char cbuf,int off,int
  len)
public boolean ready()
public void reset()
public long skip(long n)

▶FILTERWRITER

public abstract class java.io.
  FilterWriter
extends java.io.Writer
extends java.lang.Object

Fields

protected java.io.Writer out

Constructors

protected FilterWriter(Writer out)

Methods

public void close()
public void flush()
public void write(int c)
public void write(char cbuf,int off,int
  len)
public void write(String str,int off,int
  len)

▶FIXEDHEIGHTLAYOUTCACHE

public class javax.swing.tree.
  FixedHeightLayoutCache
extends javax.swing.tree.
  AbstractLayoutCache
extends java.lang.Object

Constructors

public FixedHeightLayoutCache()

Methods

public Rectangle getBounds(TreePath path,
  Rectangle placeIn)
public boolean getExpandedState(TreePath
  path)
public TreePath getPathClosestTo(int x,
  int y)
public TreePath getPathForRow(int row)

```
public int getRowCount()
public int getRowForPath(TreePath path)
public int getVisibleChildCount(TreePath
  path)
public Enumeration getVisiblePathsFrom(
  TreePath path)
public void invalidatePathBounds(
  TreePath path)
public void invalidateSizes()
public boolean isExpanded(TreePath path)
public void setExpandedState(TreePath
  path,boolean isExpanded)
public void setModel(TreeModel newModel)
public void setRootVisible(boolean
  rootVisible)
public void setRowHeight(int rowHeight)
public void treeNodesChanged(
  TreeModelEvent e)
public void treeNodesInserted(
  TreeModelEvent e)
public void treeNodesRemoved(
  TreeModelEvent e)
public void treeStructureChanged(
  TreeModelEvent e)
```

►FLATTENINGPATHITERATOR
```
public class java.awt.geom.
  FlatteningPathIterator
implements java.awt.geom.PathIterator
extends java.lang.Object
```
Constructors
```
public  FlatteningPathIterator(
  PathIterator src,double flatness)
public  FlatteningPathIterator(
  PathIterator src,double flatness,int
  limit)
```
Methods
```
public int currentSegment(float coords)
public int currentSegment(double coords)
public double getFlatness()
public int getRecursionLimit()
public int getWindingRule()
public boolean isDone()
public void next()
```

►FLOAT
```
public final class java.lang.Float
implements java.lang.Comparable
extends java.lang.Number
extends java.lang.Object
```
Fields
```
public final static float MAX_VALUE
public final static float MIN_VALUE
public final static float NaN
public final static float NEGATIVE_
  INFINITY
public final static float POSITIVE_
  INFINITY
public final static java.lang.Class
  TYPE
```
Constructors
```
public  Float(float value)
```

```
public  Float(double value)
public  Float(String s)
```
Methods
```
public byte byteValue()
public int compareTo(Float anotherFloat)
public int compareTo(Object o)
public double doubleValue()
public boolean equals(Object obj)
public static native int floatToIntBits(
  float value)
public float floatValue()
public int hashCode()
public static native float
  intBitsToFloat(int bits)
public int intValue()
public static boolean isInfinite(float v)
public boolean isInfinite()
public static boolean isNaN(float v)
public boolean isNaN()
public long longValue()
public static float parseFloat(String s)
public short shortValue()
public static String toString(float f)
public String toString()
public static Float valueOf(String s)
```

►FLOWLAYOUT
```
public class java.awt.FlowLayout
implements java.awt.LayoutManager
implements java.io.Serializable
extends java.lang.Object
```
Fields
```
public final static int CENTER
public final static int LEADING
public final static int LEFT
public final static int RIGHT
public final static int TRAILING
```
Constructors
```
public  FlowLayout()
public  FlowLayout(int align)
public  FlowLayout(int align,int hgap,
  int vgap)
```
Methods
```
public void addLayoutComponent(String
  name,Component comp)
public int getAlignment()
public int getHgap()
public int getVgap()
public void layoutContainer(Container
  target)
public Dimension minimumLayoutSize(
  Container target)
public Dimension preferredLayoutSize(
  Container target)
public void removeLayoutComponent(
  Component comp)
public void setAlignment(int align)
public void setHgap(int hgap)
public void setVgap(int vgap)
public String toString()
```

►FocusAdapter

```
public abstract class java.awt.event.
  FocusAdapter
implements java.awt.event.FocusListener
extends java.lang.Object
```

Methods
```
public void focusGained(FocusEvent e)
public void focusLost(FocusEvent e)
```

►FocusEvent

```
public class java.awt.event.FocusEvent
extends java.awt.event.ComponentEvent
extends java.awt.AWTEvent
extends java.util.EventObject
extends java.lang.Object
```

Fields
```
public final static int FOCUS_FIRST
public final static int FOCUS_GAINED
public final static int FOCUS_LAST
public final static int FOCUS_LOST
```

Constructors
```
public FocusEvent(Component source,int
  id,boolean temporary)
public FocusEvent(Component source,int
  id)
```

Methods
```
public boolean isTemporary()
public String paramString()
```

►FocusManager

```
public abstract class javax.swing.
  FocusManager
extends java.lang.Object
```

Fields
```
public final static java.lang.String
  FOCUS_MANAGER_CLASS_PROPERTY
```

Methods
```
public static void
  disableSwingFocusManager()
public abstract void focusNextComponent(
  Component aComponent)
public abstract void
  focusPreviousComponent(Component
  aComponent)
public static FocusManager
  getCurrentManager()
public static boolean
  isFocusManagerEnabled()
public abstract void processKeyEvent(
  Component focusedComponent,KeyEvent
  anEvent)
public static void setCurrentManager(
  FocusManager aFocusManager)
```

►Font

```
public class java.awt.Font
implements java.io.Serializable
extends java.lang.Object
```

Fields
```
public final static int BOLD
public final static int CENTER_BASELINE
```

```
public final static int HANGING_
  BASELINE
public final static int ITALIC
protected java.lang.String name
public final static int PLAIN
protected float pointSize
public final static int ROMAN_BASELINE
protected int size
protected int style
```

Constructors
```
public Font(String name,int style,int
  size)
private Font()
public Font(Map attributes)
```

Methods
```
public boolean canDisplay(char c)
public int canDisplayUpTo(String str)
public int canDisplayUpTo(char text,int
  start,int limit)
public int canDisplayUpTo(
  CharacterIterator iter,int start,int
  limit)
public GlyphVector createGlyphVector(
  FontRenderContext frc,String str)
public GlyphVector createGlyphVector(
  FontRenderContext frc,char chars)
public GlyphVector createGlyphVector(
  FontRenderContext frc,CharacterIterator
  ci)
public GlyphVector createGlyphVector(
  FontRenderContext frc,int glyphCodes)
public static Font decode(String str)
public Font deriveFont(int style,float
  size)
public Font deriveFont(int style,
  AffineTransform trans)
public Font deriveFont(float size)
public Font deriveFont(AffineTransform
  trans)
public Font deriveFont(int style)
public Font deriveFont(Map attributes)
public boolean equals(Object obj)
protected void finalize()
public Map getAttributes()
public Attribute getAvailableAttributes()
public byte getBaselineFor(char c)
public String getFamily()
public String getFamily(Locale l)
public static Font getFont(Map
  attributes)
public static Font getFont(String nm)
public static Font getFont(String nm,
  Font font)
public String getFontName()
public String getFontName(Locale l)
public float getItalicAngle()
public LineMetrics getLineMetrics(String
  str,FontRenderContext frc)
public LineMetrics getLineMetrics(String
  str,int beginIndex,int limit,
  FontRenderContext frc)
```

public LineMetrics getLineMetrics(char chars,int beginIndex,int limit, FontRenderContext frc)
public LineMetrics getLineMetrics(CharacterIterator ci,int beginIndex,int limit,FontRenderContext frc)
public Rectangle2D getMaxCharBounds(FontRenderContext frc)
public int getMissingGlyphCode()
public String getName()
public int getNumGlyphs()
public FontPeer getPeer()
public String getPSName()
public int getSize()
public float getSize2D()
public Rectangle2D getStringBounds(String str,FontRenderContext frc)
public Rectangle2D getStringBounds(String str,int beginIndex,int limit, FontRenderContext frc)
public Rectangle2D getStringBounds(char chars,int beginIndex,int limit, FontRenderContext frc)
public Rectangle2D getStringBounds(CharacterIterator ci,int beginIndex,int limit,FontRenderContext frc)
public int getStyle()
public AffineTransform getTransform()
public int hashCode()
public boolean hasUniformLineMetrics()
public boolean isBold()
public boolean isItalic()
public boolean isPlain()
public String toString()

▶**FONTMETRICS**
public abstract class java.awt. FontMetrics
implements java.io.Serializable
extends java.lang.Object
Fields
protected static java.awt.Font font
Constructors
protected FontMetrics(Font font)
Methods
public int bytesWidth(byte data,int off, int len)
public int charsWidth(char data,int off, int len)
public int charWidth(int ch)
public int charWidth(char ch)
public int getAscent()
public int getDescent()
public Font getFont()
public int getHeight()
public int getLeading()
public LineMetrics getLineMetrics(String str,Graphics context)
public LineMetrics getLineMetrics(String str,int beginIndex,int limit,Graphics context)

public LineMetrics getLineMetrics(char chars,int beginIndex,int limit,Graphics context)
public LineMetrics getLineMetrics(CharacterIterator ci,int beginIndex,int limit,Graphics context)
public int getMaxAdvance()
public int getMaxAscent()
public Rectangle2D getMaxCharBounds(Graphics context)
public int getMaxDecent()
public int getMaxDescent()
public Rectangle2D getStringBounds(String str,Graphics context)
public Rectangle2D getStringBounds(String str,int beginIndex,int limit, Graphics context)
public Rectangle2D getStringBounds(char chars,int beginIndex,int limit,Graphics context)
public Rectangle2D getStringBounds(CharacterIterator ci,int beginIndex,int limit,Graphics context)
public int getWidths()
public boolean hasUniformLineMetrics()
public int stringWidth(String str)
public String toString()

▶**FONTRENDERCONTEXT**
public class java.awt.font. FontRenderContext
extends java.lang.Object
Constructors
protected FontRenderContext()
public FontRenderContext(AffineTransform tx,boolean isAntiAliased, boolean usesFractionalMetrics)
Methods
public AffineTransform getTransform()
public boolean isAntiAliased()
public boolean usesFractionalMetrics()

▶**FONTUIRESOURCE**
public class javax.swing.plaf. FontUIResource
implements javax.swing.plaf.UIResource
extends java.awt.Font
extends java.lang.Object
Constructors
public FontUIResource(String name,int style,int size)
public FontUIResource(Font font)

▶**FORMAT**
public abstract class java.text.Format
implements java.lang.Cloneable
implements java.io.Serializable
extends java.lang.Object
Methods
public Object clone()
public final String format(Object obj)

```
public abstract StringBuffer format(
  Object obj,StringBuffer toAppendTo,
  FieldPosition pos)
public abstract Object parseObject(
  String source,ParsePosition status)
public Object parseObject(String source)
```

▶**FORMVIEW**
public class javax.swing.text.html.
  FormView
implements java.awt.event.
  ActionListener
extends javax.swing.text.ComponentView
extends javax.swing.text.View
extends java.lang.Object

Fields
```
public final static java.lang.String
  RESET
public final static java.lang.String
  SUBMIT
```

Constructors
```
public FormView(Element elem)
```

Methods
```
public void actionPerformed(ActionEvent
  evt)
protected Component createComponent()
protected void imageSubmit(String
  imageData)
protected void submitData(String data)
```

▶**FRAME**
public class java.awt.Frame
implements java.awt.MenuContainer
extends java.awt.Window
extends java.awt.Container
extends java.awt.Component
extends java.lang.Object

Fields
```
public final static int CROSSHAIR_
  CURSOR
public final static int DEFAULT_CURSOR
public final static int E_RESIZE_CURSOR
public final static int HAND_CURSOR
public final static int ICONIFIED
public final static int MOVE_CURSOR
public final static int NE_RESIZE_
  CURSOR
public final static int NORMAL
public final static int NW_RESIZE_
  CURSOR
public final static int N_RESIZE_CURSOR
public final static int SE_RESIZE_
  CURSOR
public final static int SW_RESIZE_
  CURSOR
public final static int S_RESIZE_CURSOR
public final static int TEXT_CURSOR
public final static int WAIT_CURSOR
public final static int W_RESIZE_CURSOR
```

Constructors
```
public static Frame()
public Frame(String title)
```

Methods
```
public void addNotify()
protected void finalize()
public int getCursorType()
public static Frame getFrames()
public Image getIconImage()
public MenuBar getMenuBar()
public synchronized int getState()
public String getTitle()
public boolean isResizable()
protected String paramString()
public void remove(MenuComponent m)
public void removeNotify()
public synchronized void setCursor(int
  cursorType)
public synchronized void setIconImage(
  Image image)
public void setMenuBar(MenuBar mb)
public void setResizable(boolean
  resizable)
public synchronized void setState(int
  state)
public synchronized void setTitle(String
  title)
```

▶**GAPCONTENT**
public class javax.swing.text.
  GapContent
implements AbstractDocument.Content
implements java.io.Serializable
extends java.lang.Object

Constructors
```
public GapContent()
public GapContent(int initialLength)
```

Methods
```
protected Object allocateArray(int len)
public Position createPosition(int
  offset)
protected int getArrayLength()
public void getChars(int where,int len,
  Segment chars)
protected Vector getPositionsInRange(
  Vector v,int offset,int length)
public String getString(int where,int
  len)
public UndoableEdit insertString(int
  where,String str)
public int length()
public UndoableEdit remove(int where,int
  nitems)
protected void resetMarksAtZero()
protected void shiftEnd(int newSize)
protected void shiftGap(int newGapStart)
protected void shiftGapEndUp(int
  newGapEnd)
protected void shiftGapStartDown(int
  newGapStart)
protected void updateUndoPositions(
  Vector positions,int offset,int length)
```

▶**GENERALPATH**

public final class java.awt.geom.
  GeneralPath
implements java.lang.Cloneable
implements java.awt.Shape
extends java.lang.Object

Fields
public final static int WIND_EVEN_ODD
public final static int WIND_NON_ZERO

Constructors
public GeneralPath()
public GeneralPath(int rule)
public GeneralPath(int rule,int
  initialCapacity)
 GeneralPath()
public GeneralPath(Shape s)

Methods
public void append(Shape s,boolean
  connect)
public void append(PathIterator pi,
  boolean connect)
public Object clone()
public synchronized void closePath()
public boolean contains(double x,double
  y)
public boolean contains(Point2D p)
public boolean contains(double x,double
  y,double w,double h)
public boolean contains(Rectangle2D r)
public synchronized Shape
  createTransformedShape(AffineTransform
  at)
public synchronized void curveTo(float
  x1,float y1,float x2,float y2,float x3,
  float y3)
public Rectangle getBounds()
public synchronized Rectangle2D
  getBounds2D()
public synchronized Point2D
  getCurrentPoint()
public PathIterator getPathIterator(
  AffineTransform at)
public PathIterator getPathIterator(
  AffineTransform at,double flatness)
public synchronized int getWindingRule()
public boolean intersects(double x,
  double y,double w,double h)
public boolean intersects(Rectangle2D r)
public synchronized void lineTo(float x,
  float y)
public synchronized void moveTo(float x,
  float y)
public synchronized void quadTo(float x1,
  float y1,float x2,float y2)
public synchronized void reset()
public void setWindingRule(int rule)
public void transform(AffineTransform at)

▶**GENERALSECURITYEXCEPTION**

public class java.security.
  GeneralSecurityException
extends java.lang.Exception

extends java.lang.Throwable
extends java.lang.Object

Constructors
public GeneralSecurityException()
public GeneralSecurityException(String
  msg)

▶**GLYPHJUSTIFICATIONINFO**

public final class java.awt.font.
  GlyphJustificationInfo
extends java.lang.Object

Fields
public final boolean growAbsorb
public final float growLeftLimit
public final int growPriority
public final float growRightLimit
public final static int PRIORITY_
  INTERCHAR
public final static int PRIORITY_
  KASHIDA
public final static int PRIORITY_NONE
public final static int PRIORITY_
  WHITESPACE
public final boolean shrinkAbsorb
public final float shrinkLeftLimit
public final int shrinkPriority
public final float shrinkRightLimit
public final float weight

Constructors
public GlyphJustificationInfo(float
  weight,boolean growAbsorb,int
  growPriority,float growLeftLimit,float
  growRightLimit,boolean shrinkAbsorb,int
  shrinkPriority,float shrinkLeftLimit,
  float shrinkRightLimit)

▶**GLYPHMETRICS**

public final class java.awt.font.
  GlyphMetrics
extends java.lang.Object

Fields
public final static byte COMBINING
public final static byte COMPONENT
public final static byte LIGATURE
public final static byte STANDARD
public final static byte WHITESPACE

Constructors
public GlyphMetrics(float advance,
  Rectangle2D bounds,byte glyphType)

Methods
public float getAdvance()
public Rectangle2D getBounds2D()
public float getLSB()
public float getRSB()
public int getType()
public boolean isCombining()
public boolean isComponent()
public boolean isLigature()
public boolean isStandard()
public boolean isWhitespace()

▶**GLYPHVECTOR**
public abstract class java.awt.font.
GlyphVector
implements java.lang.Cloneable
extends java.lang.Object
Methods
public abstract boolean equals(
GlyphVector set)
public abstract Font getFont()
public abstract FontRenderContext
getFontRenderContext()
public abstract int getGlyphCode(int
glyphIndex)
public abstract int getGlyphCodes(int
beginGlyphIndex,int numEntries,int
codeReturn)
public abstract GlyphJustificationInfo
getGlyphJustificationInfo(int glyphIndex)
public abstract Shape
getGlyphLogicalBounds(int glyphIndex)
public abstract GlyphMetrics
getGlyphMetrics(int glyphIndex)
public abstract Shape getGlyphOutline(
int glyphIndex)
public abstract Point2D getGlyphPosition(
int glyphIndex)
public abstract float getGlyphPositions(
int beginGlyphIndex,int numEntries,float
positionReturn)
public abstract AffineTransform
getGlyphTransform(int glyphIndex)
public abstract Shape
getGlyphVisualBounds(int glyphIndex)
public abstract Rectangle2D
getLogicalBounds()
public abstract int getNumGlyphs()
public abstract Shape getOutline()
public abstract Shape getOutline(float x,
float y)
public abstract Rectangle2D
getVisualBounds()
public abstract void
performDefaultLayout()
public abstract void setGlyphPosition(
int glyphIndex,Point2D newPos)
public abstract void setGlyphTransform(
int glyphIndex,AffineTransform newTX)

▶**GRADIENTPAINT**
public class java.awt.GradientPaint
implements java.awt.Paint
extends java.lang.Object
Constructors
public GradientPaint(float x1,float y1,
Color color1,float x2,float y2,Color
color2)
public GradientPaint(Point2D pt1,Color
color1,Point2D pt2,Color color2)
public GradientPaint(float x1,float y1,
Color color1,float x2,float y2,Color
color2,boolean cyclic)

public GradientPaint(Point2D pt1,Color
color1,Point2D pt2,Color color2,boolean
cyclic)
Methods
public PaintContext createContext(
ColorModel cm,Rectangle deviceBounds,
Rectangle2D userBounds,AffineTransform
xform,RenderingHints hints)
public Color getColor1()
public Color getColor2()
public Point2D getPoint1()
public Point2D getPoint2()
public int getTransparency()
public boolean isCyclic()

▶**GRAPHICATTRIBUTE**
public abstract class java.awt.font.
GraphicAttribute
extends java.lang.Object
Fields
public final static int BOTTOM_
ALIGNMENT
public final static int CENTER_BASELINE
public final static int HANGING_
BASELINE
public final static int ROMAN_BASELINE
public final static int TOP_ALIGNMENT
Constructors
protected GraphicAttribute(int
alignment)
Methods
public abstract void draw(Graphics2D
graphics,float x,float y)
public abstract float getAdvance()
public final int getAlignment()
public abstract float getAscent()
public Rectangle2D getBounds()
public abstract float getDescent()
public GlyphJustificationInfo
getJustificationInfo()

▶**GRAPHICS**
public abstract class java.awt.Graphics
extends java.lang.Object
Constructors
protected Graphics()
Methods
public abstract void clearRect(int x,int
y,int width,int height)
public abstract void clipRect(int x,int
y,int width,int height)
public abstract void copyArea(int x,int
y,int width,int height,int dx,int dy)
public abstract Graphics create()
public Graphics create(int x,int y,int
width,int height)
public abstract void dispose()
public void draw3DRect(int x,int y,int
width,int height,boolean raised)

public abstract void drawArc(int x,int y,
  int width,int height,int startAngle,int
  arcAngle)
public void drawBytes(byte data,int
  offset,int length,int x,int y)
public void drawChars(char data,int
  offset,int length,int x,int y)
public abstract boolean drawImage(Image
  img,int x,int y,ImageObserver observer)
public abstract boolean drawImage(Image
  img,int x,int y,int width,int height,
  ImageObserver observer)
public abstract boolean drawImage(Image
  img,int x,int y,Color bgcolor,
  ImageObserver observer)
public abstract boolean drawImage(Image
  img,int x,int y,int width,int height,
  Color bgcolor,ImageObserver observer)
public abstract boolean drawImage(Image
  img,int dx1,int dy1,int dx2,int dy2,int
  sx1,int sy1,int sx2,int sy2,
  ImageObserver observer)
public abstract boolean drawImage(Image
  img,int dx1,int dy1,int dx2,int dy2,int
  sx1,int sy1,int sx2,int sy2,Color
  bgcolor,ImageObserver observer)
public abstract void drawLine(int x1,int
  y1,int x2,int y2)
public abstract void drawOval(int x,int
  y,int width,int height)
public abstract void drawPolygon(int
  xPoints,int yPoints,int nPoints)
public void drawPolygon(Polygon p)
public abstract void drawPolyline(int
  xPoints,int yPoints,int nPoints)
public void drawRect(int x,int y,int
  width,int height)
public abstract void drawRoundRect(int x,
  int y,int width,int height,int arcWidth,
  int arcHeight)
public abstract void drawString(String
  str,int x,int y)
public abstract void drawString(
  AttributedCharacterIterator iterator,int
  x,int y)
public void fill3DRect(int x,int y,int
  width,int height,boolean raised)
public abstract void fillArc(int x,int y,
  int width,int height,int startAngle,int
  arcAngle)
public abstract void fillOval(int x,int
  y,int width,int height)
public abstract void fillPolygon(int
  xPoints,int yPoints,int nPoints)
public void fillPolygon(Polygon p)
public abstract void fillRect(int x,int
  y,int width,int height)
public abstract void fillRoundRect(int x,
  int y,int width,int height,int arcWidth,
  int arcHeight)
public void finalize()
public abstract Shape getClip()
public abstract Rectangle getClipBounds()

public Rectangle getClipBounds(Rectangle
  r)
public Rectangle getClipRect()
public abstract Color getColor()
public abstract Font getFont()
public FontMetrics getFontMetrics()
public abstract FontMetrics
  getFontMetrics(Font f)
public boolean hitClip(int x,int y,int
  width,int height)
public abstract void setClip(int x,int y,
  int width,int height)
public abstract void setClip(Shape clip)
public abstract void setColor(Color c)
public abstract void setFont(Font font)
public abstract void setPaintMode()
public abstract void setXORMode(Color c1)
public String toString()
public abstract void translate(int x,int
  y)

▶**GRAPHICS2D**
public abstract class java.awt.
  Graphics2D
extends java.awt.Graphics
extends java.lang.Object
Constructors
protected Graphics2D()
Methods
public abstract void addRenderingHints(
  Map hints)
public abstract void clip(Shape s)
public abstract void draw(Shape s)
public void draw3DRect(int x,int y,int
  width,int height,boolean raised)
public abstract void drawGlyphVector(
  GlyphVector g,float x,float y)
public abstract boolean drawImage(Image
  img,AffineTransform xform,ImageObserver
  obs)
public abstract void drawImage(
  BufferedImage img,BufferedImageOp op,int
  x,int y)
public abstract void drawRenderableImage(
  RenderableImage img,AffineTransform
  xform)
public abstract void drawRenderedImage(
  RenderedImage img,AffineTransform xform)
public abstract void drawString(String
  str,int x,int y)
public abstract void drawString(String s,
  float x,float y)
public abstract void drawString(
  AttributedCharacterIterator iterator,int
  x,int y)
public abstract void drawString(
  AttributedCharacterIterator iterator,
  float x,float y)
public abstract void fill(Shape s)
public void fill3DRect(int x,int y,int
  width,int height,boolean raised)
public abstract Color getBackground()

```
public abstract Composite getComposite()
public abstract GraphicsConfiguration
  getDeviceConfiguration()
public abstract FontRenderContext
  getFontRenderContext()
public abstract Paint getPaint()
public abstract Object getRenderingHint(
  Key hintKey)
public abstract RenderingHints
  getRenderingHints()
public abstract Stroke getStroke()
public abstract AffineTransform
  getTransform()
public abstract boolean hit(Rectangle
  rect,Shape s,boolean onStroke)
public abstract void rotate(double theta)
public abstract void rotate(double theta,
  double x,double y)
public abstract void scale(double sx,
  double sy)
public abstract void setBackground(Color
  color)
public abstract void setComposite(
  Composite comp)
public abstract void setPaint(Paint
  paint)
public abstract void setRenderingHint(
  Key hintKey,Object hintValue)
public abstract void setRenderingHints(
  Map hints)
public abstract void setStroke(Stroke s)
public abstract void setTransform(
  AffineTransform Tx)
public abstract void shear(double shx,
  double shy)
public abstract void transform(
  AffineTransform Tx)
public abstract void translate(int x,int
  y)
public abstract void translate(double tx,
  double ty)
```

►GraphicsConfigTemplate

```
public abstract class java.awt.
  GraphicsConfigTemplate
implements java.io.Serializable
extends java.lang.Object
```

Fields
```
public final static int PREFERRED
public final static int REQUIRED
public final static int UNNECESSARY
```

Constructors
```
public  GraphicsConfigTemplate()
```

Methods
```
public abstract GraphicsConfiguration
  getBestConfiguration(
  GraphicsConfiguration gc)
public abstract boolean
  isGraphicsConfigSupported(
  GraphicsConfiguration gc)
```

►GraphicsConfiguration

```
public abstract class java.awt.
  GraphicsConfiguration
extends java.lang.Object
```

Constructors
```
protected  GraphicsConfiguration()
```

Methods
```
public abstract BufferedImage
  createCompatibleImage(int width,int
  height)
public abstract BufferedImage
  createCompatibleImage(int width,int
  height,int transparency)
public abstract ColorModel getColorModel(
  )
public abstract ColorModel getColorModel(
  int transparency)
public abstract AffineTransform
  getDefaultTransform()
public abstract GraphicsDevice getDevice(
  )
public abstract AffineTransform
  getNormalizingTransform()
```

►GraphicsDevice

```
public abstract class java.awt.
  GraphicsDevice
extends java.lang.Object
```

Fields
```
public final static int TYPE_IMAGE_
  BUFFER
public final static int TYPE_PRINTER
public final static int TYPE_RASTER_
  SCREEN
```

Constructors
```
protected  GraphicsDevice()
```

Methods
```
public GraphicsConfiguration
  getBestConfiguration(
  GraphicsConfigTemplate gct)
public abstract GraphicsConfiguration
  getConfigurations()
public abstract GraphicsConfiguration
  getDefaultConfiguration()
public abstract String getIDstring()
public abstract int getType()
```

►GraphicsEnvironment

```
public abstract class java.awt.
  GraphicsEnvironment
extends java.lang.Object
```

Constructors
```
protected  GraphicsEnvironment()
```

Methods
```
public abstract Graphics2D
  createGraphics(BufferedImage img)
public abstract Font getAllFonts()
public abstract String
  getAvailableFontFamilyNames()
public abstract String
  getAvailableFontFamilyNames(Locale l)
```

public abstract GraphicsDevice
  getDefaultScreenDevice()
public static GraphicsEnvironment
  getLocalGraphicsEnvironment()
public abstract GraphicsDevice
  getScreenDevices()

▸GRAYFILTER
public class javax.swing.GrayFilter
extends java.awt.image.RGBImageFilter
extends java.awt.image.ImageFilter
extends java.lang.Object

Constructors
public GrayFilter(boolean b,int p)

Methods
public static Image createDisabledImage(
  Image i)
public int filterRGB(int x,int y,int rgb)

▸GREGORIANCALENDAR
public class java.util.
  GregorianCalendar
extends java.util.Calendar
extends java.lang.Object

Fields
public final static int AD
public final static int BC

Constructors
public GregorianCalendar()
public GregorianCalendar(TimeZone zone)
public GregorianCalendar(Locale aLocale)
public GregorianCalendar(TimeZone zone,
  Locale aLocale)
public GregorianCalendar(int year,int
  month,int date)
public GregorianCalendar(int year,int
  month,int date,int hour,int minute)
public GregorianCalendar(int year,int
  month,int date,int hour,int minute,int
  second)

Methods
public void add(int field,int amount)
protected void computeFields()
protected void computeTime()
public boolean equals(Object obj)
public int getActualMaximum(int field)
public int getActualMinimum(int field)
public int getGreatestMinimum(int field)
public final Date getGregorianChange()
public int getLeastMaximum(int field)
public int getMaximum(int field)
public int getMinimum(int field)
public int hashCode()
public boolean isLeapYear(int year)
public void roll(int field,boolean up)
public void roll(int field,int amount)
public void setGregorianChange(Date date)

▸GRIDBAGCONSTRAINTS
public class java.awt.
  GridBagConstraints
implements java.lang.Cloneable

implements java.io.Serializable
extends java.lang.Object

Fields
public int anchor
public final static int BOTH
public final static int CENTER
public final static int EAST
public int fill
public int gridheight
public int gridwidth
public int gridx
public int gridy
public final static int HORIZONTAL
public java.awt.Insets insets
public int ipadx
public int ipady
public final static int NONE
public final static int NORTH
public final static int NORTHEAST
public final static int NORTHWEST
public final static int RELATIVE
public final static int REMAINDER
public final static int SOUTH
public final static int SOUTHEAST
public final static int SOUTHWEST
public final static int VERTICAL
public double weightx
public double weighty
public final static int WEST

Constructors
public GridBagConstraints()
public GridBagConstraints(int gridx,int
  gridy,int gridwidth,int gridheight,
  double weightx,double weighty,int anchor,
  int fill,Insets insets,int ipadx,int
  ipady)

Methods
public Object clone()

▸GRIDBAGLAYOUT
public class java.awt.GridBagLayout
implements java.awt.LayoutManager2
implements java.io.Serializable
extends java.lang.Object

Fields
public double columnWeights
public int columnWidths
protected java.util.Hashtable comptable
protected java.awt.GridBagConstraints
  defaultConstraints
protected GridBagLayoutInfo layoutInfo
protected final static int MAXGRIDSIZE
protected final static int MINSIZE
protected final static int
  PREFERREDSIZE
public int rowHeights
public double rowWeights

Constructors
public GridBagLayout()

Methods
public void addLayoutComponent(String
  name,Component comp)

```
public void addLayoutComponent(Component
  comp,Object constraints)
protected void AdjustForGravity(
  GridBagConstraints constraints,Rectangle
  r)
protected void ArrangeGrid(Container
  parent)
public GridBagConstraints getConstraints(
  Component comp)
public float getLayoutAlignmentX(
  Container parent)
public float getLayoutAlignmentY(
  Container parent)
public int getLayoutDimensions()
protected GridBagLayoutInfo
  GetLayoutInfo(Container parent,int
  sizeflag)
public Point getLayoutOrigin()
public double getLayoutWeights()
protected Dimension GetMinSize(Container
  parent,GridBagLayoutInfo info)
public void invalidateLayout(Container
  target)
public void layoutContainer(Container
  parent)
public Point location(int x,int y)
protected GridBagConstraints
  lookupConstraints(Component comp)
public Dimension maximumLayoutSize(
  Container target)
public Dimension minimumLayoutSize(
  Container parent)
public Dimension preferredLayoutSize(
  Container parent)
public void removeLayoutComponent(
  Component comp)
public void setConstraints(Component
  comp,GridBagConstraints constraints)
public String toString()
```

►GridLayout

```
public class java.awt.GridLayout
implements java.awt.LayoutManager
implements java.io.Serializable
extends java.lang.Object
```

Constructors
```
public  GridLayout()
public  GridLayout(int rows,int cols)
public  GridLayout(int rows,int cols,int
  hgap,int vgap)
```

Methods
```
public void addLayoutComponent(String
  name,Component comp)
public int getColumns()
public int getHgap()
public int getRows()
public int getVgap()
public void layoutContainer(Container
  parent)
public Dimension minimumLayoutSize(
  Container parent)
```

```
public Dimension preferredLayoutSize(
  Container parent)
public void removeLayoutComponent(
  Component comp)
public void setColumns(int cols)
public void setHgap(int hgap)
public void setRows(int rows)
public void setVgap(int vgap)
public String toString()
```

►GuardedObject

```
public class java.security.
  GuardedObject
implements java.io.Serializable
extends java.lang.Object
```

Constructors
```
public  GuardedObject(Object object,
  Guard guard)
```

Methods
```
public Object getObject()
```

►GZIPInputStream

```
public class java.util.zip.
  GZIPInputStream
extends java.util.zip.
  InflaterInputStream
extends java.io.FilterInputStream
extends java.io.InputStream
extends java.lang.Object
```

Fields
```
protected java.util.zip.CRC32 crc
protected boolean eos
public final static int GZIP_MAGIC
```

Constructors
```
public  GZIPInputStream(InputStream in,
  int size)
public  GZIPInputStream(InputStream in)
```

Methods
```
public void close()
public int read(byte buf,int off,int len)
```

►GZIPOutputStream

```
public class java.util.zip.
  GZIPOutputStream
extends java.util.zip.
  DeflaterOutputStream
extends java.io.FilterOutputStream
extends java.io.OutputStream
extends java.lang.Object
```

Fields
```
protected java.util.zip.CRC32 crc
```

Constructors
```
public  GZIPOutputStream(OutputStream
  out,int size)
public  GZIPOutputStream(OutputStream
  out)
```

Methods
```
public void close()
public void finish()
public synchronized void write(byte buf,
  int off,int len)
```

►HASHMAP
```
public class java.util.HashMap
implements java.lang.Cloneable
implements java.util.Map
implements java.io.Serializable
extends java.util.AbstractMap
extends java.lang.Object
```
Constructors
```
public  HashMap(int initialCapacity,
  float loadFactor)
public  HashMap(int initialCapacity)
public  HashMap()
public  HashMap(Map t)
```
Methods
```
public void clear()
public Object clone()
public boolean containsKey(Object key)
public boolean containsValue(Object
  value)
public Set entrySet()
public Object get(Object key)
public boolean isEmpty()
public Set keySet()
public Object put(Object key,Object
  value)
public void putAll(Map t)
public Object remove(Object key)
public int size()
public Collection values()
```

►HASHSET
```
public class java.util.HashSet
implements java.lang.Cloneable
implements java.io.Serializable
implements java.util.Set
extends java.util.AbstractSet
extends java.util.AbstractCollection
extends java.lang.Object
```
Constructors
```
public  HashSet()
public  HashSet(Collection c)
public  HashSet(int initialCapacity,
  float loadFactor)
public  HashSet(int initialCapacity)
```
Methods
```
public boolean add(Object o)
public void clear()
public Object clone()
public boolean contains(Object o)
public boolean isEmpty()
public Iterator iterator()
public boolean remove(Object o)
public int size()
```

►HASHTABLE
```
public class java.util.Hashtable
implements java.lang.Cloneable
implements java.util.Map
implements java.io.Serializable
extends java.util.Dictionary
extends java.lang.Object
```
Constructors
```
public  Hashtable(int initialCapacity,
  float loadFactor)
public  Hashtable(int initialCapacity)
public  Hashtable()
public  Hashtable(Map t)
```
Methods
```
public synchronized void clear()
public synchronized Object clone()
public synchronized boolean contains(
  Object value)
public synchronized boolean containsKey(
  Object key)
public boolean containsValue(Object
  value)
public synchronized Enumeration elements(
  )
public Set entrySet()
public synchronized boolean equals(
  Object o)
public synchronized Object get(Object
  key)
public synchronized int hashCode()
public boolean isEmpty()
public synchronized Enumeration keys()
public Set keySet()
public synchronized Object put(Object
  key,Object value)
public synchronized void putAll(Map t)
protected void rehash()
public synchronized Object remove(Object
  key)
public int size()
public synchronized String toString()
public Collection values()
```

►HTML
```
public class javax.swing.text.html.HTML
extends java.lang.Object
```
Fields
```
public final static java.lang.String
  NULL_ATTRIBUTE_VALUE
```
Methods
```
public static Attribute
  getAllAttributeKeys()
public static Tag getAllTags()
public static Attribute getAttributeKey(
  String attName)
public static int
  getIntegerAttributeValue(AttributeSet
  attr,Attribute key,int def)
public static Tag getTag(String tagName)
```

►HTMLDOCUMENT
```
public class javax.swing.text.html.
  HTMLDocument
extends javax.swing.text.
  DefaultStyledDocument
extends javax.swing.text.
  AbstractDocument
extends java.lang.Object
```

Fields

public final static java.lang.String
  AdditionalComments

Constructors

public HTMLDocument()
public HTMLDocument(StyleSheet styles)
public HTMLDocument(Content c,
  StyleSheet styles)

Methods

protected void create(ElementSpec data)
protected Element createBranchElement(
  Element parent,AttributeSet a)
protected AbstractElement
  createDefaultRoot()
protected Element createLeafElement(
  Element parent,AttributeSet a,int p0,int
  p1)
public URL getBase()
public Iterator getIterator(Tag t)
public boolean getPreservesUnknownTags()
public ParserCallback getReader(int pos)
public ParserCallback getReader(int pos,
  int popDepth,int pushDepth,Tag insertTag)
public StyleSheet getStyleSheet()
public int getTokenThreshold()
protected void insert(int offset,
  ElementSpec data)
protected void insertUpdate(
  DefaultDocumentEvent chng,AttributeSet
  attr)
public void
  processHTMLFrameHyperlinkEvent(
  HTMLFrameHyperlinkEvent e)
public void setBase(URL u)
public void setPreservesUnknownTags(
  boolean preservesTags)
public void setTokenThreshold(int n)

▶HTMLEDITORKIT

public class javax.swing.text.html.
  HTMLEditorKit
extends javax.swing.text.
  StyledEditorKit
extends javax.swing.text.
  DefaultEditorKit
extends javax.swing.text.EditorKit
extends java.lang.Object

Fields

public final static java.lang.String
  BOLD_ACTION
public final static java.lang.String
  COLOR_ACTION
public final static java.lang.String
  DEFAULT_CSS
public final static java.lang.String
  FONT_CHANGE_BIGGER
public final static java.lang.String
  FONT_CHANGE_SMALLER
public final static java.lang.String IMG_
  ALIGN_BOTTOM
public final static java.lang.String IMG_
  ALIGN_MIDDLE

public final static java.lang.String IMG_
  ALIGN_TOP
public final static java.lang.String IMG_
  BORDER
public final static java.lang.String
  ITALIC_ACTION
public final static java.lang.String
  LOGICAL_STYLE_ACTION
public final static java.lang.String
  PARA_INDENT_LEFT
public final static java.lang.String
  PARA_INDENT_RIGHT

Constructors

public HTMLEditorKit()

Methods

public Object clone()
public Document createDefaultDocument()
protected void createInputAttributes(
  Element element,MutableAttributeSet set)
public void deinstall(JEditorPane c)
public Action getActions()
public String getContentType()
protected Parser getParser()
public StyleSheet getStyleSheet()
public ViewFactory getViewFactory()
public void insertHTML(HTMLDocument doc,
  int offset,String html,int popDepth,int
  pushDepth,Tag insertTag)
public void install(JEditorPane c)
public void read(Reader in,Document doc,
  int pos)
public void setStyleSheet(StyleSheet s)
public void write(Writer out,Document
  doc,int pos,int len)

▶HTMLFRAMEHYPERLINKEVENT

public class javax.swing.text.html.
  HTMLFrameHyperlinkEvent
extends javax.swing.event.
  HyperlinkEvent
extends java.util.EventObject
extends java.lang.Object

Constructors

public HTMLFrameHyperlinkEvent(Object
  source,EventType type,URL targetURL,
  String targetFrame)
public HTMLFrameHyperlinkEvent(Object
  source,EventType type,URL targetURL,
  String desc,String targetFrame)
public HTMLFrameHyperlinkEvent(Object
  source,EventType type,URL targetURL,
  Element sourceElement,String targetFrame)
public HTMLFrameHyperlinkEvent(Object
  source,EventType type,URL targetURL,
  String desc,Element sourceElement,String
  targetFrame)

Methods

public Element getSourceElement()
public String getTarget()

▶HTMLWRITER

public class javax.swing.text.html.
  HTMLWriter
extends javax.swing.text.AbstractWriter
extends java.lang.Object

Constructors

public HTMLWriter(Writer w,HTMLDocument
  doc)
public HTMLWriter(Writer w,HTMLDocument
  doc,int pos,int len)

Methods

protected void
  closeOutUnwantedEmbeddedTags(
  AttributeSet attr)
protected void comment(Element elem)
protected void emptyTag(Element elem)
protected void endTag(Element elem)
protected boolean isBlockTag(
  AttributeSet attr)
protected boolean matchNameAttribute(
  AttributeSet attr,Tag tag)
protected void selectContent(
  AttributeSet attr)
protected void startTag(Element elem)
protected boolean synthesizedElement(
  Element elem)
protected void text(Element elem)
protected void textAreaContent(
  AttributeSet attr)
public void write()
protected void write(String content)
protected void writeAttributes(
  AttributeSet attr)
protected void writeEmbeddedTags(
  AttributeSet attr)
protected void writeOption(Option option)

▶HTTPURLCONNECTION

public abstract class java.net.
  HttpURLConnection
extends java.net.URLConnection
extends java.lang.Object

Fields

public final static int HTTP_ACCEPTED
public final static int HTTP_BAD_
  GATEWAY
public final static int HTTP_BAD_METHOD
public final static int HTTP_BAD_
  REQUEST
public final static int HTTP_CLIENT_
  TIMEOUT
public final static int HTTP_CONFLICT
public final static int HTTP_CREATED
public final static int HTTP_ENTITY_TOO_
  LARGE
public final static int HTTP_FORBIDDEN
public final static int HTTP_GATEWAY_
  TIMEOUT
public final static int HTTP_GONE
public final static int HTTP_INTERNAL_
  ERROR

public final static int HTTP_LENGTH_
  REQUIRED
public final static int HTTP_MOVED_PERM
public final static int HTTP_MOVED_TEMP
public final static int HTTP_MULT_
  CHOICE
public final static int HTTP_NOT_
  ACCEPTABLE
public final static int HTTP_NOT_
  AUTHORITATIVE
public final static int HTTP_NOT_FOUND
public final static int HTTP_NOT_
  MODIFIED
public final static int HTTP_NO_CONTENT
public final static int HTTP_OK
public final static int HTTP_PARTIAL
public final static int HTTP_PAYMENT_
  REQUIRED
public final static int HTTP_PRECON_
  FAILED
public final static int HTTP_PROXY_AUTH
public final static int HTTP_REQ_TOO_
  LONG
public final static int HTTP_RESET
public final static int HTTP_SEE_OTHER
public final static int HTTP_SERVER_
  ERROR
public final static int HTTP_
  UNAUTHORIZED
public final static int HTTP_
  UNAVAILABLE
public final static int HTTP_UNSUPPORTED_
  TYPE
public final static int HTTP_USE_PROXY
public final static int HTTP_VERSION
protected java.lang.String method
protected int responseCode
protected java.lang.String
  responseMessage

Constructors

protected HttpURLConnection(URL u)

Methods

public abstract void disconnect()
public InputStream getErrorStream()
public static boolean getFollowRedirects(
)
public Permission getPermission()
public String getRequestMethod()
public int getResponseCode()
public String getResponseMessage()
public static void setFollowRedirects(
  boolean set)
public void setRequestMethod(String
  method)
public abstract boolean usingProxy()

▶HYPERLINKEVENT

public class javax.swing.event.
  HyperlinkEvent
extends java.util.EventObject
extends java.lang.Object

Constructors
```
public HyperlinkEvent(Object source,
   EventType type,URL u)
public HyperlinkEvent(Object source,
   EventType type,URL u,String desc)
```
Methods
```
public String getDescription()
public EventType getEventType()
public URL getURL()
```

▶**ICC_COLORSPACE**
```
public class java.awt.color.ICC_
   ColorSpace
extends java.awt.color.ColorSpace
extends java.lang.Object
```
Constructors
```
public ICC_ColorSpace(ICC_Profile
   profile)
```
Methods
```
public float fromCIEXYZ(float colorvalue)
public float fromRGB(float rgbvalue)
public ICC_Profile getProfile()
public float toCIEXYZ(float colorvalue)
public float toRGB(float colorvalue)
```

▶**ICC_PROFILE**
```
public class java.awt.color.ICC_Profile
extends java.lang.Object
extends java.lang.Object
```
Fields
```
public final static int CLASS_ABSTRACT
public final static int CLASS_
   COLORSPACECONVERSION
public final static int CLASS_
   DEVICELINK
public final static int CLASS_DISPLAY
public final static int CLASS_INPUT
public final static int CLASS_
   NAMEDCOLOR
public final static int CLASS_OUTPUT
public final static int
   icAbsoluteColorimetric
public final static int icCurveCount
public final static int icCurveData
public final static int icHdrAttributes
public final static int icHdrCmmId
public final static int icHdrColorSpace
public final static int icHdrCreator
public final static int icHdrDate
public final static int
   icHdrDeviceClass
public final static int icHdrFlags
public final static int icHdrIlluminant
public final static int icHdrMagic
public final static int
   icHdrManufacturer
public final static int icHdrModel
public final static int icHdrPcs
public final static int icHdrPlatform
public final static int
   icHdrRenderingIntent
public final static int icHdrSize
```
```
public final static int icHdrVersion
public final static int icPerceptual
public final static int
   icRelativeColorimetric
public final static int icSaturation
public final static int
   icSigAbstractClass
public final static int icSigAToB0Tag
public final static int icSigAToB1Tag
public final static int icSigAToB2Tag
public final static int
   icSigBlueColorantTag
public final static int icSigBlueTRCTag
public final static int icSigBToA0Tag
public final static int icSigBToA1Tag
public final static int icSigBToA2Tag
public final static int
   icSigCalibrationDateTimeTag
public final static int
   icSigCharTargetTag
public final static int icSigCmyData
public final static int icSigCmykData
public final static int
   icSigColorSpaceClass
public final static int
   icSigCopyrightTag
public final static int
   icSigDeviceMfgDescTag
public final static int
   icSigDeviceModelDescTag
public final static int
   icSigDisplayClass
public final static int icSigGamutTag
public final static int icSigGrayData
public final static int icSigGrayTRCTag
public final static int
   icSigGreenColorantTag
public final static int
   icSigGreenTRCTag
public final static int icSigHead
public final static int icSigHlsData
public final static int icSigHsvData
public final static int icSigInputClass
public final static int icSigLabData
public final static int icSigLinkClass
public final static int
   icSigLuminanceTag
public final static int icSigLuvData
public final static int
   icSigMeasurementTag
public final static int
   icSigMediaBlackPointTag
public final static int
   icSigMediaWhitePointTag
public final static int
   icSigNamedColor2Tag
public final static int
   icSigNamedColorClass
public final static int
   icSigOutputClass
public final static int
   icSigPreview0Tag
```

```
public final static int
  icSigPreview1Tag
public final static int
  icSigPreview2Tag
public final static int
  icSigProfileDescriptionTag
public final static int
  icSigProfileSequenceDescTag
public final static int icSigPs2CRD0Tag
public final static int icSigPs2CRD1Tag
public final static int icSigPs2CRD2Tag
public final static int icSigPs2CRD3Tag
public final static int icSigPs2CSATag
public final static int
  icSigPs2RenderingIntentTag
public final static int
  icSigRedColorantTag
public final static int icSigRedTRCTag
public final static int icSigRgbData
public final static int
  icSigScreeningDescTag
public final static int
  icSigScreeningTag
public final static int icSigSpace2CLR
public final static int icSigSpace3CLR
public final static int icSigSpace4CLR
public final static int icSigSpace5CLR
public final static int icSigSpace6CLR
public final static int icSigSpace7CLR
public final static int icSigSpace8CLR
public final static int icSigSpace9CLR
public final static int icSigSpaceACLR
public final static int icSigSpaceBCLR
public final static int icSigSpaceCCLR
public final static int icSigSpaceDCLR
public final static int icSigSpaceECLR
public final static int icSigSpaceFCLR
public final static int
  icSigTechnologyTag
public final static int icSigUcrBgTag
public final static int
  icSigViewingCondDescTag
public final static int
  icSigViewingConditionsTag
public final static int icSigXYZData
public final static int icSigYCbCrData
public final static int icSigYxyData
public final static int icTagReserved
public final static int icTagType
public final static int icXYZNumberX
```

Constructors
```
ICC_Profile()
ICC_Profile()
```
Methods
```
protected void finalize()
public int getColorSpaceType()
public byte getData()
public byte getData(int tagSignature)
public static ICC_Profile getInstance(
  byte data)
public static ICC_Profile getInstance(
  int cspace)
```

```
public static ICC_Profile getInstance(
  String fileName)
public static ICC_Profile getInstance(
  InputStream s)
public int getMajorVersion()
public int getMinorVersion()
public int getNumComponents()
public int getPCSType()
public int getProfileClass()
public void setData(int tagSignature,
  byte tagData)
public void write(String fileName)
public void write(OutputStream s)
```

▶ICC_PROFILEGRAY
```
public class java.awt.color.ICC_
  ProfileGray
extends java.awt.color.ICC_Profile
extends java.lang.Object
extends java.lang.Object
```
Constructors
```
ICC_ProfileGray()
ICC_ProfileGray()
```
Methods
```
public float getGamma()
public float getMediaWhitePoint()
public short getTRC()
```

▶ICC_PROFILERGB
```
public class java.awt.color.ICC_
  ProfileRGB
extends java.awt.color.ICC_Profile
extends java.lang.Object
extends java.lang.Object
```
Fields
```
public final static int BLUECOMPONENT
public final static int GREENCOMPONENT
public final static int REDCOMPONENT
```
Constructors
```
ICC_ProfileRGB()
ICC_ProfileRGB()
```
Methods
```
public float getGamma(int component)
public float getMatrix()
public float getMediaWhitePoint()
public short getTRC(int component)
```

▶ICONUIRESOURCE
```
public class javax.swing.plaf.
  IconUIResource
implements javax.swing.Icon
implements java.io.Serializable
implements javax.swing.plaf.UIResource
extends java.lang.Object
```
Constructors
```
public   IconUIResource(Icon delegate)
```
Methods
```
public int getIconHeight()
public int getIconWidth()
public void paintIcon(Component c,
  Graphics g,int x,int y)
```

▶**IconView**
public class javax.swing.text.IconView
extends javax.swing.text.View
extends java.lang.Object
Constructors
public IconView(Element elem)
Methods
public float getAlignment(int axis)
public float getPreferredSpan(int axis)
public Shape modelToView(int pos,Shape a,
  Bias b)
public void paint(Graphics g,Shape a)
public void setSize(float width,float
  height)
public int viewToModel(float x,float y,
  Shape a,Bias bias)
Identity
public abstract class java.security.
  Identity
implements java.security.Principal
implements java.io.Serializable
extends java.lang.Object
Constructors
protected Identity()
public Identity(String name,
  IdentityScope scope)
public Identity(String name)
Methods
public void addCertificate(Certificate
  certificate)
public Certificate certificates()
public final boolean equals(Object
  identity)
public String getInfo()
public final String getName()
public PublicKey getPublicKey()
public final IdentityScope getScope()
public int hashCode()
protected boolean identityEquals(
  Identity identity)
public void removeCertificate(
  Certificate certificate)
public void setInfo(String info)
public void setPublicKey(PublicKey key)
public String toString()
public String toString(boolean detailed)

▶**IdentityScope**
public abstract class java.security.
  IdentityScope
extends java.security.Identity
extends java.lang.Object
Constructors
protected IdentityScope()
public IdentityScope(String name)
public IdentityScope(String name,
  IdentityScope scope)
Methods
public abstract void addIdentity(
  Identity identity)

public abstract Identity getIdentity(
  String name)
public Identity getIdentity(Principal
  principal)
public abstract Identity getIdentity(
  PublicKey key)
public static IdentityScope
  getSystemScope()
public abstract Enumeration identities()
public abstract void removeIdentity(
  Identity identity)
protected static void setSystemScope(
  IdentityScope scope)
public abstract int size()
public String toString()

▶**IllegalAccessError**
public class java.lang.
  IllegalAccessError
extends java.lang.
  IncompatibleClassChangeError
extends java.lang.LinkageError
extends java.lang.Error
extends java.lang.Throwable
extends java.lang.Object
Constructors
public IllegalAccessError()
public IllegalAccessError(String s)

▶**IllegalAccessException**
public class java.lang.
  IllegalAccessException
extends java.lang.Exception
extends java.lang.Throwable
extends java.lang.Object
Constructors
public IllegalAccessException()
public IllegalAccessException(String s)

▶**IllegalArgumentException**
public class java.lang.
  IllegalArgumentException
extends java.lang.RuntimeException
extends java.lang.Exception
extends java.lang.Throwable
extends java.lang.Object
Constructors
public IllegalArgumentException()
public IllegalArgumentException(String
  s)

▶**IllegalComponentStateException**
public class java.awt.
  IllegalComponentStateException
extends java.lang.IllegalStateException
extends java.lang.RuntimeException
extends java.lang.Exception
extends java.lang.Throwable
extends java.lang.Object
Constructors
public IllegalComponentStateException()

public IllegalComponentStateException(
String s)

▶ILLEGALMONITORSTATEEXCEPTION
public class java.lang.
IllegalMonitorStateException
extends java.lang.RuntimeException
extends java.lang.Exception
extends java.lang.Throwable
extends java.lang.Object

Constructors
public IllegalMonitorStateException()
public IllegalMonitorStateException(
String s)

▶ILLEGALPATHSTATEEXCEPTION
public class java.awt.geom.
IllegalPathStateException
extends java.lang.RuntimeException
extends java.lang.Exception
extends java.lang.Throwable
extends java.lang.Object

Constructors
public IllegalPathStateException()
public IllegalPathStateException(String
s)

▶ILLEGALSTATEEXCEPTION
public class java.lang.
IllegalStateException
extends java.lang.RuntimeException
extends java.lang.Exception
extends java.lang.Throwable
extends java.lang.Object

Constructors
public IllegalStateException()
public IllegalStateException(String s)

▶ILLEGALTHREADSTATEEXCEPTION
public class java.lang.
IllegalThreadStateException
extends java.lang.
IllegalArgumentException
extends java.lang.RuntimeException
extends java.lang.Exception
extends java.lang.Throwable
extends java.lang.Object

Constructors
public IllegalThreadStateException()
public IllegalThreadStateException(
String s)

▶IMAGE
public abstract class java.awt.Image
extends java.lang.Object

Fields
public final static int SCALE_AREA_
AVERAGING
public final static int SCALE_DEFAULT
public final static int SCALE_FAST
public final static int SCALE_REPLICATE
public final static int SCALE_SMOOTH

public final static java.lang.Object
UndefinedProperty

Methods
public abstract void flush()
public abstract Graphics getGraphics()
public abstract int getHeight(
ImageObserver observer)
public abstract Object getProperty(
String name,ImageObserver observer)
public Image getScaledInstance(int width,
int height,int hints)
public abstract ImageProducer getSource()
public abstract int getWidth(
ImageObserver observer)

▶IMAGEFILTER
public class java.awt.image.ImageFilter
implements java.lang.Cloneable
implements java.awt.image.ImageConsumer
extends java.lang.Object

Fields
protected java.awt.image.ImageConsumer
consumer

Methods
public Object clone()
public ImageFilter getFilterInstance(
ImageConsumer ic)
public void imageComplete(int status)
public void resendTopDownLeftRight(
ImageProducer ip)
public void setColorModel(ColorModel
model)
public void setDimensions(int width,int
height)
public void setHints(int hints)
public void setPixels(int x,int y,int w,
int h,ColorModel model,byte pixels,int
off,int scansize)
public void setPixels(int x,int y,int w,
int h,ColorModel model,int pixels,int
off,int scansize)
public void setProperties(Hashtable
props)

▶IMAGEGRAPHICATTRIBUTE
public final class java.awt.font.
ImageGraphicAttribute
extends java.awt.font.GraphicAttribute
extends java.lang.Object

Constructors
public ImageGraphicAttribute(Image
image,int alignment)
public ImageGraphicAttribute(Image
image,int alignment,float originX,float
originY)

Methods
public void draw(Graphics2D graphics,
float x,float y)
public boolean equals(Object rhs)
public boolean equals(
ImageGraphicAttribute rhs)
public float getAdvance()

```
public float getAscent()
public Rectangle2D getBounds()
public float getDescent()
public int hashCode()
```

►**IMAGEICON**
```
public class javax.swing.ImageIcon
implements javax.swing.Icon
implements java.io.Serializable
extends java.lang.Object
```
Fields
```
protected final static java.awt.
  Component component
protected final static java.awt.
  MediaTracker tracker
```
Constructors
```
public  ImageIcon(String filename,String
  description)
public  ImageIcon(String filename)
public  ImageIcon(URL location,String
  description)
public  ImageIcon(URL location)
public  ImageIcon(Image image,String
  description)
public  ImageIcon(Image image)
public  ImageIcon(byte imageData,String
  description)
public  ImageIcon(byte imageData)
public  ImageIcon()
```
Methods
```
public String getDescription()
public int getIconHeight()
public int getIconWidth()
public Image getImage()
public int getImageLoadStatus()
public ImageObserver getImageObserver()
protected void loadImage(Image image)
public synchronized void paintIcon(
  Component c,Graphics g,int x,int y)
public void setDescription(String
  description)
public void setImage(Image image)
public void setImageObserver(
  ImageObserver observer)
```

►**IMAGINGOPEXCEPTION**
```
public class java.awt.image.
  ImagingOpException
extends java.lang.RuntimeException
extends java.lang.Exception
extends java.lang.Throwable
extends java.lang.Object
```
Constructors
```
public  ImagingOpException(String s)
```

►**INCOMPATIBLECLASSCHANGEERROR**
```
public class java.lang.
  IncompatibleClassChangeError
extends java.lang.LinkageError
extends java.lang.Error
extends java.lang.Throwable
extends java.lang.Object
```

Constructors
```
public  IncompatibleClassChangeError()
public  IncompatibleClassChangeError(
  String s)
```

►**INDEXCOLORMODEL**
```
public class java.awt.image.
  IndexColorModel
extends java.awt.image.ColorModel
extends java.lang.Object
```
Constructors
```
public static  IndexColorModel(int bits,
  int size,byte r,byte g,byte b)
public  IndexColorModel(int bits,int
  size,byte r,byte g,byte b,int trans)
public  IndexColorModel(int bits,int
  size,byte r,byte g,byte b,byte a)
public  IndexColorModel(int bits,int
  size,byte cmap,int start,boolean
  hasalpha)
public  IndexColorModel(int bits,int
  size,byte cmap,int start,boolean
  hasalpha,int trans)
public  IndexColorModel(int bits,int
  size,int cmap,int start,boolean hasalpha,
  int trans,int transferType)
```
Methods
```
public BufferedImage
  convertToIntDiscrete(Raster raster,
  boolean forceARGB)
public SampleModel
  createCompatibleSampleModel(int w,int h)
public WritableRaster
  createCompatibleWritableRaster(int w,int
  h)
public void finalize()
public final int getAlpha(int pixel)
public final void getAlphas(byte a)
public final int getBlue(int pixel)
public final void getBlues(byte b)
public int getComponents(int pixel,int
  components,int offset)
public int getComponents(Object pixel,
  int components,int offset)
public int getComponentSize()
public int getDataElement(int components,
  int offset)
public Object getDataElements(int rgb,
  Object pixel)
public Object getDataElements(int
  components,int offset,Object pixel)
public final int getGreen(int pixel)
public final void getGreens(byte g)
public final int getMapSize()
public final int getRed(int pixel)
public final void getReds(byte r)
public final int getRGB(int pixel)
public final void getRGBs(int rgb)
public int getTransparency()
public final int getTransparentPixel()
public boolean isCompatibleRaster(Raster
  raster)
```

```
public boolean isCompatibleSampleModel(
  SampleModel sm)
public String toString()
```

▶INDEXEDPROPERTYDESCRIPTOR
```
public class java.beans.
  IndexedPropertyDescriptor
extends java.beans.PropertyDescriptor
extends java.beans.FeatureDescriptor
extends java.lang.Object
```
Constructors
```
public  IndexedPropertyDescriptor(String
  propertyName,Class beanClass)
public  IndexedPropertyDescriptor(String
  propertyName,Class beanClass,String
  getterName,String setterName,String
  indexedGetterName,String
  indexedSetterName)
public  IndexedPropertyDescriptor(String
  propertyName,Method getter,Method setter,
  Method indexedGetter,Method
  indexedSetter)
 IndexedPropertyDescriptor()
 IndexedPropertyDescriptor()
```
Methods
```
public Class getIndexedPropertyType()
public Method getIndexedReadMethod()
public Method getIndexedWriteMethod()
public void setIndexedReadMethod(Method
  getter)
public void setIndexedWriteMethod(Method
  setter)
```

▶INDEXOUTOFBOUNDSEXCEPTION
```
public class java.lang.
  IndexOutOfBoundsException
extends java.lang.RuntimeException
extends java.lang.Exception
extends java.lang.Throwable
extends java.lang.Object
```
Constructors
```
public  IndexOutOfBoundsException()
public  IndexOutOfBoundsException(String
  s)
```

▶INETADDRESS
```
public final class java.net.InetAddress
implements java.io.Serializable
extends java.lang.Object
```
Constructors
```
static  InetAddress()
 InetAddress()
```
Methods
```
public boolean equals(Object obj)
public byte getAddress()
public static InetAddress getAllByName(
  String host)
public static InetAddress getByName(
  String host)
public String getHostAddress()
public String getHostName()
```

```
public static synchronized InetAddress
  getLocalHost()
public int hashCode()
public boolean isMulticastAddress()
public String toString()
```

▶INFLATER
```
public class java.util.zip.Inflater
extends java.lang.Object
```
Constructors
```
public static  Inflater(boolean nowrap)
public  Inflater()
```
Methods
```
public synchronized void end()
protected void finalize()
public synchronized boolean finished()
public synchronized int getAdler()
public synchronized int getRemaining()
public synchronized int getTotalIn()
public synchronized int getTotalOut()
public synchronized int inflate(byte b,
  int off,int len)
public int inflate(byte b)
public synchronized boolean
  needsDictionary()
public synchronized boolean needsInput()
public synchronized void reset()
public synchronized void setDictionary(
  byte b,int off,int len)
public void setDictionary(byte b)
public synchronized void setInput(byte b,
  int off,int len)
public void setInput(byte b)
```

▶INFLATERINPUTSTREAM
```
public class java.util.zip.
  InflaterInputStream
extends java.io.FilterInputStream
extends java.io.InputStream
extends java.lang.Object
```
Fields
```
protected byte buf
protected java.util.zip.Inflater inf
protected int len
```
Constructors
```
public  InflaterInputStream(InputStream
  in,Inflater inf,int size)
public  InflaterInputStream(InputStream
  in,Inflater inf)
public  InflaterInputStream(InputStream
  in)
```
Methods
```
public int available()
public void close()
protected void fill()
public int read()
public int read(byte b,int off,int len)
public long skip(long n)
```

▶INHERITABLETHREADLOCAL
```
public class java.lang.
  InheritableThreadLocal
```

extends java.lang.ThreadLocal
extends java.lang.Object

Constructors
public InheritableThreadLocal()

Methods
protected Object childValue(Object
  parentValue)

▶**INLINEVIEW**
public class javax.swing.text.html.
  InlineView
extends javax.swing.text.LabelView
extends javax.swing.text.View
extends java.lang.Object

Constructors
public InlineView(Element elem)

Methods
public AttributeSet getAttributes()
protected StyleSheet getStyleSheet()
public boolean isVisible()
protected void
  setPropertiesFromAttributes()

▶**INPUTCONTEXT**
public class java.awt.im.InputContext
extends java.lang.Object

Constructors
protected InputContext()

Methods
public synchronized void dispatchEvent(
  AWTEvent event)
public void dispose()
public synchronized void endComposition()
public Object
  getInputMethodControlObject()
public static InputContext getInstance()
public void removeNotify(Component
  client)
public boolean selectInputMethod(Locale
  locale)
public void setCharacterSubsets(Subset
  subsets)

▶**INPUTEVENT**
public abstract class java.awt.event.
  InputEvent
extends java.awt.event.ComponentEvent
extends java.awt.AWTEvent
extends java.util.EventObject
extends java.lang.Object

Fields
public final static int ALT_GRAPH_MASK
public final static int ALT_MASK
public final static int BUTTON1_MASK
public final static int BUTTON2_MASK
public final static int BUTTON3_MASK
public final static int CTRL_MASK
public final static int META_MASK
public final static int SHIFT_MASK

Constructors
 InputEvent()

Methods
public void consume()
public int getModifiers()
public long getWhen()
public boolean isAltDown()
public boolean isAltGraphDown()
public boolean isConsumed()
public boolean isControlDown()
public boolean isMetaDown()
public boolean isShiftDown()

▶**INPUTMETHODEVENT**
public class java.awt.event.
  InputMethodEvent
extends java.awt.AWTEvent
extends java.util.EventObject
extends java.lang.Object

Fields
public final static int CARET_POSITION_
  CHANGED
public final static int INPUT_METHOD_
  FIRST
public final static int INPUT_METHOD_
  LAST
public final static int INPUT_METHOD_
  TEXT_CHANGED

Constructors
public InputMethodEvent(Component
  source,int id,
  AttributedCharacterIterator text,int
  committedCharacterCount,TextHitInfo
  caret,TextHitInfo visiblePosition)
public InputMethodEvent(Component
  source,int id,TextHitInfo caret,
  TextHitInfo visiblePosition)

Methods
public void consume()
public TextHitInfo getCaret()
public int getCommittedCharacterCount()
public AttributedCharacterIterator
  getText()
public TextHitInfo getVisiblePosition()
public boolean isConsumed()
public String paramString()

▶**INPUTMETHODHIGHLIGHT**
public class java.awt.im.
  InputMethodHighlight
extends java.lang.Object

Fields
public final static int CONVERTED_TEXT
public final static int RAW_TEXT
public final static java.awt.im.
  InputMethodHighlight SELECTED_CONVERTED_
  TEXT_HIGHLIGHT
public final static java.awt.im.
  InputMethodHighlight SELECTED_RAW_TEXT_
  HIGHLIGHT
public final static java.awt.im.
  InputMethodHighlight UNSELECTED_
  CONVERTED_TEXT_HIGHLIGHT

public final static java.awt.im.
  InputMethodHighlight UNSELECTED_RAW_TEXT_
  HIGHLIGHT

Constructors
public InputMethodHighlight(boolean
  selected,int state)
public InputMethodHighlight(boolean
  selected,int state,int variation)

Methods
public int getState()
public int getVariation()
public boolean isSelected()

▶**INPUTSTREAM**
public abstract class java.io.
  InputStream
extends java.lang.Object

Methods
public int available()
public void close()
public synchronized void mark(int
  readlimit)
public boolean markSupported()
public abstract int read()
public int read(byte b)
public int read(byte b,int off,int len)
public synchronized void reset()
public long skip(long n)

▶**INPUTSTREAMREADER**
public class java.io.InputStreamReader
extends java.io.Reader
extends java.lang.Object

Constructors
public InputStreamReader(InputStream in)
public InputStreamReader(InputStream in,
  String enc)
private InputStreamReader()

Methods
public void close()
public String getEncoding()
public int read()
public int read(char cbuf,int off,int
  len)
public boolean ready()

▶**INPUTSUBSET**
public final class java.awt.im.
  InputSubset
extends java.lang.Object

Fields
public final static java.awt.im.
  InputSubset HALFWIDTH_KATAKANA
public final static java.awt.im.
  InputSubset HANJA
public final static java.awt.im.
  InputSubset KANJI
public final static java.awt.im.
  InputSubset LATIN
public final static java.awt.im.
  InputSubset LATIN_DIGITS

public final static java.awt.im.
  InputSubset SIMPLIFIED_HANZI
public final static java.awt.im.
  InputSubset TRADITIONAL_HANZI

Constructors
private InputSubset()

▶**INSETS**
public class java.awt.Insets
implements java.lang.Cloneable
implements java.io.Serializable
extends java.lang.Object

Fields
public int bottom
public int left
public int right
public int top

Constructors
public static Insets(int top,int left,
  int bottom,int right)

Methods
public Object clone()
public boolean equals(Object obj)
public String toString()

▶**INSETSUIRESOURCE**
public class javax.swing.plaf.
  InsetsUIResource
implements javax.swing.plaf.UIResource
extends java.awt.Insets
extends java.lang.Object

Constructors
public InsetsUIResource(int top,int
  left,int bottom,int right)

▶**INSTANTIATIONERROR**
public class java.lang.
  InstantiationError
extends java.lang.
  IncompatibleClassChangeError
extends java.lang.LinkageError
extends java.lang.Error
extends java.lang.Throwable
extends java.lang.Object

Constructors
public InstantiationError()
public InstantiationError(String s)

▶**INSTANTIATIONEXCEPTION**
public class java.lang.
  InstantiationException
extends java.lang.Exception
extends java.lang.Throwable
extends java.lang.Object

Constructors
public InstantiationException()
public InstantiationException(String s)

▶**INTEGER**
public final class java.lang.Integer
implements java.lang.Comparable
extends java.lang.Number

extends java.lang.Object
Fields
public final static int MAX_VALUE
public final static int MIN_VALUE
public final static java.lang.Class
  TYPE
Constructors
public Integer(int value)
public Integer(String s)
Methods
public byte byteValue()
public int compareTo(Integer
  anotherInteger)
public int compareTo(Object o)
public static Integer decode(String nm)
public double doubleValue()
public boolean equals(Object obj)
public float floatValue()
public static Integer getInteger(String
  nm)
public static Integer getInteger(String
  nm,int val)
public static Integer getInteger(String
  nm,Integer val)
public int hashCode()
public int intValue()
public long longValue()
public static int parseInt(String s,int
  radix)
public static int parseInt(String s)
public short shortValue()
public static String toBinaryString(int
  i)
public static String toHexString(int i)
public static String toOctalString(int i)
public static String toString(int i,int
  radix)
public static String toString(int i)
public String toString()
public static Integer valueOf(String s,
  int radix)
public static Integer valueOf(String s)

▶**INTERNALERROR**
public class java.lang.InternalError
extends java.lang.VirtualMachineError
extends java.lang.Error
extends java.lang.Throwable
extends java.lang.Object
Constructors
public InternalError()
public InternalError(String s)

▶**INTERNALFRAMEADAPTER**
public abstract class javax.swing.event.
  InternalFrameAdapter
implements javax.swing.event.
  InternalFrameListener
extends java.lang.Object
Methods
public void internalFrameActivated(
  InternalFrameEvent e)

public void internalFrameClosed(
  InternalFrameEvent e)
public void internalFrameClosing(
  InternalFrameEvent e)
public void internalFrameDeactivated(
  InternalFrameEvent e)
public void internalFrameDeiconified(
  InternalFrameEvent e)
public void internalFrameIconified(
  InternalFrameEvent e)
public void internalFrameOpened(
  InternalFrameEvent e)

▶**INTERNALFRAMEEVENT**
public class javax.swing.event.
  InternalFrameEvent
extends java.awt.AWTEvent
extends java.util.EventObject
extends java.lang.Object
Fields
public final static int INTERNAL_FRAME_
  ACTIVATED
public final static int INTERNAL_FRAME_
  CLOSED
public final static int INTERNAL_FRAME_
  CLOSING
public final static int INTERNAL_FRAME_
  DEACTIVATED
public final static int INTERNAL_FRAME_
  DEICONIFIED
public final static int INTERNAL_FRAME_
  FIRST
public final static int INTERNAL_FRAME_
  ICONIFIED
public final static int INTERNAL_FRAME_
  LAST
public final static int INTERNAL_FRAME_
  OPENED
Constructors
public InternalFrameEvent(
  JInternalFrame source,int id)
Methods
public String paramString()

▶**INTERNALFRAMEUI**
public abstract class javax.swing.plaf.
  InternalFrameUI
extends javax.swing.plaf.ComponentUI
extends java.lang.Object

▶**INTERRUPTEDEXCEPTION**
public class java.lang.
  InterruptedException
extends java.lang.Exception
extends java.lang.Throwable
extends java.lang.Object
Constructors
public InterruptedException()
public InterruptedException(String s)

▸**INTERRUPTEDIOEXCEPTION**
public class java.io.
  InterruptedIOException
extends java.io.IOException
extends java.lang.Exception
extends java.lang.Throwable
extends java.lang.Object

Fields
public int bytesTransferred

Constructors
public InterruptedIOException()
public InterruptedIOException(String s)

▸**INTROSPECTIONEXCEPTION**
public class java.beans.
  IntrospectionException
extends java.lang.Exception
extends java.lang.Throwable
extends java.lang.Object

Constructors
public IntrospectionException(String
  mess)

▸**INTROSPECTOR**
public class java.beans.Introspector
extends java.lang.Object

Fields
public final static int IGNORE_ALL_
  BEANINFO
public final static int IGNORE_IMMEDIATE_
  BEANINFO
public final static int USE_ALL_
  BEANINFO

Constructors
private Introspector()

Methods
public static String decapitalize(String
  name)
public static void flushCaches()
public static void flushFromCaches(Class
  clz)
public static BeanInfo getBeanInfo(Class
  beanClass)
public static BeanInfo getBeanInfo(Class
  beanClass,int flags)
public static BeanInfo getBeanInfo(Class
  beanClass,Class stopClass)
public static synchronized String
  getBeanInfoSearchPath()
public static synchronized void
  setBeanInfoSearchPath(String path)

▸**INVALIDALGORITHMPARAMETEREXCEPTION**
public class java.security.
  InvalidAlgorithmParameterException
extends java.security.
  GeneralSecurityException
extends java.lang.Exception
extends java.lang.Throwable
extends java.lang.Object

Constructors
public
  InvalidAlgorithmParameterException()
public
  InvalidAlgorithmParameterException(
  String msg)

▸**INVALIDCLASSEXCEPTION**
public class java.io.
  InvalidClassException
extends java.io.ObjectStreamException
extends java.io.IOException
extends java.lang.Exception
extends java.lang.Throwable
extends java.lang.Object

Fields
public java.lang.String classname

Constructors
public InvalidClassException(String
  reason)
public InvalidClassException(String
  cname,String reason)

Methods
public String getMessage()

▸**INVALIDDNDOPERATIONEXCEPTION**
public class java.awt.dnd.
  InvalidDnDOperationException
extends java.lang.IllegalStateException
extends java.lang.RuntimeException
extends java.lang.Exception
extends java.lang.Throwable
extends java.lang.Object

Constructors
public InvalidDnDOperationException()
public InvalidDnDOperationException(
  String msg)

▸**INVALIDKEYEXCEPTION**
public class java.security.
  InvalidKeyException
extends java.security.KeyException
extends java.security.
  GeneralSecurityException
extends java.lang.Exception
extends java.lang.Throwable
extends java.lang.Object

Constructors
public InvalidKeyException()
public InvalidKeyException(String msg)

▸**INVALIDKEYSPECEXCEPTION**
public class java.security.spec.
  InvalidKeySpecException
extends java.security.
  GeneralSecurityException
extends java.lang.Exception
extends java.lang.Throwable
extends java.lang.Object

Constructors
public InvalidKeySpecException()

```
public  InvalidKeySpecException(String
  msg).
```

►INVALIDOBJECTEXCEPTION
```
public class java.io.
  InvalidObjectException
extends java.io.ObjectStreamException
extends java.io.IOException
extends java.lang.Exception
extends java.lang.Throwable
extends java.lang.Object
```
Constructors
```
public  InvalidObjectException(String
  reason)
```

►INVALIDPARAMETEREXCEPTION
```
public class java.security.
  InvalidParameterException
extends java.lang.
  IllegalArgumentException
extends java.lang.RuntimeException
extends java.lang.Exception
extends java.lang.Throwable
extends java.lang.Object
```
Constructors
```
public  InvalidParameterException()
public  InvalidParameterException(String
  msg)
```

►INVALIDPARAMETERSPECEXCEPTION
```
public class java.security.spec.
  InvalidParameterSpecException
extends java.security.
  GeneralSecurityException
extends java.lang.Exception
extends java.lang.Throwable
extends java.lang.Object
```
Constructors
```
public  InvalidParameterSpecException()
public  InvalidParameterSpecException(
  String msg)
```

►INVOCATIONEVENT
```
public class java.awt.event.
  InvocationEvent
implements java.awt.ActiveEvent
extends java.awt.AWTEvent
extends java.util.EventObject
extends java.lang.Object
```
Fields
```
protected boolean catchExceptions
public final static int INVOCATION_
  DEFAULT
public final static int INVOCATION_
  FIRST
public final static int INVOCATION_LAST
protected java.lang.Object notifier
protected java.lang.Runnable runnable
```
Constructors
```
public  InvocationEvent(Object source,
  Runnable runnable)
```
```
public  InvocationEvent(Object source,
  Runnable runnable,Object notifier,
  boolean catchExceptions)
protected  InvocationEvent(Object source,
  int id,Runnable runnable,Object notifier,
  boolean catchExceptions)
```
Methods
```
public void dispatch()
public Exception getException()
public String paramString()
```

►INVOCATIONTARGETEXCEPTION
```
public class java.lang.reflect.
  InvocationTargetException
extends java.lang.Exception
extends java.lang.Throwable
extends java.lang.Object
```
Constructors
```
protected  InvocationTargetException()
public  InvocationTargetException(
  Throwable target)
public  InvocationTargetException(
  Throwable target,String s)
```
Methods
```
public Throwable getTargetException()
public void printStackTrace()
public void printStackTrace(PrintStream
  ps)
public void printStackTrace(PrintWriter
  pw)
```

►IOEXCEPTION
```
public class java.io.IOException
extends java.lang.Exception
extends java.lang.Throwable
extends java.lang.Object
```
Constructors
```
public  IOException()
public  IOException(String s)
```

►ITEMEVENT
```
public class java.awt.event.ItemEvent
extends java.awt.AWTEvent
extends java.util.EventObject
extends java.lang.Object
```
Fields
```
public final static int DESELECTED
public final static int ITEM_FIRST
public final static int ITEM_LAST
public final static int ITEM_STATE_
  CHANGED
public final static int SELECTED
```
Constructors
```
public  ItemEvent(ItemSelectable source,
  int id,Object item,int stateChange)
```
Methods
```
public Object getItem()
public ItemSelectable getItemSelectable()
public int getStateChange()
public String paramString()
```

▸JAPPLET
public class javax.swing.JApplet
implements javax.accessibility.
  Accessible
implements javax.swing.
  RootPaneContainer
extends java.applet.Applet
extends java.awt.Panel
extends java.awt.Container
extends java.awt.Component
extends java.lang.Object

Fields
protected javax.accessibility.
  AccessibleContext accessibleContext
protected javax.swing.JRootPane
  rootPane
protected boolean
  rootPaneCheckingEnabled

Constructors
public JApplet()

Methods
protected void addImpl(Component comp,
  Object constraints,int index)
protected JRootPane createRootPane()
public AccessibleContext
  getAccessibleContext()
public Container getContentPane()
public Component getGlassPane()
public JMenuBar getJMenuBar()
public JLayeredPane getLayeredPane()
public JRootPane getRootPane()
protected boolean
  isRootPaneCheckingEnabled()
protected String paramString()
protected void processKeyEvent(KeyEvent
  e)
public void setContentPane(Container
  contentPane)
public void setGlassPane(Component
  glassPane)
public void setJMenuBar(JMenuBar menuBar)
public void setLayeredPane(JLayeredPane
  layeredPane)
public void setLayout(LayoutManager
  manager)
protected void setRootPane(JRootPane
  root)
protected void
  setRootPaneCheckingEnabled(boolean
  enabled)
public void update(Graphics g)

▸JARENTRY
public class java.util.jar.JarEntry
extends java.util.zip.ZipEntry
extends java.lang.Object

Constructors
public JarEntry(String name)
public JarEntry(ZipEntry ze)
public JarEntry(JarEntry je)

Methods
public Attributes getAttributes()

public Certificate getCertificates()

▸JAREXCEPTION
public class java.util.jar.JarException
extends java.util.zip.ZipException
extends java.io.IOException
extends java.lang.Exception
extends java.lang.Throwable
extends java.lang.Object

Constructors
public JarException()
public JarException(String s)

▸JARFILE
public class java.util.jar.JarFile
extends java.util.zip.ZipFile
extends java.lang.Object

Fields
public final static java.lang.String
  MANIFEST_NAME

Constructors
public JarFile(String name)
public JarFile(String name,boolean
  verify)
public JarFile(File file)
public JarFile(File file,boolean verify)

Methods
public Enumeration entries()
public ZipEntry getEntry(String name)
public synchronized InputStream
  getInputStream(ZipEntry ze)
public JarEntry getJarEntry(String name)
public Manifest getManifest()

▸JARINPUTSTREAM
public class java.util.jar.
  JarInputStream
extends java.util.zip.ZipInputStream
extends java.util.zip.
  InflaterInputStream
extends java.io.FilterInputStream
extends java.io.InputStream
extends java.lang.Object

Constructors
public JarInputStream(InputStream in)
public JarInputStream(InputStream in,
  boolean verify)

Methods
protected ZipEntry createZipEntry(String
  name)
public Manifest getManifest()
public ZipEntry getNextEntry()
public JarEntry getNextJarEntry()
public int read(byte b,int off,int len)

▸JAROUTPUTSTREAM
public class java.util.jar.
  JarOutputStream
extends java.util.zip.ZipOutputStream
extends java.util.zip.
  DeflaterOutputStream
extends java.io.FilterOutputStream

extends java.io.OutputStream
extends java.lang.Object
Constructors
public JarOutputStream(OutputStream out,
  Manifest man)
public JarOutputStream(OutputStream out)
Methods
public void putNextEntry(ZipEntry ze)

▶**JarURLConnection**
public abstract class java.net.
  JarURLConnection
extends java.net.URLConnection
extends java.lang.Object
Fields
protected java.net.URLConnection
  jarFileURLConnection
Constructors
protected JarURLConnection(URL url)
Methods
public Attributes getAttributes()
public Certificate getCertificates()
public String getEntryName()
public JarEntry getJarEntry()
public abstract JarFile getJarFile()
public URL getJarFileURL()
public Attributes getMainAttributes()
public Manifest getManifest()

▶**JButton**
public class javax.swing.JButton
implements javax.accessibility.
  Accessible
extends javax.swing.AbstractButton
extends javax.swing.JComponent
extends java.awt.Container
extends java.awt.Component
extends java.lang.Object
Constructors
public JButton()
public JButton(Icon icon)
public JButton(String text)
public JButton(String text,Icon icon)
Methods
public AccessibleContext
  getAccessibleContext()
public String getUIClassID()
public boolean isDefaultButton()
public boolean isDefaultCapable()
protected String paramString()
public void setDefaultCapable(boolean
  defaultCapable)
public void updateUI()

▶**JCheckBox**
public class javax.swing.JCheckBox
implements javax.accessibility.
  Accessible
extends javax.swing.JToggleButton
extends javax.swing.AbstractButton
extends javax.swing.JComponent

extends java.awt.Container
extends java.awt.Component
extends java.lang.Object
Constructors
public JCheckBox()
public JCheckBox(Icon icon)
public JCheckBox(Icon icon,boolean
  selected)
public JCheckBox(String text)
public JCheckBox(String text,boolean
  selected)
public JCheckBox(String text,Icon icon)
public JCheckBox(String text,Icon icon,
  boolean selected)
Methods
public AccessibleContext
  getAccessibleContext()
public String getUIClassID()
protected String paramString()
public void updateUI()

▶**JCheckBoxMenuItem**
public class javax.swing.
  JCheckBoxMenuItem
implements javax.accessibility.
  Accessible
implements javax.swing.SwingConstants
extends javax.swing.JMenuItem
extends javax.swing.AbstractButton
extends javax.swing.JComponent
extends java.awt.Container
extends java.awt.Component
extends java.lang.Object
Constructors
public JCheckBoxMenuItem()
public JCheckBoxMenuItem(Icon icon)
public JCheckBoxMenuItem(String text)
public JCheckBoxMenuItem(String text,
  Icon icon)
public JCheckBoxMenuItem(String text,
  boolean b)
public JCheckBoxMenuItem(String text,
  Icon icon,boolean b)
Methods
public AccessibleContext
  getAccessibleContext()
public synchronized Object
  getSelectedObjects()
public boolean getState()
public String getUIClassID()
protected void init(String text,Icon
  icon)
protected String paramString()
public void requestFocus()
public synchronized void setState(
  boolean b)
public void updateUI()

▶**JColorChooser**
public class javax.swing.JColorChooser
implements javax.accessibility.
  Accessible

extends javax.swing.JComponent
extends java.awt.Container
extends java.awt.Component
extends java.lang.Object

Fields

protected javax.accessibility.
  AccessibleContext accessibleContext
public final static java.lang.String
  CHOOSER_PANELS_PROPERTY
public final static java.lang.String
  PREVIEW_PANEL_PROPERTY
public final static java.lang.String
  SELECTION_MODEL_PROPERTY

Constructors

public JColorChooser()
public JColorChooser(Color initialColor)
public JColorChooser(
  ColorSelectionModel model)

Methods

public void addChooserPanel(
  AbstractColorChooserPanel panel)
public static JDialog createDialog(
  Component c,String title,boolean modal,
  JColorChooser chooserPane,ActionListener
  okListener,ActionListener cancelListener)
public AccessibleContext
  getAccessibleContext()
public AbstractColorChooserPanel
  getChooserPanels()
public Color getColor()
public JComponent getPreviewPanel()
public ColorSelectionModel
  getSelectionModel()
public ColorChooserUI getUI()
public String getUIClassID()
protected String paramString()
public AbstractColorChooserPanel
  removeChooserPanel(
  AbstractColorChooserPanel panel)
public void setChooserPanels(
  AbstractColorChooserPanel panels)
public void setColor(Color color)
public void setColor(int r,int g,int b)
public void setColor(int c)
public void setPreviewPanel(JComponent
  preview)
public void setSelectionModel(
  ColorSelectionModel newModel)
public void setUI(ColorChooserUI ui)
public static Color showDialog(Component
  component,String title,Color
  initialColor)
public void updateUI()

▶JComboBox

public class javax.swing.JComboBox
implements javax.accessibility.
  Accessible
implements java.awt.event.
  ActionListener
implements java.awt.ItemSelectable

implements javax.swing.event.
  ListDataListener
extends javax.swing.JComponent
extends java.awt.Container
extends java.awt.Component
extends java.lang.Object

Fields

protected java.lang.String
  actionCommand
protected javax.swing.ComboBoxModel
  dataModel
protected javax.swing.ComboBoxEditor
  editor
protected boolean isEditable
protected KeySelectionManager
  keySelectionManager
protected boolean
  lightWeightPopupEnabled
protected int maximumRowCount
protected javax.swing.ListCellRenderer
  renderer
protected java.lang.Object
  selectedItemReminder

Constructors

public JComboBox(ComboBoxModel aModel)
public JComboBox(Object items)
public JComboBox(Vector items)
public JComboBox()

Methods

public void actionPerformed(ActionEvent
  e)
public void addActionListener(
  ActionListener l)
public void addItem(Object anObject)
public void addItemListener(ItemListener
  aListener)
public void configureEditor(
  ComboBoxEditor anEditor,Object anItem)
public void contentsChanged(
  ListDataEvent e)
protected KeySelectionManager
  createDefaultKeySelectionManager()
protected void fireActionEvent()
protected void fireItemStateChanged(
  ItemEvent e)
public AccessibleContext
  getAccessibleContext()
public String getActionCommand()
public ComboBoxEditor getEditor()
public Object getItemAt(int index)
public int getItemCount()
public KeySelectionManager
  getKeySelectionManager()
public int getMaximumRowCount()
public ComboBoxModel getModel()
public ListCellRenderer getRenderer()
public int getSelectedIndex()
public Object getSelectedItem()
public Object getSelectedObjects()
public ComboBoxUI getUI()
public String getUIClassID()
public void hidePopup()

public void insertItemAt(Object anObject,
  int index)
protected void installAncestorListener()
public void intervalAdded(ListDataEvent
  e)
public void intervalRemoved(
  ListDataEvent e)
public boolean isEditable()
public boolean isFocusTraversable()
public boolean isLightWeightPopupEnabled(
)
public boolean isPopupVisible()
protected String paramString()
public void processKeyEvent(KeyEvent e)
public void removeActionListener(
  ActionListener l)
public void removeAllItems()
public void removeItem(Object anObject)
public void removeItemAt(int anIndex)
public void removeItemListener(
  ItemListener aListener)
protected void selectedItemChanged()
public boolean selectWithKeyChar(char
  keyChar)
public void setActionCommand(String
  aCommand)
public void setEditable(boolean aFlag)
public void setEditor(ComboBoxEditor
  anEditor)
public void setEnabled(boolean b)
public void setKeySelectionManager(
  KeySelectionManager aManager)
public void setLightWeightPopupEnabled(
  boolean aFlag)
public void setMaximumRowCount(int count)
public void setModel(ComboBoxModel
  aModel)
public void setPopupVisible(boolean v)
public void setRenderer(ListCellRenderer
  aRenderer)
public void setSelectedIndex(int anIndex)
public void setSelectedItem(Object
  anObject)
public void setUI(ComboBoxUI ui)
public void showPopup()
public void updateUI()

▶JCOMPONENT
public abstract class javax.swing.
  JComponent
implements java.io.Serializable
extends java.awt.Container
extends java.awt.Component
extends java.lang.Object

Fields
protected javax.accessibility.
  AccessibleContext accessibleContext
protected javax.swing.event.
  EventListenerList listenerList
public final static java.lang.String
  TOOL_TIP_TEXT_KEY

protected transient javax.swing.plaf.
  ComponentUI ui
public final static int UNDEFINED_
  CONDITION
public final static int WHEN_ANCESTOR_OF_
  FOCUSED_COMPONENT
public final static int WHEN_FOCUSED
public final static int WHEN_IN_FOCUSED_
  WINDOW

Constructors
public JComponent()

Methods
public void addAncestorListener(
  AncestorListener listener)
public void addNotify()
public synchronized void
  addPropertyChangeListener(
  PropertyChangeListener listener)
public synchronized void
  addVetoableChangeListener(
  VetoableChangeListener listener)
public void computeVisibleRect(Rectangle
  visibleRect)
public boolean contains(int x,int y)
public JToolTip createToolTip()
protected void firePropertyChange(String
  propertyName,Object oldValue,Object
  newValue)
public void firePropertyChange(String
  propertyName,byte oldValue,byte newValue)
public void firePropertyChange(String
  propertyName,char oldValue,char newValue)
public void firePropertyChange(String
  propertyName,short oldValue,short
  newValue)
public void firePropertyChange(String
  propertyName,int oldValue,int newValue)
public void firePropertyChange(String
  propertyName,long oldValue,long newValue)
public void firePropertyChange(String
  propertyName,float oldValue,float
  newValue)
public void firePropertyChange(String
  propertyName,double oldValue,double
  newValue)
public void firePropertyChange(String
  propertyName,boolean oldValue,boolean
  newValue)
protected void fireVetoableChange(String
  propertyName,Object oldValue,Object
  newValue)
public AccessibleContext
  getAccessibleContext()
public ActionListener
  getActionForKeyStroke(KeyStroke
  aKeyStroke)
public float getAlignmentX()
public float getAlignmentY()
public boolean getAutoscrolls()
public Border getBorder()
public Rectangle getBounds(Rectangle rv)

```
public final Object getClientProperty(
  Object key)
protected Graphics getComponentGraphics(
  Graphics g)
public int getConditionForKeyStroke(
  KeyStroke aKeyStroke)
public int getDebugGraphicsOptions()
public Graphics getGraphics()
public int getHeight()
public Insets getInsets()
public Insets getInsets(Insets insets)
public Point getLocation(Point rv)
public Dimension getMaximumSize()
public Dimension getMinimumSize()
public Component
  getNextFocusableComponent()
public Dimension getPreferredSize()
public KeyStroke getRegisteredKeyStrokes(
  )
public JRootPane getRootPane()
public Dimension getSize(Dimension rv)
public Point getToolTipLocation(
  MouseEvent event)
public String getToolTipText()
public String getToolTipText(MouseEvent
  event)
public Container getTopLevelAncestor()
public String getUIClassID()
public Rectangle getVisibleRect()
public int getWidth()
public int getX()
public int getY()
public void grabFocus()
public boolean hasFocus()
public boolean isDoubleBuffered()
public boolean isFocusCycleRoot()
public boolean isFocusTraversable()
public static boolean
  isLightweightComponent(Component c)
public boolean isManagingFocus()
public boolean isOpaque()
public boolean isOptimizedDrawingEnabled(
  )
public boolean isPaintingTile()
public boolean isRequestFocusEnabled()
public boolean isValidateRoot()
public void paint(Graphics g)
protected void paintBorder(Graphics g)
protected void paintChildren(Graphics g)
protected void paintComponent(Graphics g)
public void paintImmediately(int x,int y,
  int w,int h)
public void paintImmediately(Rectangle r)
protected String paramString()
protected void processComponentKeyEvent(
  KeyEvent e)
protected void processFocusEvent(
  FocusEvent e)
protected void processKeyEvent(KeyEvent
  e)
protected void processMouseMotionEvent(
  MouseEvent e)
```

```
public final void putClientProperty(
  Object key,Object value)
public void registerKeyboardAction(
  ActionListener anAction,String aCommand,
  KeyStroke aKeyStroke,int aCondition)
public void registerKeyboardAction(
  ActionListener anAction,KeyStroke
  aKeyStroke,int aCondition)
public void removeAncestorListener(
  AncestorListener listener)
public void removeNotify()
public synchronized void
  removePropertyChangeListener(
  PropertyChangeListener listener)
public synchronized void
  removeVetoableChangeListener(
  VetoableChangeListener listener)
public void repaint(long tm,int x,int y,
  int width,int height)
public void repaint(Rectangle r)
public boolean requestDefaultFocus()
public void requestFocus()
public void resetKeyboardActions()
public void reshape(int x,int y,int w,
  int h)
public void revalidate()
public void scrollRectToVisible(
  Rectangle aRect)
public void setAlignmentX(float
  alignmentX)
public void setAlignmentY(float
  alignmentY)
public void setAutoscrolls(boolean
  autoscrolls)
public void setBackground(Color bg)
public void setBorder(Border border)
public void setDebugGraphicsOptions(int
  debugOptions)
public void setDoubleBuffered(boolean
  aFlag)
public void setEnabled(boolean enabled)
public void setFont(Font font)
public void setForeground(Color fg)
public void setMaximumSize(Dimension
  maximumSize)
public void setMinimumSize(Dimension
  minimumSize)
public void setNextFocusableComponent(
  Component aComponent)
public void setOpaque(boolean isOpaque)
public void setPreferredSize(Dimension
  preferredSize)
public void setRequestFocusEnabled(
  boolean aFlag)
public void setToolTipText(String text)
protected void setUI(ComponentUI newUI)
public void setVisible(boolean aFlag)
public void unregisterKeyboardAction(
  KeyStroke aKeyStroke)
public void update(Graphics g)
public void updateUI()
```

►JDESKTOPPANE

public class javax.swing.JDesktopPane
implements javax.accessibility.
  Accessible
extends javax.swing.JLayeredPane
extends javax.swing.JComponent
extends java.awt.Container
extends java.awt.Component
extends java.lang.Object

Constructors

public JDesktopPane()

Methods

public AccessibleContext
  getAccessibleContext()
public JInternalFrame getAllFrames()
public JInternalFrame
  getAllFramesInLayer(int layer)
public DesktopManager getDesktopManager()
public DesktopPaneUI getUI()
public String getUIClassID()
public boolean isOpaque()
protected String paramString()
public void setDesktopManager(
  DesktopManager d)
public void setUI(DesktopPaneUI ui)
public void updateUI()

►JDIALOG

public class javax.swing.JDialog
implements javax.accessibility.
  Accessible
implements javax.swing.
  RootPaneContainer
implements javax.swing.WindowConstants
extends java.awt.Dialog
extends java.awt.Window
extends java.awt.Container
extends java.awt.Component
extends java.lang.Object

Fields

protected javax.accessibility.
  AccessibleContext accessibleContext
protected javax.swing.JRootPane
  rootPane
protected boolean
  rootPaneCheckingEnabled

Constructors

public JDialog()
public JDialog(Frame owner)
public JDialog(Frame owner,boolean
  modal)
public JDialog(Frame owner,String title)
public JDialog(Frame owner,String title,
  boolean modal)
public JDialog(Dialog owner)
public JDialog(Dialog owner,boolean
  modal)
public JDialog(Dialog owner,String
  title)
public JDialog(Dialog owner,String
  title,boolean modal)

Methods

protected void addImpl(Component comp,
  Object constraints,int index)
protected JRootPane createRootPane()
protected void dialogInit()
public AccessibleContext
  getAccessibleContext()
public Container getContentPane()
public int getDefaultCloseOperation()
public Component getGlassPane()
public JMenuBar getJMenuBar()
public JLayeredPane getLayeredPane()
public JRootPane getRootPane()
protected boolean
  isRootPaneCheckingEnabled()
protected String paramString()
protected void processWindowEvent(
  WindowEvent e)
public void setContentPane(Container
  contentPane)
public void setDefaultCloseOperation(int
  operation)
public void setGlassPane(Component
  glassPane)
public void setJMenuBar(JMenuBar menu)
public void setLayeredPane(JLayeredPane
  layeredPane)
public void setLayout(LayoutManager
  manager)
public void setLocationRelativeTo(
  Component c)
protected void setRootPane(JRootPane
  root)
protected void
  setRootPaneCheckingEnabled(boolean
  enabled)
public void update(Graphics g)

►JEDITORPANE

public class javax.swing.JEditorPane
extends javax.swing.text.JTextComponent
extends javax.swing.JComponent
extends java.awt.Container
extends java.awt.Component
extends java.lang.Object

Constructors

public JEditorPane()
public JEditorPane(URL initialPage)
public JEditorPane(String url)
public JEditorPane(String type,String
  text)

Methods

public synchronized void
  addHyperlinkListener(HyperlinkListener
  listener)
protected EditorKit
  createDefaultEditorKit()
public static EditorKit
  createEditorKitForContentType(String
  type)
public void fireHyperlinkUpdate(
  HyperlinkEvent e)

```
public AccessibleContext
  getAccessibleContext()
public final String getContentType()
public final EditorKit getEditorKit()
public EditorKit
  getEditorKitForContentType(String type)
public URL getPage()
public Dimension getPreferredSize()
public boolean
  getScrollableTracksViewportHeight()
public boolean
  getScrollableTracksViewportWidth()
protected InputStream getStream(URL page)
public String getText()
public String getUIClassID()
public boolean isManagingFocus()
protected static String paramString()
protected void processComponentKeyEvent(
  KeyEvent e)
public void read(InputStream in,Object
  desc)
public static void
  registerEditorKitForContentType(String
  type,String classname)
public static void
  registerEditorKitForContentType(String
  type,String classname,ClassLoader loader)
public synchronized void
  removeHyperlinkListener(
  HyperlinkListener listener)
public void replaceSelection(String
  content)
protected void scrollToReference(String
  reference)
public final void setContentType(String
  type)
public void setEditorKit(EditorKit kit)
public void setEditorKitForContentType(
  String type,EditorKit k)
public void setPage(URL page)
public void setPage(String url)
public void setText(String t)
```

▶JFileChooser

```
public class javax.swing.JFileChooser
implements javax.accessibility.
  Accessible
extends javax.swing.JComponent
extends java.awt.Container
extends java.awt.Component
extends java.lang.Object
```

Fields

```
protected javax.accessibility.
  AccessibleContext accessibleContext
public final static java.lang.String
  ACCESSORY_CHANGED_PROPERTY
public final static java.lang.String
  APPROVE_BUTTON_MNEMONIC_CHANGED_
  PROPERTY
public final static java.lang.String
  APPROVE_BUTTON_TEXT_CHANGED_PROPERTY
public final static java.lang.String
  APPROVE_BUTTON_TOOL_TIP_TEXT_CHANGED_
  PROPERTY
public final static int APPROVE_OPTION
public final static java.lang.String
  APPROVE_SELECTION
public final static int CANCEL_OPTION
public final static java.lang.String
  CANCEL_SELECTION
public final static java.lang.String
  CHOOSABLE_FILE_FILTER_CHANGED_PROPERTY
public final static int CUSTOM_DIALOG
public final static java.lang.String
  DIALOG_TITLE_CHANGED_PROPERTY
public final static java.lang.String
  DIALOG_TYPE_CHANGED_PROPERTY
public final static int DIRECTORIES_
  ONLY
public final static java.lang.String
  DIRECTORY_CHANGED_PROPERTY
public final static int ERROR_OPTION
public final static int FILES_AND_
  DIRECTORIES
public final static int FILES_ONLY
public final static java.lang.String
  FILE_FILTER_CHANGED_PROPERTY
public final static java.lang.String
  FILE_HIDING_CHANGED_PROPERTY
public final static java.lang.String
  FILE_SELECTION_MODE_CHANGED_PROPERTY
public final static java.lang.String
  FILE_SYSTEM_VIEW_CHANGED_PROPERTY
public final static java.lang.String
  FILE_VIEW_CHANGED_PROPERTY
public final static java.lang.String
  MULTI_SELECTION_ENABLED_CHANGED_
  PROPERTY
public final static int OPEN_DIALOG
public final static int SAVE_DIALOG
public final static java.lang.String
  SELECTED_FILES_CHANGED_PROPERTY
public final static java.lang.String
  SELECTED_FILE_CHANGED_PROPERTY
```

Constructors

```
public  JFileChooser()
public  JFileChooser(String
  currentDirectoryPath)
public  JFileChooser(File
  currentDirectory)
public  JFileChooser(FileSystemView fsv)
public  JFileChooser(File
  currentDirectory,FileSystemView fsv)
public  JFileChooser(String
  currentDirectoryPath,FileSystemView fsv)
```

Methods

```
public boolean accept(File f)
public void addActionListener(
  ActionListener l)
public void addChoosableFileFilter(
  FileFilter filter)
public void approveSelection()
public void cancelSelection()
```

```
public void changeToParentDirectory()
public void ensureFileIsVisible(File f)
protected void fireActionPerformed(
  String command)
public FileFilter getAcceptAllFileFilter(
  )
public AccessibleContext
  getAccessibleContext()
public JComponent getAccessory()
public int getApproveButtonMnemonic()
public String getApproveButtonText()
public String
  getApproveButtonToolTipText()
public FileFilter
  getChoosableFileFilters()
public File getCurrentDirectory()
public String getDescription(File f)
public String getDialogTitle()
public int getDialogType()
public FileFilter getFileFilter()
public int getFileSelectionMode()
public FileSystemView getFileSystemView()
public FileView getFileView()
public Icon getIcon(File f)
public String getName(File f)
public File getSelectedFile()
public File getSelectedFiles()
public String getTypeDescription(File f)
public FileChooserUI getUI()
public String getUIClassID()
public boolean
  isDirectorySelectionEnabled()
public boolean isFileHidingEnabled()
public boolean isFileSelectionEnabled()
public boolean isMultiSelectionEnabled()
public boolean isTraversable(File f)
protected String paramString()
public void removeActionListener(
  ActionListener l)
public boolean removeChoosableFileFilter(
  FileFilter f)
public void rescanCurrentDirectory()
public void resetChoosableFileFilters()
public void setAccessory(JComponent
  newAccessory)
public void setApproveButtonMnemonic(int
  mnemonic)
public void setApproveButtonMnemonic(
  char mnemonic)
public void setApproveButtonText(String
  approveButtonText)
public void setApproveButtonToolTipText(
  String toolTipText)
public void setCurrentDirectory(File dir)
public void setDialogTitle(String
  dialogTitle)
public void setDialogType(int dialogType)
public void setFileFilter(FileFilter
  filter)
public void setFileHidingEnabled(boolean
  b)
```

```
public void setFileSelectionMode(int
  mode)
public void setFileSystemView(
  FileSystemView fsv)
public void setFileView(FileView
  fileView)
public void setMultiSelectionEnabled(
  boolean b)
public void setSelectedFile(File
  selectedFile)
public void setSelectedFiles(File
  selectedFiles)
protected void setup(FileSystemView view)
public int showDialog(Component parent,
  String approveButtonText)
public int showOpenDialog(Component
  parent)
public int showSaveDialog(Component
  parent)
public void updateUI()
```

▸JFRAME
```
public class javax.swing.JFrame
implements javax.accessibility.
  Accessible
implements javax.swing.
  RootPaneContainer
implements javax.swing.WindowConstants
extends java.awt.Frame
extends java.awt.Window
extends java.awt.Container
extends java.awt.Component
extends java.lang.Object
```

Fields
```
protected javax.accessibility.
  AccessibleContext accessibleContext
protected javax.swing.JRootPane
  rootPane
protected boolean
  rootPaneCheckingEnabled
```

Constructors
```
public  JFrame()
public  JFrame(String title)
```

Methods
```
protected void addImpl(Component comp,
  Object constraints,int index)
protected JRootPane createRootPane()
protected void frameInit()
public AccessibleContext
  getAccessibleContext()
public Container getContentPane()
public int getDefaultCloseOperation()
public Component getGlassPane()
public JMenuBar getJMenuBar()
public JLayeredPane getLayeredPane()
public JRootPane getRootPane()
protected boolean
  isRootPaneCheckingEnabled()
protected String paramString()
protected void processKeyEvent(KeyEvent
  e)
```

```
protected void processWindowEvent(
  WindowEvent e)
public void setContentPane(Container
  contentPane)
public void setDefaultCloseOperation(int
  operation)
public void setGlassPane(Component
  glassPane)
public void setJMenuBar(JMenuBar menubar)
public void setLayeredPane(JLayeredPane
  layeredPane)
public void setLayout(LayoutManager
  manager)
protected void setRootPane(JRootPane
  root)
protected void
  setRootPaneCheckingEnabled(boolean
  enabled)
public void update(Graphics g)
```

►JINTERNALFRAME

```
public class javax.swing.JInternalFrame
implements javax.accessibility.
  Accessible
implements javax.swing.
  RootPaneContainer
implements javax.swing.WindowConstants
extends javax.swing.JComponent
extends java.awt.Container
extends java.awt.Component
extends java.lang.Object
```

Fields

```
protected boolean closable
public final static java.lang.String
  CONTENT_PANE_PROPERTY
protected JDesktopIcon desktopIcon
protected javax.swing.Icon frameIcon
public final static java.lang.String
  FRAME_ICON_PROPERTY
public final static java.lang.String
  GLASS_PANE_PROPERTY
protected boolean iconable
protected boolean isClosed
protected boolean isIcon
protected boolean isMaximum
protected boolean isSelected
public final static java.lang.String IS_
  CLOSED_PROPERTY
public final static java.lang.String IS_
  ICON_PROPERTY
public final static java.lang.String IS_
  MAXIMUM_PROPERTY
public final static java.lang.String IS_
  SELECTED_PROPERTY
public final static java.lang.String
  LAYERED_PANE_PROPERTY
protected boolean maximizable
public final static java.lang.String
  MENU_BAR_PROPERTY
protected boolean resizable
protected javax.swing.JRootPane
  rootPane
```

```
protected boolean
  rootPaneCheckingEnabled
public final static java.lang.String
  ROOT_PANE_PROPERTY
protected java.lang.String title
public final static java.lang.String
  TITLE_PROPERTY
```

Constructors

```
public  JInternalFrame()
public  JInternalFrame(String title)
public  JInternalFrame(String title,
  boolean resizable)
public  JInternalFrame(String title,
  boolean resizable,boolean closable)
public  JInternalFrame(String title,
  boolean resizable,boolean closable,
  boolean maximizable)
public  JInternalFrame(String title,
  boolean resizable,boolean closable,
  boolean maximizable,boolean iconifiable)
```

Methods

```
protected void addImpl(Component comp,
  Object constraints,int index)
public void addInternalFrameListener(
  InternalFrameListener l)
protected JRootPane createRootPane()
public void dispose()
protected void fireInternalFrameEvent(
  int id)
public AccessibleContext
  getAccessibleContext()
public Color getBackground()
public Container getContentPane()
public int getDefaultCloseOperation()
public JDesktopIcon getDesktopIcon()
public JDesktopPane getDesktopPane()
public Color getForeground()
public Icon getFrameIcon()
public Component getGlassPane()
public JMenuBar getJMenuBar()
public int getLayer()
public JLayeredPane getLayeredPane()
public JMenuBar getMenuBar()
public JRootPane getRootPane()
public String getTitle()
public InternalFrameUI getUI()
public String getUIClassID()
public final String getWarningString()
public boolean isClosable()
public boolean isClosed()
public boolean isIcon()
public boolean isIconifiable()
public boolean isMaximizable()
public boolean isMaximum()
public boolean isResizable()
protected boolean
  isRootPaneCheckingEnabled()
public boolean isSelected()
public void moveToBack()
public void moveToFront()
public void pack()
protected String paramString()
```

```
public void removeInternalFrameListener(
  InternalFrameListener l)
public void reshape(int x,int y,int
  width,int height)
public void setBackground(Color c)
public void setClosable(boolean b)
public void setClosed(boolean b)
public void setContentPane(Container c)
public void setDefaultCloseOperation(int
  operation)
public void setDesktopIcon(JDesktopIcon
  d)
public void setForeground(Color c)
public void setFrameIcon(Icon icon)
public void setGlassPane(Component glass)
public void setIcon(boolean b)
public void setIconifiable(boolean b)
public void setJMenuBar(JMenuBar m)
public void setLayer(Integer layer)
public void setLayeredPane(JLayeredPane
  layered)
public void setLayout(LayoutManager
  manager)
public void setMaximizable(boolean b)
public void setMaximum(boolean b)
public void setMenuBar(JMenuBar m)
public void setResizable(boolean b)
protected void setRootPane(JRootPane
  root)
protected void
  setRootPaneCheckingEnabled(boolean
  enabled)
public void setSelected(boolean selected)
public void setTitle(String title)
public void setUI(InternalFrameUI ui)
public void setVisible(boolean b)
public void show()
public void toBack()
public void toFront()
public void updateUI()
```

▶JLABEL
```
public class javax.swing.JLabel
implements javax.accessibility.
  Accessible
implements javax.swing.SwingConstants
extends javax.swing.JComponent
extends java.awt.Container
extends java.awt.Component
extends java.lang.Object
```
Fields
```
protected java.awt.Component labelFor
```
Constructors
```
public  JLabel(String text,Icon icon,int
  horizontalAlignment)
public  JLabel(String text,int
  horizontalAlignment)
public  JLabel(String text)
public  JLabel(Icon image,int
  horizontalAlignment)
public  JLabel(Icon image)
public  JLabel()
```

Methods
```
protected int checkHorizontalKey(int key,
  String message)
protected int checkVerticalKey(int key,
  String message)
public AccessibleContext
  getAccessibleContext()
public Icon getDisabledIcon()
public int getDisplayedMnemonic()
public int getHorizontalAlignment()
public int getHorizontalTextPosition()
public Icon getIcon()
public int getIconTextGap()
public Component getLabelFor()
public String getText()
public LabelUI getUI()
public String getUIClassID()
public int getVerticalAlignment()
public int getVerticalTextPosition()
protected String paramString()
public void setDisabledIcon(Icon
  disabledIcon)
public void setDisplayedMnemonic(int key)
public void setDisplayedMnemonic(char
  aChar)
public void setHorizontalAlignment(int
  alignment)
public void setHorizontalTextPosition(
  int textPosition)
public void setIcon(Icon icon)
public void setIconTextGap(int
  iconTextGap)
public void setLabelFor(Component c)
public void setText(String text)
public void setUI(LabelUI ui)
public void setVerticalAlignment(int
  alignment)
public void setVerticalTextPosition(int
  textPosition)
public void updateUI()
```

▶JLAYEREDPANE
```
public class javax.swing.JLayeredPane
implements javax.accessibility.
  Accessible
extends javax.swing.JComponent
extends java.awt.Container
extends java.awt.Component
extends java.lang.Object
```
Fields
```
public final static java.lang.Integer
  DEFAULT_LAYER
public final static java.lang.Integer
  DRAG_LAYER
public final static java.lang.Integer
  FRAME_CONTENT_LAYER
public final static java.lang.String
  LAYER_PROPERTY
public final static java.lang.Integer
  MODAL_LAYER
public final static java.lang.Integer
  PALETTE_LAYER
```

```
public final static java.lang.Integer
  POPUP_LAYER
```
Constructors
```
public  JLayeredPane()
```
Methods
```
protected void addImpl(Component comp,
  Object constraints,int index)
public AccessibleContext
  getAccessibleContext()
public int getComponentCountInLayer(int
  layer)
public Component getComponentsInLayer(
  int layer)
protected Hashtable getComponentToLayer()
public int getIndexOf(Component c)
public static int getLayer(JComponent c)
public int getLayer(Component c)
public static JLayeredPane
  getLayeredPaneAbove(Component c)
protected Integer getObjectForLayer(int
  layer)
public int getPosition(Component c)
public int highestLayer()
protected int insertIndexForLayer(int
  layer,int position)
public boolean isOptimizedDrawingEnabled(
  )
public int lowestLayer()
public void moveToBack(Component c)
public void moveToFront(Component c)
public void paint(Graphics g)
protected String paramString()
public static void putLayer(JComponent c,
  int layer)
public void remove(int index)
public void setLayer(Component c,int
  layer)
public void setLayer(Component c,int
  layer,int position)
public void setPosition(Component c,int
  position)
```
►JLIST
```
public class javax.swing.JList
implements javax.accessibility.
  Accessible
implements javax.swing.Scrollable
extends javax.swing.JComponent
extends java.awt.Container
extends java.awt.Component
extends java.lang.Object
```
Constructors
```
public  JList(ListModel dataModel)
public  JList(Object listData)
public  JList(Vector listData)
public  JList()
```
Methods
```
public void addListSelectionListener(
  ListSelectionListener listener)
public void addSelectionInterval(int
  anchor,int lead)
public void clearSelection()
```

```
protected ListSelectionModel
  createSelectionModel()
public void ensureIndexIsVisible(int
  index)
protected void fireSelectionValueChanged(
  int firstIndex,int lastIndex,boolean
  isAdjusting)
public AccessibleContext
  getAccessibleContext()
public int getAnchorSelectionIndex()
public Rectangle getCellBounds(int
  index1,int index2)
public ListCellRenderer getCellRenderer()
public int getFirstVisibleIndex()
public int getFixedCellHeight()
public int getFixedCellWidth()
public int getLastVisibleIndex()
public int getLeadSelectionIndex()
public int getMaxSelectionIndex()
public int getMinSelectionIndex()
public ListModel getModel()
public Dimension
  getPreferredScrollableViewportSize()
public Object getPrototypeCellValue()
public int getScrollableBlockIncrement(
  Rectangle visibleRect,int orientation,
  int direction)
public boolean
  getScrollableTracksViewportHeight()
public boolean
  getScrollableTracksViewportWidth()
public int getScrollableUnitIncrement(
  Rectangle visibleRect,int orientation,
  int direction)
public int getSelectedIndex()
public int getSelectedIndices()
public Object getSelectedValue()
public Object getSelectedValues()
public Color getSelectionBackground()
public Color getSelectionForeground()
public int getSelectionMode()
public ListSelectionModel
  getSelectionModel()
public ListUI getUI()
public String getUIClassID()
public boolean getValueIsAdjusting()
public int getVisibleRowCount()
public Point indexToLocation(int index)
public boolean isSelectedIndex(int index)
public boolean isSelectionEmpty()
public int locationToIndex(Point
  location)
protected String paramString()
public void removeListSelectionListener(
  ListSelectionListener listener)
public void removeSelectionInterval(int
  index0,int index1)
public void setCellRenderer(
  ListCellRenderer cellRenderer)
public void setFixedCellHeight(int
  height)
public void setFixedCellWidth(int width)
public void setListData(Object listData)
```

public void setListData(Vector listData)
public void setModel(ListModel model)
public void setPrototypeCellValue(Object
  prototypeCellValue)
public void setSelectedIndex(int index)
public void setSelectedIndices(int
  indices)
public void setSelectedValue(Object
  anObject,boolean shouldScroll)
public void setSelectionBackground(Color
  selectionBackground)
public void setSelectionForeground(Color
  selectionForeground)
public void setSelectionInterval(int
  anchor,int lead)
public void setSelectionMode(int
  selectionMode)
public void setSelectionModel(
  ListSelectionModel selectionModel)
public void setUI(ListUI ui)
public void setValueIsAdjusting(boolean
  b)
public void setVisibleRowCount(int
  visibleRowCount)
public void updateUI()

►**JMENU**
public class javax.swing.JMenu
implements javax.accessibility.
  Accessible
implements javax.swing.MenuElement
extends javax.swing.JMenuItem
extends javax.swing.AbstractButton
extends javax.swing.JComponent
extends java.awt.Container
extends java.awt.Component
extends java.lang.Object
Fields
protected WinListener popupListener
Constructors
public JMenu()
public JMenu(String s)
public JMenu(String s,boolean b)
Methods
public JMenuItem add(JMenuItem menuItem)
public Component add(Component c)
public JMenuItem add(String s)
public JMenuItem add(Action a)
public void addMenuListener(MenuListener
  l)
public void addSeparator()
protected PropertyChangeListener
  createActionChangeListener(JMenuItem b)
protected WinListener createWinListener(
  JPopupMenu p)
public void doClick(int pressTime)
protected void fireMenuCanceled()
protected void fireMenuDeselected()
protected void fireMenuSelected()
public AccessibleContext
  getAccessibleContext()
public Component getComponent()

public int getDelay()
public JMenuItem getItem(int pos)
public int getItemCount()
public Component getMenuComponent(int n)
public int getMenuComponentCount()
public Component getMenuComponents()
public JPopupMenu getPopupMenu()
public MenuElement getSubElements()
public String getUIClassID()
public void insert(String s,int pos)
public JMenuItem insert(JMenuItem mi,int
  pos)
public JMenuItem insert(Action a,int pos)
public void insertSeparator(int index)
public boolean isMenuComponent(Component
  c)
public boolean isPopupMenuVisible()
public boolean isSelected()
public boolean isTearOff()
public boolean isTopLevelMenu()
public void menuSelectionChanged(boolean
  isIncluded)
protected String paramString()
protected void processKeyEvent(KeyEvent
  e)
public void remove(JMenuItem item)
public void remove(int pos)
public void remove(Component c)
public void removeAll()
public void removeMenuListener(
  MenuListener l)
public void setAccelerator(KeyStroke
  keyStroke)
public void setDelay(int d)
public void setMenuLocation(int x,int y)
public void setModel(ButtonModel
  newModel)
public void setPopupMenuVisible(boolean
  b)
public void setSelected(boolean b)
public void updateUI()

►**JMENUBAR**
public class javax.swing.JMenuBar
implements javax.accessibility.
  Accessible
implements javax.swing.MenuElement
extends javax.swing.JComponent
extends java.awt.Container
extends java.awt.Component
extends java.lang.Object
Constructors
public JMenuBar()
Methods
public JMenu add(JMenu c)
public void addNotify()
public AccessibleContext
  getAccessibleContext()
public Component getComponent()
public Component getComponentAtIndex(int
  i)
public int getComponentIndex(Component c)

public JMenu getHelpMenu()
public Insets getMargin()
public JMenu getMenu(int index)
public int getMenuCount()
public SingleSelectionModel
getSelectionModel()
public MenuElement getSubElements()
public MenuBarUI getUI()
public String getUIClassID()
public boolean isBorderPainted()
public boolean isManagingFocus()
public boolean isSelected()
public void menuSelectionChanged(boolean
isIncluded)
protected void paintBorder(Graphics g)
protected String paramString()
public void processKeyEvent(KeyEvent e,
MenuElement path,MenuSelectionManager
manager)
public void processMouseEvent(MouseEvent
event,MenuElement path,
MenuSelectionManager manager)
public void removeNotify()
public void setBorderPainted(boolean s)
public void setHelpMenu(JMenu menu)
public void setMargin(Insets margin)
public void setSelected(Component sel)
public void setSelectionModel(
SingleSelectionModel model)
public void setUI(MenuBarUI ui)
public void updateUI()

►JMENUITEM
public class javax.swing.JMenuItem
implements javax.accessibility.
Accessible
implements javax.swing.MenuElement
extends javax.swing.AbstractButton
extends javax.swing.JComponent
extends java.awt.Container
extends java.awt.Component
extends java.lang.Object

Constructors
public JMenuItem()
public JMenuItem(Icon icon)
public JMenuItem(String text)
public JMenuItem(String text,Icon icon)
public JMenuItem(String text,int
mnemonic)

Methods
public void addMenuDragMouseListener(
MenuDragMouseListener l)
public void addMenuKeyListener(
MenuKeyListener l)
protected void fireMenuDragMouseDragged(
MenuDragMouseEvent event)
protected void fireMenuDragMouseEntered(
MenuDragMouseEvent event)
protected void fireMenuDragMouseExited(
MenuDragMouseEvent event)
protected void fireMenuDragMouseReleased(
MenuDragMouseEvent event)

protected void fireMenuKeyPressed(
MenuKeyEvent event)
protected void fireMenuKeyReleased(
MenuKeyEvent event)
protected void fireMenuKeyTyped(
MenuKeyEvent event)
public KeyStroke getAccelerator()
public AccessibleContext
getAccessibleContext()
public Component getComponent()
public MenuElement getSubElements()
public String getUIClassID()
protected void init(String text,Icon
icon)
public boolean isArmed()
public void menuSelectionChanged(boolean
isIncluded)
protected String paramString()
public void processKeyEvent(KeyEvent e,
MenuElement path,MenuSelectionManager
manager)
public void processMenuDragMouseEvent(
MenuDragMouseEvent e)
public void processMenuKeyEvent(
MenuKeyEvent e)
public void processMouseEvent(MouseEvent
e,MenuElement path,MenuSelectionManager
manager)
public void removeMenuDragMouseListener(
MenuDragMouseListener l)
public void removeMenuKeyListener(
MenuKeyListener l)
public void setAccelerator(KeyStroke
keyStroke)
public void setArmed(boolean b)
public void setEnabled(boolean b)
public void setUI(MenuItemUI ui)
public void updateUI()

►JOPTIONPANE
public class javax.swing.JOptionPane
implements javax.accessibility.
Accessible
extends javax.swing.JComponent
extends java.awt.Container
extends java.awt.Component
extends java.lang.Object

Fields
public final static int CANCEL_OPTION
public final static int CLOSED_OPTION
public final static int DEFAULT_OPTION
public final static int ERROR_MESSAGE
protected transient javax.swing.Icon
icon
public final static java.lang.String
ICON_PROPERTY
public final static int INFORMATION_
MESSAGE
protected transient java.lang.Object
initialSelectionValue
protected transient java.lang.Object
initialValue

public final static java.lang.String
INITIAL_SELECTION_VALUE_PROPERTY

public final static java.lang.String
INITIAL_VALUE_PROPERTY

protected transient java.lang.Object
inputValue

public final static java.lang.String
INPUT_VALUE_PROPERTY

protected transient java.lang.Object
message

protected int messageType

public final static java.lang.String
MESSAGE_PROPERTY

public final static java.lang.String
MESSAGE_TYPE_PROPERTY

public final static int NO_OPTION

public final static int OK_CANCEL_
OPTION

public final static int OK_OPTION

protected transient java.lang.Object
options

public final static java.lang.String
OPTIONS_PROPERTY

protected int optionType

public final static java.lang.String
OPTION_TYPE_PROPERTY

public final static int PLAIN_MESSAGE

public final static int QUESTION_
MESSAGE

protected transient java.lang.Object
selectionValues

public final static java.lang.String
SELECTION_VALUES_PROPERTY

public final static java.lang.String
UNINITIALIZED_VALUE

protected transient java.lang.Object
value

public final static java.lang.String
VALUE_PROPERTY

protected boolean wantsInput

public final static java.lang.String
WANTS_INPUT_PROPERTY

public final static int WARNING_MESSAGE

public final static int YES_NO_CANCEL_
OPTION

public final static int YES_NO_OPTION

public final static int YES_OPTION

Constructors

public JOptionPane()

public JOptionPane(Object message)

public JOptionPane(Object message,int
messageType)

public JOptionPane(Object message,int
messageType,int optionType)

public JOptionPane(Object message,int
messageType,int optionType,Icon icon)

public JOptionPane(Object message,int
messageType,int optionType,Icon icon,
Object options)

public JOptionPane(Object message,int
messageType,int optionType,Icon icon,
Object options,Object initialValue)

Methods

public JDialog createDialog(Component
parentComponent,String title)

public JInternalFrame
createInternalFrame(Component
parentComponent,String title)

public AccessibleContext
getAccessibleContext()

public static JDesktopPane
getDesktopPaneForComponent(Component
parentComponent)

public static Frame getFrameForComponent(
Component parentComponent)

public Icon getIcon()

public Object getInitialSelectionValue()

public Object getInitialValue()

public Object getInputValue()

public int getMaxCharactersPerLineCount()

public Object getMessage()

public int getMessageType()

public Object getOptions()

public int getOptionType()

public static Frame getRootFrame()

public Object getSelectionValues()

public OptionPaneUI getUI()

public String getUIClassID()

public Object getValue()

public boolean getWantsInput()

protected String paramString()

public void selectInitialValue()

public void setIcon(Icon newIcon)

public void setInitialSelectionValue(
Object newValue)

public void setInitialValue(Object
newInitialValue)

public void setInputValue(Object
newValue)

public void setMessage(Object newMessage)

public void setMessageType(int newType)

public void setOptions(Object newOptions)

public void setOptionType(int newType)

public static void setRootFrame(Frame
newRootFrame)

public void setSelectionValues(Object
newValues)

public void setUI(OptionPaneUI ui)

public void setValue(Object newValue)

public void setWantsInput(boolean
newValue)

public static int showConfirmDialog(
Component parentComponent,Object message)

public static int showConfirmDialog(
Component parentComponent,Object message,
String title,int optionType)

public static int showConfirmDialog(
Component parentComponent,Object message,
String title,int optionType,int
messageType)

public static int showConfirmDialog(
Component parentComponent,Object message,
String title,int optionType,int
messageType,Icon icon)

```
public static String showInputDialog(
  Object message)
public static String showInputDialog(
  Component parentComponent,Object message)
public static String showInputDialog(
  Component parentComponent,Object message,
  String title,int messageType)
public static Object showInputDialog(
  Component parentComponent,Object message,
  String title,int messageType,Icon icon,
  Object selectionValues,Object
  initialSelectionValue)
public static int
  showInternalConfirmDialog(Component
  parentComponent,Object message)
public static int
  showInternalConfirmDialog(Component
  parentComponent,Object message,String
  title,int optionType)
public static int
  showInternalConfirmDialog(Component
  parentComponent,Object message,String
  title,int optionType,int messageType)
public static int
  showInternalConfirmDialog(Component
  parentComponent,Object message,String
  title,int optionType,int messageType,
  Icon icon)
public static String
  showInternalInputDialog(Component
  parentComponent,Object message)
public static String
  showInternalInputDialog(Component
  parentComponent,Object message,String
  title,int messageType)
public static Object
  showInternalInputDialog(Component
  parentComponent,Object message,String
  title,int messageType,Icon icon,Object
  selectionValues,Object
  initialSelectionValue)
public static void
  showInternalMessageDialog(Component
  parentComponent,Object message)
public static void
  showInternalMessageDialog(Component
  parentComponent,Object message,String
  title,int messageType)
public static void
  showInternalMessageDialog(Component
  parentComponent,Object message,String
  title,int messageType,Icon icon)
public static int
  showInternalOptionDialog(Component
  parentComponent,Object message,String
  title,int optionType,int messageType,
  Icon icon,Object options,Object
  initialValue)
public static void showMessageDialog(
  Component parentComponent,Object message)
public static void showMessageDialog(
  Component parentComponent,Object message,
  String title,int messageType)
public static void showMessageDialog(
  Component parentComponent,Object message,
  String title,int messageType,Icon icon)
public static int showOptionDialog(
  Component parentComponent,Object message,
  String title,int optionType,int
  messageType,Icon icon,Object options,
  Object initialValue)
public void updateUI()
```

►JPANEL
```
public class javax.swing.JPanel
implements javax.accessibility.
  Accessible
extends javax.swing.JComponent
extends java.awt.Container
extends java.awt.Component
extends java.lang.Object
```
Constructors
```
public JPanel(LayoutManager layout,
  boolean isDoubleBuffered)
public JPanel(LayoutManager layout)
public JPanel(boolean isDoubleBuffered)
public JPanel()
```
Methods
```
public AccessibleContext
  getAccessibleContext()
public String getUIClassID()
protected String paramString()
public void updateUI()
```

►JPASSWORDFIELD
```
public class javax.swing.JPasswordField
extends javax.swing.JTextField
extends javax.swing.text.JTextComponent
extends javax.swing.JComponent
extends java.awt.Container
extends java.awt.Component
extends java.lang.Object
```
Constructors
```
public JPasswordField()
public JPasswordField(String text)
public JPasswordField(int columns)
public JPasswordField(String text,int
  columns)
public JPasswordField(Document doc,
  String txt,int columns)
```
Methods
```
public void copy()
public void cut()
public boolean echoCharIsSet()
public AccessibleContext
  getAccessibleContext()
public char getEchoChar()
public char getPassword()
public String getText()
public String getText(int offs,int len)
public String getUIClassID()
protected String paramString()
public void setEchoChar(char c)
```

►JPopupMenu

```
public class javax.swing.JPopupMenu
implements javax.accessibility.
  Accessible
implements javax.swing.MenuElement
extends javax.swing.JComponent
extends java.awt.Container
extends java.awt.Component
extends java.lang.Object
```

Constructors

```
public  JPopupMenu()
public  JPopupMenu(String label)
```

Methods

```
public JMenuItem add(JMenuItem menuItem)
public JMenuItem add(String s)
public JMenuItem add(Action a)
public void addPopupMenuListener(
  PopupMenuListener l)
public void addSeparator()
protected PropertyChangeListener
  createActionChangeListener(JMenuItem b)
protected void firePopupMenuCanceled()
protected void
  firePopupMenuWillBecomeInvisible()
protected void
  firePopupMenuWillBecomeVisible()
public AccessibleContext
  getAccessibleContext()
public Component getComponent()
public Component getComponentAtIndex(int
  i)
public int getComponentIndex(Component c)
public static boolean
  getDefaultLightWeightPopupEnabled()
public Component getInvoker()
public String getLabel()
public Insets getMargin()
public SingleSelectionModel
  getSelectionModel()
public MenuElement getSubElements()
public PopupMenuUI getUI()
public String getUIClassID()
public void insert(Action a,int index)
public void insert(Component component,
  int index)
public boolean isBorderPainted()
public boolean isLightWeightPopupEnabled(
  )
public boolean isVisible()
public void menuSelectionChanged(boolean
  isIncluded)
public void pack()
protected void paintBorder(Graphics g)
protected String paramString()
public void processKeyEvent(KeyEvent e,
  MenuElement path,MenuSelectionManager
  manager)
public void processMouseEvent(MouseEvent
  event,MenuElement path,
  MenuSelectionManager manager)
public void remove(Component comp)
```

```
public void removePopupMenuListener(
  PopupMenuListener l)
public void setBorderPainted(boolean b)
public static void
  setDefaultLightWeightPopupEnabled(
  boolean aFlag)
public void setInvoker(Component invoker)
public void setLabel(String label)
public void setLightWeightPopupEnabled(
  boolean aFlag)
public void setLocation(int x,int y)
public void setPopupSize(Dimension d)
public void setPopupSize(int width,int
  height)
public void setSelected(Component sel)
public void setSelectionModel(
  SingleSelectionModel model)
public void setUI(PopupMenuUI ui)
public void setVisible(boolean b)
public void show(Component invoker,int x,
  int y)
public void updateUI()
```

►JProgressBar

```
public class javax.swing.JProgressBar
implements javax.accessibility.
  Accessible
implements javax.swing.SwingConstants
extends javax.swing.JComponent
extends java.awt.Container
extends java.awt.Component
extends java.lang.Object
```

Fields

```
protected transient javax.swing.event.
  ChangeEvent changeEvent
protected javax.swing.event.
  ChangeListener changeListener
protected javax.swing.BoundedRangeModel
  model
protected int orientation
protected boolean paintBorder
protected boolean paintString
protected java.lang.String
  progressString
```

Constructors

```
public  JProgressBar()
public  JProgressBar(int orient)
public  JProgressBar(int min,int max)
public  JProgressBar(int orient,int min,
  int max)
public  JProgressBar(BoundedRangeModel
  newModel)
```

Methods

```
public void addChangeListener(
  ChangeListener l)
protected ChangeListener
  createChangeListener()
protected void fireStateChanged()
public AccessibleContext
  getAccessibleContext()
public int getMaximum()
public int getMinimum()
```

```
public BoundedRangeModel getModel()
public int getOrientation()
public double getPercentComplete()
public String getString()
public ProgressBarUI getUI()
public String getUIClassID()
public int getValue()
public boolean isBorderPainted()
public boolean isStringPainted()
protected void paintBorder(Graphics g)
protected String paramString()
public void removeChangeListener(
  ChangeListener l)
public void setBorderPainted(boolean b)
public void setMaximum(int n)
public void setMinimum(int n)
public void setModel(BoundedRangeModel
  newModel)
public void setOrientation(int
  newOrientation)
public void setString(String s)
public void setStringPainted(boolean b)
public void setUI(ProgressBarUI ui)
public void setValue(int n)
public void updateUI()
```

▶JRADIOBUTTON

```
public class javax.swing.JRadioButton
implements javax.accessibility.
  Accessible
extends javax.swing.JToggleButton
extends javax.swing.AbstractButton
extends javax.swing.JComponent
extends java.awt.Container
extends java.awt.Component
extends java.lang.Object
```

Constructors

```
public JRadioButton()
public JRadioButton(Icon icon)
public JRadioButton(Icon icon,boolean
  selected)
public JRadioButton(String text)
public JRadioButton(String text,boolean
  selected)
public JRadioButton(String text,Icon
  icon)
public JRadioButton(String text,Icon
  icon,boolean selected)
```

Methods

```
public AccessibleContext
  getAccessibleContext()
public String getUIClassID()
protected String paramString()
public void updateUI()
```

▶JRADIOBUTTONMENUITEM

```
public class javax.swing.
  JRadioButtonMenuItem
implements javax.accessibility.
  Accessible
extends javax.swing.JMenuItem
extends javax.swing.AbstractButton
extends javax.swing.JComponent
```

```
extends java.awt.Container
extends java.awt.Component
extends java.lang.Object
```

Constructors

```
public JRadioButtonMenuItem()
public JRadioButtonMenuItem(Icon icon)
public JRadioButtonMenuItem(String text)
public JRadioButtonMenuItem(String text,
  Icon icon)
public JRadioButtonMenuItem(String text,
  boolean b)
public JRadioButtonMenuItem(Icon icon,
  boolean selected)
public JRadioButtonMenuItem(String text,
  Icon icon,boolean selected)
```

Methods

```
public AccessibleContext
  getAccessibleContext()
public String getUIClassID()
protected void init(String text,Icon
  icon)
protected String paramString()
public void requestFocus()
public void updateUI()
```

▶JROOTPANE

```
public class javax.swing.JRootPane
implements javax.accessibility.
  Accessible
extends javax.swing.JComponent
extends java.awt.Container
extends java.awt.Component
extends java.lang.Object
```

Fields

```
protected java.awt.Container
  contentPane
protected javax.swing.JButton
  defaultButton
protected DefaultAction
  defaultPressAction
protected DefaultAction
  defaultReleaseAction
protected java.awt.Component glassPane
protected javax.swing.JLayeredPane
  layeredPane
protected javax.swing.JMenuBar menuBar
```

Constructors

```
public JRootPane()
```

Methods

```
protected void addImpl(Component comp,
  Object constraints,int index)
public void addNotify()
protected Container createContentPane()
protected Component createGlassPane()
protected JLayeredPane createLayeredPane(
  )
protected LayoutManager createRootLayout(
  )
public AccessibleContext
  getAccessibleContext()
public Container getContentPane()
public JButton getDefaultButton()
```

```
public Component getGlassPane()
public JMenuBar getJMenuBar()
public JLayeredPane getLayeredPane()
public JMenuBar getMenuBar()
public boolean isFocusCycleRoot()
public boolean isValidateRoot()
protected String paramString()
public void removeNotify()
public void setContentPane(Container
  content)
public void setDefaultButton(JButton
  defaultButton)
public void setGlassPane(Component glass)
public void setJMenuBar(JMenuBar menu)
public void setLayeredPane(JLayeredPane
  layered)
public void setMenuBar(JMenuBar menu)
```

►JSCROLLBAR

```
public class javax.swing.JScrollBar
implements javax.accessibility.
  Accessible
implements java.awt.Adjustable
extends javax.swing.JComponent
extends java.awt.Container
extends java.awt.Component
extends java.lang.Object
```

Fields

```
protected int blockIncrement
protected javax.swing.BoundedRangeModel
  model
protected int orientation
protected int unitIncrement
```

Constructors

```
public  JScrollBar(int orientation,int
  value,int extent,int min,int max)
public  JScrollBar(int orientation)
public  JScrollBar()
```

Methods

```
public void addAdjustmentListener(
  AdjustmentListener l)
protected void
  fireAdjustmentValueChanged(int id,int
  type,int value)
public AccessibleContext
  getAccessibleContext()
public int getBlockIncrement(int
  direction)
public int getBlockIncrement()
public int getMaximum()
public Dimension getMaximumSize()
public int getMinimum()
public Dimension getMinimumSize()
public BoundedRangeModel getModel()
public int getOrientation()
public ScrollBarUI getUI()
public String getUIClassID()
public int getUnitIncrement(int
  direction)
public int getUnitIncrement()
public int getValue()
public boolean getValueIsAdjusting()
```

```
public int getVisibleAmount()
protected String paramString()
public void removeAdjustmentListener(
  AdjustmentListener l)
public void setBlockIncrement(int
  blockIncrement)
public void setEnabled(boolean x)
public void setMaximum(int maximum)
public void setMinimum(int minimum)
public void setModel(BoundedRangeModel
  newModel)
public void setOrientation(int
  orientation)
public void setUnitIncrement(int
  unitIncrement)
public void setValue(int value)
public void setValueIsAdjusting(boolean
  b)
public void setValues(int newValue,int
  newExtent,int newMin,int newMax)
public void setVisibleAmount(int extent)
public void updateUI()
```

►JSCROLLPANE

```
public class javax.swing.JScrollPane
implements javax.accessibility.
  Accessible
implements javax.swing.
  ScrollPaneConstants
extends javax.swing.JComponent
extends java.awt.Container
extends java.awt.Component
extends java.lang.Object
```

Fields

```
protected javax.swing.JViewport
  columnHeader
protected javax.swing.JScrollBar
  horizontalScrollBar
protected int horizontalScrollBarPolicy
protected java.awt.Component lowerLeft
protected java.awt.Component lowerRight
protected javax.swing.JViewport
  rowHeader
protected java.awt.Component upperLeft
protected java.awt.Component upperRight
protected javax.swing.JScrollBar
  verticalScrollBar
protected int verticalScrollBarPolicy
protected javax.swing.JViewport
  viewport
```

Constructors

```
public  JScrollPane(Component view,int
  vsbPolicy,int hsbPolicy)
public  JScrollPane(Component view)
public  JScrollPane(int vsbPolicy,int
  hsbPolicy)
public  JScrollPane()
```

Methods

```
public JScrollBar
  createHorizontalScrollBar()
public JScrollBar
  createVerticalScrollBar()
```

```
protected JViewport createViewport()
public AccessibleContext
  getAccessibleContext()
public JViewport getColumnHeader()
public Component getCorner(String key)
public JScrollBar getHorizontalScrollBar(
  )
public int getHorizontalScrollBarPolicy()
public JViewport getRowHeader()
public ScrollPaneUI getUI()
public String getUIClassID()
public JScrollBar getVerticalScrollBar()
public int getVerticalScrollBarPolicy()
public JViewport getViewport()
public Border getViewportBorder()
public Rectangle getViewportBorderBounds(
  )
public boolean isOpaque()
public boolean isValidateRoot()
protected String paramString()
public void setColumnHeader(JViewport
  columnHeader)
public void setColumnHeaderView(
  Component view)
public void setCorner(String key,
  Component corner)
public void setHorizontalScrollBar(
  JScrollBar horizontalScrollBar)
public void setHorizontalScrollBarPolicy(
  int policy)
public void setLayout(LayoutManager
  layout)
public void setRowHeader(JViewport
  rowHeader)
public void setRowHeaderView(Component
  view)
public void setUI(ScrollPaneUI ui)
public void setVerticalScrollBar(
  JScrollBar verticalScrollBar)
public void setVerticalScrollBarPolicy(
  int policy)
public void setViewport(JViewport
  viewport)
public void setViewportBorder(Border
  viewportBorder)
public void setViewportView(Component
  view)
public void updateUI()
```

►JSEPARATOR

```
public class javax.swing.JSeparator
implements javax.accessibility.
  Accessible
implements javax.swing.SwingConstants
extends javax.swing.JComponent
extends java.awt.Container
extends java.awt.Component
extends java.lang.Object
```

Constructors

```
public JSeparator()
public JSeparator(int orientation)
```

Methods

```
public AccessibleContext
  getAccessibleContext()
public int getOrientation()
public SeparatorUI getUI()
public String getUIClassID()
public boolean isFocusTraversable()
protected String paramString()
public void setOrientation(int
  orientation)
public void setUI(SeparatorUI ui)
public void updateUI()
```

►JSLIDER

```
public class javax.swing.JSlider
implements javax.accessibility.
  Accessible
implements javax.swing.SwingConstants
extends javax.swing.JComponent
extends java.awt.Container
extends java.awt.Component
extends java.lang.Object
```

Fields

```
protected transient javax.swing.event.
  ChangeEvent changeEvent
protected javax.swing.event.
  ChangeListener changeListener
protected int majorTickSpacing
protected int minorTickSpacing
protected int orientation
protected javax.swing.BoundedRangeModel
  sliderModel
protected boolean snapToTicks
```

Constructors

```
public JSlider()
public JSlider(int orientation)
public JSlider(int min,int max)
public JSlider(int min,int max,int
  value)
public JSlider(int orientation,int min,
  int max,int value)
public JSlider(BoundedRangeModel brm)
```

Methods

```
public void addChangeListener(
  ChangeListener l)
protected ChangeListener
  createChangeListener()
public Hashtable createStandardLabels(
  int increment)
public Hashtable createStandardLabels(
  int increment,int start)
protected void fireStateChanged()
public AccessibleContext
  getAccessibleContext()
public int getExtent()
public boolean getInverted()
public Dictionary getLabelTable()
public int getMajorTickSpacing()
public int getMaximum()
public int getMinimum()
public int getMinorTickSpacing()
public BoundedRangeModel getModel()
```

```
public int getOrientation()
public boolean getPaintLabels()
public boolean getPaintTicks()
public boolean getPaintTrack()
public boolean getSnapToTicks()
public SliderUI getUI()
public String getUIClassID()
public int getValue()
public boolean getValueIsAdjusting()
protected String paramString()
public void removeChangeListener(
  ChangeListener l)
public void setExtent(int extent)
public void setInverted(boolean b)
public void setLabelTable(Dictionary
  labels)
public void setMajorTickSpacing(int n)
public void setMaximum(int maximum)
public void setMinimum(int minimum)
public void setMinorTickSpacing(int n)
public void setModel(BoundedRangeModel
  newModel)
public void setOrientation(int
  orientation)
public void setPaintLabels(boolean b)
public void setPaintTicks(boolean b)
public void setPaintTrack(boolean b)
public void setSnapToTicks(boolean b)
public void setUI(SliderUI ui)
public void setValue(int n)
public void setValueIsAdjusting(boolean
  b)
protected void updateLabelUIs()
public void updateUI()
```

▸JSPLITPANE

```
public class javax.swing.JSplitPane
implements javax.accessibility.
  Accessible
extends javax.swing.JComponent
extends java.awt.Container
extends java.awt.Component
extends java.lang.Object
```

Fields

```
public final static java.lang.String
  BOTTOM
protected boolean continuousLayout
public final static java.lang.String
  CONTINUOUS_LAYOUT_PROPERTY
public final static java.lang.String
  DIVIDER
protected int dividerSize
public final static java.lang.String
  DIVIDER_SIZE_PROPERTY
public final static int HORIZONTAL_
  SPLIT
protected int lastDividerLocation
public final static java.lang.String
  LAST_DIVIDER_LOCATION_PROPERTY
public final static java.lang.String
  LEFT
```

```
protected java.awt.Component
  leftComponent
protected boolean oneTouchExpandable
public final static java.lang.String ONE_
  TOUCH_EXPANDABLE_PROPERTY
protected int orientation
public final static java.lang.String
  ORIENTATION_PROPERTY
public final static java.lang.String
  RIGHT
protected java.awt.Component
  rightComponent
public final static java.lang.String
  TOP
public final static int VERTICAL_SPLIT
```

Constructors

```
public  JSplitPane()
public  JSplitPane(int newOrientation)
public  JSplitPane(int newOrientation,
  boolean newContinuousLayout)
public  JSplitPane(int newOrientation,
  Component newLeftComponent,Component
  newRightComponent)
public  JSplitPane(int newOrientation,
  boolean newContinuousLayout,Component
  newLeftComponent,Component
  newRightComponent)
```

Methods

```
protected void addImpl(Component comp,
  Object constraints,int index)
public AccessibleContext
  getAccessibleContext()
public Component getBottomComponent()
public int getDividerLocation()
public int getDividerSize()
public int getLastDividerLocation()
public Component getLeftComponent()
public int getMaximumDividerLocation()
public int getMinimumDividerLocation()
public int getOrientation()
public Component getRightComponent()
public Component getTopComponent()
public SplitPaneUI getUI()
public String getUIClassID()
public boolean isContinuousLayout()
public boolean isOneTouchExpandable()
protected void paintChildren(Graphics g)
protected String paramString()
public void remove(Component component)
public void remove(int index)
public void removeAll()
public void resetToPreferredSizes()
public void setBottomComponent(Component
  comp)
public void setContinuousLayout(boolean
  newContinuousLayout)
public void setDividerLocation(double
  proportionalLocation)
public void setDividerLocation(int
  location)
public void setDividerSize(int newSize)
```

```
public void setLastDividerLocation(int
  newLastLocation)
public void setLeftComponent(Component
  comp)
public void setOneTouchExpandable(
  boolean newValue)
public void setOrientation(int
  orientation)
public void setRightComponent(Component
  comp)
public void setTopComponent(Component
  comp)
public void setUI(SplitPaneUI ui)
public void updateUI()
```

►JTABBEDPANE

```
public class javax.swing.JTabbedPane
implements javax.accessibility.
  Accessible
implements java.io.Serializable
implements javax.swing.SwingConstants
extends javax.swing.JComponent
extends java.awt.Container
extends java.awt.Component
extends java.lang.Object
```

Fields

```
protected transient javax.swing.event.
  ChangeEvent changeEvent
protected javax.swing.event.
  ChangeListener changeListener
protected javax.swing.
  SingleSelectionModel model
protected int tabPlacement
```

Constructors

```
public  JTabbedPane()
public  JTabbedPane(int tabPlacement)
```

Methods

```
public Component add(Component component)
public Component add(String title,
  Component component)
public Component add(Component component,
  int index)
public void add(Component component,
  Object constraints)
public void add(Component component,
  Object constraints,int index)
public void addChangeListener(
  ChangeListener l)
public void addTab(String title,Icon
  icon,Component component,String tip)
public void addTab(String title,Icon
  icon,Component component)
public void addTab(String title,
  Component component)
protected ChangeListener
  createChangeListener()
protected void fireStateChanged()
public AccessibleContext
  getAccessibleContext()
public Color getBackgroundAt(int index)
public Rectangle getBoundsAt(int index)
```

```
public Component getComponentAt(int
  index)
public Icon getDisabledIconAt(int index)
public Color getForegroundAt(int index)
public Icon getIconAt(int index)
public SingleSelectionModel getModel()
public Component getSelectedComponent()
public int getSelectedIndex()
public int getTabCount()
public int getTabPlacement()
public int getTabRunCount()
public String getTitleAt(int index)
public String getToolTipText(MouseEvent
  event)
public TabbedPaneUI getUI()
public String getUIClassID()
public int indexOfComponent(Component
  component)
public int indexOfTab(String title)
public int indexOfTab(Icon icon)
public void insertTab(String title,Icon
  icon,Component component,String tip,int
  index)
public boolean isEnabledAt(int index)
protected String paramString()
public void remove(Component component)
public void removeAll()
public void removeChangeListener(
  ChangeListener l)
public void removeTabAt(int index)
public void setBackgroundAt(int index,
  Color background)
public void setComponentAt(int index,
  Component component)
public void setDisabledIconAt(int index,
  Icon disabledIcon)
public void setEnabledAt(int index,
  boolean enabled)
public void setForegroundAt(int index,
  Color foreground)
public void setIconAt(int index,Icon
  icon)
public void setModel(
  SingleSelectionModel model)
public void setSelectedComponent(
  Component c)
public void setSelectedIndex(int index)
public void setTabPlacement(int
  tabPlacement)
public void setTitleAt(int index,String
  title)
public void setUI(TabbedPaneUI ui)
public void updateUI()
```

►JTABLE

```
public class javax.swing.JTable
implements javax.accessibility.
  Accessible
implements javax.swing.event.
  CellEditorListener
implements javax.swing.event.
  ListSelectionListener
implements javax.swing.Scrollable
```

implements javax.swing.event.
  TableColumnModelListener
implements javax.swing.event.
  TableModelListener
extends javax.swing.JComponent
extends java.awt.Container
extends java.awt.Component
extends java.lang.Object

Fields

protected boolean
  autoCreateColumnsFromModel
protected int autoResizeMode
public final static int AUTO_RESIZE_ALL_
  COLUMNS
public final static int AUTO_RESIZE_LAST_
  COLUMN
public final static int AUTO_RESIZE_NEXT_
  COLUMN
public final static int AUTO_RESIZE_OFF
public final static int AUTO_RESIZE_
  SUBSEQUENT_COLUMNS
protected transient javax.swing.table.
  TableCellEditor cellEditor
protected boolean cellSelectionEnabled
protected javax.swing.table.
  TableColumnModel columnModel
protected javax.swing.table.TableModel
  dataModel
protected transient java.util.Hashtable
  defaultEditorsByColumnClass
protected transient java.util.Hashtable
  defaultRenderersByColumnClass
protected transient int editingColumn
protected transient int editingRow
protected transient java.awt.Component
  editorComp
protected java.awt.Color gridColor
protected java.awt.Dimension
  preferredViewportSize
protected int rowHeight
protected int rowMargin
protected boolean rowSelectionAllowed
protected java.awt.Color
  selectionBackground
protected java.awt.Color
  selectionForeground
protected javax.swing.ListSelectionModel
  selectionModel
protected boolean showHorizontalLines
protected boolean showVerticalLines
protected javax.swing.table.JTableHeader
  tableHeader

Constructors

public JTable()
public JTable(TableModel dm)
public JTable(TableModel dm,
  TableColumnModel cm)
public JTable(TableModel dm,
  TableColumnModel cm,ListSelectionModel
  sm)
public JTable(int numRows,int
  numColumns)

public JTable(Vector rowData,Vector
  columnNames)
public JTable(Object rowData,Object
  columnNames)

Methods

public void addColumn(TableColumn
  aColumn)
public void addColumnSelectionInterval(
  int index0,int index1)
public void addNotify()
public void addRowSelectionInterval(int
  index0,int index1)
public void clearSelection()
public void columnAdded(
  TableColumnModelEvent e)
public int columnAtPoint(Point point)
public void columnMarginChanged(
  ChangeEvent e)
public void columnMoved(
  TableColumnModelEvent e)
public void columnRemoved(
  TableColumnModelEvent e)
public void columnSelectionChanged(
  ListSelectionEvent e)
protected void
  configureEnclosingScrollPane()
public int convertColumnIndexToModel(int
  viewColumnIndex)
public int convertColumnIndexToView(int
  modelColumnIndex)
protected TableColumnModel
  createDefaultColumnModel()
public void
  createDefaultColumnsFromModel()
protected TableModel
  createDefaultDataModel()
protected void createDefaultEditors()
protected void createDefaultRenderers()
protected ListSelectionModel
  createDefaultSelectionModel()
protected JTableHeader
  createDefaultTableHeader()
public static JScrollPane
  createScrollPaneForTable(JTable aTable)
public boolean editCellAt(int row,int
  column)
public boolean editCellAt(int row,int
  column,EventObject e)
public void editingCanceled(ChangeEvent
  e)
public void editingStopped(ChangeEvent e)
public AccessibleContext
  getAccessibleContext()
public boolean
  getAutoCreateColumnsFromModel()
public int getAutoResizeMode()
public TableCellEditor getCellEditor()
public TableCellEditor getCellEditor(int
  row,int column)
public Rectangle getCellRect(int row,int
  column,boolean includeSpacing)

public TableCellRenderer getCellRenderer(
int row,int column)
public boolean getCellSelectionEnabled()
public TableColumn getColumn(Object
identifier)
public Class getColumnClass(int column)
public int getColumnCount()
public TableColumnModel getColumnModel()
public String getColumnName(int column)
public boolean getColumnSelectionAllowed(
)
public TableCellEditor getDefaultEditor(
Class columnClass)
public TableCellRenderer
getDefaultRenderer(Class columnClass)
public int getEditingColumn()
public int getEditingRow()
public Component getEditorComponent()
public Color getGridColor()
public Dimension getIntercellSpacing()
public TableModel getModel()
public Dimension
getPreferredScrollableViewportSize()
public int getRowCount()
public int getRowHeight()
public int getRowMargin()
public boolean getRowSelectionAllowed()
public int getScrollableBlockIncrement(
Rectangle visibleRect,int orientation,
int direction)
public boolean
getScrollableTracksViewportHeight()
public boolean
getScrollableTracksViewportWidth()
public int getScrollableUnitIncrement(
Rectangle visibleRect,int orientation,
int direction)
public int getSelectedColumn()
public int getSelectedColumnCount()
public int getSelectedColumns()
public int getSelectedRow()
public int getSelectedRowCount()
public int getSelectedRows()
public Color getSelectionBackground()
public Color getSelectionForeground()
public ListSelectionModel
getSelectionModel()
public boolean getShowHorizontalLines()
public boolean getShowVerticalLines()
public JTableHeader getTableHeader()
public String getToolTipText(MouseEvent
event)
public TableUI getUI()
public String getUIClassID()
public Object getValueAt(int row,int
column)
protected void initializeLocalVars()
public boolean isCellEditable(int row,
int column)
public boolean isCellSelected(int row,
int column)
public boolean isColumnSelected(int
column)

public boolean isEditing()
public boolean isManagingFocus()
public boolean isRowSelected(int row)
public void moveColumn(int column,int
targetColumn)
protected String paramString()
public Component prepareEditor(
TableCellEditor editor,int row,int
column)
public Component prepareRenderer(
TableCellRenderer renderer,int row,int
column)
public void removeColumn(TableColumn
aColumn)
public void
removeColumnSelectionInterval(int index0,
int index1)
public void removeEditor()
public void removeRowSelectionInterval(
int index0,int index1)
public void reshape(int x,int y,int
width,int height)
protected void resizeAndRepaint()
public int rowAtPoint(Point point)
public void selectAll()
public void
setAutoCreateColumnsFromModel(boolean
createColumns)
public void setAutoResizeMode(int mode)
public void setCellEditor(
TableCellEditor anEditor)
public void setCellSelectionEnabled(
boolean flag)
public void setColumnModel(
TableColumnModel newModel)
public void setColumnSelectionAllowed(
boolean flag)
public void setColumnSelectionInterval(
int index0,int index1)
public void setDefaultEditor(Class
columnClass,TableCellEditor editor)
public void setDefaultRenderer(Class
columnClass,TableCellRenderer renderer)
public void setEditingColumn(int aColumn)
public void setEditingRow(int aRow)
public void setGridColor(Color newColor)
public void setIntercellSpacing(
Dimension newSpacing)
public void setModel(TableModel newModel)
public void
setPreferredScrollableViewportSize(
Dimension size)
public void setRowHeight(int newHeight)
public void setRowMargin(int rowMargin)
public void setRowSelectionAllowed(
boolean flag)
public void setRowSelectionInterval(int
index0,int index1)
public void setSelectionBackground(Color
selectionBackground)
public void setSelectionForeground(Color
selectionForeground)

```
public void setSelectionMode(int
  selectionMode)
public void setSelectionModel(
  ListSelectionModel newModel)
public void setShowGrid(boolean b)
public void setShowHorizontalLines(
  boolean b)
public void setShowVerticalLines(boolean
  b)
public void setTableHeader(JTableHeader
  newHeader)
public void setUI(TableUI ui)
public void setValueAt(Object aValue,int
  row,int column)
public void sizeColumnsToFit(boolean
  lastColumnOnly)
public void sizeColumnsToFit(int
  resizingColumn)
public void tableChanged(TableModelEvent
  e)
public void updateUI()
public void valueChanged(
  ListSelectionEvent e)
```

►JTABLEHEADER

```
public class javax.swing.table.
  JTableHeader
implements javax.accessibility.
  Accessible
implements javax.swing.event.
  TableColumnModelListener
extends javax.swing.JComponent
extends java.awt.Container
extends java.awt.Component
extends java.lang.Object
```

Fields

```
protected javax.swing.table.
  TableColumnModel columnModel
protected transient javax.swing.table.
  TableColumn draggedColumn
protected transient int draggedDistance
protected boolean reorderingAllowed
protected boolean resizingAllowed
protected transient javax.swing.table.
  TableColumn resizingColumn
protected javax.swing.JTable table
protected boolean updateTableInRealTime
```

Constructors

```
public JTableHeader()
public JTableHeader(TableColumnModel cm)
```

Methods

```
public void columnAdded(
  TableColumnModelEvent e)
public int columnAtPoint(Point point)
public void columnMarginChanged(
  ChangeEvent e)
public void columnMoved(
  TableColumnModelEvent e)
public void columnRemoved(
  TableColumnModelEvent e)
public void columnSelectionChanged(
  ListSelectionEvent e)
```

```
protected TableColumnModel
  createDefaultColumnModel()
public AccessibleContext
  getAccessibleContext()
public TableColumnModel getColumnModel()
public TableColumn getDraggedColumn()
public int getDraggedDistance()
public Rectangle getHeaderRect(int
  columnIndex)
public boolean getReorderingAllowed()
public boolean getResizingAllowed()
public TableColumn getResizingColumn()
public JTable getTable()
public String getToolTipText(MouseEvent
  event)
public TableHeaderUI getUI()
public String getUIClassID()
public boolean getUpdateTableInRealTime()
protected void initializeLocalVars()
protected String paramString()
public void resizeAndRepaint()
public void setColumnModel(
  TableColumnModel newModel)
public void setDraggedColumn(TableColumn
  aColumn)
public void setDraggedDistance(int
  distance)
public void setReorderingAllowed(boolean
  b)
public void setResizingAllowed(boolean b)
public void setResizingColumn(
  TableColumn aColumn)
public void setTable(JTable aTable)
public void setUI(TableHeaderUI ui)
public void setUpdateTableInRealTime(
  boolean flag)
public void updateUI()
```

►JTEXTAREA

```
public class javax.swing.JTextArea
extends javax.swing.text.JTextComponent
extends javax.swing.JComponent
extends java.awt.Container
extends java.awt.Component
extends java.lang.Object
```

Constructors

```
public JTextArea()
public JTextArea(String text)
public JTextArea(int rows,int columns)
public JTextArea(String text,int rows,
  int columns)
public JTextArea(Document doc)
public JTextArea(Document doc,String
  text,int rows,int columns)
```

Methods

```
public void append(String str)
protected Document createDefaultModel()
public AccessibleContext
  getAccessibleContext()
public int getColumns()
protected int getColumnWidth()
public int getLineCount()
```

```
public int getLineEndOffset(int line)
public int getLineOfOffset(int offset)
public int getLineStartOffset(int line)
public boolean getLineWrap()
public Dimension
  getPreferredScrollableViewportSize()
public Dimension getPreferredSize()
protected int getRowHeight()
public int getRows()
public boolean
  getScrollableTracksViewportWidth()
public int getScrollableUnitIncrement(
  Rectangle visibleRect,int orientation,
  int direction)
public int getTabSize()
public String getUIClassID()
public boolean getWrapStyleWord()
public void insert(String str,int pos)
public boolean isManagingFocus()
protected String paramString()
protected void processComponentKeyEvent(
  KeyEvent e)
public void replaceRange(String str,int
  start,int end)
public void setColumns(int columns)
public void setFont(Font f)
public void setLineWrap(boolean wrap)
public void setRows(int rows)
public void setTabSize(int size)
public void setWrapStyleWord(boolean
  word)
```

▶JTextComponent
```
public abstract class javax.swing.text.
  JTextComponent
implements javax.accessibility.
  Accessible
implements javax.swing.Scrollable
extends javax.swing.JComponent
extends java.awt.Container
extends java.awt.Component
extends java.lang.Object
```

Fields
```
public final static java.lang.String
  DEFAULT_KEYMAP
public final static java.lang.String
  FOCUS_ACCELERATOR_KEY
```

Constructors
```
public  JTextComponent()
```

Methods
```
public void addCaretListener(
  CaretListener listener)
public static Keymap addKeymap(String nm,
  Keymap parent)
public void copy()
public void cut()
protected void fireCaretUpdate(
  CaretEvent e)
public AccessibleContext
  getAccessibleContext()
public Action getActions()
public Caret getCaret()
```

```
public Color getCaretColor()
public int getCaretPosition()
public Color getDisabledTextColor()
public Document getDocument()
public char getFocusAccelerator()
public Highlighter getHighlighter()
public InputMethodRequests
  getInputMethodRequests()
public Keymap getKeymap()
public static Keymap getKeymap(String nm)
public Insets getMargin()
public Dimension
  getPreferredScrollableViewportSize()
public int getScrollableBlockIncrement(
  Rectangle visibleRect,int orientation,
  int direction)
public boolean
  getScrollableTracksViewportHeight()
public boolean
  getScrollableTracksViewportWidth()
public int getScrollableUnitIncrement(
  Rectangle visibleRect,int orientation,
  int direction)
public String getSelectedText()
public Color getSelectedTextColor()
public Color getSelectionColor()
public int getSelectionEnd()
public int getSelectionStart()
public String getText(int offs,int len)
public String getText()
public TextUI getUI()
public boolean isEditable()
public boolean isFocusTraversable()
public boolean isOpaque()
public static void loadKeymap(Keymap map,
  KeyBinding bindings,Action actions)
public Rectangle modelToView(int pos)
public void moveCaretPosition(int pos)
protected String paramString()
public void paste()
protected void processComponentKeyEvent(
  KeyEvent e)
protected void processInputMethodEvent(
  InputMethodEvent e)
public void read(Reader in,Object desc)
public void removeCaretListener(
  CaretListener listener)
public static Keymap removeKeymap(String
  nm)
public void removeNotify()
public void replaceSelection(String
  content)
public void select(int selectionStart,
  int selectionEnd)
public void selectAll()
public void setCaret(Caret c)
public void setCaretColor(Color c)
public void setCaretPosition(int
  position)
public void setDisabledTextColor(Color c)
public void setDocument(Document doc)
public void setEditable(boolean b)
public void setEnabled(boolean b)
```

```
public void setFocusAccelerator(char
  aKey)
public void setHighlighter(Highlighter h)
public void setKeymap(Keymap map)
public void setMargin(Insets m)
public void setOpaque(boolean o)
public void setSelectedTextColor(Color c)
public void setSelectionColor(Color c)
public void setSelectionEnd(int
  selectionEnd)
public void setSelectionStart(int
  selectionStart)
public void setText(String t)
public void setUI(TextUI ui)
public void updateUI()
public int viewToModel(Point pt)
public void write(Writer out)
```

▶JTextField
```
public class javax.swing.JTextField
implements javax.swing.SwingConstants
extends javax.swing.text.JTextComponent
extends javax.swing.JComponent
extends java.awt.Container
extends java.awt.Component
extends java.lang.Object
```
Fields
```
public final static java.lang.String
  notifyAction
```
Constructors
```
public  JTextField()
public  JTextField(String text)
public  JTextField(int columns)
public  JTextField(String text,int
  columns)
public  JTextField(Document doc,String
  text,int columns)
```
Methods
```
public synchronized void
  addActionListener(ActionListener l)
protected Document createDefaultModel()
protected void fireActionPerformed()
public AccessibleContext
  getAccessibleContext()
public Action getActions()
public int getColumns()
protected int getColumnWidth()
public int getHorizontalAlignment()
public BoundedRangeModel
  getHorizontalVisibility()
public Dimension getPreferredSize()
public int getScrollOffset()
public String getUIClassID()
public boolean isValidateRoot()
protected String paramString()
public void postActionEvent()
public synchronized void
  removeActionListener(ActionListener l)
public void scrollRectToVisible(
  Rectangle r)
public void setActionCommand(String
  command)
```

```
public void setColumns(int columns)
public void setFont(Font f)
public void setHorizontalAlignment(int
  alignment)
public void setScrollOffset(int
  scrollOffset)
```

▶JTextPane
```
public class javax.swing.JTextPane
extends javax.swing.JEditorPane
extends javax.swing.text.JTextComponent
extends javax.swing.JComponent
extends java.awt.Container
extends java.awt.Component
extends java.lang.Object
```
Constructors
```
public  JTextPane()
public  JTextPane(StyledDocument doc)
```
Methods
```
public Style addStyle(String nm,Style
  parent)
protected EditorKit
  createDefaultEditorKit()
public AttributeSet
  getCharacterAttributes()
public MutableAttributeSet
  getInputAttributes()
public Style getLogicalStyle()
public AttributeSet
  getParagraphAttributes()
public boolean
  getScrollableTracksViewportWidth()
public Style getStyle(String nm)
public StyledDocument getStyledDocument()
protected final StyledEditorKit
  getStyledEditorKit()
public String getUIClassID()
public void insertComponent(Component c)
public void insertIcon(Icon g)
protected String paramString()
public void removeStyle(String nm)
public void replaceSelection(String
  content)
public void setCharacterAttributes(
  AttributeSet attr,boolean replace)
public void setDocument(Document doc)
public final void setEditorKit(EditorKit
  kit)
public void setLogicalStyle(Style s)
public void setParagraphAttributes(
  AttributeSet attr,boolean replace)
public void setStyledDocument(
  StyledDocument doc)
```

▶JToggleButton
```
public class javax.swing.JToggleButton
implements javax.accessibility.
  Accessible
extends javax.swing.AbstractButton
extends javax.swing.JComponent
extends java.awt.Container
extends java.awt.Component
```

extends java.lang.Object

Constructors
```
public  JToggleButton()
public  JToggleButton(Icon icon)
public  JToggleButton(Icon icon,boolean
  selected)
public  JToggleButton(String text)
public  JToggleButton(String text,
  boolean selected)
public  JToggleButton(String text,Icon
  icon)
public  JToggleButton(String text,Icon
  icon,boolean selected)
```

Methods
```
public AccessibleContext
  getAccessibleContext()
public String getUIClassID()
protected String paramString()
public void updateUI()
```

►JTOOLBAR
```
public class javax.swing.JToolBar
implements javax.accessibility.
  Accessible
implements javax.swing.SwingConstants
extends javax.swing.JComponent
extends java.awt.Container
extends java.awt.Component
extends java.lang.Object
```

Constructors
```
public  JToolBar()
public  JToolBar(int orientation)
```

Methods
```
public JButton add(Action a)
protected void addImpl(Component comp,
  Object constraints,int index)
public void addSeparator()
public void addSeparator(Dimension size)
protected PropertyChangeListener
  createActionChangeListener(JButton b)
public AccessibleContext
  getAccessibleContext()
public Component getComponentAtIndex(int
  i)
public int getComponentIndex(Component c)
public Insets getMargin()
public int getOrientation()
public ToolBarUI getUI()
public String getUIClassID()
public boolean isBorderPainted()
public boolean isFloatable()
protected void paintBorder(Graphics g)
protected String paramString()
public void remove(Component comp)
public void setBorderPainted(boolean b)
public void setFloatable(boolean b)
public void setMargin(Insets m)
public void setOrientation(int o)
public void setUI(ToolBarUI ui)
public void updateUI()
```

►JTOOLTIP
```
public class javax.swing.JToolTip
implements javax.accessibility.
  Accessible
extends javax.swing.JComponent
extends java.awt.Container
extends java.awt.Component
extends java.lang.Object
```

Constructors
```
public  JToolTip()
```

Methods
```
public AccessibleContext
  getAccessibleContext()
public JComponent getComponent()
public String getTipText()
public ToolTipUI getUI()
public String getUIClassID()
protected String paramString()
public void setComponent(JComponent c)
public void setTipText(String tipText)
public void updateUI()
```

►JTREE
```
public class javax.swing.JTree
implements javax.accessibility.
  Accessible
implements javax.swing.Scrollable
extends javax.swing.JComponent
extends java.awt.Container
extends java.awt.Component
extends java.lang.Object
```

Fields
```
protected transient javax.swing.tree.
  TreeCellEditor cellEditor
protected transient javax.swing.tree.
  TreeCellRenderer cellRenderer
public final static java.lang.String
  CELL_EDITOR_PROPERTY
public final static java.lang.String
  CELL_RENDERER_PROPERTY
protected boolean editable
public final static java.lang.String
  EDITABLE_PROPERTY
protected boolean
  invokesStopCellEditing
public final static java.lang.String
  INVOKES_STOP_CELL_EDITING_PROPERTY
protected boolean largeModel
public final static java.lang.String
  LARGE_MODEL_PROPERTY
protected boolean rootVisible
public final static java.lang.String
  ROOT_VISIBLE_PROPERTY
protected int rowHeight
public final static java.lang.String ROW_
  HEIGHT_PROPERTY
protected boolean scrollsOnExpand
public final static java.lang.String
  SCROLLS_ON_EXPAND_PROPERTY
protected transient javax.swing.tree.
  TreeSelectionModel selectionModel
```

```
protected transient
  TreeSelectionRedirector
  selectionRedirector
public final static java.lang.String
  SELECTION_MODEL_PROPERTY
protected boolean showsRootHandles
public final static java.lang.String
  SHOWS_ROOT_HANDLES_PROPERTY
protected int toggleClickCount
protected transient javax.swing.tree.
  TreeModel treeModel
protected transient javax.swing.event.
  TreeModelListener treeModelListener
public final static java.lang.String
  TREE_MODEL_PROPERTY
protected int visibleRowCount
public final static java.lang.String
  VISIBLE_ROW_COUNT_PROPERTY
```

Constructors
```
public  JTree()
public  JTree(Object value)
public  JTree(Vector value)
public  JTree(Hashtable value)
public  JTree(TreeNode root)
public  JTree(TreeNode root,boolean
  asksAllowsChildren)
public  JTree(TreeModel newModel)
```

Methods
```
public void addSelectionInterval(int
  index0,int index1)
public void addSelectionPath(TreePath
  path)
public void addSelectionPaths(TreePath
  paths)
public void addSelectionRow(int row)
public void addSelectionRows(int rows)
public void addTreeExpansionListener(
  TreeExpansionListener tel)
public void addTreeSelectionListener(
  TreeSelectionListener tsl)
public void addTreeWillExpandListener(
  TreeWillExpandListener tel)
public void cancelEditing()
public void clearSelection()
protected void clearToggledPaths()
public void collapsePath(TreePath path)
public void collapseRow(int row)
public String convertValueToText(Object
  value,boolean selected,boolean expanded,
  boolean leaf,int row,boolean hasFocus)
protected static TreeModel
  createTreeModel(Object value)
protected TreeModelListener
  createTreeModelListener()
public void expandPath(TreePath path)
public void expandRow(int row)
public void fireTreeCollapsed(TreePath
  path)
public void fireTreeExpanded(TreePath
  path)
public void fireTreeWillCollapse(
  TreePath path)
```

```
public void fireTreeWillExpand(TreePath
  path)
protected void fireValueChanged(
  TreeSelectionEvent e)
public AccessibleContext
  getAccessibleContext()
public TreeCellEditor getCellEditor()
public TreeCellRenderer getCellRenderer()
public TreePath
  getClosestPathForLocation(int x,int y)
public int getClosestRowForLocation(int
  x,int y)
protected static TreeModel
  getDefaultTreeModel()
protected Enumeration
  getDescendantToggledPaths(TreePath
  parent)
public TreePath getEditingPath()
public Enumeration
  getExpandedDescendants(TreePath parent)
public boolean getInvokesStopCellEditing(
  )
public Object
  getLastSelectedPathComponent()
public TreePath getLeadSelectionPath()
public int getLeadSelectionRow()
public int getMaxSelectionRow()
public int getMinSelectionRow()
public TreeModel getModel()
protected TreePath getPathBetweenRows(
  int index0,int index1)
public Rectangle getPathBounds(TreePath
  path)
public TreePath getPathForLocation(int x,
  int y)
public TreePath getPathForRow(int row)
public Dimension
  getPreferredScrollableViewportSize()
public Rectangle getRowBounds(int row)
public int getRowCount()
public int getRowForLocation(int x,int y)
public int getRowForPath(TreePath path)
public int getRowHeight()
public int getScrollableBlockIncrement(
  Rectangle visibleRect,int orientation,
  int direction)
public boolean
  getScrollableTracksViewportHeight()
public boolean
  getScrollableTracksViewportWidth()
public int getScrollableUnitIncrement(
  Rectangle visibleRect,int orientation,
  int direction)
public boolean getScrollsOnExpand()
public int getSelectionCount()
public TreeSelectionModel
  getSelectionModel()
public TreePath getSelectionPath()
public TreePath getSelectionPaths()
public int getSelectionRows()
public boolean getShowsRootHandles()
```

```
public String getToolTipText(MouseEvent
  event)
public TreeUI getUI()
public String getUIClassID()
public int getVisibleRowCount()
public boolean hasBeenExpanded(TreePath
  path)
public boolean isCollapsed(TreePath path)
public boolean isCollapsed(int row)
public boolean isEditable()
public boolean isEditing()
public boolean isExpanded(TreePath path)
public boolean isExpanded(int row)
public boolean isFixedRowHeight()
public boolean isLargeModel()
public boolean isPathEditable(TreePath
  path)
public boolean isPathSelected(TreePath
  path)
public boolean isRootVisible()
public boolean isRowSelected(int row)
public boolean isSelectionEmpty()
public boolean isVisible(TreePath path)
public void makeVisible(TreePath path)
protected String paramString()
protected void
  removeDescendantToggledPaths(Enumeration
  toRemove)
public void removeSelectionInterval(int
  index0,int index1)
public void removeSelectionPath(TreePath
  path)
public void removeSelectionPaths(
  TreePath paths)
public void removeSelectionRow(int row)
public void removeSelectionRows(int rows)
public void removeTreeExpansionListener(
  TreeExpansionListener tel)
public void removeTreeSelectionListener(
  TreeSelectionListener tsl)
public void removeTreeWillExpandListener(
  TreeWillExpandListener tel)
public void scrollPathToVisible(TreePath
  path)
public void scrollRowToVisible(int row)
public void setCellEditor(TreeCellEditor
  cellEditor)
public void setCellRenderer(
  TreeCellRenderer x)
public void setEditable(boolean flag)
protected void setExpandedState(TreePath
  path,boolean state)
public void setInvokesStopCellEditing(
  boolean newValue)
public void setLargeModel(boolean
  newValue)
public void setModel(TreeModel newModel)
public void setRootVisible(boolean
  rootVisible)
public void setRowHeight(int rowHeight)
public void setScrollsOnExpand(boolean
  newValue)
```

```
public void setSelectionInterval(int
  index0,int index1)
public void setSelectionModel(
  TreeSelectionModel selectionModel)
public void setSelectionPath(TreePath
  path)
public void setSelectionPaths(TreePath
  paths)
public void setSelectionRow(int row)
public void setSelectionRows(int rows)
public void setShowsRootHandles(boolean
  newValue)
public void setUI(TreeUI ui)
public void setVisibleRowCount(int
  newCount)
public void startEditingAtPath(TreePath
  path)
public boolean stopEditing()
public void treeDidChange()
public void updateUI()
```

▸JVIEWPORT

```
public class javax.swing.JViewport
implements javax.accessibility.
  Accessible
extends javax.swing.JComponent
extends java.awt.Container
extends java.awt.Component
extends java.lang.Object
```

Fields

```
protected boolean backingStore
protected transient java.awt.Image
  backingStoreImage
protected boolean isViewSizeSet
protected java.awt.Point
  lastPaintPosition
protected boolean scrollUnderway
```

Constructors

```
public  JViewport()
```

Methods

```
public void addChangeListener(
  ChangeListener l)
protected void addImpl(Component child,
  Object constraints,int index)
protected boolean computeBlit(int dx,int
  dy,Point blitFrom,Point blitTo,Dimension
  blitSize,Rectangle blitPaint)
protected LayoutManager
  createLayoutManager()
protected ViewListener
  createViewListener()
protected void fireStateChanged()
public AccessibleContext
  getAccessibleContext()
public Dimension getExtentSize()
public final Insets getInsets()
public final Insets getInsets(Insets
  insets)
public Component getView()
public Point getViewPosition()
public Rectangle getViewRect()
public Dimension getViewSize()
```

```
public boolean isBackingStoreEnabled()
public boolean isOptimizedDrawingEnabled(
  )
public void paint(Graphics g)
protected String paramString()
public void remove(Component child)
public void removeChangeListener(
  ChangeListener l)
public void repaint(long tm,int x,int y,
  int w,int h)
public void reshape(int x,int y,int w,
  int h)
public void scrollRectToVisible(
  Rectangle contentRect)
public void setBackingStoreEnabled(
  boolean x)
public final void setBorder(Border
  border)
public void setExtentSize(Dimension
  newExtent)
public void setView(Component view)
public void setViewPosition(Point p)
public void setViewSize(Dimension
  newSize)
public Dimension toViewCoordinates(
  Dimension size)
public Point toViewCoordinates(Point p)
```

►JWINDOW

```
public class javax.swing.JWindow
implements javax.accessibility.
  Accessible
implements javax.swing.
  RootPaneContainer
extends java.awt.Window
extends java.awt.Container
extends java.awt.Component
extends java.lang.Object
```

Fields

```
protected javax.accessibility.
  AccessibleContext accessibleContext
protected javax.swing.JRootPane
  rootPane
protected boolean
  rootPaneCheckingEnabled
```

Constructors

```
public  JWindow()
public  JWindow(Frame owner)
public  JWindow(Window owner)
```

Methods

```
protected void addImpl(Component comp,
  Object constraints,int index)
protected JRootPane createRootPane()
public AccessibleContext
  getAccessibleContext()
public Container getContentPane()
public Component getGlassPane()
public JLayeredPane getLayeredPane()
public JRootPane getRootPane()
protected boolean
  isRootPaneCheckingEnabled()
protected String paramString()
```

```
public void setContentPane(Container
  contentPane)
public void setGlassPane(Component
  glassPane)
public void setLayeredPane(JLayeredPane
  layeredPane)
public void setLayout(LayoutManager
  manager)
protected void setRootPane(JRootPane
  root)
protected void
  setRootPaneCheckingEnabled(boolean
  enabled)
protected void windowInit()
```

►KERNEL

```
public class java.awt.image.Kernel
implements java.lang.Cloneable
extends java.lang.Object
```

Constructors

```
public static  Kernel(int width,int
  height,float data)
```

Methods

```
public Object clone()
public final int getHeight()
public final float getKernelData(float
  data)
public final int getWidth()
public final int getXOrigin()
public final int getYOrigin()
```

►KEYADAPTER

```
public abstract class java.awt.event.
  KeyAdapter
implements java.awt.event.KeyListener
extends java.lang.Object
```

Methods

```
public void keyPressed(KeyEvent e)
public void keyReleased(KeyEvent e)
public void keyTyped(KeyEvent e)
```

►KEYEVENT

```
public class java.awt.event.KeyEvent
extends java.awt.event.InputEvent
extends java.awt.event.ComponentEvent
extends java.awt.AWTEvent
extends java.util.EventObject
extends java.lang.Object
```

Fields

```
public final static char CHAR_UNDEFINED
public final static int KEY_FIRST
public final static int KEY_LAST
public final static int KEY_PRESSED
public final static int KEY_RELEASED
public final static int KEY_TYPED
public final static int VK_0
public final static int VK_1
public final static int VK_2
public final static int VK_3
public final static int VK_4
public final static int VK_5
public final static int VK_6
```

```
public final static int VK_7
public final static int VK_8
public final static int VK_9
public final static int VK_A
public final static int VK_ACCEPT
public final static int VK_ADD
public final static int VK_AGAIN
public final static int VK_ALL_
  CANDIDATES
public final static int VK_ALPHANUMERIC
public final static int VK_ALT
public final static int VK_ALT_GRAPH
public final static int VK_AMPERSAND
public final static int VK_ASTERISK
public final static int VK_AT
public final static int VK_B
public final static int VK_BACK_QUOTE
public final static int VK_BACK_SLASH
public final static int VK_BACK_SPACE
public final static int VK_BRACELEFT
public final static int VK_BRACERIGHT
public final static int VK_C
public final static int VK_CANCEL
public final static int VK_CAPS_LOCK
public final static int VK_CIRCUMFLEX
public final static int VK_CLEAR
public final static int VK_CLOSE_
  BRACKET
public final static int VK_CODE_INPUT
public final static int VK_COLON
public final static int VK_COMMA
public final static int VK_COMPOSE
public final static int VK_CONTROL
public final static int VK_CONVERT
public final static int VK_COPY
public final static int VK_CUT
public final static int VK_D
public final static int VK_DEAD_
  ABOVEDOT
public final static int VK_DEAD_
  ABOVERING
public final static int VK_DEAD_ACUTE
public final static int VK_DEAD_BREVE
public final static int VK_DEAD_CARON
public final static int VK_DEAD_CEDILLA
public final static int VK_DEAD_
  CIRCUMFLEX
public final static int VK_DEAD_
  DIAERESIS
public final static int VK_DEAD_
  DOUBLEACUTE
public final static int VK_DEAD_GRAVE
public final static int VK_DEAD_IOTA
public final static int VK_DEAD_MACRON
public final static int VK_DEAD_OGONEK
public final static int VK_DEAD_
  SEMIVOICED_SOUND
public final static int VK_DEAD_TILDE
public final static int VK_DEAD_VOICED_
  SOUND
public final static int VK_DECIMAL
public final static int VK_DELETE
public final static int VK_DIVIDE
```

```
public final static int VK_DOLLAR
public final static int VK_DOWN
public final static int VK_E
public final static int VK_END
public final static int VK_ENTER
public final static int VK_EQUALS
public final static int VK_ESCAPE
public final static int VK_EURO_SIGN
public final static int VK_EXCLAMATION_
  MARK
public final static int VK_F
public final static int VK_F1
public final static int VK_F10
public final static int VK_F11
public final static int VK_F12
public final static int VK_F13
public final static int VK_F14
public final static int VK_F15
public final static int VK_F16
public final static int VK_F17
public final static int VK_F18
public final static int VK_F19
public final static int VK_F2
public final static int VK_F20
public final static int VK_F21
public final static int VK_F22
public final static int VK_F23
public final static int VK_F24
public final static int VK_F3
public final static int VK_F4
public final static int VK_F5
public final static int VK_F6
public final static int VK_F7
public final static int VK_F8
public final static int VK_F9
public final static int VK_FINAL
public final static int VK_FIND
public final static int VK_FULL_WIDTH
public final static int VK_G
public final static int VK_GREATER
public final static int VK_H
public final static int VK_HALF_WIDTH
public final static int VK_HELP
public final static int VK_HIRAGANA
public final static int VK_HOME
public final static int VK_I
public final static int VK_INSERT
public final static int VK_INVERTED_
  EXCLAMATION_MARK
public final static int VK_J
public final static int VK_JAPANESE_
  HIRAGANA
public final static int VK_JAPANESE_
  KATAKANA
public final static int VK_JAPANESE_
  ROMAN
public final static int VK_K
public final static int VK_KANA
public final static int VK_KANJI
public final static int VK_KATAKANA
public final static int VK_KP_DOWN
public final static int VK_KP_LEFT
public final static int VK_KP_RIGHT
```

```
public final static int VK_KP_UP
public final static int VK_L
public final static int VK_LEFT
public final static int VK_LEFT_
  PARENTHESIS
public final static int VK_LESS
public final static int VK_M
public final static int VK_META
public final static int VK_MINUS
public final static int VK_MODECHANGE
public final static int VK_MULTIPLY
public final static int VK_N
public final static int VK_NONCONVERT
public final static int VK_NUMBER_SIGN
public final static int VK_NUMPAD0
public final static int VK_NUMPAD1
public final static int VK_NUMPAD2
public final static int VK_NUMPAD3
public final static int VK_NUMPAD4
public final static int VK_NUMPAD5
public final static int VK_NUMPAD6
public final static int VK_NUMPAD7
public final static int VK_NUMPAD8
public final static int VK_NUMPAD9
public final static int VK_NUM_LOCK
public final static int VK_O
public final static int VK_OPEN_BRACKET
public final static int VK_P
public final static int VK_PAGE_DOWN
public final static int VK_PAGE_UP
public final static int VK_PASTE
public final static int VK_PAUSE
public final static int VK_PERIOD
public final static int VK_PLUS
public final static int VK_PREVIOUS_
  CANDIDATE
public final static int VK_PRINTSCREEN
public final static int VK_PROPS
public final static int VK_Q
public final static int VK_QUOTE
public final static int VK_QUOTEDBL
public final static int VK_R
public final static int VK_RIGHT
public final static int VK_RIGHT_
  PARENTHESIS
public final static int VK_ROMAN_
  CHARACTERS
public final static int VK_S
public final static int VK_SCROLL_LOCK
public final static int VK_SEMICOLON
public final static int VK_SEPARATER
public final static int VK_SHIFT
public final static int VK_SLASH
public final static int VK_SPACE
public final static int VK_STOP
public final static int VK_SUBTRACT
public final static int VK_T
public final static int VK_TAB
public final static int VK_U
public final static int VK_UNDEFINED
public final static int VK_UNDERSCORE
public final static int VK_UNDO
```

```
public final static int VK_UP
public final static int VK_V
public final static int VK_W
public final static int VK_X
public final static int VK_Y
public final static int VK_Z
```

Constructors

```
public  KeyEvent(Component source,int id,
  long when,int modifiers,int keyCode,char
  keyChar)
public  KeyEvent(Component source,int id,
  long when,int modifiers,int keyCode)
```

Methods

```
public char getKeyChar()
public int getKeyCode()
public static String getKeyModifiersText(
  int modifiers)
public static String getKeyText(int
  keyCode)
public boolean isActionKey()
public String paramString()
public void setKeyChar(char keyChar)
public void setKeyCode(int keyCode)
public void setModifiers(int modifiers)
```

▶KEYEXCEPTION

```
public class java.security.KeyException
extends java.security.
  GeneralSecurityException
extends java.lang.Exception
extends java.lang.Throwable
extends java.lang.Object
```

Constructors

```
public  KeyException()
public  KeyException(String msg)
```

▶KEYFACTORY

```
public class java.security.KeyFactory
extends java.lang.Object
```

Constructors

```
protected  KeyFactory(KeyFactorySpi
  keyFacSpi,Provider provider,String
  algorithm)
```

Methods

```
public final PrivateKey generatePrivate(
  KeySpec keySpec)
public final PublicKey generatePublic(
  KeySpec keySpec)
public final String getAlgorithm()
public static KeyFactory getInstance(
  String algorithm)
public static KeyFactory getInstance(
  String algorithm,String provider)
public final KeySpec getKeySpec(Key key,
  Class keySpec)
public final Provider getProvider()
public final Key translateKey(Key key)
```

▶KEYFACTORYSPI

```
public abstract class java.security.
  KeyFactorySpi
extends java.lang.Object
```

Methods

```
protected abstract PrivateKey
  engineGeneratePrivate(KeySpec keySpec)
protected abstract PublicKey
  engineGeneratePublic(KeySpec keySpec)
protected abstract KeySpec
  engineGetKeySpec(Key key,Class keySpec)
protected abstract Key
  engineTranslateKey(Key key)
```

▶KeyManagementException

```
public class java.security.
  KeyManagementException
extends java.security.KeyException
extends java.security.
  GeneralSecurityException
extends java.lang.Exception
extends java.lang.Throwable
extends java.lang.Object
```

Constructors

```
public  KeyManagementException()
public  KeyManagementException(String
  msg)
```

▶KeyPair

```
public final class java.security.
  KeyPair
implements java.io.Serializable
extends java.lang.Object
```

Constructors

```
public  KeyPair(PublicKey publicKey,
  PrivateKey privateKey)
```

Methods

```
public PrivateKey getPrivate()
public PublicKey getPublic()
```

▶KeyPairGenerator

```
public abstract class java.security.
  KeyPairGenerator
extends java.security.
  KeyPairGeneratorSpi
extends java.lang.Object
```

Constructors

```
protected  KeyPairGenerator(String
  algorithm)
```

Methods

```
public final KeyPair genKeyPair()
public String getAlgorithm()
public static KeyPairGenerator
  getInstance(String algorithm)
public static KeyPairGenerator
  getInstance(String algorithm,String
  provider)
public final Provider getProvider()
public void initialize(int keysize)
public void initialize(int keysize,
  SecureRandom random)
public void initialize(
  AlgorithmParameterSpec params)
public void initialize(
  AlgorithmParameterSpec params,
  SecureRandom random)
```

▶KeyPairGeneratorSpi

```
public abstract class java.security.
  KeyPairGeneratorSpi
extends java.lang.Object
```

Methods

```
public abstract KeyPair generateKeyPair()
public abstract void initialize(int
  keysize,SecureRandom random)
public void initialize(
  AlgorithmParameterSpec params,
  SecureRandom random)
```

▶KeyStore

```
public class java.security.KeyStore
extends java.lang.Object
```

Constructors

```
protected  KeyStore(KeyStoreSpi
  keyStoreSpi,Provider provider,String
  type)
```

Methods

```
public final Enumeration aliases()
public final boolean containsAlias(
  String alias)
public final void deleteEntry(String
  alias)
public final Certificate getCertificate(
  String alias)
public final String getCertificateAlias(
  Certificate cert)
public final Certificate
  getCertificateChain(String alias)
public final Date getCreationDate(String
  alias)
public final static String
  getDefaultType()
public static KeyStore getInstance(
  String type)
public static KeyStore getInstance(
  String type,String provider)
public final Key getKey(String alias,
  char password)
public final Provider getProvider()
public final String getType()
public final boolean isCertificateEntry(
  String alias)
public final boolean isKeyEntry(String
  alias)
public final void load(InputStream
  stream,char password)
public final void setCertificateEntry(
  String alias,Certificate cert)
public final void setKeyEntry(String
  alias,Key key,char password,Certificate
  chain)
public final void setKeyEntry(String
  alias,byte key,Certificate chain)
public final int size()
public final void store(OutputStream
  stream,char password)
```

▶**KEYSTOREEXCEPTION**
public class java.security.
  KeyStoreException
extends java.security.
  GeneralSecurityException
extends java.lang.Exception
extends java.lang.Throwable
extends java.lang.Object
Constructors
public KeyStoreException()
public KeyStoreException(String msg)

▶**KEYSTORESPI**
public abstract class java.security.
  KeyStoreSpi
extends java.lang.Object
Methods
public abstract Enumeration
  engineAliases()
public abstract boolean
  engineContainsAlias(String alias)
public abstract void engineDeleteEntry(
  String alias)
public abstract Certificate
  engineGetCertificate(String alias)
public abstract String
  engineGetCertificateAlias(Certificate
  cert)
public abstract Certificate
  engineGetCertificateChain(String alias)
public abstract Date
  engineGetCreationDate(String alias)
public abstract Key engineGetKey(String
  alias,char password)
public abstract boolean
  engineIsCertificateEntry(String alias)
public abstract boolean engineIsKeyEntry(
  String alias)
public abstract void engineLoad(
  InputStream stream,char password)
public abstract void
  engineSetCertificateEntry(String alias,
  Certificate cert)
public abstract void engineSetKeyEntry(
  String alias,Key key,char password,
  Certificate chain)
public abstract void engineSetKeyEntry(
  String alias,byte key,Certificate chain)
public abstract int engineSize()
public abstract void engineStore(
  OutputStream stream,char password)

▶**KEYSTROKE**
public class javax.swing.KeyStroke
implements java.io.Serializable
extends java.lang.Object
Constructors
private KeyStroke()
Methods
public boolean equals(Object anObject)
public char getKeyChar()
public int getKeyCode()

public static KeyStroke getKeyStroke(
  char keyChar)
public static KeyStroke getKeyStroke(
  char keyChar,boolean onKeyRelease)
public static KeyStroke getKeyStroke(int
  keyCode,int modifiers,boolean
  onKeyRelease)
public static KeyStroke getKeyStroke(int
  keyCode,int modifiers)
public static KeyStroke getKeyStroke(
  String representation)
public static KeyStroke
  getKeyStrokeForEvent(KeyEvent anEvent)
public int getModifiers()
public int hashCode()
public boolean isOnKeyRelease()
public String toString()

▶**LABEL**
public class java.awt.Label
extends java.awt.Component
extends java.lang.Object
Fields
public final static int CENTER
public final static int LEFT
public final static int RIGHT
Constructors
public Label()
public Label(String text)
public Label(String text,int alignment)
Methods
public void addNotify()
public int getAlignment()
public String getText()
protected String paramString()
public synchronized void setAlignment(
  int alignment)
public void setText(String text)

▶**LABELUI**
public abstract class javax.swing.plaf.
  LabelUI
extends javax.swing.plaf.ComponentUI
extends java.lang.Object

▶**LABELVIEW**
public class javax.swing.text.LabelView
extends javax.swing.text.View
extends java.lang.Object
Constructors
public LabelView(Element elem)
Methods
public View breakView(int axis,int p0,
  float pos,float len)
public void changedUpdate(DocumentEvent
  e,Shape a,ViewFactory f)
public View createFragment(int p0,int p1)
public float getAlignment(int axis)
public int getBreakWeight(int axis,float
  pos,float len)
protected Font getFont()
protected FontMetrics getFontMetrics()

```
public int getNextVisualPositionFrom(int
  pos,Bias b,Shape a,int direction,Bias
  biasRet)
public float getPreferredSpan(int axis)
public void insertUpdate(DocumentEvent e,
  Shape a,ViewFactory f)
public Shape modelToView(int pos,Shape a,
  Bias b)
public void paint(Graphics g,Shape a)
public void removeUpdate(DocumentEvent
  changes,Shape a,ViewFactory f)
protected void
  setPropertiesFromAttributes()
protected void setStrikeThrough(boolean
  s)
protected void setSubscript(boolean s)
protected void setSuperscript(boolean s)
protected void setUnderline(boolean u)
public String toString()
public int viewToModel(float x,float y,
  Shape a,Bias biasReturn)
```

▶LASTOWNEREXCEPTION
```
public class java.security.acl.
  LastOwnerException
extends java.lang.Exception
extends java.lang.Throwable
extends java.lang.Object
```
Constructors
```
public  LastOwnerException()
```

▶LAYEREDHIGHLIGHTER
```
public abstract class javax.swing.text.
  LayeredHighlighter
implements javax.swing.text.Highlighter
extends java.lang.Object
```
Methods
```
public abstract void
  paintLayeredHighlights(Graphics g,int p0,
  int p1,Shape viewBounds,JTextComponent
  editor,View view)
```

▶LEASE
```
public final class java.rmi.dgc.Lease
implements java.io.Serializable
extends java.lang.Object
```
Constructors
```
public  Lease(VMID id,long duration)
```
Methods
```
public long getValue()
public VMID getVMID()
```

▶LINE2D
```
public abstract class java.awt.geom.
  Line2D
implements java.lang.Cloneable
implements java.awt.Shape
extends java.lang.Object
```
Constructors
```
protected  Line2D()
```
Methods
```
public Object clone()
```

```
public boolean contains(double x,double
  y)
public boolean contains(Point2D p)
public boolean contains(double x,double
  y,double w,double h)
public boolean contains(Rectangle2D r)
public Rectangle getBounds()
public abstract Point2D getP1()
public abstract Point2D getP2()
public PathIterator getPathIterator(
  AffineTransform at)
public PathIterator getPathIterator(
  AffineTransform at,double flatness)
public abstract double getX1()
public abstract double getX2()
public abstract double getY1()
public abstract double getY2()
public boolean intersects(double x,
  double y,double w,double h)
public boolean intersects(Rectangle2D r)
public boolean intersectsLine(double X1,
  double Y1,double X2,double Y2)
public boolean intersectsLine(Line2D l)
public static boolean linesIntersect(
  double X1,double Y1,double X2,double Y2,
  double X3,double Y3,double X4,double Y4)
public static double ptLineDist(double
  X1,double Y1,double X2,double Y2,double
  PX,double PY)
public double ptLineDist(double PX,
  double PY)
public double ptLineDist(Point2D pt)
public static double ptLineDistSq(double
  X1,double Y1,double X2,double Y2,double
  PX,double PY)
public double ptLineDistSq(double PX,
  double PY)
public double ptLineDistSq(Point2D pt)
public static double ptSegDist(double X1,
  double Y1,double X2,double Y2,double PX,
  double PY)
public double ptSegDist(double PX,double
  PY)
public double ptSegDist(Point2D pt)
public static double ptSegDistSq(double
  X1,double Y1,double X2,double Y2,double
  PX,double PY)
public double ptSegDistSq(double PX,
  double PY)
public double ptSegDistSq(Point2D pt)
public static int relativeCCW(double X1,
  double Y1,double X2,double Y2,double PX,
  double PY)
public int relativeCCW(double PX,double
  PY)
public int relativeCCW(Point2D p)
public abstract void setLine(double X1,
  double Y1,double X2,double Y2)
public void setLine(Point2D p1,Point2D
  p2)
public void setLine(Line2D l)
```

▶**LINEBORDER**
public class javax.swing.border.
  LineBorder
extends javax.swing.border.
  AbstractBorder
extends java.lang.Object

Fields
protected java.awt.Color lineColor
protected boolean roundedCorners
protected int thickness

Constructors
public LineBorder(Color color)
public LineBorder(Color color,int
  thickness)
 LineBorder()

Methods
public static Border
  createBlackLineBorder()
public static Border
  createGrayLineBorder()
public Insets getBorderInsets(Component
  c)
public Insets getBorderInsets(Component
  c,Insets insets)
public Color getLineColor()
public int getThickness()
public boolean isBorderOpaque()
public void paintBorder(Component c,
  Graphics g,int x,int y,int width,int
  height)

▶**LINEBREAKMEASURER**
public final class java.awt.font.
  LineBreakMeasurer
extends java.lang.Object

Constructors
public LineBreakMeasurer(
  AttributedCharacterIterator text,
  FontRenderContext frc)
public LineBreakMeasurer(
  AttributedCharacterIterator text,
  BreakIterator breakIter,
  FontRenderContext frc)

Methods
public void deleteChar(
  AttributedCharacterIterator newParagraph,
  int deletePos)
public int getPosition()
public void insertChar(
  AttributedCharacterIterator newParagraph,
  int insertPos)
public TextLayout nextLayout(float
  maxAdvance)
public TextLayout nextLayout(float
  wrappingWidth,int offsetLimit,boolean
  requireNextWord)
public int nextOffset(float maxAdvance)
public int nextOffset(float
  wrappingWidth,int offsetLimit,boolean
  requireNextWord)
public void setPosition(int newPosition)

▶**LINEMETRICS**
public abstract class java.awt.font.
  LineMetrics
extends java.lang.Object

Methods
public abstract float getAscent()
public abstract int getBaselineIndex()
public abstract float getBaselineOffsets(
)
public abstract float getDescent()
public abstract float getHeight()
public abstract float getLeading()
public abstract int getNumChars()
public abstract float
  getStrikethroughOffset()
public abstract float
  getStrikethroughThickness()
public abstract float getUnderlineOffset(
)
public abstract float
  getUnderlineThickness()

▶**LINENUMBERINPUTSTREAM**
public class java.io.
  LineNumberInputStream
extends java.io.FilterInputStream
extends java.io.InputStream
extends java.lang.Object

Constructors
public LineNumberInputStream(
  InputStream in)

Methods
public int available()
public int getLineNumber()
public void mark(int readlimit)
public int read()
public int read(byte b,int off,int len)
public void reset()
public void setLineNumber(int lineNumber)
public long skip(long n)

▶**LINENUMBERREADER**
public class java.io.LineNumberReader
extends java.io.BufferedReader
extends java.io.Reader
extends java.lang.Object

Constructors
public LineNumberReader(Reader in)
public LineNumberReader(Reader in,int
  sz)

Methods
public int getLineNumber()
public void mark(int readAheadLimit)
public int read()
public int read(char cbuf,int off,int
  len)
public String readLine()
public void reset()
public void setLineNumber(int lineNumber)
public long skip(long n)

►LINKAGEERROR
public class java.lang.LinkageError
extends java.lang.Error
extends java.lang.Throwable
extends java.lang.Object

Constructors
public LinkageError()
public LinkageError(String s)

►LINKEDLIST
public class java.util.LinkedList
implements java.lang.Cloneable
implements java.util.List
implements java.io.Serializable
extends java.util.
  AbstractSequentialList
extends java.util.AbstractList
extends java.util.AbstractCollection
extends java.lang.Object

Constructors
public LinkedList()
public LinkedList(Collection c)

Methods
public boolean add(Object o)
public void add(int index,Object element)
public boolean addAll(Collection c)
public boolean addAll(int index,
  Collection c)
public void addFirst(Object o)
public void addLast(Object o)
public void clear()
public Object clone()
public boolean contains(Object o)
public Object get(int index)
public Object getFirst()
public Object getLast()
public int indexOf(Object o)
public int lastIndexOf(Object o)
public ListIterator listIterator(int
  index)
public boolean remove(Object o)
public Object remove(int index)
public Object removeFirst()
public Object removeLast()
public Object set(int index,Object
  element)
public int size()
public Object toArray()
public Object toArray(Object a)

►LIST
public class java.awt.List
implements java.awt.ItemSelectable
extends java.awt.Component
extends java.lang.Object

Constructors
public List()
public List(int rows)
public List(int rows,boolean
  multipleMode)

Methods
public void add(String item)

public void add(String item,int index)
public synchronized void
  addActionListener(ActionListener l)
public void addItem(String item)
public synchronized void addItem(String
  item,int index)
public synchronized void addItemListener(
  ItemListener l)
public void addNotify()
public boolean allowsMultipleSelections()
public synchronized void clear()
public int countItems()
public void delItem(int position)
public synchronized void delItems(int
  start,int end)
public synchronized void deselect(int
  index)
public String getItem(int index)
public int getItemCount()
public synchronized String getItems()
public Dimension getMinimumSize(int rows)
public Dimension getMinimumSize()
public Dimension getPreferredSize(int
  rows)
public Dimension getPreferredSize()
public int getRows()
public synchronized int getSelectedIndex(
)
public synchronized int
  getSelectedIndexes()
public synchronized String
  getSelectedItem()
public synchronized String
  getSelectedItems()
public Object getSelectedObjects()
public int getVisibleIndex()
public boolean isIndexSelected(int index)
public boolean isMultipleMode()
public boolean isSelected(int index)
public synchronized void makeVisible(int
  index)
public Dimension minimumSize(int rows)
public Dimension minimumSize()
protected String paramString()
public Dimension preferredSize(int rows)
public Dimension preferredSize()
protected void processActionEvent(
  ActionEvent e)
protected void processEvent(AWTEvent e)
protected void processItemEvent(
  ItemEvent e)
public synchronized void remove(String
  item)
public void remove(int position)
public synchronized void
  removeActionListener(ActionListener l)
public void removeAll()
public synchronized void
  removeItemListener(ItemListener l)
public void removeNotify()
public synchronized void replaceItem(
  String newValue,int index)
public void select(int index)

public void setMultipleMode(boolean b)
public synchronized void
  setMultipleSelections(boolean b)

► **LISTDATAEVENT**
public class javax.swing.event.
  ListDataEvent
extends java.util.EventObject
extends java.lang.Object
Fields
public final static int CONTENTS_
  CHANGED
public final static int INTERVAL_ADDED
public final static int INTERVAL_
  REMOVED
Constructors
public ListDataEvent(Object source,int
  type,int index0,int index1)
Methods
public int getIndex0()
public int getIndex1()
public int getType()

► **LISTRESOURCEBUNDLE**
public abstract class java.util.
  ListResourceBundle
extends java.util.ResourceBundle
extends java.lang.Object
Constructors
public ListResourceBundle()
Methods
protected abstract Object getContents()
public Enumeration getKeys()
public final Object handleGetObject(
  String key)

► **LISTSELECTIONEVENT**
public class javax.swing.event.
  ListSelectionEvent
extends java.util.EventObject
extends java.lang.Object
Constructors
public ListSelectionEvent(Object source,
  int firstIndex,int lastIndex,boolean
  isAdjusting)
Methods
public int getFirstIndex()
public int getLastIndex()
public boolean getValueIsAdjusting()
public String toString()

► **LISTUI**
public abstract class javax.swing.plaf.
  ListUI
extends javax.swing.plaf.ComponentUI
extends java.lang.Object
Methods
public abstract Rectangle getCellBounds(
  JList list,int index1,int index2)
public abstract Point indexToLocation(
  JList list,int index)

public abstract int locationToIndex(
  JList list,Point location)

► **LISTVIEW**
public class javax.swing.text.html.
  ListView
extends javax.swing.text.html.BlockView
extends javax.swing.text.BoxView
extends javax.swing.text.CompositeView
extends javax.swing.text.View
extends java.lang.Object
Constructors
public ListView(Element elem)
Methods
public float getAlignment(int axis)
public void paint(Graphics g,Shape
  allocation)
protected void paintChild(Graphics g,
  Rectangle alloc,int index)

► **LOCALE**
public final class java.util.Locale
implements java.lang.Cloneable
implements java.io.Serializable
extends java.lang.Object
Fields
public final static java.util.Locale
  CANADA
public final static java.util.Locale
  CANADA_FRENCH
public final static java.util.Locale
  CHINA
public final static java.util.Locale
  CHINESE
public final static java.util.Locale
  ENGLISH
public final static java.util.Locale
  FRANCE
public final static java.util.Locale
  FRENCH
public final static java.util.Locale
  GERMAN
public final static java.util.Locale
  GERMANY
public final static java.util.Locale
  ITALIAN
public final static java.util.Locale
  ITALY
public final static java.util.Locale
  JAPAN
public final static java.util.Locale
  JAPANESE
public final static java.util.Locale
  KOREA
public final static java.util.Locale
  KOREAN
public final static java.util.Locale
  PRC
public final static java.util.Locale
  SIMPLIFIED_CHINESE
public final static java.util.Locale
  TAIWAN

public final static java.util.Locale
  TRADITIONAL_CHINESE
public final static java.util.Locale UK
public final static java.util.Locale US

Constructors
public Locale(String language,String
  country,String variant)
public Locale(String language,String
  country)

Methods
public Object clone()
public boolean equals(Object obj)
public static Locale getAvailableLocales(
)
public String getCountry()
public static Locale getDefault()
public final String getDisplayCountry()
public String getDisplayCountry(Locale
  inLocale)
public final String getDisplayLanguage()
public String getDisplayLanguage(Locale
  inLocale)
public final String getDisplayName()
public String getDisplayName(Locale
  inLocale)
public final String getDisplayVariant()
public String getDisplayVariant(Locale
  inLocale)
public String getISO3Country()
public String getISO3Language()
public static String getISOCountries()
public static String getISOLanguages()
public String getLanguage()
public String getVariant()
public synchronized int hashCode()
public static synchronized void
  setDefault(Locale newLocale)
public final String toString()

►**LocaleData**
public class java.text.resources.
  LocaleData
extends java.lang.Object

Methods
public static Locale getAvailableLocales(
  String key)

►**LocaleElements**
public class java.text.resources.
  LocaleElements
extends java.util.ListResourceBundle
extends java.util.ResourceBundle
extends java.lang.Object

Methods
public Object getContents()

►**LocaleElements_en**
public class java.text.resources.
  LocaleElements_en
extends java.util.ListResourceBundle
extends java.util.ResourceBundle
extends java.lang.Object

Methods
public Object getContents()

►**LocaleElements_en_US**
public class java.text.resources.
  LocaleElements_en_US
extends java.util.ListResourceBundle
extends java.util.ResourceBundle
extends java.lang.Object

Methods
public Object getContents()

►**LocateRegistry**
public final class java.rmi.registry.
  LocateRegistry
extends java.lang.Object

Constructors
private LocateRegistry()

Methods
public static Registry createRegistry(
  int port)
public static Registry createRegistry(
  int port,RMIClientSocketFactory csf,
  RMIServerSocketFactory ssf)
public static Registry getRegistry()
public static Registry getRegistry(int
  port)
public static Registry getRegistry(
  String host)
public static Registry getRegistry(
  String host,int port)
public static Registry getRegistry(
  String host,int port,
  RMIClientSocketFactory csf)

►**LogStream**
public class java.rmi.server.LogStream
extends java.io.PrintStream
extends java.io.FilterOutputStream
extends java.io.OutputStream
extends java.lang.Object

Fields
public final static int BRIEF
public final static int SILENT
public final static int VERBOSE

Constructors
private LogStream()

Methods
public static synchronized PrintStream
  getDefaultStream()
public synchronized OutputStream
  getOutputStream()
public static LogStream log(String name)
public static int parseLevel(String s)
public static synchronized void
  setDefaultStream(PrintStream newDefault)
public synchronized void setOutputStream(
  OutputStream out)
public String toString()
public void write(int b)
public void write(byte b,int off,int len)

▶LONG
public final class java.lang.Long
implements java.lang.Comparable
extends java.lang.Number
extends java.lang.Object

Fields
public final static long MAX_VALUE
public final static long MIN_VALUE
public final static java.lang.Class
 TYPE

Constructors
public Long(long value)
public Long(String s)˙

Methods
public byte byteValue()
public int compareTo(Long anotherLong)
public int compareTo(Object o)
public static Long decode(String nm)
public double doubleValue()
public boolean equals(Object obj)
public float floatValue()
public static Long getLong(String nm)
public static Long getLong(String nm,
 long val)
public static Long getLong(String nm,
 Long val)
public int hashCode()
public int intValue()
public long longValue()
public static long parseLong(String s,
 int radix)
public static long parseLong(String s)
public short shortValue()
public static String toBinaryString(long
 i)
public static String toHexString(long i)
public static String toOctalString(long
 i)
public static String toString(long i,int
 radix)
public static String toString(long i)
public String toString()
public static Long valueOf(String s,int
 radix)
public static Long valueOf(String s)

▶LOOKANDFEEL
public abstract class javax.swing.
 LookAndFeel
extends java.lang.Object

Methods
public UIDefaults getDefaults()
public abstract String getDescription()
public abstract String getID()
public abstract String getName()
public void initialize()
public static void installBorder(
 JComponent c,String defaultBorderName)
public static void installColors(
 JComponent c,String defaultBgName,String
 defaultFgName)

public static void installColorsAndFont(
 JComponent c,String defaultBgName,String
 defaultFgName,String defaultFontName)
public abstract boolean
 isNativeLookAndFeel()
public abstract boolean
 isSupportedLookAndFeel()
public static Object makeIcon(Class
 baseClass,String gifFile)
public static KeyBinding makeKeyBindings(
 Object keyBindingList)
public String toString()
public void uninitialize()
public static void uninstallBorder(
 JComponent c)

▶LOOKUPOP
public class java.awt.image.LookupOp
implements java.awt.image.
 BufferedImageOp
implements java.awt.image.RasterOp
extends java.lang.Object

Constructors
public LookupOp(LookupTable lookup,
 RenderingHints hints)

Methods
public BufferedImage
 createCompatibleDestImage(BufferedImage
 src,ColorModel destCM)
public WritableRaster
 createCompatibleDestRaster(Raster src)
public final BufferedImage filter(
 BufferedImage src,BufferedImage dst)
public final WritableRaster filter(
 Raster src,WritableRaster dst)
public final Rectangle2D getBounds2D(
 BufferedImage src)
public final Rectangle2D getBounds2D(
 Raster src)
public final Point2D getPoint2D(Point2D
 srcPt,Point2D dstPt)
public final RenderingHints
 getRenderingHints()
public final LookupTable getTable()

▶LOOKUPTABLE
public abstract class java.awt.image.
 LookupTable
extends java.lang.Object
extends java.lang.Object

Constructors
protected LookupTable(int offset,int
 numComponents)

Methods
public int getNumComponents()
public int getOffset()
public abstract int lookupPixel(int src,
 int dest)

▶MALFORMEDURLEXCEPTION
public class java.net.
 MalformedURLException

extends java.io.IOException
extends java.lang.Exception
extends java.lang.Throwable
extends java.lang.Object

Constructors
public MalformedURLException()
public MalformedURLException(String msg)

►MANIFEST
public class java.util.jar.Manifest
implements java.lang.Cloneable
extends java.lang.Object

Constructors
public Manifest()
public Manifest(InputStream is)
public Manifest(Manifest man)

Methods
public void clear()
public Object clone()
public boolean equals(Object o)
public Attributes getAttributes(String
  name)
public Map getEntries()
public Attributes getMainAttributes()
public int hashCode()
public void read(InputStream is)
public void write(OutputStream out)

►MARSHALEXCEPTION
public class java.rmi.MarshalException
extends java.rmi.RemoteException
extends java.io.IOException
extends java.lang.Exception
extends java.lang.Throwable
extends java.lang.Object

Constructors
public MarshalException(String s)
public MarshalException(String s,
  Exception ex)

►MARSHALLEDOBJECT
public final class java.rmi.
  MarshalledObject
implements java.io.Serializable
extends java.lang.Object

Constructors
public MarshalledObject(Object obj)

Methods
public boolean equals(Object obj)
public Object get()
public int hashCode()

►MATH
public final class java.lang.Math
extends java.lang.Object

Fields
public final static double E
public final static double PI

Constructors
private Math()

Methods
public static int abs(int a)
public static long abs(long a)
public static float abs(float a)
public static double abs(double a)
public static native double acos(double
  a)
public static native double asin(double
  a)
public static native double atan(double
  a)
public static native double atan2(double
  a,double b)
public static native double ceil(double
  a)
public static native double cos(double a)
public static native double exp(double a)
public static native double floor(double
  a)
public static native double
  IEEEremainder(double f1,double f2)
public static native double log(double a)
public static int max(int a,int b)
public static long max(long a,long b)
public static float max(float a,float b)
public static double max(double a,double
  b)
public static int min(int a,int b)
public static long min(long a,long b)
public static float min(float a,float b)
public static double min(double a,double
  b)
public static native double pow(double a,
  double b)
public static synchronized double random(
)
public static native double rint(double
  a)
public static int round(float a)
public static long round(double a)
public static native double sin(double a)
public static native double sqrt(double
  a)
public static native double tan(double a)
public static double toDegrees(double
  angrad)
public static double toRadians(double
  angdeg)

►MATTEBORDER
public class javax.swing.border.
  MatteBorder
extends javax.swing.border.EmptyBorder
extends javax.swing.border.
  AbstractBorder
extends java.lang.Object

Fields
protected java.awt.Color color
protected javax.swing.Icon tileIcon

Constructors
public MatteBorder(int top,int left,int
  bottom,int right,Color color)

public MatteBorder(int top,int left,int
  bottom,int right,Icon tileIcon)
public MatteBorder(Icon tileIcon)
Methods
public Insets getBorderInsets(Component
  c)
public boolean isBorderOpaque()
public void paintBorder(Component c,
  Graphics g,int x,int y,int width,int
  height)

▶**MEDIATRACKER**
public class java.awt.MediaTracker
implements java.io.Serializable
extends java.lang.Object
Fields
public final static int ABORTED
public final static int COMPLETE
public final static int ERRORED
public final static int LOADING
Constructors
public MediaTracker(Component comp)
Methods
public void addImage(Image image,int id)
public synchronized void addImage(Image
  image,int id,int w,int h)
public boolean checkAll()
public boolean checkAll(boolean load)
public boolean checkID(int id)
public boolean checkID(int id,boolean
  load)
public synchronized Object getErrorsAny()
public synchronized Object getErrorsID(
  int id)
public synchronized boolean isErrorAny()
public synchronized boolean isErrorID(
  int id)
public synchronized void removeImage(
  Image image)
public synchronized void removeImage(
  Image image,int id)
public synchronized void removeImage(
  Image image,int id,int width,int height)
public int statusAll(boolean load)
public int statusID(int id,boolean load)
public void waitForAll()
public synchronized boolean waitForAll(
  long ms)
public void waitForID(int id)
public synchronized boolean waitForID(
  int id,long ms)

▶**MEMORYIMAGESOURCE**
public class java.awt.image.
  MemoryImageSource
implements java.awt.image.ImageProducer
extends java.lang.Object
Constructors
public MemoryImageSource(int w,int h,
  ColorModel cm,byte pix,int off,int scan)

public MemoryImageSource(int w,int h,
  ColorModel cm,byte pix,int off,int scan,
  Hashtable props)
public MemoryImageSource(int w,int h,
  ColorModel cm,int pix,int off,int scan)
public MemoryImageSource(int w,int h,
  ColorModel cm,int pix,int off,int scan,
  Hashtable props)
public MemoryImageSource(int w,int h,
  int pix,int off,int scan)
public MemoryImageSource(int w,int h,
  int pix,int off,int scan,Hashtable props)
Methods
public synchronized void addConsumer(
  ImageConsumer ic)
public synchronized boolean isConsumer(
  ImageConsumer ic)
public void newPixels()
public synchronized void newPixels(int x,
  int y,int w,int h)
public synchronized void newPixels(int x,
  int y,int w,int h,boolean framenotify)
public synchronized void newPixels(byte
  newpix,ColorModel newmodel,int offset,
  int scansize)
public synchronized void newPixels(int
  newpix,ColorModel newmodel,int offset,
  int scansize)
public synchronized void removeConsumer(
  ImageConsumer ic)
public void
  requestTopDownLeftRightResend(
  ImageConsumer ic)
public synchronized void setAnimated(
  boolean animated)
public synchronized void
  setFullBufferUpdates(boolean fullbuffers)
public void startProduction(
  ImageConsumer ic)

▶**MENU**
public class java.awt.Menu
implements java.awt.MenuContainer
extends java.awt.MenuItem
extends java.awt.MenuComponent
extends java.lang.Object
Constructors
public Menu()
public Menu(String label)
public Menu(String label,boolean
  tearOff)
Methods
public MenuItem add(MenuItem mi)
public void add(String label)
public void addNotify()
public void addSeparator()
public int countItems()
public MenuItem getItem(int index)
public int getItemCount()
public void insert(MenuItem menuitem,int
  index)

```
public void insert(String label,int
  index)
public void insertSeparator(int index)
public boolean isTearOff()
public String paramString()
public void remove(int index)
public void remove(MenuComponent item)
public void removeAll()
public void removeNotify()
```

▶MENUBAR
```
public class java.awt.MenuBar
implements java.awt.MenuContainer
extends java.awt.MenuComponent
extends java.lang.Object
```
Constructors
```
public MenuBar()
```
Methods
```
public Menu add(Menu m)
public void addNotify()
public int countMenus()
public void deleteShortcut(MenuShortcut
  s)
public Menu getHelpMenu()
public Menu getMenu(int i)
public int getMenuCount()
public MenuItem getShortcutMenuItem(
  MenuShortcut s)
public void remove(int index)
public void remove(MenuComponent m)
public void removeNotify()
public void setHelpMenu(Menu m)
public synchronized Enumeration
  shortcuts()
```

▶MENUBARUI
```
public abstract class javax.swing.plaf.
  MenuBarUI
extends javax.swing.plaf.ComponentUI
extends java.lang.Object
```

▶MENUCOMPONENT
```
public abstract class java.awt.
  MenuComponent
implements java.io.Serializable
extends java.lang.Object
```
Constructors
```
public MenuComponent()
```
Methods
```
public final void dispatchEvent(AWTEvent
  e)
public Font getFont()
public String getName()
public MenuContainer getParent()
public MenuComponentPeer getPeer()
protected final Object getTreeLock()
protected String paramString()
public boolean postEvent(Event evt)
protected void processEvent(AWTEvent e)
public void removeNotify()
public void setFont(Font f)
public void setName(String name)
```

```
public String toString()
```

▶MENUDRAGMOUSEEVENT
```
public class javax.swing.event.
  MenuDragMouseEvent
extends java.awt.event.MouseEvent
extends java.awt.event.InputEvent
extends java.awt.event.ComponentEvent
extends java.awt.AWTEvent
extends java.util.EventObject
extends java.lang.Object
```
Constructors
```
public MenuDragMouseEvent(Component
  source,int id,long when,int modifiers,
  int x,int y,int clickCount,boolean
  popupTrigger,MenuElement p,
  MenuSelectionManager m)
```
Methods
```
public MenuSelectionManager
  getMenuSelectionManager()
public MenuElement getPath()
```

▶MENUEVENT
```
public class javax.swing.event.
  MenuEvent
extends java.util.EventObject
extends java.lang.Object
```
Constructors
```
public MenuEvent(Object source)
```

▶MENUITEM
```
public class java.awt.MenuItem
extends java.awt.MenuComponent
extends java.lang.Object
```
Constructors
```
public MenuItem()
public MenuItem(String label)
public MenuItem(String label,
  MenuShortcut s)
```
Methods
```
public synchronized void
  addActionListener(ActionListener l)
public void addNotify()
public void deleteShortcut()
public synchronized void disable()
protected final void disableEvents(long
  eventsToDisable)
public synchronized void enable()
public void enable(boolean b)
protected final void enableEvents(long
  eventsToEnable)
public String getActionCommand()
public String getLabel()
public MenuShortcut getShortcut()
public boolean isEnabled()
public String paramString()
protected void processActionEvent(
  ActionEvent e)
protected void processEvent(AWTEvent e)
public synchronized void
  removeActionListener(ActionListener l)
```

```
public void setActionCommand(String
  command)
public synchronized void setEnabled(
  boolean b)
public synchronized void setLabel(String
  label)
public void setShortcut(MenuShortcut s)
```

▶MENUITEMUI
```
public abstract class javax.swing.plaf.
  MenuItemUI
extends javax.swing.plaf.ButtonUI
extends javax.swing.plaf.ComponentUI
extends java.lang.Object
```

▶MENUKEYEVENT
```
public class javax.swing.event.
  MenuKeyEvent
extends java.awt.event.KeyEvent
extends java.awt.event.InputEvent
extends java.awt.event.ComponentEvent
extends java.awt.AWTEvent
extends java.util.EventObject
extends java.lang.Object
```
Constructors
```
public  MenuKeyEvent(Component source,
  int id,long when,int modifiers,int
  keyCode,char keyChar,MenuElement p,
  MenuSelectionManager m)
```
Methods
```
public MenuSelectionManager
  getMenuSelectionManager()
public MenuElement getPath()
```

▶MENUSELECTIONMANAGER
```
public class javax.swing.
  MenuSelectionManager
extends java.lang.Object
```
Fields
```
protected transient javax.swing.event.
  ChangeEvent changeEvent
protected javax.swing.event.
  EventListenerList listenerList
```
Methods
```
public void addChangeListener(
  ChangeListener l)
public void clearSelectedPath()
public Component componentForPoint(
  Component source,Point sourcePoint)
public static MenuSelectionManager
  defaultManager()
protected void fireStateChanged()
public MenuElement getSelectedPath()
public boolean
  isComponentPartOfCurrentMenu(Component c)
public void processKeyEvent(KeyEvent e)
public void processMouseEvent(MouseEvent
  event)
public void removeChangeListener(
  ChangeListener l)
public void setSelectedPath(MenuElement
  path)
```

▶MENUSHORTCUT
```
public class java.awt.MenuShortcut
implements java.io.Serializable
extends java.lang.Object
```
Constructors
```
public  MenuShortcut(int key)
public  MenuShortcut(int key,boolean
  useShiftModifier)
```
Methods
```
public boolean equals(MenuShortcut s)
public boolean equals(Object obj)
public int getKey()
public int hashCode()
protected String paramString()
public String toString()
public boolean usesShiftModifier()
```

▶MESSAGEDIGEST
```
public abstract class java.security.
  MessageDigest
extends java.security.MessageDigestSpi
extends java.lang.Object
```
Constructors
```
protected  MessageDigest(String
  algorithm)
```
Methods
```
public Object clone()
public byte digest()
public int digest(byte buf,int offset,
  int len)
public byte digest(byte input)
public final String getAlgorithm()
public final int getDigestLength()
public static MessageDigest getInstance(
  String algorithm)
public static MessageDigest getInstance(
  String algorithm,String provider)
public final Provider getProvider()
public static boolean isEqual(byte
  digesta,byte digestb)
public void reset()
public String toString()
public void update(byte input)
public void update(byte input,int offset,
  int len)
public void update(byte input)
```

▶MESSAGEDIGESTSPI
```
public abstract class java.security.
  MessageDigestSpi
extends java.lang.Object
```
Methods
```
public Object clone()
protected abstract byte engineDigest()
protected int engineDigest(byte buf,int
  offset,int len)
protected int engineGetDigestLength()
protected abstract void engineReset()
protected abstract void engineUpdate(
  byte input)
protected abstract void engineUpdate(
  byte input,int offset,int len)
```

▶**MESSAGEFORMAT**

public class java.text.MessageFormat
extends java.text.Format
extends java.lang.Object

Constructors

public MessageFormat(String pattern)
private MessageFormat()

Methods

public void applyPattern(String
  newPattern)
public Object clone()
public boolean equals(Object obj)
public final StringBuffer format(Object
  source,StringBuffer result,FieldPosition
  ignore)
public static String format(String
  pattern,Object arguments)
public final StringBuffer format(Object
  source,StringBuffer result,FieldPosition
  ignore)
public Format getFormats()
public Locale getLocale()
public int hashCode()
public Object parse(String source,
  ParsePosition status)
public Object parse(String source)
public Object parseObject(String text,
  ParsePosition status)
public void setFormat(int variable,
  Format newFormat)
public void setFormats(Format newFormats)
public void setLocale(Locale theLocale)
public String toPattern()

▶**METALBORDERS**

public class javax.swing.plaf.metal.
  MetalBorders
extends java.lang.Object

▶**METALBUTTONUI**

public class javax.swing.plaf.metal.
  MetalButtonUI
extends javax.swing.plaf.basic.
  BasicButtonUI
extends javax.swing.plaf.ButtonUI
extends javax.swing.plaf.ComponentUI
extends java.lang.Object

Fields

protected java.awt.Color
  disabledTextColor
protected java.awt.Color focusColor
protected java.awt.Color selectColor

Methods

protected BasicButtonListener
  createButtonListener(AbstractButton b)
public static ComponentUI createUI(
  JComponent c)
protected Color getDisabledTextColor()
protected Color getFocusColor()
protected Color getSelectColor()
public void installDefaults(
  AbstractButton b)

protected void paintButtonPressed(
  Graphics g,AbstractButton b)
protected void paintFocus(Graphics g,
  AbstractButton b,Rectangle viewRect,
  Rectangle textRect,Rectangle iconRect)
protected void paintText(Graphics g,
  JComponent c,Rectangle textRect,String
  text)
public void uninstallDefaults(
  AbstractButton b)

▶**METALCHECKBOXICON**

public class javax.swing.plaf.metal.
  MetalCheckBoxIcon
implements javax.swing.Icon
implements java.io.Serializable
implements javax.swing.plaf.UIResource
extends java.lang.Object

Methods

protected void drawCheck(Component c,
  Graphics g,int x,int y)
protected int getControlSize()
public int getIconHeight()
public int getIconWidth()
public void paintIcon(Component c,
  Graphics g,int x,int y)

▶**METALCHECKBOXUI**

public class javax.swing.plaf.metal.
  MetalCheckBoxUI
extends javax.swing.plaf.metal.
  MetalRadioButtonUI
extends javax.swing.plaf.basic.
  BasicRadioButtonUI
extends javax.swing.plaf.basic.
  BasicToggleButtonUI
extends javax.swing.plaf.basic.
  BasicButtonUI
extends javax.swing.plaf.ButtonUI
extends javax.swing.plaf.ComponentUI
extends java.lang.Object

Methods

public static ComponentUI createUI(
  JComponent b)
public String getPropertyPrefix()
public void installDefaults(
  AbstractButton b)
protected void uninstallDefaults(
  AbstractButton b)

▶**METALCOMBOBOXBUTTON**

public class javax.swing.plaf.metal.
  MetalComboBoxButton
extends javax.swing.JButton
extends javax.swing.AbstractButton
extends javax.swing.JComponent
extends java.awt.Container
extends java.awt.Component
extends java.lang.Object

Fields

protected javax.swing.JComboBox
  comboBox
protected javax.swing.Icon comboIcon

protected boolean iconOnly
protected javax.swing.JList listBox
protected javax.swing.CellRendererPane
  rendererPane

Constructors

MetalComboBoxButton()
public MetalComboBoxButton(JComboBox cb,
  Icon i,CellRendererPane pane,JList list)
public MetalComboBoxButton(JComboBox cb,
  Icon i,boolean onlyIcon,CellRendererPane
  pane,JList list)

Methods

public final JComboBox getComboBox()
public final Icon getComboIcon()
public boolean isFocusTraversable()
public final boolean isIconOnly()
public void paintComponent(Graphics g)
public final void setComboBox(JComboBox
  cb)
public final void setComboIcon(Icon i)
public final void setIconOnly(boolean
  isIconOnly)

▶**METALCOMBOBOXEDITOR**

public class javax.swing.plaf.metal.
  MetalComboBoxEditor
extends javax.swing.plaf.basic.
  BasicComboBoxEditor
extends java.lang.Object

Fields

protected static java.awt.Insets
  editorBorderInsets

Constructors

public MetalComboBoxEditor()

▶**METALCOMBOBOXICON**

public class javax.swing.plaf.metal.
  MetalComboBoxIcon
implements javax.swing.Icon
implements java.io.Serializable
extends java.lang.Object

Methods

public int getIconHeight()
public int getIconWidth()
public void paintIcon(Component c,
  Graphics g,int x,int y)

▶**METALCOMBOBOXUI**

public class javax.swing.plaf.metal.
  MetalComboBoxUI
extends javax.swing.plaf.basic.
  BasicComboBoxUI
extends javax.swing.plaf.ComboBoxUI
extends javax.swing.plaf.ComponentUI
extends java.lang.Object

Methods

public void configureArrowButton()
public void configureEditor()
protected JButton createArrowButton()
protected ComboBoxEditor createEditor()
protected LayoutManager
  createLayoutManager()

protected ComboPopup createPopup()
public PropertyChangeListener
  createPropertyChangeListener()
public static ComponentUI createUI(
  JComponent c)
protected void editablePropertyChanged(
  PropertyChangeEvent e)
public Dimension getMinimumSize(
  JComponent c)
protected void installKeyboardActions()
protected void installListeners()
public void installUI(JComponent c)
public boolean isFocusTraversable(
  JComboBox c)
public void layoutComboBox(Container
  parent,MetalComboBoxLayoutManager
  manager)
public void paint(Graphics g,JComponent
  c)
protected void removeListeners()
protected void selectNextPossibleValue()
protected void
  selectPreviousPossibleValue()
public void unconfigureArrowButton()
public void unconfigureEditor()
protected void uninstallKeyboardActions()
protected void uninstallListeners()
public void uninstallUI(JComponent c)

▶**METALDESKTOPICONUI**

public class javax.swing.plaf.metal.
  MetalDesktopIconUI
extends javax.swing.plaf.basic.
  BasicDesktopIconUI
extends javax.swing.plaf.DesktopIconUI
extends javax.swing.plaf.ComponentUI
extends java.lang.Object

Constructors

public MetalDesktopIconUI()

Methods

public static ComponentUI createUI(
  JComponent c)
public Dimension getPreferredSize(
  JComponent c)
protected void installComponents()
protected void installDefaults()
protected void uninstallComponents()

▶**METALFILECHOOSERUI**

public class javax.swing.plaf.metal.
  MetalFileChooserUI
extends javax.swing.plaf.basic.
  BasicFileChooserUI
extends javax.swing.plaf.FileChooserUI
extends javax.swing.plaf.ComponentUI
extends java.lang.Object

Constructors

public MetalFileChooserUI(JFileChooser
  filechooser)

Methods
protected DirectoryComboBoxModel
  createDirectoryComboBoxModel(
  JFileChooser fc)
protected DirectoryComboBoxRenderer
  createDirectoryComboBoxRenderer(
  JFileChooser fc)
protected FilterComboBoxModel
  createFilterComboBoxModel()
protected FilterComboBoxRenderer
  createFilterComboBoxRenderer()
protected JPanel createList(JFileChooser
  fc)
public PropertyChangeListener
  createPropertyChangeListener(
  JFileChooser fc)
public static ComponentUI createUI(
  JComponent c)
public void ensureFileIsVisible(
  JFileChooser fc,File f)
protected JButton getApproveButton(
  JFileChooser fc)
public String getDirectoryName()
public String getFileName()
public Dimension getMaximumSize(
  JComponent c)
public Dimension getMinimumSize(
  JComponent c)
public Dimension getPreferredSize(
  JComponent c)
public void installComponents(
  JFileChooser fc)
protected void installStrings(
  JFileChooser fc)
public void rescanCurrentDirectory(
  JFileChooser fc)
public void setDirectoryName(String
  dirname)
public void setFileName(String filename)
public void uninstallUI(JComponent c)
public void valueChanged(
  ListSelectionEvent e)

►**METALICONFACTORY**
public class javax.swing.plaf.metal.
  MetalIconFactory
implements java.io.Serializable
extends java.lang.Object
Fields
public final static boolean DARK
public final static boolean LIGHT
Methods
public static Icon
  getCheckBoxMenuItemIcon()
public static Icon
  getFileChooserDetailViewIcon()
public static Icon
  getFileChooserHomeFolderIcon()
public static Icon
  getFileChooserListViewIcon()
public static Icon
  getFileChooserNewFolderIcon()

public static Icon
  getFileChooserUpFolderIcon()
public static Icon
  getHorizontalSliderThumbIcon()
public static Icon
  getInternalFrameAltMaximizeIcon(int size)
public static Icon
  getInternalFrameCloseIcon(int size)
public static Icon
  getInternalFrameDefaultMenuIcon()
public static Icon
  getInternalFrameMaximizeIcon(int size)
public static Icon
  getInternalFrameMinimizeIcon(int size)
public static Icon getMenuArrowIcon()
public static Icon getMenuItemArrowIcon()
public static Icon getMenuItemCheckIcon()
public static Icon getRadioButtonIcon()
public static Icon
  getRadioButtonMenuItemIcon()
public static Icon getTreeComputerIcon()
public static Icon getTreeControlIcon(
  boolean isCollapsed)
public static Icon
  getTreeFloppyDriveIcon()
public static Icon getTreeFolderIcon()
public static Icon getTreeHardDriveIcon()
public static Icon getTreeLeafIcon()
public static Icon
  getVerticalSliderThumbIcon()

►**METALINTERNALFRAMEUI**
public class javax.swing.plaf.metal.
  MetalInternalFrameUI
extends javax.swing.plaf.basic.
  BasicInternalFrameUI
extends javax.swing.plaf.
  InternalFrameUI
extends javax.swing.plaf.ComponentUI
extends java.lang.Object
Fields
protected static java.lang.String IS_
  PALETTE
Constructors
public MetalInternalFrameUI(
  JInternalFrame b)
Methods
protected JComponent createNorthPane(
  JInternalFrame w)
public static ComponentUI createUI(
  JComponent c)
protected void installKeyboardActions()
public void installUI(JComponent c)
protected void replacePane(JComponent
  currentPane,JComponent newPane)
public void setPalette(boolean isPalette)
protected void uninstallKeyboardActions()
public void uninstallUI(JComponent c)

►**METALLABELUI**
public class javax.swing.plaf.metal.
  MetalLabelUI

extends javax.swing.plaf.basic.
  BasicLabelUI
extends javax.swing.plaf.LabelUI
extends javax.swing.plaf.ComponentUI
extends java.lang.Object

Fields

protected static javax.swing.plaf.metal.
  MetalLabelUI metalLabelUI

Methods

public static ComponentUI createUI(
  JComponent c)
protected void paintDisabledText(JLabel
  l,Graphics g,String s,int textX,int
  textY)

▶**METALLOOKANDFEEL**

public class javax.swing.plaf.metal.
  MetalLookAndFeel
extends javax.swing.plaf.basic.
  BasicLookAndFeel
extends javax.swing.LookAndFeel
extends java.lang.Object

Methods

protected void createDefaultTheme()
public static ColorUIResource
  getAcceleratorForeground()
public static ColorUIResource
  getAcceleratorSelectedForeground()
public static ColorUIResource getBlack()
public static ColorUIResource getControl(
)
public static ColorUIResource
  getControlDarkShadow()
public static ColorUIResource
  getControlDisabled()
public static ColorUIResource
  getControlHighlight()
public static ColorUIResource
  getControlInfo()
public static ColorUIResource
  getControlShadow()
public static ColorUIResource
  getControlTextColor()
public static FontUIResource
  getControlTextFont()
public UIDefaults getDefaults()
public String getDescription()
public static ColorUIResource
  getDesktopColor()
public static ColorUIResource
  getFocusColor()
public static ColorUIResource
  getHighlightedTextColor()
public String getID()
public static ColorUIResource
  getInactiveControlTextColor()
public static ColorUIResource
  getInactiveSystemTextColor()
public static ColorUIResource
  getMenuBackground()
public static ColorUIResource
  getMenuDisabledForeground()

public static ColorUIResource
  getMenuForeground()
public static ColorUIResource
  getMenuSelectedBackground()
public static ColorUIResource
  getMenuSelectedForeground()
public static FontUIResource
  getMenuTextFont()
public String getName()
public static ColorUIResource
  getPrimaryControl()
public static ColorUIResource
  getPrimaryControlDarkShadow()
public static ColorUIResource
  getPrimaryControlHighlight()
public static ColorUIResource
  getPrimaryControlInfo()
public static ColorUIResource
  getPrimaryControlShadow()
public static ColorUIResource
  getSeparatorBackground()
public static ColorUIResource
  getSeparatorForeground()
public static FontUIResource
  getSubTextFont()
public static ColorUIResource
  getSystemTextColor()
public static FontUIResource
  getSystemTextFont()
public static ColorUIResource
  getTextHighlightColor()
public static ColorUIResource
  getUserTextColor()
public static FontUIResource
  getUserTextFont()
public static ColorUIResource getWhite()
public static ColorUIResource
  getWindowBackground()
public static ColorUIResource
  getWindowTitleBackground()
public static FontUIResource
  getWindowTitleFont()
public static ColorUIResource
  getWindowTitleForeground()
public static ColorUIResource
  getWindowTitleInactiveBackground()
public static ColorUIResource
  getWindowTitleInactiveForeground()
protected void initClassDefaults(
  UIDefaults table)
protected void initComponentDefaults(
  UIDefaults table)
protected void initSystemColorDefaults(
  UIDefaults table)
public boolean isNativeLookAndFeel()
public boolean isSupportedLookAndFeel()
public static void setCurrentTheme(
  MetalTheme theme)

▶**METALPOPUPMENUSEPARATORUI**

public class javax.swing.plaf.metal.
  MetalPopupMenuSeparatorUI

extends javax.swing.plaf.metal.
MetalSeparatorUI
extends javax.swing.plaf.basic.
BasicSeparatorUI
extends javax.swing.plaf.SeparatorUI
extends javax.swing.plaf.ComponentUI
extends java.lang.Object

Methods
public static ComponentUI createUI(
JComponent c)
public Dimension getPreferredSize(
JComponent c)
public void paint(Graphics g,JComponent
c)

▶MetalProgressBarUI
public class javax.swing.plaf.metal.
MetalProgressBarUI
extends javax.swing.plaf.basic.
BasicProgressBarUI
extends javax.swing.plaf.ProgressBarUI
extends javax.swing.plaf.ComponentUI
extends java.lang.Object

Methods
public static ComponentUI createUI(
JComponent c)
public void paint(Graphics g,JComponent
c)

▶MetalRadioButtonUI
public class javax.swing.plaf.metal.
MetalRadioButtonUI
extends javax.swing.plaf.basic.
BasicRadioButtonUI
extends javax.swing.plaf.basic.
BasicToggleButtonUI
extends javax.swing.plaf.basic.
BasicButtonUI
extends javax.swing.plaf.ButtonUI
extends javax.swing.plaf.ComponentUI
extends java.lang.Object

Fields
protected java.awt.Color
disabledTextColor
protected java.awt.Color focusColor
protected java.awt.Color selectColor

Methods
public static ComponentUI createUI(
JComponent c)
protected Color getDisabledTextColor()
protected Color getFocusColor()
protected Color getSelectColor()
public void installDefaults(
AbstractButton b)
public synchronized void paint(Graphics
g,JComponent c)
protected void paintFocus(Graphics g,
Rectangle t,Dimension d)
protected void uninstallDefaults(
AbstractButton b)

▶MetalScrollBarUI
public class javax.swing.plaf.metal.
MetalScrollBarUI
extends javax.swing.plaf.basic.
BasicScrollBarUI
extends javax.swing.plaf.ScrollBarUI
extends javax.swing.plaf.ComponentUI
extends java.lang.Object

Fields
protected javax.swing.plaf.metal.
MetalBumps bumps
protected javax.swing.plaf.metal.
MetalScrollButton decreaseButton
public final static java.lang.String
FREE_STANDING_PROP
protected javax.swing.plaf.metal.
MetalScrollButton increaseButton
protected boolean isFreeStanding
protected int scrollBarWidth

Methods
protected void configureScrollBarColors()
protected JButton createDecreaseButton(
int orientation)
protected JButton createIncreaseButton(
int orientation)
protected PropertyChangeListener
createPropertyChangeListener()
public static ComponentUI createUI(
JComponent c)
protected Dimension getMinimumThumbSize()
public Dimension getPreferredSize(
JComponent c)
protected void installDefaults()
protected void installListeners()
protected void paintThumb(Graphics g,
JComponent c,Rectangle thumbBounds)
protected void paintTrack(Graphics g,
JComponent c,Rectangle trackBounds)
protected void setThumbBounds(int x,int
y,int width,int height)

▶MetalScrollButton
public class javax.swing.plaf.metal.
MetalScrollButton
extends javax.swing.plaf.basic.
BasicArrowButton
extends javax.swing.JButton
extends javax.swing.AbstractButton
extends javax.swing.JComponent
extends java.awt.Container
extends java.awt.Component
extends java.lang.Object

Constructors
public MetalScrollButton(int direction,
int width,boolean freeStanding)

Methods
public int getButtonWidth()
public Dimension getMaximumSize()
public Dimension getMinimumSize()
public Dimension getPreferredSize()
public void paint(Graphics g)

```
public void setFreeStanding(boolean
  freeStanding)
```

►MetalScrollPaneUI

```
public class javax.swing.plaf.metal.
  MetalScrollPaneUI
extends javax.swing.plaf.basic.
  BasicScrollPaneUI
extends javax.swing.plaf.ScrollPaneUI
extends javax.swing.plaf.ComponentUI
extends java.lang.Object
```

Methods

```
protected PropertyChangeListener
  createScrollBarSwapListener()
public static ComponentUI createUI(
  JComponent x)
public void installListeners(JScrollPane
  scrollPane)
public void installUI(JComponent c)
public void uninstallListeners(
  JScrollPane scrollPane)
public void uninstallUI(JComponent c)
```

►MetalSeparatorUI

```
public class javax.swing.plaf.metal.
  MetalSeparatorUI
extends javax.swing.plaf.basic.
  BasicSeparatorUI
extends javax.swing.plaf.SeparatorUI
extends javax.swing.plaf.ComponentUI
extends java.lang.Object
```

Methods

```
public static ComponentUI createUI(
  JComponent c)
public Dimension getPreferredSize(
  JComponent c)
protected void installDefaults(
  JSeparator s)
public void paint(Graphics g,JComponent
  c)
```

►MetalSliderUI

```
public class javax.swing.plaf.metal.
  MetalSliderUI
extends javax.swing.plaf.basic.
  BasicSliderUI
extends javax.swing.plaf.SliderUI
extends javax.swing.plaf.ComponentUI
extends java.lang.Object
```

Fields

```
protected static java.awt.Color
  darkShadowColor
protected boolean filledSlider
protected static java.awt.Color
  highlightColor
protected static javax.swing.Icon
  horizThumbIcon
protected final java.lang.String SLIDER_
  FILL
protected static java.awt.Color
  thumbColor
protected static int tickLength
```

```
protected final int TICK_BUFFER
protected static int trackWidth
protected static javax.swing.Icon
  vertThumbIcon
```

Constructors

```
public MetalSliderUI()
```

Methods

```
protected PropertyChangeListener
  createPropertyChangeListener(JSlider
  slider)
public static ComponentUI createUI(
  JComponent c)
protected int getThumbOverhang()
protected Dimension getThumbSize()
public int getTickLength()
protected int getTrackLength()
protected int getTrackWidth()
public void installUI(JComponent c)
public void paintFocus(Graphics g)
protected void
  paintMajorTickForHorizSlider(Graphics g,
  Rectangle tickBounds,int x)
protected void
  paintMajorTickForVertSlider(Graphics g,
  Rectangle tickBounds,int y)
protected void
  paintMinorTickForHorizSlider(Graphics g,
  Rectangle tickBounds,int x)
protected void
  paintMinorTickForVertSlider(Graphics g,
  Rectangle tickBounds,int y)
public void paintThumb(Graphics g)
public void paintTrack(Graphics g)
protected void scrollDueToClickInTrack(
  int dir)
```

►MetalSplitPaneUI

```
public class javax.swing.plaf.metal.
  MetalSplitPaneUI
extends javax.swing.plaf.basic.
  BasicSplitPaneUI
extends javax.swing.plaf.SplitPaneUI
extends javax.swing.plaf.ComponentUI
extends java.lang.Object
```

Methods

```
public BasicSplitPaneDivider
  createDefaultDivider()
public static ComponentUI createUI(
  JComponent x)
```

►MetalTabbedPaneUI

```
public class javax.swing.plaf.metal.
  MetalTabbedPaneUI
extends javax.swing.plaf.basic.
  BasicTabbedPaneUI
extends javax.swing.plaf.TabbedPaneUI
extends javax.swing.plaf.ComponentUI
extends java.lang.Object
```

Fields

```
protected int minTabWidth
protected java.awt.Color selectColor
```

protected java.awt.Color
selectHighlight
protected java.awt.Color
tabAreaBackground

Methods

protected int calculateMaxTabHeight(int
tabPlacement)
protected LayoutManager
createLayoutManager()
public static ComponentUI createUI(
JComponent x)
protected Color getColorForGap(int
currentRun,int x,int y)
protected int getTabLabelShiftX(int
tabPlacement,int tabIndex,boolean
isSelected)
protected int getTabLabelShiftY(int
tabPlacement,int tabIndex,boolean
isSelected)
protected int getTabRunOverlay(int
tabPlacement)
protected void installDefaults()
public void paint(Graphics g,JComponent
c)
protected void paintBottomTabBorder(int
tabIndex,Graphics g,int x,int y,int w,
int h,int btm,int rght,boolean
isSelected)
protected void
paintContentBorderBottomEdge(Graphics g,
int tabPlacement,int selectedIndex,int x,
int y,int w,int h)
protected void
paintContentBorderLeftEdge(Graphics g,
int tabPlacement,int selectedIndex,int x,
int y,int w,int h)
protected void
paintContentBorderRightEdge(Graphics g,
int tabPlacement,int selectedIndex,int x,
int y,int w,int h)
protected void paintContentBorderTopEdge(
Graphics g,int tabPlacement,int
selectedIndex,int x,int y,int w,int h)
protected void paintFocusIndicator(
Graphics g,int tabPlacement,Rectangle
rects,int tabIndex,Rectangle iconRect,
Rectangle textRect,boolean isSelected)
protected void paintHighlightBelowTab()
protected void paintLeftTabBorder(int
tabIndex,Graphics g,int x,int y,int w,
int h,int btm,int rght,boolean
isSelected)
protected void paintRightTabBorder(int
tabIndex,Graphics g,int x,int y,int w,
int h,int btm,int rght,boolean
isSelected)
protected void paintTabBackground(
Graphics g,int tabPlacement,int tabIndex,
int x,int y,int w,int h,boolean
isSelected)
protected void paintTabBorder(Graphics g,
int tabPlacement,int tabIndex,int x,int
y,int w,int h,boolean isSelected)

protected void paintTopTabBorder(int
tabIndex,Graphics g,int x,int y,int w,
int h,int btm,int rght,boolean
isSelected)
protected boolean shouldFillGap(int
currentRun,int tabIndex,int x,int y)
protected boolean shouldPadTabRun(int
tabPlacement,int run)
protected boolean shouldRotateTabRuns(
int tabPlacement,int selectedRun)
public void update(Graphics g,JComponent
c)

▶**METALTEXTFIELDUI**

public class javax.swing.plaf.metal.
MetalTextFieldUI
extends javax.swing.plaf.basic.
BasicTextFieldUI
extends javax.swing.plaf.basic.
BasicTextUI
extends javax.swing.plaf.TextUI
extends javax.swing.plaf.ComponentUI
extends java.lang.Object

Methods

public static ComponentUI createUI(
JComponent c)
public void installUI(JComponent c)
public void propertyChange(
PropertyChangeEvent e)

▶**METALTHEME**

public abstract class javax.swing.plaf.
metal.MetalTheme
extends java.lang.Object

Methods

public void addCustomEntriesToTable(
UIDefaults table)
public ColorUIResource
getAcceleratorForeground()
public ColorUIResource
getAcceleratorSelectedForeground()
protected ColorUIResource getBlack()
public ColorUIResource getControl()
public ColorUIResource
getControlDarkShadow()
public ColorUIResource
getControlDisabled()
public ColorUIResource
getControlHighlight()
public ColorUIResource getControlInfo()
public ColorUIResource getControlShadow()
public ColorUIResource
getControlTextColor()
public abstract FontUIResource
getControlTextFont()
public ColorUIResource getDesktopColor()
public ColorUIResource getFocusColor()
public ColorUIResource
getHighlightedTextColor()
public ColorUIResource
getInactiveControlTextColor()
public ColorUIResource
getInactiveSystemTextColor()

```
public ColorUIResource getMenuBackground(
  )
public ColorUIResource
  getMenuDisabledForeground()
public ColorUIResource getMenuForeground(
  )
public ColorUIResource
  getMenuSelectedBackground()
public ColorUIResource
  getMenuSelectedForeground()
public abstract FontUIResource
  getMenuTextFont()
public abstract String getName()
protected abstract ColorUIResource
  getPrimary1()
protected abstract ColorUIResource
  getPrimary2()
protected abstract ColorUIResource
  getPrimary3()
public ColorUIResource getPrimaryControl(
  )
public ColorUIResource
  getPrimaryControlDarkShadow()
public ColorUIResource
  getPrimaryControlHighlight()
public ColorUIResource
  getPrimaryControlInfo()
public ColorUIResource
  getPrimaryControlShadow()
protected abstract ColorUIResource
  getSecondary1()
protected abstract ColorUIResource
  getSecondary2()
protected abstract ColorUIResource
  getSecondary3()
public ColorUIResource
  getSeparatorBackground()
public ColorUIResource
  getSeparatorForeground()
public abstract FontUIResource
  getSubTextFont()
public ColorUIResource
  getSystemTextColor()
public abstract FontUIResource
  getSystemTextFont()
public ColorUIResource
  getTextHighlightColor()
public ColorUIResource getUserTextColor()
public abstract FontUIResource
  getUserTextFont()
protected ColorUIResource getWhite()
public ColorUIResource
  getWindowBackground()
public ColorUIResource
  getWindowTitleBackground()
public abstract FontUIResource
  getWindowTitleFont()
public ColorUIResource
  getWindowTitleForeground()
public ColorUIResource
  getWindowTitleInactiveBackground()
```

```
public ColorUIResource
  getWindowTitleInactiveForeground()
```

▶**METALTOGGLEBUTTONUI**

```
public class javax.swing.plaf.metal.
  MetalToggleButtonUI
extends javax.swing.plaf.basic.
  BasicToggleButtonUI
extends javax.swing.plaf.basic.
  BasicButtonUI
extends javax.swing.plaf.ButtonUI
extends javax.swing.plaf.ComponentUI
extends java.lang.Object
```

Fields

```
protected java.awt.Color
  disabledTextColor
protected java.awt.Color focusColor
protected java.awt.Color selectColor
```

Methods

```
public static ComponentUI createUI(
  JComponent b)
protected Color getDisabledTextColor()
protected Color getFocusColor()
protected Color getSelectColor()
public void installDefaults(
  AbstractButton b)
protected void paintButtonPressed(
  Graphics g,AbstractButton b)
protected void paintFocus(Graphics g,
  AbstractButton b,Rectangle viewRect,
  Rectangle textRect,Rectangle iconRect)
protected void paintText(Graphics g,
  JComponent c,Rectangle textRect,String
  text)
protected void uninstallDefaults(
  AbstractButton b)
```

▶**METALTOOLBARUI**

```
public class javax.swing.plaf.metal.
  MetalToolBarUI
extends javax.swing.plaf.basic.
  BasicToolBarUI
extends javax.swing.plaf.ToolBarUI
extends javax.swing.plaf.ComponentUI
extends java.lang.Object
```

Fields

```
protected java.awt.event.
  ContainerListener contListener
protected java.beans.
  PropertyChangeListener rolloverListener
```

Methods

```
protected ContainerListener
  createContainerListener()
protected MouseInputListener
  createDockingListener()
protected PropertyChangeListener
  createRolloverListener()
public static ComponentUI createUI(
  JComponent c)
protected void installListeners()
protected void installNonRolloverBorders(
  JComponent c)
```

protected void installNormalBorders(
JComponent c)
protected void installRolloverBorders(
JComponent c)
public void installUI(JComponent c)
public boolean isRolloverBorders()
protected void setBorderToNonRollover(
Component c)
protected void setBorderToNormal(
Component c)
protected void setBorderToRollover(
Component c)
protected void setDragOffset(Point p)
public void setRolloverBorders(boolean
rollover)
protected void uninstallListeners()
public void uninstallUI(JComponent c)

►METALTOOLTIPUI
public class javax.swing.plaf.metal.
MetalToolTipUI
extends javax.swing.plaf.basic.
BasicToolTipUI
extends javax.swing.plaf.ToolTipUI
extends javax.swing.plaf.ComponentUI
extends java.lang.Object

Fields
public final static int
padSpaceBetweenStrings

Constructors
public MetalToolTipUI()

Methods
public static ComponentUI createUI(
JComponent c)
public String getAcceleratorString()
public Dimension getPreferredSize(
JComponent c)
public void installUI(JComponent c)
public void paint(Graphics g,JComponent
c)

►METALTREEUI
public class javax.swing.plaf.metal.
MetalTreeUI
extends javax.swing.plaf.basic.
BasicTreeUI
extends javax.swing.plaf.TreeUI
extends javax.swing.plaf.ComponentUI
extends java.lang.Object

Constructors
public MetalTreeUI()

Methods
public static ComponentUI createUI(
JComponent x)
protected void decodeLineStyle(Object
lineStyleFlag)
protected int getHorizontalLegBuffer()
public void installUI(JComponent c)
protected boolean
isLocationInExpandControl(int row,int
rowLevel,int mouseX,int mouseY)

public void paint(Graphics g,JComponent
c)
protected void paintHorizontalPartOfLeg(
Graphics g,Rectangle clipBounds,Insets
insets,Rectangle bounds,TreePath path,
int row,boolean isExpanded,boolean
hasBeenExpanded,boolean isLeaf)
protected void paintHorizontalSeparators(
Graphics g,JComponent c)
protected void paintVerticalPartOfLeg(
Graphics g,Rectangle clipBounds,Insets
insets,TreePath path)
public void uninstallUI(JComponent c)

►METHOD
public final class java.lang.reflect.
Method
implements java.lang.reflect.Member
extends java.lang.reflect.
AccessibleObject
extends java.lang.Object

Constructors
private Method()

Methods
public boolean equals(Object obj)
public Class getDeclaringClass()
public Class getExceptionTypes()
public int getModifiers()
public String getName()
public Class getParameterTypes()
public Class getReturnType()
public int hashCode()
public native Object invoke(Object obj,
Object args)
public String toString()

►METHODDESCRIPTOR
public class java.beans.
MethodDescriptor
extends java.beans.FeatureDescriptor
extends java.lang.Object

Constructors
public MethodDescriptor(Method method)
public MethodDescriptor(Method method,
ParameterDescriptor parameterDescriptors)
MethodDescriptor()
MethodDescriptor()

Methods
public Method getMethod()
public ParameterDescriptor
getParameterDescriptors()

►MINIMALHTMLWRITER
public class javax.swing.text.html.
MinimalHTMLWriter
extends javax.swing.text.AbstractWriter
extends java.lang.Object

Constructors
public MinimalHTMLWriter(Writer w,
StyledDocument doc)
public MinimalHTMLWriter(Writer w,
StyledDocument doc,int pos,int len)

Methods

protected void endFontTag()
protected boolean inFontTag()
protected boolean isText(Element elem)
protected void startFontTag(String style)
protected void text(Element elem)
public void write()
protected void writeAttributes(
  AttributeSet attr)
protected void writeBody()
protected void writeComponent(Element
  elem)
protected void writeContent(Element elem,
  boolean needsIndenting)
protected void writeEndParagraph()
protected void writeEndTag(String endTag)
protected void writeHeader()
protected void writeHTMLTags(
  AttributeSet attr)
protected void writeImage(Element elem)
protected void writeLeaf(Element elem)
protected void writeNonHTMLAttributes(
  AttributeSet attr)
protected void writeStartParagraph(
  Element elem)
protected void writeStartTag(String tag)
protected void writeStyles()

►MissingResourceException

public class java.util.
  MissingResourceException
extends java.lang.RuntimeException
extends java.lang.Exception
extends java.lang.Throwable
extends java.lang.Object

Constructors

public MissingResourceException(String
  s,String className,String key)

Methods

public String getClassName()
public String getKey()

►Modifier

public class java.lang.reflect.Modifier
extends java.lang.Object

Fields

public final static int ABSTRACT
public final static int FINAL
public final static int INTERFACE
public final static int NATIVE
public final static int PRIVATE
public final static int PROTECTED
public final static int PUBLIC
public final static int STATIC
public final static int STRICT
public final static int SYNCHRONIZED
public final static int TRANSIENT
public final static int VOLATILE

Methods

public static boolean isAbstract(int mod)
public static boolean isFinal(int mod)

public static boolean isInterface(int
  mod)
public static boolean isNative(int mod)
public static boolean isPrivate(int mod)
public static boolean isProtected(int
  mod)
public static boolean isPublic(int mod)
public static boolean isStatic(int mod)
public static boolean isStrict(int mod)
public static boolean isSynchronized(int
  mod)
public static boolean isTransient(int
  mod)
public static boolean isVolatile(int mod)
public static String toString(int mod)

►MouseAdapter

public abstract class java.awt.event.
  MouseAdapter
implements java.awt.event.MouseListener
extends java.lang.Object

Methods

public void mouseClicked(MouseEvent e)
public void mouseEntered(MouseEvent e)
public void mouseExited(MouseEvent e)
public void mousePressed(MouseEvent e)
public void mouseReleased(MouseEvent e)

►MouseDragGestureRecognizer

public abstract class java.awt.dnd.
  MouseDragGestureRecognizer
implements java.awt.event.MouseListener
implements java.awt.event.
  MouseMotionListener
extends java.awt.dnd.
  DragGestureRecognizer
extends java.lang.Object

Constructors

protected MouseDragGestureRecognizer(
  DragSource ds,Component c,int act,
  DragGestureListener dgl)
protected MouseDragGestureRecognizer(
  DragSource ds,Component c,int act)
protected MouseDragGestureRecognizer(
  DragSource ds,Component c)
protected MouseDragGestureRecognizer(
  DragSource ds)

Methods

public void mouseClicked(MouseEvent e)
public void mouseDragged(MouseEvent e)
public void mouseEntered(MouseEvent e)
public void mouseExited(MouseEvent e)
public void mouseMoved(MouseEvent e)
public void mousePressed(MouseEvent e)
public void mouseReleased(MouseEvent e)
protected void registerListeners()
protected void unregisterListeners()

►MouseEvent

public class java.awt.event.MouseEvent
extends java.awt.event.InputEvent
extends java.awt.event.ComponentEvent

extends java.awt.AWTEvent
extends java.util.EventObject
extends java.lang.Object

Fields
public final static int MOUSE_CLICKED
public final static int MOUSE_DRAGGED
public final static int MOUSE_ENTERED
public final static int MOUSE_EXITED
public final static int MOUSE_FIRST
public final static int MOUSE_LAST
public final static int MOUSE_MOVED
public final static int MOUSE_PRESSED
public final static int MOUSE_RELEASED

Constructors
public MouseEvent(Component source,int
  id,long when,int modifiers,int x,int y,
  int clickCount,boolean popupTrigger)

Methods
public int getClickCount()
public Point getPoint()
public int getX()
public int getY()
public boolean isPopupTrigger()
public String paramString()
public synchronized void translatePoint(
  int x,int y)

►MouseInputAdapter
public abstract class javax.swing.event.
  MouseInputAdapter
implements javax.swing.event.
  MouseInputListener
extends java.lang.Object

Methods
public void mouseClicked(MouseEvent e)
public void mouseDragged(MouseEvent e)
public void mouseEntered(MouseEvent e)
public void mouseExited(MouseEvent e)
public void mouseMoved(MouseEvent e)
public void mousePressed(MouseEvent e)
public void mouseReleased(MouseEvent e)

►MouseMotionAdapter
public abstract class java.awt.event.
  MouseMotionAdapter
implements java.awt.event.
  MouseMotionListener
extends java.lang.Object

Methods
public void mouseDragged(MouseEvent e)
public void mouseMoved(MouseEvent e)

►MultiButtonUI
public class javax.swing.plaf.multi.
  MultiButtonUI
extends javax.swing.plaf.ButtonUI
extends javax.swing.plaf.ComponentUI
extends java.lang.Object

Fields
protected java.util.Vector uis

Methods
public boolean contains(JComponent a,int
  b,int c)
public static ComponentUI createUI(
  JComponent a)
public Accessible getAccessibleChild(
  JComponent a,int b)
public int getAccessibleChildrenCount(
  JComponent a)
public Dimension getMaximumSize(
  JComponent a)
public Dimension getMinimumSize(
  JComponent a)
public Dimension getPreferredSize(
  JComponent a)
public ComponentUI getUIs()
public void installUI(JComponent a)
public void paint(Graphics a,JComponent
  b)
public void uninstallUI(JComponent a)
public void update(Graphics a,JComponent
  b)

►MulticastSocket
public class java.net.MulticastSocket
extends java.net.DatagramSocket
extends java.lang.Object

Constructors
public MulticastSocket()
public MulticastSocket(int port)

Methods
public InetAddress getInterface()
public int getTimeToLive()
public byte getTTL()
public void joinGroup(InetAddress
  mcastaddr)
public void leaveGroup(InetAddress
  mcastaddr)
public void send(DatagramPacket p,byte
  ttl)
public void setInterface(InetAddress inf)
public void setTimeToLive(int ttl)
public void setTTL(byte ttl)

►MultiColorChooserUI
public class javax.swing.plaf.multi.
  MultiColorChooserUI
extends javax.swing.plaf.ColorChooserUI
extends javax.swing.plaf.ComponentUI
extends java.lang.Object

Fields
protected java.util.Vector uis

Methods
public boolean contains(JComponent a,int
  b,int c)
public static ComponentUI createUI(
  JComponent a)
public Accessible getAccessibleChild(
  JComponent a,int b)
public int getAccessibleChildrenCount(
  JComponent a)

public Dimension getMaximumSize(
  JComponent a)
public Dimension getMinimumSize(
  JComponent a)
public Dimension getPreferredSize(
  JComponent a)
public ComponentUI getUIs()
public void installUI(JComponent a)
public void paint(Graphics a,JComponent
  b)
public void uninstallUI(JComponent a)
public void update(Graphics a,JComponent
  b)

►MultiComboBoxUI
public class javax.swing.plaf.multi.
  MultiComboBoxUI
extends javax.swing.plaf.ComboBoxUI
extends javax.swing.plaf.ComponentUI
extends java.lang.Object
Fields
protected java.util.Vector uis
Methods
public boolean contains(JComponent a,int
  b,int c)
public static ComponentUI createUI(
  JComponent a)
public Accessible getAccessibleChild(
  JComponent a,int b)
public int getAccessibleChildrenCount(
  JComponent a)
public Dimension getMaximumSize(
  JComponent a)
public Dimension getMinimumSize(
  JComponent a)
public Dimension getPreferredSize(
  JComponent a)
public ComponentUI getUIs()
public void installUI(JComponent a)
public boolean isFocusTraversable(
  JComboBox a)
public boolean isPopupVisible(JComboBox
  a)
public void paint(Graphics a,JComponent
  b)
public void setPopupVisible(JComboBox a,
  boolean b)
public void uninstallUI(JComponent a)
public void update(Graphics a,JComponent
  b)

►MultiDesktopIconUI
public class javax.swing.plaf.multi.
  MultiDesktopIconUI
extends javax.swing.plaf.DesktopIconUI
extends javax.swing.plaf.ComponentUI
extends java.lang.Object
Fields
protected java.util.Vector uis
Methods
public boolean contains(JComponent a,int
  b,int c)

public static ComponentUI createUI(
  JComponent a)
public Accessible getAccessibleChild(
  JComponent a,int b)
public int getAccessibleChildrenCount(
  JComponent a)
public Dimension getMaximumSize(
  JComponent a)
public Dimension getMinimumSize(
  JComponent a)
public Dimension getPreferredSize(
  JComponent a)
public ComponentUI getUIs()
public void installUI(JComponent a)
public void paint(Graphics a,JComponent
  b)
public void uninstallUI(JComponent a)
public void update(Graphics a,JComponent
  b)

►MultiDesktopPaneUI
public class javax.swing.plaf.multi.
  MultiDesktopPaneUI
extends javax.swing.plaf.DesktopPaneUI
extends javax.swing.plaf.ComponentUI
extends java.lang.Object
Fields
protected java.util.Vector uis
Methods
public boolean contains(JComponent a,int
  b,int c)
public static ComponentUI createUI(
  JComponent a)
public Accessible getAccessibleChild(
  JComponent a,int b)
public int getAccessibleChildrenCount(
  JComponent a)
public Dimension getMaximumSize(
  JComponent a)
public Dimension getMinimumSize(
  JComponent a)
public Dimension getPreferredSize(
  JComponent a)
public ComponentUI getUIs()
public void installUI(JComponent a)
public void paint(Graphics a,JComponent
  b)
public void uninstallUI(JComponent a)
public void update(Graphics a,JComponent
  b)

►MultiFileChooserUI
public class javax.swing.plaf.multi.
  MultiFileChooserUI
extends javax.swing.plaf.FileChooserUI
extends javax.swing.plaf.ComponentUI
extends java.lang.Object
Fields
protected java.util.Vector uis
Methods
public boolean contains(JComponent a,int
  b,int c)

```
public static ComponentUI createUI(
  JComponent a)
public void ensureFileIsVisible(
  JFileChooser a,File b)
public FileFilter getAcceptAllFileFilter(
  JFileChooser a)
public Accessible getAccessibleChild(
  JComponent a,int b)
public int getAccessibleChildrenCount(
  JComponent a)
public String getApproveButtonText(
  JFileChooser a)
public String getDialogTitle(
  JFileChooser a)
public FileView getFileView(JFileChooser
  a)
public Dimension getMaximumSize(
  JComponent a)
public Dimension getMinimumSize(
  JComponent a)
public Dimension getPreferredSize(
  JComponent a)
public ComponentUI getUIs()
public void installUI(JComponent a)
public void paint(Graphics a,JComponent
  b)
public void rescanCurrentDirectory(
  JFileChooser a)
public void uninstallUI(JComponent a)
public void update(Graphics a,JComponent
  b)
```

►MultiInternalFrameUI

```
public class javax.swing.plaf.multi.
  MultiInternalFrameUI
extends javax.swing.plaf.
  InternalFrameUI
extends javax.swing.plaf.ComponentUI
extends java.lang.Object
```

Fields

```
protected java.util.Vector uis
```

Methods

```
public boolean contains(JComponent a,int
  b,int c)
public static ComponentUI createUI(
  JComponent a)
public Accessible getAccessibleChild(
  JComponent a,int b)
public int getAccessibleChildrenCount(
  JComponent a)
public Dimension getMaximumSize(
  JComponent a)
public Dimension getMinimumSize(
  JComponent a)
public Dimension getPreferredSize(
  JComponent a)
public ComponentUI getUIs()
public void installUI(JComponent a)
public void paint(Graphics a,JComponent
  b)
public void uninstallUI(JComponent a)
```

```
public void update(Graphics a,JComponent
  b)
```

►MultiLabelUI

```
public class javax.swing.plaf.multi.
  MultiLabelUI
extends javax.swing.plaf.LabelUI
extends javax.swing.plaf.ComponentUI
extends java.lang.Object
```

Fields

```
protected java.util.Vector uis
```

Methods

```
public boolean contains(JComponent a,int
  b,int c)
public static ComponentUI createUI(
  JComponent a)
public Accessible getAccessibleChild(
  JComponent a,int b)
public int getAccessibleChildrenCount(
  JComponent a)
public Dimension getMaximumSize(
  JComponent a)
public Dimension getMinimumSize(
  JComponent a)
public Dimension getPreferredSize(
  JComponent a)
public ComponentUI getUIs()
public void installUI(JComponent a)
public void paint(Graphics a,JComponent
  b)
public void uninstallUI(JComponent a)
public void update(Graphics a,JComponent
  b)
```

►MultiListUI

```
public class javax.swing.plaf.multi.
  MultiListUI
extends javax.swing.plaf.ListUI
extends javax.swing.plaf.ComponentUI
extends java.lang.Object
```

Fields

```
protected java.util.Vector uis
```

Methods

```
public boolean contains(JComponent a,int
  b,int c)
public static ComponentUI createUI(
  JComponent a)
public Accessible getAccessibleChild(
  JComponent a,int b)
public int getAccessibleChildrenCount(
  JComponent a)
public Rectangle getCellBounds(JList a,
  int b,int c)
public Dimension getMaximumSize(
  JComponent a)
public Dimension getMinimumSize(
  JComponent a)
public Dimension getPreferredSize(
  JComponent a)
public ComponentUI getUIs()
public Point indexToLocation(JList a,int
  b)
```

```
public void installUI(JComponent a)
public int locationToIndex(JList a,Point
  b)
public void paint(Graphics a,JComponent
  b)
public void uninstallUI(JComponent a)
public void update(Graphics a,JComponent
  b)
```

▶MULTILOOKANDFEEL
```
public class javax.swing.plaf.multi.
  MultiLookAndFeel
extends javax.swing.LookAndFeel
extends java.lang.Object
```
Methods
```
public static ComponentUI createUIs(
  ComponentUI mui,Vector uis,JComponent
  target)
public UIDefaults getDefaults()
public String getDescription()
public String getID()
public String getName()
public boolean isNativeLookAndFeel()
public boolean isSupportedLookAndFeel()
protected static ComponentUI uisToArray(
  Vector uis)
```

▶MULTIMENUBARUI
```
public class javax.swing.plaf.multi.
  MultiMenuBarUI
extends javax.swing.plaf.MenuBarUI
extends javax.swing.plaf.ComponentUI
extends java.lang.Object
```
Fields
```
protected java.util.Vector uis
```
Methods
```
public boolean contains(JComponent a,int
  b,int c)
public static ComponentUI createUI(
  JComponent a)
public Accessible getAccessibleChild(
  JComponent a,int b)
public int getAccessibleChildrenCount(
  JComponent a)
public Dimension getMaximumSize(
  JComponent a)
public Dimension getMinimumSize(
  JComponent a)
public Dimension getPreferredSize(
  JComponent a)
public ComponentUI getUIs()
public void installUI(JComponent a)
public void paint(Graphics a,JComponent
  b)
public void uninstallUI(JComponent a)
public void update(Graphics a,JComponent
  b)
```

▶MULTIMENUITEMUI
```
public class javax.swing.plaf.multi.
  MultiMenuItemUI
extends javax.swing.plaf.MenuItemUI
```

```
extends javax.swing.plaf.ButtonUI
extends javax.swing.plaf.ComponentUI
extends java.lang.Object
```
Fields
```
protected java.util.Vector uis
```
Methods
```
public boolean contains(JComponent a,int
  b,int c)
public static ComponentUI createUI(
  JComponent a)
public Accessible getAccessibleChild(
  JComponent a,int b)
public int getAccessibleChildrenCount(
  JComponent a)
public Dimension getMaximumSize(
  JComponent a)
public Dimension getMinimumSize(
  JComponent a)
public Dimension getPreferredSize(
  JComponent a)
public ComponentUI getUIs()
public void installUI(JComponent a)
public void paint(Graphics a,JComponent
  b)
public void uninstallUI(JComponent a)
public void update(Graphics a,JComponent
  b)
```

▶MULTIOPTIONPANEUI
```
public class javax.swing.plaf.multi.
  MultiOptionPaneUI
extends javax.swing.plaf.OptionPaneUI
extends javax.swing.plaf.ComponentUI
extends java.lang.Object
```
Fields
```
protected java.util.Vector uis
```
Methods
```
public boolean contains(JComponent a,int
  b,int c)
public boolean containsCustomComponents(
  JOptionPane a)
public static ComponentUI createUI(
  JComponent a)
public Accessible getAccessibleChild(
  JComponent a,int b)
public int getAccessibleChildrenCount(
  JComponent a)
public Dimension getMaximumSize(
  JComponent a)
public Dimension getMinimumSize(
  JComponent a)
public Dimension getPreferredSize(
  JComponent a)
public ComponentUI getUIs()
public void installUI(JComponent a)
public void paint(Graphics a,JComponent
  b)
public void selectInitialValue(
  JOptionPane a)
public void uninstallUI(JComponent a)
public void update(Graphics a,JComponent
  b)
```

►MULTIPANELUI
public class javax.swing.plaf.multi.
  MultiPanelUI
extends javax.swing.plaf.PanelUI
extends javax.swing.plaf.ComponentUI
extends java.lang.Object
Fields
protected java.util.Vector uis
Methods
public boolean contains(JComponent a,int
  b,int c)
public static ComponentUI createUI(
  JComponent a)
public Accessible getAccessibleChild(
  JComponent a,int b)
public int getAccessibleChildrenCount(
  JComponent a)
public Dimension getMaximumSize(
  JComponent a)
public Dimension getMinimumSize(
  JComponent a)
public Dimension getPreferredSize(
  JComponent a)
public ComponentUI getUIs()
public void installUI(JComponent a)
public void paint(Graphics a,JComponent
  b)
public void uninstallUI(JComponent a)
public void update(Graphics a,JComponent
  b)

►MULTIPIXELPACKEDSAMPLEMODEL
public class java.awt.image.
  MultiPixelPackedSampleModel
extends java.awt.image.SampleModel
extends java.lang.Object
Constructors
public MultiPixelPackedSampleModel(int
  dataType,int w,int h,int numberOfBits)
public MultiPixelPackedSampleModel(int
  dataType,int w,int h,int numberOfBits,
  int scanlineStride,int dataBitOffset)
Methods
public SampleModel
  createCompatibleSampleModel(int w,int h)
public DataBuffer createDataBuffer()
public SampleModel
  createSubsetSampleModel(int bands)
public int getBitOffset(int x)
public int getDataBitOffset()
public Object getDataElements(int x,int
  y,Object obj,DataBuffer data)
public int getNumDataElements()
public int getOffset(int x,int y)
public int getPixel(int x,int y,int
  iArray,DataBuffer data)
public int getPixelBitStride()
public int getSample(int x,int y,int b,
  DataBuffer data)
public int getSampleSize()
public int getSampleSize(int band)
public int getScanlineStride()

public int getTransferType()
public void setDataElements(int x,int y,
  Object obj,DataBuffer data)
public void setPixel(int x,int y,int
  iArray,DataBuffer data)
public void setSample(int x,int y,int b,
  int s,DataBuffer data)

►MULTIPOPUPMENUUI
public class javax.swing.plaf.multi.
  MultiPopupMenuUI
extends javax.swing.plaf.PopupMenuUI
extends javax.swing.plaf.ComponentUI
extends java.lang.Object
Fields
protected java.util.Vector uis
Methods
public boolean contains(JComponent a,int
  b,int c)
public static ComponentUI createUI(
  JComponent a)
public Accessible getAccessibleChild(
  JComponent a,int b)
public int getAccessibleChildrenCount(
  JComponent a)
public Dimension getMaximumSize(
  JComponent a)
public Dimension getMinimumSize(
  JComponent a)
public Dimension getPreferredSize(
  JComponent a)
public ComponentUI getUIs()
public void installUI(JComponent a)
public void paint(Graphics a,JComponent
  b)
public void uninstallUI(JComponent a)
public void update(Graphics a,JComponent
  b)

►MULTIPROGRESSBARUI
public class javax.swing.plaf.multi.
  MultiProgressBarUI
extends javax.swing.plaf.ProgressBarUI
extends javax.swing.plaf.ComponentUI
extends java.lang.Object
Fields
protected java.util.Vector uis
Methods
public boolean contains(JComponent a,int
  b,int c)
public static ComponentUI createUI(
  JComponent a)
public Accessible getAccessibleChild(
  JComponent a,int b)
public int getAccessibleChildrenCount(
  JComponent a)
public Dimension getMaximumSize(
  JComponent a)
public Dimension getMinimumSize(
  JComponent a)
public Dimension getPreferredSize(
  JComponent a)

```
public ComponentUI getUIs()
public void installUI(JComponent a)
public void paint(Graphics a,JComponent
  b)
public void uninstallUI(JComponent a)
public void update(Graphics a,JComponent
  b)
```

►MULTISCROLLBARUI
```
public class javax.swing.plaf.multi.
  MultiScrollBarUI
extends javax.swing.plaf.ScrollBarUI
extends javax.swing.plaf.ComponentUI
extends java.lang.Object
```
Fields
```
protected java.util.Vector uis
```
Methods
```
public boolean contains(JComponent a,int
  b,int c)
public static ComponentUI createUI(
  JComponent a)
public Accessible getAccessibleChild(
  JComponent a,int b)
public int getAccessibleChildrenCount(
  JComponent a)
public Dimension getMaximumSize(
  JComponent a)
public Dimension getMinimumSize(
  JComponent a)
public Dimension getPreferredSize(
  JComponent a)
public ComponentUI getUIs()
public void installUI(JComponent a)
public void paint(Graphics a,JComponent
  b)
public void uninstallUI(JComponent a)
public void update(Graphics a,JComponent
  b)
```

►MULTISCROLLPANEUI
```
public class javax.swing.plaf.multi.
  MultiScrollPaneUI
extends javax.swing.plaf.ScrollPaneUI
extends javax.swing.plaf.ComponentUI
extends java.lang.Object
```
Fields
```
protected java.util.Vector uis
```
Methods
```
public boolean contains(JComponent a,int
  b,int c)
public static ComponentUI createUI(
  JComponent a)
public Accessible getAccessibleChild(
  JComponent a,int b)
public int getAccessibleChildrenCount(
  JComponent a)
public Dimension getMaximumSize(
  JComponent a)
public Dimension getMinimumSize(
  JComponent a)
public Dimension getPreferredSize(
  JComponent a)
```

```
public ComponentUI getUIs()
public void installUI(JComponent a)
public void paint(Graphics a,JComponent
  b)
public void uninstallUI(JComponent a)
public void update(Graphics a,JComponent
  b)
```

►MULTISEPARATORUI
```
public class javax.swing.plaf.multi.
  MultiSeparatorUI
extends javax.swing.plaf.SeparatorUI
extends javax.swing.plaf.ComponentUI
extends java.lang.Object
```
Fields
```
protected java.util.Vector uis
```
Methods
```
public boolean contains(JComponent a,int
  b,int c)
public static ComponentUI createUI(
  JComponent a)
public Accessible getAccessibleChild(
  JComponent a,int b)
public int getAccessibleChildrenCount(
  JComponent a)
public Dimension getMaximumSize(
  JComponent a)
public Dimension getMinimumSize(
  JComponent a)
public Dimension getPreferredSize(
  JComponent a)
public ComponentUI getUIs()
public void installUI(JComponent a)
public void paint(Graphics a,JComponent
  b)
public void uninstallUI(JComponent a)
public void update(Graphics a,JComponent
  b)
```

►MULTISLIDERUI
```
public class javax.swing.plaf.multi.
  MultiSliderUI
extends javax.swing.plaf.SliderUI
extends javax.swing.plaf.ComponentUI
extends java.lang.Object
```
Fields
```
protected java.util.Vector uis
```
Methods
```
public boolean contains(JComponent a,int
  b,int c)
public static ComponentUI createUI(
  JComponent a)
public Accessible getAccessibleChild(
  JComponent a,int b)
public int getAccessibleChildrenCount(
  JComponent a)
public Dimension getMaximumSize(
  JComponent a)
public Dimension getMinimumSize(
  JComponent a)
public Dimension getPreferredSize(
  JComponent a)
```

```
public ComponentUI getUIs()
public void installUI(JComponent a)
public void paint(Graphics a,JComponent
  b)
public void uninstallUI(JComponent a)
public void update(Graphics a,JComponent
  b)
```

►MultiSplitPaneUI
```
public class javax.swing.plaf.multi.
  MultiSplitPaneUI
extends javax.swing.plaf.SplitPaneUI
extends javax.swing.plaf.ComponentUI
extends java.lang.Object
```
Fields
```
protected java.util.Vector uis
```
Methods
```
public boolean contains(JComponent a,int
  b,int c)
public static ComponentUI createUI(
  JComponent a)
public void finishedPaintingChildren(
  JSplitPane a,Graphics b)
public Accessible getAccessibleChild(
  JComponent a,int b)
public int getAccessibleChildrenCount(
  JComponent a)
public int getDividerLocation(JSplitPane
  a)
public int getMaximumDividerLocation(
  JSplitPane a)
public Dimension getMaximumSize(
  JComponent a)
public int getMinimumDividerLocation(
  JSplitPane a)
public Dimension getMinimumSize(
  JComponent a)
public Dimension getPreferredSize(
  JComponent a)
public ComponentUI getUIs()
public void installUI(JComponent a)
public void paint(Graphics a,JComponent
  b)
public void resetToPreferredSizes(
  JSplitPane a)
public void setDividerLocation(
  JSplitPane a,int b)
public void uninstallUI(JComponent a)
public void update(Graphics a,JComponent
  b)
```

►MultiTabbedPaneUI
```
public class javax.swing.plaf.multi.
  MultiTabbedPaneUI
extends javax.swing.plaf.TabbedPaneUI
extends javax.swing.plaf.ComponentUI
extends java.lang.Object
```
Fields
```
protected java.util.Vector uis
```
Methods
```
public boolean contains(JComponent a,int
  b,int c)
```

```
public static ComponentUI createUI(
  JComponent a)
public Accessible getAccessibleChild(
  JComponent a,int b)
public int getAccessibleChildrenCount(
  JComponent a)
public Dimension getMaximumSize(
  JComponent a)
public Dimension getMinimumSize(
  JComponent a)
public Dimension getPreferredSize(
  JComponent a)
public Rectangle getTabBounds(
  JTabbedPane a,int b)
public int getTabRunCount(JTabbedPane a)
public ComponentUI getUIs()
public void installUI(JComponent a)
public void paint(Graphics a,JComponent
  b)
public int tabForCoordinate(JTabbedPane
  a,int b,int c)
public void uninstallUI(JComponent a)
public void update(Graphics a,JComponent
  b)
```

►MultiTableHeaderUI
```
public class javax.swing.plaf.multi.
  MultiTableHeaderUI
extends javax.swing.plaf.TableHeaderUI
extends javax.swing.plaf.ComponentUI
extends java.lang.Object
```
Fields
```
protected java.util.Vector uis
```
Methods
```
public boolean contains(JComponent a,int
  b,int c)
public static ComponentUI createUI(
  JComponent a)
public Accessible getAccessibleChild(
  JComponent a,int b)
public int getAccessibleChildrenCount(
  JComponent a)
public Dimension getMaximumSize(
  JComponent a)
public Dimension getMinimumSize(
  JComponent a)
public Dimension getPreferredSize(
  JComponent a)
public ComponentUI getUIs()
public void installUI(JComponent a)
public void paint(Graphics a,JComponent
  b)
public void uninstallUI(JComponent a)
public void update(Graphics a,JComponent
  b)
```

►MultiTableUI
```
public class javax.swing.plaf.multi.
  MultiTableUI
extends javax.swing.plaf.TableUI
extends javax.swing.plaf.ComponentUI
extends java.lang.Object
```

Fields

protected java.util.Vector uis

Methods

public boolean contains(JComponent a,int b,int c)

public static ComponentUI createUI(JComponent a)

public Accessible getAccessibleChild(JComponent a,int b)

public int getAccessibleChildrenCount(JComponent a)

public Dimension getMaximumSize(JComponent a)

public Dimension getMinimumSize(JComponent a)

public Dimension getPreferredSize(JComponent a)

public ComponentUI getUIs()

public void installUI(JComponent a)

public void paint(Graphics a,JComponent b)

public void uninstallUI(JComponent a)

public void update(Graphics a,JComponent b)

▶**MultiTextUI**

public class javax.swing.plaf.multi. MultiTextUI

extends javax.swing.plaf.TextUI

extends javax.swing.plaf.ComponentUI

extends java.lang.Object

Fields

protected java.util.Vector uis

Methods

public boolean contains(JComponent a,int b,int c)

public static ComponentUI createUI(JComponent a)

public void damageRange(JTextComponent a, int b,int c)

public void damageRange(JTextComponent t, int p0,int p1,Bias firstBias,Bias secondBias)

public Accessible getAccessibleChild(JComponent a,int b)

public int getAccessibleChildrenCount(JComponent a)

public EditorKit getEditorKit(JTextComponent a)

public Dimension getMaximumSize(JComponent a)

public Dimension getMinimumSize(JComponent a)

public int getNextVisualPositionFrom(JTextComponent t,int pos,Bias b,int direction,Bias biasRet)

public Dimension getPreferredSize(JComponent a)

public View getRootView(JTextComponent a)

public ComponentUI getUIs()

public void installUI(JComponent a)

public Rectangle modelToView(JTextComponent a,int b)

public Rectangle modelToView(JTextComponent t,int pos,Bias bias)

public void paint(Graphics a,JComponent b)

public void uninstallUI(JComponent a)

public void update(Graphics a,JComponent b)

public int viewToModel(JTextComponent a, Point b)

public int viewToModel(JTextComponent t, Point pt,Bias biasReturn)

▶**MultiToolBarUI**

public class javax.swing.plaf.multi. MultiToolBarUI

extends javax.swing.plaf.ToolBarUI

extends javax.swing.plaf.ComponentUI

extends java.lang.Object

Fields

protected java.util.Vector uis

Methods

public boolean contains(JComponent a,int b,int c)

public static ComponentUI createUI(JComponent a)

public Accessible getAccessibleChild(JComponent a,int b)

public int getAccessibleChildrenCount(JComponent a)

public Dimension getMaximumSize(JComponent a)

public Dimension getMinimumSize(JComponent a)

public Dimension getPreferredSize(JComponent a)

public ComponentUI getUIs()

public void installUI(JComponent a)

public void paint(Graphics a,JComponent b)

public void uninstallUI(JComponent a)

public void update(Graphics a,JComponent b)

▶**MultiToolTipUI**

public class javax.swing.plaf.multi. MultiToolTipUI

extends javax.swing.plaf.ToolTipUI

extends javax.swing.plaf.ComponentUI

extends java.lang.Object

Fields

protected java.util.Vector uis

Methods

public boolean contains(JComponent a,int b,int c)

public static ComponentUI createUI(JComponent a)

public Accessible getAccessibleChild(JComponent a,int b)

public int getAccessibleChildrenCount(JComponent a)

```
public Dimension getMaximumSize(
  JComponent a)
public Dimension getMinimumSize(
  JComponent a)
public Dimension getPreferredSize(
  JComponent a)
public ComponentUI getUIs()
public void installUI(JComponent a)
public void paint(Graphics a,JComponent
  b)
public void uninstallUI(JComponent a)
public void update(Graphics a,JComponent
  b)
```

►MultiTreeUI
```
public class javax.swing.plaf.multi.
  MultiTreeUI
extends javax.swing.plaf.TreeUI
extends javax.swing.plaf.ComponentUI
extends java.lang.Object
```
Fields
```
protected java.util.Vector uis
```
Methods
```
public void cancelEditing(JTree a)
public boolean contains(JComponent a,int
  b,int c)
public static ComponentUI createUI(
  JComponent a)
public Accessible getAccessibleChild(
  JComponent a,int b)
public int getAccessibleChildrenCount(
  JComponent a)
public TreePath
  getClosestPathForLocation(JTree a,int b,
  int c)
public TreePath getEditingPath(JTree a)
public Dimension getMaximumSize(
  JComponent a)
public Dimension getMinimumSize(
  JComponent a)
public Rectangle getPathBounds(JTree a,
  TreePath b)
public TreePath getPathForRow(JTree a,
  int b)
public Dimension getPreferredSize(
  JComponent a)
public int getRowCount(JTree a)
public int getRowForPath(JTree a,
  TreePath b)
public ComponentUI getUIs()
public void installUI(JComponent a)
public boolean isEditing(JTree a)
public void paint(Graphics a,JComponent
  b)
public void startEditingAtPath(JTree a,
  TreePath b)
public boolean stopEditing(JTree a)
public void uninstallUI(JComponent a)
public void update(Graphics a,JComponent
  b)
```

►MultiViewportUI
```
public class javax.swing.plaf.multi.
  MultiViewportUI
extends javax.swing.plaf.ViewportUI
extends javax.swing.plaf.ComponentUI
extends java.lang.Object
```
Fields
```
protected java.util.Vector uis
```
Methods
```
public boolean contains(JComponent a,int
  b,int c)
public static ComponentUI createUI(
  JComponent a)
public Accessible getAccessibleChild(
  JComponent a,int b)
public int getAccessibleChildrenCount(
  JComponent a)
public Dimension getMaximumSize(
  JComponent a)
public Dimension getMinimumSize(
  JComponent a)
public Dimension getPreferredSize(
  JComponent a)
public ComponentUI getUIs()
public void installUI(JComponent a)
public void paint(Graphics a,JComponent
  b)
public void uninstallUI(JComponent a)
public void update(Graphics a,JComponent
  b)
```

►Naming
```
public final class java.rmi.Naming
extends java.lang.Object
```
Constructors
```
private  Naming()
```
Methods
```
public static void bind(String name,
  Remote obj)
public static String list(String name)
public static Remote lookup(String name)
public static void rebind(String name,
  Remote obj)
public static void unbind(String name)
```

►NegativeArraySizeException
```
public class java.lang.
  NegativeArraySizeException
extends java.lang.RuntimeException
extends java.lang.Exception
extends java.lang.Throwable
extends java.lang.Object
```
Constructors
```
public  NegativeArraySizeException()
public  NegativeArraySizeException(
  String s)
```

►NetPermission
```
public final class java.net.
  NetPermission
extends java.security.BasicPermission
extends java.security.Permission
```

extends java.lang.Object
Constructors
public NetPermission(String name)
public NetPermission(String name,String
  actions)

▶**NoClassDefFoundError**
public class java.lang.
  NoClassDefFoundError
extends java.lang.LinkageError
extends java.lang.Error
extends java.lang.Throwable
extends java.lang.Object
Constructors
public NoClassDefFoundError()
public NoClassDefFoundError(String s)

▶**NoninvertibleTransformException**
public class java.awt.geom.
  NoninvertibleTransformException
extends java.lang.Exception
extends java.lang.Throwable
extends java.lang.Object
Constructors
public NoninvertibleTransformException(
  String s)

▶**NoRouteToHostException**
public class java.net.
  NoRouteToHostException
extends java.net.SocketException
extends java.io.IOException
extends java.lang.Exception
extends java.lang.Throwable
extends java.lang.Object
Constructors
public NoRouteToHostException(String
  msg)
public NoRouteToHostException()

▶**NoSuchAlgorithmException**
public class java.security.
  NoSuchAlgorithmException
extends java.security.
  GeneralSecurityException
extends java.lang.Exception
extends java.lang.Throwable
extends java.lang.Object
Constructors
public NoSuchAlgorithmException()
public NoSuchAlgorithmException(String
  msg)

▶**NoSuchElementException**
public class java.util.
  NoSuchElementException
extends java.lang.RuntimeException
extends java.lang.Exception
extends java.lang.Throwable
extends java.lang.Object
Constructors
public NoSuchElementException()

public NoSuchElementException(String s)

▶**NoSuchFieldError**
public class java.lang.NoSuchFieldError
extends java.lang.
  IncompatibleClassChangeError
extends java.lang.LinkageError
extends java.lang.Error
extends java.lang.Throwable
extends java.lang.Object
Constructors
public NoSuchFieldError()
public NoSuchFieldError(String s)

▶**NoSuchFieldException**
public class java.lang.
  NoSuchFieldException
extends java.lang.Exception
extends java.lang.Throwable
extends java.lang.Object
Constructors
public NoSuchFieldException()
public NoSuchFieldException(String s)

▶**NoSuchMethodError**
public class java.lang.
  NoSuchMethodError
extends java.lang.
  IncompatibleClassChangeError
extends java.lang.LinkageError
extends java.lang.Error
extends java.lang.Throwable
extends java.lang.Object
Constructors
public NoSuchMethodError()
public NoSuchMethodError(String s)

▶**NoSuchMethodException**
public class java.lang.
  NoSuchMethodException
extends java.lang.Exception
extends java.lang.Throwable
extends java.lang.Object
Constructors
public NoSuchMethodException()
public NoSuchMethodException(String s)

▶**NoSuchObjectException**
public class java.rmi.
  NoSuchObjectException
extends java.rmi.RemoteException
extends java.io.IOException
extends java.lang.Exception
extends java.lang.Throwable
extends java.lang.Object
Constructors
public NoSuchObjectException(String s)

▶**NoSuchProviderException**
public class java.security.
  NoSuchProviderException

extends java.security.
  GeneralSecurityException
extends java.lang.Exception
extends java.lang.Throwable
extends java.lang.Object
Constructors
public NoSuchProviderException()
public NoSuchProviderException(String
  msg)

►NOTACTIVEEXCEPTION
public class java.io.NotActiveException
extends java.io.ObjectStreamException
extends java.io.IOException
extends java.lang.Exception
extends java.lang.Throwable
extends java.lang.Object
Constructors
public NotActiveException(String reason)
public NotActiveException()

►NOTBOUNDEXCEPTION
public class java.rmi.NotBoundException
extends java.lang.Exception
extends java.lang.Throwable
extends java.lang.Object
Constructors
public NotBoundException()
public NotBoundException(String s)

►NOTOWNEREXCEPTION
public class java.security.acl.
  NotOwnerException
extends java.lang.Exception
extends java.lang.Throwable
extends java.lang.Object
Constructors
public NotOwnerException()

►NOTSERIALIZABLEEXCEPTION
public class java.io.
  NotSerializableException
extends java.io.ObjectStreamException
extends java.io.IOException
extends java.lang.Exception
extends java.lang.Throwable
extends java.lang.Object
Constructors
public NotSerializableException(String
  classname)
public NotSerializableException()

►NULLPOINTEREXCEPTION
public class java.lang.
  NullPointerException
extends java.lang.RuntimeException
extends java.lang.Exception
extends java.lang.Throwable
extends java.lang.Object
Constructors
public NullPointerException()
public NullPointerException(String s)

►NUMBER
public abstract class java.lang.Number
implements java.io.Serializable
extends java.lang.Object
Methods
public byte byteValue()
public abstract double doubleValue()
public abstract float floatValue()
public abstract int intValue()
public abstract long longValue()
public short shortValue()

►NUMBERFORMAT
public abstract class java.text.
  NumberFormat
extends java.text.Format
extends java.lang.Object
Fields
public final static int FRACTION_FIELD
public final static int INTEGER_FIELD
Methods
public Object clone()
public boolean equals(Object obj)
public final StringBuffer format(Object
  number,StringBuffer toAppendTo,
  FieldPosition pos)
public final String format(double number)
public final String format(long number)
public abstract StringBuffer format(
  double number,StringBuffer toAppendTo,
  FieldPosition pos)
public abstract StringBuffer format(long
  number,StringBuffer toAppendTo,
  FieldPosition pos)
public static Locale getAvailableLocales(
)
public final static NumberFormat
  getCurrencyInstance()
public static NumberFormat
  getCurrencyInstance(Locale inLocale)
public final static NumberFormat
  getInstance()
public static NumberFormat getInstance(
  Locale inLocale)
public int getMaximumFractionDigits()
public int getMaximumIntegerDigits()
public int getMinimumFractionDigits()
public int getMinimumIntegerDigits()
public final static NumberFormat
  getNumberInstance()
public static NumberFormat
  getNumberInstance(Locale inLocale)
public final static NumberFormat
  getPercentInstance()
public static NumberFormat
  getPercentInstance(Locale inLocale)
public int hashCode()
public boolean isGroupingUsed()
public boolean isParseIntegerOnly()
public abstract Number parse(String text,
  ParsePosition parsePosition)
public Number parse(String text)

```
public final Object parseObject(String
  source,ParsePosition parsePosition)
public void setGroupingUsed(boolean
  newValue)
public void setMaximumFractionDigits(int
  newValue)
public void setMaximumIntegerDigits(int
  newValue)
public void setMinimumFractionDigits(int
  newValue)
public void setMinimumIntegerDigits(int
  newValue)
public void setParseIntegerOnly(boolean
  value)
```

►NUMBERFORMATEXCEPTION
```
public class java.lang.
  NumberFormatException
extends java.lang.
  IllegalArgumentException
extends java.lang.RuntimeException
extends java.lang.Exception
extends java.lang.Throwable
extends java.lang.Object
```
Constructors
```
public  NumberFormatException()
public  NumberFormatException(String s)
```

►OBJECT
```
public class java.lang.Object
extends java.lang.Object
```
Methods
```
protected native Object clone()
public boolean equals(Object obj)
protected void finalize()
public final static native Class
  getClass()
public native int hashCode()
public final native void notify()
public final native void notifyAll()
public String toString()
public final native void wait(long
  timeout)
public final void wait(long timeout,int
  nanos)
public final void wait()
```

►OBJECTINPUTSTREAM
```
public class java.io.ObjectInputStream
implements java.io.ObjectInput
implements java.io.
  ObjectStreamConstants
extends java.io.InputStream
extends java.lang.Object
```
Constructors
```
public  ObjectInputStream(InputStream in)
protected  ObjectInputStream()
```
Methods
```
public int available()
public void close()
public void defaultReadObject()
```

```
protected boolean enableResolveObject(
  boolean enable)
public int read()
public int read(byte b,int off,int len)
public boolean readBoolean()
public byte readByte()
public char readChar()
public double readDouble()
public GetField readFields()
public float readFloat()
public void readFully(byte data)
public void readFully(byte data,int
  offset,int size)
public int readInt()
public String readLine()
public long readLong()
public final Object readObject()
protected Object readObjectOverride()
public short readShort()
protected void readStreamHeader()
public int readUnsignedByte()
public int readUnsignedShort()
public String readUTF()
public synchronized void
  registerValidation(ObjectInputValidation
  obj,int prio)
protected Class resolveClass(
  ObjectStreamClass v)
protected Object resolveObject(Object
  obj)
public int skipBytes(int len)
```

►OBJECTOUTPUTSTREAM
```
public class java.io.ObjectOutputStream
implements java.io.ObjectOutput
implements java.io.
  ObjectStreamConstants
extends java.io.OutputStream
extends java.lang.Object
```
Constructors
```
public  ObjectOutputStream(OutputStream
  out)
protected  ObjectOutputStream()
```
Methods
```
protected void annotateClass(Class cl)
public void close()
public void defaultWriteObject()
protected void drain()
protected boolean enableReplaceObject(
  boolean enable)
public void flush()
public PutField putFields()
protected Object replaceObject(Object
  obj)
public void reset()
public void useProtocolVersion(int
  version)
public void write(int data)
public void write(byte b)
public void write(byte b,int off,int len)
public void writeBoolean(boolean data)
public void writeByte(int data)
```

```
public void writeBytes(String data)
public void writeChar(int data)
public void writeChars(String data)
public void writeDouble(double data)
public void writeFields()
public void writeFloat(float data)
public void writeInt(int data)
public void writeLong(long data)
public final void writeObject(Object obj)
protected void writeObjectOverride(
  Object obj)
public void writeShort(int data)
protected void writeStreamHeader()
public void writeUTF(String data)
```

▶OBJECTSTREAMCLASS

```
public class java.io.ObjectStreamClass
implements java.io.Serializable
extends java.lang.Object
```

Fields
```
public final static java.io.
  ObjectStreamField NO_FIELDS
```

Constructors
```
private  ObjectStreamClass()
 ObjectStreamClass()
```

Methods
```
public Class forClass()
public ObjectStreamField getField(String
  name)
public ObjectStreamField getFields()
public String getName()
public long getSerialVersionUID()
public static ObjectStreamClass lookup(
  Class cl)
public String toString()
```

▶OBJECTSTREAMEXCEPTION

```
public abstract class java.io.
  ObjectStreamException
extends java.io.IOException
extends java.lang.Exception
extends java.lang.Throwable
extends java.lang.Object
```

Constructors
```
protected  ObjectStreamException(String
  classname)
protected  ObjectStreamException()
```

▶OBJECTSTREAMFIELD

```
public class java.io.ObjectStreamField
implements java.lang.Comparable
extends java.lang.Object
```

Constructors
```
public  ObjectStreamField(String n,Class
  clazz)
 ObjectStreamField()
private  ObjectStreamField()
 ObjectStreamField()
```

Methods
```
public int compareTo(Object o)
public String getName()
```

```
public int getOffset()
public Class getType()
public char getTypeCode()
public String getTypeString()
public boolean isPrimitive()
protected void setOffset(int offset)
public String toString()
```

▶OBJECTVIEW

```
public class javax.swing.text.html.
  ObjectView
extends javax.swing.text.ComponentView
extends javax.swing.text.View
extends java.lang.Object
```

Constructors
```
public  ObjectView(Element elem)
```

Methods
```
protected Component createComponent()
```

▶OBJID

```
public final class java.rmi.server.
  ObjID
implements java.io.Serializable
extends java.lang.Object
```

Fields
```
public final static int ACTIVATOR_ID
public final static int DGC_ID
public final static int REGISTRY_ID
```

Constructors
```
public  ObjID()
public  ObjID(int num)
private  ObjID()
```

Methods
```
public boolean equals(Object obj)
public int hashCode()
public static ObjID read(ObjectInput in)
public String toString()
public void write(ObjectOutput out)
```

▶OBSERVABLE

```
public class java.util.Observable
extends java.lang.Object
```

Constructors
```
public  Observable()
```

Methods
```
public synchronized void addObserver(
  Observer o)
protected synchronized void clearChanged(
  )
public synchronized int countObservers()
public synchronized void deleteObserver(
  Observer o)
public synchronized void deleteObservers(
  )
public synchronized boolean hasChanged()
public void notifyObservers()
public void notifyObservers(Object arg)
protected synchronized void setChanged()
```

▶OPERATION

```
public class java.rmi.server.Operation
extends java.lang.Object
```

Constructors

public Operation(String op)

Methods

public String getOperation()
public String toString()

►**OPTION**

public class javax.swing.text.html.
  Option
extends java.lang.Object

Constructors

public Option(AttributeSet attr)

Methods

public AttributeSet getAttributes()
public String getLabel()
public String getValue()
public boolean isSelected()
public void setLabel(String label)
protected void setSelection(boolean
  state)
public String toString()

►**OPTIONALDATAEXCEPTION**

public class java.io.
  OptionalDataException
extends java.io.ObjectStreamException
extends java.io.IOException
extends java.lang.Exception
extends java.lang.Throwable
extends java.lang.Object

Fields

public boolean eof
public int length

Constructors

OptionalDataException()
OptionalDataException()

►**OPTIONPANEUI**

public abstract class javax.swing.plaf.
  OptionPaneUI
extends javax.swing.plaf.ComponentUI
extends java.lang.Object

Methods

public abstract boolean
  containsCustomComponents(JOptionPane op)
public abstract void selectInitialValue(
  JOptionPane op)

►**OUTOFMEMORYERROR**

public class java.lang.OutOfMemoryError
extends java.lang.VirtualMachineError
extends java.lang.Error
extends java.lang.Throwable
extends java.lang.Object

Constructors

public OutOfMemoryError()
public OutOfMemoryError(String s)

►**OUTPUTSTREAM**

public abstract class java.io.
  OutputStream
extends java.lang.Object

Methods

public void close()
public void flush()
public abstract void write(int b)
public void write(byte b)
public void write(byte b,int off,int len)

►**OUTPUTSTREAMWRITER**

public class java.io.OutputStreamWriter
extends java.io.Writer
extends java.lang.Object

Constructors

public OutputStreamWriter(OutputStream
  out,String enc)
public OutputStreamWriter(OutputStream
  out)
private OutputStreamWriter()

Methods

public void close()
public void flush()
public String getEncoding()
public void write(int c)
public void write(char cbuf,int off,int
  len)
public void write(String str,int off,int
  len)

►**OVERLAYLAYOUT**

public class javax.swing.OverlayLayout
implements java.awt.LayoutManager2
implements java.io.Serializable
extends java.lang.Object

Constructors

public OverlayLayout(Container target)

Methods

public void addLayoutComponent(String
  name,Component comp)
public void addLayoutComponent(Component
  comp,Object constraints)
public float getLayoutAlignmentX(
  Container target)
public float getLayoutAlignmentY(
  Container target)
public void invalidateLayout(Container
  target)
public void layoutContainer(Container
  target)
public Dimension maximumLayoutSize(
  Container target)
public Dimension minimumLayoutSize(
  Container target)
public Dimension preferredLayoutSize(
  Container target)
public void removeLayoutComponent(
  Component comp)

►**PACKAGE**

public class java.lang.Package
extends java.lang.Object

Constructors

 Package()
private Package()

Methods
```
public String getImplementationTitle()
public String getImplementationVendor()
public String getImplementationVersion()
public String getName()
public static Package getPackage(String
  name)
public static Package getPackages()
public String getSpecificationTitle()
public String getSpecificationVendor()
public String getSpecificationVersion()
public int hashCode()
public boolean isCompatibleWith(String
  desired)
public boolean isSealed()
public boolean isSealed(URL url)
public String toString()
```

►PACKEDCOLORMODEL
```
public abstract class java.awt.image.
  PackedColorModel
extends java.awt.image.ColorModel
extends java.lang.Object
```

Constructors
```
public PackedColorModel(ColorSpace
  space,int bits,int colorMaskArray,int
  alphaMask,boolean isAlphaPremultiplied,
  int trans,int transferType)
public PackedColorModel(ColorSpace
  space,int bits,int rmask,int gmask,int
  bmask,int amask,boolean
  isAlphaPremultiplied,int trans,int
  transferType)
```

Methods
```
public SampleModel
  createCompatibleSampleModel(int w,int h)
public boolean equals(Object obj)
public WritableRaster getAlphaRaster(
  WritableRaster raster)
public final int getMask(int index)
public final int getMasks()
public boolean isCompatibleSampleModel(
  SampleModel sm)
```

►PAGEFORMAT
```
public class java.awt.print.PageFormat
implements java.lang.Cloneable
extends java.lang.Object
```

Fields
```
public final static int LANDSCAPE
public final static int PORTRAIT
public final static int REVERSE_
  LANDSCAPE
```

Constructors
```
public PageFormat()
```

Methods
```
public Object clone()
public double getHeight()
public double getImageableHeight()
public double getImageableWidth()
public double getImageableX()
public double getImageableY()
```

```
public double getMatrix()
public int getOrientation()
public Paper getPaper()
public double getWidth()
public void setOrientation(int
  orientation)
public void setPaper(Paper paper)
```

►PAINTEVENT
```
public class java.awt.event.PaintEvent
extends java.awt.event.ComponentEvent
extends java.awt.AWTEvent
extends java.util.EventObject
extends java.lang.Object
```

Fields
```
public final static int PAINT
public final static int PAINT_FIRST
public final static int PAINT_LAST
public final static int UPDATE
```

Constructors
```
public PaintEvent(Component source,int
  id,Rectangle updateRect)
```

Methods
```
public Rectangle getUpdateRect()
public String paramString()
public void setUpdateRect(Rectangle
  updateRect)
```

►PANEL
```
public class java.awt.Panel
extends java.awt.Container
extends java.awt.Component
extends java.lang.Object
```

Constructors
```
public Panel()
public Panel(LayoutManager layout)
```

Methods
```
public void addNotify()
```

►PANELUI
```
public abstract class javax.swing.plaf.
  PanelUI
extends javax.swing.plaf.ComponentUI
extends java.lang.Object
```

►PAPER
```
public class java.awt.print.Paper
implements java.lang.Cloneable
extends java.lang.Object
```

Constructors
```
public Paper()
```

Methods
```
public Object clone()
public double getHeight()
public double getImageableHeight()
public double getImageableWidth()
public double getImageableX()
public double getImageableY()
public double getWidth()
public void setImageableArea(double x,
  double y,double width,double height)
```

public void setSize(double width,double
  height)

►PARAGRAPHVIEW
public class javax.swing.text.html.
  ParagraphView
extends javax.swing.text.ParagraphView
extends javax.swing.text.BoxView
extends javax.swing.text.CompositeView
extends javax.swing.text.View
extends java.lang.Object

Constructors
public ParagraphView(Element elem)

Methods
protected SizeRequirements
  calculateMinorAxisRequirements(int axis,
  SizeRequirements r)
public void changedUpdate(DocumentEvent
  e,Shape a,ViewFactory f)
public AttributeSet getAttributes()
public float getMaximumSpan(int axis)
public float getMinimumSpan(int axis)
public float getPreferredSpan(int axis)
protected StyleSheet getStyleSheet()
public boolean isVisible()
public void setParent(View parent)
protected void
  setPropertiesFromAttributes()

►PARAGRAPHVIEW
public class javax.swing.text.
  ParagraphView
implements javax.swing.text.TabExpander
extends javax.swing.text.BoxView
extends javax.swing.text.CompositeView
extends javax.swing.text.View
extends java.lang.Object

Fields
protected int firstLineIndent

Constructors
public ParagraphView(Element elem)

Methods
protected void adjustRow(Row r,int
  desiredSpan,int x)
public View breakView(int axis,float len,
  Shape a)
protected SizeRequirements
  calculateMinorAxisRequirements(int axis,
  SizeRequirements r)
public void changedUpdate(DocumentEvent
  changes,Shape a,ViewFactory f)
protected int
  findOffsetToCharactersInString(char
  string,int start)
protected boolean flipEastAndWestAtEnds(
  int position,Bias bias)
public float getAlignment(int axis)
public int getBreakWeight(int axis,float
  len)
protected int getClosestPositionTo(int
  pos,Bias b,Shape a,int direction,Bias
  biasRet,int rowIndex,int x)

protected View getLayoutView(int index)
protected int getLayoutViewCount()
protected int
  getNextNorthSouthVisualPositionFrom(int
  pos,Bias b,Shape a,int direction,Bias
  biasRet)
protected float getPartialSize(int
  startOffset,int endOffset)
protected float getTabBase()
protected TabSet getTabSet()
protected View getViewAtPosition(int pos,
  Rectangle a)
protected int getViewIndexAtPosition(int
  pos)
public void insertUpdate(DocumentEvent
  changes,Shape a,ViewFactory f)
protected void layout(int width,int
  height)
protected void loadChildren(ViewFactory
  f)
public float nextTabStop(float x,int
  tabOffset)
public void paint(Graphics g,Shape a)
public void removeUpdate(DocumentEvent
  changes,Shape a,ViewFactory f)
protected void setFirstLineIndent(float
  fi)
protected void setJustification(int j)
protected void setLineSpacing(float ls)
protected void
  setPropertiesFromAttributes()

►PARAMETERBLOCK
public class java.awt.image.renderable.
  ParameterBlock
implements java.lang.Cloneable
implements java.io.Serializable
extends java.lang.Object

Fields
protected java.util.Vector parameters
protected java.util.Vector sources

Constructors
public ParameterBlock()
public ParameterBlock(Vector sources)
public ParameterBlock(Vector sources,
  Vector parameters)

Methods
public ParameterBlock add(Object obj)
public ParameterBlock add(byte b)
public ParameterBlock add(char c)
public ParameterBlock add(short s)
public ParameterBlock add(int i)
public ParameterBlock add(long l)
public ParameterBlock add(float f)
public ParameterBlock add(double d)
public ParameterBlock addSource(Object
  source)
public Object clone()
public byte getByteParameter(int index)
public char getCharParameter(int index)
public double getDoubleParameter(int
  index)

```
public float getFloatParameter(int index)
public int getIntParameter(int index)
public long getLongParameter(int index)
public int getNumParameters()
public int getNumSources()
public Object getObjectParameter(int
  index)
public Class getParamClasses()
public Vector getParameters()
public RenderableImage
  getRenderableSource(int index)
public RenderedImage getRenderedSource(
  int index)
public short getShortParameter(int index)
public Object getSource(int index)
public Vector getSources()
public void removeParameters()
public void removeSources()
public ParameterBlock set(Object obj,int
  index)
public ParameterBlock set(byte b,int
  index)
public ParameterBlock set(char c,int
  index)
public ParameterBlock set(short s,int
  index)
public ParameterBlock set(int i,int
  index)
public ParameterBlock set(long l,int
  index)
public ParameterBlock set(float f,int
  index)
public ParameterBlock set(double d,int
  index)
public void setParameters(Vector
  parameters)
public ParameterBlock setSource(Object
  source,int index)
public void setSources(Vector sources)
public Object shallowClone()
```

►PARAMETERDESCRIPTOR
```
public class java.beans.
  ParameterDescriptor
extends java.beans.FeatureDescriptor
extends java.lang.Object
```
Constructors
```
public  ParameterDescriptor()
  ParameterDescriptor()
```

►PARSEEXCEPTION
```
public class java.text.ParseException
extends java.lang.Exception
extends java.lang.Throwable
extends java.lang.Object
```
Constructors
```
public  ParseException(String s,int
  errorOffset)
```
Methods
```
public int getErrorOffset()
```

►PARSEPOSITION
```
public class java.text.ParsePosition
```

```
extends java.lang.Object
```
Constructors
```
public  ParsePosition(int index)
```
Methods
```
public boolean equals(Object obj)
public int getErrorIndex()
public int getIndex()
public int hashCode()
public void setErrorIndex(int ei)
public void setIndex(int index)
public String toString()
```

►PARSER
```
public class javax.swing.text.html.
  parser.Parser
implements javax.swing.text.html.parser.
  DTDConstants
extends java.lang.Object
```
Fields
```
protected javax.swing.text.html.parser.
  DTD dtd
protected boolean strict
```
Constructors
```
public  Parser(DTD dtd)
```
Methods
```
protected void endTag(boolean omitted)
protected void error(String err,String
  arg1,String arg2,String arg3)
protected void error(String err,String
  arg1,String arg2)
protected void error(String err,String
  arg1)
protected void error(String err)
protected void flushAttributes()
protected SimpleAttributeSet
  getAttributes()
protected int getCurrentLine()
protected int getCurrentPos()
protected void handleComment(char text)
protected void handleEmptyTag(TagElement
  tag)
protected void handleEndTag(TagElement
  tag)
protected void handleEOFInComment()
protected void handleError(int ln,String
  msg)
protected void handleStartTag(TagElement
  tag)
protected void handleText(char text)
protected void handleTitle(char text)
protected TagElement makeTag(Element
  elem,boolean fictional)
protected TagElement makeTag(Element
  elem)
protected void markFirstTime(Element
  elem)
public synchronized void parse(Reader in)
public String parseDTDMarkup()
protected boolean
  parseMarkupDeclarations(StringBuffer
  strBuff)
protected void startTag(TagElement tag)
```

►**PARSERDELEGATOR**
public class javax.swing.text.html.
  parser.ParserDelegator
extends java.lang.Object
Constructors
public ParserDelegator()
Methods
protected static DTD createDTD(DTD dtd,
  String name)
public void parse(Reader r,
  ParserCallback cb,boolean ignoreCharSet)
protected static void setDefaultDTD()

►**PASSWORDAUTHENTICATION**
public final class java.net.
  PasswordAuthentication
extends java.lang.Object
Constructors
public PasswordAuthentication(String
  userName,char password)
Methods
public char getPassword()
public String getUserName()

►**PASSWORDVIEW**
public class javax.swing.text.
  PasswordView
extends javax.swing.text.FieldView
extends javax.swing.text.PlainView
extends javax.swing.text.View
extends java.lang.Object
Constructors
public PasswordView(Element elem)
Methods
protected int drawEchoCharacter(Graphics
  g,int x,int y,char c)
protected int drawSelectedText(Graphics
  g,int x,int y,int p0,int p1)
protected int drawUnselectedText(
  Graphics g,int x,int y,int p0,int p1)
public Shape modelToView(int pos,Shape a,
  Bias b)
public int viewToModel(float fx,float fy,
  Shape a,Bias bias)

►**PERMISSION**
public abstract class java.security.
  Permission
implements java.security.Guard
implements java.io.Serializable
extends java.lang.Object
Constructors
public Permission(String name)
Methods
public void checkGuard(Object object)
public abstract boolean equals(Object
  obj)
public abstract String getActions()
public final String getName()
public abstract int hashCode()

public abstract boolean implies(
  Permission permission)
public PermissionCollection
  newPermissionCollection()
public String toString()

►**PERMISSIONCOLLECTION**
public abstract class java.security.
  PermissionCollection
implements java.io.Serializable
extends java.lang.Object
Methods
public abstract void add(Permission
  permission)
public abstract Enumeration elements()
public abstract boolean implies(
  Permission permission)
public boolean isReadOnly()
public void setReadOnly()
public String toString()

►**PERMISSIONS**
public final class java.security.
  Permissions
implements java.io.Serializable
extends java.security.
  PermissionCollection
extends java.lang.Object
Constructors
public Permissions()
Methods
public void add(Permission permission)
public Enumeration elements()
public boolean implies(Permission
  permission)

►**PHANTOMREFERENCE**
public class java.lang.ref.
  PhantomReference
extends java.lang.ref.Reference
extends java.lang.Object
Constructors
public PhantomReference(Object referent,
  ReferenceQueue q)
Methods
public Object get()

►**PIPEDINPUTSTREAM**
public class java.io.PipedInputStream
extends java.io.InputStream
extends java.lang.Object
Fields
protected byte buffer
protected int in
protected int out
protected final static int PIPE_SIZE
Constructors
public PipedInputStream(
  PipedOutputStream src)
public PipedInputStream()

Methods
```
public synchronized int available()
public void close()
public void connect(PipedOutputStream
  src)
public synchronized int read()
public synchronized int read(byte b,int
  off,int len)
protected synchronized void receive(int
  b)
```

►PipedOutputStream
```
public class java.io.PipedOutputStream
extends java.io.OutputStream
extends java.lang.Object
```
Constructors
```
public  PipedOutputStream(
  PipedInputStream snk)
public  PipedOutputStream()
```
Methods
```
public void close()
public synchronized void connect(
  PipedInputStream snk)
public synchronized void flush()
public void write(int b)
public void write(byte b,int off,int len)
```

►PipedReader
```
public class java.io.PipedReader
extends java.io.Reader
extends java.lang.Object
```
Constructors
```
public  PipedReader(PipedWriter src)
public  PipedReader()
```
Methods
```
public void close()
public void connect(PipedWriter src)
public synchronized int read()
public synchronized int read(char cbuf,
  int off,int len)
public synchronized boolean ready()
```

►PipedWriter
```
public class java.io.PipedWriter
extends java.io.Writer
extends java.lang.Object
```
Constructors
```
public  PipedWriter(PipedReader snk)
public  PipedWriter()
```
Methods
```
public void close()
public synchronized void connect(
  PipedReader snk)
public synchronized void flush()
public void write(int c)
public void write(char cbuf,int off,int
  len)
```

►PixelGrabber
```
public class java.awt.image.
  PixelGrabber
implements java.awt.image.ImageConsumer
```
```
extends java.lang.Object
```
Constructors
```
public  PixelGrabber(Image img,int x,int
  y,int w,int h,int pix,int off,int
  scansize)
public  PixelGrabber(ImageProducer ip,
  int x,int y,int w,int h,int pix,int off,
  int scansize)
public  PixelGrabber(Image img,int x,int
  y,int w,int h,boolean forceRGB)
```
Methods
```
public synchronized void abortGrabbing()
public synchronized ColorModel
  getColorModel()
public synchronized int getHeight()
public synchronized Object getPixels()
public synchronized int getStatus()
public synchronized int getWidth()
public boolean grabPixels()
public synchronized boolean grabPixels(
  long ms)
public synchronized void imageComplete(
  int status)
public void setColorModel(ColorModel
  model)
public void setDimensions(int width,int
  height)
public void setHints(int hints)
public void setPixels(int srcX,int srcY,
  int srcW,int srcH,ColorModel model,byte
  pixels,int srcOff,int srcScan)
public void setPixels(int srcX,int srcY,
  int srcW,int srcH,ColorModel model,int
  pixels,int srcOff,int srcScan)
public void setProperties(Hashtable
  props)
public synchronized void startGrabbing()
public synchronized int status()
```

►PixelInterleavedSampleModel
```
public class java.awt.image.
  PixelInterleavedSampleModel
extends java.awt.image.
  ComponentSampleModel
extends java.awt.image.SampleModel
extends java.lang.Object
```
Constructors
```
public  PixelInterleavedSampleModel(int
  dataType,int w,int h,int pixelStride,int
  scanlineStride,int bandOffsets)
```
Methods
```
public SampleModel
  createCompatibleSampleModel(int w,int h)
public SampleModel
  createSubsetSampleModel(int bands)
```

►PKCS8EncodedKeySpec
```
public class java.security.spec.
  PKCS8EncodedKeySpec
extends java.security.spec.
  EncodedKeySpec
extends java.lang.Object
```

Constructors
public PKCS8EncodedKeySpec(byte
  encodedKey)

Methods
public byte getEncoded()
public final String getFormat()

►PLAINDOCUMENT
public class javax.swing.text.
  PlainDocument
extends javax.swing.text.
  AbstractDocument
extends java.lang.Object

Fields
public final static java.lang.String
  lineLimitAttribute
public final static java.lang.String
  tabSizeAttribute

Constructors
public PlainDocument()
protected PlainDocument(Content c)

Methods
protected AbstractElement
  createDefaultRoot()
public Element getDefaultRootElement()
public Element getParagraphElement(int
  pos)
protected void insertUpdate(
  DefaultDocumentEvent chng,AttributeSet
  attr)
protected void removeUpdate(
  DefaultDocumentEvent chng)

►PLAINVIEW
public class javax.swing.text.PlainView
implements javax.swing.text.TabExpander
extends javax.swing.text.View
extends java.lang.Object

Fields
protected java.awt.FontMetrics metrics

Constructors
public PlainView(Element elem)

Methods
public void changedUpdate(DocumentEvent
  changes,Shape a,ViewFactory f)
protected void drawLine(int lineIndex,
  Graphics g,int x,int y)
protected int drawSelectedText(Graphics
  g,int x,int y,int p0,int p1)
protected int drawUnselectedText(
  Graphics g,int x,int y,int p0,int p1)
protected final Segment getLineBuffer()
public float getPreferredSpan(int axis)
protected int getTabSize()
public void insertUpdate(DocumentEvent
  changes,Shape a,ViewFactory f)
public Shape modelToView(int pos,Shape a,
  Bias b)
public float nextTabStop(float x,int
  tabOffset)
public void paint(Graphics g,Shape a)

public void preferenceChanged(View child,
  boolean width,boolean height)
public void removeUpdate(DocumentEvent
  changes,Shape a,ViewFactory f)
public int viewToModel(float fx,float fy,
  Shape a,Bias bias)

►POINT
public class java.awt.Point
implements java.io.Serializable
extends java.awt.geom.Point2D
extends java.lang.Object

Fields
public int x
public int y

Constructors
public Point()
public Point(Point p)
public Point(int x,int y)

Methods
public boolean equals(Object obj)
public Point getLocation()
public double getX()
public double getY()
public void move(int x,int y)
public void setLocation(Point p)
public void setLocation(int x,int y)
public void setLocation(double x,double
  y)
public String toString()
public void translate(int x,int y)

►POINT2D
public abstract class java.awt.geom.
  Point2D
implements java.lang.Cloneable
extends java.lang.Object

Constructors
protected Point2D()

Methods
public Object clone()
public static double distance(double X1,
  double Y1,double X2,double Y2)
public double distance(double PX,double
  PY)
public double distance(Point2D pt)
public static double distanceSq(double
  X1,double Y1,double X2,double Y2)
public double distanceSq(double PX,
  double PY)
public double distanceSq(Point2D pt)
public boolean equals(Object obj)
public abstract double getX()
public abstract double getY()
public int hashCode()
public abstract void setLocation(double
  x,double y)
public void setLocation(Point2D p)

►POLICY
public abstract class java.security.
  Policy

extends java.lang.Object
Methods
public abstract PermissionCollection
  getPermissions(CodeSource codesource)
public static Policy getPolicy()
public abstract void refresh()
public static void setPolicy(Policy
  policy)

▶POLYGON
public class java.awt.Polygon
implements java.io.Serializable
implements java.awt.Shape
extends java.lang.Object
Fields
protected java.awt.Rectangle bounds
public int npoints
public int xpoints
public int ypoints
Constructors
public Polygon()
public Polygon(int xpoints,int ypoints,
  int npoints)
Methods
public void addPoint(int x,int y)
public boolean contains(Point p)
public boolean contains(int x,int y)
public boolean contains(double x,double
  y)
public boolean contains(Point2D p)
public boolean contains(double x,double
  y,double w,double h)
public boolean contains(Rectangle2D r)
public Rectangle getBoundingBox()
public Rectangle getBounds()
public Rectangle2D getBounds2D()
public PathIterator getPathIterator(
  AffineTransform at)
public PathIterator getPathIterator(
  AffineTransform at,double flatness)
public boolean inside(int x,int y)
public boolean intersects(double x,
  double y,double w,double h)
public boolean intersects(Rectangle2D r)
public void translate(int deltaX,int
  deltaY)

▶POPUPMENU
public class java.awt.PopupMenu
extends java.awt.Menu
extends java.awt.MenuItem
extends java.awt.MenuComponent
extends java.lang.Object
Constructors
public PopupMenu()
public PopupMenu(String label)
Methods
public void addNotify()
public void show(Component origin,int x,
  int y)

▶POPUPMENUEVENT
public class javax.swing.event.
  PopupMenuEvent
extends java.util.EventObject
extends java.lang.Object
Constructors
public PopupMenuEvent(Object source)

▶POPUPMENUUI
public abstract class javax.swing.plaf.
  PopupMenuUI
extends javax.swing.plaf.ComponentUI
extends java.lang.Object

▶PRINTERABORTEXCEPTION
public class java.awt.print.
  PrinterAbortException
extends java.awt.print.PrinterException
extends java.lang.Exception
extends java.lang.Throwable
extends java.lang.Object
Constructors
public PrinterAbortException()
public PrinterAbortException(String msg)

▶PRINTEREXCEPTION
public class java.awt.print.
  PrinterException
extends java.lang.Exception
extends java.lang.Throwable
extends java.lang.Object
Constructors
public PrinterException()
public PrinterException(String msg)

▶PRINTERIOEXCEPTION
public class java.awt.print.
  PrinterIOException
extends java.awt.print.PrinterException
extends java.lang.Exception
extends java.lang.Throwable
extends java.lang.Object
Constructors
public PrinterIOException(IOException
  exception)
Methods
public IOException getIOException()

▶PRINTERJOB
public abstract class java.awt.print.
  PrinterJob
extends java.lang.Object
Constructors
public PrinterJob()
Methods
public abstract void cancel()
public abstract PageFormat defaultPage(
  PageFormat page)
public PageFormat defaultPage()
public abstract int getCopies()
public abstract String getJobName()
public static PrinterJob getPrinterJob()

```
public abstract String getUserName()
public abstract boolean isCancelled()
public abstract PageFormat pageDialog(
  PageFormat page)
public abstract void print()
public abstract boolean printDialog()
public abstract void setCopies(int
  copies)
public abstract void setJobName(String
  jobName)
public abstract void setPageable(
  Pageable document)
public abstract void setPrintable(
  Printable painter)
public abstract void setPrintable(
  Printable painter,PageFormat format)
public abstract PageFormat validatePage(
  PageFormat page)
```

▸PRINTJOB
```
public abstract class java.awt.PrintJob
extends java.lang.Object
```
Methods
```
public abstract void end()
public void finalize()
public abstract Graphics getGraphics()
public abstract Dimension
  getPageDimension()
public abstract int getPageResolution()
public abstract boolean lastPageFirst()
```

▸PRINTSTREAM
```
public class java.io.PrintStream
extends java.io.FilterOutputStream
extends java.io.OutputStream
extends java.lang.Object
```
Constructors
```
public  PrintStream(OutputStream out)
public  PrintStream(OutputStream out,
  boolean autoFlush)
```
Methods
```
public boolean checkError()
public void close()
public void flush()
public void print(boolean b)
public void print(char c)
public void print(int i)
public void print(long l)
public void print(float f)
public void print(double d)
public void print(char s)
public void print(String s)
public void print(Object obj)
public void println()
public void println(boolean x)
public void println(char x)
public void println(int x)
public void println(long x)
public void println(float x)
public void println(double x)
public void println(char x)
public void println(String x)
```

```
public void println(Object x)
protected void setError()
public void write(int b)
public void write(byte buf,int off,int
  len)
```

▸PRINTWRITER
```
public class java.io.PrintWriter
extends java.io.Writer
extends java.lang.Object
```
Fields
```
protected java.io.Writer out
```
Constructors
```
public  PrintWriter(Writer out)
public  PrintWriter(Writer out,boolean
  autoFlush)
public  PrintWriter(OutputStream out)
public  PrintWriter(OutputStream out,
  boolean autoFlush)
```
Methods
```
public boolean checkError()
public void close()
public void flush()
public void print(boolean b)
public void print(char c)
public void print(int i)
public void print(long l)
public void print(float f)
public void print(double d)
public void print(char s)
public void print(String s)
public void print(Object obj)
public void println()
public void println(boolean x)
public void println(char x)
public void println(int x)
public void println(long x)
public void println(float x)
public void println(double x)
public void println(char x)
public void println(String x)
public void println(Object x)
protected void setError()
public void write(int c)
public void write(char buf,int off,int
  len)
public void write(char buf)
public void write(String s,int off,int
  len)
public void write(String s)
```

▸PRIVILEGEDACTIONEXCEPTION
```
public class java.security.
  PrivilegedActionException
extends java.lang.Exception
extends java.lang.Throwable
extends java.lang.Object
```
Constructors
```
public  PrivilegedActionException(
  Exception exception)
```
Methods
```
public Exception getException()
```

```
public void printStackTrace()
public void printStackTrace(PrintStream
  ps)
public void printStackTrace(PrintWriter
  pw)
```

►PROCESS
```
public abstract class java.lang.Process
extends java.lang.Object
```

Methods
```
public abstract void destroy()
public abstract int exitValue()
public abstract InputStream
  getErrorStream()
public abstract InputStream
  getInputStream()
public abstract OutputStream
  getOutputStream()
public abstract int waitFor()
```

►PROFILEDATAEXCEPTION
```
public class java.awt.color.
  ProfileDataException
extends java.lang.RuntimeException
extends java.lang.Exception
extends java.lang.Throwable
extends java.lang.Object
```

Constructors
```
public  ProfileDataException(String s)
```

►PROGRESSBARUI
```
public abstract class javax.swing.plaf.
  ProgressBarUI
extends javax.swing.plaf.ComponentUI
extends java.lang.Object
```

►PROGRESSMONITOR
```
public class javax.swing.
  ProgressMonitor
extends java.lang.Object
```

Constructors
```
public  ProgressMonitor(Component
  parentComponent,Object message,String
  note,int min,int max)
private  ProgressMonitor()
```

Methods
```
public void close()
public int getMaximum()
public int getMillisToDecideToPopup()
public int getMillisToPopup()
public int getMinimum()
public String getNote()
public boolean isCanceled()
public void setMaximum(int m)
public void setMillisToDecideToPopup(int
  millisToDecideToPopup)
public void setMillisToPopup(int
  millisToPopup)
public void setMinimum(int m)
public void setNote(String note)
public void setProgress(int nv)
```

►PROGRESSMONITORINPUTSTREAM
```
public class javax.swing.
  ProgressMonitorInputStream
extends java.io.FilterInputStream
extends java.io.InputStream
extends java.lang.Object
```

Constructors
```
public  ProgressMonitorInputStream(
  Component parentComponent,Object message,
  InputStream in)
```

Methods
```
public void close()
public ProgressMonitor
  getProgressMonitor()
public int read()
public int read(byte b)
public int read(byte b,int off,int len)
public synchronized void reset()
public long skip(long n)
```

►PROPERTIES
```
public class java.util.Properties
extends java.util.Hashtable
extends java.util.Dictionary
extends java.lang.Object
```

Fields
```
protected java.util.Properties defaults
```

Constructors
```
public  Properties()
public  Properties(Properties defaults)
```

Methods
```
public String getProperty(String key)
public String getProperty(String key,
  String defaultValue)
public void list(PrintStream out)
public void list(PrintWriter out)
public synchronized void load(
  InputStream inStream)
public Enumeration propertyNames()
public synchronized void save(
  OutputStream out,String header)
public synchronized Object setProperty(
  String key,String value)
public synchronized void store(
  OutputStream out,String header)
```

►PROPERTYCHANGEEVENT
```
public class java.beans.
  PropertyChangeEvent
extends java.util.EventObject
extends java.lang.Object
```

Constructors
```
public  PropertyChangeEvent(Object
  source,String propertyName,Object
  oldValue,Object newValue)
```

Methods
```
public Object getNewValue()
public Object getOldValue()
public Object getPropagationId()
public String getPropertyName()
```

```
public void setPropagationId(Object
  propagationId)
```

▶PROPERTYCHANGESUPPORT

```
public class java.beans.
  PropertyChangeSupport
implements java.io.Serializable
extends java.lang.Object
```

Constructors

```
public  PropertyChangeSupport(Object
  sourceBean)
```

Methods

```
public synchronized void
  addPropertyChangeListener(
  PropertyChangeListener listener)
public synchronized void
  addPropertyChangeListener(String
  propertyName,PropertyChangeListener
  listener)
public void firePropertyChange(String
  propertyName,Object oldValue,Object
  newValue)
public void firePropertyChange(String
  propertyName,int oldValue,int newValue)
public void firePropertyChange(String
  propertyName,boolean oldValue,boolean
  newValue)
public void firePropertyChange(
  PropertyChangeEvent evt)
public synchronized boolean hasListeners(
  String propertyName)
public synchronized void
  removePropertyChangeListener(
  PropertyChangeListener listener)
public synchronized void
  removePropertyChangeListener(String
  propertyName,PropertyChangeListener
  listener)
```

▶PROPERTYDESCRIPTOR

```
public class java.beans.
  PropertyDescriptor
extends java.beans.FeatureDescriptor
extends java.lang.Object
```

Constructors

```
public  PropertyDescriptor(String
  propertyName,Class beanClass)
public  PropertyDescriptor(String
  propertyName,Class beanClass,String
  getterName,String setterName)
public  PropertyDescriptor(String
  propertyName,Method getter,Method setter)
 PropertyDescriptor()
 PropertyDescriptor()
```

Methods

```
public Class getPropertyEditorClass()
public Class getPropertyType()
public Method getReadMethod()
public Method getWriteMethod()
public boolean isBound()
public boolean isConstrained()
public void setBound(boolean bound)
```

```
public void setConstrained(boolean
  constrained)
public void setPropertyEditorClass(Class
  propertyEditorClass)
public void setReadMethod(Method getter)
public void setWriteMethod(Method setter)
```

▶PROPERTYEDITORMANAGER

```
public class java.beans.
  PropertyEditorManager
extends java.lang.Object
```

Methods

```
public static synchronized
  PropertyEditor findEditor(Class
  targetType)
public static synchronized String
  getEditorSearchPath()
public static synchronized void
  registerEditor(Class
  targetType,Class editorClass)
public static synchronized void
  setEditorSearchPath(String path)
```

▶PROPERTYEDITORSUPPORT

```
public class java.beans.
  PropertyEditorSupport
implements java.beans.PropertyEditor
extends java.lang.Object
```

Constructors

```
protected  PropertyEditorSupport()
protected  PropertyEditorSupport(Object
  source)
```

Methods

```
public synchronized void
  addPropertyChangeListener(
  PropertyChangeListener listener)
public void firePropertyChange()
public String getAsText()
public Component getCustomEditor()
public String
  getJavaInitializationString()
public String getTags()
public Object getValue()
public boolean isPaintable()
public void paintValue(Graphics gfx,
  Rectangle box)
public synchronized void
  removePropertyChangeListener(
  PropertyChangeListener listener)
public void setAsText(String text)
public void setValue(Object value)
public boolean supportsCustomEditor()
```

▶PROPERTYPERMISSION

```
public final class java.util.
  PropertyPermission
extends java.security.BasicPermission
extends java.security.Permission
extends java.lang.Object
```

Constructors

```
public  PropertyPermission(String name,
  String actions)
```

Methods
public boolean equals(Object obj)
public String getActions()
public int hashCode()
public boolean implies(Permission p)
public PermissionCollection
  newPermissionCollection()

▶**PROPERTYRESOURCEBUNDLE**
public class java.util.
  PropertyResourceBundle
extends java.util.ResourceBundle
extends java.lang.Object

Constructors
public PropertyResourceBundle(
  InputStream stream)

Methods
public Enumeration getKeys()
public Object handleGetObject(String key)

▶**PROPERTYVETOEXCEPTION**
public class java.beans.
  PropertyVetoException
extends java.lang.Exception
extends java.lang.Throwable
extends java.lang.Object

Constructors
public PropertyVetoException(String
  mess,PropertyChangeEvent evt)

Methods
public PropertyChangeEvent
  getPropertyChangeEvent()

▶**PROTECTIONDOMAIN**
public class java.security.
  ProtectionDomain
extends java.lang.Object

Constructors
public ProtectionDomain(CodeSource
  codesource,PermissionCollection
  permissions)

Methods
public final CodeSource getCodeSource()
public final PermissionCollection
  getPermissions()
public boolean implies(Permission
  permission)
public String toString()

▶**PROTOCOLEXCEPTION**
public class java.net.ProtocolException
extends java.io.IOException
extends java.lang.Exception
extends java.lang.Throwable
extends java.lang.Object

Constructors
public ProtocolException(String host)
public ProtocolException()

▶**PROVIDER**
public abstract class java.security.
  Provider

extends java.util.Properties
extends java.util.Hashtable
extends java.util.Dictionary
extends java.lang.Object

Constructors
protected Provider(String name,double
  version,String info)
  Provider()

Methods
public synchronized void clear()
public Set entrySet()
public String getInfo()
public String getName()
public double getVersion()
public Set keySet()
public synchronized void load(
  InputStream inStream)
public synchronized Object put(Object
  key,Object value)
public synchronized void putAll(Map t)
public synchronized Object remove(Object
  key)
public String toString()
public Collection values()

▶**PROVIDEREXCEPTION**
public class java.security.
  ProviderException
extends java.lang.RuntimeException
extends java.lang.Exception
extends java.lang.Throwable
extends java.lang.Object

Constructors
public ProviderException()
public ProviderException(String s)

▶**PUSHBACKINPUTSTREAM**
public class java.io.
  PushbackInputStream
extends java.io.FilterInputStream
extends java.io.InputStream
extends java.lang.Object

Fields
protected byte buf
protected int pos

Constructors
public PushbackInputStream(InputStream
  in,int size)
public PushbackInputStream(InputStream
  in)

Methods
public int available()
public synchronized void close()
public boolean markSupported()
public int read()
public int read(byte b,int off,int len)
public long skip(long n)
public void unread(int b)
public void unread(byte b,int off,int
  len)
public void unread(byte b)

►**PUSHBACKREADER**
public class java.io.PushbackReader
extends java.io.FilterReader
extends java.io.Reader
extends java.lang.Object

Constructors
public PushbackReader(Reader in,int
  size)
public PushbackReader(Reader in)

Methods
public void close()
public void mark(int readAheadLimit)
public boolean markSupported()
public int read()
public int read(char cbuf,int off,int
  len)
public boolean ready()
public void reset()
public void unread(int c)
public void unread(char cbuf,int off,int
  len)
public void unread(char cbuf)

►**QUADCURVE2D**
public abstract class java.awt.geom.
  QuadCurve2D
implements java.lang.Cloneable
implements java.awt.Shape
extends java.lang.Object

Constructors
protected QuadCurve2D()

Methods
public Object clone()
public boolean contains(double x,double
  y)
public boolean contains(Point2D p)
public boolean contains(double x,double
  y,double w,double h)
public boolean contains(Rectangle2D r)
public Rectangle getBounds()
public abstract Point2D getCtrlPt()
public abstract double getCtrlX()
public abstract double getCtrlY()
public static double getFlatness(double
  x1,double y1,double ctrlx,double ctrly,
  double x2,double y2)
public static double getFlatness(double
  coords,int offset)
public double getFlatness()
public static double getFlatnessSq(
  double x1,double y1,double ctrlx,double
  ctrly,double x2,double y2)
public static double getFlatnessSq(
  double coords,int offset)
public double getFlatnessSq()
public abstract Point2D getP1()
public abstract Point2D getP2()
public PathIterator getPathIterator(
  AffineTransform at)
public PathIterator getPathIterator(
  AffineTransform at,double flatness)
public abstract double getX1()

public abstract double getX2()
public abstract double getY1()
public abstract double getY2()
public boolean intersects(double x,
  double y,double w,double h)
public boolean intersects(Rectangle2D r)
public abstract void setCurve(double x1,
  double y1,double ctrlx,double ctrly,
  double x2,double y2)
public void setCurve(double coords,int
  offset)
public void setCurve(Point2D p1,Point2D
  cp,Point2D p2)
public void setCurve(Point2D pts,int
  offset)
public void setCurve(QuadCurve2D c)
public static int solveQuadratic(double
  eqn)
public void subdivide(QuadCurve2D left,
  QuadCurve2D right)
public static void subdivide(QuadCurve2D
  src,QuadCurve2D left,QuadCurve2D right)
public static void subdivide(double src,
  int srcoff,double left,int leftoff,
  double right,int rightoff)

►**RANDOM**
public class java.util.Random
implements java.io.Serializable
extends java.lang.Object

Constructors
public Random()
public Random(long seed)

Methods
protected synchronized int next(int bits)
public boolean nextBoolean()
public void nextBytes(byte bytes)
public double nextDouble()
public float nextFloat()
public synchronized double nextGaussian()
public int nextInt()
public int nextInt(int n)
public long nextLong()
public synchronized void setSeed(long
  seed)

►**RANDOMACCESSFILE**
public class java.io.RandomAccessFile
implements java.io.DataInput
implements java.io.DataOutput
extends java.lang.Object

Constructors
public RandomAccessFile(String name,
  String mode)
public RandomAccessFile(File file,
  String mode)

Methods
public native void close()
public final FileDescriptor getFD()
public native long getFilePointer()
public native long length()
public native int read()

```
public int read(byte b,int off,int len)
public int read(byte b)
public final boolean readBoolean()
public final byte readByte()
public final char readChar()
public final double readDouble()
public final float readFloat()
public final void readFully(byte b)
public final void readFully(byte b,int
  off,int len)
public final int readInt()
public final String readLine()
public final long readLong()
public final short readShort()
public final int readUnsignedByte()
public final int readUnsignedShort()
public final String readUTF()
public native void seek(long pos)
public native void setLength(long
  newLength)
public int skipBytes(int n)
public native void write(int b)
public void write(byte b)
public void write(byte b,int off,int len)
public final void writeBoolean(boolean v)
public final void writeByte(int v)
public final void writeBytes(String s)
public final void writeChar(int v)
public final void writeChars(String s)
public final void writeDouble(double v)
public final void writeFloat(float v)
public final void writeInt(int v)
public final void writeLong(long v)
public final void writeShort(int v)
public final void writeUTF(String str)
```

►RASTER

```
public class java.awt.image.Raster
extends java.lang.Object
```

Fields

```
protected java.awt.image.DataBuffer
  dataBuffer
protected int height
protected int minX
protected int minY
protected int numBands
protected int numDataElements
protected java.awt.image.Raster parent
protected java.awt.image.SampleModel
  sampleModel
protected int sampleModelTranslateX
protected int sampleModelTranslateY
protected int width
```

Constructors

```
protected  Raster(SampleModel
  sampleModel,Point origin)
protected  Raster(SampleModel
  sampleModel,DataBuffer dataBuffer,Point
  origin)
protected  Raster(SampleModel
  sampleModel,DataBuffer dataBuffer,
```

```
  Rectangle aRegion,Point
  sampleModelTranslate,Raster parent)
```

Methods

```
public static WritableRaster
  createBandedRaster(int dataType,int w,
  int h,int bands,Point location)
public static WritableRaster
  createBandedRaster(int dataType,int w,
  int h,int scanlineStride,int bankIndices,
  int bandOffsets,Point location)
public static WritableRaster
  createBandedRaster(DataBuffer dataBuffer,
  int w,int h,int scanlineStride,int
  bankIndices,int bandOffsets,Point
  location)
public Raster createChild(int parentX,
  int parentY,int width,int height,int
  childMinX,int childMinY,int bandList)
public WritableRaster
  createCompatibleWritableRaster()
public WritableRaster
  createCompatibleWritableRaster(int w,int
  h)
public WritableRaster
  createCompatibleWritableRaster(Rectangle
  rect)
public WritableRaster
  createCompatibleWritableRaster(int x,int
  y,int w,int h)
public static WritableRaster
  createInterleavedRaster(int dataType,int
  w,int h,int bands,Point location)
public static WritableRaster
  createInterleavedRaster(int dataType,int
  w,int h,int scanlineStride,int
  pixelStride,int bandOffsets,Point
  location)
public static WritableRaster
  createInterleavedRaster(DataBuffer
  dataBuffer,int w,int h,int
  scanlineStride,int pixelStride,int
  bandOffsets,Point location)
public static WritableRaster
  createPackedRaster(int dataType,int w,
  int h,int bandMasks,Point location)
public static WritableRaster
  createPackedRaster(int dataType,int w,
  int h,int bands,int bitsPerBand,Point
  location)
public static WritableRaster
  createPackedRaster(DataBuffer dataBuffer,
  int w,int h,int scanlineStride,int
  bandMasks,Point location)
public static WritableRaster
  createPackedRaster(DataBuffer dataBuffer,
  int w,int h,int bitsPerPixel,Point
  location)
public static Raster createRaster(
  SampleModel sm,DataBuffer db,Point
  location)
public Raster createTranslatedChild(int
  childMinX,int childMinY)
```

```
public static WritableRaster
  createWritableRaster(SampleModel sm,
  Point location)
public static WritableRaster
  createWritableRaster(SampleModel sm,
  DataBuffer db,Point location)
public Rectangle getBounds()
public DataBuffer getDataBuffer()
public Object getDataElements(int x,int
  y,Object outData)
public Object getDataElements(int x,int
  y,int w,int h,Object outData)
public final int getHeight()
public final int getMinX()
public final int getMinY()
public final int getNumBands()
public final int getNumDataElements()
public Raster getParent()
public int getPixel(int x,int y,int
  iArray)
public float getPixel(int x,int y,float
  fArray)
public double getPixel(int x,int y,
  double dArray)
public int getPixels(int x,int y,int w,
  int h,int iArray)
public float getPixels(int x,int y,int w,
  int h,float fArray)
public double getPixels(int x,int y,int
  w,int h,double dArray)
public int getSample(int x,int y,int b)
public double getSampleDouble(int x,int
  y,int b)
public float getSampleFloat(int x,int y,
  int b)
public SampleModel getSampleModel()
public final int
  getSampleModelTranslateX()
public final int
  getSampleModelTranslateY()
public int getSamples(int x,int y,int w,
  int h,int b,int iArray)
public float getSamples(int x,int y,int
  w,int h,int b,float fArray)
public double getSamples(int x,int y,int
  w,int h,int b,double dArray)
public final int getTransferType()
public final int getWidth()
```

►RASTERFORMATEXCEPTION

```
public class java.awt.image.
  RasterFormatException
extends java.lang.RuntimeException
extends java.lang.Exception
extends java.lang.Throwable
extends java.lang.Object
```

Constructors
```
public RasterFormatException(String s)
```

►READER

```
public abstract class java.io.Reader
extends java.lang.Object
```

Fields
```
protected java.lang.Object lock
```
Constructors
```
protected  Reader()
protected  Reader(Object lock)
```
Methods
```
public abstract void close()
public void mark(int readAheadLimit)
public boolean markSupported()
public int read()
public int read(char cbuf)
public abstract int read(char cbuf,int
  off,int len)
public boolean ready()
public void reset()
public long skip(long n)
```

►RECTANGLE

```
public class java.awt.Rectangle
implements java.io.Serializable
implements java.awt.Shape
extends java.awt.geom.Rectangle2D
extends java.awt.geom.RectangularShape
extends java.lang.Object
```
Fields
```
public int height
public int width
public int x
public int y
```
Constructors
```
public static  Rectangle()
public  Rectangle(Rectangle r)
public  Rectangle(int x,int y,int width,
  int height)
public  Rectangle(int width,int height)
public  Rectangle(Point p,Dimension d)
public  Rectangle(Point p)
public  Rectangle(Dimension d)
```
Methods
```
public void add(int newx,int newy)
public void add(Point pt)
public void add(Rectangle r)
public boolean contains(Point p)
public boolean contains(int x,int y)
public boolean contains(Rectangle r)
public boolean contains(int X,int Y,int
  W,int H)
public Rectangle2D createIntersection(
  Rectangle2D r)
public Rectangle2D createUnion(
  Rectangle2D r)
public boolean equals(Object obj)
public Rectangle getBounds()
public Rectangle2D getBounds2D()
public double getHeight()
public Point getLocation()
public Dimension getSize()
public double getWidth()
public double getX()
public double getY()
public void grow(int h,int v)
```

```
public boolean inside(int x,int y)
public Rectangle intersection(Rectangle
  r)
public boolean intersects(Rectangle r)
public boolean isEmpty()
public void move(int x,int y)
public int outcode(double x,double y)
public void reshape(int x,int y,int
  width,int height)
public void resize(int width,int height)
public void setBounds(Rectangle r)
public void setBounds(int x,int y,int
  width,int height)
public void setLocation(Point p)
public void setLocation(int x,int y)
public void setRect(double x,double y,
  double width,double height)
public void setSize(Dimension d)
public void setSize(int width,int height)
public String toString()
public void translate(int x,int y)
public Rectangle union(Rectangle r)
```

►RECTANGLE2D

```
public abstract class java.awt.geom.
  Rectangle2D
extends java.awt.geom.RectangularShape
extends java.lang.Object
```

Fields

```
public final static int OUT_BOTTOM
public final static int OUT_LEFT
public final static int OUT_RIGHT
public final static int OUT_TOP
```

Constructors

```
protected  Rectangle2D()
```

Methods

```
public void add(double newx,double newy)
public void add(Point2D pt)
public void add(Rectangle2D r)
public boolean contains(double x,double
  y)
public boolean contains(double x,double
  y,double w,double h)
public abstract Rectangle2D
  createIntersection(Rectangle2D r)
public abstract Rectangle2D createUnion(
  Rectangle2D r)
public boolean equals(Object obj)
public Rectangle2D getBounds2D()
public PathIterator getPathIterator(
  AffineTransform at)
public PathIterator getPathIterator(
  AffineTransform at,double flatness)
public int hashCode()
public static void intersect(Rectangle2D
  src1,Rectangle2D src2,Rectangle2D dest)
public boolean intersects(double x,
  double y,double w,double h)
public boolean intersectsLine(double x1,
  double y1,double x2,double y2)
public boolean intersectsLine(Line2D l)
```

```
public abstract int outcode(double x,
  double y)
public int outcode(Point2D p)
public void setFrame(double x,double y,
  double w,double h)
public abstract void setRect(double x,
  double y,double w,double h)
public void setRect(Rectangle2D r)
public static void union(Rectangle2D
  src1,Rectangle2D src2,Rectangle2D dest)
```

►RECTANGULARSHAPE

```
public abstract class java.awt.geom.
  RectangularShape
implements java.lang.Cloneable
implements java.awt.Shape
extends java.lang.Object
```

Constructors

```
protected  RectangularShape()
```

Methods

```
public Object clone()
public boolean contains(Point2D p)
public boolean contains(Rectangle2D r)
public Rectangle getBounds()
public double getCenterX()
public double getCenterY()
public Rectangle2D getFrame()
public abstract double getHeight()
public double getMaxX()
public double getMaxY()
public double getMinX()
public double getMinY()
public PathIterator getPathIterator(
  AffineTransform at,double flatness)
public abstract double getWidth()
public abstract double getX()
public abstract double getY()
public boolean intersects(Rectangle2D r)
public abstract boolean isEmpty()
public abstract void setFrame(double x,
  double y,double w,double h)
public void setFrame(Point2D loc,
  Dimension2D size)
public void setFrame(Rectangle2D r)
public void setFrameFromCenter(double
  centerX,double centerY,double cornerX,
  double cornerY)
public void setFrameFromCenter(Point2D
  center,Point2D corner)
public void setFrameFromDiagonal(double
  x1,double y1,double x2,double y2)
public void setFrameFromDiagonal(Point2D
  p1,Point2D p2)
```

►REFERENCE

```
public abstract class java.lang.ref.
  Reference
extends java.lang.Object
```

Constructors

```
 Reference()
 Reference()
```

Methods
```
public void clear()
public boolean enqueue()
public static Object get()
public boolean isEnqueued()
```

▶**REFERENCEQUEUE**
```
public class java.lang.ref.
  ReferenceQueue
extends java.lang.Object
```
Constructors
```
public  ReferenceQueue()
```
Methods
```
public Reference poll()
public Reference remove(long timeout)
public Reference remove()
```

▶**REFLECTPERMISSION**
```
public final class java.lang.reflect.
  ReflectPermission
extends java.security.BasicPermission
extends java.security.Permission
extends java.lang.Object
```
Constructors
```
public  ReflectPermission(String name)
public  ReflectPermission(String name,
  String actions)
```

▶**REMOTEEXCEPTION**
```
public class java.rmi.RemoteException
extends java.io.IOException
extends java.lang.Exception
extends java.lang.Throwable
extends java.lang.Object
```
Fields
```
public java.lang.Throwable detail
```
Constructors
```
public  RemoteException()
public  RemoteException(String s)
public  RemoteException(String s,
  Throwable ex)
```
Methods
```
public String getMessage()
public void printStackTrace(PrintStream
  ps)
public void printStackTrace()
public void printStackTrace(PrintWriter
  pw)
```

▶**REMOTEOBJECT**
```
public abstract class java.rmi.server.
  RemoteObject
implements java.rmi.Remote
implements java.io.Serializable
extends java.lang.Object
```
Fields
```
protected transient java.rmi.server.
  RemoteRef ref
```
Constructors
```
protected  RemoteObject()
protected  RemoteObject(RemoteRef newref)
```

Methods
```
public boolean equals(Object obj)
public RemoteRef getRef()
public int hashCode()
public String toString()
public static Remote toStub(Remote obj)
```

▶**REMOTESERVER**
```
public abstract class java.rmi.server.
  RemoteServer
extends java.rmi.server.RemoteObject
extends java.lang.Object
```
Constructors
```
protected  RemoteServer()
protected  RemoteServer(RemoteRef ref)
```
Methods
```
public static String getClientHost()
public static PrintStream getLog()
public static void setLog(OutputStream
  out)
```

▶**REMOTESTUB**
```
public abstract class java.rmi.server.
  RemoteStub
extends java.rmi.server.RemoteObject
extends java.lang.Object
```
Constructors
```
protected  RemoteStub()
protected  RemoteStub(RemoteRef ref)
```
Methods
```
protected static void setRef(RemoteStub
  stub,RemoteRef ref)
```

▶**RENDERABLEIMAGEOP**
```
public class java.awt.image.renderable.
  RenderableImageOp
implements java.awt.image.renderable.
  RenderableImage
extends java.lang.Object
```
Constructors
```
public  RenderableImageOp(
  ContextualRenderedImageFactory CRIF,
  ParameterBlock paramBlock)
```
Methods
```
public RenderedImage
  createDefaultRendering()
public RenderedImage createRendering(
  RenderContext renderContext)
public RenderedImage
  createScaledRendering(int w,int h,
  RenderingHints hints)
public float getHeight()
public float getMinX()
public float getMinY()
public ParameterBlock getParameterBlock()
public Object getProperty(String name)
public String getPropertyNames()
public Vector getSources()
public float getWidth()
public boolean isDynamic()
public ParameterBlock setParameterBlock(
  ParameterBlock paramBlock)
```

▶RENDERABLEIMAGEPRODUCER
```
public class java.awt.image.renderable.
  RenderableImageProducer
implements java.awt.image.ImageProducer
implements java.lang.Runnable
extends java.lang.Object
```
Constructors
```
public  RenderableImageProducer(
  RenderableImage rdblImage,RenderContext
  rc)
```
Methods
```
public synchronized void addConsumer(
  ImageConsumer ic)
public synchronized boolean isConsumer(
  ImageConsumer ic)
public synchronized void removeConsumer(
  ImageConsumer ic)
public void
  requestTopDownLeftRightResend(
  ImageConsumer ic)
public void run()
public synchronized void
  setRenderContext(RenderContext rc)
public synchronized void startProduction(
  ImageConsumer ic)
```

▶RENDERCONTEXT
```
public class java.awt.image.renderable.
  RenderContext
implements java.lang.Cloneable
extends java.lang.Object
```
Constructors
```
public  RenderContext(AffineTransform
  usr2dev,Shape aoi,RenderingHints hints)
public  RenderContext(AffineTransform
  usr2dev)
public  RenderContext(AffineTransform
  usr2dev,RenderingHints hints)
public  RenderContext(AffineTransform
  usr2dev,Shape aoi)
```
Methods
```
public Object clone()
public void concetenateTransform(
  AffineTransform modTransform)
public Shape getAreaOfInterest()
public RenderingHints getRenderingHints()
public AffineTransform getTransform()
public void preConcetenateTransform(
  AffineTransform modTransform)
public void setAreaOfInterest(Shape
  newAoi)
public void setRenderingHints(
  RenderingHints hints)
public void setTransform(AffineTransform
  newTransform)
```

▶RENDERINGHINTS
```
public class java.awt.RenderingHints
implements java.lang.Cloneable
implements java.util.Map
extends java.lang.Object
```

Fields
```
public final static Key KEY_ALPHA_
  INTERPOLATION
public final static Key KEY_
  ANTIALIASING
public final static Key KEY_COLOR_
  RENDERING
public final static Key KEY_DITHERING
public final static Key KEY_
  FRACTIONALMETRICS
public final static Key KEY_
  INTERPOLATION
public final static Key KEY_RENDERING
public final static Key KEY_TEXT_
  ANTIALIASING
public final static java.lang.Object
  VALUE_ALPHA_INTERPOLATION_DEFAULT
public final static java.lang.Object
  VALUE_ALPHA_INTERPOLATION_QUALITY
public final static java.lang.Object
  VALUE_ALPHA_INTERPOLATION_SPEED
public final static java.lang.Object
  VALUE_ANTIALIAS_DEFAULT
public final static java.lang.Object
  VALUE_ANTIALIAS_OFF
public final static java.lang.Object
  VALUE_ANTIALIAS_ON
public final static java.lang.Object
  VALUE_COLOR_RENDER_DEFAULT
public final static java.lang.Object
  VALUE_COLOR_RENDER_QUALITY
public final static java.lang.Object
  VALUE_COLOR_RENDER_SPEED
public final static java.lang.Object
  VALUE_DITHER_DEFAULT
public final static java.lang.Object
  VALUE_DITHER_DISABLE
public final static java.lang.Object
  VALUE_DITHER_ENABLE
public final static java.lang.Object
  VALUE_FRACTIONALMETRICS_DEFAULT
public final static java.lang.Object
  VALUE_FRACTIONALMETRICS_OFF
public final static java.lang.Object
  VALUE_FRACTIONALMETRICS_ON
public final static java.lang.Object
  VALUE_INTERPOLATION_BICUBIC
public final static java.lang.Object
  VALUE_INTERPOLATION_BILINEAR
public final static java.lang.Object
  VALUE_INTERPOLATION_NEAREST_NEIGHBOR
public final static java.lang.Object
  VALUE_RENDER_DEFAULT
public final static java.lang.Object
  VALUE_RENDER_QUALITY
public final static java.lang.Object
  VALUE_RENDER_SPEED
public final static java.lang.Object
  VALUE_TEXT_ANTIALIAS_DEFAULT
public final static java.lang.Object
  VALUE_TEXT_ANTIALIAS_OFF
public final static java.lang.Object
  VALUE_TEXT_ANTIALIAS_ON
```

Constructors
```
public  RenderingHints(Map init)
public  RenderingHints(Key key,Object
  value)
```
Methods
```
public void add(RenderingHints hints)
public void clear()
public Object clone()
public boolean containsKey(Object key)
public boolean containsValue(Object
  value)
public Set entrySet()
public boolean equals(Object o)
public Object get(Object key)
public int hashCode()
public boolean isEmpty()
public Set keySet()
public Object put(Object key,Object
  value)
public void putAll(Map m)
public Object remove(Object key)
public int size()
public String toString()
public Collection values()
```

▶REPAINTMANAGER
```
public class javax.swing.RepaintManager
extends java.lang.Object
```
Constructors
```
public  RepaintManager()
```
Methods
```
public synchronized void addDirtyRegion(
  JComponent c,int x,int y,int w,int h)
public synchronized void
  addInvalidComponent(JComponent
  invalidComponent)
public static RepaintManager
  currentManager(Component c)
public static RepaintManager
  currentManager(JComponent c)
public Rectangle getDirtyRegion(
  JComponent aComponent)
public Dimension
  getDoubleBufferMaximumSize()
public Image getOffscreenBuffer(
  Component c,int proposedWidth,int
  proposedHeight)
public boolean isCompletelyDirty(
  JComponent aComponent)
public boolean isDoubleBufferingEnabled()
public void markCompletelyClean(
  JComponent aComponent)
public void markCompletelyDirty(
  JComponent aComponent)
public void paintDirtyRegions()
public synchronized void
  removeInvalidComponent(JComponent
  component)
public static void setCurrentManager(
  RepaintManager aRepaintManager)
public void setDoubleBufferingEnabled(
  boolean aFlag)
```
```
public void setDoubleBufferMaximumSize(
  Dimension d)
public synchronized String toString()
public void validateInvalidComponents()
```

▶REPLICATESCALEFILTER
```
public class java.awt.image.
  ReplicateScaleFilter
extends java.awt.image.ImageFilter
extends java.lang.Object
```
Fields
```
protected int destHeight
protected int destWidth
protected java.lang.Object outpixbuf
protected int srccols
protected int srcHeight
protected int srcrows
protected int srcWidth
```
Constructors
```
public  ReplicateScaleFilter(int width,
  int height)
```
Methods
```
public void setDimensions(int w,int h)
public void setPixels(int x,int y,int w,
  int h,ColorModel model,byte pixels,int
  off,int scansize)
public void setPixels(int x,int y,int w,
  int h,ColorModel model,int pixels,int
  off,int scansize)
public void setProperties(Hashtable
  props)
```

▶RESCALEOP
```
public class java.awt.image.RescaleOp
implements java.awt.image.
  BufferedImageOp
implements java.awt.image.RasterOp
extends java.lang.Object
```
Constructors
```
public  RescaleOp(float scaleFactors,
  float offsets,RenderingHints hints)
public  RescaleOp(float scaleFactor,
  float offset,RenderingHints hints)
```
Methods
```
public BufferedImage
  createCompatibleDestImage(BufferedImage
  src,ColorModel destCM)
public WritableRaster
  createCompatibleDestRaster(Raster src)
public final BufferedImage filter(
  BufferedImage src,BufferedImage dst)
public final WritableRaster filter(
  Raster src,WritableRaster dst)
public final Rectangle2D getBounds2D(
  BufferedImage src)
public final Rectangle2D getBounds2D(
  Raster src)
public final int getNumFactors()
public final float getOffsets(float
  offsets)
public final Point2D getPoint2D(Point2D
  srcPt,Point2D dstPt)
```

public final RenderingHints
  getRenderingHints()
public final float getScaleFactors(float
  scaleFactors)

▸**RESOURCEBUNDLE**
public abstract class java.util.
  ResourceBundle
extends java.lang.Object
Fields
protected java.util.ResourceBundle
  parent
Constructors
public ResourceBundle()
Methods
public final static ResourceBundle
  getBundle(String baseName)
public final static ResourceBundle
  getBundle(String baseName,Locale locale)
public static ResourceBundle getBundle(
  String baseName,Locale locale,
  ClassLoader loader)
public abstract Enumeration getKeys()
public Locale getLocale()
public final Object getObject(String key)
public final String getString(String key)
public final String getStringArray(
  String key)
protected abstract Object
  handleGetObject(String key)
protected void setParent(ResourceBundle
  parent)

▸**RGBIMAGEFILTER**
public abstract class java.awt.image.
  RGBImageFilter
extends java.awt.image.ImageFilter
extends java.lang.Object
Fields
protected boolean
  canFilterIndexColorModel
protected java.awt.image.ColorModel
  newmodel
protected java.awt.image.ColorModel
  origmodel
Methods
public IndexColorModel
  filterIndexColorModel(IndexColorModel
  icm)
public abstract int filterRGB(int x,int
  y,int rgb)
public void filterRGBPixels(int x,int y,
  int w,int h,int pixels,int off,int
  scansize)
public void setColorModel(ColorModel
  model)
public void setPixels(int x,int y,int w,
  int h,ColorModel model,byte pixels,int
  off,int scansize)
public void setPixels(int x,int y,int w,
  int h,ColorModel model,int pixels,int
  off,int scansize)

public void substituteColorModel(
  ColorModel oldcm,ColorModel newcm)

▸**RMICLASSLOADER**
public class java.rmi.server.
  RMIClassLoader
extends java.lang.Object
Constructors
private RMIClassLoader()
Methods
public static String getClassAnnotation(
  Class cl)
public static Object getSecurityContext(
  ClassLoader loader)
public static Class loadClass(String
  name)
public static Class loadClass(URL
  codebase,String name)
public static Class loadClass(String
  codebase,String name)

▸**RMISECURITYEXCEPTION**
public class java.rmi.
  RMISecurityException
extends java.lang.SecurityException
extends java.lang.RuntimeException
extends java.lang.Exception
extends java.lang.Throwable
extends java.lang.Object
Constructors
public RMISecurityException(String name)
public RMISecurityException(String name,
  String arg)

▸**RMISECURITYMANAGER**
public class java.rmi.
  RMISecurityManager
extends java.lang.SecurityManager
extends java.lang.Object
Constructors
public RMISecurityManager()
Methods
public void checkPackageAccess(String
  pkgname)

▸**RMISOCKETFACTORY**
public abstract class java.rmi.server.
  RMISocketFactory
implements java.rmi.server.
  RMIClientSocketFactory
implements java.rmi.server.
  RMIServerSocketFactory
extends java.lang.Object
Constructors
public RMISocketFactory()
Methods
public abstract ServerSocket
  createServerSocket(int port)
public abstract Socket createSocket(
  String host,int port)

```
public static synchronized
  RMISocketFactory getDefaultSocketFactory(
  )
public static synchronized
  RMIFailureHandler getFailureHandler()
public static synchronized
  RMISocketFactory getSocketFactory()
public static synchronized void
  setFailureHandler(RMIFailureHandler fh)
public static synchronized void
  setSocketFactory(RMISocketFactory fac)
```

▸RoundRectangle2D

```
public abstract class java.awt.geom.
  RoundRectangle2D
extends java.awt.geom.RectangularShape
extends java.lang.Object
```

Constructors
```
protected  RoundRectangle2D()
```

Methods
```
public boolean contains(double x,double
  y)
public boolean contains(double x,double
  y,double w,double h)
public abstract double getArcHeight()
public abstract double getArcWidth()
public PathIterator getPathIterator(
  AffineTransform at)
public boolean intersects(double x,
  double y,double w,double h)
public void setFrame(double x,double y,
  double w,double h)
public abstract void setRoundRect(double
  x,double y,double w,double h,double
  arcWidth,double arcHeight)
public void setRoundRect(
  RoundRectangle2D rr)
```

▸RSAPrivateCrtKeySpec

```
public class java.security.spec.
  RSAPrivateCrtKeySpec
extends java.security.spec.
  RSAPrivateKeySpec
extends java.lang.Object
```

Constructors
```
public  RSAPrivateCrtKeySpec(BigInteger
  modulus,BigInteger publicExponent,
  BigInteger privateExponent,BigInteger
  primeP,BigInteger primeQ,BigInteger
  primeExponentP,BigInteger primeExponentQ,
  BigInteger crtCoefficient)
```

Methods
```
public BigInteger getCrtCoefficient()
public BigInteger getPrimeExponentP()
public BigInteger getPrimeExponentQ()
public BigInteger getPrimeP()
public BigInteger getPrimeQ()
public BigInteger getPublicExponent()
```

▸RSAPrivateKeySpec

```
public class java.security.spec.
  RSAPrivateKeySpec
```

```
implements java.security.spec.KeySpec
extends java.lang.Object
```

Constructors
```
public  RSAPrivateKeySpec(BigInteger
  modulus,BigInteger privateExponent)
```

Methods
```
public BigInteger getModulus()
public BigInteger getPrivateExponent()
```

▸RSAPublicKeySpec

```
public class java.security.spec.
  RSAPublicKeySpec
implements java.security.spec.KeySpec
extends java.lang.Object
```

Constructors
```
public  RSAPublicKeySpec(BigInteger
  modulus,BigInteger publicExponent)
```

Methods
```
public BigInteger getModulus()
public BigInteger getPublicExponent()
```

▸RTFEditorKit

```
public class javax.swing.text.rtf.
  RTFEditorKit
extends javax.swing.text.
  StyledEditorKit
extends javax.swing.text.
  DefaultEditorKit
extends javax.swing.text.EditorKit
extends java.lang.Object
```

Constructors
```
public  RTFEditorKit()
```

Methods
```
public Object clone()
public String getContentType()
public void read(InputStream in,Document
  doc,int pos)
public void read(Reader in,Document doc,
  int pos)
public void write(OutputStream out,
  Document doc,int pos,int len)
public void write(Writer out,Document
  doc,int pos,int len)
```

▸RuleBasedCollator

```
public class java.text.
  RuleBasedCollator
extends java.text.Collator
extends java.lang.Object
```

Constructors
```
public  RuleBasedCollator(String rules)
  RuleBasedCollator()
```

Methods
```
public Object clone()
public int compare(String source,String
  target)
public boolean equals(Object obj)
public CollationElementIterator
  getCollationElementIterator(String
  source)
```

```
public CollationElementIterator
  getCollationElementIterator(
  CharacterIterator source)
public CollationKey getCollationKey(
  String source)
public String getRules()
public int hashCode()
```

▶**RUNTIME**
```
public class java.lang.Runtime
extends java.lang.Object
```
Constructors
```
private  Runtime()
```
Methods
```
public Process exec(String command)
public Process exec(String command,
  String envp)
public Process exec(String cmdarray)
public Process exec(String cmdarray,
  String envp)
public void exit(int status)
public native long freeMemory()
public native void gc()
public InputStream
  getLocalizedInputStream(InputStream in)
public OutputStream
  getLocalizedOutputStream(OutputStream
  out)
public static Runtime getRuntime()
public void load(String filename)
public void loadLibrary(String libname)
public void runFinalization()
public static void runFinalizersOnExit(
  boolean value)
public native long totalMemory()
public native void traceInstructions(
  boolean on)
public native void traceMethodCalls(
  boolean on)
```

▶**RUNTIMEEXCEPTION**
```
public class java.lang.RuntimeException
extends java.lang.Exception
extends java.lang.Throwable
extends java.lang.Object
```
Constructors
```
public  RuntimeException()
public  RuntimeException(String s)
```

▶**RUNTIMEPERMISSION**
```
public final class java.lang.
  RuntimePermission
extends java.security.BasicPermission
extends java.security.Permission
extends java.lang.Object
```
Constructors
```
public  RuntimePermission(String name)
public  RuntimePermission(String name,
  String actions)
```

▶**SAMPLEMODEL**
```
public abstract class java.awt.image.
  SampleModel
```

```
extends java.lang.Object
```
Fields
```
protected int dataType
protected int height
protected int numBands
protected int width
```
Constructors
```
public static  SampleModel(int dataType,
  int w,int h,int numBands)
```
Methods
```
public abstract SampleModel
  createCompatibleSampleModel(int w,int h)
public abstract DataBuffer
  createDataBuffer()
public abstract SampleModel
  createSubsetSampleModel(int bands)
public abstract Object getDataElements(
  int x,int y,Object obj,DataBuffer data)
public Object getDataElements(int x,int
  y,int w,int h,Object obj,DataBuffer data)
public final int getDataType()
public final int getHeight()
public final int getNumBands()
public abstract int getNumDataElements()
public int getPixel(int x,int y,int
  iArray,DataBuffer data)
public float getPixel(int x,int y,float
  fArray,DataBuffer data)
public double getPixel(int x,int y,
  double dArray,DataBuffer data)
public int getPixels(int x,int y,int w,
  int h,int iArray,DataBuffer data)
public float getPixels(int x,int y,int w,
  int h,float fArray,DataBuffer data)
public double getPixels(int x,int y,int
  w,int h,double dArray,DataBuffer data)
public abstract int getSample(int x,int
  y,int b,DataBuffer data)
public double getSampleDouble(int x,int
  y,int b,DataBuffer data)
public float getSampleFloat(int x,int y,
  int b,DataBuffer data)
public int getSamples(int x,int y,int w,
  int h,int b,int iArray,DataBuffer data)
public float getSamples(int x,int y,int
  w,int h,int b,float fArray,DataBuffer
  data)
public double getSamples(int x,int y,int
  w,int h,int b,double dArray,DataBuffer
  data)
public abstract int getSampleSize()
public abstract int getSampleSize(int
  band)
public int getTransferType()
public final int getWidth()
public abstract void setDataElements(int
  x,int y,Object obj,DataBuffer data)
public void setDataElements(int x,int y,
  int w,int h,Object obj,DataBuffer data)
public void setPixel(int x,int y,int
  iArray,DataBuffer data)
```

```
public void setPixel(int x,int y,float
  fArray,DataBuffer data)
public void setPixel(int x,int y,double
  dArray,DataBuffer data)
public void setPixels(int x,int y,int w,
  int h,int iArray,DataBuffer data)
public void setPixels(int x,int y,int w,
  int h,float fArray,DataBuffer data)
public void setPixels(int x,int y,int w,
  int h,double dArray,DataBuffer data)
public abstract void setSample(int x,int
  y,int b,int s,DataBuffer data)
public void setSample(int x,int y,int b,
  float s,DataBuffer data)
public void setSample(int x,int y,int b,
  double s,DataBuffer data)
public void setSamples(int x,int y,int w,
  int h,int b,int iArray,DataBuffer data)
public void setSamples(int x,int y,int w,
  int h,int b,float fArray,DataBuffer data)
public void setSamples(int x,int y,int w,
  int h,int b,double dArray,DataBuffer
  data)
```

►Scrollbar

```
public class java.awt.Scrollbar
implements java.awt.Adjustable
extends java.awt.Component
extends java.lang.Object
```

Fields

```
public final static int HORIZONTAL
public final static int VERTICAL
```

Constructors

```
public static  Scrollbar()
public  Scrollbar(int orientation)
public  Scrollbar(int orientation,int
  value,int visible,int minimum,int
  maximum)
```

Methods

```
public synchronized void
  addAdjustmentListener(AdjustmentListener
  l)
public void addNotify()
public int getBlockIncrement()
public int getLineIncrement()
public int getMaximum()
public int getMinimum()
public int getOrientation()
public int getPageIncrement()
public int getUnitIncrement()
public int getValue()
public int getVisible()
public int getVisibleAmount()
protected String paramString()
protected void processAdjustmentEvent(
  AdjustmentEvent e)
protected void processEvent(AWTEvent e)
public synchronized void
  removeAdjustmentListener(
  AdjustmentListener l)
public void setBlockIncrement(int v)
```

```
public synchronized void
  setLineIncrement(int v)
public void setMaximum(int newMaximum)
public void setMinimum(int newMinimum)
public void setOrientation(int
  orientation)
public synchronized void
  setPageIncrement(int v)
public void setUnitIncrement(int v)
public void setValue(int newValue)
public synchronized void setValues(int
  value,int visible,int minimum,int
  maximum)
public void setVisibleAmount(int
  newAmount)
```

►ScrollBarUI

```
public abstract class javax.swing.plaf.
  ScrollBarUI
extends javax.swing.plaf.ComponentUI
extends java.lang.Object
```

►ScrollPane

```
public class java.awt.ScrollPane
extends java.awt.Container
extends java.awt.Component
extends java.lang.Object
```

Fields

```
public final static int SCROLLBARS_
  ALWAYS
public final static int SCROLLBARS_AS_
  NEEDED
public final static int SCROLLBARS_
  NEVER
```

Constructors

```
public  ScrollPane()
public  ScrollPane(int
  scrollbarDisplayPolicy)
```

Methods

```
protected final void addImpl(Component
  comp,Object constraints,int index)
public void addNotify()
public void doLayout()
public Adjustable getHAdjustable()
public int getHScrollbarHeight()
public int getScrollbarDisplayPolicy()
public Point getScrollPosition()
public Adjustable getVAdjustable()
public Dimension getViewportSize()
public int getVScrollbarWidth()
public void layout()
public String paramString()
public void printComponents(Graphics g)
public final void setLayout(
  LayoutManager mgr)
public void setScrollPosition(int x,int
  y)
public void setScrollPosition(Point p)
```

►ScrollPaneLayout

```
public class javax.swing.
  ScrollPaneLayout
```

implements java.awt.LayoutManager
implements javax.swing.
  ScrollPaneConstants
implements java.io.Serializable
extends java.lang.Object

Fields
protected javax.swing.JViewport colHead
protected javax.swing.JScrollBar hsb
protected int hsbPolicy
protected java.awt.Component lowerLeft
protected java.awt.Component lowerRight
protected javax.swing.JViewport rowHead
protected java.awt.Component upperLeft
protected java.awt.Component upperRight
protected javax.swing.JViewport
  viewport
protected javax.swing.JScrollBar vsb
protected int vsbPolicy

Methods
public void addLayoutComponent(String s,
  Component c)
protected Component
  addSingletonComponent(Component oldC,
  Component newC)
public JViewport getColumnHeader()
public Component getCorner(String key)
public JScrollBar getHorizontalScrollBar(
)
public int getHorizontalScrollBarPolicy()
public JViewport getRowHeader()
public JScrollBar getVerticalScrollBar()
public int getVerticalScrollBarPolicy()
public JViewport getViewport()
public Rectangle getViewportBorderBounds(
  JScrollPane scrollpane)
public void layoutContainer(Container
  parent)
public Dimension minimumLayoutSize(
  Container parent)
public Dimension preferredLayoutSize(
  Container parent)
public void removeLayoutComponent(
  Component c)
public void setHorizontalScrollBarPolicy(
  int x)
public void setVerticalScrollBarPolicy(
  int x)
public void syncWithScrollPane(
  JScrollPane sp)

▶SCROLLPANEUI
public abstract class javax.swing.plaf.
  ScrollPaneUI
extends javax.swing.plaf.ComponentUI
extends java.lang.Object

▶SECURECLASSLOADER
public class java.security.
  SecureClassLoader
extends java.lang.ClassLoader
extends java.lang.Object

Constructors
protected SecureClassLoader(ClassLoader
  parent)
protected SecureClassLoader()

Methods
protected final Class defineClass(String
  name,byte b,int off,int len,CodeSource
  cs)
protected PermissionCollection
  getPermissions(CodeSource codesource)

▶SECURERANDOM
public class java.security.SecureRandom
extends java.util.Random
extends java.lang.Object

Constructors
public SecureRandom()
public SecureRandom(byte seed)
protected SecureRandom(SecureRandomSpi
  secureRandomSpi,Provider provider)

Methods
public byte generateSeed(int numBytes)
public static SecureRandom getInstance(
  String algorithm)
public static SecureRandom getInstance(
  String algorithm,String provider)
public final Provider getProvider()
public static byte getSeed(int numBytes)
protected final int next(int numBits)
public synchronized void nextBytes(byte
  bytes)
public synchronized void setSeed(byte
  seed)
public void setSeed(long seed)

▶SECURERANDOMSPI
public abstract class java.security.
  SecureRandomSpi
implements java.io.Serializable
extends java.lang.Object

Methods
protected abstract byte
  engineGenerateSeed(int numBytes)
protected abstract void engineNextBytes(
  byte bytes)
protected abstract void engineSetSeed(
  byte seed)

▶SECURITY
public final class java.security.
  Security
extends java.lang.Object

Constructors
private Security()

Methods
public static int addProvider(Provider
  provider)
public static String
  getAlgorithmProperty(String algName,
  String propName)
public static String getProperty(String
  key)

public static Provider getProvider(
  String name)
public static Provider getProviders()
public static int insertProviderAt(
  Provider provider,int position)
public static void removeProvider(String
  name)
public static void setProperty(String
  key,String datum)

►**SECURITYEXCEPTION**
public class java.lang.
  SecurityException
extends java.lang.RuntimeException
extends java.lang.Exception
extends java.lang.Throwable
extends java.lang.Object
Constructors
public SecurityException()
public SecurityException(String s)

►**SECURITYMANAGER**
public class java.lang.SecurityManager
extends java.lang.Object
Fields
protected boolean inCheck
Constructors
public SecurityManager()
Methods
public void checkAccept(String host,int
  port)
public void checkAccess(Thread t)
public void checkAccess(ThreadGroup g)
public void checkAwtEventQueueAccess()
public void checkConnect(String host,int
  port)
public void checkConnect(String host,int
  port,Object context)
public void checkCreateClassLoader()
public void checkDelete(String file)
public void checkExec(String cmd)
public void checkExit(int status)
public void checkLink(String lib)
public void checkListen(int port)
public void checkMemberAccess(Class
  clazz,int which)
public void checkMulticast(InetAddress
  maddr)
public void checkMulticast(InetAddress
  maddr,byte ttl)
public void checkPackageAccess(String
  pkg)
public void checkPackageDefinition(
  String pkg)
public void checkPermission(Permission
  perm)
public void checkPermission(Permission
  perm,Object context)
public void checkPrintJobAccess()
public void checkPropertiesAccess()
public void checkPropertyAccess(String
  key)

public void checkRead(FileDescriptor fd)
public void checkRead(String file)
public void checkRead(String file,Object
  context)
public void checkSecurityAccess(String
  target)
public void checkSetFactory()
public void checkSystemClipboardAccess()
public boolean checkTopLevelWindow(
  Object window)
public void checkWrite(FileDescriptor fd)
public void checkWrite(String file)
protected native int classDepth(String
  name)
protected int classLoaderDepth()
protected ClassLoader currentClassLoader(
)
protected Class currentLoadedClass()
protected native Class getClassContext()
public boolean getInCheck()
public Object getSecurityContext()
public ThreadGroup getThreadGroup()
protected boolean inClass(String name)
protected boolean inClassLoader()

►**SECURITYPERMISSION**
public final class java.security.
  SecurityPermission
extends java.security.BasicPermission
extends java.security.Permission
extends java.lang.Object
Constructors
public SecurityPermission(String name)
public SecurityPermission(String name,
  String actions)

►**SEGMENT**
public class javax.swing.text.Segment
extends java.lang.Object
Fields
public char array
public int count
public int offset
Constructors
public Segment()
public Segment(char array,int offset,
  int count)
Methods
public String toString()

►**SEPARATORUI**
public abstract class javax.swing.plaf.
  SeparatorUI
extends javax.swing.plaf.ComponentUI
extends java.lang.Object

►**SEQUENCEINPUTSTREAM**
public class java.io.
  SequenceInputStream
extends java.io.InputStream
extends java.lang.Object

Constructors

```
public  SequenceInputStream(Enumeration
  e)
public  SequenceInputStream(InputStream
  s1,InputStream s2)
```

Methods

```
public int available()
public void close()
public int read()
public int read(byte b,int off,int len)
```

▶SERIALIZABLEPERMISSION

```
public final class java.io.
  SerializablePermission
extends java.security.BasicPermission
extends java.security.Permission
extends java.lang.Object
```

Constructors

```
public  SerializablePermission(String
  name)
public  SerializablePermission(String
  name,String actions)
```

▶SERVERCLONEEXCEPTION

```
public class java.rmi.server.
  ServerCloneException
extends java.lang.
  CloneNotSupportedException
extends java.lang.Exception
extends java.lang.Throwable
extends java.lang.Object
```

Fields

```
public java.lang.Exception detail
```

Constructors

```
public  ServerCloneException(String s)
public  ServerCloneException(String s,
  Exception ex)
```

Methods

```
public String getMessage()
public void printStackTrace(PrintStream
  ps)
public void printStackTrace()
public void printStackTrace(PrintWriter
  pw)
```

▶SERVERERROR

```
public class java.rmi.ServerError
extends java.rmi.RemoteException
extends java.io.IOException
extends java.lang.Exception
extends java.lang.Throwable
extends java.lang.Object
```

Constructors

```
public  ServerError(String s,Error err)
```

▶SERVEREXCEPTION

```
public class java.rmi.ServerException
extends java.rmi.RemoteException
extends java.io.IOException
extends java.lang.Exception
extends java.lang.Throwable
extends java.lang.Object
```

Constructors

```
public  ServerException(String s)
public  ServerException(String s,
  Exception ex)
```

▶SERVERNOTACTIVEEXCEPTION

```
public class java.rmi.server.
  ServerNotActiveException
extends java.lang.Exception
extends java.lang.Throwable
extends java.lang.Object
```

Constructors

```
public  ServerNotActiveException()
public  ServerNotActiveException(String
  s)
```

▶SERVERRUNTIMEEXCEPTION

```
public class java.rmi.
  ServerRuntimeException
extends java.rmi.RemoteException
extends java.io.IOException
extends java.lang.Exception
extends java.lang.Throwable
extends java.lang.Object
```

Constructors

```
public  ServerRuntimeException(String s,
  Exception ex)
```

▶SERVERSOCKET

```
public class java.net.ServerSocket
extends java.lang.Object
```

Constructors

```
private  ServerSocket()
public  ServerSocket(int port)
public  ServerSocket(int port,int
  backlog)
public  ServerSocket(int port,int
  backlog,InetAddress bindAddr)
```

Methods

```
public Socket accept()
public void close()
public InetAddress getInetAddress()
public int getLocalPort()
public synchronized int getSoTimeout()
protected final void implAccept(Socket s)
public static synchronized void
  setSocketFactory(SocketImplFactory fac)
public synchronized void setSoTimeout(
  int timeout)
public String toString()
```

▶SHAPEGRAPHICATTRIBUTE

```
public final class java.awt.font.
  ShapeGraphicAttribute
extends java.awt.font.GraphicAttribute
extends java.lang.Object
```

Fields

```
public final static boolean FILL
public final static boolean STROKE
```

Constructors

```
public  ShapeGraphicAttribute(Shape
  shape,int alignment,boolean stroke)
```

Methods

```
public void draw(Graphics2D graphics,
  float x,float y)
public boolean equals(Object rhs)
public boolean equals(
  ShapeGraphicAttribute rhs)
public float getAdvance()
public float getAscent()
public Rectangle2D getBounds()
public float getDescent()
public int hashCode()
```

►SHORT

```
public final class java.lang.Short
implements java.lang.Comparable
extends java.lang.Number
extends java.lang.Object
```

Fields

```
public final static short MAX_VALUE
public final static short MIN_VALUE
public final static java.lang.Class
  TYPE
```

Constructors

```
public  Short(short value)
public  Short(String s)
```

Methods

```
public byte byteValue()
public int compareTo(Short anotherShort)
public int compareTo(Object o)
public static Short decode(String nm)
public double doubleValue()
public boolean equals(Object obj)
public float floatValue()
public int hashCode()
public int intValue()
public long longValue()
public static short parseShort(String s)
public static short parseShort(String s,
  int radix)
public short shortValue()
public static String toString(short s)
public String toString()
public static Short valueOf(String s,int
  radix)
public static Short valueOf(String s)
```

►SHORTLOOKUPTABLE

```
public class java.awt.image.
  ShortLookupTable
extends java.awt.image.LookupTable
extends java.lang.Object
extends java.lang.Object
```

Constructors

```
public  ShortLookupTable(int offset,
  short data)
public  ShortLookupTable(int offset,
  short data)
```

Methods

```
public final short getTable()
public int lookupPixel(int src,int dst)
public short lookupPixel(short src,short
  dst)
```

►SIGNATURE

```
public abstract class java.security.
  Signature
extends java.security.SignatureSpi
extends java.lang.Object
```

Fields

```
protected final static int SIGN
protected int state
protected final static int
  UNINITIALIZED
protected final static int VERIFY
```

Constructors

```
protected  Signature(String algorithm)
```

Methods

```
public Object clone()
public final String getAlgorithm()
public static Signature getInstance(
  String algorithm)
public static Signature getInstance(
  String algorithm,String provider)
public final Object getParameter(String
  param)
public final Provider getProvider()
public final void initSign(PrivateKey
  privateKey)
public final void initSign(PrivateKey
  privateKey,SecureRandom random)
public final void initVerify(PublicKey
  publicKey)
public final void setParameter(String
  param,Object value)
public final void setParameter(
  AlgorithmParameterSpec params)
public final byte sign()
public final int sign(byte outbuf,int
  offset,int len)
public String toString()
public final void update(byte b)
public final void update(byte data)
public final void update(byte data,int
  off,int len)
public final boolean verify(byte
  signature)
```

►SIGNATUREEXCEPTION

```
public class java.security.
  SignatureException
extends java.security.
  GeneralSecurityException
extends java.lang.Exception
extends java.lang.Throwable
extends java.lang.Object
```

Constructors

```
public  SignatureException()
public  SignatureException(String msg)
```

►SIGNATURESPI

```
public abstract class java.security.
  SignatureSpi
extends java.lang.Object
```

Fields

protected java.security.SecureRandom
appRandom

Methods

public Object clone()
protected abstract Object
engineGetParameter(String param)
protected abstract void engineInitSign(
PrivateKey privateKey)
protected void engineInitSign(PrivateKey
privateKey,SecureRandom random)
protected abstract void engineInitVerify(
PublicKey publicKey)
protected abstract void
engineSetParameter(String param,Object
value)
protected void engineSetParameter(
AlgorithmParameterSpec params)
protected abstract byte engineSign()
protected int engineSign(byte outbuf,int
offset,int len)
protected abstract void engineUpdate(
byte b)
protected abstract void engineUpdate(
byte b,int off,int len)
protected abstract boolean engineVerify(
byte sigBytes)

►SignedObject

public final class java.security.
SignedObject
implements java.io.Serializable
extends java.lang.Object

Constructors

public SignedObject(Serializable object,
PrivateKey signingKey,Signature
signingEngine)

Methods

public String getAlgorithm()
public Object getObject()
public byte getSignature()
public boolean verify(PublicKey
verificationKey,Signature
verificationEngine)

►Signer

public abstract class java.security.
Signer
extends java.security.Identity
extends java.lang.Object

Constructors

protected Signer()
public Signer(String name)
public Signer(String name,IdentityScope
scope)

Methods

public PrivateKey getPrivateKey()
public final void setKeyPair(KeyPair
pair)
public String toString()

►SimpleAttributeSet

public class javax.swing.text.
SimpleAttributeSet
implements java.lang.Cloneable
implements javax.swing.text.
MutableAttributeSet
implements java.io.Serializable
extends java.lang.Object

Fields

public final static javax.swing.text.
AttributeSet EMPTY

Constructors

public SimpleAttributeSet()
public SimpleAttributeSet(AttributeSet
source)
private SimpleAttributeSet()

Methods

public void addAttribute(Object name,
Object value)
public void addAttributes(AttributeSet
attributes)
public Object clone()
public boolean containsAttribute(Object
name,Object value)
public boolean containsAttributes(
AttributeSet attributes)
public AttributeSet copyAttributes()
public boolean equals(Object obj)
public Object getAttribute(Object name)
public int getAttributeCount()
public Enumeration getAttributeNames()
public AttributeSet getResolveParent()
public int hashCode()
public boolean isDefined(Object attrName)
public boolean isEmpty()
public boolean isEqual(AttributeSet attr)
public void removeAttribute(Object name)
public void removeAttributes(Enumeration
names)
public void removeAttributes(
AttributeSet attributes)
public void setResolveParent(
AttributeSet parent)
public String toString()

►SimpleBeanInfo

public class java.beans.SimpleBeanInfo
implements java.beans.BeanInfo
extends java.lang.Object

Methods

public BeanInfo getAdditionalBeanInfo()
public BeanDescriptor getBeanDescriptor()
public int getDefaultEventIndex()
public int getDefaultPropertyIndex()
public EventSetDescriptor
getEventSetDescriptors()
public Image getIcon(int iconKind)
public MethodDescriptor
getMethodDescriptors()
public PropertyDescriptor
getPropertyDescriptors()

public Image loadImage(String
 resourceName)

►SIMPLEDATEFORMAT
public class java.text.SimpleDateFormat
extends java.text.DateFormat
extends java.text.Format
extends java.lang.Object

Constructors
public SimpleDateFormat()
public SimpleDateFormat(String pattern)
public SimpleDateFormat(String pattern,
 Locale loc)
public SimpleDateFormat(String pattern,
 DateFormatSymbols formatData)
 SimpleDateFormat()

Methods
public void applyLocalizedPattern(String
 pattern)
public void applyPattern(String pattern)
public Object clone()
public boolean equals(Object obj)
public StringBuffer format(Date date,
 StringBuffer toAppendTo,FieldPosition
 pos)
public Date get2DigitYearStart()
public DateFormatSymbols
 getDateFormatSymbols()
public int hashCode()
public Date parse(String text,
 ParsePosition pos)
public void set2DigitYearStart(Date
 startDate)
public void setDateFormatSymbols(
 DateFormatSymbols newFormatSymbols)
public String toLocalizedPattern()
public String toPattern()

►SIMPLETIMEZONE
public class java.util.SimpleTimeZone
extends java.util.TimeZone
extends java.lang.Object

Constructors
public SimpleTimeZone(int rawOffset,
 String ID)
public SimpleTimeZone(int rawOffset,
 String ID,int startMonth,int startDay,
 int startDayOfWeek,int startTime,int
 endMonth,int endDay,int endDayOfWeek,int
 endTime)
public SimpleTimeZone(int rawOffset,
 String ID,int startMonth,int startDay,
 int startDayOfWeek,int startTime,int
 endMonth,int endDay,int endDayOfWeek,int
 endTime,int dstSavings)

Methods
public Object clone()
public boolean equals(Object obj)
public int getDSTSavings()
public int getOffset(int era,int year,
 int month,int day,int dayOfWeek,int
 millis)

public int getRawOffset()
public synchronized int hashCode()
public boolean hasSameRules(TimeZone
 other)
public boolean inDaylightTime(Date date)
public void setDSTSavings(int
 millisSavedDuringDST)
public void setEndRule(int month,int
 dayOfWeekInMonth,int dayOfWeek,int time)
public void setEndRule(int month,int
 dayOfMonth,int time)
public void setEndRule(int month,int
 dayOfMonth,int dayOfWeek,int time,
 boolean after)
public void setRawOffset(int
 offsetMillis)
public void setStartRule(int month,int
 dayOfWeekInMonth,int dayOfWeek,int time)
public void setStartRule(int month,int
 dayOfMonth,int time)
public void setStartRule(int month,int
 dayOfMonth,int dayOfWeek,int time,
 boolean after)
public void setStartYear(int year)
public String toString()
public boolean useDaylightTime()

►SINGLEPIXELPACKEDSAMPLEMODEL
public class java.awt.image.
 SinglePixelPackedSampleModel
extends java.awt.image.SampleModel
extends java.lang.Object

Constructors
public static
 SinglePixelPackedSampleModel(int
 dataType,int w,int h,int bitMasks)
public SinglePixelPackedSampleModel(int
 dataType,int w,int h,int scanlineStride,
 int bitMasks)

Methods
public SampleModel
 createCompatibleSampleModel(int w,int h)
public DataBuffer createDataBuffer()
public SampleModel
 createSubsetSampleModel(int bands)
public int getBitMasks()
public int getBitOffsets()
public Object getDataElements(int x,int
 y,Object obj,DataBuffer data)
public int getNumDataElements()
public int getOffset(int x,int y)
public int getPixel(int x,int y,int
 iArray,DataBuffer data)
public int getPixels(int x,int y,int w,
 int h,int iArray,DataBuffer data)
public int getSample(int x,int y,int b,
 DataBuffer data)
public int getSamples(int x,int y,int w,
 int h,int b,int iArray,DataBuffer data)
public int getSampleSize()
public int getSampleSize(int band)
public int getScanlineStride()

```
public void setDataElements(int x,int y,
   Object obj,DataBuffer data)
public void setPixel(int x,int y,int
   iArray,DataBuffer data)
public void setPixels(int x,int y,int w,
   int h,int iArray,DataBuffer data)
public void setSample(int x,int y,int b,
   int s,DataBuffer data)
public void setSamples(int x,int y,int w,
   int h,int b,int iArray,DataBuffer data)
```

▶SIZEREQUIREMENTS

```
public class javax.swing.
   SizeRequirements
implements java.io.Serializable
extends java.lang.Object
```

Fields

```
public float alignment
public int maximum
public int minimum
public int preferred
```

Constructors

```
public SizeRequirements()
public SizeRequirements(int min,int
   pref,int max,float a)
```

Methods

```
public static int adjustSizes(int delta,
   SizeRequirements children)
public static void
   calculateAlignedPositions(int allocated,
   SizeRequirements total,SizeRequirements
   children,int offsets,int spans)
public static void
   calculateTiledPositions(int allocated,
   SizeRequirements total,SizeRequirements
   children,int offsets,int spans)
public static SizeRequirements
   getAlignedSizeRequirements(
   SizeRequirements children)
public static SizeRequirements
   getTiledSizeRequirements(
   SizeRequirements children)
public String toString()
```

▶SKELETONMISMATCHEXCEPTION

```
public class java.rmi.server.
   SkeletonMismatchException
extends java.rmi.RemoteException
extends java.io.IOException
extends java.lang.Exception
extends java.lang.Throwable
extends java.lang.Object
```

Constructors

```
public SkeletonMismatchException(String
   s)
```

▶SKELETONNOTFOUNDEXCEPTION

```
public class java.rmi.server.
   SkeletonNotFoundException
extends java.rmi.RemoteException
extends java.io.IOException
extends java.lang.Exception
```

```
extends java.lang.Throwable
extends java.lang.Object
```

Constructors

```
public SkeletonNotFoundException(String
   s)
public SkeletonNotFoundException(String
   s,Exception ex)
```

▶SLIDERUI

```
public abstract class javax.swing.plaf.
   SliderUI
extends javax.swing.plaf.ComponentUI
extends java.lang.Object
```

▶SOCKET

```
public class java.net.Socket
extends java.lang.Object
```

Constructors

```
protected Socket()
protected Socket(SocketImpl impl)
public Socket(String host,int port)
public Socket(InetAddress address,int
   port)
public Socket(String host,int port,
   InetAddress localAddr,int localPort)
public Socket(InetAddress address,int
   port,InetAddress localAddr,int localPort)
public Socket(String host,int port,
   boolean stream)
public Socket(InetAddress host,int port,
   boolean stream)
private Socket()
```

Methods

```
public synchronized void close()
public InetAddress getInetAddress()
public InputStream getInputStream()
public InetAddress getLocalAddress()
public int getLocalPort()
public OutputStream getOutputStream()
public int getPort()
public synchronized int
   getReceiveBufferSize()
public synchronized int
   getSendBufferSize()
public int getSoLinger()
public synchronized int getSoTimeout()
public boolean getTcpNoDelay()
public synchronized void
   setReceiveBufferSize(int size)
public synchronized void
   setSendBufferSize(int size)
public static synchronized void
   setSocketImplFactory(SocketImplFactory
   fac)
public void setSoLinger(boolean on,int
   linger)
public synchronized void setSoTimeout(
   int timeout)
public void setTcpNoDelay(boolean on)
public String toString()
```

▶SOCKETEXCEPTION

```
public class java.net.SocketException
```

```
extends java.io.IOException
extends java.lang.Exception
extends java.lang.Throwable
extends java.lang.Object
```
Constructors
```
public  SocketException(String msg)
public  SocketException()
```

►SOCKETIMPL
```
public abstract class java.net.
  SocketImpl
implements java.net.SocketOptions
extends java.lang.Object
```
Fields
```
protected java.net.InetAddress address
protected java.io.FileDescriptor fd
protected int localport
protected int port
```
Methods
```
protected abstract void accept(
  SocketImpl s)
protected abstract int available()
protected abstract void bind(InetAddress
  host,int port)
protected abstract void close()
protected abstract void connect(String
  host,int port)
protected abstract void connect(
  InetAddress address,int port)
protected abstract void create(boolean
  stream)
protected FileDescriptor
  getFileDescriptor()
protected InetAddress getInetAddress()
protected abstract InputStream
  getInputStream()
protected int getLocalPort()
protected abstract OutputStream
  getOutputStream()
protected int getPort()
protected abstract void listen(int
  backlog)
public String toString()
```

►SOCKETPERMISSION
```
public final class java.net.
  SocketPermission
implements java.io.Serializable
extends java.security.Permission
extends java.lang.Object
```
Constructors
```
public static  SocketPermission(String
  host,String action)
 SocketPermission()
```
Methods
```
public boolean equals(Object obj)
public String getActions()
public int hashCode()
public boolean implies(Permission p)
public PermissionCollection
  newPermissionCollection()
```

►SOCKETSECURITYEXCEPTION
```
public class java.rmi.server.
  SocketSecurityException
extends java.rmi.server.ExportException
extends java.rmi.RemoteException
extends java.io.IOException
extends java.lang.Exception
extends java.lang.Throwable
extends java.lang.Object
```
Constructors
```
public  SocketSecurityException(String s)
public  SocketSecurityException(String s,
  Exception ex)
```

►SOFTBEVELBORDER
```
public class javax.swing.border.
  SoftBevelBorder
extends javax.swing.border.BevelBorder
extends javax.swing.border.
  AbstractBorder
extends java.lang.Object
```
Constructors
```
public  SoftBevelBorder(int bevelType)
public  SoftBevelBorder(int bevelType,
  Color highlight,Color shadow)
public  SoftBevelBorder(int bevelType,
  Color highlightOuter,Color
  highlightInner,Color shadowOuter,Color
  shadowInner)
```
Methods
```
public Insets getBorderInsets(Component
  c)
public boolean isBorderOpaque()
public void paintBorder(Component c,
  Graphics g,int x,int y,int width,int
  height)
```

►SOFTREFERENCE
```
public class java.lang.ref.
  SoftReference
extends java.lang.ref.Reference
extends java.lang.Object
```
Constructors
```
public  SoftReference(Object referent)
public  SoftReference(Object referent,
  ReferenceQueue q)
```
Methods
```
public Object get()
```

►SPLITPANEUI
```
public abstract class javax.swing.plaf.
  SplitPaneUI
extends javax.swing.plaf.ComponentUI
extends java.lang.Object
```
Methods
```
public abstract void
  finishedPaintingChildren(JSplitPane jc,
  Graphics g)
public abstract int getDividerLocation(
  JSplitPane jc)
```

```
public abstract int
  getMaximumDividerLocation(JSplitPane jc)
public abstract int
  getMinimumDividerLocation(JSplitPane jc)
public abstract void
  resetToPreferredSizes(JSplitPane jc)
public abstract void setDividerLocation(
  JSplitPane jc,int location)
```

►SQLEXCEPTION

```
public class java.sql.SQLException
extends java.lang.Exception
extends java.lang.Throwable
extends java.lang.Object
```

Constructors

```
public  SQLException(String reason,
  String SQLState,int vendorCode)
public  SQLException(String reason,
  String SQLState)
public  SQLException(String reason)
public  SQLException()
```

Methods

```
public int getErrorCode()
public SQLException getNextException()
public String getSQLState()
public synchronized void
  setNextException(SQLException ex)
```

►SQLWARNING

```
public class java.sql.SQLWarning
extends java.sql.SQLException
extends java.lang.Exception
extends java.lang.Throwable
extends java.lang.Object
```

Constructors

```
public  SQLWarning(String reason,String
  SQLstate,int vendorCode)
public  SQLWarning(String reason,String
  SQLstate)
public  SQLWarning(String reason)
public  SQLWarning()
```

Methods

```
public SQLWarning getNextWarning()
public void setNextWarning(SQLWarning w)
```

►STACK

```
public class java.util.Stack
extends java.util.Vector
extends java.util.AbstractList
extends java.util.AbstractCollection
extends java.lang.Object
```

Constructors

```
public  Stack()
```

Methods

```
public boolean empty()
public synchronized Object peek()
public synchronized Object pop()
public Object push(Object item)
public synchronized int search(Object o)
```

►STACKOVERFLOWERROR

```
public class java.lang.
  StackOverflowError
extends java.lang.VirtualMachineError
extends java.lang.Error
extends java.lang.Throwable
extends java.lang.Object
```

Constructors

```
public  StackOverflowError()
public  StackOverflowError(String s)
```

►STATEEDIT

```
public class javax.swing.undo.StateEdit
extends javax.swing.undo.
  AbstractUndoableEdit
extends java.lang.Object
```

Fields

```
protected javax.swing.undo.StateEditable
  object
protected java.util.Hashtable postState
protected java.util.Hashtable preState
protected final static java.lang.String
  RCSID
protected java.lang.String undoRedoName
```

Constructors

```
public  StateEdit(StateEditable anObject)
public  StateEdit(StateEditable anObject,
  String name)
```

Methods

```
public void end()
public String getPresentationName()
protected void init(StateEditable
  anObject,String name)
public void redo()
protected void removeRedundantState()
public void undo()
```

►STREAMCORRUPTEDEXCEPTION

```
public class java.io.
  StreamCorruptedException
extends java.io.ObjectStreamException
extends java.io.IOException
extends java.lang.Exception
extends java.lang.Throwable
extends java.lang.Object
```

Constructors

```
public  StreamCorruptedException(String
  reason)
public  StreamCorruptedException()
```

►STREAMTOKENIZER

```
public class java.io.StreamTokenizer
extends java.lang.Object
```

Fields

```
public double nval
public java.lang.String sval
public int ttype
public final static int TT_EOF
public final static int TT_EOL
public final static int TT_NUMBER
public final static int TT_WORD
```

Constructors
```
private  StreamTokenizer()
public  StreamTokenizer(InputStream is)
public  StreamTokenizer(Reader r)
```
Methods
```
public void commentChar(int ch)
public void eolIsSignificant(boolean
  flag)
public int lineno()
public void lowerCaseMode(boolean fl)
public int nextToken()
public void ordinaryChar(int ch)
public void ordinaryChars(int low,int hi)
public void parseNumbers()
public void pushBack()
public void quoteChar(int ch)
public void resetSyntax()
public void slashSlashComments(boolean
  flag)
public void slashStarComments(boolean
  flag)
public String toString()
public void whitespaceChars(int low,int
  hi)
public void wordChars(int low,int hi)
```

►STRING
```
public final class java.lang.String
implements java.lang.Comparable
implements java.io.Serializable
extends java.lang.Object
```
Fields
```
public final static java.util.Comparator
  CASE_INSENSITIVE_ORDER
```
Constructors
```
public  String()
public  String(String value)
public  String(char value)
public  String(char value,int offset,int
  count)
public  String(byte ascii,int hibyte,int
  offset,int count)
public  String(byte ascii,int hibyte)
private  String()
public  String(byte bytes,int offset,int
  length,String enc)
public  String(byte bytes,String enc)
public  String(byte bytes,int offset,int
  length)
public  String(byte bytes)
public  String(StringBuffer buffer)
private  String()
```
Methods
```
public char charAt(int index)
public int compareTo(String
  anotherString)
public int compareTo(Object o)
public int compareToIgnoreCase(String
  str)
public String concat(String str)
public static String copyValueOf(char
  data,int offset,int count)
```

```
public static String copyValueOf(char
  data)
public boolean endsWith(String suffix)
public boolean equals(Object anObject)
public boolean equalsIgnoreCase(String
  anotherString)
public void getBytes(int srcBegin,int
  srcEnd,byte dst,int dstBegin)
public byte getBytes(String enc)
public byte getBytes()
public void getChars(int srcBegin,int
  srcEnd,char dst,int dstBegin)
public int hashCode()
public int indexOf(int ch)
public int indexOf(int ch,int fromIndex)
public int indexOf(String str)
public int indexOf(String str,int
  fromIndex)
public native String intern()
public int lastIndexOf(int ch)
public int lastIndexOf(int ch,int
  fromIndex)
public int lastIndexOf(String str)
public int lastIndexOf(String str,int
  fromIndex)
public int length()
public boolean regionMatches(int toffset,
  String other,int ooffset,int len)
public boolean regionMatches(boolean
  ignoreCase,int toffset,String other,int
  ooffset,int len)
public String replace(char oldChar,char
  newChar)
public boolean startsWith(String prefix,
  int toffset)
public boolean startsWith(String prefix)
public String substring(int beginIndex)
public String substring(int beginIndex,
  int endIndex)
public char toCharArray()
public String toLowerCase(Locale locale)
public String toLowerCase()
public String toString()
public String toUpperCase(Locale locale)
public String toUpperCase()
public String trim()
public static String valueOf(Object obj)
public static String valueOf(char data)
public static String valueOf(char data,
  int offset,int count)
public static String valueOf(boolean b)
public static String valueOf(char c)
public static String valueOf(int i)
public static String valueOf(long l)
public static String valueOf(float f)
public static String valueOf(double d)
```

►STRINGBUFFER
```
public final class java.lang.
  StringBuffer
implements java.io.Serializable
extends java.lang.Object
```

Constructors
```
public  StringBuffer()
public  StringBuffer(int length)
public  StringBuffer(String str)
```
Methods
```
public synchronized StringBuffer append(
  Object obj)
public synchronized StringBuffer append(
  String str)
public synchronized StringBuffer append(
  char str)
public synchronized StringBuffer append(
  char str,int offset,int len)
public StringBuffer append(boolean b)
public synchronized StringBuffer append(
  char c)
public StringBuffer append(int i)
public StringBuffer append(long l)
public StringBuffer append(float f)
public StringBuffer append(double d)
public int capacity()
public synchronized char charAt(int
  index)
public synchronized StringBuffer delete(
  int start,int end)
public synchronized StringBuffer
  deleteCharAt(int index)
public synchronized void ensureCapacity(
  int minimumCapacity)
public synchronized void getChars(int
  srcBegin,int srcEnd,char dst,int
  dstBegin)
public synchronized StringBuffer insert(
  int index,char str,int offset,int len)
public synchronized StringBuffer insert(
  int offset,Object obj)
public synchronized StringBuffer insert(
  int offset,String str)
public synchronized StringBuffer insert(
  int offset,char str)
public StringBuffer insert(int offset,
  boolean b)
public synchronized StringBuffer insert(
  int offset,char c)
public StringBuffer insert(int offset,
  int i)
public StringBuffer insert(int offset,
  long l)
public StringBuffer insert(int offset,
  float f)
public StringBuffer insert(int offset,
  double d)
public int length()
public synchronized StringBuffer replace(
  int start,int end,String str)
public synchronized StringBuffer reverse(
  )
public synchronized void setCharAt(int
  index,char ch)
public synchronized void setLength(int
  newLength)
public String substring(int start)
```

```
public synchronized String substring(int
  start,int end)
public String toString()
```

▶STRINGBUFFERINPUTSTREAM
```
public class java.io.
  StringBufferInputStream
extends java.io.InputStream
extends java.lang.Object
```
Fields
```
protected java.lang.String buffer
protected int count
protected int pos
```
Constructors
```
public  StringBufferInputStream(String s)
```
Methods
```
public synchronized int available()
public synchronized int read()
public synchronized int read(byte b,int
  off,int len)
public synchronized void reset()
public synchronized long skip(long n)
```

▶STRINGCHARACTERITERATOR
```
public final class java.text.
  StringCharacterIterator
implements java.text.CharacterIterator
extends java.lang.Object
```
Constructors
```
public  StringCharacterIterator(String
  text)
public  StringCharacterIterator(String
  text,int pos)
public  StringCharacterIterator(String
  text,int begin,int end,int pos)
```
Methods
```
public Object clone()
public char current()
public boolean equals(Object obj)
public char first()
public int getBeginIndex()
public int getEndIndex()
public int getIndex()
public int hashCode()
public char last()
public char next()
public char previous()
public char setIndex(int p)
public void setText(String text)
```

▶STRINGCONTENT
```
public final class javax.swing.text.
  StringContent
implements AbstractDocument.Content
implements java.io.Serializable
extends java.lang.Object
```
Constructors
```
public  StringContent()
public  StringContent(int initialLength)
```
Methods
```
public Position createPosition(int
  offset)
```

public void getChars(int where,int len,
  Segment chars)
protected Vector getPositionsInRange(
  Vector v,int offset,int length)
public String getString(int where,int
  len)
public UndoableEdit insertString(int
  where,String str)
public int length()
public UndoableEdit remove(int where,int
  nitems)
protected void updateUndoPositions(
  Vector positions)

▶STRINGINDEXOUTOFBOUNDSEXCEPTION

public class java.lang.
  StringIndexOutOfBoundsException
extends java.lang.
  IndexOutOfBoundsException
extends java.lang.RuntimeException
extends java.lang.Exception
extends java.lang.Throwable
extends java.lang.Object

Constructors
public StringIndexOutOfBoundsException()
public StringIndexOutOfBoundsException(
  String s)
public StringIndexOutOfBoundsException(
  int index)

▶STRINGREADER

public class java.io.StringReader
extends java.io.Reader
extends java.lang.Object

Constructors
public StringReader(String s)

Methods
public void close()
public void mark(int readAheadLimit)
public boolean markSupported()
public int read()
public int read(char cbuf,int off,int
  len)
public boolean ready()
public void reset()
public long skip(long ns)

▶STRINGSELECTION

public class java.awt.datatransfer.
  StringSelection
implements java.awt.datatransfer.
  ClipboardOwner
implements java.awt.datatransfer.
  Transferable
extends java.lang.Object

Constructors
public StringSelection(String data)

Methods
public synchronized Object
  getTransferData(DataFlavor flavor)
public synchronized DataFlavor
  getTransferDataFlavors()

public boolean isDataFlavorSupported(
  DataFlavor flavor)
public void lostOwnership(Clipboard
  clipboard,Transferable contents)

▶STRINGTOKENIZER

public class java.util.StringTokenizer
implements java.util.Enumeration
extends java.lang.Object

Constructors
public StringTokenizer(String str,
  String delim,boolean returnTokens)
public StringTokenizer(String str,
  String delim)
public StringTokenizer(String str)

Methods
public int countTokens()
public boolean hasMoreElements()
public boolean hasMoreTokens()
public Object nextElement()
public String nextToken()
public String nextToken(String delim)

▶STRINGWRITER

public class java.io.StringWriter
extends java.io.Writer
extends java.lang.Object

Constructors
public StringWriter()
public StringWriter(int initialSize)

Methods
public void close()
public void flush()
public StringBuffer getBuffer()
public String toString()
public void write(int c)
public void write(char cbuf,int off,int
  len)
public void write(String str)
public void write(String str,int off,int
  len)

▶STUBNOTFOUNDEXCEPTION

public class java.rmi.
  StubNotFoundException
extends java.rmi.RemoteException
extends java.io.IOException
extends java.lang.Exception
extends java.lang.Throwable
extends java.lang.Object

Constructors
public StubNotFoundException(String s)
public StubNotFoundException(String s,
  Exception ex)

▶STYLECONSTANTS

public class javax.swing.text.
  StyleConstants
extends java.lang.Object

Fields
public final static java.lang.Object
  Alignment

```
public final static int ALIGN_CENTER
public final static int ALIGN_JUSTIFIED
public final static int ALIGN_LEFT
public final static int ALIGN_RIGHT
public final static java.lang.Object
  Background
public final static java.lang.Object
  BidiLevel
public final static java.lang.Object
  Bold
public final static java.lang.Object
  ComponentAttribute
public final static java.lang.String
  ComponentElementName
public final static java.lang.Object
  ComposedTextAttribute
public final static java.lang.Object
  FirstLineIndent
public final static java.lang.Object
  FontFamily
public final static java.lang.Object
  FontSize
public final static java.lang.Object
  Foreground
public final static java.lang.Object
  IconAttribute
public final static java.lang.String
  IconElementName
public final static java.lang.Object
  Italic
public final static java.lang.Object
  LeftIndent
public final static java.lang.Object
  LineSpacing
public final static java.lang.Object
  ModelAttribute
public final static java.lang.Object
  NameAttribute
public final static java.lang.Object
  Orientation
public final static java.lang.Object
  ResolveAttribute
public final static java.lang.Object
  RightIndent
public final static java.lang.Object
  SpaceAbove
public final static java.lang.Object
  SpaceBelow
public final static java.lang.Object
  StrikeThrough
public final static java.lang.Object
  Subscript
public final static java.lang.Object
  Superscript
public final static java.lang.Object
  TabSet
public final static java.lang.Object
  Underline
```

Constructors

```
static  StyleConstants()
```

Methods

```
public static int getAlignment(
  AttributeSet a)
public static Color getBackground(
  AttributeSet a)
public static int getBidiLevel(
  AttributeSet a)
public static Component getComponent(
  AttributeSet a)
public static float getFirstLineIndent(
  AttributeSet a)
public static String getFontFamily(
  AttributeSet a)
public static int getFontSize(
  AttributeSet a)
public static Color getForeground(
  AttributeSet a)
public static Icon getIcon(AttributeSet
  a)
public static float getLeftIndent(
  AttributeSet a)
public static float getLineSpacing(
  AttributeSet a)
public static float getRightIndent(
  AttributeSet a)
public static float getSpaceAbove(
  AttributeSet a)
public static float getSpaceBelow(
  AttributeSet a)
public static TabSet getTabSet(
  AttributeSet a)
public static boolean isBold(
  AttributeSet a)
public static boolean isItalic(
  AttributeSet a)
public static boolean isStrikeThrough(
  AttributeSet a)
public static boolean isSubscript(
  AttributeSet a)
public static boolean isSuperscript(
  AttributeSet a)
public static boolean isUnderline(
  AttributeSet a)
public static void setAlignment(
  MutableAttributeSet a,int align)
public static void setBackground(
  MutableAttributeSet a,Color fg)
public static void setBidiLevel(
  MutableAttributeSet a,int o)
public static void setBold(
  MutableAttributeSet a,boolean b)
public static void setComponent(
  MutableAttributeSet a,Component c)
public static void setFirstLineIndent(
  MutableAttributeSet a,float i)
public static void setFontFamily(
  MutableAttributeSet a,String fam)
public static void setFontSize(
  MutableAttributeSet a,int s)
public static void setForeground(
  MutableAttributeSet a,Color fg)
public static void setIcon(
  MutableAttributeSet a,Icon c)
```

```
public static void setItalic(
  MutableAttributeSet a,boolean b)
public static void setLeftIndent(
  MutableAttributeSet a,float i)
public static void setLineSpacing(
  MutableAttributeSet a,float i)
public static void setRightIndent(
  MutableAttributeSet a,float i)
public static void setSpaceAbove(
  MutableAttributeSet a,float i)
public static void setSpaceBelow(
  MutableAttributeSet a,float i)
public static void setStrikeThrough(
  MutableAttributeSet a,boolean b)
public static void setSubscript(
  MutableAttributeSet a,boolean b)
public static void setSuperscript(
  MutableAttributeSet a,boolean b)
public static void setTabSet(
  MutableAttributeSet a,TabSet tabs)
public static void setUnderline(
  MutableAttributeSet a,boolean b)
public String toString()
```

▶**STYLECONTEXT**
```
public class javax.swing.text.
  StyleContext
implements AbstractDocument.
  AttributeContext
implements java.io.Serializable
extends java.lang.Object
```
Fields
```
public final static java.lang.String
  DEFAULT_STYLE
```
Constructors
```
public StyleContext()
```
Methods
```
public synchronized AttributeSet
  addAttribute(AttributeSet old,Object
  name,Object value)
public synchronized AttributeSet
  addAttributes(AttributeSet old,
  AttributeSet attr)
public void addChangeListener(
  ChangeListener l)
public Style addStyle(String nm,Style
  parent)
protected MutableAttributeSet
  createLargeAttributeSet(AttributeSet a)
protected SmallAttributeSet
  createSmallAttributeSet(AttributeSet a)
public Color getBackground(AttributeSet
  attr)
protected int getCompressionThreshold()
public final static StyleContext
  getDefaultStyleContext()
public AttributeSet getEmptySet()
public Font getFont(AttributeSet attr)
public Font getFont(String family,int
  style,int size)
public FontMetrics getFontMetrics(Font f)
```

```
public Color getForeground(AttributeSet
  attr)
public static Object getStaticAttribute(
  Object key)
public static Object
  getStaticAttributeKey(Object key)
public Style getStyle(String nm)
public Enumeration getStyleNames()
public void readAttributes(
  ObjectInputStream in,MutableAttributeSet
  a)
public static void readAttributeSet(
  ObjectInputStream in,MutableAttributeSet
  a)
public void reclaim(AttributeSet a)
public static void
  registerStaticAttributeKey(Object key)
public synchronized AttributeSet
  removeAttribute(AttributeSet old,Object
  name)
public synchronized AttributeSet
  removeAttributes(AttributeSet old,
  Enumeration names)
public synchronized AttributeSet
  removeAttributes(AttributeSet old,
  AttributeSet attrs)
public void removeChangeListener(
  ChangeListener l)
public void removeStyle(String nm)
public String toString()
public void writeAttributes(
  ObjectOutputStream out,AttributeSet a)
public static void writeAttributeSet(
  ObjectOutputStream out,AttributeSet a)
```

▶**STYLEDEDITORKIT**
```
public class javax.swing.text.
  StyledEditorKit
extends javax.swing.text.
  DefaultEditorKit
extends javax.swing.text.EditorKit
extends java.lang.Object
```
Methods
```
public Object clone()
public Document createDefaultDocument()
protected void createInputAttributes(
  Element element,MutableAttributeSet set)
public void deinstall(JEditorPane c)
public Action getActions()
public Element getCharacterAttributeRun()
public MutableAttributeSet
  getInputAttributes()
public ViewFactory getViewFactory()
public void install(JEditorPane c)
```

▶**STYLESHEET**
```
public class javax.swing.text.html.
  StyleSheet
extends javax.swing.text.StyleContext
extends java.lang.Object
```
Constructors
```
public StyleSheet()
```

Methods
public void addRule(String rule)
public Color getBackground(AttributeSet a)
public BoxPainter getBoxPainter(AttributeSet a)
public AttributeSet getDeclaration(String decl)
public Font getFont(AttributeSet a)
public Color getForeground(AttributeSet a)
public static int getIndexOfSize(float pt)
public ListPainter getListPainter(AttributeSet a)
public float getPointSize(int index)
public float getPointSize(String size)
public Style getRule(Tag t,Element e)
public Style getRule(String selector)
public AttributeSet getViewAttributes(View v)
public void loadRules(Reader in,URL ref)
public void setBaseFontSize(int sz)
public void setBaseFontSize(String size)
public Color stringToColor(String str)
public static AttributeSet translateHTMLToCSS(AttributeSet htmlAttrSet)

▶SwingPropertyChangeSupport
public final class javax.swing.event.SwingPropertyChangeSupport
extends java.beans.PropertyChangeSupport
extends java.lang.Object

Constructors
public SwingPropertyChangeSupport(Object sourceBean)

Methods
public synchronized void addPropertyChangeListener(PropertyChangeListener listener)
public synchronized void addPropertyChangeListener(String propertyName,PropertyChangeListener listener)
public void firePropertyChange(String propertyName,Object oldValue,Object newValue)
public void firePropertyChange(PropertyChangeEvent evt)
public synchronized boolean hasListeners(String propertyName)
public synchronized void removePropertyChangeListener(PropertyChangeListener listener)
public synchronized void removePropertyChangeListener(String propertyName,PropertyChangeListener listener)

▶SwingUtilities
public class javax.swing.SwingUtilities

implements javax.swing.SwingConstants
extends java.lang.Object

Constructors
private SwingUtilities()

Methods
public static Rectangle computeDifference(Rectangle rectA, Rectangle rectB)
public static Rectangle computeIntersection(int x,int y,int width,int height,Rectangle dest)
public static int computeStringWidth(FontMetrics fm,String str)
public static Rectangle computeUnion(int x,int y,int width,int height,Rectangle dest)
public static MouseEvent convertMouseEvent(Component source, MouseEvent sourceEvent,Component destination)
public static Point convertPoint(Component source,Point aPoint,Component destination)
public static Point convertPoint(Component source,int x,int y,Component destination)
public static void convertPointFromScreen(Point p,Component c)
public static void convertPointToScreen(Point p,Component c)
public static Rectangle convertRectangle(Component source,Rectangle aRectangle, Component destination)
public static Component findFocusOwner(Component c)
public static Accessible getAccessibleAt(Component c,Point p)
public static Accessible getAccessibleChild(Component c,int i)
public static int getAccessibleChildrenCount(Component c)
public static int getAccessibleIndexInParent(Component c)
public static AccessibleStateSet getAccessibleStateSet(Component c)
public static Container getAncestorNamed(String name,Component comp)
public static Container getAncestorOfClass(Class c,Component comp)
public static Component getDeepestComponentAt(Component parent, int x,int y)
public static Rectangle getLocalBounds(Component aComponent)
public static Component getRoot(Component c)
public static JRootPane getRootPane(Component c)
public static void invokeAndWait(Runnable doRun)

public static void invokeLater(Runnable
doRun)
public static boolean isDescendingFrom(
Component a,Component b)
public static boolean
isEventDispatchThread()
public static boolean isLeftMouseButton(
MouseEvent anEvent)
public static boolean
isMiddleMouseButton(MouseEvent anEvent)
public final static boolean
isRectangleContainingRectangle(Rectangle
a,Rectangle b)
public static boolean isRightMouseButton(
MouseEvent anEvent)
public static String layoutCompoundLabel(
JComponent c,FontMetrics fm,String text,
Icon icon,int verticalAlignment,int
horizontalAlignment,int
verticalTextPosition,int
horizontalTextPosition,Rectangle viewR,
Rectangle iconR,Rectangle textR,int
textIconGap)
public static String layoutCompoundLabel(
FontMetrics fm,String text,Icon icon,int
verticalAlignment,int
horizontalAlignment,int
verticalTextPosition,int
horizontalTextPosition,Rectangle viewR,
Rectangle iconR,Rectangle textR,int
textIconGap)
public static void paintComponent(
Graphics g,Component c,Container p,int x,
int y,int w,int h)
public static void paintComponent(
Graphics g,Component c,Container p,
Rectangle r)
public static void updateComponentTreeUI(
Component c)
public static Window windowForComponent(
Component aComponent)

►SyncFailedException
public class java.io.
SyncFailedException
extends java.io.IOException
extends java.lang.Exception
extends java.lang.Throwable
extends java.lang.Object
Constructors
public SyncFailedException(String desc)

►System
public final class java.lang.System
extends java.lang.Object
Fields
public final static java.io.PrintStream
err
public final static java.io.InputStream
in
public final static java.io.PrintStream
out

Constructors
private static System()
Methods
public static native void arraycopy(
Object src,int src_position,Object dst,
int dst_position,int length)
public static native long
currentTimeMillis()
public static void exit(int status)
public static void gc()
public static String getenv(String name)
public static Properties getProperties()
public static String getProperty(String
key)
public static String getProperty(String
key,String def)
public static SecurityManager
getSecurityManager()
public static native int
identityHashCode(Object x)
public static void load(String filename)
public static void loadLibrary(String
libname)
public static native String
mapLibraryName(String libname)
public static void runFinalization()
public static void runFinalizersOnExit(
boolean value)
public static void setErr(PrintStream
err)
public static void setIn(InputStream in)
public static void setOut(PrintStream
out)
public static void setProperties(
Properties props)
public static String setProperty(String
key,String value)
public static synchronized void
setSecurityManager(SecurityManager s)

►SystemColor
public final class java.awt.SystemColor
implements java.io.Serializable
extends java.awt.Color
extends java.lang.Object
Fields
public final static java.awt.SystemColor
activeCaption
public final static java.awt.SystemColor
activeCaptionBorder
public final static java.awt.SystemColor
activeCaptionText
public final static int ACTIVE_CAPTION
public final static int ACTIVE_CAPTION_
BORDER
public final static int ACTIVE_CAPTION_
TEXT
public final static int CONTROL
public final static java.awt.SystemColor
control
public final static java.awt.SystemColor
controlDkShadow

```
public final static java.awt.SystemColor
  controlHighlight
public final static java.awt.SystemColor
  controlLtHighlight
public final static java.awt.SystemColor
  controlShadow
public final static java.awt.SystemColor
  controlText
public final static int CONTROL_DK_
  SHADOW
public final static int CONTROL_
  HIGHLIGHT
public final static int CONTROL_LT_
  HIGHLIGHT
public final static int CONTROL_SHADOW
public final static int CONTROL_TEXT
public final static int DESKTOP
public final static java.awt.SystemColor
  desktop
public final static java.awt.SystemColor
  inactiveCaption
public final static java.awt.SystemColor
  inactiveCaptionBorder
public final static java.awt.SystemColor
  inactiveCaptionText
public final static int INACTIVE_
  CAPTION
public final static int INACTIVE_CAPTION_
  BORDER
public final static int INACTIVE_CAPTION_
  TEXT
public final static int INFO
public final static java.awt.SystemColor
  info
public final static java.awt.SystemColor
  infoText
public final static int INFO_TEXT
public final static int MENU
public final static java.awt.SystemColor
  menu
public final static java.awt.SystemColor
  menuText
public final static int MENU_TEXT
public final static int NUM_COLORS
public final static int SCROLLBAR
public final static java.awt.SystemColor
  scrollbar
public final static int TEXT
public final static java.awt.SystemColor
  text
public final static java.awt.SystemColor
  textHighlight
public final static java.awt.SystemColor
  textHighlightText
public final static java.awt.SystemColor
  textInactiveText
public final static java.awt.SystemColor
  textText
public final static int TEXT_HIGHLIGHT
public final static int TEXT_HIGHLIGHT_
  TEXT
public final static int TEXT_INACTIVE_
  TEXT
```

```
public final static int TEXT_TEXT
public final static int WINDOW
public final static java.awt.SystemColor
  window
public final static java.awt.SystemColor
  windowBorder
public final static java.awt.SystemColor
  windowText
public final static int WINDOW_BORDER
public final static int WINDOW_TEXT
```

Constructors
```
private  SystemColor()
```
Methods
```
public PaintContext createContext(
  ColorModel cm,Rectangle r,Rectangle2D
  r2d,AffineTransform xform,RenderingHints
  hints)
public int getRGB()
public String toString()
```

▶**SYSTEMFLAVORMAP**
```
public final class java.awt.datatransfer.
  SystemFlavorMap
implements java.awt.datatransfer.
  FlavorMap
extends java.lang.Object
```
Constructors
```
private  SystemFlavorMap()
```
Methods
```
public static DataFlavor
  decodeDataFlavor(String atom)
public static String decodeJavaMIMEType(
  String atom)
public static String encodeDataFlavor(
  DataFlavor df)
public static String encodeJavaMIMEType(
  String mimeType)
public static FlavorMap
  getDefaultFlavorMap()
public synchronized Map
  getFlavorsForNatives(String natives)
public synchronized Map
  getNativesForFlavors(DataFlavor flavors)
public static boolean isJavaMIMEType(
  String atom)
```

▶**TABBEDPANEUI**
```
public abstract class javax.swing.plaf.
  TabbedPaneUI
extends javax.swing.plaf.ComponentUI
extends java.lang.Object
```
Methods
```
public abstract Rectangle getTabBounds(
  JTabbedPane pane,int index)
public abstract int getTabRunCount(
  JTabbedPane pane)
public abstract int tabForCoordinate(
  JTabbedPane pane,int x,int y)
```

▶**TABLECOLUMN**
```
public class javax.swing.table.
  TableColumn
```

implements java.io.Serializable
extends java.lang.Object
extends java.lang.Object

Fields

protected javax.swing.table.
 TableCellEditor cellEditor
protected javax.swing.table.
 TableCellRenderer cellRenderer
public final static java.lang.String
 CELL_RENDERER_PROPERTY
public final static java.lang.String
 COLUMN_WIDTH_PROPERTY
protected javax.swing.table.
 TableCellRenderer headerRenderer
protected java.lang.Object headerValue
public final static java.lang.String
 HEADER_RENDERER_PROPERTY
public final static java.lang.String
 HEADER_VALUE_PROPERTY
protected java.lang.Object identifier
protected boolean isResizable
protected int maxWidth
protected int minWidth
protected int modelIndex
protected transient int
 resizedPostingDisableCount
protected int width

Constructors

public TableColumn()
public TableColumn(int modelIndex)
public TableColumn(int modelIndex,int
 width)
public TableColumn(int modelIndex,int
 width,TableCellRenderer cellRenderer,
 TableCellEditor cellEditor)

Methods

public synchronized void
 addPropertyChangeListener(
 PropertyChangeListener listener)
protected TableCellRenderer
 createDefaultHeaderRenderer()
public void disableResizedPosting()
public void enableResizedPosting()
public TableCellEditor getCellEditor()
public TableCellRenderer getCellRenderer(
)
public TableCellRenderer
 getHeaderRenderer()
public Object getHeaderValue()
public Object getIdentifier()
public int getMaxWidth()
public int getMinWidth()
public int getModelIndex()
public int getPreferredWidth()
public boolean getResizable()
public int getWidth()
public synchronized void
 removePropertyChangeListener(
 PropertyChangeListener listener)
public void setCellEditor(
 TableCellEditor anEditor)

public void setCellRenderer(
 TableCellRenderer aRenderer)
public void setHeaderRenderer(
 TableCellRenderer aRenderer)
public void setHeaderValue(Object aValue)
public void setIdentifier(Object
 anIdentifier)
public void setMaxWidth(int maxWidth)
public void setMinWidth(int minWidth)
public void setModelIndex(int anIndex)
public void setPreferredWidth(int
 preferredWidth)
public void setResizable(boolean flag)
public void setWidth(int width)
public void sizeWidthToFit()

▶**TableColumnModelEvent**

public class javax.swing.event.
 TableColumnModelEvent
extends java.util.EventObject
extends java.lang.Object

Fields

protected int fromIndex
protected int toIndex

Constructors

public TableColumnModelEvent(
 TableColumnModel source,int from,int to)

Methods

public int getFromIndex()
public int getToIndex()

▶**TableHeaderUI**

public abstract class javax.swing.plaf.
 TableHeaderUI
extends javax.swing.plaf.ComponentUI
extends java.lang.Object

▶**TableModelEvent**

public class javax.swing.event.
 TableModelEvent
extends java.util.EventObject
extends java.lang.Object

Fields

public final static int ALL_COLUMNS
protected int column
public final static int DELETE
protected int firstRow
public final static int HEADER_ROW
public final static int INSERT
protected int lastRow
protected int type
public final static int UPDATE

Constructors

public TableModelEvent(TableModel
 source)
public TableModelEvent(TableModel
 source,int row)
public TableModelEvent(TableModel
 source,int firstRow,int lastRow)
public TableModelEvent(TableModel
 source,int firstRow,int lastRow,int
 column)

public TableModelEvent(TableModel
  source,int firstRow,int lastRow,int
  column,int type)

Methods
public int getColumn()
public int getFirstRow()
public int getLastRow()
public int getType()

▸**TableUI**
public abstract class javax.swing.plaf.
  TableUI
extends javax.swing.plaf.ComponentUI
extends java.lang.Object

▸**TableView**
public abstract class javax.swing.text.
  TableView
extends javax.swing.text.BoxView
extends javax.swing.text.CompositeView
extends javax.swing.text.View
extends java.lang.Object

Constructors
public TableView(Element elem)

Methods
protected SizeRequirements
  calculateMinorAxisRequirements(int axis,
  SizeRequirements r)
protected TableCell createTableCell(
  Element elem)
protected TableRow createTableRow(
  Element elem)
protected View getViewAtPosition(int pos,
  Rectangle a)
protected void layoutColumns(int
  targetSpan,int offsets,int spans,
  SizeRequirements reqs)
protected void layoutMinorAxis(int
  targetSpan,int axis,int offsets,int
  spans)
protected void loadChildren(ViewFactory
  f)

▸**TabSet**
public class javax.swing.text.TabSet
implements java.io.Serializable
extends java.lang.Object

Constructors
public TabSet(TabStop tabs)

Methods
public TabStop getTab(int index)
public TabStop getTabAfter(float
  location)
public int getTabCount()
public int getTabIndex(TabStop tab)
public int getTabIndexAfter(float
  location)
public String toString()

▸**TabStop**
public class javax.swing.text.TabStop
implements java.io.Serializable

extends java.lang.Object
Fields
public final static int ALIGN_BAR
public final static int ALIGN_CENTER
public final static int ALIGN_DECIMAL
public final static int ALIGN_LEFT
public final static int ALIGN_RIGHT
public final static int LEAD_DOTS
public final static int LEAD_EQUALS
public final static int LEAD_HYPHENS
public final static int LEAD_NONE
public final static int LEAD_THICKLINE
public final static int LEAD_UNDERLINE

Constructors
public TabStop(float pos)
public TabStop(float pos,int align,int
  leader)

Methods
public boolean equals(Object other)
public int getAlignment()
public int getLeader()
public float getPosition()
public int hashCode()
public String toString()

▸**TagElement**
public class javax.swing.text.html.
  parser.TagElement
extends java.lang.Object

Constructors
public TagElement(Element elem)
public TagElement(Element elem,boolean
  fictional)

Methods
public boolean breaksFlow()
public boolean fictional()
public Element getElement()
public Tag getHTMLTag()
public boolean isPreformatted()

▸**TextAction**
public abstract class javax.swing.text.
  TextAction
extends javax.swing.AbstractAction
extends java.lang.Object

Constructors
public TextAction(String name)

Methods
public final static Action augmentList(
  Action list1,Action list2)
protected final JTextComponent
  getFocusedComponent()
protected final JTextComponent
  getTextComponent(ActionEvent e)

▸**TextArea**
public class java.awt.TextArea
extends java.awt.TextComponent
extends java.awt.Component
extends java.lang.Object
Fields
public final static int SCROLLBARS_BOTH

```
public final static int SCROLLBARS_
   HORIZONTAL_ONLY
public final static int SCROLLBARS_NONE
public final static int SCROLLBARS_
   VERTICAL_ONLY
```

Constructors
```
public static  TextArea()
public  TextArea(String text)
public  TextArea(int rows,int columns)
public  TextArea(String text,int rows,
   int columns)
public  TextArea(String text,int rows,
   int columns,int scrollbars)
```

Methods
```
public void addNotify()
public void append(String str)
public synchronized void appendText(
   String str)
public int getColumns()
public Dimension getMinimumSize(int rows,
   int columns)
public Dimension getMinimumSize()
public Dimension getPreferredSize(int
   rows,int columns)
public Dimension getPreferredSize()
public int getRows()
public int getScrollbarVisibility()
public void insert(String str,int pos)
public synchronized void insertText(
   String str,int pos)
public Dimension minimumSize(int rows,
   int columns)
public Dimension minimumSize()
protected String paramString()
public Dimension preferredSize(int rows,
   int columns)
public Dimension preferredSize()
public void replaceRange(String str,int
   start,int end)
public synchronized void replaceText(
   String str,int start,int end)
public void setColumns(int columns)
public void setRows(int rows)
```

►TEXTATTRIBUTE
```
public final class java.awt.font.
   TextAttribute
extends java.lang.Object
```

Fields
```
public final static java.awt.font.
   TextAttribute BACKGROUND
public final static java.awt.font.
   TextAttribute BIDI_EMBEDDING
public final static java.awt.font.
   TextAttribute CHAR_REPLACEMENT
public final static java.awt.font.
   TextAttribute FAMILY
public final static java.awt.font.
   TextAttribute FONT
public final static java.awt.font.
   TextAttribute FOREGROUND
```

```
public final static java.awt.font.
   TextAttribute INPUT_METHOD_HIGHLIGHT
public final static java.awt.font.
   TextAttribute JUSTIFICATION
public final static java.lang.Float
   JUSTIFICATION_FULL
public final static java.lang.Float
   JUSTIFICATION_NONE
public final static java.awt.font.
   TextAttribute POSTURE
public final static java.lang.Float
   POSTURE_OBLIQUE
public final static java.lang.Float
   POSTURE_REGULAR
public final static java.awt.font.
   TextAttribute RUN_DIRECTION
public final static java.lang.Boolean
   RUN_DIRECTION_LTR
public final static java.lang.Boolean
   RUN_DIRECTION_RTL
public final static java.awt.font.
   TextAttribute SIZE
public final static java.awt.font.
   TextAttribute STRIKETHROUGH
public final static java.lang.Boolean
   STRIKETHROUGH_ON
public final static java.awt.font.
   TextAttribute SUPERSCRIPT
public final static java.lang.Integer
   SUPERSCRIPT_SUB
public final static java.lang.Integer
   SUPERSCRIPT_SUPER
public final static java.awt.font.
   TextAttribute SWAP_COLORS
public final static java.lang.Boolean
   SWAP_COLORS_ON
public final static java.awt.font.
   TextAttribute TRANSFORM
public final static java.awt.font.
   TextAttribute UNDERLINE
public final static java.lang.Integer
   UNDERLINE_ON
public final static java.awt.font.
   TextAttribute WEIGHT
public final static java.lang.Float
   WEIGHT_BOLD
public final static java.lang.Float
   WEIGHT_DEMIBOLD
public final static java.lang.Float
   WEIGHT_DEMILIGHT
public final static java.lang.Float
   WEIGHT_EXTRABOLD
public final static java.lang.Float
   WEIGHT_EXTRA_LIGHT
public final static java.lang.Float
   WEIGHT_HEAVY
public final static java.lang.Float
   WEIGHT_LIGHT
public final static java.lang.Float
   WEIGHT_MEDIUM
public final static java.lang.Float
   WEIGHT_REGULAR
```

public final static java.lang.Float
  WEIGHT_SEMIBOLD
public final static java.lang.Float
  WEIGHT_ULTRABOLD
public final static java.awt.font.
  TextAttribute WIDTH
public final static java.lang.Float
  WIDTH_CONDENSED
public final static java.lang.Float
  WIDTH_EXTENDED
public final static java.lang.Float
  WIDTH_REGULAR
public final static java.lang.Float
  WIDTH_SEMI_CONDENSED
public final static java.lang.Float
  WIDTH_SEMI_EXTENDED

Constructors
protected TextAttribute(String name)

Methods
protected Object readResolve()

►TextComponent
public class java.awt.TextComponent
extends java.awt.Component
extends java.lang.Object

Fields
protected transient java.awt.event.
  TextListener textListener

Constructors
 TextComponent()

Methods
public synchronized void addTextListener(
  TextListener l)
public synchronized int getCaretPosition(
)
public synchronized String
  getSelectedText()
public synchronized int getSelectionEnd()
public synchronized int
  getSelectionStart()
public synchronized String getText()
public boolean isEditable()
protected String paramString()
protected void processEvent(AWTEvent e)
protected void processTextEvent(
  TextEvent e)
public void removeNotify()
public synchronized void
  removeTextListener(TextListener l)
public synchronized void select(int
  selectionStart,int selectionEnd)
public synchronized void selectAll()
public synchronized void
  setCaretPosition(int position)
public synchronized void setEditable(
  boolean b)
public synchronized void setSelectionEnd(
  int selectionEnd)
public synchronized void
  setSelectionStart(int selectionStart)
public synchronized void setText(String
  t)

►TextEvent
public class java.awt.event.TextEvent
extends java.awt.AWTEvent
extends java.util.EventObject
extends java.lang.Object

Fields
public final static int TEXT_FIRST
public final static int TEXT_LAST
public final static int TEXT_VALUE_
  CHANGED

Constructors
public TextEvent(Object source,int id)

Methods
public String paramString()

►TextField
public class java.awt.TextField
extends java.awt.TextComponent
extends java.awt.Component
extends java.lang.Object

Constructors
public static TextField()
public TextField(String text)
public TextField(int columns)
public TextField(String text,int
  columns)

Methods
public synchronized void
  addActionListener(ActionListener l)
public void addNotify()
public boolean echoCharIsSet()
public int getColumns()
public char getEchoChar()
public Dimension getMinimumSize(int
  columns)
public Dimension getMinimumSize()
public Dimension getPreferredSize(int
  columns)
public Dimension getPreferredSize()
public Dimension minimumSize(int columns)
public Dimension minimumSize()
protected String paramString()
public Dimension preferredSize(int
  columns)
public Dimension preferredSize()
protected void processActionEvent(
  ActionEvent e)
protected void processEvent(AWTEvent e)
public synchronized void
  removeActionListener(ActionListener l)
public synchronized void setColumns(int
  columns)
public void setEchoChar(char c)
public synchronized void
  setEchoCharacter(char c)
public void setText(String t)

►TextHitInfo
public final class java.awt.font.
  TextHitInfo
extends java.lang.Object

Constructors
private TextHitInfo()
Methods
public static TextHitInfo afterOffset(
  int offset)
public static TextHitInfo beforeOffset(
  int offset)
public boolean equals(Object obj)
public boolean equals(TextHitInfo
  hitInfo)
public int getCharIndex()
public int getInsertionIndex()
public TextHitInfo getOffsetHit(int
  delta)
public TextHitInfo getOtherHit()
public int hashCode()
public boolean isLeadingEdge()
public static TextHitInfo leading(int
  charIndex)
public String toString()
public static TextHitInfo trailing(int
  charIndex)

►**TextLayout**
public final class java.awt.font.
  TextLayout
implements java.lang.Cloneable
extends java.lang.Object
Fields
public final static CaretPolicy DEFAULT_
  CARET_POLICY
Constructors
public TextLayout(String string,Font
  font,FontRenderContext frc)
public TextLayout(String string,Map
  attributes,FontRenderContext frc)
public TextLayout(
  AttributedCharacterIterator text,
  FontRenderContext frc)
  TextLayout()
Methods
protected Object clone()
public void draw(Graphics2D g2,float x,
  float y)
public boolean equals(Object obj)
public boolean equals(TextLayout rhs)
public float getAdvance()
public float getAscent()
public byte getBaseline()
public float getBaselineOffsets()
public Shape getBlackBoxBounds(int
  firstEndpoint,int secondEndpoint)
public Rectangle2D getBounds()
public float getCaretInfo(TextHitInfo
  hit,Rectangle2D bounds)
public float getCaretInfo(TextHitInfo
  hit)
public Shape getCaretShape(TextHitInfo
  hit,Rectangle2D bounds)
public Shape getCaretShape(TextHitInfo
  hit)

public Shape getCaretShapes(int offset,
  Rectangle2D bounds,CaretPolicy policy)
public Shape getCaretShapes(int offset,
  Rectangle2D bounds)
public Shape getCaretShapes(int offset)
public int getCharacterCount()
public byte getCharacterLevel(int index)
public float getDescent()
public TextLayout getJustifiedLayout(
  float justificationWidth)
public float getLeading()
public Shape getLogicalHighlightShape(
  int firstEndpoint,int secondEndpoint,
  Rectangle2D bounds)
public Shape getLogicalHighlightShape(
  int firstEndpoint,int secondEndpoint)
public int
  getLogicalRangesForVisualSelection(
  TextHitInfo firstEndpoint,TextHitInfo
  secondEndpoint)
public TextHitInfo getNextLeftHit(
  TextHitInfo hit)
public TextHitInfo getNextLeftHit(int
  offset,CaretPolicy policy)
public TextHitInfo getNextLeftHit(int
  offset)
public TextHitInfo getNextRightHit(
  TextHitInfo hit)
public TextHitInfo getNextRightHit(int
  offset,CaretPolicy policy)
public TextHitInfo getNextRightHit(int
  offset)
public Shape getOutline(AffineTransform
  tx)
public float getVisibleAdvance()
public Shape getVisualHighlightShape(
  TextHitInfo firstEndpoint,TextHitInfo
  secondEndpoint,Rectangle2D bounds)
public Shape getVisualHighlightShape(
  TextHitInfo firstEndpoint,TextHitInfo
  secondEndpoint)
public TextHitInfo getVisualOtherHit(
  TextHitInfo hit)
protected void handleJustify(float
  justificationWidth)
public int hashCode()
public TextHitInfo hitTestChar(float x,
  float y,Rectangle2D bounds)
public TextHitInfo hitTestChar(float x,
  float y)
public boolean isLeftToRight()
public boolean isVertical()
public String toString()

►**TextUI**
public abstract class javax.swing.plaf.
  TextUI
extends javax.swing.plaf.ComponentUI
extends java.lang.Object
Methods
public abstract void damageRange(
  JTextComponent t,int p0,int p1)

```
public abstract void damageRange(
  JTextComponent t,int p0,int p1,Bias
  firstBias,Bias secondBias)
public abstract EditorKit getEditorKit(
  JTextComponent t)
public abstract int
  getNextVisualPositionFrom(JTextComponent
  t,int pos,Bias b,int direction,Bias
  biasRet)
public abstract View getRootView(
  JTextComponent t)
public abstract Rectangle modelToView(
  JTextComponent t,int pos)
public abstract Rectangle modelToView(
  JTextComponent t,int pos,Bias bias)
public abstract int viewToModel(
  JTextComponent t,Point pt)
public abstract int viewToModel(
  JTextComponent t,Point pt,Bias
  biasReturn)
```

►TEXTUREPAINT

```
public class java.awt.TexturePaint
implements java.awt.Paint
extends java.lang.Object
```

Constructors

```
public  TexturePaint(BufferedImage txtr,
  Rectangle2D anchor)
```

Methods

```
public PaintContext createContext(
  ColorModel cm,Rectangle deviceBounds,
  Rectangle2D userBounds,AffineTransform
  xform,RenderingHints hints)
public Rectangle2D getAnchorRect()
public BufferedImage getImage()
public int getTransparency()
```

►THREAD

```
public class java.lang.Thread
implements java.lang.Runnable
extends java.lang.Object
```

Fields

```
public final static int MAX_PRIORITY
public final static int MIN_PRIORITY
public final static int NORM_PRIORITY
```

Constructors

```
public  Thread()
public  Thread(Runnable target)
public  Thread(ThreadGroup group,
  Runnable target)
public  Thread(String name)
public  Thread(ThreadGroup group,String
  name)
public  Thread(Runnable target,String
  name)
public  Thread(ThreadGroup group,
  Runnable target,String name)
```

Methods

```
public static int activeCount()
public final void checkAccess()
public native int countStackFrames()
```

```
public static native Thread
  currentThread()
public void destroy()
public static void dumpStack()
public static int enumerate(Thread
  tarray)
public ClassLoader getContextClassLoader(
  )
public final String getName()
public final int getPriority()
public final ThreadGroup getThreadGroup()
public void interrupt()
public static boolean interrupted()
public final native boolean isAlive()
public final boolean isDaemon()
public boolean isInterrupted()
public final synchronized void join(long
  millis)
public final synchronized void join(long
  millis,int nanos)
public final void join()
public final void resume()
public void run()
public void setContextClassLoader(
  ClassLoader cl)
public final void setDaemon(boolean on)
public final void setName(String name)
public final void setPriority(int
  newPriority)
public static native void sleep(long
  millis)
public static void sleep(long millis,int
  nanos)
public synchronized native void start()
public final void stop()
public final synchronized void stop(
  Throwable obj)
public final void suspend()
public String toString()
public static native void yield()
```

►THREADDEATH

```
public class java.lang.ThreadDeath
extends java.lang.Error
extends java.lang.Throwable
extends java.lang.Object
```

►THREADGROUP

```
public class java.lang.ThreadGroup
extends java.lang.Object
```

Constructors

```
private  ThreadGroup()
public  ThreadGroup(String name)
public  ThreadGroup(ThreadGroup parent,
  String name)
```

Methods

```
public int activeCount()
public int activeGroupCount()
public boolean allowThreadSuspension(
  boolean b)
public final void checkAccess()
public final void destroy()
public int enumerate(Thread list)
```

```
public int enumerate(Thread list,boolean
  recurse)
public int enumerate(ThreadGroup list)
public int enumerate(ThreadGroup list,
  boolean recurse)
public final int getMaxPriority()
public final String getName()
public final ThreadGroup getParent()
public final void interrupt()
public final boolean isDaemon()
public synchronized boolean isDestroyed()
public void list()
public final boolean parentOf(
  ThreadGroup g)
public final void resume()
public final void setDaemon(boolean
  daemon)
public final void setMaxPriority(int pri)
public final void stop()
public final void suspend()
public String toString()
public void uncaughtException(Thread t,
  Throwable e)
```

►THREADLOCAL

```
public class java.lang.ThreadLocal
extends java.lang.Object
```

Constructors

```
public  ThreadLocal()
```

Methods

```
public Object get()
protected Object initialValue()
public void set(Object value)
```

►THROWABLE

```
public class java.lang.Throwable
implements java.io.Serializable
extends java.lang.Object
```

Constructors

```
public  Throwable()
public  Throwable(String message)
```

Methods

```
public native Throwable fillInStackTrace(
  )
public String getLocalizedMessage()
public String getMessage()
public void printStackTrace()
public void printStackTrace(PrintStream
  s)
public void printStackTrace(PrintWriter
  s)
public String toString()
```

►TIME

```
public class java.sql.Time
extends java.util.Date
extends java.lang.Object
```

Constructors

```
public  Time(int hour,int minute,int
  second)
public  Time(long time)
```

Methods

```
public int getDate()
public int getDay()
public int getMonth()
public int getYear()
public void setDate(int i)
public void setMonth(int i)
public void setTime(long time)
public void setYear(int i)
public String toString()
public static Time valueOf(String s)
```

►TIMER

```
public class javax.swing.Timer
implements java.io.Serializable
extends java.lang.Object
```

Fields

```
protected javax.swing.event.
  EventListenerList listenerList
```

Constructors

```
public  Timer(int delay,ActionListener
  listener)
```

Methods

```
public void addActionListener(
  ActionListener listener)
protected void fireActionPerformed(
  ActionEvent e)
public int getDelay()
public int getInitialDelay()
public static boolean getLogTimers()
public boolean isCoalesce()
public boolean isRepeats()
public boolean isRunning()
public void removeActionListener(
  ActionListener listener)
public void restart()
public void setCoalesce(boolean flag)
public void setDelay(int delay)
public void setInitialDelay(int
  initialDelay)
public static void setLogTimers(boolean
  flag)
public void setRepeats(boolean flag)
public void start()
public void stop()
```

►TIMESTAMP

```
public class java.sql.Timestamp
extends java.util.Date
extends java.lang.Object
```

Constructors

```
public  Timestamp(int year,int month,int
  date,int hour,int minute,int second,int
  nano)
public  Timestamp(long time)
```

Methods

```
public boolean after(Timestamp ts)
public boolean before(Timestamp ts)
public boolean equals(Timestamp ts)
public boolean equals(Object ts)
public int getNanos()
public void setNanos(int n)
```

```
public String toString()
public static Timestamp valueOf(String s)
```

▶TIMEZONE

```
public abstract class java.util.
  TimeZone
implements java.lang.Cloneable
implements java.io.Serializable
extends java.lang.Object
```

Fields

```
public final static int LONG
public final static int SHORT
```

Constructors

```
public  TimeZone()
```

Methods

```
public Object clone()
public static synchronized String
  getAvailableIDs(int rawOffset)
public static synchronized String
  getAvailableIDs()
public static synchronized TimeZone
  getDefault()
public final String getDisplayName()
public final String getDisplayName(
  Locale locale)
public final String getDisplayName(
  boolean daylight,int style)
public String getDisplayName(boolean
  daylight,int style,Locale locale)
public String getID()
public abstract int getOffset(int era,
  int year,int month,int day,int dayOfWeek,
  int milliseconds)
public abstract int getRawOffset()
public static synchronized TimeZone
  getTimeZone(String ID)
public boolean hasSameRules(TimeZone
  other)
public abstract boolean inDaylightTime(
  Date date)
public static synchronized void
  setDefault(TimeZone zone)
public void setID(String ID)
public abstract void setRawOffset(int
  offsetMillis)
public abstract boolean useDaylightTime()
```

▶TITLEDBORDER

```
public class javax.swing.border.
  TitledBorder
extends javax.swing.border.
  AbstractBorder
extends java.lang.Object
```

Fields

```
public final static int ABOVE_BOTTOM
public final static int ABOVE_TOP
public final static int BELOW_BOTTOM
public final static int BELOW_TOP
protected javax.swing.border.Border
  border
public final static int BOTTOM
public final static int CENTER
```

```
public final static int DEFAULT_
  JUSTIFICATION
public final static int DEFAULT_
  POSITION
protected final static int EDGE_SPACING
public final static int LEFT
public final static int RIGHT
protected final static int TEXT_INSET_H
protected final static int TEXT_SPACING
protected java.lang.String title
protected java.awt.Color titleColor
protected java.awt.Font titleFont
protected int titleJustification
protected int titlePosition
public final static int TOP
```

Constructors

```
public  TitledBorder(String title)
public  TitledBorder(Border border)
public  TitledBorder(Border border,
  String title)
public  TitledBorder(Border border,
  String title,int titleJustification,int
  titlePosition)
public  TitledBorder(Border border,
  String title,int titleJustification,int
  titlePosition,Font titleFont)
public  TitledBorder(Border border,
  String title,int titleJustification,int
  titlePosition,Font titleFont,Color
  titleColor)
```

Methods

```
public Border getBorder()
public Insets getBorderInsets(Component
  c)
public Insets getBorderInsets(Component
  c,Insets insets)
protected Font getFont(Component c)
public Dimension getMinimumSize(
  Component c)
public String getTitle()
public Color getTitleColor()
public Font getTitleFont()
public int getTitleJustification()
public int getTitlePosition()
public boolean isBorderOpaque()
public void paintBorder(Component c,
  Graphics g,int x,int y,int width,int
  height)
public void setBorder(Border border)
public void setTitle(String title)
public void setTitleColor(Color
  titleColor)
public void setTitleFont(Font titleFont)
public void setTitleJustification(int
  titleJustification)
public void setTitlePosition(int
  titlePosition)
```

▶TOOLBARUI

```
public abstract class javax.swing.plaf.
  ToolBarUI
extends javax.swing.plaf.ComponentUI
```

extends java.lang.Object

▶TOOLKIT
public abstract class java.awt.Toolkit
extends java.lang.Object

Fields
protected final java.util.Map
  desktopProperties
protected final java.beans.
  PropertyChangeSupport
  desktopPropsSupport

Methods
public void addAWTEventListener(
  AWTEventListener listener,long eventMask)
public synchronized void
  addPropertyChangeListener(String name,
  PropertyChangeListener pcl)
public abstract void beep()
public abstract int checkImage(Image
  image,int width,int height,ImageObserver
  observer)
protected abstract ButtonPeer
  createButton(Button target)
protected abstract CanvasPeer
  createCanvas(Canvas target)
protected abstract CheckboxPeer
  createCheckbox(Checkbox target)
protected abstract CheckboxMenuItemPeer
  createCheckboxMenuItem(CheckboxMenuItem
  target)
protected abstract ChoicePeer
  createChoice(Choice target)
protected LightweightPeer
  createComponent(Component target)
public Cursor createCustomCursor(Image
  cursor,Point hotSpot,String name)
protected abstract DialogPeer
  createDialog(Dialog target)
public DragGestureRecognizer
  createDragGestureRecognizer(Class
  abstractRecognizerClass,DragSource ds,
  Component c,int srcActions,
  DragGestureListener dgl)
public abstract DragSourceContextPeer
  createDragSourceContextPeer(
  DragGestureEvent dge)
protected abstract FileDialogPeer
  createFileDialog(FileDialog target)
protected abstract FramePeer createFrame(
  Frame target)
public abstract Image createImage(String
  filename)
public abstract Image createImage(URL
  url)
public abstract Image createImage(
  ImageProducer producer)
public Image createImage(byte imagedata)
public abstract Image createImage(byte
  imagedata,int imageoffset,int
  imagelength)
protected abstract LabelPeer createLabel(
  Label target)

protected abstract ListPeer createList(
  List target)
protected abstract MenuPeer createMenu(
  Menu target)
protected abstract MenuBarPeer
  createMenuBar(MenuBar target)
protected abstract MenuItemPeer
  createMenuItem(MenuItem target)
protected abstract PanelPeer createPanel(
  Panel target)
protected abstract PopupMenuPeer
  createPopupMenu(PopupMenu target)
protected abstract ScrollbarPeer
  createScrollbar(Scrollbar target)
protected abstract ScrollPanePeer
  createScrollPane(ScrollPane target)
protected abstract TextAreaPeer
  createTextArea(TextArea target)
protected abstract TextFieldPeer
  createTextField(TextField target)
protected abstract WindowPeer
  createWindow(Window target)
public Dimension getBestCursorSize(int
  preferredWidth,int preferredHeight)
public abstract ColorModel getColorModel(
)
public static synchronized Toolkit
  getDefaultToolkit()
public final synchronized Object
  getDesktopProperty(String propertyName)
public abstract String getFontList()
public abstract FontMetrics
  getFontMetrics(Font font)
protected abstract FontPeer getFontPeer(
  String name,int style)
public abstract Image getImage(String
  filename)
public abstract Image getImage(URL url)
public int getMaximumCursorColors()
public int getMenuShortcutKeyMask()
protected static Container
  getNativeContainer(Component c)
public abstract PrintJob getPrintJob(
  Frame frame,String jobtitle,Properties
  props)
public static String getProperty(String
  key,String defaultValue)
public abstract int getScreenResolution()
public abstract Dimension getScreenSize()
public abstract Clipboard
  getSystemClipboard()
public final EventQueue
  getSystemEventQueue()
protected abstract EventQueue
  getSystemEventQueueImpl()
protected void
  initializeDesktopProperties()
protected Object
  lazilyLoadDesktopProperty(String name)
protected void loadSystemColors(int
  systemColors)

public abstract boolean prepareImage(
    Image image,int width,int height,
    ImageObserver observer)
public void removeAWTEventListener(
    AWTEventListener listener)
public synchronized void
    removePropertyChangeListener(String name,
    PropertyChangeListener pcl)
protected final synchronized void
    setDesktopProperty(String name,Object
    newValue)
public abstract void sync()

►TOOLTIPMANAGER
public class javax.swing.ToolTipManager
implements java.awt.event.
    MouseMotionListener
extends java.awt.event.MouseAdapter
extends java.lang.Object

Fields
protected boolean
    heavyWeightPopupEnabled
protected boolean
    lightWeightPopupEnabled

Constructors
ToolTipManager()

Methods
public int getDismissDelay()
public int getInitialDelay()
public int getReshowDelay()
public boolean isEnabled()
public boolean isLightWeightPopupEnabled(
)
public void mouseDragged(MouseEvent
    event)
public void mouseEntered(MouseEvent
    event)
public void mouseExited(MouseEvent event)
public void mouseMoved(MouseEvent event)
public void mousePressed(MouseEvent
    event)
public void registerComponent(JComponent
    component)
public void setDismissDelay(int
    microSeconds)
public void setEnabled(boolean flag)
public void setInitialDelay(int
    microSeconds)
public void setLightWeightPopupEnabled(
    boolean aFlag)
public void setReshowDelay(int
    microSeconds)
public static ToolTipManager
    sharedInstance()
public void unregisterComponent(
    JComponent component)

►TOOLTIPUI
public abstract class javax.swing.plaf.
    ToolTipUI
extends javax.swing.plaf.ComponentUI
extends java.lang.Object

►TOOMANYLISTENERSEXCEPTION
public class java.util.
    TooManyListenersException
extends java.lang.Exception
extends java.lang.Throwable
extends java.lang.Object

Constructors
public TooManyListenersException()
public TooManyListenersException(String
    s)

►TRANSFORMATTRIBUTE
public final class java.awt.font.
    TransformAttribute
implements java.io.Serializable
extends java.lang.Object

Constructors
public TransformAttribute(
    AffineTransform transform)

Methods
public AffineTransform getTransform()

►TREEEXPANSIONEVENT
public class javax.swing.event.
    TreeExpansionEvent
extends java.util.EventObject
extends java.lang.Object

Fields
protected javax.swing.tree.TreePath
    path

Constructors
public TreeExpansionEvent(Object source,
    TreePath path)

Methods
public TreePath getPath()

►TREEMAP
public class java.util.TreeMap
implements java.lang.Cloneable
implements java.io.Serializable
implements java.util.SortedMap
extends java.util.AbstractMap
extends java.lang.Object

Constructors
public TreeMap()
public TreeMap(Comparator c)
public TreeMap(Map m)
public TreeMap(SortedMap m)

Methods
public void clear()
public Object clone()
public Comparator comparator()
public boolean containsKey(Object key)
public boolean containsValue(Object
    value)
public Set entrySet()
public Object firstKey()
public Object get(Object key)
public SortedMap headMap(Object toKey)
public Set keySet()
public Object lastKey()

```
public Object put(Object key,Object
   value)
public void putAll(Map map)
public Object remove(Object key)
public int size()
public SortedMap subMap(Object fromKey,
   Object toKey)
public SortedMap tailMap(Object fromKey)
public Collection values()
```

►TreeModelEvent

```
public class javax.swing.event.
   TreeModelEvent
extends java.util.EventObject
extends java.lang.Object
```

Fields
```
protected int childIndices
protected java.lang.Object children
protected javax.swing.tree.TreePath
   path
```

Constructors
```
public  TreeModelEvent(Object source,
   Object path,int childIndices,Object
   children)
public  TreeModelEvent(Object source,
   TreePath path,int childIndices,Object
   children)
public  TreeModelEvent(Object source,
   Object path)
public  TreeModelEvent(Object source,
   TreePath path)
```

Methods
```
public int getChildIndices()
public Object getChildren()
public Object getPath()
public TreePath getTreePath()
public String toString()
```

►TreePath

```
public class javax.swing.tree.TreePath
implements java.io.Serializable
extends java.lang.Object
extends java.lang.Object
```

Constructors
```
public  TreePath(Object path)
public  TreePath(Object singlePath)
protected  TreePath(TreePath parent,
   Object lastElement)
protected  TreePath(Object path,int
   length)
protected  TreePath()
```

Methods
```
public boolean equals(Object o)
public Object getLastPathComponent()
public TreePath getParentPath()
public Object getPath()
public Object getPathComponent(int
   element)
public int getPathCount()
public int hashCode()
public boolean isDescendant(TreePath
   aTreePath)
```

```
public TreePath pathByAddingChild(Object
   child)
public String toString()
```

►TreeSelectionEvent

```
public class javax.swing.event.
   TreeSelectionEvent
extends java.util.EventObject
extends java.lang.Object
```

Fields
```
protected boolean areNew
protected javax.swing.tree.TreePath
   newLeadSelectionPath
protected javax.swing.tree.TreePath
   oldLeadSelectionPath
protected javax.swing.tree.TreePath
   paths
```

Constructors
```
public  TreeSelectionEvent(Object source,
   TreePath paths,boolean areNew,TreePath
   oldLeadSelectionPath,TreePath
   newLeadSelectionPath)
public  TreeSelectionEvent(Object source,
   TreePath path,boolean isNew,TreePath
   oldLeadSelectionPath,TreePath
   newLeadSelectionPath)
```

Methods
```
public Object cloneWithSource(Object
   newSource)
public TreePath getNewLeadSelectionPath()
public TreePath getOldLeadSelectionPath()
public TreePath getPath()
public TreePath getPaths()
public boolean isAddedPath()
public boolean isAddedPath(TreePath path)
```

►TreeSet

```
public class java.util.TreeSet
implements java.lang.Cloneable
implements java.io.Serializable
implements java.util.SortedSet
extends java.util.AbstractSet
extends java.util.AbstractCollection
extends java.lang.Object
```

Constructors
```
private  TreeSet()
public  TreeSet()
public  TreeSet(Comparator c)
public  TreeSet(Collection c)
public  TreeSet(SortedSet s)
```

Methods
```
public boolean add(Object o)
public boolean addAll(Collection c)
public void clear()
public Object clone()
public Comparator comparator()
public boolean contains(Object o)
public Object first()
public SortedSet headSet(Object
   toElement)
public boolean isEmpty()
public Iterator iterator()
```

public Object last()
public boolean remove(Object o)
public int size()
public SortedSet subSet(Object
  fromElement,Object toElement)
public SortedSet tailSet(Object
  fromElement)

►TreeUI
public abstract class javax.swing.plaf.
  TreeUI
extends javax.swing.plaf.ComponentUI
extends java.lang.Object

Methods
public abstract void cancelEditing(JTree
  tree)
public abstract TreePath
  getClosestPathForLocation(JTree tree,int
  x,int y)
public abstract TreePath getEditingPath(
  JTree tree)
public abstract Rectangle getPathBounds(
  JTree tree,TreePath path)
public abstract TreePath getPathForRow(
  JTree tree,int row)
public abstract int getRowCount(JTree
  tree)
public abstract int getRowForPath(JTree
  tree,TreePath path)
public abstract boolean isEditing(JTree
  tree)
public abstract void startEditingAtPath(
  JTree tree,TreePath path)
public abstract boolean stopEditing(
  JTree tree)

►Types
public class java.sql.Types
extends java.lang.Object

Fields
public final static int ARRAY
public final static int BIGINT
public final static int BINARY
public final static int BIT
public final static int BLOB
public final static int CHAR
public final static int CLOB
public final static int DATE
public final static int DECIMAL
public final static int DISTINCT
public final static int DOUBLE
public final static int FLOAT
public final static int INTEGER
public final static int JAVA_OBJECT
public final static int LONGVARBINARY
public final static int LONGVARCHAR
public final static int NULL
public final static int NUMERIC
public final static int OTHER
public final static int REAL
public final static int REF
public final static int SMALLINT
public final static int STRUCT

public final static int TIME
public final static int TIMESTAMP
public final static int TINYINT
public final static int VARBINARY
public final static int VARCHAR

Constructors
private Types()

►UID
public final class java.rmi.server.UID
implements java.io.Serializable
extends java.lang.Object

Constructors
public UID()
public UID(short num)
private UID()

Methods
public boolean equals(Object obj)
public int hashCode()
public static UID read(DataInput in)
public String toString()
public void write(DataOutput out)

►UIDefaults
public class javax.swing.UIDefaults
extends java.util.Hashtable
extends java.util.Dictionary
extends java.lang.Object

Constructors
public UIDefaults()
public UIDefaults(Object keyValueList)

Methods
public synchronized void
  addPropertyChangeListener(
  PropertyChangeListener listener)
protected void firePropertyChange(String
  propertyName,Object oldValue,Object
  newValue)
public Object get(Object key)
public Border getBorder(Object key)
public Color getColor(Object key)
public Dimension getDimension(Object key)
public Font getFont(Object key)
public Icon getIcon(Object key)
public Insets getInsets(Object key)
public int getInt(Object key)
public String getString(Object key)
public ComponentUI getUI(JComponent
  target)
public Class getUIClass(String uiClassID,
  ClassLoader uiClassLoader)
public Class getUIClass(String uiClassID)
protected void getUIError(String msg)
public Object put(Object key,Object
  value)
public void putDefaults(Object
  keyValueList)
public synchronized void
  removePropertyChangeListener(
  PropertyChangeListener listener)

▶UIMANAGER
public class javax.swing.UIManager
implements java.io.Serializable
extends java.lang.Object
Methods
public static void
  addAuxiliaryLookAndFeel(LookAndFeel laf)
public static synchronized void
  addPropertyChangeListener(
  PropertyChangeListener listener)
public static Object get(Object key)
public static LookAndFeel
  getAuxiliaryLookAndFeels()
public static Border getBorder(Object
  key)
public static Color getColor(Object key)
public static String
  getCrossPlatformLookAndFeelClassName()
public static UIDefaults getDefaults()
public static Dimension getDimension(
  Object key)
public static Font getFont(Object key)
public static Icon getIcon(Object key)
public static Insets getInsets(Object
  key)
public static LookAndFeelInfo
  getInstalledLookAndFeels()
public static int getInt(Object key)
public static LookAndFeel getLookAndFeel(
)
public static UIDefaults
  getLookAndFeelDefaults()
public static String getString(Object
  key)
public static String
  getSystemLookAndFeelClassName()
public static ComponentUI getUI(
  JComponent target)
public static void installLookAndFeel(
  LookAndFeelInfo info)
public static void installLookAndFeel(
  String name,String className)
public static Object put(Object key,
  Object value)
public static boolean
  removeAuxiliaryLookAndFeel(LookAndFeel
  laf)
public static synchronized void
  removePropertyChangeListener(
  PropertyChangeListener listener)
public static void
  setInstalledLookAndFeels(LookAndFeelInfo
  infos)
public static void setLookAndFeel(
  LookAndFeel newLookAndFeel)
public static void setLookAndFeel(String
  className)

▶UNDOABLEEDITEVENT
public class javax.swing.event.
  UndoableEditEvent
extends java.util.EventObject

extends java.lang.Object
Constructors
public UndoableEditEvent(Object source,
  UndoableEdit edit)
Methods
public UndoableEdit getEdit()

▶UNDOABLEEDITSUPPORT
public class javax.swing.undo.
  UndoableEditSupport
extends java.lang.Object
Fields
protected javax.swing.undo.CompoundEdit
  compoundEdit
protected java.util.Vector listeners
protected java.lang.Object realSource
protected int updateLevel
Constructors
public UndoableEditSupport()
public UndoableEditSupport(Object r)
Methods
public synchronized void
  addUndoableEditListener(
  UndoableEditListener l)
public synchronized void beginUpdate()
protected CompoundEdit
  createCompoundEdit()
public synchronized void endUpdate()
public int getUpdateLevel()
public synchronized void postEdit(
  UndoableEdit e)
public synchronized void
  removeUndoableEditListener(
  UndoableEditListener l)
public String toString()
protected void _postEdit(UndoableEdit e)

▶UNDOMANAGER
public class javax.swing.undo.
  UndoManager
implements javax.swing.event.
  UndoableEditListener
extends javax.swing.undo.CompoundEdit
extends javax.swing.undo.
  AbstractUndoableEdit
extends java.lang.Object
Constructors
public UndoManager()
Methods
public synchronized boolean addEdit(
  UndoableEdit anEdit)
public synchronized boolean canRedo()
public synchronized boolean canUndo()
public synchronized boolean
  canUndoOrRedo()
public synchronized void discardAllEdits(
)
protected UndoableEdit editToBeRedone()
protected UndoableEdit editToBeUndone()
public synchronized void end()
public synchronized int getLimit()

```
public synchronized String
  getRedoPresentationName()
public synchronized String
  getUndoOrRedoPresentationName()
public synchronized String
  getUndoPresentationName()
public synchronized void redo()
protected void redoTo(UndoableEdit edit)
public synchronized void setLimit(int l)
public String toString()
protected void trimEdits(int from,int to)
protected void trimForLimit()
public synchronized void undo()
public void undoableEditHappened(
  UndoableEditEvent e)
public synchronized void undoOrRedo()
protected void undoTo(UndoableEdit edit)
```

▶**UNEXPECTEDEXCEPTION**
```
public class java.rmi.
  UnexpectedException
extends java.rmi.RemoteException
extends java.io.IOException
extends java.lang.Exception
extends java.lang.Throwable
extends java.lang.Object
```
Constructors
```
public  UnexpectedException(String s)
public  UnexpectedException(String s,
  Exception ex)
```

▶**UNICASTREMOTEOBJECT**
```
public class java.rmi.server.
  UnicastRemoteObject
extends java.rmi.server.RemoteServer
extends java.rmi.server.RemoteObject
extends java.lang.Object
```
Constructors
```
protected  UnicastRemoteObject()
protected  UnicastRemoteObject(int port)
protected  UnicastRemoteObject(int port,
  RMIClientSocketFactory csf,
  RMIServerSocketFactory ssf)
```
Methods
```
public Object clone()
public static RemoteStub exportObject(
  Remote obj)
public static Remote exportObject(Remote
  obj,int port)
public static Remote exportObject(Remote
  obj,int port,RMIClientSocketFactory csf,
  RMIServerSocketFactory ssf)
public static boolean unexportObject(
  Remote obj,boolean force)
```

▶**UNKNOWNERROR**
```
public class java.lang.UnknownError
extends java.lang.VirtualMachineError
extends java.lang.Error
extends java.lang.Throwable
extends java.lang.Object
```

Constructors
```
public  UnknownError()
public  UnknownError(String s)
```

▶**UNKNOWNGROUPEXCEPTION**
```
public class java.rmi.activation.
  UnknownGroupException
extends java.rmi.activation.
  ActivationException
extends java.lang.Exception
extends java.lang.Throwable
extends java.lang.Object
```
Constructors
```
public  UnknownGroupException(String s)
```

▶**UNKNOWNHOSTEXCEPTION**
```
public class java.net.
  UnknownHostException
extends java.io.IOException
extends java.lang.Exception
extends java.lang.Throwable
extends java.lang.Object
```
Constructors
```
public  UnknownHostException(String host)
public  UnknownHostException()
```

▶**UNKNOWNHOSTEXCEPTION**
```
public class java.rmi.
  UnknownHostException
extends java.rmi.RemoteException
extends java.io.IOException
extends java.lang.Exception
extends java.lang.Throwable
extends java.lang.Object
```
Constructors
```
public  UnknownHostException(String s)
public  UnknownHostException(String s,
  Exception ex)
```

▶**UNKNOWNOBJECTEXCEPTION**
```
public class java.rmi.activation.
  UnknownObjectException
extends java.rmi.activation.
  ActivationException
extends java.lang.Exception
extends java.lang.Throwable
extends java.lang.Object
```
Constructors
```
public  UnknownObjectException(String s)
```

▶**UNKNOWNSERVICEEXCEPTION**
```
public class java.net.
  UnknownServiceException
extends java.io.IOException
extends java.lang.Exception
extends java.lang.Throwable
extends java.lang.Object
```
Constructors
```
public  UnknownServiceException()
public  UnknownServiceException(String
  msg)
```

►UNMARSHALEXCEPTION
public class java.rmi.
  UnmarshalException
extends java.rmi.RemoteException
extends java.io.IOException
extends java.lang.Exception
extends java.lang.Throwable
extends java.lang.Object
Constructors
public UnmarshalException(String s)
public UnmarshalException(String s,
  Exception ex)

►UNRECOVERABLEKEYEXCEPTION
public class java.security.
  UnrecoverableKeyException
extends java.security.
  GeneralSecurityException
extends java.lang.Exception
extends java.lang.Throwable
extends java.lang.Object
Constructors
public UnrecoverableKeyException()
public UnrecoverableKeyException(String
  msg)

►UNRESOLVEDPERMISSION
public final class java.security.
  UnresolvedPermission
implements java.io.Serializable
extends java.security.Permission
extends java.lang.Object
Constructors
public UnresolvedPermission(String type,
  String name,String actions,Certificate
  certs)
Methods
public boolean equals(Object obj)
public String getActions()
public int hashCode()
public boolean implies(Permission p)
public PermissionCollection
  newPermissionCollection()
public String toString()

►UNSATISFIEDLINKERROR
public class java.lang.
  UnsatisfiedLinkError
extends java.lang.LinkageError
extends java.lang.Error
extends java.lang.Throwable
extends java.lang.Object
Constructors
public UnsatisfiedLinkError()
public UnsatisfiedLinkError(String s)

►UNSUPPORTEDCLASSVERSIONERROR
public class java.lang.
  UnsupportedClassVersionError
extends java.lang.ClassFormatError
extends java.lang.LinkageError
extends java.lang.Error

extends java.lang.Throwable
extends java.lang.Object
Constructors
public UnsupportedClassVersionError()
public UnsupportedClassVersionError(
  String s)

►UNSUPPORTEDENCODINGEXCEPTION
public class java.io.
  UnsupportedEncodingException
extends java.io.IOException
extends java.lang.Exception
extends java.lang.Throwable
extends java.lang.Object
Constructors
public UnsupportedEncodingException()
public UnsupportedEncodingException(
  String s)

►UNSUPPORTEDFLAVOREXCEPTION
public class java.awt.datatransfer.
  UnsupportedFlavorException
extends java.lang.Exception
extends java.lang.Throwable
extends java.lang.Object
Constructors
public UnsupportedFlavorException(
  DataFlavor flavor)

►UNSUPPORTEDLOOKANDFEELEXCEPTION
public class javax.swing.
  UnsupportedLookAndFeelException
extends java.lang.Exception
extends java.lang.Throwable
extends java.lang.Object
Constructors
public UnsupportedLookAndFeelException(
  String s)

►UNSUPPORTEDOPERATIONEXCEPTION
public class java.lang.
  UnsupportedOperationException
extends java.lang.RuntimeException
extends java.lang.Exception
extends java.lang.Throwable
extends java.lang.Object
Constructors
public UnsupportedOperationException()
public UnsupportedOperationException(
  String message)

►URL
public final class java.net.URL
implements java.io.Serializable
extends java.lang.Object
Constructors
public URL(String protocol,String host,
  int port,String file)
public URL(String protocol,String host,
  String file)

```
public  URL(String protocol,String host,
  int port,String file,URLStreamHandler
  handler)
public  URL(String spec)
public  URL(URL context,String spec)
public  URL(URL context,String spec,
  URLStreamHandler handler)
```

Methods

```
public boolean equals(Object obj)
public final Object getContent()
public String getFile()
public String getHost()
public int getPort()
public String getProtocol()
public String getRef()
public synchronized int hashCode()
public URLConnection openConnection()
public final InputStream openStream()
public boolean sameFile(URL other)
protected void set(String protocol,
  String host,int port,String file,String
  ref)
public static synchronized void
  setURLStreamHandlerFactory(
  URLStreamHandlerFactory fac)
public String toExternalForm()
public String toString()
```

►URLCLASSLOADER

```
public class java.net.URLClassLoader
extends java.security.SecureClassLoader
extends java.lang.ClassLoader
extends java.lang.Object
```

Constructors

```
public  URLClassLoader(URL urls,
  ClassLoader parent)
public  URLClassLoader(URL urls)
public  URLClassLoader(URL urls,
  ClassLoader parent,
  URLStreamHandlerFactory factory)
```

Methods

```
protected void addURL(URL url)
protected Package definePackage(String
  name,Manifest man,URL url)
protected Class findClass(String name)
public URL findResource(String name)
public Enumeration findResources(String
  name)
protected PermissionCollection
  getPermissions(CodeSource codesource)
public URL getURLs()
public static URLClassLoader newInstance(
  URL urls,ClassLoader parent)
public static URLClassLoader newInstance(
  URL urls)
```

►URLCONNECTION

```
public abstract class java.net.
  URLConnection
extends java.lang.Object
```

Fields

```
protected boolean allowUserInteraction
```

```
protected boolean connected
protected boolean doInput
protected boolean doOutput
protected long ifModifiedSince
protected java.net.URL url
protected boolean useCaches
```

Constructors

```
protected  URLConnection(URL url)
```

Methods

```
public abstract void connect()
public boolean getAllowUserInteraction()
public Object getContent()
public String getContentEncoding()
public int getContentLength()
public String getContentType()
public long getDate()
public static boolean
  getDefaultAllowUserInteraction()
public static String
  getDefaultRequestProperty(String key)
public boolean getDefaultUseCaches()
public boolean getDoInput()
public boolean getDoOutput()
public long getExpiration()
public static FileNameMap getFileNameMap(
  )
public String getHeaderField(String name)
public String getHeaderField(int n)
public long getHeaderFieldDate(String
  name,long Default)
public int getHeaderFieldInt(String name,
  int Default)
public String getHeaderFieldKey(int n)
public long getIfModifiedSince()
public InputStream getInputStream()
public long getLastModified()
public OutputStream getOutputStream()
public Permission getPermission()
public String getRequestProperty(String
  key)
public URL getURL()
public boolean getUseCaches()
protected static String
  guessContentTypeFromName(String fname)
public static String
  guessContentTypeFromStream(InputStream
  is)
public void setAllowUserInteraction(
  boolean allowuserinteraction)
public static synchronized void
  setContentHandlerFactory(
  ContentHandlerFactory fac)
public static void
  setDefaultAllowUserInteraction(boolean
  defaultallowuserinteraction)
public static void
  setDefaultRequestProperty(String key,
  String value)
public void setDefaultUseCaches(boolean
  defaultusecaches)
public void setDoInput(boolean doinput)
public void setDoOutput(boolean dooutput)
```

```
public static void setFileNameMap(
  FileNameMap map)
public void setIfModifiedSince(long
  ifmodifiedsince)
public void setRequestProperty(String
  key,String value)
public void setUseCaches(boolean
  usecaches)
public String toString()
```

►**URLDecoder**
```
public class java.net.URLDecoder
extends java.lang.Object
```
Methods
```
public static String decode(String s)
```

►**URLEncoder**
```
public class java.net.URLEncoder
extends java.lang.Object
```
Constructors
```
private static  URLEncoder()
```
Methods
```
public static String encode(String s)
```

►**URLStreamHandler**
```
public abstract class java.net.
  URLStreamHandler
extends java.lang.Object
```
Methods
```
protected abstract URLConnection
  openConnection(URL u)
protected void parseURL(URL u,String
  spec,int start,int limit)
protected void setURL(URL u,String
  protocol,String host,int port,String
  file,String ref)
protected String toExternalForm(URL u)
```

►**UTFDataFormatException**
```
public class java.io.
  UTFDataFormatException
extends java.io.IOException
extends java.lang.Exception
extends java.lang.Throwable
extends java.lang.Object
```
Constructors
```
public  UTFDataFormatException()
public  UTFDataFormatException(String s)
```

►**Utilities**
```
public class javax.swing.text.Utilities
extends java.lang.Object
```
Methods
```
public final static int drawTabbedText(
  Segment s,int x,int y,Graphics g,
  TabExpander e,int startOffset)
public final static int getBreakLocation(
  Segment s,FontMetrics metrics,int x0,int
  x,TabExpander e,int startOffset)
public final static int getNextWord(
  JTextComponent c,int offs)
```

```
public final static Element
  getParagraphElement(JTextComponent c,int
  offs)
public final static int getPositionAbove(
  JTextComponent c,int offs,int x)
public final static int getPositionBelow(
  JTextComponent c,int offs,int x)
public final static int getPreviousWord(
  JTextComponent c,int offs)
public final static int getRowEnd(
  JTextComponent c,int offs)
public final static int getRowStart(
  JTextComponent c,int offs)
public final static int\
  getTabbedTextOffset(Segment s,
  FontMetrics metrics,int x0,int x,
  TabExpander e,int startOffset)
public final static int
  getTabbedTextOffset(Segment s,
  FontMetrics metrics,int x0,int x,
  TabExpander e,int startOffset,boolean
  round)
public final static int
  getTabbedTextWidth(Segment s,FontMetrics
  metrics,int x,TabExpander e,int
  startOffset)
public final static int getWordEnd(
  JTextComponent c,int offs)
public final static int getWordStart(
  JTextComponent c,int offs)
```

►**VariableHeightLayoutCache**
```
public class javax.swing.tree.
  VariableHeightLayoutCache
extends javax.swing.tree.
  AbstractLayoutCache
extends java.lang.Object
```
Constructors
```
public  VariableHeightLayoutCache()
```
Methods
```
public Rectangle getBounds(TreePath path,
  Rectangle placeIn)
public boolean getExpandedState(TreePath
  path)
public TreePath getPathClosestTo(int x,
  int y)
public TreePath getPathForRow(int row)
public int getPreferredWidth(Rectangle
  bounds)
public int getRowCount()
public int getRowForPath(TreePath path)
public int getVisibleChildCount(TreePath
  path)
public Enumeration getVisiblePathsFrom(
  TreePath path)
public void invalidatePathBounds(
  TreePath path)
public void invalidateSizes()
public boolean isExpanded(TreePath path)
public void setExpandedState(TreePath
  path,boolean isExpanded)
public void setModel(TreeModel newModel)
```

```
public void setNodeDimensions(
  NodeDimensions nd)
public void setRootVisible(boolean
  rootVisible)
public void setRowHeight(int rowHeight)
public void treeNodesChanged(
  TreeModelEvent e)
public void treeNodesInserted(
  TreeModelEvent e)
public void treeNodesRemoved(
  TreeModelEvent e)
public void treeStructureChanged(
  TreeModelEvent e)
```

►Vector

```
public class java.util.Vector
implements java.lang.Cloneable
implements java.util.List
implements java.io.Serializable
extends java.util.AbstractList
extends java.util.AbstractCollection
extends java.lang.Object
```

Fields

```
protected int capacityIncrement
protected int elementCount
protected java.lang.Object elementData
```

Constructors

```
public  Vector(int initialCapacity,int
  capacityIncrement)
public  Vector(int initialCapacity)
public  Vector()
public  Vector(Collection c)
```

Methods

```
public synchronized boolean add(Object o)
public void add(int index,Object element)
public synchronized boolean addAll(
  Collection c)
public synchronized boolean addAll(int
  index,Collection c)
public synchronized void addElement(
  Object obj)
public int capacity()
public void clear()
public synchronized Object clone()
public boolean contains(Object elem)
public synchronized boolean containsAll(
  Collection c)
public synchronized void copyInto(Object
  anArray)
public synchronized Object elementAt(int
  index)
public Enumeration elements()
public synchronized void ensureCapacity(
  int minCapacity)
public synchronized boolean equals(
  Object o)
public synchronized Object firstElement()
public synchronized Object get(int index)
public synchronized int hashCode()
public int indexOf(Object elem)
public synchronized int indexOf(Object
  elem,int index)
```

```
public synchronized void insertElementAt(
  Object obj,int index)
public boolean isEmpty()
public synchronized Object lastElement()
public int lastIndexOf(Object elem)
public synchronized int lastIndexOf(
  Object elem,int index)
public boolean remove(Object o)
public synchronized Object remove(int
  index)
public synchronized boolean removeAll(
  Collection c)
public synchronized void
  removeAllElements()
public synchronized boolean
  removeElement(Object obj)
public synchronized void removeElementAt(
  int index)
protected void removeRange(int fromIndex,
  int toIndex)
public synchronized boolean retainAll(
  Collection c)
public synchronized Object set(int index,
  Object element)
public synchronized void setElementAt(
  Object obj,int index)
public synchronized void setSize(int
  newSize)
public int size()
public List subList(int fromIndex,int
  toIndex)
public synchronized Object toArray()
public synchronized Object toArray(
  Object a)
public synchronized String toString()
public synchronized void trimToSize()
```

►VerifyError

```
public class java.lang.VerifyError
extends java.lang.LinkageError
extends java.lang.Error
extends java.lang.Throwable
extends java.lang.Object
```

Constructors

```
public  VerifyError()
public  VerifyError(String s)
```

►VetoableChangeSupport

```
public class java.beans.
  VetoableChangeSupport
implements java.io.Serializable
extends java.lang.Object
```

Constructors

```
public  VetoableChangeSupport(Object
  sourceBean)
```

Methods

```
public synchronized void
  addVetoableChangeListener(
  VetoableChangeListener listener)
public synchronized void
  addVetoableChangeListener(String
```

propertyName,VetoableChangeListener
listener)
public void fireVetoableChange(String
propertyName,Object oldValue,Object
newValue)
public void fireVetoableChange(String
propertyName,int oldValue,int newValue)
public void fireVetoableChange(String
propertyName,boolean oldValue,boolean
newValue)
public void fireVetoableChange(
PropertyChangeEvent evt)
public synchronized boolean hasListeners(
String propertyName)
public synchronized void
removeVetoableChangeListener(
VetoableChangeListener listener)
public synchronized void
removeVetoableChangeListener(String
propertyName,VetoableChangeListener
listener)

►VIEW
public abstract class javax.swing.text.
View
implements javax.swing.SwingConstants
extends java.lang.Object
Fields
public final static int BadBreakWeight
public final static int
ExcellentBreakWeight
public final static int
ForcedBreakWeight
public final static int GoodBreakWeight
public final static int X_AXIS
public final static int Y_AXIS
Constructors
public View(Element elem)
Methods
public View breakView(int axis,int
offset,float pos,float len)
public void changedUpdate(DocumentEvent
e,Shape a,ViewFactory f)
public View createFragment(int p0,int p1)
public float getAlignment(int axis)
public AttributeSet getAttributes()
public int getBreakWeight(int axis,float
pos,float len)
public Shape getChildAllocation(int
index,Shape a)
public Container getContainer()
public Document getDocument()
public Element getElement()
public int getEndOffset()
public float getMaximumSpan(int axis)
public float getMinimumSpan(int axis)
public int getNextVisualPositionFrom(int
pos,Bias b,Shape a,int direction,Bias
biasRet)
public View getParent()
public abstract float getPreferredSpan(
int axis)

public int getResizeWeight(int axis)
public int getStartOffset()
public View getView(int n)
public int getViewCount()
public ViewFactory getViewFactory()
public void insertUpdate(DocumentEvent e,
Shape a,ViewFactory f)
public boolean isVisible()
public abstract Shape modelToView(int
pos,Shape a,Bias b)
public Shape modelToView(int p0,Bias b0,
int p1,Bias b1,Shape a)
public Shape modelToView(int pos,Shape a)
public abstract void paint(Graphics g,
Shape allocation)
public void preferenceChanged(View child,
boolean width,boolean height)
public void removeUpdate(DocumentEvent e,
Shape a,ViewFactory f)
public void setParent(View parent)
public void setSize(float width,float
height)
public abstract int viewToModel(float x,
float y,Shape a,Bias biasReturn)
public int viewToModel(float x,float y,
Shape a)

►VIEWPORTLAYOUT
public class javax.swing.ViewportLayout
implements java.awt.LayoutManager
implements java.io.Serializable
extends java.lang.Object
Methods
public void addLayoutComponent(String
name,Component c)
public void layoutContainer(Container
parent)
public Dimension minimumLayoutSize(
Container parent)
public Dimension preferredLayoutSize(
Container parent)
public void removeLayoutComponent(
Component c)

►VIEWPORTUI
public abstract class javax.swing.plaf.
ViewportUI
extends javax.swing.plaf.ComponentUI
extends java.lang.Object

►VIRTUALMACHINEERROR
public abstract class java.lang.
VirtualMachineError
extends java.lang.Error
extends java.lang.Throwable
extends java.lang.Object
Constructors
public VirtualMachineError()
public VirtualMachineError(String s)

►VMID
public final class java.rmi.dgc.VMID
implements java.io.Serializable

extends java.lang.Object
Constructors
public VMID()
Methods
public boolean equals(Object obj)
public int hashCode()
public static boolean isUnique()
public String toString()

▶**VOID**
public final class java.lang.Void
extends java.lang.Object
Fields
public final static java.lang.Class
  TYPE
Constructors
private Void()

▶**WEAKHASHMAP**
public class java.util.WeakHashMap
implements java.util.Map
extends java.util.AbstractMap
extends java.lang.Object
Constructors
public WeakHashMap(int initialCapacity,
  float loadFactor)
public WeakHashMap(int initialCapacity)
public WeakHashMap()
Methods
public void clear()
public boolean containsKey(Object key)
public Set entrySet()
public Object get(Object key)
public boolean isEmpty()
public Object put(Object key,Object
  value)
public Object remove(Object key)
public int size()

▶**WEAKREFERENCE**
public class java.lang.ref.
  WeakReference
extends java.lang.ref.Reference
extends java.lang.Object
Constructors
public WeakReference(Object referent)
public WeakReference(Object referent,
  ReferenceQueue q)

▶**WINDOW**
public class java.awt.Window
extends java.awt.Container
extends java.awt.Component
extends java.lang.Object
Constructors
Window()
public Window(Frame owner)
public Window(Window owner)
Methods
public void addNotify()

public synchronized void
  addWindowListener(WindowListener 1)
public void applyResourceBundle(
  ResourceBundle rb)
public void applyResourceBundle(String
  rbName)
public void dispose()
protected void finalize()
public Component getFocusOwner()
public InputContext getInputContext()
public Locale getLocale()
public Window getOwnedWindows()
public Window getOwner()
public Toolkit getToolkit()
public final String getWarningString()
public boolean isShowing()
public void pack()
public boolean postEvent(Event e)
protected void processEvent(AWTEvent e)
protected void processWindowEvent(
  WindowEvent e)
public synchronized void
  removeWindowListener(WindowListener 1)
public void show()
public void toBack()
public void toFront()

▶**WINDOWADAPTER**
public abstract class java.awt.event.
  WindowAdapter
implements java.awt.event.
  WindowListener
extends java.lang.Object
Methods
public void windowActivated(WindowEvent
  e)
public void windowClosed(WindowEvent e)
public void windowClosing(WindowEvent e)
public void windowDeactivated(
  WindowEvent e)
public void windowDeiconified(
  WindowEvent e)
public void windowIconified(WindowEvent
  e)
public void windowOpened(WindowEvent e)

▶**WINDOWEVENT**
public class java.awt.event.WindowEvent
extends java.awt.event.ComponentEvent
extends java.awt.AWTEvent
extends java.util.EventObject
extends java.lang.Object
Fields
public final static int WINDOW_
  ACTIVATED
public final static int WINDOW_CLOSED
public final static int WINDOW_CLOSING
public final static int WINDOW_
  DEACTIVATED
public final static int WINDOW_
  DEICONIFIED
public final static int WINDOW_FIRST

```
public final static int WINDOW_
  ICONIFIED
public final static int WINDOW_LAST
public final static int WINDOW_OPENED
```
Constructors
```
public WindowEvent(Window source,int id)
```
Methods
```
public Window getWindow()
public String paramString()
```

▸**WRAPPEDPLAINVIEW**
```
public class javax.swing.text.
  WrappedPlainView
implements javax.swing.text.TabExpander
extends javax.swing.text.BoxView
extends javax.swing.text.CompositeView
extends javax.swing.text.View
extends java.lang.Object
```
Constructors
```
public WrappedPlainView(Element elem)
public WrappedPlainView(Element elem,
  boolean wordWrap)
```
Methods
```
protected int calculateBreakPosition(int
  p0,int p1)
public void changedUpdate(DocumentEvent
  e,Shape a,ViewFactory f)
protected void drawLine(int p0,int p1,
  Graphics g,int x,int y)
protected int drawSelectedText(Graphics
  g,int x,int y,int p0,int p1)
protected int drawUnselectedText(
  Graphics g,int x,int y,int p0,int p1)
protected final Segment getLineBuffer()
public float getMaximumSpan(int axis)
public float getMinimumSpan(int axis)
public float getPreferredSpan(int axis)
protected int getTabSize()
public void insertUpdate(DocumentEvent e,
  Shape a,ViewFactory f)
protected void loadChildren(ViewFactory
  f)
public float nextTabStop(float x,int
  tabOffset)
public void paint(Graphics g,Shape a)
public void removeUpdate(DocumentEvent e,
  Shape a,ViewFactory f)
public void setSize(float width,float
  height)
```

▸**WRITABLERASTER**
```
public class java.awt.image.
  WritableRaster
extends java.awt.image.Raster
extends java.lang.Object
```
Constructors
```
protected WritableRaster(SampleModel
  sampleModel,Point origin)
protected WritableRaster(SampleModel
  sampleModel,DataBuffer dataBuffer,Point
  origin)
```

```
protected WritableRaster(SampleModel
  sampleModel,DataBuffer dataBuffer,
  Rectangle aRegion,Point
  sampleModelTranslate,WritableRaster
  parent)
```
Methods
```
public WritableRaster
  createWritableChild(int parentX,int
  parentY,int w,int h,int childMinX,int
  childMinY,int bandList)
public WritableRaster
  createWritableTranslatedChild(int
  childMinX,int childMinY)
public WritableRaster getWritableParent()
public void setDataElements(int x,int y,
  Object inData)
public void setDataElements(int x,int y,
  Raster inRaster)
public void setDataElements(int x,int y,
  int w,int h,Object inData)
public void setPixel(int x,int y,int
  iArray)
public void setPixel(int x,int y,float
  fArray)
public void setPixel(int x,int y,double
  dArray)
public void setPixels(int x,int y,int w,
  int h,int iArray)
public void setPixels(int x,int y,int w,
  int h,float fArray)
public void setPixels(int x,int y,int w,
  int h,double dArray)
public void setRect(Raster srcRaster)
public void setRect(int dx,int dy,Raster
  srcRaster)
public void setSample(int x,int y,int b,
  int s)
public void setSample(int x,int y,int b,
  float s)
public void setSample(int x,int y,int b,
  double s)
public void setSamples(int x,int y,int w,
  int h,int b,int iArray)
public void setSamples(int x,int y,int w,
  int h,int b,float fArray)
public void setSamples(int x,int y,int w,
  int h,int b,double dArray)
```

▸**WRITEABORTEDEXCEPTION**
```
public class java.io.
  WriteAbortedException
extends java.io.ObjectStreamException
extends java.io.IOException
extends java.lang.Exception
extends java.lang.Throwable
extends java.lang.Object
```
Fields
```
public java.lang.Exception detail
```
Constructors
```
public WriteAbortedException(String s,
  Exception ex)
```

Methods
```
public String getMessage()
```

▶**WRITER**
```
public abstract class java.io.Writer
extends java.lang.Object
```
Fields
```
protected java.lang.Object lock
```
Constructors
```
protected  Writer()
protected  Writer(Object lock)
```
Methods
```
public abstract void close()
public abstract void flush()
public void write(int c)
public void write(char cbuf)
public abstract void write(char cbuf,int
  off,int len)
public void write(String str)
public void write(String str,int off,int
  len)
```

▶**X509CERTIFICATE**
```
public abstract class java.security.cert.
  X509Certificate
implements java.security.cert.
  X509Extension
extends java.security.cert.Certificate
extends java.lang.Object
```
Constructors
```
protected  X509Certificate()
```
Methods
```
public abstract void checkValidity()
public abstract void checkValidity(Date
  date)
public abstract int getBasicConstraints()
public abstract Principal getIssuerDN()
public abstract boolean
  getIssuerUniqueID()
public abstract boolean getKeyUsage()
public abstract Date getNotAfter()
public abstract Date getNotBefore()
public abstract BigInteger
  getSerialNumber()
public abstract String getSigAlgName()
public abstract String getSigAlgOID()
public abstract byte getSigAlgParams()
public abstract byte getSignature()
public abstract Principal getSubjectDN()
public abstract boolean
  getSubjectUniqueID()
public abstract byte getTBSCertificate()
public abstract int getVersion()
```

▶**X509CRL**
```
public abstract class java.security.cert.
  X509CRL
implements java.security.cert.
  X509Extension
extends java.security.cert.CRL
extends java.lang.Object
```

Constructors
```
protected  X509CRL()
```
Methods
```
public boolean equals(Object other)
public abstract byte getEncoded()
public abstract Principal getIssuerDN()
public abstract Date getNextUpdate()
public abstract X509CRLEntry
  getRevokedCertificate(BigInteger
  serialNumber)
public abstract Set
  getRevokedCertificates()
public abstract String getSigAlgName()
public abstract String getSigAlgOID()
public abstract byte getSigAlgParams()
public abstract byte getSignature()
public abstract byte getTBSCertList()
public abstract Date getThisUpdate()
public abstract int getVersion()
public int hashCode()
public abstract void verify(PublicKey
  key)
public abstract void verify(PublicKey
  key,String sigProvider)
```

▶**X509CRLENTRY**
```
public abstract class java.security.cert.
  X509CRLEntry
implements java.security.cert.
  X509Extension
extends java.lang.Object
```
Methods
```
public boolean equals(Object other)
public abstract byte getEncoded()
public abstract Date getRevocationDate()
public abstract BigInteger
  getSerialNumber()
public abstract boolean hasExtensions()
public int hashCode()
public abstract String toString()
```

▶**X509ENCODEDKEYSPEC**
```
public class java.security.spec.
  X509EncodedKeySpec
extends java.security.spec.
  EncodedKeySpec
extends java.lang.Object
```
Constructors
```
public  X509EncodedKeySpec(byte
  encodedKey)
```
Methods
```
public byte getEncoded()
public final String getFormat()
```

▶**ZIPENTRY**
```
public class java.util.zip.ZipEntry
implements java.lang.Cloneable
implements java.util.zip.ZipConstants
extends java.lang.Object
```
Fields
```
public final static int DEFLATED
public final static int STORED
```

Constructors
```
public  ZipEntry(String name)
public  ZipEntry(ZipEntry e)
 ZipEntry()
 ZipEntry()
```
Methods
```
public Object clone()
public String getComment()
public long getCompressedSize()
public long getCrc()
public byte getExtra()
public int getMethod()
public String getName()
public long getSize()
public long getTime()
public int hashCode()
public boolean isDirectory()
public void setComment(String comment)
public void setCompressedSize(long csize)
public void setCrc(long crc)
public void setExtra(byte extra)
public void setMethod(int method)
public void setSize(long size)
public void setTime(long time)
public String toString()
```

▶ZipException
```
public class java.util.zip.ZipException
extends java.io.IOException
extends java.lang.Exception
extends java.lang.Throwable
extends java.lang.Object
```
Constructors
```
public  ZipException()
public  ZipException(String s)
```

▶ZipFile
```
public class java.util.zip.ZipFile
implements java.util.zip.ZipConstants
extends java.lang.Object
```
Constructors
```
public  ZipFile(String name)
public  ZipFile(File file)
```
Methods
```
public void close()
public Enumeration entries()
public ZipEntry getEntry(String name)
public InputStream getInputStream(
  ZipEntry entry)
public String getName()
public int size()
```

▶ZipInputStream
```
public class java.util.zip.
  ZipInputStream
implements java.util.zip.ZipConstants
extends java.util.zip.
  InflaterInputStream
extends java.io.FilterInputStream
extends java.io.InputStream
extends java.lang.Object
```

Constructors
```
public  ZipInputStream(InputStream in)
```
Methods
```
public int available()
public void close()
public void closeEntry()
protected ZipEntry createZipEntry(String
  name)
public ZipEntry getNextEntry()
public int read(byte b,int off,int len)
public long skip(long n)
```

▶ZipOutputStream
```
public class java.util.zip.
  ZipOutputStream
implements java.util.zip.ZipConstants
extends java.util.zip.
  DeflaterOutputStream
extends java.io.FilterOutputStream
extends java.io.OutputStream
extends java.lang.Object
```
Fields
```
public final static int DEFLATED
public final static int STORED
```
Constructors
```
public  ZipOutputStream(OutputStream out)
```
Methods
```
public void close()
public void closeEntry()
public void finish()
public void putNextEntry(ZipEntry e)
public void setComment(String comment)
public void setLevel(int level)
public void setMethod(int method)
public synchronized void write(byte b,
  int off,int len)
```

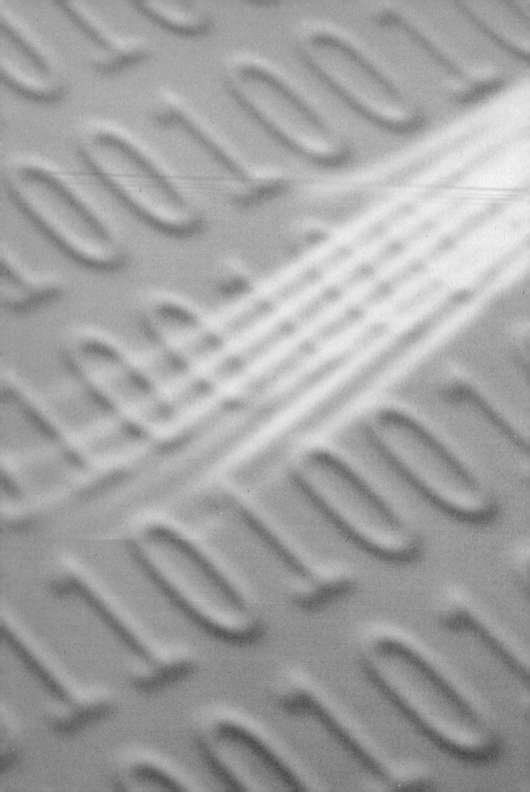

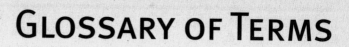

GLOSSARY OF TERMS

A

abstract   Retaining the essential features of some thing, process, or structure. The opposite of concrete.

abstract class   A class that contains abstract methods. Abstract classes cannot be instantiated.

abstract method   A method that is declared but not implemented. Abstract methods are used to ensure that subclasses implement the method.

Abstract Window Toolkit (AWT)   The collection of Java classes that allows you to implement platform-independent (hence *abstract*) GUIs.

ActiveX   A set of technologies that uses controls (formerly known as OCXs and VBXs) based on the Component Object Model (COM). COM is used throughout Microsoft's desktop applications for communication and automation. Integrating a Web browser with ActiveX controls extends the Microsoft desktop across the Internet.

adapter class   A class that implements all the methods of an interface. You then subclass the adapter class and only override the necessary methods from the original interface. Adapter classes are frequently used when listening for events.

additive colors   The set of primary colors (red, green, and blue) from which all other colors can be created by mixing.

API   See *Application Programming Interface.*

applet   A Java program that appears to be embedded in a Web document.

appletviewer   A JDK utility that displays only Java applets from HTML documents; as opposed to a Web browser, which shows applets embedded in Web documents.

Application Programming Interface (API)   A set of methods, functions, classes, and libraries provided by a language or operating system to help application developers write applications without needing to reinvent low-level functions. All of the standard Java packages combined form the Java Core API.

argument   A parameter passed to a method.

array   A group of variables of the same type that can be referenced by a common name. An array is an object with length as its public data member holding the size of the array. It can be initialized by a list of comma-separated expressions surrounded by curly braces.

atomic   Indivisible or uninterruptible. In the context of multithreading, it is an operation (statement, code block, or even an entire method) that cannot be interrupted. Code that accesses composite data structures shared with other threads usually must protect its critical sections by making them atomic.

autocommit A method to turn off and on transaction processing. When autocommit is off, transactions can be undone using the `rollback()` method, or the database can be updated using the `commit()` method. When autocommit is on, transactions are automatically committed after each statement.

AWT See *Abstract Window Toolkit.*

B

base class The superclass from which each class in a set of classes inherits members.

baseline The imaginary line on which text is drawn.

BDK See *Beans Development Kit.*

bean A reusable software component created with a specific naming convention to define the properties and events it understands. It can be manipulated visually within a builder tool.

BeanInfo A bean support class that defines information about the bean with the same base name.

Beans Development Kit (BDK) A Sun tool that helps Java developers create reusable components (Beans) through the inclusion of introductory documentation, a tutorial, sample Beans, and a test container.

big-endian An internal ordering of data bytes in memory. Big-endian ordering is also called *network ordering.* In the big-endian ordering, high bytes of a word are stored first in memory. RISC and Motorola processors use the big-endian byte ordering; Intel *x*86 processors use the little-endian byte ordering.

black box The concept of a functional entity whose internals are wholly irrelevant. A black box is characterized by the type of inputs it takes, the type of outputs produced, and the circumstances under which these outputs are generated (that is, the black box function).

blitting To BLIT (Block Image Transfer). In graphical systems, the high-speed, rectangular copy operations often performed by dedicated accelerator hardware. Moving a window, scrolling a window's contents, and rendering text are examples of operations that rely heavily on blitting.

block A section of source code beginning with a {, ending with a }, and containing statements in between.

boolean A variable that can assume only the values `true` or `false`. Booleans can be used to represent things that have a binary state, such as alive/dead, connected/disconnected, same/not the same, open/closed, and so on.

break statement   One of the flow-breaking statements. Without a label, control will be transferred to the statement just after the inner-most enclosing loop or `switch` statement. With a label, control will be transferred to the enclosing statement or block of statements carrying the same label.

buffer   In the narrow sense, an amount of storage set aside to temporarily hold and/or accumulate some information, such as write and read disk buffers and frame buffers. In the wider sense, any decoupling system that desynchronizes two entities; that is, a system that lets the entities run at their own speeds or frequencies.

bytecode verifier   Part of Java's security precautions, the bytecode verifier checks that the bytecodes can be executed safely by the Java Virtual Machine (VM).

bytecodes   Compiled Java code. Bytecodes are portable instructions that can be executed by any Java Virtual Machine (VM).

C

Call Level Interface (CLI)   An interface to perform SQL calls to databases. A CLI consists of method calls to the database that return values and result sets. The SQL statement is embedded in the calls. For example, the call `execute` takes the SQL string as a string parameter.

case clause   A part of a `switch` statement. The clause consists of the `case` keyword, followed by a constant expression, a colon, and one or more statements. See also *switch statement*.

casting   Explicitly coercing a value from one datatype to another.

CGI   See *Common Gateway Interface*.

class   A description of a specific kind of Java object, including the instructions that are particular to it.

class file   A binary file containing Java bytecodes. The Java compiler generates a class file from source code for each Java class.

class library   A collection of pre-fabricated classes that the programmer can use to build applications more rapidly. Java's class library is the Core API. In Java, these are also called *packages*.

class loader   The part of the Java Virtual Machine (VM) that fetches classes from the client file system or from across the network.

class variable   A variable within a class that is available for use by the class itself. Only one copy of the variable exists, and the class variable is unique to all instances of the class within the program.

CLI   See *Call Level Interface*.

client   An entity that relies on another (*server*) entity to accomplish some goal. Clients can be as simple as classes calling on other classes or (more frequently) client programs calling on server programs across a network.

client/server application model An application model commonly employed in networked environments. The monolithic application program is split into two halves; one half running on the server machine, the other running on the client machines. The client/server model is used as a solution in multiuser systems where central resources must be shared/changed/consulted by many.

Common Gateway Interface (CGI) A standard interface between Web servers and other server programs. The server programs are usually used to process database requests and generate HTML documents on the fly.

Common Object Request Broker Architecture (CORBA) An Object Management Group (OMG) standard that defines an Interface Definition Language (IDL) that is vendor- and language-neutral. The IDL is used to create a contract between a client and server implementation.

compiler A utility that reads the commands in a source file, interprets each command, and creates a new file containing equivalent byte-codes (or in the case of a C compiler, creates a file with native machine code instructions).

concrete Opposite of *abstract*.

conditional statement A statement for selective execution of program segments, such as the `if` and `switch` statements.

constructor A method that creates an instance of the class to which it belongs.

continue statement One of the flow-breaking statements. Without a label, control will be transferred to the point immediately after the last statement in the enclosing loop body. With a label, control will be transferred to the end of the enclosing loop body carrying the same label.

convolve filter A type of image-processing filter that combines the pixels located around a central pixel to form the new central pixel. Different weights are assigned to each neighbor in a 3 x 3 matrix. The resulting pixel is the weighted average of all pixels.

CORBA See *Common Object Request Broker Architecture*.

critical section In the context of multithreaded systems, any section of code that needs to take precautions to avoid corrupting data structures shared with other threads. When implemented correctly, only one thread will be inside a critical section of code at any given point in time.

D

daisy chaining The concept of building on a simpler I/O class with something that offers more capabilities.

data hiding The ability to hide data within a class. Any changes to the hidden data from outside the class, if permitted at all, must be via methods.

datatype The specific type of data stored in variables; for example, `int` variables hold whole numbers, `char` variables hold individual alphanumeric characters, and `String` variables hold groups of alphanumeric characters.

debugger A utility that can monitor and suspend the execution of a program so that the state of the running program can be examined.

decoupling The avoidance of a direct link between two entities by inserting a third entity (an interface, a buffer, or a whole subsystem). Decoupling introduces an extra level of flexibility for the price of a slight reduction in performance. A hallmark of a well-designed software system is the loose coupling between its subsystems (achieved by a multitude of decoupling techniques).

default clause An optional part of a `switch` statement. It consists of the `default` keyword, followed by a colon, and one or more statements. See also *switch statement*.

default constructor A constructor that is automatically available to a class that does not define its own constructor.

deprecated methods Methods that were supported in previous releases of the Java Development Kit (JDK) but are not the preferred ones in the current release. Future releases may drop the methods altogether.

design pattern A reusable, standard approach to a design problem. This is different from algorithms in that design patterns address higher-level issues and usually describe solutions in structural/relationship terms.

destructor A method that is called to delete an object from memory. Java does not support destructors directly.

dial-up connection An Internet connection that is established by a leaf machine dialing a modem connected to a host that is connected to the Internet 24 hours a day.

disassembler A utility that displays the meaning of instructions in a compiled file. The Java disassembler (`javap`) shows what the Java Virtual Machine (VM) will do when it runs a class file of bytecodes.

DLL See *dynamic link library*.

DNS See *Domain Name System*.

do statements One of the loop statements. The loop body is executed once, and then the conditional expression is evaluated. If it evaluates to `true`, the loop body is re-executed and the conditional expression is retested. It will be repeated until the conditional expression evaluates to `false`.

documentation comment A comment block that will be used by `javadoc` to create documentation.

Domain Name System (DNS) A distributed Internet database that can resolve textual Internet addresses to their real numeric forms. The DNS is organized as a hierarchy with each node responsible for a subset of the Internet host address namespace (hence distributed database).

double buffering In general, the use of two buffers to allow one buffer to be constructed while the other is being used. Double buffering is used in animation to display one animation frame while the next is being drawn off-screen. Double buffering can also be used in the context of I/O logic to decouple the algorithm's performance from the performance limits of the I/O device (referred to as being *I/O-bound*).

dynamic link library (DLL) An executable library module, usually in binary form as an external file, that will be loaded during the run time of a program on an as-needed basis.

E

ECMAScript See *JavaScript*.

else clause An optional clause for an `if` statement. If the conditional expression of an `if` statement is evaluated to `false`, the statement or block of statements of the `else` clause will be executed.

encapsulation Embedding both data and code into a single entity.

event A system-generated object for when something interesting happens. Java components serve as sources for events such as key presses, mouse clicks, or changes to bean properties.

event-driven programming Programming in response to external events, like key presses, mouse clicks, and timer tick, typically as a result of user input.

exception An abnormal condition that disrupts normal program flow.

expression A combination of terms that evaluates to a single data value.

extend See *subclass*.

F

factory A design pattern for creating instances of a class without using a constructor.

File Transfer Protocol (FTP) The Internet protocol that allows users to download publicly accessible files from any Internet machine that accepts FTP connections. FTP also allows users to transfer files from their machine to another machine on the Internet.

final   A modifier that indicates a class, method, or variable is not changeable.

finalizer   A method that is called immediately before a class is garbage-collected.

flow-breaking statement   A statement for breaking the flow of execution. These include `break`, `continue`, and `return` statements.

flow-control statement   A statement for flow control. These include conditional, loop, and flow-breaking statements.

flushing   Final writing of any output data left in a write buffer. Closing files and streams flush their data buffers automatically (this is one of the reasons to close files and streams).

for statements   One of the loop statements. The initialization part is executed, followed by the evaluation of the conditional expression. If the expression evaluates to `true`, the loop body is executed, followed by the execution of the increment part. This cycle is repeated if the conditional expression evaluates to `true`.

fractal   In graphics, a recursively self-similar structure of infinite complexity. Contradictory to their definition, fractals can often be generated by very simple, finite equations or algorithms.

frame   In the context of GUIs, the graphical outline of a window. In the context of data communications, another word for *packet*.

frame header   The collection of fields at the start of a frame (packet) that contain nonuser data necessary for the fluent and efficient operation of the protocol. A typical frame header field is the checksum field that allows a receiver to check whether received data arrived as sent.

frame rate   Frequency at which new images are displayed in animation sequences or film. Typical rates range from 24Hz to 60Hz. Rates are measured in frames per second (fps).

framework   A reusable pattern for creating common classes of applications.

friendly   Used to describe the default access protection when missing any of the access keywords of `private`, `protected`, or `public`.

FTP   See *File Transfer Protocol*.

G

garbage collection   A feature of automatic memory management that discards unused blocks of memory, freeing the memory for new storage.

GIF See *Graphics Interchange Format.*

graphical user interface (GUI)
The mouse-driven, iconic interface to modern computer operating systems. Also called *windows, icons, menus, and pointer (WIMP)* interface.

Graphics Interchange Format (GIF) A standard format for storing compressed images.

GUI See *graphical user interface.*

H

hashtable A list-storing mechanism that uses key-value pairs; also a class in the `java.util` package.

HCI See *human-computer interface.*

HTML See *Hypertext Markup Language.*

HTTP See *Hypertext Transfer Protocol.*

human-computer interface (HCI) A broad concept comprising the physical and nonphysical interaction between people and computers. Ergonomics is a physical facet of HCI. Graphical user interface (GUI) design is a (mainly) nonphysical aspect of HCI.

Hypertext Markup Language (HTML) The language in which Web documents are written. Java applets appear embedded in HTML documents.

Hypertext Transfer Protocol (HTTP) The application protocol used by the World Wide Web for requesting, transmitting, and receiving Web documents.

I

IAB See *Internet Architecture Board.*

IDDE See *Integrated Development and Debugging Environment.*

IDE See *Integrated Development Environment.*

identifier A name the programmer gives to a class, variable, or method. Identifiers have restrictions on leading characters.

IDL See *Interface Definition Language.*

if statement One of the two types of conditional statements. It consists of the `if` keyword, followed by a conditional expression enclosed in a pair of parentheses, and a statement (or block of statements) to be executed when the conditional expression evaluates to `true`. It may be followed by an optional `else` clause consisting of the `else` keyword and a statement (or block of statements) to be executed when the conditional expression evaluates to `false`.

image filtering   The process of altering (generally improving) a digital image. This can be as simple as changing a picture's overall brightness or as complicated as applying an optical correction to minimize a flaw in the physical optics of the device that made the picture (as was done with the Hubble telescope, for instance).

inheritance   The ability to write a class that extends the definition of a superclass. The new class inherits the member variables and member functions (or methods) of this superclass. The new class may override the behavior it is inheriting.

inner classes   Classes that are defined within other classes, much in the way methods are defined within those classes. Inner classes have the same scope and access as other variables and methods defined within the same class. Their existence is hidden from view behind the enclosing class.

instance   An instance of a class; in other words, an object.

instance variable   A variable within a class; a new copy of which is available for storage in each instance of that class. Each object of that class has its own copy of the instance variable (as opposed to a class variable).

instantiation   The process of creating an object instance of a class.

Integrated Development and Debugging Environment (IDDE)   The same as an Integrated Development Environment (IDE), but with built-in debugging features; IDDE programs include Sun's Java WorkShop and Symantec's Café.

Integrated Development Environment (IDE)   A program that aids in application development by providing a graphical environment that combines all the tools required to write code.

interface   A formal set of method and constant declarations that must be defined by the classes that implement it.

Interface Definition Language (IDL)   A system that enables Java programs to communicate with CORBA (Common Object Request Broker Architecture) systems.

Internet Architecture Board (IAB)   One of the Internet standards bodies that applies the final technical review to any new proposed Internet standard (in the form of Request for Comments, or RFCs).

Internet Protocol (IP)   The core Internet protocol on which all other application-level Internet protocols build. Some of the counterintuitive characteristics of IP are that it does not guarantee delivery of data and that it can only transfer data in maximum 64KB chunks.

Internet Service Provider (ISP)
An organization (commercial or not) that allows users to hook up their machine to the Internet via a permanent or dial-up connection.

interpreter A utility that reads the commands in a file, then interprets and executes each command one at a time.

introspection A mechanism that allows classes to publish the operations and properties they support and a mechanism to support the discovery of such mechanisms.

IP See *Internet Protocol.*

ISP See *Internet Service Provider.*

J

Java Archive (JAR) file Like a tar or zip file, a file that holds an aggregate of files. These may be signed by their creator to permit greater access to the user.

Java Core API Java's class library. It contains core language features and methods for tasks such as networking, I/O, and graphics.

Java Database Connectivity (JDBC) Defines a set of Java classes and methods to interface with databases.

Java Developers Kit (JDK) The set of Java development tools distributed (for free) by Sun Microsystems. The JDK consists mainly of

the Core API classes (including their source), a Java compiler (written in Java), and the Java Virtual Machine (VM) interpreter.

Java Electronic Commerce Framework (JECF) A standard that provides support for Java applet-based shopping and other financial transactions.

Java Naming and Directory Interface (JNDI) A Java API that provides naming and directory functionality.

Java Server A full-featured Web server program that can be extended via plug-in servlets.

Java Virtual Machine (VM) The system that loads, verifies, and executes Java bytecodes.

JavaBeans API An API for the creation of reusable components. Through bridges, these Java objects can link with objects created in other languages, including ActiveX, OpenDoc, and several other industry standards. A Java "Bean" is a single reusable software component.

JavaOS An operating system written mostly in the Java language, which incorporates the Java Virtual Machine (VM) and classes.

JavaScript A separate programming language loosely related to Java. JavaScript can be coded directly in an HTML document, which makes the JavaScript source code part of the document itself.

The standardized form of Java-Script is called ECMAScript.

JavaStation The Network Computer developed by Sun Microsystems, which uses JavaOS (the Java operating system).

JDBC See *Java Database Connectivity.*

JDK See *Java Developers Kit.*

JECF See *Java Electronic Commerce Framework.*

Jeeves Early code name for a complete Web server written in Java. See *Java Server.*

JIT compiler See *Just-in-Time (JIT) compiler.*

JNDI See *Java Naming and Directory Interface.*

JPEG (Joint Photography Engineering Group) file A compressed graphics file format. JPEG images may be compressed in a "lossy" fashion that sacrifices image detail for smaller image size, or in a "lossless" method, where information about the image is retained, but the file size increases accordingly.

Just-in-Time (JIT) compiler A compiler that converts verified byte-codes to native processor instructions before execution and can significantly improve Java application performance.

K

keyword A word that has a special meaning for the Java compiler, such as a datatype name or a program construct name.

L

LayoutManager A Java class that handles preprogrammed layout styles for the graphical user interface (GUI) components.

life-cycle methods Applet methods, such as `init()`, that you do not call directly; the browser calls them for you.

literal An actual value such as "35" or `"Hello"`, as opposed to an identifier, which is a symbol for a value.

little-endian An internal ordering of data bytes in memory. In the little-endian ordering, low bytes of the word are stored first in memory. In the big-endian ordering, high bytes of a word are stored first in memory. RISC and Motorola processors use the big-endian byte ordering; Intel *x*86 processors use the little-endian byte ordering.

loop statement A statement for the repeated execution of program segments. These include `for`, `while`, and do statements.

M

marshaling   The process of assembling and disassembling parameters to and from remote objects and methods is collectively called marshaling and unmarshaling the parameters.

member   The generic term for data or code entities within a class.

member function   See *method*.

member variable   A variable that is part of a class.

message   A method call.

method   A function or routine that is part of a class. Also called a *member function*.

microJava   A medium-end Sun microchip that runs Java natively.

MIME format   See *Multipurpose Internet Mail Extension* format.

modifier   Alters aspect of access to classes, methods, and variables.

multidimensional array   An array of arrays. It can be nonrectangular. A multidimensional array can be initialized by grouping comma-separated expressions with nested curly braces.

multiple inheritance   The ability to write a class that inherits the member variables and methods (member functions) of more than one class. See also *inheritance*.

Multipurpose Internet Mail Extension (MIME) format
An extension of the standard Internet e-mail format to allow the inclusion (as file attachments) of content other than plain text. It is typically used for the newer multimedia types like audio/video clips, but it is generally capable of handling any binary file format.

multithreading   The means to concurrently perform multiple tasks independently of each other.

N

namespace   A set of rules allowing the generation of valid names or labels. For example, the e-mail address syntax, US state number license plate format, and global telephone numbering systems define namespaces. Namespace also means the boundaries that can be accessed by a program. The operating system (or the Java Virtual Machine) defines the namespace for a program.

namespace partitioning   A set of rules to structure a namespace. The Java package namespace partitioning rules structure the namespace into a collection of nonoverlapping trees.

native method   Code that is native to a specific processor. On Windows 95, native methods refer to code written specifically for Intel *x*86 processors.

nesting   The "Russian dolls" effect of repeatedly wrapping or layering entities around other entities. In graphical user interface (GUI) design, widgets are often nested in container widgets that themselves are nested in bigger containers and so on.

Netscape Plug-Ins   Netscape Communications has created a standard interface to extend its Navigator browser product line. Products adhering to the specification are called Netscape Plug-Ins.

Network Computer   A computer that meets the Network Computer Platform specification, which is designed based on the "network as the computer system" concept.

Network News Transfer Protocol (NNTP)   The Internet protocol behind the newsgroup reading programs. NNTP manages daily threads of discussion in some 15,000 "news" groups, such as `comp.lang.java.programmer`.

network ordering   See *big-endian*.

NNTP   See *Network News Transfer Protocol*.

null   A value that means *no object*, which can be held by an object variable.

O

object   A software "thing" that has characteristics (state) and behavior (methods).

object pointer   In C++ and Delphi, an object variable that points to a specific memory location.

object variable   A name for an object. It may refer to an object or be null.

object-oriented programming (OOP)   Programming that focuses on these independent objects and their relationships to other objects, rather than using a top-down, linear approach (as with traditional Pascal or C).

octet   Another term for the 8-bit byte. Used only in the data communications world.

ODBC   See *Open Database Connectivity*.

OOP   See *object-oriented programming*.

opcode   Short for operation code. It is an integer representing the code for an operation.

Open Database Connectivity (ODBC)   A specification for connecting databases; the ODBC is a C interface. ODBC is based on the X/Open SQL Command Level Interface (CLI).

overloaded methods   Methods defined multiple times, each definition having the same name but accepting different parameters, either in number or type. The compiler knows which method to call based on the parameters it is passed.

P

package   A collection of related classes.

packet   A unit of communication. A packet can contain mostly user data, or it can be a pure protocol management packet (that is, containing no user data whatsoever).

packet-switched   A type of web-structured (as opposed to star- or ring-structured) data communications network that uses datagram packets as its building block packet type. Examples are the global X.25 packet-switching network and the Internet.

parent class   See *superclass*.

persistence   The ability of a Java object to record its state so it can be reproduced in the future, perhaps in another environment.

persistent object stores   Database-independent, object-oriented storage systems for storing various types of objects, such as video, audio, and graphics.

picoJava   Low-end Sun Microsystems microchip that runs the Java language.

pipe   An abstract data connection between (typically) two processes or threads. Process A writes data to Process B via a pipe. Process B needs to read the data from the pipe to receive any data.

polymorphism   The ability of a single object to operate on many different types.

POP   See *Post Office Protocol*.

Post Office Protocol (POP)   The Internet protocol that handles e-mail collection.

primitive   A datatype that is not represented by an object.

properties   Describe attributes associated with a component in a graphical user interface (GUI), such as color, size, and the string to be used as a label.

protocol   The set of rules and the structures of legal packets that are used to provide some communication service between two computers. Common examples are TCP/IP, Z-Modem, Kermit, SLIP, PPP, X.25, and IBM SNA.

Q

Quicksort   A binary sorting algorithm used by the Collections API.

R

RAD   See *Rapid Application Development*.

Rapid Application Development (RAD)   A kind of development tool that enables programmers to create sophisticated programs quickly.

reader   Similar to an input stream (used in I/O programming), but the basic unit of data is a Unicode character.

recursive   Self-calling. A recursive method calls itself repeatedly, either directly or indirectly.

registers   Known areas in a microprocessor for keeping small pieces of information like a pointer to the next instruction, the results of an addition, and so on. Usually, registers are in the microprocessor and can be accessed much faster than memory.

Remote Method Invocation (RMI)   The set of APIs for a Java program to call objects and methods that reside outside the current runtime environment or namespace.

rendering   Computer graphics jargon for drawing (used as both a verb and a noun).

request and response headers   Terms used to denote the ASCII-readable multiline headers of the HTTP protocol. The HTTP protocol consists of client (browser) requests followed by Web server (site) responses.

result set   The most common operations on a database are queries that return data. This data,

which consists of many rows and columns, is called a result set.

return statement   One of the flow-breaking statements. It is used to return control to the caller from within a method or constructor. Before the control is passed back to the caller, all of the `finally` clauses of the enclosing `try` statements are executed, from the innermost `finally` clause to the outermost one.

RMI   See *Remote Method Invocation*.

root class   In general, any class that acts as the superclass for a subhierarchy. An entire inheritance hierarchy, like Java's, has a single absolute root class: class `Object`.

router   A device in a packet-switched network that can accept packets and decide to which of its many output ports it should forward the packet to bring the packet a step closer to its final destination.

S

schema   A description of data elements in a database and their relationships. Primarily used by database designers, developers, and administrators.

SecurityManager   A Java class that restricts access to files, the network, or other parts of the system for security purposes.

separator   An unselectable line that appears on menus for decorative purposes.

serialization   The process whereby an object records itself by writing out the values that describe its state. *Deserialization* is the process of restoring serialized objects.

server   An entity whose sole purpose is to serve clients (either sequentially or in parallel) by providing them with some kind of well-defined service, such as searching a database or accepting mail messages.

servlet   A mini server-side program, similar to an applet, defined in the Java Servlet API.

Servlet API   An API that makes it possible to create programs that can run within the context of a Java-enabled server.

signature   A method's unique profile, consisting of its name, argument list, and return type. If two methods with the same name have the slightest difference in their argument lists, they are considered totally unrelated as far as the compiler is concerned.

signed classes   Classes and applets that can be traced to the company who developed them. This is achieved by keeping a tamper-proof electronic signature in the .class file. The technology for this scheme is in development.

Simple Mail Transfer Protocol (SMTP)   The Internet protocol behind e-mail delivery. See also *Post Office Protocol (POP)*.

single inheritance   The ability to write a class that inherits the member variables and methods (member functions) from a single class. See also *inheritance*.

sink   The final destination for data moving through a stream.

SMTP   See *Simple Mail Transfer Protocol (SMTP)*.

socket   A software interface that connects an application to the network.

source file   A text file containing human-readable instructions. A Java source file is a text file written in the Java programming language.

stack   A list-storing mechanism that uses the last-in, first-out (LIFO) metaphor. Also, a class in the `java.util` package.

state   An unambiguous, non-overlapping mode of "being"; for example, the binary states *on* and *off*.

statement   A line of source code ending with a semicolon (;). If multiple statements need to be placed together, they would be placed within a block, delineated with curly braces.

stream   An abstract concept used in the context of I/O programming to represent a linear, sequential flow of bytes of input or output data. A program can read from *input streams* (that is, read the data a stream delivers to it) and write to *output streams* (that is, transfer data to a stream).

streaming   Term used to denote audio, video, and other Internet content that is distributed in real time and does not need to be downloaded.

stub   A method with no body. It satisfies the compiler's need for completeness and leaves space for you to define the method specifics later.

subclass   A class that descends or inherits (*extends* in Java terminology) from a given class. Subclasses are more specialized than the classes they inherit from.

superclass   A class from which a given class inherits. This can be its immediate parent class or can be more levels away. Superclasses become more and more generic as you travel up the inheritance hierarchy and, for this reason, can often be abstract.

switch statement   A multiway selection statement. The integer expression is evaluated, and the first case clause whose constant expression evaluated to the same value is executed. The optional default clause is executed if there is no case clause matching the

value. The break statement is usually used as the last statement of a case clause so that the control will not continue on to statements of the next case clause.

T

TCP   See *Transmission Control Protocol (TCP)*.

telephony   Applications that combine telecommunications and multimedia computer technologies.

thread   A single flow of control within a program, similar to a process (or a running program) but easier to create and destroy than a process because less resource management is involved. Each thread must have its own resources, such as the program counter and the execution stack, as the context for execution. However, all threads in a program share many resources, such as memory space and opened files.

tokenizing   A common technique used to reduce the complexity of textual input.

tool tip   A pop-up box that describes an item's purpose. It appears when the cursor dwells (rests) over an area designated with a defined tip.

transaction processing   A general term used in the context of databases to denote, among other things, consistency, recoverability, and data integrity of relational databases. A transaction consists of multiple SQL (Structured Query Language) commands that read and update databases.

Transmission Control Protocol (TCP) The connection-oriented protocol built on top of the Internet Protocol (IP). TCP guarantees delivery of data and can handle arbitrary amounts of data.

U

UDP See *User Datagram Protocol (UDP)*.

Unicode An international character-mapping scheme (see `http://www.unicode.org` for more information).

Uniform Resource Locator (URL) A string that identifies the location of a resource and the protocol used to access it.

unmarshaling See *marshaling*.

untrusted applets Applets downloaded from a network whose source cannot be traced or trusted. These applets need to be verified before they are executed because they could contain malicious virus programs.

URL See *Uniform Resource Locator (URL)*.

User Datagram Protocol (UDP) A protocol between Internet Protocol (IP) and Transmission Control Protocol (TCP). It allows IP-style

datagrams to be sent to a port on a machine (instead of just a machine).

V

vector A list-storing mechanism that continually resizes itself, as space allocation needs to be changed. Also, a class in the `java.util` package.

Virtual Machine See Java Virtual Machine (VM).

W

Web browser A viewer program used by the client machine to display Web documents.

Web server A network server that, upon request, transmits Web documents via HTTP (Hyptertext Transfer Protocol).

Web site A set of Web documents belonging to a particular organization. A Web site may share a server machine with other sites or may extend across several machines.

while statements One of the loop statements. The conditional expression is first evaluated. If it evaluates to `true`, the loop body is executed, and the conditional expression is reevaluated. It will cycle through the testing of the conditional expression and the execution of the loop body until the conditional expression evaluates to `false`.

widgets   From "window gadgets," a generic term for graphical user interface (GUI) elements like buttons, scrollbars, radio buttons, text input fields, and so on.

windows, icons, menus, and pointer (WIMP)   See *graphical user interface (GUI)*.

World Wide Web (WWW)

A huge collection of interconnected hypertext documents on the Internet.

writer   Similar to an output stream (used in I/O programming), but the basic unit of data is a Unicode character.

Z

ZIP   Like a tar or jar file, a file that holds an aggregate of files, usually compressed.

INDEX

Note: Page numbers in *italics* refer to figures; page numbers in **bold** refer to primary discussion of the topic. Also check the Appendix, which is not included in this index.

SYMBOLS AND NUMBERS

A

B

I

K

O

P

U

V

About the Contributors

Some of the best—and best-selling—Sybex authors have contributed chapters from their current books to *Java 2 Complete*.

Philip Heller contributed material from *Java 2 Developer's Handbook*.

Philip is a software consultant, Java instructor, and novelist. A lifelong San Francisco Bay Area resident, he worked for both Sun and NeXT in the early years.

Simon Roberts contributed material from *Java 2 Developer's Handbook*.

Simon is a Java course developer and software engineer for Sun. A resident of Denver, he began his computing career writing machine code and has been teaching programming for the past decade.

John Zukowski contributed material from *Mastering Java 2*.

John is a Software Mage with MageLang Institute, a Java training firm. He is author of *Java AWT Reference*, *Borland JBuilder: No Experience Required*, and the Focus on Java online guide at The Mining Co., `http://java.miningco.com`. His latest book, *John Zukowski's Definitive Guide to Swing for Java 2*, is due out this Spring.

Laurence Vanhelsuwé contributed material from *Mastering Java Beans*.

Laurence is a self-taught independent software engineer. He has worked on such diverse technologies as X.25 WAN routers, Virtual Reality flight simulation, Postscript, and real-time, digitized, video-based traffic analysis. He expects Java to revolutionize computer science by leveling the computing landscape into one pan-Java playing field.

Steven Holzner contributed chapters from *Java 2: In Record Time*.

Steve is one of the most prolific programming authors around. With more than 48 books to his credit—including numerous best-sellers—he has taught more than a million people how to program, reaching people in 15 different languages. Recent titles include *Mastering Visual J++ 1.1*, *Visual J++ 1.1: No Experience Required*, *Visual C++ 6: No Experience Required*, *Java 2: No Experience Required*, and *Mastering Netscape IFC*, all from Sybex. Steve was formerly a faculty member at Cornell University and contributing editor at *PC Magazine*.

SYBEX BOOKS ON THE WEB

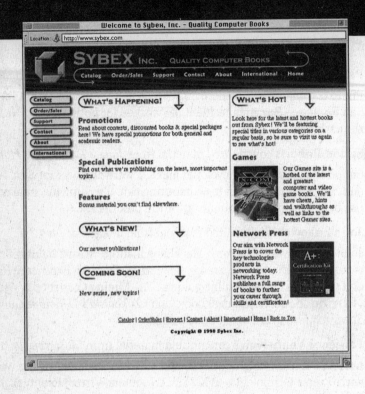

A t the dynamic and informative Sybex Web site, you can:

- · view our complete online catalog
- · preview a book you're interested in
- · access special book content
- · order books online at special discount prices
- · learn about Sybex

www.sybex.com

SYBEX Inc. • 1151 Marina Village Parkway
Alameda, CA 94501 • 510-523-8233